# A HISTORY
# OF THE
# WORLD

## IN THE
## TWENTIETH
## CENTURY

J. A. S. GRENVILLE

# A HISTORY
# OF THE
# WORLD

IN THE

## TWENTIETH
## CENTURY

The Belknap Press of
Harvard University Press,
Cambridge, Massachusetts

1994

*Library of Congress Cataloging-in-Publication Data*

Grenville, J. A. S. (John Ashley Soames), 1928–
    A history of the world in the twentieth century / J. A. S. Grenville.
        p.   cm.
    Includes bibliographical references and index.
    ISBN 0-674-39960-9
    1. History. Modern--20th century.   1. Title.
D421.G65 1994                                                      94-8591
909.82--dc20                                                         CIP

# CONTENTS

# LIST OF MAPS

# LIST OF ILLUSTRATIONS

# PREFACE

Interest in world history has grown enormously in recent years. Jet travel has shrunk the globe. People are now less confined to their own part of the world than ever before. Migrations have resulted in multicultural societies on every continent; different ethnic groups have a desire to learn more about each other. Another major reason for the growth of interest is that events and developments in any part of the world – wars, revolutions, the movement of trade, changes in economic conditions – impact on the rest of the world.

To write a world history is a formidable task. I began sixteen years ago, adding to the islands of knowledge I had researched in the previous twenty-five years of academic study. In 1980 the first part of the *Collins History of the World in the Twentieth Century*, covering mainly Europe, Asia and the United States from 1900 to 1945, was published by Fontana Press and has since been widely used. Twelve years later I reached the 1990s and widened the scope of the history to Africa, Latin America and Australasia. I am grateful to Stuart Proffitt for his encouragement and for suggesting that the first volume should be revised and that the work should now cover the twentieth century in one volume. His support has made the realisation of my original concept possible.

One way of writing world history is to concentrate on general movements affecting the world as a whole, to describe the underlying forces of history – population growth, increasing literacy, the technological revolution, for instance – to reveal how the twentieth century became the 'age of the masses'. A number of excellent books have appeared based on this approach. But if we ignore the fact that our world in the twentieth century is a world of nations we leave out of account one of the mainsprings of historical change in this century.

Clearly we have to deal with the enormous impact made by social and economic changes in the twentieth century across national frontiers, the consequences of industrialisation, the clashes of cultures as the West came to dominate Africa and Asia, reactions and counter-reactions making themselves felt to the present day. The varied responses to conflict, change and maladjustments were not confined in the twentieth century to national borders: the appeals of socialism and communism, of totalitarian state organisation, of Western parliamentary government, of fascism and Nazism, all crossed land frontiers and the oceans and continents of the world.

What a writer of world history cannot do without seriously distorting its understanding is simply to ignore and discard national frontiers and national influences beyond a country's frontiers. International co-operation was and still is too weak to reduce national frontiers to no more than historical and cultural boundaries. On the other hand, though world trade has made nations more dependent on each other for their prosperity and perhaps even survival, this interdependence is not a relationship of free equals, great and small! The moment we analyse more closely the actual nature of that interdependence we come back to questions of national power. That is why a world history cannot make 'interdependence' the central theme.

In this century technological and scientific advances have resulted in startling transformations: journeys have been made to the moon by lone astronauts; more usefully the masses can be carried by air from one continent to another in a few hours; communication by the single political leader with millions by means of radio, and later television too, has profoundly affected the conduct of politics; from artillery projectiles capable of killing a hundred people at once we have moved to the capability of obliterating several millions with a barrage of nuclear missiles. And yet, accepting the twentieth century in its way as a revolutionary stage of historical change, it was not the first nor is it likely to be the last such stage. Historical change has not in the past come about by gradual steps; the pace quickens and slackens.

The first half of the twentieth century was a period during which intercontinental rivalries frequently played a role in world history, but we have to be precise in showing the interrelationships. Industrial power ceased to be a virtual European monopoly. Two devastating wars occurred in Europe and the first furthered the partial triumph of the new revolutionary ideology of communism. The problems of eastern Asia were both a consequence of Western impact and the result of Asian conflicts. They are too frequently viewed through Western eyes alone. After 1945, the part played by Western Europe, important though it remains, shrinks when viewed within a global perspective. The significance in world affairs of Africa, the Middle East and Latin America increased. The nations of these continents asserted their national rights and imposed on the most powerful nations of the world a sense of the limits of their own power.

I have put forward no startling new theories or hypotheses about world history. Space limits what can be written on any one topic: some have had to be omitted altogether, since only by means of a degree of selectivity can anything be written in depth and I have preferred to do this rather than to provide an encyclopaedic account of many more subjects. On the subjects I have written about I have endeavoured to keep abreast of present research so far as this is humanly possible.

*A technical note*: First, some basic statistics are provided of population, trade and industry in various countries for purposes of comparison. They are often taken for granted. Authorities frequently disagree on these in detail; they should therefore be regarded as indicative rather than absolutely precise. A comparison of standards of living between countries is not an exact science. I have given per capita figures of the gross national product (GNP) as a very rough guide; but these represent only averages in societies where differentials of income may be great; furthermore they are expressed in U.S. dollars and so are dependent on exchange rates; actual costs of living also vary widely between countries; the per capita GNP can not therefore be simply translated into comparative standards of living and provide but a rough guide. Secondly, the transliteration from Chinese to Roman lettering presents special problems. The Pinyin system of romanisation was officially adopted by China on 1 January 1979 for international use, replacing the Wade-Giles system. Thus where Wade-Giles had Mao Tse-tung and Teng Hsaio-ping, Pinyin gives Mao Zedong and Deng Xiaoping. For clarity's sake, the usage in this book is not entirely consistent: the chosen form is Pinyin, but Wade-Giles is kept for certain older names where it is more easily recognisable, for example Shanghai, Chiang Kai-shek and the Kuomintang. Peking changes to the Pinyin form Beijing after the communist takeover.

The onerous task of typing was expertly undertaken by Miss Gillian Briggs and Mrs S. Atkins. I have consulted numerous colleagues, too many to list. I hope they will accept a collective word of thanks.

An author who has Peter James as an editor is fortunate indeed. He tackled the formidable manuscript with zest. His many queries have rooted out ambiguities and mistakes, and the book is very much better as a result of his efforts. Caroline Wood's picture research has added to our understanding of twentieth-century history; the illustrations are not included just to enliven a page of text. Overall editorial control has been exercised by Philip Gwyn Jones with just the right combination of firmness and flexibility. The support by all concerned at HarperCollins on so large a project has been all that an author could wish for. My wife has lived with me while I, for months at a time, lived with the manuscript. I cannot find adequate words to thank her for her constant support, but dedicate the book to her.

*The School of History, The University of Birmingham.*

# PART I

---

*Social Change and*
*National Rivalry in the*
*West, 1900–1914*

jet travel, radio, television, telephones, cars, nuclear weapons

state more centralized, nationalism, widening franchise, better medical care for workers, pensions, universal education, democracy gaining ground, greater value of the rule of law / impartial justice, imperial expansion, colonialization of Africa/Asia, population explosion,

# CHAPTER 1

## The World in the Twentieth Century

Historical epochs do not coincide strictly with centuries. The French Revolution in 1789, not the year 1800, marked the beginning of a new historical era. The beginning of the twentieth century too is better dated to 1871, when Germany became unified, or the 1890s, when international instability became manifest in Europe and Asia and a new era of imperial rivalry which the Germans called *Weltpolitik* began. On the European continent Germany had become by far the most powerful military nation and was rapidly advancing industrially. In eastern Asia during the 1890s a modernised Japan waged her first successful war of aggression against China. In the Americas the foundations were laid for the emergence of the United States as a superpower later in the century. The United States no longer felt secure in isolation. Africa was finally partitioned between the European powers. These were some of the portents indicating the great changes to come in the new century. There were many more.

Modernisation was creating new industrial and political conflict and dividing society. The state was becoming more centralised, its bureaucracy grew and achieved control to an increasing degree over the lives of the individual. Social tensions were weakening the tsarist Russian Empire and during the first decade of the twentieth century Russia was defeated by Japan. The British Empire was at bay and Britain was seeking support, not certain which way to turn. Fierce nationalism, the build-up of vast armies and navies, and unquestioned patriotism that regarded war as an opportunity to prove manhood rather than a catastrophe characterised the mood as the new century began. Boys played with their tin soldiers and adults dressed up in the finery of uniforms. The rat-infested mud of the trenches and machine guns mowing down tens of thousands of young men as yet lay beyond the imagination. Soldiering was still glorious, chivalrous and glamorous. But the early twentieth century also held the promise of a better and more civilised life in the future.

In the Western world civilisation was held to consist not only of cultural achievements but also of moral values. Despite all the rivalries of the Western nations, wanton massacres of ethnic minorities, such as that of the Armenians by the Turks in the 1890s, aroused widespread revulsion and prompted great-power intervention. The pogroms in Russia and Romania against the Jews were condemned by civilised peoples, including the Germans, who offered help and refuge despite the growth of anti-Semitism at home. The Dreyfus affair outraged Queen Victoria and prompted Émile Zola to mobilise a powerful protest movement in France; the Captain's accusers were regarded as representing the corrupt elements of the Third Republic. Civilisation to contemporary observers seemed to be moving forward. Before 1914 there was no good reason to doubt that history was the story of mankind's progress, especially that of the white European branch.

There was a sense of cultural affinity among the

aristocracy and bourgeoisie of Europe. Governed by monarchs who were related to each other and who tended to reign for long periods or, in France, by presidents who changed too frequently to be remembered for long, the well-to-do felt at home anywhere in Europe. The upper reaches of society were cosmopolitan, disporting themselves on the Riviera, in Paris and in Dresden; they felt that they had much in common and that they belonged to a superior civilisation. Some progress was real. Increasingly, provision was made to help the majority of the people who were poor, no doubt in part to cut the ground from under socialist agitators and in part in response to trade union and political pressures brought about by the widening franchise in the West. Pensions and insurance for workers were first instituted in Germany under Bismarck and spread to most of the rest of Western Europe. Medical care too improved in the expanding cities. Limits were set on the hours and kind of work children were allowed to perform. Universal education became the norm. The advances made in the later nineteenth century were in many ways extended after 1900.

Democracy was gaining ground in the new century. The majority of men were enfranchised in Western Europe and the United States. The more enlightened nations understood that good government required a relationship of consent between those who made the laws and the mass of the people who had to obey them. The best way to secure co-operation was through the process of popularly elected parliamentary assemblies, which allowed the people some influence – government by the will of the majority, at least in appearance. The Reichstag, the French Chambers, the Palace of Westminster, the two Houses of Congress, even the Russian Duma, all met in splendid edifices intended to reflect their importance. In the West the trend was thus clearly established early in the century against arbitrary rule. However much national constitutions differed, another accepted feature of the civilised polity was the rule of law, the provision of an independent judiciary meting out equal justice to rich and poor, the powerful and the weak. Practice might differ from theory, but justice was presented as blindfolded: justice to all, without favours to any.

Equal rights were not universal in the West. Working people were struggling to form effective unions so that, through concerted strike action, they could overcome their individual weakness when bargaining for decent wages and conditions. Only a minority, though, were members of a union. In the United States in 1900, only about 1 million out of more than 27 million workers belonged to a labour union. Unions in America were male dominated and, just as in Britain, women had to form their own unions. American unions also excluded most immigrants and black workers.

Ethnic minorities were discriminated against even in a political system such as that of the United States which prided herself as the most advanced democracy in the world. Reconstruction after the Civil War had bitterly disappointed the black Americans in their hopes of gaining equal rights. Their claims to justice remained a national issue for much of the twentieth century.

All over the world there was discrimination against a group which accounted for half the earth's population – women. It took the American suffragette movement half a century to win in 1920 the right to vote. In Britain the agitation for women's rights took the drastic form of public demonstrations after 1906, but not until 1918 did women over thirty years of age gain the vote, and those aged between twenty-one and thirty had to wait even longer. But the acceptance of votes for women in the West had already been signposted before the world war. New Zealand in 1893 was the first country to grant women the right to vote in national elections; Australia followed in 1908. But even as the century comes to an end there are countries in the Middle East where women are denied this basic right. Moreover, this struggle represents only the tip of the iceberg of discrimination against women on issues such as education, entry into the professions, property rights and equal pay for equal work. Incomplete as emancipation remains in Western societies, there are many countries in Asia, Latin America, Africa and the Middle East where women are still treated as inferior, the chattels of their fathers or husbands. In India, for example, orthodox Hindu marriage customs were not changed by law until 1955. As for birth-control education, which began in the West in the nineteenth century, freeing women from the burden of repeated pregnancies, it did not reach the women of the Third World until late this century – though it is there that the need is greatest.

The limited progress towards equal rights achieved in the West early in the twentieth century was not mirrored in the rest of the world. Imperialism in Africa and Asia saw its final flowering as the nineteenth century drew to a close. The benefits brought to the indigenous peoples of Africa and Asia by the imposition of Western rule and values was not doubted by the majority of white people. 'The imperialist feels a profound pride in the magnificent heritage of empire won by the courage and energy of his ancestry,' wrote one observer in 1899; '. . . the spread of British rule extends to every race brought within its sphere the incalculable benefits of just law, tolerant trade, and considerate government.'

In 1900 Europeans and their descendants who had settled in the Americas, Australasia and southern Africa looked likely to dominate the globe. They achieved this tremendous extension of power in the world because of the great size of their combined populations and because of the technological changes which collectively are known as the industrial revolution. One in every four human beings lived in Europe, some 400 million out of a total world population of 1600 million in 1900. If we add the millions who had left Europe and multiplied in the Americas and elsewhere, more than one in every three human beings was European or of European descent. The Europeans ruled a great world empire with a population in Africa, Asia, the Americas and the Pacific of nearly 500 million by 1914. To put it another way, before 1914 only about one in three people had actually avoided being ruled by Europeans and their descendants, most of whom were unshaken in their conviction that their domination was natural and beneficial and that the only problem it raised was to arrange it peacefully between them.

To the Asians and Africans, the European presented a common front with only local variations: some spoke German, others French or English. There are several features of this common outlook. First, there was the Westerner's feeling of superiority, crudely proven by his capacity to conquer other peoples more numerous than the invading European armies. Vast tracts of land were seized by the Europeans at very small human cost to themselves from the ill-equipped indigenous peoples of Asia and Africa. That was one of the main reasons for the extension of European power over other regions of the world. Since the mid-nineteenth century the Europeans had avoided fighting each other for empire, since the cost of war between them would have been of quite a different order.

Superiority, ultimately proven on the battlefield, was, the European in 1900 felt, but one aspect of his civilisation. All other peoples he thought of as uncivilised, though he recognised that in past ages these peoples had enjoyed a kind of civilisation of their own, and their artistic manifestations were prized. China, India, Egypt and, later, Africa were looted of great works of art. Most remain to the present day in the museums of the West.

A humanitarian European impulse sought to impose on the conquered peoples the Christian religion, including Judaeo-Christian ethics, and Western concepts of family relationships and conduct. At his best the Western coloniser was genuinely paternalistic. Happiness, he believed, would follow on the adoption of Western ways, and the advance of mankind materially and spiritually would be accomplished only by overcoming the prejudice against Western thought.

From its very beginning, profit and gain were also powerful spurs to empire. In the twentieth century industrialised Europe came to depend on the import of raw materials for its factories; Britain needed vast quantities of raw cotton to turn into cloth, as well as nickel, rubber and copper. As her people turned her into the workshop of the world in the nineteenth century, so she relied on food from overseas, including grain, meat, sugar and tea, to feed the growing population. Some of these imports came from the continent of Europe close by, the rest from far afield – the Americas, Australasia and India. As the twentieth century progressed, oil imports assumed an increasing importance. The British mercantile marine, the world's largest, carried all these goods across the oceans. Colonies were regarded by Europeans as essential to provide secure sources of raw materials; just as important, they provided markets for industrialised Europe's output.

Outside Europe only the United States matched, and indeed exceeded, the growth of European industry in the first two decades of the twentieth century. Europe and the United States accounted for virtually all the world trade in manufactured goods, which doubled between 1900 and 1913. There was a corresponding increase in demand for raw materials and food supplied by the Americas, Asia and the less industrialised countries of Europe. Part of Europe's wealth was used to develop resources in other areas of the world: railways everywhere, manufacture and mining in Asia, Africa and

North and South America; but Europe and the United States continued to dominate in actual production.

Global competition for trade increased colonial rivalry for raw materials and markets, and the United States was not immune to the fever. The division of Asia and Africa into outright European colonies entailed also their subservence to the national economic policies of the imperial power. Among these were privileged access to colonial sources of wealth, cheap labour and raw materials, domination of the colonial market and, where possible, shutting out national rivals from these benefits. Thus the United States was worried at the turn of the century about exclusion from what was believed to be the last great undeveloped market in the world – China. In an imperialist movement of great importance, Americans advanced across the Pacific, annexing Hawaii and occupying the Philippines in 1898. The United States also served notice of her opposition to the division of China into exclusive economic regions. Over the century a special relationship developed between America and China that was to contribute to the outbreak of war between the United States and Japan in 1941, with all its consequences for world history.

By 1900 most of Africa and Asia was already partitioned between the European nations. With the exception of China, what was left – the Samoan islands, Morocco and the frontiers of Togo – caused more diplomatic crises than was warranted by the importance of such territories.

Pride in an expanding empire, however, was not an attitude shared by everyone. There was also an undercurrent of dissent. Britain's Gladstonian Liberals in the 1880s had not been carried away by imperialist fever. An article in the *Pall Mall Gazette* in 1884 took up the case for indigenous peoples. 'All coloured men', it declared, 'seem to be regarded as fair game,' on the assumption that 'no one has a right to any rule or sovereignty in either hemisphere but men of European birth or origin'. During the Boer War (1899–1902) a courageous group of Liberals challenged the prevailing British jingoism. Lloyd George, a future prime minister, had to escape the fury of a Birmingham crowd by leaving the town hall disguised as a policeman. Birmingham was the political base of Joseph Chamberlain, the Colonial Secretary who did most to propagate the 'new imperialism' and to echo Cecil Rhodes's call for the brotherhood of the 'Anglo-Saxon races',

supposedly the British, the Germans and white Americans of British or German descent. Americans, however, were not keen to respond to the embrace.

After the Spanish–American War of 1898 the colonisation of the Philippines by the United States led to a fierce national debate. One of the most distinguished and eloquent leaders of the Anti-Imperialist League formed after that war denounced US policies in the Philippines and Cuba in a stirring passage,

> This nation cannot endure half republic and half colony – half free and half vassal. Our form of government, our traditions, our present interests and our future welfare, all forbid our entering upon a career of conquest.

Clearly, then, there was already opposition to imperialism on moral grounds by the beginning of the twentieth century. The opponents' arguments would come to carry more weight later in the century. Morality has more appeal when it is also believed to be of practical benefit. As the nineteenth century came to an end competition for empire drove each nation on, fearful that to lose out would inevitably lead to national decline. In mutual suspicion the Western countries were determined to carve up into colonies and spheres of influence any remaining weaker regions.

The expansion of Western power in the nineteenth and early twentieth century carried with it the seeds of its own destruction. It was not any 'racial superiority' that had endowed Western man with a unique gift for organising society, for government or for increasing the productivity of man in the factory and on the land. The West took its knowledge to other parts of the world, and European descendants had increased productivity in manufacturing industries in the United States beyond that of their homelands. But high productivity was not a Western monopoly: the Japanese were the first to prove, later in the century, that they could exceed Western rates.

The Wars of American Independence demonstrated that peoples in one region of the world will not for ever consent to be ruled by peoples far distant. By 1900 self-government and separate nationhood had been won, through war or through consent, by other descendants of Europeans who had become Australians, Brazilians, Argentinians,

Canadians and, soon, South Africans. These national rebellions were led by white Europeans. It remained a widespread European illusion that such a sense of independence and nationhood could not develop among the black peoples of Africa in the foreseeable future. A people's capacity for self-rule was crudely related to 'race' and 'colour', with the white race on top of the pyramid, followed by the 'brown' Indians, who, it was conceded, would one distant day be capable of self-government. At the bottom of the pile was the 'black' race. The 'yellow' Chinese and Japanese peoples did not fit easily into the colour scheme, not least because the Japanese had already shown an amazing capacity to Westernise. Fearful of the hundreds of millions of people in China and Japan, the West thus conceived a dread of the yellow race striking back – the 'yellow peril'.

The spread of European knowledge undermined the basis of imperialist dominance. The Chinese, the Japanese, the Koreans, the Indians and the Africans would all apply this knowledge, and goods would be manufactured in Tokyo and Hong Kong as sophisticated as those produced anywhere else in the world. A new sense of nationalism would be born, resistant to Western dominance and fighting it with Western scientific knowledge and weapons. When independence came, older traditions would reassert themselves and synthesise with the new knowledge to form a unique amalgam in each region. The world remains divided and still too large and diverse for any one group of nations, or for any one people or culture, to dominate.

All this lay in the future, the near future. Western control of most of the world appeared in 1900 to be unshakeable fact. Africa was partitioned. All that was left to be shared out were two nominally independent states, Morocco and Egypt, but this involved little more than tidying up European spheres of influence. Abyssinia alone had survived the European attack.

The Ottoman Empire, stretching from Balkan Europe through Asia Minor and the Middle East to the Indian Ocean, was still an area of intense rivalry among the European powers. The independent states in this part of the world could not resist European encroachment, both economic and political, but the rulers did succeed in retaining

*The public execution of a 'Boxer' after suppression of the Rising.*

some independence by manoeuvring between competing European powers. The partition of the Middle East had been put off time and time again because in so sensitive a strategic area, on the route to India, Britain and Russia never trusted each other sufficiently to strike any lasting bargain, preferring to maintain the Ottoman Empire and Persia as impotent buffer states between their respective spheres of interest. Much farther to the east lay China, the largest nation in the world, with a population in 1900 of 400 million.

When Western influence in China was threatened by the so-called Boxer rising in 1900, the West acted with a show of solidarity. An international army was landed in China and 'rescued' the Europeans. Europeans were not to be forced out by 'native' violence. The Western powers' financial and territorial hold over China tightened, though they shrank from the responsibility of directly ruling the whole of China and the hundreds of millions of Chinese living there. Instead, European influence was exerted indirectly through Chinese officials who were ostensibly responsible to a central Chinese government in Peking. The Western Europeans detached a number of trading posts from China proper, or acquired strategic bases along the coast and inland and forced the Chinese to permit the establishment of semi-colonial international settlements. The most important, in Shanghai, served the Europeans as a commercial trading centre. Britain enlarged her colony of Hong Kong by forcing China to grant her a lease of the adjacent New Territories in 1898. Russia sought to annex extensive Chinese territory in the north.

With hindsight it can be seen that by the turn of the century the European world empires had reached their zenith. Just at this point, though, a non-European Western power, the United States, had staked her first claim to power and influence in the Pacific. But Europe could not yet, in 1900, call in the United States to redress the balance which Russia threatened to upset in eastern Asia. That task was undertaken by an eastern Asian nation – Japan. Like China, Japan was never conquered by Europeans. Forced to accept Western influence by the Americans in the mid-nineteenth century, the Japanese were too formidable to be thought of as 'natives' to be subdued. Instead the largest European empire, the British, sought and won the alliance of Japan in 1902 on terms laid down by the Japanese leaders.

Europe's interests were global, and possible future conflicts over respective imperial spheres preoccupied its leaders and those sections of society with a stake in empire. United, their power in the world was overwhelming. But the states of Europe were not united. Despite their sense of common purpose in the world, European leaders saw themselves simultaneously ensnared in a struggle within their own continent, a struggle which, each nation believed, would decide whether she would continue as a world power.

The armaments race and competition for empire, with vast standing armies facing each other and the new battleship fleets of Dreadnoughts were symptoms of increasing tension rather than the cause of the great war to come. Historians have endlessly debated why the West plunged into such a cataclysmic conflict. Social tensions within each country and the fears of the ruling classes, especially in the Kaiser's Germany, indirectly contributed to a political malaise during a period of great change. But as an explanation why war broke out in 1914 the theory that a patriotic war was 'an escape forward' to evade conflict at home fails to carry conviction even in the case of Germany. It seems almost a truism to assert that wars have come about because nations simply do not believe they can go on coexisting. It is nevertheless a better explanation than the simple one that the *prime* purpose of nations at war is necessarily the conquest of more territory. Of Russia and Japan that may have been true in the period 1900–5. But another assumption, at least as important, was responsible for the Great War. Among the then 'great powers', as they were called in the early twentieth century, there existed a certain fatalism that the growth and decline of nations must inevitably entail war between them. The stronger would fall on the weaker and divide the booty between them. To quote the wise and experienced British Prime Minister, the third Marquess of Salisbury, at the turn of the century,

You may roughly divide the nations of the world as the living and the dying. . . . the weak states are becoming weaker and the strong states are becoming stronger. . . . the living nations will gradually encroach on the territory of the dying and the seeds and causes of conflict among civilised nations will speedily appear. Of course, it is not to be supposed that any one of the living nations will be allowed to have the monopoly of curing or cutting up these unfortunate patients and the controversy is as to who shall have the privilege of doing so, and in what measure he shall do it. These things may introduce causes of fatal difference between the great nations whose mighty armies stand opposed threatening each other. These are the dangers I think which threaten us in the period that is coming on.

In 1900 there were some obviously dying empires, and the 'stronger nations' competing for their territories were the European great powers and Japan. But during the years immediately preceding the Great War the issue had changed. Now the great powers turned on each other in the belief that some must die if the others were to live in safety. Even Germany, the strongest of them, would not be safe, so the Kaiser's generals believed, against the menace of a combination of countries opposing her. That was the fatal assumption which more than anything led to the 1914–18 war. It was reducing the complexity of international relations to a perverse application of Darwinian theory.

The First World War destroyed the social cohesion of pre-war continental Europe. The Austro-Hungarian and Ottoman Empires broke up; Germany, before 1914 first among the continental European countries, was defeated and humiliated; Italy gained little from her enormous sacrifices; the tsarist Russian Empire disintegrated, and descended into civil war and chaos. In their despair people sought new answers to the problems that threatened to overwhelm them, new ideals to replace respect for kings and princes and the established social order. In chaos a few ruthless men were able to determine the fate of nations, ushering in a European dark age in mid-century. Lenin, Trotsky and Stalin were able to create a more efficient and crueller autocracy than that of the Romanovs. The new truths were held to be found in the works of Karl Marx as interpreted by the Russian dictators, who imposed their ideas of communism on the people. In Italy disillusionment with parliamentary government led to fascism. In Germany, democracy survived by a narrow margin but was demolished when her people despaired once more in the depression of the early 1930s. Hitler's doctrine of race then found a ready response, and his successes at home and abroad confirmed him in power.

Different though their roots were, what these dictators had in common was the rejection of Judaeo-Christian ethics, a contempt for the sanctity of human life, for justice and for equality before the law. They accepted the destruction of millions of people in the belief that it served desirable ends. They were responsible for a revolution in thought and action that undid centuries of progress.

Stalin and Hitler were not the first leaders to be responsible for mass killings. During the First World War, the Turks had massacred Armenians, ethnic hatred inflamed by fears that in war the Armenians would betray them. Stalin's calculated killing of 'class enemies' and his murderous purges of those from whom he suspected opposition were the actions of a bloody tyrant, by no means the first in history. The ruthless exploitation of slave labour, the murder of the Polish officers during the Second World War and the expulsion of whole peoples from their homes revealed the depths to which an organised modern state was capable of sinking. But nothing in the history of a Western nation equals the Nazi state's application of its theories of good and bad races which ended with the carefully planned factory murder of millions of men, women and children, mostly Jews and gypsies. There were mass killings of 'inferior Slavs', Russians and Poles, and those who were left were regarded as fit only to serve as labour for the German masters.

The Nazi evil was ended in 1945. But it had been overcome only with the help of the communist power of the Soviet Union. As long as Stalin lived, in the Soviet Union and her satellite states the rights of individuals counted for little. In Asia, China and her neighbours had suffered war and destruction when the Japanese, who adopted from the West doctrines of racial superiority, forced them into their cynically named 'co-prosperity sphere'. The ordeal was not over for China when the Second World War ended. Civil war followed until the victory of the communists. Mao Zedong imposed his brand of communist theory on a largely peasant society for three decades. Many millions perished in the terror he unleashed, the class war and as a result of experiments designed to create an abundant communist society. In Asia too the regime of Pol Pot in Cambodia provided a more recent example of inhumanity in the pursuit of ideological theories amounting to genocide.

By the close of the century the tide finally turned against communist autocracy and dictatorship. The suffering and oppression all over the world in the twentieth century was much greater than it had been in the nineteenth. Only the minority whose standards of living improved, who lived in freedom in countries where representative government remained an unbroken tradition, had the promise of progress fulfilled through greater abundance of wealth. But even in these fortunate societies few families were untouched by the casualties of the wars of the twentieth century. Western societies were spared the nightmare after 1945 of a third world war, which more than once seemed possible, though they were not spared war itself. These wars, however, involved far greater suffering to the peoples living in Asia, Africa and the Middle East than to the West.

The Cold War had divided the most powerful nations in the world into opposing camps. The West saw itself as the 'free world' and the East as the society of the future, the people's alliance of the communist world. They were competing for dominance in the rest of the world, in Africa, Asia, the Middle East and Latin America, where the West's overwhelming influence was challenged by the East. That struggle dominated the second half of the century. Regional conflicts in the world came to be seen through the prism of the Cold War. Within the two blocs differences also arose, of which the most serious was the quarrel between the Soviet Union and China, which further complicated developments in Asia. That the Cold War never turned to a real war between its protagonists was largely due to MAD, the doctrine of mutual assured destruction. Both sides had piled up nuclear arsenals capable of destroying each other and much of the world, and there was no sure defence against all the incoming missiles. Mutual assured destruction kept the dangerous peace between them. The battle for supremacy was fought by other means, including proxy wars between nations not possessing the 'bomb' but armed and supported by the nuclear powers.

The abiding strength of nationalism from the nineteenth century right through the twentieth has generally been underestimated by Western historians. Hopes of peace for mankind and a lessening of national strife were aroused by the formation of the League of Nations after the Great War of 1914–18. But long before the outbreak of the Second World War the principle of 'collective security' had broken down when the undertakings

to the League by its member states clashed with perceived national interests. The United Nations began with a burst of renewed hope after the Second World War but could not bridge the antagonisms of the Cold War. Both the League and the UN performed useful international functions but their effectiveness was limited whenever powerful nations refused their co-operation.

Despite growing global interdependence on many issues, including trade, the environment and health, national interests were narrowly interpreted rather than seen as secondary to the interests of the international community. Nationalism was not diminished in the twentieth century by a shrinking world of mass travel and mass communication, by the universal possession of cheap transistor radios and the widespread availability of television nor by any ideology claiming to embrace mankind. To cite one obvious example, the belief that the common acceptance of a communist society would obliterate national and ethnic conflict was exploded at the end of the century, and nationalism was and still is repressed by force all over the world. Remove coercion, and nationalism re-emerges in destructive forms.

But the world since 1945 has seen some positive changes too. Nationalism in Western Europe at least has been transformed by the experiences of the Second World War and the success of co-operation. A sign of better times is the spread of the undefended frontier. Before the Second World War the only undefended frontier between two sovereign nations was the long continental border between Canada and the United States. By the closing years of the century all the frontiers between the nations of the European Community were undefended. Today the notion of a war between France and Germany or between Germany and any of her immediate neighbours has become virtually unthinkable; a conflict over the territories they possess is inconceivable, as is a war prompted by the belief that coexistence will not be possible. To that extent the international climate has greatly changed for the better. But the possibility of such wars in the Balkans, in eastern Europe, in Asia, Africa and the Middle East remains ever present.

No year goes by without one or more wars occurring somewhere in the world, many of them savage civil wars. What is new in the 1990s is that these wars no longer bring the most powerful nations of the world into indirect conflict with each other. The decision of Russia and the United States to cease arming and supplying opposing contestants in the Afghan civil wars marked the end of an indirect conflict that had been waged between the Soviet Union and the United States since the Second World War in Asia, the Middle East, Africa and Latin America. But this understanding will not banish wars. Intervention, whether by a group of nations acting under UN sponsorship or by a major country acting as policeman, is costly. UN resources are stretched to the limits by peacekeeping efforts in Cyprus, Cambodia, Yugoslavia and other trouble-spots. No universal peacekeeping force exists. Intervention would therefore be likely only when the national interests of powerful countries were involved, as they were in the Gulf in 1991. It would be less likely, unfortunately, where the motive was purely humanitarian.

The world's history is interwoven with migrations. The poor and the persecuted have left their home-land for other countries. The great movement of peoples from eastern to western Europe and further west across the Atlantic to the United States, Canada, the Argentine, Australasia and South Africa continued throughout the nineteenth century, most of the emigrants being unskilled workers from rural areas. But this free movement of peoples, interrupted by the First World War, was halted soon after its close. In countries controlled by Europeans and their descendants quotas were imposed, for example by the United States Immigration Act of 1924, denying free access to further immigrants from Europe. These countries so arranged their immigration policies that they slowed down to a trickle or excluded altogether the entry of Asians and Africans. In the United States the exclusion of Asians from China and Japan had begun well before 1914. They had been welcome only when their labour was needed. The same attitude became clear in Britain where immigration of West Indians was at first encouraged after 1945, only to be restricted in 1962. The demand for labour, fluctuating according to the needs of a country's economy, and the strength of racial prejudice have been the main underlying reasons for immigration policies. While the West restricted intercontinental migrations after the First World War, within Asia the movement continued, with large population transfers from India, Japan and Korea to Burma, Malaya, Ceylon, Borneo and Manchuria. Overseas Chinese in Asia play a crucial role, as do Indian traders in sub-Saharan Africa.

After the Second World War there were huge migrations once more in Asia, Europe and the Middle East. Millions of Japanese returned to their homeland. The partition of the Indian subcontinent led to the largest sudden and forced migration in history of some 25 million from east to west and west to east. At the close of the war in Europe, West Germany absorbed 20 million refugees and guest-workers from the East. Two million from Europe migrated to Canada and to Australia; 3 million North Koreans fled to the South.

The United States experienced a changing pattern of immigration after the Second World War. More than 11 million people were registered as entering the country between 1941 and 1980. The great majority of immigrants had once been of European origin. After 1945 increasing numbers of Puerto Ricans and Filipinos took advantage of their rights of entry. There was a large influx of Hispanics from the Caribbean; in addition probably as many as 5 million illegal immigrants crossed the Mexican border to find low-paid work in burgeoning California. The proportion of Europeans fell to less than one-fifth of the total number of immigrants. The second-largest ethnic influx came from Asia – Taiwan, Korea and, after the Vietnam War, Vietnam. The United States has become more of a multicultural society than ever before. But, unlike most blacks and Hispanics, the Asians have succeeded in working their way out of the lower strata of American society.

Although the migration of Europeans to Africa south of the Sahara after 1945 was less spectacular in terms of numbers – probably less than a million in all – their impact as settlers and administrators on the history of African countries was crucial for the history of the continent.

One of the most significant developments in the Middle East after 1945 was the creation of a whole new nation, the State of Israel. Proportionally, migration into Israel saw the most rapid population increase of any post-war state. Under the Law of Return any Jew from any part of the world had the right to enter and enjoy immediate citizenship. Between May 1948 and June 1953 the population doubled and by the end of 1956 had tripled to 1,667,000.

There are no accurate statistics relating to the peoples of the world who, since 1945, have been driven by fear, hunger or the hope of better opportunities to migrate. They probably exceed 80 million. As the century draws to a close more than 10 million are still refugees without a country of their own; political upheavals and famines create more refugees every year. The more prosperous countries of the world continue to erect barriers against entry from the poor countries and stringently examine all those who seek asylum. In Europe, the Iron Curtain has gone but an invisible curtain has replaced it to stop the flow of migration from the East to the West, from Africa across the Mediterranean, from the poor South of the world to the North.

The only real solution is to assist the poor countries to develop so that their populations have a hope of rising standards of living. The aid given by the wealthy has proved totally inadequate to meet these needs, and loans have led to soaring debt repayments. The commodities the Third World has to sell have generally risen in price less than the manufacturing imports it buys. The natural disadvantage is compounded by corruption, economic mismanagement, the waste of resources on the purchase of weapons, wars and the gross inequalities of wealth. But underlying all these is the remorseless growth of population, which vitiates the advances that are achieved.

There has been a population explosion in the course of the twentieth century. It is estimated that 1200 million people inhabited planet earth in 1900. By 1930 the figure reached 2000 million, in 1970 it was 3600 million and by the end of the century the world's population is expected to total 6000 million. Most of that increase, some 90 per cent, has taken place in the Third World, swelling the size of cities like Calcutta, Jakarta and Cairo to many millions. The inexorable pressure of population on resources has bedevilled all efforts to improve standards of living in the poorest regions of the world, such as Bangladesh. The gap between the poor parts of the world and the rich widened rather than narrowed. Birth-control education is now backed by Third World governments, but, apart from China's draconian application of it, it has not yet made an impact on reducing the acceleration of population growth. Despite the suffering caused, wars and famines inflict no more than temporary dents on the upward curve. Only the experience with Aids may prove different, if no cure is found: in Africa the disease is widespread, and in Uganda it has

infected one person in every six. The one positive measure of population control is to achieve economic and social progress in the poorest countries of the world. With more than 800 million people living in destitution the world is far from being in sight of this goal.

At the end of the twentieth century many of the problems that afflicted the world at its beginning remain unresolved. The prediction of Thomas Robert Malthus in his *Essay on the Principle of Populations* published in 1798 that, unless checked, the growth of population would outrun the growth of production still blights human hopes for progress and happiness in the Third World. According to one estimate, a third of all children under five, some 150 million, in the Third World are undernourished and prey to disease. Of the 122 million children born in 1979, one in ten were dead by the beginning of 1981. In Africa there are still countries where one child in four does not survive to its first birthday. In Western society, too rich a diet has led to dramatic increases in heart disease. In the Third World, according to the UN Secretary-General in 1989, 500 million go hungry and every year there are 10 million more. The Brandt report, *North–South: A Programme for Survival* (1980), offered an even higher estimate, and declared that there was 'no more important task before the world community than the elimination of hunger and malnutrition in all countries'. No one can calculate the figures with any accuracy. The world community has reacted only to dramatic televised pictures of suffering and famine, for example in the Horn of Africa, but there is no real sense of global agreement on the measures necessary to tackle the problem. Now that the Third World is politically independent, the former Western colonial powers are conveniently absolved from direct responsibility.

The political independence of the once Western-dominated globe represents an enormous change, one which occurred much more rapidly than was expected in the West before the Second World War. But in many countries independence did not lead to better government or the blessings of liberty. Third World societies were not adequately prepared, their wealth and education too unequally distributed to allow any sort of democracy to be established – although this was accomplished in India. But on the Indian subcontinent, as elsewhere in the former colonial states, ethnic strife and blood-

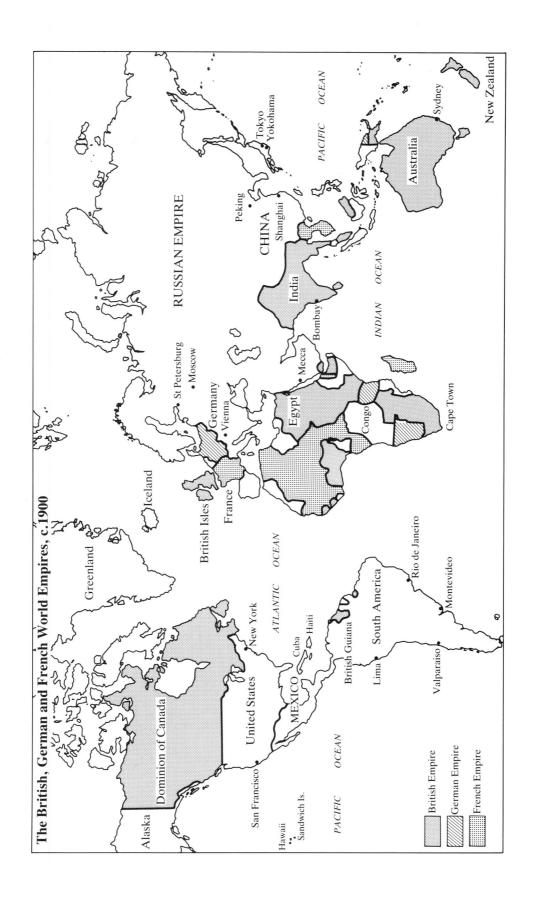

**The British, German and French World Empires, c.1900**

Greenland

Alaska

Dominion of Canada

United States

San Francisco

Hawaii

Sandwich Is.

*PACIFIC OCEAN*

MEXICO

Cuba

Haiti

New York

*ATLANTIC OCEAN*

British Guiana

Lima

South America

Valparaiso

Rio de Janeiro

Montevideo

Iceland

British Isles

France

Germany

Vienna

St Petersburg

Moscow

RUSSIAN EMPIRE

Mecca

Egypt

Congo

Cape Town

Bombay

*INDIAN OCEAN*

India

CHINA

Peking

Shanghai

Tokyo

Yokohama

*PACIFIC OCEAN*

Australia

Sydney

New Zealand

British Empire

German Empire

French Empire

shed persist. Corruption, autocracy and the abuse of human rights remain widespread.

In eastern Asia at the beginning of the century the partition of China seemed to be at hand, and Japan already claimed to be the predominant power. But China proved too large to be absorbed and partitioned. The military conflict between Japan and her Pacific neighbours ended only in 1945. By the close of the twentieth century she has emerged as an economic superpower decisively influencing world economic relations. China, economically still weak, but developing rapidly remains by far the largest and most populous unified nation in the world. By the end of the century the last foreign outposts taken from her before the twentieth century, Hong Kong and Macao, will become part of her national territory again. Apart from Vietnam and North Korea, China in 1993 is the last communist state in the world.

At the beginning of the century Karl Marx had inspired socialist thinking and indeed much political action in the Western world. The largest socialist party in 1900 was in the Kaiser's Germany. But these socialist parties believed that the road to power lay through constitutional means. Revolutionaries were on the fringe, one of them the exiled Lenin in Zurich, their prospects hopeless until the First World War transformed them and created the possibility of violent revolutions in the east. By the end of the century, in an overwhelmingly peaceful revolution communism and the cult of Marxism–Leninism has been discredited in the Soviet Union. Whatever takes its place will change the course of the next century. The unexpected revolutions that swept through central and Eastern Europe from 1989 to 1991 were on the whole no less peaceful. In every corner of the globe the autocratic, bureaucratic state faced a powerful challenge. The comparative economic success and social progress achieved by the West through the century proved desirable to the rest of the world, as did its institutions, especially the 'free market' and 'democracy' with a multi-party system. But how will these concepts be transferred to societies which have never practised them?

'Freedom', 'democracy' and the 'free market' are simple concepts but their realisation is beset by ambiguity. In societies lately subjected to autocratic rule, how much freedom can be allowed without risking disintegration into anarchy and disorder? There is no Western country which permits a free market to function without restraint, without protecting the interests of workers and consumers. These institutional restraints, embodied for example in the successful 'social market economy' of Germany, have taken years to develop. How large a role should the state play? Not everything can be privatised, and certainly not instantly. How large a welfare system needs to be created? 'Communism' too has lost precise meaning. Communism in China today is very different from the communism of thirty years ago, now that private enterprises are flourishing. Labels change their meaning. Nor do simple slogans provide the answers.

At the beginning of the century one could believe that a better world was gradually emerging. History was the story of progress. For some this meant that socialist ideals would lead to a utopia before the century had come to an end. In mid-century that faith in human progress and in the inevitable march of civilisation was shattered. The power of National Socialism and its destructive master-race doctrine were broken; it was the end of an evil empire but not the end of tyranny. At the close of the century there is a little more cause for optimism. The horrors, corruption and inefficiency of autocracy, with its denial of humanity, lie exposed. But the problems that face mankind as a new era of history begins remain daunting. With the collapse of the Soviet model of communist autocracy there superficially appears to be a consensus in the world (except in China) that only 'democracy' and the 'market economy' can reconcile the people and their government and master the complex economic requirements of today's societies if progress is to be achieved and the people are to be deflected from revolution. Is it then the 'end of history', an end to the great ideological debate about the direction in which mankind is going to travel? Can we be more sure about our future? The world is far too diverse for that to be likely. New apparent certainties will no more survive immutably than did the old.

Right to the end the great events of the century did not turn out the way contemporaries expected. Having considered some of the overall changes, comparing the beginning of the century and the end, the chapters that follow will recount the tumultuous history that lies between.

# CHAPTER 2

# The German Empire: Achievement and Excess

Imperial Germany symbolised success. Created in three victorious wars, she had replaced France as the first military power in Europe. The Prussian spirit was seen to be matched by astonishing progress in other directions. In all branches of education and scientific discovery, the German Empire stood second to none. In manufacture, German industry grew by leaps and bounds. The secret of her success seemed to lie in the Prussian genius for organisation and in the orderliness and self-discipline of her hard-working people. There were a lot of them, too – nearly 67 million in 1913; this made the Germans the second-largest nation of Europe, well ahead of France and Britain, and behind only the vast population of Russia.

By the turn of the century Germany had become a predominantly industrial nation, with large cities. For every German working on the land, two were engaged in manufacture on the eve of the First World War. Once far behind Britain in coal production, by 1914 Germany had almost closed the gap, and after the United States and Britain was the third industrial power in the world. Coal, iron and steel, produced in ever larger quantities, provided the basis for Germany's leap forward, challenging Britain's role as Europe's leader.

Between 1871 and 1914 the value of Germany's agricultural output doubled, the value of her industrial production quadrupled and her overseas trade more than tripled. Germany's progress aroused anxieties among her neighbours, but there was also co-operation and a recognition that the progress of one European nation would, in fact, enrich the others. Germany was catching up with Britain, the pioneer of the industrial revolution, but Britain and Germany were also important trading partners.

Unlike Britain, the German Empire was transformed in a relatively short time from a well-ordered, mainly rural country to a modern industrial nation. In contrast with her industrial progress, the pace of Germany's political development was slow, deliberately retarded by its ruling men. The government of the Prussian–German Monarchy after 1871 was a mixture of traditional mid-nineteenth-century institutions, together with an imperial parliament – the Reichstag – more in harmony with the new democratic age. But the old traditional Junker society found allies after 1871 among the big industrialists in its opposition to the advance of democracy. The cleavage so created between the powerful few and the rest of society, in the name of maintaining the power of the Crown, was responsible for the continuation of social and political divisions in Wilhelmine Germany down to the outbreak of war.

The constitutional arrangements for the German Empire of 1871 did nothing to heal these divisions. On the contrary, Bismarck, their creator, intended to block any possibility that the old Prussia should be submerged by the new Germany. In Britain during the period of rapid industrialisation half a century earlier, the ruling wealthier groups of society had, in the end, acquiesced in the necessary political and social adjustments and admitted the

**Coal, Iron and Steel Production in Germany and Britain**
(*annual averages*)

|  | 1875–9 | | 1910–13 | |
| --- | --- | --- | --- | --- |
|  | Germany | Britain | Germany | Britain |
| Coal and lignite (*million metric tons*) | 49.9 | 135.7 | 251.5 | 292.0 |
| Pig iron (*thousand metric tons*) | 1,791.0 | 6,483.0 | 14,829.0 | 9,792.0 |
| Steel (*million metric tons*) | 0.97 (1880–4) | 1.82 | 15.34 | 6.94 |

less wealthy to participate in government through radical electoral reform; not so in Prussia.

The German Empire consisted of a federation of twenty-five states; the largest was the kingdom of Prussia with a population in 1890 of some 30 million; it overshadowed the second largest state, Bavaria, with a population of 5.5 million. By preserving state parliaments and extensive state rights, Bismarck not only appeased the feelings of the other states, but above all preserved Prussia's own position. In Prussia, the parliament elected on a mid-nineteenth-century three-class system, not even by secret ballot, ensured the permanent predominance of the landed aristocracy, the Junkers, and also of the wealthy merchants and industrialists, and the socially conservative groups. Whereas some other states introduced democratic franchises, Prussia retained her totally undemocratic parliament until 1917.

The Reichstag for the empire as a whole was an entirely separate parliamentary body, democratically elected by universal manhood suffrage. The basis of parliamentary power lies in parliament's control of the purse-strings of government. But Bismarck had done his best to draw the teeth of parliamentary control. In the first place most of the imperial budget was spent on the military; by various means annual control over the army budget was removed from the Reichstag. The Reich's increasing expenditure in the twentieth century necessitated asking for more money from the Reichstag, which then acquired more significance for government.

The power to raise taxes was divided between the democratically elected Reichstag and the undemocratic Prussian (and other state) parlia-

ments. The Reichstag controlled only indirect taxes, the rate of custom duties, duties on tobacco, sugar, brandy, salt, which weighed most heavily on the poor. Taxes on income and property could be voted only in the state parliaments. The Reichstag was thus virtually powerless to secure greater social justice through the introduction of more progressive taxation of the wealthy and the landed Junkers. These groups in their turn were determined to resist all attacks on their privileged position from the Reichstag, and as long as they could preserve the constitutional settlement with its divided parliaments they were able to block all serious attempts at constitutional reform. Bismarck wanted to ensure that there would never be parliamentary government on the British model.

The constitution of 1871 also gave tremendous powers to the emperor; he alone could appoint and dismiss the chancellor; he was supreme commander of the military forces and final arbiter of war and peace. The chancellor was nominally responsible to the Federal Council formed by delegates from the federal states – the Bundesrat – but this Council exercised no real power. The system so devised could operate as long as the Reichstag demanded no real control over government policies.

In fact the Reichstag was far from quiescent. By refusing to increase indirect taxation it could deny the imperial government the money it needed. 'Government', however, is rather a misnomer for the frequently chaotic executive of Wilhelmine Germany. The heads of the army, the navy and the civil branches of government and administration were often in conflict. The chancellor had to attempt to find a consensus and, if he succeeded in doing so, either to circumvent the Kaiser altogether or to win his consent. Sometimes the chancellor was too late, and the impressionable Kaiser had been led in a different direction already. After Bismarck no chancellor succeeded in dominating the state.

The Reichstag's political leaders too were in an isolated position. They debated vigorously and bargained with the chancellor, but their actions were not tempered by the responsibility of office. Divorced from government, the parties of the left, centre and right lacked the incentive of reaching workable and stable compromises. The parties of the left were insistently calling for reform and an end to the privilege so entrenched in Prussia. The conservative right, or agrarians as they were called, demanded tariffs on the import of grain to protect themselves. The left opposed tariffs because they meant dearer food for the people. So it became increasingly difficult for the chancellors of the empire to find majorities for the budget and other legislation from the shifting coalitions of parties from the centre to the right which they tried to form for their support after 1890; meanwhile the support of the Reichstag became indispensable in the new century as government expenditure on the navy, the army and the colonies rose rapidly. The scope of political manoeuvre available to the chancellor was, furthermore, narrowed by the growth of the Social Democratic Party; it had become, by 1912, the largest single party with 110 seats out of a total of 391.

**Reichstag Election, 1912** (*number of seats*)

| | |
|---|---|
| Conservatives & Free Conservatives | 57 |
| National Liberals | 45 |
| Progressives | 42 |
| Centre | 91 |
| Social Democrats | 110 |
| Nationalities | 33 |
| Anti-Semitic | 13 |

The Social Democratic Party was denounced as revolutionary, its members as 'enemies of the state' – an extraordinary and unwarranted attack on a party operating fully within the law. The defeat of social democracy was the main purpose of the

Conservatives and the men surrounding the Kaiser. They could not conceive of including the Social Democrats within the fabric of the political state. This was more understandable while the Social Democratic Party was indeed Marxist and revolutionary. But as the twentieth century advanced the great majority of the party members in 1913, led by the pragmatic Friedrich Ebert, had become democratic socialists working for gradual reform; their Marxist revolutionary doctrine was becoming more a declaration of outward faith than actual practice, or immediate expectation. In a number of the state parliaments, Social Democrats had already joined coalitions with Liberals to form a responsible base for governments, thus abandoning their revolutionary role. But in Prussia this was unthinkable.

One consequence of the narrow outlook of the Conservatives was that they would never consent to constitutional change which would have made the chancellor and his ministers responsible to the Reichstag as the government in Britain was to Parliament. The Conservatives thus had no alternative but to leave power, in theory at least, ultimately in the hands of the Kaiser. The Kaiser's pose as the 'All Highest' was ridiculous, and even the fiction could not be maintained when, after the Kaiser's tactless *Daily Telegraph* interview in 1908, when he claimed that he had helped Britain during the Boer War, his own ministers sought to restrain him.

Kaiser Wilhelm II did not have the strength to lead Germany in the right direction. He was an intelligent man of warm and generous impulse at times, but he was also highly emotional and unpredictable. He felt unsure of his fitness for his 'divine calling', and posed and play-acted. This was a pity as his judgement was often intuitively sound. He did not act unconstitutionally, leaving control of policy to his ministers and military men. But when, in an impasse or conflict between them, the decision was thrust back to him, he occasionally played a decisive role. More usually he was manipulated by others, his vanity making him an easy victim of such tactics. He wanted to go down as the people's Kaiser and as the Kaiser of peace; also as the emperor during whose reign the German Empire became an equal of the world's greatest powers. His contradictory aims mirrored a personality whose principal traits were not in harmony with each other.

The Kaiser, and the Conservative–industrial alliance, were most to blame for the divisiveness of German society and politics. There was constant

*Kaiser Wilhelm II and General Helmuth von Moltke, who as Chief of the General Staff was responsible for carrying through the Schlieffen Plan. After an ignominious performance at the Marne, he was relieved of his command in November 1914 and replaced by von Falkenhayn.*

talk of crisis, revolution or pre-emptive action by the Crown to demolish the democratic institutions of the Reich. Much of this was hysterical.

But the Wilhelmine age in German development was not entirely bleak. The judiciary remained substantially independent and guaranteed the civil rights of the population and a free press; there was a growing understanding among the population as a whole that Kaiser Wilhelm's pose as the God-ordained absolute ruler was just play-acting. Rising prosperity was coupled with the increasing moderation of the left and the growth of trade unions. The political education of the German people proceeded steadily, even if inhibited by the narrowly chauvinistic outlook of so many of the schoolmasters and university professors, by the patronage of the state as an employer, and by the Crown as a fount of titles, decorations and privileges. Significantly, the anti-Conservative political parties on the eve of 1914 commanded a substantial majority, even though they could not work together.

The deep political and social divisions never really threatened Germany with violence and civil

war in the pre-war era. Over and above the conflict, the German people, including the Social Democrats, felt a strong sense of national pride in the progress of the 'fatherland'. Furthermore the last peacetime chancellor of imperial Germany, Theobald von Bethmann Hollweg, recognised that constitutional reform was a matter of time. But there was not sufficient time.

The Social Democrats, the Progressives and Centre, who had won a majority in the 1912 elections, demanded a constitutional monarchy responsible to the Reichstag. The Conservatives chose to regard this challenge as provoking a constitutional crisis, threatening the Wilhelmine state. But did they unleash a war deliberately to preserve their position and to avoid reform? To be sure, there were Conservatives and militarists who saw a successful war as a means of defeating democratic socialism. The Chancellor, Bethmann Hollweg, was not one of them. Nevertheless it was an element in the situation that the Kaiser and his supporters saw themselves in a hostile world surrounded by enemies at home and abroad. There developed in the increasingly militarised court a wild and overheated atmosphere, a fear and pessimism about the future. While German society as a whole had good reasons for confidence and satisfaction on the eve of the war, the increasingly isolated coterie around the Kaiser suffered more and more from hysterical nightmares inimical to cool judgement.

They were carried forward in 1914 by a tide of events they had themselves done much to create. In the summer of 1914 war was seen as a last desperate throw to stave off Germany's otherwise inevitable decline. Bethmann Hollweg laid the blame for the outbreak of war on cosmic forces, on the clash of imperialism and nationalism, and specifically on British, French and Russian envy of Germany's progress. Germany, so he claimed, could have done little to change this. But did her growth of power make the struggle in Europe inevitable or did her own policies contribute to war and her 'encirclement'?

Twenty-six years earlier, in 1888, at the time of the accession of Wilhelm II, Germany appeared not only secure but on the threshold of a new expansion of power, world power. The contrast of mood and expectations between then and 1914 could not have been greater. Bismarck had raised German power to the position where Berlin was the centre of diplomacy. European affairs revolved around the triangular-alliance relationship of Berlin, St Petersburg and Vienna. Bismarck had accomplished this by convincing Europe that Germany's power would be used only in her own defence, that Germany was a satiated nation, looking for no more territorial expansion, and that he would join with other peace-loving nations to preserve the general peace of Europe. After twenty years of peace, Germany's pacific intent could not seriously be doubted. Bismarck followed this policy to avoid what Bethmann Hollweg three decades later in August 1914 claimed to be inevitable, the formation of a hostile coalition to check the growth of German power in Europe and the world.

All this fundamentally changed in 1890 after the Kaiser's dismissal of Bismarck. The harm was not done by dropping the 'old pilot'. Bismarck was not indispensable. What proved so harmful to Germany's interests was that the basic aim of his policy in Europe was deliberately abandoned. Germany's leaders were blinded by a vision of *Weltpolitik*. They forcefully argued that the German Empire could not be content with her position on the European continent alone but must become a 'world power', otherwise her decline would be certain. Germany, so they thought, needed colonies, world markets, the certainty of securing raw materials, a merchant marine, and a navy no one would dare challenge, to protect her overseas commerce. They placed themselves at the head of, and stimulated further, the chauvinism of some sections of German society. No wonder that fear of Germany in the end bound together her neighbours in alliance against her. One of the most consistent advocates of this *Weltpolitik* from its inception was Admiral Alfred von Tirpitz.

The one overmastering purpose of Tirpitz's life was to build up a great German battleship fleet that would match on the high seas the primacy of the army on the land. He pursued this aim with tenacity and political skill. The Kaiser was obsessed with being respected and loved by the British. What better way to achieve this than to build up a rival navy, he thought, and so supported Tirpitz. The trouble was that a large navy in addition to a large army entailed heavy expenditures. Was it really necessary? Tirpitz set out to persuade the Reichstag. The first Navy Law was passed in March 1898. Tirpitz had claimed that it was a matter of survival to protect Germany's interests on the high seas; without their defence in the new age of *Weltpolitik* German decline was certain. For Foreign Minister Prince von Bülow, the navy would be a means of pressurising the European imperial powers, who had got there first, into making way for Germany, so that she too would have her 'place in the sun'. But how could the German navy hope to catch up with the large navies of France, Russia and above all Britain?

To meet the arguments that to attempt to build a large offensive fleet was a waste of German effort, Tirpitz developed facile and yet, to his contemporaries, plausible theories. He postulated that given Britain's widespread global commitments a German battleship fleet only two-thirds of the size of the British would suffice for victory, provided the German fleet was concentrated in the North Sea. Then there was his famous risk theory: Britain might strike at the incomplete German battleship fleet as Nelson had struck at the enemy in Copenhagen. Therefore until her fleet was large enough Germany would pass through a period of risk. During this period she must avoid war. Tirpitz calculated that this risk period would end in 1920, by which time, if his construction programme were adhered to, Germany would possess sixty battleships. Then what? Tirpitz publicly argued that the fleet would act as a deterrent, so ensuring Britain's neutrality in any future conflict; indeed he and others claimed that Britain would respect and only deal 'fairly' with Germany when Germany possessed enough naval force to impress on her the dangers of conflict. With Britain deterred from acting against her, Germany's plans for continental hegemony could be realised. Tirpitz professed to believe, taking a longer view, that since empires came and went in history, there would come the time for a new global share-out of territory; then Germany would be able to take her proper place only if she possessed a navy strong enough. Secretly he wrote that the fleet would need to defeat the British navy in war before Britain would cease to oppose Germany's rise to world power. Did Tirpitz believe in all his theories or just in a large navy? Were the theories really no more than propaganda to persuade the Kaiser and the Reichstag to accept the burdens of constructing the navy? Probably Tirpitz, like so many dynamic men of action, convinced himself by arguments first devised to persuade others.

Tirpitz's campaign of persuasion was certainly very successful. To the industrialists supplying the steel and to the owners of the shipyards, the battleship fleet plan could be presented as both patriotic and highly profitable. The cause of the navy was popularised among the people through a Navy League; the Pan-Germans were wooed as were all those who believed in Germany's *Weltpolitik*, from patriotically ardent professors to Reichstag deputies. One harmful consequence of all this propaganda, not actually welcome to Tirpitz while Germany passed through the risk years, was that German chauvinism was greatly increased. The difficulty of persuading the Reichstag to grant more money also added to the empire's constitutional difficulties and this, in turn, aroused the fears of Germany's rulers. Tirpitz's navy helped to stimulate a belligerent, restless spirit of dissatisfaction. The direct impact on Anglo-German relations was considerable too during the years of the 'naval race' after the launch of the first Dreadnought-class battleships in 1906, though it was not the naval challenge as such that brought Britain to the side of France and Russia. The British government knew it could maintain a margin of superiority over Germany and outbuild whatever the Germans could manage. But there was a fear that Germany might

*Europe prepares for Armageddon. The Krupps 'Cannon Workshop No. 5' in Essen here turns out 15-inch guns for Germany's new 'Super-Dreadnoughts'.*

soon launch herself on a general course of aggression endangering the whole European continent.

It was clear for all the world to see that the leaders of Wilhelmine Germany did not regard the German Empire any longer as satiated. The Germans saw no *moral* reason why they should be denied a 'place in the sun'. There were plenty of good practical reasons which would have made more responsible men hesitate.

While the Kaiser and the navy looked into the yonder of the wider world, the military had their eyes firmly fixed on the problem of how Germany in the centre of Europe could overcome the disadvantage of facing two enemies, Russia and France, at the same time and emerge dominant. The outcome was the Schlieffen Plan, which laid down that the bulk of the German army should be thrown against the French army, leaving the east for two months only lightly defended against the Russians.

The Schlieffen Plan was remarkable for two aspects of German official thinking: the complete disregard for international morality, in the interests of military advantage; and the excessive faith the German military mind placed on theoretical planning that disregarded the human factor and the unexpected. Despite its increasing remoteness from reality, the Schlieffen Plan acquired the authority of Holy Writ. It was the work of Count Alfred von Schlieffen, Chief of the German General Staff from 1891 to 1906. In all its versions, beginning with the first plan of 1899, Belgian neutrality would be violated – although Germany was a party to its perpetual guarantee. This would be justified by 'military necessity', claimed Schlieffen, and no one dared dispute that the General's plan overrode any treaty obligations. Schlieffen saw as his model Hannibal's victory at Cannae, achieved 2000 years earlier by turning both flanks of the Romans. Schlieffen's plan, however, concentrated on one wing, the right wing only, which would sweep around the French armies, 'crush the enemy's flanks . . . and complete the destruction by attack upon his rear'. The plan assumed that the French in the centre would not withdraw in time; that the war in the west could be won before the Russians could be ready to mount a serious offensive in the east; that France would be defeated more or less precisely in thirty-nine days and would then seek peace. The plan was based on many unsupported political and military assumptions. It was in truth a desperate gamble designed to achieve victory on one front in what was from the beginning a three-front war (Germany against France in the west, Germany against Russia in the east, Austria–Hungary against Russia in the south-east).

Imperial Germany began to give expression to her new post-Bismarckian orientation of foreign policy in 1890 by abandoning the alliance with Russia and drawing closer to England. Her intention was to regain a 'free hand' and exploit international rivalries to advance Germany's global objectives. Republican France and tsarist Russia thereupon drew together in alarm and concluded a defensive alliance directed against the possibility of German aggression (page 28). Fear of Germany was the main rationale of this otherwise incongruous alliance.

The policy of the 'free hand', of exploiting international differences, was thought out by one of Bismarck's pupils and erstwhile admirers, the publicity-shy head of the political section of the German Foreign Ministry, Baron von Holstein. To exploit Germany's freedom while the other powers confronted each other also became the guiding motive of policy during the years presided over by Bernhard von Bülow as Foreign Minister and Chancellor (1897–1909). These were fateful years for Germany. At the turn of the century a number of pro-German British ministers, led by the Colonial Secretary Joseph Chamberlain, were seeking a closer alignment with Germany as a counter to Russia's global expansion. There probably never was a possibility that Britain would have been ready to sign a formal alliance with Germany during the years 1898 to 1901, but she was ready to work in close collaboration with Germany. The chance for a far-reaching Anglo-German entente was rejected by Holstein and Bülow except on the impossible terms that Britain should share portions of her empire with Germany. The Germans expected the hard-pressed British to become more amenable later. The British found another way and managed without Germany's support. As Prime Minister Lord Salisbury had foretold in 1898 when speaking to the German Ambassador, 'You ask too much for your friendship.'

The 'other way' for Britain was to reach compromise settlements with imperial rivals. That was achieved with the French in the spring of 1904. The settlement involved allowing France predominance in Morocco. It was German policy that began turning the Anglo-French settlement of their differences into a partnership against Germany. The

Germans also had rights in Morocco and were not going to be ignored. The Kaiser made a dramatic visit to Tangier in 1905 and promised to support the Sultan of Morocco against the French. It is unlikely that the German military were looking for a pretext for war against France while France's ally, Russia, was internationally impotent, having to face the consequences of her unsuccessful war against Japan both abroad and at home. The Kaiser and Bülow in any case did not want war. Their aim was to bully France and Britain and to frighten them out of their recent entente. The result was the opposite. The Germans gained nothing from the conference which they convened at Algeciras in 1906 to deal with the Moroccan question, and British and French officers began secret discussions on military co-operation. French fears of Germany were strengthened.

But in 1905 the Kaiser's personal diplomacy did lead to one spectacular scoop. Constantly on the move, the Kaiser was cruising in his yacht just north of Stockholm in the Bay of Björkö; there he met the Tsar from close-by Russian Finland and talked him into signing a German–Russian alliance. In St Petersburg and Berlin the ministers were aghast. The Russian ministers would not abandon the French alliance against Germany. The treaty was stillborn.

Four years later in 1909, the Germans more successfully bullied Russia during the Bosnian crisis (page 59) and in 1911 attempted to coerce the French again over Morocco (page 30). The ineptitude of German policy is striking. The threats of war were bluff. Despite Germany's military superiority during these years, the Kaiser and his ministers did not wish to unleash an aggressive war. As long as the leaders of imperial Germany felt themselves to be stronger than their country's neighbours, they maintained the peace. Aggression was to stem from a growing sense of weakness, from the conviction after 1912 that Germany's superiority was slipping away.

Bülow's disastrous direction of German foreign policy came to an end with his resignation in 1909. He was succeeded as chancellor by Bethmann Hollweg. The dour philosophical new chancellor was conscious of, and opposed to, the excesses of German policy, of the naval programme and of the wilder shores of *Weltpolitik*. He hoped by patient diplomacy to allay the fears of Germany's neighbours and, above all, to improve relations with Britain. He began with the right ideas but soon found that in Wilhelmine Germany others, besides the responsible chancellor, had the ear of the Kaiser and could nullify the chancellor's efforts. British attempts, initiated by Richard Haldane and Winston Churchill in 1912, to cool down the naval competition all failed. British naval arrangements with France and Russia to share the defence of the oceans followed in 1914. In this way Germany herself tightened the coalition formed to contain her.

Bethmann Hollweg's efforts had also been undermined by the Secretary of State for Foreign Affairs, Alfred von Kiderlen-Wächter, who in 1911 turned France's attempts to increase her hold over Morocco into a second trial of strength and another international crisis. A German gunboat was sent to Agadir in Morocco to frighten the French. British reaction was unambiguous: Britain would stand by France if Germany attacked her. The Kaiser was all the more annoyed as this had not been his intention; finally the Germans withdrew from the Moroccan affair with 'compensation' – a strip of African territory which France relinquished to Germany. But there was no hiding the fact that imperial Germany had suffered a humiliating diplomatic defeat.

The Moroccan setback only reinforced Germany's desire to become stronger. It also drove her to support her one reliable ally, Austria–Hungary, and so to link Germany's fate with that of the Habsburgs. Germany's leaders were unwilling to contemplate a future based on their own calculations of a *relative* decline of power. General Ludendorff, the second most influential planner after the Chief of Staff General Moltke (the younger), urged a preventive war before it was too late. The year 1912 marks the turning point in the once confident thinking of the Kaiser and his entourage. By now they recognised that the possibility of building a German fleet sufficiently large to inflict defeat on Britain on the seas was a pipedream. Germany could not match Britain's naval construction. The naval race was lost for all to see. With it *Weltpolitik* faded.

Much more immediate and serious for Germany was the situation on the continent of Europe. The Habsburg ally appeared in dire straits, weakened by the dispute among the nationalities composing the empire. Russia had recovered from defeat by Japan and was launched on a colossal programme of military expansion and preparedness. With so little to show for so much effort in the cause of *Weltpolitik*, with the position of the Habsburg monarchy weakening, and Russia's strengthening in the Balkans where her protégés were in the ascendant after their victory in the first Balkan war, with more Social Democrats in the Reichstag after the elections of 1912 than ever before, an air of desperation can be discerned in the attitudes of the Kaiser's military advisers.

Bethmann Hollweg, from 1912 to 1914, consistently worked for better Anglo-German relations, but his efforts to detach Britain from her support of France failed. He did not rule out war as a solution to Germany's problems in Europe but it would need to be a war for what he saw as the right objectives, the survival of Germany as the strongest continental power, providing a base also for a share of imperial world power; diplomatically, he believed, this would mean loosening the Triple Entente and neutralising Britain. In its illusions Bethmann Hollweg's policy was as disastrous as his predecessor Bülow's had been.

The army command was clearly growing jittery in 1912. Bethmann Hollweg could still count on Tirpitz and his ever-unready navy to aid him in urging a delay in bringing about conflict. The desirability of launching a preventive war against France and Russia was discussed by the Kaiser and his principal military advisers, meeting in a so-called war council, in December 1912. The Kaiser had had one of his periodical belligerent brainstorms, this time brought about by a warning received from Britain that she would not leave France in the lurch if Germany attacked her. Nothing aroused the Kaiser to greater fury than to be scorned by Britain. But the secret meeting of 8 December 1912 did no more than postpone war. A consensus among all those present was achieved in the end; Admiral Tirpitz had opposed the army, which urged that war should be unleashed quickly; all in the end agreed to wait but not for much beyond 1914. They were also agreed that Germany would lose all chance of defeating Russia and France on land if the war was longer delayed. Speedier Russian mobilisation would make the Schlieffen Plan inoperable because Russia would be able to overwhelm Germany's weak screen of defence in the east before the German army in the west could gain its victory over France.

The most sinister aspect of the meeting of December 1912 was the cynical way in which the Kaiser's military planned to fool the German people and the world about the true cause of the war. It was to be disguised as a defensive war against Russia in support of the Habsburg Empire. In the coming months, they agreed, the German people should be prepared for war.

Still, a war postponed is a war avoided. Bethmann Hollweg was not yet convinced or finally committed. Wilhelm II could and, in July 1914, actually did change his mind. As the German Chief of Staff rightly observed, what he feared was not 'the French and the Russians as much as the Kaiser'.

Nevertheless, in 1913 the needs of the army did become first priority; a bill passed by the Reichstag increased the hitherto fairly static standing army by calling up an additional 136,000 conscripts. This measure was designed to bring the peacetime strength of the army to nearly 800,000 men by the autumn of 1914.

Bethmann Hollweg scored one success. The abrasive *Weltpolitik* overseas was downgraded. Instead, Germany now pushed her interests in Asia Minor and Mesopotamia and developed her new friendship with Turkey. The projected Berlin-to-Baghdad railway was to be the economic artery of this Germany's new imperial commercial sphere. The intrusion of German interests in the Middle East was not unwelcome to Britain since Germany would help to act as a buffer against Russian expansion.

In the Balkans, where a second Balkan war had broken out in 1913, Bethmann Hollweg and the British Foreign Secretary Sir Edward Grey worked together to localise the conflict and to ensure a peaceful outcome. The Kaiser's conference of December 1912 had at least made it much easier for Bethmann Hollweg to follow a pacific policy in 1913 and he could show some success for it, though not a weakening of Britain's support for France, his main objective. Nevertheless, the drift to war in Germany was unmistakable. Her leaders were accustoming themselves to the idea of a war, persuaded by the seemingly irrefutable logic of the military. In the end, in the summer of 1914, Bethmann Hollweg too would be carried forward with the Kaiser over the brink.

# CHAPTER 3

# Republican France during the 'Belle Epoque'

The German Empire symbolised to contemporaries in 1900 discipline, union and progress; France was generally seen as a country divided, whose politicians' antics could scarcely be taken seriously, a society sinking into corruption and impotence. The malevolence of that corruption had been demonstrated in the highest reaches of the army, the Church and politics by the Dreyfus affair, the innocent Captain having been found in 1899 yet again guilty of espionage. The slander against the Jews living in France achieved a degree of viciousness not seen anywhere in a civilised country. Only Russia could compete. Yet the better-off flocked to France. Paris was acknowledged as perhaps the most beautiful city in the world, certainly the artistic capital of Europe. The Riviera was becoming the holiday playground of European society.

Foreigners of course realised that there was more to France than the surface glitter of Paris and the Riviera. Few of them could understand a country so varied, so divided and so individualistic. Governments changed so frequently that in any other country such a state of affairs would have meant the nation was close to chaos, ungovernable. Yet in everyday life France was a stable country, with a strong currency and well ordered. Monarchial Europe looked askance at republican France with her official trappings derived from the revolution of 1789. Yet France was far more stable than she seemed and by 1914 had achieved a quite remarkable recovery as a great power.

Can we now discern more clearly how government and society functioned in France, something which so clearly mystified contemporaries?

The key to an understanding of this question is that the majority of Frenchmen wished to deny their governments and parliaments the opportunities to govern boldly, to introduce new policies and change the course of French life. France was deeply conservative. What most Frenchmen wanted was that nothing should be done that would radically alter the existing state of affairs in town and country or touch their property and savings. Thus the Republic became the symbol of order, the best guarantee of the *status quo* against those demanding great changes. The monarchist right were now the 'revolutionaries', something they had in common with the extreme left.

One explanation for this innate conservatism is that France did not experience the impact of rapid population growth and rapid industrialisation. For close on half a century from 1866 to 1906 the occupations of the majority of the working population altered only gradually. Whereas in 1866 half the working population was engaged in agriculture,

**Population** (*millions*)

|         | 1880 | 1900 | 1910 |
|---------|------|------|------|
| France  | 37.4 | 38.4 | 39.2 |
| Germany | 45.2 | 56.4 | 64.9 |

**French and German Coal, Iron and Steel Production** (*annual averages*)

|  | 1880–4 | | 1900–4 | | 1910–13 | |
|---|---|---|---|---|---|---|
|  | France | Germany | France | Germany | France | Germany |
| Coal and lignite (*million metric tons*) | 20.2 | 65.7 | 33.0 | 157.5 | 39.9 | 247.5 |
| Pig iron (*thousand metric tons*) | 1,518.0 | 2,893.0 | 2,665.0 | 7,926.0 | 4,664.0 | 14,829.0 |
| Steel (*million metric tons*) | 0.46 | 0.97 | 1.7 | 7.7 | 4.09 | 15.34 |

fisheries and forestry, by 1906 it was still nearly 43 per cent. Employment in industry during the same years scarcely changed at all, from 29 per cent to 30.6 per cent. The tariff protected what was in the main a society of small producers and sellers. In industry small workshops employing less than five people predominated, as did the old-established industrial enterprises of clothing and textiles. But this is not the whole picture. Productivity on the land and in industry rose. New industries such as electricity, chemicals and motorcars developed with considerable success. France possessed large iron reserves in French Lorraine which enabled her to become not only an exporter in iron but also a steel producer. Large works were built at Longwy on the Luxembourg frontier, and the Le Creusot works rivalled Krupps as armament manufacturers. Coal mining in the Pas de Calais developed rapidly in response; but France remained heavily dependent on Britain and Germany for coal imports to cover all her needs. Production figures show that France, with a stable population, was overtaken dramatically as an industrial nation by Germany, whose population increased (see tables). For this reason France's success in maintaining her position in exports and production, judged per head of population, can easily be overlooked.

In one respect – the provision of capital finance for Europe – France won first place, and the large proportion of her total investment overseas which went to Russia between 1890 and 1914 became a major factor in international relations.

The majority of Frenchmen did not wish to face the fact that new problems were arising which required new solutions; they saw the 'defence' of the Republic in terms of combating the political aims of the Church and the army. But in the early twentieth century the growth and concentration of industry and a new militancy among groups of workers also threatened the Republic from the left. The majority groups of the parliamentary lower Chamber were determined to defeat these threats from the extreme right or the left. Political power depended on the management of the elected Chamber; governments came and went, but the legislation prepared by the Chamber provided the necessary continuity. Actual office was confined to a number of leading politicians who reappeared in ministry after ministry. In this scheme of things few Frenchmen cared how many ministries were formed. Their frequency in itself was a healthy obstacle to too much government, for Frenchmen had singularly little faith in their politicians.

There existed side by side with the elected government an administration with an ethos of its own and which had little connection with the demo-cratic roots of government. This centralised administration had been little modified through all the constitutional change since its creation in 1800 by Napoleon. It made the head of state the chief executive, while the prefects were the state's representatives and administrators in each of the ninety geographical departments into which France was divided. They were appointed, and could be transferred or dismissed, by the Ministry of the Interior.

The prefects dealt directly with each ministry and on the whole kept aloof from politics; they were hand-picked administrators who carried out the decrees of the state. Each prefect in his department had his own administration which could be appealed against only by putting the case to the Council of

State in Paris. The prefects were not, of course, elected; they deliberately did not grow local roots but represented, in theory at least, an impersonal justice. They were powerful men who controlled enormous patronage in their department; they could make appointments to many paid posts from archivists to some grades of schoolteachers, tax collectors and small tobacco and post-office staff. They stood at the head of the social hierarchy, and were a guarantee of stability and conservatism. In this way France was at one and the same time both highly centralised but also decentralised; for the ordinary Frenchman 'government' in practice meant what the prefect and his administration did, not what was happening in far-off Paris. France has had the good fortune to attract to this type of higher administrative service, over a long period of time, many capable men.

The Republic stood for the defence of property and a well-ordered, static society. At the same time it was identified in the minds of its supporters as the bastion of the enlightenment and so, curiously, despite their frozen attitude towards the desirability of social change, republicans saw themselves as the people who believed in progress and the modern age. This was only possible because they could identify an 'enemy to progress' in the Church and its teachings. More passion was expended on the question of the proper role of the Church and the state during the first three decades of the Third Republic than on social questions. In every village the secular schoolteacher represented the Republic and led the ranks of the enlightened; the priest led the faithful; the Church demanded liberty to care for the spiritual welfare of Catholics not only in worship but also in education. Republicans decried the influence of the Church as obscurantist and resisted especially its attempts to capture the minds of the rising generation of young Frenchmen.

The Church was supported by the monarchists, most of the old aristocracy and the wealthier sections of society; but 'class' division was by no means so complete and simple as this suggests: the Church supporters were not just the rich and powerful. The peasantry was divided: in the west and Lorraine, they were conservative and supported the Church; elsewhere anti-clericalism was widespread. In the towns, the less well-off middle classes and lower officials were generally fervid in their anti-clericalism. Their demand for a 'separation' of state and Church meant in practice that the Church should lose certain rights, most importantly, its right to separate schools. The Catholic Church in France by supporting the losing monarchial cause was responsible in good part for its own difficulties. In the 1890s the Vatican wisely decided on a change and counselled French Catholics to 'rally' to the Republic and to accept it; but the *ralliement* was rejected by most of the French Catholic bishops and the Church's monarchist supporters. The Dreyfus affair polarised the conflict with the Church, the monarchists and the army on one side and the republicans on the other. Whether one individual Jewish captain was actually guilty or not of the espionage of which he stood accused seemed to matter little when the honour of the army or Republic was at stake.

Dreyfus' cause united all republicans and they triumphed. In May 1902, though the electoral vote was close, the republicans won some 370 seats and the opposition was reduced to 220. There now followed three years of sweeping legislation against the Church. Church schools were closed wholesale; a number of religious orders were banned; in 1904 members of surviving religious orders were banned from teaching. In December 1905 a Law of Separation between Church and state was passed. This law represents both the culmination of republican anti-clericalism and the beginning of a better relationship. Freedom of worship was guaranteed and, despite the opposition of the Vatican, the bitter struggle was gradually brought to a close. Anti-clericalism declined, and the monarchist right lost its last opportunity of enlisting mass support with the help of the Church. Extreme anti-clerical governments were now followed by more moderate republicans in power.

French governments before 1904 remained dependent not on one party but on the support of a number of political groupings in the Chamber; these groups represented the majority of socially conservative voters: the peasants who owned their land, shopkeepers, craftsmen, civil servants and pensioners with small savings. Governments were formed around groups of the centre, sometimes veering more to the 'left' and sometimes to the 'right'. But 'left' in the French parliamentary sense did not mean socialism. Once the predominant groupings of radical republicans had succeeded in defeating the Church, their radicalism was mild indeed. They stood for defending the interests of the peasant land proprietors, the shopkeepers, the less well-off in society; their socialism went no further than wishing to introduce a graduated income tax. The radical republicans were not in fact in the least radical but were 'firmly attached to the principle of private property' and rejected 'the idea of initiating class struggles among our citizens'. Their reforming record down to 1914 was indeed meagre. Even progressive income tax had to wait until 1917 before it became effective.

Socialism developed late but rapidly in France. Jean Jaurès and the more orthodox Marxist, Jules Guesde, led the parliamentary party, which gained 103 deputies and 1 million votes in the elections of 1914. But they never shared power with the parties of the centre for two reasons: the Socialist Party adhered to the line laid down in the International Socialist Congress of 1904 by refusing to co-operate in government with bourgeois parties, and in any case it was excluded by all the anti-socialist groups, which could unite on this one common enmity.

Besides the extreme left, the extreme right was also ranged against the Republic. From the debris of the Dreyfus case there had emerged a small group of writers led by Charles Maurras who formed the Comité de l'Action Française. Under the cloak of being a royalist movement, Maurras' ideas were really typical of some aspects of later fascism; fanatically anti-democratic and anti-parliamentarian, he hated Protestants, Jews, Freemasons and naturalised Frenchmen. An aristocratic elite would rule the country and destroy the socialism of the masses. The Action Française movement could not really appeal to the masses with its openly elitist aims. Yet it appealed to a great variety of supporters. Pius X saw in the movement an ally against the godless Republic; its hatreds attracted the support of the disgruntled, but it did not become a significant political movement before the war of 1914. The Action Française enjoyed notoriety through its daily paper of the same name, distributed by uniformed toughs, the so-called *Camelots du roi*; uninhibited by libel laws, the paper outdid the rest of the press in slander.

Far more significant than right extremists was the revolutionary workers' movement known as syndicalism, which emerged during the early years of the twentieth century. The factory worker had become a significant and growing element of society between 1880 and 1914. The trade unions, or *syndicats*, really got under way in the 1890s. Unlike the parliamentary Socialists, the syndicalists believed that the worker should have no confidence in the parliamentary Republic, which was permanently dominated by the propertied. The unions were brought together in the Confédération Générale du Travail (CGT). By 1906 the CGT firmly adhered to a programme of direct action, of creating the new state not through parliament but by action directly affecting society; its ultimate weapon, its members believed, would be the general strike. They accepted violence also as a justifiable means to bring about the 'social revolution'. The attitude of the CGT had much in common with the British phase of revolutionary trade unionism in the 1830s. Although most workers did not join the syndicalist CGT – only some 7 per cent in 1911 – nevertheless with 700,000 members their impact was considerable; they organised frequent violent strikes which were then ruthlessly put down by the army. The syndicalists declared they would not fight for the Republic and on 27 July 1914 demonstrated against war. Socialism, by being divided as a movement – for syndicalists rejected any community of interest with parliamentary Socialists – was much weakened in France. The result was a deep alienation of a large group of working men from the Third Republic. The defence of the fatherland, the almost unanimous patriotism in 1914 against the common enemy, was to mask this alienation for a time.

The assertiveness of France in the wider world stands in remarkable contrast to the conservatism of French society at home. The national humiliation and defeat at German hands in the war of 1870–1 did not turn France in on herself; the growing disparity between French and German power after 1870, whether looked at in terms of population or industrial production, did not, as might be expected, inhibit France's efforts abroad.

During the Bismarckian years from 1871 to 1890, France was isolated in Europe by the Iron Chancellor's diplomacy. Even so, a sense of security began to return. The rest of Europe was not likely again to stand by idly if Germany chose to attack France once more. To protect themselves against the danger of a German hegemony in Europe the other powers would seek to check Germany. French weakness thus gave to France paradoxically a certain international strength. But every French leader also knew that France could only count on help if she were the victim of aggression; no ally would ever be willing to risk war with Germany merely in order to help France recover the lost territories of Alsace-Lorraine. The cry for *revanche* was a stance, a sentiment, and in any case grew gradually weaker; it never became the basis of practical policies.

The choice confronting France towards the end of the nineteenth century was clear. A policy of reconciliation and trust in imperial Germany could have been followed. This would have been based on the fact that Germany had not exploited her superior strength for twenty-five years to foist another ruinous war on France. Alternatively, France could follow a deterrent policy. Unable ever to be strong enough to match Germany alone, she could with the help of an ally contain her by making the chances of success for Germany in war much more hazardous. This was the policy generally followed by the governments of the Third Republic after 1890. They first sought an alliance with tsarist Russia, and after its conclusion in 1894 made its maintenance the bedrock of French foreign policy. The alliance made it possible for France to continue to conduct policy as a great power despite her relative inferiority in population and production. Reliance on good relations with Germany would have made her dependent on her goodwill, a weaker and in the end junior partner as long as relationships were seen purely in terms of national power.

The path to the alliance with Russia was smoothed by the large loans raised on the Paris money market which Russia needed for her industrial and military development. From close on 3000 million francs in 1890 they rose to 12,400 million francs in 1914, representing between a third and a quarter of the total of France's foreign investments.

At the heart of the Franco-Russian alliance lay the military convention, concluded in 1892 and ratified in 1894. This stated that if France were attacked by Germany or by Italy supported by Germany, then Russia would attack Germany with all her forces; and that if Russia were attacked by Germany, or by Austria supported by Germany, then France would fight Germany with all her forces (Article 1). That was a clear though strictly defined and limited defensive-alliance commitment for both sides against a German attack. Of equal practical importance was the second article, on mobilisation, because mobilisation in conditions of modern warfare leads almost inevitably to war. According to this article, if any one of the Triple Alliance powers mobilised, that is Italy, Austria or Germany,

then France and Russia would immediately mobilise. The practical consequences of the first and second article did not coincide. The French realised that the second article might very well undo the careful limitation (restricting the contingency to conflict with Germany) of the first. Under the first article France was not committed to go to war if Austria and Russia alone fought; but under the second article she was bound to mobilise if Austria did so, and this mobilisation would lead to German mobilisation and in this way to certain war between France and Germany. Thus in practice France could become involved in war with Germany over an Austro-Russian quarrel. Both sides had grave misgivings that the alliance would either prove worthless or drag one side into war over the national ambition of the other. Yet there was one common interest: fear of having to face Germany in isolation.

In other respects Russian and French ambitions did not coincide. Russia had her eyes on the Balkans, the Middle East and China, the French on Africa and the Mediterranean. Russia's rivals were Japan, Austria and Britain and France's rivals in different regions of the world were Britain and Italy for a time, then Germany over Morocco. Before 1912 neither Russia nor France was in the slightest interested in engaging in a great European war of life and death merely as a consequence of the other power's expansionist desires in the Balkans or Morocco. Before 1912 the French invariably advised the Russians to exercise caution and warned them against the use of the alliance to push national regional interests. The Russians for their part gave exactly the same advice. This happened when the French asked for and failed to secure Russian support against Britain in the 1890s and Germany in 1905 and 1911; the Russians similarly got no help from France in Asia in 1904 and 1905 or in the Balkans during the Bosnian crisis in 1909 (page 59).

What then kept the alliance alive despite these setbacks? It was the threat which was felt both in Russia and France of imperial Germany's growing might and the fear that Germany with her ally Austria–Hungary was seeking continental hegemony.

It is a remarkable fact that France's relative weakness on the European continent before 1914 did not throw her whole diplomacy on the defensive. On the contrary, successive French governments followed well-thought-out expansionist aims overseas and, to the bafflement of their German neighbours, refused to be intimidated. Only the threat of war led them to draw back when clashing with Britain in 1898 at Fashoda over control of the Sudan and the Upper Nile. But French colonial policy had enormously extended the French Empire from the 1880s to the turn of the century: in West Africa, in North Africa (where Tunis was added to Algeria) and in eastern Asia in Indo-China. This policy drew for support on no popular enthusiasm. Colonies excited few Frenchmen. It was the work of but a small number of politicians, explorers and soldiers. But when in consequence of colonial expansion there occurred a clash with a European neighbour, then ardent patriotism would sweep through the country. Until 1903 this animosity was directed far more against Britain, which blocked French imperial ambitions, than against Germany. During the Boer War (1899–1902) no country exceeded France in expressions of popular hatred of Britain.

Then in 1905 occurred an extraordinary and unanticipated change. Germany suddenly loomed large as the obstacle to French colonial ambitions and Britain became the friend. This was partly accidental and partly a deliberate result of French and German policies. The French were determined to gain control of Morocco, which would round off her large African empire stretching from Tunisia and Algeria through the Saharan desert hinterland to French West Africa. In April 1904 the French Foreign Minister, Théophile Delcassé, reached a comprehensive settlement with Britain over rival colonial interests all over the world. The main purpose was to gain Britain's consent to French predominance in Morocco, in return for which France would cease to make difficulties for Britain as the occupying power of Egypt.

The only two major international crises France faced after the agreement with Britain were due to French attempts to make good that bargain. The Germans, who also had treaty rights, had been left in the cold. Belatedly, in 1905, they reacted with a visit to Tangier by the Kaiser, emphasising dramatically Germany's interests in the future of the Sultan's dominions. What was really at issue for the Germans, however, was not the future of Morocco but France's new international position. France had escaped from the Bismarckian shackles of isolation, first by concluding an alliance with Russia in 1894 and now by reaching agreement with Britain and establishing the *entente cordiale*. To the Germans it seemed that their position of strength was an illusion and that the tables were being turned on Germany herself, now threatened with isolation and 'encirclement'. They used the Moroccan issue in 1905 and again in 1911 to attempt to tear asunder the alliances and alignments France had constructed.

The Germans in 1905 timed their diplomatic strike extremely well. With Russia fully engaged in an unsuccessful war in China, and her navy annihilated by the Japanese, the Russians were in no condition to provide any military support to France. The French military staff had always recognised that because of Russia's slower mobilisation, the German armies would all be hurled against France at the outset of the war. This was in fact the essence of the Schlieffen Plan, which sought to meet the dangers for Germany of a two-front war by defeating France before Russia could be ready to advance in the east. So, conversely, from the French point of view the vital importance of Russia's military role would be to strike against Germany as soon as possible after the outbreak of war and thus relieve the outnumbered French. In 1901 the Russian General Staff had promised to begin their offensive even before they were fully mobilised, on the eighteenth day after the outbreak of war.

It was clear to the French in 1905 that the Russians could no longer fulfil this commitment. A year later the Russian General Staff formally confirmed this. The new entente partner, Britain, was no substitute for Russia. The British refused a formal alliance commitment and warned the French right down to 1914 that they could not count on British military support. Even if British support did materialise it would be confined to 100,000 men. Until Russia had recovered sufficiently to resume her military commitment to France in 1912, France found herself in a position of desperate military inferiority. Yet this fact did not alter her basic policy in Morocco.

The French appeared to give way in 1905. The Germans demanded the removal of the architect of the Moroccan policy, Foreign Minister Delcassé; the French government obliged by forcing him to resign. The French also agreed to a conference to be held at Algeciras in 1906. But when the powers assembled at the conference, France's special position in Morocco was recognised by the majority of powers, whose support had been secured by Delcassé's earlier diplomacy. Similarly in 1911 during the second Moroccan crisis Germany failed in her main objective. France's alliance and alignments held. Again France showed her willingness to acknowledge German claims by ceding other colonial French territory to the Germans in compensation. But she secured Morocco. Britain, alarmed by Germany's bellicosity, also drew closer to France. But the Kaiser did not in 1905 or in 1911 press German policy to the point of war.

The following year in 1912 Raymond Poincaré, a tough nationalist, impeccable republican, orthodox anti-clerical and conservative in social questions, became premier, and subsequently president in 1913. Army appropriations were increased; even so in 1913 the French army of 540,000 would be facing a German army of 850,000 if war should break out – a catastrophic prospect. To reduce this gap a bill lengthening service in the French army from two to three years became law in 1913. The French Chamber had turned away from the left Socialists, and the army became more respectable in the eyes of the leading politicians in power, as it had proved a valuable and reliable instrument in crushing strikes and revolutionary syndicalism. Poincaré was determined that France should never find herself at the mercy of Germany. A strong alliance with Russia became the most cherished objective of his diplomacy. So he reversed earlier French policy and assured the Russians in 1912 that they could count on French support if their Balkan policy led to conflict with Austria–Hungary; if Germany then supported her ally, France would come to the aid of Russia. This was a most significant new interpretation and extension of the original Franco-Russian alliance of 1894; it ceased to be wholly defensive. Poincaré also encouraged the Russians to reach naval agreements with the British.

Against the growing power of Germany Poincaré saw that France was faced with a grim choice: either to abandon her status as a great power and to give in to German demands (the manner of their presentation had been amply demonstrated during the Moroccan crisis of 1911); or to strengthen her own forces and draw as close as she could to her Russian ally (even at the risk of being sucked into war by purely Russian Balkan interests) and to the British entente partner. In staff conversations the Russians in 1912 agreed to resume their offensive military role and to start their attack on East Prussia on the fifteenth day of mobilisation. France had come through her years of 'risk' giving up very little. The other side of the coin is that imperial Germany had not exploited her military superiority during the years from 1905 to 1911 by launching a so-called 'preventive' war.

The years from 1912 to 1914 marked a vital change. Fatalism about the inevitability of war was spreading among those who controlled policy, and ever larger armies were being trained for this eventuality on all sides of the continent. With Poincaré as France's president, Russia would not again be left in the lurch by her ally whenever Russia judged her vital interest to be at stake in the Balkans and the Ottoman Empire. But French diplomacy conflicted increasingly with public sentiment. There was strong domestic opposition to strengthening the army; foreign dangers, the left believed, were being deliberately exaggerated by the right. On the very eve of war in 1914, the French elections gave the majority to the pacifist groups of the left. But it was too late. Poincaré's support for Russia did not waver during the critical final days before the outbreak of war and was a crucial factor in the decision the Tsar and his ministers took to mobilise, which made war inevitable in 1914.

# CHAPTER 4

# Italy: Aspirations to Power

What happens when a parliamentary constitution is imposed on an underdeveloped society? The answer is not without relevance to conditions in the Third World in the twentieth century. Italy provides an interesting early case history. In population size Italy, Austria–Hungary France and Britain belong to the same group of larger European nations; but the differences between their development and power are striking. The greater part of Italy, especially the south, was in the late nineteenth century among the poorest and most backward regions of Europe. But her rulers in the north imposed parliamentary constitutional government on the whole of Italy, over the more developed as well as the undeveloped regions. Furthermore, a highly centralised administration was devised dividing the whole country into sixty-nine provinces, each governed by a prefect responsible to the minister of the interior.

Parliamentary institutions suited well enough the north-western region of Italy, formerly the kingdom of Piedmont, the most advanced region of Italy, where parliamentary government had taken root before unification. The problem arose when the Piedmontese parliamentary system was extended to the whole of Italy in 1861; it was now intended to cover the very different traditions and societies of the former city states, the papal domains and the Neapolitan kingdom. It was a unity imposed from above. For many decades 'unity' existed more on paper than in reality. Italy had the appearance of a Western European parliamentary state.

A closer look at the Italian parliament shows how very different it was from Britain's. To begin with, only a very small proportion, 2 per cent, of Italians were granted the vote. This was gradually extended until in 1912 manhood suffrage was introduced. But in the intervening half-century, the small electorate had led to the management of parliament by government; a few strong men dominated successive administrations. There were no great political parties held together by common principles and beliefs, just numerous groups of deputies. The dominating national leaders contrived parliamentary majorities by striking bargains with political groups, by bribes of office or by the promise of local benefits. When a government fell, the same leaders would strike new bargains and achieve power by a slight shuffling of political groupings.

In such a set-up, parliamentary deputies came to represent not so much parties as local interests; their business was to secure benefits for their electors. Politicians skilled in political deals dominated the oligarchic parliamentary system from 1860 to 1914. (In the early twentieth century Giovanni Giolitti became the leading politician.) These leaders can be condemned for their undeniable political corruption as well as for undermining the principles of constitutional parliamentary and, eventually, democratic government. The ordinary voter could scarcely be aroused in defence of parliament which seemed to assemble only for the benefit of politicians and special-interest groups.

On the other hand the particular conditions of

recently united Italy have to be taken into account. It had a strong tradition of local loyalties. Central government was regarded as an alien force. The difficulty of building bridges between the political oligarchy of those who ruled and the mass of the people was great. Outside Piedmont there was little tradition of constitutional parliamentary government of any sort. At the time of unification three-quarters of the population could neither read nor write. The poverty of southern and central Italy was in great contrast to the progress of the north. And the enmity of the papacy, which had lost its temporal dominion, meant that Catholics obedient to the pope were alienated from the state and would not participate in elections. In a country so rent by faction and regional rivalry as well as so backward, it can be argued that the firm establishment of unity and the solid progress achieved represented in themselves a notable success. The franchise was extended, and illiteracy greatly reduced so that by 1911 almost two-thirds of the population could read and write; in the south the proportion of literate to illiterate was reversed.

Politics cannot be divorced from society and poverty. Compared to France and Britain, Italy was a poor country; the greater part of Italy, especially the south, was caught in the poverty trap of a backward agrarian economy. A larger proportion of the population remained dependent on agriculture right down to the First World War than in any other Western European country, including France. Some agricultural progress was achieved as landowners and peasants turned to exporting olive oil, fruit and wine, but protection against the influx of low-cost wheat from the Americas benefited principally the great landowners of the south, while high food costs bore most heavily on the poorest landless labourers. The masses of the south were exploited in the interests of the north. Deforestation, exhaustion of the soil and soil erosion, taxation and overpopulation forced some of the peasantry to emigrate in search of a less harsh life elsewhere in Europe or across the Atlantic. During every year of the 1890s, on average 280,000 people left Italy, rather more than half this number to go overseas; this human stream rose to 600,000 a year in the first decade of the twentieth century and reached 873,000 in 1913, by which time about two-thirds went overseas, principally to the United States. No European state suffered so great an exodus of its population in the early twentieth century. By 1927,

the Italian government calculated there were more than 9 million Italians living abroad, where they formed concentrated communities: among them, half a million in New York, 3.5 million in the United States as a whole, 1.5 million in the Argentine and 1.5 million in Brazil.

The alliance between northern industry and the large and frequently absentee landowners growing wheat in the south impoverished the mass of the peasantry: protected by a high tariff, these landowners were able to farm large tracts of land inefficiently and wastefully without penalty; unlike in France, no class of peasant proprietors, each with his own plot of land, would emerge. Almost half the peasants had no land at all; many more held land inadequate even for bare subsistence.

By the turn of the century, there was a growing recognition that there was a 'southern question' and that the policies of United Italy had been devised to suit the conditions of the north; special state intervention would be necessary to help the south. In December 1903 Giolitti, when prime minister, expressed the will of the government to act: 'To raise the economic conditions of the southern provinces is not only a political necessity, but a national duty,' he declared in parliament. Genuine efforts were made by legislation to stimulate industrial development in the Naples region, to improve agriculture and reform taxation, build railways and roads, improve the supply of clean water and, above all, to wage a successful campaign against the scourge of malaria. But too little was done to improve the wealth of the peasants and to increase peasant proprietorship; the middle class was small and, in the absence of industry, mainly confined to administration and the professions. Government help on the economic front was but a drop in the ocean of widespread poverty and backwardness. Despite the undoubted progress, the gap between the north and south continued to widen. Little would be achieved until after the Second World War, but even in the last quarter of the twentieth century the problem of the south persists.

Italian industrialisation was handicapped by the lack of those indigenous resources on which the industrialisation of Britain, France and Germany was based: the amount of coal in Italy was negligible and there was little iron ore. But helped by protection (since 1887), Italian industry developed in the north. The first decade of the twentieth century was (apart from the brief depression of 1907 to

1908) a period of exceptionally fast growth, overcoming the depression of the 1890s. Textile production, led by silk, rapidly expanded in Piedmont and Lombardy and dominated exports. Large quantities of coal had to be imported but as a source of energy coal was supplemented by the exploitation of hydroelectrical power, in which large sums were invested. Italy also entered into the 'steel age', building up her steel production to close on a million metric tons by the eve of the First World War, a quantity five times as large as in the 1890s. A start was made, too, in promising new twentieth-century industries in typewriters (Olivetti), cars (Fiat), bicycles and motorcycles. A chemical industry producing fertilisers rapidly developed. State aid, in the form of special legislation aiding shipbuilding or by stimulating demand through railway construction and through tariff protection, contributed to this spurt of industrialisation in the early twentieth century. The banks provided investment funds; the help of tourist income and the money sent back by Italians abroad enabled a greater investment to be made than was earned by the industrial and agricultural production of the country.

### Population (millions)

|  | 1900 | 1910 |
| --- | --- | --- |
| Italy | 32.4 | 34.7 |
| France | 38.4 | 39.2 |

**Italian Production** (annual averages)

|  |  | Italy | France |
| --- | --- | --- | --- |
| Raw-cotton consumption (thousand metric tons) | 1895–1904 | 125.7 | 174.0 |
|  | 1905–13 | 186.0 | 231.0 |
| Raw-silk output (thousand metric tons) | 1895–1904 | 53.6 | 7.9 |
|  | 1905–13 | 43.5 | 6.8 |
| Pig-iron output (thousand metric tons) | 1900–4 | 47.0 | 2,665.0 |
|  | 1910–13 | 366.0 | 4,664.0 |
| Steel output (million metric tons) | 1900–4 | 0.15 | 1.7 |
|  | 1910–13 | 0.83 | 4.09 |
| Electric-energy output (million kilowatt hours) | 1901 | 220.0 | 340.0 |
|  | 1913 | 2,200.0 | 1,800.0 |

But a weakness of Italy's industrialisation was its concentration in three north-western regions, Piedmont (Turin), Lombardy (Milan) and Liguria (Genoa), thus widening further the gap between administrative political unification and industrial economic unification.

The growth of industry in the north led, as elsewhere in Europe, to new social tensions as factory workers sought to better their lot or simply to protest at conditions in the new industrial centres. During the depression of 1897 and 1898 riots spread throughout Italy, culminating in violence and strikes in Milan. They were met by fierce government repression. But the year 1900 saw a new start, a much more promising trend towards conciliation. The Socialist Party was prepared to collaborate with the Liberal parliamentarians and accept the monarchy and constitution in order to achieve some measure of practical reform. This was the lesson they learnt from the failure of the recent violence in Milan. Giolitti, who became prime minister for the second time in 1903, saw the involvement of the masses in politics as inevitable and so sought to work with the new forces of socialism and to tame them in political combinations. But he looked beyond this to genuine social and fiscal reforms.

The rise of socialism in the 1890s had one beneficial result for the embattled state. It alarmed the Church and led to a revision of the papal interdiction against such activities as participation in government and parliamentary elections. The temporal rights of the Church – the 'occupation' of Rome – were becoming a question of history rather than one of practical politics. Pope Leo XIII expressed the Church's concern for the poor and urged social reform as a better alternative to repressive conservativism on the one hand and atheistic socialism on the other. The Church was coming to terms with twentieth-century society. His successor, Pope Pius X, though more conservative, in 1904 permitted Catholics to vote wherever Socialists might otherwise be elected. This marked the cautious beginning of collaboration between Church and state, and a beginning too in creating a Catholic political force (Christian Democrat) to keep the Socialists out of power in collaboration with other groups.

Catholic support was welcome to Giolitti. His progressive social views did not mean he wished to allow Socialists a decisive voice in government.

From 1903 onwards the Socialists were split into violently hostile factions: a minority, the reformists, were still ready to collaborate within the constitutional framework and to work for practical reform; the majority, the syndicalists, were intent on class revolution to be achieved by direct action and violence through syndicates or trade unions. The weapon which they hoped would overthrow capitalist society was the general strike. The split into reformist socialists, revolutionary socialists and syndicalists further weakened the Socialists, faced in the new century with the overwhelmingly difficult task of changing a well-entrenched capitalist state. The great strikes of 1904, 1907 and 1908 were defeated, the Socialist Party in parliament was small, the forces of law and order strong; a Catholic labour movement, too, successfully diverted a minority of peasants and industrial workers from socialist trade unions.

The absence of strong parties and the commanding position established by a few politicians were the most noteworthy characteristics of Italian political life before the First World War. The Catholic political group was embryonic, unlike those in neighbouring France and Germany. Italian socialism could not overcome the handicap of the fierce factional struggles which characterised the emergence of socialism in Europe. Regionalism, the Church and the backwardness of much of the country also prevented the development of a broadly based conservative party. So government was dominated by the 'liberal' groupings of the centre, agreeing only on the maintenance of law, order and national unity, and bound by a common opposition to conservative extremism and revolutionary socialism. Were these characteristics of Italian political life the inevitable consequence of this stage of uneven national development, of the continuing regional particularism of a sharply differentiated society and of a limited franchise? Or should the arrested form of parliamentary government be regarded as forming the roots of the later fascist dictatorship and the corporate state? It is not helpful to look upon Giolitti as a precursor of Benito Mussolini. The two men and their policies must be examined in the context of the conditions of their own times. The shattering experience of the First World War separated two eras of modern Italian history, Giolitti's from Mussolini's.

Giolitti was a politician of consummate skill in parliamentary bargaining. He followed broad and consistent aims. The first was to master the whirlpool of factions and to reconcile the broad masses of workers and peasants with the state, to accept the upsurge of mass involvement in politics and industrial life and to channel it away from revolution to constructive co-operation. 'Let no one delude himself that he can prevent the popular classes from conquering their share of political and economic influence,' he declared in a remarkable parliamentary speech in 1901. He clearly accepted the challenge and saw it as the principal task of those who ruled to ensure that this great new force should be harnessed to contribute to national prosperity and greatness. He was not prepared to accept revolutionary violence, yet repression, he recognised, would only lead to unnecessary bloodshed, create martyrs and alienate the working man.

Giolitti utilised the revulsion against the strikes of 1904 to increase his parliamentary support by calling for a new election which he fought on a moderate platform. His tactics succeeded and he never, down to 1914, lost the majority of support he then gained. But this support was based as much on the personal loyalty and dependence on political favours of individual deputies as on agreement with any broad declaration of policy. His management of parliament (and the electoral corruption) undeniably diminished its standing and importance.

Enjoying the support of King Victor Emmanuel III, Giolitti's power was virtually unfettered for a decade. He used it to administer the country efficiently, to provide the stability which enabled Italy in the favourable world economic conditions to make progress and modernise her industry. His concern for the south was genuine, and state help pointed the way. In order to preserve the state, Giolitti appeased the left and claimed to be a conservative. His most startling move towards the politics of the masses, away from those of privilege, was to introduce a bill in 1911 to extend the electorate to all males. The bill became law in 1912. It was not so much the new extension of the franchise which undermined Giolitti's hold over his parliamentary majority: he secured the return of a large majority in the new parliament of 1913. What transformed Italian politics was the unleashing of ardent nationalism by the war with Turkey in 1911 which Giolitti had started in quite a different spirit of cool calculation.

*

It was Italy's misfortune to be diverted in the twentieth century from the path of highly necessary internal development to a policy of nationalism and aggressive imperialism. Italy lacked the resources and strength for an expansionist foreign policy. But for her own ambitions, Italy could have remained as neutral as Switzerland.

Italy was favoured by her geographical position in that she did not lie in the path of the hostile European states confronting each other. Luckily for Italy, her military forces represented to her neighbours a 'second front' which they were most anxious to avoid opening while facing their main enemy elsewhere. However little love they had for Italy, they were therefore anxious to preserve Italian neutrality and even willing to purchase her benevolence with territorial rewards. Thus the diplomatic tensions and divisions of Europe were extraordinarily favourable to Italy's security, which her own military strength could not have ensured.

One of the most virulent forms of nationalism is that known as 'irredentism', the demand to bring within the nation areas outside the national frontier inhabited by people speaking the same language. There were two such regions adjoining the northern Italian frontier: Trentino and Trieste. Both were retained by Austria–Hungary after the war with Italy in 1866. A third area, Nice and Savoy, which had been ceded to France in return for French help in the war of unification, also became the target of irredentist clamour. Besides this irredentism, Italian leaders also wished to participate in the fever of European imperialism. Surrounded on three sides by the sea, Italians looked south across the Mediterranean to the North Africa shore where lay the semi-autonomous Turkish territories of Tunis and Tripolis and perceived them as a natural area of colonial expansion. They saw to the west the island of Corsica, now French, but once a dependency of Genoa; to the east, across the Adriatic, the Ottoman Empire was the weakening ruler of heterogeneous Balkan peoples.

All these possibilities for expansion presented Italian governments with choices as to which neighbours would be friends and which enemies. Italian foreign policy from 1878 to 1915 is really the story of Rome's manoeuvres between the powers to secure the particular prize or objective of the moment. It is this national 'egoism' which gives Italian policy the appearance of faithlessness and inconsistency. But it would be facile to make the moral judgement that Italian nationalism was either better or worse than that of the other European powers. What can be said with certainty is that it served Italian interests ill, but then it would have required vision and statesmanship of the highest order to have resisted the imperialist urge which swept over all the European powers.

The French occupation of Tunis in 1881 brought Italy a year later into the Austro-German alliance group, and a Triple Alliance was concluded in 1882. Italy remained a formal member of this alliance down to the First World War, but it helped her achieve her territorial ambitions hardly at all. At the turn of the century she made further agreements with France and Britain whereby the spheres of interest along the North African coast were divided. The 'tariff war' between France and Italy ended. Meanwhile Italy had established a protectorate in east Africa and dreamt of conquering Abyssinia. These ambitions were checked in a most humiliating way when the Abyssinians, the 'natives', defeated an Italian force at the battle of Adowa in 1896. The Italians, however, did not lose their appetite for influence and empire. Austria–Hungary's annexation of Bosnia in 1908 stimulated the Italians to search for compensation in the far-flung and loosely controlled Ottoman Empire. But the terrible Messina earthquake in December 1908 riveted national attention on Sicily for a while.

The Italians did not wait very long, however. The Moroccan crisis of 1911 between France and Germany pointed to the North African coast as a region where the Europeans would complete their colonisation soon. Perhaps, some Italians feared, the Germans foiled in Morocco would descend on Tripoli instead. Giolitti's 'imperialism' was much more opportunist. He was more interested in the effect which the agitation for colonial expansion had on his domestic position than in imperialism as such. He regarded the nationalists as just another group to be appeased at home, another group to be brought into his broad parliamentary front of supporters. When he assessed the international situation in 1911 he concluded that Italy would get away with the seizure of Tripoli. His domestic hold on power would be much strengthened by a successful little war.

In October 1911 the Italians, after declaring war on Turkey, landed troops in Tripoli. A month later Giolitti announced the annexation of Libya. But the Turks refused to give in. The Italians now escalated the war, attacking in April 1912 the Dardanelles and occupying a number of Aegean islands. By October 1912 the Turks had had enough and the war ended.

The consequences of the war were, however, far from over. As peace was signed, Montenegro, Serbia, Bulgaria and Greece began a new war, the first Balkan war, attacking Turkey. Italy's policy cannot be said to have caused the Balkan wars but her success, and Turkey's proven isolation, had certainly encouraged the Balkan states. Setting the Balkans alight was the last thing Giolitti wanted, yet that is what occurred. Just as serious were the reactions at home. Giolitti desired only limited expansion, but a reversion to a cautious pacific policy had been difficult. The nationalists thirsted for more colonies, more territory. And so it came about that Giolitti had unleashed a political force more powerful than he could control.

# CHAPTER 5

# The British Empire: Premonitions of Decline

At the height of her imperial greatness, there is discernible in the Edwardian Britain of the early twentieth century a new mood of uncertainty, even of apprehension about the future. Why should this be so?

British society had shown itself remarkably successful in adapting to new conditions brought about by the industrial revolution. The inevitable social changes were taking place without violence. Britain had passed peacefully through some two decades of difficult economic conditions. The apprehensive mood was related more to her future role in the world. On the face of it the British Empire was the most powerful in the world: the navy 'ruled the waves'; Britain's wealth was matched by no other European state; a war in South Africa had been brought to a successful end in 1902, though it had not enhanced Britain's military reputation. Superficially the Edwardian age was elegant and opulent, the King giving a lead to fashionable society and doing little else, despite the myth about his influence on affairs of state. But it was obvious that in the years to come Britain would face great changes.

The effects of trade on British industry were widely discussed. It was argued that British industrial management was not good enough. If British industrialists did not wake up, authors of books like *Made in Germany* (1896) and the *American Invaders* (1902) warned, Britain would be overtaken and become a second-rate industrial power.

People feared another depression and rightly sensed that British industry was lagging behind that of the United States and Germany. This can indeed be seen in the comparative growth in value of manufactured exports of the world's three leading industrial nations.

Britain's economic performance during the years from 1900 to 1914 showed several weaknesses. The 'first' industrial revolution was spreading to the less developed world. A textile industry was being built up in Japan and India. But Britain continued to rely on a few traditional industries such as cotton textiles, which for a time continued to grow strongly because of worldwide demand. Then the coal industry, employing more than a million men in 1914, still dominated the world's coal export trade due to the fortunate fact that British coal mines were close to the sea, making possible cheap transportation to other parts of the world. Together with iron and steel, coal and textiles accounted for the greater

**Value of Exports** (*US$ millions, 1913 prices*)

|  | 1899 | | 1913 | |
|---|---|---|---|---|
|  | Manu-factures | All exports | Manu-factures | All exports |
| Britain | 479 | 912 | 624 | 969 |
| Germany | 437 | 691 | 925 | 1285 |
| United States | 272 | 1366 | 535 | 1850 |

part of Britain's exports. After 1900 British exporters found increasing difficulty in competing with Germany and the United States in the developing industrial countries. At home, foreign manufacturers invaded the British market. The speed of the American and German growth of production is very striking. This success was partly due to the increasing disparity between Britain's, Germany's and America's populations.

**Population** (*millions*)

|               | 1880 | 1900 | 1910 | 1920  | 1930  |
|---------------|------|------|------|-------|-------|
| Britain*      | 35.6 | 44.3 | 45   | 46.9  | 45.8  |
| Germany       | 45.2 | 56.4 | 64.9 | 59.2  | 64.3  |
| United States | 50.2 | 89.4 | 92.0 | 118.1 | 138.4 |

* Including Ireland and Northern Ireland respectively.

The story these statistics told was one people felt in their bones. Of course it would be mistaken to believe that Britain and her industry was set on an inevitable course of rapid decline. There were successful 'new' industries of the 'second' industrial revolution, such as the chemical and electrical industry. Britain was still in 1914 immensely strong and wealthy because of the continuing expansion of her traditional textile industry and large coal reserves, the world dominance of her mercantile marine, her investment income from overseas and the reputation of the insurance and banking institutions which made the City of London the financial centre of the world. But there was already in 1900 a doubt as to whether Britain would move sufficiently fast in changing conditions to maintain her leading industrial place in the world.

Then industrialists felt doubts about the continuing co-operation of labour. The trade union movement had revealed a new militancy which posed a threat to industrial peace. The movement was no longer dominated by the skilled artisans sharing the values of the Victorian middle class. The new unions of the poor working men formed in the last two decades of the nineteenth century looked to the state for decisive support, for a redistribution of wealth.

The Labour political movement also emerged during the last decade of the nineteenth century, though the ultimate break between 'Liberal' and 'Labour' politics did not take place until after the First World War. In 1900 the trade union movement became convinced that involvement in parliamentary politics was now necessary if the working man was to improve his standard of life. The Labour Representation Committee, embracing a broad alliance of socialist parties and trade unions, was formed in 1900. In the election later that year two Labour candidates succeeded in winning seats in the House of Commons. The founders of the Labour movement were practical men who realised that in the foreseeable future Labour members would be in a minority. They resolved accordingly that they would co-operate with any party ready to help labour. In Britain, the Labour Party was prepared to work within the parliamentary system, and turned its back on revolution and violence. In turn it became accepted, and enjoyed the same freedom as other political parties.

The Conservatives, who were in power until the close of 1905, followed cautious social–political policies. A state system of primary and secondary schools was introduced, partly because of the belief that it was their better educational provisions that were enabling America and Germany to overtake Britain in industrial efficiency. When the Liberals came to power in 1906 their attitude to social and economic reforms was equally half-hearted, much of the party still believing in self-help and a minimum of state paternalism. The surprise of the new Parliament of 1906 was the election of fifty-three Labour members, though that number owed much to an electoral arrangement with the Liberals. Among this Labour group were a few genuine socialists, such as Keir Hardie and Ramsay MacDonald, who had nothing in common with the Liberals; but other Labour members were less interested in socialism than in securing legislation to benefit the working men – for example the Trade Disputes Bill which protected union funds from employers' claims for compensation after strikes.

In 1908 Herbert Asquith succeeded to the premiership. In the same year, one of the few major reforms was introduced – old-age pensions, which removed fear of the workhouse from the aged. The famous budget of 1909, however, sparked off a political crisis. Introduced by the Liberal chancellor of the Exchequer, David Lloyd George, it increased indirect taxes on spirits and tobacco – which was unpopular with the poor – but also modestly increased the burdens on the better-off. The House of Lords – quite unjustly – sensed in these measures the thin edge of the wedge that would destroy their privileges. The Liberals pressed the issue of constitutional reform as a means of reviving the party's popularity in the country. The power of the Conservative-dominated House of Lords to veto bills passed by the Liberal majority in the Commons was to be curtailed so that within the life of one Parliament the House of Commons majority would prevail.

An impasse was reached in Britain's political life, not dissimilar from that in imperial Germany at about the same time. Should the conservative hereditary lords have the power to block even the mild reforming legislation of an elected Liberal majority? Unlike in Germany, the constitutional turmoil was resolved. In November 1909 the House of Lords threw out the budget with the intention of submitting the issue to the electorate. This readiness by government and Parliament to accept the wishes of the people on the one hand and

the constitutional monarch's acceptance of the same verdict (though George V did insist unnecessarily on *two* elections) on the other was the essential difference between imperial Germany and Britain. The Liberal tactic of taking the constitutional issue to the country misfired. They lost their overall majority and now ran neck and neck with the Conservatives. By the close of the second election in December 1910, each party had precisely the same strength in the House of Commons. But the Liberals, supported by Labour members and the Irish Nationalists, commanded a substantial majority over the Conservatives. The House of Lords in the summer of 1911 gave their assent to the bill limiting their powers. No social upheaval threatening the influence of wealth and property followed. But common sense, and a respect for the wishes of the majority of the House of Commons on which parliamentary constitutional government was based, prevailed. Britain would continue to follow the political and social path of evolution, not revolution.

*A suffragette demonstration in Britain, May 1913. As is evident here, the movement often brought sexes and social classes together in common cause.*

A National Insurance Bill of 1911 covered most workers against ill health, but only those in the cyclical building and engineering trades against unemployment. What Liberal policies did not do was to satisfy the working man who resented paying (with employers) compulsorily for national insurance and whose real wage in the recent years had not risen. The years 1911 and 1912 witnessed an unprecedented number of strikes and an increase in the power of the trade unions. The Liberal Party did not win the support of organised industrial labour. Nor did it seize the chance to earn the gratitude of potential women voters by granting their enfranchisement. The Liberals, for all Lloyd George's dash and clamour as chancellor of the Exchequer, were simply not ready to embark on bold social policies.

Many prominent British politicians believed that the future safety and prosperity of Britain depended on revitalising and drawing together the strength of the empire. Only in this way, they thought, could Britain hope to face the other great powers on an equal footing. But the questions were also asked: Will the empire last? Does it rest on permanent foundations or is it only a political organism in a certain state of decomposition? Will the younger nations, as they grow to maturity, be content to remain within it, or will they go the way of the American Colonies before them . . . ?

The 400 million peoples of the British Empire had reached different stages of advancement to independence by the close of the nineteenth century. The division of the empire was largely on racial lines. The white people of the empire, where they predominated or even formed a significant minority of the country, were granted 'self-government', only a step short of total independence. In practice, 'self-government' was brought about by applying the pattern of British parliamentary government to these countries; this, together with a federal structure, created the Dominions: Canada in 1867, New Zealand in 1876, the Commonwealth of Australia in 1901 and, in 1909, seven years after the conclusion of the bitter Boer War, the Union of South Africa. The responsibility to protect the 'native' inhabitants of lands conquered and colonised by Europeans was recognised by Britain. But little that was effective was done by the imperial government in London. Indians in Canada, Maoris in New Zealand and Aborigines in Australia were largely left to struggle alone for their rights. In southern Africa, the black Africans formed the majority of the inhabitants but democratic rights were denied them and they were left to the control of the white peoples. British governments in London were not prepared to jeopardise their relations with the white ruling inhabitants. Racial discrimination was a grievous flaw in the British Empire, though a paternalistic concern for the 'natives' was perfectly genuine. Those parts of the empire not granted self-government were controlled and ruled in a bewildering variety of ways, more the result of accident than design, as Crown Colonies (in the Caribbean and West Africa, for instance) or indirectly through local rulers – as, originally, in the Indian States, and later in the Malay States and the protectorates of tropical Africa. Of these 'realms in trust' the most populous and extensive was India. Ruled by British viceroys under the Crown as a separate empire, some 300 million Indians were Britain's responsibility from 1858 until 1947.

In 1900, a British Empire which did not include India would have seemed as unlikely as London without the Tower. But already the voice of India had been heard calling for autonomy and independence. In 1885 the first Indian National Congress had met. Those who gathered represented the Western viewpoint and admired the British. But rule by the British was seen as alien rule, and independence through the stage of Dominion status as an achievable goal for the future. The British brought unity, external and internal peace to India, and with the active co-operation of those Indians who had traditionally ruled the various states, established an incomparable administration all over the subcontinent. It was made possible by the marriage of Anglo-Indian traditions. But India was exploited too. Little was done for the masses of the poor. Economically, India was a dependency of Britain. The splendour of the British Raj never stilled British doubts about their role, so strongly reinforced by the Indian mutiny of 1857; the British were conscious that they, a mere handful of aliens, were ruling over millions of people. Would the people always so consent? In 1905 a senior member of the British ruling caste of India summed up the general view held by those responsible for British policy in India: British rule, he wrote, rested on 'its character for justice, toleration and careful consideration of native feeling', but it was also based on bayonets, on the maintenance of an 'adequate' force of British soldiers in India and the absolute command of the sea. If Britain weakened, her domination of India would come to an end through an uprising, perhaps helped along by a hostile foreign power, in all probability Russia. That was regarded as the ultimate disaster.

The dynamic Colonial Secretary, Joseph Chamberlain, was the principal advocate of an imperial movement for greater unity. In his great 'tariff reform' campaign from 1903 to 1905 he sought to win British support for a protected and preferential empire market which he believed would cement imperial relationships; but, as it would also have entailed higher food prices for the British people, he failed to carry the whole country. In a different way, the attempt to create a more unified system of imperial defence also failed; the self-governing Dominions were not willing to give up their independence. The cause of imperial unity was destined to fail. But in the era from 1900 to 1945, the British Empire remained very much a reality, as the prodigious effort in two great wars was to show. Co-operation between the Dominions and the mother country, however, was voluntary, based on a variety of changing institutions devised to meet no more than immediate needs.

The most striking aspect of Britain's world position in 1900 was the contrast between the appearance of her world power and its reality. Anyone looking at a map of the world with the British Empire painted red might well think that Britain dominated the world. This was certainly not the case.

The security of the British Isles and the empire came to depend on three circumstances: in North America on peaceful good relations; in eastern Asia on the assistance of an ally; in Europe on a continued 'balance of power' between the great continental nations.

Even with the largest navy, Britain could not continue relying entirely on her own strength and on temporary allies whose own interests happened to coincide with Britain's at any particular moment of crisis. There was a widespread feeling that Britain was over-committed and that some change of course in her foreign relations would be essential. There were those who favoured an alliance with Germany. But the Germans proved coy. They saw no advantage in helping Britain against Russia, except perhaps if Britain were to pay the price of sharing her empire with Germany. An alliance was never really on the cards and discussions about such a possibility ceased in 1902.

Others thought the sensible course for Britain would be to reduce the number of potential opponents all over the world. A successful start was made by removing all possibility of conflict with the United States. On the British side, the readiness to defend British interests in the Americas by force, against the United States if necessary, was abandoned in the new century. The British government signified its willingness to trust the United States by allowing the Americans control of the future Panama Canal, by withdrawing the British fleet from the Caribbean, and by leaving the Dominion of Canada, in practice, undefended. On the United States' side the idea that the absorption of Canada was part of the United States' manifest destiny faded. Plans for war were for some time still drawn up by the military on both sides of the Atlantic; but the political realities were quite different. In the twentieth century it really became unthinkable that Britain and the United States would ever go to war against each other again.

Britain liquidated with equal success the long-drawn-out imperial rivalry with France in many parts of the world. As late as 1898 it had seemed possible that Britain and France would be at war again, as they had been in the early nineteenth century. There was very little love for Britain in France, where Britain was most bitterly condemned during the South African War. But the French government made its prime objective the control of Morocco. Eventually, in April 1904, Delcassé, the French Foreign Minister, was ready to secure British support by settling amicably all outstanding imperial differences with Britain. German threats against France, in 1905 and later, turned this settlement into one involving British promises of support against Germany, though never an alliance in peacetime; the increasingly intimate relations between France and Britain became known as the *entente cordiale*.

Britain's attempt to reach a settlement with her most formidable opponent in the world arena, Russia, was far less successful. Russia's occupation of Manchuria in China, which began in 1900, alarmed the British government. The China market was seen as vital to Britain's future prosperity. Unable to check Russia, or to trust her, Britain concluded an alliance with Japan in 1902.

This alliance marks a significant stage in the history of Western imperialism. In the division of empire the European powers had been locked in rivalry and confrontation one against the other, though this rivalry had not led to war between them since the mid-nineteenth century. It was the Africans and Chinese, the peoples whose lands were parcelled up, who had suffered the ravages of war. The Europeans, though fiercely competitive among themselves, acted in this their last phase of expanding imperialism on the common assumption that it was their destiny to impose European dominion on other peoples. Now, for the first time in the new century, a European power had allied with an Asiatic power, Japan, against another European power, Russia.

In the Middle East Britain was determined to defend against Russia those territorial interests which in 1900, before the age of oil had properly begun, were largely strategic: the road to India which ran through the Ottoman Empire, Persia and landlocked mountainous Afghanistan. India was the greatest possession and jewel of the British Empire and tsarist Russia was credited by the British with the ultimate desire of ousting Britain from India and of seeking to replace Britain as the paramount power of southern Asia. The defence of India and Britain's own supremacy in southern Asia had been the foremost objective of British policy in the nineteenth century and remained so in the new century.

But it became increasingly difficult to defend the 'buffer states' which kept Russia away from the classic land-invasion route to India. The Ottoman Empire, once dominated by British influence, had turned away from Britain. No British government could easily have come to the defence of an empire which under the Sultan Abdul Hamid, 'the Damned', had murdered defenceless Christian Armenians in Asia Minor. In Persia, Russia's influence was steadily advancing.

In 1904 occurred a dramatic change. Russia became embroiled in war with Japan over China (page 58). Her military weakness became apparent to the world. Tsarist Russia desperately needed years of peace after 1905 to recover. The British Foreign Secretary, Sir Edward Grey, therefore found the Russians more ready in 1907 to reach an agreement with Britain to partition their imperial spheres of interests in the Middle East. But Grey believed this agreement only provided a temporary respite.

British security in Europe had been based on an effective balance of power on the continent. It had been a part of Britain's traditional policy to seek to prevent any one power gaining the mastery of continental Europe. After the defeat of Napoleon there seemed to be no serious possibility that any single nation either harboured such ambitions or could carry them through. But around 1905 doubts began to arise as to whether this fundamental condition of safety might not be passing. Germany's ambitious plans of naval expansion were being seriously noted. Germany's aggressive reaction in 1905 to the Anglo-French deal over Morocco aroused graver fears that Germany might be contemplating another war against France. Britain gave unhesitating support to France. From 1905 to 1914 the golden thread of British policy was to endeavour to preserve the peace, but in any case to avoid the possibility of a German hegemony of the continent which would result from a German victory over much weaker France.

Accordingly, on the one hand British policy towards Germany was pacific and the prospect of helping her achieve some of her imperial ambitions was held out to her as long as she kept the peace. But she was warned that, should she choose to attack France in a bid for continental hegemony, she could not count on the British standing aside even if Britain were not directly attacked. The Liberal Cabinet from 1906 to 1914 was not united, however, though Grey's policy of growing intimacy with France in the end prevailed. Several Liberal ministers were more anti-Russian than anti-German; strongly pacific, they saw no cause for war with Germany or anyone. Grey went his own way of constructing a barrier against the threat of Germany, supported by the two prime ministers of the period, Campbell-Bannerman and Asquith, and a small group of ministers. In secret discussions between the French and British military staffs, military plans were drawn up after the second Moroccan crisis of 1911 to land a British army of 150,000 men in France if Germany invaded France. At the same time Grey continued to emphasise that the French should place no reliance on Britain as there could be no formal alliance between the two countries. It was a curious policy dictated partly by differences among his ministerial colleagues and partly by Grey's own desire to play a mediating role in present and future conflicts. This compromise between 'alliance' and the 'free hand' in fact worked quite well down to the outbreak of war in 1914. Grey made a notable contribution to calming Europe during the Bosnian crisis of 1909 (page 65) and in collaborating with Germany during the Balkan wars in 1912 and 1913 in order to help preserve European peace.

Alarm at Germany's intentions nevertheless grew in Britain from 1910 onwards. In the public mind this had much to do with the expansion of the German navy. Efforts to moderate the peace – the War Secretary, Richard Haldane, visited Berlin for this purpose early in 1912 and Winston Churchill, First Lord of the Admiralty, called for a 'naval holiday' in 1913 – all came to nothing. The German ministers in return had demanded that Britain should tie her hands in advance and promise to remain neutral if Germany went to war with France. The Germans continued to be warned that Britain, in her own interests, would stand by France if France found herself attacked by the numerically superior German military machine. This threat, rather than Germany's naval challenge, motivated British policy. As Grey put it in 1912, Britain was in no danger of being involved in a war 'unless there is some Power, or group of Powers in Europe which has the ambition of achieving . . . the Napoleonic policy'.

The British government knew that it possessed the resources to keep pace with any increase in Germany's naval construction. By 1914 Britain had twenty new super-battleships of the Dreadnought class, against Germany's thirteen; in older battleships Britain's superiority was even greater – twenty-six to Germany's twelve. By making arrangements with France to concentrate this fleet in home waters, leaving the Mediterranean to be defended by the French fleet, British naval superiority over Germany was assured and, also significantly, her ties with France were strengthened.

Still trying at the same time to assure Germany of Britain's general goodwill, Grey concluded two agreements with her in 1913 and 1914. The first, a rather dubious one, divided up two Portuguese colonies in Africa, Mozambique and Angola, allowing Germany a good share should Portugal choose to dispose of these possessions. The other agreement helped Germany to realise plans for the final sections of the Berlin–Baghdad railway project and so facilitated German commercial penetration of Asia Minor and Mesopotamia. It was concluded on the very eve of the outbreak of war in Europe.

Grey endeavoured to steer a difficult middle path. He had met the Russian threat by the agreements of 1907, just as his predecessor in the Foreign Office, Lord Lansdowne, had removed the imperial rivalry with France in 1904 by a general settlement. But the British never thought that agreements with Russia, unlike the French settlement, would allow more than breathing space from her inexorable pressure. Yet in every one of these agreements made to protect Britain's empire there was a price which the British Cabinet would have preferred not to pay. To protect her enormous stake in China, Britain had concluded the alliance with Japan in 1902 sanctioning Japanese aggression in Korea and making war in eastern Asia with Russia more likely. After Japan's victory in 1904–5, Japan was set on the road to dominate China. Then there was the agreement with France over Morocco and Egypt in 1904, which was bound to offend Germany. Britain would have preferred to appease Germany by allowing her a share of Morocco. The French would not allow that. So Britain once more gained her imperial objective – predominance in Egypt – at the cost of increasing tensions in Europe. The most striking example of Britain protecting her empire at the cost of international tension was the settlement reached with Russia. With the conclusion of this agreement with Russia in 1907 over spheres of influence in the Middle East, Sir Edward Grey, the British Foreign Secretary, well understood that the Germans would increasingly feel 'encircled'.

The question that has to be asked is why, if Russia continued to be considered even after 1907 to present the main threat to the heart of the British Empire in Asia, did Britain go to war with Germany in 1914? There were no direct Anglo-German territorial disputes or differences over spheres of influence that were not capable of settlement. It is not easy to answer that question but there are clues in what Grey wrote and said. Agreement with Russia rather than enmity bought time. Then looking to the future, how could Britain best maintain her position as a great power in Europe? She certainly wanted the peace of Europe to be maintained. But Grey feared that Britain might be faced with too powerful a combination of countries in Europe in coalition against her. However, he also repeatedly warned against Britain becoming dependent on Germany.

Britain's distrust of Germany was certainly growing in the Edwardian period. The Kaiser was regarded as over-emotional and unstable. German manufacturers were competing with the British in the world. Of course Germany was an excellent market for British goods, something that was taken for granted. Above all, the German naval build-up touched the public to the quick. As Sir Eyre Crowe, a senior member of the Foreign Office, put it in 1907, a hostile Germany was disregarding the 'elementary rules of straightforward and honourable dealing' and Britain would have to defend her position in the world, her naval supremacy and the European balance of power. Still, there were others who deplored the Germanophobia, among them the bankers, industrialists, politicians and many ordinary people who preferred the 'clean' Germans to their Latin neighbours with their supposedly more dubious morals and awful lavatories. Tsarist autocratic Russia, with her record of abusing human rights, was regarded as the one European country which not only threatened Britain in Asia but least shared British democratic ideals and respect for human rights.

Grey did not share the Germanophobia, but he believed it essential to preserve and strengthen the entente with France as the primary objective of British policy in Europe. He hoped to gain some influence over French policy in return for supporting France against unreasonable German behaviour. He could not hope to exercise such influence over German policy. As it turned out he could exercise little influence over the French either. But it was the bedrock of Grey's policy that friendly relations with Germany should never be established at the expense of France. In the end it meant that Britain was more influenced by French objectives than the other way around. To please the French and Russians in 1914, Grey for instance consented to Anglo-Russian naval conversations which unnecessarily but dramatically increased German fears of encirclement. On the eve of 1914 the well-informed Grey perceptively assessed German apprehensions:

The truth is that whereas formerly the German Government had aggressive intentions ... they are now genuinely alarmed at the military preparation in Russia, the prospective increase in her military forces and particularly at the intended construction at the instance of the French Government and with French money of strategic railways to converge on the German Frontier.

Yet for all these insights, when the crisis came in July 1914. Grey's mediating efforts, limited as they were by previous constraints, proved unavailing.

On the eve of the Great War, the most serious problem facing the British government seemed to be not abroad but at home: the question of maintaining the unity of the United Kingdom. Ireland was Britain's heel of Achilles. British governments had been too slow in attempting to satisfy Irish national feeling by devolution or limited 'home rule'. Ireland's problems had been allowed to languish until after the elections of December 1910. Now the decline of the Liberals' fortunes forced Asquith into more active collaboration with the Irish Nationalist Party in the House of Commons. Not for the first time the Irish held the parliamentary balance of power. The Liberals with the support of the Irish Nationalists had staked their future on reforming the House of Lords. Asquith in return was committed to home rule for Ireland. In April 1912 he introduced the Home Rule Bill in the Commons. Ulster Protestant militants, strong in the north of Ireland, were determined to kill the bill or at least to demand partition. Sinn Fein, the Irish republican movement, was equally determined to preserve a united Ireland. Both sides raised private armies which on the eve of the Great War in 1914 threatened to plunge a part of the United Kingdom into civil war. The outbreak of the war gave Asquith the opportunity of postponing the Irish confrontation. What with suffragettes resorting to spectacular demonstrations to gain the vote for women, industrial unrest, Ireland seemingly on the brink of civil war, Britain presented a picture of disarray. It was deceptive. A united Britain and Empire entered the Great War of 1914.

# CHAPTER 6

## The Emergence of the United States as a World Power

The emergence of the United States as a superpower by the mid-twentieth century is one of the most striking changes of modern history. The state of the American economy and America's decision as to where and in what manner to intervene in any part of the globe have profoundly affected every continent. The United States came to wield an influence such as no other single nation has exercised before. What is striking is that this impact on the world has been so recent, scarcely predating the turn of the century. How did it come about and where are the roots of American world power?

The growth of the population, and of the industrial and agricultural production of the United States, were phenomenal. Their sustained increase through the nineteenth and twentieth centuries, overcoming two depressions in the mid-1870s and the mid-1890s as well as the serious depression of the 1930s, is one of the 'economic wonders' of modern history. There was a contemporary awareness of America's good fortune, and 'growth' was both expected and regarded as the unique 'American way'. When we compare the population growth of the United States with that of the European great powers, we see clearly how relatively sudden the transformation of the United States into the present-day colossus has been. In 1880 the total population of the United States was about the same as Germany's ten years later and only 5 million more than Germany's at the same time. Thus in population the United States only just ranked in

the same league as the largest of the European nations. But, from then on, the United States' rapid outdistancing of previously comparable countries was one fundamental reason for the emergence of the United States as a superpower.

**Population** (*millions*)

|                | 1880 | 1900 | 1920  | 1930  |
|----------------|------|------|-------|-------|
| United States  | 50.2 | 89.4 | 118.1 | 138.4 |
| Germany        | 45.2 | 56.4 | 59.2  | 64.3  |

A crucial factor in this growth of population was another feature of the New World, the large-scale emigration from Europe. Driven largely by poverty and the hope of a better life a great mass of humanity flooded into the United States, more than 13 million between 1900 and 1914 alone. Most of them were peasants from central and southern Europe. The majority of these 'new immigrants' (to distinguish them from the 'old' immigrants from Britain, Ireland, Germany and Scandinavia) settled in the towns where they preferred to join their countrymen who had kept close together in the cities and found unskilled industrial work. Immigrants contributed significantly to the growth of major cities, reinforced economic expansion and helped to bring about the mass market which is characteristic of twentieth-century America. Of the 13 million, more than a million were Jews leaving the pogrom-ridden

Coming to America. Ellis Island was the gateway to the New World for immigrants from Europe. Between 1881 and 1910, 17,729,545 settlers were admitted to the United States and of these more than 90 per cent came from Europe. The picture (left) shows a dining room, c.1900, for those who were detained for further questioning. Others were cleared to pass on swiftly (top); they settled in tenement flats and lived in cramped conditions (right), almost invariably with fellow-immigrants from their 'homeland'.

Russian Empire; they helped to make New York into one of the great clothing manufacturing centres of America.

The rich cultural variety of the United States, the diversity of ethnic groups from west and east, as well as the sheer numbers of immigrants, are among the unique features of America's national growth. America, as one historian put it, was less a 'melting pot' – intermarriage and common allegiances did not speedily obliterate national differences of origin – than a 'salad bowl'. All the same, the fusion of peoples of every national origin and religion and, over a much longer period, the fusion of the races black and white, into a national community has proved a more powerful force than national and racial differences and conflict.

In the twentieth century the shared experiences of two world wars were powerful influences in making for more toleration and mutual acceptance – one of the most significant aspects of the development of the United States for world history.

The immigrants added immensely to the vitality of the United States. Starting from nothing, they and their descendants acquired new skills and an education. The United States was the country where the accident of a father's social status mattered least in the Western world. As far as the blacks were concerned, this generalisation did not hold true. As long ago as 1868 some of the framers of the fourteenth amendment of the constitution sought to protect the rights of blacks. The amendment declared that Americans enjoyed equal rights and equality before the law and specifically laid down that no state could 'deprive any person of life, liberty, or property, without due process of law'. However, as a protection of the civil rights of the blacks the fourteenth amendment proved worthless because it was not enforced. It was used instead by the rising industrialists and financiers to amass greater fortunes and influence through combinations and mergers.

The age distribution of the immigrants and their tendency to have larger families than the American-born kept the increase of population at a much higher level than could otherwise be sustained. America was in reality, and in self-image, a young country constantly renewing herself. At the turn of the century, the United States had just recovered from the depression of the mid-1890s, and Americans faced the twentieth century with much optimism believing, rightly as it turned out, that

*An assembly line in a Ford car factory, 1913. Henry Ford (1863–1947) is said to have died with a stop-watch in his hand.*

their country was on the threshold of industrial expansion and the accumulation of wealth. Between 1900 and 1914 manufacturing production nearly doubled and overtook agriculture as the main source of national wealth. The traditional America was a nation of farmers, artisans and small businessmen. The America of the twentieth century was predominantly industrial, with the growth of cities, and railways linking the industrial midwest and the east. Industry was increasingly dominated by the giant corporations such as John D. Rockefeller's Standard Oil Company or the Trusts of J. Pierpont Morgan, though small businesses also persisted. The absolute growth of population, the opening up of virgin lands in the west, made possible simultaneously a great expansion of agricultural output despite the population movement to the towns. This increasing output was more than enough to feed the growing American population and leave sufficient to export. Meat packing and food canning became important industries. The vast continent of the United States was singularly blessed in all its resources – fertile land, forests, coal, iron and oil. Their simultaneous successful development provided the dynamic of American economic growth which no European nation could match, and meant that Americans were less dependent on imports or exports than any other advanced Western nation.

In the early twentieth century, American business nevertheless expanded American exports to industrialised Europe, seeing this as a necessary insurance against a glut in the market at home – yet these exports were only a small proportion of America's total production, which was protected at home by a high tariff. In the early twentieth century the application of electricity as a new energy source provided a further boost, and electrical machinery together with automobiles – Henry Ford alone producing 125,000 cars a year by 1913, half the nation's total output – were the 'new industries' maintaining America's lead as the world's first industrial power.

America's explosive growth was not achieved without severe political and social tensions. This was the other side of the optimism expressed at the turn of the century about the future. People began to ask who would control the destinies of the United States. Would it be the new breed of immensely successful and wealthy financiers and businessmen? Was not their influence already the main reason for the corruption of government, no longer a government for and by the people but for the good of business? The cleavage between the rich and poor appeared to widen as the Vanderbilts, Morgans, Rockefellers and Harrimans displayed their wealth.

The western farmers were exposed to the vagaries of the seasons and also to the increases and falls of world grain prices. A good harvest could drive the prices farther down and the farmers seeking a cause for their misfortunes focused on the high interest they had to pay on the loans they needed – the result, as they saw it, of government dominated by the industrial east. The southern United States remained relatively stagnant, unable to diversify when, after the worldwide drop in cotton prices, cotton could no longer yield the same profit as before the Civil War.

The American workers in the mines and factories also tried to organise to meet the increased power of business. Socialism as a political force had developed in the United States as well as in Europe during the nineteenth century, and for a short while after 1872 the headquarters of Marx's First International was in New York. But the Socialist Labor Party of North America could not establish itself as a serious force in politics. In the early twentieth century, under the charismatic leadership of Eugene V. Debs, the Social Democratic Party attempted to win over the worker from trade union economic bargaining to politics, but was unsuccessful on a national scale, though Debs, when he became a presidential candidate, secured almost 900,000 votes. When labour unions expanded it was under the direction of men like Samuel Gompers who rejected political socialism as utopian and saw themselves as practical men seeking to improve the wages and conditions of labour day by day without ulterior ends in view. In 1886 they organised the American Federation of Labor but in the 1890s found that union militancy could not prevail against the employers supported by the federal government. There were some successes to set against the failures, with the gradual introduction of maximum working hours and the ending of the abuse of child labour. Theodore Roosevelt, when president, showed more sympathy for the workers. Strikes of national concern, like the coal strike in Pennsylvania in 1902, were no longer settled by the federal government siding with the employers. President Roosevelt intervened and refused to back the mine owners, who had to concede higher wages. Roosevelt's action was characteristic of one aspect of a new spirit collectively known as the Progressive Movement.

But Roosevelt's outlook was not shared by all the states, which had retained extensive rights under the constitution. In 1903 and 1904 the Governor of the state of Colorado, for instance, had mobilised the militia, jailed the union leaders of the striking copper miners and beaten down the strikes with violence and bloodshed; and in all this he was eventually supported by the Supreme Court. Gompers himself was imprisoned by federal courts after another strike and denounced as a dangerous rabble-rouser subverting the law. Against this onslaught of employers, and with business dominating the courts and the state governments, Roosevelt could do little. Though the American Federation of Labor expanded from half a million to 2 million members by 1914, it could scarcely hold its own. Only the boom brought about by the Great War and the shortage of labour enabled the more moderate unions to gain acceptance and to negotiate better terms for workers. But the mass of the unskilled and the blacks remained largely outside the unions. The AFL's successes were mainly won on behalf of the skilled craft unions and the semi-skilled.

After the depressed 1880s and mid-1890s the farmers, who had been a major force behind the rising challenge to eastern business dominance, became quiescent. From 1897 until 1914 they enjoyed a short 'golden age' of prosperity, the *value* of their crops doubling during this period.

Looking at the United States as a whole, the only safe generalisation is that the problems which forced themselves on the attention of people varied enormously from one region to another, as did the responses of those in power in any particular state. Thus, in contrast to the conduct of Colorado's government, the Governor of Wisconsin, Robert M. La Follette, passed many practical reforms in his state, as did Woodrow Wilson after becoming governor of New Jersey in 1911.

'Progressive' became a loose label denoting little more than a recognition of the many varied ills besetting American society and politics during years of rapid change and a desire to remedy whichever of these ills a particular progressive felt to be the most injurious. The ills were well publicised by a new breed of journalists who proudly accepted what was meant to be an insulting description of their work – 'The Muckrakers'. Their targets were manifold – political corruption, the inequality of wealth, the domination of politics by big business; they investigated most aspects of American life; they attacked the doctrine of freedom which allowed the grasping entrepreneur to develop America at too great a price; they stressed the undermining of democracy; and argued the need for more regulatory government, not less.

In domestic politics the president's powers are limited by the rights of the two Houses of Congress, the Senate and the House of Representatives, and by the Supreme Court, the final arbiter of any dispute about constitutional rights. What President Theodore Roosevelt and his successors – the more conservative William Howard Taft, and then the Democrat Woodrow Wilson – actually achieved in legislation was less important than the fact that the presidency gave a reforming lead and so helped to change the climate of American public opinion. The Progressives were successful in the passage of child-labour laws in over forty states, and of laws governing the working conditions of women, but their attempts to clean up politics and smash the power of party machines failed. Lack of supervision to ensure enforcement also weakened much of the social legislation passed. After the Great War was over, in 1919, one reform dear to many Progressives, Prohibition (of alcoholic drinks), was enacted by Congress nationwide. Here too a large gap soon became apparent between law and actual observance.

Theodore Roosevelt was the first president of the United States to play a role as world statesman. As in his domestic policy, where he was inhibited by political constraints, so in his 'world' diplomacy he was circumscribed by America's lack of military power and the unwillingness of American people to make sacrifices to back up a 'large' American foreign policy. Superficially Roosevelt succeeded in drawing international attention to the United States and to his own role as diplomatist. In this respect his greatest achievement was to act in 1905 as mediator between the Japanese and Russians and to host the peace conference at Portsmouth, New Hampshire, ending the Russo-Japanese War. The United States next played a part in the international Moroccan conference at Algeciras in 1906. The following year, in a characteristically ostentatious gesture, Roosevelt sent the newly constructed United States Navy on a world cruise to show the flag. Roosevelt made America's presence felt. But what really lay behind these great-power posturings was apprehension that the conditions which had given the United States security for the past century were passing away.

For this feeling, which actually anticipated dangers that still lay in the future, there were two principal reasons: the likely direction of European imperialism and the consequences of America's own flirtation with imperialism at the turn of the century. Both can be seen clearly at work during the course of a war just won, the 'splendid little' Spanish–American war of 1898.

The American response to European imperialism, which had led to the partition of Africa and China, was to try to anticipate a serious challenge to the Monroe Doctrine, with its Declaration of US opposition to any further European colonial extension within the Western hemisphere. What if the Europeans next sought to extend their influence in the Caribbean and Central America and so surrounded the United States with armed bases? Captain A. T. Mahan, in his day the most influential writer and proponent of the importance of sea power, was writing at this time that such a danger did exist since crucial strategic regions of significance in world trade would inevitably become areas of great-power rivalry. One such artery of trade would be the canal (later Panama Canal) which it was

*A prescient view of American imperialism from the satirical German magazine* Kladderadatch, *1894.*

planned to construct across the isthmus of Central America. The backward and weak independent Caribbean island states were also easy prey for any intending European imperialist. The island of Cuba, lying close to the mainland of Florida was, then as now, a particularly sensitive spot. Before the war with Spain, Cuba was a Spanish colony, in chronic rebellion and anarchy. The war on the island was barbarous as most guerrilla wars are apt to be, and American opinion, genuinely humanitarian, was inflamed by the popular 'yellow' press. But the hidden aspect of the situation as seen by the administration was that a weak Spain as the sovereign power on the island might be replaced by an aggressive Britain or Germany.

A group of Americans, including a number of senior naval officers, Theodore Roosevelt (then an up-and-coming politician) and Senator Henry Cabot Lodge, discussed ways and means of taking precautionary action before these dangers materialised. They were later seen as 'imperialists' or 'expansionists' and indeed this was the practical outcome of their ideas, but their motivation was essentially defensive – to preserve American security in the coming conditions of the twentieth century.

Imperialism was inextricably bound up with this defensive attitude. The Americans intervened and made themselves the gendarmes of the Caribbean. After the war with Spain in 1898, Cuba, though proclaimed an independent republic, became a virtual protectorate of the United States. A US naval base was constructed on the island and the land needed for it was ceded to the United States. This American presence was intended to ensure that no European power could take over Cuba or reach the inner naval defences of the United States before meeting the US Navy in the western Atlantic. The United States also imposed conditions on Cuba

which allowed the United States to intervene in case of internal discord. Another Caribbean island, Puerto Rico, was simply annexed for similar strategic reasons. In 1904 Theodore Roosevelt extended the right of the United States to act as a policeman throughout Central and Latin America, invoking the Monroe Doctrine as justification. By helping the Panamanian revolutionaries against Colombia in 1903, Roosevelt established another American protectorate in all but name in the new state of Panama. Nor did the United States hesitate to intervene in the independent republics of Dominica and Nicaragua. Although Woodrow Wilson, when he became president, attempted to revert to the earlier spirit of inter-American collaboration, he did not himself hesitate to intervene in Mexico from 1914 to 1916.

In contrast to the advanced industrialised and agriculturally developed North American continent, the habitable regions of South America supported a growing population in, for the most part, abject poverty. (For a fuller discussion of Latin America see Part XIV.) The descendants of the Spaniards and Portuguese and the immigrants from Europe who formed the minority of inhabitants enjoyed the wealth and political power of the American 'republics'. There was much variety in the politics and society of Latin America. Their revolutions, though, had been revolutions from above in the early nineteenth century. The new states remained authoritarian, despite their elaborate constitutions modelled on the French or American, and their professed ideals of democracy, with a few notable exceptions, proved a façade for governments based on force: they were governments of the generals or of dictators who commanded the military forces of the state. Violence was the language of politics. Trade with Europe, especially (in the later nineteenth century) with Britain and Germany, was considerably greater than with the United States, to which there was much hostility, on account of her claims to pre-eminence in the Americas. The possibility of 'Yankee' interference was the object of particular Latin American suspicion and animosity.

In 1900 strategic planners in the United States clearly saw the discrepancy between the pretensions of the Monroe Doctrine and the inability of the United States to exert any military and naval influence south of the Amazon in Brazil. What if the partition of Africa were followed by European domination of South and Central America? In fact the

The Americas, 1990

conflicts in Europe, the Mediterranean and Near East, in Africa and in Asia absorbed the military resources of the European Western powers. Britain, the major European power with colonies and commercial interests in Latin America and an empire extending from colonies in the Caribbean to the Dominion of Canada in the north, furthermore made clear her intention not to challenge the United States' claim for regional supremacy. At the turn of the century Britain and the United States signed the Hay–Pauncefote Treaty which granted the United States the sole right of defence of the future Panama Canal. This was followed by Britain withdrawing her fleet from the Caribbean and settling all outstanding disputes with the United States. Britain could not afford to risk the enmity of the United States as well when her interests were more endangered at home, first by Russia then by Germany, in the Mediterranean, in Asia and in Europe. And so a war between Britain and the United States became increasingly unthinkable as the twentieth century progressed. In this way the conflicts of the European powers in the early years of the twentieth century continued to serve the security of the United States in her hemisphere.

But in the Pacific and eastern Asia the United States became more deeply involved and exposed. US interests in the trade of China date back to the foundations of the American republic herself. Not until the close of the nineteenth century, however, did the United States acquire a territorial stake in the Pacific. The annexation of Hawaii in 1898 could still just about be fitted in with the notion that the island was an essential offshore base of defence for the western seaboard of the United States. There could be no such claim for the annexation of the Philippines after the Spanish–American War of 1898. An American army crushed the Filipino struggle for independence (1899–1902). This was imperialism. The United States staked her claim

for a share of the China market whose potential was overestimated. The appearance of the United States in eastern Asia as a Western colonial power aroused the alarm of Japan and marks the origins of a new conflict in eastern Asia in the twentieth century. Theodore Roosevelt had recognised that the Philippines were indefensible; they were, to use his words, America's 'heel of Achilles'.

In the military sense, America's role as a world power was potential rather than actual during the first decade and a half of the twentieth century. The American army was small – adequate to deal with Indians and Mexicans; her warships in the 1880s had been called in Congress a collection of washtubs. How soon the United States could turn military potential into reality is illustrated by the amazingly rapid construction of the modern US Navy. In the 1890s American naval power was puny, just enough to cope with Spain's antiquated warships; by 1920, the United States Navy could match the British. But to exercise world power requires not only the means – and no one could doubt in the early twentieth century America's capacity – but also the will. Before 1914, it did not seem realistic to suppose that the United States would become involved in war over the conflicts of the other Western powers. The American people saw no need for war. The large navy, which could ensure the security of the North American continent and its approaches, and the small professional army indeed point to the overwhelmingly defensive attitude of the United States. How nevertheless she was to be involved in war in 1917 will be examined in a later chapter (pages 116–19). But it was only with great reluctance that Americans came to accept that the United States' circumstances had fundamentally changed from the times when George Washington could advise that the United States should not entangle her fortunes in the rivalries of Europe.

# CHAPTER 7

## The Russian Empire: Absolutism and Adaptation

As the world entered the twentieth century there was a large question mark over the largest Western state, the Russian Empire. The total size of Russia's population remained ahead of the United States'. But in industrial development Russia lagged behind the Western world. She was what would be termed today a vast underdeveloped country, stretching from the European frontiers with Germany and Austria–Hungary through the Middle East and Asia to the shores of the Pacific Ocean. The only nation larger than Russia was China, which in 1900 seemed on the verge of disintegration. Would Russia also disintegrate in the new century? Would revolution sweep away the Romanov dynasty, or would Russian autocracy prevail and continue to send the largest army in the world to conquer more and more territory and continue to incorporate more and more nationalities into the Russian Empire? Russia possessed all the resources of iron and coal to turn her into a major industrial power. How would her neighbours be able to resist Russian expansion as she modernised?

### Population (*millions*)

|  | 1880 | 1900 | 1910 | 1920 | 1940 |
|---|---|---|---|---|---|
| Russia | 97.1 | 132.1 | 155.7 | 145.3 | 195.0 |
| United States | 50.2 | 84.4 | 102.4 | 118.1 | 150.6 |

Her potential threat to the interests and security of all the countries surrounding her hung over them all, and increased in proportion to the actual growth of Russian power in the nineteenth and twentieth century.

By 1914 some hundred distinct national peoples had been incorporated into Russia. This made her the largest and most varied multinational empire. Government was highly centralised and absolute loyalty to the tsar was demanded of every national group. The predominant Russian people, the largest single population group by far, believed in the superiority of their culture, their Orthodox form of Christianity and the superiority of Slavs. The tsar sought to impose Russification on the other peoples and to suppress other religions. The Orthodox Church also formed a pillar of the tsar's autocracy and justified it as ordained by God. The most persistently persecuted minority were the Jews, who were deliberately made scapegoats for the ills besetting Russia. Anti-Semitism and discrimination, and even persecution of Jews, were endemic throughout Europe, but most virulent in Russia. Liberal and progressive European opinion was shocked and offended by the tsarist regime's treatment of the Jews.

It is difficult to look objectively at the history of Russia during the period of the last Tsar's rule, 1894 to 1917, knowing what followed. Was the development of Russia in the reign of Nicholas II a kind of blind alley bound to lead to collapse and revolution and the triumph of the Bolsheviks, or was she already on the road to reform and change before the outbreak of the First World War? An affirmative answer to the question of fundamental change can most confidently be given when industrialisation is considered. Rapid acceleration in the growth of the Russian economy began some forty years later than in the United States. Growth was uneven during the period 1890 to 1914, rapid in the 1890s when it more than doubled, was checked by a serious depression during the early years of the twentieth century, then from 1910 onwards resumed rapid expansion until the war. Not before 1928 would the Soviet Union again reach that level of production and so recover from war, revolution and civil war. Industrialisation was purposefully promoted by the state and masterminded in the 1890s by Sergei Witte, the Minister of Finance. He recognised that to maintain her status as a great power, Russia must break with past traditions and catch up with her rapidly industrialising European neighbours. A protective tariff (1891), a stable currency linked to gold, and high interest rates attracted massive foreign capital, especially from France, and encouraged capital formation in Russia. The expansion of railways had a widespread and stimulating effect on industrial growth. Besides the small workshops which in 1915 still employed two-thirds of all those employed in industry, there had also developed large-scale and modern industry.

**Russian Production** (*annual averages*)

|  | 1880–4 | 1900–4 | 1910–13 |
|---|---|---|---|
| Railways (*kilometres*) | 22,865 (1880) | 53,234 (1900) | 70,156 (1913) |
| Raw-cotton consumption (*thousand metric tons*) | 127.6 (1879–84) | 281.2 (1895–1904) | 388.5 (1905–13) |
| Pig-iron output (*thousand metric tons*) | 477.0 | 2,773.0 | 3,870.0 |
| Steel output (*million metric tons*) | 0.25 | 2.35 | 4.20 |
| Oil output (*thousand metric tons*) | 764.0 | 10,794.0 | 10,625.0 |
| Coal and lignite output (*million metric tons*) | 3.7 | 17.3 | 30.2 |

The statistics set out in the table give some indication of Russian economic growth.

It must also be remembered that population growth was very rapid during these years so that the increase calculated per head of population was much less impressive. But because Russia was so large, her total production ranked her in world terms by 1913 the fifth industrial power after the United States, Germany, Great Britain and France.

In 1913, in comparison with the United States, Russia still lagged far behind. She was also behind Germany and Britain, but Russian output became comparable to that of France and Austria–Hungary in a number of leading industries. With a population four times as large as that of France, Russia only achieved roughly the same total industrial production. All these figures on the one hand show Russia's great progress since 1890 compared with earlier decades, while on the other hand they reveal that in comparison with the United States, Germany and Britain, she remained backward and the gap was still wide.

Even in 1914 Russian society remained overwhelmingly rural. Precise classification is extremely difficult as many workers in factories retained their ties with their village and returned seasonally at harvest time. But not less than 80 per cent of the population were peasants, or muzhiki, who led a hard life, close to subsistence and dependent on weather and harvests. Religion was their solace but less a reasoned Christianity than ritual and superstition. More than half the peasantry were illiterate. Oppressed, the muzhiki symbolised the Russian masses revering the tsar as father and autocrat, yet, when driven by hunger and deprivation, resorting to violence and destruction. Those peasants recently forced by destitution into the crowded tenements or factory barracks of St Petersburg and other industrial centres to work even lived separated from their families.

At the heart of the problem of a Russia seeking to modernise and move into the twentieth century lay this vast peasantry. It was mainly on their heads too that the burden of industrialisation had to be placed, because they provided a cheap labour force and generated the necessary surplus of wealth which made investment in new and expanding industries possible. Exports of agricultural produce had to provide the greater part of capital to pay for all that the state spent on the huge army, on administration and on industry. In the early twentieth century the heavily burdened peasantry was ripe for large-scale violent protests. In town and country sporadic violence was to turn into the explosion of 1905.

The year 1905 marks a turning point in the history of Russia. The peasantry looted and burnt the countryside and appropriated the landlords' land. The immediate reason was the loss of authority suffered by the tsarist autocracy during the Russo-Japanese War (page 88). Violence also flared in St Petersburg and the towns. The defeat of the Russian armies in China and the despatch of the Russian fleet to the bottom of the ocean by the Japanese at the battle of Tsushima in May 1905 weakened the hold of the autocratic Tsar and his ministers.

The capital, St Petersburg, became the scene of violence and brutal repression. It was the enigmatic leadership of a charismatic priest, Father Georgei Gapon, who had initially worked for the tsarist regime, that led to bloodshed. As trade unions were forbidden in Russia the tsarist authorities developed an ingenious scheme to provide a safety valve for industrial grievances and a link with the government workers. Associations, carefully guided in their loyalty to the Tsar and led by reliable supporters of autocracy were promoted. One of these associations, formed with the blessings of the Ministry of the Interior, was Gapon's in St Petersburg. Gapon proved an unreliable supporter. He organised a mass strike and in January 1905 the whole of industrial St Petersburg was shut down by strikes. On what became known as Bloody Sunday, 22 January, he led to the Winter Palace a huge demonstration of workers, their wives and children, perhaps as many as 200,000 in all, dressed in their Sunday best, to seek redress of their grievances from the Tsar. At the Narva Gate the head of the procession was met by Cossacks, who charged with drawn sabres at the masses before them, maiming and killing indiscriminately; soldiers fired into the crowd. Killing continued all morning. Several hundred, possibly as many as 1000, innocent people perished. The spell of a beneficent tsar was broken. The Tsar would never entirely recover his authority or the faith and veneration of the masses who had seen him as their 'little father'.

Throughout the borderlands – Poland, Baltic, Finland and the Caucasus – there followed widespread unrest and insurrection. To the earlier victims of assassination now, in February 1905, was added another illustrious victim, the Grand Duke Sergei, the Tsar's uncle. Terrorism, strikes, student agitation and a rioting peasantry, together with the defeated and demoralised army and navy, added up to a picture of Russian autocracy in complete disarray. The prospect of disaffected armed forces on which autocracy relied was a spectre reinforced in June 1905 by the celebrated mutiny of the battleship *Potemkin* in Odessa harbour. Russian autocracy had reached a critical point: the Tsar could go on shooting and follow a policy of harsh repression or seek to master the situation by some timely concession and reform. He chose the latter, though at heart he remained a convinced, unbending autocrat.

Yet from the low point of his reign in 1905 to the outbreak of the war nine years later the Tsar ·managed better than many would have foretold at the outset. For a short while he placed the able Sergei Witte in charge of the immediate crisis. Witte had a true, if cynical appreciation of the problem of governing the empire. 'The world should be surprised that we have any government in Russia, not that we have an imperfect government,' he remarked in July 1905. Witte was convinced that chaos would follow if the Tsar's rule was allowed to fail; the nationalities and the conflict of classes would tear Russia apart. Autocracy was the only answer to lawlessness and dissolution. Faced with so much popular opposition, Witte saw clearly enough that the Tsar must either now resort to repression far more bloody than any that had preceded or put himself at the head of the 'reform' movement and limit its scope. Above all the Tsar must stop drifting in a sea of indecision. Witte's personal inclination was for the maintenance of undiluted autocracy but he recognised that this was not likely to succeed, and the Tsar had neither the nerve nor the stomach for total repression. The Tsar gave way to those who argued that a form of constitutionalism should be introduced. A renewed wave of strikes in October overcame his final resistance. The outcome was the October Manifesto of 1905.

In the previous February, Nicholas had declared that he would call into being a consultative assembly, to be known as the Duma. In August the complicated method of election was announced which allowed as little influence as possible to the disaffected workers. Now the October Manifesto promised to bring to life a genuinely parliamentary body with whom the Tsar would share power. No law would be promulgated without the consent of the Duma.

These promises made no impression on the workers who had formed themselves into soviets, or workers' councils, spontaneously. In St Petersburg and Moscow they openly called on the army to come to the side of the revolutionary movement. But the loyalty of the army to the Tsar was never seriously in doubt, the soviets were dispersed, their leaders arrested, and gradually during 1906 in town and country the tide of revolution passed.

With the need for compromise pressing, the Tsar soon showed his true colours. There were four meetings of the parliamentary assembly: the Duma of 1906, the second Duma of 1907, the third from 1907 to 1912, and the last from 1912 to 1917. In the first Duma, a new party emerged, the Constitutional Democratic Party, or Kadets as they were known. They were moderate and liberal and hoped on the basis of the October Manifesto to transform Russian autocracy into a genuine Western parliamentary constitutional government. Together with the moderate left, they outnumbered the revolutionary socialists, who had mostly boycotted the Duma, and the ultra-conservatives. But the Tsar would have nothing to do with a constitutional party or their leader Pavel Miliukov. After the short second Duma, which saw a strengthening of revolutionary socialists, the Tsar simply changed the electoral rules, ensuring tame conservative majorities in the third and fourth Dumas.

The opportunity of transforming Russia into a genuinely constitutional state by collaborating with moderate liberal opinion was spurned by the Tsar. As long as Nicholas II reigned, genuine constitutional change on the Western model was blocked. In 1917 the liberals as well as autocracy would be swept away by the forces of revolution. Yet before the war the actual hold of the various revolutionary socialist parties over the urban workers and the peasants was tenuous. Therein lies the extent of the lost opportunity to modernise and transform Russia while avoiding the terrible violence which after 1917 accompanied that process.

Despite the undoubted political repression and reactionary policies of the Tsar and his ministers, there was also a genuine effort made to tackle some of Russia's basic problems and so to cut the ground from under the widespread discontent. In 1906 the Tsar entrusted power to a ruthless but able man,

Peter Stolypin, as chairman of the Council of Ministers, a position he held until his assassination in 1911. Stolypin lived up to his reputation as a 'strong man', and through draconian measures such as military court martials executed hundreds and smothered revolutionary agitation. There were also, of course, revolutionary attacks on government officials whose victims equally ran into many hundreds killed and wounded. Stolypin launched a war on terrorism. He suppressed the rights of the nationalists; the Jews again particularly suffered, associated as they were in the Tsar's mind with sedition and socialism.

It took no great discernment to recognise that something needed to be done to help the peasantry. In November 1905 the peasants' redemption payments for the land they farmed were cancelled (as from 1907). This made it possible for a peasant to become the legal proprietor of the land. But as most of the land was held within the organisation of a village commune (*mir*), his freedom was still heavily circumscribed. The change Stolypin aimed at was a transformation of the existing communes into a whole new class of peasant proprietors, each farming his own land, not in strips as before, but consolidated into one viable farm.

The independent well-to-do peasant proprietors were already a phenomenon, especially in western Russia. The purpose of the land reform associated with Stolypin's name was to increase their number in all parts of Russia. Legislation passed in 1906, 1910 and 1911 facilitated the redistribution of land within the commune and gave the right to the peasant to secede from the commune and claim the land he farmed. How successful did these reforms prove? The problem of Russian agriculture was gigantic, due to over-population, lack of capital, lack of knowledge and simple peasant resistance to change. It has been calculated that by 1916 about 2 million households had left the communes and set up their own farms. It was no more than a beginning, but a significant one. But since by 1916 more than 80 per cent of the land was already being farmed by peasants, redistribution of land by taking it away from the larger landlords and the Church could no longer solve the continuing problem of land hunger caused by over-population. The peasantry was being divided between the richer, the poorer and the landless peasant driven into the towns to swell discontent there. Rapid industrialisation promoted by the state, the spread of education,

*Nicholas II with his family (including four nephews) in January 1916. His wife (not in the photograph) and children were murdered with him eighteen months later. To the left of the Tsar an officer is in attendance. On the extreme right of the picture is the Tsarevitch; next to him the Grand Duchess Anastasia.*

political agitation, the continuing increase of the population all produced severe social tensions.

Nicholas II was quite unequal to the Herculean task of ruling Russia. He was more and more dominated by his wife, the Empress Alexandra, devoted but equally narrow-minded, and she in turn was influenced by the 'magic' of Rasputin, whose spiritual healing was alleviating the agonies of their son, the sick Tsarevich.

Yet by the eve of the 1914 war a succession of energetic ministers such as Witte and Stolypin had brought about some change. Higher agricultural prices and reforms did benefit rural Russia and pacify the peasants. But in the towns the standard of living of the workers did not improve. Workers had gained limited rights to form trade unions. Bad conditions and an increasing political awareness that change was necessary and possible led after 1910 to strikes. The only answer the government

knew was repression, which reached its horrifying peak in the Lena goldfields in 1912 when the troops killed 170 miners striking for higher wages. 1913 and 1914 saw a renewal of massive strikes especially in St Petersburg and Moscow and, significantly, they became increasingly political.

Faced with these internal disorders, the Tsar and his ministers had to weigh, during that fateful July of 1914, the question of war and peace. Would war release a patriotic spirit that would drown the voice of revolution; or would it spark off the great upheaval? The Tsar's agonising over the fateful mobilisation order indicates vividly how he was fully aware that he might be signing the death warrant of his autocratic rule, perhaps his dynasty. Certainly during these last critical weeks, decisions which required the utmost coolness of judgement were being taken under the daily tensions of unrest much more immediate and severe than those facing the Kaiser in Berlin. How had the Tsar allowed Russia to be brought to so dangerous an international position in 1914 when what Russia most needed was peace?

Throughout the nineteenth century Russian foreign and imperial policy sought, generally speaking, the lines of least resistance. Hence the great expansive drive into central Asia and the extension of Russian territory and power to the Sea of Japan with the establishment of Vladivostok as a naval port rather than expansion into western Europe. In western Europe, Russia followed a policy of maintaining good relations with Prussia and Austria–Hungary. The three kingdoms shared a common conservatism and would each be endangered by the revival of nationalism in Poland, that unfortunate kingdom having been partitioned between them in the eighteenth century. In Asia, by the third quarter of the nineteenth century, Russia came in conflict with British imperial interests on a very wide front. In Europe, Russia never ceased to fear that the effect of a hostile occupation of Constantinople and the Straits would be to close the maritime routes of southern Russia and, worse, to provide a springboard for an attack on Russia herself. Yet despite this vital interest Russia always shrank from provoking a coalition of powers against her by attempting to conquer the region. So faced with powerful neighbours in Europe, Russia for a century had followed a path of caution.

The co-operation with Germany and Austria was first breached in 1887 when the Three Emperors' Alliance was not renewed and then more decisively in 1890 when the Germans refused to extend the separate Russo-German 'Insurance' treaty. This was not because the Russians wanted to change the direction of their policy fundamentally, but because the new course had been inaugurated by Wilhelm II, whose advisers persuaded him after the fall of Bismarck not to renew the Russian alliance (page 19). The Russians felt themselves menaced by their isolation, especially when simultaneously Germany drew closer to Russia's imperial rival in Asia, Britain. Fear of isolation drove the Russians reluctantly into the defensive alliance with France in 1894.

During the next five years, little reference was made to the alliance, though France became increasingly important as the provider of foreign loans. The alliance had so far proved of little use and in the new century the French seemed anxious to come to an amicable settlement with Britain just at a time when Russia was faced with the prospect of grave complications in China.

Russia was determined to leave her own way open to the exploitation of Manchuria and northern China while keeping the other European powers and Japan away from the Russian frontiers in eastern Asia. As so frequently happens, a sense of weakness and a desire to defend territory and interests led the Russians into *offensive* action. Following the German appearance on the Chinese mainland when they seized the port of Kiaochow in 1897, the Russians countered by forcing the Chinese to lease to them strategically important Port Arthur. During the years from 1898 to 1903 Russia penetrated deeply into northern China. The peaceful policy advocated by Witte of working with the Chinese and seeking economic dominance with the help of a Russian-constructed and -controlled Manchurian railway was abandoned. The Boxer rising in 1900 gave Russia the opportunity to occupy large parts of northern China under the guise of rescuing the Europeans and suppressing the Boxers. At the same time Russia also sought to dominate the neighbouring kingdom of Korea.

The military expansion of Russia in eastern Asia greatly alarmed the Japanese (page 87). With Britain's alliance in 1902, the Japanese were sure that they could not be overwhelmed by a European coalition if they chose to resist Russia. They demanded that Russia withdraw. The Tsar and his ministers knew in 1904 that they faced war unless they withdrew. But with their own sense of 'white' superiority – they referred to the Japanese as baboons – it seemed unthinkable to Nicholas II that he should give way to mere Asiatics. The Minister of the Interior even thought that 'a little victorious war' would calm the revolutionary agitation at home.

War broke out in February 1904. There were two unexpected results. The first was the Japanese surprise attacks on the Russian fleet at Port Arthur during the night of 8/9 February 1904 without the benefit of a declaration of war. The second was that the Japanese won. Russia's military, and even more her naval, performance during the Russo-Japanese war presented a sorry spectacle. Port Arthur finally fell to the Japanese troops investing it in January 1905. In February and March 1905 the Japanese inflicted heavy defeats on Russia's land forces in Manchuria at Mukden. The crowning disaster was the annihilation of Russia's European

Baltic battlefleet which had sailed halfway round the world to the straits separating Korea and Japan only to be sunk at the battle of Tsushima on 27 May 1905.

The war ended by compromise. The Japanese were equally anxious to end the war once they had gained their objective. With the help of Theodore Roosevelt's mediation, the peace of Portsmouth was concluded on 5 September 1905. Russian influence in southern Manchuria and Korea was at an end. She remained predominant in northern Manchuria and outer Mongolia. In peaceful agreement with Japan, Russia's frontier of interest in China was now drawn.

No doubt the revolutionary outbreaks at home had persuaded the Tsar to accept this humiliation. Even more compelling was the necessity of rebuilding the army and navy in the face of the ever present danger of European complications. The menace to the security of the empire in Europe was not a limited one but threatened its very existence.

Russia had no choice but to remain conciliatory and pacific in Europe. The French had to be told that Russia for the time being was militarily in no position to fulfil the military obligations of the alliance (page 29). In the Balkans, the policy of friendly co-operation with the Habsburgs was continued. The empire had to have peace. In August 1907, agreement with Britain settling their imperial rivalries in Persia, Afghanistan and Tibet removed the greatest immediate dangers of conflict. Peaceful relations with all her neighbours, agreements of compromise rather than active extension of Russia's influence – those were the guidelines for the Russian foreign ministers during the years from 1906 to 1908. For a brief period the 'Russian threat' loomed less darkly in Europe and Asia.

From 1909 to 1914 the rapid recovery, reorganisation and planned enlargement of the Russian army alarmed her neighbours. Unlike the German army, the Russian – and this may cause surprise – was never simply the bastion of class privilege. The nobility and gentry played a prominent role as officers but two out of every five officers up to the rank of colonel had risen from the peasantry or lower-middle class. The fathers of many officers had been serfs. The industrial upsurge and the recovery of agriculture rapidly increased the income of the state during these years and together with foreign loans from France enabled the government to budget for the huge additional expenditure on the army, on the navy and on new railway construction.

By 1914, it has been calculated that Russia was already spending more than Germany on her army and navy; when the armaments programme was completed in 1917 the Russian army on paper would enjoy overwhelming superiority with a peacetime strength of nearly 2 million men; what is more, by 1917 they could be mobilised in eighteen days, against Germany's fifteen days. The Schlieffen Plan, which was based on quickly defeating France before Russia was ready to attack Germany (page 21), would then be done for; France could not be defeated in three days. Germany, thrown on the defensive, would be overwhelmed. To be sure, this gloomy prognostication by the German military staff left out of account Russia's poor planning, inefficient command structure and wasteful military expenditure. It also took no account of her lack of communications or her industrial weakness. But there can be no doubt that at the time the German military leadership was thrown virtually into panic by believing that Germany's conditions of safety would soon vanish. The 'Russian danger' was greatly exaggerated in Berlin in 1914.

In 1908 the Balkan fuse was lit. The resumption of Austro–Russian tension in the Balkans began paradoxically with an agreement between the Russian Foreign Minister Alexander Izvolski and Count Aehrenthal, the Habsburg Foreign Minister. Both wished to score some external success to revive the flagging status of their respective empires. Izvolski desired to change the 'rule' of the Straits of Constantinople, which closed them to all warships when Turkey was at peace, to a new rule which would allow Russian warships to pass them. Russia had always regarded control of the Straits as one of her most vital interests. Aehrenthal, less ambitious, wished to convert the occupation of the two Turkish provinces of Bosnia and Herzegovina into an actual annexation. They promised each other mutual support. In October 1908 Aehrenthal collected his side of the bargain, but British opposition prevented the Russians from realising their objective (page 43). The 'Bosnian crisis' marks a turning point in the relations of the powers before 1914. Slav Serbia, resenting the annexation of Bosnia–Herzegovina, appealed to Russia for support; Austria relied on Germany. No one was ready to fight. But good relations between Austria and Russia were at an end. Also ended was the Austro–Russian understanding to settle their imperial rivalries in the Balkans. Now they intrigued against each other and the fuse leading to war in 1914 was lit.

Other European nations with their own ambitions added to the breakdown of stability in the Balkans. The Ottoman Empire was attempting to reform itself after the Young Turk revolution of 1908. But Turkey was weak. Italy attacked Turkey in 1911 and annexed Tripoli. The small Balkan states, equally greedy, wanted Turkish territory in Europe and were ready to fight each other over the spoils.

Turkish weakness, Balkan nationalism and the rivalry of Austria and Russia destabilised south-east Europe.

At first the Balkan states went to war against Turkey. The Balkan League of Serbia, Bulgaria, Greece and Montenegro attacked the Turks in October 1912 and defeated them. As a result of the war Serbia greatly increased her territory, to the alarm of Austria. All the great European powers stepped in to supervise the peace and Russia had to agree to Austrian demands limiting Serbia's gains.

But hardly had the question been settled in London in May 1913 when the members of the Balkan League fought each other. Bulgaria now attacked Serbia and Greece; Montenegro, Romania and Turkey joined Serbia and Greece in attacking Bulgaria. Bulgaria was forced to make peace and yield many of her gains from the first Balkan war.

The conflicts of the Balkan states would have mattered comparatively little outside their own region of the world, but for the effects on Austria–Hungary (pages 61–66) and on Russia. There was little consistency about Russian policy in the Balkans. Strong Pan-Slav feelings motivated Russia's ambassadors in the Balkans and these were backed by sections of public opinion within Russia. But the official line taken by Sergei Sazonov, Izvolsky's successor at the Foreign Ministry in St Petersburg, was caution. The result of the Balkan

wars was to weaken Russia's position as well as Austria's. For Russia the future appeared full of uncertainties in the Balkans. The eventual alignment of the individual Balkan states, with Austria–Hungary and Germany on the one side and Russia and France on the other, was unpredictable. Only Serbia was still Russia's firm ally and that was not for love of Russia but due to her enmity of Austria–Hungary.

These uncertainties made the Russians much more nervous about the future of the Straits of Constantinople. They were not only vital strategically but, with the upsurge of the Russian economy, they also formed an increasingly important link in the chain of Russia's trade with the rest of the world. Three-quarters of her grain exports were shipped from the Black Sea through the Straits, and grain constituted some 40 per cent of Russia's total export trade. The Russians wished the Turks to remain the guardians as long as they did not fall under hostile influence until the Russians were strong enough to control them. Germany now had become a double threat: as Austria–Hungary's ally and, since 1909, as Turkey's 'friend'. The appointment of a German general, Liman von Sanders in November 1913 to command the army corps stationed in Constantinople greatly alarmed St Petersburg. Russian protests this time worked. General von Sanders was promoted to the rank of field marshal, which made him too grand merely to command troops in Constantinople.

On the plus side for the Russians was the attitude of the French who in 1912 strongly revived the Franco–Russian alliance (pages 29–30). But Russian policy would in the end be dictated by Russian interests. Until Russia's military reorganisation was completed, and while still faced with strikes and unrest at home, Russia wanted to avoid war. That was still the view of the Council of Ministers called to debate the question in January 1914 just a few months before the outbreak of war.

# CHAPTER 8

# *The Closing Decades of the Habsburg Empire*

The Habsburg Empire had been a formidable European power for more than four centuries. Was its disintegration in the twentieth century the inevitable consequence of the two most powerful currents of modern history: nationalism and industrialisation? These threatened respectively the common bond of loyalty which the nationalities composing the Dual Monarchy felt for the dynasty and the acceptance of an existing social order. In many ways industrialisation and nationalism were contradictory forces in Austria–Hungary. The large market of the empire and free trade within it helped industrial progress; socialism, which grew with industrial expansion, also called for an allegiance that cut across the ethnic differences of nationality. Nationalism, on the other hand, was divisive and threatened to break up the empire. But nationalism contained the seeds of conflict within itself. There could be no easy agreement in a part of Europe where the nationalities were so intermingled as to what precise national frontiers should be drawn, or who should form the majority in a state or which peoples must acquiesce in remaining a minority. There would be conflicts and tensions however matters were arranged and the majority of

the emperor's subjects felt 'better the devil we know'. There was much to be said for the supranational solution which the Habsburg Monarchy represented. Multinational states break apart when the central power is weakened beyond point of recovery. This did not happen in the Habsburg Empire until 1918. In defeated Russia, Lenin and Trotsky were able to restore the authority of the central power through civil war, but no such Habsburg recovery was possible in 1918. Nevertheless it took four years of devastating war to break Habsburg power and the cohesion of the Monarchy.

It has frequently been claimed that central power had been eroded half a century earlier with the constitutional settlement of 1867. But the settlement stood the test of time when judged by central European standards. The greatest threat to the Monarchy was Hungarian independence. After 1867 there was no longer a serious possibility of this. The extensive rights which the Magyars were granted in the historic kingdom of Hungary reconciled them to the unity of the empire under the personal link of the emperor–king. For the Magyars the continuation of the empire meant that the entire power of the Monarchy was available to defend their position against external and internal enemies.

The settlement of 1867 granted to each half of the empire its own government with control of internal affairs; this included, importantly, powers to decide what rights were to be conceded to the other nationalities living within the jurisdiction of

**Austria-Hungary's Population**
*(in millions)*

| 1900 | 1910 |
|------|------|
| 46.9 | 52.4 |

the kingdom of Hungary and Cis-Leithania, as the Austrian half of the empire was officially called. But the central power of the empire remained strong and real after 1867. Finance, foreign affairs and military matters remained the responsibility of the imperial ministries in Vienna, whose ministers were chosen by the emperor. The emperor was commander-in-chief of the imperial army. In another important way this unique imperial constitution actually strengthened central power. The democratic constitutional trend of the nineteenth and twentieth century could not be entirely halted in the empire. But franchise concessions were granted for the separate parliaments sitting in Vienna and Budapest. In Austria the year 1907 saw the introduction of manhood suffrage. The Magyars refused to accept any substantial reforms. But the Hungarian parliament exercised much more real power over the Hungarian government than the Austrian over the Austrian government. There existed no parliament for the empire as a whole which could influence or control the crucially important joint imperial ministries.

Indirect parliamentary influence was in theory provided for by the system of the 'delegations', representatives of the Austrian and Hungarian parliaments meeting separately and together (in theory) to deal with questions affecting the joint ministries. In practice, what concerned the delegations mainly was finance, customs, commercial policy and the contributions to the common budget to be paid by Austria and by Hungary. These questions were settled, after much wrangling based on obvious self-interest, for ten years at a time. The emperor's 'reserved' powers in foreign and military affairs remained virtually absolute through his choice of ministers and refusal to take notice of any parliamentary disapproval. His power would not have been so completely preserved in the twentieth century, and with it a strong central power, but for the dualism of the empire and so the absence of a single imperial parliament. Consequently imperial policies in war and foreign affairs were conducted by just a handful of men. These included the heads of the three joint ministries, with the minister of foreign affairs presiding; on important occasions the prime minister of Hungary, who had a constitutional right to be consulted on questions of foreign policy, and other ministers were invited to join in the discussion.

Among some of the Slavs, dualism was seen as

a device for excluding the Slav majority from their rightful and equal place in the empire. By dividing the empire, the Magyars and Germans constituted the majority each in their own half. The majority of the 21 million Slavs (approximate 1910 figures) in the empire as a whole was thus turned into minorities.

Of course the 'Slavs' were not unified in religion, social structure or tradition. The rivalries and hostilities between them were at least as important as their supposedly common interests. The Magyar–German compromise of 1867 led to parallel small compromises within each half of the empire. In Austria, the Polish gentry were given privileges at the expense of the Ruthenes; the Czechs were from time to time allowed special rights; but Serb, Croat and Slovene cultural development was restricted. The struggle between German-speaking Habsburg subjects and the other nationalities was bitter at the local level and in parliament, but it was not, as in Hungary, systematic government policy. In Hungary, the Magyars allowed a special status to the Croats but excluded the Slovaks and Serbs and Romanians from any share of power or from exercising autonomous rights.

**Nationalities of the Dual Monarchy, 1910**

|  | Austria | Hungary |
| --- | --- | --- |
| Germans | 9,950,000 | 2,037,000 |
| Czechs | 6,436,000 | – |
| Poles | 4,968,000 | – |
| Romanians | 275,000 | 2,949,000 |
| Ruthenians | 3,519,000 | 473,000 |
| Serbs & Croats | 783,000 | 2,939,000 |
| Italians | 768,000 | – |
| Slovenes | 1,253,000 | – |
| Slovaks | – | 1,968,000 |
| Magyars | – | 9,945,000 |

The politics of 'Austria' and of Hungary also diverged in other respects in the twentieth century. In Austria one striking development was the emergence of a socialist party led by Victor Adler which gained a sizeable parliamentary following in 1907. Austrian politics were marred by the antics of the German nationalists and the anti-Semitic Christian Socialists inspired by Karl Lueger. Conflicts between nationalists in Austria frequently paralysed parliament. The industrialised and prosperous Czechs demanded autonomy. The Germans in Bohemia sought to keep the Czechs in an inferior national status. The focus of the struggle was over the official use of language. When the emperor's ministers made concessions to the Czechs, the Germans refused co-operation to the government and when concessions were made to the Germans the Czechs went into bitter opposition. In any case parliament was regarded by the emperor as no more than an 'advisory body'.

The introduction of manhood suffrage in Austria in 1907 was intended to break the nationality deadlock. For a brief time the Social Democrats sat together, irrespective of national origin, whether German or Czech. It did not last. From 1908 to 1914 the old nationality conflict reasserted itself with as much vehemence as before. The conflict of the national parties reduced the parliament in its splendid and imposing building in Vienna to impotence. With such a record, parliamentary government could win little respect among the population as a whole.

In Hungary, extensive franchise reforms were blocked by the Magyar gentry as likely to undermine Magyar predominance. Relations with the non-Magyar nationalities remained bad down to 1914. Repression was the only policy consistently adopted. Hungarian politics revolved around largely unsuccessful attempts to modify the compromise of 1867 so that the Magyars could gain greater control over the army. But this was fiercely resisted by Francis Joseph, who threatened force against any Hungarian government or parliament seeking to tamper with the royal prerogatives.

When now we marvel at the continued resilience of the Habsburg Empire, despite national and constitutional conflicts, which seemed to increase rather than diminish during the last years of peace, we tend to overlook one question. Who had anything to gain from driving the conflict to extremes and threatening the Habsburg Empire with disintegration? Not the Magyars, not the Germans, nor the Poles, who enjoyed greater liberties under Austrian than Russian and German rule; not the Jews, whose talents transformed cultural Vienna; not the Czechs

who believed their own security necessitated the empire; not even the majority of Serbs and Croats in the annexed provinces of Bosnia and Herzegovina. Everywhere the mass of the peasantry was attached to the Habsburg dynasty. Agitation for independence, whether of Czech or southern Slavs, was largely the work of a minority among the more educated. The great majority of Francis Joseph's subjects wanted the empire to continue even though they differed so bitterly on the kind of empire they wanted. Meanwhile the dynasty and its central power, the imperial civil service and administration, and the imperial army all carried out their duties sustained by the common consent of the great majority of the people.

Francis Joseph had won the affection of his subjects simply by always having been there. His family misfortunes bravely borne, his simplicity and honesty, and pride in his robustness in very old age combined to make him the most respected and venerated monarch in Europe. And all this despite the fact that he had made war on his own subjects in 1849 (Hungary) and had lost all the wars in which Austria had engaged since his accession against Italy, France and Prussia. It was a remarkable achievement.

During the last years of the nineteenth and during the early twentieth century, the empire emerged as a modern state. In Hungary the administration was virtually Magyarised. This applied also to the judicial administration. But the country enjoyed a high reputation for justice, with admittedly the important exception of what were seen as 'political' offences. The kingdom of Hungary was Magyar: patriotism meant Magyar patriotism; dissent from this view was treated harshly. But, despite this fierce attempt to Magyarise the nationalities on the peripheries of the kingdom, the policy met with little success; the nationalities preserved their identities. In the Austrian half of the empire the governments sought to arrive at settlements between Germans, Czechs and Poles acceptable to all sides, but with little lasting success.

That the empire was on the whole so well governed was in no small part due to an incorruptible and, on the whole, intelligent and fair-minded bureaucracy of civil servants and jurists. It is true that in the Austrian half of the empire the Germans constituted some 80 per cent of the civil servants though by population they were entitled only to a third. The much better education of the Germans accounts for some of this predominance. In Hungary deliberate Magyarisation led to more than 90 per cent of government service being in Hungarian-speaking hands. In the central imperial administration the Germans also played the major role, with more than half the civil servants German-speaking. But one can certainly not speak of a totally German-dominated imperial administration. In the principal joint ministries of the empire, Francis Joseph ensured that the three common ministers never came from the same half of the Monarchy. The senior Foreign Ministry was held in turn by a Saxon German, a Hungarian, an Austrian German, a Pole, a Hungarian and an Austrian German.

To say when we turn to the economic development of the empire that it was disappointingly slow in the latter part of the nineteenth and early twentieth century implies a comparison with western and northern Europe. But the empire's centre was in the Balkans, the grain-producing Hungarian plain. Within the empire lay regions such as the Czech provinces, which achieved a development comparable to the most advanced areas of Europe, and such poverty-stricken provinces as Galicia.

The empire thus provides great contrasts between comparative wealth and stark poverty. Agricultural backwardness and an increasing population condemned the peasants of Galicia to continuous poverty. Large-scale emigration was one consequence. (The empire's population grew from 46.9 million in 1900 to 52.4 million in 1910.) In Bohemia, and in upper and lower Austria, agriculture, as well as industry, turned these regions into the most prosperous in the empire. In Hungary the owners of the great landed estates led the way to the introduction of better farming methods. The central Hungarian plain became one of the granaries of Europe. The imperial customs union, freeing all trade within the empire, opened up to Hungary's agriculture the market of the more industrialised Austrian half of the empire.

In the twentieth century Austria–Hungary achieved a fast rate of industrial growth in the favoured regions. Nevertheless the empire as a whole lagged far behind the more advanced western and northern European nations. Regional variations were as marked in industrial as in agricultural development. The most successful agricultural parts of the empire were also the most industrially advanced: upper and lower Austria, Bohemia, Moravia and

Silesia and Hungary proper. Industrialisation had made little impact in Galicia, Dalmatia or Transylvania. In 1911, textiles and clothing, tobacco and foodstuffs together with wood, leather and paper accounted for nearly two-thirds of the Austrian half of the empire's industrial output. But imperial policies of free trade within the empire tended to maintain these regional differences of progress and backwardness. On the other hand, it needs to be remembered that without state aid in the development of the railways, without good administration and internal peace and security throughout the empire, the economic conditions of the people would have been far worse than they actually were.

## Austria-Hungary's Production
*(annual averages)*

|  | 1900–4 | 1910–13 |
|---|---|---|
| Raw-cotton consumption *(thousand metric tons)* | 135.4 (1895–1904) | 191.4 (1905–13) |
| Coal and lignite output *(million metric tons)* | 38.8 | 50.7 |
| Pig-iron output *(thousand metric tons)* | 1,425.0 | 2,204.0 |
| Steel output *(million metric tons)* | 1.2 | 2.46 |

It is remarkable that the empire, beset by so many problems internally, backward in economic development and also poor, achieved a high reputation in the arts and was still acknowledged to be one of the great powers of Europe. The Monarchy's universities were second to none, the musical, literary and theatrical life of Vienna, Budapest and Prague, and the renown of Freud and Liszt and Strauss, were celebrated throughout the Western world. The Monarchy's status as a great power had been diminished, it is true, but not extinguished by defeats in the nineteenth-century continental wars that created united Italy and Germany. In 1900 the empire was still considered one of the foremost military powers of Europe, a bulwark against the possibility of the Russian or German dominance of south-eastern Europe. The territorially large Habsburg Empire was thus a major element in the pre-1914 European balance of power whose disappearance, the other powers felt, would create grave new problems.

Actually the empire's military capacity was overrated. The perennial lack of funds was one reason for its weakness. Another unique problem was that it was largely officered by German-speaking Austrians and a smaller number of Hungarians; the troops themselves were composed of all the nationalities and spoke in many languages. Even worse was the incompetence of the General Staff. Only in the two years before the war of 1914 was the army increased to a potential wartime strength of 1.5 million men. Military and economic weakness made the Monarchy's foreign ministers cautious and conservative.

There is a shape, logic and consistency to Habsburg foreign policy in the nineteenth century with its emphasis on the importance of tradition and of dynastic rule and its opposition to nationalism. The loss of the Italian provinces was therefore seen as a particularly heavy blow. If the neighbours of the Habsburg Empire, Romania and Serbia, followed the example of Piedmont in the wars of Italian unification, justifying their efforts by an appeal to the right of national self-determination, then the Habsburg Empire must disintegrate altogether. Serbia cast in the role of Piedmont was the nightmare vision that drove the Emperor and his ministers to stake the future of the empire on the field of battle in July 1914. But they also recognised that the real threat had not been Piedmont but Piedmont in alliance with France in 1859 and with Prussia in 1866. The real threat in 1914 was felt to be not Serbia but Serbia in alliance with Russia.

Security and integrity are basic objectives of any state's foreign policy. But the great powers of pre-1914 Europe also considered it axiomatic that they should possess spheres of influence and control beyond their own state frontiers. In the nineteenth century the Habsburgs were forced to abandon their traditional role of influence first in the Italian and then in the German states. By the twentieth century the only 'frontier' left open was the Balkan. Not to suffer a third defeat on this last frontier was seen as a matter of vital importance for the future of the empire.

With the decline of the Ottoman Empire in Europe the future of the Balkan peoples, divided and intermingled in religious beliefs, in tradition, in culture and in socio-economic structure, preoccupied the European great powers. But the Balkan states pursued policies of their own and were locked in rivalry over the disposition of the still Turkish or formerly Turkish lands.

Once Russia had recovered from defeat in the Far East, the attention of St Petersburg reverted to the Balkans and a rediscovery of Russia's Slav mission. A much more active Russian policy now coincided with a new period of Ottoman weakness caused by the internal upheavals of the Young Turk movement (1908 to 1910). It also coincided with the growing ambitions and rivalries of the Balkan states, themselves casting covetous eyes on Macedonia and other territories still ruled by the Turk. The Balkans were becoming a powder barrel. Austro-Russian co-operation might have contained these tensions. Instead Russia's ambitious ministers at the various Balkan capitals were adding to the growing turmoil. The turning point came in 1908/9.

In the Monarchy, the Foreign Minister Count Aehrenthal was a well-known advocate of a policy of co-operation and agreement with Russia. He regarded Austria–Hungary as a 'satiated' state that needed no more territories and no more Slavs. But as a final step of consolidation – almost a technical consolidation – whose purpose was to regularise and remove all uncertainty, he wished to convert the Monarchy's position in Bosnia–Herzegovina from that of the permanently occupying power (since 1878) to one of sovereignty. He was prepared to pay compensation to the Turks and to give up the occupation of another Turkish territory, the strategically important land known as Novipazar. This withdrawal would also convince the Russians that Austria–Hungary had abandoned all thought of territorial expansion. Talks were arranged with the Russian Foreign Minister, Alexander Izvolski. Their famous, and unrecorded, conversation took place at the castle of Buchlau in 1908. From the available evidence it seems clear that the whole basis of these talks was the intention to strengthen Austro-Russian co-operation. Izvolski said that Russia would diplomatically support Austria–Hungary's wish to annex Bosnia–Herzegovina. In return he asked for, and obtained, Aehrenthal's promise of diplomatic support for a Russian proposal to the powers to change the rule of the Straits (page 59). Aehrenthal soon after, while Izvolski toured western Europe and had not even time to consult the Tsar about the Buchlau 'bargain', announced the annexation of Bosnia–

Herzegovina to Europe. Izvolski was furious. He had no success with his attempt to change the rule of the Straits: Britain rejected the proposal outright. To save face, Izvolski now claimed he had been tricked by Aehrenthal.

From here on the threads lead to the catastrophe of 1914. Out of the breakdown of relations between Izvolski and Aehrenthal grew the prolonged Bosnian crisis. Serbia's nationalist feelings had been wildly aroused by the Monarchy's annexation of Bosnia and Herzegovina, inhabited by many Serbs. Russia backed Serbia and was insistent on 'compensation' for Serbia; also that the Monarchy should submit the whole question of annexation to a conference of powers. With the German ally's support, Aehrenthal refused both demands. Russia and Britain and France backed away. Serbia did not. In 1909 Serbia and Austria–Hungary came close to war, with Russia acting as Serbia's protector. In reality neither Russia nor any of the powers were ready for war in 1909. One cannot help speculating how different a course history might have taken if Austria–Hungary had used her superior strength to defeat Serbia then. As it was, Izvolski drew back. On Germany fell the odium of having threatened Russia with a peremptory note that unless she recognised the annexation at once, Germany would not hold the Monarchy back from attacking Serbia. Izvolski could now claim that the German 'ultimatum' forced Russia to give way. More important, the crisis marked the end of tolerably good Austro-Russian relations. Were their Balkan differences really so irreconcilable? The collision of the two empires was due to miscalculation rather than deliberate intent. In 1909 Russia was the more aggressive of the two states.

The Russian diplomats in the years after 1909 redoubled their efforts to re-establish Russia's damaged prestige among the Balkan states. These moves coincided with the intrigues and national ambitions of the Balkan states themselves, whose policies in the end could not be controlled by the Russians.

In 1911 the Italians made war on the Ottoman Empire (page 35). This started a new period of continuous Balkan tensions. In 1912 the Habsburgs believed that the Russians had inspired a Balkan League of Greece, Serbia, Montenegro and Bulgaria to attack Turkey. These states had temporarily buried their own disputes over Macedonia and other territorial disputes to grab more lands from Turkey. Then they in turn fell out over the booty in 1913 when Bulgaria attacked Serbia and Greece and was herself defeated by a new alliance of Balkan states (page 60).

Apart from the certainty of Austro-Serb enmity, there were no other certainties in the Balkans during the last years before 1914. Neither Russia nor the Monarchy could be sure at any point of crisis which of the other Balkan states would side with whom. The unhappy consequence for the peace of Europe was that Russia and Austria–Hungary felt equally threatened by the diplomatic intrigues of the other! Russia, with promises of French support, was both fearful and active. The Dual Monarchy could never assume that the German ally would stand behind her. As for Italy, her alliance was nominal. Italy was regarded as a potential enemy. So the Habsburgs felt unsure of the future.

Austria–Hungary's bitter opponent, Serbia, had emerged greatly enlarged from the two Balkan wars. In 1913, by helping to create independent and friendly Albania, Austria–Hungary succeeded in checking Serbia's further expansion to the Adriatic. This was achieved not so much by the 'conference of European' powers as by the Dual Monarchy's own threats delivered to Serbia. Count Leopold Berchtold, Aehrenthal's successor at the Foreign Ministry since 1912, learnt from these experiences that Austria–Hungary must needs rely on her own firmness. Behind Serbia stood Russia. But Francis Joseph and his ministers believed that firm diplomacy could still break the hostile ring of states and Russia's manifest design to encircle the Monarchy, provided Germany loyally backed the Habsburg Empire. Sarajevo changed all that.

# CHAPTER 9

## *Over the Brink: The Five-week Crisis, 28 June to 1 August 1914*

The Great War disrupted and destroyed lives on a scale never known before. More than 60 million men were mobilised and 8.5 million were killed, 21 million were wounded and in every town and village in Europe the blinded and maimed victims served as daily reminders decades after the war was over. In every town and village war memorials commemorate the names of those who gave their lives for their country. The war which involved millions and for which millions suffered was launched by the decision of just a few men negotiating and conspiring in secret. They bear a heavy responsibility. What made these men act the way they did? Were they aware of what they were doing, or did they just muddle into war through confusion and error?

There was a widespread illusion about the course the war would take. The troops left for the front believing that they would be home by Christmas. With the new mass armies it was thought that the war would be decided by the devastating battles fought at the outset. But no one expected that this would be just another war, like those of the mid-nineteenth century, ending with the victors exacting some territorial and financial punishment from the vanquished and leading to a new balance of power. There was, however, no illusion about what was at stake. Grey's famous words about the lights going out all over Europe expressed a sentiment that would have been well understood in Paris, Berlin, Vienna and St Petersburg. Bethmann Hollweg gloomily predicted the toppling of thrones

and the victory of socialism. In Vienna, the future existence of the Habsburg Monarchy was felt to be at stake: defeat would lead to her dissolution. Tsarist Russia was beset by serious internal disturbances and French society was deeply divided on the eve of the war. There were no illusions about the devastating consequences of this war from which a new world would emerge. There were hesitations on the brink of war. It was then too late. How had the powers allowed the crisis caused initially by a terrorist crime, the assassination of an archduke, the heir to the Habsburg throne, to escalate until there was no way out but a devastating European war? There seems to be no obvious connection between the murder committed by a young man in Bosnia and the clash of armies of millions.

The assassination of the Archduke Francis Ferdinand in Sarajevo on 28 June 1914 was the work of a handful of Bosnian youths who had romantically dedicated their lives to Serb nationalism and had been greatly influenced by the Russian terrorists in exile. They received their weapons from the secret Serbian conspiratorial Black Hand organisation headed by Colonel Dragutin Dimitrijević, who was also in charge of army secret intelligence. The Bosnian youths, who had spent some time in Belgrade, had been helped across the Serb frontier by Serbian agents. The Prime Minister of Serbia, Nikola Pašić, and King Alexander were powerless against the army officers and the Black Hand. But Pašić did send a vague warning to Vienna that

*Gavrilo Princip is seized by police, moments after mortally wounding Archduke Francis Ferdinand and his wife.*

the Archduke would be in danger when he visited Sarajevo.

The amateur assassins almost bungled their task. On the morning of 28 June, the first attempt failed and the bomb thrown by one of the six conspirators exploded under the car following the Archduke. Incredibly the Archduke, his wife and the Governor of Bosnia drove through the open streets again the same afternoon. When the Archduke's chauffeur hesitated which way to go, by mere chance one of the conspirators, Gavrilo Princip, found himself opposite the Archduke's stationary car. He aimed two shots at the Archduke and the Governor of Bosnia; they mortally wounded Francis Ferdinand and his wife.

The government of Serbia did not want war in 1914, for the country had not yet recovered from the exertions of the Balkan wars. But the government could not control the army nor prevent the secret societies from fomenting and aiding anti-Habsburg movements in Bosnia and Herzegovina. The assassination of the Archduke was unwelcome news to the government, for the King and his government would now be called to account for

allowing anarchical political conditions which gave the terrorists their base and power.

In Vienna, the Dual Monarchy's foreign minister, Count Berchtold, before those fateful shots at Sarajevo had given no serious thought to war. He did not judge the internal state of the Habsburg Monarchy as so desperate. Serbia and Russia would surely be restrained by firm Austro-Hungarian diplomacy backed by imperial Germany. The Habsburgs could continue to rely upon the divisions and mutual antagonisms of their Slav subjects. The Slovenes were Catholics and loyal to the Crown. The Croats were Catholics too, and union with the Greek Orthodox Serbs was opposed by the majority of them. Nor were the Serbs in favour of any general union of southern Slavs, 'Yugoslavia', which would place them in the minority of such a new state. They dreamt of a 'Greater Serbia', but this would have placed the Croats in a minority! The idea of 'Yugoslavia' had won the adherence of only a minority of students and intellectuals. The majority of the southern Slavs had no thought of leaving the Habsburg Monarchy in 1914.

Every Austro-Hungarian minister since 1909

realised that the threat to the existence of the Habs-burg Empire was due not to the challenge of any of the small Balkan states such as Serbia, but to Russia utilising Balkan discontents against the Dual Monarchy. That is why the misunderstanding and dispute between Russia and Austria–Hungary – the so-called Bosnian crisis – is such a significant milestone on the road to war.

Russia had been forced to back down when faced with Germany's determined support of Austria–Hungary. In this way, the changed status of two provinces in the Balkans – which made no real difference to the map of Europe – led to disastrous consequences out of all proportion to the issues involved. Henceforth, the good Austro-Russian understanding, designed to prevent the two powers from becoming so entangled in local Balkan conflicts that thereby they could be dragged into hostility with each other, was broken by crises that threatened the peace of Europe. Rivalry, suspicion and intrigue in the Balkans replaced the co-oper-ation of former years. The final crisis was occasioned by the assassination of the Archduke.

In Vienna, news of the assassination entirely changed the attitude of Berchtold and the majority of the Monarchy's ministers. A diplomatic offensive was no longer thought enough. Habsburg prestige was now so seriously involved that, unless Serbia was 'punished', the empire's role as a great power would be at an end. Serbia could not be allowed to get away with this last and most serious provocation by sheltering behind Russia. If the Monarchy could prove that Russian protection could not save Serbia from her wrath, the lesson would not be lost on the other Balkan states and Austria–Hungary's international position of power would be reasserted. Berchtold concluded that Serbia's hostility must be broken and that only Serbian submission to the will of the Monarchy should be allowed to save her from war and conquest.

There were three obstacles. The Austro-Hungarian army was not ready for war: it would need more than a month to prepare. The Chief of Staff, Conrad von Hötzendorf, moreover, pointed out that, if Russia intervened, the Austro-Hungarian army would need German military co-operation to cope successfully with a war on two fronts, the Serbian and Russian. The Monarchy's ministers were in any case convinced that the Monarchy could not risk war with Russia unless the German ally stood side by side with Austria–

Hungary in war. Would the imperial German government support the Monarchy now? The third obstacle to war was internal, the opposition of the Hungarian Prime Minister, Count Tisza.

On 4 July 1914, the Council of Ministers, meeting in Vienna, decided that the first step was to ascertain the attitude of the Kaiser and his ministers. Count Hoyos was sent to Berlin with a personal letter from the Emperor Francis Joseph to the Kaiser, and a set of questions from the Monarchy's ministers. They did not beat about the bush, but wanted to know whether Germany would come to Austria–Hungary's help if Russia chose to intervene on behalf of Serbia. They also explained what was in store for Serbia. Serbia would be eliminated 'as a power factor in the Balkans'.

From a variety of recorded conversations, some of which have only recently come to light, it is possible to gain close insights into what the Kaiser and Bethmann Hollweg and the military thought. For two years and more there had been mounting fears about the planned expansion of Russian military power. The weakness of the Habsburg Monarchy became increasingly apparent, and there were serious doubts about her future after the old Emperor's death, which could not be long delayed. There were also nagging doubts about Austria–Hungary's loyalty to the alliance with Germany. Would the alliance survive if Germany once again forced the Monarchy to desist from doing what she thought imperative for her survival – to show she was stronger than Serbia and would not tolerate Serbian hostility? Imperial Germany felt she needed the support of Austria–Hungary if the mass Russian Slav armies were to be checked. A war with Russia arising out of an Austro-Serb conflict would ensure the Monarchy's support. A war starting between Germany and Russia, or Germany and France, might not find Austria–Hungary on Germany's side. Then there was a calculation of quite a different kind. Bethmann Hollweg hoped to weaken, perhaps even to break up, the alignment of Russia, France and Britain. Bethmann Hollweg's calculations were all based on 'ifs'. If Russia should decide to back Serbia and then applied to Paris for backing, and if France then refused to risk war with Germany so that Russia might threaten Austria–Hungary with war, Russia would discover that the French alliance was, in reality, worthless. *If* all this happened then Germany would be in a position to win back Russia's friendship, perhaps even her alliance. If, on the other hand, it should come to war, then better now than later. But the Dual Monarchy must initiate the war so that at home it could be presented as being fought in defence of Germany's ally against tsarist Russia. Russia would be cast in the role of aggressor.

The critical discussions between the Kaiser, Bethmann Hollweg and the military took place immediately after the arrival of Count Hoyos in Berlin. The decision, when it was reached, was not the Kaiser's alone. That is a myth which was believed for a long time. The decision was to back Austria–Hungary to the hilt, with German military support if necessary, should Russia intervene to prevent the Dual Monarchy from dealing with Serbia. The Habsburg ministers were given a free hand to settle with Serbia in any way they thought appropriate. That was the message to Vienna on 6 July, the Kaiser's famous 'blank cheque'. The Habsburg ministers were also urged to act quickly against Serbia while the governments of Europe were still shocked by the assassinations at Sarajevo. In Germany, the Chief of Staff, General Moltke, continued his health cure at the spa of Karlsbad. Admiral Tirpitz stayed away from Berlin and the Kaiser departed on his yacht to cruise in the North Sea. Everything was done to avoid an air of crisis, to camouflage the impending Habsburg action. Why? It could only have been to allay British, Russian and French suspicions that Germany secretly stood behind Austria–Hungary. A diplomatic triumph for Austria–Hungary and Germany was still preferable to war. Europe was to be faced with a sudden *fait accompli*.

What went wrong? In Vienna the ministers were not unanimous, even after receiving the German assurances. Count Tisza, the powerful Hungarian Prime Minister, remained opposed to war at their meeting on 7 July and the following week gave way only on condition that the Dual Monarchy first agreed not to annex any Serbian territory after the expected victory. Tisza, a Magyar, wanted to see no more Slavs added to the population of the empire. Then there was further delay as the army asked for more time. Berchtold used it to compile a justificatory dossier of Serbia's recent wrongdoings for presentation to the chancelleries of Europe when the time for action eventually came. Then Berchtold decided to wait until the French President, Poincaré, and the French Prime Minister,

René Viviani, had ended their visit to St Petersburg. Thereby he hoped that Austria would act at the very moment when Russia would find it more difficult to consult her French ally.

More than three weeks had now elapsed since the assassination of Francis Ferdinand at Sarajevo. The Austrians had worked in greatest secrecy, and Europe had been lulled into a false sense of calm. On 23 July the Austro-Hungarian ultimatum was presented in Belgrade, and in just six days Europe plunged headlong from peace to certain war. On 25 July, Serbia mobilised her army and, in a cleverly worded reply later that day, appeared to accept many of the Austrian demands, although not to the point of submitting Serbia to Austrian supervision. The same evening, the Austro-Hungarian Ambassador left Belgrade and Austria–Hungary mobilised against Serbia. Even though the Austro-Hungarian army would not be ready for another three weeks, Austria–Hungary declared war on 28 July, and to make war irrevocable bombarded Belgrade on 29 July.

Between the break of diplomatic relations and the actual declaration of war, Sir Edward Grey attempted mediation and sent proposals to Berlin in an attempt to preserve the peace of Europe. Bethmann Hollweg wanted no such interference and Grey's efforts came to nothing. When the Kaiser learnt how the Serbians had replied to the ultimatum, he was personally delighted. So much for the myth that he was thirsting to go to war. He immediately wrote a note on the morning of 28 July from his palace in Potsdam, expressing his evident relief that now there was no longer any need for war – 'On the whole the wishes of the Danube Monarchy have been acceded to, every cause for war has vanished' – and he added that he was ready to mediate. But by then Bethmann Hollweg and Berchtold had instigated the Austro-Hungarian declaration of war on Serbia which the Kaiser heard about later that day. Bethmann Hollweg now made every effort to localise the war. On 30 July, he urged Vienna to exchange views with St Petersburg. He resisted calls for mobilisation in Berlin and he initiated the Kaiser's personal telegrams appealing to the Tsar not to mobilise.

The weak Tsar was under pressure from his own military advisers to mobilise. The French military, too, were urging mobilisation and the French Ambassador in St Petersburg, Maurice Paléologue,

**Europe in 1914**

ICELAND

GREAT BRITAIN &
IRELAND

*ATLANTIC*

*OCEAN*

Dublin •

• London

BELGIUM

*Seine*

• Paris

FRANCE

LUX.

NORWAY

Oslo

*NORTH*

*SEA*

SWEDEN

Stockholm

Helsinki

FINLAND

RUSSIA

DENMARK

Copenhagen

NETHER-
LANDS

*Elbe*

• Berlin

• Warsaw

GERMANY

Cologne

*Rhine*

*Danube*

• Prague

Vienna

HUNGARY

AUSTRIA

Budapest

SWITZ.

• Munich

*Rhône*

ITALY

Belgrade

ROMANIA

• Bucharest

SERBIA

BULGARIA

Sofia

PORTUGAL

• Madrid

SPAIN

GIBRALTAR
(British)

Spanish Protectorate

Morocco
(French
Protectorate)

CORSICA
(French)

Rome •

MONTE-
NEGRO

SARDINIA
(Italian)

SICILY

Algiers

ALGERIA
(French)

GREECE

Athens

ALBANIA

DODECANESE
(Italian)

TURKEY

CRETE
(Greek)

*MEDITERRANEAN SEA*

TUNISIA
(French)

Tripoli •

TRIPOLITANIA
(Italian)

CYRENAICA
(Italian)

EGYPT

0                    1000 miles

0              1000 km

pressed their views on the Foreign Minister, Sazonov. The French General Staff was terrified that war would begin in the west and find the Russians unprepared. Russia, if she went to war, could count on French support; the Tsar had known this for certain ever since the visit of President Poincaré and Prime Minister Viviani to St Petersburg (20–23 July). But the Russians, in so vital a question for the empire, would reach their own decisions just as the Austrians had had to do.

The reaction of the Tsar, Sazonov and his ministers was to seek to 'localise' the crisis in a way neither Germany nor Austria–Hungary had in mind. When Bethmann Hollweg spoke of 'localisation', he meant that the Dual Monarchy should be allowed to dictate terms to Serbia. The Tsar and Sazonov, on the other hand, hoped that Germany and the other powers would stand aside while Russia supported Serbia to prevent Austria–Hungary from attacking Serbia. To the Russians, the Austrian ultimatum to Serbia was hurling down the gauntlet. But could Russia risk war now? There was much civil disturbance and there were large-scale strikes; the army would be in a much stronger position three years later. The news of the ultimatum reached Sazonov on the morning of 24 July. His first reaction was to advise the Serbians to surrender to Austrian demands and not to fight. But later that afternoon, the Russian Council of Ministers agreed to recommend to the Tsar a 'partial' mobilisation against Austria–Hungary only. Russian involvement in the fate of Serbia was also officially announced. The line was now to put pressure on Austria–Hungary.

The following day, 25 July, the Tsar at an imperial council confirmed the need for preparatory military measures in anticipation of partial mobilisation. By 26 July, these secret preparations were in full swing. The news of the Austrian declaration of war on Serbia and bombardment of Belgrade on 29 July threw St Petersburg into a frenzy. The Tsar agreed to a general mobilisation, but after receiving the Kaiser's telegram changed this to a 'partial mobilisation', against Austria only. In reality, though, the Tsar's motive was to avoid pushing Germany into mobilisation – partial or total made no difference, for the Austro-Hungarian–German alliance and campaign plans would necessitate German mobilisation anyway. It was too late in Berlin to continue playing the game of 'localising' the Austro-Serbian war. With the military in Berlin now also in a frenzy,

Moltke insisting on the need to mobilise, Bethmann Hollweg and the Kaiser could not resist the 'military imperative' much longer. On 31 July, the Russian military persuaded the Tsar that a 'partial mobilisation' was technically impossible, and Nicholas II consented to general mobilisation. But the nature of German military planning had made war inevitable after the Russian partial mobilisation on 29 July.

The very concept of the Schlieffen Plan was responsible for the situation that mobilisation meant war. Its implications may not have been grasped fully by the Kaiser and Bethmann Hollweg in July. But in militaristic Wilhelmine Germany, the generals' views on military necessity were conclusive. Until the moment of Russian mobilisation, Moltke, the Chief of Staff, was ready to leave control to Chancellor Bethmann Hollweg. But, when on 30 July it became clear that the Chancellor's policy of frightening Russia into acquiescence had failed, there was not a moment to lose. France had to be defeated before Russia could complete her mobilisation. The German onslaught must now start without delay against Belgium and France. Ultimatums were sent to Russia and France and war was declared with unseemly haste on Russia on 1 August 1914, on France two days later. The German invasion of Belgium was followed by a British ultimatum and declaration of war on 4 August.

It was the same Schlieffen Plan which was responsible for forcing the pace in St Petersburg and Paris. That the Germans would at the outset turn the mass of their armies against France and not Russia was known. The Russian–French military plans were constructed accordingly, with the promise of an early Russian offensive to relieve pressure on the French. That is why the French military were so worried about 'partial mobilisation' against Austria–Hungary. In the event of war they wanted Russia's military effort to be directed against the main enemy, Germany. No wonder Paléologue was urging full mobilisation in St Petersburg. In this way was Bethmann Hollweg's diplomatic 'offensive' matched by the offensive strategy of the German General Staff with its aim of destroying the French will to resist by seeking total victory in the west.

Behind the 'governments' – the handful of men who made the decisions in Berlin, Vienna, Paris and St Petersburg – stood populations willing to fight for Republic, King and Emperor. Only a tiny minority dissented. For the largest Socialist Party

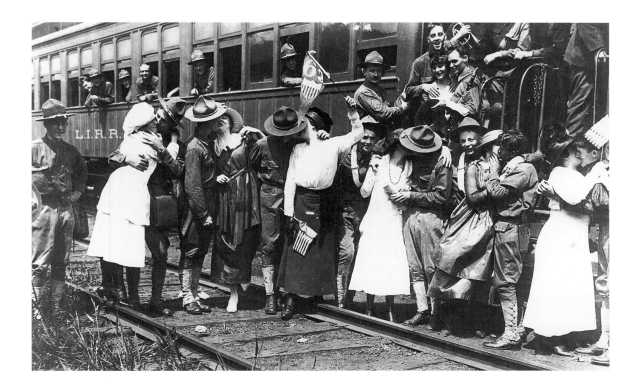

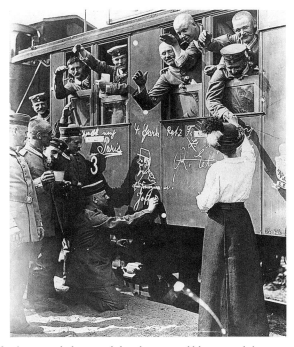

*To Arms. Marching off to war with no conception of what lay in store for them, everybody expected that the war would be over and the troops home by Christmas. In August 1914, all the combatants looked equally optimistic – witness the French,* left, *and the Germans,* right. *Even in 1917, the soldiers of the last nation to enter the First World War – the United States – still seemed gleeful, despite being poorly trained and ill-equipped* (top).

in Europe, the German, the war was accepted as being fought against tsarist Russian aggression. The different nationalities of the Dual Monarchy all fought for the Habsburgs, the French socialists fought as enthusiastically in defence of their fatherland ruthlessly invaded by the Germans.

The responsibility for starting the conflict in July and August must rest primarily on the shoulders of Germany and Austria–Hungary. Russia and France reacted and chose to fight rather than to withdraw from the confrontation, which would have left the diplomatic victory to Germany and Austria–Hungary. Whether they had wisely interpreted their national interests is another question. For Britain it was a preventive war. Not directly threatened by Germany, Britain was looking to the future and what that future would hold for her if Germany were able to gain the mastery of continental Europe. But Britain's was a 'preventive' war in quite a different sense to Germany's. The British government had done everything possible to prevent war from breaking out, but could not afford to stand aside.

Yet Britain cannot be absolved from blame. War broke out in 1914 not only as a consequence of the shots at Sarajevo. The tensions that had been building up in Europe and the wider world for two decades and more had created the frame of mind that led the European chancelleries along a fatal path. For Britain, faced with the relative decline of her power, the problem of defending her empire loomed ever larger. She negotiated a division of interests with France of territory – Morocco and Egypt – that did not exclusively belong to either. Russia also was appeased for a time. Inevitably fears and hostilities in Europe were raised. British foreign secretaries were well aware of this and would have preferred it not to be so. But Britain's immediate interests were placed before international harmony. That is the darker thread that ran through British policy. During the last decade before the war Britain too tended to follow Bismarckian *Realpolitik*. Just as she wanted to avoid imperial clashes with Russia, so too Britain feared that the entente with France

might not prove strong enough to prevent Germany and France reaching a settlement of their differences. Then Britain would have been isolated in the world. British policy was too compromised to allow Grey in the summer of 1914 a strong mediating role. But, given German war plans and the small size of the British army at the outset, the hope that London might influence decisively the course of events in Europe during July 1914 was an illusion anyway.

Nowhere were domestic political considerations the decisive influence. The war was about national power, and ambitions, and also fears as to how national power would in the future be exercised. Russia was not satisfied with her already huge empire. France was conscious of her secondary status in Europe which, if she were left without an ally, would leave her at Germany's mercy. Austria–Hungary wished to annihilate Slav hostility beyond her frontiers. For imperial Germany, a future in which her military power was no longer superior to the combined military forces of her potential enemies was not to be tolerated. This had to be averted by diplomacy or so-called 'preventive' war. Germany's own diplomacy had contributed much to the French and British feelings of insecurity. It had finally placed her in the unenviable position of being on bad relations with her neighbours in the east and the west. The working out of the Schlieffen Plan saddled her with the guilt of violating a small neutral state and with the necessity to strike the first blow, for it was Germany who had to declare war in order to keep to the timetable of the famous war plan. What the coming of the war in 1914 reveals is how a loss of confidence and fears for the future can be as dangerous to peace as the naked spirit of aggression that was to be the cause of the Second World War a quarter of a century later. A handful of European leaders in 1914 conceived national relationships crudely in terms of power and conflict, and the future in terms of a struggle for survival in competition for the world. For this, millions had to suffer and die.

# PART II

The Response of China and
Japan to Western Dominance

# CHAPTER 10

## *China in Disintegration, 1900–1929*

About one-fifth of humanity lives in China, the most populous nation of the world. But until the nineteenth century, though in touch with the West, China followed her own path of historical development unaffected by Western contact. Some features of this historical development are remarkable.

The hugeness of China in land area and population makes it all the more extraordinary that for more than a thousand years a concept of unity was maintained. Other peoples were absorbed as China expanded. The ethnic origin of some of these peoples survives to the present day in the form of national minorities with which about one in eighteen Chinese identify – though intermarriage has obliterated the majority. In traditional China, to be considered Chinese was not a matter of race or nationality in the Western sense but depended on an acceptance of Chinese customs and culture. Those who did not accept them – even people within Chinese frontiers – were considered 'barbarian'. The living traditions of Chinese culture were so strong that they absorbed the alien peoples who conquered China and so turned them into Chinese. These included the Mongol dynasty and, in the mid-seventeenth century, the Manchus who ruled from then until the revolution of 1911 as the Ch'ing dynasty. Foreign peoples were incorporated by conquest or else absorbed by China when they conquered the empire from without. The political and cultural continuity of China persisted, overcoming periods of internal rebellion and war:

integration, not disintegration, was the dominant theme of more than a millennium of Chinese history until the mid-nineteenth century. But how should historians interpret the century that followed?

If we stop the clock in 1925 it would certainly seem that the disintegration of China had proceeded so far that the long tradition of the national unity of the Chinese Empire could never be restored. It was then a country torn by internal strife, economically bound to the West and Japan, yet without significant progress, as far as the mass of Chinese were concerned, to show for Western economic penetration, politically divided, and with parts of China dominated by foreign powers. From the later Ch'ing period in the 1840s until the close of the civil war in 1949, China knew no peace and passed through a number of phases of disintegration which no single ruler who followed the Ch'ing dynasty after 1911 could halt. But from the perspective of the 1990s the picture looks quite different again. The Chinese Empire is unified once more and has reasserted her right to recover territories once Chinese or over which suzerainty was asserted. Tibet has been reabsorbed already. After the Second World War, China wanted to eliminate all foreign penetration and special privileges in her country – Japanese, Russian, British, American, French and Portuguese. But the total eradication of foreign rights and settlements secured by earlier 'unequal' treaties could not be achieved in 1945 or 1949. The British Crown Colony of Hong Kong, as it turned out, proved of inestimable economic value as a trading partner. Nevertheless, faced with the expiry in 1997 of the lease of the so-called New Lands (without which the rest of Hong Kong would become untenable), China successfully insisted on regaining sovereignty over the whole colony. China now takes her place among the world's great powers and her rulers control the whole of mainland China. The ancient traditions of China were overlaid by Western democratic ideals, coupled with national self-assertion, imperial claims and after 1917 the ideology of Marxism, influences which were in many respects antagonistic to one another. Yet there has evolved, too, some common ground: it seems as if China has absorbed some features from each to form a unique Chinese blend, in which one constant is a readiness to change and modify. But in the process China has been transformed.

The essence of the traditional culture of China, dating from the age of Confucius in the sixth century before Christ, was to emphasise the wholeness of the universe in which the ultimate goal of all people was to strive together to achieve harmony and universal peace. Harmony was to be attained by the individual's virtue and understanding, and by the right ordering of the family where the older enjoyed seniority over the younger, and men over women, and every member of the family accepted his or her obligations and responsibilities; the right ordering of the state would then follow. The theory of state was based on the family, on the affection between its members, extended to relationships between families to the community and between communities to the whole empire. The ruler of the empire ruled by the Mandate of Heaven. By his deeds he showed whether he enjoyed that mandate and when the people deemed that he did not, then it was their duty to rebel and to depose their ruler. The Confucian tradition is idealistic: it is centred not in religion and a belief in a God creator assuming an entity separate from the wholeness of the universe, but in humanity and a concern to bring about harmonious relationships between each individual and between rulers and ruled. It emphasises virtue and happiness and the values of humanism. Its focus is on the individual family unit tilling its soil; and in a vast land overwhelmingly peopled by peasants it thus strengthened local economic and social responsibility. But the millions of family units were part of a whole ruled over by an emperor

and his officials. This was the utopian vision of harmony.

The emperor's role was that of a virtuous head of his family of all the Chinese people; and as a father his powers were not restricted. In practice his powers were delegated to the class of scholar–officials, China's unique contribution to government, an elite group selected by a system of examinations and drawn from each region of the empire in proportion to the population. A body of censors was responsible for investigating corruption in administration. In the localities a gentry, again selected by examinations rather than birth, acted as intermediaries between the imperial officials and the people, holding the people under their influence and raising local defence forces for their protection whenever necessary. The Confucian spirit extolled contentment rather than change and development, and it is a mistake to apply Western yardsticks of progress and technical innovation or use them to make contrasts unfavourable to Chinese history. Within traditional technology China coped with almost a tripling of her population from 150 million in 1700 to 420 million by the early nineteenth century, maintaining living standards just above subsistence level at all times, except when natural disasters struck. Does that compare so unfavourably with contemporary efforts by the less economically developed parts of the Indian continent, Africa and Latin America where population increases lead to famine, and natural disasters to death?

In the nineteenth century a double crisis threatened the cohesion and stability of China and undermined traditional China and the rule of the Ch'ing dynasty. A great blow to central authority was the defeat of the Manchu Ch'ing dynasty by the invasion of the 'barbarians' of the West. The West saw an opportunity to trade in China and made wars to force their way in. The British fought the Opium Wars (1839–42) and China ceded her territory (Hong Kong) and was forced to accept the opening of her trade to Britain. An even more fundamental cause of unrest was that population growth was no longer matched by an increase in the lands under cultivation. Amid the general distress occurred the greatest rising in world history – the Taiping Rebellion of 1850–64 – which led to huge destruction and to the loss of between 20 and 30 million lives. The rising was mastered in the end by gentry-led regional armies. China was thereby pushed along a path where regional independence and strength asserted themselves against central authority. During this period and later in the nineteenth century other Western nations followed the British example and secured concessions; and so began a process whereby the Western powers acquired territorial settlements, colonies, leases, rights to trade in 'treaty ports', and concessions in some eighty towns on the coast and inland. The foreigners not only enjoyed immunity from Chinese government but in their settlements in effect ruled over the Chinese inhabitants as well. The largest, the foreign settlements of Shanghai, in 1928 comprised a Chinese population of more than 1 million subordinated to 35,000 Westerners. China was not only defeated and forced to accept the 'unequal treaties' by the West, but during the last decade of the nineteenth century was attacked by Japan as well.

The impact of the West and Japan as well as China's internal upheavals led Chinese intellectuals to question China's future role. Yet their initial reaction was to seek to preserve Chinese traditions. China should strengthen herself through the adoption of Western industrial and military techniques. But little real headway could be made materially. It was not Confucian tradition which blocked the path but economic reality. China remained a peasant society with a surface scratch of industrial development, largely in the foreign-dominated enclaves. The movement of 'self-strengthening' was nowhere near sufficient to counter the forces of disintegration. The Ch'ing dynasty under the formidable Empress Dowager Tz'u-hsi attempted in a last spasm to adopt Western techniques in government and education, but always with the underlying conservative purpose of strengthening traditional China. The reforms were undertaken in the wake of the disastrous Boxer rising of 1900, which attempted to throw out Western influence – economic, political, territorial and religious – by force and was in its turn crushed by a Western international army joined by the Japanese. China was placed further in debt to the West and lost control over even more territory since the Russians refused to leave northern China and Manchuria. Then the Chinese had to stand aside as Russia and Japan in 1904 and 1905 fought each other for dominance over this portion of China (page 58). China was breaking apart into foreign spheres of influence; simultaneously the regions were asserting their autonomy from central government. In 1908 the Empress died and the strength of the Ch'ing dynasty was spent. If the misery of the condition of the country and its people could prove such a thing, then the Ch'ing dynasty had lost its Heavenly Mandate.

Among the small group of conservative intellectuals and administrators there were some who under the impact of the experience of their own lifetime looked at the world beyond China more realistically and knowledgeably. They contrasted Japanese success in maintaining national independence, in throwing off discriminatory treaties in their homeland and in inflicting military defeat on a great Western power with China's weakness and helplessness. China had, in theory, preserved her sovereignty over all but small portions of her empire. The reality, however, was different since foreigners controlled her commerce, built her railways and established industries under their ownership. (Here, though, it is necessary to distinguish the few Westerners who were dedicated to serving the interests of China as they saw them. These were officials like Robert Hart, head of the Maritime Customs Service, who warned in the aftermath of the Boxer rising that the Western powers should take care how they treated the Chinese: 'a China in arms will be a big power at some future day', he wrote; the Western powers should make sure that 'the China of the future might have something to thank us for and not to avenge'.) There were some Chinese reformers who sensed that China stood at the parting of the ways. China could emulate Japan or suffer the fate of India and south-east Asia, then part of the colonial empires of the Dutch, the British and the French.

Many of these reformers had received part of their education in Japan or the West. Yan Fu, one of the most important, spent time not only in Japan but also in England. In his writings he contrasted the Chinese ideals of harmony and stability with Western encouragement of the thrusting individual, competition and the goal of progress. Yan Fu translated into Chinese seminal Western works on politics and the economy, books by T. H. Huxley, John Stuart Mill and Adam Smith among them. His translations and his own advocacy stimulated demands for a break with Confucian traditions and the adoption of a Western-style form of constitutional government. Another reformer of great influence in the first decade of the twentieth century was Liang Qichao, the intellectual leader of the

*China looks to the West.*

young Chinese progressives, who wrote extensively about Western political leaders and thinkers in the hope of opening up a new world to the Chinese and thus transforming them into a new people. In its last years, not so much directly influenced by the reformers but reacting to the same stimuli – a desire to strengthen China against the foreigner – the Ch'ing dynasty promulgated reforms thick and fast, promising the gradual introduction of constitutional government, a process which when set in motion was to lead to its own downfall and the revolution of 1911.

Thousands of students in the first decade of the twentieth century travelled and studied abroad. Their ideas were far more radical than those of the reformers. Their goal was a revolution against the 'foreign' Ch'ing dynasty and the establishment of a republic. They identified with another Western-educated revolutionary, Dr Sun Yat-sen. A farmer's son, like many Chinese he had emigrated abroad joining, at the age of twelve, his brothers in Hawaii. He was educated in a British missionary school there and, later, in Hong Kong, where he graduated in medicine. He did not practise long as a doctor, instead seeing that his task was to awaken China to revolution. In breach of Chinese tradition, Sun Yat-sen encouraged the Chinese to view themselves as a distinctive race. The removal of the foreign Manchu Ch'ing dynasty provided a focus for the revolutionary movement. Sun Yat-sen wished to create a modern Chinese nation state, with a constitution based on that of the United States together with some Chinese traditions grafted on to it such

as a control branch of government – the old censors, under a new name. In Japan he founded the revolutionary League of Common Alliance, an organised political movement which in 1912 joined with other groups to form the Kuomintang or Nationalist Party. Not until after his death in 1925, however, did the Kuomintang play a leading role in China's history.

Sun Yat-sen summed up his political programme and aims in three principles: first, the restoration of the Chinese identity, which came to mean the removal of both the 'foreign' Manchu dynasty and foreign imperialism. China, Sun Yat-sen said, lacked a national spirit; the 400 million people of China were 'just a heap of loose sand', and China the weakest and poorest nation – 'other men are the carving knife and serving dish; we are the fish and meat'. China must seek its salvation by espousing nationalism and so avert the catastrophe of 'China being lost and our people being eliminated'. The foreign oppression, he pointed out, was not just political, which was easily recognised, but economic, transforming China 'into a colony of the foreign powers'. The second principle was democracy, by which he meant the creation of a strong executive central power and the ultimate sovereignty of the people expressed in an electoral process. The third principle, socialism, was the vaguest; in theory it stood for landownership equalisation and some state control to prevent the abuse of monopoly capitalist power, but since the Kuomintang drew support from businessmen, the principle was blurred. Sun Yat-sen developed these ideas throughout his political life though in his own lifetime they found little application.

The advocates of Westernisation always faced one serious emotional and intellectual problem. The very people they wished to emulate showed their belief in Chinese inferiority. Foreign residents, whether missionaries or merchants, only too frequently looked down on the Chinese, regarding their culture as pagan. The roles of the civilised and the barbarians were reversed. In Shanghai there were parks reserved exclusively for the Westerners, characteristic of the racial prejudice of the time. The Christian missionaries saw themselves engaged in saving souls otherwise lost to heathen ways. So the Chinese reacted to Western ways with both admiration and intense hostility. The political and economic behaviour of the Western powers could only strengthen that hostility.

The course of the revolution of 1911, which soon

ended the monarchy, was not determined by Sun Yat-sen, though a Chinese republic did come into being. A strong Chinese nation dedicated to the objectives of his loose Alliance movement did not emerge when the revolution had succeeded in its first task of overthrowing the Manchus. The membership of Sun Yat-sen's party amounted to only a few thousand within China. More significant in determining the subsequent course of events were the men of influence in the provinces – the merchants and the gentry – who took advantage of constitutional reform to assert the independence of the provinces in the newly elected assemblies. The spark for starting the revolution was provided by a rising of a small group of revolutionary soldiers in Wuchang in central China in October 1911 with only the weakest links with Sun Yat-sen's Alliance. Sun Yat-sen at the time was in Denver in the United States. The rising could easily have been suppressed. But so weak had the power of the central government become that province after province in October and November 1911 declared its independence from the central court government. Hostility to the dynasty was widespread. The court turned to Yuan Shikai, recently a governor-general of a northern province, where he had built up a modern Chinese Northern Army.

Yuan Shikai was in retirement when the revolution broke out; the dynasty saw him now as the only man considered capable of commanding the loyalty of the officers of the Northern Army, whose military strength might still re-establish the dynasty's authority. Yuan Shikai, however, was determined to be his own master. He negotiated with the revolutionaries. They agreed to his assuming the presidency of the Chinese republic provided he could secure the abdication of the Ch'ing dynasty. In February 1912 the abdication decree was published and in March 1912 Yuan Shikai became the first president of China as the man most acceptable to the provincial gentry and merchants. These men were basically conservative, and Sun Yat-sen's revolutionary movement was abhorrent to them. There was to be no social revolution. The republic and its new parliament representing the unity of China were frail institutions. During the last four years of Yuan Shikai's life, from 1912 to 1916, he ruled more and more as a military dictator through the army and shortly before his death attempted to revive the monarchy with himself as emperor. Through his

hold over the army, the provinces were unable to assert complete independence from Peking. But Yuan Shikai could establish no genuine national unity and with his death the disintegration of China accelerated.

The years from 1916 to 1928 mark the warlord era in modern Chinese history. To the outside world the republic of China was governed from Peking. In reality this was just one of the hundreds of governments, each headed by a warlord with a personal army which had gained control of an area sometimes small, sometimes covering a whole province. The warlords intrigued and fought each other in hundreds of wars throughout twelve years of constant strife and bloodshed. These twelve years mark the furthest stage of China's disintegration. The peasants suffered from merciless pillage, tax oppression, destruction of their property and bloodshed.

This same period, however, also saw more positive developments. The combination of China's misfortunes internal and external welded together a new national movement which tried to recapture the objectives set by Sun Yat-sen but totally disregarded after the revolution of 1911.

Foreign encroachments on Chinese integrity provoked the strongest reaction among the young students and intellectuals. Peking University became the centre of the intellectual ferment and participated in what became known as the New Culture Movement. Japan's Twenty-one Demands in January 1915 took advantage of the preoccupation of the European powers with winning the war in Europe to demand of the Chinese government its practical subordination to Japan (page 89). In China they were met with a storm of protest. An even greater outburst of indignation greeted the decisions of the Paris Peace Conference in 1919. China was an ally, yet Japan had been accorded the right to take over Germany's extensive concessions in the province of Shantung, and the warlord government in Peking, representing China, had accepted this transfer of what was after all still Chinese territory.

The fourth of May 1919 is an important date in the history of modern China. It was later seen as marking the moment when China reasserted her national identity once more in angry response to imperialism. Some 3000 students in Peking University launched a national protest movement which took its name from that date. The government had arrested some students and the protest was directed equally against the government and national humiliation. In the burst of publications that followed, the May the Fourth movement had a powerful effect on stimulating the young intellectuals to reject the social and political traditions of old China, including the Confucian ideals of duty and filial obedience and the subordination of women. A boycott of Japanese goods in turn led to the organisation of Chinese labour in the ports. But the intellectual revolution also had a divisive effect as the mass of the countryside and the peasantry was virtually untouched by the fever for change.

During the warlord period there occurred not only the intellectual ferment making a decisive break with the traditional past but also the revival of one political party, the Kuomintang, and the establishment of a new party, the Communist Party; their rivalry divided China during the 1930s and 1940s. They began by joining forces, the communists in obedience to orders from Moscow. Then in the 1930s and 1940s they fought a triangular struggle – together against the Japanese invader, and also against each other. That struggle reached its climax during the years following the defeat of Japan in 1945 and China was once more divided by civil war. In 1949 the era of war ended at last and mainland China was set on the course of national unity. So although the actual power the Kuomintang and the Communist Party exerted beyond their base in Canton was weak in the early 1920s, and they

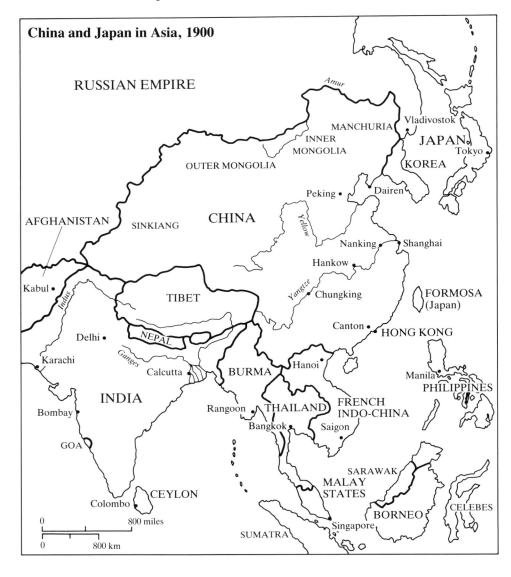

**China and Japan in Asia, 1900**

too were dependent on the protection of a warlord, they emerged to dominate contemporary Chinese history.

In 1923 Sun Yat-sen was looking for ways to strengthen his enfeebled Kuomintang Party, which was nominally ruling Canton but in reality was dependent on the local warlord. He turned for help to the tiny Communist Party, numbering less than a thousand members. The Comintern welcomed any opportunity to strike a blow against Western imperialism and agents were sent from Moscow. The co-operation of Sun Yat-sen and his Russian advisers soon bore fruit. Sun Yat-sen adapted his principles to the new situation and the Comintern ordered the Chinese communists not to form an alliance but to subordinate their interests and fuse with the Kuomintang. The communists, now forming the left wing of the Kuomintang, never lost their sense of identity. The party, with the help of Russian advice, was reorganised, and communist influence among Chinese labour working for Western interests rapidly grew; strikes were fomented and supported. In the countryside too the Kuomintang made headway among the peasants in encouraging the seizure of landlord's land.

The right wing of the Kuomintang controlled the national revolutionary army it was organising. The task was assigned to one of Sun Yat-sen's loyal young followers, Chiang Kai-shek. In 1923 Chiang Kai-shek went to Moscow to study the new Soviet Red Army. On his return he was placed in charge of training the officers of the Kuomintang's revolutionary army. In 1925 Sun Yat-sen died. There was no obvious successor. For a time the party continued under a collective leadership amid increasing strains between the left and the right. But Chiang Kai-shek soon made clear his opposition to the left of the Kuomintang. Chiang Kai-shek turned against the socialist plans of his communist allies. He also vied for the assistance of the propertied and for help from the West. Meanwhile the communists in following Moscow's orders fared disastrously. In April 1927 the Nationalists and their supporters crushed organised workers in Shanghai and shot protesters. In the countryside peasant risings were bloodily put down. By the end of that year the break between the communists and Nationalists was complete. Driven

out of the towns, the communists established base areas in remote regions. Mao Zedong, then in his thirties, created the most important in Jiangxi. Here the Red army was trained by Zhou Enlai and taught to help and not plunder the peasants. Other significant reforms ended the sale of girls into forced marriages, while the peasants' greatest need was land reform. After five years, surrounded by Chiang's forces, the base became untenable. Daringly at night on 16 October 1934, leaving behind a rearguard and the sick and wounded, the communists broke through the encirclement and fought their way north for six thousand miles on the epic 'Long March'. Yet it was not civil war that dominated the 1930s but the Japanese invasion in 1937. Once more, fervent national feelings created a sense of unity in resisting the brutal aggressor. Before his decisive breach he utilised the strength of the communists to support the northern military expedition started in 1926 to convert what was a local government into a national one. It was a tremendous feat to sweep successfully north from their base in southern China to Peking. There was some hard fighting; some warlords agreed to accept Chiang Kai-shek's authority on behalf of the Nationalist government now established in a new capital in Nanking.

Chiang Kai-shek took care at this stage not to offend the Western powers in China. He smashed the anti-Western movement of the communists in the Kuomintang. He set himself as his first task to gain military control over China. But, though his success had been astonishing, he had not broken the power of all the warlords and by the close of the 1920s controlled less than half of China. In 1930 he quelled a rising in the north in large-scale battles. Thereafter the remaining warlords and Chiang Kai-shek's government agreed to tolerate each other. China was far more unified, but a new military struggle was opening up between the Kuomintang and the communists. Simultaneously Japan took advantage of China's weakness to seize Manchuria in 1931. In the end Chiang Kai-shek, faced with the Japanese war and simultaneous civil conflict with the communists, failed to create the national unity of China which was Sun Yat-sen's testament to his followers.

# CHAPTER 11

## *The Emergence of Japan, 1900–1929*

The continent of Asia can be divided into three regions, each in a different relationship to the West. Southern and south-east Asia was, by the close of the nineteenth century, partitioned by the European powers and the United States and constituted the most populous and important parts of the Western world empires. In eastern Asia, China had fallen under a different kind of Western control, remaining semi-independent, but with large areas under foreign economic control, while some parts of China had also fallen under foreign territorial control. Also part of eastern Asia were the islands of Japan.

Japan's history is strikingly different from the rest of Asia. Japan had been forced open by the American warships of Commodore Perry in the mid-nineteenth century and exposed to the pressures of the Western powers backed by guns. They refused to permit Japan to follow her own course in isolation and demanded, as a Western right, that Japan open her markets to trade with the West. The rulers of Japan, the Tokugawa Shoguns, could not match the military power of the West and so had to concede. After 200 years of virtual isolation, imposed by the Shoguns to protect her from Western influence, Japan then lay exposed and virtually helpless. Like China, she was forced to accede to 'unequal treaties', providing Western merchants with economic advantages and special territorial privileges which set aside Japan's rights to rule over all the people settled in her country. Yet half a century later, by the early twentieth

century, the Western powers agreed to abrogate the 'unequal treaties' and Japan developed a military power not only capable of defeating her much larger neighbour, China, but also one of the Western great powers, Russia. The foundations of a modern state had been laid and Japan stood on the threshold of replacing Western dominance in eastern Asia. By the fourth quarter of the twentieth century, though her military power was modest and her Asian territorial empire broken by the West, Japan had become an industrial superpower second only to the United States.

Japan was the only Asian nation to achieve this astonishing transformation within the short span of a little more than a hundred years from the 1860s to the 1990s. But the perspective of the 1990s should not lead us to the conclusion that Japan represents a unique progressiveness among the otherwise stagnant and overwhelmingly peasant societies of Asia. Today, for instance, Taiwan, Singapore and South Korea are showing that they are capable of following Japan's industrial 'miracle', mainland China's growth is also accelerating. In the later nineteenth century the Japanese reformers, reacting to the West, tended to think of 'Western' as one overall formula for human progress and national power. Everything was seen as part of this same phenomenon and there was at first little understanding of what differentiated the Western nations from each other socially, politically or economically. So too, the West used to think of Asia's history in an undifferentiated way. The 'slowness' of

China's 'modernisation' was sometimes compared with the speed of Japan's, thereby applying the same Western yardstick to two totally different societies, the one a vast land empire of 420 million people at the turn of the century, the other a group of compact islands with a population of some 30 million. The contrast of physical conditions, even leaving aside questions of culture and historical development, is far greater than that between the British Isles and Russia. Even to compare Russia and China is likely to lead to fog rather than illumination. That is not to deny that there are common cultural influences which affected Asia, just as there are common features of Western culture.

Japan from the sixth century onwards owed much to the Korean and Chinese civilisations adopting and adapting the religions of China – Buddhism of Indian origin and Chinese Taoism – and the philosophy of Confucius. Indeed some aspects of Confucianism, with its emphasis on hierarchical family relationships and the obligations owed to those more senior, retained a stronger hold in modern Japan than in China. The Tokugawa shoguns had been the real rulers of feudal Japan since the early seventeenth century with the emperors fulfilling largely ceremonial functions. The shoguns sought to preserve a static, hierarchical society dominated by the warrior caste of *samurai*, a Japan free from the contagion of the outside world. For two and a half centuries they appeared to succeed. Confucianism with its emphasis on the duty inferiors owed to their superiors and the ideal of harmony in a hierarchical society was an ideology well suited to the shogunate. According to the Confucian ideal the officials' task was to enrich and enlighten the people; in practice they acted as the bureaucracy of an authoritarian state. At the same time the ruling elites of Japan, though imbued with the conservative Confucian beliefs, also showed themselves open to new ideas where they demonstrably contributed to the increase of wealth. Economic and social change from the early nineteenth century on, however, eroded the orderly traditional society. To internal strains were added external ones all pointing to the need for a stronger state, an ending of the shogunate era and a centralised nation built around a restored monarch.

The urgent need for such strengthening was brought home to the Japanese by the forcible appearance of the West. Japan's response under the last of the Shoguns was to make an effort to catch up with Western military technology. The industrialisation of Japan had its beginning not in the setting up of a textile mill, but in a shipyard in 1863 capable of building steam warships. The process was much accelerated after the 1868 revolution known as the Meiji Restoration. The requirements of armaments and attempts to gain self-sufficiency created the Osaka Ironworks (1881) and at about the same time steel-making by the Krupp method was started. Heavy industry was expanded originally to meet these national defence needs before a single railway line was constructed. National defence never lost this primacy of concern in Japan, at least not until after the Second World War. Her population lived in compact territories which made arousing a sense of national consciousness and patriotism easier than in the vast area of China. The revolution which overthrew the Shogunate and started the Meiji era was a turning point in this respect too, as in other aspects of the modernisation of Japan. The great feudal domains were abolished and the people were now subject to the imperial government, which strengthened its central authority in many ways in the 1870s and 1880s.

The rapid progress achieved by Japan had its origins nevertheless in the period before 1868. There already existed large groups of educated people – the former warriors (the *samurai*), merchants and craftsmen, who had obtained some Western technological knowledge through contacts at the port of Nagasaki, where the Dutch merchants were allowed to remain under rigid supervision – and they formed a reservoir of people with a capacity to learn and adapt to new Western skills. The revolution of 1868 brought to power a remarkable group of *samurai* statesmen. They restored the monarch to his ancient pinnacle; but the emperor was no mere figurehead. He was advised by a small group, later a council of elders, or *genro*, who wielded enormous power. He listened to their advice, but at times of differences between his *genro* his own views were decisive, and at critical moments of Japanese history the emperor actively used his prerogative as final arbiter. Below the emperor and the *genro* council, which had no formal place in the constitution, a Western structure of government with a prime minister, cabinet and an elected parliament was set up in the last decades of the nineteenth century. Despite the outward style of Western government, Japan was not democratic but was ruled by a few prominent leaders. The Meiji Restoration was no social revolution but a revolution from above.

These Meiji oligarchs presented to the world a picture of a close group acting behind a faceless, godlike emperor. In reality they were men of powerful personality and sometimes fundamentally clashing policies who fought each other when critical decisions, especially on Japan's relations with the rest of the world, had to be reached, both in the *genro* council and through their nominees in the government and in the army and navy. Once the emperor's decision was made, the ruling group accepted this resolution of their conflict. During the last three decades of the nineteenth century some six oligarchs, mainly members of two clans of the Choshu and Satsuma, transformed Japan by introducing widespread changes, military, naval, industrial, economic and educational. The increasing government expenditure and beginnings of industrialisation nurtured by the state, the construction of railways, were all based on the improving productivity of the Japanese farmer. His standard of living was held back, however, to provide the margin of capital for this early industrial modernisation.

By the turn of the century, the young reformers of the 1860s had become elder statesmen. Pre-eminent among this small group were Ito Hirobumi and Yamagata Aritomu. Ito was Japan's elder statesman and the best-known Japanese in the West. He had travelled and studied in the West and was responsible for Japan's representative constitution. Field Marshal Yamagata had created the modern Japanese army, which proved victorious in the wars with China in 1894–5 and with Russia in 1904–5. He was opposed to Ito's policies at home, and Ito's more pacific approach to foreign affairs. In 1909 Ito was assassinated in Korea; soon Yamagata's influence also weakened when after 1914 the surviving *genro* grew old and were replaced by new power groups.

One feature of Japan's emergence as a world power can be discerned from early on: a ruthless disregard for personal pride when it conflicted with the higher interests of national defence and survival in the face of Western pressure. The natural reaction of peoples treated as inferior by the Westerner is to become assertive, even over-assertive, of the worth of their own race. The Japanese became deeply sensitive to issues of race and reacted with anger to American discrimination against Japanese immigration. It was seen as a humiliating slight. Nor did it help when later Hollywood portrayed 'orientals' as crafty and cruel villains. But in the 1880s a Japanese official could write that, if Japan were to survive as a nation, then:

> having accepted the hypothesis that the physical and mental constitution of our Japanese is inferior to that of European peoples, it follows that in the event that we persist on an inferior racial level there is a danger that we may soil the historical record of our blameless Empire. What, then, can we do? The only solution is to improve our racial quality by means of intermarriage [with the white race]. When we marry European women there is an additional benefit in the custom of following a meat diet.

Ito wished to have the expert opinion of the famous Social Darwinist, Herbert Spencer, who tactfully advised against intermarriage since, as he explained, it destroys racial characteristics and breaks down the integrity of personality. (Needless to add, this was all part of the pseudo-racial science of the nineteenth century, an unwarranted extension to human beings of Darwin's theories about animals, the survival of the fittest, namely those best able to adapt to the changing conditions of their physical environment. To seek falsely to apply such observations to human qualities helped to lead to some terrible perversions in the twentieth century.) What Japanese concerns do illustrate is the length to which Japan's leaders were prepared to go to ensure that the Japanese nation should not succumb to the West. This was the mainspring of Japanese thinking and of the policies adopted during the Meiji Restoration and after.

In foreign relations 1895 is a year of great importance for Japan. During the period from the first diplomatic contacts down to 1894 the Japanese had preserved their independence from the West. Indeed a start was made in negotiating treaties with the European powers that would lead in due course to the abrogation of the wounding special treaties. The treaties had placed the Europeans in Japan beyond Japanese authority on the grounds that the Japanese lacked the civilisation to be entrusted with applying their laws to Europeans. But one reason why the West did not attempt to carve out spheres of interests or colonies in Japan as in China is to be found in the fact that the Europeans were impressed by Japanese progress in adopting

Western ways and by their consequent growing strength. But what was more important during these critical early decades was that the West did not regard the commercial possibilities and the market of Japan as nearly as important as China's for the future. Japan's neighbour, tsarist Russia, deliberately rejected a policy of penetrating Japan in favour of the exploitation of China. The same was true of the other Western powers. At the turn of the century the scramble for European concessions was reaching its height in China, and Britain's place as the paramount power in eastern Asia was being challenged. The Colonial Secretary, Joseph Chamberlain, declared, 'our interests in China are so great, our proportion of the trade is so enormous and the potentialities of that trade are so gigantic that I feel no more vital question has ever been presented for the decision . . . of the nation'. The West's image of China protected Japan and contributed to the very different development of the two nations after the incursion of the West into eastern Asia.

In 1895 Japan had just brought to a victorious conclusion a war with China over the question of the suzerainty of Korea. As part of her peace terms she had forced China into territorial concessions. This step by the Japanese into what the European powers wished to keep as their preserve led to an angry reaction by France, Germany and Russia, which demanded that Japan give up her territorial spoils in China. It was with a national sense of humiliation that the Japanese rulers bowed to this pressure.

The Japanese, who had lived at peace with China for close on a thousand years, had learned from the West that a great power must acquire an empire and exercise power beyond the national frontier. But Japan was not treated as an equal. This realisation marks a turning point in the Japanese outlook. It was necessary carefully to study every move; Japan would succeed only by the judicious use of force coupled with guile and then only if the Western powers were divided and so could not combine against her.

A complex two-tier decision-making process developed from 1901, after which time no individual genro led the government; policy was first discussed between the different groups in the government and then by the genro. This reinforced the tendency to discuss fully all aspects, advantages and disadvantages, of every important policy decision. The

Emperor was the supreme authority. The genro were expected in the end to submit to him an agreed decision for his formal consent. But in the Meiji era the Emperor's influence was considerable and he could to some degree steer and prolong genro discussions on important issues on which there were differences of opinion. In its fullest and most constructive form this deliberate way of reaching group decisions after long and careful discussion lasted until about the First World War, when the advancing age of the surviving genro weakened their influence. The influence of Emperor Meiji's descendants did not match his own. His son, whose reign lasted from 1912 to 1926, was weak in health and mind; his grandson, Emperor Hirohito, was supreme only in theory but followed until 1945 the advice of Japan's military and political leaders. The post-Meiji emperors were kept aloof from any real role in the making of decisions. In later decades the Japanese looked back on the Meiji era as a period of brilliant success abroad as well as at home, a golden age.

Japan's policy towards the eastern Asian mainland from 1900 until the outbreak of the Great War in Europe illustrates both circumspection and ultimately boldness. There was an attempt to steer a middle course between the exponents of expansion and the more cautious groups who wished to strengthen Japan in Korea by means of commerce and influence rather than outright territorial control. With the acceptance of the alliance Britain offered in January 1902 – after long debate and scrutiny – the Japanese leaders knew that, if it came to war with Russia, Japan could count on Britain's military help if any other power joined Russia against her. By diplomacy the Japanese had ensured that they would not be blocked by a united European front aligned against her as in 1895. The genro decided for war in February 1904. But in launching a war against Russia the mood was not one of arrogance. The Japanese leaders knew they were taking a carefully calculated risk. They hoped to do well enough to gain Japan's most important aims: expansion of territory on the Asian mainland and security for Japan and her empire. Specifically the Japanese were determined to achieve dominance over Korea and southern Manchuria.

The genro at the time they decided on war were already considering how the war might be ended in good time. There was no expectation that Russia could be completely defeated. Russia was not

*The Russo-Japanese War of 1904–5 as seen from opposing sides. Before the conflict began, the Russians were confident that they would crush the 'yellow devils' easily* (left). *The Japanese woodcut* (right) *celebrates a more tangible triumph, the naval victory in the Straits of Tsushima on 27 May 1905.*

brought to the point where she could not have continued the war, although her navy was annihilated and Japan also won spectacular successes on land (page 58). Yet the Japanese too were exhausted by the war and, through President Theodore Roosevelt's mediation, secured a peace treaty which brought them great gains. These gains, however, fell short of their expectations. There were riots in Japan when the peace terms became known in September 1905. The Japanese people wanted Russia to acknowledge defeat by paying reparation. The Russians refused to do so and the *genro* knew that Japan, her financial resources weakened, was in no position to continue the war in the hope of exacting better terms. On 5 September 1905 the Peace of Portsmouth was concluded.

Japan did not use military force again for a quarter of a century and thereby risk all she had gained in her wars with China and with Russia. By the time of the Meiji Emperor's death in 1912, Japan had won international recognition as a great power. Her alliance with Britain was renewed, her 'special' position in northern China acquiesced in, as well as her outright annexation of Korea. Internally too, Japan had made great strides during the forty-five years of the Meiji Emperor's reign.

But on the negative side there were tensions building up in Japan. There was pressure from below among the more prosperous and influential merchants, administrators, landowners and the educated elites, all desiring some share in power; they resented the fact that an entrenched oligarchy ruled Japan from behind the scenes and monopolised all the important positions in the state. Within

the oligarchy too there was growing conflict between the party-based governments demanding independence of the *genro*, and the *genro* who advised the emperor on all questions of importance. For a time the *genro* continued to exercise their traditional function. But the army, its prestige raised by success in the Russo-Japanese War, won a new place with the right to present its views to the emperor directly, so bypassing the civilian governments. The remarkable unity that had been achieved during the founding years of the Meiji era under the leadership of the emperor and the *genro* existed no longer in the 1920s and 1930s. Instead, powerful rival groups sought to dominate policy. In the absence of the *genro* and a strong emperor, Japan lacked any supreme body to co-ordinate her domestic and foreign policies. The beginnings of strife between labour and employers was also making itself felt as Japan became more industrialised in the early twentieth century. The educated Japanese became vulnerable to a cultural crisis of identity. Should Japanese ways be rejected totally? Western dress and conformity with Western customs became general among the progressives. There also occurred a nationalist–patriotic reaction. The Japanese elites were obliged to choose between Japanese tradition and Western ways, or to find some personal compromise between the two.

The First World War and its consequences brought about a decisive change in the international power relations of eastern Asia. The period was also one of economic industrial boom for Japan, whose earlier development provided the basis for rapid expansion. Japan benefited, second only to the United States, from the favourable conditions created by the Allies' needs at war and their disappearance as strong competitors in Asian markets. The First World War enabled Japan to emerge as an industrial nation.

Japan joined the Allied side in the war in 1914 after careful deliberation. China, after the revolution of 1911, was showing increasing signs of losing her national cohesion (pages 81–83). For Japan, the war in Europe provided an opportunity to strengthen and extend her position, especially in Manchuria. But behind Japanese expansion there was also a 'defensive' motivation similar to the earlier imperialism of the West and similar as well to fears expressed by American strategic planners (page 49). What would happen when the war was over? The *genro* Yamagata was convinced that the great war among the Western powers would be followed by a global racial struggle, a struggle between 'the yellow and white races'; Japan would therefore have 'to make plans to prevent the establishment of a white alliance against the yellow races'. He looked to friendly relations with Russia and the avoidance of hostility with the United States. Critical was the relationship with China. Here Yamagata sought the best of all worlds: the practical establishment of Japan's senior partnership in a friendly alliance. Japan should seek to 'instil in China a sense of abiding trust in us'. China and Japan, 'culturally and racially alike', might then preserve their identity when competing with the 'so-called culturally advanced white races'. When the Japanese made their Twenty-one Demands on China in 1915, the Chinese naturally regarded the Japanese from quite a different point of view – more as enemies than friends (page 81). In their first form the demands amounted to a claim for a Japanese protectorate, including insistence on employing Japanese 'advisers' in financial, military and administrative affairs in the Chinese government. Until the close of the First World War there was little the Western powers could do to restrain Japan, beyond diplomatic pressure.

In the Taisho (meaning 'great righteousness') era from the Meiji Emperor's death in 1912 until the death of his son in 1926, it seemed that, despite Japanese assertiveness in China during the Great War, the overall trend would be towards greater liberalisation and peace. The *genro* were ceasing to play so critical a role, especially after Yamagata's

death in 1922, and one great obstacle towards constitutional parliamentary development was thereby removed. The new Emperor was weak and the powers of the government increased. Yet, as developments after 1926 were to show very clearly, in the end the 'liberal' Taisho period marked only a transition to a more illiberal and authoritarian state than had developed in the Meiji era. There were signs too that Taisho was 'liberal' only in a very restricted sense. Industrial expansion, first fostered by the state, was later handed over to a few large business enterprises still pre-eminent today. These huge business empires, the *zaibatsu*, were conducted paternalistically and required loyalty from their employees from the cradle to the grave. Links between big business and the state remained unusually close. There was no possibility of the growth of a strong and independent democratic labour movement under such industrial conditions.

Distress arose in Japan at the end of the war due to the phenomenal rise in the price of rice, the country's staple food; this led to serious riots all over Japan in the summer of 1918. Troops repressed the violence in the towns and villages with great severity. Hundreds of people were killed and thousands more arrested. The collapse of the war boom in 1921 led to further repression of any signs of socialism or of attempts by labour to organise. The devastating Tokyo earthquake in September 1923 became the pretext for arresting Koreans, communists and socialists who were accused of plotting to seize power. Many were lynched by 'patriotic gangs'. The police were given authority to arrest and imprison anyone suspected of subversive thoughts, and many were brutally treated. Compulsory military training of Japanese youth was seen as a good way to counteract 'dangerous thoughts'. Thus the 1930s cannot be seen as a complete reversal of the Taisho period.

In Japan's relations with the world too there is more continuity than at first appears. On the one hand the Russian Revolution of 1917 and the emergence of the United States as a world power had repercussions of enormous importance in eastern Asia. The Soviet leaders succeeded for a time in forging an alliance with Chinese Nationalists in a joint drive against Western and Japanese imperialism (page 179). On the other hand, the United States was calling for a new deal for China and an end to the pre-war power alliances, particularly the Anglo-Japanese alliance, which had enormously

*The aftermath of the Tokyo earthquake of 1 September 1923. Strong winds had fanned the fires and made two-thirds of the population homeless. Some 74,000 people are believed to have lost their lives.*

strengthened Japan's position in Asia. But the Japanese government, beset by severe economic problems in the 1920s, and dependent on American trade, was in no position to resist the United States. This became clear at the Washington Conference in 1921–2. Several treaties were signed, placing the security of the eastern Pacific and the integrity of China on a multinational basis. The Japanese were obliged to return to China the Shantung province gained at the Paris Peace Conference (page 81). A naval limitations treaty placed Japan in a position inferior to Britain and the United States, which were allowed five battleships each compared to Japan's three. Finally, Japan became a co-signatory to the nine-power treaty to seek to uphold the unity of China. It is true that Japan also received private assurances recognising her special interests in Manchuria; nevertheless the Washington Treaties placed a considerable check on any Japanese unilateral action in China.

The 'spirit of Washington', as the great-power co-operation in eastern Asia came to be described, proved as unsuccessful in the long run as the 'spirit of Locarno' in Europe (pages 145–6). Foreign Minister Kijuro Shidehara became identified with Japan's pacific policy in Asia and he loyally did his best to act in its spirit. But there were ominous signs of the troubles to come. With the passing of *genro* control the army became more independent and chafed under the consequences of Japan's new foreign policy. Great-power co-operation proved singularly ineffective in China and certainly did not reduce either that country's internal conflict or its anti-imperialist feelings. Good relations with the United States were seriously harmed by the passage of an immigration law in 1924 which excluded the Japanese, further strengthening the military view that the United States had become Japan's most likely enemy. The rise of Chinese nationalism and Chiang Kai-shek's thrust to the north in 1926 were seen as threats to Japan's position in Manchuria.

The new Emperor Hirohito, whose reign began in December 1926, chose Showa, 'enlightened peace', as the name of his era. But the domestic and international difficulties besetting Japan were to make the coming years a period of war and violence.

# PART III

The Great War, Revolution
and the Search for Stability

# CHAPTER 12

# The Great War – I:
# War without Decision, 1914–1916

The shape of the future world after August 1914 would now be decided by force. At the outset of the war all the major nations launched offensives to knock out the enemy quickly, and every one of these offensives had failed by the autumn of 1914 with great loss of life. War ended four years later not by defeat of the armies in the field alone, as in the wars of the nineteenth century, but with the breakdown of the political and economic structure of the defeated, their societies weakened or shattered.

On the eastern war-front in August 1914 the two Russian armies assigned to invade East Prussia were badly led. Fulfilling their undertaking to the French, the Russian armies, superior in numbers, invaded East Prussia. After some initial Russian success General von Hindenburg was called from retirement to take command of the German defence and he selected General Ludendorff as his chief of staff. The myth of Hindenburg the heroic war leader was born. At the battle of Tannenberg on 28 and 29 August one Russian army was practically destroyed; the other was mauled in a subsequent engagement – the battle of the Masurian Lakes – but was able to withdraw to Russia in good order. Tannenberg is celebrated by the Germans in the tradition of the ancient Teutonic knights defeating hordes of Slavs. What followed was as important as the battle itself and is less heroically Wagnerian. The pursuing German army of the second Russian army was in its turn thrown back by the Russians. The end result of the year's fighting was heavy casualties on both sides and neither a German nor a Russian decisive victory but a stalemate.

Farther south, the Russians more than balanced their defeat in Prussia by proving their military superiority over the Habsburg armies. Austria–Hungary had launched an offensive into Polish Russia and in September suffered a crushing defeat; almost half (400,000) of the Austro-Hungarian army was lost and the Russians occupied Galicia. Russia also suffered heavy casualties, a quarter of a million men. The 'forgotten' war in the east for three long years from 1915 to 1917 sapped Germany's military strength by forcing a division of Germany's armies between the two major fronts east and west. German victory came too late in the east to save her.

Another military campaign which is forgotten, though it cost France 300,000 casualties, was the 1914 French offensive into Lorraine. The French initiative came to be overshadowed by the German breakthrough in north-west France. In accordance with the (modified) Schlieffen Plan the German armies attacked Belgium and were pouring into France in a great enveloping move. At the frontier the French armies were beaten and the small British army, right in the path of the Germans, withdrew from Mons having suffered heavy casualties. The French Commander-in-Chief, General Joffre, did not lose his nerve despite these almost overwhelming reverses. The French armies withdrew in good order and escaped encirclement.

As the Germans rapidly advanced, their offensive

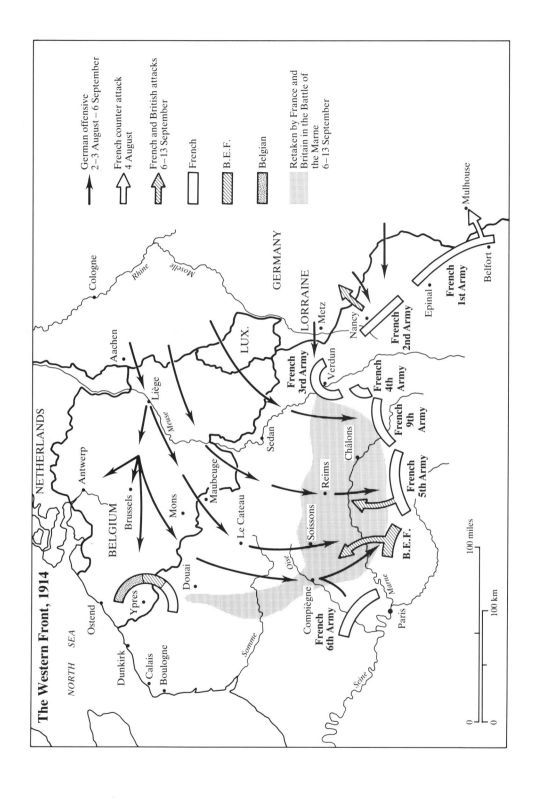

# The Western Front, 1914

German offensive
2–3 August – 6 September

French counter attack
4 August

French and British attacks
6–13 September

French

B.E.F.

Belgian

Retaken by France and
Britain in the Battle of
the Marne
6–13 September

NETHERLANDS

NORTH SEA

BELGIUM

GERMANY

LUX.

LORRAINE

Cologne

Rhine

Moselle

Aachen

Liège

Meuse

Antwerp

Brussels

Mons

Maubeuge

Le Cateau

Sedan

Verdun

Metz

Nancy

Epinal

Mulhouse

Belfort

French
1st Army

French
2nd Army

French
3rd Army

French 4th
Army

French
9th
Army

Châlons

Reims

Soissons

French
5th Army

B.E.F.

Compiègne

French
6th Army

Oise

Marne

Paris

Seine

Somme

Douai

Ypres

Ostend

Dunkirk

Calais

Boulogne

100 miles

100 km

*Enlisting Patriotism. Wartime posters – a British one of 1914 (right); a German one urging 'Keep At It!' (left).*

ran out of steam. General Gallieni, appointed to defend Paris, now conceived of a counterstroke. The Germans had wheeled in before Paris. Joffre and Gallieni halted the retreat and counterattacked. The outcome was the battle of the Marne, won by the French during the period 6 to 13 September. Now it was the German turn to withdraw; they halted 100 kilometres from Paris having established a firm defence. The battles spread and raged to the west, all the way to Flanders, in a 'race to the sea' as the armies attempted to outflank each other. The British, French and Germans suffered heavy casualties in these epic struggles around Ypres. By the end of November 1914, the machine gun, the trenches and barbed wire finally proved the strength of the defensive. The western front was now dead-locked. The French had already suffered heavy casualties in the fighting in north-west France, with 380,000 killed and 600,000 wounded. This was matched by casualties on the German side. Yet it was only a beginning. The war in the west would from now on be won not by superior strategy, nor by movement and rapid encirclement, but by the slow process of attrition. The Great War had turned into the first 'industrial war' to be won as decisively on the home front, producing ever vaster quantities of guns and munitions, as in the field.

In Britain the Liberal government of Asquith at first preserved most civic freedoms. There was no conscription. Two million men volunteered in response to Kitchener's appeal for a New Army. But soon there were doubts whether the war could be won by peacetime-style government. In the spring of 1915 the government was being blamed for a shortage of munitions. Asquith strengthened

the government by bringing in the Conservatives; Labour, too, was found a place. A small War Committee took over a tighter direction. Lloyd George, the new Minister of Munitions, built up a network of control over raw materials and manufacturing industry. War supplies improved and national economic planning was seen to work, which after the war boosted the claims of the socialists. The war could not be fought in the traditions of previous victorious struggles. That became clear when conscription for military service was introduced early in 1916. Even so 1916 did not bring the expected victory. The politicians sought a new leader to direct the war with more ruthless purpose and energy. In December 1916 the fiery and charismatic Welshman, Lloyd George, replaced Asquith and headed a coalition government for the remainder of the war.

During the years of the war the individual lost many rights as hope of a quick victory vanished. In accepting state direction, organised labour co-oper-ated with the national government, and a political 'truce' was proclaimed in Britain as in other belligerent countries. Due in no small measure to Lloyd George's skill, the dominant style was that of co-operation rather than coercion, of preserving constitutional parliamentary government rather than resorting to authoritarian rule.

In France President Poincaré called for a 'sacred union' in defence of the fatherland. Patriotism for the anti-clerical republic was sanctified. Political and social issues which had rent the republic before were now subordinated in face of the common enemy invading France for a second time. Symboli-cally the veteran socialist leader, Jean Jaurès, who had so fervently denounced militarism and had worked for Franco-German reconciliation, was assassinated by a nationalist fanatic on the very eve of the war. He too would have joined with his fellow socialists in the defence of France.

For France, invaded and losing large tracts of the country right at the beginning of the war, it could not be 'business as usual' – the inappropriate words of calm coined by Winston Churchill across the Channel – because from the start France was in imminent danger of defeat. That is why the French were the first to establish a government of national unity representing all parties from left to right.

Although the war was fought on French soil, and the loss of industrial north-western France was serious, the French improvised war production and relied on financial and material aid from Britain and the United States. Shortages of food and of necessities sent prices soaring. Increasingly authori-tarian control of production, allocation of labour and distribution had to be undertaken by the state.

The first of the belligerents to organise their production and manpower, however, were the Germans. The British naval blockade reducing essential supplies from overseas – though war materials continued to pass through neutral ports, Scandinavian and Dutch – made careful planning all the more essential. Substitute (*Ersatz*) materials were invented with scientific skill and ingenuity. As the general staff, with an almost characteristic lack of prudence, had made no plans for a long-drawn-out war, the war the Germans had to fight, it was a 'civilian', Walter Rathenau, in August 1914, who was responsible for setting up a centralised organisa-tion to ensure the supply of essential raw materials.

In Germany too the political parties closed ranks to support the nation at war. Only a small minority of socialists continued to oppose the war. The Kaiser responded emotionally, declaring that 'I do not know parties any more, only Germans.' He actually received the Social Democratic leaders in his palace and they were happy to shake hands with their Kaiser. Who would have believed a year earlier such a thing would happen? Until 1916 the *Burgfrieden* (literally 'Courtpeace', another typically Wagnerian phrase) held, but then tensions began to appear and a larger group of socialists began to oppose the war. The Reichstag, unfettered, debated war aims and the conduct of government, culminating in the famous peace resolution of July 1917: 'The Reichstag strives for a peace of understanding and lasting reconciliation of nations. Such a peace is not in keeping with forcible annexations of territory . . .' But it turned out that, if German armies were to prove victorious, the Reichstag did not expect its resolution to be taken too literally.

In any case, the Chancellor was dependent not on the Reichstag but increasingly on the High Command. The Kaiser, too, became more and more of a shadow. After Hindenburg and Ludendorff had been appointed to the High Command, they demanded in 1917 the dismissal of the Chancellor Bethmann Hollweg. He was too independent. His successors were nonentities and Germany practi-cally fell under a Hindenburg–Ludendorff military dictatorship during the last year and a half of the war.

If Austria–Hungary had been on the verge of dissolution through the disaffection of the Habsburg's Slav subjects this would certainly have shown itself when the Monarchy's Slav neighbours – the Russians and Serbs – went to war. In Vienna and Budapest there was much concern. The Serb, Ruthene and Czech populations were lukewarm in their war effort. Some Czechs and Poles formed their own Legions, which fought for the Allies. But there were no large-scale defections, let alone national uprisings. Croats, Slovenes, Italians, Romanians fought bravely side by side with Germans, Austrians and Magyars, and so did many Poles and Czechs.

The Austro–Hungarian army was a unique multinational force. But in one respect it was not unique: the incompetence of its leadership. The ordinary soldiers suffered appalling hardships, and

*News of the sinking of the passenger liner,* Lusitania, *on 7 May 1915, reaches England. Relatives await news of survivors at the Cunard shipping line's London offices.*

casualties during the first nine months of the war exceeded 2 million. Even so, new conscripts allowed fresh armies to be formed. In 1915, facing war on three fronts with Russia, Romania and Italy, the Monarchy was too weak to meet all her enemies, and substantial German armies were needed to sustain the ally. The 'national' division between Austria and Hungary also impeded the war effort. The Hungarians refused to go short of grain and profited by raising prices to the Austrian half of the Monarchy, which went hungry. War production, concentrated in Bohemia, was inefficient. But the multinational army fought on doggedly, though new recruits failed to maintain its strength, sapped by the losses in the field. In 1916 the aged Emperor Francis Joseph died. His successor Charles believed the Monarchy was close to collapse, having over-taxed its strength, and he was soon secretly trying to make peace. The army remained loyal to the dynasty virtually to the end.

New weapons killed in new ways: attacks from Zeppelins from the air and poison gas on land. Far more serious in its effect of spreading war to non-combatants was the conflict on the oceans. Germany attempted to break the effects of the British-imposed blockade by ordering in 1915 her submarines to sink all belligerent and neutral ships which entered a 'war zone' around the British Isles. To avoid capture the submarines torpedoed, without warning, boats bound for Britain. On 7 May 1915 the Germans sank the British passenger liner *Lusitania*; almost 2000 crew and passengers, including women and children, lost their lives. World opinion, especially in the United States, was outraged. 128 Americans had been among those who had lost their lives. Germany's excuse that starving women and children in Germany were victims of Britain's food blockade was always flimsy. The submarine campaign failed completely in its objective. It failed to cut off vital supplies from reaching France and Britain and it failed to frighten the neutral countries from continuing to expand their trade with the Allies.

Germany launched a propaganda campaign of hatred directed especially against Britain. This had little effect on those actually engaged on the battle-fronts. Much to the embarrassment of the generals on both sides, the German and Allied troops on the western front spontaneously stopped fighting on Christmas Day 1914, exchanged gifts and even played football between the trenches. There was little hatred, even a good deal of fellow feeling. The soldiers knew that there was no way out of the war except through death or injury or victory.

The Great War differed from the Second World War in one very important respect. There were no planned atrocities committed by the military on prisoners of war or on civilians. Wartime propaganda was, for the most part, lies. There were no savage Huns killing Belgian priests, nuns and babies, nor Belgian civilians behind the lines gouging out the eyes of wounded Germans. The Red Cross was respected in all countries, including tsarist Russia. Brutalities no doubt occurred but they were isolated. The record of the Germans in Belgium, Russia, Poland and elsewhere during the First World War in no way supports the conclusion that the Germans did not respect human rights or regarded the conquered peoples as inferiors. There were no mass murders of civilian populations as occurred during the Second World War. There was this much substance to early Allied propaganda that during the first two months of the war trigger-happy German troops did kill several hundred innocent Belgian civilians who were falsely accused of atrocities which German propaganda had led the troops to expect. The German Army Command in Belgium quickly brought the situation under control and the occupation was humanely conducted by the German military authorities, though there was undeniable hardship. The blot on this record was the forced deportation of some 60,000 Belgians in 1916 to work in German factories. Though it was wartime, the socialists in the Reichstag loudly protested; the deportations ceased, and by the summer of 1917 the great majority of the Belgians had been sent home again. In Belgium herself no coercion was exercised to force Belgian industry to work for the German war effort, though factories were dismantled. Only the miners, with the permission of the Belgian government, continued to produce coal.

Both among the Belgians and in occupied Russian Poland, the Germans and Austrians attempted to win over the population to their cause. The Poles were promised an independent state at least in form, though in practice such an independent Poland would have become a German satellite. There was no maltreatment. The Poles of Prussia and of the Habsburg Monarchy fought with much loyalty for Germany and the Habsburgs, seeing tsarist Russia as the oppressor.

Unquestionably the worst atrocity against defenceless civilians occurred in Turkey against the Christian Armenian people in 1915 and 1916. When the war went badly for the Turks in 1915 and the Russians were pushing into Anatolia, the Russians attempted to inflame and exploit Armenian nationalism against the Turks. An Armenian Legion fought for the Russians and an Armenian puppet government was set up. The Turks, uncertain of the loyalty of the Armenian population in Asia Minor, committed the worst atrocity of the war by ordering the wholesale deportation of the Armenians from the lands adjoining the battlefront to Syria. Armenian historians accuse the Turks of genocide against their people. Turkish historians admit that huge massacres took place but deny that the Turkish government intended them to happen. Sporadic large-scale massacres had already taken place before 1914, shocking Western Europe. What is certain is that the tragedy of 1915 and 1916 was on an ever greater scale. The forced deportation of men, women and children caused the deaths of tens of thousands through starvation and disease. Some (by no means all) of the Turks reverted to outright massacres on the spot. There are no reliable figures for those who perished. They vary, according to whether the sources are Turkish or Armenian, from 200,000 to more than 2 million. Of the 1.6 million Armenians between a half and three-quarters of a million perished. In the 'progressive' twentieth century the Armenian massacres were a precursor of even more extensive and cold-blooded massacres.

The five great nations of Europe went to war in 1914 not for any specific territorial gains. It was not a 'limited' war in the post-Napoleonic nineteenth-century manner. The war was a gigantic contest between them to determine their power in Europe and the wider world. It belongs with the wars of international insanity of the first half of the twentieth century. When that contest was decided, it was widely believed, it would inevitably bring about also the ruin of the imperial world ambitions of the defeated and provide new imperial prospects of conquest and influence for the victors. The illusion was fostered that this contest would settle the power struggle for ever. Hence the phrase 'the war to end wars'.

For two small nations there was no choice. Serbia was guilty of provoking Austria–Hungary and then in 1914, when faced with the Austrian ultimatum, fought for her independence. The Belgians were guilty of nothing. Their misfortune was their strategic position between France and Germany. Both French and German military planners wanted to march through Belgian territory, but Britain had prevented France from taking the initiative. Belgium wished to preserve her neutrality. The King of the Belgians, even after the invasion of his country, remained suspicious of both sides. He claimed he was defending the little bit of Belgium still free from German occupation as a neutral and not as an ally of Britain and France.

In the Balkans another small nation, Greece, was finally brought into the war in 1917 by France and Britain against the wishes of the King of Greece. Britain and France sent a military expedition to Salonika in October 1915 and then attempted to coerce the pro-German King Constantine into war on the Allied side. Although not as blatant as German aggression in Belgium, it was another violation of the rights of a small nation.

A number of European countries chose and were allowed to remain neutral throughout the war: the Netherlands, Denmark, Sweden, Norway, Switzerland and Spain. Their sympathies between the contestants were divided. They had benefited from the balance of power and so they would have preferred to see the war ended in the way that President Wilson, who led the most powerful of the neutrals, the United States, hoped, with the conclusion of a compromise peace. The European neutrals were too weak to insist on their 'neutral rights', the freedom to trade. The Dutch government, for instance, had to guarantee that the goods imported to the Netherlands from across the seas and passing through the British blockade would not be re-exported to Germany. In fact the neutrals did well as centres of trade to the belligerents during the first three years of the war. The 'illegal' trade between the Scandinavian countries, the Netherlands and Germany was enormous. It was no secret to the British and French authorities that a profitable trade even from their own countries by way of neutral countries was being conducted with Germany.

Some industries in neutral countries experienced a great boom. The Spanish coal mines in Asturias and textile mills in Catalonia supplied the French. Dutch industry developed; the Swiss found a ready market for clocks, machines and textiles. The shortage of food made farming highly profitable. But in the last two years of the war, while the farmers and some industrialists continued to do well, the standard of living of the mass of the workers in the neutral countries of Europe fell with soaring food prices.

The United States was by far the most important and powerful of the neutrals from 1914 to 1917, the only great power in the world not at war. The feeling of most Americans was that the war in Europe was but one further chapter in the history of the folly of European nations; it reinforced in their view the wisdom of the Founding Fathers in establishing the American Republic and separating her destiny from the rivalries of Europe. In Europe, Frenchmen, Englishmen, Italians and Russians were fighting the Germans, Austrians and Hungarians. During the Easter rising in Dublin in 1916 some Irishmen were fighting the English too; in the United States their descendants lived at peace with each other. Americans were convinced that they were building a higher civilisation and from this stemmed a genuine desire to help her neighbours on the American continent and in the world attain the blessings of liberty. This too was the faith of President Wilson. It helps to explain the missionary style of American diplomacy.

Wilson's moralising certainly led to some decidedly contradictory behaviour. The United States intervened on her own continent, sending troops to the countries of weaker neighbours in Mexico, Haiti, Santo Domingo and Nicaragua to establish American supremacy and naval bases in the Caribbean. But this was not seen as anything at all like European 'imperialism'. The purpose of the United States was 'pure': to teach her badly governed neighbours the benefits of American democracy. If people were enlightened and were given a free choice then Americans believed they would choose the American way.

In August 1914 Wilson issued a neutrality proclamation. Both Allied and German propaganda sought to persuade the American people that right and justice were on their side. The Germans emphasised that they were fighting a despotic and cruel regime in Russia, whose persecution of the Jews had already led to a great exodus of immigrants to the United States. The British dwelt on the rights of small nations and the dangers to a peaceful Europe if the Kaiser and Prussian militarism were to get away with breaking treaties and attacking weaker neighbours. The behaviour of the countries at war made a deep impression on the United

States and nothing more so than Germany's warfare against defenceless merchant vessels and even passenger liners. The President took his stand legalistically on 'neutral rights', the right of Americans to travel the oceans safely and of American merchant ships to trade with Europe. Wilson protested at Britain's conduct of the blockade and Germany's ruthless submarine warfare designed to cut off the British Isles from the world's arteries of trade essential to her war effort. Wilson's protests were effective. Rather than risk an American declaration of war, the German government desisted from attacking American ships in 1915 and on 1 September also pledged not to sink any more Allied passenger liners, which had also led to the loss of American lives. But meanwhile the loss of American lives and the ruthlessness of German warfare had swung the majority of American opinion in favour of the Allied cause. But this was sentiment, not action; the Americans also stood behind their President in wishing to keep out of the war.

The Americans saw no reason, however, why they should not profit from the huge increase of trade brought about by the war. While Germany was just about able to maintain her trade with the United States through neutrals, US trade with the Allies increased fourfold. By 1916 that trade was calculated at a staggering $3214 million, whereas trade with Germany and the neutrals amounted to a little over $280 million. The war resulted in a great expansion of American industry. During the war years Ford developed a mass market for motor cars and trucks. It was the beginning of the motor revolution, which matched in importance the earlier railway revolution in transport. Free from the burdens of war, the United States developed new technologies and more efficient methods of industrial manufacture, outdistancing the European nations more and more. As the Allies used up their capital to purchase from the United States, America herself replaced Britain as the principal source of capital to other nations. American prosperity came to depend on Allied purchases and, when these could no longer be met by payment, the prohibition against loans to the belligerents was relaxed. However, Britain's command of the sea prevented the Germans importing goods directly through their ports from overseas, though supplies did reach them through neutral ports (page 97). America's response to Allied needs meant that her economic strength was thrown predominantly behind the

Allied cause long before she formally abandoned neutrality.

There was no reason for the United States to go to war. She was still safe from European attack and was constructing a navy designed to be as powerful as any in the world to guarantee that safety in the future. She coveted no more territory. But already Americans perceived weaknesses in their position. The growth of Japanese power in Asia, no longer checked by the Europeans, threatened American interests in Asia. Even more worrying appeared to be the prospect of the European conflict ending in the complete victory of one side or the other. That would destroy the global balance of power. Would not the United States then be faced with the threat of a European superpower? American naval war plans before April 1917 were intended to meet that danger and not the possibility of joining on the Allied side. It made sense that Wilson would attempt to preserve the European balance by attempting to persuade the belligerents to conclude a compromise peace. But all his efforts in 1915 and 1916 failed. They failed for a simple reason. As long as the Germans occupied Belgium and northern France, they felt themselves at least partially victorious, but the Allies would contemplate no peace unless Germany gave up all her conquests. This would have made the sacrifices of Germany all in vain. In truth, neither side was ready to conclude a peace that might prove merely temporary. The only way they could conceive of ensuring a durable peace was through total defeat of the enemy.

When the first two months of the war did not lead to the expected decision, France, Britain and Russia and Germany and Austria–Hungary hoped to strengthen their position by winning new allies and opening up new war-fronts to threaten their enemies. The Germans were the first to be successful in this respect, persuading the Turks to attack Russia and enter the war in October 1914. The Turkish decision not only widened the area of conflict but also profoundly changed the history of the Middle East. The future of the Middle East became a bargaining counter between the powers at war. Britain invaded Mesopotamia to secure the oilfields, and supported an Arab revolt. Less successful was a British and French naval attack on the Dardanelles repelled by the Turks in February and March 1915. However an attack on Turkey was still seen by Churchill and Lloyd George as the best way of striking a decisive blow in a war deadlocked in the west but immensely costly in human life. In April 1915 British and French troops landed on the Gallipoli peninsula with the object of capturing Constantinople. But the Turks defended resolutely, and the Anglo-French campaign was a failure. Turkish and Allied losses were heavy before the Allies finally decided on evacuation, which they completed in January 1916. The Ottoman Empire did not play a decisive role in the war: the Turkish participation on the losing side resulted in her dismemberment and the dramatic growth of Arab nationalism.

Ottoman territory was held out as a bait during the war in order to keep one ally, Russia, in the war. In the famous 'secret treaties', Britain and France in 1915 promised Constantinople and the Straits to Russia. Other portions of the empire were promised to Italy as colonies by the treaty of London (April 1915) to induce the Italians to join the Allies and attack Austria–Hungary to the north.

Though nominally partners of the Triple Alliance with Germany and Austria–Hungary, the Italians had declared their neutrality in August 1914. They were for the next nine months wooed by both sides. The Italian government in the end chose war for territorial gain alone, though the politicians were divided whether or not to go to war. The government blatantly sought to extract the best bid, an attitude dignified by Prime Minister Salandra as conforming to *sacro egoismo*. What was decisive for Italy was a determination to complete her 'liberation' and to wrest from Austria–Hungary the Italian-speaking lands of the Trentino and Trieste. But her appetite was larger than this; the Italian government hoped also to acquire the German-speaking South Tyrol, as well as influence and territory in the Balkans and Ottoman territory in Asia Minor. The Austrians felt they were being blackmailed. 'Against brigands such as the Italians are now, no diplomatic swindle would be excessive,' secretly wrote the Austrian Prime Minister. The Allies offered the most. In May 1915 the Italians declared war on Austria–Hungary and so quite unnecessarily entered a war that was to prove for the Italians immensely costly in human life and material resources.

For the Balkan states the Great War provided an opportunity to start a third Balkan war for the satisfaction of Balkan territorial ambitions. Bulgaria in September 1915 joined the war on the side of Germany and Austria–Hungary with the promise of large territorial gains, including Serbian Macedonia. A year later, in August 1916, Romania was promised by the Allies Romanian-speaking Transylvania and part of the Austro–Hungarian Empire as well as other territories, and she declared war to secure them.

In eastern Asia, Japan's chosen policy was to strengthen her position in China. She declared war on Germany in August 1914, captured Germany's Chinese colonial sphere and then presented to China the Twenty-One Demands to assure herself a predominant position (page 89). The war begun by Germany, Austria–Hungary, Russia, France and Britain for one set of reasons widened to include other nations, all of whom, with the exception of the United States, saw in it an opportunity for extending their territorial empires.

In each of the belligerent countries there were some politicians who after the failure to win the war in 1914 looked towards the conclusion of a compromise peace. But, despite President Wilson's efforts to build a bridge between the combatants through mediation, the generals and the governments conceived only of a peace ended on the victor's terms. This attitude, as much as the outbreak of the war itself, changed the course of world history. In Berlin, Chancellor Bethmann Hollweg at times viewed the unfolding drama in terms of Greek tragedy; it would be disastrous for civilisation whether Germany won or lost. In victory, would he be able to keep in check crude concepts of military conquest?

In the plans for a peace following a German victory which Bethmann Hollweg drew up in September 1914, he tried to create a new Europe, at least a new continental Europe, because he could not conceive defeating Britain, only of isolating her through the defeat of Russia and France. He said he wished to conclude a so-called 'Bismarckian' peace of limited annexation. On the other hand he was convinced that France and Russia must be so weakened that they would never be able to threaten Germany again. Belgium, and even a coastal strip of northern France, would have to fall under direct or indirect German control. Through the creation of autonomous states, carved out of the Russian Empire, but made dependent on Germany, Russia would be pushed far to the east. A continental economic custom union would bring prosperity to all, and reconcile continental Europe to German hegemony while excluding Britain. All this he called 'Middle Europe'. To satisfy imperial ambitions, the German African colonies would be augmented with French and Belgian colonial possessions to form German 'Middle Africa'. The base of Germany's political and economic power would, however, have lain in her domination of continental Europe. There was to be no return to the balance of power. This meant in practice the destruction of Russia and France as great powers and a compromise peace with Britain which would acknowledge Germany's continental domination – hardly a limited Bismarckian peace!

Russian aims were both specifically territorial and absolute. The Russian government wished to fulfil what it regarded as Russia's 'historic mission' of acquiring Constantinople and control of the Straits. What this involved was the final destruction of Ottoman power and its replacement by a Russian domination of the Balkans, Asia Minor and as much of the Middle East as France and Britain would allow.

All Allied war aims were dependent on defeating Germany. With Germany eliminated as a great power, the reduced Habsburg Empire and the smaller Balkan states presented no problem to Russia. The rivalry of allies would be more serious than the ambitions of former enemies. We can gain a glimpse of Russian aims. According to the French Ambassador's memoirs, the Russian Foreign Minister, Sazonov, told him on 20 August 1914 that the 'present war is not the kind of war that ends with a political treaty after a battle of Solferino or Sadowa'; Germany must be completely defeated.

> My formula is a simple one, we must destroy German imperialism. We can only do that by a series of military victories so that we have a long and very stubborn war before us. . . . But great political changes are essential if . . . the Hohenzollern are never again to be in a position to aspire to universal dominion. In addition to the restitution of Alsace-Lorraine to France, Poland must be restored, Belgium enlarged, Hanover reconstituted, Slesvig returned to Denmark, Bohemia freed, and all the German colonies given to France, England and Belgium, etc. It is a gigantic programme. But I agree with you that we ought to do our utmost to realise it if we want our work to be lasting.

It is a commonplace to compare the peace of Brest-Litovsk of March 1918, which the Germans imposed on the hapless Russians, with Versailles, and to conclude that the Germans only justly received what they had meted out to others. The reverse is also true. The Russians had every intention of treating the Germans as harshly as the Germans treated Russia in defeat. When we compare the 'war aims', it becomes rather hazardous to pass comparative moral judgements on them.

The French government also wanted to impose conditions on the defeated so that they would remain victors for all foreseeable time. The French, alone among the great powers, were fighting the same enemy for the second time for national survival. French territorial demands were limited to Alsace-Lorraine and colonies. But French requirements went far beyond that, beyond the restoration of Belgium, to the imposition of terms that as Viviani, the French Prime Minister, declared to the Chamber of Deputies in December 1914, would destroy Prussian militarism. The economic imbalance between Germany and France was to be righted by territorial cessions and by forcing the Germans to transfer wealth – gold – to France under the heading of 'reparations'. Germany would be made to 'pay for the war', to weaken her and to strengthen her neighbours.

The British approach was more pragmatic, avoiding commitments as far as possible. There was no desire whatever to reconstitute Hanover! Indeed there were no war aims formulated at all during the first two years of the war, except for the restoration of Belgian independence, since this had been the principal ostensible reason for going to war. Little thought was given to the terms to be imposed on defeated Germany, far more on what favourable inducements might entice Germany's allies to abandon her. There was no desire to break up the Habsburg Empire. But the one recurring theme, the destruction of the war spirit of the principal enemy, was frequently proclaimed. General Sir William Robertson, Chief of the Imperial General Staff, in a speech to munition workers in April 1917, summed up this uncompromising outlook: 'Our aim is, as I understand it, to deal German despotism such a blow as will for generations to come prevent a recurrence of the horrors of the last two and a half years.' But this did not mean exactly what the Russians and French had in mind. Britain's prime minister, Lloyd George, as well as

Arthur Balfour, the Foreign Secretary, were convinced that Germany's great power on the continent could not be permanently diminished. The best hope for peace was the emergence of a peaceful democratic post-war Germany. Thus Germany should not be driven to seek revenge to recover territory won from her. Unjust and harsh treatment of defeated Germany would only sow the seeds of future conflict. Britain's leaders looked to a close alliance with the United States to guarantee the maintenance of peace. Later differences which emerged with France over the right policy to adopt are clearly foreshadowed in British war aims. These were only 'absolute' on one point: the security of the British Empire from any future German challenge. Germany would not be permitted again to compete with Britain's naval supremacy. As for other war aims, they were to be formulated by Britain during the war in response to the demands of allies, or would-be allies, or in pursuit of military objectives. The latter led to the encouragement of the Arab revolts against the Turks, for instance, and so to the post-war transformation of the Middle East.

Were these war aims only formulated during the course of war to justify to the people an increasingly bloody, but basically irrational, war, as has so often been asserted? Or do they represent a continuity of assumptions held since before the war? They are indeed all of a piece. That is not to say that France would have gone to war for Alsace-Lorraine, or Germany in order to dominate Belgium, or Russia for Constantinople. The territorial aspirations were but a reflection of a more deep-rooted belief: that the balance of power could not last, that either Germany and her allies or Britain, France and Russia must dominate, that sooner or later a supreme struggle between the powers on the continent would be inevitable. Russia was convinced that either she or a Habsburg Empire supported by Germany would dominate the Balkans. The struggle could not be avoided. No one 'stumbled' into war. Nor would any power stumble out of it. The end would be brought about by military imperatives.

The attempts of the belligerent nations to win a decision in 1915 and 1916 all failed at a cost in human life never before experienced. Both sides on the western front attempted to break through the other's carefully prepared defences. For the soldiers this meant leaving the security of their own trench and advancing across a 'no-man's land' raked by machine-gun fire to the enemy trench protected by barbed wire and bayonets. If you were lucky artillery had cleared something of a path before you and disorganised the defence, but it was rarely totally effective. If good fortune favoured you, you actually reached the enemy trench; others only moved a few yards beyond their own trench before falling to the enemy fire. French and British offensives were launched by Joffre and Haig in the spring of 1915. No breakthrough was achieved; the little territory gained was no compensation for the appalling losses. In the autumn of 1915 the Allies renewed their offensive, ending again without any worthwhile gain; 242,000 men were lost by the Allies in that autumn offensive alone. New recruits were nevertheless still increasing the size of the armies.

On the eastern front German troops in 1915 were now essential to sustain the Austro-Hungarian front as well as their own. In successive Austrian and German offensives from January to September 1915 the Russians suffered heavy defeats, were driven from all German territory as well as Habsburg Galicia and gave up a large area of the Russian Empire including Russian Poland. The Russian retreat demoralised the army. The Germans and Austrians captured more than a million prisoners and the Russians had lost another million men. But the Russian war effort was not broken. By enormous effort on the home industrial front and by the raising of new troops the Russian front-line strength reached 2 million once again in 1916. Some 4 million men had by then been lost. The tsarist government, despite the vast reserve of population, was incapable of doing more than making good the losses. The Russian armies that would by sheer numbers steamroller over Germany and Austria–Hungary never materialised in the First World War as they were to in the Second. That nightmare vision for the Germans which had been so powerful an influence on them in deciding for war in 1914 was illusory.

Before 1915 was ended the first of the nations to have gone to war in August 1914 was crushed. Serbia was overwhelmed by a joint Bulgarian, German and Austrian attack.

The new front created by Italy's entry into the war in May 1915 resembled the fighting in France rather than in Russia. Although the Italians enjoyed a superiority over the Austrians, they suffered heavy

*Images of War. Thoughts of home on the Russian front* (left). *The imperial Austro-Hungarian army suffers casualties after an unsuccessful assault* (right). *The Kaiser's troops attempt one last onslaught at Villers Bretonneux on the western front in March 1918 – without success* (top right). *Will new men and weapons bring victory? A Canadian division is supported by a Mark IV tank* (top left).

casualties in a series of offensives during the course of 1915 without coming near to winning any decisive battles or achieving a breakthrough. Here too the short glorious war that was expected proved an illusion and Italy was locked in costly battles of attrition. It was easier to enter the war than to leave it with profit.

The central powers (Germany, Austria–Hungary, Turkey and Bulgaria) planned to carry on the war in 1916 so that through attrition the enemy would be exhausted. The German commander in the west, General Falkenhayn, calculated that if the Germans attacked the fortress of Verdun, then the French would sacrifice their manpower to hold on to it. This would break France's military morale.

Verdun became associated with the doggedness of its French hero defender Pétain, who, like Hindenburg, was to play a critical political role in post-war Europe for which he was unsuited. Falkenhayn failed to take Verdun or to limit German casualties by the use of artillery as he had planned. By the year's end German casualties – a third of a million men – were almost as heavy as the French losses of 362,000 men.

During the summer months until the autumn of 1916 the British and French armies not committed to Verdun launched their great offensive on the Somme intending to bring victory. The casualties suffered in hurling men against well-prepared positions were horrifying. The German army was not beaten but, refusing to yield territory in tactical withdrawals, also suffered enormous casualties. The French, British and Germans sacrificed more than a million men. British casualties alone exceeded 400,000, French 190,000 men, and the Germans around 500,000. Still there was no decision.

The Somme offensive in the west was part of a co-ordinated inter-Allied plan to attack the central powers. Only the Russians in 1916 gained a great victory. General Brusilov's summer offensive was an overwhelming success, destroying the independent Austro-Hungarian war effort. The Austro-Hungarian army lost more than 600,000 men in casualties or as prisoners, the Germans 150,000. But Russia, too, failed to defeat Germany in the east. Russian casualties were heavy and multiplied during the fighting from August to September. As it turned out, though no one expected it at the time, the Brusilov offensive was to be the last major Russian military effort before the outbreak of the revolution in Russia. The central powers did score one easy military success in the east in 1916 after the halting of the Russian offensive: the defeat of Romania. Her supplies of foodstuffs and oil now became available to the central powers.

While the war was being fought, during the winter of 1916 and the following spring of 1917, new forces were at work which changed its course fundamentally: American intervention and the Russian Revolution.

# CHAPTER 13

# War and Revolution in the East, 1917

The upheavals in Russia during 1917 changed the history of the world. Russia broke with the evolutionary Western path of national development. The birth of communist power was seen by Lenin, its founder, as the means by which not only the vast lands and peoples of Russia would be transformed but also the world. For seven decades Lenin was revered by half the world as its spiritual guide despite the bitter dissensions among communist countries as to which was the rightful heir. His vision of communism as a world force was realised less than twenty-five years after his death.

One of the fascinations of history is that it shows how a man, in many ways very ordinary, with ordinary human weaknesses, making mistakes and bewildering his contemporaries with the inconsistencies of his actions, can exert enormous influence on his own times and on the world decades later. Napoleon and Hitler caused devastation. Napoleon left some good behind him; Hitler, nothing but destruction. Lenin's reputation today has suffered with the demise of the Soviet Union, once elevated by propaganda he is now stripped of myth, but the impact of his ideas was enormous.

The success of Lenin's revolution, and the birth and growth of Soviet power, exercised great appeal as well as revulsion. Lenin's achievement was that he gave concrete expression to the theories of Karl Marx. The Russian Revolution appeared as the beginning of the fulfilment of Marx's 'scientific' prophecy that capitalist society was heading for its inevitable collapse and that the 'proletariat', the workers hitherto exploited, would take over and expropriate the exploiters. The poor shall inherit this world, not the next. That was obviously an intoxicating message. Of course Marx had written his great works in the mid-nineteenth century. Some 'adjustments' of his predictions were necessary to square them with the realities of the early twentieth century.

In Germany, where Marx's teachings had the largest political following, and where a powerful Social Democratic Party emerged, the lot of the working man was improving, not getting worse as Marx had predicted. The collapse of capitalism did not after all seem imminent. Some German socialists asked whether the party should not concentrate on securing practical benefits for the workers and accept the political system meanwhile. This became the policy of the majority of the party. The British Labour movement was clearly taking this direction too. In France the doctrine of industrial and class strife leading to revolution had limited appeal outside the towns. Marx's apocalyptic vision of capitalism in its last throes bore little relevance to conditions in the most industrialised countries. But Lenin was not disconcerted. He sharply condemned all the 'revisionists' and compromises with the 'exploiting' bourgeois society. He found much later the answer to the paradox in the book of an English radical on the nature of imperialism. J. A. Hobson believed that the drive for empire by the European states was caused by the need of advanced Western countries to find new profitable markets for investment. Lenin elaborated and went further. Imperialism, he wrote, was the last stage of capitalism. It postponed the fulfilment of Marx's prophecy. Because the Asiatic and African labourer was cruelly exploited, employers could afford to pay their European workers more. But the extension of the capitalist world could only postpone, not avert, its collapse. The proletariat must steel itself for the ultimate takeover and not compromise. The class struggle, as Marx taught, was the driving force of historical evolution. Anything that lessened the class struggle was treachery against the proletariat.

Lenin's views were so extreme, ran so much counter to the world in which he lived, that the majority of socialists ridiculed him when they were not accusing him of seeking to divide the socialist movement. Those who were not socialists did not take him seriously. His following, even among Russian socialists right up to the revolution of November 1917, was only a minority one.

This fanatical believer in the victory of the proletariat and castigator of bourgeois capitalist society and its intelligentsia of professors, lawyers and administrators had himself been born into the strata of society he virulently condemned. More important, its privileges had given him the education and freedom indispensable to his early success. The founder of communism indubitably sprang from the Russian tsarist middle class, to the embarrassment of some of his Soviet biographers. His real name was Vladimir Ilyich Ulyanov. He assumed the name of Lenin later to confuse the tsarist police. He was born in 1870. His mother was the daughter of a retired doctor who had become a small landowner. His father exemplified success and social mobility in nineteenth-century Russia: he had made his way from humble origins to the post of provincial director of schools, a position in the Russian civil service entitling him to be addressed 'Excellency'. Lenin was not 'of the people'.

Lenin was only sixteen when his father suddenly died. A year later an unnatural tragedy blighted family life. The eldest son of this eminently respectable family, Alexander, a student in St Petersburg, had become involved in a terrorist conspiracy to assassinate the Tsar. Apprehended, he was tried and hanged. Lenin now began to study and enquire into his brother's beliefs and actions, which were a naive and violent response to autocracy in the tradition of Russian terrorism. But in Russia there

was not yet guilt by association. The family was treated with consideration. Lenin was accepted to study law in the University at Kazan. However, he was soon involved in student protests and was expelled. For three years he read and studied and became engrossed in the radical writings of his time.

It was during this period that he first discovered in Karl Marx's writings a revolutionary philosophy and a goal which, according to Marx, was a scientific certainty. He spent his life working out the right policies and tactics for Marxists to follow in order to realise the goals of the proletarian revolution. Unlike many other socialists, his faith in Marx's prediction was absolute, akin to that following a religious revelation. This faith and certainty gave him strength, but Lenin saw no point in martyrdom. His brother's gesture had been heroic but useless. The leader must preserve himself and avoid danger. It was an aspect of Lenin's ice-cold rationality – despite his attacks on the intelligentsia – that he ignored taunts that he sent others into danger while he himself enjoyed domesticity and safety abroad in London, Geneva and Zurich.

A remarkable feature of tsarist Russia at this time is that despite police surveillance of political suspects – and Lenin was undoubtedly a suspect – no political opponent was condemned for his thoughts, as later in communist countries, but only for his deeds. Even then punishment by later standards was frequently lenient. The death penalty was limited to those involved in assassination, political murders or plotting such murders. If sentenced to dreaded fortress imprisonment a man's health could be broken. The lesser sentence of exile to Siberia bears no relationship to the labour camps of Stalin's Russia. The inhospitable climate was a hardship but there was no maltreatment. Lenin, for instance, when later on he was sentenced, was free to live in a comfortable household and to study and read.

But before this he was allowed a second chance and after three years of waiting and petitioning was readmitted to Kazan University. He was thus able to complete his university studies before moving as a fully fledged lawyer to the capital, St Petersburg. Here he plunged into political activities and became a leading member of a small group of socialists. Adopting the agitational techniques of the Lithuanian Jewish socialist organization, the Bund, the St Petersburg socialists determined to spread the message of Marxism by involving themselves in trade union agitation on behalf of workers. Lenin and his associates agitated successfully among the textile workers. The police stepped in. Eventually Lenin was sentenced to three years exile in Siberia. In 1900 he was permitted to return to European Russia. He had matured as a revolutionary. He believed he could best promote the revolution by leaving Russia, as so many socialist émigrés had done before him, and to organise from safety in the West. Perhaps the police authorities were happy to get rid of him. In any event, Lenin in 1900 received the required permission to leave his country. Except for a few months in Russia after the outbreak of the revolution in 1905, Lenin spent the years before his return to Russia in April 1917 mainly as an exile in Switzerland.

Abroad, he developed the organisation of his revolutionary party based on his own uncompromising ideology. In the process he quarrelled with the majority of Russian and international socialists and finally split the Russian Democratic Socialist Party. His faction, which at the Second Party Congress in Brussels and London in 1903 managed to gain a majority, became known as the 'majority' or Bolsheviks, and the minority took the name of Mensheviks, although soon the fortunes were reversed and until 1917 the Mensheviks constituted the majority of the party. It is easier to define the Bolsheviks' ideas than the Mensheviks'. The Bolsheviks thought that leadership was established by the power of Lenin's personality and the hardness and sharpness of his mind and at each point of crisis had to be re-established. Lenin imbued the Bolsheviks with his own uncompromising revolutionary outlook. There was to be no co-operation with the 'bourgeois' parties, unless for tactical reasons it were expedient to support them briefly and then only as 'the noose supports a hanged man'. Lenin believed a broadly based mass party run by the workers would go the way of the Labour Party in Britain and weakly compromise. Only a small elite could understand and mastermind the seizure of power by the proletariat. The party must be centralised and unified. Lenin therefore sought to build up this party of dedicated revolutionaries who would agitate among the masses and take advantage of all opportunities, having but one goal, the socialist revolution.

The Mensheviks were never as united as the Bolsheviks nor were they led by any one man of commanding personality. In turn they accused Lenin of dictatorial behaviour. The Mensheviks developed their own Marxist interpretations. Accepting Marx's stages of development, they believed that Russia must pass through a bourgeois capitalist stage before the time would be ripe for the socialist revolution. And so when Russia embarked on the constitutional experiment after 1905, they were prepared to support the constitutional Kadet party in the Duma (page 56). Despite their Marxist authoritarian revolutionary ideology, the leadership in practice softened the line of policy. Lenin was never very consistent about his tactics, but his driving passion for the socialist revolution, his ruthless pursuit of this one goal when others in the party wavered and were distracted, gave him ultimate victory over the Mensheviks, who endlessly debated and advocated freedom of speech for all – even for Lenin, who was determined to undermine their authority. What true revolutionary in any case cared for 'majorities' and 'minorities'? Rule by the majority Lenin contemptuously regarded as a liberal bourgeois concept.

Within Russia herself the adherents of the supporters of the Social Democratic Party had little appreciation of why the Mensheviks and Bolsheviks were quarrelling in face of the common enemy of autocracy. It was not among the rank and file, small in Russia in any case, that their differences mattered. The Bolsheviks had no more than 20,000 members as late as February 1917. In any case it was neither Mensheviks nor Bolsheviks who won the greatest popular support but the Socialist Revolutionaries. Formed in 1901, they looked to the much more numerous peasants rather than to the urban workers. Some carried on the tradition of terror; a special group organised assassinations and thereby satisfied the demand for immediate revolutionary action. In the long run the revolution of the peasantry would occur. Other Socialist Revolutionaries, acting as a reforming party, would press for liberal constitutional reforms and laws to protect the peasants. These liberal reforms would pave the way to socialism later. The Socialist Revolutionary terrorist and party wings were never really co-ordinated. The phenomenon became evident in Ireland too.

The revolution of 1905 took the Bolsheviks and Mensheviks by surprise. At the outset they had only a small following among the workers, the Bolsheviks probably only a few hundred. Lenin did not affect its course. Nine years later, the outbreak of the

First World War appeared to mark the end of international socialism as one after the other the national socialist parties placed their countries before the brotherhood of the proletariat. Some socialists formed a pacifist wing; with them Lenin had nothing in common. Only a small band of revolutionaries gathered around Lenin. He was briefly imprisoned as a Russian spy in Austrian Poland at the outbreak of the war but was released to rejoin the other socialist exiles in Switzerland. The Social Democrat Party in Russia had dwindled from its peak of some 150,000 members in 1907 to probably less than 50,000 in 1914 and only a small minority of them were Bolsheviks. But Lenin's supreme self-assurance and confidence in Marx's analysis enabled him to survive disappointments and setbacks. For him the conflict among the imperialists was the opportunity the socialists had been waiting for. He hoped for the defeat of Russia and the exhaustion of the imperialists. Then he would turn the war between nations into a civil war that would end with the mass of peoples united in their aim of overthrowing their rulers and establishing the 'dictatorship of the proletariat'.

Lenin's view of the war and of the role of the socialists did not persuade even the left wing of the socialists who met in conferences in Switzerland at Zimmerwald in 1915 and Kienthal in the following year. The majority wished to bring the war to a compromise end, with international friendship and no annexations, and so espoused a pacifist stand. Lenin attracted only a handful to his side, among them the brilliant and fiery young Trotsky, who had inspired the workers' councils – the soviets – which had sprung up during the 1905 revolution. Trotsky believed in revolutionary action, in a 'permanent revolution'. He forecast that the bourgeois first stage would flow into the socialist second stage. Lenin closely shared Trotsky's views, believing he would witness the socialist revolution in his lifetime. When the new revolution did occur, however, in February 1917, the events took him once more by surprise.

The overthrow of tsarism took place with startling speed. For the army of 6.5 million men in the field, 1916 had closed with hope for the future. The Russian army, after suffering some 7 million casualties, had nevertheless proved more than a match for the Austrian army. Indeed, only the great power of the German army had stood in the way of total Habsburg disaster. The Germans proved formid- able foes, but they were now outnumbered and the plans for a co-ordinated offensive east, west and south on the Italian front held out the promise that the central powers could be overwhelmed in 1917. The severe problems of weapons and munitions for the Russian army had been largely overcome by a prodigious Russian industrial effort during 1916 After the heavy losses sustained in the third year of war the rank and file in the army viewed war with stoicism and resignation rather than with the *élan* and enthusiasm of the early months. But it was not an arms demoralised and ready to abandon the front. The 'home front' was the first to collapse.

The hardship suffered by the workers and their families in the cities swollen in numbers by the industrial demands of the war effort was felt in the winter of 1916/17 to be becoming insupportable. The ineffectual government was being blamed. The Tsar had assumed personal responsibility for leading the armies and spent most of his time after the summer of 1915 at army headquarters. He had left behind the Empress Alexandra, a narrow-minded, autocratic woman. The 'ministers' entrusted with government were little more than phantoms. The infamous Rasputin, on the other hand, was full of energy until murdered in December 1916 – an event greeted with much public rejoicing.

The rioting that spontaneously broke out in Petrograd – formerly St Petersburg – early in March (23 February by Russian dating) 1917 was not due to the leadership of the socialist exiles. Their organisation within the country had suffered severely when early in the war the tsarist government smashed the strike movement. Yet unrest in Petrograd and Moscow had been growing. Only a proportion of the workers in war industries had received wage rises to compensate them for the rapid rises in the price of food and other necessities. Other workers and the dependent families of the soldiers at the front were placed in an increasingly desperate position. The peasants were withholding food from the towns and were unwilling to accept paper money, which bought less and less. The railway system was becoming more inefficient as the war continued, unable to move grain to the towns in anything like sufficient quantities. Dissatisfaction turned on the supposedly 'German' Empress and the administration and government which permitted such gross mismanagement. The revolution in March 1917 succeeded because the garrison troops of the swollen army were not loyal and would not blindly follow the command of the Tsar as they had done in peacetime.

Quite fortuitously the Duma had begun one of its sessions at the very time when this new unrest began. Among the professional classes, the gentry and the army generals, the Duma leaders had gained respect, even confidence, as faith in the Tsar's autocracy and management of the war rapidly diminished. The feeling of country and towns was still patriotic. Everyone was suffering – gentry, workers, peasants and the professional classes. The war against the invader should be won. But at the same time an alleviation of the hardships that the population was suffering especially food shortages, must be dealt with now, without delay. There seemed no contradiction. The Duma was the one institution which provided continuity and embodied constitutional authority. Under the pressure of striking workers and increasing anarchy in Petrograd, the Duma attempted to gain control over the situation. Its leaders advised the Tsar to abdicate. The Tsar, lacking all support, hesitated only a short while before giving up his throne. His brother declined the poisoned chalice when offered the crown. Once the decisive break of the Tsar's abdication had been achieved there could be no saving of the dynasty. The Duma also gave up meeting, handing over all authority to a small group of men who became the provisional government, composed of mainly moderate liberals and presided over by a benign figure of the old school, Prince Lvov. The new government contained one Socialist Revolutionary, Alexander Kerensky, whose co-operation, however, was sincere and who set himself the goal of revitalising the war effort by winning over the Russian people with a programme of broad reform and freedom.

From the start, the provisional government did not enjoy undisputed authority. In Petrograd, as in 1905, a Council of Soviets of Workers' and Soldiers' Deputies sprang up, claiming to speak on behalf of the workers and soldiers throughout Russia. They were not ready to rule. But they asserted the right to watch over the provisional government and to act as they pleased in the interests of 'political freedom and popular government'. The provisional government sought the co-operation of the Petrograd Soviet and had to agree to permit the garrison troops, who had taken the side of the revolution, to remain in Petrograd. Henceforth this disaffected

force was under the control of the Petrograd Soviet and could not be moved. The provisional government also agreed to the establishment of soldiers' councils throughout the army, and the Soviet published their famous 'Order number one' decreeing that they should be set up in every army unit by election. But the Soviet, dominated by Mensheviks and Socialist Revolutionaries, was quite incapable of providing for the coherent government of Russia and had no intention either of replacing the provisional government or of seeking an early end to the war other than through a Russian victory. Two leading Bolsheviks at this time, Lev Kamenev and Joseph Stalin, were ready to co-operate with the 'bourgeois' revolution.

The Soviets of Workers' and Soldiers' Deputies and the Soviets of Peasant Deputies were dominated by the Socialist Revolutionaries and had no thought of ruling the country. However, the provisional government also found it increasingly difficult to prevent the country sinking into anarchy. Only the army at the war-fronts stood firm. At home the provisional government spoke of agrarian reform, order, freedom and victory. A new, freely elected parliament would be called to decide on Russia's future and provide a government based on the democratic wishes of the people. But meanwhile the provisional government lacked the power and the means to improve the conditions of the people. In the worsening situation in May 1917, the provisional government insisted that rivalry with the Soviets must cease and that socialist representatives of the Soviets enter the 'bourgeois' government. The Soviets agreed to share power in a coalition and the fusion seemed to be consummated when Alexander Kerensky, as war minister, became its leading member.

These developments were anathema to Lenin. With the assistance of the German High Command, who naturally wished to further the disintegration of Russia, Lenin reached Petrograd in April, having travelled from Switzerland by way of Germany. Lenin had no scruples about accepting the aid of the German class enemy. Soon, he believed, revolution would engulf Germany too. What mattered now was to win back the Russian socialists to the correct revolutionary path, even though he led the minority Bolsheviks. The socialist revolution, Lenin believed, could be thwarted by the collaboration of socialists and the bourgeois government. With relentless energy, overcoming what proved to be temporary failures, he changed the revolutionary tide.

For Lenin the mass upheaval taking place in Russia was more than a 'bourgeois' revolution. He believed the revolutionary upsurge would pass beyond the bourgeois to the socialist stage without pause. In his 'April theses' Lenin argued that the provisional government was the great antagonist already of the 'republic' of Soviet workers and poor peasants taking shape among the grass roots of society. This view was rejected by the Socialist Revolutionaries, by the Mensheviks and at first by many of the Bolsheviks as well. But Lenin won the Bolsheviks over and thereby became the principal architect of the course that the revolution took in November. Lenin's first aim was to destroy the provisional government. With agitation of 'all land to the peasants' and 'all power to the soviets', he helped the revolutionary process along. But Lenin was not the actual cause of the increasing lawlessness; he could only fan the already existing flames. The economic situation was daily getting more out of hand. Inflation was increasing by leaps and bounds. The provisional government was entirely ineffectual in halting the slide into chaos at home. The one hope left for it was the army.

Kerensky appointed a new commander-in-chief, General Kornilov, and ordered a fresh offensive in Galicia. The army responded, made some progress at first, but was then routed when facing an attack in turn. Meanwhile, in July, while the offensive was still in progress, fresh disorders in Petrograd, supported by thousands of sailors from Kronstadt, looked like the beginning of the new revolution. Lenin, however, regarded an uprising at this time as premature. The Bolshevik leadership was divided in its response and hesitated to give a lead to the masses. The rising proved a total failure. The provisional government branded Lenin a German spy and ordered his arrest. He was forced into hiding and later fled to Finland. The prospect of an early Bolshevik revolution now seemed remote. Yet despite the ruin of his hopes, Lenin's diagnosis that Russia was in the grip of a continuing revolutionary ferment proved, in the end, to be correct.

The turn of events in September aided the Bolsheviks. General Kornilov was marching on Petrograd with troops with the avowed intention of destroying the Bolsheviks and dissension and defeatism in the armies' rear. Kerensky ordered Kornilov to lay down his command. Kornilov refused and proclaimed himself the saviour of the nation. Kerensky now appealed for armed help from all the people, including the Bolsheviks. Kornilov's march on Petrograd ended in fiasco, but the Bolshevik militia, the Red Guards, retained their arms. Lenin now set about the overthrow of the provisional government. In the Petrograd Soviet the Bolsheviks in September 1917 at last enjoyed a majority. Lenin returned to Petrograd in October in disguise. He won over the Central Committee of the Bolshevik Party to his view that the time was now ripe for an armed insurrection. The task of organising the rising was assigned by the Petrograd Soviet to a military revolutionary committee. Trotsky was its leading spirit. To this threat, Kerensky and the provisional government reacted complacently and too late.

On the Bolshevik side there was not much confidence either. Trotsky's armed men were largely untrained. Nevertheless Trotsky organised them to seize power on 25 October (Russian date), 7 November (Western). Bolshevik strength, feeble as it was, proved enough. Kerensky could not find sufficient troops to defend his government.

With the seizure of the Winter Palace, where the provisional government was in session, the virtually bloodless revolution was over. The insurrection had been deliberately timed so that it coincided with the assembly of the second All-Russian Congress of Soviets of Workers' and Soldiers' Deputies. The Bolsheviks, who were in the majority, dominated the proceedings. Until the time when a constituent assembly was elected and met, the Congress entrusted the executive to a provisional workers' and peasants' government, thus regularising the power won by Lenin and his associates. But the hold of power by the Bolsheviks was precarious. It might last a day, a week or longer. They could be overwhelmed by a few hundred troops or outside powers. Lenin's achievement was to solidify Bolshevik power until it embraced the greater part of the former Russian Empire.

Had this birth of communist power fulfilled the 'scientific' forecasts of Karl Marx as Lenin believed? Was it a realisation of the inevitable historical process of class conflict according to Marxian theory? Lenin had to adapt Marx to fit the fact that the revolution had first succeeded in an overwhelmingly peasant country. But he believed, thus squaring these facts with Marx's analysis, that the revolution in backward Russia would not survive

*Revolutionary Russia.* Top: *July 1917, demonstrators scatter outside the Duma in Petrograd as the Provisional Government seeks to hold on to power. In the confusion a Bolshevik regiment standing guard at the Taurida Palace fires on other Bolsheviks trying to seize it.*
Opposite: *Lenin's urban supporters, Petrograd, 1917.* Above: *after the October Revolution, the Bolsheviks take the plaudits of the crowd. Stalin is at the extreme right of the photograph; Trotsky is the second from the left.*

without the international socialist revolution, without the proletarian revolution, especially in neighbouring Germany. Russia had but provided the spark. The advanced industrialised West, with its large proletariat would, so he thought, take over the leadership of the world revolution. In fact, the Russian crisis had its immediate cause in the war – not in a general world crisis of capitalism, but in the specific failing of Russian autocracy and of the provisional government to provide for the successful economic and military management of the war. Tsarism first and Kerensky next were destroyed by inflation, by lack of food in the towns and by the general hardships inflicted on a people without an end to war in sight or sustained victories to show for their immense sacrifices.

The second All-Russian Congress of Soviets had called for a just and democratic peace without annexations and indemnities, and had also abolished the landlords' ownership of land. Bolshevik propaganda in the army and the lawless state of the countryside, where the peasants seized the land, added to Russia's state of anarchy. The invading German armies, with their appeal to the subject nationalities, Ukrainians, Georgians, Poles and the Baltic peoples, threatened Russia with territorial disintegration. Lenin's insistence on peace with the

Germans at any price appeared suicidal even to his closest collaborators. Fighting ceased and armistice negotiations were formally completed early in December 1917. Meanwhile, Lenin in November had permitted elections for the Constituent Assembly to be held. When it met in January 1918 the Bolsheviks found they had not obtained a majority. Out of a possible 520 deputies the Bolsheviks had only gained 161, and the Socialist Revolutionaries, with 267 deputies, held an absolute majority. Lenin now turned his back on this 'sovereign' assembly and the whole democratic process. The assembly was adjourned and prevented from gathering again.

Trotsky was sent to negotiate peace terms with the Germans. At Brest-Litovsk he prevaricated and made fine speeches. Lenin and the Bolshevik leaders pinned their hopes on the coming German revolution, spurred on by revolutionary propaganda among the German troops. The Germans lost patience with Trotsky's intoxication with his own intellectual brilliance and occupied large regions of western Russia virtually without resistance. Trotsky thereby almost destroyed the revolution in its infancy. On 3 March 1918, the Russians, on Lenin's insistence, and overruling Trotsky's tactics, accepted the peace terms of Brest-Litovsk which

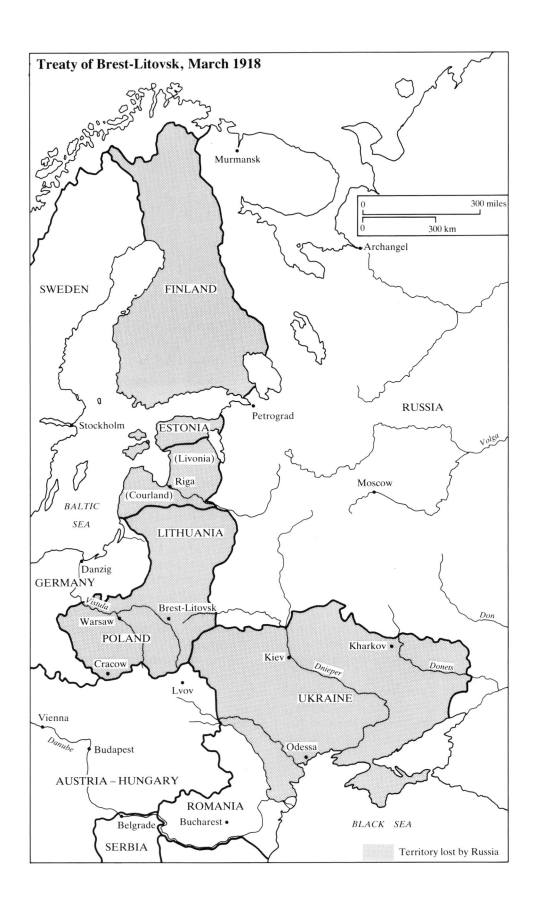

**Treaty of Brest-Litovsk, March 1918**

SWEDEN

FINLAND

Murmansk

Archangel

0       300 miles

0       300 km

RUSSIA

*Volga*

Stockholm

Petrograd

ESTONIA

(Livonia)

Riga

Moscow

(Courland)

*BALTIC
SEA*

LITHUANIA

Danzig

GERMANY

*Vistula*

Brest-Litovsk

*Don*

Warsaw

POLAND

Kiev

Kharkov

*Dnieper*

*Donets*

Cracow

Lvov

UKRAINE

Vienna

*Danube*

Budapest

Odessa

AUSTRIA – HUNGARY

ROMANIA

Belgrade

Bucharest

*BLACK SEA*

SERBIA

▒ Territory lost by Russia

*Lenin, November 1917.*

dispossessed Russia of a large part of her former Empire. Lenin had cajoled and bullied his colleagues on the Central Committee into accepting the harsh terms. Then he had to fight again to achieve its ratification by the Congress of the Bolshevik Party.

Peace with Germany gave Lenin and the Bolsheviks a breathing space, and saved the Bolshevik revolution. Lenin still confidently expected the war among the Western nations to turn into the great civil war and victory for the proletariat. But meanwhile the revolutionary spark had to be kept alive. It was now threatened by anarchy and by civil war from the opponents of the Bolsheviks, aided by Russia's former allies, who hoped somehow to bring her back into the war. In the succeeding years of war and famine, the Russian people were to suffer even more than they had suffered during the course of the First World War itself. But at the end of this period, the first communist nation was firmly established in a world very different from the one imagined by Lenin at the time of revolution and one which presented problems of a kind entirely different to those for which the two chief founders of communist power, Lenin and Trotsky, had prepared themselves in rigorous Marxist analysis.

# CHAPTER 14

# The Great War – II:
# The End of War in the West, 1917–1918

If the war had come to an end in 1917, if the conflict had been decisively won by either the Allies or the central powers eighteen months earlier, then for certain the history of the world would have been very different. Instead the war went on. Neither a compromise peace nor a decision on the western front could be attained. European society had withstood the strains of war for more than two and a half years extraordinarily well, much better than anyone thought likely in the beginning. In the third year, the toll of destruction finally began to crack the political and social cohesion of Russia, the largest of the European powers; nor could even the militarily stronger Western countries escape the consequences of the conflict. The year 1917 marked as great a change in the direction of world history as did 1914.

From the start the war had not been entirely European. With the entry of Turkey into the war in 1914 the destiny of the Middle East was bound up in the war's outcome. In what, from the point of view of the war itself, was a sideshow, the British launched offensives in 1916, 1917 and 1918 against the Turks and at the end of the war became the predominant military power in this region of the world. They were now bound to agreements and promises to the French (the Sykes–Picot agreement) to divide influence with them after the war; to the Arabs they had held out prospects of independence; and to the Zionists, who under Chaim Weizmann's leadership were working for a Jewish State, 'a National Home of the Jewish People' in

Palestine. From these origins in the First World War developed the Middle East conflicts which have continued down to the present day.

From the start, too, eastern Asia was involved in the war. On the pretext of pursuing the war against Germany, Japan began by occupying the German colonial sphere in China in 1914, and went on to attempt to gain predominance over a much greater part of China while the European powers were locked in devastating conflict thousands of miles away. On the continent of Africa the war seemed only to result in a rearrangement of colonies: a further chapter in the history of imperialism. Yet the new 'mandates' of the League of Nations over former German colonies held out eventual promise of independence for the African people. Peace treaties did not end these worldwide repercussions of the war. National aspirations which were intensified during the war continued to ferment when the war was over.

Nineteen-seventeen was a momentous year in world history. Two events almost coincided: the Russian Revolution and the United States' entry into the war. By becoming a belligerent and assuming world commitments, the United States was in decisive breach of the advice of George Washington and the Founding Fathers of the Republic. After the war, the American people tried to treat this as an aberration and return to normalcy and 'isolation'. But Americans could not escape involvement in global affairs in the twentieth century as they perceived their security and prosperity threatened by events elsewhere in the world.

Because of the realities of American politics, the decision for war rested on the shoulders of one man, President Wilson. Wilson's Secretary of State, Robert Lansing, was a convinced interventionist on the Allied side long before Wilson reached the same conclusion. He saw the war in Europe as a fight for democracy against the warlike Prussian Junker spirit. Lansing's views did not much affect the President one way or the other. He listened more to his friend and personal emissary, Colonel Edward M. House. But Wilson was very much his own man, supremely confident of his good judgement at a time when in questions of foreign policy, of peace and of war, the presidency was virtually supreme. There can be no doubt that his personal sympathies lay with the democracies. The overthrow of the Tsar in March 1917 therefore removed one obstacle to the United States' siding with the Allies. Nor can there be any doubt that from the start of the war in Europe the actual interpretation of American neutrality enormously favoured the Allied cause in providing financial credit and war supplies, even though Germany managed to secure some American imports through the neutral Scandinavian ports and Holland. Still, US policy was not even-handed and did not exemplify Wilson's own call to the American people to 'act and speak in the true spirit of neutrality'. In November 1916, Wilson narrowly won a second term as president, using such slogans as 'He kept us out of war'. Was Wilson cynically playing politics when during the campaign he declared, 'I am not expecting this country to get into war,' although five months later he led the United States into war?

The charge of insincerity cannot be simply dismissed. Wilson's change of stance in April 1917, his public enthusiasm for the rightness and justice of the noble cause of war, was not what he felt; he hated war, and his efforts to keep the United States out of the war before February 1917 were genuine. To claim that the United States did not behave as a proper neutral from 1914 to 1917, that Wilson hoped to frustrate a German victory by assisting the Allies, that he legalistically stretched the concept of America's neutral rights, condoning British infractions and harshly condemning German violations of these rights, does not prove that Wilson desired or expected the United States to enter the war and was willing to sacrifice American lives for the Allied cause. Wilson knew there was a risk of

war. From the outset the Germans had been left in no doubt, and were indeed themselves in no doubt, that to resume unrestricted submarine warfare against American ships supplying the Allies would lead to war with the United States. Expecting to win the war before America could carry military weight in Europe, the Kaiser, urged by the German military, nevertheless on 9 January 1917 finally chose to use this weapon.

Wilson had wished to save America's strength so as to ensure a just and permanent peace after war was over. The war, he believed, would leave the world exhausted, ready to listen to his words of reason. To gain his end, he had attempted as a first step to lead the warring nations to a compromise peace through his personal mediation. But war was nevertheless eventually forced on him by the German military leaders.

On 22 January 1917, after the failure of his last effort to mediate, Wilson still proclaimed a vision of a 'peace without victory' and a new world order or League of Nations to ensure that peace would prevail. Nine days later the Germans publicly announced their intention to attack all neutral shipping. Wilson could not ignore the challenge, but his reaction stopped short of war. The next blow to his attempt to keep out of war was the revelation of the so-called Zimmermann Telegram, a message from the German Foreign Minister to the Mexicans encouraging them to go to war with the United States and to recover their lost territories in alliance with Germany. The telegram had been intercepted by British intelligence and published on 1 March. Anger and indignation swept America. A few days later American cargo ships were sunk without warning by German submarines. Still Wilson hesitated. In the confidential documents and private papers of this time there is no hint of enthusiasm for war on Wilson's part, though his Cabinet were now unanimously in favour. But on 2 April 1917 Wilson submitted to Congress a request to recognise that Germany had made war on the United States, which both Houses of Congress approved on 6 April 1917.

Even so, President Wilson still maintained a separate status on behalf of the United States. He did not simply join the alliance; the United States became an 'associated power', Wilson thereby retaining a free diplomatic hand. He would pursue his goal of arriving at a just peace by other means. The American people were not making war on the

German people but on their militarily crazed rulers. Wilson's faith in American democracy made him believe rather naively that he could appeal to the peoples to follow his ideals if the governments of the Allies or former enemies should place obstacles in the way of the just peace he envisioned.

The United States was not ready for war in April 1917. Her military preparations, especially her great naval expansion, as well as her war plans, had been designed to secure American safety against the eventual victors of the First World War, whether led by Britain or Germany. Some military men believed the Germans could land more than a million men in the United States should they decide to invade her; the navy estimate was a more sober 200,000. The US Navy thus built a great battleship fleet 'second to none' – that is, equal in size to the British – to protect the United States from invasion after the First World War had ended. America's military preparations were particularly ill-suited for the war she now joined. The Allies did not need any more battleships, but they were desperately short of troops on the western front. Wilson had forbidden war plans of intervention in the First World War before April 1917; now everything had to be improvised.

The impact of American military intervention in Europe was not felt for a year. Not until May 1918 were American forces, under General John Pershing's command, strong enough to affect the fighting on the western front. It was just such a breathing space the German High Command had counted on to force Britain and France to their knees.

Along the battlefields of France the year 1917 again brought no result but continued to grind up hundreds of thousands of men and their weapons. General Robert Georges Nivelle, who had replaced Joffre in all but name as French commander-in-chief, planned a great spring offensive to be co-ordinated with Russian and Italian offensives. The British army had now grown to 1,200,000 men and the French to 2,000,000; together with the Belgians the Allies now enjoyed a superiority of 3,900,000 over 2,500,000 Germans. The Germans stood on the defensive in the west but frustrated the French and British efforts in the spring and summer of 1917 to break through their lines and rout their armies. Nivelle's failure resulted in widespread demoralisation among the French troops. The French nation which had withstood so much

in two and a half years of war appeared, during the spring of 1917, to lose her cohesion and unity of purpose. Soldiers mutinied, bitter at the spectacle of Paris, with its cafés and boulevards and smart ladies untroubled by war. Bitterness and despair, fear of mutilation and death, reopened old wounds of social schism.

The collapse of French morale was localised and General Henri Philippe Pétain's skilful handling of the situation, and the belief he instilled that the war would in future be fought with more consideration for the value of human life, brought the mutinies under control. Of the 30,000 to 40,000 mutineers forty-nine were shot to serve as an example. In the summer of 1917 the 'sacred union', the French political truce, ended. Following the lead of Russian Bolsheviks, French socialists now spoke of compromise peace. At this critical juncture President Raymond Poincaré chose as head of government, hated though he was by the socialists, the seventy-six-year-old veteran politician Georges Clemenceau, who embodied the spirit of fighting the war to victory. The country responded once more.

For the British and Canadians who bore the brunt of the fighting during the summer and autumn of 1917 it was a bitter year, and their commander Field Marshal Lord Haig was criticised for the unprecedented losses sustained in the offensives in Flanders. In November he reached the deserted village of Passchendaele less than ten miles from his starting point. Passchendaele came to symbolise the apparently pointless slaughter. There was no longer any romance in war.

By the autumn of 1917 three of the now six great powers at war were on the point of military and economic collapse. The Austrian half of the Dual Monarchy was desperately short of food; the Habsburg army could not without German help sustain the war on all fronts. The new Emperor Charles I was secretly seeking a way out of the war. On the other side, the Italians were also soon in desperate plight. Suffering 340,000 casualties, the Italian army was defeated at the battle of Caporetto in October 1917, but with some British and French help recovered to man a new line of defence.

One of the great powers, Russia, did collapse. The revolution that overthrew the Tsar in March 1917 had not taken her out of the war immediately. The new provisional government intended to fight it more energetically and successfully than before. But Alexander Kerensky, War Minister of the government and later its leader, could not with fine speeches make up for Russia's exhaustion and the mismanagement of the 'home front'. The Russian summer offensive which he ordered turned into a rout. In November 1917 the Bolsheviks seized power and called for peace immediately 'without annexations and without indemnities'. Russia was out of the war, a stunning blow for the Allies.

Nineteen-seventeen was a disastrous year for the Allies. Only on the oceans did they win what for Britain and France was a battle for survival. The Germans only once seriously challenged the battle-ship might of the British navy. The resulting battle of Jutland in May 1916 was claimed by both sides as a victory, but the German fleet did not again challenge the British navy whereas Britain continued to rule above the waves and maintain her blockade of Germany. The real danger to the Allies was the 'blockade' imposed below the water's surface by German submarines. At first it looked as though the Germans would sink enough ships to knock Britain and France out of the war by cutting the Atlantic supply line, for they sank 212 ships in February 1917 and a record 335 ships, totalling 847,000 tons, in April. By convoying ships losses were reduced to 107 ships by December. This was the damage that some 100 German submarines inflicted. What would have happened if the Germans had before the war concentrated on this effective offensive weapon instead of wasting resources on the prestigious German battleship fleet? They were to repeat the error in the Second World War.

During the grim winter of 1917 and 1918, wide-spread disaffection and doubts whether the war could ever be won led to new calls for peace from all sides. Lenin had nothing to lose by calling the labouring masses in Europe to revolution and to bring to an end the capitalist imperialist war of their masters. Lloyd George, determined to fight until the German rulers were defeated, responded, to still the doubts in Britain, by delivering a speech in January 1918 to the British Trades Union Congress. Its keynote was moderation and an insistence that the central powers give up all their conquests so that the sanctity of treaties be upheld. Lloyd George's speech was overshadowed a few days later, on 8 January 1918, by President Wilson's famous Four-teen Points setting out in a similar way the basis of peace. The worldwide appeal of the Fourteen Points lay in their lofty design for a new era of international relations. The world led by the United States and Wilson's 'new diplomacy' would 'be made fit and safe to live in'; every nation would 'determine its own institutions, be assured of justice and fair dealing by the other peoples of the world as against force and selfish aggression'. But the specific Russian, British and American peace proclamations, with their insistence on the restoration of conquered territory, all presupposed the defeat of Germany. No German could regard as a 'compromise' giving up all the territory still firmly occupied.

In 1918 it appeared likely that the Allies would be defeated rather than Germany. The generals Hindenburg and Ludendorff had established a virtual dictatorship in Germany and marshalled all resources in a country exhausted by war. In March 1918 Ludendorff mounted a tremendous offensive in the west; during April, May and June German troops broke through and once more came close to Paris. The cost in casualties was again huge: 800,000 Germans and more than a million Allied troops. This turned out to be imperial Germany's last bid for victory, though the Allies, commanded now by Marshal Ferdinand Foch, did not know it.

The Allied counter-offensives found a weakened enemy losing the will to fight. The greatest defeatism was not, however, to be found on the battlefront but among the so recently revered German generals, Hindenburg and Ludendorff. Germany's allies were collapsing in September 1918. The Turkish army was defeated in Palestine. The Bulgarians could not resist an Allied advance from Greece and requested an armistice. Though Austrian troops were still stoutly defending the Italian front, the Dual Empire was disintegrating and its various nationalities were proclaiming their independence. In France, the arrival of new masses of fresh American troops had not only blunted Germany's earlier thrust against Paris, but filled the German High Command with a sense of hope-lessness. Successful Allied offensives broke their last will to resist.

Ludendorff, towards the close of September 1918, demanded that the government in Berlin should secure an immediate armistice to save the army. In Berlin the politicians tried to win a little time. Later Ludendorff propagated the lie, so useful to the Nazis, that the army had been 'stabbed in the back'. The truth is that Ludendorff wished to end a war that was militarily lost while the army still preserved its discipline and cohesion. He got his way. On 11 November 1918 the last shot was fired in France.

# CHAPTER 15

# *Peacemaking in an Unstable World, 1918–1923*

The history of the period from the armistice in November 1918 until the conclusion of the majority of the peace treaties a year later has a dual aspect. On the one hand the victors, assembled in Paris, argued about peace terms to be imposed on Germany and her allies; they knew that after four years of war and all the changes it had brought about, the people of the West longed for an immediate and a stable peace. At Paris too, decisions would be taken to reconstruct the map not only of Europe, but also of the Middle East, Africa and China. A new framework of conducting international relations would be created by establishing the League of Nations. All this represents just one side of the historical development of this critical period.

The other side of the picture was that eastern, central and southern Europe was daily becoming more disorganised; in Turkey a nationalist revolution would reject the peace terms altogether; China continued to disintegrate, rent by internal dissension and the pressure of the Japanese and the West. The future of Russia and the ultimate size of the territories that would fall under Soviet control was one of the biggest uncertainties of all. With the end of the war and the collapse of the defeated rulers there was a threat of anarchy. National and social conflicts erupted in revolution. In Russia the war had not ended in time to save the country from internal violence. For how much of the rest of Europe was it now too late as well? No previous war had ended in such chaos. The peacemakers

thus did not preside over an empty map of the world waiting for settlement in the light of their decisions reached around the conference table.

The great powers no longer disposed of huge victorious armies. These were being rapidly demobilised and war-weary peoples were not ready to allow their leaders to gather fresh mass armies. The leaders who mattered, the 'big three' – Wilson, Lloyd George and Clemenceau – as the representatives of democracies were dependent on assemblies and electorates and became increasingly conscious of the limits of their ability simply to follow the dictates of their own reasoning. Another 'Europe' and 'Asia' was taking shape beyond the control of the victors at Paris. It was shaped by its own local antagonisms.

When the peace conference opened on 18 January 1919, just two months after the signing of the armistices with Turkey, Austria, Hungary and Germany, obviously the problem that most weighed on Wilson, Clemenceau and Lloyd George was the future of Germany. The armistice terms had been harsh, but fell short of demanding unconditional surrender. The German government had applied to Wilson for an armistice on the basis of the Fourteen Points, after Ludendorff and Hindenburg had suddenly declared that the army was in no condition to hold out a moment longer. In accordance with Wilson's clearly expressed reply that the terms to be imposed on Germany would be harsher still if the Kaiser remained in power, the generals themselves had co-operated in persuading the

Kaiser to abdicate and depart for exile in the Netherlands. And they were also ready to co-operate with the new government of Social Democrats in Berlin headed by Friedrich Ebert. Hindenburg and his generals brought the German armies home from France and Belgium in excellent order. They were received more as victors than as defeated troops by the German population. But, once on German soil, these once great armies simply dissolved; they did not wait to be demobilised according to plans which did not exist. They just went home. Only in the east, in Poland and the Baltic, were there still army units left, sufficiently powerful in the chaotic conditions of this region of Europe caught up in civil wars and national conflicts to constitute a decisive military factor. To combat Bolshevism the Allied armistice conditions actually required the Germans to remain in occupation of the eastern and Baltic territories until Allied troops could be spared to take over their responsibilities as guardians against the 'reds'.

Despite the changes in Germany and the proclamation of a republic, the Allied attitude in Paris did not noticeably alter. Whether 'Junkers' or 'Social Democrats', the Allies continued to regard them as arrogant and dangerous Germans and treated them accordingly. But they also dealt with the Germans at a distance, rejecting the responsibility of occupying the country and confining themselves to the strategic occupation of part of the Rhineland alone. Considering the condition of threatening anarchy, the Allies continued to be haunted by the fear that the Germans only wanted to use the armistice as a breathing space to reorganise and resume the war. Such thoughts had indeed crossed Ludendorff's now disordered mind and the possibility of resisting should the peace terms prove unacceptable was discussed by Hindenburg and the Social Democratic government. The answer was obvious. There were no German armies any longer in existence in 1919 that could hope to put up a defence even against the reduced strength of the Allied armies. Yet the Allies kept up the fiercest pressure during the weeks of the armistice. The blockade was maintained from November 1918 through that winter until March 1919; later this proved a good propaganda point for the Nazis, who exaggerated Allied callousness.

During that first winter and spring of 1918/19, Germany was left to survive as best as she could. The new democratic republic, soon known as the Weimar Republic after the town in which its constitution-making parliament met, could not have had a worse start. Within Germany herself, a vacuum of power, similar to that in Russia in 1917, which rival groups sought to fill, threatened stability. Everyone was aware of the parallel, not least the new chancellor Ebert. But Ebert, once a humble saddle-maker, was a politician of considerable experience and strength. He was determined not to be cast in the role of the Russian Kerensky. For Ebert, the most important tasks ahead were to establish law and order, revive industry and agriculture so that the German people could live, preserve German unity and ensure that the 'revolution' that had begun with the Kaiser's departure should itself lead to the orderly transfer of power to a democratically elected parliamentary assembly. Ebert was tough, and determined that Germany should become a parliamentary democracy and not a communist state. This was a programme which won the support of the army generals, who recognised that the Social Democratic republic would be both the best immediate defence against anarchy and Bolshevism and a screen acceptable to the Allies behind which Germany's traditional forces could regroup.

The compact reached between the army command and the Social Democratic government of the Republic in order to counter the danger of a Bolshevik revolution has been much criticised. Why did the Social Democrats leave the revolution half-finished, retain the army and the imperial administration, and leave society and wealth undisturbed? Did they not thereby seal their own doom and pave the way for the Nazis a decade later? With hindsight one may legitimately ask would Germany's future have been better with a 'completed' communist revolution? The question is deceptively simple. It is unlikely that the Allies would have allowed the communists to retain power in Germany; an extensive Allied occupation might then have resulted after all. The breakdown of order within Germany left the sincerely democratic socialists isolated and so forced them to seek co-operation with the forces that had upheld the Kaiser's Germany hitherto. They had no other practical alternative.

There can be no doubt, either, that a communist seizure of power would have represented the will of only a small minority of Germans; the great majority, including the workers, did not desire to emulate Bolshevik Russia. All over Germany in

*Revolution Infects Germany.* Left: *Karl Liebknecht, founder, with Rosa Luxemburg, of the Spartacus League, which in 1919 became the German Communist Party.* Right: *Rosa Luxemburg herself, the fiery Polish revolutionary with a humane vision. She was taken prisoner with Liebknecht and murdered on 15 January 1919. A third prisoner was more fortunate: Wilhelm Pieck survived to become first president of the German Democratic Republic (East Germany) in October 1949.* Above: *street fighting in Berlin during the Spartacist rising in January 1919.*

November 1918 'workers' and soldiers' councils' formed themselves spontaneously; the Russian model of the 'soviet' was quite consciously followed by those who organised these bodies. The movement began in Kiel where sailors of the imperial navy mutinied, unwilling at the end of the war to risk their lives senselessly to satisfy their officers' sense of honour. The officers had planned to take the Grand Fleet out to sea to engage the British in one last glorious suicidal battle. From Kiel the setting up of German soviets spread to Hamburg and other parts, then to Berlin and the rest of Germany. But not all these self-proclaimed soldiers' and workers' councils, which claimed to speak for the people, were in favour of a Bolshevik state. In many, the more moderate socialists predominated and those who before the armistice had been opposed to war (Independent Socialists) now joined with the majority who had supported war. In others the Independent Socialists allied with the Spartacists, the name the communist faction led by Karl Liebknecht and Rosa Luxemburg had assumed.

In Berlin, the capital, the crucial struggle between the socialist factions was decided. Ebert had assumed the chancellorship, constitutionally accepting this office from Prince Max von Baden, the last imperial chancellor. His fellow socialist, Philipp Scheidemann, in the confusion that followed proclaimed a republic to anticipate Liebknecht. Liebknecht simultaneously proclaimed the 'socialist republic' to his followers. Ebert would have preferred a constitutional monarchy, but now the die was cast. Ebert and Scheidemann won over the Independent Socialists with concessions that would allow the Berlin Soldiers' and Workers' Council 'all power' until the constituent parliament met. The constituent parliament was elected early in January 1919 and assembled in Weimar in February to begin its labours of drawing up one constitution for the whole of Germany.

All this gives a false impression of orderliness. During the winter and spring following the armistice it was uncertain whether Ebert would survive. Germany was torn by political strife of unprecedented ferocity, and separatist movements in several regions even suggested that Germany might disintegrate and so follow the fate of the Habsburg Empire. In the second-largest state, Bavaria, political strife was unfolding. The Independent Socialist leader Kurt Eisner had led a revolution of workers and soldiers in Munich, proclaimed the republic of Bavaria, and deposed the royal house of Wittelsbach. All over Germany the princes disappeared. They had counted for so little, their disappearance made little impact now. Eisner's republic was not communist. Though he had been opposed to the war, he was at one with Ebert in desiring a democratic Bavaria, in a Germany of loosely 'federated' states. Elections duly held in January and February 1919 in Bavaria resulted in the defeat of Eisner's Independent Socialist Party. On his way to the Bavarian parliament to lay down office, Eisner was brutally murdered in the street. This was the signal for civil war in Bavaria, which slid into anarchy and extremism.

December 1918 and January 1919 were the decisive months in Berlin, too. There the Spartacists decided to carry the revolution further than the Social Democrats were prepared to go. The Spartacists attempted an insurrection in December, seizing Berlin's public buildings, and the Social Democrats, still having no efficient military force of their own, appealed to the army. Irregular volunteer army units were formed, the so-called Free Corps; all sorts of freebooters, ex-officers and men enjoying violence joined; there were few genuine Social Democrats among these paramilitary units. The scene was set for fighting among the factions, for bloodshed and brutality. The Spartacist rising was put down and Liebknecht and Rosa Luxemburg were murdered as they emerged from their hiding place. The rising followed by strikes and fresh disorders seriously threatened Ebert's government in the new year of 1919 (page 134).

In Bavaria there were three rival governments – two Bolshevik and one majority Socialist. The showdown came in Bavaria in April 1919. The moderate Socialists called on the Free Corps units in Bavaria for military assistance. The Bolsheviks were bloodily suppressed and in Munich many innocent people lost their lives. It was a tragedy for Germany and the world that the Weimar Republic was founded in bloodshed, that the Social Democrats had to call on the worst anti-democratic elements in the state for support. This left a legacy of suspicion and bitterness among the working people, split the Socialists and so in the end helped the right-wing extremists to power. The communists blamed the Social Democrats, the Social Democrats the communists. Democracy had triumphed but at what proved to be a heavy price.

*

In Paris there was a keen awareness that to delay the making of peace would endanger stability even further. Germany should be presented with the terms and given a short period for a written submission embodying their reply. There should be no meaningful negotiations with the Germans. Better a 'dictated' peace quickly than a long-drawn-out wrangle that allowed the Germans to exploit Allied differences. It was a remarkable achievement that despite these serious differences – the French, in particular, looked for more extensive territorial guarantees and reparations – in the short space of four months an agreed treaty was presented to the

Germans on 7 May 1919. This represented the compromises reached by Wilson, Lloyd George and Clemenceau. The Italians took little part, deeply offended and dissatisfied with their territorial gains in general and the rejection of their claim for Fiume in particular. There was no set agenda for the negotiations in Paris. The crucial decisions were taken by Wilson, Lloyd George and Clemenceau and then the details were left to the experts who accompanied the statesmen in large numbers.

Clemenceau was aware of France's basic weakness, inferior in population and industrial production to a Germany that was bound to recover. How to provide then for French security? The break-up and partition of Germany were not seriously considered, though a separate Rhineland would have served French interests. Germany, albeit deprived of Alsace-Lorraine and of territory in the east, remained intact as potentially the most powerful European continental state.

One of the few undertakings of the Allies, and incorporated in the Fourteen Points, was to reconstitute an independent Polish nation and so to undo the eighteenth-century partition of Poland by Russia, Austria and Prussia. The carrying out of this pledge created great difficulties in redrawing Germany's eastern frontier. The German city of

Left: *Lloyd George, Orlando, Clemenceau and Wilson at the Versailles conference, 1919.* Below: *Parisians celebrate the news of the armistice, November 1918.*

**Peace Settlements, 1919–1923**

ICELAND
1918

NORWAY

SWEDEN

FINLAND
1917

Oslo

Stockholm

Helsinki

GREAT BRITAIN

ATLANTIC

NORTH
SEA

ESTONIA
1918

1920

SOVIET
UNION
1917

LATVIA
1918

IRELAND

OCEAN

Dublin

1920

DANZIG
1919/20

Elbe

Berlin

LITHUANIA
1918

1920

1921

EAST PRUSSIA

London

1919

GERMANY

• Warsaw

1921

POLAND

Cologne

Rhine

CZECHOSLOVAKIA

1918

1918

BESSARABIA

Seine

1920

Paris

1919

FRANCE

AUSTRIA

1919

HUNGARY
1922

1920

ROMANIA

Rhône

1919

Bucharest

1920

PORTUGAL

• Madrid

SPAIN

CORSICA

ITALY

• Rome

YUGOSLAVIA

1919

BULGARIA

ALBANIA

1923

TURKEY
1922 Republic

SARDINIA

1923

GREECE

Tangier

GIBRALTAR

Athens

Algiers

SICILY

CRETE

MEDITERRANEAN   SEA

Tripoli

0                    1000 miles

0            1000 km

Danzig was separated from Germany and turned into an autonomous free city for which the League of Nations accepted certain responsibilities and over which Poland enjoyed specific rights. The wedge of Polish territory to the sea created the 'Polish corridor' which henceforth separated Germany from East Prussia. In parts of Silesia a plebiscite in March 1921 and the League decision in 1922 decided where the precise frontier with Poland ran. But the peace treaty placed several million German-speaking peoples under foreign rule. In the west, apart from Alsace-Lorraine and two small territories which became Belgian, Germany lost no territory; the Saarland, with its valuable coal, was placed under the League, and the French were granted the rights to the mines with the provision that after fifteen years a plebiscite would allow the population to choose their own future.

An important guarantee of French security was the requirement that the Germans were not permitted to fortify or station troops in the Rhineland; all the German territory west of the Rhine and bridgeheads across the Rhine, moreover, were occupied by the Allies for fifteen years and evacuation would only occur in three stages every five years if Germany fulfilled the treaty conditions of Versailles. But Clemenceau never lost sight of the fact that France remained, even after these German losses, inferior to her neighbour in population and industrial potential, and therefore militarily as well in the longer term. Clemenceau realised that France would need the alliance of Britain and the United States even more after 1918. France had been gravely weakened by the war. With Bolshevik Russia no longer contributing to the balance of Europe as tsarist Russia had done before 1914, German preponderance on the continent of Europe had potentially increased. Clemenceau understood, and some basic facts bear out what he foresaw.

**Population** (*millions*)

|                | 1920  | 1930  | 1940       |
| -------------- | ----- | ----- | ---------- |
| France         | 38.8  | 41.2  | 41.3       |
| Germany        | 59.2  | 64.3  | 67.6(1937) |
| Britain        | 44.3  | 46.9  | 48.2       |
| Russia         | 155.3 | 179.0 | 195.0      |
| Poland         | 26.0  | 29.5  | 31.5       |
| Czechoslovakia | 12.9  | 13.9  | 14.7       |
| Yugoslavia     | 12.4  | 14.4  | 16.4       |
| Austria        | 6.5   | 6.6   | 6.7        |
| Hungary        | 7.9   | 8.6   | 9.3        |

But Clemenceau struggled in vain with Wilson and Lloyd George in Paris to secure more permanent guarantees than were provided by the occupation of the Rhineland, which remained sovereign German territory. He accepted in the end that Germany could not be diminished further in the west; that France could not attain the Rhine frontier. He feared that, if he refused, Britain and the United States would cease all post-war support of France. In place of 'territorial' guarantees, France was offered a substitute: the promise of a post-war alliance with Britain and the United States. This treaty, concluded in June 1919, was conditional upon the consent of the Senate of the United States. As it turned out, Clemenceau had received payment with a cheque that bounced, though Wilson at the time was confident that the Senate would approve.

It became from the French point of view all the more vital to write into the treaty provisions for restricting the German army and armaments and

**Coal including Lignite and Steel Production, 1920–1939**
(*million metric tons*)

|         | Coal and Lignite | | | | Steel | | | |
| ------- | ----- | ----- | ----- | ----- | ---- | ---- | --- | ---- |
|         | 1920  | 1929  | 1933  | 1939  | 1920 | 1929 | 1933 | 1939 |
| Britain | 233.0 | 262.0 | 210.4 | 235.0 | 9.2  | 9.8  | 7.1 | 13.4 |
| France  | 25.3  | 55.0  | 48.0  | 50.2  | 2.7  | 9.7  | 6.5 | 8.0  |
| Germany | 220.0 | 337.0 | 237.0 | 400.0 | 7.8  | 16.2 | 7.6 | 23.7 |

to have the means of supervising these provisions to see that they were carried out. But for how long could this be maintained? The German army was reduced to a professional force of 100,000 men, a size appropriate for only the smallest of European states. Such a force was not even adequate to ensure internal security. Add to this a few obsolete warships, the Grand Fleet having under the armistice conditions been already interned in British waters, a prohibition to build an air force, an Allied control commission to supervise the production of light armaments that the Germans were permitted to manufacture and the total picture is one of Germany reduced to military impotence. Finally, Germany lost all her colonies.

In Germany there was a tremendous outcry. But already in 1919, among the military and the more thoughtful politicians, it was realised that the sources of Germany's strength would recover and her industries revive. As memories of the war receded, opportunities would arise to modify or circumvent the restrictions imposed on Germany by the 'dictated' Versailles Treaty. The German public especially focused their anger on the 'war guilt' article of the treaty. It was misunderstood and considered out of context. It stated that Germany had imposed war on the Allies by her aggression and that of her allies. Today, looking at the July crisis of 1914, there can be no real doubt that Germany and Austria–Hungary were the 'aggressors', though their motives and justification can be debated still. What the Germans could not be expected to know was that this article (231) and the one that followed represented a compromise between the Allies on the question of reparations.

The French and British wished the Germans to pay the 'whole cost' of the war. North-eastern France, once France's industrial region, had been devastated while Germany was untouched. Britain and France had incurred heavy war debts which the United States insisted had to be repaid. France and Britain had to be satisfied with the controversial article 231 whereby Germany and her allies accepted responsibility for causing all the loss and damage because of her aggression. But in article 232 the Germans were not required actually to pay for all these losses and damages, that is 'the whole cost of the war'. The Germans would have to pay only for losses caused to civilians and their property. This represented a victory for Wilson; Allied public opinion would be appeased by the 'war guilt' clause.

Little thought was extended to German public opinion. No agreement on a total sum was reached. This was left for a Reparations Commission to determine by May 1921. The Germans were presented with the treaty draft on 7 May 1919. Their voluminous protests and counter-proposals delivered on 29 May were considered, a small number of concessions made. They were then presented with the unalterable final draft in the form of a virtual ultimatum on 16 June. Unable to resume the war, the Germans formally accepted and signed the treaty on 28 June 1919. They began as they were to continue: evading its terms. A week earlier, the German fleet, interned in Scapa Flow, was scuttled by the crews.

Had the Allies acted wisely in their treatment of Germany? The financial thinking of the Allies, led by the United States, lacked realism. Reparations and war debts, the growth of trade and employment were international and not purely German problems. John Maynard Keynes, the distinguished economist, who had been sent to Paris to serve as one of Britain's financial experts, later in his famous book on the peace treaty, *The Economic Consequences of the Peace*, condemned the financial provisions. The total amount of reparations payable by Germany fixed in May 1921 – 132,000,000,000 gold marks – was actually not so excessive. But only a prosperous, stable Germany in a relatively free international market could contribute to general European prosperity. Lloyd George understood that to 'punish' Germany financially would create a powerful competitor in export markets as Germany sought the means to pay. If there were to be security from Germany in the longer term, then one way was to reduce German power by dividing the country; but this offended prevailing views of nationality. The other way was to ensure that Germany's political development would lead to a fundamental change of attitudes: genuine democracy coupled with a renunciation of nationalist aspirations. Instead the peace weakened the democratic movement and heightened nationalist feelings.

Besides Germany and Austria–Hungary the other great power defeated in war was Russia. The West was perplexed by the Russian problem. Lenin's Russia was openly hostile both to the victors and the vanquished of 1918. They were all, in Lenin's eyes, imperialist bourgeois powers ripe for revolution. There were voices in the West which called for an all-out effort to kill the poisonous influence of Red Russia from the outset. But there was also sympathy for her plight. Confused attempts were made by France, Britain and the United States to provide support for the anti-Bolshevik forces in Russia and so the West became embroiled, though only feebly, in the chaos of the Russian Civil War (page 179).

The communist seizure of power in November 1917 had initially gained control only of Petrograd and Moscow. That seizure was not given the stamp of approval by the rest of Russia. Lenin had allowed elections for a constitutional parliament, arranged by Kerensky's provisional government. This 'constituent assembly' which met in January 1918 was the most representative ever elected, and the mass of the peasantry turned to the Socialist Revolutionaries who constituted the majority of the elected representatives. Only a quarter of them were Bolsheviks. Lenin had no intention of allowing the assembly to undo the Bolshevik revolution. The assembly was forcibly dispersed on his orders. It was the end of any genuine democratic process. During 1918 Lenin was determined that the Bolsheviks should seize power throughout Russia, and dealt ruthlessly with opposition and insurrection against Bolshevik rule. Lenin was not held back by any moral scruple. He saw as the greater goal the success of the communist revolution, even though a majority of the people were too backward to understand it. Every other consideration had to be subordinated then to the secure achievement of Bolshevik power, which would act as a torch to set alight revolution in the more advanced West. Lenin's eyes were fixed on the world. Without a world revolution, he believed, the purely Russian Revolution would not survive.

Lenin met the force of opponents with force and terror. The terrorist police which Lenin set up in December 1917 was called the Cheka. This organisation was given the right to kill opponents and even those suspected of opposition, without benefit of trial, by summary execution. The authority of the state now stood behind the exercise of brute lawless power. No questions would be asked and the killing of some innocents was accepted as inevitable in the interests of the consolidation of communist power in Russia – 'the great goal'. Lenin's successors were to accept such exercise of terror, which reached its climax under Stalin in the

1930s, not as a temporary necessity in conflict but as a permanent part of Soviet control over the population.

Soviet terror included the killing of the Tsar and his family in July 1918. Soviet ferocity was partly responsible for resolute centres of opposition to the Bolsheviks. Already before the peace of Brest-Litovsk some of the non-Russian peoples around the whole periphery of the old Russian Empire had shown a desire for independence. With German help in 1918, states were being formed in the Baltic (Lithuania, Latvia, Estonia); Finland became completely independent and the local Bolshevik forces were defeated; the Ukraine became an independent state; in central Asia independence was claimed by the peoples living in these regions; only Poland had been promised her independence and sought to make good her claims and, much more, to create a large Polish nation by carving out territories from Russia proper. In opposition to 'Red' Petrograd, to Moscow and the central region controlled by the Bolsheviks, other Russian forces, led by tsarist generals, formed in many parts of Russia, sometimes in co-operation but also sometimes in conflict with local nationalist forces. These disparate military groups and armies became known collectively as White Russians, which suggested they possessed more coherence than was actually the case. In many regions there was a complete breakdown of law and order and independent brigand armies looted and lived off the countryside.

Among these independent and lawless armies one of the strangest was the Czech Legion (of some 50,000 officers and men) which had been formed in Russia from prisoners of war to fight for the Allied cause. After the Russian peace with Germany the Czech Legion attempted to leave Russia by way of the Trans-Siberian railway and the port of Vladivostok in Siberia. Fearing Bolshevik intentions, they came into open conflict with the Bolsheviks sent to disarm them. In Siberia they then formed a nucleus around which White Russian forces gathered. The self-proclaimed Supreme Ruler of Russia at the head of these partly disciplined and frequently insubordinate troops was Admiral Kolchak. The Allies had first intervened in Russia in the hope of reopening a war front in the east in order to relieve pressure on the western front. After the conclusion of the war with Germany, Britain and France were unsure whether the Bolsheviks or the Whites would ultimately gain power. Lloyd George's instincts at Paris were sound in that he did not wish to make an enemy of the Bolsheviks. He proposed Allied 'mediation' between the Russians fighting each other quite irreconcilably. British intervention was small and limited. The French made a more determined but useless attempt, co-operating with White forces in the Ukraine from a base in Odessa. The Japanese landed a large force in Siberia, pursuing imperialist ambitions of their own; and the Americans a smaller force at Vladivostok, ostensibly to rescue the Czech Legion but really to watch the Japanese. Allied intervention was too small to make a significant impact on the outcome of the civil war in Russia.

Lenin left it to Trotsky as commissar for war to create a Red Army to complete the conquest of the former Russian Empire and defeat all the opposing forces. Their disunity made it easier for Trotsky to defeat first one opponent and then the next. Nevertheless his achievement in recreating an army for the revolution was remarkable. Army discipline was reintroduced, as was the death penalty. Trotsky was no less ruthless than Lenin in the draconian measures he was ready to take to achieve discipline. Former tsarist officers were recruited to provide the necessary expertise and 'political commissars' were attached to the units to ensure that the armies would continue to fight for the right cause.

Lenin ended the period of civil war in 1920 partly by compromise and partly by conquest. He recognised the independence of the Baltic states of Finland, Estonia, Latvia and Lithuania. Poland was for communist Russia the most critical region. Poland was the gateway to Germany, and so, Lenin believed, the gateway to world revolutions. But the Poles proved too strong for the Red Army, though not strong enough to defeat it decisively. The war between Poland and Russia lasted from the spring of 1920 until the following October. Given only limited Allied help, the Poles were really left to win or lose by themselves. At first they succeeded spectacularly and reached Kiev in the Ukraine. The Red Army then drove them back and for a time Lenin hoped to overrun Poland altogether and to instal a puppet communist government. But at the gates of Warsaw the Red Army was defeated in turn and Lenin in 1921 accepted Polish independence. The remainder of the Russian Empire was successfully brought under communist control and the short-lived independent states of the Ukraine, Georgia and Transcaucasia were forcibly incorporated in the Soviet Union.

Communist Russia had failed to spread the revolution. The sparks that led to short-lived communist takeovers in Hungary and Bavaria were quickly extinguished. Russia had also failed to thrust through Poland to the West. Equally the West had failed either to overthrow the Bolsheviks or to befriend them. For two decades from 1921 to 1941 the Soviet Union remained essentially cut off, a large self-contained empire following her own road to modernisation and living in a spirit of hostile coexistence with the West.

Up to the last year of the war the Allies did not desire to destroy the Habsburg Empire, which was seen as a stabilising influence in south-eastern Europe. Wilson's Fourteen Points had promised 'autonomous' development to the peoples of the empire, not independence. Reform, not destruction, was the aim of the West. Within the Monarchy itself the spirit of national independence among the Slavs had grown immensely, stimulated by the Bolshevik revolution and the Russian call for the national independence of all peoples. Now the Czechs and Slovaks wished to form a national unit within a Habsburg federal state where each nation would enjoy equal rights. The Slovenes, Croats and Serbs of the Monarchy wished to form an independent Yugoslav nation and the Ruthenes demanded freedom from Polish dependence. The Habsburg dynasty and ruling classes could not respond adequately to these aspirations even in the Austrian half of the Monarchy; it was unthinkable that the Magyars would accept a sufficiently liberal policy to win over the Slavs, or even that they could have done so as late as 1917. The Monarchy was tied to dualism. Outside the Monarchy, émigrés were winning the support of the Allies for the setting up of independent nations. As the Monarchy weakened under the impact of war, so these émigré activities grew more important.

In 1918 Wilson became gradually converted to the view that the Czechoslovaks and Yugoslavs were oppressed nationalities whose efforts for freedom deserved sympathy and support. Before the conclusion of the armistice, the Czechoslovaks had won Allied recognition as an 'Allied nation', Poland had been promised independence, and the Yugoslav cause, though not accorded the same recognition, had at any rate become well publicised. When Austria–Hungary appealed to Wilson for an armistice on the basis of the Fourteen Points in October 1918, Wilson replied that the situation had changed and that autonomy for the other nationalities was no longer sufficient. This was strictly true. With defeat, the Hungarians and the Slavs all hastened to dissociate themselves from the Germans. Poland and Yugoslavia declared their independence as did the Hungarians. The German Austrians only had one option left, to dissociate Austria from the dynasty, and declare German Austria a republic. The revolution in Vienna was bloodless as Charles I withdrew.

The Habsburg Empire broke apart before the armistice on 3 November 1918 and there was no way the Allies could have brought her together again. But in no other part of the world was it more difficult to reconcile Wilson's ideals of national self-determination and national frontiers as the different peoples of the Balkans did not live in tidily delineated lands. There would always be people who formed majorities and minorities. The defeat of the dominant Austrians and Hungarians now determined that they and not the Slavs, Romanians and Italians would constitute new minorities within the 'successor states' of the Habsburg Empire.

The Allies at Paris modified the central Europe that had been created by strong national leaders in respect to frontiers, attempted to ensure good treatment of minorities and enforced punitive conditions on the defeated Hungarians and German Austrians; in its essentials, however, power had been transferred to the new nations already. Austria was reduced to a small state of 6.5 million inhabitants. The peace treaties forbade their union with Germany. The principle of national self-determination was violated as far as the defeated were concerned. The Italians had been promised the natural frontier of the Brenner Pass, even though this meant incorporating nearly a quarter of a million German-speaking Tyrolese into Italy. The new Czechoslovak state was granted its 'historic frontiers' which included Bohemia, and another 3.5 million German-speaking Austrians and also Ruthenes were divided between the Czechs and Poles and separated from the Ukraine. Hungary was reduced to the frontiers where only Magyars predominated. Hungary was now a small state of some 8 million, nearly three quarters of a million Magyars being included in the Czechoslovak state. The Hungarians remained fiercely resentful of the enforced peace, and their aspirations to revise the peace treaties aroused the fears of neighbouring Romania, Czechoslovakia and Yugoslavia.

A peace settlement in the Near East eluded the 'peacemakers' altogether. With the defeat of the Ottoman Empire and the Turkish acceptance of an armistice on 30 October 1918, the Arab people had high hopes of achieving their independence. The Americans, British and French were committed by public declarations to the goal of setting up governments which would express the will of the peoples of the former Turkish Empire. But Britain and France had also during the war secretly agreed on a division of influence in the Middle East. To complicate the situation still further, the British government had promised the Zionists 'the establishment in Palestine of a National Home for the Jewish people' in what became known as the Balfour Declaration (2 November 1917). How were all these conflicting aspirations now to be reconciled? Wars and insurrections disturbed Turkey and the Middle East for the next five years.

The Arabs were denied truly independent states except in what became Saudi Arabia. The other Arab lands were placed under French and British tutelage as 'mandates' despite the wishes of the inhabitants. Iraq and Palestine became British mandates and Syria and Lebanon, French. Within a few years, the Arab states of Syria, Lebanon, Transjordan and Iraq emerged but remained firmly under British and French control.

Peace with Turkey proved even more difficult to achieve. The Sultan's government had accepted the peace terms of the Treaty of Sèvres in August 1920, but a Turkish general, Mustafa Kemal, the founder of modern Turkey, led a revolt against the peace terms. The Greeks, meanwhile, were seeking to fulfil their own ambitions and landed troops in Turkish Asia Minor. The disunity of the Allies added to the confusion and made the enforcement of the Treaty of Sèvres quite impossible. By skilled diplomacy – by dividing the Anglo-French alliance, and by securing supplies from the French and Russians – Kemal gathered and inspired a Turkish national movement to free Turkey from the foreign invasions. He defeated the Greeks in September 1922 and then turned on the British troops stationed in the Straits of Constantinople. In October 1922 Lloyd George, unsupported by his former allies, was forced to accept Kemal's demands for a revision of the peace treaty. This was accomplished by the Lausanne Conference and a new treaty in July 1923

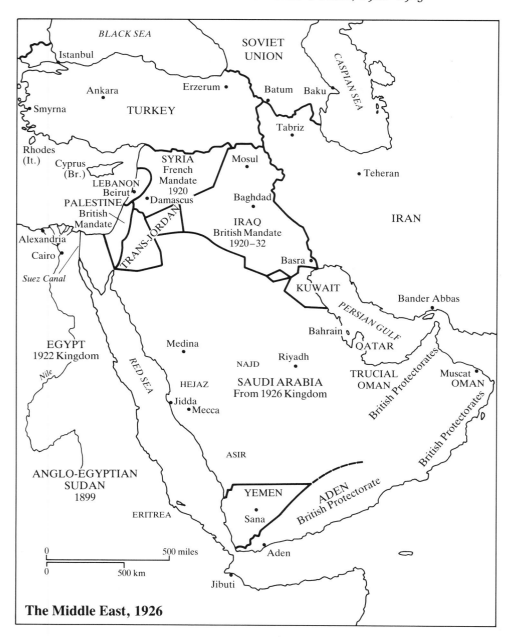

**The Middle East, 1926**

which freed Turkey from foreign occupation and interference. Shortly afterwards Turkey was proclaimed a republic and Kemal became the first president. Of all the defeated powers, Turkey alone challenged successfully the terms of peace the Allies sought to impose.

It was clear to President Wilson that the effort of reaching peace had involved unsatisfactory compromises and that Allies and former enemies were both deeply dissatisfied with some of the terms. One ally, Italy, had left the conference over the decision not to yield the port of Fiume to her, and the Italians returned only for the formal concluding ceremonies. The Japanese were offended by their failure to have a 'racial equality' clause incorporated in the Covenant of the League of Nations. The Hungarians and Germans did not regard the treaties as just and were determined to revise them. Wilson nevertheless pinned his hope for the future on the League of Nations.

The real purpose of the League of Nations was

to find a better way of solving disputes that could lead to war than by the kind of devastating conflict through which the world had just passed. In the League great states and small states were to find security with justice. Within ten years of its founding, these high hopes seemed unlikely to be fulfilled. Britain, France and the United States would not risk war in the 1930s to uphold the League's ideals when the aggressors were other great powers – Japan, Italy and Germany and the Soviet Union. The strength of the League depended on its members and not on the rules and procedures laid down; to be sure, if these had been applied and observed they would most likely have preserved peace. At the heart of the Covenant of the League lay article Ten whereby all the members undertook to preserve the existing independence of all other members. Furthermore, if there were aggression against a member or a threat of such aggression, then the Council of League would 'advise' on the best way in which members could fulfil their obligations. Possible sanctions of increasing severity were set out in other articles which, if adopted, would hurt the aggressor. The weakness of the League was that each member could in effect decide whether or not to comply with a Council request to apply sanctions. Furthermore the Council, consisting of permanent great-power members, together with some smaller states, could act only unanimously, so that any one of its members could block all action. The League was not a world government, lacked all armed force and remained dependent on the free co-operation of its members to behave according to its principles and to join with others in punishing those states that did not.

It was a heavy blow to the League when the United States in the end repudiated Wilson's efforts. Before a treaty to which the United States is a party can be valid, a two-thirds majority of the Senate has to vote in its favour. There were genuine misgivings about the wide-ranging but unique commitment of article X, whereby the United States would literally be obliged 'to preserve' the independence of every nation in the world. The President might have won the necessary majority if he had dealt tactfully with the opposition. But he would not admit the obvious gap between the utopian aims of the League and realistic national policies. Wilson rejected the compromise of accepting Senate reservations to the treaty and toured the country in September 1919 to appeal over the heads of the Senate to the people. On his return to Washington, he suffered a severe stroke. The chance of compromise with the Senate was now lost for certain. The treaty without amendments was lost twice when the Senate voted in November 1919 and March 1920. But this did not mean that the United States was as yet 'isolationist'. The United States would have joined the League with no more reservations than in practice the other great powers demanded for themselves. The treaty of alliance with France signed together with Britain at Paris in 1919 (page 126) is often lost sight of in Wilson's débâcle over the League. It was Wilson who lost all interest in it. For him it was a question of the League or nothing. The alliance treaty between the United States, France and Britain, if it had been ratified by the Senate, could have altered subsequent history. Opponents of universal and vague commitments to the League, like the powerful Senator Henry Cabot Lodge, were in favour of this treaty of alliance or, as it was called, Guarantee. But the treaty was never submitted to a Senate vote.

The presidential elections of 1920 reflected the new mood of the people. With the slogan 'Return to Normalcy' the Republican candidate Warren Harding won by a large margin over the Democratic candidate. The American people turned their backs on Wilson's leadership and Wilson's vision of America's mission in the world.

The conditions for a stable peace had not been laid by 1920. The French, deprived of the treaty of Guarantee, were well aware how far Europe was from achieving any balance of power, which hitherto had kept the peace. Much now depended on the attitude which the British would take to the issues of the continent; much, too, would depend on the course of German history. Nor had any reconciliation of conflicting interests been achieved in Asia (page 205). The Japanese had secured Germany's former rights in China in the province of Shantung and so incensed the Chinese delegation in Paris that it refused to sign the treaty of Versailles. The sure foundations of peace had thus not been achieved at Paris in 1919. Perhaps it was unrealistic to expect they would be.

# CHAPTER 16

# Democracy on Trial: Weimar Germany

Even before the outbreak of the war, the more discerning conservatives such as Bethmann Hollweg recognised that imperial Germany must move in the direction of a more broadly based constitutional monarchy. The Kaiser, the big landed and industrial interests and the powerful military frustrated progressive constitutional policies. Then it happened with the imminence of defeat facing Germany in November 1918: the Social Democrats joined the cabinet of Prince Max von Baden; government, it was intended, should in future be dependent on a Reichstag majority. The great change from a semi-authoritarian to a parliamentary democracy had taken place without a revolution. The revolution had been anticipated and made unnecessary. The Kaiser had left for exile in Holland with his little-loved family and the consequent vacuum of power had to be filled.

The peaceful transfer of power was almost successful and there can be no doubt that this is what the vast majority of the German people desired. They did not want to suffer a civil war and bloodshed on top of the defeat. They feared revolution, especially of the kind that had occurred in neighbouring Russia. Indeed, deeply disillusioned by the suddenness of defeat, they cared little about politics altogether, wanted law and order and to keep their possessions. This 'silent majority' showed an extraordinary capacity to get on with their own lives regardless of the wild men, the battalions of mutinied sailors and armed bands of various political persuasions rushing around in lorries. Life in Berlin during the early days of the republic went on with everyday orderliness. If shooting occurred, people sheltered in doorways, while in neighbouring streets others shopped, ate and amused themselves as usual. Prussia had been renowned for her public orderliness. No one in their lifetime had experienced violence on the streets. Now the ordinary German coped with the breakdown of his orderly world by simply ignoring the disorder and turning the other way. It was admirable in one sense. In another, this lack of interest was a dangerous omen for the building of a democratic state. A few years later the majority of Germans would equally easily avert their eyes from Nazi and communist thuggery in the streets and from violence to the rights of their fellow citizens in Hitler's time.

Political democracy requires that the majority feel a concern for their rights and the rights of others and are ready to defend them. In Germany in the early years of the Weimar Republic it was possible for the committed few who did not shrink from using force to threaten to take over control of the state, jeopardising peaceful change. When on 9 November 1918, Prince Max von Baden announced the abdication of the Kaiser and handed over his office to Ebert who thereby became chancellor 'on the basis of the constitution', the German people were pleased to learn not that there had been a 'revolution', but that the revolution had been pronounced as having occurred unbeknown to all but a few. The Social Democrats had long ago given up any real intention of seeking revolution. Like the British Labour Party they were intent on gradual parliamentary and democratic change. They had become the true heirs of the liberals of '1848' including taking pride in German nationalism. They had supported the war. No less a personage than Field Marshal von Hindenburg, who represented the traditions of the Prussian army, testified that Ebert was sound and 'loved his fatherland'.

But this kind of 'tame' revolution did not satisfy the more politically active. In imitation of the Russian example, 'soldiers' and workers' councils' sprang up all over Germany (page 123). Ebert humoured them, knowing that the parliamentary constituent assembly he planned would soon give the government of the Reich a solidly based and legal foundation. Then, too, the Social Democratic government was so weak that it had no military forces of its own to resist any group seeking to wrest control from it. The Spartacists' insurrections in December 1918 and January 1919, followed by political strikes and disorders, although fomented by a revolutionary party with only little support among the workers, nevertheless posed a serious threat to the Ebert government. With the support of the army command and irregular Free Corps bands of soldiers the violence of the extreme left was met with counter-violence and lawless terror. The two Spartacist (communist) leaders, Rosa Luxemburg and Karl Liebknecht, were murdered. Violence continued in other parts of Germany especially in Berlin and Munich. The Free Corps units, fanatical opponents both of democracy and of Bolshevism and the forerunners of those who were to support the Nazis, everywhere, with excessive brutality, suppressed the militant left.

The Social Democratic government and the Republic survived. What had maintained it in power was the tacit alliance between Field Marshal von Hindenburg and General Wilhelm Groener, the army Chief of Staff, with Ebert and his government. Their motives for co-operating with the socialist government were to maintain German unity and to prevent the 'patriotic' German Social Democrats from being driven from power by the Bolshevik 'internationalists'. They also believed that the traditions of the Prussian army represented the 'best' of Germany and that the new emerging Germany could be imbued with these qualities provided the Reichswehr retained a position of power in the state.

It was a misfortune that the Social Democrats were inevitably stained by the misdeeds of military excess. The communists had not been suppressed, only prevented from seizing power. The communists were never to gain as many votes as the Social Democrats, but as the Social Democrats weakened from their high-water mark of support of 38 per cent of the electorate in 1919, the Communist Party, benefiting from the depression, recovered to secure 13 per cent of the vote in 1930, which in the last free elections in November 1932 rose to 17 per cent. By then the Social Democratic support had sunk to 20 per cent. Figures do not fully reveal how this split of the socialists handicapped the strengthening of the democratic parliamentary Republic in the 1920s. The growth of the Communist Party to the left of the Social Democrats competing for the working man's vote sapped the will of the Social Democratic politicians to lead the governments of the Republic boldly, even though they formed the single largest party in the Reichstag throughout the 1920s. After 1919 they enjoyed no absolute majority, so had they wished to govern they would have had to form coalitions with the 'bourgeois' parties of the centre and moderate right. This, of course, they feared would lay them open to the cry of having 'betrayed' the working class. The early experiences of the Republic also reinforced their conclusion that the danger to her democratic existence arose from an extreme left, that is, a communist takeover.

We know better now; but the sudden and huge expansion of the Nazi vote between 1928 and 1932 was entirely unforeseen. The Social Democrats were afraid of losing votes to the political left by collaborating with the 'bourgeois' parties in coalition governments; only one of the sixteen chancellors after 1920 was a Social Democrat. Between November 1922 until June 1928 (except for a brief period of three months in 1923) – that is, for the greater part of the life of the parliamentary Republic they had done so much to create – the Social Democrats refused to participate in government at all. The parties of the centre and moderate right formed the basis of all the coalition governments, sometimes seeking to strengthen their position in the absence of the Social Democrats by seeking the more extreme-right support of the Nationalists. Even so, every one of the coalitions without the Social Democrats was a minority government. They generally lasted only a few months. The major political parties from the Conservatives to the Centre Party were either hostile or lukewarm about the new Republic even before the National Socialists became significant. The only genuine parliamentary party fully supporting democracy among the non-socialist 'bourgeois' parties was the German Democratic Party, whose support significantly dwindled during the 1920s. Though the Social Democratic leaders recognised that they had most to lose from the destruction of the democratic Republic, their own shortsighted political attitude contributed to the spectacle of government instability which lowered the esteem of parliamentary government in the eyes of the German people when that esteem was already being constantly assailed by the anti-democratic political parties.

The difficulties under which the Weimar laboured during its early years were very evident. It is therefore all the more remarkable how much was nevertheless constructively achieved. The constituent assembly met in February 1919 in Germany's capital of culture, the little town of Weimar, where Germany's two greatest poets, Goethe and Schiller, had lived. Berlin was politically too unsettled and dangerous for lengthy parliamentary deliberations. The majority of the National Assembly belonged to the Social Democratic Party, the Centre Party and the successors of the old Liberal Party.

The constitution-making was completed by August 1919. In the spirit of '1848', the inalienable rights of the individual to basic freedoms – free speech, equality before the law, freedom of religion – were set out; so were political rights of free speech and assembly, but the latter could be set aside, for the president was given emergency powers to restore public order if it were seriously disturbed or threatened. The legislators were still living under the shadow of the danger of communist coups and the ability of the president to act quickly and decisively seemed essential. Only later did it turn out that the considerable powers granted to the president would pave the way for the destruction of the democratic republic. The president himself was to be elected every seven years by a direct popular vote, like the president of the United States. There was no separation of powers as in the American constitution, yet his powers, which included that of appointing the chancellor, meant that the Weimar constitution also differed from the British form of parliamentary government. The chancellor had to win the majority support of the Reichstag; if he failed, the president could dissolve the Reichstag and call new elections. The introduction of proportional representation was one of the most significant features of the constitution. It led to a multiplicity of parties and inevitable coalition governments. The old pre-1918 states – Prussia, Bavaria and the smaller states – retained their own governments but with lesser powers. The constitution emphasised the sovereignty of the people and the right of all adult men and women to vote. There could be no doubt that the intention of the constitution was to replace the old authoritarian state with a 'scientifically' constructed democracy.

The flaws of the constitution have been touched on here and are frequently stressed. But they were not the real reason for the failure of political democracy in Germany. The reasons for this failure are not to be found in the shortcomings of legal documents but in the shortcomings of the politicians of the Weimar period and in the reactions of the German people to the problems that faced them. It is perfectly true that the army remained profoundly anti-democratic in attitude despite its oath of loyalty to the republic. So was the higher civil service on the whole. No doubt many judges were politically biased when dealing leniently with the many political crimes of the right and harshly with the few of the left. But they did not play an active role in seeking the overthrow of the republic. During its brief years, Weimar also appointed and promoted to high administrative and judicial positions sincere democrats who would never have secured such appointments in imperial Germany. All discrimination on grounds of politics or religion was ended. Given time, these newcomers would have increased and enjoyed a growing influence in the state. But time was too short.

The army was a special case. The Social Democrats treated the army High Command and the officers as indispensable pillars of the republic. They shared as patriotic Germans a false veneration for the gods of yesterday such as Hindenburg. There was little excuse for this after the behaviour of the Chief of the Army, General Hans von Seeckt, in the spring of 1920. A right-wing plot to overthrow the Republic, supported by Free Corps units near Berlin, came to fruition in March 1920. Led by a General Lüttwitz, the troops actually entered Berlin and installed a Prussian bureaucrat, Wolfgang Kapp, as chancellor. Why was the government of

Ebert so weak? It had at its disposal the regular army. To Ebert's astonishment, Seeckt refused to defend the government, declaring that the 'Reichswehr does not shoot on the Reichswehr'. Ebert and the government ignominiously fled from Berlin to the safety of southern Germany. The trade unions ordered a general strike. In Berlin some civil servants continued to function, others obeyed the government's call and refused to work under the new, self-appointed Chancellor. But the banks supplied no funds. While there was no military opposition to Kapp's seizure of power, the country was industrially paralysed, and few people would positively co-operate, though the army continued to remain 'neutral'. Nevertheless Kapp quickly recognised that he could not govern in such circumstances. A few days after his arrival in Berlin, he 'resigned' and withdrew with his troops. Ebert returned. The weakness of the Social Democrats was now shown clearly, for they neither dismissed the disloyal head of the army, nor attempted to remove from the service of the Republic those who had disobeyed the government's call to strike. The whole affair was quickly dismissed as a ridiculous adventure. But the extremists on the right did not abandon their war against the Republic of 'traitors'.

Why did the army not back the right-wing insurrectionists like Kapp? It was not for love of the Republic, or of the Social Democrats, that is clear. For the army, the Republic was necessary to deal with the Allies, who were in occupation of the Rhineland. The French still enjoyed overwhelming military strength and could occupy parts of Germany at will, as they did in 1920, 1921 and 1923. Seeckt and the army High Command knew that the French would certainly not stand idly by if the legal democratic German government were overthrown by the generals. That would be the signal for intervention. It was therefore as unrealistic to support a man like Kapp as it would have been to bring the Kaiser back.

Besides attempted coups and violence from left and right, every German was affected by the unprecedented experience of hyperinflation. The murder in June 1922 by a young nationalist of the 'Jew' Foreign Minister Walter Rathenau undermined internal and foreign confidence in the political stability of Weimar Germany with inevitably disastrous consequences for Germany's financial standing as well. The final blow to German financial stability was delivered by the Germans themselves.

It was due not to reparations payments made by Germany but to the decision of the government to organise passive resistance when the French, in response partly to the threatened political disintegration of Weimar Germany and evasion of reparations, occupied the Ruhr in January 1923 (page 144). The consequent industrial standstill in the Ruhr and the relief paid by the government to the Germans who had no income now could be met only by printing more money since the government was reluctant to increase taxation sufficiently to meet the bill. By the autumn of 1923 paper money was practically worthless. A tram ticket cost millions of marks. All goods, including food, became scarce. No one wanted paper money that might lose half its value in a day. Somehow people survived with ingenuity. The pensioner and the weakest members of society suffered the most. Unemployment soared. Only those who had property and understood how to manipulate credit became rich. Industrialists like Hugo Stinnes amassed factories

*Germany suffered hyper-inflation in 1923; this woman is finding banknotes more profitable to burn as fuel than to spend on fuel.*

and mines paid for in worthless currency. The inflation left an indelible impression.

For ordinary people the effect was as bad as the communism they had so feared and resisted. Their savings were wiped out. The middle classes saw their modest accumulation of wealth, saved from the war years, being lost. The long-term consequences of the war were now really felt. And more and more people were saying that it was all the fault of the republic, both the lost war and the lost money. The general misery provided fertile soil for extremists. In the autumn of 1923 the attitude and questionable loyalty of the Chief of the Army, Seeckt, was perhaps the most disturbing feature of the situation. The communists believed Germany to be ripe for revolution and attempted to start it in Saxony and Thuringia. Separatism was still a potent force in Bavaria and a new name, Adolf Hitler, came to national attention when he attempted and failed to seize power in Munich. But in this hour of crisis for democracy and the republic, Gustav Stresemann, a political leader of the more moderate right, an ex-monarchist, an ex-supporter of the war of 1914 and of Germany's plans to achieve continental European hegemony, was entrusted with guiding Weimar's foreign relations.

Stresemann led the small People's Party. The Social Democrats agreed to his appointment as chancellor in August 1923 and joined the parties of the centre and moderate right in briefly forming a grand government coalition. In November, he became foreign minister in a new government and remained in this post through every successive government until his death. Historical controversy surrounds the evaluation of Stresemann's role in the Weimar Republic. Was he a blatant nationalist, even still an expansionist? There can be no doubt that he did wish to free Germany from the remaining restrictions of the Versailles Treaty: reparations, foreign occupation and military limitations. He followed pacific policies openly, yet was ready secretly and deceitfully, by any practical means, to reach his goals in making Germany respected and powerful. His aims included the restoration of German territory lost to Poland in the east, and the former colonies too: in short a return to pre-1914 Germany before the folly of the German leaders and the lost war threw away Germany's peaceful ascendancy in Europe. But it is mistaken to see in Stresemann a precursor of Hitler. He was at heart a conservative and an old-fashioned nationalist. He

learnt from the war experience that Germany could not 'conquer' Europe. To attempt this would create another coalition against her. He was realistic and accepted limits to German power. His powerful and respected Germany would be one of Europe's great powers, not the *only* great power. Germany in the aftermath of defeat he compared to Austria after the defeat of Napoleon. Like Metternich, he would recover his country's position and prestige. He succeeded in doing so during the course of the next six years until his untimely death in October 1929.

Stresemann had the courage to do the politically unpopular. Despite the nationalist patriotic clamour against the French and the diktat of Versailles, he recognised that Germany was only ruining her economic recovery at home and her reputation abroad. His policy was that of sweet reasonableness, a policy of 'fulfilment', as it became known. Germany would now freely accept the Versailles Treaty, seek peace and friendship with France and renounce any future claim to recover Alsace-Lorraine and any part of territory lost in the west. The French should feel secure and so, to prove their own acceptance of the entirely new spirit of reconciliation, would show their confidence by giving up the remaining guarantees of her security – the occupation of the Rhineland and the Allied commission supervising German disarmament. He called off passive resistance and allowed the French President, Poincaré, the illusion of victory and German submission. The French were not so naive as to accept all these protestations of love at their face value. But the British were delighted at this promising turn of events. They wanted the war to be over and peace and goodwill instantly to reign. British foreign secretaries were more suspicious of the French than of the Germans, though one of them at least, Austen Chamberlain, recognised clearly enough that French militancy was the result of their feeling of insecurity. Yet he too grasped at the opportunity of avoiding an Anglo-French alliance. Instead he underwrote a general Western European security treaty suggested by Stresemann to head off any possibility of an Anglo-French alliance and drafted with the help of the British Ambassador in Berlin. The outcome was the Locarno Treaties of 16 October 1925. France and Germany undertook to respect each other's territories and frontiers and to accept them as final. This treaty of Mutual Guarantee, which included Belgium, was also signed by Britain and Italy. Britain

*The Treaty of Locarno, signed on 16 October 1925 by Stresemann, Briand and Baldwin, amongst others. The new spirit of peace it engendered proved less than durable.*

and Italy guaranteed that they would come to the immediate aid of any country attacked by the other signatories of Locarno. But Stresemann had refused to extend Locarno to cover Germany's eastern frontiers with Czechoslovakia and Poland, nor would Britain guarantee the post-Versailles frontiers in the east as she had done in the west. Although Germany also signed arbitration treaties at the same time with Poland and Czechoslovakia, they did not form part of the Locarno security system. Stresemann's hardly realistic long-term aim was to revise the eastern frontier peacefully making use of

Germany's economic preponderance.

In return for renouncing territorial changes at the expense of France Stresemann won concessions from the Allies. Reparations were scaled down in 1924 and 1929 (page 145). Stresemann aimed to get rid of them altogether. Germany was admitted to the League of Nations in 1926 and given a permanent seat on the Council. Stresemann joined on condition that Germany too need never fight to back up the League if she chose not to do so. The Allied commission supervising German disarmament was withdrawn. Stresemann never lived to see the fulfilment of one of his most cherished objectives – the complete Allied evacuation of all German territory – but before his death he had secured agreement that the Rhineland would be evacuated in 1930. With his French opposite number, Aristide Briand, Stresemann gave publicity to the new Franco-German friendship, the essence of the so-called 'spirit of Locarno', even though in private Stresemann was continually demanding more concessions than France would grant. As for Briand, he believed the French had no alternative but to make the best of German protestations and promises.

At home, too, the years from 1924 to 1927 were a brief golden period for the Republic. The currency was stabilised. The promise of peace at home and abroad enabled the hardworking Germans to attract large American loans which covered the cost of reparations. American efficiency and methods of manufacture were successfully adopted by German industry. Business concerns combined and formed themselves into huge cartels in steel, chemicals and the electrical goods industries. Export flourished. Trade unions, too, enjoyed freedom and for the first time the positive protection of the state. These were the brief years of prosperity and had they continued the German people might well have come to value more their new republican democracy. Instead, as the economic crisis which began among the farmers and spread to industry hit Germany, a majority of the electorate in the early 1930s turned to parties which sought totalitarian solutions.

## CHAPTER 17

# *Britain, France and the United States from War to Peace*

The democracies of the West were tested in the period after the war. If they failed to retain the active support of the people, then others were ready to take over power. To the right, fascist movements and later the Nazi movement developed, promising new solutions. To the left, the communists pointed to the Soviet Union and the new society being created there as the right goal for all progressive peoples.

Before the Great War the triumph of liberal democracy had seemed certain in the West. Even Russia had begun to establish embryonic parliamentary institutions, and Italy had extended the vote to all adult males. The war, that ended with the victory of the democracies, might have been expected to confirm the superiority of the parliamentary form of government. The tide first turned against democracy in Russia after the revolution of 1917, in Italy in the 1920s with Mussolini and the emergence of the fascists. Forms of fascism spread to a number of the new Balkan successor states of the Habsburg Empire. Czechoslovakia was the shining exception, a bastion of Western liberal ideas and institutions in Eastern and central Europe. The most critical question was whether Germany would become a liberal democracy (Chapter 16).

The immediate danger from the Bolsheviks faded. The Polish defeat of the Red Army in 1920 halted any dream of spreading revolution with the Red Army in the vanguard. Lenin and Stalin did not lose their sense of isolation and insecurity. On the contrary, they expected the capitalist West to turn on communist Russia and crush her. In foreign relations the initiative nevertheless passed out of the hands of the Kremlin. Soviet policy in the 1920s was directed to increasing the difficulties of 'imperialist' Britain by encouraging the colonial peoples, especially in Asia, to struggle for independence. Another objective was to divide the Western democratic nations from each other; separate agreements of technical and military co-operation were concluded with the government of Weimar Germany (Rapallo, 1922; Berlin, 1926). Even while co-operating, however, the third prong of Soviet policy, surreptitiously masterminded by the Comintern, was to promote internal disruption within the Western democracies with the objective of weakening them and so making it a safer world for the first and only communist state – Russia. In Weimar politics the German Communist Party exerted a harmful influence on the attempts to construct a parliamentary democracy. Thus although the Soviet Union lacked the strength to endanger peace in Europe *directly*, communist tactics in the democratic states and fear of communism were among the formative influences of the 1920s.

The communists were weakest in the country which they had mistakenly believed would lead the 'capitalist assault' on the Soviet Union one day. There was never any danger between the two world wars that Britain would deviate from her evolutionary democratic path. The tradition of parliament, the impartial administration of the law and civic freedoms of the individual were too deeply embedded in the British way of life to be overthrown by any authoritarian movement. But, within the constitutional framework accepted by all except small minorities, the struggle for what came to be called 'social justice' increased. Working people demanded the satisfaction of basic economic rights; they called for state intervention to assure them of these rights should this prove necessary; they wanted work, a decent wage and adequate support for themselves and their families when out of work or unable to work due to sickness; they expected the ending of bad housing and, as they became increasingly aware of their disadvantaged position in society, a better future for their children. Industry, the manufacturers and the mine owners all looked back to before the war and wanted to be rid of all wartime government control and direction, though not subsidies when forthcoming.

What government wanted depended on party. The majority of the Conservatives believed in market forces to remedy the economic difficulties, in sound money and in a balanced budget. Government's business in the direct control of industry, they believed, was to divest itself as rapidly as possible of such controls as had been brought in during the war. The Labour Party had scarcely begun in the 1920s to translate socialist aspirations into practical policies. That work was not done until the 1930s. Meanwhile the Labour Party knew clearly what it did not want: communism on the Russian model. The small British Communist Party was refused affiliation to the Labour Party and in the mid-1920s communists could no longer be individual members of the Labour Party. The Labour Party, supported by the Trades Union Congress, sought power within the constitution knowing that to be tainted with communism would drive away moderate political support and so condemn the party in British politics to a minor role. The Labour Party was successful in becoming the main opposition party, and held office on its own twice during this period, briefly in 1924 as a minority government and from 1929 until the financial débâcle of 1931.

Labour prospered on the decay of the once great Liberal Party. The Liberal Party had simply lost its identity, its reforming policies absorbed by the Conservatives to the right, with Labour to the left offering a more plausible dynamic alternative to Conservative rule. The working man's vote in the industrial towns swung to Labour; many Liberal supporters deserted liberalism for the Conservatives, giving the latter an almost unbroken hold of power in the inter-war years. The Liberals in the post-war years had neither great national causes nor political leaders who could command a mass personal following as Gladstone had once done. Lloyd George appeared the obvious candidate; the man through whose energy and leadership Britain's war effort had been galvanised to victory; Lloyd George had then become a leader on the world stage at the Paris Peace Conference. His standing in 1919 was indeed high. As prime minister of a coalition government of those Liberals who followed him and the Conservatives, the elections of December 1918 gave the Conservative-Lloyd-George-Liberal coalition parties a landslide victory. The Liberals under Asquith, who opposed them, won no more than twenty-eight seats. Labour, with 2.3 million votes and sixty-three seats, for the first time became the main opposition party. This election marked a profound change in British politics. The results, moreover, reflected a greatly enlarged electorate. For the first time the vote was exercised by women over thirty; having proven during the war that they could do a man's job on the land and in factories, women could no longer be denied the vote.

For a time Lloyd George's personal ascendancy obscured the collapse of Liberal support in the country. He had agreed with his coalition partner, Andrew Bonar Law, the leader of the Conservatives, that the Conservatives would support 159 Liberal candidates, and the majority, 133, were elected as a result. Nevertheless the Conservatives predominated over Lloyd Georgian Liberals in the coalition by almost three to one. This meant Lloyd George was at the mercy of Conservative support. They would drop him for a Conservative leader when he ceased to be an electoral asset. And that is what they did in 1922.

An immediate problem facing post-war Britain was Ireland. 'Home Rule' was no longer enough for the Irish nationalists, whose cause had been spectacularly enhanced by the Easter rising in Dublin in 1916. The Sinn Fein fought the general election of December 1918, won all but four seats outside Ulster, and met in Dublin – those members not in prison – in a self-constituted Irish parliament which promptly declared the whole of Ireland an independent republic. Bloodshed, guerrilla war and the breakdown of law and order followed. The

*Irish Republican Army rebels take to the streets of Dublin in July 1922 to show their strength.*

Troubles began in 1919. Allied with Sinn Fein was the Irish Republican Army which attacked the armed police (Royal Irish Constabulary), and the British volunteer troops known as the Black and Tans. The IRA attempted to force the British government in London to recognise Irish independence. It was the worst sort of violent conflict – civil war, without battle lines, carried on by ambush, assassination and murder on both sides.

Two problems stood in the way of a solution: Lloyd George's refusal to grant total independence without any link with Britain, and the attitude of the six counties of Ulster, where a majority of Protestants fiercely defended the integrity and union of the British Isles, refusing to be merged with the predominantly Catholic south. An attempted British solution of December 1920 did not satisfy the south. Atrocities on both sides multiplied. But an appeal by the King in June 1921 led to a truce and a negotiated settlement that December. The Irish Free State became a Dominion and so remained within the British Empire, and the six counties of Ulster were granted the right to vote themselves out of independent Ireland and so remain a part of the United Kingdom. But the Irish leaders in London, in accepting partition, brought about a new civil war in Ireland in 1922 with those who rejected the treaty. Not until the spring of 1923 was Ireland at peace, with partition a fact. Yet the seeds of conflict tragically remained.

Dominion status in practice meant independence. The other British Dominions asserted their own independence, though the personal links between Dominion leaders such as South Africa's General Smuts and the British political leaders remained close and every Dominion except the Irish Free State independently joined Britain in declaring war on Germany in September 1939. As significant as this insistence of the right of the 'white Dominions' to exercise independence was Britain's declared intention to extend dominion status to the 'brown empire'. During the war, in 1917, the British government had declared that its aim was 'responsible government' for India. Fourteen years later, in 1931, a viceroy of India had advanced this to 'Dominion status' for India eventually. No one in Britain believed this would come about for a generation or two. But the major Indian independence party, the Congress Party, agitated for independence to be conceded quickly.

During the 1930s Mahatma ('great-souled') Gandhi had launched his remarkable movement of non-violent passive resistance to the British–Indian authorities. He served notice to the Raj that India could not be ruled in the long run without the consent of the Indian masses. And these masses of the poor of India were responding to a Western-educated lawyer, now turned into a holy man and skilled politician all in one, walking the length and breadth of India with little more than a loincloth and a stick. The emaciated figure of the frail Gandhi was as powerful a symbol for change as the strutting militaristic dictators of Europe. His teaching of how the poor and powerless could force the hand of the powerful and armed has proved to be one of the most potent influences in the world of the twentieth century.

Violence in Ireland and mass protest movements in India did not complete Britain's difficulties. Nearer home British governments from 1920 down to the present day became preoccupied with Britain's relative industrial decline, the threat of falling living standards and, most of all, the miseries of unemployment. Britain was not a happy land between the wars. The problem was deep-seated and arose from a combination of changes. Britain had increasingly derived earnings from trading as well as manufacture to offset the cost of importing food and raw materials. After a short post-war boom world trade contracted, particularly in the 1930s, and the earnings from carrying the world's trade fell correspondingly. There was no demand for more ships, and the shipyards of Scotland and north-eastern England became symbols of the deepest depression and unemployment.

World patterns of trade were also changing. Britain's traditional trade in textiles and other goods to the empire suffered as the poor of the world became even poorer. As raw material prices fell with slackening industrial activity so the poorest parts of the world earned less and less; this in turn gave them less to spend on British goods. Then textile factories, the first stage of industrialisation, were springing up in India and Japan and with their low labour costs drove Britain out of many traditional markets. Actually Britain was remarkably successful in developing the industries of the second industrial revolution, the chemical, electrical and motor industries. But these successes could not take up the slack of Britain's pre-war traditional exports.

The coal industry was one of the worst affected. The mines were not efficient, and demand for coal slackened with declining industrial activity in Europe and the competition of oil. The powerful miners' union saw nationalisation as the solution which would enable the numerous privately owned mines to be developed on a national basis. The mine owners, faced with declining profits, argued for increasing hours and cutting wages. But the owners' case was weakened by the fact that they had not used their large profits of the war years to modernise the mines. The mines had then been under state control and the miners were embittered when Lloyd George returned them to their owners' control in 1921. A miners' strike failed to win better terms. In 1925 a strike was narrowly averted when the government paid a temporary subsidy to the mines to prevent wage cuts and set up an inquiry. The report of this inquiry (the Samuel Commission) the following year found much in favour of the miners' view but rejected nationalisation and suggested that less drastic cuts in wages were probably inevitable. The miners were anxious to avoid a strike which would bring hardship to themselves, but in negotiating with the owners refused to countenance any further cut in wages or increase in hours. At the end of April 1926 the government subsidy came to an end and the mine owners now locked out the miners.

The importance of the dispute with the miners lay in the fact that it led to the General Strike of 1926, the most widespread and dramatic breakdown of Britain's industrial relations for a century. It lasted only nine days from 3 to 12 May 1926. But these days manifested Britain's division into the labouring class and the middle and upper classes, who for the main part wished to break the strike. There was more involved than a strike of miners. The Trades Union Congress involved itself and in doing so involved organised labour on the one hand and the Prime Minister Stanley Baldwin and the British government on the other. Its sincere intention was to facilitate a compromise settlement between the mine owners and the miners. When these efforts foundered the TUC used its industrial muscle to call out on strike key industries, including transport. The government countered by putting into practice carefully worked-out emergency measures to keep the essential services going. The TUC's attempt to force the government to coerce the mine owners failed, though the rank and file overwhelmingly supported the call to strike. What was the strike really about then? It certainly was not an attempt to bring about a revolution. It was not purely industrial either. At the end of the General Strike, which the TUC called off, the miners were left to fight their own battle, which lasted several bitter months.

In the 1920s and 1930s Conservative-dominated

*The British General Strike of 1926. Armoured cars escort a food convoy down the East India Dock Road in London.*

governments of the Lloyd George, Baldwin and Chamberlain era were socially conscious and anxious to pass measures which would protect the sick and unemployed and help the poor. Their finance was orthodox, believing the country was best served by sound money and balanced budgets but not by direct control of industry. The minority Labour government of 1924 was just as orthodox in financial questions as the Conservatives. Neither Conservatives nor Labour followed policies of confrontation and even the General Strike was not a confrontation that either side had been keen to invite. What would be held against the governments of the inter-war years was the persistence of 1 million unemployed, and much higher numbers during the most severe years of depression, concentrated above all in the north of the country. No government knew how to 'cure' this unemployment in the prevailing international conditions. It was the biggest argument against 'democracy', yet the great majority of the British electorate turned neither to fascism nor to communism.

France emerged the victor from the Great War, but no country, excepting Russia, had suffered more physical damage, human and material. In the struggle for power on the European continent,

*Prime Minister Stanley Baldwin of Britain, an adept at pouring oil on troubled water.*

France was the loser. Population losses had been such that there were now three Germans for every two Frenchmen. French industry had been devastated in northern France. The war had deeply scarred the towns and countryside of this region, whereas no battles, apart from the early encounters in East Prussia, had been fought on German soil. One in every five Frenchmen had been mobilised during the war (one in eight in Britain), 1.4 million killed and another three-quarters of a million permanently invalided. Put another way, it has been calculated that for every ten men between the ages of twenty and forty-five, two were killed, one was totally invalided and three were incapacitated for long periods of time, leaving only four available for work. The French governments faced the common problems of demobilisation and changeover from wartime and industrial controls to a peacetime economy. In addition the French had to cope with the task of reconstruction in the war-torn regions of France.

The acquisition of Alsace-Lorraine and the utilisation of the Saar mines were important compensations for the losses suffered, but did not cancel them out. Financially France was in a difficult plight. The government had financed the war not by taxes but largely by making loans at home and receiving loans from Britain and the United States. After the war, yet more money had to be found for reconstruction and invalid or widows' pensions. France was dependent on the goodwill of the United States and Britain. She was also dependent on receiving reparations from Germany to cover the gap between what she could earn and what she spent. French needs and policies in the 1920s have not received the understanding and sympathy they deserve. In British judgement, the French were acting vindictively and arrogantly towards defeated Germany, and thus were responsible in part for Germany's fervent nationalism and for delaying a 'normalisation' and pacification of Western Europe. Britain came to see her role not as an ally of France so much as a mediator between France and 'helpless' Germany in the interests of creating a new balance of power. This British attitude of 'conditional' support could only strengthen France's anxieties about her long-term security once Germany had revived her strength.

For France the 'German problem' was insoluble, because France *alone* could not enforce any solution in the long run. Britain and the United States could express their disapproval effectively by applying financial pressure on a weakened French economy. But the exaction of reparations from Germany was for France not only a necessary financial operation. Far more was involved. Nothing less than the question of whether Germany would be required, and if necessary forced, by the Allies to abide by all the terms of the Treaty of Versailles. On that issue depended the security of France. If Germany could set aside reparations with impunity, then why not also the military restrictions and finally the territorial clauses of Versailles? Marshal Foch had expressed these deep fears when he called the Treaty of Versailles no more than a twenty-year truce. France had already lost one pillar of her security when the Senate of the United States failed to ratify the treaty of Guarantee (page 132), and Britain, too, according to its original terms, had backed out. The second pillar of her security was the Allied (including her own) right to occupy the Rhineland zones and to continue to do so beyond the five-, ten- and fifteen-year periods specified if Germany did not fulfil her obligations under the Treaty of Versailles. After the failure of the treaty of Guarantee, the French were naturally all the more determined to maintain their rights. In the third pillar, the League of Nations, the French realistically did not place much faith.

In March 1921, with the Germans appearing to be evading the military and financial obligations placed on them, the French, with Britain's blessing and co-operation, occupied three industrial German towns. Almost immediately afterwards the Germans were presented with the total reparations bill of 132 billion gold marks (£6600 million) and a method of payment. The Germans gave way. Reparations were regularly resumed until the end of 1922. Then the Germans defaulted once again and disputed with Poincaré, by then prime minister, the amounts due and already delivered. Despite British disapproval, French and Belgian troops occupied the industrial Ruhr in January 1923, ostensibly with the object of collecting what was due. The more important objective was to weaken Germany's reviving power by occupying her most important industrial region. French uncertainties about Germany's ultimate intentions had been increased by the murder of Rathenau, by the political instability of the country and by what appeared to be deliberate attempts to evade her obligations (page 136).

The French move was no sudden reaction but the result of a carefully thought-out policy. It separated her from Britain, as the Germans could not fail to note, and they exploited the split successfully in the 1920s. The German government called an industrial boycott in the Ruhr, thereby providing the French with a reason for staying there; only the German coal owners refused to behave so patriotically and continued delivering coal to the French. The ruin of German finances, which was the consequence of Germany's decision to order industrial passive resistance in the Ruhr, was a victory of sorts for Poincaré. In outward appearance his resistance to British mediating pressure seemed justified too. He demanded that the Germans call off their industrial boycott before fresh negotiations over reparations could be started to resolve the underlying problem that had led to the occupation. In September 1923 the new Stresemann government abandoned resistance and agreed to resume reparations payments (page 137).

All along, however, reparations had been only part of the reason for the conflict. The French felt too weak to control the Germans single-handed. The year 1923–4 marked France's last effort to attain what she had failed to secure at Versailles, a means of checking the future threat of German preponderance in Europe. France failed in 1924 and had to bow to the pressure of the United States and Britain. This was marked by her agreement that experts should work out a new reparations settlement which, when accepted by Germany, would leave France no excuse to stay in the Ruhr. The American expert Charles G. Dawes gave his name to the reparations plan of 1924; it did not fix a final total but, as expected, scaled down the immediate annual payments and coupled payment to a loan to the Germans. The Germans accepted the plan and with the restoration of the value of their currency became internationally creditworthy. Poincaré fell from power. Briand, who returned to power, had no option but to end the occupation. All efforts meanwhile which the French had made to encourage separation in the Rhineland failed.

The French had to make the best of the situation. The outcome was the European reconciliation of Locarno. Briand and Stresemann to all outward appearances had buried wartime enmities. In the Locarno Treaties, signed on 16 October 1925, the Germans renounced any desire to change their western frontier with France and so accepted the loss of Alsace-Lorraine. Britain and Italy guaranteed the western frontiers and the continued demilitarisation of Rhineland against a 'flagrant breach', and engaged themselves to aid the victim of aggression whether France or Germany. The British congratulated themselves that their original Versailles obligations were now lessened, since 'flagrant' was an adjective open to different interpretation. The French sadly noted that they had secured British support not in an equal Anglo-French alliance but with Britain in her new role as mediator and arbitrator. Much would therefore depend on the view Britain took of any particular situation.

France was left with no secure allies. Her position was worse than in 1914 when Russia, militarily, had been a powerful and reliable ally. She had a new alliance with Poland and Czechoslovakia, but these two countries could not be relied on to fight for French security nor France for theirs, for there was a 'catch' in the European security arrangements. The Germans had refused to include their eastern frontier with Czechoslovakia and Poland in the Locarno Treaties package (page 138). Britain and Italy did not act as guarantors of these frontiers, either. The Germans had signed arbitration treaties with Czechoslovakia and Poland separately, but they were worth little. The Germans could still resort to force if arbitration did not give them what they wanted. Only the separate alliances of Poland and Czechoslovakia with France might deter Germany. But now by the terms of the Locarno Treaties France would be arraigned as the aggressor if the French army sought to come to the aid of their eastern allies by the only means available to them – an attack on Germany. Britain was to exercise this 'leverage' to the full when, thirteen years later, France declared herself ready to aid her Czech ally against Germany in 1938. Britain then insisted that, should such an eventuality lead to war with Germany, she was not bound to help France (page 242).

In the new spirit of conciliation, France also relinquished prematurely her territorial guarantees permitted by Versailles, the occupation of the Rhineland zones. In order to prove their goodwill, Britain and France had pulled out their last troops by 1930. The 'goodwill' and 'faith' were not justified, as the later experience of the 1930s was to show. Briand played this last card of defusing the

German problem by seeking to make Germany and France the nucleus of a 'new Europe', but in vain.

Where, then, was the most serious single flaw in the way in which Britain and France, with American financial connivance, dealt with Germany? Was the right policy coercion or conciliation? Both were tried, with some good results and some bad. We cannot rerun history to discover what would have happened if there had been greater or less coercion. But the basic fault of Allied policy lay in not maintaining Anglo-French unity after the war. Allied policy of either coercion or conciliation should have been based on strength, on the capacity and determination to preserve peace if ever again threatened by Germany. The French realised this and tried to act as if they were strong. It was Britain which basically undermined this stance. Horrified by the Great War and the millions of dead and maimed, she attempted to withdraw and limit her European commitments. At Locarno she had refused to guarantee the frontiers of Poland and Czechoslovakia, an open invitation to German revisionism. This was true even in Western Europe. While Britain acknowledged that her strategic 'frontier' now ran along the Rhine, the British Cabinet was not willing to match this concept militarily by maintaining a British army capable of defending this supposedly 'joint' frontier. France alone stood as guardian of the European frontiers of Versailles, and France by herself was too weak for that role. Briand's policy of reconciliation was sincere enough; it seemed also the only way left to achieve French security.

Despite the grave uncertainties of France's European position, and weakness of her international financial position, she achieved a spectacular domestic recovery in the 1920s. The majority of Frenchmen resisted the siren call of those on the right, the fascist Action Française, or the Communist Party on the extreme left, who sought to overthrow the institutions of the Third Republic.

The elections of November 1919 were won by groups of the conservative right allied in a Bloc National. Led by an ex-socialist, Alexandre Millerand, its commanding figure was Clemenceau, the 'father of victory'. Behind the Bloc stood big business interests and the mass of voters, especially the peasantry frightened by the Bolshevist bogey. They approved of a policy of dealing sternly with Germany; exacting reparations rather than paying taxes. Once elected, the Bloc National reverted to the tradition of the Third Republic in denying the presidency to Clemenceau in 1920. They preferred a weak president, only this time overdid it in electing a man who a few months later had to retire into a mental home. Clemenceau's career too was ended.

The work of reconstruction was begun in north-eastern France and with government credits there was enough to do to ensure full employment in the 1920s. Some concessions were also made to the workers in legislating for an eight-hour day and conceding collective bargaining. But control of industry was handed back to the owners. The government was firmly opposed to nationalisation and socialism. Among industrial workers after the war there was much discontent. Their wages had not kept pace with rising prices. The main French trade union – the Confédération Générale du Travail – was determined to challenge the government in a series of large, well-organised strikes. The socialist-inspired strikes were as much political as economic. Confident of the army and of majority electoral support, the government would not yield; the unions had no chance and lost. In 1920 French socialism split, as it did elsewhere in Europe. The communists formed their own party and separate trade union. The 'democratic' socialists, led by Léon Blum, and democratic trade unions organised themselves also. The split of the 'left' was mirrored by a split on the right, Poincaré's policies having failed to produce the expected results in 1923.

The elections of 1924 gave power to a grouping of centre radicals and socialists, the so-called Cartel des Gauches. The Bloc National formed the main opposition to the right, and the small Communist Party to the left, but the presence of the communists to their left, bitterly critical, had the effect of inhibiting the socialists from collaborating with the radicals of the centre. The split of French socialism thus deprived the large socialist electorate from exercising an influence in the government of the Republic commensurate with their strength. It was a formula for sterility. Meanwhile the undoing of the Cartel government was its inability to master the financial situation. The franc fell precipitously in value. While American loans were reaching Germany, the French inability and refusal to negotiate a debt settlement with the United States closed the American money market to the French. In 1926, the Chamber turned once more to the strong man of French politics, Poincaré. Poincaré was granted special powers to restore France to financial health, which he promptly succeeded in doing by raising

*Passengers crowd on to a Parisian locomotive during a rail strike in May 1920.*

taxes and cutting expenditure. France now experienced a few golden years of progress and prosperity until the effects of the worldwide slump made themselves seriously felt in France in 1933.

In industrial strength and influence the United States had emerged as a world power by the close of the First World War. But victory left the American people disillusioned with the role of world leadership which Wilson had sought to thrust upon them. Yet during the 1920s and 1930s there was no way in which the Americans could opt out of world affairs and return to what appeared only in retrospect as a golden past of American self-sufficiency.

The immediate post-war mood favoured a rapid return to freeing the individual American from all constraints of wartime control and freeing business too to get on with the job of expanding American prosperity. An amiable conservative Republican politician, Warren G. Harding, had been elected to the White House in November 1920 on a campaign slogan which reflected the public mood precisely: 'less government in business and more business in government'. Businessmen were no longer depicted as the 'robber barons' ruthlessly amassing wealth but as the new patriotic leaders who would benefit the average American. On 4 March 1921 Harding was inaugurated. Big business was brought into government with the appointment of Andrew

Mellon, one of the richest men of the United States, whose wealth was exceeded only by Rockefeller and Ford, as secretary of the Treasury. Mellon's fortune was founded on banking, channelling money into steel, railroads and a wide range of industry. There were other appointments of men of proven ability: Herbert Hoover, Henry Wallace and, as secretary of state to take charge of foreign affairs, a brilliant lawyer, Charles Evans Hughes. Unfortunately Harding made grave errors too in rewarding political cronies of his own state, Ohio. The 'Ohio gang' were to surround Harding in 1923 during the last months of his administration with some of the worst and most spectacular scandals of corruption in the history of American government.

The early boom which had absorbed the ex-servicemen in 1919 collapsed in 1920 and the depression lasted until 1922. But then followed seven years of remarkable economic expansion and rising industrial prosperity led by the growth of the automobile industry, electrical machinery and appliances and building. Yet the decade was to close with the most severe and longest-lasting economic collapse in American history. The 1920s did not turn out to be the new era of never-ending prosperity.

With hindsight the weaknesses of the 1920s can be discerned. Industry, enjoying the protection of a high tariff, had over-expanded as its productivity had increased. Wages had failed to keep pace with the increases in production. Big business had successfully defeated the great waves of strikes that spread across the country in 1919 by characterising the strikers and their leaders as Bolsheviks. Acts of terrorism in the cities were blamed on the 'radicals' and communists. Anti-labour hysteria swept the country. Aliens were arrested as suspected communists though few were actually deported. The most celebrated case of prosecution of suspected radicals arousing worldwide interest was the arrest and conviction in 1920 of two anarchists, Nicola Sacco and Bartolomeo Vanzetti, for robbery and murder. Liberals insisted that their trial was a travesty of justice and called for their release. They were executed all the same in 1927.

Intolerance and hysteria extended to other minorities: the vulnerable blacks as well as Jews and Catholics. The racial prejudice of the whites and competition for work in the cities exploded in racial riots in some twenty cities in 1919. Before the Great War the great majority of blacks had lived in the South. During the war half a million blacks sought an escape from poverty by migrating to the industrial cities of the North. Wilson's efforts to establish democracy and self-determination in Europe stood in glaring contrast to intolerance and discrimination at home. In the south the Ku Klux Klan greatly expanded its violent activities.

One of the most extraordinary aspects of American government in the era of financial and industrial 'freedoms' of the 1920s was the invasion of people's privacy and right to lead the life they chose through the enactment of Prohibition. Congress had passed the law in 1919 over Wilson's veto. The law could never be properly enforced as ordinary citizens constantly broke it by surreptitiously consuming liquor. On the now illegal manufacture and transportation of alcoholic drinks gangster empires flourished. The most notorious, Al Capone's, in Chicago, with its aura of violence and series of street murders undertaken by rival gangs, became as much a symbol of America in the 1920s as jazz and the stolid respectability of President John Calvin Coolidge, who had succeeded to the presidency in August 1923 on the death of Harding. Related to the attitude of intolerance was the change in immigration laws. They too exhibited a racial aspect of discrimination. Immigration from eastern Asia was cut off. Quotas for immigrants were now established, which

*The St Valentine's Day Massacre of 14 February 1929. Mobsters mow down mobsters, and Chicago's name is mud world-wide.*

favoured the British, Germans, Irish and Scandinavians as against the 'new immigrants' from central and southern Europe. The era of virtually free entry to the United States from Europe was over. Something special which the United States stood for – a haven from persecution – was ended.

American soldiers returned from Europe believing they had won the war for the Allies, and their President sailed home believing he had put the world on the road to peace and prosperity. Dreams turned sour. The American people now wanted to get on with their own lives, to own a home, a Model-T Ford and a refrigerator. The Hollywood dream industry started on its phenomenal growth. In the inter-war years more and more Americans questioned why the United States had involved herself at all in the war. The overwhelming feeling was that the American continent was far enough away from the storm centres of Europe and Asia to enjoy geographical security. There was thus no reason why Americans should again sacrifice their lives for other nations. They needed no large army. Their security could be guaranteed by a navy powerful enough to meet any challenge.

*Beer is poured down the drain during the Prohibition years in the USA. Even the children here look displeased.*

International naval disarmament was welcomed as it would allow less to be spent on the United States Navy. President Harding bowed to the public revolt on armaments expenditure. Secretary of State Hughes was spectacularly successful in hosting a naval disarmament conference in Washington. The British too were anxious to turn their backs on the war and reduce armaments expenditure. The outcome of the conference was a treaty in which Britain and the United States agreed to limit their battleship strength to 500,000 tons each and Japan to 300,000 tons. It was said that the Washington Conference between November 1921 and February 1922 sank more ships than all the naval battles of the war put together. As there were no American or British naval bases anywhere close to Japan and American and British naval defences spanned the Atlantic and Mediterranean too, the apparent Japanese inferiority was not so real. At that same conference, in further treaties, the Americans hoped to ensure that China would remain free and independent. More important, the Japanese government itself decided to withdraw from Siberia and China. The treaties provided the illusion of peace in eastern Asia without solving the underlying conflicts, just as the later Locarno Treaties created the illusion of peace in Europe. The climax came in 1928 with the Briand-Kellogg treaty 'outlawing' war. They could be dismissed as harmless were it not for the fact that they lulled the West into a false sense of security. No doubt many people wished to be lulled.

Americans did not speak of 'isolationism' in the 1920s, but of 'America first'. Even the mid-westerner knew that the United States could not be separated from the rest of the world. What Americans demanded was that in dealings with the rest of the world it was the duty of Congress and the administration to take care of American interests and not to meddle in the world concerns of the League of Nations. Above all America should not be dragged into conflicts by concluding a military alliance with any other country but should preserve a 'free hand' confident in her ability to defend her interests. It was an attitude based on confidence.

**Principal Allied Debtors and Creditors, November 1918** (*dollars*)

|  | Owed to USA | Owed to Britain | Owed to France | Total debt | Total due |
|---|---|---|---|---|---|
| United States | – | – | – | – | 7,078 |
| Britain | 3,696 | – | – | 3,696 | 7,014 |
| France | 1,970 | 1,683 | – | 3,653 | 2,237 |
| Russia | 188 | 2,472 | 955 | 3,615 | – |
| Italy | 1,031 | 1,855 | 75 | 2,961 | – |
| Belgium | 172 | 434 | 535 | 1,141 | – |
| Other states | 21 | 570 | 672 | 1,263 | – |

In fact the American administrations involved the United States more in problems of international diplomacy than the American people would have approved of.

One aspect of 'America first' was the insistence on collecting all the moneys lent mainly to France and Britain but also to the other Allies, during the Great War. Since Europe remained in desperate need of American loans, the administration could pressurise the wartime allies by closing the American money market to those nations which defaulted. One of the curious results of this outlook was the treatment of Germany. When the United States at length concluded a separate peace with her former enemy only token reparations were demanded. Consequently Germany had free access to the American money market. American financial orthodoxy in the 1920s had the effect of dragging out the reparations problem which did so much to unsettle Europe.

Americans did play a major role in 1924 and 1930 and gave a lead in sorting out the reparation question, but rejected the British suggestion that German reparations should be linked to Allied indebtedness. It would have created a very much healthier international financial climate if both large reparations and large debts had been cancelled altogether. Many of these lessons were learnt only after the Second World War. A narrow, nationalistic approach to international finance and trade in the end harmed the United States as much as it did any other country; for it contributed to the great collapse of 1929 and to the depression of the 1930s and so, indirectly, to the rise of Hitler and the outbreak of the Second World War.

# CHAPTER 18

# Italy and the Rise of Fascism

The world of the twentieth century sharply differs from that of the nineteenth. The twentieth century is the age of the masses. Those who govern have the opportunity for the first time to communicate directly with those they govern. The mass-circulation newspapers, the radio, the cinema and, after the Second World War, television created entirely new conditions of government. Contemporaries were not slow to recognise this. Those who ruled could create images of themselves, of their policies and objectives, of society and the world around them and so seek to lead and manipulate the masses. Mass persuasion became an essential ingredient of government; and the techniques of the art were seriously studied and consciously applied by elected governments and totalitarian regimes alike; the British Prime Minister Stanley Baldwin used the radio effectively during the General Strike of 1926 by broadcasting to the nation; President Roosevelt started his famous 'fireside chats'; and the totalitarian leaders, Stalin, Mussolini and Hitler, put on gigantic displays which could be 'witnessed' by millions through the cinema. Mussolini's and Hitler's raucous speeches became familiar to every Italian and German; they were amplified by loudspeakers erected in public places in case anyone turned off their radio at home. Mass participation in politics was a fact in the post-war world.

The minority of the politically and economically privileged not unnaturally felt alarmed and threatened by this new age which was dawning. In countries with strong traditions of representative government and democratically inspired institutions this new force of the 'masses' might be won over and representative institutions so adapted to win their allegiance to them. This is essentially what happened in Britain and the United States in the 1920s and 1930s and, less convincingly, in France too. In the Soviet Union the mass of people were brought into harmony with the rulers by propaganda, appeals to communist idealism and, where this did not suffice, by force and terror. The revolution created an entirely new class of privileged and bound these to the regime. But those who had possessed social, political and economic privilege in pre-war Russia overwhelmingly lost it. It was a total revolution, and its spectre haunted the majority of Western societies where communist parties only gained the allegiance of a determined minority of society. The communist appeal to the masses, and their use of the masses, had to be effectively countered if communist revolutions were to be avoided. But how far were existing institutions strong enough to cope with this onslaught? The danger from the extreme left was generally exaggerated as it was unknown and could not therefore be measured. The weaknesses of existing representative forms of government to deal with national problems, however, became glaringly clear to everyone. The soldiers returning from the hardships of a long war to the unsettled conditions of post-war Europe, with its endemic under-employment as economies readjusted from war to peace, were disillusioned.

Besides the unsettled post-war conditions, the fears of Bolshevik revolutions and mass participation in politics, there is a fourth new element in the post-war situation: the expectations of expanding national frontiers and financial reparations that would follow victory and recompense the people for the sacrifices of war. The victors did not experience such rewards. Neither territorial increases nor reparations could compensate for the immense human loss and material damage of the war. The defeated in any case lacked the means to compensate the victors adequately. Among the defeated powers the sense of loss now suffered made the sacrifices of war seem all the more unbearable. Unrequited nationalism was a powerful destabilising force in post-war Europe. It differed from the pre-1914 variety in that it was not just expansionist; it also was fed by the fury felt at the injustices real and imagined of the outcome of the Great War and the peace settlements. That the defeated powers should harbour such resentments was to be expected.

Among the victorious nations the Italians particularly suffered from this malaise. They referred to the 'mutilated' peace that had not given them what they believed they deserved. The Ottoman Empire had been defeated by the Allies, but the Greeks, British and French were the intended principal beneficiaries. The sorest point of all was that Italy, despite her sacrifices in the war, had not replaced the Habsburgs as the paramount Balkan power. At the peace conference the flashpoint of Italian resentment came when Italian claims to the Italian-speaking port of Fiume, formerly in the Habsburg Empire, were rejected by her allies. Gabriele D'Annunzio, poet and professional patriot, thereupon took the law into his own hands and with government connivance and indications of royal support in 1919 seized Fiume at the head of an army of volunteers. The outburst of super-patriotism, bravado and violence, the dictatorial rabble-rousing techniques of balcony-oratory which D'Annunzio adopted made him the Duce on whom Mussolini modelled his own political style.

Whenever representative institutions had no established hold there was a tendency towards authoritarian forms of government which promised to meet the multiplicity of problems. The particular movement which became known to the world as fascism first reached power in post-war Italy. There are a number of general reasons for its rise: it developed in response to problems and opportunities facing the West in the twentieth century and arose out of the Great War. But its success at the same time has to be studied in purely Italian terms. The form that fascism later took varied so much from one country to another as the movement spread in the 1930s to Austria, Hungary, Romania, France, Portugal and Spain that historians dispute the usefulness of applying a common label. Today fascism as a description has been further debased by being applied to almost anything of which the Marxist left disapproves.

What can it be said to have had in common before the Second World War? Fascism was a movement designed to secure the support of the masses for a leader without the intermediary of a democratically elected parliament. It was a substitute for democracy, giving the masses the illusion of power without the reality. Thus, though violently anti-communist, fascism appeared to support the existing social and economic hierarchy of society and so appealed to the right. Fascism made a virtue of destroying the powers of parties and divisions in the state. It stood for 'strength through unity' at the expense of civil liberties. The cult of the leader was fostered by the leader above all and his principal lieutenants. Fascism was a chauvinist male-oriented movement assigning women to the role of child-bearing and raising a family. It was stridently nationalist. The leader, with virtually unlimited powers, stood at the apex of a party, a private army and a bureaucracy. Violence against opponents cowed possible opposition. The fascist army and bureaucracy of course ensured that tens of thousands would have a vested interest in preserving the fascist state. Here loyalty to the movement, not social standing, provided an avenue of advancement to the unscrupulous and the ambitious.

In Italy, as elsewhere, fascism derived its strength as much from what it was against as from what it was for. In detail this varied according to the tactical need of the movement to attain and then retain power. It was a totalitarian response to new social forces and to change and to discontents real and imagined, both personal and national. Parliamentary government had functioned very imperfectly already before the war (pages 31–2). The conduct of the war did not enhance parliament's prestige. The disaster of the battle of Caporetto was blamed on civilian mismanagement. The mass of impoverished Italians in the south, and the agricultural and the urban workers in the north, half a century after unification still did not identify themselves with the parliamentary state set up by Piedmont, depending as it did on local favours and corruption.

Government was by personalities rather than by leaders of parties. Manhood suffrage, introduced in 1912, and proportional representation in 1919, undermined the way in which parliament and government had previously been managed. The two biggest parties which emerged from the elections of 1919 with more than half the seats between them, the Catholic Popular party (100 seats) and the Socialists (156), were both incapable of providing the basis of a stable coalition with the Liberal and Nationalist Parties to the left of centre or the right of centre. The Socialists were divided between the communists and the more moderate socialists in 1921. Since 1919 neither wing wished to collaborate with government and both spoke the language of revolution. The Catholic Popular Party had been formed with the tacit support of the Pope to fight socialism. But it was not a class party. The majority were genuinely reformist, advocating the distribution of the landed estates to the peasantry. It was a mass party relying on the support of the agricultural labourer in the south, just as the Socialist strength lay in the industrial towns of the north. But the Popular Party also included conservative and extreme-right supporters. Their support of government policies was accordingly unpredictable. The five governments between 1918 and 1922 were consequently faced with parliamentary paralysis and no sound base on which to build a majority. Giovanni Giolitti dominated the last years of Italian parliamentary life.

Against the Catholics and Socialists, Giolitti enlisted the help of Mussolini's fascists, who in the elections of May 1921 with his electoral support gained thirty-five deputies out of more than 500. It was a modest parliamentary beginning for the fascists. But, without Giolitti, Mussolini and his party would have remained a negligible constitutional force. In the streets, however, the fascists had already made their violence felt. They flourished on the seed-bed of industrial and agricultural discontent. There was large-scale post-war unemployment. On the land the peasantry took possession of uncultivated parts of the large landed estates. In the towns militant unionism demanded higher wages and in some instances in 1920 occupied factories. It was not the beginning of revolution.

*Benito Mussolini. Oratorical flourishes and heroical posturing on the doorstep; sexual frolics indoors.*

Higher wages were conceded, the standard of living of the urban worker rose appreciably despite higher prices. Real wages were between a quarter and a third higher in 1922 than in 1919, and by the autumn of 1922 unrest subsided. It was at this point that Mussolini came to power, claiming to have saved the country from the imaginary threat of Bolshevism and offering fascism as an alternative.

Mussolini succeeded in attracting attention to himself in his pose as statesman and Duce. He made Italy seem more important in international affairs than her weak industrial resources and military strength warranted. It was an image built up with skill to mislead a gullible world until the image was shattered when the ineptitude of Mussolini's armies were revealed on every front during the Second World War. The success of fascism lay largely in creating such myths, which after 1925 become identified with the public personality Mussolini created of himself.

Benito Mussolini was born to genuinely 'proletarian' parents on 29 July 1883 in the small town of Predappio in the poor east-central region of Italy, the Romagna. His father was a blacksmith and named his son Benito after the Mexican revolutionary leader Juarez. From youth onwards, Mussolini admired rebellious violence against the 'establishment' of schoolmasters; and as he became older he rebelled against the better off and privileged. He experienced poverty, and his hatred of privilege turned him into an ardent socialist. He left Italy and spent some time in Switzerland under socialist tutelage. He then accepted both the internationalist and pacifist outlook of the socialists. Yet in 1904 he returned to Italy to serve his obligatory time in the army and clearly enjoyed army life and discipline. It was the first and not the only inconsistency in his development. For a time he took a post as a teacher. But above all Mussolini saw himself as a socialist political agitator. He rose to prominence in the pre-war Italian Socialist Party, belonging to the most extreme revolutionary wing. He denounced nationalism as a capitalist manifestation and was briefly imprisoned for his activities in seeking to hinder the war effort during Italy's Libyan war with Turkey, 1911–12 (page 35). His imprisonment brought him into favour with the revolutionary socialists who controlled the Socialist Party in 1912. They appointed Mussolini to the editorship of *Avanti*, the socialist newspaper.

Consistency and loyalty to friends and principles was not a strong trait in Mussolini. War, that is international violence, later attracted him. Mussolini was no pacifist by nature. So all went well with his efforts as a socialist editor until shortly after the outbreak of the Great War. Then, to the anger of the Socialists who condemned the capitalist war and demanded non-intervention, Mussolini switched and started banging the drum of nationalism and patriotism in *Avanti*. The Socialists thereupon ousted him from the editorship. Mussolini then founded his own paper in November 1914, the *Popolo d'Italia*, and campaigned for intervention.

Without political connections his influence, however, was negligible. He served in the army from 1915 to 1917, was wounded and, on release from the army, returned to patriotic journalism.

Mussolini observed the impotence and weakness of parliamentary government after the war and saw it as an opportunity for him to form and lead an authoritarian movement; with its help he might then play an important role in the state, something he had so far failed to do.

A meeting in Milan addressed by Mussolini of some 200 of his followers in March 1919 marks the formal beginning of the fascist movement. The movement in the beginning expressed its hostility to property and to capitalist industry and followed the line of French syndicalism in advocating worker control of industry – 'economic democracy' – and so tried to win the urban workers' support. Yet in its early years the money flowing in to support it, and to fund Mussolini's own newspaper, came from Milan industrialists. The landowners too intended to use his bands of ruffians – the *squadristi* – against peasants. Mussolini's personal inclinations were probably socialist still in 1919, but in his bid for power he was ready to trim his sails and operate in the interests of property to secure the support of industrialists and landowners. He had become a pure opportunist and adventurer.

Fascism was the main beneficiary of the ineffectual trade union activities, the occupation of the factories in the summer of 1920 and the Socialists' appeals to workers to engage in a general strike. During the winter of 1920 and the following spring, bands of fascists in their black shirts both in the towns and in the countryside attacked all forms of labour organisations, socialist councils, socialist newspapers, even cultural societies. Opponents were beaten and tortured. The 'red shirts' offered resistance and street battles ensued. Liberal Italy and the Church, while condemning all violence, connived at the destruction of socialist organisations by the fascists. Since the government appeared powerless to restore law and order, the fascists came to be regarded as the protectors of property by the middle classes and not as the principal disturbers of the peace, which they were.

The rapid growth of violent bands of fascists, swelled by the followers of D'Annunzio, whose escapade in Fiume had collapsed, could no longer be effectively controlled by Mussolini and at this stage, in 1921, was unwelcome to him. Mussolini had entered parliament as the leader of a small party and sought power in alliance with either one of the two large parties, the Catholic Popular Party or the Socialists. He chose the Socialists temporarily to capture the mass votes of the urban workers. But the leaders of the fascist bands were outraged at this 'betrayal'. Mussolini even lost the leadership of the party for a short time. The fascists continued their violence in the cities and the countryside. Mussolini also nourished the belief of the parliamentary Liberals that he would co-operate with them against the socialist left.

Mussolini played the anti-Bolshevik card for all he was worth. The call by the Socialists in July 1922 for a general strike in a bid to stop the increasing lawlessness and drift to the right provided a semblance of justification for Mussolini's claims. The strike call was a failure but increased the desire for tough measures against the workers. The support the fascists were given was particularly strong from those groups – artisans, white-collar workers and shopkeepers, the lower-middle class – who saw their status threatened and usurped by the demands of the workers. The army despised the parliamentary regime, which was obliged to reduce their swollen wartime strength. Mussolini's strident nationalism naturally appealed to them. Prefects and civil servants in the provinces too connived at fascist violence and were hedging their bets in case the fascists should one day come to power. Giolitti's policy of non-interference in disputes which he believed would blow themselves out was a clever tactic as far as weakening the strength of the trade unions and socialists was concerned. Strikes diminished. Any danger the left had posed was rapidly vanishing. But the low government profile also created a power vacuum which the fascists filled until they themselves openly defied law and order and even threatened the state itself. Without government weakness, without the parliamentary paralysis which prevented the liberal centre from forming a stable coalition, the fascists could never have gained power. While the politicians connived and jockeyed for power, divided as much by ambition as policy, administration throughout the country was becoming anarchic.

The fascists chose the month of October 1922 to seize power from the unstable liberal administrations. Their plan was first to stage uprisings in the provinces which would capture prefectures and post offices and cut off Rome from the surrounding countryside thus paralysing government, and then to march on Rome with armies of 'blackshirts' and throw out the government by force if intimidation did not suffice. Conveniently for Mussolini his one rival Duce, D'Annunzio, who might have claimed the leadership, fell on his head from a balcony after quarrelling with his mistress. It was rumoured that the poet's fall had been assisted. A touch of opera was never entirely absent from the dramatic moments of Italian history.

Yet a fascist victory was far from certain. It was a great gamble, as Mussolini knew while he waited in Milan, a fascist stronghold not too far from the Swiss frontier, in case of failure. The King, Victor Emmanuel III, held the key to the situation. Loyalty to the dynasty was strong and it seems most probable that the army, though infiltrated by fascists from the highest-ranking officers to the most junior, would have responded to his lead and command. But there was nothing heroic about Victor Emmanuel. He did not put army loyalty to the test. Although a constitutional monarch, he must increasingly have lost confidence in the jockeying politicians and in the corruption of the electoral system. When his ministers finally found the courage to resist the threats of the fascists, the King refused them his backing and in doing so handed Italy over to Mussolini.

The government in Rome, after receiving news of the fascist uprising, of the seizure of government buildings in the provinces, was at first undecided how to act. It had already resigned in the process of another reshuffle but in the interim remained in charge. After a night of alarm, Luigi Facta, the temporary Prime Minister, having secured assurances of the loyalty of the army garrison in Rome, decided with the support of his ministers on a firm stand. The army was ordered to stop the fascist attempt to seize Rome. Early on the morning of 28 October 1922 an emergency decree was published which amounted to a proclamation of martial law. To this decree the King refused his assent and so it was revoked. The way was now open to Mussolini to state his terms. He demanded that he be asked to head the new government. The King's action had left the state without power at this critical moment. The government was discredited and so was the Crown when Mussolini, arriving comfortably in Rome in a railway sleeping-car on the morning of 30 October, accepted from the King the commission to form a new government. Thus the march on Rome occurred *after* and not before Mussolini's assumption of the premiership. There was never in fact a 'seizure' of power – though fascist historiography embroidered and glorified the event – only a *threat* to seize power. The fascists also did not *march* on Rome but were conveyed in special trains to the capital and there reviewed by the King and the Duce before being quickly packed off home on 31 October. Yet without the threat of seizing power Mussolini would not have achieved his ends. The threat was real, though whether he would have succeeded if he had attempted to seize control of Rome is another, much more debatable, question.

Now that Mussolini was in power he had no programme to place before parliament. He had concerned himself solely with the problem of how to attain power. Should he complete the 'revolution' now, as the fascist militants expected, or should he manipulate the parliamentary system and seek to govern at least pseudo-constitutionally? Should the Fascist Party replace the state or should it be subordinated to the state? These important questions, often asked, are in fact somewhat unreal. What mattered to Mussolini now that he had attained power was to retain as much of it personally in his hands for as long as possible. He had no principles or methods and despite talk of a new corporative state all relationships with existing institutions and organisations possessing some power in the state were subordinated to his will. His own fascist backers in this sense posed as much of an obstacle to him as political opponents, the monarchy, the papacy, the army and the bureaucracy. 'Policy' was what Mussolini felt best served his interests in dealing with every group.

Did Mussolini establish a 'totalitarian' regime? The monarchy was preserved, and the Church and the armed forces enjoyed some independence, while the independence of parliament was virtually destroyed. But Mussolini avoided a sudden revolutionary break; he allowed some degree of independence, believing this to serve his interests. He lacked in any case the iron will, utter ruthlessness and total inhumanity of Hitler. Rather than make the Fascist Party supreme, Mussolini preferred to leave some delegated power in the hands of rival interest groups so that his task of domination would be made easier. Mussolini understood in his early years before self-delusion blinded

him that some voluntary limits on his exercise of power would make him more acceptable and so strengthen his hold over government. The Duce was a complex character whose undoubted arrogance and insensitivity was complemented by intelligence and unusual political skill.

In October 1922 Mussolini made himself the head of a government which looked not so different to previous government coalitions based on personal bargaining. Included were the Catholics and Conservatives. Mussolini, in addition to holding the premiership, was also minister of the interior and his own foreign minister. He won an overwhelming vote of confidence in parliament for this government. His objective of breaking the political power of other parties by inveigling the majority to co-operate with him in national tasks was attained slowly but surely. When he felt sufficiently strong and secure, he backed a fascist bill for parliamentary 'reform', the Acerbo bill. In place of proportional representation this bill established that the party gaining most votes (as long as these amounted to at least 25 per cent of the total) should automatically secure two-thirds of all the seats in the Chamber of Deputies. Since the fascists were infiltrating and taking over the provincial administrations, they would be able to ensure in any case that more than a quarter of the votes were cast for the list of government candidates. The bill passed in November 1923 made certain that Mussolini would have at his disposal a permanent majority of deputies ready to do his will. The morale of any intending opposition parties was consequently undermined. Intimidation played its part in persuading the deputies lamely to consent to Mussolini's retention of power by legal and constitutional means. He always hinted he could act differently, especially as he now had a private army, the former fascist bands, which had been transformed into a voluntary militia of national security paid for by the state and swearing allegiance to the Duce, not the King.

The elections of April 1924 were a triumph for Mussolini. Intimidation and corruption to a degree not practised before secured for his candidates two-thirds of all the votes cast. The year 1924 was the last, nevertheless, in which Mussolini could have been driven from power. There was a revulsion of feeling in the country when a socialist deputy, Giacomo Matteotti, was murdered by a fascist gang after he had attacked the corrupt elections in parliament. Mussolini was taken aback by the sense of outrage; he was accused in parliament in June 1924 of being an accomplice of murder, and a group of opposition deputies withdrew in protest. But the King did nothing. Mussolini rode out this, his first and last serious storm before his fall in 1943. In 1926 his regime became more openly totalitarian with the suppression of the free press.

Just as Mussolini did not wish to be dependent on a genuine representative assembly, so he did not intend to be at the mercy of fascist followers more revolutionary than he. In December 1922 he created a Grand Council of Fascism over which he presided and which he dominated. In October 1926 it was the turn of the independence of the Fascist Party to be undermined; all elections within the party were henceforth ended; the party was organised from above with Mussolini as its supreme head. Within two years the party was bureaucratised and its violent activities outside the law curbed.

The Pope and the Catholic Church were another powerful and independent focus of power in the state. With remarkable skill, Mussolini, an avowed atheist, succeeded in reducing the political influence of the Church. It had not been so hostile to fascism as might have been expected, since it saw in fascism a bulwark against atheistic communism and socialism. The threat of socialism had already brought the Church back into the politics of the Italian state before the war (page 33). Mussolini built on this reconciliation of state and Church. The outcome of long negotiations from 1926 to 1929 was the Lateran Accords; by recognising papal sovereignty over the Vatican City, the state returned to the papacy a token temporal dominion in Italy; furthermore Catholicism was recognised as the sole religion of the state, and much of the anti-clerical legislation was repealed. The treaty won for the Church a position in Italy it had not enjoyed since unification. Judged as *Realpolitik* Vatican diplomacy was successful. But what of the moral standing of the Church? It was to be compromised even more when the Vatican attempted to preserve Catholic interests in Germany by concluding a concordat with Hitler in 1933. Temporary advantages led to long-term damage. The Church was inhibited from taking a clear moral stand and from condemning outright the crimes against humanity which the dictators in the end committed. Official Catholic protest tended to be muted (more so under Pius XII after 1939 than under Pius XI) though individual priests, including the Pope, sought to protect persecuted individuals.

The positive contribution of fascism was supposed to be the introduction of the 'corporate state'. This was based on the idea that, instead of being fought out, conflicts of interest were to be negotiated under the guidance of the state in bodies known as corporations. Thus in 1925 the employers' federation and the fascist trade unions recognised each other as equal partners, and corporations to settle differences in many different branches of industry, agriculture and education were envisaged. A huge bureaucratic structure was built up under a Ministry of Corporations. The industrialists nevertheless largely preserved their autonomy from the state. Not so the representatives of labour – labour was now represented in the corporations by fascist bureaucrats. The workers were exploited and even their basic right to move from one job to another without official permission was taken away. Real wages fell sharply, and fascism, despite some spectacular schemes such as the expansion of wheat-growing in the 1930s, and drainage of marsh land, could not propel the under-developed economy forward. Economically, Italy remained backward and labour ceased to make social advances. The increasing fascist bureaucracy, moreover, was a heavy burden to bear. Massive propaganda showing happy Italians and the Duce stripped to the waist in the fields might fool foreigners but could not better the lot of the poor.

The cult of the Duce was substituted for genuine progress. He posed as world leader, as the greatest military genius and economic sage, as the man who had transformed the civilised Italian people into conquering Romans. His conquests in the 1920s were meagre, however. In Libya and Somalia his troops fought savagely to reduce poorly armed tribesmen. After ten years of fighting they were subjected. In no way was this a glorious military episode. In the Balkans and the Middle East there was little he could do without British and French acquiescence. He tried in 1923, defying the League of Nations by seizing the island of Corfu from the Greeks, using as a pretext the murder of an Italian in Greece. But Britain and France intervened and, after finding a face-saving formula, Mussolini had to withdraw. He did, however, secure Fiume for Italy in the following year. All in all it was not very heroic. For the rest, Mussolini unsuccessfully tried to exploit Balkan differences and sought the limelight by signing many treaties. Before the rise of

Hitler, Mussolini had few real opportunities to exploit Western differences in order to fulfil his designs of imperial grandeur. So he was misjudged abroad as a sensible statesman in the 1920s. Conservatives even admired the superficial order he had imposed on Italy's rich and varied life. The 1930s were to reveal to the world what his opponents in Italy and the colonies had already learnt to their cost – the less benevolent aspects of Mussolini's rule.

# PART IV

*The Continuing World Crisis,*
*1929–1939*

# CHAPTER 19

# The Depression, 1929–1939

The despair of poverty is hard to imagine for those who have never suffered it. A decade after the conclusion of the Great War the era of the great depression began, reducing millions of people in the advanced Western world to the levels of grinding poverty suffered throughout the twentieth century by humanity in Asia, South America and Africa. The peoples living in the empires of the West now fell even below the barest subsistence levels as the price they could obtain for their raw materials dropped precipitously. Their economies were dependent on the demand of the West. Whatever befell the industrialised West, the effects on the poor of what we now call the Third World were even more catastrophic. The great depression, usually considered solely in terms of the ills affecting the industrialised countries, should be seen in its worldwide setting. At the time only one country appeared immune – the Soviet Union, where industrial production increased. It was a persuasive argument to some that communism provided the only solution to the periodic booms and depressions which bedevilled the trade cycle. But in the Soviet Union, Stalin's state planning actually imposed hardships as great and greater than anything happening in the West (Chapter 20).

The impact of the economic crisis on politics and society was immense in the West, second only to that of the Great War. The effect of the depression was aggravated by its occurring before the trauma of the Great War had been overcome. It is the shortness of time that elapsed between one shock and the next that gives the years from 1919 to 1939 their particular characteristic when compared with the long period of growing prosperity in the West before 1914 and the growth that occurred during the thirty-five years after 1945. In contrast, 1919 to 1939 came to be viewed as a 'continuing world crisis'. The industrial depression that began in 1929 had been preceded by an agricultural depression dating from 1921, not really overcome in the mid-1920s, and then rapidly deepening after 1926. The 'boom years' of industrial expansion of the 1920s thus were not as uniformly prosperous as often supposed. For all its startling psychological repercussions, the Wall Street crash on 'black Tuesday', 29 October 1929, did not cause the depression. The Western world, despite its attempts to return to the 'normality' of the pre-1914 years, was unable to do so after the Great War. Indeed, in this desire to return to the past there was an insufficient recognition of how enormously the war had dislocated the workings of the world economy. No radical new international financial initiatives were believed to be required to cope with the situation. Instead each nation sought to return to pre-war practices, some like Britain to the gold standard, sound money and balanced budgets.

The new problem of Allied war debts and German reparations did necessitate a fresh approach and international discussion and co-operation. During the 1920s, before 1931 when all these payments came practically to a halt, the international settlements followed a circular route of German

*The Global Depression.* Left: *in China, as everywhere, the common denominator is destitution.* Right: *an unemployed war veteran in Hanover in 1932 has little to thank Weimar democracy for.* Below left: *an American family escapes the Oklahoma 'dust bowl' in June 1938.* Below right: *a French soup kitchen at Ivry in 1934.*

*Anxious New Yorkers mill around Wall Street during the Crash of October 1929 wondering how bad it's going to get.*

reparations payments constantly scaled down, making possible the payment of Allied debts to the United States also scaled down, while American loans to Germany, exceeding German reparations payments, completed the circle. This was not very sensible financially, but the actual sums involved, though not the principal cause of the breakdown of world trade, contributed to the disruption of international finance by the end of the decade. The causes of the depression are so complex that they remain a matter of lively debate among experts. It is best here to make a number of brief points.

Study of the economic development of each Western nation reveals how far the depression of the 1930s had causes going back even before the First World War. As has been seen, Britain, for example, continued to rely on textile, coal and ship-building industries of the first industrial revolution, and was shifting only slowly, too slowly, to industries of the more advanced technology of the twentieth century. This lack of progress caused continuous and heavy unemployment even during the 1920s, when only in one year did unemployment drop below 10 per cent of the workforce.

The United States provided a contrast with the massive growth of new consumer industries such

as the automobile industry and with unemployment at around only 4 per cent. The problem here was that these new industries did not produce necessities and the decision not to buy a new car because of a lack of faith in the future could produce a sudden reversal of fortunes in manufacturing industry. But it was not until 1931 that unemployment became the serious kind of problem that it had been in Britain throughout the 1920s. The French economy was different again, with half the population engaged in agriculture. But post-war reconstruction favoured the rise of new industries (as in Germany after the Second World War) and by 1930 France had emerged strengthened, even requiring foreign labour to augment the native labour force. The effect of the worldwide depression was stagnation throughout the 1930s.

In Germany the impact of the world economic crisis was conditioned by the particular experiences of Germans since the lost war. Having once experienced hyperinflation which made money worthless (page 136), the German government was determined to preserve sound money regardless of the cost in terms of unemployment. Agricultural prosperity had suffered a serious setback some two years before in 1929, while German industry boomed. The later 1920s saw the formation of large industrial cartels and the introduction of new technology. Germany not only financed this modernisation by attracting loans from the United States but also paid off reparations from loans. Other American loans financed unproductive municipal projects such as town halls and swimming baths. Much of this loan capital could be recalled at short notice and when this happened in 1929 the German economy, already affected by declining international markets, threatened to spin out of control. The largest Western percentage of unemployed was Germany's in 1932 with 30 per cent out of work.

The state of the United States economy was the common denominator in the world economic crisis. The American economy had assumed such importance that the other Western economies depended on its good health. There is thus pretty general agreement that the origins of great worldwide depression are to be sought in the United States. With the American economy running down, the prices of raw materials slumped; markets all over the world contracted as a result. When the United States reduced the flow of capital abroad, and in 1930 created a prohibitive tariff which prevented the European powers from selling their goods in the United States, the rest of the world could no longer cope.

There were weaknesses in the economic structure of European nations which had already made themselves felt, as in Britain, before 1929. The American recession turned these problems into one of the most severe crises these countries had ever experienced. The depression proved to be not just a short downturn in the business cycle, as had been expected. The bad year from 1929 to 1930 was followed by an even worse year in 1931. When 1932 brought no relief, hope of an automatic upturn collapsed. World economic conditions did improve from the low point of 1931–2 but only gradually. The world depression continued down to the Second World War, which, like the First, transformed economic activity and absorbed the unemployed to feed the war machine. So long and deep a depression was a new experience and governments were frequently at a loss as to how best to handle the economic problems of their day. Sometimes, as in Germany from 1931 to 1933, they made matters worse.

The depression also provided a test for the different forms of government by which the peoples of the world were ruled. The performance of different governments was inevitably judged by ordinary people according to how effective they perceived them to be in finding remedies for the ills of depression, unemployment foremost among them. In people's minds, the communist, the various fascist and Nazi 'models', the conduct of the democratic governments, as well as colonial rule, could in these circumstances be uniquely compared.

Any government and political system which happened to exist during the early depression years was bound to be blamed for the widespread misery. But those authoritarian governments that were already firmly established by 1929 were in a better position to maintain themselves by brute force and to manipulate the attitudes of the masses through propaganda. Popular discontent could no longer threaten the Soviet system of communist rule. The Western colonial empires were under firm military control. Mussolini stifled protest: strikes were prohibited by law; the Italian state set low rates of interest; and the Institute for Industrial Reconstruction was created in January 1933 to assist Italian banks, which in turn led to the state assuming direct responsibility for a range of industry from shipping to steel. Unemployment in Italy nevertheless remained stubbornly high in the early 1930s and the standard of living persistently low. Yet there was no open criticism as Mussolini advertised himself, photographed stripped to the waist with spade in hand and working on public works projects such as draining the marshes or extending land for wheat cultivation.

Hitler came to power during the most serious period of depression and he quickly consolidated dictatorial power. Nevertheless it was his evident success in reducing unemployment in Germany from 6 million in October 1933 to just over 4 million a year later and 2.8 million in 1935 that so increased national popular support for him. Rearmament and army expansion after 1936 virtually eliminated unemployment in Germany. Whatever evils came to be associated with Hitler's rule in the eyes of the German people, they gave Hitler credit for 'curing' unemployment. Hitler recognised that he could turn the prevailing despair to his advantage if he could infuse a spirit of action, convey his understanding and concern for the plight of the unemployed and actually put people to work. His success was not instantaneous; it was achieved, moreover, by forcibly destroying the independence of labour. It was achieved, too, in the face of traditional banking advice. Hitler listened to the Keynesian-type econ-omists in Germany who had met with rejection by Brüning (page 199). Hjalmar Schacht, who returned as president of the Reichsbank, created large paper credits. Money was spent on new super-highways – the *Autobahnen*, which had military value – on expanding rearmament and on support for agriculture. The Nazi economy was tightly controlled by the state in order to achieve self-sufficiency in agriculture – and as far as possible in industry – without replacing the actual private ownership of industry or the land.

At the price of liberty, the Nazi economy from 1933 to 1939 was remarkably successful in main-taining stable prices, full employment eventually and a modest rise in the standard of living of the working man. Rearmament was not allowed to cut standards of living drastically. Hitler was anxious to win and retain German support by providing economic and social benefits, and used violence only against open opponents from the beginning and against the Jews from 1938. The authoritarian models' good points, which were proclaimed by their own captive press, radio and film, impressed the unemployed in the democracies more than the bad. Democratic governments requiring the co-operation of parliament looked less effective and more cumbersome by comparison.

Poincaré's government of national union had restored French finances to health in 1926 (page 146). The elections of 1928 had given the right a great victory, but his retirement a year later, sick and worn out, marked the end of an era in which France had attempted to reassert her standing as a great power in Europe, and coincided also with the time when the depression became more serious worldwide. French governments after Poincaré lost their stability once more: between 1929 and 1934 they lasted an average of three or four months. Albert Lebrun, elected president in 1932, remained until the fall of France in 1940, but he was a colourless politician who gave no kind of lead. At first the strength of France's financial position seemed to make her immune, alone among the Western nations, from the débâcle following the crash in October 1929 in the United States. Throughout 1930 unemployment remained low. But in the autumn of 1931 the slump and unemploy-ment finally spread to France. French governments now sought by financial 'orthodoxy' to meet the

crisis, simultaneously cutting pensions, salaries and public expenditure. The cessation of German repar-ation payments in 1931, coupled with the Americans' continuing insistence on repayment of debts, compounded the difficulty. Despite devaluing once in 1928, successive governments until 1936 added to France's problems by refusing to devalue an overvalued franc which made the task of exporting increasingly hard. During the worst years from 1933 to 1934 the survival of the Republic herself seemed very doubtful. Big business and the extreme right admired the fascist model as an authoritarian solution behind which they could operate profitably. Among politicians of the right, Pierre Laval and André Tardieu as well as Marshal Pétain, the hero of Verdun, inclined towards some sort of authoritarian resolution for the troubles and divisions of the Republic.

The unpopular measures of successive French governments in a parliamentary Chamber of predominantly centre and left-wing parties, as well as fear of communism, played into the hands of the right. The socialists led by Léon Blum would not join any coalition government which included the 'bourgeois' Radical-Socialists, whose main support came from the conservative peasantry and the middle classes and whose aims were not in the least socialist. The communists under Maurice Thorez meanwhile followed the Moscow line of the Comin-tern, which ordered them to regard the Democratic Socialist Party as their greatest enemy. So govern-ments were formed mainly by the Radical parliamentary leaders seeking alignments to the right. The impact of the depression gravely weak-ened and divided the left, with the communists until 1934 pursuing an apparently insane tactic of undermining the stability of the Republic that might well have helped fascism to power in France as it had done earlier in Germany. The realisation of the folly of the Moscow course dawned on Thorez and in 1934 he became a leading and successful advocate of changing it.

The years 1933 and 1934 also saw the growth in France of paramilitary fascist 'leagues' whose bands of rowdies brawled in the streets of Paris like Nazi stormtroopers. There was the royalist Action Française, the oldest of the leagues founded before the First World War. Another was the Jeunesses Patriotes composed mainly of students. François Coty, the perfume millionaire, financed the Solidarité Française and a fascist journal, *L'Ami du peuple*. The most important of these leagues was the Croix de Feu, made up of war veterans led by Colonel de la Rocque, whose main aim was the negative one of overthrowing the parliamentary Republic. Royalism, extreme Catholicism, anti-Semitism, other movements inspired by Mussolini's and Hitler's example, all had little in common except a determination to undermine the Republic. With this aim the politically opposite Communist Party at first also agreed, and the communists were even ready to work in parallel with fascists to achieve this object. The leagues were supported by numerous vicious Parisian newspapers which were constantly stirring up popular hatred against the legislators.

At the worst possible moment, with the government discredited by its instability and inept handling of the depression, with financial hardship deepening and polarising class antagonism, the politicians were smeared with the taint of corruption by what became known as the Stavisky scandal. Stavisky was a swindler who had through the years floated a number of bonds and shares which defrauded the investors. Although arrested, he had enjoyed a strange immunity from trial, in the meantime making more money from shady deals. In January 1934 he had finally shot himself and the police, who could have saved his life, allowed him to die. It was rumoured that his death had shielded highly placed politicians and the police from the revelation of their involvement in his crimes and in these allegations there was undoubtedly some truth. All the anti-parliamentary forces seized on the scandal to make a concerted effort to overthrow not only the government but the Republic. The members of the various leagues were summoned in their thousands on to the streets of Paris to oust the politicians. The climax was reached during the night of 6 February 1934 when street battles raged in Paris, the police and Garde Mobile narrowly gaining the upper hand. Hundreds of demonstrators were wounded, some seriously, and it is surprising that the death toll – some eighteen people – was relatively small. The supposedly strong government under the Radical Prime Minister Édouard Daladier turned out to be weak after all and promptly resigned. The Republic was saved by a few of its resolute defenders among the Paris police, by luck and above all by the total disunity of the leaders of the right. There was no Hitler or even Mussolini among them.

Weak French governments which could find no solution to the political, social and economic prob-

lems succeeded each other during the next two years. The elections of May 1936, however, seemed to herald a turning point: the parties of the left – the Socialists and communists – together with the Radicals had by then formed an electoral alliance, the Popular Front. This extraordinary change had been made possible by the *volte face* of the French Communist Party. In June 1934 the communists and Socialists had overcome their mutual suspicions to join in a United Front to fight fascism. The reasons for the change have fascinated historians, for the communists had regarded the Democratic Socialists, or 'social fascists' as they called them, as their worst enemies. They accused them of leading the proletariat away from the true goal of communist revolution under the guise of representing the working people's class interests. The fascists, on the other hand, could be recognised as the enemy of the proletariat and were but a passing phenomenon associated with the later stages of capitalism before its inevitable demise.

Outside the Soviet Union, some of the communist parties which subscribed to the Soviet-controlled Comintern began to question these doctrinaire views. How could all Social Democrats be regarded as enemies when they were fighting the same foe as in Austria, where the Social Democrats forcibly resisted the authoritarian clerical Dollfuss government and were in 1934 bombarded in Vienna into submission (page 219)? In Germany Hitler's Nazis looked like consolidating their power. Communists languished in concentration camps, their party organisation smashed up. There was a serious danger that fascism would win power in other European countries. The French communist leader, Maurice Thorez, became especially fearful of a fascist triumph in France. The French Communist Party took the lead in creating a new United Front with the socialists. They could not have openly disobeyed the Comintern in Moscow. But the Soviet leadership was divided and persuaded by the brilliant Bulgarian communist leader, George Dimitrov, the hero of the Reichstag fire trial,[1] to allow some latitude and experimentation of tactics. From the summer of 1934 onwards Thorez pushed on, the Soviet leaders acquiescing. The socialist and communist trade unions merged. Not satisfied with a socialist alliance alone, Thorez

---

[1] For the Reichstag fire, see page 201. Dimitrov was among those in Berlin accused of organising the fire; he defied and taunted the Nazis and was acquitted.

*Riots in Paris on 6 February 1934 on the Place de la Concorde. But the republic survives.*

extended the alignment even further to include the 'bourgeois' Radicals, and so turned the United Front into the much broader Popular Front. The electoral pact of the three parties – Socialist, communist and Radical – gave the Popular Front electoral victory over the right in the spring of 1936 and brought Léon Blum to power as prime minister. Though the Radicals did least well, the communists gained greatly and the three parties together won 378 seats against the right's 220. The electoral arrangements, rather than a large shift in the voting, had achieved this result. But French society remained more divided than ever. This polarisation was as important as the election results. Léon Blum had taken no part in the elections. He had been nearly beaten to death in the street when fanatics of the Action Française had set upon him. He was fortunately rescued by building workers who happened to be nearby. That was the other side of French politics.

The right now assailed Blum, who headed the Popular Front government, not only for serving as a cover for the communists, but also as an alien, as a Jew. In few countries outside Nazi Germany was anti-Semitism as crude and virulent as in some sections of French society. Blum was sensitive to these attacks; he followed in the socialist traditions of pacifism and humane consideration for the poor. He could never quite rise above the viciousness of the onslaught on him and too self-consciously sought to prove himself a patriot and conciliator. In his Cabinet when facing opposition he was prone to indecision and weakness, as became very clear when the Popular Front government in Madrid appealed to France for help at the outset of the Spanish Civil War (page 225). There was every reason why the French Popular Front government should help republican Spain with arms, not only on ideological grounds but also because a fascist victory threatened to encircle France. This too was Blum's view. But the outcry of the right and the weakness of his Radical and Socialist ministerial colleagues changed Blum's mind and he reversed his earlier decision to respond to Madrid's appeal.

In domestic affairs, Blum's government scored one spectacular success. At the time that he took office, France was hit by a huge wave of strikes and factory sit-ins. Discontent with low wages and poor working conditions in industry and on the land had finally led to this confrontation which served notice to the politicians that as in other Western countries – except, of course, in fascist Italy and Nazi Germany – organised labour demanded basic rights and higher wages. The employers and propertied were thoroughly frightened. Blum brought the employers and the trade unionists – the Confédération Générale du Travail – together at his official residence, the Hôtel Matignon on Sunday, 7 June. After a night's discussion there emerged a package: a substantial wage increase, two weeks' paid holiday, a forty-hour week and, most important of all, the employers' acceptance of the trade unions' bargaining rights; in return the unions would persuade the workers to end their sit-ins and the strikes. Believing themselves on the verge of social revolution, parliament rushed this constructive legislation through in a few days – an uncharacteristic show of good sense and urgency. Industrial peace was restored for a time. But the impact of the Blum government on the health of the economy was small, despite the belated devaluation of the franc in October 1936. Blum was determined to work pacifically, by seeking the co-operation of big business and high finance, which loathed all his government stood for. There was to be no enforced socialism. After a year, the stagnating economy and price rises had wiped out much of the advantage the workers had gained by wage rises.

*Premier Léon Blum with his wife, among friends, in July 1936.*

Soon after coming to office, Blum banned the 'leagues'. This proved as ineffectual as in Germany in 1932. The leagues assumed a new 'legitimate' political garb – but the street brawling continued as before. A particularly violent clash between the communists and the right in March 1937 ended in bloodshed; it horrified Blum and damaged the reputation of the Popular Front. Blum was ready to resign immediately but carried on in the end. He resigned three months later, in June 1937, disillusioned and frustrated in his domestic and foreign policies, when a hostile Senate, dominated by the Radicals, refused to give him the powers he had asked for so that his government could deal with the financial crisis. For a further year a hollowed-out Popular Front continued. The disunity of the left, its weakness, the bitterness of class war, which even took the form of making it fashionable on the right to mouth 'better Hitler than Blum', allowed government to fall into the hands of a coalition of the disunited Radicals and the right. Édouard Daladier in April 1938 emerged as another supposedly 'strong' man whose actual performance belied his reputation. His finance minister, Paul Reynaud, tried to restore the economy by increased taxation and a longer working week. The employers, recovered from the early days of the Popular Front, were able to redress the balance again in their favour but at the expense of social bitterness. The repercussions for world peace of France's feebleness were immense. It was a misfortune that all this occurred when across France's eastern frontier a determined and ruthless dictator was taking full advantage of the French political and social crisis.

Political division at the centre of government in the years between the wars did not lie at the root of Britain's social and economic difficulties. Indeed it is difficult to think of any two decades of British history where there was such unanimity. The Liberal Party never recovered sufficiently to provide an alternative government. The role was taken over by the Labour Party. Labour had briefly formed a minority government in 1924, and then again from 1929 to 1931. Just three years after the conclusion of the General Strike, Baldwin in May 1929 went to the country confident of electoral victory. The total Labour vote (8.4 million) was slightly lower than the Conservative (8.7 million), but the constituency electoral system gave Labour more seats, 289 against the Conservatives' 260, while lack of proportional representation penalised the Liberals who, despite their 5.3 million votes, gained only 59 seats. But the really perverse fact of the election of 1929 was that there was less practical difference between Ramsay MacDonald's brand of Labour policies and the policies of the Conservatives than between the policies of either party and those of the Liberals. It was the Liberals who put forward a radically different economic strategy masterminded by the most famous economic thinker of the age, John Maynard Keynes. He and others produced the pre-election plan *Britain's Industrial Future*, which advocated government spending as the spearhead to industrial revival. 'We Can Conquer Unemployment' was Lloyd George's more popular election version of this plan. Lloyd George, with his own 'brains trust' behind him, was ready to provide the British people with their 'New Deal'. But there was to be no political comeback for Lloyd George. His new remedies were never tried, at least not until after the Second World War.

Labour became the alternative to the Conservatives. Its leadership was anxious not to present the party as too socialist, let alone as revolutionary, as the communists had no electoral appeal. The left wing of the Labour movement found itself isolated, shunned both by the communists who were following the Comintern line of fighting the 'social fascists' and by the bulk of the trade unions and the moderate Labour right. Despite Ramsay MacDonald's commitment to a Labour Party whose theoretical aim was to transform capitalism into socialism, as leader of the party he saw this as some very distant objective, certainly not practical politics in 1929. From that day to the present, the precise definition of what should constitute the Labour's definition of 'democratic socialism' rent the party. The predominant majority of the Labour Party always stood behind leaders who warned that to embrace far-reaching socialist measures, such as bringing the greater part of industry under state control, would alienate the electorate and condemn the party to permanent opposition. The move to the left needed to be gradual and pragmatic.

In fact the Labour minority government which MacDonald formed in June 1929 largely excluded the Labour left. The electoral programme had soft-pedalled socialism and the whole issue of public ownership, except for the coal industry (and even the Conservatives were to move eventually towards some form of state supervision over the coal industry); quite likely Labour owed its electoral success to this stance of 'respectability'. Philip Snowden, Chancellor of the Exchequer; was as orthodox, as sternly opposed to unbalanced budgets and as fearful of inflation as any Conservative chancellor. It is true that MacDonald's government might have been ousted if it had followed policies on which the Conservatives and Liberals would have combined against Labour. The survival of the government was his first priority. But it must also be noted that MacDonald held back from radical policies – such as new measures for dealing with unemployment – which would have secured Liberal support.

The single biggest problem facing Britain at home throughout the 1920s was unemployment, which persisted at over 1 million, more than 10 per cent of the labour force. This average for the whole country does not reveal its full seriousness, since unemployment was far more severe in the Clydeside of Scotland and Tyneside in north-east England where shipbuilding was in the doldrums, in the coal-mining valleys of South Wales, in Ulster and in the textile region of south Lancashire. Whole regions were blighted, sunk in poverty with unemployment persisting year after year. The famous hunger marches to London in the 1930s helped to draw the 'forgotten' regions to the attention of the more prosperous Midlands and southern England. It brought home to the man in the street the desperate and seemingly hopeless plight of the unemployed. The coming to power of the Labour government was followed within a few weeks by the Wall Street crash. The effects of the American depression soon spread to Britain. Unemployment rapidly rose. The government attempted nothing that might have stemmed this rise. Within the government Oswald Mosley, taking his cue from Keynes, recommended radical measures to deal with unemployment. He resigned from the government in May 1930 having failed to persuade his colleagues, and eventually left the party after his motion against government unemployment policies was defeated at the party conference in October and further efforts to change the party's policies proved fruitless. His authoritarian inclinations have obscured the question whether his economic judgements were sound. Once considered a potential leader of the Labour Party, he came to lead instead the British Union of Fascists and left the mainstream of British politics.

*The indomitable British MP Ellen Wilkinson leading the Jarrow hunger marchers on the road to London, October 1936.*

Labour's meagre legislative record, with unemployment rising to 2.8 million by the summer of 1931, had severely weakened MacDonald's standing in both the country and in the Labour Party when the financial crisis hit London. The Labour government had sought to follow financial policies acceptable to the orthodox bankers and adopted a course above parties – thus diminishing its independence of action. Policy recommendations were left to commissions and committees of experts. These orthodox financiers now recommended that government expenditure be cut by lowering wages of government employees, by reducing unemployment benefits and by raising new taxation. MacDonald's colleagues baulked, but eventually agreed to most of these measures. They went much against the grain even of the Labour moderates. When MacDonald insisted, on the advice of the bankers, on the full cuts, a minority of the Cabinet backed by the General Council of the Trades Union Congress, which opposed all cuts, would not accept further economies. The realisation was growing that the government in simply giving in to the financiers would separate itself from the bulk of the Labour movement. If the policy were necessary, would it not be better to have left it to the Opposition?

At the suggestion of the bankers, who urged MacDonald that the prime need was to restore international confidence in the government – a loan from the United States was said to be conditional on sufficiently stringent government economies – MacDonald and Snowden had already conferred with the leaders of the Opposition. At the height of the crisis King George V played a leading role in persuading MacDonald, Baldwin and the Liberals to join in a new 'national government'. Lloyd George, who might have blocked a coalition led by MacDonald, was in hospital. On 24 August 1931 the King's personal appeal was 'loyally' acceded to, such was still the inherent influence of the Crown. MacDonald on the next day headed a new national government with Baldwin serving under him. Only three Labour Cabinet ministers, including Snowden, followed MacDonald. The Labour Party formally rejected the national government and voted for a new leader. At the general election which followed in October 1931 the Labour Party suffered a devastating defeat. They could hold only fifty-two seats. The Conservatives won a corresponding victory of 471 seats and so an absolute majority. The Liberals were soon as badly split as Labour; after supporting the national government for a time about half the sixty-eight MPs in 1932 turned against it. MacDonald's National Labour following was reduced to thirteen. In all but name, Britain was ruled by the Conservatives until 1940. MacDonald had genuinely believed in a financial crisis and had been panicked into action which the Labour Party regarded as a betrayal.

What was the domestic record of the Conservative-National administrations, MacDonald's (1931–5), Baldwin's (1935–7) and Neville Chamberlain's (1937–40), in meeting the social and industrial ills of Britain? There can be no doubt that these governments followed policies which they believed would most effectively alleviate the distress of unemployment and would cure the sickness from which the British economy suffered. They did care. But their political philosophy and economic thinking precluded them from following the communist or fascist totalitarian remedies. They also rejected the notion that government could initiate public spending sufficiently large to mop up unemployment regardless of other harmful effects on the economy such spending would have had. The fact that the national government with its tiny Liberal and Labour components in parliament but backed by the overall Conservative majority could act decisively without fear of parliamentary defeat in itself helped to restore confidence. MacDonald, followed by Baldwin in 1935, presided over their cabinets as prime minister, but the rising star was Neville Chamberlain, who became chancellor of the Exchequer in the depth of the depression in November 1931. Winston Churchill might have become the real force in these governments of the 1930s had he not quarrelled with Baldwin and the Conservative majority when the Conservatives were still in opposition over how to deal with the problem of Indian nationalism. The Labour government supported by Baldwin wished to make concessions; Churchill thundered against appeasing Indian nationalism and resigned from the Conservative shadow Cabinet. It was a tragic misjudgement not only as regards India but possibly in its effect on world history. Churchill was politically isolated in the 1930s and when he warned against appeasing Hitler, most of the Conservatives did not listen.

The later 1930s belonged to Chamberlain not Churchill. Chamberlain tackled the economic problem with the characteristic vigour he had already displayed as minister of health in the 1920s. Nevertheless government policies were pretty cautious. They were less spectacular, but arguably more effective, than Roosevelt's in America. Chamberlain sought to create conditions which would allow British industry to revive. Recovery was not, however, all a matter of government economic planning. Equally important was the behaviour of the British people – those in employment – who by their spending gradually helped to lift Britain out of the slump.

Already in September 1931 Britain had gone off the gold standard and devalued her currency by a quarter so as to make British exports more competitive. She followed the United States in adopting a protective tariff to discourage competitive imports from abroad; a limited degree of imperial preference was agreed by the Imperial Economic Conference at Ottawa of July/August 1932, which lowered mutual tariffs in the Commonwealth, stimulating empire trade. Currency control was introduced and not eased until 1979 (it was abolished soon after). Cheap credit stimulated the domestic economy, especially in the house-building trade. Schemes of direct government subsidies and marketing boards also greatly aided the British farmer. The government sought to rationalise and produce a more uniform system of unemployment benefits. The intentions were good, but the resulting family 'means tests', which investigated whether a whole family had sufficient for its needs even if one of its members was out of work, came to symbolise the heartless bureaucracy of what was intended as a sensible policy. The echoes of the resulting bitterness made themselves felt for decades.

Class distinction was more acceptable to the man in the street in good times, or in the war when common hardships and dangers were being shared by the upper and lower classes in the trenches. In the 1930s the increasing division between rich and poor, employed and unemployed, left bitter memories of Conservative rule that not even Winston Churchill's personal popularity could overcome in 1945. The Prince of Wales, by his well-publicised concern for the misery of the unemployed, did something to bridge the gap. The abdication crisis of November and December 1936, which forced Edward VIII to renounce the throne unless he gave up his proposed marriage to the divorced Mrs Simpson, was seen by some embittered working men as a manoeuvre to get rid of a king who sympathised with them.

Unemployment, nevertheless, in the mid-1930s

was slowly declining. It never reached the proportions of German and American unemployment at their peak in 1932–3, and fell steadily from 1933 to 1937 from just under 3 million to 1.7 million. Even with rearmament getting under way thereafter, it did not fall below 1 million and since it was heavily concentrated in the depressed areas it actually varied from 26 per cent in Northern Ireland and 24 per cent in Wales to 6 per cent in the Midlands. Such gestures as subsidising the completion of the liner *Queen Mary* on the Clyde and other limited public schemes could not touch the hard-core unemployment problems of these regions. This, rather than the fact that total production in 1934 exceeded the level of 1929, was what made the deepest impact on the public mind in the 1930s.

**Unemployment** (*percentage of total labour force*)

|      | Britain | Germany | United States |
|------|---------|---------|---------------|
| 1923 | 8.1     | 9.6     | 2.4           |
| 1930 | 11.2    | 15.3    | 8.7           |
| 1931 | 15.1    | 23.3    | 15.9          |
| 1932 | 15.6    | 30.1    | 23.6          |
| 1933 | 14.1    | 26.3    | 24.9          |
| 1934 | 11.9    | 14.9    | 21.7          |
| 1935 | 11.0    | 11.6    | 20.1          |
| 1936 | 9.4     | 8.3     | 16.9          |
| 1937 | 7.8     | 4.6     | 14.3          |
| 1938 | 9.3     | 2.1     | 19.0          |

One serious consequence of the depression was that the democracies became preoccupied with problems at home. Chamberlain saw rearmament as a waste of national resources. Gradually recovery was proceeding. For those in work living standards were rising rather than falling. War threatened the better way of life governments were seeking to achieve for their peoples. But it was the war effort that alone 'cured' unemployment in Britain and the United States.

The social consequences of the depression, the despair of the unemployed, the failure to provide adequately for the poor and the sick, the undernourishment of millions of children, unhealthy slum housing and many other ills in the early years of the 1930s turned the mass of people on the continent of Europe towards a search for new solutions. Since Stalin's Russia appeared to have found the answer to banishing the capitalist trade cycle, communism attracted millions. Their support was given not only for materialistic but also for idealistic reasons. Communists fought fascism and in claiming to provide a better and healthier life for the poor acted in a way that seemed ethical and good. The realities of Stalin's tyrannical regime were unknown to many, overlooked or explained away. Mussolini and Hitler were seen by other millions as the saviours who would restore a sense of national unity, orderly government and employment to their people. They had many admirers outside Italy and Germany, even some in Britain. The deep divisions and the turmoil in France discredited parliamentary government in this part of Europe too. In Britain, the Labour government had ignominiously fallen, though Parliament itself survived the crisis. Humane and democratic socialism was everywhere the main victim. Such desperate conditions, millions of people felt, demanded not compromise but radical remedies. The left battled the right politically, in Spain even on the battlefield. But there was at least one country in Europe where humanity, democracy and social progress were safe and which did not follow the pattern of most of the rest of the continent.

Sweden had not bypassed the depression, but the economic slump led to the establishment of a democratic form of government which determined the social and economic policies of the country for almost six decades. Before 1932, the socialist parties on the one side and the liberals and conservatives on the other were evenly divided, and coalition governments frequently had to make do with parliamentary minorities. The same weakness, however, was not evident in the strong economic development of Sweden during the second half of the 1920s. She was ceasing to be a predominantly agricultural country: her steel, ballbearings and other advanced industrial products like telephones were in worldwide demand, in addition to her older exports such as woodpulp and matches. Nonetheless, in this large, under-populated northern region of Europe, farming continued to play an important role in the 1930's.

*Modernity on Endless Trial. Sweden has, for most of the twentieth century, been the quintessentially modern collectivist European nation-state. In the 1930s this formerly tradition-bound and orthodox country transformed itself into a model of innovation, organization and liberty. The state positively encouraged healthy living (top right), new freedoms (right), less divisive, punitive punishment – as in this hotel-like prison (left), and a minimum standard of living for all, which included durable, comfortable modern housing (top). But the* fin-de-siècle *mood brings re-evaluation, even here.*

The impact of the depression, at its height in 1932 and 1933, was devastating. One in three of the workforce was unemployed; many farmers could no longer meet their mortgages and were forced to sell. But Sweden recovered relatively quickly from the crash compared to the rest of Europe and she was politically strong and stable. The credit for this must go largely to the coalition administration of the Farmers' Party and the Social Democrats, led by the Social Democrat Per Albin Hansson. Hansson, born in 1885, was self-educated, having left school at the age of twelve. At eighteen he founded the Social Democratic Youth Movement. Prime minister in September 1932, he proved himself an outstanding parliamentary tactician and an able national leader, remaining continuously in office until his death in 1946. The compromise reached with the Farmers' Party was to abandon free trade and to promise minimum farm prices and other supports. For the industrial unemployed, relief works were launched and industrial revival encouraged. In the first three years of the administration, bills to promote active state intervention were passed, regulating the working hours of agricultural labourers, statutory holidays and unemployment insurance. The simple slogan was to make Sweden 'a home for all her people' and so to create social harmony.

By 1939 Sweden's unemployment problem had been solved and the plans for a welfare state had been worked out. The Social Democrats, since their election victory in 1936, had become the dominant political force in the country. The war postponed the extension of social welfare, but from 1946 to 1950 the reforms were enacted, including comprehensive old-age pensions, child allowances, health insurance and educational reforms. The Swedish people were to be safeguarded from 'cradle to grave', in sickness and in health. The socialist element of the government policies was to tax the better-off heavily to pay for the welfare state and to redistribute income, rather than to try to nationalise private industry. For once a utopian vision seemed to correspond to reality. Sweden and her people prospered. Swedish research, technology and design were second to none. After the death of Hansson, Targe Erlander succeeded to the premiership (1946–69). The Social Democratic dominance for all but six years since 1932 came to an end only in 1992.

Sweden exemplified a distinctive and much admired social, political and cultural way of life. The emphasis on closeness to nature and on individual choice and liberty extended to the sphere of sexual permissiveness long before it did so in the rest of Europe. In many areas of social reform Sweden was the pioneer. The Swedes enjoyed one of the highest standards of living in Europe, along with the Swiss, the Norwegians, the Finns, the Germans and the people of Luxembourg. Swedish society was egalitarian and unshakeably democratic, although it had to make readjustments in the early 1990s.

On Franklin Delano Roosevelt came to rest the hopes of those who continued to pin their faith on liberalism and democracy in the 1930s as providing a better answer to the world's ills than totalitarian leadership. Roosevelt's New Deal was to be the answer to those who in the crisis despaired of reconciling freedom with the measures necessary to bring about economic recovery. Keynes wrote in December 1933 that Roosevelt had made himself 'the trustee for those in every country who seek to mend the evils of our condition. If you [Roosevelt] fail, rational change will be gravely prejudiced throughout the world, leaving orthodoxy or revolution to fight it out.' The shortcomings of the New Deal are very evident to historians today. Unemployment remained obstinately high. It fell from some 13 million in 1933 to under 8 million in 1937 but it rose again to 9.5 million in 1939. In fact Roosevelt's administrations failed to 'cure' the blight and waste of human resources until the United States geared industry to war. But the attitude of the President and administration, brilliantly publicised, gave renewed hope to the nation and provided leadership without the destruction of democracy. There is thus a stark contrast between the general psychological impact of the New Deal and the real success of the many different laws, special agencies and programmes which constituted it.

The depression provided Roosevelt with the opportunity of attaining and retaining political power for more than a decade until his death in 1945. But its onset destroyed the political power of his predecessor at the White House, Herbert Hoover. Hoover in 1929 had begun his term at the moment of highest confidence. The failure of his economic policies to halt the steep rise in unemployment shattered his reputation. He had a clear concept of the role of the state. He wished to limit federal powers, which he warned would throttle individual initiative. He was by conviction a conservative, though he was willing to adopt new ways to stimulate business. His inability, nevertheless, to halt the steep slide into depression did more than discredit him personally, it also discredited the whole philosophy of minimal state intervention. But Hoover did act to contain the effects of the onset of the depression. He appealed to businessmen not to contract their activities and to maintain their workforce. He appealed to the banks to extend credit. Besides such exhortations, federal policies were limited – though in the right direction. The nation should help herself by enlightened *voluntary* co-operation between the different interest groups. Prosperity 'lay just around the corner'.

When the voluntary approach did not work, Hoover took more energetic steps to influence the economy. He persuaded the bankers to establish a National Credit Corporation in October 1931; the strong banks were to assist the weak and failing ones. But banks continued in their thousands to close their doors. Business confidence was not restored. In 1931 Hoover belatedly halted international financial chaos for a time by calling for a year's moratorium of Allied debts to the United States; German reparations also ceased in practice. Hoover broke with his traditions by establishing the Reconstruction Finance Corporation in 1932, empowered to make loans to banks and financial institutions. That summer he accepted a Congressional bill to advance federal loans to individual states to provide unemployment reliefs and public works. The federal budget, despite his misgivings, allowed for more state expenditure than income. But the funds thus pumped into the economy were overshadowed by the stringent credit policies followed by the banks, paradoxically because they were better supervised and receiving financial support. The net result was that from 1929 to 1934 the American money supply contracted by nearly a third, inevitably deepening the depression and increasing unemployment.

Roosevelt had no basic understanding of the overall management of the economy and in the election campaign of 1932 attacked President Hoover for his unbalanced budgets, promising as one of his remedies for the depression to cut federal spending by a quarter! Roosevelt's electrifying inaugural address of 4 March 1933 reveals the other, psychological side of his mixture of ideas together making up the promised New Deal. He

*The Great Communicator. US President Franklin D. Roosevelt about to speak to the people in 1937 during one of his 'fireside chats'.*

cautioned against unnecessary fear, attacked the 'unscrupulous money changers' and vigorously promised action: 'our greatest primary task is to put people to work'. He was now determined to put into practice what a year earlier he had called 'bold persistent experimentation'. If something fails, he declared, admit it frankly and try something else, but 'above all try something. The millions who are in want will not stand by silently forever while the things to satisfy their needs are within easy reach.'

Roosevelt spoke to the ordinary people and they were at last convinced that the new president was not prepared to capitulate to seemingly uncontrollable economic forces, to the inexorable workings of the business cycle. Roosevelt exuded confidence, charm and sincerity. There was something else about him. Crippled by polio in 1921, he had lost the use of his legs. Now, as president, he personified the fact that adversity could be triumphantly overcome. Quite possibly one consequence of his serious disability was that he developed a new homely touch in politics, a charisma in the eyes of the mass of the people that became an invaluable asset to him. The pampered child of wealthy Americans, privately educated at the best schools and at Harvard, Roosevelt bore a famous family name. And indeed he modelled himself on his famous relative Theodore.

His early political career advanced by easy progression from the Senate of the state of New York, to a junior place in the Navy Department in Wilson's administration. Then to the governorship of New York State when already stricken with polio. The Republicans seemed firmly in power in the 1920s, but the depression gave the Democrats their chance and Roosevelt secured the nomination in 1932. Roosevelt was happiest when active. During the first Hundred Days of his own administration he initiated measure after measure, backed by a bevy of academics and politicians who served as his think tank, or brains trust as it was then called. One associate who knew him well described Roosevelt's mind as 'fly-paper'. There was a tremendous array of New Deal policies, Washington became the centre and source of new federal powers hitherto undreamt of, and a vast sprawling bureaucracy administered the programmes. The public's thirst for action was satisfied. Thirst too was slaked by the Twenty-first Amendment in February 1933, ratified by the States in December. It was the end of Prohibition. 'Happy Days are here again'.

An emergency banking act restored confidence in the banks and in June 1933 deposits were insured by the Federal Deposit Insurance. In May 1933 the Agricultural Adjustment Act (AAA) tried to raise farm prices by paying federal subsidies to farmers for reducing production; marketing agreements were supervised by the federal authorities. In June 1933 the National Industrial Recovery Act (NIRA) created corporate committees representing the public, management and labour to establish codes on production, prices and competition. Labour was aided by the laying down of maximum hours and minimum wages and by being conceded the right to join a trade union, which at last gave a great impetus to the unionisation of the less skilled workers. Underlying NIRA was a belief in national planning. But the biggest businesses dominated the codes, as government supervision was small.

Among the most celebrated early measures was the creation of the Tennessee Valley Authority (TVA) in May 1933, which established government authority over a vast impoverished region containing a hydroelectric dam and fertiliser factories. The Authority promoted scientific agriculture, prevented flooding and engaged in a variety of social programmes to aid the poor. Another part of the NIRA Act established the Public Works Administration with a fund of $3.3 billion. Under the

Secretary of the Interior, Harold Ickes, it was set up to promote construction which was in the public interest, and employed during its first year 1 million men. But Ickes was cautious in his approach; not so ex-social worker Harry Hopkins. Hopkins worked for speedy aid to restore the morale of the unemployed. The Civilian Works Administration run by the indefatigable Hopkins employed 4 million people on public works schemes and cost $2000 million in 1933 to 1934. Roosevelt thought this was too much and abolished it in the spring of 1934. His own programme in 1933 was the Civilian Conservation Corps, which offered American unemployed young men from the cities work in army-style camps in the countryside. 300,000 lived in over a thousand camps planting trees and working in rural areas. Other New Deal measures sought to supervise and regulate Stock Exchange dealings and financiers.

The work of many minds, the New Deal measures were not intended to introduce 'socialism'. Roosevelt attempted to make capitalism work better, to use the power of representative democratic government to secure social justice for all the people. Despite the measures comprising the New Deal, the United States' unemployment figures disappointingly showed only gradual improvement. The reason for this is not now difficult to find. Congress and the President in 1933 and in 1934 were not prepared to tolerate large deficit budgets. Funds spent on the programmes of the New Deal were balanced by savings secured by reducing veterans' allowances, curtailing unemployment reliefs and discharging government employees. What one hand gave, the other took away, and federal deficits increased only gently in 1933 and 1934. The federal government had played a larger role and Roosevelt was genuinely responsive to the needs of the poor; but in the end practical achievements when seen against the vastness of the problem proved insufficient to 'cure' unemployment.

The New Deal policies ran into trouble in 1935. While the Congressional elections of 1934 had strengthened the reformers, the Supreme Court took a conservative view of constitutional rights. In May 1935 the Court invalidated the National Industrial Recovery Act as an unconstitutional delegation of power and regulation of business. Roosevelt's administration was already moving towards changes in the New Deal and so did not

*The Scourge of Unemployment. Among the public works programmes authorized by the Emergency Relief Appropriation Act passed by the US Senate in 1935, the Works Progress Administration (WPA) was one of the most successful. It spawned almost a million and a half individual projects as varied as building highways, financing vaudeville shows and circuses, and hiring writers and artists. By the time the scheme ended in 1943 more than eight million had been in its employ. Pictured are:* below, *a free lunch project in Utah;* left, *sewer construction;* and right, *brick-making.*

attempt to re-enact any parts of the National Industrial Recovery Act. The attempt to co-operate with business had not led to the expected beneficial results. The New Deal legislation of 1935 to 1936 sought to reform business practices and to destroy concentrations of business power. Another important decision was to create many more jobs – 'work relief' – by setting up the Works Progress Administration under Harry Hopkins and providing it with large funds, $1.47 billion on average in a full year (1936–40). Besides public works, Hopkins created projects for out-of-work artists and writers. The latter collected information and wrote guide books. Many suddenly discovered a new vocation for writing. Nearly one and a half million projects were set up which at different periods of time employed a total of more than 8.5 million people, during its years of operation. Even so, all these programmes absorbed only one-third of the unemployed.

One of the most significant reforms of the New Deal era was the introduction – belated in comparison to other Western nations – of basic welfare policies such as old-age pensions. The passage of the Social Security Act in August 1935, inspired by the efforts of Frances Perkins, provided – besides federal old-age pensions – unemployment insurance and help to the less privileged. Many of the poorest sections of American society were still excluded, but the act marked a beginning on which later expansion could be built. The growth of labour unions and recognition of their rights by the National Labor Relations Act (Wagner Act) further limited business power. All in all, the New Deal had redistributed power in the community and greatly increased that of the federal government.

In November 1936 Roosevelt was re-elected to a second term by a bigger victory than in 1932, gaining 61 per cent of the popular vote. He represented the non-revolutionary change the majority of voters wished to see. His biggest personal political setback occurred soon after the election, when he attempted to change the composition of the Supreme Court, which threatened his New Deal legislation. He requested Congress to legislate that the Supreme Court could be enlarged by the president appointing an additional supplementary justice for every existing justice over the age of seventy who did not wish to retire. But Congress refused to tamper with the Court in this way. Nevertheless Roosevelt's complaints of the Court's unresponsiveness to social needs seems to have produced a change of attitude; the Court ceased to be the conservative obstacle to New Deal legislation after 1936. In any case, gradually Roosevelt's nominees came to predominate as the older judges retired.

That the New Deal was not even larger in scope was not so much due to the attacks of its opponents as to the policies of the administration itself. Roosevelt never could abandon his belief in a 'sound money' policy. He favoured keeping spending within well-controlled limits. A recession in 1937 was followed by a slow recovery, but even in 1940 15 per cent of the workforce remained jobless. Yet America in 1940 was very different from when Roosevelt first entered the White House. He had sought reform and change, but not a revolution of the capitalist system. His bold approach, his faith in democracy and his desire to help the ordinary people, the disadvantaged and the poor, not only brought hope where there had been despair, but significantly changed American society and attitudes.

# CHAPTER 20

# Soviet Russia: 'Communism in Transition'

The Soviet leadership, after the departure in 1922 of the Japanese, the last foreign troops on Soviet territory, was able to fashion and create Soviet society free from outside interference. The Allies had withdrawn. The Whites were defeated. Bolshevik armies had established control over the Caucasus region, central Asia and the whole of Siberia during 1920 and 1921. With the end of the Civil War, and Russia's own foreign war with Poland – fighting stopped in October 1920 – not only was Soviet revolutionary power established, but for two decades, until Hitler's invasion of 1941, the expected concerted capitalist attack did not materialise. It never in fact materialised as the Soviet Union eventually fought Germany in alliance with capitalist Britain and the United States. But the fear that the halfhearted Allied intervention immediately after the revolution was not the end but the precursor of an attempt by the capitalist world to liquidate the first communist state powerfully influenced the Soviet Union's foreign policy throughout the period. It placed her, according to such calculations, in a desperate situation of weakness and inferiority.

To preserve Soviet power every weapon appeared to be justifiable. Britain and the West were to be weakened by pursuit of a vigorous anti-imperialist policy in Asia and the Middle East. Western communist parties, members of the Comintern (the First Congress of the Third International was convened by Lenin in Moscow in March 1919) were to join the struggle for the survival of the Soviet Union, however much such a policy might conflict with a purely national interest. Simultaneously, foreign relations with the West were conducted so as to exploit divisions between them. Arrangements for mutual military and technical aid were developed with Weimar Germany after the signature of the Treaty of Rapallo in April 1922. Such a policy was combined with the apparently contradictory support for the German Communist Party's attacks on the 'social fascists' which contributed to the fall of Weimar and the coming to power of the Nazis. Even when the German communists became the first victims of Nazi violence, they held to the doctrinal correctness of the analysis that the overthrow of bourgeois socialists had brought the communist revolution a step closer.

The imminent danger of foreign intervention was thus as much an illusion of the Soviet leaders in the 1920s as the expectation of communist revolution spreading in the West which, as late as 1921, the Soviet leadership still believed was the only hope of Russia's survival. But, for anyone living in Russia in the winter of 1920/1, there could be no illusion about the country's virtually total collapse after six years of war and civil war. Then a new disaster struck: in the summer of 1921 the grain crop failed. Added to the millions killed in war, countless more millions now died of starvation and disease. This time the West 'intervened' in a humanitarian mission of relief. In March 1921, even before the actual famine, Lenin told the Tenth Congress of the Communist Party, 'We are living in such conditions of impoverishment and ruin that for a time everything must be subordinated to this fundamental consideration – at all costs to increase the quantity of goods . . .' Principal among them were food and medicine. The aid of Hoover's American Relief Administration was therefore later accepted. Yet all such efforts had only a limited effect in the face of the scale of the disaster. No understanding of the early years of Soviet rule is possible without an appreciation of the suffering of the Russian people amid mounting chaos such as had not occurred in the history of Europe in modern times. Foreign military intervention, albeit halfhearted, contributed to the general breakdown.

Lenin, whose authority towered above that of his frequently arguing lieutenants, heading a Communist Party which at first was only small, sought to establish some sort of stable basis on which communism could be built. Between 1919 and 1922 the Bolshevik Party became a mass movement of 700,000 members, by no means all of whom were still revolutionary. In Lenin's policies there was little consistency – they were more reactions to successive emergencies. During the Civil War the Red Army of 5 million men as well as the workers in the cities had to be fed. The term 'war communism' is used to decribe the measures taken during the years from July 1918 to 1921 which were as extreme as was the situation facing Lenin. A Supreme Council of National Economy had already been created in December 1917 to take over such industry and finance as it considered necessary and to plan centrally the Soviet economy. After June 1918, industrial enterprises were rapidly nationalised and workers and managers subjected to rigid control. As money became virtually valueless with the collapse of the economy, theorists saw one advantage in the misfortune: communism might be attained not gradually but in one leap; state industries could now be 'purely' planned – the money economy abolished and with it all private enterprise and trade.

The key problem of the war-communist period was how to secure food from the peasants, whose alliance with the urban proletariat Lenin had declared to be essential to the success of the revolution. The value of money had been reduced to almost nothing; the factories were not producing goods that could be bartered. The peasants obstinately clung to the ownership of their land and refused to join state farms. Lenin at first attempted to divide the peasants, the poor from the better off – the kulaks, or exploiters, as they were called. This no doubt succeeded in spreading hatred in the villages but it did not yield grain. Then he wooed the so-called 'middle peasants' – the supposedly less poor (these categorisations corresponded to policy tactics rather than realities: only one in a hundred peasant households employed more than one labourer). Force was applied since the state could give nothing to the peasants in exchange for what were defined as 'surpluses'. With the utmost ruthlessness, detachments were sent into the countryside to seize food. Peasants were shot for resisting expropriation. Villages were searched, peasants left destitute. Bolshevik punitive expeditions attempted to overcome peasant resistance and violence. The excesses of war communism were encouraged by Lenin. The only answer he could find as the crisis deepened in early 1920 was even more ruthless pressure on the peasants. Those who were accused of retaining food were condemned as 'enemies of the people'. The Civil War above all, and the policies of war communism resulting from it, led, however, to the total collapse of what remained of the Russian agricultural and industrial economy. Transport had broken down and there was a large exodus from the starving towns and idle factories back to the country.

During his years of power, Lenin never wavered from his insistence on the supreme authority of the party and centralised control. No sectional interest of workers or peasants organised in the form of trade unions should act as a counterpoise to the party. Power was to be retained by the centre with iron discipline. In this he was strongly supported by Trotsky, who wished to rebuild Russia by mobilising the people under military discipline. Under the harsh realities of the Civil War and its aftermath Lenin had given up his earlier views that once the revolution had succeeded the state would begin to wither away and socialism would evolve by the spontaneous enthusiasm and work of the masses. He convinced himself that it was necessary to replace the revolution with a one-party state. But as he conceived it there was flexibility; especially after 1921 'non-party' specialists were encouraged. The bureaucracy was an inevitable outcome of the centralised state, though it deeply worried Lenin during the last months of his life. He began to alter course in 1921–2 and simultaneously government employees were drastically reduced. It was also Lenin who urged the use of force and terror where other means failed to achieve the desired ends. However much he criticised the consequences of the direction of state policy, the foundations of the Soviet state had been laid by Lenin.

While it is true that Lenin permitted debate within and outside the higher echelon of the party as in newspapers, men of the old guard, such as Lev Kamenev, Grigori Zinoviev, Aleksei Rykov, Nikolai Bukharin and Leon Trotsky, who differed on the right policies to be followed, ultimately had to obey the party line once Lenin had reached a decision. On the issue whether there could be any but a one-party state no debate was possible. The Tenth Party Congress, held in March 1921, passed the resolution 'On Party Unity', which though it did not stifle all debate and criticism forbade the formation within the party of any political groups 'with separate platforms, striving to a certain degree to segregate and create their own group discipline' and then to publish views not authorised by the party. The famous Paragraph Seven of this resolution empowered the Central Committee by two-thirds majority to expel from the party members of the Central Committee who diverged, and so to banish them into political exile. The weapon for stifling any dissident view not favouring the leader or group of leaders in power had been forged. Stalin later made full use of it to eliminate anyone he chose to accuse of factionalism.

In March 1921, simultaneously with the resolution on party unity, came the about-turn of Lenin's policy – the inauguration of the slogan New Economic Policy (NEP), coined to cover the dramatic reversal. The conviction that ever-increasing ruthlessness, especially in extracting food from the peasantry, was threatening the whole country's coherence must have been taking shape for some time. It was a mutiny of the sailors in the fortress of Kronstadt early in March 1921, bloodily repressed, which Lenin claimed 'was the flash which lit up reality better than anything else'. But the decision had already been taken by him following peasant riots and workers' strikes in the previous months.

The New Economic Policy began when the Tenth Party Congress passed a resolution replacing the seizure of surplus food with a less onerous and a properly regulated 'tax in kind'. Any further surplus the peasant could market freely. Three years later in 1924 the tax in kind became a money

payment. Free trading and, with it, a money economy revived. Small-scale production by not more than twenty workers was allowed once again. Large industries continued under state ownership with few exceptions. The vast majority of production was by state enterprises or by individual artisans. Between 1921 and 1926, the mixed industrial economy, part private part state, recovered so that by 1926 the level of production of 1913 had been reached. In agriculture, individual peasants farmed more than 98 per cent of the land sown. Agriculture recovered from the low levels of 1921 and 1922, but the amount left over from peasant consumption was less than in 1913; yet the need for grain to feed the expanding urban population and for export to provide capital grew much faster than the traditional peasant agriculture supplied. Nor were the peasants imbued with enthusiasm for socialism despite attempts to arouse a sense of common solidarity against the better-off peasants, the kulaks. A peasant farming his land traditionally, and encouraged to improve his standard of living by having stimulated in him a desire for profit, was not likely to accept the ideals of communism. The more successful a peasant, the less socialist he became. NEP on the land helped to save Russia from starvation, but did not provide the surplus to allow the economy to advance rapidly.

A complementary element of the more liberal economic approach of NEP in the 1920s was the tightening of party discipline and centralism. Cultural concessions, for instance, were made to the non-Russian nationalities, but not at the expense of centralised party and military control. The Tenth Party Congress of March 1921, which saw the beginnings of NEP, also, as has been noted, passed the resolutions against factions within the party. The swollen Communist Party itself was purged of some 200,000 members considered unreliable to the Bolshevik ideals. Lenin warned that the revolutionary old guard must hold together through all the transitional phases of communism, even those like NEP which marked a retreat from socialist objectives. How temporary would the retreat have to be? That was a fundamental and contentious issue. As long as Lenin remained the indisputable leader, however much debate and individual criticism took place within the party, great changes of policy were still possible without destroying the cohesion of the party or without producing a savage fight, literally to the death, between Lenin's lieutenants. Lenin's own premature death so early in the formation of the state was therefore of enormous significance.

The struggles of the revolution and war had sapped Lenin's strength. Towards the end of 1921 he fell seriously ill. In May 1922 at the age of fifty-two he suffered a serious stroke which paralysed his right side. By October he had recovered sufficiently to resume a partial workload. In December 1922 his health again deteriorated and on 21 January 1924 he died. Of particular interest during his last weeks of active work from the end of 1922 to 4 January 1923 are the notes he dictated which together comprise what was called his 'testament'. In these memoranda he stressed the need to strengthen the unity of the Central Party Committee, and characterised the strengths and weaknesses of six leading members of the party. The characterisation of Stalin, who having 'become the General Secretary has accumulated enormous power in his hands and I am not sure whether he will be able to use this power with due care', was especially important in view of the question who should succeed Lenin. During his illness he was outraged by Stalin's attempt to cut him off from influence in January 1923, a year before his death. He urged Stalin's dismissal and replacement by a new general secretary 'more tolerant, more loyal and less capricious'. It was too late. Lenin was too ill to act as unquestioned leader any longer. He had also criticised Trotsky, though describing him as the other leading personality of the party, for 'non-Bolshevism', for 'his too far-reaching self-confidence' and as too much attracted to pure administration. What was the purpose of this critical testament? Lenin was preoccupied by what would happen after his death. He concluded that no single one of the Bolshevik leadership could be designated as his successor. By his frank criticisms of all his lieutenants he was arguing for his own solution to the succession. This was to increase the Central Committee to fifty, even a hundred persons, by adding industrial workers and peasants close to the feeling of the rank and file of the party and for this body to control and supervise the collective leadership.

But following Lenin's death no stable collective leadership in fact took over. Stalin, who had been appointed general secretary with Lenin's support in 1922 to bring order to the organisation of the party, transformed this important but secondary position into a vehicle for the advancement of his personal power. His work for the party before this elevation had shown him to be ruthless and a good organiser. To these qualities he added cunning and a sense of timing in political intrigue. Using his powers to the full, he promoted to key posts men who would follow him and strengthened his position further by removing others who supported rivals.. Among the old guard, Trotsky was widely disliked for his arrogance, intellectual brilliance and showmanship. Stalin aligned himself with Zinoviev to undermine Trotsky's influence. In a little more than five years, he had ousted all the prominent former leadership. But he was not Lenin's undisputed heir; nor did he enjoy the veneration granted to the late leader. Stalin encouraged a Lenin cult. He then kept himself at the top by the ruthless liquidation of all real and potential rivals who might conceivably challenge his control. Not until the end of the Great Terror in 1938 did any challenge to Stalin's supreme control become unthinkable. Yet his paranoid fear of plots and conspiracies beset him to the end of his life.

Lenin tolerated party discussion; Stalin could not stifle it in the 1920s as the better-known, more prominent Soviet leaders still overshadowed him. He supported a moderate internal economic policy, upheld NEP and identified himself with Lenin's policies after his death. Appealing to party unity, while packing key positions with his supporters, Stalin was ready to take on the most prestigious of the old Bolshevik leaders. The big quarrel with Trotsky occurred at the end of 1923 and early 1924 after Trotsky's attacks on the old guard. Trotsky was effectively defeated at the Thirteenth Party Congress in January 1924. Together with Zinoviev, president of the Comintern, whose power base was the Leningrad party, and Kamenev, chairman of the Moscow Soviet, Stalin had already made himself the leading member of the triumvirate controlling the party, the key to controlling the country. Trotsky had published a book, *Lessons of October*, in which he bitterly attacked the credentials of Zinoviev and Kamenev, who had been 'Right' Bolsheviks opposed to the October Revolution in 1917. In his denunciation Trotsky implied that such shortcomings were responsible for the failure of revolution beyond the Soviet Union, for instance in Germany. The triumvirate countered by stressing the long-standing quarrel between Trotsky and Lenin about 'permanent' revolution, which Trotsky had fervently advocated; and Stalin enunciated the slogan 'socialism in one country'. Stalin declared more realistically that the Soviet Union *had* survived and claimed that the conditions existed in Russia for the complete construction of socialism; this he saw as the primary task. The policies of communists in other countries too were therefore expected in practice to make this their primary objective, subordinating national considerations to the strengthening of the Soviet Union.

Trotsky and Stalin were not so far apart as their polemics made it appear. At moments of great danger, such as the Soviet leaders believed existed in 1927 and 1928, Trotsky was just as ready as Stalin to place the safety of the Soviet Union first. In this respect they were both heirs of Lenin's *Realpolitik*. In the power struggle in the top echelon of the party, Stalin calculated that a moderate line would be the most successful, while Trotsky assumed the mantle of the ardent, unquenchable revolutionary and the champion of 'democracy' within the party. The genuineness of Trotsky's democratic sentiments was never tested, for he never wielded supreme power. He was certainly no less ruthless than Stalin in his readiness to subordinate means to an end. But Stalin's control of the party machine secured Trotsky's gradual elimination. In January 1925 Trotsky lost the argument of his *Lessons of October* and the Central Committee deprived him of his nominal leadership of the Red Army.

Stalin now pushed from key control two other members of the Politburo, his fellow triumvirates, Kamenev and Zinoviev. Instead he allied with those who fully backed the NEP, Nikolai Bukharin, a long-standing companion of Lenin and editor of *Pravda*, and two other Politburo members, Aleksei Rykov and Mikhail Tomsky. But Trotsky, Kamenev and Zinoviev still retained their places on the Politburo, at least until 1926. That year the three men, calling themselves the United Opposition, mounted attacks on Comrade Stalin's capacity to unite the party and on the economic state of the country and bureaucracy. Stalin expelled all three from the Politburo and purged their supporters Trotsky's further attacks on Stalin and the organisation of an open demonstration against the leadership in November 1927 led to his and Zinoviev's and many of their followers' exclusion from the party in December 1927. A year later Trotsky was expelled from Russia.

Two years later it was the turn of the 'Right' opposition. Bukharin lost control of the Comintern at the end of 1928 and in 1929 and 1930 Tomsky and Rykov were replaced (page 186). All eventually died violently, victims of Stalin's purges of the mid-1930s. But it is simplistic to reduce the struggles at the centre of power to Stalin's completely cynical manoeuvrings to reach the top. Three deep concerns formed just a part of the immense nexus of problems associated with 'communism in transition': transforming a predominantly peasant society into an industrial power capable of catching up with the capitalist West, while keeping the goal of a communist society in view; at the same time the leadership was anxiously scanning the international horizon for an impending attack by the capitalist nations; as disastrous was the possibility that their own imperialist rivalry would start a second world war involving Russia in the maelstrom. Any one problem was in itself gigantic; together they were truly baffling. And there were no models to follow. Marxism was based on revolution in an advanced industrial nation, not an overwhelmingly peasant society. Lenin, when confronted with practical problems, had made bewildering changes of policy, justifying each with fresh doctrinal pronouncements. The mark of the dominant leader was his capacity radically to change policy and *retain* power. After Lenin, only Stalin as it turned out could do that. But this does not mean that he changed policy merely for the sake of discrediting his rivals or that he had plotted in advance first a policy to the 'right' and then to the 'left'.

Stalin's own uncertainty about his ability to hold on to supreme power in the face of the policies he felt it necessary to pursue is indeed the basic explanation of his murderous purges of the 1930s. He linked the survival of the communist regime with his own survival as undisputed leader. He wanted to be regarded as infallible; for proof he presented an unending stream of wrongdoers who in public trials confessed their errors and were shot. Their confessions to foreign conspiracies were intended to underline the mortal dangers to which the Soviet Union was exposed, but saved from by Stalin's vigilance. At the same time an understanding of Soviet policies is not possible without the assumption that there were deep and genuine problems, that more than one plausible option of action presented itself; and even granted that Stalin never lost sight of his tenure of power and would stop at nothing to maintain it, he was also concerned to discover the *right* policy to follow.

Stalin had reached the leadership group through Lenin's own selection and Lenin had an eye for remarkable men to act as the founding members of the new state. Unlike Lenin and the rest of the Bolshevik leadership, Stalin spent the years of preparation not in comfortable and argumentative exile, but in Russia herself, in constant danger and engaged in organizing the party when not in tsarist prison or Siberian exile. In Stalin, the cobbler's son born in Georgia in December 1879, Lenin saw a hardened, totally dedicated revolutionary leader, painstaking, and an effective organiser. Stalin showed a total disregard for 'conventions' of the law and civil rights when they impeded what he deemed necessary. As a young revolutionary in tsarist days he was lawless in a cause; in power he became lawless without restraint, filling the prisons, the places of execution and the labour camps in the 1930s and later with millions of people innocent of any crime except to arouse Stalin's suspicions. The apparently benign, modest and down-to-earth leader – it was easy for the Stalin cult to portray him as the father of his people just as the tsars before him had been – had turned into a monstrous tyrant.

Stalin was a consummate actor who could hide his true nature and if he chose charm those who had dealings with him, just as he was to charm Churchill and Roosevelt when the three leaders met during the Second World War. He was capable of carefully weighing alternatives, of calculating the risks and proceeding rationally, of outwitting his enemies at home and abroad. Secretive, suspicious, malevolent and lacking Lenin's intellect, he made himself into Lenin's heir and saw himself as such. His crimes were immense. His mistakes brought the whole country close to catastrophe in 1930 and in 1941, yet both he and the Soviet Union survived. During the Stalin era, there occurred the decisive shift that was to propel the Soviet Union from being a backward country to a state capable of grinding down and, during the latter part of the Second World War, overwhelming Germany. The industrial and military transformation of Russia, the creation of tens of thousands of technically proficient men, of administrators and doctors from a backward peasant society, though at immense sacrifice, was the achievement of the Stalin era from 1929 to his death in 1953.

\*

That the New Economic Policy had to be a 'transitional' phase in the construction of communism was obvious, unless communism itself was to abandon its Marxist goals. NEP had brought about an amazing recovery but was it capable of continuing at its previous pace of growth, after the first five years, given the low base from which it had started? Would the Soviet Union not merely catch up with tsarist pre-war production but decisively move beyond it? Then how could NEP enable the Soviet Union to acquire the sinews of the modern industrial state with an iron and steel industry, machinery and armaments, improved transportation and adequate power? A vast network of electric power stations was one of Lenin's pet dreams. With a 'mixed' economy would too many resources be swallowed up in providing the consumer with his needs rather than investing for the future? Had the essentially tsarist agricultural methods reached the limit of their productive capacity? On purely economic grounds, leaving aside ideological considerations, there were powerful arguments for a change of policy at the point when NEP failed to provide for the economic growth desired by the Bolshevik leadership.

During the winter of 1927 and 1928 the peasants reacted to increased taxes, low official prices, threats against the offence of hoarding and simply a lack of goods to buy by hanging on to their grain. Industrial investment had already speeded up industrialisation, the 'selfishness' and 'petty-bourgeois' behaviour of the kulaks in Stalin's judgement threatened the whole economy. Violence against the peasant to extract the grain needed to feed the towns was again resorted to in 'emergency' measures. The peasantry from rich to poor were hard hit in 1928 and alienated from the Soviet regime, though it was obviously the kulaks and better-off peasants who had most grain and so suffered the most. After the summer of 1928 Stalin faced the prospect of annual crises to purchase sufficient grain unless some fundamental changes were effected in dealing with the peasantry and agricultural productivity. Stalin had little love for the Russian peasantry, which he believed was holding the country to ransom.

Industrial expansion was jeopardised by the crisis in agriculture. If the peasantry were to be appeased, more goods would need to be released for their consumption. This was in contradiction to a policy of catching up rapidly with the advanced capitalist countries. No Soviet leader ever lost sight of

Russia's comparative weakness, which was believed to offer a temptation to the capitalist nations to attack her. The more relaxed attitudes of the mid-1920s, which also affected foreign policy – the slogan here used to describe Soviet aims was 'peaceful coexistence' – came to an end in 1927 and 1928. The Soviet leadership was beset by acute new fears that some concerted onslaught on the Soviet Union was imminent. The Soviet policy in China of supporting the nationalist revolution of Chiang Kai-shek had collapsed when Chiang turned on his former communist partners (page 83). Relations with Britain had deteriorated, and Britain, France and Poland were credited with plans to launch an offensive against the Soviet Union. There was a sense that the breathing space in Europe and the Far East could be short. The worldwide depression added a new element of uncertainty.

We have little indication of Stalin's thinking during this or any other period. One can plausibly surmise that in 1928 and 1929 he was still much concerned with rivals and criticisms of his policies and economic developments, which were certainly not going well. The problem of the change of course of the economic and social policies of the Soviet state has been debated by historians and we may never be able to fathom what perceptions and plans were Stalin's at any precise moment. Certainly a vociferous group of his supporters was calling for rapid industrialization and Stalin leant on them in his struggle with opponents of the policy. At what point in particular did he regard NEP as an obstacle to be cleared away if the pace of Russian industrialisation and its direction were to conform to his own objectives? If industrialisation were to be pushed ahead rapidly, the necessary investment would not significantly come from foreign loans, or even significantly from exports of grain, but from the higher productivity of workers and peasants and a holding back of consumption by them. In plain English, the industrial advance was achieved at the sacrifice of their own living standards, the work being rewarded with only low real wages. Long-term state planning by the State Planning Commission was certainly well under way and resources were increasingly transferred to large-scale industrial projects. By 1926 the increasing shortages of goods led to multi-pricing of the same goods in 'commercial' shops or at artificially low prices but strictly rationed. Despite rises in wages the actual cost of

living rose much more steeply and in the opinion of one economic historian, Alec Nove, the 'fact still seems to be clear: 1933 was the culmination of the most precipitous peacetime decline in living standards known in recorded history'. While there was none of the unemployment that plagued Western economies at the time, the great industrial leap forward was accompanied by mass misery and hunger.

A 'maximum' version of the First Five-Year Plan was adopted by the Sixteenth Party Congress in 1929. Industrial output was intended to increase more than twofold and agricultural output to rise by half. The industrial growth actually achieved fell far short of such unrealisable targets. In trying to fulfil them there was huge waste and confusion. Coercion and regulation were necessary means to drive industrialisation forward especially in the primitive regions of Russia, the Urals and Siberia, where for military strategic reasons new industrial complexes were set up. The emphasis was on heavy industry, iron and steel, and machinery. The First Five-Year Plan, declared to be fulfilled a year in advance, actually fell short of its target in most industrial sections. But great iron and steel works were being constructed, the gigantic Dnieper dam was built and the engineering industry greatly expanded. The basis of a modern industry had been constructed.

The Second Five-Year Plan (1933–7) brought improvements for the Russian people. The economic sacrifices demanded of the people were not as harsh and there was greater emphasis on producing goods for consumption. Planning became more efficient and a greater self-sufficiency was achieved. After 1937 the massive switch to arms production once more created new bottlenecks and shortages. Control over the labour force became much harsher. Workers were tied in 1940 to their place of work and absenteeism became a crime. Industrially the Soviet Union in a decade and a half had been transformed and proved strong enough to withstand the shock of the German invasion. Statistics should always be considered with caution and this is especially true of Soviet statistics. But the figures shown in the table indicate and reflect the change of Soviet Russia's industry. Whether Soviet statistics are to be relied on is an open question.

The results were in any case impressive, the human cost equally enormous. Enthusiasm for building socialism was replaced by terror and

### Soviet Russia's Industrial Growth

|  | 1928 | 1940 | 1950 |
|---|---|---|---|
| Electricity (*milliard Kwhs*) | 5.0 | 48.3 | 91.2 |
| Steel (*million metric tons*) | 4.3 | 18.3 | 27.3 |
| Oil (*million metric tons*) | 11.6 | 31.1 | 37.9 |
| Coal (*million metric tons*) | 35.5 | 166.0 | 261.1 |
| Machine-tools (*thousands*) | 2.0 | 58.4 | 70.6 |
| Tractors (*thousands*) | 1.3 | 31.6 | 116.7 |
| Mineral fertiliser (*million metric tons*) | 0.1 | 3.2 | 5.5 |
| Leather footwear (*million pairs*) | 58.0 | 211.0 | 203.0 |

coercion. Ideals of socialist equality did not inhibit Stalin from decreeing differential rewards. With much stick, and the carrot of high rewards for successful skilled piece-work, he drove the mass of new peasant workers in industry to pull Russia out of the morass. Socialism could not be built in a society predominantly peasant and backward, Stalin believed. Nor could a backward Soviet Union survive, surrounded as she was by enemies. But the arbitrary murderous excesses of Stalin's rule in the 1930s bear no relation to the achievement of such goals. On the contrary, they gravely jeopardised progress. In dealing with the peasantry and agriculture his policies led to disaster. Here the 'revolution from above' not only inflicted enormous hardship on the majority of the population, the peasantry, but also failed in its purpose to 'modernise' agriculture on a scale similar to industry.

Stalin's cure for Russia's backward agriculture was to transform the small scattered peasant holdings into large farms collectively and co-operatively farmed. In theory this was sound. In practice productivity slumped when the individual peasant's personal ownership of his lands and his livestock was abolished. The peasants did not voluntarily give up their land and join collective farms. By 1928 less than three acres in a hundred of sown land were cultivated by collective or state farms. At the beginning of that year Stalin organised from his own secretariat the forcible seizure of grain as the peasants were unwilling to part with it for the artificially low prices laid down. It was a return to the methods of war communism. Bukharin, Rykov and Tomsky, once Stalin's allies against the Trotsky 'left', as has been seen, attacked Stalin from May 1928 onwards when they realised he intended to continue the emergency measures. Bukharin in particular condemned Stalin's dictatorial pretensions, declaring, 'We stand by the principle of collective action and refuse to accept the principle of control by a single individual, no matter how great his authority.' Stalin countered by savagely attacking Bukharin as a right-wing deviationist. Between February and July 1929 the political standing of the three leaders was progressively undermined and the expulsion from the Politburo of Tomsky and Bukharin in November 1929 marked the elimination of their opposition to Stalin's industrial and agricultural plans. (Rykov retained his membership of the Politburo until 1930.)

From the summer of 1929 Stalin issued party directives to secure more grain for state purchase at low prices. The kulaks were singled out as the most prosperous and therefore pressure on them would, it was thought, yield a good return. Not only their grain but their farms too began to be seized. NEP was breaking up. On 7 November 1929 Stalin signalled the drive for forcible collectivisation at the greatest possible speed. He characteristically declared that the middle peasants as well as the poor peasants had turned to the collective farms. The continuing crisis caused by the difficulty of getting grain was a crucial reason for the sudden urgency, but behind Stalin's assault also lay a long-felt suspicion of peasants as reliable allies of the urban proletariat.

Between the Bolsheviks and the peasants there was a large gap. The notion of petty-peasant proprietorship simply did not fit into the communist model of the future classless society. Stalin saw even the poorest peasant defending his possession of land and animals as exhibiting the characteristics of the 'petty-capitalist class'. As long as the landed peasant persisted in Russian society, Stalin believed, a communist state would never be built. He may have calculated that by ruining the more prosperous peasants, the kulaks, by defining them as a class to be destroyed, all the peasants would be taught the lesson that successful private enterprise held no future for them. Certainly party leaders believed that they could stir up class war between the poor peasant and the kulak and so gain some peasant support. 'Kulak' was, moreover, an entirely elastic definition and could be extended to any peasant; those too obviously poor could simply be labelled as kulak sympathisers. Under the cover of the supposed kulak enemy, land could be seized, peasants expelled and sent by cattle trucks to Siberia, and the whole peasantry could be terrorised. Without forcible measures to overcome the agricultural crisis, Stalin believed, the *acceleration* of industrialisation would fail, and one of his close supporters improbably claimed that all industrial growth would come to a standstill halfway through the Five-Year Plan if industrialisation was not accelerated.

Plans for the acceleration of industrial production went hand in hand with plans for the acceleration of collectivisation of the peasant farms. From the summer of 1929 onwards the peasants were being pressurised by party representatives in the villages to join the collective farms. The peasants reacted with suspicion or outright hostility. Although progress was made, the attitude of the bulk of the peasantry undoubtedly remained negative. Nevertheless by October 1929 collectives were farming almost one acre in eleven of sown land. Forcible procurement of grain meanwhile by party task forces over the whole country were securing results. In the autumn of 1929 Stalin, supported by Molotov

and Kaganovich, determined to break all resistance to a great leap forward and to the mass discontent that coercion in the procurement of grain was producing.

It was in part wishful thinking and in part a command that collectivisation was to be quickly achieved regardless of what resistance remained. In December 1929 mass 'dekulakisation' began. Stalin decreed their 'elimination as a class'. Elimination of the individual peasant defined as kulak did not yet mean death, except in the case of those categorised as the most active counter-revolutionaries, but meant the confiscation of his property and imprisonment or the deportation of the whole family to Siberia, where with a few tools they began to farm again. Some kulaks were allowed to remain in their locality and were integrated into the collective system. The whole programme was carried through with the utmost violence and barbarity and in total disregard of human rights. Many perished through deprivation or suicide. It was an enormous tragedy almost totally hidden from Western view. The miseries of the depression do not compare with the human disaster that unfolded in Stalin's Russia.

The result in the countryside was chaos. More than half the peasant farmers had been collectivised by the spring of 1930. As the time for spring sowing approached, reports from the countryside came back to Moscow that the forcible collectivisation was preparing the way for an unparalleled disaster. There was much peasant resistance, including uprisings. The new collectives were unlikely to produce a fraction of the food produced by the

*Farming like machines without machines in the Soviet Union: a collective in the Volga basin, c. 1930.*

individual peasants before collectivisation. Stalin, faced with disastrous failure, compromised. In the face of so great a failure, his own standing could be jeopardised. He published an article, 'Dizzy with Success'. Local party workers were blamed for the excesses; coercion was wrong; those peasants who wished to leave the collective farms could do so. But instead of the expected few there was a mass exodus; more than half the peasants left the collectives and took back some of their land to farm. The best land the collective farmers retained.

To counter this unexpected turn of events, Stalin in the summer of 1930 ordered a resumption of forcible collectivisation. There was no let-up this time. By 1935, 94 per cent of the crop area of land was collectivised. The results in productivity were appalling. The peasants slaughtered their animals; the collectives were inefficient; the yield of crops dropped and party purges and coercion could not relieve the food shortages. The conditions of the early 1930s revived the experiences of the early 1920s. There were widespread famines and millions perished. The situation would have been even worse if Stalin had not learnt one lesson from the winter of 1929/30 and the widespread peasant violence and resistance to collectivisation. The collectivised peasants were permitted small plots and to own a few animals from 1930 onwards. After 1932 they were even allowed to sell food privately over and above the quota to be delivered to the state at state prices. The private peasant plot became an important element in the supply of milk and meat. Agriculture recovered slowly from the onslaught, but there was no leap forward as occurred in the industrial sector. The pre-1928 levels were only just attained again, though the population had grown in the meantime. Economically Stalin's collectivisation did not solve Russia's need for growth of agricultural production before the German invasion in 1941 dealt a devastating blow. Even Stalin had to compromise with the peasantry in allowing some private production and sale or face the prospect of permanent conditions of famine.

The enormous tensions created by Stalin's industrial and agricultural policies from 1929 to 1934 were accompanied by a policy of terrorisation to thwart any possible opposition. Propaganda sought to raise Stalin to the public status of a demi-god, the arbiter of every activity of society – art, literature, music, education, Marxist philosophy. Terror

tactics were not new under Soviet rule. Show trials, which turned those who were constructing the new Russia into scapegoats for failures, had begun in 1928. We know so little of the inner workings of Soviet government that historians have been reduced to surmise. It appears that Stalin's power was not absolute between 1928 and 1934 and that the failures, especially in agriculture, were weakening his position. Perhaps a straw in the wind was the curious fact that the Seventeenth Party Congress early in 1934 changed his title from that of 'General Secretary' to just 'Secretary' of the party. Was this a rebuke against his attempt to gather all power in his hands? Was the leader of the Leningrad party, Sergei Kirov, who was also a member of the Politburo and hitherto a Stalin supporter, among those who attempted to clip Stalin's wings? That December 1934 Kirov was murdered and Western experts suspect that Stalin was implicated. That he acted as pallbearer at Kirov's funeral is no evidence to the contrary. The first mass terror-wave of arrests and executions followed. Then there was a pause, just as there had been with collectivisation. Stalin in 1936 even promulgated a constitution guaranteeing every conceivable human and civic right! It was no more than a façade that misled only the most gullible. Then the arrests and executions were resumed. The years from 1936 to 1938 are known as the Great Terror. At the end, Stalin emerged as the undisputed dictator whom none could resist.

Stalin turned on the elite of communist society, the party functionaries, the army officers from the junior to the commander in chief, the technocrats and managers. The world learnt only a little from the show trials of the prominent leaders, the 'fathers' of the revolution, who were now paraded to confess publicly their sins, confessions secured beforehand by torture and threats. Not only they, but also their wives and associates, were murdered. Nothing like this had ever occurred before. Behind the benign façade of Stalin's smile there existed a paranoiac tyrant who had convinced himself that he alone could lead Russia and who disregarded all human cost. Stalin may have been 'mad' according to some definitions, but he acted with cold and ruthless calculation. The victims of these purges have never been counted. Dekulakisation, the famine and the purges claimed millions of victims. No one was safe. Death, exile or incarceration in the huge complex of labour camps was the fate of anyone who fell under suspicion. The material loss to Russia of

Above: *in 1935, the benign dictator, Stalin, suffers the adulation of two grateful subjects from a collective farm in Tajikistan, while the purges continue apace.* Right: *At Kirov's funeral, December 1934, Stalin, implicated in Kirov's murder, is pre-eminent amongst the mourners, among them the equally hypocritical Molotov, Voroshilov and Kalinin.*

skilled people was incalculable. The grip of the secret police under the hated Beria was not loosened until after Stalin's death. There were thousands willing to do Stalin's bidding and commit all these crimes. He justified them by claiming there were conspiracies with outside Western powers, with Japan, Germany, Britain and France, to sabotage and attack the Soviet Union. Did he believe it? Stalin thought it theoretically possible and that was enough.

Stalin had little experience of foreign travel. Behind his notion of Russia's correct foreign policy two assumptions or principles can be discerned: Russia's defence in a hostile capitalist world must come first at all costs; secondly, the behaviour of other powers could be deduced by a Leninist analysis. Not only were these powers motivated by a joint hostility to the only communist state, but they were also locked in an imperial struggle for supremacy among themselves. Thus Soviet theoreticians, including Stalin in the 1920s, believed in

the likelihood of war between Britain and the United States. But this was not seen, as might be expected, as benefiting the Soviet Union, for a great war anywhere might force Soviet involvement against her will. Later in the early 1930s, Stalin hoped that rivalry in eastern Asia would lead the United States to check Japanese expansion in China. But Soviet hopes were disappointed by American non-intervention during the Manchurian crisis of 1931–3 (page 213).

The Soviet view of the West was grotesquely distorted. The Western social democrats were cast in the role of 'right deviationists' or 'social fascists' from 1929 to 1934, more dangerous than the real fascists. The Nazis were seen as a short-lived right-wing excess against which the workers would soon react. There was a lingering fear of Poland and her ally, capitalist France, and of 'hostile' Britain. Thus from the West as well as from Asia, the Soviet Union appeared to be in continuing and great danger.

From 1934 to 1938 there was some readjustment of Soviet policy and a rapprochement with the

Western democracies. The Soviet Union was accepted finally by the United States when Roosevelt agreed to establish diplomatic relations in 1933. In 1934 the Soviet Union joined the League of Nations, and the Commissar for Foreign Affairs, Maxim Litvinov, now preached the need for collective security against Hitler's Germany and Mussolini's Italian expansionist policies. The genuine search for peace did not mean, however, that the Soviet Union was ready to go to war in alliance with the Western democracies against Germany. Rather, the Russians wanted to avoid a war breaking out altogether, and believed a firm stand would deter Hitler and Mussolini. If it did not, as it did not in September 1939, the Soviet leaders were determined to avoid being involved in war themselves. If there had to be a war – a situation full of danger for Russia – then at least it should be confined to a war between the Western powers. As long as Nazi Germany could be prevented from turning *first* on Russia, then the Soviet Union would remain neutral and appease Germany to any extent necessary to preserve peace. But the nightmare of the Soviet leadership was a reverse of that situation, that France and Britain would stand aside while Hitler conquered *Lebensraum* in the east. What is more, would the Ukrainians and Georgians and other non-Russian nationalities fight for Russia, when the people were suffering from such terrible communist repression? While socialism was still in transition, Russia could not afford war without risking the very survival of socialism.

The Soviet Union attempted to create a 'barrier of peace' by signing non-aggression treaties with her neighbours, of whom the most important was Poland. Until the autumn of 1938 Hitler employed no direct violence near Russia's borders. In eastern Asia the threat of war was met by a combination of policies, in the first place by appeasing Japan: in 1935 Russia sold her interest in the Chinese Eastern Railway to the Japanese puppet state of Manchukuo. It was lessened, furthermore, by encouraging Chiang Kai-shek's nationalist resistance to Japan in the hope that Japan would then be too busy fighting China to turn on Russia as well. When necessary, however, the Soviet Union did not hesitate to resist militarily any direct Japanese attacks on Soviet spheres of influence, on the People's Republic of Mongolia and along the Russo–Chinese frontier. There was full-scale fighting between Soviet and Japanese troops in 1938 and in

the summer of 1939. These were no mere 'incidents'. Marshal Zhukov in 1939 had the advantage of modern tanks and troops far better armed than the Japanese. The Japanese suffered a severe defeat and left behind 18,000 dead. Thereafter they avoided open conflict with Russia. The Soviet Union and Japan in fact remained at peace until it suited Stalin, shortly before Japan's surrender, to attack the Japanese in China in 1945.

In the West, the Soviet Union did what she could to persuade France and Britain to stand up to Hitler and Mussolini. The menace they presented to peace and so to the Soviet Union was belatedly recognised in 1934. The Soviet Union then signed a treaty of mutual assistance with France in May 1935 to strengthen the deterrent alignment. The Soviet Union also joined in the League's ineffectual sanctions to deter Mussolini from conquering Abyssinia. In 1934 the new United Front tactics were acquiesced in when France herself seemed in danger of succumbing to fascism (page 165). But at the same time the communist leadership was always conscious of and never wished to repeat the experiences of the First World War when Russia was cast in the role of providing military relief to the West and in the effort went down in defeat. Russian policy aimed to maintain a careful balance and to avoid war by encouraging the will of France and Britain to resist. In line with this overall strategy the Russian help afforded to the Republican side during the Spanish Civil War was carefully limited to exclude any possible risk of war. It was left to the Comintern to organise the International Brigades to fight as volunteers on the Republican side. But Soviet technical advisers, tanks, aircraft and supplies played a crucial role in the war (page 230).

The year 1937 saw Stalin's military purge at its height. Russia was more unready than ever to face military attack from the West. The Soviet Union almost frantically attempted to construct a diplomatic peace front in 1938. It failed. Britain and France went to Munich in September and consented to the partition of Czechoslovakia (page 244). The Russians meanwhile had promised to support the Czechs only to the extent of their limited treaty obligations. Whatever Russian aid might have been forthcoming if the Czechs had fought, it appears certain that Stalin would not have risked war with Germany. The tendency of the Western powers to give way to the Nazis did not alter Soviet policy but reinforced its objectives to avoid war;

simultaneously Soviet diplomats sought to stiffen French and British resistance to Hitler by warning their governments that Hitler meant to defeat them. Stalin's faith in 'collective security', probably never strong, did not survive after the German occupation of Czechoslovakia in March 1939. It was unlikely that peace could much longer be preserved between Hitler and his neighbours and his prime objective remained to stop the Soviet Union from going to war. And so after simultaneous and secret negotiations with France and Britain on the one hand and Germany on the other – a double insurance policy – Stalin, having delayed as long as he dared, concluded a non-aggression pact with Germany on 23 August 1939. There were a few anxious days while Stalin waited to see whether Britain would actually fulfil her alliance obligations to Poland. Stalin had calculated correctly and kept the Soviet Union at peace. The Germans extracted a price in requiring supplies from the Soviet Union. To that extent Stalin became the most active proponent of appeasement. The war that began in September 1939, Stalin believed, afforded the Soviet Union a long breathing space during which communism would strengthen the Soviet Union's capacity to meet the dangers still to come. But the breathing space he had actually won lasted barely two years.

# CHAPTER 21

# The Failure of Parliamentary Democracy in Germany and the Rise of Hitler, 1920–1934

In retrospect there can be no minimising the importance of one historical date – 30 January 1933, when Adolf Hitler was appointed chancellor of Germany by President von Hindenburg. Within eight years of his coming to power, Germany had conquered continental Europe from the Channel coast to the gates of Moscow. It was not a conquest and occupation such as had occurred in the Great War. In German-occupied Europe some 10 million people, including 2 million children, were deliberately murdered. Hitler's Reich was a reversion into barbarism. Racism as such was nothing new, nor was it confined to Germany. These doctrines attracted groups of supporters in most of Europe, including France and Britain, in South America and in the United States. But it was in Germany that the resources of a modern industrial state enabled criminal leaders to murder and enslave millions. Until the concentration camps revealed their victims the world was inclined to believe that a country once in the forefront of Western culture, the Germany of Goethe, could not so regress. This faith in civilisation was misplaced. How was it possible? For just one of the more easily discernible parts of the explanation we must turn to the politics of Weimar Germany, which failed to provide stable governments until political democracy ceased to function altogether after the onset of the economic crisis of 1929.

From 1920 to 1930 no party was strong enough on its own to form a government and enjoy the necessary majority in parliament. But until 1928 a majority in parliament either favoured or at least tolerated the continuation of the parliamentary system of government. The Communist Party was too weak in its parliamentary representation to endanger the Republic during the middle years of Weimar prosperity from 1924 to 1928; its strength was appreciably smaller than that of the deputies of the moderate Socialist Party. Indeed the Socialists steadily gained votes and deputies in the Reichstag. From 100 in May 1924 their representation increased to 153 in 1928. Significantly the Communist Party fell in the same period from 62 to 54 Reichstag deputies. On the extreme anti-democratic right the Nazis did even worse in parliamentary elections; in May 1924 there were 32 Nazis elected to the Reichstag and in 1928 only 12. Even the conservatives, the Nationalist Party, who formed the opposition for most of the time from 1918 to 1930, declined from 95 to 73.

Weimar Germany appeared to gain in strength. This was not really so. The Nazis were winning adherents wherever there was distress. Even during the years of comparative prosperity, many of the farmers did not share the benefits of industrial expansion. Then governments were discredited by their short life-spans – on average only eight months. Parties appeared to be locked in purely selfish battles of personal advantage. The Social Democratic Party must share in the blame for the instability of the Weimar coalition governments. It preferred to stay in opposition and not to participate in the business of ruling the country. The difficulties

*Prussian honour is allied to the new barbarism at the official opening ceremony of the first sitting of the Reichstag during the Thousand-Year Reich, 21 March 1933. Hitler and Hindenburg sit side-by-side at the Garrison Church of Potsdam; as ever, Hitler eschews uniform when appearing alongside the bemedalled Field Marshal.*

of any party with socialist aspirations joining a coalition were genuinely great. Coalition meant compromise on policy. In any coalition with the centre and moderate right the Social Democrats could not hope to pass socialist measures and they were afraid that co-operation with the 'bourgeois' parties would discredit them with their electoral base, which consisted mainly of urban workers and trade unionists. From an electoral party point of view these tactics appeared to pay off as their increasing representation in the Reichstag shows. But the price paid was the discrediting of parliamentary government, for the exclusion from government of both the Nationalists and the communists and the absence of the Socialists meant that the coalitions of the centre and mainly moderate right were minority governments at the mercy of the Socialists.

In government there was thus a permanent sense of crisis, the coalition partners who formed the governments, especially the smaller parties, becoming more concerned about how the unpopularity of a particular government policy might affect their own supporters than about the stability of government as a whole. This situation imperilled the standing of the whole parliamentary democratic system. After 1925 there seemed to be only one method by which the parties of the centre and

moderate right, saddled with the responsibility of government, could logically attain stability and a majority and that was to move further to the right. So its right wing came to predominate the Centre Party, enabling the conservatives, the Nationalist Party, to join coalition cabinets with them. The coalition cabinets were also very much cabinets of 'personalities' relying on presidential backing and only loosely connected with, and dependent on, the backing of the Reichstag parties. The close link between party and government, as existed in Britain, was lacking in the Weimar working of the constitution. Indeed it did not so much 'work' as function by one expedient after another.

When in 1928 the Socialists at last joined a broad coalition excluding the more extreme right they seemed to be remedying their earlier mistaken policy; but it was very late in the history of the parliamentary Republic. The coalition partners, especially the Centre Party, had already moved so far to the right that they now felt ill at ease working with the Socialists under a Socialist chancellor. This so-called grand coalition had the utmost difficulty holding together for the two years (1928–30) the government lasted, plunging from one internal crisis to the next. The influence of the brilliantly successful Foreign Minister, Gustav Stresemann, just managed to keep the right wing of the coalition in government. To carry through his diplomacy of persuading the Allies to relax their grip on Germany, he needed a stable government behind him. But the coalition did not survive his death in October 1929.

The three years from 1928 to 1930 were critical in the decline of Weimar Germany. Economic distress was becoming severe among the small farmers. Then followed the Wall Street crash and its chain reaction in Europe. Industrial output contracted and unemployment soared (page 164). The Nazis were able to capitalise on the grievances of the small farmers and then as the depression widened and deepened they exploited the resentments of the lower-middle classes, the shopkeepers and white-collar workers who were facing uncertainties and financial hardships and who feared a Bolshevik revolution from the unemployed industrial workers. On the political scene, the conservative Nationalist Party was excluded from power by the 'grand coalition' which in 1928 supported a broader-based government. The Nationalists in that year had fallen under the leadership of a wealthy industrialist and publisher, Alfred Hugenberg, who hated Weimar democracy and socialism equally. The Nationalists had not done well in the elections of 1928. The effect of their setback was to encourage Hugenberg to look to the more extreme right for votes. In the wings, the small, violent and racialist Nazi Party stood on the threshold of achieving mass support.

The first opportunity for the Nazis to make a significant electoral impact in the Reichstag elections came in 1930. The economic crisis had broken up the Socialist-led grand coalition. The partners of that coalition could not agree whether employers or the workers should suffer from the government's only remedy to the crisis, the cutting back of expenditure. Like the majority of the Labour Party in Britain, the Social Democrats could not remain in a government which reduced unemployment benefits. President von Hindenburg now called on the leader of the Centre Party, Heinrich Brüning, to lead a new government. There were threats that the President would dispense with the Reichstag's approval and resort to emergency decrees provided for in the constitution if it rejected Brüning's savage deflation. This happened within a few weeks and Brüning now staked his future on dissolving the Reichstag and on a new election. Its unexpected result and its political consequences ushered in the

final phase of Weimar democracy. The vote of the Nazis increased from some 810,000 in 1928 to nearly 6.5 million in the September 1930 election. They increased their representation from 12 to 107, just behind the Socialists, who had 143, and nudged ahead of the Communists, who had 77, to become the second largest party. The conservative Nationalists lost half their support.

It would still perhaps have been just possible to stabilise the political fortunes of Weimar, but Brüning's financial 'cures' killed any chance of this happening. Confidence throughout the country in the ability of the politicians to solve the crisis ebbed away. Economists of the Keynesian school of thought met with complete rejection in the Brüning era. (The Nazis lent them a more ready ear.) There was an alternative policy of expansion and of credit and of state help to put the unemployed to work. Financially the country was sliding into a position where administrators felt that something had to be done. In parliament, the Social Democrats, under the great shock of the National Socialist landslide, backed the minority Brüning government from the benches of the opposition as far as they could. Brüning's preference was for authoritarian, austere government, and with Hindenburg's backing he governed by emergency presidential decrees.

Hindenburg did not want Hitler to come to power. He felt a strong antipathy for the 'Bohemian corporal' (he was actually a Bavarian corporal), a violent uncouth Austrian who shared none of Hindenburg's own Prussian Junker qualities. When Hindenburg was elected president in 1925 by a narrow margin over the candidate of the Socialists and Centre, the spectacle of an avowed monarchist and legendary war hero, the most decorated and honoured of the Kaiser's field marshals, heading a republic seemed incongruous indeed. But the seventy-seven-year-old symbol of past glories did his job decently enough, even raising the respectability of the Republic by consenting to serve as her head. But all his life he had been trained to believe in command and leadership, and the spectacle of parliamentary bickering and the musical chairs the politicians were playing in and out of government appeared to him a travesty of what Germany needed.

Nevertheless the Field Marshal could be relied on to honour his oath to the republican constitution. This gave him the constitutional right to act in an emergency, and he believed, not without justification, that the destructive behaviour of the political parties during the economic crisis of 1929 to 1930 had created a crisis of government. The Young Plan, which fixed the total amount of reparations at 121 thousand million Marks to be paid in instalments over fifty-nine years, was assailed by the Nazis and the right. In 1932, however, at Lausanne, the amount was reduced to 3000 thousand million Marks. Brüning's attempt to court Nationalist opinion and aid the stricken economy by announcing an Austro-German customs union in 1931 failed because the Allies declared that it broke the Versailles Treaty, which prohibited the union of Austria and Germany. Thus dissatisfied, German nationalism was further increased. The army now enjoyed great influence and the attention of historians has been especially focused on the few men, including Hindenburg's son, who increasingly gained the old gentleman's confidence and influenced his decisions.

Brüning governed with austere authority, complete integrity and disastrous results. Raising taxes and reducing salaries was naturally unpopular, all the more so as the economic crisis deepened. Unemployment rose from 2.25 million in 1930 to over 6 million in 1932. Brüning in April 1932 tried to curb street violence by banning all the private armies such as the SA, the SS and the Stahlhelm. His intentions were good but this measure too was largely ineffectual as the organisations survived without openly wearing uniforms. At the depth of the crisis in 1932 the presidential term of office expired. Hindenburg was deeply chagrined not to be re-elected unopposed. Hitler chose to stand against him and lost, but more significant than his failure was the fact that more than 13 million had voted for him. Hindenburg had secured over 19 million votes but was so old that he could not last much longer. Shortly after the presidential elections in May 1932 Hindenburg dropped Brüning. Franz von Papen became chancellor, enjoying no support in the Reichstag or the country. Less than a year was left before Hitler assumed power over Germany. How had he, a complete unknown only eleven years earlier, achieved this transformation? To understand Hitler's rise we must now look at this aspect of Weimar Germany's politics: how Hitler managed to challenge successfully the whole democratic basis of the state.

Fewer than three out of every hundred Germans voted for the Nazis at the national election of 1928 and that was after seven years of unceasing Nazi propaganda. But the Nazis had built an organisational base and increased the party's membership significantly. Nazi ideology was no consistent or logically developed theory such as Marxism claimed to be. There was nothing original about any of its aspects. It incorporated the arrogant nationalistic and race ideas of the nineteenth century, specifically the anti-Semitic doctrines and the belief in German uniqueness and Germany's world mission, together with elements of fascism and socialism, for in its early days the National Socialist Workers' Party wooed the urban worker.

The National Socialists, or Nazis for short, had grown out of one of the many small racialist and nationalist groups already flourishing in Germany – one organised in Munich by a man called Anton Drexler. His name would have remained insignificant but for Hitler's association with the group. Under Hitler's leadership from July 1921 onwards, the party was opportunistic, seeking to grow strong on all the resentments felt by different sections of the German people: the small farmers, who suffered from the agricultural depression and, later, inflation; the middle class, whose status was threatened and whose savings had been wiped out; unemployed workers; those industrialists at the other end of the scale who were the declared enemies of socialism even in its mildest form; theologians, mainly Protestant, who saw in Nazism a spiritual revival against Weimar materialism. The extreme nationalism of the Nazis made a strong appeal.

Few of those who were early supporters accepted all the disparate objectives that Nazism purported to stand for, but every group of supporters was prepared to discount, overlook or accept as the 'lesser evil' those things it inwardly disapproved of. They saw in Hitler and his movement what they wished to see. This same attitude also accounts for the still widely held view that there was a 'good Hitler' who cured unemployment and unified Germany, and a 'bad Hitler' who persecuted the Jews, made war and ignored justice when dealing with individuals and minority groups. That attitude expresses the feelings of those who brought the Nazis to power and maintained them; it assumes that one does not have to judge the 'whole' but can accept the evils for the sake of the benefits.

Nazism exploited the backward-looking conservatism that flourished in Germany after the disillusionment of defeat in 1918. Paradoxically

Hitler imposed a revolution of values and attitudes that plunged German society into accelerating change after 1933. But what some of those Germans who supported him saw in Hitler in the 1920s was a return to an old virtuous Germany, a simpler Germany that had never really existed. Part of this turning back can be seen in Hitler's emphasis on the need for a healthy people to live close to the land. It was erroneously argued that modern Germany lacked land and space for a 'healthy' expansion of the people. Hence the obsession with gaining *Lebensraum*, and Hitler's plans for satisfying these 'needs' in the east. Hitler, too, dwelt obsessively on the medieval image of the Jew as an alien, a parasite, who produced nothing but lived on the work of others. 'Work' was ploughing the land, the sweat of the brow, not sitting in banks and lending money. Yet he also had sound instincts which led him to accept some modern economic concepts as a way out of the miseries of the last Weimar years. The discredited race doctrines of the nineteenth century were reinforced and amplified in the study of a new race biology. The ideology of race lent a spurious cohesion to all the Nazi policies.

This was a turning back on the age of reason. Numerous organizations from the large veteran association, the Stahlhelm, to small so-called *völkisch* groups embraced strident nationalism and a mystical Teutonic secular faith. None saw in Weimar's parliamentary democracy anything but a shameful subordination of the German nation to alien foreign domination. It was identified also with the Jews, who played a small but distinguished role in its constitutional, administrative, economic and artistic life, although they formed only 1 per cent of the nation's population. They were besmirched by Nazi calumnies that they were war profiteers and corrupters. More significant than the slanders themselves is the wide credence which lies won in Germany.

The counterpart to this support for right-wing extremism in its various forms was the lack of positive support and understanding by the majority of Germans for the spirit of parliamentary democracy. In the 1920s anti-democratic ideas were not only propagated by the communists and by the ignorant and ill-educated, but found strong support among the better-off, middle-class youth, especially within the student unions and universities. Stresemann's success in dismantling the punitive aspects of Versailles won no acclaim because his methods were peaceful and conciliatory, as they had to be if they were to succeed in the years immediately after the war. The notion that a democracy tolerates different ideas and different approaches to solving problems was instead condemned as disunity, as the strife and chaos of parties. The parties themselves – apart from the totalitarian-oriented Nazi and Communist Parties – rarely understood that they had to place the well-being of the whole nation before narrow party interests, that even while they attacked each other they had to acknowledge a common framework and defend above all parliamentary democracy itself. Democracy was regarded as representing the lowest common denominator of politics, the rule of the masses. Fascism and Nazism also appealed to the elitists, who saw themselves as leading the masses.

The educated and better-off followers feared above everything 'social revolution'; they preferred the Nazi promise of 'national revolution' which would, they thought, enhance their career opportunities. What made the Nazis so successful was precisely the combination of physical force in the streets, which was welcomed by anti-communists, and the support of the 'professionals' in the army, civil service, the Churches and education. They, the supposedly educated elite, had helped to undermine Weimar democracy even in the years of prosperity and made Nazism respectable. In the absence of strong positive support, democracy – and with it the rule of law – is dangerously exposed. It could not survive the economic blizzard of 1929 to 1932, which was not the root cause of its downfall but more the final blow. Nevertheless there were regions of Germany that did not succumb to the tidal wave of Nazism even in 1933; this is true of the strongly Catholic Rhineland and Bavaria. In the big industrial cities, too, such as Berlin and Hamburg, most factory workers in the beginning continued to support the Social Democrats and the communists. The rise of the Nazis to power was not the inevitable consequence of the lost war, of inflation and depression. It was not automatic, the result of the inexorable working out of the disadvantages besetting Germany after 1918. Hitler succeeded because a sufficient mass of German people, including many in leading positions of society, chose to support what he stood for. While he did not reveal all his aims, he did reveal enough to be rejected by anyone believing in democracy and basic human rights. Among mainly young Nazi thugs there were many fanatical and warped idealists. Other supporters were opportunists joining a bandwagon for reasons of personal gain. Many saw in Hitler a saviour who would end Germany's 'humiliation' and the 'injustices' of Versailles.

No preparation for power was stranger or more unlikely than Adolf Hitler's. He lived for fifty-six years, from his birth in the small Austrian town of Braunau on 20 April 1889 until his suicide on 30 April 1945 in his bunker under the Reich Chancellery in Berlin. During the last twelve years of his life he dominated first Germany and then most of continental Europe. His impact on the lives of millions was immense, responsible as he was for immeasurable human misery. He believed mankind to be engaged in a colossal struggle between good and evil and he made this hysterical fantasy come true more nearly than any single man had done before. Yet nothing in the first thirty years of his life pointed to the terrible impact he would make on history. The historian searches in vain for anything extraordinary in his early life.

*Mein Kampf* 'My Struggle', which Hitler wrote during his short spell of imprisonment in 1924, glamorised his past, and recent research has shown his account to be unreliable. Hitler suffered no hardship other than the consequences of his own early restless way of life. His father was a conscientious customs official who died when he was fourteen years old; his mother was devoted and did her best for her son, whose attachment to her was deep. But Hitler could not accustom himself to regular work, even during his secondary school days. Supported financially by his mother, he drifted into a lonely way of life, avoiding all regular work, aspiring to be an artist. He attempted to gain entrance to the Academy of Fine Arts in Vienna but was rejected, as were the majority of applicants. Nevertheless, in his nineteenth year he moved to the Habsburg capital. His mother had recently died from cancer; Hitler had cared for her during the final traumatic phase, aided by a Jewish doctor to whom he expressed his gratitude.

For the next two years the money left him by his parents and an orphan's pension provided him with an adequate income. He could indulge his fancies; he read a great deal and impractically designed grandiose buildings in the backroom of his lodgings. He continued in this lonely and irregular lifestyle; soon all the money he had inherited was spent.

There is little reliable information about his next two years. He disappeared from view, living in poverty without attempting regular work, relying on charity and boarding in cheap hostels. It would seem probable that he still dreamt of becoming an architect, and more importantly imbibed the crude anti-Semitic and racialist ideas current in Vienna at that time. In May 1913, in his twenty-fourth year, he moved to Munich, Bavaria's artistic capital. He lived there by selling sketches and watercolours, executed with care and photographic accuracy, pleasing pictures of no great artistic merit. He could, then, be fairly described as self-educated but without discipline, with sufficient artistic skill to have earned his living as an engraver or poster designer had he desired regular work. He was essentially a loner, who had established no deep relationships, and he was already filled with resentments and hatreds which came to be centred more and more on the Jews.

The outbreak of the Great War he later regarded as the turning point in his life. He volunteered for the Bavarian army with enthusiasm. He already saw himself as a Pan-German, and not a loyal subject of the multinational Habsburgs, whom he detested. During the war he was wounded and awarded the Iron Cross First Class; he served as a despatch messenger, though in those days communications were passed mainly on foot along the small distances from trench to trench or from one command post to another. It is notable that he was never promoted beyond the rank of corporal, despite the desperate need for NCOs, a reflection of his superior's view that Corporal Hitler was not a suitable leader of men. When he returned to Munich after the war at the age of twenty-nine, his lack of formal qualification and education was typical of millions for whom the future looked grim. But it is from this point on that his hitherto insignificant and unsuccessful life took a fantastic new turn.

For a start, his interest in politics and loyalty commended him to the new Reichswehr. The army retained him in a division for 'military education'. One of his tasks was to investigate and infiltrate dubious, possibly left-wing, political groups. In this way he came to join Drexler's small German Workers' Party, more a pub-debating society than a genuine party. The transformation of Hitler now began. As a political agitator and an orator who could move his audiences to emotion and hysteria with the violence of his language, Hitler discovered a new vocation. He did not of course see himself as the leader of Germany at this stage, but rather as the propagandist who would help to power the extreme nationalists – men like Ludendorff who would rescue Germany from 'Bolshevism' and the Jews and who would break the shackles of Versailles.

Hitler fulminated against the world Jewish conspiracy, Wall Street and 'Bolshevism', and against the injustices of Versailles, until out of Drexler's debating club a real party emerged with 55,000 supporters by 1923. From 1921 Hitler led that party, renamed the National Socialist German Workers' Party (or by its German initials NSDAP). Hitler the rabid rabble-rousing politician had arrived, a fact made possible only by the totally chaotic political condition of Bavaria where a disparate right had bloodily defeated an equally disparate left (page 123). In November 1923 Hitler misjudged the situation and sought to seize power for the forces of the right in much the same way as Lenin had seized control of Petrograd with a few devoted revolutionaries. His attempted Munich *Putsch* ended ignominiously, Hitler fleeing when the police opened fire. Ludendorff alone, with more courage than good sense, marched through the cordon of police. Hitler had expected that he would seize power without bloodshed and that the police and army would rally to the Ludendorff–Hitler alliance. Later he recognised that failure had saved him. Had he succeeded in gaining control and marched on 'Red Berlin' as he intended, the government would not have capitulated to a fanatic and extremist. Nor, as the Army High Command knew, would the French, who had entered the Ruhr, have tolerated for a moment a coup led by a man who so stridently denounced the Versailles Treaty; the French, moreover, still possessed the strength and determination to prevent such a coup. Hitler might then have been finished for good.

Hitler turned his trial for treason, conducted in Bavaria by judges who sympathised with his cause, into a personal propaganda triumph. Sentenced to the minimum term of five years' imprisonment, he actually only served a few months. While in prison he started writing *Mein Kampf* and after his release he began to rebuild the party which was to carry him to power. The Munich *Putsch* had convinced him that the Nationalist right could not be trusted and was too feeble. He would be the leader, not they. From 1925 to 1928 there were two important developments: a steady but slow growth of membership

of the Nazi Party and continuing bitter internal disputes among the leaders, notably Joseph Goebbels, Julius Streicher and the Strasser brothers, Gregor and Otto. Hitler was handicapped by a ban on his making public speeches until May 1928, and he did not dare defy it for fear of being deported from Germany as an Austrian citizen. He nevertheless sought to create a tight, national Nazi organisation, insisting on absolute obedience to himself. Right up to the final triumph of 30 January 1933, when he became chancellor, there was a real threat of defections from the Nazi Party he led.

In 1925 Hitler judged that the established government was too strong to be seized by force. He changed his tactics. He would follow the legal, constitutional road by entering Reichstag elections to gain a majority, and only then establish his dictatorship. He never showed anything but contempt for the Reichstag and, though leader of the party, would never himself take part in its proceedings. He advised his followers 'to hold their nose' when in the Reichstag. During the period from 1925 to 1928 he built up his party as a virulent propaganda machine, insisted that he alone should lead it, without requiring the advice of leading party personalities, for it was an essential element of his plans to cultivate the cult of the Führer or Leader. The party membership reached 97,000 in 1929. Was the economic crisis then not the real cause of this sudden success? The economic crisis which overtook the world is usually dated from the time of the Wall Street crash in 1929. But this is misleading (see Chapter 19). By the winter of 1927–8 distress was already felt in Germany among the small agricultural farmers and workers in north-west Germany and by artisans and small shopkeepers especially. The Nazi party made considerable headway in rural districts in local and state elections in 1929 at the expense of the traditional Conservative and Nationalist Parties.

In that same year with the economic crisis deepening, the conservative Nationalist, Hugenberg, hoped to gain power by forming a broad alliance of the right and using Hitler to win the support of those masses which the conservatives had failed to attract. A vicious campaign was launched against the Young reparations plan of 1929. The reparations and the politicians of Weimar were blamed for Germany's economic ills. The economic and Nationalist assault proved explosive. But the German electorate's reaction in the Reichstag elec-

*Who would have considered Hitler the man of destiny as the Nazi Party faithful congregated in Nuremberg for the third Party rally in 1927? Despite the ceremonial pomp, the NSDAP only polled 810,000 votes the following year, winning just twelve seats in the Reichstag.*

tion of September 1930 was not what Hugenberg expected: the Nationalists lost heavily and the Nazis made their first breakthrough at the level of national elections, winning 107 seats to become the second-largest party after the Socialists. In a little more than two years their electoral support had increased from 810,000 to 6.5 million.

The period from 1930 to the end of January 1933 was in many ways the most testing for Hitler. Industrialists, however, began to hedge their bets and substantial financial contributions began flowing into Nazi funds. The propaganda campaign against Weimar became ever more vicious. Support among the industrial workers in the big cities could not be won over; the Catholic south remained largely immune too. Although originating in Bavaria, the Nazis gained the greatest following in rural northern Germany. The white-collar workers, the rural voters and elements of what is rather unsatisfactorily labelled the middle class, especially those threatened by Brüning's financial measures with a drop in their standard of living, were the new Nazi voters. The Nazis and Nationalists did all in their power to discredit Weimar democracy. Papen, the new Chancellor in June 1932, hoped to gain Hitler's sympathetic support by lifting the ban

*Weimar Germany, 1932, on the brink of collapse. Communist and Nazi flags jostle for space in this Berlin tenement.*

on the SA (Sturm Abteilung, or stormtroopers) and, in July, by illegally ousting the socialist government of Prussia.

Papen's Cabinet of 'Barons', as it became known from the titled nonentities of which it was composed, enjoyed no support in the Reichstag. The effect of the two elections which Papen induced Hindenburg to call in July and November 1932 in an unsuccessful attempt to secure some support in the country and parliament were the coffin nails of democracy, for those parties which were determined to destroy the Weimar republic between them won a comfortable majority in the Reichstag. The Nazis in July won 230 seats and 37 per cent of the vote, becoming the largest single party; in the election of November 1932 they held on to 33 per cent of the electorate, saw their seats drop to 196, but remained the largest party; the Nationalists secured almost 9 per cent, and the communists 17 per cent (100 seats) – nor did the three anti-democratic parties have any scruples about acting together. The Socialists slipped from 133 seats to 121. Papen had gambled on making the Nazis more amenable by inflicting an electoral defeat on them. The Nazis did indeed suffer a setback in November 1932. Papen was pleased, but Hitler had lost only a battle, not a war. On 17 November Papen resigned. Hitler thought his moment had come. Summoned to Hindenburg, he was told by the Field Marshal that he would be considered as chancellor only if he could show that a parliamentary majority backed him and that unlike Papen he could govern without special presidential decrees. Such conditions, Hindenburg and Hitler perfectly well knew, could not be met. They amounted to a rejection of Hitler.

Hindenburg wanted his favourite, Papen, back. Papen planned to prorogue the Reichstag and change the constitution. However, General Kurt von Schleicher, who represented the right of the Army High Command and who had played an influential political role behind the scenes, persuaded Hindenburg that Papen's plans would lead to civil war and that the army had lost confidence in Papen's ability to control the situation. With obvious reluctance Hindenburg appointed Schleicher on 2 December 1932 to head the last pre-Hitler government. Schleicher's own solution was to try to split the Nazi Party and to win the support of Gregor Strasser and his more left-wing section of the party. Strasser, who was very influential as the head of the party's political organisation,

had become disillusioned with Hitler's tactics of demanding total power and his adamant refusal to share power with coalition partners. Despite evidence of falling Nazi support in the November 1932 election, Hitler won. Strasser made the task easier for him by resigning from the party in early December 1932 after bitterly quarrelling with Hitler, who accused him of treachery. Hindenburg's opposition and internal disputes made many Nazis feel that their chance of gaining power was ebbing away. But Hitler was proved right only a few weeks later. Schleicher announced his government's programme for relieving unemployment and distress; wages and benefits were raised, but even so the divided Reichstag was united on one issue alone – to refuse Schleicher their backing. Papen meanwhile ensured that the only outcome of Schleicher's failure would be a new coalition ostensibly led by Hitler but which Papen expected to control.

Hindenburg was cajoled into concluding that the parliamentary crisis could be ended only by offering the chancellorship to Hitler, the leader of the largest party, even though Hitler had not set foot in the Reichstag as a parliamentary leader. The ins and outs of the final intrigues that overcame Hindenburg's obvious reluctance are still debated by historians. Papen and the conservative and Nationalist right totally misjudged and underestimated Hitler. They believed they could tame him, that he would have to rely on their skills of government. Instead Hitler ended the parliamentary crisis in short order by doing what he said he would do, that is by crushing the Weimar constitution and setting up a totalitarian state. But Papen's intrigues were merely the final blow to the already undermined structure of Weimar's democracy; it cannot be overlooked that Hitler, whose party had openly proclaimed that it stood for the destruction of the Weimar constitution, had won one-third of the votes in November 1932; this meant a higher proportion of electors supported the Nazi Party than had supported any other single party at previous post-1920 Reichstag elections. Given the multiplicity of parties and the system of proportional representation a greater electoral victory than the Nazis achieved is difficult to conceive. It was not backstairs diplomacy alone then that brought Hitler to power, but also the votes of millions of people which made his party the largest in the Reichstag by far. In November 1932 the Nazis had polled 11,737,000 votes against 7,248,000 of the second-largest party, the Social Democrats.

There is a strong contrast between the long wait for power and the speed with which Hitler silenced and neutralised all opposition to establish a totalitarian regime. The destruction of Weimar democracy, and the civic rights that were guaranteed by the constitution to all German citizens was accomplished behind a legal façade which stilled the consciences of all those in the state who should have resisted. The reasons for the lack of opposition had their roots in the past. The elites which led the German state – the majority of administrators, civil servants, the army, the Churches too – had followed a long tradition of defaming democracy; Hitler's anti-Semitism and his attacks on minorities were nothing new in their thinking. This weakness is as noteworthy as Hitler's rise. All the more honour to the minority who refused to accept the changes and actively resisted or left the country. Almost half the German electorate was prepared to support Hitler in the hope of better times, to be brought about by a 'national revolution' and an end to Weimar and disunity.

The Nazis occupied only three posts in the coalition Cabinet. Hitler was chancellor; Hermann Göring was placed in charge of Prussia as minister without portfolio and Prussian minister of the interior under Vice-Chancellor Papen; and Wilhelm Frick was minister of the interior. The government posts had been carefully arranged so that the army and the Foreign Ministry, as well as other key ministries, were not under Nazi control. Papen and the Nationalists soon discovered that Hitler was not inhibited from exercising control by the constitutional niceties that had been devised to restrain him. This was no Weimar coalition government!

The easy, almost effortless path to total dictatorial power makes melancholy reading. The setting alight of the Reichstag on 27 February 1933, probably by the unbalanced Dutchman van der Lubbe alone – though there can be no certainty – became the pretext for an emergency decree signed by Hindenburg suspending personal liberties and political rights.

Hitler had insisted on new elections as a condition for accepting office, intending to gain an absolute majority, and he meant to make sure of it. Accordingly, despite Papen's supposed seniority, Göring seized control of Prussia, which comprised two-thirds of Germany, and under cover of the emergency decree terrorised the opponents of the Nazis. After an electoral campaign of unparalleled violence and intimidation, with Joseph Goebbels manipulating press and radio to help secure a Nazi victory, the Nazis just failed to gain the expected overall majority. Their votes, rose to over 17 million; the Socialists held on to over 7 million votes and the Communists, despite the Nazi campaign, polled 4.8 million votes; the Centre Party secured nearly 4.5 million and the Nationalists (DNVP) a disappointing 3.1 million. But, together with the Nationalists, the Nazis could muster a majority against all other parties, sufficient to govern with the support of the Reichstag. This was obviously not Hitler's aim. He sought dictatorial power and a change of the constitution, but this required a two-thirds majority and shrewdly he wished to proceed in a pseudo-legal way to assure himself of the support of the country afterwards.

Not a single communist deputy of the 81 elected could take his seat. All were already in the hands of the Gestapo (Geheime Staats Polizei, or Secret State Police) or being hunted down. More than twenty of the Socialists also were under arrest or prevented from attending. Still Hitler needed the support of the Nationalists and so to reassure them and the army and the President, he staged an opening ceremony of the Reichstag in the shrine of monarchical Junkerdom, the old garrison church of Potsdam where Frederick the Great lay buried. But even with the communists prevented from voting and the Nationalists voting on his side, Hitler still lacked the two-thirds majority he needed. It will always be to the shame of the members of the once great Centre Party that they tempered their principles and threw in their lot with Hitler, and agreed to vote for his dictatorial law. They lost the will to resist, and the leadership later came to an

### Reichstag Elections, 5 March 1933

|  | seats | percentage of votes |
|---|---|---|
| National Socialists (NSDAP) | 288 seats | 43.9% |
| Nationalists (DNVP) | 52 seats | 8% |
| Centre (Zentrum) | 74 seats | 11.2% |
| Socialists (SPD) | 120 seats | 18.3% |
| Communists (KPD) | 81 seats | 12.3% |
| Others | 32 seats | 6.3% |

*The Reichstag sits, 23 March 1933. All seems orderly in this Nazi propaganda photo; there is no hint of the violence and intimidation that succeeded in burying democracy with the passing of the Enabling Law that day. Göring presides over proceedings from the chair in the top right.*

agreement to secure Catholic interests. It was left to the Socialist Party alone to vote against Hitler's so-called Enabling Law, which acquired its two-thirds majority on 23 March 1933 with the stormtroopers howling vengeance outside the Reichstag on anyone who dared to oppose Hitler's will.

Now Hitler was able to put his aims into practice with far less restraint. Under the sinister application of the term *Gleischaltung* (co-ordination or literally a switch used to bring one current in line with another), a vague all-embracing aim was set out forcibly to subordinate all the activities of German society – government, administration, the free press and trade unions – to Nazi bodies set up specially to supervise them. Thus while in some cases the old institutions remained, they were subject to new Nazi controls. The whole process was haphazard and new Nazi organisations proliferated, frequently in rivalry with each other as well. Hitler in the final resort would decide between conflicting authorities. Until he did so there was the inevitable chaos and infighting. For a time he might decide it best not to interfere too much in a particular administrative branch or, for example, leave the High Command of the army intact. The complete process of *Gleisch-*

*altung* would be applied later to the army also. Hitler insisted on his own final say, on maintaining some of the traditional structures as long as he thought this tactically necessary to overcome misgivings among broad sections of the German people or powerful groups such as the army. His revolution would be complete but gradual. The Nazi state was thus no efficient monolith. Within the overall framework of acceptance of the Führer as leader, rivalries flourished and independent policies were still pursued for short periods. During the early years there were even islands of legality and normality to confuse opinion at home and abroad.

Among the first steps that Hitler took was to abolish the independent powers of the federal states in March 1933. In April a decree purged the civil service of Jews and those of Jewish descent, and of anyone whom the Nazis deemed to oppose the regime's aims. In Prussia a quarter of the higher civil service was dismissed, including judges who were supposed to be irremovable. The Supreme Court in Leipzig secretly debated whether they should make a protest at this unconstitutional act and decided on discretion. No wonder the German public was misled by the seeming legality of these new 'laws'. During the course of the summer of

1933, the remaining independent parties were disbanded. The communist leaders were already in the new concentration camps. The Vatican now decided to conclude a treaty – the Concordat – with Hitler in a misguided effort to protect Catholic interests. The independent trade unions were quickly brought to heel and suppressed, and the workers enrolled in the Nazi Labour Front. The press and broadcasting were placed under Goebbels's direction. The universities did not put up any real resistance either. There were famous professors like the philosopher Martin Heidegger who, at least for a short time, gave public support to the Nazi movement. Some became ardent Nazis out of conviction; many, opportunistically, for the sake of their careers.

Thus there were many who tried to please the new rulers. Academics participated in the famous burning of the books by Jewish and anti-Nazi authors. Many of Germany's internationally known scientists, writers and artists joined the 'national revolution' of the Nazis. Nor were theologians immune from the Nazi corruption: Christ became an Aryan even. The dismissed Jews, such as Albert Einstein, began to leave the country. So did a few Christian Germans, including the Nobel Prize-winning writer Thomas Mann. Germany's other literary giant, who had also won the Nobel Prize for literature, Gerhart Hauptmann, remained in Nazi Germany, adorning the new regime.

Hitler was sensitive to German public opinion. The German people, he understood, would need to be 'educated' to accept the harshness and final brutality in stages. So, when Jews were dismissed from the civil service, some were granted their state pensions provided they had completed at least ten years of service. Those Jews who had fought in the First World War or whose sons or fathers had died in the war were temporarily excepted from dismissal at Hindenburg's request. Terror was exercised against specific opponents. Dachau was the first concentration camp, established near Munich in 1933 by Heinrich Himmler, head of the Bavarian political police. It became the model for others, and by the summer of 1933 at least 30,000 Germans were held in concentration camps. Himmler soon advanced to become the Reichsführer of the SS (Schutzstaffel) and head of the police throughout the Reich. The courts and police also continued to function.

Germany was left as a mosaic where the normal process of law and administration continued to function fairly in some instances. In other areas the Nazis or the terror arm of the SS were supreme, and no appeal to the courts was possible. Jewish students were for a time permitted to continue their university studies on a quota system. Until 1938, some Jewish businesses continued to function, though many went bankrupt. 'I always go as far as I dare and never farther,' Hitler told a meeting of party leaders in April 1937. So Hitler, at the same time as he breached the vital principles of basic civic rights, gave the outward appearance of acting mildly and reasonably, and always in conformity with proper 'laws'. And did not the person of President Hindenburg guarantee decency? The German people did not realise how completely the President had lost all power. But knowledge of the concentration camps was a deterrent to any thought of opposition from all except the most courageous.

Hitler was especially careful to appease the army. He assured it of an independent status and of its position as the sole armed force in the state. The army wished to draw on the young stormtroopers whom it would train as a large armed force that could quickly augment the regular army in time of crisis. This meant the subordination of the SA to the needs of the army. The head of the stormtroopers, Ernst Röhm, had entirely different ideas. The stormtroopers were not only a separate army in the state, but he saw them under his command as the untainted force which would carry through the complete Nazi revolution in opposition to Hitler, who appeared willing to compromise with the old elements of power, the army and industrialists. Hitler reacted ruthlessly and, with the help of the Reichswehr during what became known as the Night of the Long Knives on 30 June 1934, had Röhm and many senior officers of the SA murdered. The same opportunity was taken to murder General von Schleicher, Gregor Strasser and two of Papen's close associates, as a warning to Papen's nationalist 'allies'. Hitler, with the connivance of the army, had now openly set himself above the law.

On 2 August 1934, Hindenburg, the one man probably still more popular than Hitler, died. He was buried at a great funeral ceremony and for the last time Hitler took a back seat. With Hindenburg were laid to rest symbolically the last vestiges of the Prussian Junker and military traditions of honour and service. The moment Hindenburg died, Hitler took another important step towards supreme power. A decree announced that the offices of president and chancellor were merged in one person, Hitler, who now became the Führer and Reich Chancellor. The Reichswehr generals, believing that they would still control all military decisions, did not oppose Hitler's demand that the army should swear a personal oath of loyalty to him as head of state. Enormous power was now concentrated in Hitler's hands. But still he moved with caution, step by step, accepting that he would need time to achieve his goals.

The year 1934 also witnessed the belated small beginnings of protest against the implications of Nazi anti-Semitism though only as far as it affected the Church's own administration, and the largely unsuccessful attempts by Hitler to subordinate the Protestant Church. That Hitler did not choose immediately to crush the opposition of the Confessional Protestant Church movement and other protests, however, was due not to moderation, as people mistakenly thought, but to his caution, his wish to dominate only gradually all spheres of German life. He bided his time.

Hitler had a clear view of priorities. At home the most important issue was unemployment. If he could get the out-of-work back into factories and construction, enable the small businesses to become sufficiently profitable again and provide security and promotion opportunities for civil servants and army officers, their support for him would be sure. If he failed on the economic front, he would be likely to fail all along the line. That is why Hitler was prepared to tolerate the continuation of Jewish businesses, to allow Jewish salesmen to remain prominent in the export trade until 1938, and to make use of unorthodox financial management to achieve a rapid reduction of the unemployed; real incomes would cease to fall.

Between March 1933 and March 1934 unemployment fell by over 2 million, in part but not wholly due to the ending of recession. Able men served Hitler, including the brilliant financial expert, Hjalmar Schacht, whom the Führer appointed president of the Reichsbank. Plans worked out in advance by Hitler's economic advisers were now put into action. With guaranteed prices for their produce, farmers recovered during the first

three years of the regime; small businesses were helped with state spending; taxes were reduced; grants were made to industry to install new machinery; work was created in slum clearance and housing and *Autobahn* construction. The economy was stimulated out of recession. Though wages did not rise in real terms, security of employment was a greater benefit for the wage-earners. The pursuit of autarky or self-sufficiency helped the construction, chemical, coal and iron and steel industries. The industrialists welcomed the opportunities for expansion and increased profit and applauded the destruction of free trade unions. But industry lost its independence as its barons became dependent on state orders and state allocation of resources. The First and Second Four-Year Plans imposed state controls severely limiting the capitalist economy. Armament expenditure remained relatively low from 1933 to 1935, but from then on was rapidly increased, putting Germany on a war footing and eliminating unemployment. Belts had to be tightened, – 'guns before butter' – but it was too late for any opposition to loosen the Nazi hold on power; there was in any case no opposition that could any longer command a mass following.

By 1934 Hitler's regime had established a sufficient base of power and secured enough willing co-operation of 'experts' in the administration, business and industry as well as the army for his Nazi state to function, though often with much confusion. The Nazi ideologues and fanatics had formed an alliance with the educated and skilled who served them. Without them the Nazis could not have ruled Germany. What German history of this period shows is that parliamentary democracy and the rule of law, once established, will not inevitably continue. If they are not defended, they can be destroyed – not only by violent revolution, but more subtly by determined and ruthless men adopting pseudo-legal tactics.

And what of the outside world – they too not only gave Hitler the concessions he demanded or unilaterally took by breaking treaties but in 1936 handed him the spectacular triumph of holding the Olympic Games, dedicated to freedom and democracy, in Berlin.

# CHAPTER 22

# The Mounting Conflict in Eastern Asia, 1928–1937

It is often said that the Second World War began in China in 1931. According to this view the global rise of fascism first blossomed into external aggression when Japan attacked China; then the tide of war spread to Europe and Africa, to Abyssinia and Spain, until Hitler unleashed the Second World War by marching into Poland in 1939. Undeniably there was some interdependence of European and Asian events in the 1930s. Britain and the United States were in a sense sandwiched between conflicts on the European continent and eastern Asia, with vast interests bound up in the future of both worlds, West and East. But to view the earlier history of eastern Asia from the point of view of the European war of 1939 is to see that history from a Western focus, and thus to distort it. The problems of eastern Asia were coming to a head irrespective of the rise of fascism and Nazism. The problems of Europe, too, had entirely independent roots. 'Interdependence' between Asia and Europe before the critical months of 1940 and 1941 has thus been exaggerated.

It is important to recognise also that seen through Japanese and Chinese eyes Western policies appeared to change with confusing rapidity in the first three decades of the twentieth century. Conscious of their military and industrial weakness in comparison with the West, the Chinese and Japanese accordingly had to calculate how best to adapt to constantly shifting external conditions. Critical too was the question of what their relationship to each other should be. All these problems

arising from 'modernisation' and changing external and internal Asian relationships were to reach explosive intensity during the 1930s. The different strands can be seen more clearly if separated.

In Japan the orderly coherent structure of national government and decision-making began to fall apart in 1930. Extremism and lawlessness and a decentralisation of power occurred. Japan's disintegration was political and internal. In China there was physical disintegration. No 'government' of the 'republic' of China could rule the whole vast country. Foreign control had been established over China's principal ports during the nineteenth and twentieth century and over Manchuria, Outer Mongolia and Tibet. To add to these setbacks Chiang Kai-shek and his Kuomintang Party became involved in civil war after breaking with the communists. Then there were constant conflicts between the greater and lesser warlords who ruled much of China as military–feudal commanders in the 1930s. Chiang Kai-shek fought some of these warlords but was never strong enough really to control them or their armies. Most made their peace with him, however, by assenting to nominal allegiance to Chiang Kai-shek and his government of the Republic of China, while continuing to rule independently over their fiefs large and small.

From 1928 to 1937, while Chiang Kai-shek established his capital and government in Nanking, no unified Chinese republic really existed; his reforms had made an impact on urban life but did not reach millions of peasants. His vision of a unified China which as yet bore no relationship to reality. To the Western world he nevertheless embodied China; his ambassadors were accredited to other countries and represented China at the League of Nations in Geneva. Here it was that Chiang Kai-shek sought to mobilise the help of the Western powers when in 1931 the Japanese began transforming their special rights in Manchuria into outright occupation and control of the whole province. The issue appeared to be a simple one for the Western powers of supporting the League and China against Japanese aggression. The contrast between the real condition of China and her international legal position, together with her image in the eyes of the public in the Western world, was one critical factor in the eastern Asia crisis of the 1930s.

The struggle between a central power claiming to speak for and to rule China and regional and provincial rulers was nothing new in modern Chinese history; or, to put it more briefly, the contest between integration and disintegration had been going on for decades and continued until 1949. China's chronic weakness had allowed the European powers to establish colonies and special rights in Shanghai and other treaty ports. Since the beginning of the century the Japanese leaders had been conscious of a great divide in their options for a China policy. Japan could identify with China as a fellow Asian nation and help her to achieve independence from the 'white' imperialists; or she could copy the Western imperialists and join them in acquiring colonial possessions and 'spheres of influence' in China. To combine with China against the West meant certain conflict with the far more powerful Western powers. Japan's best interests seemed to be served by emulating the Western powers and joining in the scramble for China. This meant participating fully in Western great-power diplomacy, which Japan did when concluding an alliance with Britain in 1902. Britain for her part welcomed the Japanese alliance to check Russia and to preserve her own position in China. After the Russo-Japanese war three years later Japan acquired her own considerable empire by annexing Korea and by replacing Russia and carving out a sphere of interest in southern Manchuria. During the next fifteen years the Japanese sought to extend their influence in northern China in agreement with the Russians and at China's expense. The First World War gave Japan her biggest opportunity and

for the first time her ambition now encompassed controlling the government of China itself. But hostile Chinese and international reactions forced the Japanese to withdraw from these extreme pretensions. This was a blow. Worse was the army's profitless Siberian intervention from 1918 to 1922. It had brought neither glory nor gain.

The Japanese in the 1920s then appeared ready to limit their empire to what they already held with the acknowledgement of the Western powers, and beyond this to work with the Western powers within an agreed framework of international treaties, military and territorial. At the Washington Conference of 1921–2 this framework was set up. Japan, as has been noted (page 149), accepted an inferior ratio of battleships to Britain and the United States (3:5:5), but this inferiority was counterbalanced by the agreement of Britain and the United States not to build any naval bases in the Western Pacific. Then the Japanese also signed the Nine-Power Treaty (1922) whereby the powers undertook 'to respect the sovereignty, the independence, and the territorial and the administrative integrity of China', and not to take 'advantage of conditions in China' to seek special rights or create 'spheres of influence'. But what of existing rights? The Western powers were not about to relinquish their rights in Shanghai. Japan also interpreted the treaty as not affecting her existing rights and 'special interests' which, the United States had acknowledged in the past, she should exercise wherever her own territories were close to China's.

Since the opening of the twentieth century the United States had tried to secure the consent of the other powers with interests in China to two propositions. First, they should allow equal economic opportunity to all foreign nations wishing to trade in China (the Open Door). The behaviour of the foreign nations, however, showed that this 'equal opportunity' was not extended to the Chinese themselves, who did not exercise sovereign power over all Chinese territory. Secondly, the United States urged that China should not be further partitioned (respect for sovereignty and territorial integrity), but in practice the United States had acknowledged Japan's special rights and spheres of influence. The second proposition was more a moral hope than real politics. These principles nevertheless were not abandoned. They were reasserted in the 1920s and 1930s.

For Japan, the Washington treaties of 1921–2

stabilised international conduct towards disintegrating China and lessened the chance of conflict with the Western powers. Japan would now maintain her existing rights against a new possible threat, Bolshevik Russia, without fear of conflict with Britain and the United States. A third reason for Japan's peaceful adaptation to the entirely new postwar world was her inability to compete in a naval race with the United States. Japanese finances were exhausted. Japan was dependent on the West to a degree matched by few modern nations. Her capacity to modernise was at the mercy of the Western powers, especially the United States. A Japanese journalist in 1929 summed up Japan's position, reflecting views widely held at the time: 'Japan is a country whose territory is small and whose resources are scarce. It has to depend upon other countries for securing such materials. Furthermore, to sustain the livelihood of its excessive population, Japan finds it imperative to place a high priority upon exporting its products abroad.'

Yet surprisingly the worldwide depression hit Japan less seriously than the West. Japan had an industrious and well-organised people to further economic progress. With the help of a large devaluation of her currency, she had pulled out of the slump by 1932. But now the need for capital, especially from the United States, and for raw materials (cotton, coal, iron ore and oil) from abroad became increasingly essential. The Japanese believed that their own continued economic existence, the ability of the nation to progress, depended on developing the resources of Manchuria (where the Japanese could secure some of the raw materials they needed) and on continued access to the American market. The heavy rearmament programme launched in 1936 and the needs of the military in China, moreover, could not be sustained without American imports of scrap metal and oil. Thus the poverty of resources was Japan's heel of Achilles.

Recognition of this weakness united the Japanese leadership in the military, business, diplomacy, bureaucracy and politics in one aim: that Japan had to maintain her economic empire in China. Four-fifths of all her overseas investment at the close of 1929 were in China. On the importance of China there was no difference between the 'pacific' 1920s and the militaristic 1930s. The rift occurred between the leaders who argued that Japan could achieve this while staying within the legal framework of treaties and concessions held in common with the West, and those who wished to extend the Japanese economic empire not only at China's expense but regardless too of Western economic interests in China. The whole of eastern Asia and south-eastern Asia would become a Japanese-dominated empire serving Japan's interests under the high-sounding guise of a co-operative Japanese commonwealth of Asian nations called the Greater Asia Co-prosperity Sphere. Foreign Minister Matsuoka of the later 1930s, looking at Western behaviour with its earlier emphasis on imperialism and its later support for the League of Nations, simply derided it as a cynical way of changing the rules of international law to suit the West's own selfish interests. 'The Western Powers had taught the Japanese the game of poker,' he once remarked, but then, 'after acquiring most of the chips they pronounced the game immoral and took up contract bridge.'

One significant strand in Japanese thinking about the world was the belief that only by her own endeavours would Japan be accepted as an equal of the 'white' world powers, which did not treat her as an equal. She was still in the process of catching up militarily and industrially with the leading Western nations; to survive among the world powers she must grow in strength or go under. Since the days of Meiji, Japan, for all her later talk of Asian co-operation against the West, did not seek a new role as the leading anti-imperialist nation; she wanted to join the imperialist powers and foresaw a partition of the whole world among them. In that partition Japan and her empire would dominate Asia. Now inevitably this set her on a collision course with Western possessions and economic interests in Asia. Against the European imperialist nations, Japan, though weaker than their combined strength, had a chance of success. Just as the weaker United States in the eighteenth century had made herself dominant in the Western hemisphere – a parallel not lost on Japan – by taking advantage of Europe's distress, of Europe's great internecine wars, so Japan in the twentieth century would profit from the conflicts of Europe. But unlike in the eighteenth century, there was one great power not so affected by these conflicts and standing aside from them and that was the United States. The fulfilment of Japanese ambitions came to depend on the United States.

American policy in Asia in the twentieth century

has been beset by some confusion and contradictions. Paradoxically, one basic tenet of American policy – to uphold the unity and national independence of China in the face of Japanese and European ambitions of piecemeal territorial partition – triumphed in 1949 with the communist victory. For the first time in the century the Chinese mainland was then fused into a genuine national unity. What the Americans had always maintained, that China rightly belonged to the Chinese, had come about. China was set on the road to joining the world's great nations. Only a vestigial presence today remains of the former Western imperial era – Portuguese Macao and British Hong Kong – and both outposts are due to return to full Chinese control by the end of the century. The Chinese became masters of their own internal economic development, their trading relations and their policy towards the outside world. The fulfilment of the Americans' objectives was followed by more than two decades of bitter dispute between the United States and China, including war in Korea. One reason for past ambiguities in US policy was that it was rooted in the genuine desire for eventual Chinese unity on the one hand and equal commercial opportunities for all Western powers on the other. During the 1920s and 1930s the United States was determined to participate in a share of China's market, whose potential was believed to be of critical importance for future Western prosperity.

In 1930 American investment in China, concentrated in Shanghai, was less than American investment in Japan. The Japanese had also acquired rights and privileges, especially in southern Manchuria, based on the Japanese control of the south Manchurian railway and the concessions that went with it. But these rights in Manchuria could not compare with the outright colonial possessions of the European powers acquired by force from a weak China in the nineteenth century, or the semi-colonial 'extra-territorial rights' which the Europeans and Japanese enjoyed in the treaty ports. In southern Manchuria, Japanese control was not absolute but had to be attained by manipulating China's difficulties and working through the local Manchurian warlord. Thus, what came to be regarded as the 'nation's lifeline' was threatened by chaotic conditions and the internal conflicts of China. The Japanese in the 1920s considered China's claims to Manchuria to be purely nominal,

arguing that without Japan's defeat of Russia Manchuria would have been annexed by Russia in 1905 and that Japan's presence in Manchuria for a quarter of a century had ensured peace there. That was not the view of the United States, which upheld China's sovereignty over Manchuria; it should be preserved for a future time when China had overcome her internal problems.

But successive American presidents from Theodore to Franklin Roosevelt never contemplated the possibility that America's commercial or strategic interests were sufficiently large in China to justify the United States' defending them by force of arms and so risking war with Japan. It was not in defence of *American* interests in China that the Pacific War of 1941 to 1945 was fought. For Franklin Roosevelt much wider and more fundamental issues were at stake. These were based on American ideological assumptions which were neither shared nor understood in Japan. The fascinating account of American – Japanese relations from 1939 to 1941 needs to be told later where it belongs chronologically (pages 271–9).

With the onset of the depression after 1927, Japan was beset by additional problems. Though industry recovered more quickly than elsewhere in the world, the farmers suffered severely. The domestic silk industry provided an important additional income for the peasantry and the price of silk plunged in the United States. The countryside became the breeding ground for militarism. A strident nationalism, a sort of super Japanese patriotism with a return to emperor-worship, marks the 1930s. It unified most of the Japanese people. Harsh repression in any case ensured broad conformity, and the educational system was geared to uphold military national values. The more 'liberal' tendencies of the 1920s, which saw a strengthening of the Diet, of political parties, of the influence of big business (the *zaibatsu*) on politics, of the civilian politicians as against the military, was engulfed by the new militaristic nationalism.

All these changes occurred without any formal changes in the Meiji constitution. It had never been a part of that constitution to guarantee personal liberties and thereby to limit the powers of the state. Whenever necessary, censorship and control were instituted. The Japanese were taught to obey the state, and patriotism centred on the veneration of the emperor. But it was characteristic of formal

Japanese institutions and laws that they allowed for enormous flexibility and change in practice. The fount of all power, however, remained the emperor. This meant that whichever group succeeded in speaking in his name could wrap itself in his unchallengeable authority. The Meiji Emperor had taken a real role in the decisions of crucial national policies on the advice of his elder statesmen, the *genro*. The position of his successors was weaker. Emperor Hirohito was elevated to an object of worship and, as a god, was thereby moved away from practical influence on national affairs. Temperamentally gentle and scholarly, the emperor followed rather than controlled the tide of events.

But, despite the introduction of universal male suffrage, Japan was not about to turn into a parliamentary constitutional state in the 1920s. She was ruled from above. Her uniqueness as a society, 'blending emperor-worship and authority with elected institutions, would not be essentially changed by any democratic demands. A Peace Preservation Law imposed severe prison penalties on anyone who even advocated such a change. So the description of the 1920s as the years of Taisho Democracy is a misnomer. The people were not prepared or encouraged to think that they should decide the policies of the state through their elected parties in the parliament. Thus the political parties had no real roots and were the easy victims of military reaction in the 1930s.

There was of course a real difference between the policies pursued by the Japanese in the 1920s and those followed in the 1930s. That difference was due to the change of balance among the groups that exercised power in the state. The army and navy were not subject to the control of the government but, through the right of separate access to the emperor, constituted a separate position of power. The informal *genro* had co-ordinated civilian and military aspects of national affairs. With the passing of the original *genro* through the deaths of its members, no other body advising the emperor was ever again able to exercise such undisputed overall control. The civilian politicians, leaning for support on parliament and backed by some moderates in the army and navy, in the 1920s seemed to have gained the upper hand over the more extreme officers in the navy and army. This split in the military between extremists and moderates indeed made possible their predominance. It found expression in Shidehara's foreign policy and especi-

ally in the naval disarmament treaties of the Washington Conference. But both in the Kwantung army stationed in Manchuria and in the navy a violent reaction to civilian control was forming.

From 1928 until 1936 the leadership groups were caught in cross-currents of violent conflict. They were no longer able to provide a unified Japanese policy. So there is the contrast between the outwardly unified nation embodied in the emperor's supremacy and the breakdown of government culminating in the assassination of those politicians who had fallen foul of nationalist extremists. The army was no longer under unified control. The army command in Tokyo was rent by conspiracies to encourage the Kwantung army to act on its own in Manchuria regardless of the policy of the government. In 1928 the Kwantung army attempted to seize military control over Manchuria and so to anticipate Chiang Kai-shek's attempts to extend his rule by conquest or diplomacy. Chiang Kai-shek might decide to strike a deal with the Manchurian warlord at the expense of Japan's ambitions. The Japanese Kwantung Army Command organised the warlord's murder by blowing up the train on which he was travelling. Although at the time there was an aggressive Japanese government in power in Tokyo which was certainly ready to use military force in China to prevent northern China from falling under Chiang Kai-shek's control, the Kwantung army had overreached itself and its attempt to take over Manchuria was disavowed. The murdered warlord's son took over control of the Chinese Manchurian administration and army. A much more moderate Japanese government came to power in 1929 and the pacific Shidehara returned to the Foreign Ministry. The army smarted under its humiliation. But the Kwantung army was not punished – the colonel in command was merely retired – and two years later, in September 1931, it struck again more effectively.

Meanwhile the new Cabinet of Prime Minister Hamaguchi was soon involved in a confrontation with the navy. The government had consented to a new treaty of naval limitation at the London Conference of 1930, this time applying to cruisers. The Japanese navy had not secured the ratio of cruisers which the Chief of the Naval General Staff, Admiral Kato Kanji, and those naval officers who supported him considered indispensable. The Navy Minister, another admiral, supported the Prime Minister, who won after months of bitter debate.

The split into factions even within the armed services themselves is illustrated by this whole episode. It ended tragically when a nationalist fanatic shot Hamaguchi, who lingered several months before succumbing to his wounds.

In September 1931 the insubordination of the Kwantung garrison army in Manchuria attracted the attention of the world. Its plot to seize Manchuria by force from theoretical Chinese suzerainty and the warlord's actual control was an ill-kept secret. The government in Tokyo was powerless. Shidehara received worthless assurances from the War Minister that the plot would be quashed. In fact there was sympathy within the Army General Staff for the plotters. During the night of 18 and 19 September the Japanese themselves blew up the tracks of the South Manchurian Railway just outside Mukden in Manchuria. On this flimsy pretext the Kwantung army attacked the Chinese and occupied Mukden. The Japanese army in Korea now concerted with the Kwantung army and units crossed into Manchuria. Soon the whole of Manchuria was under military administration.

If this action had been the work of only the middle-ranking subordinate officers of the Kwantung army, as was thought for a long time to be the case, then the government in Tokyo might have re-established its authority. We now know that this authority had already been severely undermined by the lack of confidence of the military in the general course of policy adopted. The conspiracy at Mukden extended to the army leadership in Tokyo. Government was disintegrating. Shidehara tried to hide this fact from the outside world and to make the diplomatic best of it. The difficulty which Shidehara and the politicians, supported by big business, faced was also in part self-made. While they strongly disapproved of the armies' insubordination and interference in politics, as well as their resort to force, they held in common with the army the belief in Japan's China destiny. The army was pursuing essentially the same goals as they. Only their means differed.

Internally the army was out of control and followed its own policy of solving Japan's China policy by force. In February 1932 it set up a puppet state which it called Manchukuo and so declared that Manchuria was severed from Chinese sovereignty. Then it placed the last boy emperor of the ousted Manchu dynasty, with the unlikely name of Henry Pu-yi, on the puppet throne. Possibly the motive for this bizarre move was to have a useful symbol under their control who might be put forward as a Japanese-backed emperor of China. What is certain is that during the next few years the army's ambitions were not limited to securing Japan's rights in southern Manchuria. The Kwantung army was soon extending Japanese influence beyond Manchuria, which was completely conquered by 1933. The Great Wall, the ancient traditional defensive boundary which the Chinese had built to keep out the northern barbarians, proved no barrier to the Japanese. The Japanese army crossed the Great Wall along the railway line running from Mukden in Manchuria to Peking.

Chiang Kai-shek's Nationalist government was far too weak to oppose the Kwantung army by force. In many provinces warlords persisted in exercising power and the communists, from the bases they had established, disputed the Kuomintang's right to speak for and unite China. Resistance against Japan would be hopeless unless China could first be effectively united, and this became Chiang Kai-shek's first priority. He was therefore glad of a truce, which the Japanese were ready to conclude with the Nationalist government in May 1933. Chiang Kai-shek concentrated his forces against the communist stronghold in the south, to crush peasant uprisings and the Red Army. He almost succeeded in the autumn of 1934. But the Red Army broke through the encircling Nationalist armies and set out on the epic Long March, a military manoeuvre without parallel in the annals of history. The Red Army and the communist political and administrative cadres, about 80,000 people in all, sought safety from the pursuing Nationalist forces by walking a long circuitous route to the last-surviving communist base in the north-west of China. They had to fight all the way. The distance which this army covered, through mountains and swamps, in heat and freezing cold, was almost 6000 miles. The Long March took just over a year to accomplish and of the 80,000 who had set out possibly only 9000 reached Yan'an in Shaanxi in October 1935, though others joined on the way. In this province Mao Zedong then rebuilt the communist movement from an initial nucleus of 20,000 to the eventual millions that drove Chiang Kai-shek's armies from the mainland in 1949.

The Kwantung army meanwhile was not idle. It was rapidly expanded from 10,000 officers and men in 1931 to 164,000 in 1935 and by 1941 it had

*Chinese Communist leader Mao Zedong on the arduous Long March of nearly 6000 miles, 16 October 1934–20 October 1935. Of the 80,000 who set out, only some 9000 reached the sanctuary of Yan'an.*

reached an astonishing strength of 700,000. These figures alone provide a graphic illustration of the escalation of Japan's military effort in China. Chiang Kai-shek did not declare war on the Japanese; nor did the Tangku truce in May 1933 between the Nationalist Chinese and the Japanese stop the Kwantung army. By the end of 1935 large regions of northern China and Inner Mongolia were occupied. This brought the Japanese army into contact with the Soviet Union along hundreds of miles of new frontier. The Kwantung army regarded Soviet Russia as the real menace to Japan's aspirations in eastern Asia: Russia alone could put a modern army of millions into the field of battle on land. The Chinese the Japanese disregarded as a serious military force. But just because there were no real obstacles to expansion in China, it was difficult for the Army General Staff to decide where to stop. They argued that the war in China should be limited so that the army could concentrate on the Soviet Union. Other officers wanted first to expand in China. It was the latter who won out in July 1937 when a clash of local Chinese and Japanese troops on the Marco Polo Bridge outside Peking became the Japanese excuse for launching a full-scale war on China.

Chiang Kai-shek had used the years from 1933 to 1937 to consolidate the power of the Kuomintang in the rest of China with some success. But the Western image of republican Chinese democracy was removed from reality. Chiang's regime was totalitarian, with its own gangs and terror police and an army held together by fear and harsh discipline. Supported by intellectuals as the only rallying point for anti-Japanese resistance, and by big business and the landlords as the bulwark against communism, Chiang ruled the country through harshness and corruption. The peasantry were the principal and most numerous victims. Chiang prided himself on having copied techniques of government from Mussolini and Hitler. German military advisers were attached to his army. He also cultivated American friendship by his attitude to business and his welcome to American educators and missionaries. The achievements of the Kuomintang in modernising China during a decade of reforms from 1928 to 1937 also should not be overlooked. Industry grew, communications improved, new agricultural techniques raised produce, education was extended. The cities benefited the most. Tens of millions of peasants, however, remained sunk in abject poverty. Further progress in modernising and unifying China was terminated by the all-out war launched by Japan in 1937.

The educated elite in particular displayed a sense of national pride in the face of internal conflicts and foreign aggression. Trade boycotts were organised against the Japanese and students demonstrated. Groups argued that the Kuomintang and the communists should form a new united front to fight the Japanese. Chiang Kai-shek's priority, however, was to follow Mao to the base he had recently set up in Yenan and smash the 'bandits', before turning to meet the Japanese aggression. He sent Zhang Xueliang, called the Young Marshal, to Xi'an in the province of Shensi with the intention that he should march his troops to Yenan and liquidate the communist stronghold. What happened then is one of the most astonishing episodes in the Chinese war. The Young Marshal installed in Xi'an with his army had ideas of his own. Mao skilfully undermined his loyalty to Chiang Kai-shek appealing to him to make common front against the Japanese. The Young Marshal then looked for allies and sought the support of the powerful warlord in the neighbouring Shansi province; he found him guarded but not unsympathetic. When in October 1936 Chiang Kai-shek left

Nanking and flew to Xi'an to rally the generals against the communist 'traitors' the response was lukewarm. So in early December 1936 Chiang Kai-shek returned to Xi'an hoping for better success.

The Young Marshal now brought matters to a head. He probably saw himself as replacing Chiang Kai-shek in a united national movement against the Japanese who were starting a full-scale military drive in the north. On 12 December the Young Marshal's troops stormed Chiang's headquarters just outside Xian, killed many of his bodyguards and took Chiang Kai-shek himself captive. Two weeks later he was released and allowed to fly back to Nanking. He owed his release, and possibly his life, to the intervention of Mao Zedong. It was an extraordinary turn of events. Mao had received a telegram from Moscow conveying Stalin's advice that Mao should form a united front with Chiang Kai-shek against the Japanese. Mao sent Zhou Enlai to Xi'an to negotiate, to propose that the communists unite in the fight against the Japanese with Chiang Kai-shek and to offer to subordinate their forces. Zhou Enlai also persuaded the Young Marshal that Chiang Kai-shek was the only possible leader of a 'united' China. A formal communist offer in February 1937 was not officially accepted by Chiang Kai-shek, but the military effort of the Kuomintang did switch to resisting the Japanese.

As for the Young Marshal, he was arrested and imprisoned. But the 'Xi'an incident' did mark the beginning of cooperation at least in theory between the Kuomintang and Mao's communist forces. After the Japanese had resumed a full-scale war in the summer of 1937, the two sides reached agreement that the 30,000 soldiers of the Chinese Red Army should become the Eighth Route Army under nominal Kuomintang control. It was not a union of spirit, but a tactical move on both fronts and Mao retained control of the communist base areas.

Of all the Western powers, Britain had most at stake in China. Her total trade and commercial investment in China were very large in 1930, just exceeding Japan's. Together, Britain and Japan dominated all foreign investment in China, accounting for 72 per cent of the total. The United States' investment was far behind at 6 per cent, about the same as France's. No other power had any significant investment. The most sensitive point of Western interests and influence was the great city of Shanghai. The Western powers and the Japanese held 'concessions' there which virtually removed the heart of the city and its port from Chinese control. In January 1932 the Japanese bombed the Chinese district, army reinforcements attacked the Chinese parts of Shanghai, meeting fierce resistance from a Chinese army.

The conflict in China was now brought home to the ordinary people in the West. For the first time the cinema newsreels showed the effects of modern warfare. People were horrified by the sufferings inflicted on civilian populations and by the terror bombing from Japanese planes on the hapless Chinese. This new image of war, which was to become even more familiar after the outbreak of the Spanish Civil War in 1936, had a tremendous impact on public opinion. It produced contradictory currents. It provoked a revulsion against war, thus underpinning later attempts at conciliating Hitler in Europe. The public also identified with the sufferers and therefore cast attackers in the role of aggressors to be stopped. China was seen as the innocent victim. The Japanese did incalculable harm to their cause by adopting such a ruthless style of warfare within the range of Western cameramen.

When the League of Nations met to consider China's appeal immediately after the Japanese launched their operation in Manchuria, public opinion in the West sided with China. There was an element of wishful thinking that the League of Nations would be able to punish the aggressor by using the machinery of sanctions set up to provide for collective security. Governments were urged to support the League. But the League of Nations could not fulfil such unrealistic expectations. To oppose Japan by military force on the Chinese mainland would have required an enormous military effort. Who would be ready in the midst of deep depression to raise and supply the large armies? Alternatively, by a great effort and with large funds the Chinese armies might be better equipped and led. Germany was doing all she could in providing military advice to Chiang Kai-shek's forces. The political divisions of China, however, made it difficult in 1932 and 1933 to conceive of any effective check on Japan.

The British Foreign Office and the American State Department had a more realistic appreciation of the situation. With so much at stake, the British attitude to Japan was ambiguous. Chinese nationalism threatened Britain's imperialist interests as much as Japan's. In the United States it was clear from the start that American material interests were not sufficient to justify the possibility of conflict with Japan or even a trade embargo, which would have deeply injured Japan. That remained the view of official America throughout the 1930s. Yet there was a genuine sense of outrage that Japan had offended against the ethical code that should dictate how she was to conduct her relations with neighbours. She had broken solemn treaties, and this was to be condemned. Secretary of State Henry Stimson issued a famous statement on 7 January 1932 that became known as the Stimson Doctrine – much to President Hoover's chagrin since, he claimed, he had first thought of it. The United States, it declared, would not recognise any treaties or situations brought about in violation of earlier treaties. The United States thus refused to accept all Japanese attempts to regularise her control of Manchuria. The League endorsed this view a little later.

The League of Nations meanwhile had sent Lord Lytton as British chairman of a commission to investigate on the spot Chinese claims and Japanese counter-claims. His report in October 1932 largely condemned the Japanese military action and suggested a compromise solution which would have given Manchuria autonomy while preserving Japanese rights. In February 1933 these recommendations were accepted by the League Assembly; the Japanese delegation thereupon left the League Assembly and never returned. The League of Nations had pinned its hopes on conciliation and when this failed had nothing more to offer in the absence of will on the part of Britain and the United States to back further action. The League suffered greatly in prestige. This in itself did not bring a general war between the other powers nearer; indeed it might have served a useful purpose if the peoples in the democratic countries had thereby gained a greater sense of realism. Too often the call to 'support the League' was believed to be all that was required; it could be comfortably combined with pacifism and a refusal to 'fight for king and country'. Many preferred to believe that they did not need to shoulder the responsibilities of peacekeeping or make the sacrifices required to check aggression – that was the job of the League. An ardent desire for peace and further wishful thinking thus led to blame being transferred to the League of Nations.

In Japan itself the success of the Kwantung army and the failure of the League had important effects too. A wave of patriotism and ultra-nationalism swept the population. Japanese governments now seemed to those Japanese patriots much too cautious. Patriotic secret societies, with sometimes only a few hundred members, sought to influence policy decisively. One method was to assassinate ministers who, in the societies' view, did not follow patriotic policies. Frustrated army officers joined such societies and there were repeated attempts to stage military coups. Several prominent ministers were murdered. This reign of terror did succeed in intimidating many opponents of extremism. The army meanwhile did not try to put its own house in order – at least not until several hundred officers and rebellious troops in February 1936 had seized the whole government quarter of Tokyo and assassinated a number of Cabinet ministers. All this was done in the name of the Emperor. The Japanese navy now played a leading part in putting down the insurrection. But it proved no victory for moderation. From then on, civilian ministers came to be even more dominated by the military. Japan was set on an expansionist course. Although Britain and the United States did not wish to fight Japan, in the last resort the issue of peace with the West would depend on whether Japan's aims in China were limited or whether ambition would drive her on to seek to destroy all Western influence in eastern and southern Asia. That day came perceptibly closer when, in July 1937, the Japanese resumed full-scale warfare with China.

# CHAPTER 23

## *The Crumbling Peace, 1933–1936*

In chess what matters is the result, the endgame. The opening moves and the middle play are all directed to achieving such a superiority of position that the endgame is preordained, the annihilation of the opponent. The analogy holds for Hitler's foreign policy. Much confusion of interpretation is avoided if one essential point is grasped: Hitler never lost sight of his goal – wars of conquest that would smash Soviet Russia, and subordinate France and the smaller states of the continent of Europe to the domination of a new Germany. This new order would be based on the concept of race. 'Races' like the Jews were so poisonous that there was literally no place for them in this new Europe. Other inferior races would be handled ruthlessly: the Slavs would not be permitted any national existence and could only hope for a servile status under their Aryan masters. Logically this biological foreign policy could not be confined to Europe alone. From the mastery of the European continent, the global conflict would ensue. Hitler was vague about details; this would be a task for his successors and future generations. But he took some interest in German relations with Japan in the 1930s because he recognised that Japan's war in Asia and threat to British interests could be exploited. He preferred to concentrate on the 'limited' task of gaining mastery of the European continent.

It is interesting to compare Hitler's aims with those of his Weimar and Wilhelmine predecessors. The desire for predominance on the continent of Europe was shared by both Wilhelmine Germany in 1914 and Hitler's Germany of the 1930s. The foreign policy of Weimar's Germany, like Hitler's, included secret rearmament and the objective of restoring German military power by abolishing the restrictions imposed by the Treaty of Versailles. Furthermore, Weimar's foreign policy was ultimately directed towards recovering the territories lost to Poland. (It is difficult to see how this could actually have been achieved without a war on Poland; but as Weimar Germany was not prepared to risk war with Poland's ally, France, it seems unlikely that Weimar's policies could have forced Poland to relinquish territory and her special rights in Danzig.)

Differences between Hitler's policy and earlier policies are also very evident. Wilhelmine Germany was brought to the point of launching war only after years of trying to avoid such a war; she rejected even the notion of 'preventive' war when the opportunity was most favourable, in 1904–5 (page 22). The final decision for war was reached only when the ostensible leader, the Kaiser, desperately and unsuccessfully backtracked, seeking to reverse earlier policies of forcing the tensions of August 1914 to a crisis point in the hope that Russia and France would yield. In 1914, furthermore, an alternative to war was always considered both possible and desirable. War would become unnecessary if the alliance between France and Russia 'encircling' Germany could have been broken by the threat of force alone. Even when Wilhelmine Germany made peace plans in the autumn of 1914 in the flush of early victories, the German leaders did not contemplate the enslavement of peoples or mass murder. Wilhelmine Germany's vision was a utopian one of a prosperous Europe led by a powerful Germany. Her occupation policies, moreover, show that she did not regard non-German people as inferior or as her perpetual enemies. Of course what appeared as utopia to the German leaders, a Pax Germanica, was intolerable to her neighbours.

When we next contrast Hitler's aims with those of Stresemann the differences are equally great. Weimar Germany was not bent on either racialist barbarism or continental domination. The reconciliation with France was genuine, as was Stresemann's assumption that another European war with France and Britain would spell Germany's ruin. A realistic objective, he believed, was for Germany to recover the position she had held as a great power before 1914. To strive for more was to make the mistake that had led other powers to combine against imperial Germany and so had brought about the catastrophic defeat of Germany and the harsh peace. The essence then of Stresemann's diplomacy was to win as much for Germany as possible without provoking the slightest chance of war. It followed that his 'weapon' was to make repeated pleas for trust and reconciliation. He never threatened war. His policy was at times devious but also essentially sincere in that avoidance of war was his real aim. He conducted Weimar's diplomacy with extraordinary skill and considerable success, overcoming many difficulties. Tragically it was Hitler who became the heir of Germany's much improved international position; furthermore he derided Weimar's achievements as the work of the 'November criminals'.

Many historians have commented on Hitler's political skills and on his extraordinary personality, which won the support and allegiance of the majority of German people. This achievement cannot be minimised. But his skill in building up German power and in conducting German foreign policy can very easily be exaggerated. It is a commonplace since the publication of A. J. P. Taylor's *The Origins of the Second World War* to discredit the findings of the Nuremberg War Crimes Tribunal that Hitler and his associates carefully and precisely planned their aggressions culminating in the attack on Poland in September 1939. It is true that Hitler was following no such *precise* and *detailed* plan of aggression. He clearly reacted to events and, as the

documents show, was ready at times to be flexible when it came to timing and detail. After all he could not totally disregard contemporary circumstances or the policies of the other powers, nor could he foretell what opportunities would arise for Germany to exploit.

But all this does not lead to the opposite conclusion that he had no plan. That is totally to misunderstand Hitler. No one can read *Mein Kampf*, or his other writings and the few existing documents expressing his views, without being struck by their general consistency. His actions, moreover, conformed to the broad plans he laid down. This was no mere coincidence. Unlike his predecessors, Hitler was working towards one clear goal: a war, or several wars, which would enable Germany to conquer the continent of Europe. Once a dictator has acquired sufficient power internally there is nothing difficult about launching a war. The difficulty lies in winning it, and in getting right the timing of aggression. The task of preserving peace, of solving conflicts, of deciding when war cannot be avoided because of the ambitions and aggressions of other nations – that requires skill and good judgement. Hitler was not prepared to compromise his ultimate goal. Only to a very limited degree, as will be seen, was he prepared to modify the steps by which he intended to attain this goal. Hitler showed a greater degree of skill as a propagandist by hiding his true objectives for a time when in power. His repeated assurances that he was making his 'last territorial demands' fooled some people abroad, as well as the majority of Germans, who certainly did not imagine they would be led again into another war against Britain, France, Russia and the United States.

With hindsight, it is easy to ask and to answer the question why Hitler and resurgent Germany were not stopped before German power had become so formidable that it was too late, except at the cost of a devastating war. Equally, there can be little doubt that British and French policy between the wars and, more especially, in the 1930s was disastrous. But the real interest of these years lies in the contrast between a single-minded Hitler bent on a war of conquest from the start and the reaction of his neighbours who were uncertain of his ultimate intentions, who had to grapple with the problem of how best to meet ill-defined dangers abroad, while facing economic and social difficulties at home. The leaders of the Western democracies, moreover, were incessantly concerned with the problems of domestic political rivalries and divisions within their own parties. In France political divisions had escalated into violence and greatly weakened the capacity of unstable governments to respond decisively to the German danger. In the circumstances it is perhaps all the more remarkable that a real attempt on the level of diplomacy was made by the French to check Hitler. In Britain, despite the overwhelming parliamentary strength won by the nationalist government in 1931, continuing widespread distress and unemployment gave the Conservatives much cause for concern from an electoral point of view. Foreign policy also played a considerable role in the November election of 1935. Baldwin reflected the public mood by simultaneously expressing Conservative support for the League of Nations while reassuring the electorate that there would be no great rearmament. After another electoral victory in 1935, almost as massive as the 1931 landslide, the Conservatives had most to fear from their own supporters, and from one in particular, Winston Churchill, who from the backbenches constantly attacked the government's weak response to German rearmament.

When, on coming to power, Hitler accelerated German rearmament in defiance of the Versailles Treaty, he was in fact taking no real risk. The lack of effective Allied reaction during the period from 1933 to 1935 was not due to the finesse of Hitler or of his diplomats, nor even to Hitler's deceptive speeches proclaiming his peaceful intentions. The brutal nature of the Nazi regime in Germany revealed itself quite clearly to the world with the information leaking out of beatings and concentration camps, and these impressions were reinforced by the exodus of distinguished, mainly Jewish, refugees. Britain tolerated Hitler's illegal actions just as rearmament in the Weimar years had been accepted. France, though much more alarmed than Britain by the development of German military strength, would not take action without the certainty of British support in case such actions should lead to war with Germany. But until 1939 British governments refused to back France unless France herself were attacked by Germany. The French army would have been much stronger than Germany's in 1933 and 1934 at the outset of any war, but France's military and industrial potential for war was much weaker.

It is not quite accurate either to ascribe the failure of the French response to a totally defensive military strategy symbolised by the great Maginot fortress line. It was rather that the French had reached a conclusion diametrically opposite to the Germans. The French did not believe that a lightning strike by her own armies before Germany had a chance to mobilise her greater manpower and industry for war could bring rapid victory. In short, the French abandoned the notion of a limited punitive military action such as they had undertaken in the Ruhr ten years earlier (page 144). Any military response, so the French High Command advised the governments of the day, could lead to general war; therefore, it could not be undertaken without extensive prior mobilisation placing France on a war footing. This left the French governments with no alternative but diplomacy, aimed at aligning allies against Germany in order to exert pressure in time of peace. But no British government was prepared to face another war unless Britain's national interests were clearly imperilled to the point where her very survival as a great power was at stake.

This nexus between the rejection of any limited military response and Britain's and France's perfectly understandable desire to avoid outright war unless there was an attack on their territories, or a clear threat of one, made possible Hitler's rake's progress of treaty violations and aggressions until the serious crisis over Czechoslovakia in September 1938. All Hitler required was the nerve to seize where there would be no resistance. He had only to push against open doors, and occasionally to display temporary hesitations and tactical withdrawals from his original intentions. Even these were probably unnecessary.

A disarmament conference under the auspices of the League was proceeding in Geneva when Hitler came to power. It served as a useful smokescreen for the Nazis. The Germans argued a seemingly reasonable case. It was up to the other powers to disarm to Germany's level, or Germany should be allowed to rearm to theirs. The French could never willingly give their blessing to this proposition, so they were placed in the position of appearing to be the unreasonable power, blocking the progress of negotiations which the British wished to succeed for they had no stomach for increasing armaments expenditure in the depth of the depression. The British argued that some agreement, allowing but limiting German rearmament, was better than none.

The French, however, refused to consent to German rearmament. In fact it made no difference whether the British or the French policy was pursued. In April 1933 the German delegate to the disarmament negotiations confidentially briefed German journalists, telling them that, while Germany hoped to secure the consent of the other powers to a standing army of 600,000, she was building the army up to this size anyway. Hitler was giving rearmament first priority, regardless of the attitude of other nations, though any cover which Anglo-French disagreements gave for his own treaty violations was naturally welcome to him. In June 1933 he happily signed a four-power treaty proposed by Mussolini which bound Britain, France, Germany and Italy, in no more than platitudes of goodwill, to consult with each other within the framework of the League.

In Germany, meanwhile, a National Defence Council had been secretly set up in April 1933 to co-ordinate military planning. It would take time to build up the necessary infrastructure – to set up and equip factories to manufacture large quantities of tanks, planes and the weapons of mechanised warfare. The lack of swift early progress was an inherent problem of complex modern rearmament, as Britain was to discover to her cost later on. So it is erroneous to cite the slow start of German rearmament as good evidence that Hitler was not preparing for war from the beginning. Financial responsibility for providing the regime with all the credit it needed belonged to Hjalmar Schacht, who was appointed head of the Reichsbank by Hitler when the incumbent showed reluctance to abandon orthodox financial practice. Hitler in February 1933 secretly explained to the army generals and to the Nazi elite that the solution to Germany's problems could be found only in the conquest of territory in the east. It is clear that Hitler did not expect France simply to stand by and allow Germany to aggrandise her power in the east. 'I will grind France to powder,' he told the visiting Prime Minister of Hungary in June 1933. But until a superior German military strength could be built up, Hitler explained to his associates, he would have to talk the language of peace. In fact he coupled peaceful gestures, such as offers of friendship to France in the autumn of 1933, with decidedly bellicose action.

Deeds were more convincing than words. In October 1933, in a deliberately aimed blow at the League of Nations, Germany withdrew from the disarmament conference at Geneva and from the League of Nations as well. Hitler then sought approval by a plebiscite and claimed in November that 95 per cent of the German people had expressed their approval in the ballot box. The world is today quite familiar with this device of totalitarian regimes whereby astounding statistical unanimity is expressed. In 1933, it is probable that the majority of Germans believed Hitler's claim. They were undoubtedly elated by Hitler's handling of this aspect of the Versailles diktat – Germany would no longer be pushed around. What followed? An outburst of anger by the other powers? Talk of sanctions? The British government decided Germany should be conciliated and coaxed back to Geneva, and put pressure on the French to make concessions.

Hitler's priorities in 1933 and 1934 were clear: first rearmament and conscription, then a Nazi takeover in Austria and the return of the Saar, and at home the consolidation of power. Although Hitler's next diplomatic move startled Europe it was obvious *Realpolitik*. He wished to weaken the two-front threat posed by the alliance between Poland and France. And so in January 1934 he concluded a non-aggression pact with Poland, thereby renouncing German claims to Danzig and to the Polish corridor, the strip of territory separating East Prussia from the rest of Germany. It was no more than a temporary expedient. It shows how little faith the Poles placed in the French alliance. In April 1934 the French broke off further disarmament discussions with Germany. French political weakness at home after the Stavisky scandal (page 166) turned this apparently new tough stand into an empty gesture. French policy had no teeth. French ministers were under no illusions about Hitler's intentions, but a preventive war before German rearmament had reached an unassailable point was again rejected. So all that was left was diplomacy; but the mood was profoundly pessimistic, and although France would seek closer ties with Britain, little headway was made until 1936.

The Foreign Minister, Louis Barthou, made a determined effort for some months in 1934 to revive France's Eastern and Danubian alliances and alignments of the 1920s and to couple this pressure on Germany with the offer to bind Germany to an 'Eastern Locarno', whereby the Soviet Union, Germany, Poland, Czechoslovakia, the Baltic states and Finland would all guarantee each other's territories and promise to assist one another. This pact was to be linked to the League of Nations. No one can deny that Barthou was a man of real energy, but the idea of an 'Eastern Locarno' was pure moonshine. Hitler had rather cleverly pre-empted Poland's possible involvement. Poland preferred to maintain her own non-aggression treaty with Russia and with Germany and to retain a free hand. Hitler would not agree either. Although he did not feel bound by treaties, he preferred, for the sake of public feeling at home and in order not to antagonise Germany's neighbours prematurely, to sign no unnecessary treaties which he would have to break later on.

More promising was France's rapprochements in 1934 with Russia and with Italy, which were to bear fruit in 1935. Barthou also sought to draw closer to Yugoslavia. His diplomacy was tragically cut short in October 1934 when he met King Alexander in Marseilles. A Croat terrorist assassinated both Alexander and Barthou, an event dramatically captured by the newsreel cameras. His successor, Pierre Laval, who was to play an infamous role in the wartime Vichy government, in 1935 pursued Barthou's policy skilfully. Barthou had wooed Mussolini for Italy's friendship and even an alliance for France. In 1934 and 1935 this was a realistic aim – though Mussolini was notoriously fickle and impulsive – but, militarily speaking, the Italian alliance was of decidedly limited value.

Although Mussolini had hoped that Germany would follow the fascist path of Italy, he was not so sure about Hitler personally. Hitler for his part admired the Duce, who, so he thought, was trying to make something of the Italian people. The Duce was seen by Hitler as a ruthless man of action who like himself believed in superior force. His framed photograph stood on Hitler's desk in Munich in 1931. (Frederick the Great and Bismarck were the two other leaders whom Hitler acknowledged as worthy predecessors.) Mussolini's admiration for Hitler was not uncritical. He patronised him and sent him advice; there were times when Mussolini suspected Hitler might be mad. Many Italian fascists naturally resented Germany's emphasis on Nordic racialism and the supposed superiority of light-skinned blonds over swarthy Latins. In Italy there was no tradition of anti-Semitism. Indeed few Jews lived there. Mussolini's objection to anti-Semitism was not moral; he simply did not believe in the value of

Hitler's racial theories and thought that his diatribes against the Jews were impolitic. In June 1934 Mussolini and Hitler met in Venice. Mussolini stage-managed the whole visit to impress Hitler with his superiority. Hitler looked decidedly drab in his raincoat. He was seen to be the junior partner.

They discussed the questions over which German-Italian conflict might arise, the agitation of the German-speaking inhabitants in the South Tyrol and the future of the Austrian Republic. Hitler said he was ready to abandon the Germans of the South Tyrol in the interests of Italian friendship, but Mussolini remained suspicious as the irredentist movement was encouraged by Nazi Party officials. More immediately serious was Hitler's pressure on Chancellor Engelbert Dollfuss to resign and allow an internal takeover by the Austrian Nazi movement. Dollfuss reacted robustly. The Austrian Nazis were now conspiring to seize power.

Austria, with a population of 6.5 million, was one of Europe's smallest nations. Some 3.5 million former German Austrians were now subjects of the Italians and the Czechs. Austria had not exactly been created by the Allies at Paris; she consisted of what was left of the Habsburg Empire after the territories of all the successor states had been decided upon. The Austrian state made very little economic sense with her large capital in Vienna and impoverished provinces incapable of feeding the whole population. Economically the Republic had been kept afloat only by loans arranged through the League of Nations, whose representatives supervised the government's finances. The depression had hit Austria particularly hard and unemployment soared. Not surprisingly it was in Vienna in 1931 that the general European banking collapse began. This impoverished state was also deeply divided politically and socially. Austrian labour was united behind the Social Democratic Party, which supported the parliamentary constitution and rejected the solutions both of revolutionary communism and of fascism. On the right, supported by the Catholic Church, stood the Christian Social Party and groups of right-wing nationalist extremists. For a short while from 1918 to 1920 the Social Democrats had held power. After 1920, although the Social Democrats maintained their strength they no longer commanded an absolute majority. Except for a year from 1929 to 1930, the *Bürgerblock*, a coalition of Christian Socials and Nationalist and Pan-German parties, was in power until the extinc-

tion of the multi-party system in 1934. The only
issue that united this coalition was a common hatred
of labour and socialism.

So deep were the political and social divisions
that the danger of civil war was always close. The
(Catholic) Christian Socials favoured authoritarian
solutions, and their fascist and Nazi allies set up
paramilitary organisations such as the SA, the SS
and the Heimwehr. The Social Democrats also
sought to defend themselves by enrolling armed
workers in a Republican Defence Corps. Meanwhile many Austrians regarded their state as a
wholly artificial creation; loyalties were provincial
rather than national. There were many Austrians
who looked towards a union with Germany.
Austria's internal problems were exacerbated by her
more powerful neighbours. Germany posed a threat
to her independence. But Mussolini would defend
Austrian independence only if Austria modelled
herself on the fascist state. He specifically insisted
that the Social Democrats should be excluded from
participation in politics. Dollfuss, who became chancellor in May 1932, leant increasingly on the Duce's
support against the Nazis. In the spring and summer
he banned the Communist Party, the Republican
Defence Corps and the Nazis, and a few months
later, early in 1934, banned the Social Democrat
Party as well. The Social Democrats determined to
oppose this attack on their existence. They offered
armed resistance when their strongholds were
attacked. They were then brutally beaten into
submission during a brief civil war in February
1934. Democratic Europe was particularly shocked
by the bombardment of the municipal blocks of
flats of the workers in Vienna. In fact, Dollfuss had
destroyed the one political force able to resist the
Nazis, who were the real threat to Austria's independence.

The Austrian Nazi conspiracy to take over power
came to fruition in July 1934. The Nazis seized the
government buildings in Vienna and forced their
way into Dollfuss's office and there murdered him.
Although Dollfuss had lost much of the support of
the ordinary people, no one rallied to the Nazis.
The coup failed. Kurt Schuschnigg was appointed
chancellor and promised to continue the policies of
Dollfuss. Whether Hitler had connived at this Nazi

Below: *the murdered Austrian Chancellor, Dollfuss, lies in state,
July 1934.* Above: *battle-scarred workers' housing in Vienna, during
a lull in the civil disturbances of 1934.*

conspiracy and, if so, how far remains uncertain. But, coming as it did just a month after his visit to Venice, Mussolini was outraged and rushed troops to the Brenner frontier, warning Hitler not to interfere in Austria. For a few years longer Austria lived on under Mussolini's protection.

In Britain, the growing turbulence in Europe and in Asia alarmed even a government as committed to pacific solutions as that led by Ramsay MacDonald. Even before Hitler had come to power, the famous 'ten-year rule' was scrapped. It had been adopted in 1919 to save on armaments expenditure and postulated that such expenditure should be based on the assumption that there would be no war for ten years. But there was no real move to rearm for several years after 1932. Throughout the 1920s and in the 1930s, too, every British government, Labour and Conservative, believed that to spend money on arms would worsen Britain's economic plight, making her weaker and less able to resist aggression. It was a perverse and paradoxical conclusion. In February 1933, the Cabinet was informed of the gross military deficiency on land, sea and air caused by a decade of inadequate finance, but the Chancellor of the Exchequer and future Prime Minister, Neville Chamberlain, replied, 'today financial and economic risks are far the most serious and urgent that the country has to face . . . other risks have to be run until the country has had time and opportunity to recuperate and our financial situation to improve.' The depression was Hitler's best ally. When Churchill in Parliament attacked the government's neglect of Britain's security, especially in the air, Anthony Eden, Under Secretary of State at the Foreign Office, replied that the solution was to persuade the French to disarm so that Germany would limit her rearmament. Otherwise 'they could not secure for Europe that period of appeasement which is needed'. And, speaking in Birmingham, Chamberlain added, 'it is our duty by every effort we can make, by every influence we can exert, to compose differences, and to act as mediators to try and devise methods by which other countries may be delivered from this great menace of war'. These speeches from the government side in 1933 encapsulate the main tenets of British policy over the next few years.

Something, but too little, was done for defence. The great fear was that the new form of aerial warfare would lead to devastation and huge civilian casualties. German superiority in the air could thus become a potent form of blackmail. Increased defence spending was accordingly concentrated on the air force. Curiously, though, it was spent not on defensive fighter planes but on bombers. The thinking behind this was that the 'bombers would always get through' anyway. The only credible form of defence was to build up a deterrent bomber force that could carry the war to the enemy. Deterrence was preferable to war. In the Far East, the construction of the Singapore naval base was resumed, even though neglect of the British fleet meant that there would be no warships to send east if trouble simultaneously occurred in Europe. Worst affected by the parsimony of defence expenditure was the British army. In the event of war, only a token force could be despatched to France. This limited military commitment to the defence of the European continent was adhered to by governments and critics until 1939. On the French would rest the main burden of containing Germany on land, even though political conditions in France raised grave doubts about the capacity of the French army to deal with the Germans.

Provided one overlooks many mistaken assumptions, British foreign policy followed its own logic. Both France and Germany needed to be restrained. Britain would mediate between them. Even though Hitler secretly and openly defied treaties, Britain would go far to conciliate Germany and assure her that 'reasonable' rearmament would be acceptable to the other powers. When Eden visited Berlin in February 1934 he attempted to persuade Hitler to return to the League, and thought him sincere in wishing to conclude a disarmament convention. Eden's policy was to gain Hitler's signature to a treaty which would permit German rearmament but also, by its very provisions, place a limit on it. When the British government in July 1934 announced rearmament in the air, the search for an Anglo-German agreement did not slacken. Hitler was outwardly cautious during the six months from the summer of 1934, which opened with the failure of the Nazis in Austria and ended in January 1935 with the holding of the plebiscite in the Saar which would decide that region's future.

The Saar was 'brought home' to the Reich by votes through the ballot box and not by force, under the supervision of the League of Nations. Dr Goebbels had, however, mounted a great propaganda campaign and so ensured a Nazi 'yes' vote of 90 per cent. Hitler's prestige was further enhanced.

In the spring of 1935 Hitler was simply waiting for a good opportunity to announce the reintroduction of conscription and Germany's open repudiation of the military restrictions of the Versailles Treaty. Everyone, of course, already knew that they had been 'secretly' broken for years. Indeed a British defence White Paper, published in March 1935, which justified modest British rearmament by referring to Germany's 'illegal' rearmament, provided the kind of pretext Hitler sought. It was followed by the approval of the French Chamber on 15 March 1935 to extend military service from one to two years. On the very next day Hitler sprang a 'Saturday surprise', repudiated the Locarno Treaties, proclaimed conscription in Germany and 'revealed' the existence of the Luftwaffe. Britain's reaction was characteristically weak. Sir John Simon, the Foreign Secretary, and Anthony Eden, Minister for League Affairs, hastened to Berlin to exchange views with Hitler. The Führer was now ready to receive them. With conscription in the bag, Hitler could afford to be affable. Britain's conciliatory gesture vitiated the meeting of the other Locarno powers at Stresa a short while later in April 1935. Hitler's unilateral breach of Versailles and Locarno was condemned and the need to uphold treaties spelt out in the final communiqué. Significantly Mussolini had lined up with Britain and France and not with Germany. The League then joined in the condemnation.

If Hitler was impressed by this united front – and there is no reason to believe he was much – any apprehensions he might have felt were soon dispelled by the British government. Without consulting her French ally, Britain signified that Germany could also breach the Versailles limitations on her naval development by concluding the Anglo-German Naval Agreement in June 1935. This now permitted Germany to develop her formidable 'pocket' battleships and submarines; all Germany undertook was not to construct a fleet whose total tonnage would exceed 35 per cent of the combined fleets of the British Commonwealth. Even so this treaty also held out the eventual prospect of equality with Britain in submarines. Hitler did not have to push open doors, they were flung open for him. Already Hitler was considering his next step, the remilitarisation of the Rhineland in violation of that part of the Versailles Treaty which France held dear as a guarantee of her own security.

Had he moved in the summer of 1935 he would almost certainly have got away with that too – but the cautious streak in his make-up gained the upper hand. There would be a much better opportunity in 1936 when Mussolini was looking for German support instead of opposing her.

The Stresa meeting in April 1935 was not only concerned with Germany. Mussolini was himself planning a breach of the League Covenant, at Abyssinia's expense. The French were willing to connive at Mussolini's aggression. They were searching for a diplomatic bargain to gain Mussolini's support against Hitler. Foreign Minister Laval had paved the way when he visited Rome in January 1935. Mussolini and Laval then agreed that France and Italy would check Hitler's militaristic ambitions. On the question of Abyssinia, Laval appears to have reassured the Duce that France would not impede Italy. But at Stresa Mussolini was left in no doubt about the strength of British public feeling if Italy should attack Abyssinia. The final Stresa communiqué, which upheld the sanctity of treaties and condemned Germany's breach of them, carefully avoided reference to any but *European* conflicts. What was left undone was more important. The powers realised that Hitler's next step would be to remilitarise the Rhineland. But the three Stresa powers, Italy, Britain and France, took no decisions on how this threat might be met in time. The British government remained more anxious to conciliate than to warn.

In the autumn of 1935 Europe's attention was fixed not on Hitler but on Mussolini's war of aggression waged against Abyssinia, the practically defenceless kingdom of Emperor Haile Selassie. Mussolini felt he had adequately prepared the ground diplomatically with France and Britain and that in view of the German danger, which he exploited, the two democracies would acquiesce. The British government, he believed, would defy pro-League outbursts of public opinion. But Mussolini had miscalculated the British government's resolve in an election year. Throughout 1935 he built up a huge army, eventually reaching 650,000 men, with modern weapons and poison gas, to overcome the Abyssinian tribesmen. On 3 October 1935 he launched his war on Abyssinia. The Italian army after some initial success became bogged down. The democratic world admired the plucky resistance of the underdog. At Geneva the League condemned Italy as an aggresor and voted

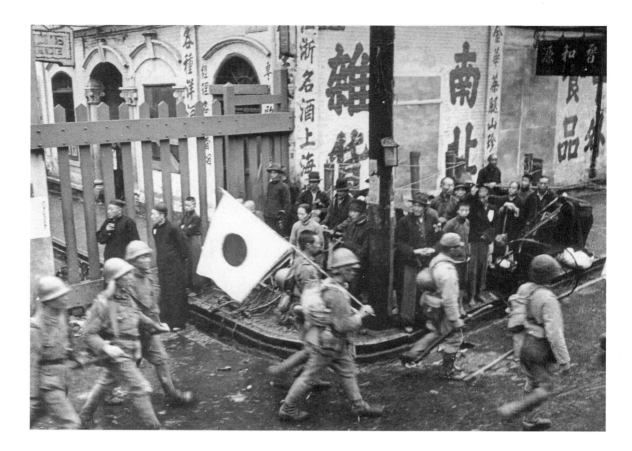

*The World Re-Arms. Armies begin to march again during the 1930s, as the League of Nations and 'collective security' fail to sustain peaceful equilibrium. In Asia, the Japanese invade Manchuria (1931–3) and the Chinese prove no match for them (top). Then in 1937 they move further into the Chinese heartlands (left). Meanwhile, in Africa, Mussolini conquers Abyssinia. The picture (right) shows Italian troops entering Gondar, capital of the Amhar province, in 1935.*

for sanctions. But sanctions were not rigidly imposed nor did they include oil, necessary to fuel Italy's war machine. In any case Italy had stockpiled oil in Africa in expectation of sanctions. Sanctions proved an irritant, the main result of which was to create a patriotic reaction in Italy herself.

In Britain in June 1935, Ramsay MacDonald finally retired and Stanley Baldwin became prime minister. Sir Samuel Hoare, who replaced Sir John Simon at the Foreign Office, conferred with Laval in December 1935 on partition plans of Abyssinia which, it was hoped, would bring the war to an end through secret mediation between Mussolini and the Abyssinians. The so-called Hoare-Laval Pact was a 'compromise' plan which would have given Mussolini a large part of Abyssinia. He might well have accepted such a solution but when the French leaked the agreement in Britain there was a great public protest that the League was being betrayed and the aggressor rewarded. The British Cabinet, finding itself in an embarrassing position after fighting an election on the issue of support for the League, placed the blame on Hoare and refused to endorse the proposals he and Laval had agreed upon. Hoare resigned on 19 December 1935. That is how Anthony Eden, who had himself favoured compromise, now inherited the Foreign Office.

Mussolini resumed his military campaign, and his troops occupied Addis Ababa in May 1936. The war was being conducted in the most barbarous fashion. The Abyssinians had no means of defence against air attack or poison gas. The brutality of the Italian occupation and the suppression of tribesmen still resisting in 1937 was a precursor of Nazi terror in occupied Europe during the Second World War. Thousands of defenceless Abyssinians were massacred, while Haile Selassie made his dignified protests in Geneva. The war had brought Mussolini cheap glory, but it also isolated him and drove him to seek closer relations with Germany.

The disunity of the 'Stresa front' made Hitler's next move, the remilitarisation of the Rhineland, even less risky than it appeared to be. Hitler later was to call his boldness in March 1936 the great turning point when he had 'bluffed' the French. It was not a real turning point, but just another step along the road he had already successfully followed. Hitler was looking for a new pretext. The Franco-Soviet pact, concluded in 1934, provided it (page 190). When the French Chamber ratified the treaty, Hitler on 7 March 1936 declared it to be contrary

to the Locarno Treaties and ordered the Wehrmacht to move into the demilitarised zone of the Rhineland. In its final timing Hitler's move came as a surprise, but the occupation of the Rhineland had been anticipated and discussed. French ministers were clear they could not react with anything but immediate protests and later on possible recourse to the machinery of League sanctions. The Chief of the Army General Staff, General Maurice Gamelin, insisted that no military moves were possible without prior full-scale mobilisation, placing more than 1 million Frenchmen under arms. He pointed out to the French ministers that there was no immediate striking force available. The British, meanwhile, were not prepared to consider mere German troop movements into the Rhineland zone as sufficient reason for a military counterstroke.

Thus France, rent by internal conflict, could not and Britain would not consider stopping Hitler. Hitler, for his part, was careful to enter the Rhineland with only a small force of lightly armed Wehrmacht troops. Rather like rearmament, the open remilitarisation of the Rhineland had been preceded by 'secret' remilitarisation as the so-called 'police' already stationed in the demilitarised zone were in fact trained infantry. The total force of 'police' and Wehrmacht amounted to less than 40,000 men and could not possibly threaten France.

*German troops re-enter the Rhineland in 1936 – with horses still more in evidence than tanks. Here, in Heidelberg, they are greeted with flowers by proud Germans.*

But Hitler was not bluffing. He had no intention of accepting defeat had the French marched. It is a myth that all that was required to humiliate Hitler in March 1936 was a French show of strength. In the hastily drawn-up final war plans, the German troops were to withdraw as far as the Ruhr and there to stay and fight. But in view of earlier French political and military decisions it was obvious that the only French counter-moves would be diplomatic.

These counter-moves were handled with skill by the French Foreign Minister, Pierre Flandin. He proposed to the British that economic and military sanctions be applied to force Hitler to withdraw. But Eden was looking for mediation. The British Cabinet had ruled out force. Flandin's sanction plan raised the spectre of war with Germany. But tortuous negotiations in London and Geneva did not this time end entirely without result. The expected League condemnation was the usual empty gesture. But Flandin extracted from the British government an avowal that Britain still stood by her Locarno commitment to France and Belgium. The British Cabinet had been pushed by the French further than it wished to go in the direction of a strictly *defensive* Anglo-French alliance backed up by staff talks in place of the more flexible Locarno agreements (page 137). Arguably, therefore, Hitler had lost more than he gained by his Rhineland coup. There was now a much closer Anglo-French alignment and Britain began to rearm, though still at far too slow a pace. On the debit side, Belgium reverted to absolute neutrality.

Nineteen-thirty-six was to be the year of international goodwill. Berlin was host to the Olympic Games that year. Defiance of treaties and the Nuremberg laws proved no obstacle to the holding of the Games in Berlin. Hitler wanted the world to come to Berlin and admire the National Socialist state. No effort was spared to make the Games a spectacular success. For the duration of the Games

*The Berlin Olympic Games, 1936. Fraülein Fleischer has just thrown the javelin further than any other woman. She receives her gold medal and a handshake from the Führer.*

anti-Jewish propaganda was toned down in Berlin. Hitler, moreover, assured the Olympic Committee that there would be no discrimination between 'Aryans' and 'non-Aryans'. Even Jewish sporting organisations were allowed to function. It was of course discomfiting that the outstanding athlete of the games was the black Jesse Owens. Nazi commentators explained this success, embarrassing to racial doctrines of superiority, by stressing that blacks were racially lower in the scale of development and hence naturally faster. Nevertheless, for Hitler the holding of the Games in Berlin served as an international recognition of his regime.

# CHAPTER 24

# The Spanish Civil War and Europe, 1936–1939

The Spanish Civil War, to many contemporaries outside Spain, represented a great struggle between the totalitarian forces of the fascist right against the resistance of the Republic, whose legitimate government was composed of the Popular Front parties defending democracy. The war as it dragged on indeed came to resemble such an ideological contest. This was because, unlike earlier internal Spanish conflicts, the Civil War occurred at a time of deep European division, when fascism, democracy and communism were seen to be moving towards some sort of showdown, which it was thought would decide the fate of Europe. Fascism had spread from Italy to Germany and Eastern Europe. Fascism, so its fervent opponents believed, should be finally stopped in Spain. The battle in Spain was seen as marking the turning point of victory or defeat for the fascists. This was a popular illusion. Governments, communist, democratic or fascist, understood better that events in Spain were a secondary problem. The real question mark hanging over the future of the rest of Europe was how Hitler's Germany and Mussolini's Italy would act in Europe and in Africa. Would they be satisfied with a negotiated revision of the Versailles settlement, or was Europe facing a new contest for supremacy as in 1914–18?

For the major governments of Europe, Spain was a sideshow and policy towards Spain was subordinated to other more important policy objectives. In France and Britain in particular (even in the Soviet Union), there consequently developed a schism between passionate popular feeling, especially among intellectual adherents of the broad left, and governments which appeared incapable of acting against the fascist menace. In Spain, the simple line of ideological division, as seen from abroad, was exploited by both sides since foreign volunteers, and even more so foreign supplies, played a critical part in military success. The warring factions in Spain became known simply as the insurgent Nationalists (the right) and the Loyalists defending the Republic (the left). The battle lines between the parties were not so simple, and the defenders of the Republic, particularly, were deeply divided. On the right the analogy with fascism was not a simple one either. That is not to deny fascist elements in their policies.

The rise of contemporary fascism and communism in the 1920s influenced the political struggle in Spain herself. Mussolini's movement had served as a model to some Spaniards, although the dictator of the 1920s, Primo de Rivera, owed only a slight ideological debt to Mussolini. Socialism and Marxism and anarchism, rather than communism of the Stalinist variety, won adherents in Spain also. But Spanish traditions were strong too. Although political contest assumed some of the forms of the great European ideological schisms of the twentieth century, its roots lay also in the conditions of Spain and in the evolution of past social and political tensions. In searching for the origins of the Civil War the purely Spanish causes always lie just under the surface and explain why in 1936 Spain was split into two warring sides which inflicted savage cruelties on each other during the course of the conflict.

In the north the Republicans held most of Asturias and the Basque region; Catalonia, with the large city of Barcelona, became a Republican stronghold; Valencia and the whole Mediterranean coast and central Spain, the eastern regions of Andalucia and New Castile with the capital of Madrid were also Republican regions. The other bigger cities, except for Seville and Saragossa, were republican too. Western Spain, western Aragon, Old Castile, León and the south – mainly the arid and agricultural regions of Spain – fell into the hands of the Nationalists. Within each of the regions of Spain controlled by Nationalists and Republicans, there were minorities who adhered to the opposite side and so were subject to murderous reprisals. The Church, an object of Republican hatred, suffered grievously in the Republican areas. Landless peasants recruited in the south by the socialists and anarchists were exposed to Nationalist terror.

If we look back no further than to the nineteenth century, the contest over how Spain was to be governed was already splitting the country and leading to civil wars. The more extreme monarchists, supported by the Church, fought the constitutionalists and liberal monarchists who then enjoyed the support of much of the army. Superimposed on this constitutional conflict was the desire of the northern regions for autonomy: they opposed attempts to centralise and unify these regions which enjoyed extensive local rights and traditions. Spain's internal turbulence did not come to an end during the last quarter of the nineteenth century with the establishment of the constitutional monarchy and the granting of universal male suffrage. The votes of the peasants in the countryside were managed by the wealthy and by local men of influence. Despite the liberal constitution, the parliamentary system did not embody the hopes of all the reformers: rather the whole parliamentary democracy appeared something of a sham. Popular discontent was further increased by Spain's poor showing abroad. The loss of colonies, the war with the United States at the turn of the century and the failures of her imperial policies in Morocco, where the Spanish army also suffered defeats, weakened the authority of government.

Besides the constitutional conflict, the problem of the regions and the failures of foreign and imperial policies, Spanish industrialisation, though slow, was concentrated in the north and so added to regional particularism as well as leading to bitter economic conflict between worker and employer. Spain was a very poor country, and suffered perennially from the agricultural problem of her landless and impoverished peasantry. In the early twentieth century, socialism made headway in Spain. As in France, the movement was divided and the anarcho-syndicalists who believed in direct action had won many adherents among the workers of the north and some of the peasants in the south. The strength of their main trade union organisation, the CNT, lay in Catalonia and especially in Barcelona. (Before 1936, however, the Communist Party was small.)

On more than one occasion in the early twentieth century Spain seemed to be poised on the brink of civil war; Barcelona, the capital of Catalonia, was a focal point of bloodshed and civil conflict. The civil guard, hated by the workers, kept unrest just in check by ruthless force and imprisonment. Spain was disintegrating amid warring factions, while the politicians of the Cortes, the Spanish parliament, proved unable to provide effective and stable governments. In September 1923, repeating a pattern familiar in the nineteenth century, an army general seized power to bring peace to Spain and save her from monarchist politicians. Compared with other dictators, this general, Primo de Rivera, was an attractive figure. The King, Alfonso XIII, acquiesced in the overthrow of the constitution. Primo de Rivera followed a policy of repression of politicians, the Socialist Party, anarchists and supporters of Catalan regionalism. But the socialist trade union, the UGT, became a mainstay of the regime. He also inaugurated public works which, in the 1920s, seemed to promise some economic progress. Yet by 1930 he had exhausted his credit and lost support in the army, and the King dismissed him. The King himself did not long survive. The cities had turned against him and he left for exile in 1931.

The second Republic was then established without violence or bloodshed. Its history was brief and filled with mounting political and social conflict. The left had drawn together, temporarily as it turned out, to take charge of the country. But it was characteristic of the politics of the left and the right that, once the electoral victory was won by electoral pacts, rivalry between the parties would thereafter prevent any coalition from providing stable government.

First, until the end of 1933, the Republic was governed by a coalition of the left and moderate Republicans under the leadership of Manuel Azaña. He sought to solve the regional question by granting autonomy to the Catalans; he promoted educational reform, and plunged into a programme of agricultural reform which achieved little. In the summer of 1932, there was an abortive generals' rising against the government of the Republic. It was a fiasco.

What caused the greatest bitterness was the anti-clerical legislation of the government, which regarded the Church as the bulwark of reaction. It drove moderate supporters who were faithful Catholics into opposition. The anarchists stirred up the workers in violent strikes which the government suppressed with bloodshed, thus alienating supporters on the left. As in the last days of the Weimar Republic the moderate politicians, of whom Azaña was an example, were assailed by extremists on the left and right, and even the more moderate Socialists looked fearfully over their shoulders lest supporting the government should lose them the allegiance of their followers to those political groups further to the left, especially the anarchists. During the election of November 1933, the left no longer fought by means of electoral agreements. It was the turn of the right to strike such bargains, forming a common opposition to the government's anti-clerical legislation. Gil Robles founded CEDA, a confederation of right-wing Catholic groups. A new electoral pact, with the radicals changing sides and now supporting CEDA, gave the centre–right a resounding victory. From 1934 to 1936 the republic struggled on amid mounting tensions towards civil war.

The coalition government of the centre supported by CEDA reversed the 'progressive' aspects of the legislation of Azaña's government. With the roles reversed, the miners in Asturias, under the united leadership of socialists, communists and anarchists began a general strike in October 1934 and seized Oviedo, the provincial capital. Simultaneously there occurred an abortive separatist rising in Catalonia. The government retaliated by using the Foreign Legion and Moorish troops from Morocco bloodily to suppress the Asturian rising. The shootings and tortures inflicted on the miners increased the extreme bitterness of the workers, while there was

strong Catholic feeling against the godless Marxist conspiracy. Both the left and right were strengthening their following. Among groups of the right, José Antonio, son of Primo de Rivera, attracted increasing support to the Falange Party, which he had founded in 1933 and which came closest to a fascist party in Spain. But in the election of February 1936 the parties of the left, which were out of power, organised an effective electoral pact and presented themselves as the Popular Front. Its cry was that the Republic was in danger and that the parties of the right were fascist. The parties of the right called on the electorate to vote for Spain and against revolution. Spanish politics had become so polarised that neither the parties of the right nor those of the left were ready to accept the 'democratic' verdict of the people. The Popular Front combination gave the left the parliamentary victory, but the country was almost equally split between left and right in the votes cast. What was now lacking was a strong grouping of the centre, a majority who believed in a genuine democratic peace and parliamentary institutions.

The familiar spectacle of the united left achieving electoral victory, and then falling into division when they got to power, was repeated in the spring and summer of 1936. The left-wing socialists, led by Largo Caballero, rejected all co-operation with left 'bourgeois' governments; Caballero continued the Popular Front but would not serve in the government. He was supported by the communists; but despite all his revolutionary language, he had no plans for revolution. On the right, however, plans were drawn up to forestall the supposed revolution of the left. The generals justified their July 1936 rising on precisely these grounds. Attacked by those who should have supported the Republic, the government was too weak to suppress the generals' rising as easily as in 1932. But the right, on its own, was unable to wrest power from the government, either electorally or by force. It called on the army to restore conservative order and to uphold the values and position of the Church. And the army assumed this task in an action that had more in common with nineteenth-century Spanish tradition and the military seizure of power by Primo de Rivera in 1923, than with Nazi or fascist takeovers which were backed by their own paramilitary supporters, the army standing aside.

The government of the left in 1931–2 had offended army feeling by attempting its reform, replacing many officers with those whose loyalty to the Republic seemed certain. A large number of such promotions after the victory of the Popular Front in 1936 offended the traditionalist officers, and General Francisco Franco, 'banished' to the military governorship of the remote Canary Islands, protested that such unfair practices offended the dignity of the army. The leader of the officers' conspiracy was not Franco, however, but General José Sanjurjo, and General Emilio Mola was its chief organiser. The army itself was divided between those ready to overthrow the Republic and those still prepared to serve it. Franco himself hesitated almost to the last moment. The increasing disorder in Spain – the lawlessness and violence of demonstrations of the left, which the government seemed unable to control – finally decided the army conspirators in July 1936 to carry out a military coup, 'planned' since the previous April, to take over Spain.

Franco had finally thrown in his lot with the conspirators and secretly, on 18 July, left the Canary Islands to take charge of the army in Africa. On 13 July, the murder of a well-known anti-Republican politician by members of the Republican Guard provided a further pretext for the military rising, which had actually already been set in motion. A day early, on 17 July, the army rose in Morocco. General Mola had ordered the risings to begin in Morocco on 18 July and the garrisons in mainland Spain to take power a day later. But the risings on the mainland also began earlier, on the 18th, and the following day spread to Spain's two largest cities, Madrid and Barcelona. Here the risings were successfully suppressed. Thus the army failed to take over the whole of Spain in one swift action. Within a short time the Nationalist and Republican zones were becoming clear. Their respective military resources were fairly equally balanced in metropolitan Spain with about half the army and most of the air force and much of the fleet siding with the government of the Republic.

What decisively tipped the balance was the help Hitler and Mussolini gave to Franco, providing transport planes to ferry the African army to the peninsula. Franco decided not to risk crossing by sea. The Republican fleet's doubtful capacity was thus not tested. The disorganisation on the Republican side extended to the air force, which made no efforts to intercept the German and Italian transport planes. The Nationalists speedily dominated the

west and much of the south. By the end of July, Burgos in the north had become the capital of Nationalist Spain. Mola had set up there a junta of generals. However, it was Franco who was accepted by all the generals as their commander-in-chief; by the end of September he was also declared head of the Spanish state as well as of the government. This marked the beginning of a long, undisputed hold on absolute power which was to last until his death thirty-nine years later in 1975.

As the Nationalists captured Republican-held territory, prominent Republican leaders, civil and military, were murdered in their tens of thousands. Terror was a weapon used to cow working-class populations. On the Republican side attacks were indiscriminately directed against the Church. The Church's political identification with the right (except in the Basque provinces) was beyond doubt, but the Church had not participated in the uprising. Twelve bishops and thousands of priests and monks were murdered. Many thousands suspected of sympathy with the Nationalists were summarily executed. The government of the Republic could not control its followers in this bloody lawlessness. The bitter hatreds of the fratricidal war have, not surprisingly, lived on as long as survivors of both sides remain to recall the atrocities of three years of war. These murders on both sides have been estimated by Professor Hugh Thomas to total a ghastly 130,000 (75,000 committed by the Nationalists and 55,000 by the Republicans). To these losses must be added deaths in battle – 90,000 Nationalists and 110,000 Republicans – and death from all other causes, about 500,000, out of a total population of 25 million.

The Republicans had the difficult task of welding together an effective central government in Madrid from all the disparate forces of the left, and a cohesive army from the many military formations that had gathered spontaneously. The communists, declaring that the 'revolution' had to be postponed, joined the moderate Socialists and Republicans. Largo Caballero headed a Popular Front government in the autumn of 1936 which even the anarchists, dominant in Catalonia and Barcelona, joined. But the left could not maintain unity through the war. Their 'fraternal' strife, with the communists fighting the anarchists and the anti-Stalinist Marxists (known by their initials as POUM), was the main cause of the ultimate defeat of the Republic. On the other side, despite the heterogeneous

*The Spanish Civil War.* Above left: *General Franco receives the fascist salute from the nursing staff of a Nationalist hospital.* Above right: *Republican militiamen celebrate their defence of Madrid.* Left: *Republican soldiers like this one at the Aragon front fought on, despite inferior resources, to the bitter end.* Right: *POUM, a Trotskyist party, calls on the peasants to rise up to claim their land.*

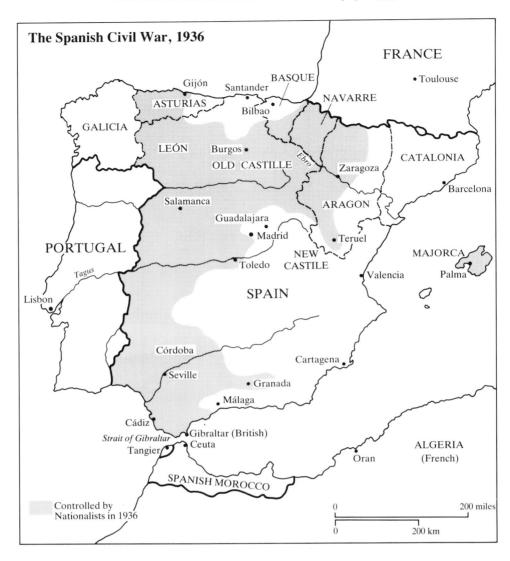

**The Spanish Civil War, 1936**

Controlled by
Nationalists in 1936

0          200 miles

0          200 km

political complexion of the Nationalists, Franco and the army dominated and created an effective unity and an impressive fighting force.

German and Italian help had been critical in the early stages of the war and favoured Franco's advance to the gates of Madrid. But massive Soviet military assistance including planes and tanks saved Madrid in November 1936. Britain and France, ostensibly with German, Soviet and Italian agreement, set up a Non-Intervention Committee whose undertaking not to send weapons to either side was honoured only by the two Western democracies. The Germans sent tanks and experts and the notorious Condor Legion, which, with a hundred planes, played an important role and horrified the

democracies by bombing defenceless towns. The wanton destruction of Guernica (26 April 1937) symbolised the terror of war on civilians. The lesson was not lost on the British who week after week saw on their cinema screens the horrible effects of those air raids. Not surprisingly it strengthened the desire of the British people to keep out of a general war and to support those politicians who were trying to do so, though the committed did go to fight in Spain. Mussolini sent over 70,000 volunteer troops. The Russians, from headquarters in Paris, organised the volunteer International Brigades and sent tanks and planes. All this foreign aid succeeded in staving off defeat for either side, but it was not sufficient to ensure a victory.

After the Nationalist advances in August to October 1936, the Republic still held half of Spain – the whole east and south-east, as well as a strip in the north. Madrid remained in government hands, having repulsed the Nationalist advance. In 1937 the Nationalists finally overcame Basque resistance in the north. In Madrid the government was reorganised to take a stronger line against dissidents. The communists, whose strength rapidly grew, took a lead in fighting against the POUM and the anarchists. Caballero was replaced as premier by a socialist professor, Dr Juan Negrín. By now the Republicans had organised a well-disciplined army. In the winter of 1937 the Republican army launched an offensive against the Nationalists. Franco's counter-offensive, however, recovered all the lost territory and went on to split the Republic in half, separating Barcelona and Catalonia from central and southern Spain. The defeat of the Republic appeared imminent. Unexpectedly the Republicans won a short-lived victory in the summer of 1938, but then in the autumn suffered a catastrophic defeat when Franco counterattacked. Internationally the Republic simultaneously sustained devastating blows. France, which intermittently had allowed arms to pass the Pyrenees frontier, closed it, and Stalin gave up sending aid to the Republic. Franco's victories and the desertion of the Soviet Union and France doomed the Republic. In January 1939 Barcelona fell. Still Negrín inspired the final resistance. The Republic came to an end in confusion, with part of her own armed forces in rebellion. At the end of March 1939, Madrid finally capitulated to Franco's army.

The Spanish Civil War was over. It had dragged on with enormous loss of life. Refugees now flooded across the Pyrenees into France. But Europe's attention was only momentarily fixed on the final agony. War between the European powers had been only narrowly averted in the autumn of 1938, and now in March 1939 Hitler again held the centre of the stage. The world would soon turn upside down. The communists, seen by the left-wing idealists as the real opponents of the fascists and Nazis in Spain, would that same year, in September 1939, praise Hitler and condemn the imperialist–capitalist Western democracies for going to war to check Nazi expansion in Europe.

# CHAPTER 25

## The Outbreak of War in Europe, 1937–1939

Responsibility is a portmanteau word covering many different meanings. All the nations in a complex international society are to some degree involved with each other and in that sense share 'responsibility' for the most important international events such as war. In that sense, too, it is both true and misleading to conclude that Hitler's Germany was not alone responsible for the outbreak of war in 1939 – misleading when responsibility is equated with blame, and blame, like responsibility, is considered something to be shared out between all the nations involved. Such an analysis of responsibility for the outbreak of the second great war in Europe, however, confuses more than it illuminates. This point is vividly brought out when we compare the attitudes of Hitler and Chamberlain as revealed in accounts not at the time intended for the general public.

Hitler, in September 1939, posed before the German people as the injured party, as acting in *defence* of Germans persecuted by Poles, and in response to actual Polish attacks across the frontier (in fact secretly organised by the Gestapo). Hitler knew this pose was a blatant lie. Since coming to power he had built up the armed forces of the Reich, not simply to gain his ends by the bluff of overawing Germany's weaker neighbours: the Wehrmacht and Luftwaffe were fighting instruments prepared for real use. Although not precisely certain of the right timing, Hitler intended all along to pass from a policy of piecemeal territorial acquisition by blackmail to actual wars of conquest. In

September 1938, he was frustrated when he could not make war on Czechoslovakia. A year later he was not again deterred. On 23 November 1939, a few weeks after war began, he summoned the chiefs of the armed services and explained that he had not been sure whether to attack first in the East or in the West (it should be noted that it was not a question of either/or); but Polish resistance to his demands had decided the issue:

> One will blame me [for engaging in] war and more war. I regard such struggle as the fate of all being. No one can avoid the fight if he does not wish to be the inferior. The growth of population requires a larger living space. My aim was to bring about a sensible relationship between population size and living space. This is where the military struggle has to begin. No people can evade the solution of this task unless it renounces and gradually succumbs. That is the lesson of history. . . .[1]

There can be no reasonable doubt now, with hindsight and the evidence available, that while Hitler remained in power he intended passing from the phase of preparation for war to actual wars of conquest, and that the purpose of these conquests was the aggrandisement of Germany herself, and the reduction of the conquered nations who would

[1] Max Domarius, *Hitler Reden und Proklamationen*, Vol. 2, pp. 1421–6.

retain a separate existence only as satellites. The dominated people would all have to conform to Hitler's racialist plan for the New Order of Europe. This racialist basis of Nazi policy meant not that Hitler aimed at a Wilhelmine German domination of Europe, but that he planned a European revolution entailing mass population movements in the East, murder and the enslavement of 'inferior' races. For Hitler, then, the question of war and peace was a question of timing, of choosing the moment which promised the greatest chance of success.

As has been seen, the French, whose assessment of Hitler's aims tended to be more realistic than that of the British, would not in any case risk war with Germany without a cast-iron guarantee of Britain's backing. Even then doubts about France's survival as a great power if she were further weakened by heavy losses of men and reserves made Frenchmen look at the prospect with horror. What was true of France was also true of Germany's smaller neighbours. As for the Soviet Union she shared no frontier with Germany and hoped to contain her by deterrence in association with the Western powers; but that policy was bluff since the Soviet alternative to the failure of deterrence was not war but a truce, an accommodation with Germany. The United States was fervently prodemocratic (and Roosevelt gave eloquent expression to these beliefs) but equally fervently neutral if it should come to war in Europe. That gave Britain the key role.

Until the spring of 1939, Neville Chamberlain dominated the Cabinet as few prime ministers had before him. He was Hitler's most formidable protagonist. Chamberlain too, though subject to public opinion and the pressure of his colleagues, would have to decide when to accept that general European war was inevitable, unless Britain were simply to stand by while Hitler secured the domination of the European continent. The conquest of Poland would have been followed by other conquests, though no one can be sure in what direction Hitler would have struck *first* and so what precise sequence he would have followed. Nor did he intend to spare a hostile and independent Britain. When Hitler passed from 'cold' war to 'hot' war, Chamberlain reluctantly accepted that a great European war would become inevitable if civilisation in Europe and Britain's independence and security were to survive.

Chamberlain's attitude stands in stark contrast to Hitler's. Chamberlain abhorred war. He belonged to the generation of the Great War. Humanitarian feelings were the positive motivations of his life. He wished to better the lot of his fellow men, to cure the ills, in particular unemployment, which still beset Britain's industrial life. War, to him, was the ultimate waste and negation of human values. He believed in the sanctity of individual human life and rejected the crude notions of a people's destiny, purification through violence and struggle, and the attainment of ends by brute force. He had faith in the triumph of reason and, believing himself to be fighting the good fight for peace, he was prepared to be patient, tenacious and stubborn, drawing on inner resources to maintain a personal optimism even when conditions all around pointed the other way. To the very end he hoped for some miracle that would ensure a peaceful outcome. Only a week away from war at the end of August 1939 he expressed his feelings in a private letter to his sister Hilda, 'I feel like a man driving a clumsy coach over a narrow cracked road along the face of a precipice . . . I sat with Annie [Mrs Chamberlain] in the drawing room, unable to read, unable to talk, just sitting with folded hands and a gnawing pain in the stomach.'[1] When Chamberlain spoke to the nation over the BBC at the outbreak of war, he, unlike Hitler, could say with sincerity:

> You can imagine what a bitter blow it is to me that all my long struggle to win peace has failed. Yet I cannot believe that there is anything more or anything different that I could have done and that would have been more successful. His [Hitler's] action shows convincingly that there is no choice of expecting that this man will ever give up his practice of using force to gain his will. He can only be stopped by force.

There is no meaningful way in which Chamberlain's responsibility for war can be discussed or compared on the same basis as Hitler's, any more than a man who violently attacks his neighbour is less responsible for his action because of the weakness of the police force.

This is not to suggest of course that the origins of the war in Europe can be reduced to a contrast between two men, Hitler and Chamberlain. Hitler

[1] Chamberlain to Hilda, 27 August 1939, Chamberlain Papers, University of Birmingham, England.

could not safely wage war without the assurance that rearmament had progressed sufficiently – an assurance which required the co-operation of industry and the management of finance. Nor could he totally ignore technical military considerations. He needed the co-operation of the army. The overlapping party and state machinery of government, and the gearing of the economy to war preparations under Hermann Göring's overall direction, created many problems. The 'court' of leading Nazis around the Führer – Himmler, Goebbels, Hess, Bormann, Göring, and lesser sub-leaders such as Rosenberg, Ribbentrop, Ley – were engaged in bitter infighting, jockeying for Hitler's favour and a more influential place in the hierarchy. German policymaking was not monolithic; various highly placed people and organisations influenced policy. Hitler certainly had the last word on all major issues, but took care to try and carry the leaders of the army, industry and the mass of the people with him. His speeches were a torrent of untruths, carefully calculated; he was well aware that war with Britain and France was widely regarded with apprehension.

The many dimensions of British policy and all influences shaping it are just as complex, though different. Party political considerations play an important role in the making of policy in a parliamentary democracy. Governments were more directly affected by public feeling, which could be freely expressed, unlike in Germany. Decisions in Britain were taken by committees, the supreme government committee being the Cabinet, which met at the prime minister's residence. Chamberlain's control was never dictatorial as Hitler's was. Chamberlain's ascendancy over his ministerial colleagues was at its height in 1938, but he could not act without carrying them with him – resignations had to be contained to the single minister in disagreement. In 1939, Chamberlain's influence lessened as the assumption behind his policies was seen to be more and more at variance with unfolding events in Europe. Belated rearmament was a particular handicap, narrowing Britain's policy options.

There was one further, striking difference between German and British policy. Hitler paid relatively little attention to his two 'allies', Italy and Japan, and fashioned policy without allowing their reactions to affect his own decisions. Not so the British government, which, while taking the lead in the framing of the policy in the West, could not ignore France's reactions and later Poland's. Britain stood at the centre of the Commonwealth, and the views of Canada, South Africa, Australia and New Zealand also made themselves felt.

The greatest difference between Britain's and Germany's position derived from Britain's role not only as a European but as a world power with imperial interests in every continent. These interests were each supported by different politicians and pressure groups which conflicted with each other when the priorities of policies came to be resolved. Britain's commitments to defend Australia, New Zealand and India from the Japanese threat were as absolute as considerations of security at home which required Britain to stand by France if she were attacked by Germany. The Defence Requirements Committee, specifically assigned the task of analysing Britain's military needs, came to a clear decision when it reported to the Cabinet in February 1934 that Germany was 'the ultimate potential enemy against whom all our "long range" defence policy must be directed'.

For many years none of Britain's armed forces would be strong enough to meet all potential enemies. At first there were only two of these: Germany in Europe, rapidly arming, and Japan in Asia. With the outbreak of the Italian-Abyssinian war and Britain's support for League sanctions there was now a third potential enemy with naval forces in the Mediterranean – Italy. The need to defend every British possession was equally absolute. How then was the lack of resources to be matched to these requirements? That was the task of diplomacy. The real question was not whether or not to 'appease', but which nation to stand up to and which to conciliate. In the Far East much would depend on the attitude of the United States. Britain's situation via-à-vis the United States in Asia was similar to that of France vis-à-vis Britain in Europe. France could not risk war with Germany without British support; Britain could not afford to contemplate war with Japan without the guarantee of American support unless driven into war in defence of the territory of the empire and Commonwealth. In Europe also, Britain could only act defensively. Her air force, intended as a deterrent, lagged behind the strength of the German air force and so its deterrent value never materialised. It did not even figure in Hitler's calculations: Germany made great efforts towards self-sufficiency (autarky) under Göring's Four-Year Plan after 1936, though Hitler recognised that, without conquests, self-sufficiency could not be completely attained. Nevertheless, dependence on foreign supplies was reduced and to that extent the damage which a British blockade by sea could inflict much lessened. How then did Britain conceive a war with Germany might be conducted so that it would end in Germany's defeat?

The one consistent military assumption that the politicians in the British Cabinet made until February 1939 was the extraordinary one that Britain needed no large army to fight Germany on the continent. Chamberlain, as chancellor of the Exchequer, argued that there was not enough money to expand all three services and everyone, except the Chiefs of Staff, agreed that the British public would never accept that Britain should, as in 1914–18, send an army of millions to France and Belgium. The French realised that they could not opt out of providing the land army to repel Germany. All the heavy casualties would thus fall on them. No wonder that in the circumstances they sought to protect their depleted manhood by reliance on the Maginot Line and felt some bitterness towards their British ally.

While the British and French service chiefs were agreed that the most dangerous enemy would be a rearmed Germany, their policy towards Italy was never co-ordinated. When France wanted to conciliate Mussolini in 1935, Britain gave no backing and in January 1939 the reverse occurred. British attention, moreover, and French too, was not exclusively fixed on Germany. From 1931 to 1933 Japanese aggression in Manchuria and the question of support for the League of Nations occupied the attention of the public and of governments. Alarm at Germany's growing armament was next diverted by the Italian–Abyssinian war in 1935. Hitler was singularly lucky at having these 'diversions' during his years of military preparations. In just the same way the remilitarisation of the Rhineland, Germany's own 'backyard', soon came to be overshadowed by the outbreak of the Spanish Civil War. While Hitler incessantly worked in his foreign policy to extend and strengthen Germany, he was simultaneously transforming the country from inside with increasing emphasis on Nazi ideology and the militarisation of the whole of society. German women were admonished to 'give' the Führer many babies, the soldiers of the future. The Führer cultivated the image of the lone leader on whom rested all the burdens of his people. He was occasionally shown more humanly in the company of children and dogs. But the existence of his blonde mistress, Eva Braun, was one of the best-kept secrets of the Third Reich.

The middle 1930s were years of feverish preparation for the great moment when Nazi Germany would consummate Hitler's revolution and establish the new racial order in Europe. The preparations were still taking place within the frontiers of Germany, though party propaganda was reaching out and spawning local parties not only in Austria but as far afield as Latin America. Within Germany, incessant propaganda was directed against one arch-opponent in Nazi demonology, the Jews. Despite widespread anti-Semitism Hitler felt he had to move with caution so as not to arouse sympathy for the Jews: many good 'Aryans' knew at least 'one good' Jew and did not grasp the literal meaning of the SA bands' obscene shout, *Judah verrecke*, 'perish the Jew'. The Jews were bewildered. Many saw themselves as patriotic Germans, tied to German culture, and thought the Hitler phenomenon was mere summer's madness. The tide of emigration was slow. They could transfer only a fraction of their possessions out of the country. Opportunities of earning a living abroad were restricted, and the language and customs were strange. Most German Jews hung on. Despite all the discrimination against them they continued to enjoy the protection of the law from common violence. By and large they were not physically molested before November 1938. Nevertheless the screw was being turned more tightly year by year.

The notorious anti-Semitic Nuremberg laws, first proclaimed at the Nazi Party rally in 1935, and in subsequent years constantly extended, were but a logical step in the direction of the new Nazi world which Hitler and his followers were creating. The persecution of the Jews was not an accidental blemish of Hitler's government, which, it has been mistakenly argued, should be seen as just another aggressive nationalist German regime. Without hatred of Jews and the relentless persecution waged against them, the core of Nazi ideology collapses. In 1935 all Jews remaining in the civil service were dismissed. The definitions of 'full' Jew, 'half' Jew or *Mischlinge* – 'mixtures' of various degrees – were determined not by a man's baptism or personal belief but by descent. Three Jewish grandparents made the second-generation descendants all Jews.

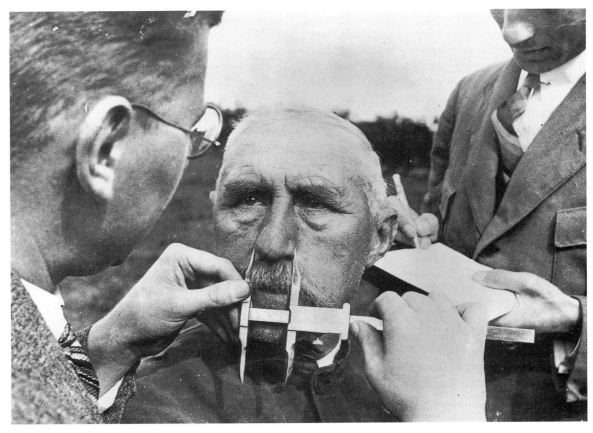

*Eugenics Rampant. A German has his credentials as an Aryan measured by calliper rule.*

The definition thus was racial, based on pseudo-science, not religious. The 'full' Jews, or 'Non-Aryans' as they were called, felt the total weight of persecution from the very start. The only *temporary* exception was made in cases where Jews were married to Aryans and there were 'mixed' children from the marriage. Pressure was placed on the Christian partner to divorce the Jewish spouse. Some did so. Other German wives and husbands protected their partner and children with the utmost courage and loyalty throughout the years of persecution and so saved their lives, for the war ended before Hitler could take measures against them. These brave people came from every walk of life and included officers in the armed forces and at least one admiral. Their behaviour alone should serve as a caution against crude generalisations about the 'German character', even though they formed, like the active resistance, only a tiny minority of the population. The Nuremberg laws made the German Jews second-class citizens officially and forbade further marriages between Jews and non-Jews and any sexual relations between Aryans and Jews. This latter crime was called *Rassenschande* and death sentences were passed where Jewish men were accused. Over a period of time Jews were removed from all professional contact with non-Jews. Only in business activities were Jews permitted to carry on until 1938, since it was feared that their sudden removal would harm the German economy. This concession was not due to Hitler's moderation – rather it is an indication that he was prepared to countenance a tactical delay while never deviating one inch from his ultimate ideological goals.

This pressure on the helpless small German Jewish population in 1933 – there were about 500,000 racially defined as Jews – drove them into increasing isolation and hardship. Even so they did not emigrate to Palestine or elsewhere fast enough. The majority of German Jews wanted to stay in their homes and in their country, whose cultural heritage, the works of Lessing, Goethe and Beethoven, they cherished. German culture was their culture. Not in moments of blackest nightmare could they imagine that in the twentieth century in Western Europe women and children would be murdered in factories of death. They were not, after all, stuck in the Middle Ages. Many Jews were still living in reasonable comfort, and for the most part relationships with their fellow Germans were correct and occasionally even friendly. But official discrimination steadily increased; Jews were expelled by the autumn of 1938 from all professions, they could no longer study in universities, and their shops were compulsorily purchased and Aryanised. It was by then clear that there was no future for young Jews, but the older generation expected to live out the rest of their days in Germany on their pensions and savings. During the summer of 1938, however, the Nazi leadership had decided to take far harsher measures against the Jews. First it was the turn of Jews from Poland who had not acquired German citizenship to be expelled brutally overnight. Then concentration camps were readied inside Germany. The German people would be given a practical demonstration of how to treat their Jewish neighbours as their enemies. Only a pretext was needed.

It was provided on 7 November 1938 by the fatal shooting of the third secretary of the German Embassy in Paris. The perpetrator was a half-crazed young Jew whose parents (of Polish origin) had just been deported; perhaps there were other reasons too. Paradoxically, the diplomat, Ernst von Rath, was no Nazi. After news of Rath's death reached Germany on the afternoon of 9 November, a pogrom all over Germany was launched. Synagogues were set on fire, Jewish shop-windows smashed. With typical black humour, Berliners dubbed the 9 November 'Kristallnacht', the night of crystals. Gangs of ruffians roamed the streets and entered Jewish apartments – it was a night of terror. Jewish men were arrested in their homes on the following day and incarcerated in concentration camps. A recently discovered entry in Goebbels's diary fully implicates Hitler, thus adding more evidence, if any were needed, that no major action could be undertaken in the Reich without the Führer's explicit approval. It so happened that 9 November was the annual occasion when all the Nazi leaders met to commemorate the abortive *Putsch* of 1923. In Munich, Goebbels wrote in his diary:

I report the situation to the Führer. He decides: let the demonstrations continue. Pull back the police. The Jews should be made to feel the wrath of the people. . . . As I head for the hotel, I see the sky is blood-red. The synagogue is burning. . . . the Führer has ordered 20,000–30,000 Jews to be arrested immediately.

The purpose of the great November pogrom of 1938 was to force the remaining Jews into emigration. A visa to a foreign country gained release from concentration camps. The question is often asked: why did Hitler try to force the Jews out of Germany even after the war began? Does this mean he would have preferred this solution to murdering them later? We do not know exactly what was in Hitler's mind but it is safe to conclude that humanitarian considerations did not come into his calculations on so central a question as his hatred of the Jews. He certainly was sensitive to German public feeling and presumably concluded that the German people were not ready to back his rule with increasing enthusiasm if he simply massacred all Jews, men, women and children *within Germany*.

During the war, vain efforts were made to preserve the secrecy of the death camps. Hitler wished to remove physically all Jews from the territory ruled by him. Emigration would 'export' anti-Semitism. And when he had won his wars the Jews would be done for in any case, as Nazi policies in all occupied Europe were to show during the war. After November 1938 the Jews in panic belatedly attempted to leave: the civilised world debated but could not agree to absorb the remaining 300,000. But tens of thousands of people were saved, with the 'children's transports' to Britain forming a poignant part of these emigrants. Many children said goodbye to the one parent who was permitted to come to the railway station in Germany. Most of these children never saw their parents again. The exodus was made possible by the response of thousands of concerned individuals who collected money and pressurised their reluctant governments to let the refugees in.

The Jewish persecution by bureaucratic machine involved and implicated more and more Germans in the criminal activities of the Nazi regime under pseudo-legislative cover. Opposition became more risky as the grip of the totalitarian state tightened. There were still a few who spoke out openly, like the Protestant pastor Martin Niemöller, and were placed in concentration camps. Amid the general enthusiasm for the Nazis, it must be remembered that there were many too who were terrorised into silence.

The Jews were the most obvious and open targets of persecution. But there were hundreds of thousands of others who suffered. In ruthless pursuit of the supposedly racially healthy German *Volk*, laws were passed in 1933 which permitted mass sterilisation of those deemed able to pass on genetic defects, such as medical handicaps, epilepsy and deafness, mental defects or even social defects, one of which was identified as drunkenness and another as habitual criminality. Not only were pregnancies aborted and sterilisation ordered for the individual affected, but the whole family, including young adolescents, were sterilised. Convicted homosexuals were incarcerated in concentration camps. In the interests of 'racial hygiene' it was then but a step to proceed to murder the handicapped during the war under the pretence that they were being released from their suffering – this was the 'euthanasia' programme. But, as with the murder of the Jews, Hitler decided that the extermination of 'lives not worthy of life' would have to wait for the cover of war. Racial discrimination after 1935 was also suffered by the 22,000 gypsies living in Germany. They too, men, women, children and babies, together with the tens of thousands of Polish and European gypsies, were designated for extermination.

Hitler was still telling the German people that he wanted peace and desired no more than to bring home to the Reich those German people living beyond the German frontier: not just the people of course but also the lands in which they were living. At a meeting of his military commanders and in the presence also of the Foreign and War Ministers in his Chancellery on 5 November 1937 Hitler spoke his mind. Colonel Hossbach recorded the meeting. The aims Hitler expressed contained nothing new; they were all familiar from his previous statements and writings. He referred to the need to realise these aims within six to eight years at the latest. The German *race* needed space in the east to expand and multiply or it would be doomed to decline. More land and resources were an economic necessity. The solution to Germany's problems could be found only by using force. Beyond the years 1943-5 the rearmament of Germany's enemies would exceed the ageing equipment of the German military. Germany had to assume the enmity of Britain and France. Hitler speculated on international complications like a civil war in France or a war between the Mediterranean powers which would divide Germany's enemies to her advantage. As a first step, a strategic necessity was an 'attack' on Austria and Czechoslovakia. It was therefore obvious that rearmament expenditure could not be reduced. The immediate objective of winning Austria and Czechoslovakia, however, would be attained by a little war conducted with lightning speed; and Hitler assured the generals that this would not lead to general war.

What is noteworthy about Hitler's policy from 1937 to 1939 is the acceleration of pace – his reluctance simply to await events and to exploit suitable opportunities. He became more confident and reckless; he wanted to carry through his grand design without waiting much longer. He became obsessed with his health, nerves and stomach disorders. He was ageing and would do so rapidly during the war. Such independence as the army had retained, as a professional body whose independent judgement was expressed on the military feasibility of Hitler's plans, was an obstacle to their realisation. The Commander-in-Chief of the Wehrmacht as well as the War Minister were forced to resign early in 1938. Hitler assumed personal supreme control with his own military staff by replacing the War Ministry with the Oberkommando der Wehrmacht (OKW, or High Command of the Armed Forces). The General Staff of the Army was subordinated to the OKW. The army was purged of generals unenthusiastic about Nazi plans, though opposition to them from within the officer corps was not silenced. The Foreign Minister Konstantin von Neurath was also replaced – by an ardent Nazi, Joachim von Ribbentrop – and the diplomatic service was purged. Before embarking on action, Hitler had thus powerfully strengthened his authority.

Hitler had no immediate plans for the annexation of independent Austria. Yet within a few weeks it was a fact. The events as they unfolded made possible a quick finish to Austria's independence and convinced Hitler in the spring of 1938 that the tide was running more swiftly and favourably towards Germany's destiny than he had thought. He had wished to cow Austria into satellite status without, for the time being, openly destroying her independence. From 1936 to February 1938 he succeeded well with the Austrian Chancellor Schuschnigg, who was finally summoned to his mountain retreat

*Scapegoating the Jews.* Above: *the incineration of Jewish, 'degenerate' and 'un-German' books, May 1933.* Top right: *Viennese Jews scrub the paving stones in the public humiliation that swiftly followed the* Anschluss, *March 1938.* Top left: *The shell of Königsberg's synagogue, burnt out during* Kristallnacht, *9/10 November 1938.*

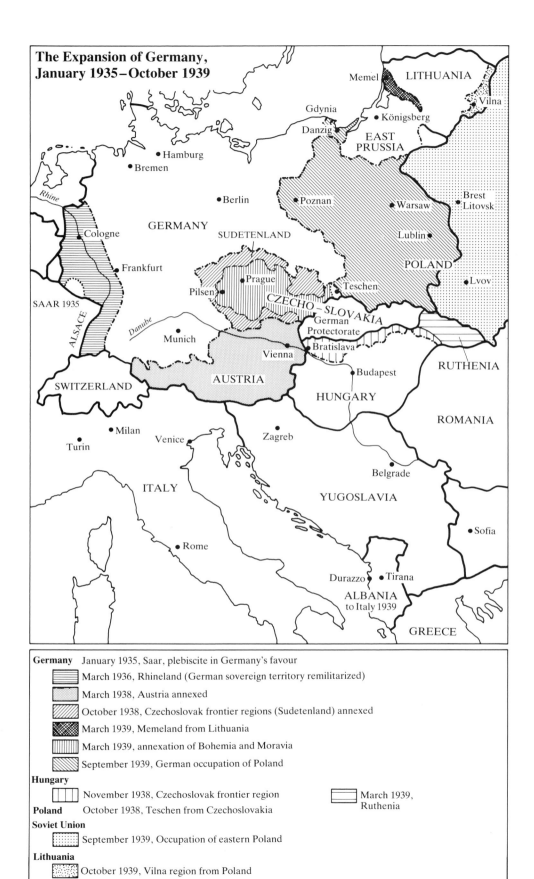

**The Expansion of Germany, January 1935–October 1939**

Memel
LITHUANIA
Vilna
Gdynia
Königsberg
Danzig
EAST PRUSSIA
Hamburg
Bremen
Rhine
Berlin
Poznan
Brest Litovsk
Warsaw
GERMANY
SUDETENLAND
Cologne
Lublin
POLAND
Frankfurt
Prague
Pilsen
CZECHO-SLOVAKIA
Teschen
Lvov
SAAR 1935
Danube
German Protectorate
ALSACE
Munich
Bratislava
RUTHENIA
Vienna
SWITZERLAND
AUSTRIA
Budapest
HUNGARY
ROMANIA
Milan
Venice
Zagreb
Turin
Belgrade
ITALY
YUGOSLAVIA
Sofia
Rome
Durazzo
Tirana
ALBANIA to Italy 1939
GREECE

**Germany** January 1935, Saar, plebiscite in Germany's favour

March 1936, Rhineland (German sovereign territory remilitarized)

March 1938, Austria annexed

October 1938, Czechoslovak frontier regions (Sudetenland) annexed

March 1939, Memeland from Lithuania

March 1939, annexation of Bohemia and Moravia

September 1939, German occupation of Poland

**Hungary**

November 1938, Czechoslovak frontier region

March 1939, Ruthenia

**Poland** October 1938, Teschen from Czechoslovakia

**Soviet Union**

September 1939, Occupation of eastern Poland

**Lithuania**

October 1939, Vilna region from Poland

at Berchtesgaden a month before the *Anschluss* to be bullied into agreeing to make far-reaching further concessions to the Nazis in Austria entailing the certain erosion of what independence had remained. Deserted by Mussolini, he had little choice but to agree to German demands.

Mussolini preferred a German alignment ever since his conflict with Britain over Italian aggressions in Abyssinia and involvement in Spain. He was jealous of German success, but in 1936 bombastically claimed that European affairs now revolved around the Axis of Berlin and Rome. He visited Hitler in September 1937 and was very impressed by the spectacle of Germany's might and flattered by the Führer's attentions. He had already secretly removed his objection to German dominance over Austria and had been assured that her independence would not be too blatantly destroyed.

That is one reason why Hitler as late as 28 February 1938 sought an 'evolutionary' Austrian course. But Schuschnigg in the end would not play the game; the rabbit bolted. When he returned to Austria he announced he would hold a plebiscite on 13 March, intending to ask the people whether they desired independence or union with Germany. Despite the suppression of the socialists and trade unions, who had no love for Schuschnigg, their vote would certainly have been cast against Hitler's Germany. Hitler demanded a 'postponement' of the plebiscite. Schuschnigg conceded and resigned. But now the President would not appoint the National Socialist nominee in his place, a new demand. Göring, given responsibility for the Austrian Nazi takeover, had completed the military preparations. On 12 March 1938 the Wehrmacht crossed the frontier; Hitler followed close behind. There was no military opposition. Hitler was received in Linz with cheers and flowers by part of the population. He decided on an instantaneous acceleration of his plans. Instead of a gradual fusion of the two countries, complete union, or the *Anschluss*, was announced on 13 March and later approved by a charade of a plebiscite.

It all happened so quickly that international reaction in the first place consisted merely of some ineffectual protests. But this ruthless expansion of Germany's frontiers forced the British and French governments into a fresh stock-taking.

In February 1938 Eden resigned and Halifax replaced him at the Foreign Office. Eden had resigned over the immediate difference of opinion with Prime Minister Chamberlain on whether Mussolini should be appeased before he had given concrete proof of abiding by international undertakings and withdrawing troops from Spain. Eden was testing the specific, the good faith of the dictators, while Chamberlain was following a grand design of foreign policy and was ready to subordinate 'secondary' questions to its fulfilment. Chamberlain's grand design for peace and stability involved working separately on Hitler and Mussolini. His ideas had already been clearly formulated the previous November 1937 when he sent Halifax, then Lord President of the Council and not Foreign Secretary, on a mission to Hitler. Halifax, according to the official British record, told Hitler that England accepted 'possible alterations in the European order which might be destined to come about with the passage of time. Amongst these questions were Danzig, Austria, Czechoslovakia. England was interested to see that any alterations should come through the course of peaceful evolution . . .' The German record is more pointed and has Halifax expressing the view that he 'did not believe that the *status quo* had to be maintained under all circumstances'. As further baits to persuade Germany into the paths of peace, Chamberlain was prepared to make economic concessions and even envisaged some eventual African colonial appeasement.

Privately Chamberlain explained to his sister Ida that he regarded the visit as a great success because it had created an atmosphere which would make possible discussions with Germany on 'the practical questions involved in a European settlement':

What I wanted to do was to convince Hitler of our sincerity and to ascertain what objectives he had in mind . . . Both Hitler and Göring said separately and emphatically that they had no desire or intention of making war and I think we may take this as correct at any rate for the present. Of course they want to dominate Eastern Europe; they want as close a union with Austria as they can get without incorporating her in the Reich and they want much the same thing for the Sudeten Deutsch as we did for the Uitlanders in the Transvaal. . . . But I don't see why we shouldn't say to Germany give us satisfactory assurances that you won't use force to deal with the Austrians and Czecho-Slovakians and we will give you similar assurances that we won't use force to prevent the changes you want, if you can get them by peaceful means. . . .[1]

The flaws in Chamberlain's reasoning were several and serious. First, it was wrong that Hitler was pursuing a nationalist foreign policy which could be satisfied by limited territorial adjustments. Down to the outbreak of war in 1939 Chamberlain failed to comprehend the central racialist kernel of Hitler's policy and therefore the significance of the persecution of the Jews. There is one interesting piece of evidence about this in an unpublished private letter. His sister Hilda had passed the absurd information to him that it was possible for Jews to be admitted to the Hitler Youth, and Chamberlain replied in July 1939:

I had no idea that Jews were still allowed to work or join such organisations as the Hitler Youth in Germany. It shows, doesn't it, how much sincerity there is in the talk of racial purity. I believe the persecution arose out of two motives: a desire to rob the Jews of their money and a jealousy of their superior cleverness.[2]

Chamberlain, unlike Churchill, did not have warm feelings for Jews in general. He wrote that he did not regard them as a 'lovable people' but condemned their persecution: 'I don't care about them myself' but that was not sufficient reason to explain pogroms. Chamberlain failed to grasp early on the limitless nature of Hitler's demands. He worked for a 'reasonable' settlement so that a great war would be seen as a needless and criminal sacrifice of life.

The second flaw, which led to the taint of moral guilt, was that Chamberlain believed in the justification of the greater good, or more precisely the avoidance of the greater evil, which for him was a general war. This played into Hitler's hands. Hitler intended to secure the maximum advantages at minimum cost. He would thus without risk of general war provide Germany with a strong base before launching his ultimate wars of conquest. The sacrifices Chamberlain called for, moreover, were not of British territory. It would be the Austrians,

Czechs and other 'foreigners' who would actually suffer the consequences. So too the colonial concessions in Africa would be offered largely at the expense of Portugal and Belgium and, far more importantly, would have placed racist Nazis in control of black peoples whom they looked on as subhumans. It is doubtful whether Chamberlain really grasped this fact.

The third flaw was the weakening of Britain's allies, actual and potential, on the continent. But Chamberlain was essentially right when he assessed the United States as an unlikely ally at the outset of any war in Europe. Whatever Roosevelt might say, he was the prisoner of an overwhelmingly isolationist Congress. Also Chamberlain was right that no reliance could be placed on the Soviet Union, which was not ready for war and would not fight Germany in alliance with Britain and France as long as she could divert the German attack from her own territory.

By the spring of 1938 the Anglo-French alliance had reached a pretty low point. The British Cabinet was forging ahead with the grand design of Chamberlain's peace policy, intermittently consulting French ministers. A consistent British policy was followed throughout 1938. It was obvious that the German-speaking inhabitants of Czechoslovakia would be the next target. Germany was informed that the November 1937 assurances to Hitler still held (page 241). Britain was willing to come to an agreement over the Sudeten question on Germany's terms provided this could be accomplished peacefully. The new French government of Prime Minister Édouard Daladier and Foreign Minister Georges Bonnet was promised the support of the British alliance if Germany launched an unprovoked attack on France. The sting in this seemingly satisfactory guarantee was that it was not extended to the case where France declared war on Germany in fulfilment of her commitment to the Franco-Czechoslovakian alliance. In this way the British alliance became a potent weapon which Chamberlain and Halifax used to force the French into line behind a policy of concessions to Germany at Czechoslovakia's expense. Not that the French had much spirit of resistance given the pessimism of General Gamelin and the British attitude. French policy too was to reach agreement with Germany. The French consistently sought to influence British policy, without ever taking a position in advance of Britain's which risked war. France, the ministers

---

[1] Chamberlain to Ida Chamberlain, 26 November 1937, Chamberlain Papers.
[2] Chamberlain to Hilda Chamberlain, 30 July 1939, Chamberlain Papers.

had decided in March 1938, 'could only react to events, she could not take the initiative'.

In dealing with Germany, Britain offered the carrot and the stick. The colonial, territorial and economic carrots dangled before the Germans have already been noted. The 'stick' consisted of refusing to bind Britain to neutrality if Hitler did resort to force. Chamberlain declared in the House of Commons after the *Anschluss*,

> His Majesty's Government would not however pretend that, where peace and war are concerned, legal obligations are alone involved and that if war broke out it would be likely to be confined to those who have assumed obligations. It would be quite impossible to say where it might end and what Governments might become involved.

It was a clear warning to Hitler not to attack Czechoslovakia, though secretly the Cabinet had already concluded that there was no way in which Czechoslovakia could be helped militarily.

British policy from March 1938 until September 1938 thus put pressure on all who might precipitate a conflict – the French, the Germans and, not least, the Czechs if they resisted German demands. Chamberlain got his way because the military were only too aware of Britain's woeful weakness, especially in the air; the Dominions counselled peace; and British public opinion, however indignant about Hitler, was overwhelmingly for peace as well. These pressures corresponded to Chamberlain's innermost convictions that his mission was to save the peace of Europe.

Plans for attacking Czechoslovakia were discussed by Hitler and the generals in April 1938. To ensure that Czechoslovakia would receive no support, a crisis was to be worked up. At the end of May Hitler declared to his generals his 'unshakeable will that Czechoslovakia shall be wiped off the map'. He signed a military directive which set a final date, 1 October 1938. He had been infuriated by indications that Czechoslovakia would not tamely submit as Austria had done. Rumours of German military moves had in May led to a partial Czech mobilisation and warnings from Britain and France. Hitler had actually been anticipated, and he raged at the public loss of face. He was not yet ready to smash Czechoslovakia but soon would be – that mixed 'racial' state was for him a monstrosity that challenged his ideology of racial purity.

Among all the Eastern European states, only Czechoslovakia had retained her Western democratic constitution – an added reason to make it unfit for German partnership. Another sin was the prominent support Czech statesmen gave to the ideals of the League of Nations. Czechoslovakia, largely because of her national composition, faced grave difficulties as a new successor state. In 1930 the country was inhabited by 7.1 million Czechs, 3.3 million Germans, 2.6 million Slovaks, 720,000 Hungarians, 569,000 Ruthenes, 100,000 Poles and a smaller number of Romanians and Yugoslavs. The cohesion of the state depended on the co-operation of Slovaks and Czechs as symbolised by the founding fathers, Thomas Masaryk and Eduard Beneš. The peasantry of Slovakia was administered mainly by the more educated Czechs, which caused discontent and the creation of a Slovak People's party, led by Father Hlinka, demanding autonomy. But the most serious difficulty was caused by relations with the German-speaking ex-Habsburg population living in Bohemia and Moravia and along the frontiers with Germany and the new Austria. Most of the Germans, once the masters, now resented their subordination to the 'Slav' state. Czech suspicions of German loyalties and attempts to favour Czech education and discriminate against Germans aroused anger and resentment.

The depression of the 1930s and the consequent economic crisis sharpened nationality conflicts as both Slovaks and Sudeten Germans blamed the Czechs. It coincided with the rise of Hitler, whose movement inspired imitations. In Bohemia and Moravia Konrad Henlein led the German National Front, which claimed rights for the Germans within the state, but secretly in 1938 worked for its disruption and union with Germany. Meanwhile Hitler publicly proclaimed that he would 'protect' the Sudeten Germans, who were unable to protect themselves. But not all Germans were enamoured of the Nazis. A significant minority of Social Democrats opted for Czechoslovakia out of hatred for Hitler, as the Austrian Social Democrats had also done. In 1938 the Czechs made far-reaching attempts to satisfy the German minority in negotiations with Henlein. But as Henlein had been told at a meeting with Hitler always to ask for more than the Czechs would accede to, these negotiations were doomed. Despite the genuine catalogue of internal difficulties, the 'multinational' army was patriotic and loyal and Czechoslovakia was in no danger of internal disruption. It was Hitler's aggression and Anglo-French diplomacy that destroyed Czechoslovakia in two stages, in September 1938 and in March 1939.

The agony of Czechoslovakia had its counterpart in Chamberlain's triumphant reception after saving the peace in September 1938. For the first time the Western democracies had been brought to the brink of war. The German Army High Command was alarmed as well by Hitler's tactics and warned Hitler that the Wehrmacht was not ready for war against France and Czechoslovakia. In August 1938 Colonel Ludwig Beck, the Chief of the Army General Staff, courageously resigned in protest at Hitler's insistence that Czechoslovakia must be attacked regardless of the risks of war with France. His successor was General Halder. In August both Halder and Beck plotted against Hitler and planned to arrest him before he could plunge Germany into war. The attitude of the majority of the army, including General von Brauchitsch, the Commander-in-Chief, makes it extremely doubtful whether the plot would have succeeded had it ever materialised. It depended in part on the appeal sent to London secretly urging Chamberlain to stand firm. Not unreasonably, Chamberlain was not prepared to risk the issue of war and peace on the success of a few conspirators in Germany who were trying to remove a powerful and popular dictator.

Chamberlain was pursuing his own peaceful policy. He induced the Czech government to 'invite' Lord Runciman early in August to assist as 'mediator' in the negotiations between the Czech government and Henlein. In view of Hitler's instructions to Henlein not to reach a settlement the mission was futile from the start. On 7 September Henlein broke off the negotiations. Hitler now deliberately worked for his pretext to attack Czechoslovakia, having carefully made all the necessary military preparations. The last stage of the German propaganda campaign began with Hitler's attack on the Czech President Beneš in a speech to the faithful at Nuremberg. But Chamberlain now began to interfere with Hitler's well-laid plans. Chamberlain's personal diplomacy, his flight to visit Hitler at Berchtesgaden on 15 September, caught the public imagination not only in Britain but also in Germany. He had come to find out what Hitler wanted. The crisis would be solved by diplomacy not force. The Czechs were diplomatically bludgeoned into agreeing on the cession of the Sudeten region

to Germany and the French were persuaded to desert their Czech ally. But when Chamberlain met Hitler with these fruits of his diplomacy on a second occasion in Godesberg, the Führer refused to give up the use of force and Chamberlain broke off the negotiations. The Czechs mobilised. It looked as if war might still result.

What made Hitler draw back on the brink at the end of September and forgo his *Blitzkrieg* or 'lightning war'? We can only surmise. He delivered another almost unbelievably insulting speech abusing Beneš on 26 September. But the likelihood of war with France and Britain made Hitler hesitate. A probable major influence on his decision not to force a war was the 'unsatisfactory' state of German public opinion. Watching the dramatic newsreels, the German cinema audiences applauded the old gentleman with his umbrella so determined to struggle for peace. The Germans feared the consequences of another war with Britain and France. And so Hitler allowed Mussolini the glory of arranging for a peaceful outcome. A conference was called at Munich and Hitler, Mussolini, Daladier and Chamberlain assembled on 29 September. By the early hours of 30 September the formalities of arranging for a German occupation of the Sudeten areas between 1 and 10 October were agreed and a few other details such as a declaration that what was left of Czechoslovakia would be guaranteed once the Poles and Hungarians too were satisfied. Chamberlain even got Hitler to sign the piece of paper he waved at the airport on his return to Britain promising to settle all future Anglo-German differences by diplomacy. The Czechs were not allowed to participate. Nor the Russians, who in 1938 were still the sworn Bolshevik enemies of Nazi Germany.

The new rump Czech-Slovak state did not last long, although she tried to avoid all offence in Germany. The Slovak autonomy movement proved disruptive and in March 1939 Hitler browbeat the Czech President Hacha in Berlin to sign away what was left of the independence of his country. Göring threatened that he would otherwise obliterate Prague with bombs. The Czech will to resist had already been broken at Munich. On 15 March 1939 the Wehrmacht moved in and Hitler hastened to Prague to savour his new triumph. But his cynical breach of the Munich settlement caused an immense revulsion in the West and the crowds which had so recently applauded Chamberlain on

*Mussolini's last appearance as Hitler's equal took place at the Munich Conference in September 1938.*

*But will Hitler honour his signature? On his return from Munich, British Prime Minister Neville Chamberlain waves the 'Anglo-German' agreement promising peace.*

his triumphant return from Munich demanded that something should now be done to stop Hitler. Thirty-five well-equipped Czechoslovak divisions were lost to the French ally. Could the French without a 'second front' in the east still check Germany on land? Fears were voiced in the British Cabinet that France might even abandon the British alliance and make the best terms she could with Germany. These worries drove both the Cabinet and the military advisers of the government to accept the need for a continental commitment. At the end of March 1939 plans were approved which would double the strength of the British Territorial Army from thirteen to twenty-six divisions.

Britain's foreign policy now had to be aligned to the recently perceived shift in the balance of power on the European continent. After initial hesitations Chamberlain responded in a speech he delivered in Birmingham on 17 March 1939. He accused Hitler of breaking his word and taking the law into his own hands, and asked rhetorically, 'Is this the end of an old adventure or is it the beginning of a new? Is this the last attack upon a small state or is it to be followed by others? Is this, in effect, a step

in the direction of an attempt to dominate the world by force?' In London, the Cabinet insisted on steps to create a deterrent alliance to save the peace if it could still be saved. They believed that only the threat of force might stop Hitler. Rumours of an impending German ultimatum to Romania, false as it turned out, served as the initial impetus which led to a unilateral Anglo-French guarantee, announced on 31 March 1939, to defend Romania and Poland against German aggression. Although Chamberlain continued to place faith in conciliating Hitler, he too was converted to the need for a deterrent alliance. Halifax and the Cabinet also urged that the alliance of the Soviet Union, too, should be sought. A sceptical Chamberlain had to give way. The long and weary Anglo-French–Soviet negotiations which followed lasted until 23 August 1939 when Stalin decided that Soviet interests were best served by concluding a non-aggression treaty with Nazi Germany instead (page 248).

If Britain's negotiations with Russia and her guarantee (and later alliance) with Poland prove anything, it is that the British never sought to

*March 1939: German troops march into the Hradcany Castle in Prague, seat of Czechoslovakia's president.*

embroil the Germans in a war with Russia while they themselves stood aside. Hitler could have invaded Russia on a broad front only by way of Poland or Romania, and Britain's policy had put up a barrier which could not be breached without involving Britain and France in war as well. It was ironic that the Western democracies should now be aligned with authoritarian Poland, having sacrificed democratic Czechoslovakia.

It has been argued that Britain and France were unnecessarily dragged into war by the March 1939 guarantees to Poland. Hitler, so this reasoning runs, would have followed the attack on Poland with an invasion of the Soviet Union. Would this not have been in Britain's and France's interest? The speculation about benefit is highly dubious. The evidence, moreover, is by no means so conclusive. At various times after Munich Hitler spoke of having to strike at France first before turning eastwards, on other occasions of finishing Poland first. He hoped by coercion and cajolery to keep Britain neutral. Logically the strategy of the lightning war suggested a

quick campaign against Poland, then France, before resuming the war in the East again. In any case this was the path Hitler eventually followed. Our uncertainty concerns only his timing and strategic priorities.

Hitler's well-tried step-by-step policy of aggrandisement entered a new phase in 1939. He recognised that further bloodless successes were unlikely; he welcomed the opportunity of war, preferably against a small, weaker neighbour. Britain and France fought in September 1939 not because Hitler had *then* forced war on *them*. They fought because there could no longer be any doubt about the pattern of Hitler's violent diplomacy nor about his ultimate goals. It would have been madness to allow him to pick off his victims one by one and to choose his time for overpowering them while reassuring those whose turn had not yet come. Belatedly, by September 1939, Hitler was no longer able to call the tune. For Chamberlain, Hitler's choice of how to settle his Polish demands was the ultimate test.

The intricate diplomacy of the powers from March to September 1939 can only be briefly summarised here. The British and French governments were still seeking a settlement with Hitler and were even prepared to make far-reaching concessions to him after March 1939. They had accepted his seizure of Memel on the Baltic only a week after his entry into Prague. Poland, moreover, had not been guaranteed unconditionally. Her frontiers were not regarded as inviolate. As in the case of Czechoslovakia, if Hitler made 'reasonable' demands the Western powers hoped that the Poles would be 'reasonable' too. What the two Western powers ruled out, however, was that Hitler should simply seize what he wanted by launching with impunity a war against Poland.

In October 1938 Poland was first approached by the Nazi Foreign Minister Ribbentrop with demands that she return Danzig to Germany, create an extra-territorial corridor to East Prussia and join with Italy and Japan in the anti-communist alignment known as the Anti-Comintern Pact. Then in January 1939 the Polish Foreign Minister Colonel Beck visited Hitler and was offered a junior partnership as Germany's ally, with promises of Czech territory and the Soviet Ukraine. During the earlier Czech crisis Hitler had already been helpful in permitting the Poles to acquire the Czech territory of Teschen. It seems that because of Poland's strong anti-communist past, and the 'racial' mixture of Balt and Slav in her population, Hitler was ready to see the 'best' Polish elements as a suitable ally. Fervent anti-Semitism and the Polish government's desire to force Poland's own Jewish population into emigration was another link between them. But the Poles proved stubborn. They overestimated the worth of their own army and with a population of more than 34 million regarded themselves as almost a great European power. The cession of territory was anathema to them; in Polish history cession of territory had been the prelude to partition.

Hitler had offered the Poles what amounted to an alliance in the East. Later during the war against the Soviet Union other Slav nations, the Slovaks and Croats, were to become allies. Does this mean that Hitler was flexible about his definition of 'subhumans' other than the Jews? Might Poland have been spared the carnage that followed? For 3 million Poles who were Jews the outcome would have been no different; for the rest of the Poles, of whom another 3 million were murdered, the great

majority would probably have survived the war as the Czechs did. But in the longer term Hitler was inflexible. The new greater German Reich after victory would have annexed large tracts of land in the East for 'living space'. These territories would have been 'racially cleansed' and resettled by Germans. Some Slav *Untermenschen* might have been retained as slave labour; Poles, Ukrainians and Russians capable of being Germanised would have been absorbed; of the millions driven out, few would have survived sickness and starvation. But the rejection by the Poles of Hitler's offers as late as 1938 sealed their immediate fate.

Beck's rejection and the Anglo-French guarantee determined Hitler to smash the Poles at the first opportunity. In May 1939 Germany and Italy ostentatiously signed the bombastically named Pact of Steel, which by its terms committed Italy to go to war whenever Hitler chose that Germany would fight, despite the Duce's explanations that Italy would not be ready for war for another three years. The conquest of Abyssinia and the more recent occupation of little Albania by Italian troops (in April 1939) were one thing, war with France and Britain quite a different prospect. The alliance nevertheless served the purpose of dashing any

*As Molotov signs the Nazi-Soviet Non-Aggression Pact on 23 August 1939, Ribbentrop and Stalin look on.*

hopes Chamberlain might have had left of detaching Italy from Germany after his own abortive attempt to achieve this on a visit to Rome the previous January. It was intended to pressurise Britain into neutrality. Far more important was the conclusion on 23 August of a Nazi–Soviet Pact, which Hitler hoped would convince Britain and France that it was useless to fight for Poland.

August 1939 turned out to be the last full month of peace. The crisis started when Poland insisted on her treaty rights in Danzig and Hitler chose to regard this as a provocation. However, Danzig was not the real issue; nor even was the future of the territory lying between East Prussia and the rest of Germany – the Polish corridor. Rather, it was that Hitler could not tolerate an independent Poland which blocked his road to *Lebensraum* in the East. The Poles were not impressed either by efforts at intimidating them by the Nazis on the one hand and pressure to be 'reasonable' exerted by Britain and France on the other. They had no intention of suffering the fate of Czechoslovakia. But the Chamberlain Cabinet in London and Daladier's government vainly hoped that the dispute was about no more than Danzig and the corridor and that war could be avoided if Poland gave way.

However, from Hitler's point of view, war with France and Britain would only be postponed, not avoided, that is postponed until he decided that the balance of power was most advantageously in Germany's favour. To the extent that one can fathom Hitler's mind, war with Poland was by now a certainty. He told his commanders-in-chief on 22 August that the destruction of Poland was necessary even if it meant conflict with Britain and France. He added that he did not believe it likely that Britain and France would go to war. What was desirable, politically and militarily, was not a settling of all accounts, but concentration on single tasks. Hitler had no intention of allowing the British or French any role as mediators.

According to Hitler's original plans, the attack on Poland was to begin on 26 August. On 25 August at 3 p.m. the order to attack was given and then, much to the annoyance of the Wehrmacht, counter-manded at 7 p.m. when the final troop movements were already under way. The attack was postponed by Hitler for a few days. How significant was the postponement? Was there a real chance of peace somehow missed by lack of communication or misunderstanding? Chamberlain was aware of the

parallel with July 1914. In a personal letter to Hitler on 22 August he made it clear that Britain would stand by her Polish commitments regardless of the German–Soviet Pact. Hitler received the letter on 23 August. The flurry of negotiations principally between London and Berlin during the last days of peace were undertaken by Britain to induce Germany and Poland to negotiate the differences over Danzig and the corridor. In that respect there was a parallel between the Czech crisis of 1938 and the Polish crisis. Britain and France would have acquiesced in any territorial gains Germany succeeded in obtaining from Poland without use of force. Mere German blackmail had become almost an acceptable fact of life as far as diplomacy was concerned. But if Germany attacked Poland to gain her ends by force then there was no doubt that Britain would support Poland by declaring war on Germany. The British Cabinet knew no other policy was possible and that the country would not accept another Munich, especially with the Poles, unlike the Czechs, fighting for their country. In France, Daladier firmly controlled his government and Bonnet, the Foreign Minister, counted for little now; there was no doubt here too that an actual German invasion of Poland meant war.

That is not to say that Britain and France wanted to fight Germany. Quite the contrary; the two governments were ready to talk and negotiate as long as Hitler did not actually attack. There was no certainty in their minds that he would actually go to war – so talk they did from 25 August until the outbreak of war with Poland, and even for two days beyond that. Only Hitler was sure that he was going to attack Poland and that his military timetable allowed only a few days' leeway. He used these days not to make any genuine attempt to draw back from the war with Poland, but to try to persuade Britain and France to abandon her. He wanted to postpone war with them until after Poland had been defeated and so avoid, if he could, a war on two fronts. Hitler concentrated on Britain. The 25 August was the most dramatic day of the crisis in Berlin. At 1.30 p.m. Hitler talked to the British Ambassador, Nevile Henderson, and he put on a very good act; he declared that he wanted to live on good terms with Britain, that he would personally guarantee her world empire, that Germany's colonial demands were limited and that his offer of a general settle-ment would follow the solution of the Polish–German disputes, which in any case he was determined to settle. This, he emphasised, was his last offer. He overdid it a little, stretching credulity too far by confiding to Henderson that once the Polish question was out of the way he would conclude his life as an artist and not as a war-maker.

About half an hour after Henderson had left the Chancellery in Berlin to fly with this offer to London, Hitler ordered the attack on Poland to commence the following day. The war machine was set in motion at 3 p.m. At 5.30 p.m. Hitler received the French Ambassador to tell him Germany wanted to live at peace with France and that the issue of peace and war was up to the French. But Hitler was unsettled that afternoon by the news of the imminent conclusion of the Anglo-Polish alliance, and by Mussolini's message revealing his unwillingness to join Germany in war. In London, meanwhile, the news that the Soviet Union and Germany had signed a treaty, and that the Anglo-French alliance negotiations with Russia had thus ended in failure, meant that nothing now stood in the way of the formal conclusion of the Anglo-Polish alliance, which was signed on 25 August. It promised Poland that Britain would go to war with Germany if Germany attacked Poland. In Berlin it was dawning on Hitler that Britain might not simply desert Poland the very moment Germany attacked her. Then in the late afternoon of 25 August Mussolini informed Hitler that Italy did not have the resources to go to war.

Not surprisingly Hitler now thought it prudent to give his 'offer' to Britain a chance of being accepted and not to jeopardise his overture by simultaneously attacking Poland. Hitler did not rely on Henderson alone. Göring had initiated the use of an unofficial emissary, Birger Dahlerus, a Swedish businessman, who shuttled between London and Berlin from 25 to 30 August. After his first return from London he saw both Göring and Hitler; unwittingly he became a tool of Hitler's diplomacy to detach Britain from Poland. If that succeeded, then France also could be counted on to remain out of the war. The British reply on 28 August to Hitler's 'last' offer was to welcome the opportunity of an Anglo-German settlement, but not at Poland's expense. Instead, the British Cabinet urged direct Polish–German negotiations, offered to act as mediators and informed Hitler that the Poles were willing to enter such negotiations. Germany was warned against the use of force. Henderson saw Hitler on the 28th and again on the evening of

29 August when Hitler angrily conceded direct negotiations – solely, so he claimed, to prove his desire for lasting friendship with Britain. Such proof, he hoped, would dissuade the British from supporting an unreasonable Poland. As Goebbels recorded in his diary, Hitler's aim was 'to decouple Warsaw from London and still find an excuse to attack'.

Hitler demanded that a special envoy must reach Berlin the very day following, on 30 August. Henderson was upset by the peremptory German reply. He gave as good as he got, shouting back at Hitler and warning him that Britain was just as determined as Germany and would fight. The British Cabinet refused to 'mediate' what amounted to an ultimatum. The German demands were unknown yet Hitler was insisting that the Poles should come immediately to Berlin to settle all that Germany required within a time limit of only a few hours. The time limit was ignored in London and discussions about starting direct negotiations were still proceeding on 31 August. Hitler's time limit for a Polish plenipotentiary to present himself in Berlin expired at midnight on 30 August. The Poles were not prepared to rush cap in hand to Hitler.

Polish policy has been characterised as crazy and suicidal. How could the Poles hope to maintain their independence sandwiched, as they were, between Germany and the Soviet Union? But such an argument denies small nations a policy of independence, which in practice they have retained. How can they be expected to give in without at least attempting to resist? Nevertheless it is perfectly true that Poland's military situation in September 1939 was hopeless. The Poles overrated their capacity to resist in the short term. So did the French Commander-in-Chief, General Gamelin, who expected the Poles to be able to hold out until the following spring. The Poles also counted on effective help from France and Britain. There was logic and reason in Poland's refusal to contemplate significant concessions to Germany in 1939. The recent example of Czechoslovakia showed only too clearly that independence could not be bought for long by making concessions to Hitler. Once started on that road, the Poles believed with good reason, the end at best would be that they might be permitted to remain Germany's satellite. So they reasoned that if the Germans intended the destruction of Polish independence, it would be better to fight them at the outset with Britain and France as allies than to accept piecemeal subordination to Germany and to risk the loss of the French and British alliance. Furthermore, there was just the possibility that Hitler's objectives were limited to Danzig and access through the Polish corridor. For such aims alone, Hitler, so they thought, might not risk a great European war. But if his aims were not limited, then Poland's only choice was to submit or fight. Accordingly the Polish government came to the conclusion that Poland's national interests were best served by resisting Hitler's territorial demands, by holding tight and so testing his real intentions. Hitler's determination, the Poles vainly hoped, might crack if his policy was based on bluff.

Did this Polish attitude then dash hopes of a peaceful settlement? That would have been so only to the extent that, if the Polish government had submitted to *whatever* Hitler demanded in August 1939, then France and Britain would have had no cause for war in September 1939. But while the British Cabinet and the French government were anxious for the Poles to explore all possibilities of a peaceful settlement with Germany by opening direct negotiations with Hitler, they did not expect the Poles simply to submit to time limits and the threat of force. Hitler, too, would have to demonstrate Germany's desire for peace by putting forward reasonable terms for a settlement, and by negotiating in a reasonable way without ultimatums.

At first sight he appeared to be putting forward what in London and Paris might be considered 'reasonable' terms. The German demands were embodied in sixteen points; they struck the British Ambassador in Berlin as moderate, when he *eventually* heard what they were! They included the immediate takeover by Germany of Danzig and a plebiscite later in the corridor to decide whether it was to remain Polish or become German, with the loser being granted extra-territorial rights across the strip of territory. But the method of negotiation belied the apparent moderation of the sixteen points. They were drawn up in strict secrecy and not communicated until *after* the time set for the appearance in Berlin of a Polish plenipotentiary with full powers to negotiate. In fact they first reached the ears of the British Ambassador just after midnight – in the early hours of 31 August. Henderson had called on the German Foreign Minister, Ribbentrop, who after a stormy discussion pulled a piece of paper out of his pocket and then read the sixteen demands aloud in German, according to Henderson, at 'top speed'. Ribbentrop added that since no Pole had arrived they were superseded anyway. He refused the Ambassador's request for a copy. Henderson was astonished at this breach of diplomatic practice and had to rely on his memory for the gist of the proposals.

Henderson in Berlin, and Halifax in London, nevertheless tried to persuade the Poles to act quickly to open discussions in Berlin. Not until noon on 31 August did Dahlerus, the innocent intermediary, who was being used by Göring and Hitler in an attempt to keep Britain out of the war, communicate the full terms to the British and Polish ambassadors in Berlin. All the efforts of the professional and amateur diplomats were in vain. The sixteen points and Hitler's diplomatic manoeuvres in August were designed to provide an alibi to put the Poles in the wrong and so justify war to the German people. Furthermore, Hitler almost to the last seemed to have had some hopes that, if the Poles could be shown to be unreasonable, then France and Britain would refuse to live up to their alliance commitments. He intended to drive a wedge between Poland and her Western allies. But in the last resort he was prepared to risk war with France and Britain rather than abandon the war he was preparing to launch against Poland. The first order to the Wehrmacht to attack Poland at 4.35 a.m. on 1 September reached the Army High Command at 6.30 a.m. on 31 August, that is several hours *before* the full text of the 'moderate' proposals was communicated to the British and Polish ambassadors in Berlin. It was finally confirmed by Hitler at 4 p.m., little more than three hours after the full text of the sixteen points was first revealed.

Would Hitler have accepted a settlement based on these demands if the Poles had rushed cap in hand to Berlin and agreed to everything? This would have avoided a war with Britain and France, which at this stage Hitler did not want. On the other hand Hitler was driven by his conviction that the Wehrmacht, navy and Luftwaffe needed a *Feuertaufe*, a baptism of fire, to maintain their fighting fibre. The German people too had to be taught to accept a real war, not be softened into believing that every victory would be bloodless. Hitler did not hesitate for long. If war with Poland risked a great European war, that risk had to be taken. As Henderson later wrote in his memoirs, the conclusion that Hitler did not want to negotiate at all on the basis of these proposals is inescapable.

The invasion of Poland began at 4.45 a.m. on 1

September. Now it is true that in both Paris and London, while Poland fought back, the ministers were still clutching at hopes of restoring peace even less substantial than straws. Mussolini offered again, as at the time of Munich, his mediation and held out hopes that another conference of the powers might be called. But the British Cabinet made it a firm precondition that Germany should first withdraw her troops from Poland. As Hitler would never have accepted this, Mussolini told the British and French that there was no point in his attempting further mediation. Meanwhile, between Paris and London, there was an extraordinary lack of co-ordination on the very eve of the war. On 1 September, Germany was warned about the consequences of war on Poland only by Britain. On 2 September, Chamberlain faced a hostile and suspicious House of Commons. Was another Munich in the making? But there was no chance that Britain and France this time could avoid war. On 3 September, separate British and French ultimatums led to the declaration of war on Germany, the French actually going to war a few hours after the British, though they did not start attacking Germany for a while longer, and then only ineffectually.

There could be no other outcome but a European war once Hitler had decided to attack Poland. Not a single country in Europe wished to attack Germany, but in September 1939 the British and French governments were forced to the conclusion that they must fight in their own defence and not allow Hitler to pick off one European state after another. There can be little doubt that this is precisely what Hitler would have done had he been allowed his war against the Poles. Hitler's aggression against Poland, despite the clear warnings he received of its consequences on the one hand and the perception of the British and French governments of his real intentions after the unprecedented concessions to his demands in the previous year on the other, thus led to the outbreak of the second great European war within twenty-five years of the first.

# PART V

---

*The Second World War*

# CHAPTER 26

# Germany's Wars of Conquest in Europe, 1939–1941

During the first two years of war, Germany won a series of victories on the continent of Europe that staggered the world and made the Wehrmacht appear invincible. Apprehensive at the outset, the German people were intoxicated by military success; all that Hitler had done appeared justified by this unanticipated and brilliant outcome. The nightmare that the experiences of the First World War would be repeated seemed for the Germans no more than a bad dream in 1940. Europe learned the reality of the *Blitzkrieg*. The Wehrmacht used the tactics of speedy penetration by tanks, followed by mechanised infantry and then more slowly by infantry on foot, supported closely by the Luftwaffe; towns were subjected to indiscriminate air raids, and the terrorised populations jammed the roads to escape the advancing Germans. The *Blitzkrieg* required careful planning, a well-co-ordinated command structure and highly disciplined, well-equipped troops. The armed forces, from the most senior officers to the newest conscript, served Hitler's cause, which they identified with Germany's, with efficiency and the utmost devotion. The home front supplied the means. It was their war, too, though Hitler's lightning wars did not require the entire mobilisation of the home front as in Britain. Women were not conscripted and luxury items continued to be produced to keep the Germans happy. Military victory alone made possible the horrors that Hitler's regime inflicted on the millions of people who, as a result, fell into Germany's grasp.

In September 1939 Poland was conquered; in April 1940, Denmark and Norway; during May the Netherlands and Belgium; and then in June 1940 the greatest victory of all, France was defeated. With France prostrate, Britain withdrew from the continent of Europe. Did not the 'good' which Hitler had achieved outweigh the 'bad'? – so many Germans now reasoned. Hitler even publicly offered peace to Britain. In July 1940 the war, so it seemed, was virtually over, an astonishingly short war rather than the expected long and bloody struggle, leaving Germany victorious. Why were these German dreams shattered so soon?

Hitler was not satisfied with what he had achieved so far. He had not won sufficient *Lebensraum* in the East or the undisputed hegemony of Europe. Any 'peace' for him now would have been tactical and short-lived. Everything he said to his associates, either secretly at the time or in conversations and writings before, points to the fact that he regarded the victory in the West as only a prelude to greater conquests. Plans for a great fleet had been carried forward not with a view to winning the continental European war but with an eye to the wars after that, including the world war with the British Empire and the United States. The struggle would continue as long as Hitler lived and until Europe was racially transformed and world power was won; but naturally Hitler preferred to proceed according to his own timetable. The Germans were not allowed for long to enjoy the fruits of victory, the victory parades accompanied by champagne and other luxuries

*Warsaw capitulates to the Germans on 27 September 1939. Polite formalities are on display here, but millions of Poles were to die at German hands during the occupation.*

looted from France. After the war was finally over in 1945, Hitler's megalomania was rightly seen as Germany's undoing. Her defeat then was so complete that it is easy to overlook the fact that four years earlier it had been a much more close-run thing.

Germany's defeat of Poland was rapid. Surrounded Warsaw resisted until 27 September 1939. Badly led, the Poles bravely fought the Wehrmacht, which enjoyed overwhelming strength. In the earliest days of the war, the Luftwaffe destroyed the Polish air force, mostly on the ground. Any chance the Poles had of holding out a little longer was lost when the Russians on 17 September invaded from the east in accordance with their secret agreement with Germany of the previous August (page 248). Still it was no walkover. The Poles inflicted heavy casualties and the Wehrmacht was in no fit state to switch immediately to the west and to attack France in November 1939 as Hitler desired.

Hitler's public 'peace' proposals to Britain and France early in October 1939, after the victorious Polish campaign, were almost certainly meant for German public opinion. He would not, of course, have rejected the idea that Britain should accept and withdraw from involvement on the continent. Then France could not have continued the war on her own and would have been in his power even without a battle. Did Britain contemplate any sort of peace? Had Chamberlain altogether abandoned his previous policies? Much recent manuscript material, including Chamberlain's private papers, add to our knowledge of the so-called 'phoney war' period in the West. There remain gaps in our knowledge. But, whatever differences of opinion may have existed, peace terms involving the eventual abandonment of France were unthinkable in 1939.

Militarily, on land and in the air, the war scarcely got started in terms of real fighting on the western front. The French were not ready to take *quick* offensive action against the weak screen of German troops facing them behind the incomplete fortifications of the Siegfried line. By the time the army was fully mobilised and in a state of readiness for offensive action – had the Commander-in-Chief,

Maurice Gamelin, desired it – the Polish campaign was drawing to its close and the German High Command was rushing reinforcements westwards from Poland. The military inaction on land corresponded to the doctrine, Poland notwithstanding, that the army which attacked would be forced to suffer huge casualties. All the advantage was believed to lie with the defence behind such powerfully constructed fortifications as the Maginot line. In preparing the defence of France one section of the front – the Franco-Belgian frontier to the Channel – had been left 'open', designed to act as a limited region for offensive manoeuvre. But when the Belgians returned to a position of complete neutrality in 1936 this strategy was more difficult to execute. The Anglo-French campaign plan of 1939–40 was nevertheless designed to meet the expected German advance through Belgium, by a forward movement of their own into Belgium the moment the Germans attacked that country; no earlier move was possible as the Belgians fearfully clung to absolute neutrality.

These military assumptions about how best to conduct the war were paralleled by political assumptions held by Chamberlain about the war and its likely outcome. It would be ended, if possible, without great sacrifice of life by imposing a strict blockade on Germany. The British and French governments even considered blowing up the sources of Germany's oil supplies in Romania and the Soviet Caucasus. With neutral Scandinavia, the Balkan states and the Soviet Union delivering oil and other essential raw materials, the British blockade by sea was far less effective than during the First World War. It did not seriously impede Hitler's intended lightning strikes against the West. For fear of massive reprisals, the French and British dropped nothing more lethal than pamphlets on the industrial Ruhr. But then Chamberlain did not believe that the war would be won by military force. In December 1939 he wrote to the Archbishop of Canterbury, 'I feel before another Christmas comes the war will be over, and then the troubles will really begin!' What was in his mind when he wrote that? Was it that he expected reasonable negotiations and a peace treaty? He certainly thought that the war would end in a stalemate and that, once the Germans were convinced that they could not win, they would negotiate for peace. The war would be won on the home front. Chamberlain was certainly anxious whether the British people would stand for

a long stalemated kind of war. He feared there was in Britain a 'peace at any price' party whose influence might become powerful. He thought it probable nevertheless that the German home front would crack first, forcing Hitler into the wrong policy of attack!

Whether all aspects of 'appeasement' completely ended after the outbreak of war in September 1939 poses questions which can as yet be answered only tentatively. The future situations which Chamberlain envisaged were hypothetical and no one can say for certain how he, his Cabinet colleagues, Parliament or the country would have reacted to events which never happened. From existing evidence we can reasonably conclude that Chamberlain would never have consented to peace on Hitler's terms; also that Chamberlain thought Britain and France would not be able to impose a Carthaginian peace on Germany. Indeed he would have been likely to insist on Hitler's removal from any real exercise of power in Germany. He appears to have thought that some reshuffle of power setting Hitler aside might offer a solution. 'Until he disappears and his system collapses there can be no peace,' he wrote a week after the outbreak of the war. Chamberlain's assumptions were mistaken. Events turned out very differently, when what was to him unthinkable occurred and the French armies collapsed. Only then did the pre-war illusions on which policies had been based for so long finally collapse.

While at sea Britain had the better of the war, serious fighting on land began not on the frontiers of France but in Norway. Winston Churchill had rejoined the Cabinet as First Lord of the Admiralty at the beginning of the war and was anxious that some visible blow be struck at Germany's war effort. The attack by the Soviet Union on Finland on 30 November 1939 seemed to provide a good pretext and opportunity. British experts calculated that Swedish iron ore was vital to the German war machine. During the winter months it was shipped through the Norwegian port of Narvik. For weeks under Chamberlain's chairmanship the cabinet discussed the possibility of an operation which would disrupt its flow. The favourite idea was to help the Finns against the Russians by sending volunteers who would, on the way so to speak, control the railway line from northern Sweden to the coast. This scheme made use of the public indignation in the West about Russia's attack to

*Well-equipped Finnish troops successfully resist Russian attacks during the winter of 1939.*

damage both Germany and the Soviet Union, which was seen as Germany's partner in the European war of aggression. The Finns successfully resisted the ill-prepared Soviet troops for weeks, inflicting heavy casualties on them in what became known as the Winter War.

The French too were keen to fight, but not in France. They agreed in February 1940 to a joint Anglo-French expedition of 'volunteers' to aid the Finns and occupy the strategic northern railway. British scruples about infringing neutral rights, and Norway's terrified adherence to neutrality – the Norwegians did not wish to give Germany an excuse for invasion – led to delays, until finally the British decided to mine the waters off Narvik through which the ore ships sailed (though only until spring had opened the other route by way of the Baltic, blocked by ice in the winter). Before an expedition could be sent to the Finns, however, they were defeated, making peace on 12 March 1940. French politicians were so outraged at the inability of the government to help that Daladier's ministry fell; the more militant Paul Reynaud became prime minister. Chamberlain's own fall was delayed by another month and historically was far more important.

The public was tiring of the phoney war and the easy successes of the dictators, Hitler and Stalin. Poland and now Finland had fallen. Fortunately the British Cabinet (unlike the French) never contemplated any steps that might lead to outright war with the Soviet Union as well, even though, or perhaps because, the Soviet Union represented a far greater threat to Britain's imperial interests than to France. Chamberlain was singularly unlucky in some of his public utterances. After Munich he had rashly repeated the phrase about 'peace in our time'. Early in April 1940 he coined one phrase too many when he told the nation that Hitler 'has missed the bus'. It was Britain that missed the bus. After relatively small forces had secretly begun the operation at sea on 3 April 1940, the main force following during the night of 7 and 8 April, the Germans in a daring move occupied all Norway's major ports, including the capital, Oslo, on 9 April. The Norwegians resisted and inflicted casualties, especially on the German warships making for Oslo's harbour. But Germany's attack was almost entirely successful, even though it was not a complete surprise to Britain and France. The British navy missed the German. Executing the policy decided on by the Cabinet, the Royal Navy on 8 April was proceeding to lay mines in Norwegian territorial waters accompanied by a small force of troops which was ready to land in Norway should the Germans retaliate by invading. In fact they had already anticipated the British move. The instructions to the British force were unclear and reveal Britain's moral dilemma about landing in Norway if the Norwegians chose to resist. In many ways the Norway fiasco was an 'honourable' defeat.

The question arose whether Britain and France could defeat Hitler with such a sense of 'honour'. Only in the extreme north, in Narvik, were Anglo-French forces able to inflict a temporary setback to the small German forces far from their base. The British navy sank the German destroyers in the port and a month later Narvik was reoccupied. After Dunkirk, these forces had to be withdrawn and the whole of Norway fell under German occupation. Nevertheless German naval losses had been so severe that in July 1940 there was no surface fleet in active service; only a few lighter warships were undamaged.

The most important political consequence of so evidently acting too late once again in Norway was the fall of the Chamberlain Cabinet, and the outcome – surprising at the time of the crisis – was that Winston Churchill became prime minister on 10 May 1940 of a national government joined by Labour and the Liberals. With the passage of time the adulation of Churchill as war leader has rightly given place to a more critical and detailed assessment of his role in policy making at home, in foreign relations and in military strategy, which together make up what is called the conduct of the war. Churchill's shortcomings do now stand revealed. But this does not totally alter the older picture of him. By filling in the shadows, showing his mistakes as well as his successes, Churchill becomes more real and believable. The shadows only bring into sharper relief the predominance of that galvanising spirit, the enormous energy and undaunted faith in final victory which became an asset of inestimable value to Britain and to the war effort of the whole alliance. And, despite wartime restrictions, Churchill still led a democracy rooted in Parliament, and was dependent upon the support of the people. The nation thrilled to the rhetoric of his radio speeches and sensed that Britain now had a war leader who was at last a match for Hitler. Churchill, more than any single man, sustained national morale and hope

*Winston Churchill, 1941.*

in the future.

It is therefore all the more remarkable that the secrets now emerging from private papers and official records reveal how insecure Churchill's position really was during the first four months of his administration. Chamberlain was no broken reed. His government had actually won what amounted to a vote of confidence, though many Conservatives had abstained or voted with the Opposition. It was Chamberlain who was deeply injured by so many of his former supporters turning against him. It was he who decided that for the 'duration' what was required was a truly national government. But he would remain leader of the Conservative Party and quite possibly thought that he might return to power when sanity returned and that the time might come when his unrivalled experience would be used to bring back peace. As yet he had no inkling of the cancer that, within a few weeks, turned him into an invalid and caused his death early in November 1940. Churchill was prime minister, but Chamberlain and Halifax remained the most powerful Conservatives in the Cabinet. When Churchill first presented himself to the House of Commons, it was Chamberlain whom the Conservatives loudly cheered. Chamberlain was soon to earn those cheers for far more than his readiness to accept second place under Churchill.

\*

Norway was a serious defeat for the Allied war effort. The Norwegian fjords could now serve as ideal bases for the German submarines threatening to sever the lifeline of war supplies crossing the Atlantic from the United States. The most shattering blow of all was the defeat of France, on whose armies the containment of Germany overwhelmingly rested. It seemed unthinkable that a great power like France would succumb as quickly and as totally to the onslaught of the *Blitzkrieg* as smaller nations like Poland and Norway had done. Yet that is what occurred.

The military débâcle of the Allied campaign in France can only be briefly summarised. The total strength of the German army on the one hand and the French, British, Belgian and Dutch forces on the other were roughly comparable, as were the numbers of tanks on each side. Arguably the French had the edge in the quality of their tanks and artillery. Germany achieved superiority in the air but this in itself was not decisive and, contrary to popular belief, the Maginot line, to which so much blame came to be attached, was of advantage to the Allies: it deterred the Germans from attacking more than half the frontier and it could be held by a relatively small force. This meant that the Allies did not have to concentrate on the Franco-German border but could predict that the main battles would occur in the regions not covered by the Maginot line. They could not, or rather should not, have been taken by surprise. The Allies then had apparently good reason for quiet confidence before the Germans opened the offensive.

The Allies realised that the obvious route of invasion lay through the north, the Netherlands and Belgium, and made all their plans accordingly. The Germans, when they attacked, should not be allowed to turn industrial northern France immediately into a battle zone as they had done in the First World War. The French and British forces would, and did, have time to meet the German thrust in Belgium before it reached France. The Maginot line ran alongside the whole frontier with Germany, alongside that of Luxembourg and alongside the southern tip of the Belgian frontier. Just beyond was the heavily wooded Ardennes region, believed by the Allies to be impassable to any major German offensive with tanks, and this section of the front was lightly held. Beyond the Maginot line to the sea, one careful calculation – others did not differ appreciably – indicated that forty French divisions

and nine British were facing two German armies totalling seventy-four divisions. But alongside the Allies another twenty-two Belgian divisions were expected to fight, even discounting ten Dutch divisions which were quickly overwhelmed. The purely Anglo-French/German disparity would have disappeared if thirty-five French and one British division had not been allotted to the Maginot line and upper Rhine. The total German and combined French and British forces were roughly comparable. Germany's success was based not on superiority of numbers or equipment but on taking and choosing the offensives and in so distributing the German divisions that (as in chess) they would appear in overwhelming strength at the weak point of the Allied front. The massed, co-ordinated use of armour would ensure that the initial breakthrough could be exploited with great speed.

As has been noted, the Allies anticipated no major thrust through the Ardennes and the Germans achieved complete surprise there. The second unexpected development was the direction of the thrust. Even now the French High Command thought in terms of 1914. They thought the Germans would continue straight from Sedan in a south-westerly direction for Paris. Instead, in a great arc the massed Panzers co-ordinated with aircraft followed by infantry, turned west towards the Channel coast at Abbeville, and north-west to Boulogne, Calais and in the direction of Dunkirk. The BEF (the British Expeditionary Force) and northern French armies were now caught in a nutcracker, with one German army pressing them through Belgium and the other swinging behind their rear. It was like a mirror image of the Schlieffen Plan and had the advantage that the wheel to the coast was a finite and limited distance, whereas Schlieffen's arc had been huge, and of virtually indefinite length. Had the Wehrmacht attacked in November 1939, the plan would then have corresponded to Anglo-French expectations of an offensive predominantly through Belgium, the old Schlieffen formula.

In short, German victory was due to the brilliance of the amended war-plan carried out in May 1940, its successful execution by the German High Command and the fighting qualities of the well-trained troops, particularly the Panzer divisions. Obversely, Allied failure was primarily a failure of strategy. French armies were thrown into total confusion, their generals lost control over communications and over the movements of whole armies. No soldier can successfully fight in such a situation, except in local actions. Later, the generals and politicians were quick to blame all sorts of factors – the communists, sabotage, poor equipment, low morale – as having greatly contributed to defeat. The blame must lie overwhelmingly with Gamelin and the Allied generals themselves.

The devastating timetable of defeat can be tersely set out. On 10 May 1940 the Germans launched the western offensive, simultaneously attacking the Netherlands, Belgium and Luxembourg. The terror-bombing and destruction of Rotterdam added a new term to the war vocabulary. The French and British troops moved forward according to a plan which, as it turned out, placed them more securely in the noose. On 13 May the Germans broke through on the Meuse. The French Prime Minister Reynaud telephoned Churchill the following day telling him that the situation was grave, and on the 15th that the battle was lost, the way to Paris open.

The first rift now appeared between the British and French conduct of the war. The French wanted the outcome of the whole war to depend on the battle for France. Churchill already foresaw that if indeed the battle for France was lost the war would go on. There would then be the battle for Britain before Hitler could win. So 15 May 1940 is an important date. Reynaud appealed to Britain to throw the whole of her air force into the battle as the only chance left to stop the Germans. Churchill and the Cabinet were ready to send further squadrons of fighters to France. But twenty-five squadrons would be retained as indispensable for the defence of Britain, as the Commander-in-Chief of Fighter Command, Air Marshal Sir Hugh Dowding, insisted that this represented the minimum necessary protection. On 15 May, to Reynaud's desperate plea, Churchill responded: 'we would do everything we could, but we could not denude England of her essential defences'.

On 16 May Churchill crossed the Channel to see the situation for himself and to infuse some of his fighting spirit into Reynaud's government. As the full disaster became evident, there was near panic in Paris in the ministries and government. Gamelin was dismissed and replaced by General Weygand on 19 May. But Hitler slowed the advance to the Channel. He did not wish to risk his tanks in unsuitable terrain; to Göring and his *Luftwaffe* was to be

left a share in annihilating the trapped British. The tanks were temporarily halted. General de Gaulle, of later fame, managed a small-scale counterattack on 17 May but it could not affect the outcome of the battle. In the north the BEF and French divisions were retreating in good order – much too slowly. On 20 May Reynaud had brought Marshal Pétain into his new government. Defeat was in the air. On 24 May the German Panzers reached the coast at Abbeville on the mouth of the Somme. The Allied northern armies were now cut off.

The story of the French capitulation is well known. Increasingly the French began to blame the British for not throwing their last reserves into the battle. They could not conceive how Britain would continue the war without France. Churchill was back in Paris on 23 May to discover how the northern Allied armies including the BEF might be saved. It was trapped, he reported back to the War Cabinet in London the next day. On 25 May, General Lord Gort, the commander of the BEF, in spite of instructions on the 19th from Churchill and the Chiefs of Staff to link with the French, independently began the manoeuvre, subsequently approved, that eventually made it possible to save the British divisions, and many French troops too, from the beaches of Dunkirk. Weygand's planned counter-offensive against the German flanks never had a chance; there were no French forces left who could seriously threaten the Germans. Meanwhile in Paris on the night of 25 May Pétain and other members of the government were already searching for a way to conclude a separate peace with Germany. Prime Minister Reynaud was despatched to London to sound out British reactions to peace initiatives. That same day contingency arrangements to evacuate the BEF were acted on.

The last week of May 1940 was one of the most critical and dramatic periods of the Second World War. The full story of British Cabinet deliberations on possible peace negotiations with Hitlerite Germany, some of which were so secret that their record was kept in a separate and special file, are extraordinarily interesting in the light of later history.[1] Churchill's 'finest hour' was to come: Britain withstood the German Blitz, later that summer and autumn. Government and people were

---

[1] The file of the relevant Cabinet Records is kept at the Public Record Office, London, 65/13.

determined to repel invasion from their shores. In Churchill's speeches the spirit of resolution and the will to fight were accurately encapsulated. Yet the 'finest hour' might never have struck.

The picture of Churchill as the indomitable war leader towering over colleagues is so deeply etched in the history of the Second World War that it comes as a surprise that his position as prime minister during the first weeks of office was far weaker than that enjoyed by any of his predecessors since the fall of Lloyd George. Chamberlain probably at first saw Churchill as the best war leader for the duration of the conflict and he was also the one Conservative whom Labour and Liberals could agree to serve under. Churchill presided over a small War Cabinet of five. Neville Chamberlain and Halifax, the two most powerful Conservatives, were now joined by two Labour Party ministers, Clement Attlee and Arthur Greenwood. But Churchill was regarded with much suspicion by many Conservatives, who continued to look to Chamberlain for guidance. Within the War Cabinet, Chamberlain's role was still decisive. If he sided with Halifax against Churchill, given the continued party loyalty Chamberlain still enjoyed and the overwhelming strength of the Conservatives in the House of Commons, Churchill would not be able to make his views prevail even with the support of Labour and its two representatives in the War Cabinet. The government might then break up – as the French did – with disastrous results at a moment of crisis. This political reality has to be borne in mind when assessing what Churchill, Chamberlain, Halifax, Attlee and Greenwood said during the long hours of Cabinet discussion in May 1940. What was at stake was more than the fate of a government. Whether Britain would remain in the war, the future of Western Europe and the course of world history would be affected by the outcome.

Halifax, the Foreign Secretary, made a determined bid to persuade the War Cabinet to sanction peace feelers. The Cabinet had authorised him on 24 May to try to discover what terms might keep Mussolini out of the war. But Halifax went beyond his brief when he spoke to the Italian Ambassador on 25 May.[1] He reported back to the Cabinet on the morning of Sunday, 26 May, that the Italian Ambassador had sounded him out on whether the

British government would agree to a conference; according to the Ambassador, Mussolini's principal wish was to secure peace in Europe, and he wanted Italian and British issues to be looked at as 'part of a general European settlement'. Halifax agreed emphatically and replied that peace and security in Europe were equally Britain's main object and that 'we should naturally be prepared to consider any proposal which might lead to this provided our liberty and independence were assured'.[2] In this way efforts to keep Italy out of the war – efforts which the Cabinet had already sanctioned involved seeking Roosevelt's good offices – were being widened to draw in Germany and France in an attempt to reach a general peace. Halifax now wanted to secure the authorisation of the Cabinet to seek the Duce's mediation for this purpose. Churchill opposed Halifax; the Prime Minister's instincts were sound. Even if 'decent' terms were offered in May 1940 they would have been no safeguard against fresh demands later, once Britain was at Hitler's mercy. Churchill also knew that if he consented to the commencement of any negotiations it might then prove impossible to fight on. He was therefore determined by any and all means to block Halifax's manoeuvres.

After the Cabinet meeting on Sunday morning of 26 May Churchill lunched with the French Prime Minister Paul Reynaud, who had flown over from France. Churchill urged him to keep France in the war. Reynaud, according to Churchill, 'dwelt not obscurely upon the possible French withdrawal from the war'. Reynaud's immediate request was that negotiations should be started to keep Italy out of the war by bribing Mussolini with offers including the neutralisation of Gibraltar and Suez as well as the demilitarisation of Malta. But Churchill wanted no approach to Italy. He knew how easily this could slide into peace negotiations with Germany. He told Reynaud that Britain would not give up on any account but would rather go down fighting than be enslaved to Germany.

After further discussions with the French Prime Minister, the British Cabinet reassembled in the afternoon. Halifax urged that the mediation of Mussolini be sought; Hitler, he observed, might not present such unreasonable terms. Churchill repeatedly opposed such a move. In the diary Cham-

---

1    Record of conversation Halifax and Bastiani, 25 May 1940, Cabinet 65/13, PRO.

2    Record of conversation Halifax and Bastiani, 25 May 1940, Cabinet 65/13, PRO.

berlain kept of these vital hours he records Churchill as saying, 'It was incredible that Hitler would consent to any terms that we could accept though if we could get out of this jam by giving up Malta and some African colonies he would jump at it. But the only safe way was to convince Hitler that he could not beat us. We might do better without the French than with them if they tied us to a conference into which we should enter with our case lost beforehand.' What are we to make of Churchill's remark that 'he would jump' at the chance of getting out of the war? If this one remark is considered alone it might appear that not much separated Churchill from Halifax. But Churchill's actions throughout these critical days, and all the arguments he marshalled, make it absurd to suppose that he had any other intention but that of defeating Halifax and of winning over the remaining Cabinet ministers in order to fight on. An approach to Mussolini, Churchill warned, would not only be futile but would involve Britain in 'deadly danger'; 'let us therefore avoid being dragged down the slippery slope with France'.

Nevertheless in making an effort to appear reasonable, by apparent concessions to Halifax's arguments, Churchill was manoeuvred into a dangerous corner at the Cabinet meeting on the following day, 27 May. He reiterated his view that no attempt should be made to start any negotiations by way of Mussolini. Halifax, who was a formidable opponent, now accused Churchill of inconsistency, saying that when on the previous day he had asked him whether he were satisfied that if matters vital to Britain's independence were unaffected he would be prepared to discuss terms, Churchill had then replied that 'he would be thankful to get out of our present difficulties on such terms, provided we retained the essentials and the elements of our vital strength, even at the cost of some cession of territory'. Yet now, Halifax pointed out, Churchill spoke only of fighting to a finish. Churchill was flustered; he attempted to reconcile what could not be reconciled by saying, 'If Herr Hitler were prepared to make peace on the terms of the restoration of the German colonies and the overlordship of Central Europe, that was one thing. But it was quite unlikely that he would make any such offer.' Halifax immediately followed up his advantage, pressing Churchill by asking him whether he would be willing to discuss Hitler's terms. Churchill rather feebly responded that 'He would not join France

in asking for terms; but if he were told what the terms offered were, he would be prepared to consider them.' The Cabinet ended. Churchill had gained just one important point: Britain would not initiate direct negotiations with Hitler.[‡]

The Cabinet met again on 28 May. Halifax once more, on the pretext of starting negotiations to keep Italy out of the war, was trying to find a way of discussing peace with Hitler's Germany. The War Cabinet well understood this. The real difference between Halifax and Churchill was simple. Halifax believed the war already lost; to fight on would entail useless sacrifice. What he actually said was that Britain might get better terms before France left the war and before Britain's aircraft factories were bombed by the Luftwaffe. The Italian Embassy now wanted to know, Halifax said, whether 'we should like mediation by Italy'. Churchill retorted that Britain could not negotiate from weakness; 'the position would be entirely different when Germany had made an unsuccessful attempt to invade the country', he added, and he argued that even if defeated later Britain would get no worse terms than now. A nation that went down fighting would rise again whereas those that tamely surrendered were finished. Any negotiations, furthermore, would undermine the nation's morale. Churchill was supported by both Attlee and Greenwood. The cold, calculating Foreign Secretary thought that Churchill was indulging in rhetorical heroics. But the decisive voice was Chamberlain's.

Chamberlain had been deeply shocked by the débâcle in France. The basis on which he had previously conducted the war had been shattered. In his diary a little over a week before these crucial Cabinet discussions he had noted that he expected a German ultimatum, and that it might be necessary to fight on but that 'We should be fighting only for better terms not for victory.' Chamberlain thought with Halifax that realism could only lead to the conclusion that the war was lost. But he jibbed at bribing Mussolini while Britain and Germany remained at war. On the issue of whether Mussolini's help should be invoked to bring Germany, France and Britain to the conference table his views fluctuated. Halifax worked hard on him to get him to force Churchill's hand. Chamberlain, however, attempted to reconcile Halifax and Churchill. In addressing the Cabinet, Chamberlain said on 28

‡ Cabinet Record, 27 May 1940, 65/13, PRO.

May, 'He felt bound to say that he was in agreement with the Foreign Secretary in taking the view that if we thought it was possible that we now get terms, which, although grievous, would not threaten our independence, we should be right to consider such terms.' But, he added, he did not think the French idea of an approach to Mussolini would produce 'decent terms', especially with France in Hitler's grasp. Chamberlain therefore said he had come to the conclusion that an 'approach to Italy was useless at the present time, it might be that we should take a different view in a short time, possibly even a week hence'. Churchill had won, at least for the time being.

One cannot say with certainty what would have happened if Chamberlain, not Churchill, had been prime minister. Halifax might then have carried the day. The impression the documents leave is that Chamberlain had acted less from conviction than out of loyalty to the Prime Minister. The Cabinet adjourned at 6.15 p.m. Churchill had called a meeting of the ministers not in the War Cabinet to his room in the House of Commons that evening. He told them that 'of course whatever happens at Dunkirk, we shall fight on'. He reported back to the reassembled War Cabinet at 7 p.m. that his message had been greeted with enthusiasm. Churchill then agreed to a long and tactful message to be sent to Reynaud explaining that Halifax's 'formula' prepared on the occasion of Reynaud's visit two days previously, which had contemplated asking Mussolini to act as mediator, was now dead; 'we are convinced that at this moment when Hitler is flushed with victory . . . it would be impossible for Signor Mussolini to put forward proposals for a conference with any success'.[*]

Churchill's victory would not be final as long as Halifax remained in the Cabinet and could influence Chamberlain. Indeed the following day the Foreign Secretary challenged Churchill's fighting despatch to Lord Gort. Halifax wanted a despatch sent that left to Gort's judgement the decision whether to surrender the BEF. 'It would not be dishonourable to relinquish the struggle in order to save a handful of men from massacre.' Churchill was not strong enough to offer outright opposition to such defeatism but evaded the issue by asking for time to consider the position. The evacuation from Dunkirk soon made any reconsideration unnecessary. Churchill was successfully playing for time.

In mid-June 1940, with the imminent withdrawal of France from the war, there were more anxious moments for Churchill. In July Hitler in a speech finally called on Britain to be reasonable and to make peace. At the same time he mocked Churchill, whose position was still far from assured. On 2 August, the King of Sweden secretly offered his mediation but the Cabinet on 7 August approved Halifax's reply which made Germany's withdrawal from all her conquests a precondition.[†] The full story of continuing attempts by those under Churchill to seek peace remains to be told but there is no reason to doubt Chamberlain's continued loyalty to the Prime Minister. It enabled Churchill to survive and at least to neutralise his opponents.

Chamberlain was incapacitated in the summer of 1940. Inoperable cancer was diagnosed. It was Chamberlain's terminal illness and resignation from the government in October 1940 that transformed Churchill's position. He now became leader of the party and in November 1940, when Chamberlain died, he paid tribute to Chamberlain's sincerity. During those critical first weeks of his administration he had owed much to him. Britain had survived. The Chiefs of Staff in a grave report in May 1940 had not rated Britain's chances very highly, concluding that 'Germany has most of the cards; but the real test is whether the morale of our fighting personnel and civil populations will counterbalance the numerical and material advantages which Germany enjoys. We believe it will.' That Britain had fought back was due to a unified people, to the Royal Air Force, the Royal Navy and the army, whose morale remained intact. This unity would have been severely tested if Churchill's leadership had been repudiated at the heart of government. But the doubts and divisions within the War Cabinet remained a well-kept secret until long after the war was over. In December 1940, Churchill reconstructed the War Cabinet and sent Halifax to Washington as ambassador, bringing Eden into the Cabinet as foreign secretary. But we must now retrace our steps to the course the war took during the last days of May and the summer of 1940.

*

---

* Cabinet Record, 28 May 1940, 65/13, PRO.

† Cabinet Record, 7 August 1940, 65/14, PRO.

Dunkirk. The Germans blundered, the British improvised and the French fought stubbornly to defend the beachhead. That is why 338,226 British, French and other Allied soldiers were able to escape the French coast when the Cabinet in London had already given most of them up for lost; waiting to embark was tense for all (above); the relief at reaching English shores unbounded (right). The evacuation began on 24 May and ended on 4 June. Eva Braun, Hitler's mistress, no doubt gloated over the 40,000 who did fall into German hands. This photo (left) of British prisoners was found in her private collection after her death.

On 28 May Leopold, King of the Belgians, capitulated, ignoring the contrary advice of his ministers. The evacuation of the BEF had begun the previous day. Every possible boat, including paddle pleasure steamers, was pressed into service. The Royal Navy conducted the evacuation, and some air cover could be provided by the air force. Göring's Luftwaffe strafed the boats and the men waiting on the beaches. But the calm seas favoured the Allies. The evacuation went on day after day until 3 June. A total of 338,226 Allied troops were snatched from certain capture, including 139,097 Frenchmen, but all the equipment was lost. To the south the war went on in France, and Britain even sent reinforcements to encourage the French. But Weygand viewed the situation as nearly hopeless. The French were given a few days' grace while the German divisions redeployed.

On 10 June 1940 Mussolini – having contemptuously rejected Roosevelt's earlier offer of good offices (page 262) – declared war on an already beaten France. Even so the French forces along the Italian frontier repulsed the Italian attacks. But the Germans could not be held. On 14 June they entered Paris. The government had fled to Bordeaux and was seeking release from the British alliance so that it could negotiate separately with Germany. Churchill at first replied that Britain would be willing to grant this wish provided the powerful French fleet were sent to British ports. Hard on the heels of this response, General de Gaulle, who had come to Britain to call on the French to continue the fight from a base still free from the enemy, telephoned from London an extraordinary proposal. Britain, as evidence of solidarity, was now offering to all Frenchmen an 'indissoluble union' of the United Kingdom and the 'French Republic'. Churchill had been sceptical from the first about whether this dramatic gesture would have much effect in Bordeaux and so keep France in the war. In Bordeaux Reynaud favoured acceptance but the French Cabinet never considered the idea seriously. During these critical days there remained much doubt about Britain's actual conditions for releasing France from her alliance. The final agonies ended with Pétain replacing Reynaud as prime minister. He immediately began armistice negotiations. On 22 June the French accepted the German terms and later signed them in the same railway carriage in which Marshal Foch had accepted the German capitulation at the end

*A photo that none would have thought possible ten months previously. It depicts Hitler arriving on a surprise early morning visit one June day in 1940 to satisfy his curiosity about Parisian architecture. He found much to criticize.*

of the First World War.

France was divided into occupied and unoccupied areas. The whole Atlantic coast came under German control. South and south-eastern France was governed by Pétain from a new capital established in Vichy. The colonial empire remained under the control of Vichy. The French sought to ensure that their fleet would not be used by Germany against Britain. The armistice provided that it would be disarmed under German supervision. Not unreasonably the British Cabinet remained unsure whether or not the Germans would in the end seize the fleet. For Britain the war had become a fight for national survival. In one of the most controversial military actions of the war, British forces attacked units of the French fleet at

Mers-el-Kebir on 3 July, after the French Admiral refused a British ultimatum requiring him to follow one of four courses, each of which would have denied the Germans use of these warships. The British action cost the lives of 1297 French sailors so recently their allies. It was an indication that Churchill would pursue the war with all the ruthlessness necessary to defeat a ruthless enemy. Vichy decided not to declare war but to break off diplomatic relations with Britain.

In London, General de Gaulle rallied the small Free French Forces. But the great majority of Frenchmen and most of the colonial empire accepted the legitimacy of Vichy and Pétain. Vichy France remained an important strategic factor in Britain's calculations, so de Gaulle was not granted the status of the leader of a French government in exile, even though such Polish, Dutch and Belgian governments had been recognised. He deeply resented this as an insult to the honour of France as now embodied in his movement.

The course of the war from the fall of France to December 1941 needs to be followed in three separate strands. First there was the actual conflict between Britain and Germany and Italy on land, sea and air. The most critical of the struggles was the battle in the air. Hitler believed that unless he won command of the air he could not, in the face of the strong British fleet, successfully mount Operation Sea Lion, codename for his invasion of the British Isles. On 10 July the preliminary of the Battle of Britain started over the Straits of Dover, then in mid-August the main attack switched to British airfields. The Luftwaffe could use some 2500 bombers and fighters in the battle. Britain's first-line fighter strength was some 1200 fighters. The radar stations on the coast which gave warning of the approach of the German planes and the cracking of the German operational code, as well as the superior Hurricanes and Spitfires, of which 660 could be used, were to Britain's advantage. But had the Germans persisted in their attacks on airfields they might nevertheless have succeeded in their aim of destroying Britain's air strength. Instead the German attack switched to cities. London was heavily raided on 7 September in reprisal for an RAF raid on Berlin. On 15 September it was clear that the German air force had failed to establish command of the air and two days later Hitler abandoned plans for the invasion of England. But now

the night raids against cities were causing tremendous damage to London and other British towns. On 14 November 1940 Coventry was blitzed. The night raids continued, but for all their damage, for all the loss of life they caused, they were not a decisive factor in the outcome of the war. The people emerged from the air-raid shelters to work in the war factories.

More critical was the war at sea. Although Britain controlled the surface of the oceans, submarine warfare once again brought her into desperate danger by disrupting essential supplies from America. The submarine threat reached its most serious peak between March and July 1941. The losses of British tonnage were heavy, but the United States increasingly assumed a belligerent attitude in guarding the convoys on her side of the Atlantic. The Germans never won what Churchill called the battle of the Atlantic.

On land Britain at first won spectacular victories in Africa during General Wavell's campaigns against the Italians in the spring of 1941. With the help of Dominion troops from South Africa, Australia and New Zealand as well as Indian troops, a much larger Italian army was defeated and chased out of Libya and Cyrenaica. In East Africa Abyssinia was freed and Haile Selassie restored to his throne. Hitler responded by sending General Erwin Rommel and an Afrika Korps to assist the Italians in the western desert. Wavell was forced back to the Egyptian frontier.

Britain had weakened her forces in the Middle East by sending an expedition to Greece. Mussolini had attacked Greece in October 1940 to show Hitler that he too could act independently. Unfortunately he could win no battles and soon the Greeks were chasing the Italians into Albania. In April 1941, Hitler came to Mussolini's rescue once more. By the end of the month the Greeks were defeated and the British expeditionary force withdrew. Britain's last forces were defeated in Crete which was spectacularly captured at the end of May 1941 by German paratroopers, who, however, suffered heavy casualties in the operation.

The second strand of the period from June 1940 to the end of 1941 is formed by the growing informal alliance between Britain and the United States. During Britain's 'finest hour', she did not stand alone. Besides the forces of her European Allies who had formed new fighting units in Britain she enjoyed from the beginning of the war the full support of the Dominions, all of whom had chosen to stand by Britain. Only Eire (Ireland) declared her neutrality. The support of the Dominions and empire was an important addition to Britain's ability to wage war. But without the United States Britain's survival would have been problematical. Until the fall of France, President Roosevelt was convinced that to make available the capacities of American industry to provide war supplies to Britain and France would be sufficient to ensure an Allied victory. In the mid-1930s Congress had attempted to prevent the United States from playing a role similar to that of the First World War by passing the Neutrality Laws in 1935, 1936 and 1937 so that the United States would not be 'dragged' into war. This legislation denied belligerents the right to purchase arms and munitions or secure American credit for such purposes. In November 1939, Roosevelt secured the repeal of some of its provisions. Belligerents could now obtain arms and munitions provided they paid for them and transported them home in their own ships ('cash and carry'). Britain and France took immediate advantage of the opportunity. Germany, lacking the means to transport purchases to Europe, could not do so.

The collapse of American neutrality was rapid. Roosevelt was determined to help Britain in every way possible to continue the war against Germany once he became convinced in July 1940 that Britain was not about to be knocked out of the war. Congress, concerned to keep the United States out of the war, was the major impediment. Bypassing Congress, Roosevelt agreed in September 1940 to Churchill's repeated pleas for fifty First World War destroyers in return for leases on naval bases in the British West Indies. He also obtained a formal promise from the British government never to surrender the British fleet to the Germans. But he felt it politically essential during the presidential election of the autumn of 1940 to promise the American people simply, 'Your boys are not going to be sent into any foreign wars.' When the votes were counted in November, Roosevelt's victory was decisive.

Following the election, Churchill appealed to Roosevelt for all-out aid. He wanted arms and ships and planes if Britain were to match Germany's strength. Roosevelt did his best to marshal American public opinion, declaring in a speech on 30 December 1940 that the United States would become the 'arsenal of democracy'. The Lend–Lease Act (March 1941) made all these goods available to Britain without payment. By May 1941 Roosevelt had concluded that the United States would have to enter the war, but given the attitude of Congress and of the majority of the American people he wanted Germany to fire the first shot. Hitler did not oblige. He cleverly avoided treating the United States as a hostile state even though the US Navy was now convoying merchant vessels – British, American and neutral – halfway across the Atlantic, and was occupying Iceland. In August 1941 Roosevelt met Churchill off Newfoundland and they jointly enunciated the principles on which a post-war settlement (known as the Atlantic Charter) would be based after the final destruction of the Nazi tyranny. Roosevelt and Congress supported all such unneutral behaviour partly out of hatred of Nazi rule but above all because the safety of the United States depended on Britain's successful resistance. Roosevelt and Congress had virtually placed the United States in a state of undeclared war against Germany, but did not cross the rubicon of declared all-out war until after the attack by Japan in December 1941 – and then it was Germany which first declared war on the United States.

The third decisive strand of these years was the transformation of the Nazi–Soviet partnership into hostility, marked by the beginning of the great war which Germany launched against Russia on 22 June 1941. Since 23 August 1939, when the Nazi–Soviet Non-Aggression Pact had been concluded, Stalin had avoided being drawn into war against Germany. Military unpreparedness in 1939 would have made war even more catastrophic for Russia then than in 1941: the West would have remained behind their defensive line leaving Russia to face the full force of the Wehrmacht. If the Wehrmacht had succeeded in defeating the Soviet Union, admittedly a hypothetical question, the military picture of the Second World War would have been totally different. Stalin in 1939 had no wish, of course, to save the Western democracies. He wanted to protect Russia and never lost his belief in the ultimate hostility of the Western capitalist powers. From the Soviet point of view the pact with the Germans had other advantages in enabling her to take on Japan without fear of a German attack in Europe. The Japanese were stunned by Hitler's U-turn of policy. Left isolated, they hastened their own undeclared war with the Soviet Union on the borders of Manchuria and Mongolia and were defeated. The

Non-Aggression Pact also brought other gains for Russia. In a secret additional protocol the Russians secured German acknowledgement of the Russian sphere of interest in Eastern Europe. The Baltic states, Finland, Estonia, Latvia and Lithuania, fell into Russia's sphere. Russia also expressed her 'interest' in Bessarabia, then part of Romania. Poland was partitioned 'in the event of a territorial and political rearrangement' taking place, a fine circumlocution for the imminent German attack on Poland.

Germany's unexpectedly rapid defeat of the Poles nevertheless surprised and alarmed the Russians, who extensively mobilised and entered Poland on 17 September 1939. But Hitler did not plan to attack the Soviet Union next. France was to be defeated first. Stalin in any case was confident that he could 'appease' Hitler. A new Soviet–German treaty of friendship was concluded on 28 September, adjusting the Polish partition in favour of the Germans. The Russians also denounced France and Britain as responsible for continuing the war. From the end of September 1939 to June 1941, the Soviet Union supplied Germany with grain, oil and war materials.

In this way the Soviet Union, though officially neutral, became aligned with Germany. The faithfulness with which Stalin carried out his part of the bargain indicates his fear of being exposed to Germany's demonstrated armed might and he expected no real help from the West. Fears of Allied hostility, especially now that the Soviet Union was collaborating with Germany economically, were well founded. Until May 1940, when the German victories in the West revealed the desperate weakness of their own position, the British and French were considering not only sending volunteers to Finland, but also stopping the flow of oil from the Baku oilfields by bombing them or by some other means. Fortunately, the kind of action which could have led to war with the Soviet Union was never taken by France and Britain.

Soviet aggression in 1939 and 1940 was in part pure aggrandisement to recover what had once belonged to the Russian Empire and more, but also to improve Russia's capacity for defence. The Baltic states were occupied without a war. But the Finns refused to accept Soviet proposals for naval bases and a shift of the frontier on the Karelian isthmus, which was only twenty miles from Leningrad. In return Finland was offered Soviet territory. The three months Soviet–Finnish War from 30 November 1939 to 12 March 1940 that followed did nothing to enhance Russia's military prestige. Hitler must have well noted her military incompetence, but her turn had not yet come, and Germany did nothing to help the 'Nordic' Finnish defenders against the Russian Slavs. Stalin was undoubtedly severely shaken by Hitler's victory in France, but he did not show it. On the contrary, he was in June 1940 unexpectedly tough, demanding that Romania return Bessarabia to Russia and, for good measure, the province of Bukovina. He wished to anticipate German dominance in a strategic region bordering on the Soviet Union. Hitler put pressure on Romania to comply. But secretly he had already made his first plans for the invasion of Russia.

Fears in the Kremlin of German dominance in the Balkans led to a sharp deterioration of good relations. This became evident when Molotov, the Soviet Foreign Minister, visited Berlin in November 1940. Molotov's demands infuriated Hitler and reinforced his determination to 'smash' Russia. Yet at the same time Stalin was anxious not to give Germany any pretext for attack and loyally fulfilled to the bitter end all Russia's economic undertakings to deliver war materials. When the Germans struck on 22 June 1941, the Soviet forces were totally unprepared. Despite all the information on the impending German onslaught reaching Stalin from spies and from the Allies, he either disbelieved it as an Allied plot to involve the Soviet Union in war or was afraid to take precautionary military counter-measures for fear of provoking the Germans. His failure in June 1941 was perhaps one of the most extraordinary displays of weakness by this hard and ruthless dictator.

Hitler's decision to launch his war on Russia marks a great turning point in the Second World War and made his ultimate defeat certain when he failed to destroy Russia militarily in this new *Blitzkrieg* during the first few months. Previous German military successes had made him overconfident. The war with the Soviet Union in fact repeated the 'war of attrition' which alone had brought the First World War to an end. Of course the Russian war from 1941 to 1945 was a war of dramatic movement, unlike the trench warfare on the western front – but its effect in destroying millions of soldiers and huge quantities of material in the end bled the Third Reich to death. Why did

Hitler attack the Soviet Union?

After the fall of France, Hitler hoped Britain would sue for peace. After the failure of the Luftwaffe in the battle of Britain, Hitler for the time being abandoned the alternative of subjugating the British Isles militarily. He also failed in October 1940 to win Franco's and Pétain's support for a joint Mediterranean strategy of destroying Britain's Mediterranean power. Hitler now reasoned that the war against Russia, which he had all along intended to wage as the centrepiece of his ideological faith and territorial ambition, should be launched before Britain's defeat. It was to serve the additional, though not primary, purpose of convincing Britain that it was useless to continue the war any longer. Hitler gave the order to prepare Operation Barbarossa on 18 December 1940.

A series of brief Balkan campaigns in the spring of 1941 ensured that the invasion of Russia would be undertaken on a broad front without any possibility of a hostile flank. Fear of Germany, together with hostility to Russia, had turned Romania, Hungary and Slovakia into more or less enthusiastic junior German partners who all declared war on Russia, as did Italy and Finland. They felt safe under Germany's military umbrella. Bulgaria, though practically occupied by German troops, remained neutral. Greece was also involved since Mussolini had decided on his own little war of conquest. In the end German troops had to rescue the Italian army and so Greece was occupied. Hitler thought Yugoslavia too was in the bag when the Regent, Prince Paul, signed a treaty with Germany in March 1941. But there was a revolt against the Regent and the new government repudiated the German alignment. Yugoslavia's resistance did not last long. The Germans attacked on 6 April and the Hungarians faithlessly joined in three days later. In less than two weeks Yugoslav resistance was overpowered. Until recently it was believed that these two wars against Yugoslavia and Greece, though minor for Germany, had momentous consequences by delaying the attack on the Soviet Union – a delay that meant the Wehrmacht ground to a halt in front of Moscow in the bitter winter of 1941/2. In fact the Greek and Yugoslav military diversion was too slight to affect significantly the time it took to assemble the huge build-up of men, equipment and supplies for the Russian invasion. In the early hours of 22 June 1941 the Germans launched the attack in the air with approximately 190 German and satellite divisions. The Soviet Union was thereby given no choice but to enter into an alliance with Britain and, later, into alignment with the United States as well. The consequences of this new war unleashed by Hitler proved momentous for the course of world history.

# CHAPTER 27

## *The China War and the Origins of the Pacific War, 1937–1941*

The Pacific War grew out of Japan's China War renewed in 1937. Though there are doubts about how far the Japanese pre-planned a large-scale conflict, a small incident became for the Japanese the starting point for an all-out war against China. It was essentially the future of China that four years later led Japan to war with the United States. The decision for war was taken in Tokyo in September 1941 because the United States was seen as the enemy unalterably opposed to Japan's concept of her right to a dominant role in China and eastern Asia. The only chance for peace was a change in the course of American policy as perceived by the Japanese, and this did not happen. The Japanese leaders believed that the choice before them was to fulfil the task of conquest or to acquiesce in Japan's national decline. Why, the Japanese wondered, should the United States of all nations deny Japan the right to an Asian Monroe Doctrine?

But the course of events that led to war was not so straightforward when looked at in depth, and raises fascinating questions. Was the Japanese perception of US policy correct? Britain and the United States, moreover, were not the only two strong Western powers with interests in eastern Asia. From the beginning of Japan's expansion in China, the only country capable of challenging Japan's army on land with an army of millions other than Nationalist China was Russia. At the time, in the mid-1930s, the Japanese military asked themselves whether Japan's empire could ever be completely safe without first removing the potential Russian threat. Should therefore a war against her northern neighbour precede the efforts to control China? Indeed, might an alliance with China against the Soviet Union be possible? And if the Soviet Union was to be fought, or checked from interfering in Japan's China policy, then might not Europe help – calling in the old world to balance the new?

Such a view corresponded with the traditions of Japanese foreign policy. From 1902, until its dissolution at the Washington Conference two decades later, Japan had enjoyed the support of the Anglo-Japanese alliance. In the new conditions of the 1930s, Hitler's Germany was the obvious counterweight to Bolshevik Russia. The history of German–Japanese relations from 1936, when Japan first joined the Anti-Comintern Pact, to the close of the Second World War is another important theme for study: how the Germans and Japanese viewed this relationship, and whether the British and more importantly American perceptions of that relationship were accurate. The origins of the war in Asia are less well understood than the origins of the war in Europe.

The roots of the conflict lie in the militaristic–spiritual values that Japanese education inculcated. During the 1930s these values were translated into politics by the small group of military, naval and political leaders who exercised power. They now controlled a highly centralised bureaucratic state, having reversed the earlier broadening of political participation which had taken place during the so-called era of Taisho 'democracy' of the 1920s (page 89). Men like Prince Konoe, prime minister in 1937–9 and 1940–1, believed that Japan had a right to achieve equality with other great powers. Unlike the United States and the British Empire, Japan lacked the necessary resources within her own tightly packed islands to fulfil the role of a great power. She was a have-not nation, so some Japanese argued, claiming only the opportunity for prosperity and strength to which her advanced culture, civilisation and capacity for modern technical development entitled her. For Konoe's foreign minister, Matsuoko, Japan's international conduct was also a question of national pride. No Japanese must accept the insulting, inferior role the Western imperialists assigned to him. Only by showing forceful courage would the West ever be convinced of the equality of Japan. The view of many American politicians was precisely the counterpart of this; the Japanese would give way if shown a firm hand.

Confrontation was unavoidable given the Japanese leaders' concept of their national honour's requirements. They saw themselves as guiding a unique people with a divine emperor. While Western *Realpolitik* was certainly practised by Japanese policymakers, the ultimate factor deciding national policy was not rational policy but chauvinism masquerading as spiritual values. The Chief of the Japanese Naval General Staff, for instance, urged in 1941 that Japan should wage war to remain true to the spirit of national defence, saying, 'even if we might not win the war, this noble spirit of defending the fatherland will be perpetuated and our posterity will rise again and again'. The 'spirit' of war itself was glorified; a nation which denied this spirit and did not rise against injustice would deserve to decay. The 'injustice' referred to was America's denial that Japan had the sole right to shape China's destiny. All this chauvinistic spirituality was not the inevitable heritage of Japanese beliefs. There were opposing views, socialist, pacific views based on different Japanese traditions. The moods of governments of the 1930s and 1940s mark a distinctive period in Japanese history, as the post-1945 changes in attitude further confirm.

Britain and the United States formally protested at Japanese aggression in China, but there was no thought in the 1930s of resisting it by force so long as only China was involved. Japan, moreover, stressed the anti-communist aspect of her policy

when concluding the Anti-Comintern Pact with Germany in November 1936. The following summer of 1937 was decisive in the policies pursued by the Kwantung and Manchurian armies. In June Russia's capability to hinder Japanese objectives in China was tested. There was more sporadic fighting on the borders with Russia in 1938. The fighting capacity of the Soviet Union had recovered sufficiently from Stalin's purges of the armed forces to inflict a severe defeat on the Japanese army at Nomonhan in August 1939. More than 18,000 Japanese were killed (page 190). This evidence of Soviet strength, coming close on the heels of the German–Soviet Non-Aggression Pact, led the Japanese to revise their estimate that Russia was too weak to interfere in China. The Soviet Union became an important factor in Japan's calculations. Meanwhile the die in China had long been cast, but the Japanese army, despite its victorious advances, could not bring the China War to an end.

The Japanese army had continued to interfere and expand its influence in northern China from 1933 to 1937, but in the whole of northern China the Japanese garrison was only 6000 men. Then, near Peking, on an ancient bridge, Chinese and Japanese soldiers clashed in July 1937. The Marco Polo Bridge incident was in itself minor; exactly how a small number of Japanese and Chinese troops came to clash is still obscure. There is no evidence (unlike in Manchuria in 1931) that the Japanese army had planned war against China and provoked the conflict. There were divided counsels in Tokyo. The hawks won. At first, sharp local actions were undertaken in the expectation that Nationalist China would be overawed. Full-scale war ensued when Chiang Kai-shek chose to resist instead. The war quickly spread from northern China. The Japanese attacked Shanghai and by December 1937 the Nationalist capital of Nanking had fallen. Japanese reinforcements had been rushed to China. In the Shanghai–Nanking operation the Japanese suffered 70,000 casualties and the Chinese at least 370,000. By then 700,000 Japanese troops were engaged in China. After 1938 close to 1 million Japanese troops were fighting some 3 million Chinese troops. The Japanese troops behaved with the utmost brutality, massacring, raping and looting. The fall of Nanking was not the end of the war, as the Japanese hoped, but its beginning. Although one of the world's most devastating wars, the China War is little known in the West. It became a three-

Japan's War in Asia, 1937–1945

SOVIET UNION

MONGOLIA

MANCHUKUO
1931–45

CHINA

Peking

1938

KOREA

Chungking

Nanking

Shanghai

BURMA

1944

FORMOSA

Hong Kong
Dec. 1941

PHILIPPINES
1942

MARIANAS
ISLANDS

PACIFIC
OCEAN

Guam

THAILAND

FRENCH
INDO-CHINA
1940

1942

MALAYA

BORNEO

1942

SOLOMON
ISLANDS

SUMATRA

CELEBES

NETHERLANDS EAST INDIES

NEW
GUINEA

1942
JAVA

JAPANESE EMPIRE

Tokyo

KAMCHATKA

Japanese Empire and occupied land to 1938

Japanese conquests until 1942

0          1000 miles

0          1000 km

AUSTRALIA

sided struggle between the Chinese communists, the Chinese Nationalists and the Japanese. The communists' main priority was to gain control over as much of the territories evacuated by the Nationalists as they could. The Nationalist Chinese armies bore the brunt of the regular fighting.

The sinking of the US naval vessel, *Panay*, and damage to the British *Ladybird* in December 1937 directly involved the two Western powers in the conflict. Since the autumn of 1937 Roosevelt had been searching for some effective counterblast to German, Italian and now Japanese aggression. He gave expression to his desire for 'positive endeavours to preserve peace' in his well-known 'Quarantine' speech in Chicago on 5 October 1937. He called on the peace-loving nations to make a 'concerted effort' in opposition to the lawless aggressors; that lawlessness, he declared, was spreading and the aggressors, like sick patients, should be placed in 'quarantine'. It was rousing stuff but meant little in concrete terms. The depression preoccupied the United States and Britain at home. Neither Congress in America nor Parliament in Britain would contemplate war with Japan. After the *Panay* incident, and before full Japanese apologies were received, Roosevelt for a short while had considered economic sanctions without calling them such. He was to return to this policy in 1940 and 1941 with devastating results.

Meanwhile, the powers with interests in China had met in Brussels but the conference assembled there could achieve nothing. Britain would not act without US backing, or in advance of American policy. The needs of the Dominions, Australia and New Zealand, for adequate protection or peace in the Pacific were obvious. But Britain could not match the worldwide defence requirements of her Commonwealth with her available military resources, which had been neglected for years. As the crisis mounted in Europe the British navy was needed in home waters and the Mediterranean and could not be spared for Singapore. Although recognising clearly the threat Japan posed to British interests in China and Asia, a cautious policy had to be followed: conciliation and firmness without risking war at a time of European dangers. In 1939 the Japanese blockaded the British concession in Tientsin, demanding that Britain in effect abandon Nationalist China. It was a serious crisis but the simultaneous threat of war in Europe decided the British Cabinet in June 1939 to reach a compromise with Japan.

The first tentative shift of American policy, nevertheless, did occur just after Britain's climb-down in the summer of 1939. Of fundamental importance for the history of eastern Asia was that for a decade the United States felt somewhat uncritically anti-Japanese, while Chiang Kai-shek became almost an American folk hero.

The Prime Minister, Prince Fumimaro Konoe, would have liked to bring the war in China to an end but his 'solution' implied Chinese acceptance of Japan as the senior member of the Asian 'family'. That is how the Japanese deluded themselves that their aggression was really for the good of all the Asian people. The vastness of Chinese territory denied the Japanese army the possibility of conquering the whole of China, even after eight years of warfare. Within the huge areas they did occupy, despite the utmost barbarity of the occupation, which would have been unthinkable in the Meiji era, much of the countryside remained under communist or Nationalist control. The Japanese for the most part could make their occupation effective only in the towns and along the vital railway lines.

Encouraged by moral and some material American support, Chiang Kai-shek refused all peace terms which would have subjugated China in the manner of Japan's Twenty-One Demands. In November 1938 Konoe sought to make it clear to Chiang Kai-shek, and the world, that Japan would never leave China. Japan would establish a New Order in Asia through the economic, political and cultural union of Japan, Manchukuo and China. The New Order served notice to the Western powers that there would be no room for Western interests of the kind that had existed in China before. Early in 1939 Konoe resigned. It is certainly mistaken to see him as a peaceful moderate, though he endeavoured to avoid war with the United States without abandoning Japan's anti-Western policy in east Asia. German victories in Europe from September 1939 to July 1940 greatly strengthened the impatient military. With the abolition of political parties Japan became more authoritarian.

In July 1940 Konoe headed a second government. Japan drew closer to Germany, concluding, as a result of Foreign Minister Matsuoka's urging, the Three-Power Pact (Italy was also a signatory) on 27 September 1940. It purported to be an agreement on the division of the world. Japan recognised Germany's and Italy's leadership in the establishment of a 'new order in Europe'; Germany and

Italy recognised the 'leadership of Japan in the establishment of a new order in Greater Asia'. With the reservation of Japanese neutrality towards the Soviet Union, the three powers promised to help each other by all means, including military, if attacked by a 'Power at present not involved in the European War or in the Sino-Japanese Conflict'. That article (three) pointed to the United States. What was the purpose of the alliance? Both the Japanese and the Germans at the time hoped it would act as a deterrent against the United States involving herself in a war over Asian issues. Hitler, furthermore, hoped Japan would attack Britain, thus increasing the pressure on Britain to make peace with Germany or to face even worse military complications in defence of her empire. In Tokyo, in all probability without Berlin having any knowledge of it, the German Ambassador in an additional exchange of notes with Matsuoka conceded to the Japanese a good deal of flexibility in the honouring of their obligations to help Germany militarily if in fact the United States went to war with Germany alone and not with Japan.

The existence of the treaty made a deep impression on Roosevelt, who saw it as confirmation that all the aggressors in Europe and Asia were linked in one world conspiracy of aggression. That this was *not* so in fact Roosevelt discovered when the Japanese–American confrontation had reached the point in September 1941 at which war was seen by the Japanese as the only way out. But the prime cause of US–Japanese tension was not the German–Japanese alliance. That lacked all substance on the Japanese side. Konoe instructed the Japanese Embassy in Washington in September 1941 to tell the United States that, if she went to war with Germany in Europe, Japan would not feel herself bound to declare war on her in the Pacific but that the 'execution of the Tripartite Pact shall be independently decided'.

The story of how the United States and Japan came to be engaged in the Pacific War is a twisted and tangled one. Roosevelt did not want a war in the Pacific, believing that the defeat of Nazi Germany should take priority. Hitler urged the Japanese to strike at the British Empire in Asia, thereby weakening Britain's capacity to oppose him in Europe and the Mediterranean. If the Japanese decided they had to attack the United States simultaneously, they were assured of Germany's alliance. What the Japanese wanted was to finish the war in China and not have to take on America as well.

In Britain both Chamberlain before May 1940 and Churchill afterwards wished to avoid the extension of war in the Pacific. In 1940 and 1941 Britain was engaged in fighting in the Mediterranean and the Middle East to preserve her power there. The Dominions of New Zealand and Australia, moreover, clamoured for adequate defence in eastern Asia; that defence would best be served by peace and deterrence. But Churchill believed that for deterrence to have credibility the United States and Britain would need to form a counterpart to the Triple Alliance of Japan, Germany and Italy, so that Japan would realise that her expansion beyond the limits which Britain and the United States were prepared to accept in south-east Asia would result in war. Thus both Churchill's and Roosevelt's thinking was based on the theory of deterrence. Except that Roosevelt, dependent upon support in Congress, could not go so far as to threaten war or to ally with Britain.

The mutual policies of deterrence – of the Japanese on the one hand, and of the United States and Britain on the other – totally failed in their purpose. The United States was not deterred by Japan's alliance with Germany and Italy from continuing to play a role as an eastern Asian power. Indeed she stepped up her support for Chiang Kai-shek. Without Nationalist Chinese resistance, the ever-growing pretensions of Japan's co-prosperity sphere would become a reality, placing Western interests completely at Japan's mercy. For Britain, the vital regions were those bordering on the British Empire in Malaya, Burma and India. In this way the French colonies of Indo-China, the Netherlands East Indies, independent Thailand and the American Philippines came to be seen as the key areas to be defended against Japan. But the 'firm' policy towards Japan eventually adopted by the United States to impede Japanese expansion triggered off among Japan's leaders an almost fatalistic response that war with the United States and Britain was preferable to the kind of peace, a return to the Washington peace structure of the 1920s, which the two Western powers sought. The crux was China. Britain and the United States were not prepared to accept Japanese domination over China. Roosevelt held to the simple truth that China was for the Chinese. Furthermore, if the Japanese were allowed to achieve their aims in China no Western interests in eastern Asia would be safe.

The course of US policy from 1940 to 1941 was nevertheless not clear or consistent. It is sometimes difficult to fathom precisely what was in Roosevelt's mind. He was sensitive to American public opinion, which increasingly demanded tough measures, short of war, to restrain Japan from ousting US commerce from China. Yet, with war raging across the Atlantic, Roosevelt genuinely wished to preserve peace in the Pacific for as long as possible, though not on Japan's terms. The United States possessed powerful retaliatory economic weapons: the American market for Japanese goods, American raw materials essential to Japan, including oil, and capital for Japanese industry. Secretary of State Cordell Hull advised caution in applying any economic sanctions; but some of Roosevelt's other advisers, including the powerful Secretary of the Treasury, Henry Morgenthau, believed that Japan would have to accept American conditions for a just settlement in China once the United States made use of her economic muscle, for oil and raw materials were essential to sustain a Japanese war against the West. Roosevelt followed an uncertain middle course. In July 1939, the Japanese were informed that the treaty of commerce with the United States would be terminated in January 1940. This was the first tentative application of economic pressure and shocked the Japanese leaders. After its termination it would be possible to impose sanctions other than 'moral embargoes'.

With the defeat of the Netherlands and France by Germany in the summer of 1940, the chances of peace in the Pacific grew less. French and Dutch possessions in south-east Asia now became tempting targets for Japan, which cast covetous eyes particularly on the Netherlands East Indies with their valuable raw materials of tin, rubber and oil. But the American administration made clear that it would regard any change in the *status quo* of these European possessions as endangering American interests and peace in the Pacific. In 1940 Japan increased the pressure on France and Britain to block aid to China. Vichy France had to accept the stationing of Japanese troops in northern Indo-China and for a time Britain agreed to close the Burma Road along which supplies had been sent to Nationalist China. If the United States were not prepared to use her economic weapons, then, the British argued, there was nothing left for them to do but to attempt to appease Japan.

In July 1940, Roosevelt took a second step to apply economic pressure on Japan. He ordered that the export of petrol suitable for aviation fuel be restricted, in addition to lubricants and high-grade scrap metal. Although this was a very limited embargo, there were those in Washington who, as it turned out, rightly foretold that turning the screw would not make for peace but would lead the Japanese in desperation to attack the Netherlands East Indies. Roosevelt was well aware of the danger and characteristically wanted to apply some pressure but not push Japan too hard. The Tripartite Pact which Japan, Germany and Italy concluded in September 1940 hardened Roosevelt's attitude (page 275). In a speech soon after the conclusion of the pact, Roosevelt declared, 'No combination of dictator countries of Europe and Asia will stop the help we are giving to … those who resist aggression, and who now hold the aggressors far from our shores.' All the same, from the summer of 1940 to the summer of 1941 Roosevelt attempted to dampen down the crisis in the Pacific. He gave some additional help to China, but also urged restraint on Japan. He also made it clear that he was still willing and anxious to negotiate a settlement. Meanwhile he rejected Churchill's urging that the United States and Britain should jointly take steps so that the Japanese should be left in no doubt that further aggression in Asia meant war.

Negotiations got under way in Washington between the Japanese Ambassador Nomura and Secretary of State Cordell Hull in the spring of 1941. Meanwhile, the Japanese signed a neutrality pact with the Soviet Union and were extending their military bases to southern Indo-China in the obvious direction of the Netherlands East Indies. A crucial decision was taken in Tokyo that affected the whole course of world history. The plan to strike north from China and join Germany in the war against the Soviet Union was rejected. Japan would advance to the south to secure the raw materials vital to her own needs. An imperial conference on 2 July 1941 gave its final seal of approval to that decision. The goal was the Dutch East Indies. Japan did not wish to go to war with the United States and the British Empire. Her diplomats would try to convince London and Washington that for her this was a question of survival. If Britain and the United States, however, opposed the southern drive, the Japanese Empire would not shrink from war either.

THE CHINA WAR AND THE ORIGINS OF THE PACIFIC WAR, 1937–1941

Roosevelt proposed that, if Japan withdrew from southern French Indo-China, the raw materials she needed could be guaranteed by the powers and the region would be neutralised. What impressed the Japanese more was the order freezing Japanese funds in the United States and an American trade embargo which, despite Roosevelt's initial intentions, included oil. But Roosevelt's object was still to avoid war in the Pacific, while somehow getting the United States in on the side of Britain in Europe. After the German invasion of Russia during the summer of 1941, he also ordered that ways be found to provide all-out aid to the Soviet Union.

So when in mid-August 1941 Nomura suggested the continuation of informal negotiations to settle American–Japanese differences, Roosevelt gladly agreed. Nomura suggested a meeting between Prime Minister Konoe and the American President. Roosevelt was excited by the idea, but followed the advice of the State Department and insisted that first the Japanese government should accept a number of basic propositions: they should desist from a southern drive of conquest (that is, in the direction of the Netherlands East Indies), they should agree to withdraw troops from China and to give up any economic discrimination, and they should detach themselves from the Tripartite Pact. All but one of these preconditions were entirely unacceptable to the Japanese. They might have been willing to halt their southern expansion on their own terms, but not to make any but token withdrawals from China.

What the Americans were really demanding was the Japanese abandonment of the basic tenets of their co-prosperity sphere. The negotiations dragged on through October and November. The gulf between the Japanese and American concepts of the future peace of eastern Asia was as wide as ever, despite the search by the diplomats for some middle ground. As late as mid-November 1941, Roosevelt was searching without success for a compromise which would lead to a postponement of war for at least six months. This shows that for Roosevelt, in any case, Germany still came first, but his judgements proved very changeable.

In Tokyo the basic countdown to war was decided upon at the Imperial Conference which took place on 6 September 1941. Prime Minister Konoe opened the meeting saying that Japan must complete her war preparations, but that diplomacy should be given a last chance to resolve peacefully the prob-

lems facing her. If diplomacy failed, and only a limited time could be allowed for its success, then Japan must fight a war of self-defence. The United States' conditions for a settlement, involving not only a barrier to the southern drive of Japan but also American insistence that Japan withdraw her troops from China and abandon her demands for exclusive economic control, were, Konoe claimed, tantamount to denying Japan's right to exist as an equal and Asian power. Without oil and a certain source of essential raw materials Japan was at the mercy of foreign powers. That was her interpretation of the American proposals for a peaceful settlement. The Chief of Naval Staff, Admiral Osami Nagano, moreover, was confident that the Japanese navy's early victories would place Japan in an 'invincible position' even in a long war. The Japanese Army Chief of Staff urged the opening of hostilities as soon as possible while Japan still enjoyed a relative military advantage. The tone of the conference was therefore that war with the United States and Britain would become inevitable unless American policy rapidly altered course. In October, Konoe resigned and made way for a new government headed by General Hideki Tojo, a clear indication that the moment for war was drawing close.

The outcome of these Tokyo conferences became known in Washington from the intercepted instructions cabled from Tokyo to Ambassador Nomura, who was still negotiating with Cordell Hull in Washington. The Japanese code had been broken by the Americans, who were now privy to the Japanese secrets. The Americans thus learnt that the Japanese had a time limit in mind for the success of these negotiations. Furthermore, that there could be no question of any genuine Japanese withdrawal from China and that when the time limit expired the Japanese army and navy would extend the war by continuing their drive southward against the Dutch and British possessions. What was not clear to the Americans was whether the Japanese intended to attack the United States simultaneously in the Pacific. The Americans, therefore, were aware while negotiating that unless they were prepared to abandon China war would become inevitable. The Japanese might be brought to compromise on their 'southern' drive in return for American neutrality but not on the issue of the war in China. The Hull–Nomura negotiations were thus unreal, maintained on the American side

*Pearl Harbor, 7 December 1941.*

mainly in the hope of delaying the outbreak of war.

It is in this light that Roosevelt's remarks at a policy conference which took place on 25 November must be judged. Roosevelt by this time regarded war as virtually inevitable, observing, 'The question now was how we should manoeuvre them into the position of firing the first shot without allowing too much danger to ourselves.' But the well-known Hull Note of the following day, sent in reply to an earlier Japanese note, was couched in the form of a 'tentative outline' to serve as a 'basis for agreement'. It set out America's ideas for a settlement point by point. The Japanese could look forward to a normalisation of trade and access to raw materials in return for peace in eastern Asia; the Japanese must promise to respect the territorial integrity of all her neighbours; the 'impossible' American condition from the Japanese point of view was that

both Japan and the United States should give up their special rights in China and that Japan should withdraw all her military forces from China and Indo-China.

At the Imperial Conference in Tokyo on 1 December 1941, this note was placed before the assembled Japanese leaders as if it were an ultimatum. It was a deliberate misrepresentation by the Japanese themselves, intended to unite the ministers. Differences were now indeed reconciled. The decision was reached to attack Britain, the Netherlands and the United States simultaneously.

The Japanese sent a formal declaration of war to Washington, intending it to be delivered fifty minutes before the carrier planes of Admiral Yamamoto's task force, which was at that moment secretly making for Pearl Harbor, attacked America's principal naval base in the Pacific. Unfortunately, the

Japanese Embassy was slow in deciphering the message and so the Japanese envoys appeared at the State Department almost an hour after the start of the Pearl Harbor attack on the United States fleet. That made 7 December 1941 an unintentional, greater 'day of infamy'. In two hours 360 carrier-based planes from Yamamoto's fleet sank or damaged seven battleships, the pride of America's Pacific fleet.

Japan had decided to start the war having clearly set a time limit for negotiations in September. It was self-deception to believe that the United States was about to make war on Japan after Hull's note on 26 September, even if Roosevelt thought war virtually inevitable. There is no evidence that Congress would have allowed the President to declare war for the sake of China or of any non-American possessions in Asia attacked by the Japanese. The traumatic loss of lives and ships, the fact and manner of the Japanese attack, now ensured a united American response for war. For Churchill a great cloud had lifted. With the United States in the war, he knew for certain that Hitler would now be defeated. Furthermore the United States found herself simultaneously at war with Germany, not by resolution of Congress, which might still have been difficult to secure, but by Hitler's own decision to declare war on America. In this way it came about that in December 1941 all the great powers of the world were at war.

# CHAPTER 28

## *The Ordeal of the Second World War*

The Second World War was the last world war to be fought with conventional weapons and the first to end with the use of the nuclear bomb, which raised the threat that any third world war could end in the destruction of the majority of the human population. The Second World War also became a new kind of total warfare with the deliberate killing of many millions of civilian non-combatants.

The major technical advance was aerial warfare. That cities could be reduced to rubble from the air the Germans first demonstrated in Spain in 1937 with the destruction of Guernica. In 1939 it was the turn of Warsaw, and in 1940 Coventry suffered a similar fate. Britain and the United States from 1942 to 1945 retaliated with mass bombing of the majority of Germany's cities. The results of such raids were to cause heavy casualties to civilian populations and widespread destruction. The Allied bombing of Dresden, crammed with refugees from the East, just before the war ended has been singled out for particular condemnation. By February 1945 the devastation of German cities no longer affected the outcome of the war. The impact on the capacity of a country to wage war despite such bombing was throughout the war less than anticipated. The Germans fought on in desparation. There was no alternative. Fear, especially of Russian revenge, maintained the resistance. Nor did the devastation prevent the rapid expansion of war production in Germany. Was the great loss of human life – post-war official Germany calculated that 593,000

civilians were killed – justified by the military results?

Vengeance on the Allied side was a subsidiary motive for the bombing offensive. For mere vengeance the lives of more than 50,000 aircrew and an enormous industrial war effort would not have been expended. Photographic reconnaissance of the destruction of the industrial Ruhr region and other cities seemed at the time to justify these raids as crippling blows against Germany's capacity to wage war. There can be no doubt that German resources were destroyed and wasted in reconstruction and that this weakened Germany's war effort. But one cannot quantify what contribution the air war made to bringing the war to an end, or how much longer it would have lasted if mass 'carpet' bombing had not been adopted. It did not reach its most devastating dimensions until 1944, and by then the German armies had already been defeated and could only delay the inevitable end. But there can be little doubt that more specific strategic bombing of, for instance, synthetic fuel plants and communications did impede the German war effort from 1944 to 1945 and that the brilliant German Armaments Minister, Albert Speer, could no longer make good the losses within the frontier of a shrinking Reich. Important, too, was the fact that before the invasion of France in 1944 the land war waged by the Allies was minor relative to the struggle on the eastern front. The bombing offensive was the only major weapon available to wage a war whose impact would be felt by the Germans until the Allied military build-up was sufficient to defeat the German armies in the West.

During the Second World War the distinction between combatants and non-combatants was not so much blurred as deliberately ignored. The factory worker was seen as a combatant. In most contemporary eyes, as the war progressed, this justified his destruction and the destruction of his home from the air. Children, women, the old and the sick were killed and maimed in this new type of warfare. The Germans, Japanese and Italians went beyond even what in the Second World War came to be considered legitimate warfare against all those involved in the war effort. What would have been in store for Europe, Asia and Africa if Germany and Japan had won the war can be seen from their ruthlessly brutal behaviour as occupying powers. The contrast with the First World War in this respect could not be greater. Murder and terror became deliberate acts of policy.

The destruction of towns and villages during the German military campaigns and the machine-gunning of fleeing columns of refugees was just a beginning. Hitler's Reich was no respecter of the human values of those regarded as belonging to lesser races, or of the lives of the Germans themselves. The 'euthanasia' programme, for example, was designed to murder 'useless' incurably ill or mentally handicapped German men, women and children. Many thousands of gypsies, classified as 'non-Aryans', were murdered in Auschwitz. Jehovah's Witnesses, whose faith would not allow them to be subservient to Hitler's commands, were persecuted and killed, as were countless other civilians of every nationality who were defined as opponents of the ideals of the regime. Hostages were picked off the streets in the occupied countries and shot in arbitrary multiples for the resistance's killing of German soldiers. Offences against the occupying powers were punishable by death at the discretion of the local military authorities. To hide partisans or Jews meant the death penalty if discovered or denounced. For the Jews in Europe, who were not so much opponents as defenceless victims, a unique fate awaited: physical destruction, as foretold in Hitler's Reichstag speech of 30 January 1939.

Yet, side by side with these horrors, the German armies fighting the Allied armies in the West behaved conventionally too and took prisoners who were, with some notable exceptions, treated reason-ably. In Russia, however, the German army became increasingly involved with the specially formed units attached to the army commands which committed atrocities on a huge scale. Here there was to be no 'honourably' conducted warfare.

More than 3 million Russian prisoners of war in German hands died through exposure and famine. Himmler, who as head of the SS organisation wielded ever-increasing power, later in the war recognised the waste of manpower involved, and Russian prisoners of war and civilians were used as forced labour in German war industries. Many died from exhaustion. On the Allied side, some 300,000 German prisoners of war in Russian hands never returned to Germany. There was also the Soviet murder of Polish officers at Katyn, their bodies discovered by the Germans in mass graves in April 1943. The full horror of this slaughter was only revealed by Russia's new leaders in September 1992. The orders to shoot Polish officers and civilians in prison for suspected enmity to the Soviet Union were signed in March 1940 by Stalin himself and by three Politburo comrades, Voroshilov, Molotov and Mikoyan, at the suggestion of Beria, chief of the secret police. In the forest of Katyn, near Smolensk, 4421 Polish officers were shot. They were only a small proportion of the total victims. Another 17,436 soldiers and civilians were murdered as well. All the Soviet leaders, Khrushchev, Brezhnev and Gorbachev, were told of the dark secret in the files, which were kept in a special safe. Brezhnev minuted, 'Never to be opened'; Gorbachev passed on some information to the Polish government. The Yeltsin government revealed the full account of the murders.

Japanese troops also became brutalised. To be taken prisoner was regarded as a disgrace. Allied prisoners of war were treated inhumanely by the Japanese military authorities, and thousands of them died. Many were employed together with forced Asian labour on such projects as the construction of the Burma–Siam railway. By the time that death line was completed in October 1943, 100,000 Asians and 16,000 Europeans had lost their lives.

The horrors and ordeals, the depravity and brutality behind the battlefronts, the mass murder of millions are an inseparable part of the history of the Second World War. But the historian, confronted with such enormities, must not allow the atrocities simply to become merged into one impenetrable blackness. The separate strands have to be analysed if some understanding is to be reached of why civilisation collapsed on so vast a scale. Nor can the atrocities be set aside by the misguided argument that those on one side cancel out those on the other.

In Poland, and then in Russia, the German conquerors displayed a degree of barbarism which has no parallels with Germany's conduct during the First World War. In the 1930s, for tactical reasons, Hitler had been prepared to work with the Poles, and his view of them was quite favourable. The authoritarian Polish state, the Polish brand of anti-Semitism and official Poland's anti-Bolshevism made them, in Hitler's eyes, suitable junior partners. But Poland's courageous resistance in 1939 changed all that. With the exception of the Jews, who were all seen as destroyers of the Aryan race, Hitler's views of what to do with other 'races' such as Slavs was opportunistic. He cared nothing for their lives. In destroying the Polish intelligentsia he was not so much following a racial policy as taking what he regarded as the most efficacious practical steps to root out the strong sense of Polish nationalism. The same 'racial' inconsistency is noticeable in the treatment of the Ukrainian population. Vengeance for the slightest resistance to his will was a dominant element of Hitler's character. With the exception of the parts of the Soviet Union which the Germans occupied, no state, once independent, was treated worse than the Polish. Hitler planned that the Poles should lose their national existence altogether. Intellectual leaders and members of the professions were murdered wholesale. Polish culture and national consciousness were to be wiped out. Parts of western Poland were annexed by Germany and settled with 'German' farmers, mainly the so-called *Volksdeutsche*, ethnic Germans who for generations had lived in Eastern Europe.

The greater part of the rest of Poland was organised as a colony called the General Government of the Occupied Polish Territories headed by Hans Frank, a fanatical, brutal Nazi since the earliest days of the party. In this colony the Poles were to rise to positions no higher than workers. Frank described his fief in November 1940 as 'a gigantic labour camp in which everything that signifies power and independence rests in the hands of the Germans'. Frank, typically for the strife-torn Nazi German administration, himself engaged in much infighting with the SS, who obeyed no one except the leader, Heinrich Himmler. The Ukraine, with

Frank's General Government, was selected by the SS for the majority of the sites of the extermination camps, such as Treblinka. Frank approved of the murder of the Jews, objecting to their settlement in the General Government. In December 1941 he declared, 'Gentlemen, I must ask you to arm yourselves against all feelings of pity. We must destroy the Jews wherever we meet them wherever possible.'

The majority of the Polish people were expected to survive so long as they served their German masters and lost all national consciousness. What the Nazis had in store for the Jews was so incredible that, even when the facts leaked out, most of the Jews still surviving in German-occupied Europe could not believe it, nor was the horror fully grasped abroad. Indeed the hell the Nazis created in the death camps of the East, like hell itself, is so far removed from human experience as to be scarcely real and credible. The Holocaust forms one of the most difficult aspects of modern history to explain and understand.

Hitler's ultimate intention about the fate of the Jews before 1941 remains a subject of intense historical debate. From all the available evidence, however, some definite conclusions are possible. In conditions of peace, that is before the outbreak of war in 1939, he could not order the mass murder of German, Austrian and Czech Jews within Germany. If the German sphere was to be made *Judenrein*, free of Jews, their forced emigration was the only option. For Hitler, the Jews had another possible value; they could be used to blackmail the West. He believed National Socialist propaganda that behind the scenes the Jews were influential in pulling the strings of policy in Washington, London and Paris. His aim was to conquer continental Europe piecemeal. The next target was Poland. In January 1939 he therefore threatened in his well-known Reichstag speech that the Jews would perish if Britain, France and the United States resisted his aggression on the continent by unleashing a general war.

Until Germany attacked the Soviet Union in June 1941, there seemed to be a small chance of a Western peace. Jews in Germany and conquered Europe were still allowed to live. Hitler liked to keep options open: alternative solutions to isolate the Jews and drive them out of Europe altogether were considered, such as the plan to banish them to Madagascar. That from the start he had no moral inhibition against mass murder, if that should prove the best course, cannot be doubted. During the summer and autumn of 1941, millions of 'Bolshevik Jews', the mortal enemy in his eyes, were added to the millions of European Jews already under German control, and mass emigration or expulsion overseas was no longer a possibility. Nor, with so much non-Jewish slave labour falling into German hands, Hitler calculated, would Jewish slave labour be needed. The option of mass murder as the final solution now became the most desired and practical course.

As Hitler's own pep talks to the generals during the spring of 1941 show, on the eve of the attack on Russia, the 'racial' war was now being openly launched. That spelt doom for the Jews, the race which Hitler hated and saw as a pestilence in human society. He could now repeat his Reichstag speech of January 1939, this time as a justification to the German people for the destruction of Jewry. In the light of this analysis Nazi policies can be seen to have followed a path that had inevitably to end in genocide.

By every means available the Nazis attempted before 1939 to 'clear' Germany of Jews by forcing them to emigrate. The Germans were not alone in following such policies. The Poles, too, before the war hoped to 'solve' their Jewish problem by promoting forced emigration of the Polish Jews. Anti-Semitism was virulent all over Europe and in the United States. But discrimination was not a part of government policy in any Western country, offending as it does against basic civil rights and freedoms. Entry of Jews to settle outside Germany was restricted. Unemployment was everywhere high so any increase of labour was not welcomed, especially if caused by immigrants deprived of their money and possessions. Nevertheless, can guilt be turned away from Nazi Germany by blaming her neighbours for not enabling more Jews to leave Germany before their later destruction? It is true that Western governments were preoccupied with their own problems during the depression years. And it always has to be remembered that before 1942 no government in the West could conceive what 'Final Solution' lay in store for the Jews on the German-dominated continent.

Britain, holding the League Mandate for Palestine and having promised the Jews a National Home there (page 130), had a special responsibility to aid the Jews. Until German persecution became more severe, the majority of German Jews, however, did not wish to emigrate to Palestine. When they desperately sought to leave Germany after November 1938 and would have gladly escaped to Palestine, the British government was more concerned to safeguard its vital strategic interests in the Middle East. Palestine had become a cauldron of conflict between Arab and Jew and the British occupiers. In Arab eyes both the Jews and the British authorities were European colonisers of Arab lands. The Arabs, moreover, could see that the increased Jewish immigration had its roots in European anti-Semitism, which strengthened Zionism. British governments tried to extricate themselves from these conflicting interests without satisfying either the Zionists or the Arabs. Finally, in May 1939 the British government took the decision that the Arabs would have to be appeased by promising to limit Jewish immigration to 75,000 over the next five years and, after that, the government promised the Arabs that further immigration would be subject to the consent of the Arab majority.

Public opinion and voluntary organisations before 1939 gave the efforts to rescue the Jews a dynamism which governments lacked. Germany's European neighbours, and the United States and Latin America, accepted German and Austrian Jews in tens of thousands. Although the Nazis were ready at first to expedite their exit even after the war broke out, the exodus was slowed down to a trickle by the war. In all, more than half the German Jews, some 280,000, succeeded in finding refuge between 1933 and 1939, many, however, only temporarily as Hitler overran the continent. The Jews so saved came from Germany and from the countries – Austria and Czechoslovakia – occupied by Hitler before the outbreak of war in 1939. They represented only a very small proportion of Europe's total Jewish population.

In Poland in 1940 many Polish Jews were killed wantonly, and the whole Jewish population was herded into ghettos, as in the Middle Ages, by fencing off or building a wall around a part of a city and leaving the Jews to fend for themselves. The two largest were in Warsaw and Lodz. In the ghettos the Germans could secure what was practically slave labour to supply the German armies. Undernourished and overcrowded, the ghetto population was decimated by disease and exhaustion. The planned massacre designed to kill every last Jew was begun on the day, 22 June 1941, when the German armies invaded the Soviet Union. These terrible killings of men, women and children in Russia, machine-gunned next to the open graves they had been forced to dig, had been deliberately worked out beforehand. It is not conceivable that they were undertaken without Hitler's knowledge. Hitler's full brutality is revealed by the record of a Führer Conference held at his headquarters on 16 July 1941 in which he spoke of his aims and referred to Russian orders to start partisan warfare behind the German front. Hitler saw in this order 'some advantages for us; it enables us to exterminate everyone who opposes us'. The actual task for the open-air killings was assigned to special SS detachments, the *Einsatzgruppen*. The German army, too, became heavily implicated in the mass murder. Nazi ideology had come to be widely accepted by ordinary people. Hitler and a small leadership group could not have committed such crimes without thousands of active helpers and an uncaring attitude to the victims by many more even where it was not actually hostile. The Final Solution in the Soviet Union avoided all need for transport and special camps or ghettos.

In Poland, the Jews were not perishing fast enough. Then the destruction had to be planned of the Jews remaining in German-occupied Europe, and of the Jews living in the countries of Germany's allies. After discussions among the Nazi leaders an order to Heydrich, a subordinate of Himmler, was issued by Göring on 31 July 1941 to draw up plans for the destruction – the so-called Final Solution – of non-Russian Jewry on a systematic basis. In accordance with these instructions Heydrich called the notorious conference on 20 January 1942 of senior administrators from the various Reich ministries who would be involved and which took its name from Wannsee, a favourite picnic area just outside Berlin where they met. It was assumed that the Jews in the rest of Europe could not be massacred as in Russia. Though there were several concentration camps in Germany herself, these could kill only tens of thousands, not millions! The greatest concentration of Jews was already in Poland, so to Poland and the East the Jews were to be transported: 'Europe will be combed from west to east.' What 'resettlement' really meant was clear from the record of the conference: 'the Jews capable of work will be led into these areas in large labour columns to build roads, whereby doubtless a large part will fall away through natural reduction

... The inevitable remainder will have to be dealt with appropriately, since it represents a natural selection which upon liberation is to be regarded as a germ cell of a new Jewish development.'

No one present could doubt that what was being planned was indeed mass murder. Adolf Eichmann of the SS, who was present and was one of the principal organisers of the Holocaust, later testified that the atmosphere was one of general agreement; no one raised difficulties or moral objections. The eastern ghettos now became transit stations as the plans were implemented. The construction of the Auschwitz extermination camp had already begun before the Wannsee Conference. Others followed, among them Chelmo, Belzec, Sobibor, Treblinka. These camps of mass murder were specifically equipped to kill thousands *every day*, generally in large gas chambers. The 'selection' of those to be murdered as unfit to work was done on arrival from the rail transports arriving straight at the camps; the remainder, a smaller number and never the old, the sick or children, were allowed to survive some weeks longer. There were only very few long-term survivors.

Mass murder was so huge in extent that historians cannot tell for certain even to the *nearest million* how many people perished. Despite the virtual hopelessness of their situation in some ghettos and camps, a few Jews did resist, and with such weapons as could be smuggled in fought against German troops, thus at least selling their lives dearly. The whole world learnt of the Jewish rising of the Warsaw ghetto in April and May 1943 and its destruction. Less well known were risings in a number of extermination camps, in Treblinka in August 1943 and Sobibor in October of the same year, for instance. A few thousand more Jews were able to escape into the forests in Poland and the Ukraine, and operated as partisan units. They were not always welcome, and they were sometimes killed by their compatriots as well as by the Germans. Before the war was over, between 5 and 6 million Jews had been murdered. Nazi ideology was so widespread that it is unrealistic to limit responsibility for these crimes to Hitler and his henchmen. While Germans, soldiers, the SS and officials were overwhelmingly responsible, they were aided in their work of destruction by some sections of the conquered peoples of Europe in every country.

In Germany knowledge was widespread, brought home by soldiers and SS on leave from the East.

*Survivors of the Warsaw Ghetto Rising of April 1943 are chaperoned by the Wehrmacht out of the city to be killed soon after.*

How much the Germans were actually told can be seen from an article written by Goebbels and published in the 'respectable' weekly journal *Das Reich* on 16 November 1941. That world Jewry started the war, he wrote, was proven beyond dispute:

> The Jews wanted their war, and now they have it. What is now coming true is the Führer's prophecy of 30 January 1939, in his speech to the Reichstag, when he said that if international Finance Jewry once more succeeded in driving the peoples into a world war, the result would not be the bolshevising of the world and thereby the victory of the Jews, but the destruction of the Jewish race in Europe. We are now witnessing the fulfilment of that prophecy, and a destiny is being realised which is harsh but more than deserved. Feelings of sympathy or pity are entirely inappropriate ... [Jewry] according to its law, 'an eye for an eye, a tooth for a tooth', is now perishing.

The demand of the German authorities that all Jews be handed over for the terrible Final Solution being prepared for them was one of the deepest moral challenges faced by occupied Europe and Germany's allies during the Second World War. There was not one response that was uniquely French, Polish, Dutch or Hungarian. The response was multi-faceted. There was the 'official' collaboration of governments – and even this was not uniform – and then there was the response of institutions, the Churches above all, and of ordinary people. In every corner of Europe there were some individuals who risked their lives to shelter Jews. Otherwise, the Jews who survived in Germany were mainly those in mixed Jewish–Christian marriages. They too were on the list for murder but they came last in the plan for the Final Solution and the war was over before they could be exterminated as well. Several hundred Jews were hidden from humanitarian motives or managed with forged papers to pass themselves off as Aryan. The Christians who protected Jews in Germany were heroic, their number pitifully small – far fewer than in Poland or other occupied countries. In Germany the opportunities for the non-privileged Jews (those not married to Christian spouses with offspring) to survive were so slight as to be negligible in practice.

Poles and Jews had lived for centuries together, but in separate communities. Even in 1931, most of the 3 million Jews in Poland were largely unassimilated, although those who were assimilated were well represented in the professions and the middle class. Under the Nazi occupation anti-Semitism was reinforced by propaganda, but there were Poles who, though they did not like Jews, helped them because they hated the Germans more. There were also Poles who actively assisted the Germans to round up Jews. Several thousand Poles, however, out of feelings of pity, hid Jews at great risk to themselves, for the penalty was death. It has been estimated that between 50,000 and 100,000 Polish Jews survived, some fighting as partisans or with the Red Army. In Warsaw 15,000 found hiding places, many more than in Berlin. Had more Germans made efforts to protect the Jews, Hitler would have found it far more difficult to carry out the Holocaust.

In the Netherlands, Belgium, France and, above all, Italy the Jews stood a better chance of survival. Many Jews were hidden in homes, in monasteries and in villages. Official Vichy France, however, gave some aid to the Germans in rounding up the Jews, including French citizens of Jewish faith, for transportation to the death camps in the East. Uniquely, all but 500 of about 7000 Jews living in Denmark were rescued by the Danish resistance by being ferried across to Sweden. The Danish resistance had been alerted to their imminent deportation by Dr Duckwitz, a courageous German official in Copenhagen who had learnt of their intended fate from a leak passed on by someone in the Gestapo. The fate of the Danish Jews who did not escape was extraordinary. The Nazi rulers in Berlin maintained the fiction that Denmark had remained a sovereign country and the Danes were therefore permitted to continue to protect all Danish citizens, including Danish Jews. The 500 Danish Jews were deported to the privileged ghetto of Theresienstadt, where they were housed separately in much better conditions than the other Jews. They remained in contact with the Danish authorities, who insisted on providing for them to the end of the war. None was transported to the extermination camps further east and almost all of them survived and returned to Denmark after the liberation. They were the fortunate exception. Dr Duckwitz also survived and is honoured as 'one of the righteous' at Yad Vashem, the Holocaust Memorial in Jerusalem.

Germany's ally, Italy, on the other hand, in practice protected Jews despite Mussolini's anti-Jewish legislation. Until Italy's capitulation and the consequent German occupation, the Italian military authorities in their Croatian zone and in the Italian zone of France prevented both German troops and police from arresting Jews for transportation east or murder by the Croatian Ustachi on the spot. The Italian army would have nothing to do with the brutal mass murder of the Jews being instigated by the Germans and their 'allies' and either sabotaged orders or simply refused to carry them out. Feelings of humanity and decency were not extinct.

In occupied Europe local police could be found to do the dirty work of the Germans for them. In some cases they would have been shot had they disobeyed. In others the work was done with enthusiasm. The public silence of the Pope and the Vatican and of the *German* Protestant Churches signifies a massive moral failure. In contrast, in Holland Catholic churches and many Protestant churches read protests from the pulpit after the first Dutch transport of Jews. Priests and pastors, wherever Germany held power, suffered martyrdom for their personal protest. Bishop Galen of Münster publicly condemned the murder of some 60,000 to 80,000 feeble-minded and incurably ill Germans in the so-called 'euthanasia' programme: Hitler feared that the people's war effort might be undermined by an open onslaught on religious beliefs. A strong public movement by the *German* Churches and military might also, therefore, have saved countless Jewish lives. Hitler and his regime were sensitive to, and watched, the reactions of the German people. There was no such public movement as, for instance, in the Netherlands.

The importance and nature of resistance to the Nazis within Germany herself and in Nazi-dominated Europe varied enormously. Conspiratorial by necessity, it came into the open in acts of violent sabotage and several attempts on Hitler's life, the most spectacular – the 20 July 1944 plot – almost succeeding when an explosive charge went off a few feet from Hitler at his headquarters in East Prussia. The composition of the resistance ranged from members of the pre-Nazi Weimar political parties to individuals moved by moral considerations. Thus in Munich a small group of students and teachers who called themselves the White Rose distributed, until they were caught and executed, thousands of leaflets condemning the barbarities of the Nazis. But the only resistance that had the power actually to remove Hitler came from within the army and culminated in the bomb plot of 20 July 1944. The officers involved saw clearly that the war was lost and hoped by removing Hitler to be able to make peace with the Western allies while keeping the Russians out of Germany. Others were less materialistically motivated. Had Hitler been killed, the plot might have succeeded, though Britain and America would certainly have refused to make peace on any terms other than unconditional surrender.

Successful armed resistance, tying down considerable numbers of German troops, was carried out by Tito's partisans in Yugoslavia. And in France,

## Holocaust Victims and Survivors

|  | Victims | Survivors (after 1939) |
|---|---|---|
| Germany | 165,000 | 20,000 |
| (Austria) | 65,000 | 6,000 |
| France | 76,000 | 230,000 |
| Belgium | 28,500 | 36,000 |
| Netherlands | 102,000 | 38,000 |
| Denmark | 116 | 7,380 |
| Norway | 760 | 1,000 |
| Italy | 6,500 | 29,500 |
| Greece | 59,000 | 12,700 |
| Poland pre 1939 frontier | 2,700,000 | |
| post 1939 frontier | 1,600,000 | 50,000 |
| Soviet Union pre 1939 frontier | 1,000,000 | |
| post 1939 frontier | 2,100,000 | |
| Czechoslovakia 1937 frontier | 260,000 | 40,000 |
| (Slovakia) | 65,000 | 20,000 |
| Romania | 211,200 | 381,200 |
| Bulgaria | 11,000 | 50,000 |
| Yugoslavia | 65,000 | 14,500 |
| Hungary | 550,000 | 290,000 |

These approximate statistics of the Holocaust have been calculated primarily on the basis of *Dimension des Völkermords*, editor W. Benz (Munich 1991).

while Pétain and the Vichy regime enjoyed overwhelming support, a sizeable minority joined the French resistance, undertaking sabotage and supplying a 'secret army' which returned aircrew shot down in France and Belgium on an escape route back to England by way of neutral Spain. In the East, Russian partisans acted as auxiliaries of the Red Army and interrupted the supply routes of the Wehrmacht. But in occupied Europe there was not one simple struggle against Nazi Germany. Among the resistance fighters themselves there was conflict after the communists joined the resistance after Hitler's invasion of the Soviet Union in June 1941.

The struggle in Yugoslavia between the royalist Colonel Mihailović and the communist leader, Tito, led to civil war between them as well as war against the Germans. In Poland, the Home Army was as bitterly opposed to the Polish communist partisans as to the common German enemy. Here Stalin had the last word. The Polish government in exile in London and the Home Army, which took its orders from London, attempted to frustrate or at least impede Stalin's plans to bring Poland under communist control. In August 1944, as the Red Army reached the River Vistula, the Home Army began to rise in Warsaw against the Germans. Their intention was to prove to the world that Poles, not the Russians, had liberated the Polish capital. The Poles seized half the city and fought bitterly for two months until their capitulation to the Germans on 2 October. Warsaw was entirely destroyed. Soviet help was cynically withheld by Stalin. Only during the last stages were Russian supplies dropped; they could only prolong the doomed struggle, resulting in the deaths of still more Polish Home Army fighters holding out in the sewers of the city. The Soviet command had even prevented Polish units fighting with the Red Army from battling their way to the city. Soviet airfields were closed to relief flights from the West. Surrender terms were finally agreed by the Home Army with the Germans on 2 October 1944 and three days later General Bor-Komorowski, with the exhausted remnants of the fighters, gave up the struggle. Surprisingly the Home Army were well treated as prisoners of war probably in order to increase hatred between the Poles and the Russians.

During the early stages of the rising auxiliary SS units committed terrible atrocities against the civilian population, until regulars were brought in to crush resistance. The total (mainly civilian) casualties in Warsaw reached about 200,000. The Germans lost some 2000 killed and 9000 wounded. Polish military casualties were far higher: 17,000 killed or missing and 9000 wounded. Politically and militarily the anti-communist Polish underground had been destroyed, leaving a vacuum which Stalin was able to fill with communists ready to follow Soviet orders. The Warsaw rising marked one more milestone in the tragedy of Poland and signalled to the rest of the world the ruthlessness of which Stalin was capable in furtherance of the Soviet Union's post-war plans.

In the West this conflict between the communist and anti-communist resistance did not flare into civil war but a similar pattern emerges. As the defeat of Nazi Germany drew close, the resistance was as concerned with questions of post-war political power as with fighting the Germans. The Nazi answer to all resistance from whatever quarter was terror.

Houses were burnt to the ground in reprisals and people not involved in the resistance were killed wholesale. The destruction of the village of Oradour-sur-Glane in France and of Lidice in Czechoslovakia, and the massacres which took place there, are among the best known of such barbarities. But these were just two of the thousands of atrocities that became a common occurrence in German-occupied Europe. The terrible reprisals taken by the German occupiers raise the question whether the Allies should have actively encouraged resistance and parachuted agents into the occupied countries, many of whom lost their lives. Was the sabotage to the German war effort sufficiently great to justify this policy? It is impossible to balance such an equation, or to estimate the importance of maintaining morale on the continent, of sustaining belief that Hitler's Germany would be beaten. All over Europe, from northern Italy to Norway, large German forces were tied down. The Nazi New Order could not be imposed anywhere unchallenged, and the German forces could not relax their vigilance amid populations of which significant sections were hostile. Even though the active resistance was a minority, it made an impact out of proportion to its numbers.

The Japanese had been at war since 1937. They sought to justify their wars of expansion at home and abroad both as self-defence and as fulfilling a mission of liberating Asia from Western imperialism. In its place Japan would build a Greater East Asia Co-Prosperity Sphere. The Japanese, to emphasise the solidarity of eastern Asia against the West, chose to call the war they had launched the Greater East Asian War. The real intentions of the Japanese leaders can be deduced from the decisions taken at secret conferences in Tokyo rather than from the rhetoric of their propaganda. First consideration in all the conquered regions was to be given to military needs. Local economies were to be strictly controlled and independence movements discouraged. No industry was to be developed in the southern region, which was to become the empire's source of raw materials and a market for her goods. The Japanese saw themselves as the superior people who possessed the right to subordinate and exploit the conquered peoples. Everywhere propaganda and indoctrination sought to reinforce the superiority of everything Japanese. For the indigenous peoples, foreign Western rule was replaced by more brutal foreign Japanese rule. Japanese colonialism had taken the place of Western imperialism. The 'natives' were regarded as inferiors.

Even before the war had been launched a secret conference in Tokyo on 20 November 1941 settled the general principle of Japanese occupations. Local administrations were to be utilised as far as possible, but each territory was placed under military government and subordinated to Japan's needs. The Japanese government never worked out any really coherent plan for the future of eastern Asia. Some territories of particular strategic importance such as Malaya would remain under direct Japanese control; others, the Philippines and Burma, were promised eventual 'independence' but only if they became co-operative satellite states. Japanese attempts to win over the mass of Asian peoples to support the war against their former colonial masters was almost totally a failure. The great majority of the ordinary people did not see the conflict as *their* war. Equally, there was little active support for the departed Westerners against the Japanese, except in the Philippines. In Burma, and especially in the Philippines, sections of the population became vehemently anti-Japanese. But on the whole the peoples saw themselves as suffering from a war between two foreign masters struggling for ultimate control over them. In India, as has been seen, the political leaders sought to make use of the situation to promote genuine independence.

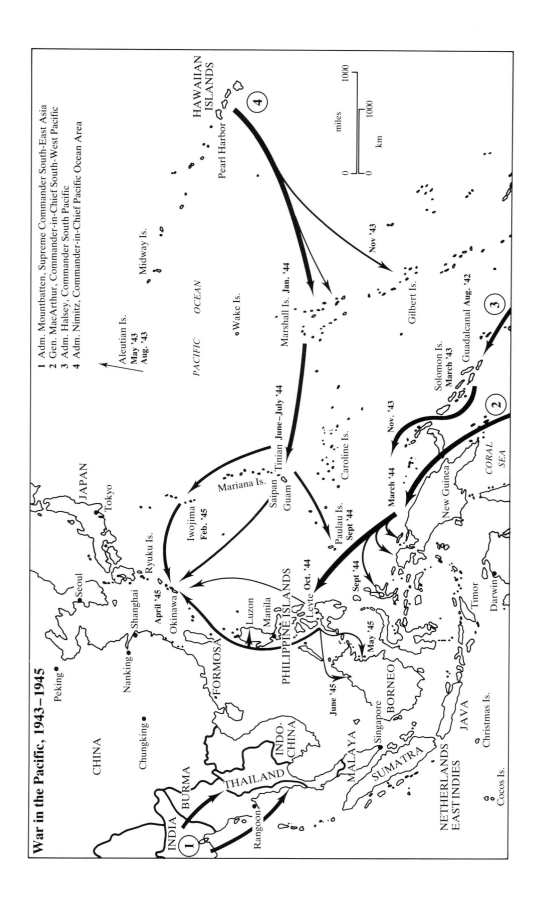

# War in the Pacific, 1943–1945

1 Adm. Mountbatten, Supreme Commander South-East Asia
2 Gen. MacArthur, Commander-in-Chief South-West Pacific
3 Adm. Halsey, Commander South Pacific
4 Adm. Nimitz, Commander-in-Chief Pacific Ocean Area

HAWAIIAN ISLANDS

Pearl Harbor

PACIFIC OCEAN

Midway Is.

Wake Is.

Gilbert Is.

Nov. '43

Aleutian Is.
May '43
Aug. '43

Marshall Is. Jan. '44

Guadalcanal Aug. '42

Solomon Is.
March '43

Nov. '43

JAPAN

Tokyo

Seoul

Shanghai

Nanking

Peking

Chungking

CHINA

Ryuku Is.

April '45

Okinawa

Iwojima
Feb. '45

Mariana Is.

Saipan
Guam

Tinian June–July '44

Caroline Is.

Paulau Is.
Sept '44

March '44

New Guinea

CORAL SEA

FORMOSA

Luzon
Manila

PHILIPPINE ISLANDS

Leyte Oct. '44

Sept '44

Timor

Darwin

INDIA

BURMA

THAILAND

Rangoon

INDO-CHINA

MALAYA

Singapore

SUMATRA

BORNEO

JAVA

NETHERLANDS
EAST INDIES

Christmas Is.

Cocos Is.

May '45

June '45

1000

miles

1000

km

0

0

Of all the peoples under Japanese rule, the Chinese suffered the most – both in China and wherever Chinese communities had settled in south-eastern Asia. In Singapore after her fall, there was a terrible bloodbath of Chinese and at least 5000 were massacred. Japanese barbarities against the Chinese population, which constituted about a third of the total population of Malaya, drove them into armed resistance. Japanese terror tactics thus proved counter-productive. But though undeniably harsh, and though atrocities were committed, the Japanese did not emulate their German allies in resorting to an irrational and carefully planned and executed policy of extermination of whole peoples. With the Japanese as masters instead of the Europeans, local administrations continued to function smoothly, with the indigenous junior administrators carrying out the orders of their new masters. With the need to fight the war, the Japanese left the social order intact and tried to preserve the *status quo*. To win over the population and channel nationalist feelings, they set up Japanese-controlled mass movements. The constant emphasis on Japanese superiority, however, alienated the local populations.

Some nationalist leaders because of their great popularity, like Sukarno in Indonesia, were able to gain a degree of genuine independence in return for promising to rally the people to co-operate with the Japanese war effort. More concessions were promised to the Burmese and Filipinos in 1943 as the war began to go badly for the Japanese. In August 1943 Burma was proclaimed independent, but in alliance with Japan and at war with the Allies. In October the Japanese sponsored an independent Philippine republic and in the same month Bose proclaimed a provisional Indian government in exile. In mainland China puppet governments had been set up from the first; Manchuria had been transformed into Manchukuo in 1932 with its own emperor Pu-yi; another Japanese-controlled government of China was set up in Nanking in 1938. But plunder, rape and massacre were routinely perpetrated by the Japanese troops in China. Despite a veneer of local autonomy in some regions under Japanese occupation, the reality of the co-prosperity sphere was not liberation but Japanese domination and imperial exploitation.

In 1942 the Japanese had won large territories in Asia at small cost. The Americans prepared their counter-offensive across the Pacific, straight at the Japanese heartland. This is how Japan was defeated while her armies still occupied the greater part of what had been conquered at the outset of the war. The fall of the Japanese-held island of Saipan, in July 1944, placed American bombers within range of Tokyo. The Americans hoped to bomb the Japanese into submission. The massive indiscriminate raids brought huge destruction on the flimsily constructed Japanese houses. On 10 March 1945 one of the most devastating air raids of the whole war was launched against Tokyo. The fire storm created destroyed close on half the city and caused 125,000 casualties. In May and June 1945 the bomber offensive spread to sixty other major towns throughout Japan.

On 6 August 1945, for the first time, a new weapon was used, the atom bomb that devastated Hiroshima. The destruction and suffering were appalling. Most of the city was destroyed and more than 70,000 people were killed immediately. About the same number were to succumb to a new man-made illness, radiation sickness. For decades the atom bomb claimed victims from among the survivors. The casualties from the spring raid on Tokyo by fleets of Super-Flying Fortresses were greater, but what filled the whole world with awe and horror was that a single plane dropping just one bomb from out of the blue sky could produce such suffering and destruction. A second bomb was dropped on Nagasaki three days later, again causing great loss of life. In the face of such a war the Japanese surrendered.

The Second World War was waged simultaneously in Asia, Europe and North Africa by huge armed forces on all sides, backed by tanks and aircraft in numbers hitherto unknown and, in its closing stages, with a new weapon releasing the devastating power of nuclear fission. The destruction and maiming on a global scale consequently exceeded anything known before. The war caused not only many millions of dead and wounded, but also inflicted on millions more forcible population migrations and wholesale destruction of towns and villages – a sum total of virtually unimaginable human misery.

As the tide of the war turned, the German people increasingly suffered the ravages of war. The losses on the eastern front alone matched the bloodbath of the First World War on all fronts. The great majority of the German war dead died fighting

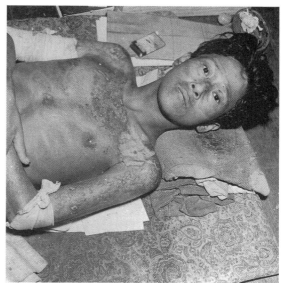

On 9 August 1945, the mushroom cloud rose 60,000 feet into the sky (left). Below lay Nagasaki. Once the cloud cleared, little was left intact in the city save the Catholic Cathedral (below). *The lucky people were those who were killed outright. Makeshift shelters housed the survivors* (right), *but medics were flummoxed by new injuries and new diseases like 'radiation sickness', which claimed many more lives in the years to come, and afflicted the unborn.*

in Russia. The Bomber Commands of the Allies inflicted terrible devastation as city after city was laid waste during the last months of the war. Above all else, the German people feared the Russians, bent on revenge for the German invaders' actions in Russia. Ethnic Germans and German colonisers fled from the advancing Russian armies, retreating into Germany. The Sudeten Germans, who had lived in Czechoslovakia before 1938, were driven out. Most of the Germans living in Polish-occupied eastern German regions from East Prussia to Silesia – assigned to the Poles for administration in compensation for territorial losses to the Soviet Union – were driven out or fled in terror from the Poles and Russians. 'Orderly and humane' population transfers were sanctioned by the Allied Potsdam Conference in the summer of 1945. But the mass exodus of 15 million people immediately after the war was certainly not orderly and was frequently inhumane. Pent-up hatreds against the Germans burst out and were vented not only on the guilty supporters of Hitler's regime but also, indiscriminately, on tens of thousands of innocent people, on children and the sick. The exodus from Eastern and central Europe began during the last months of the war and continued after the war was over. Although relatively few were deliberately murdered, in all as many as 2 million Germans are estimated to have died as a result of the privations they suffered.

Mere statistics cannot convey the tragedies which befell almost every family in Europe. The Soviet Union suffered the most: at least 20 million military and civilian people died – a staggering figure. Germany's dead numbered between 4.5 and 5 million. Proportionately to their population, the Jews suffered the most; only a minority of those in Europe at the outbreak of the war survived to its end. For Britain, France and Italy, however, the Second World War casualties did not repeat the bloodbath of the First World War. British military and civilian deaths totalled 450,000, to which must be added those of the empire: 120,000. The French figures are approximately 450,000 dead; the Italians lost 410,000 dead. Yugoslav, Hungarian, Polish and Romanian losses were heavy. In central Europe, the Poles suffered far more even than their neighbours. American deaths on the European and Pacific fronts were 290,000. No one knows how many million Chinese died in the war; the figure may well be in excess of 10 million; about 2 million Japanese are estimated to have lost their lives in the war. The physical destruction has largely been made good in the years since the war. But the loss of lives will continue to be mourned as long as the generations that experienced the war are still alive. The ordeal of the Second World War also serves a lasting warning to future generations of what national aggression and the intolerance of peoples can lead to.

# CHAPTER 29

# The Victory of the Allies, 1941–1945

The war that began in September 1939 has been called the European War, in contrast to the World War that ensued when the Soviet Union, the United States and Japan became involved in 1941. Militarily there is an obvious reason for seeing 1941 as a dividing line. In Asia, the China War being waged since 1937 was a separate conflict until it was widened into the Pacific War by Japan's attack on Pearl Harbor. In Europe Hitler's invasion of the Soviet Union marks a turning point in the course of the war. But in a deeper sense the global implications of Hitler's attack on Poland in 1939 were there from the beginning. Long before Germany declared war on the United States, the USA was throwing her support behind Britain and actually engaging in warfare in the battle of the Atlantic. Then Nazi–Soviet 'friendship', affirmed in August 1939, was clearly nothing but a temporary expedient. Hitler did not abandon his goal of winning living-space in the East and conquering 'Jewish-Bolshevism'. The outcome of the war between Germany and Russia would decide whether the Soviet Union or Germany would emerge as a superpower in the second half of the twentieth century.

In 1940 and 1941 Britain on her own was incapable of inflicting serious damage on Germany. Was her survival as a belligerent therefore of much importance? Without the war in the East, it is difficult to imagine how Britain could have launched even a destructive bomber offensive against Germany. Not only was much of the German air force fighting the Russians, but had the war against Russia not continued, and so frustrated his plans, Hitler would have diminished the size of his victorious continental army and transferred the main German war effort to building up an air force which in sheer size alone would probably have overwhelmed the Royal Air Force. Hitler was never able to realise this plan as Germany's war resources continued to be fully stretched in holding the eastern front. Britain was the only Western European democracy left in 1940. Her refusal to accept the apparent logic of the military situation saved post-war Western Europe from suffering the fate either of continued German overlordship or of a future under Stalin's Red Army if, as seems more probable, the Soviet Union had won the war. Instead democratic Britain provided the link, and later the base, for an Anglo-American counter-offensive in Western Europe that created the conditions for recovery free from the totalitarian control of the left or the right. Without Britain still fighting from 1940 to 1941, the likelihood of an American involvement in the European theatre of the war was remote.

The powers victorious in the Second World War recognised that they would be faced with world problems and worldwide confrontations after the war was over. The future of the millions who were largely tacit observers of the war, the subjects of the colonial European empires, or under Japanese rule, would be dependent on its outcome. A new world was in the making and its history would have been different had Germany and Japan instead of the Soviet Union and the United States emerged as the post-war superpowers.

The size and destructive capability of the armies which fought on each side during the Second World War exceeded even those of the Great War of 1914–18. Behind the fighting fronts, the industrial war was waged, pouring out guns, tanks, aircraft and ships. One of the most intriguing aspects of the war was that of spies and of science. Secrecy about the espionage war has only partially been lifted. Much may never be known. Generalisations are therefore particularly hazardous. It does appear, however, that despite spectacular coups, the achievement of the spies in affecting the course of the war was less than might have been expected. The decision-makers could never be certain whether in the world of deceit and intrigue in which the various espionage networks operated the information obtained was real or planted. The success of espionage and counter-espionage meant that they tended to cancel each other out. One of the best-known illustrations of this was the failure of Richard Sorge, the master spy working for the Russians in Tokyo, to convince Moscow that his information from the German Embassy of Hitler's intentions and the timing of the invasion of the Soviet Union was true. On the Allied side a more demonstrable espionage success, was the breaking of the German code machine Enigma, used by Germany's armed forces. The Poles had built a replica and just before the start of the war passed its secret to the British, who continued the deciphering work at Bletchley Park. The Germans never suspected that their codes were not totally secure. The ability to read these codes contributed to the Allied capacity to meet the German onslaughts in the air, on the sea and on land.

There can be no uncertainty about the advantage the Allies derived from their successful application of science to warfare. Radar was in use early in the war in both Germany and Britain; Germany was probably ahead in its development at the outset of the war. But during 1940–1 small airborne radar sets were produced in Britain which allowed night fighters to defend cities during the Blitz. Airborne radar also became an indispensable adjunct to the Allied bomber offensive, enabling the bombers to pinpoint their targets at night. At sea, advanced types of radar gave the Allies a decisive advantage against German submarines in the spring of 1943 and helped to turn the tide of battle in their favour.

But the scientific breakthrough that did most to shape the future was the atomic bomb; the decision at the end of the war to use this weapon brought about the rapid Japanese surrender.

Allied scientists from many nations, British, American, French, Danish, Italian and German too (for German refugees played a crucial role), made the construction of a nuclear bomb possible. It was eventually in the United States that science was matched by the technical know-how and the immense production facilities necessary for its manufacture were provided. First tested in the empty spaces of the New Mexican desert, the bomb was dropped just three weeks later in August 1945 over Hiroshima.

An early indication of Allied suspicions about the likely post-war attitude of the Soviet Union can be seen in the decision not to share the secrets of nuclear development with the USSR. Indeed, despite an agreement with Britain, the United States sought to retain a monopoly on the manufacture of these awesome weapons. The Soviets were well aware they would need to develop their own atomic bomb and in 1942, despite the immediate German threat, pressed ahead vigorously with their own research. The Danish atomic scientist Niels Bohr advised Roosevelt that the Russians would succeed in building their own bomb some time after the Americans did so. Would it not be better to share secrets with them and to work for international control? The Russians made their own bomb in 1949. The atom spy Klaus Fuchs had provided some help but the Russians could eventually have built their own bomb in any case. It seems unlikely that the course of Stalin's policy would have differed much even if the Americans had passed on the atomic secrets. German atomic research – despite the eminence of some of the scientists ready to work for the Nazis – lagged behind. Hitler, according to Armaments Minister Albert Speer, was not prepared to earmark the vast resources necessary to make the bomb, regarding nuclear physics as 'Jewish physics'. Instead the Germans did devote great resources to the development of new rockets, which by themselves could have no decisive effect on the war. The outcome was the pilotless plane, the V-1, and the advanced supersonic rocket, the V-2, against which there was no defence when it came into use in 1944. But the later combination of Allied and German science, the new delivery system and new explosive force – in other words, rocket technology and nuclear weapons – led to our present-day nuclear-missile age.

In the summer of 1940 it was difficult to see how Germany's victorious armies would ever be defeated. But by attacking the Soviet Union in June 1941 and then declaring war that December on the United States the balance *potentially* swung against Germany. Allied superiority was only potential in the sense that it depended on Britain and Russia not being defeated. The United States would make her military weight felt in Europe only in 1943 and 1944.

For Britain the danger of invasion finally passed in 1941. With Germany fully engaged in the East, there remained no possibility of her mounting an invasion of the British Isles as well. But this did not mean that there was no longer any danger that Britain might be forced to submit. She remained beleaguered, dependent for longer-term survival on supplies reaching her from overseas, above all from the United States. Her own resources, great though they were when fully mobilised, were not sufficient both to sustain the war effort and to feed all the people. For Britain's success in mobilising her material and human resources much credit must go to Ernest Bevin, a leading trade unionist who had entered Churchill's national government as minister of labour in 1940. The British people accepted an unprecedented degree of direction of labour and of rationing. Even so, supplies from overseas became increasingly essential. Lend–Lease made possible the purchase of war supplies in the United States without payment of cash. But they still had to reach Britain.

The conflict at sea, the battle of the Atlantic, was therefore as vital to Britain as the land battles had been to France in 1940. The acute shortage of shipping and the sinkings by German U-boats made 1941 and 1942 the years when Britain survived by the narrowest margin. Before Pearl Harbor on 7 December 1941, Hitler had given orders that American vessels supplying Britain and their escorting US warships were not to be attacked. His hands had been tied. After Pearl Harbor he welcomed the outbreak of war between Japan and the US, and declared war on the Americans himself, removing the restrictions on the U-boat war in the Atlantic. Now, he thought, Britain would be forced to her knees. In November 1942 U-boats sank 729,000 tons, and for the year as a whole almost

8 million tons or 1664 ships. These losses were inflicted by about 200 submarines and could no longer be made good. New methods of defence, including the use of radar during the winter of 1942/3 gradually mastered the menace, though losses remained heavy. The submarine was the greatest threat. Germany's surface fleet was not sufficiently strong to challenge Britain's supremacy. Hitler's battleships were eliminated after some spectacular engagements. The *Graf Spee* sank in 1939, the *Bismarck* in 1941 and the powerful *Tirpitz* by air attack in 1944. Supplies were carried across the Atlantic by convoys. By far the most hazardous route for these merchant vessels was from Scotland and Iceland to Murmansk to aid Russia. But by the end of 1943 not only had the Germans lost the battle of the seas, they had also sustained defeats on land from which there would be no recovery. The darkest years of the war were over for Britain. Churchill's contribution to maintaining British morale would be difficult to overestimate.

Britain's warfare with Italy and Germany on land in 1941 and 1942, judged by the numbers of men engaged, was secondary when compared with the millions of German and Russian troops locked in battle in the Soviet Union. Yet strategically the region of the eastern Mediterranean, known loosely as the Middle East and lying between neutral Turkey and the Italian colony of Libya, was the vital one. During the inter-war years it was dominated by Britain and France not as outright colonial powers but as the powers holding League Mandates. Both Britain and France had problems with their Mandates. From 1936 onwards, Arab militancy forced Britain to station 30,000 troops in Palestine. But after the British government's decision in 1939 to restrict the immigration of the Jews there was relative calm until 1944.

Hitler's Arab policy was ambiguous. While welcoming Arab hostility to Britain, the Nazis were not prepared to give unequivocal promises of future independence to the Arab states. But Arab attitudes were determined by Arab hostility to Britain and France as the occupying powers. Thus Egypt, nominally independent, and though being 'defended' by Britain, was pro-German during the war and was actually occupied by Britain. Iraq, Britain's Mandate, achieved independence in 1930 under British sponsorship but was closely linked to Britain economically and militarily. What was important to Britain was that Iraq and her eastern neighbour, Persia, were the major suppliers of oil in the region.

Britain's Middle Eastern dominance was seriously threatened in 1941 by Germany. Germany's victory over France stimulated Arab nationalism. The Vichy French authorities in the Lebanon and Syria, moreover, were not pro-British in their sympathies; while in Iraq, a group which favoured Germany staged a military coup and drove out the regime in power which had been friendly to Britain. Turkey, fearful of German power, decided on neutrality and so did not, as expected, join Britain. If Hitler had followed his Balkan campaigns in the spring of 1941 by advancing into the Middle East, there would have been no sufficiently strong British forces to oppose the Germans. Instead, Hitler attacked the Soviet Union in June 1941. Germany might nevertheless have reached Persia and the Persian Gulf by way of southern Russia. But Russia's defence of the Caucasus blocked that path. Britain, meanwhile, despite her militarily weak position, decided on offensive action. Together with Free French troops, a relatively small British force invaded Syria and the Lebanon and overcame Vichy French resistance. Britain intervened in Iraq and restored the pro-British regime. Persia was also

invaded in conjunction with the Russians. In Persia and the Arab world, including Egypt, Britain had secured her strategic interests by force against local political nationalist groups. From her point of view, Arab national feelings could not be permitted to jeopardise the war effort.

In North Africa on the western frontiers of Egypt, Britain and Dominion troops fought the Axis. The fortunes of this desert war varied dramatically until October 1942 when the battle of Alamein finally broke the offensive power of General Erwin Rommel and the Afrika Korps. General Bernard Montgomery had built up an army of 195,000 men with a thousand tanks, almost double the size of the German–Italian army. At Alamein he outgunned and outwitted Rommel, who had to withdraw hastily.

Britain's Alamein victory ended the disastrous sequence of British defeats. A trap was sprung. Rommel's line of retreat was being simultaneously cut off by Anglo-American landings at his rear. There had been much inter-Allied dispute on where an Anglo-American force could best strike against Hitler's Europe in 1942. Roosevelt and the American generals favoured an assault on France. Their reasoning was political as well as military. Stalin was pressing for a 'second front' to relieve

*The Battle of El Alamein of 23 October 1942 was the first decisive land battle the British won in the Second World War.*

Black Military Service. An aspect of the story of the twentieth century still not fully told is the contribution made by black servicemen to all of the wars in which the United States has taken part. During the First World War, 370,000 were enlisted, but they were rigidly segregated (though separate regiments of the 92nd Division served with French troops). In the Second World War, one million black American men served in the armed forces alongside several thousand black women. Again segregated, they were mainly assigned service roles. Above: the most senior black officer, Brigadier-General Benjamin O. Davis, inspects combat troops in England in October 1942. The all-black 93rd Division served in the Pacific. The gun crew of Battery "B" 598th Field Artillery 92nd Division (below) on the banks of the Arno, Italy, 1 September 1944. In 1948, President Truman ended segregation by executive order. During the Korean War, all races were integrated in the armed forces.

pressure in the East by forcing the Germans to transfer forty divisions to the West. But the Americans were quite unrealistic about the time needed for so difficult an undertaking. An unsuccessful commando raid on Dieppe in August 1942 showed how hard it would be to establish a bridgehead. Shortage of landing craft meant that no more than ten Allied divisions could have been sent across the Channel in 1942. Churchill and the British Chiefs of Staff were in any case opposed to a premature invasion of France. Agreement was eventually reached that an Anglo-American force should land in Vichy French North Africa in November 1942. General Dwight Eisenhower commanded this whole operation, codenamed Torch. At first the Vichy French forces resisted the landings but then agreed to an armistice. The Allies were thus able to occupy French Morocco and Algeria virtually unopposed.

Hitler responded to the Allied invasion of North Africa by sending his troops into the hitherto unoccupied regions of Vichy France. Britain had always feared that this would happen and that the French fleet would then fall into German hands. In fact the French fleet in Toulon eluded a German takeover by scuttling itself. Hitler also sent in troops from Sicily to occupy French Tunisia in North Africa. Rommel, meanwhile, fought and retreated westwards from Libya. The real fighting between the Allies and the Italian and German forces then occurred in Tunisia and lasted until May 1943, when a total of 150,000 troops (both Italian and German) finally capitulated. It was a major victory for the Anglo-American forces. Even so, the scale of the fighting in North Africa cannot be compared with that of the Russian front. Here the main war on land was being waged.

On 22 June 1941 the greatest military force Hitler had ever assembled invaded the Soviet Union. The German armies – north, centre and south – which launched the attack totalled 117 divisions with 22 divisions in reserve. They were supported by fourteen Romanian divisions. With the Panzers racing ahead in best *Blitzkrieg* tradition, the Soviet armies in the west were to be smashed by a three-pronged attack. The army of the north drove through the former Baltic states with Leningrad as their goal. The German army of the centre made its thrust in the direction of Smolensk and Moscow, and the army group south invaded the Ukraine. The purpose of these deep thrusts was to encircle and to destroy the Red Army in western Russia, and to prevent a Russian retreat into the vastness of Soviet territory. The victorious German armies expected to control European Russia from the Volga to Archangel. A 'military frontier' could then be established against Asiatic Russia, where the Japanese ally later might be encouraged to colonise parts of Siberia. Territorially Germany almost achieved her objective of conquering the whole of European Russia in 1941 and 1942. Yet the Soviet Union was not defeated and the *Blitzkrieg* turned into a war of attrition, during which the greater Soviet reserves of manpower and the increasing output of her armament industry turned the tide of the war against Hitler's Germany.

After the initial and spectacular victories of the battles of the frontiers during the first weeks of the war, when the Germans took hundreds of thousands of Russian prisoners and whole Russian armies disintegrated, the German generals and Hitler disagreed which of the three offensives was to be the main effort. Thus already in August of 1941 the basic weakness of Germany's latest *Blitzkrieg* became evident. Speaking to Goebbels on 18 August, Hitler bitterly complained about the failures of military intelligence before the war. Instead of the expected 5000 tanks, the Soviets disposed of 20,000. Goebbels reflected that had the true strength of the Soviet Union been known, 'Perhaps we would have drawn back from tackling the questions of the East and Bolshevism which had fallen due.' What a momentous 'perhaps', on which the whole course of the war was to depend! During the first six weeks the Germans lost 60,000 dead; newspaper columns in Germany were filled with small black iron crosses announcing a son or husband fallen for Führer and Fatherland. As the Germans penetrated the Soviet Union the already vast front from the Black Sea to the Baltic of more than 500 miles lengthened even further. The same tactics that had worked in the 'confined' space of France failed in the vastness of the Soviet Union. Though Stalin was completely stunned by the German attack, not expecting it, despite all warnings, to be launched before 1942, huge Russian reserves of manpower and the setting up of industrial complexes beyond the Urals meant that the Soviet military capacity to resist was not destroyed.

But Stalin's fear of provoking Germany by taking adequate preparatory measures had left the Soviet

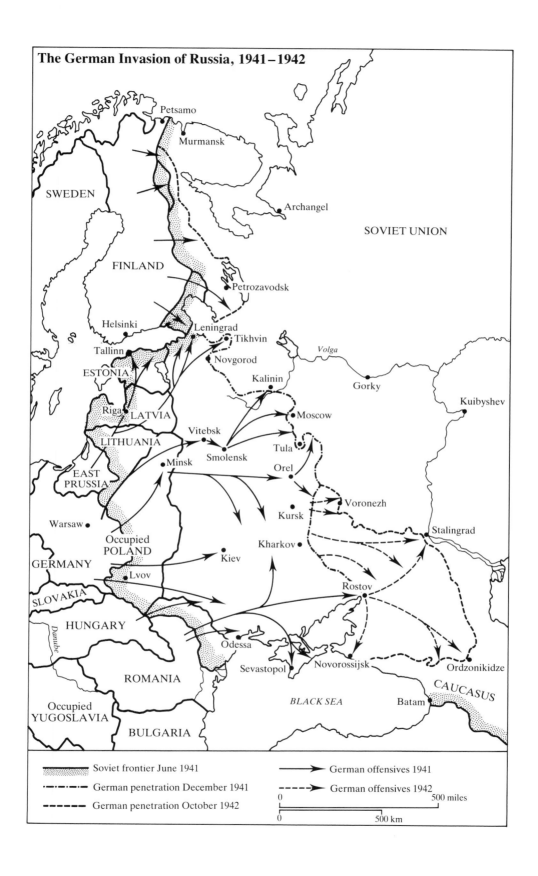

**The German Invasion of Russia, 1941–1942**

SWEDEN

Petsamo

Murmansk

Archangel

SOVIET UNION

FINLAND

Petrozavodsk

Helsinki

Leningrad

Tikhvin

*Volga*

Tallinn

Novgorod

ESTONIA

Kalinin

Gorky

Riga

LATVIA

Moscow

Kuibyshev

LITHUANIA

Vitebsk

Tula

Minsk

Smolensk

Orel

EAST
PRUSSIA

Kursk

Voronezh

Warsaw

Stalingrad

Occupied
POLAND

Kiev

Kharkov

GERMANY

Lvov

SLOVAKIA

Rostov

HUNGARY

*Danube*

Odessa

Ordzonikidze

ROMANIA

Sevastopol

Novorossijsk

*CAUCASUS*

Occupied
YUGOSLAVIA

*BLACK SEA*

Batam

BULGARIA

| | Soviet frontier June 1941 | | German offensives 1941 |
|---|---|---|---|
| | German penetration December 1941 | | German offensives 1942 |
| | German penetration October 1942 | | |

0                    500 miles

0                    500 km

armies unprepared and exposed to German encirclements at the outset. The Germans captured more than 3 million prisoners between June and December 1941. But if the Soviet Union could avoid actual defeat in 1941 and 1942 it would then become impossible for the German armies to defeat the more numerous Soviet armies, whose weapons matched, and in the case of the T-34 tank even outclassed, those of the Germans. First the autumn rains and the mud and then the winter weather caught the German armies unprepared. Not only did the troops freeze during the particularly severe winter of 1941/2, but much of the mechanised equipment became unusable in the Arctic frosts. Russia's two greatest cities, Leningrad and Moscow, were the goals of the central and northern German armies. Leningrad was almost surrounded by the Germans and the Finns.

The siege of Leningrad is one of the epics of the Second World War. It lasted from September 1941 to January 1944. During the siege 641,803 people died from hunger and disease alone. The Soviet spirit of resistance was not broken. Almost three-quarters of a million German troops were bogged down around the city for 900 days. The Germans were also denied the capture of Moscow, although they reached the southern suburbs. Germany's defeats were not due to 'General Winter' alone, but owed much to the skill and heroism of the Soviet forces facing the invaders. The German High Command was forced to admit that for the first time a *Blitzkrieg* had failed. The war was not over in the East; the war of attrition which had defeated Germany in 1914–18 and which Hitler had done everything to escape was just beginning.

There are occasions when secret intelligence plays a crucial role in war. The Soviets had a spy in Tokyo, Richard Sorge, a German press correspondent who had predicted the date of the German attack almost to the day. The warning appears to have fallen on deaf ears. But when he passed on the information that the Japanese would strike south and not attack the Soviet Union just before his arrest as a spy, and Japanese military inactivity confirmed his tip off, Stalin, though still suspicious, gradually withdrew those troops facing the Japanese after the Siberian campaigning season was over (Sorge was imprisoned and executed in 1944). With the help of these troops and other reinforcements, Marshal Zhukov, the most outstanding general on the Soviet side during the war, organised the defence of Russia's capital. In December 1941 fresh Soviet divisions counterattacked and the Germans were forced to give up territory, but their own retreat was orderly. They were not routed or captured in huge numbers as the Russians had been. Although the Russians probably did not yet enjoy superiority in men or materials on the Moscow front, the Germans were severely disadvantaged by the length of and lack of adequate rail and road supply lines to their own troops.

Stalin's own mistakes in carrying on the Russian offensives in the spring of 1942, believing the German armies virtually beaten, led to major military disasters on the Kharkov front in the south in May and June 1942 and in the Crimea. Hundreds of thousands more Soviet troops were lost. Stalin, expecting the Germans to renew their main drive on Moscow, concentrated Russian reserves on the central front. Instead the main German blow was delivered in the south. The Crimea, including Sevastopol, was taken. The Germans drove forward to the city of Stalingrad on the Volga, intending to cut off the whole of Russia south of that city including the oil-rich Caucasus, which formed the gateway to Persia.

In the ruins of Stalingrad the Russians, fighting from house to house, made their stand. The battle lasted from mid-August to mid-November 1942. Stalin and Hitler were locked in a titanic proxy struggle for supremacy. Hitler decided that Stalingrad would be taken come what may and that Germany would not withdraw. Stalin sent Zhukov to mastermind the defence of the city regardless of casualties. Most of the city was taken by the Germans in October, and the Russian defenders were denied reinforcements as fresh divisions were being husbanded in preparation for a great counter-offensive. On 19 November 1942 the Russians launched their attack and encircled the 200,000 men of Germany's Sixth Army fighting in Stalingrad. Hitler ordered the Sixth Army to stand fast. Losing the opportunity to link up with the German armies to the rear it was doomed. Fierce fighting continued until the 91,000 survivors including Field Marshal von Paulus surrendered on 31 January 1943. The Wehrmacht had been decisively defeated, and, more than that, the myth of Hitler's infallible military genius had been exploded. The world felt Stalingrad marked a turning point in the war. Soviet strength would increase as Germany's diminished. By the summer of 1943 the Russians

*The Battle for Stalingrad, August 1942–January 1943. Every house, every factory a fortress. The German Army was never to recover from its defeat and Hitler's reputation as the 'greatest military leader of all times' was finally shattered.*

had also won superiority in the air, with thousands of planes engaged on each side.

Had there been wholesale defections from the forced union of Soviet Socialist Republics the whole prospect of the war might have changed. The almost unbelievable number of prisoners that the Germans took in 1941 suggests not only military defeat but also large-scale desertions. But Hitler resisted those of his advisers who wished to utilise this anti-communist and anti-Russian sentiment. The peasants hungered for land and for release from the collective farms. A captured Russian general, Andrei Vlasov, even offered to raise an army from prisoners of war to fight Stalin's Russia. But Hitler's racist fanaticism stood in the way of winning the war by these means. European Russia was designated as colonial territory, eventually to be depopulated as necessary to provide room for the New German settlers. The Slavs were 'subhumans'; nearly 3 million were sent to Germany to work as virtual slave labour. With the Germans ransacking the Russian territories they occupied, the early welcome which they received turned to hatred. Partisan resistance increased behind German lines and was met by ruthless terror. Only too late in 1943 and 1944 did Himmler try to change a German policy bound to alienate the local population and to recruit for the German army from among the minorities. Meanwhile Stalin skilfully appealed to Russian patriotism and encouraged all the peoples of the Soviet republics to turn out the invaders.

Hitler tenaciously clung to one hope even when surrounded in his bunker in burning Berlin in April 1945, that the 'unholy' and unnatural alliance between Britain, the United States and the Soviet Union would fall apart and that the Western powers would recognise that he was fighting the common Bolshevik enemy. There is not the slightest evidence that Roosevelt or Churchill would for one moment have contemplated any kind of pact with Hitler. Though Churchill, more so than Roosevelt, foresaw that there would be post-war conflict with the Soviet Union, his conviction of the need to destroy the evils of Nazism was unshakeable. The holding together of the grand alliance was a precondition of victory.

Was this also Stalin's perception of British policy? Did Stalin, pathologically suspicious of the motives of all possible enemies, have any faith in Britain's determination to fight Hitler's Germany to the finish? Despite Churchill's immediate and unqualified promise of support the moment the Germans invaded Russia, suspicion of any antagonist past, present or future was second nature to Stalin. The continuing delays in the opening of a second front in France through 1942, then 1943, must have confirmed his fears that the reason for delay was mainly political not military. He bitterly complained to Churchill, charging him with breaches of faith. The Soviet archives are only just being opened and the workings of Stalin's mind remain a matter of conjecture. But he may well have concluded that the West was deliberately prolonging the war to weaken the Soviet Union in the bloodbath of the eastern front in order to dictate the future from a position of strength. The longer European Russia remained in German hands, the more difficult it would be to re-establish communist autocracy over the non-Russian peoples. Hence it became for Stalin almost a test of Britain's good faith that Russia's right to her *1941* frontiers should be accepted by Britain and the United States and not become a matter of negotiation after the war was won. The 1941 frontiers included the additional territory the Soviet Union had acquired as a result of the deal struck with Nazi Germany: eastern Poland, the Baltic states, Bessarabia and northern Bukovina, and also the territories taken from Finland after the Soviet–Finnish War.

The British position at first was to reject any frontier changes until after the war was over and peace negotiations took place. Roosevelt, mindful of his own Polish minority in America and of the condemnation of the 'secret deals' of the First World War, at first resisted even more firmly European frontier discussions. But Churchill and Eden were anxious to appease Stalin at a time when the Red Army was bearing the brunt of the war on land. An Anglo-Russian agreement for jointly waging war against Germany had been signed in Moscow on 12 July 1941; on 26 May 1942 it was replaced by a formal twenty-year alliance. Churchill also responded courteously to Stalin's angry and wounding messages about the lack of a second front. But there was much apprehension in London that Stalin might lose confidence in his Western allies. Everything was avoided that might add to his suspicions. This had one important consequence. Discussions with emissaries from the German resistance, or with representatives sent by Himmler's SS to bargain over the lives of the Hungarian Jews, were avoided for fear that they would compromise Britain and lead Stalin to the wrong conclusion that a separate peace was being considered.

Among Hitler's entourage were advisers and allies who urged him to seek a separate peace with the Soviet Union. But the struggle against the Bolsheviks and Jews lay at the core of his ideology. He would contemplate no peace with his arch-enemies the Bolshevik Jews as he saw them. His barbarity in Russia and the carrying through of the Final Solution while the war was being lost militarily show that ideology ultimately dominated Hitler's actions when *Realpolitik* would have served the interests of the Third Reich. As for Stalin it is possible that he welcomed the West's belief that he had an alternative to war with Germany for it would make Britain and the United States more willing to accede to Russia's military and political demands.

The question of the future of Poland was the most difficult for Britain and the United States to solve. The Polish government in exile demanded that the independence of its state be restored within the frontiers of 1939, that is of pre-war Poland.

But Stalin had already annexed and incorporated in the Soviet Union the portions of Poland occupied in September 1939 and insisted on a post-war Poland 'friendly' to the Soviet Union. With the Red Army inevitably overrunning Poland there was little in effect the United States and Britain could do to force Stalin to renounce territory which he claimed as Soviet already. The Polish government in exile in London was in a hopeless situation. General Sikorski, who headed the Polish government in exile in London, had at first tried to work with the Russians. He had signed an agreement for Russo-Polish co-operation with Stalin in 1941, but from the first two issues clouded Polish–Soviet relations: the question of Poland's eastern frontier and the thousands of missing Polish officers who should have re-emerged from Russian prisoner-of-war camps after the 1941 agreement had been concluded. The corpses of Polish officers found by the Germans near Smolensk in the Katyn forest provided a grisly explanation for their disappearance and ruptured relations between the Polish government and the Kremlin in April 1943. The Russians formed their own Polish military units and an embryonic rival Polish government, the Union of Polish Patriots.

The fate of Poland was virtually decided at the first summit conference when Roosevelt, Churchill and Stalin met in Teheran in Persia from 28 November to 1 December 1943. There was no formal agreement, but Churchill agreed on behalf of Britain, and Roosevelt personally acquiesced too, to the Soviet Union's retaining eastern Poland as far as the Curzon line (the armistice line between Poland and Russia proposed by the British Foreign Secretary Lord Curzon in 1920) and that Poland should be compensated with German territory east of the rivers Oder and Neisse. At the Yalta Conference more than a year later (4–11 February 1945), with Poland by then overrun by the Red Army, despite some ambiguities in the official declarations Stalin secured his territorial ambitions at Poland's expense. For his part Stalin promised that he would allow all the liberated peoples in Eastern and central Europe to choose their own governments freely and democratically. Power had passed to a Polish provisional government which was based in the Soviet Union and which some 'London' Poles were permitted to join. At Teheran and Yalta, military needs and realities, as well as hopes for post-war co-operation, decided Churchill and Roosevelt to accept Stalin's demands that Soviet conditions concerning the future frontiers of Russia be met in all but formal treaty from before the conclusion of the war.

Until 1945 there was little link between the war waged in Europe and Africa and the war waged by Japan, Britain, China and the United States in eastern and south-eastern Asia. The Soviet Union was not a party to the Pacific war until shortly before its end. Japan and the Soviet Union signed a neutrality treaty in April 1941 and the two countries remained at peace until Russia declared war on Japan just one week before Japan's surrender.

Roosevelt and Churchill never wavered from their early determination after Japan's attack on Pearl Harbor in December 1941 that despite the military disasters in eastern Asia the defeat of Germany must come first. Japan's victories came as a tremendous shock to British and Dominion public opinion. The Western empires of the Dutch, French and British and the American hold on the Philippines collapsed in just a few weeks and the whole region fell for the first time under the control of one power, Japan.

In Malaya, Britain had constructed the Singapore naval base and Churchill had insisted on sending to it two battleships, the *Prince of Wales* and the *Repulse*, intending thereby to deter the Japanese from going to war. The British commanded in Malaya 89,000 troops, including 37,000 Indian, 19,000 British and 15,000 Australians. In the Netherlands East Indies 35,000 Dutch regular troops were stationed. The Americans had posted 31,000 regulars to the Philippines. But the British, Dutch and American troops were poorly equipped. Air defence in particular was inadequate, which gave the Japanese a decisive advantage. The Japanese almost immediately after the outbreak of the war sank the *Prince of Wales* and the *Repulse* from the air. There were now no battleships left to oppose them. The attack on Pearl Harbor had knocked out the capacity of the United States fleet to challenge Japan's offensive. The capture of Guam and Wake islands denied the United States naval bases beyond Hawaii. In Malaya the well-equipped and skilfully led Japanese army began the invasion on 8 December and, though only 60,800 in strength, overwhelmed the British defence forces, which finally capitulated in Singapore on 15 February 1942. Some 80,000 troops under British command surrendered, a stunning military defeat when added

to the shock provoked by the sinking of the *Repulse* and *Prince of Wales*. The fall of Singapore was also a great psychological blow which undermined the faith of Asian peoples in 'white' superiority.

General Douglas MacArthur defended the Philippines. The Japanese gained air control and their invading army defeated the Americans, who withdrew to the Bataan peninsula in January 1942; the Americans finally had to surrender their last fortress defence on 9 April with 70,000 troops, a disaster comparable to Singapore, except that the defence had been long drawn out and skilfully conducted. Simultaneously with the invasion of Malaya, another Japanese army crossed from Thailand into Burma and by the end of April had driven the weak British forces into India. The Netherlands East Indies were captured between January and March 1942. Throughout these five months of victorious campaigns the Japanese had suffered only some 15,000 killed and wounded and had taken more than ten times as many Allied troops prisoner. The whole of south-east Asia had fallen under Japanese domination.

British rule seemed to be threatened now at the very heart of the empire, British India. The position was regarded as sufficiently desperate for the British Cabinet to send out Sir Stafford Cripps with a promise to the leaders of the Indian Congress Party that India would be granted independence after the war. A constituent assembly would be called to decide whether she would remain within or outside the Commonwealth. Meanwhile, during the war, the Congress Party would be granted some participation in but not control of government. Congress rejected the proposals, partly because Cripps also offered to the Muslim League the possibility of secession for the predominantly Muslim parts of India (later Pakistan). Gandhi, India's greatest voice of non-violent opposition, now called on Britain simply to 'quit India'. He expected non-violence to defeat Britain and Japan and to win India for the 385 million Indians. The Viceroy of India reacted with repression and arrested the Congress leaders and Gandhi. India did not rise against the British, and the Indian army fought under British command against the Japanese. The Japanese also created an Indian 'liberation' army from prisoners of war mainly taken at Singapore and founded the Indian Independence League. In 1943 an Indian nationalist, Subhas Chandra Bose, ex-president of the Indian Congress, took over the Indian 'government' operating with the Japanese. Though Bose had a good deal of success among Indians beyond British control, his impact within India was limited and never threatened British rule. The problem of Indian independence was now shelved until the war was won.

Militarily the Japanese expansion in the Pacific and south-east Asia was checked by the summer of 1942. In the naval battle of the Coral Sea in May 1942 Japan's thrust towards Australia was blunted when the Japanese attack on Port Moresby in New Guinea was called off as a result of the naval engagement. Far more serious for the Japanese was the failure of their attack on the American-held Midway Island. Admiral Yamomoto was in overall command of the most powerful fleet of battleships, aircraft carriers, cruisers, destroyers and submarines the Japanese had ever assembled. Its task was not only to cover the Japanese landing force, but to destroy the remaining US Pacific fleet. But the Americans had broken the Japanese code and were well prepared when the fleets clashed in June. It was a naval battle dominated by the aircraft carriers on both sides. The Japanese lost four of their eight aircraft carriers whereas the Americans lost only one. The Japanese broke off the battle and from then on had lost the initiative in the Pacific. It was now certain that the American war effort, once fully developed, would overwhelm Japan eventually. Just as in Europe, where Hitler's *Blitzkrieg* had failed finally in 1942, so did Japan's oriental *Blitzkrieg* now fail in its purpose of forcing her principal enemies to accept her claim to predominance in eastern and southern Asia.

The American counter-offensive in the Pacific began in August 1942 with the American attack on the tiny Japanese-held island of Guadalcanal, one of the Solomon group of islands. The fighting between the American marines and the defending Japanese was ferocious and casualties on both sides were heavy, until the Americans overwhelmed the fanatical defenders. This was to become the pattern of the remorseless Pacific war until Japan's surrender.

The Japanese war with Britain, the Dominions and the United States brought relief to the Chinese, who had been at war with the Japanese alone since 1937. Chiang Kai-shek now avoided active battles with the Japanese as far as possible. His eyes were firmly set on the future when, with the Anglo-American defeat of the Japanese, he would gain mastery over all China, including the communists, his theoretical allies against Japan. Despite the growing corruption of the Kuomintang and the inefficiency of Chiang Kai-shek's armies, the United States based her hopes for the future peace and progress of eastern Asia on the emergence of a strong and democratic Chinese republic linked in friendship to the United States. Roosevelt did not wish to see the restoration of the pre-war special rights of Europe in China or the re-establishment of the European empires in eastern Asia. In January 1945 he expressed his hopes to his Secretary of State that United States policy 'was based on the belief that despite the temporary weakness of China and the possibility of revolutions and civil war, 450 million Chinese would someday become united and modernised and would be the most important factor in the whole Far East'.

The problem during the last two years of the land war in Asia was to get Chiang Kai-shek's armies to put up any resistance at all to the Japanese, who renewed their offensives and occupied large new areas of eastern China in 1944. The Japanese overran the American-built airfields from which they had been bombed. Chiang Kai-shek meanwhile positioned half a million of his best troops in the north to contain the communists and was preserving his armies for a future war of supremacy in China after the Western powers had defeated Japan. Throughout 1944 the tension between Roosevelt and Chiang Kai-shek grew. Roosevelt had little faith in the Chinese leader. He wished to force on him the appointment of an American general to command all the Chinese armies and to bring about effective co-operation between the communists and the Kuomintang against the Japanese. A China policy that would reconcile China and serve America's global interests continued to elude the United States.

During the course of 1943 the tide of war turned decisively against Japan, Italy and Germany. The enormous industrial resources of the United States alone, when fully mobilised for war, exceeded all that Germany, Japan and their allies could produce together. The Soviet Union was by now more than a match for the military strength Germany had built up in the east. It was only the tenacity and skill of Germany's armies, despite Hitler's disastrous interferences as at Stalingrad, that enabled

Germany to stave off defeat for so long. Germany did not collapse even when the ordinary man in the street knew the war was lost and had no confidence left in Hitler's promised 'wonder' weapons. She fought to the bitter end, until Hitler had shot himself and the crushing superiority of the Allied armies closing in from all sides made further resistance a physical impossibility. Until close to the end of the war, Hitler's regime could still successfully terrorise and kill anyone who openly refused orders to fight to the last. Equally important was German fear of Russian conquest and occupation. Nazi propaganda had successfully indoctrinated the German people into believing that the Russian subhumans from the east would destroy, loot and kill and that it was better to die resisting than to fall into Russian hands. Early experiences of the Russian armies when they first invaded East Prussia appeared to confirm this belief.

But a separate peace with the West, the principal hope of those who during the later stages of the war had plotted against Hitler, was not a possibility. In practice the Western Allies could follow no other policy than to demand that Germany must surrender unconditionally on *all* fronts simultaneously. The actual phrase 'unconditional surrender' emerged during discussions between Roosevelt and Churchill when they met at Casablanca in January 1943 to co-ordinate and agree on Anglo-American strategy. Roosevelt gave it official public backing in speaking to the press. It meant that Britain and the United States would not entertain any bargaining over peace terms with Germany, Italy and Japan and would fight until complete military victory had been achieved.

It has been argued that the call for unconditional surrender made the enemies of the Allies fight more fanatically to the bitter end and that the war might have been shortened by a more flexible Allied attitude. The evidence of Germany's and Italy's behaviour in 1944 and 1945 does not support this view. The Italians were able to overthrow Mussolini and in fact negotiate their surrender, whereas Hitler's grasp over Germany remained so complete, and his own attitude so utterly uncompromising, that no negotiated peace was possible short of Germany's total collapse, even if any of the Allies had desired to negotiate for peace. The advantages of having proclaimed as a war aim 'unconditional surrender' on the other hand were solid. Allied differences on how to treat a conquered Germany

could be kept secret since the Allied public had been satisfied by the demand of 'unconditional surrender'. Moreover, Roosevelt and Churchill hoped that the call for unconditional surrender would reassure Stalin in the absence of an early second front. In January 1943 Britain's and America's military effort on land did not compare with that of Russia, where the final phase of the Stalingrad battle was raging.

Within the Grand Alliance, or United Nations as all the countries fighting Germany came to be called, there was an inner Anglo-American alliance. A joint strategic body, the Combined Chiefs of Staff, was set up soon after Pearl Harbor to provide a forum for debate on strategy and eventual decision-making. Joint Anglo-American commands were created as necessary. There are no parallels in modern history of such close co-ordination of policy as was achieved by the United States and Britain during the last three and a half war years. It was based on the trust and working relationships at the top between Roosevelt and Churchill. Stalin would never have agreed to a joint command, and the Soviet Union remained an outsider fighting her own war with Germany, which engaged in 1942 and 1943 two-thirds of the total number of German divisions.

Joint Anglo-American planning bodies did not mean, however, that there was perfect harmony. The American military argued for a concentration of all effort on the earliest possible cross-Channel attack on France and so a blow at Germany's vitals. Churchill and his British military advisers warned against any premature landings, which might fail. Roosevelt, fearful in 1942 of the possibility that the Soviet forces might collapse unless some of the German forces were diverted, was inclined to listen to Stalin's appeals more sympathetically. Churchill mollified Stalin, convincing him that the projected landings in Vichy North Africa were a genuine second front. The successful completion of these operations in May 1943 was too late to allow for a switching of resources necessary to mount a cross-Channel attack in 1943. Churchill argued in favour of a Mediterranean strategy and attacking Italy, the 'soft underbelly' of the Axis. Churchill's reasons were based on his appraisal of military alternatives. The Germans were weakest in the Mediterranean and if the Allies carried the war into the Balkans then the German armies would be trapped between them and the Russians. The Allies, moreover, would

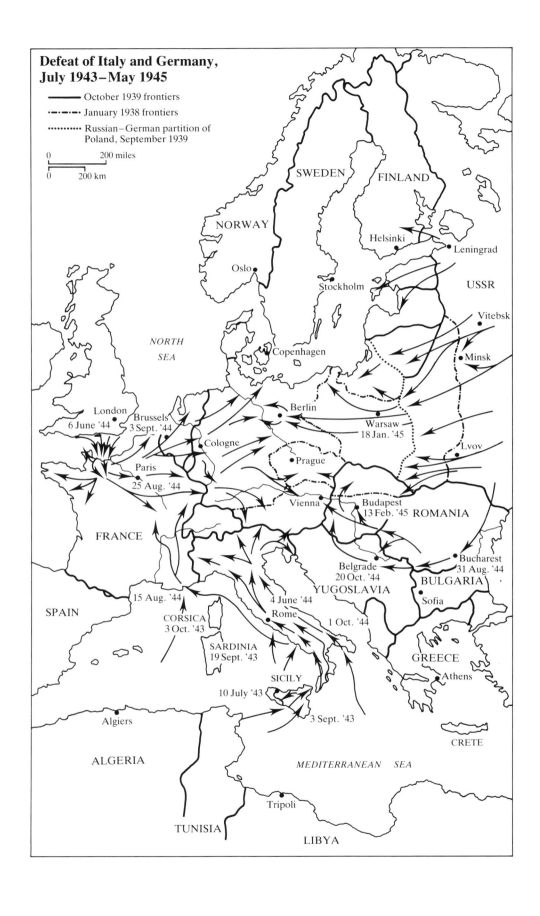

**Defeat of Italy and Germany,
July 1943 – May 1945**

——— October 1939 frontiers
—·—·— January 1938 frontiers
············· Russian–German partition of
Poland, September 1939

0          200 miles
0          200 km

SWEDEN

FINLAND

NORWAY

Helsinki

Leningrad

Oslo

USSR

Stockholm

Vitebsk

NORTH
SEA

Copenhagen

Minsk

London
6 June '44

Brussels
3 Sept. '44

Berlin

Warsaw
18 Jan. '45

Cologne

Lvov

Paris
25 Aug. '44

Prague

FRANCE

Vienna

Budapest
13 Feb. '45   ROMANIA

15 Aug. '44

4 June '44

Belgrade
20 Oct. '44

Bucharest
31 Aug. '44

SPAIN

CORSICA
3 Oct. '43

Rome

1 Oct. '44

YUGOSLAVIA

BULGARIA

Sofia

SARDINIA
19 Sept. '43

GREECE

SICILY

Athens

10 July '43

3 Sept. '43

Algiers

CRETE

ALGERIA

MEDITERRANEAN    SEA

Tripoli

TUNISIA

LIBYA

be able to link with Tito's Yugoslav partisans. The Americans wanted to concentrate all forces on an attack on France, but agreed that the North African forces could be used to invade Sicily next.

The rapid fall of Sicily to the Anglo-American forces in July 1943 marked the end of Mussolini's hold on power. The fascist leaders and King Victor Emmanuel could see the writing on the wall. The way out for Italy was to jettison the German alliance and to change sides if possible. Military defeat and the imminent invasion of Italy had weakened Mussolini's position sufficiently to make it possible to overthrow him. The Duce was dismissed from his office not by a popular revolution but by the King and his fascist collaborators on 24 and 25 July 1943. He was then imprisoned until rescued by the Germans. The King appointed Marshal Pietro Badoglio as Mussolini's successor. But Badoglio and the fascist leaders failed to save Italy from becoming a battleground. Despite the promise to continue the war, German suspicions were aroused and reinforcements were sent to Italy. The new regime held secret negotiations with the Allies, but did not persuade them to land in northern Italy to enable the Italians to avoid a German occupation. The Anglo-American plan envisaged occupying only southern Italy. This made it possible for the Germans to seize the remainder of Italy when Italy's surrender was made public on 8 September 1943. Naples was reached by the Allies on 1 October. The Germans by then had established a strong defensive line across the Italian peninsula. The King and the Italian government fled south behind the Allied lines and then declared war on Germany, while Hitler restored Mussolini to act as a puppet dictator over the republic he had proclaimed. Until the close of the war in May 1945, the Allied armies had to fight their way gradually north, piercing heavily fortified lines which the Germans created in their path. Meanwhile a guerrilla war was fought in the north by the partisans, whose aim was not only to drive out the Germans but also to bring about radical social change in Italy.

Mussolini did not survive the military defeat of his ally. Captured by Italian partisans, he, together with his mistress, was executed by them. The Italian campaign did not prove to be a rapid success and entailed some of the heaviest fighting of the war. But Hitler's decision to defend Italy and so keep the Allies as far as possible away from south Germany diverted many divisions to her defence and to the defence of the Balkans, which had become vulnerable.

While in July 1943 the British and American armies invaded Sicily, the largest tank battle of the war was being waged at Kursk on the Russian front. The German attack on the Russian salient was beaten back by Marshal Zhukov. It was the last occasion on which the Germans were able to mount a major offensive in Russia. Both sides suffered huge casualties, but the Russian armour had proved superior and the Russians, unlike the Germans, could make good such losses. Successive Russian offensives drove the German armies back in heavy fighting into Poland, but they halted the Russians on the River Vistula. The Warsaw rising (1 August –2 October 1944) did not induce the Red Army at all costs to reach the Polish capital. In mid-September Russian attempts to advance were repelled by the Germans, who remained in control of Warsaw until the end of the year. Further south, Russian armies advanced from the Ukraine into Romania, Bulgaria, Yugoslavia and Hungary. As in Italy, new governments attempted to change from the German to the Russian side. But the Germans were still strong enough to remove the Hungarian Regent Admiral Horthy from power and to make a stand against the Russian armies. Budapest did not surrender to the Russians until February 1945. But Hitler could no longer in 1944 place the bulk of his armies to defend the eastern front.

On 6 June 1944 under General Dwight Eisenhower's supreme command the successful cross-Channel invasion of France began. The tremendous obstacles to this enterprise had been overcome by meticulous planning and brilliant execution. Beaches and bases were won and by the end of July 1944 1.5 million men had been landed in France. After the battle of Normandy, Paris was taken on 25 August and the German troops were pursued as they retreated from France. A landing in southern France against the depleted German forces there enabled the Allies rapidly to liberate most of France. The Allies reached the southern Netherlands and the northern Franco-German frontier between Aachen and Trier in September.

Meanwhile Hitler had launched his promised wonder weapons, the pilotless aircraft-bomb, the V-1, and the missile bomb, V-2, against London. The attacks by these new weapons on London and

*An immense armada brought the Allied invasion forces to the Normandy beaches, 6 June 1944.*

Antwerp in the summer and autumn of 1944 did much damage but could not alter the course of the war. The last of these ingenious bombs hit Antwerp in March 1945.

One problem that could not await any longer for solution was who was to be recognised as representing the free government of France. There could be no question that Pétain's Vichy regime had forfeited all its claims by collaborating with the Germans. Of all the countries that had been overrun by the Germans, France was the most important, the only indubitable pre-war great power. Yet ironically it was the one ally not represented by a government in exile in London. The Free French, who had rallied to General de Gaulle in 1940 and formed their own administration in London, were recognised only as the French Committee of National Liberation. De Gaulle felt his inferior status deeply. But it cannot be denied that his status corresponded to reality in that the majority of Frenchmen in France and in the French Empire accepted Pétain's authority. Not that this would

have stopped the British and Americans in wartime from according recognition to de Gaulle. Expediency, however, persuaded them not to challenge Vichy France openly. A powerful French fleet after all was still in Vichy hands in 1942. When the Allies made their North African landings in November 1942, Operation Torch, it was with the Vichy authorities there that secret negotiations were conducted to avoid the hostility of the French army units stationed there. Admiral Darlan, who happened to be in Algiers, decided to support the Americans. Soon after that he was assassinated. De Gaulle was regarded as something of an embarrassment; but despite Allied intrigues he succeeded in reasserting his leadership over all the Free French.

Roosevelt was particularly averse to committing himself to de Gaulle, who reacted by asserting all the more strongly his rights and those of France. The disparity between the reality of the French position and de Gaulle's behaviour struck Churchill and Roosevelt at the time as incongruous. But Churchill, with more imagination, insight and sympathy

*Liberation.* Left: *in Belfort, France, in November 1944, an American GI receives a warm welcome.* Right: *In Paris, the penalty for taking a German lover during the Occupation was public humiliation.*

than Roosevelt, urged after the Allied invasion of France in June 1944 that de Gaulle's administration should be recognised as the provisional government of France. Such recognition nevertheless was delayed until October 1944. The manner in which de Gaulle had been treated by the 'Anglo-Saxon' powers made the deepest impression on him and still rankled years later. The restoration of France to great-power status, and her independence from Anglo-American dominance, became almost an obsession with de Gaulle in the post-war years.

The war was clearly drawing to a close in the autumn of 1944. But stiff German resistance frustrated a quick victory. In the East, the Germans continued to fight fiercely. In the West, they were even able to inflict temporary reverses on the Allies. Montgomery made a bold attempt in September 1944 to cross the lower Rhine at Arnhem with the help of parachute divisions dropped in advance, but just short of Arnhem the Germans were able to halt his thrust. The Allied armies, however, were slowly pushing on to the Rhine along a broad front and had reached practically the whole length of the German frontier by mid-December. The Germans had still one surprise left. Powerful German divisions, led by tanks, together with what was left of the Luftwaffe in the West, opened an offensive through the Ardennes on 16 December 1944. The Germans advanced sixty miles before they were halted. It was their last offensive of the war.

With the imminent collapse of Hitler's Germany, agreement with the Russians on the military division of the territories the Allies would occupy, and on the post-war delimitation of frontiers and spheres of influence, took on a new urgency. In October 1944, Churchill flew to Moscow. Russian armies were by then already in Romania and Bulgaria and a British force was about to enter Greece. Churchill in Moscow proposed to Stalin a division of influence in the Balkan states. Stalin readily consented. But the resulting agreement was little more than a piece of paper. The Red Army would dominate Romania, Bulgaria and Hungary as it advanced towards Greater Germany. But Stalin allowed Britain freedom of action in Greece, provided a broadly based government including communists was formed in that country. British troops who landed in Greece soon found themselves fighting the communist-organised partisans. The uneasy peace established by the British force was to be shattered two years later in 1947 by civil war. Despite Stalin's promises to respect the sovereignty and the rights of self-determination of the nations of central Europe and the Balkans, in his mind there was always one overriding qualification: the free choice of the people would be forcefully set aside if it led, as was likely, to anti-Soviet governments. Only Greece and Yugoslavia were able after the war to assert their independence from Soviet control. The realities of Soviet 'freedom' were already apparent before the war with Germany was even won. A division of Europe was emerging between the Soviet-controlled territory of Eastern, central and south-eastern Europe and the West.

Roosevelt's hope of achieving some solid understanding between the three world powers, Britain, the Soviet Union and the United States, was severely tested by Soviet behaviour in 1944 and 1945. He pinned his hopes on creating a new international organisation – the United Nations – under the tutelage and based on the agreement of Britain, the Soviet Union and the United States. But Stalin was making unreasonable demands. All sixteen Soviet Republics were to be among the founder members of the United Nations. He also insisted that the six permanent members of the proposed council of the United Nations should be able to exercise an all-inclusive veto, that is to say, have the right to a veto when disputes were being dealt with in which they themselves were involved. The Dumbarton Oaks Conference which had met to organise the United Nations thus ended in September 1944 without agreement on these vital issues. What was seen as Stalin's intransigence brought the United States and Britain more closely together.

In Quebec, Churchill and Roosevelt met that same month, September 1944, to devise their joint military and political strategy. Plans were made to move troops from Italy into Istria and Austria ahead of Russian troops. To help Britain economically, Roosevelt also agreed to continue Lend–Lease during the time that would elapse between the defeat of Germany and the defeat of Japan. Britain's likely post-war economic weakness was thus fore-shadowed: Britain would not remain an equal superpower with the United States and the Soviet Union. Britain and the United States next agreed to co-operate in the military and civilian development of atomic energy and, significantly, to exclude the Soviet Union from sharing this information.

The future of Germany was another subject of primary importance discussed at Quebec. Roosevelt's advisers had prepared both a 'soft' plan for peace terms and the famous plan associated with the name of the Secretary of the Treasury, Henry Morgenthau, which intended to deprive Germany of her major industries, reduce the German standard of living and turn her into an agricultural country. At first Churchill was violently opposed to this 'hard' option. It would too clearly be repeating the error of the First World War. A prosperous Europe could not develop without German economic recovery. But in return for concessions for the continuation of American economic aid to Britain he finally assented to 'converting Germany into a country primarily agricultural and pastoral in its character'. What were Roosevelt's motives in advocating a course that would have been so disastrous for European recovery? He spoke of punishing the German people for their wars of aggression; more important to him was to win Stalin's co-operation by reassuring the Soviet leader that the Western Allies would not try to rebuild Germany as a bulwark against Russia. In the autumn of 1944 Roosevelt's hand was greatly strengthened by his re-election as president. He would not have to enter peace negotiations without the certainty of public support as Wilson had done in 1919.

At Yalta in February 1945 Stalin, Roosevelt and Churchill finally met together again for the first time since Teheran. Roosevelt and Churchill arrived with some 700 officials. The photograph of the three leaders in front of the tsarist Livadia Palace implied an equality that did not exist. Roosevelt as a head of state was seated in the centre flanked on his left by Stalin and on his right by Churchill. Roosevelt's exhaustion and illness were plain to see, a shocking transformation from the confident President pictured only fifteen months earlier at Teheran. He was in a hurry and wanted the conference to be quickly over. He telegraphed to Churchill that it ought not to last more than five or six days. Churchill replied, 'Even the Almighty took seven.' In the event it lasted eight days from 4 to 11 February 1945.

Roosevelt was determined to come to terms with the Soviet leader and saw in Churchill almost as great an obstacle to establishing a good post-war partnership between them as Stalin himself. He had even been reluctant to meet Churchill in Malta before flying on to the Crimea for fear that Uncle Joe would interpret this as the Anglo-Saxons ganging up on him. The peaceful future of the world rested, as Roosevelt saw it, on a good Soviet–American understanding founded on trust. He regarded Churchill's 'Victorian' imperialism and his lifelong anti-communism as outdated in the post-war world.

As for Churchill, he felt keenly on the eve of Germany's defeat that Europe was in danger from the overbearing, immensely powerful Russian bear. He was looking to a less rosy future than Roosevelt was, in a world in which a United Nations organisation could no more be relied upon to preserve peace with justice than the League of Nations had been. He wanted to dilute the bilateral relationship between the United States and Russia that Roosevelt was trying to establish. Like Talleyrand at Vienna in 1814, conscious of Britain's comparative weakness Churchill tried to bring in another European ally, France. He failed. De Gaulle was not invited and would henceforth refer to the Yalta carve-up with bitterness and blame the 'Anglo-Saxons' for it.

The only concession Churchill did win, finally gaining Roosevelt's support for it, was to secure for France participation on the Allied Control Commission for Germany, which was to co-ordinate Allied rule over the defeated Reich. France would thus have her own occupation zone and her own sector in Berlin. On reparations there was an acceptance that the Soviet Union had a special claim but the final amount was left to a commission to propose. Perhaps the most significant thing about Yalta was what was *not* discussed and agreed. The question of Germany's future was really shelved. Churchill and Roosevelt had moved away from turning Germany into a 'pastoral' country. The dismemberment of Germany was *not* now determined. The destitute plight of the Germans, so Stalin may well have calculated, would strengthen communism throughout Germany. To gain material ends, he was ready to make promises which would appear as major concessions. He agreed to modify the Soviet stand on the organisation of the United Nation, whose success was closest to Roosevelt's heart. But Roosevelt had incautiously told him that

American troops would be withdrawn from Europe within two years. Stalin therefore knew that he had only to wait until 1947; no military threat would then be able to stop him from doing whatever he then deemed to be in the Soviet interest.

The debate about Poland occupied much of the conference and was the most vexed. History did not have the same meaning for Churchill, Roosevelt and Stalin. Stalin looked at the frontiers of post-Versailles Europe through different eyes. For the West, 1937 was the last year that was 'normal', when the political geography of Europe reflected the peace settlements reached after the First World War. After 1937, Hitler first blackmailed the West and then redrew the map of Europe by force. For Russia, international injustice predated Hitler and had occurred after she had lost the war in 1917. The settlement then of the post-1918 Versailles era represented the humiliating acceptance of the superior force of the capitalist West at a time of Soviet weakness.

From her own perspective, the Soviet Union had simply not in her infancy had the necessary strength to regain Russia's 'just' frontiers. And so she had to acquiesce in the detaching of the Baltic provinces, which became independent states – Latvia, Lithuania and Estonia. Large territories were also carved out of what was formerly imperial Russia to create the Polish state, which included many Ukrainians and White Russians. Bessarabia was detached and added to Romania. As Stalin saw it, the frontiers of 1918–20 were those imposed on Russia; they were neither 'just' nor settled. He took advantage of the war between Germany, Poland, Britain and France in 1939–40 to put right what he believed were past wrongs by first making deals with Hitler. By 1941, with the absorption of eastern Poland, the three Baltic states and Bessarabia, Russia had regained most of her 'historic' frontiers. Stalin claimed that the Russian frontiers of 1941 should be regarded as the settled ones and not those of 1921 or 1937; he was prepared to consider only minor concessions. With remarkable consistency, he took his stand on this issue in discussions and negotiations with his Western allies from the earliest to the last months of the war.

The Czechs in 1943 had arranged their own settlement over the frontiers and future government of their country. Beneš, head of the exiled government in London, after the Munich experience of 1938 was not prepared to rely on Western support again. He did not allow a confrontation to develop between the communist-led Moscow Czechs and the London Western-oriented Czechs and accepted certain Soviet conditions and some loss of territory. But the Poles in London had not made their peace with Moscow. On the contrary, relations between the Polish government in exile and Moscow were little short of outright hostility, and had been aggravated by the establishment in Lublin of a communist-dominated provisional government.

Beyond Russia's frontiers the smaller nations in an arc from the Baltic to the Balkans had recently acted, in Stalin's view, as the springboard of aggression from the West against the Soviet Union. He insisted to Roosevelt and Churchill that they must not be allowed again to serve as hostile bridges to the heart of Russia. Soviet security, he emphasised, would depend on guarantees that they would be 'friendly' to the Soviet Union and would act in co-operation with her. What, however, did 'friendly' mean? To Stalin it meant that they could not remain capitalist, with anti-Russian governments based on the kind of society that had existed before the war; only societies transformed by a social revolution would be 'friendly' in the long term. The Western leaders rejected this link between the social and economic composition of the Soviet Union's neighbours and her own security. They in turn insisted on free elections, meaning that the people of the nations in question should be allowed to choose the kind of government and society they desired.

The prospect of reconciling these opposite views was slight. From Stalin's point of view the West had no business to dictate the social and political reconstruction of Poland, Czechoslovakia, Romania, Bulgaria or Hungary, any more than he himself wished to dictate the shape which the societies and politics of France, Italy, Belgium and the Netherlands should take. In these countries, Moscow had instructed the communist parties to work constructively in coalitions dominated by non-communists. He expected a *quid pro quo*. The West saw the issue in simple terms of democracy and self-determination.

For the Polish government in London the relationship with the Soviet Union was one of understandable enmity. The Russians had invaded Poland in September 1939 and now were annexing a large part of eastern Poland. The mass graves of 4421 Polish officers, shot in the back of the head by the Russians, had been discovered in 1943 in the forests of Katyn by German occupying forces and exploited by Joseph Goebbels for Nazi propaganda purposes (page 281). This unforgettable atrocity tormented Polish-Soviet relations. During the Second World War, Poland had been the conquered nation which, with Russia, had endured the most. Should she also become the nation that would now be made to suffer the consequences of victory? Britain and the United States agreed at Yalta to accept the Curzon line, with some deviations, as Poland's eastern frontier, thus giving a third of her pre-war territory to the Soviet Union. This, the London Polish government felt, was a betrayal. Churchill and Roosevelt had been driven to the reluctant conclusion that they had no realistic alternative. The Red Army occupied Poland and could not be forced to withdraw unless the Anglo-American armies were prepared to fight. Stalin for his part was well aware of the bitterness of the Polish government in London, which constituted an obvious danger to the Polish settlement he had in mind. The Poles were traditionally anti-Russian. They would not be allowed to assert their freedom at Russia's expense.

The major tussle was over the western boundary of Poland. Stalin had promised the communist Lublin government that the frontier would be marked by the Western Neisse. It was agreed that Poland would receive Pomerania and the larger half of East Prussia. Churchill and Roosevelt held out for the Eastern Neisse, which would not have assigned the whole of Silesia to Poland in addition. This question was left open to be settled later. These territories were only to be 'administered' by Poland until the conclusion of a final peace treaty with Germany.

Despite these calculations Stalin signed the Declaration on Liberated Europe at Yalta. According to its provisions the Allies would act as trustees, reaffirming the principle of the Atlantic Charter – the right of all peoples to choose the form of government under which they would live – and ensuring the restoration of sovereign rights and self-government to those peoples who had been forcibly deprived of them by the aggressor nations. Interim governments representing all democratic elements were to be set up, followed later by governments established 'through free elections'. This apparently unambiguous undertaking was ambiguous after all because it permitted only 'democratic and anti-Nazi parties' to put up candidates.

The Soviet Union twisted this to suit her own purpose of securing communist-dominated governments.

Churchill and Roosevelt wanted more specific arrangements for Poland to ensure that the Lublin provisional government, subservient to Moscow, would be replaced by a broad coalition, including exiled Polish leaders from the London-based government. The British and American ambassadors in Moscow, together with the Soviet Foreign Minister Vyacheslav Molotov, were to facilitate negotiations between the rival Polish governments in Lublin and London. Once a unified provisional government had been established, free elections were to be held. The suspicious Stalin had agreed to this for the sake of Allied unity before the final defeat of Germany. As the Red Army was in occupation of Poland he held all the cards and believed that there were enough loopholes in the Yalta agreement to ensure Soviet control in reality. For the Soviet Union an independent Poland in the post-war world was likely to be a hostile Poland, so her future was for Stalin a critical issue. Yalta had only papered over the cracks between West and East.

One reason why Roosevelt had been conciliatory in dealing with Stalin, frequently isolating Churchill, was his anxiety to secure Soviet help against the large Japanese armies deployed in China and in the Japanese home islands. The future of the atom bomb was still in doubt. Roosevelt told Stalin nothing about the progress that had been made. Actually, through agents, Stalin was already well informed. But it still appeared likely in February 1945 that the defeat of Japan would require bitter fighting, culminating in the invasion of mainland Japan, fanatically defended by the Japanese. Stalin at Yalta agreed to the Soviet Union's entry into the Pacific war two or three months after the defeat of Germany, but he named his price. With American lives at stake, Roosevelt did not allow anti-imperialist sentiments to stand in the way. Stalin demanded that Japan should relinquish southern Sakhalin and the Kurile Islands and that China should concede the warm-water port of Dairen and use of the Manchurian railway. The former imperial rights that tsarist Russia had enjoyed in China before 1904 were to be restored to the Soviet Union. The Chinese were not consulted, though in one part of their secret agreement it was stated that Chiang Kai-shek's consent was to be secured; but elsewhere, inconsistently, another paragraph was included: 'The Heads of the three Great Powers have agreed that these claims of the Soviet Union shall be unquestionably fulfilled after Japan has been defeated.' Stalin also promised to support efforts to bring about the co-operation of the Chinese Nationalists and the communists. For him this had the advantage of preventing the far more numerous Nationalists from simply attempting to wipe out the communists once the war with Japan was over.

Although Roosevelt had conceded Soviet predominance in Manchuria, he believed he had done his best to strengthen the post-war position of a weak China and that he had reduced the risk of civil war. The actual consequences of his diplomacy turned out differently and Harry S. Truman, his successor, did not welcome the last-minute Soviet declaration of war on Japan. Roosevelt in public spoke of Yalta as a triumph and a new beginning which would see the replacing of alliances and spheres of influence by the new international organisation of the United Nations. In private he was far more doubtful whether Stalin would fulfil what he had promised. But the war against Japan was still to be won and in the new year of 1945 he would contemplate no confrontation with the Soviet Union in Eastern or central Europe. Co-operation with her was possible, he believed, but he was at one with Churchill in concluding that firmness in dealing with Stalin was equally necessary. Roosevelt was not duped by Stalin but he could see no peaceful future unless coexistence could somehow be made to work. It was best to express confidence rather than misgivings.

Churchill's conscience was troubled by the Yalta agreement, which had once again partitioned Britain's brave wartime ally Poland. The shadow of appeasement, of Munich and Czechoslovakia lay not far behind and there was discontent in the House of Commons where a hard core of votes were cast against what had been concluded at Yalta. Poland was potentially damaging politically, a sensitive spot for Churchill at home. Internationally that spring of 1945, with the defeat of Germany in sight, his apprehensions also grew, as he contemplated a prostrate Western Europe and Britain being left to face the Soviets alone. The Americans, he feared, would withdraw to concentrate on the war in the Pacific. At Yalta, he had not been able to influence the outcome as the third and equal partner, because Roosevelt and Stalin had negotiated directly with

The Occupation Zones of Germany and Austria, 1945

each other. The Soviets had secretly agreed to help defeat Japan so it was tempting, especially for the Americans, to appease the Soviet Union in Europe. In the war theatre, General Eisenhower also appeared too trusting of the Russians, ready to concert military strategy with his Soviet counterparts, rather than to occupy as much of northern Germany as could be captured and then to drive on to Berlin, as Churchill urged in March 1945.

Stalin meanwhile was accusing the West of secretly arranging for the German armies to stop fighting on the western front while they continued to resist the Russians ferociously all along the eastern battle zones. This was indeed partially true. The German forces were disintegrating in the West,

with many soldiers deserting. Cities and towns surrendered to Anglo-American forces, disobeying Hitler's senseless orders to fight to the last, and the German High Command would have liked to reach a separate military surrender in the West. This was rejected. This did not mean that Churchill was complacent about the threat he discerned from the Soviet advance deep into Western Europe.

Churchill kept up a barrage of warnings in telegrams to Roosevelt. He urged that Stalin be treated firmly and made to adhere to the Yalta engagements. At Yalta, he cabled to Roosevelt, they had sided with Russia on the question of her western border. 'Poland has lost her frontier. Is she now to lose her freedom?' Churchill asked rhetorically. For Roosevelt too the Poles were a sensitive domestic political issue: there were 6 million Americans of Polish descent in the United States. But at the time he was anxious to secure Soviet co-operation to found the United Nations. He was therefore inclined to more conciliatory tactics to avoid alienating Stalin and so jeopardising his vision of a new world order. He also wanted to make sure of the promised Soviet help against Japan. Nevertheless he joined Churchill in firm appeals to Stalin.

On 12 April 1945 Roosevelt suffered a stroke so severe that he died shortly afterwards. He had responded with a growing sense of urgency to the threat posed by the totalitarian states. He recognised that freedom and democracy were being endangered throughout the world. His 'Quarantine' speech in 1937 had marked an important stage in his realisation that domestic problems at home would have to take second place to world problems. Working within the context of an overwhelming isolationist sentiment, Roosevelt had provided the indispensable, if at times devious, leadership which placed on the American people the burden of accepting the role of the United States as a superpower. In his post-war plans he worked for Soviet–American understanding, and for the creation of a viable United Nations organisation. He placed the United States on the side of independence for the peoples of Asia, including the dismantling of the European empires. He pinned his hopes on China achieving unity and stability. In Western Europe he was ready to provide American support to bring about a recovery that would enable these liberated nations, together with Britain, to safeguard their own freedoms. But he was under no illusions that all this had already actually been achieved. The behaviour of Stalin's Russia filled him with anxiety, yet it was an anxiety not without hope for the future. For all his limitations, Roosevelt's contribution to the reorientation of America's vision of her responsibilities in the world was all important. The news of his death came as a shock to the world. A half-crazed Hitler buried in his Berlin bunker saw it as the miracle that might save his Reich from defeat. By then the final offensives in the East and West were striking into the heart of Germany.

In March 1945 the American and British armies crossed the Rhine. During April they passed well beyond the military demarcation zones agreed at Yalta. Suspicion of Russian intentions was high and Churchill urged that the Anglo-American forces should withdraw only when the Russians had fulfilled their undertakings. It had been agreed that Berlin, although deep within the Russian zone of Germany, should be occupied by the United States, Britain and the Soviet Union, as well as France. But would the Soviets, once they had taken Berlin, honour their obligations?

The final Soviet offensives began in January 1945. Hitler ordered fanatical resistance on all fronts and the adoption of a 'scorched earth' policy. If Germany were not victorious, he concluded, the German people had not proved themselves worthy of the ideals of the Aryan race. He thus condemned Germany to senseless destruction. With Goebbels and Bormann at his side, he issued streams of orders from his underground headquarters in Berlin. But his orders were no longer unquestioningly obeyed. Armaments Minister Albert Speer attempted to prevent Germany's industry from being totally destroyed. He was looking beyond Hitler and defeat to Germany's recovery. Himmler tried to save his skin by seeking to negotiate an end to the war. Göring, who was in southern Germany, fancied himself as Hitler's successor, but an angry Hitler ordered the Field Marshal's arrest. The Reich ended in intrigue, ruins, bloodshed and shabby farce. Hitler concluded his life marrying his mistress, and on 30 April they both committed suicide. Goebbels and his wife then killed themselves with all their children. On 2 May Berlin surrendered to Soviet troops. Despite Germany's rapid disintegration, Admiral Karl Dönitz, nominated by Hitler as new leader of the Reich, took over as head of state observing legal niceties. He even formed a new 'government'. It lasted but a few days. On 7 May Germany unconditionally surrendered on all fronts. Britain and the United States now confronted the Soviet Union amid the ruins of continental Europe. Thus began a new era of international realities and conflict.

The sudden death of Roosevelt was a great blow for Churchill. While the Prime Minister's influence over the peace settlements had diminished, his special relationship with Roosevelt, an old friendship and appeals to past loyalties still counted for something. But would the new inexperienced President listen to the advice of the elder statesman, as Churchill now directed his warnings about Russia to Truman? He sent a cable to Truman expressing his foreboding that an 'iron curtain is being drawn down on their front', his first use of this phrase, which was to become famous later when he uttered it in public at Fulton in March 1946. He wanted Truman to come to London to co-ordinate a show-down with Stalin at a new conference. Truman rejected the idea as signalling to Stalin that the Anglo-Americans were ganging up against him.

Churchill further urged Truman to delay imple-menting the agreements reached on the respective occupation zones of Germany and not to withdraw the Allied forces which held territory deep in the zone assigned to the Soviet Union. It would be a bargaining counter and at least force the Russians to relinquish control over the whole of Berlin. But Truman was his own man. He was not enamoured of the Russians, to put it mildly, yet he was deter-mined to honour previous agreements, so that he could hold Stalin, so he thought, to what the Russians had undertaken. If Churchill had prevailed, the Cold War would have begun earlier, more of Germany would have been kept out of the Soviet sphere, and the West would not have become entangled in Berlin; alternatively, Stalin would have had to give way in central Europe. But a major difficulty of standing up to the Russians at this early date was public opinion in the West, where an unbounded admiration was felt for the Red Army, which had played the major role on land in the defeat of the Wehrmacht.

Far from co-ordinating policy with Churchill, Truman sought a direct Soviet–American under-standing on all the issues not settled at Yalta, to which end he sent Harry Hopkins to Moscow in May 1945. Churchill was upset by this move, which left Britain out in the cold. He was anxious to secure settlements with the Soviet Union concerning fron-tiers and spheres of influence before the British and American armies on the continent had been demobilised, for he feared that if such settlements were delayed the Russians would be able to do what they wanted. Truman and his advisers were more anxious to establish the United Nations as an insti-tution that would ensure peace and solve all future world problems. It was a case of realism versus idealism.

The conference to negotiate the United Nations Charter convened in San Francisco on 25 April 1945. The Americans feared that the UN would be stillborn unless Russian co-operation could be won. The problem of how the veto would operate on the Security Council had not finally been settled at Yalta, and Molotov's widening of its application was creating difficulties. It was common ground that the five permanent members – the United States, the Soviet Union, Britain, France and China – could veto any *action*; the dispute was about whether the veto also applied to a discussion, an examination or a recommendation concerning an issue brought before the Security Council. If it did, any one of the permanent members could stop a dispute from even being considered. The Russian attitude, however, was understandable given that the West looked like enjoying a permanent majority in the General Assembly. In addition the question of whether any government could represent Poland raised the unsolved Polish question once more.

It was to straighten out these and other differ-ences that Truman sent Hopkins to Moscow in May. At their meetings, Stalin cleverly tried to drive a wedge between the United States and Britain, while Hopkins listened sympathetically. Stalin certainly got the better of the bargain. His concession that the Polish government would be widened by the admission of some of the London Polish leaders still left the communists in a dominant position. Hopkins meanwhile accepted as sincere Stalin's promise not to interfere in Polish affairs, especially during the holding of 'free elections', and to show respect for individual rights and liberties. Yet when Stalin refused to release Poles he had arrested for what he described as 'diversionist' activities, the reality behind the words became only too clear. Hopkins was also anxious to gain confir-mation of the secret agreement concerning the Far East reached at Yalta. Stalin promised to attack the Japanese on 8 August 1945 and to respect Chinese sovereignty in Manchuria. On the veto issue which was blocking progress on the UN Charter, Stalin made genuine concessions and the final agreements reached in San Francisco represented a complicated compromise of the American and Soviet view (page 373). It made possible the completion of negoti-ations for the Charter on 25 June 1945.

Hopkins returned from his mission in early June, with the way now clear for the summit meeting in Potsdam. Truman's idea that he should meet Stalin alone before being joined by the British Prime Minister was angrily rejected by Churchill, who was adamant that he was not 'prepared to attend a meeting which was a continuation of a conference between yourself and Marshal Stalin'. He insisted on a simultaneous meeting on equal terms.

The Potsdam Conference was the final confer-

*The 'Big Three' at the Potsdam Conference, 17 July–2 August 1945. Soon hereafter only Stalin among the wartime leaders remained at the helm of his country.*

ence, and the longest, of the Grand Alliance. It lasted from 17 July to 2 August 1945, forming a bridge between the world at war and the coming peace. Churchill had hoped Britain would recapture part of her lost influence, that the inexperienced new President would listen to the elder statesman. De Gaulle was again snubbed; although France was to become a member of the Control Commission for Germany, French representatives were not invited to join in discussions over Germany. Agreement was reached on many post-war issues, especially the Allied treatment of Germany, but suspicion between the Allies had grown. The military necessity of holding together was gone. The relationship between East and West lacked trust and, in the personal contact between the big three, Churchill, later Clement Attlee, Truman and Stalin, the old sense of comradeship was lacking. Despite the rounds of dinners and receptions, there was a palpable absence of warmth. Averell Harriman, US Ambassador in Moscow, tried to make a friendly remark to Stalin at Potsdam: 'Marshal, you must be very proud now to be in Berlin.' He received the rather disconcerting reply, 'Tsar Alexander got to Paris' – a reference to Alexander I, who with the allies entered Paris on the defeat of Napoleon in 1814. Distrust was to widen as the agreements reached at Potsdam were broken. The West accused the Soviet Union of bad faith; this made little

impression on Stalin, who faced the enormous task of rebuilding the Soviet Union and tightening the dictatorial reins once more so that his regime would survive the capitalist external threat which he perceived.

Stalin did not trust the West and the West did not trust him. That was very clearly shown by the fact that Britain and the United States had been building the atomic bomb in great secrecy, without sharing their knowledge with their Soviet ally during the war. The Russians too had been secretly engaged on making a bomb, but the Americans got there first. After hearing that an experimental bomb had been successfully tested in New Mexico on 16 July, Truman obliquely referred to this success in talking to Stalin, without specifically mentioning that an atomic bomb would soon be dropped on Hiroshima. Stalin did not betray his anxiety that the United States had tilted the balance of power in her favour. Churchill was elated. The atomic bomb would redress the balance: despite the strength of the Red Army, Stalin no longer had all the cards in his hands. After Stalin had returned to the Kremlin, he ordered Soviet scientists to redouble their efforts to make a Soviet atomic bomb. Now that the world knew it could be done, the basic obstacles were more industrial than scientific, the difficulty of extracting the fissionable materials. Klaus Fuchs helped the Soviet scientists to reach their goal in 1949, but they would no doubt have solved the problems, without him, albeit perhaps a little later.

On the whole Stalin could be well satisfied with the outcome of the conference at Potsdam. Churchill did not stay to the end. He returned to be in London when the outcome of the general election was announced. He was replaced on 28 July in Potsdam by Clement Attlee and the redoubtable Ernest Bevin, the new foreign secretary, who in the last days of the conference conducted most of the negotiations for Britain. Truman also left most of the critical bargaining to his Secretary of State James Byrnes. The Polish issue once more proved highly contentious. There was much argument about Poland's western frontier. To the end Stalin insisted on the Western Neisse, facing the West with a *fait accompli*. Bevin and Byrnes had to accept this but did so with the proviso that these German territories were only to be 'administered' by Poland and a final settlement of the western frontier would have to await the signature of the peace treaty with Germany. In fact the provisional was to prove permanent.

The Polish agreement was part of a deal whereby the Soviet Union reluctantly accepted the American proposal on reparations. From a reparations point of view, Stalin had wanted to have Germany treated as a whole so that he could participate in spoils from the West and the industrial Ruhr as well as take away all that could be moved from the Soviet zone – in other words, so that he could get the best of both worlds. But he had to be satisfied with a formula that left each of the occupying powers to take reparations from her own zone. The reparation claims of Poland too would have to be met from the Soviet share. In addition, the Soviet Union would receive 10 per cent of industrial capital equipment taken as reparations by the West and a further 15 per cent in exchange for food and raw materials from the East. The agreement soon led to bitter recriminations.

Stalin did better on the question of the reconstituted Polish government. The London Poles were pressurised into accepting a settlement which incorporated some London ministers in the communist-dominated government in Warsaw. Poland would not emerge again from communist rule and Soviet domination for two generations.

The redrawing of Poland's frontiers only ratified what had already happened on the human level.

Millions of Poles moved west to the Polish side of the Curzon line. Millions of Germans too had fled westward from the Red Army and the Polish forces, as well as from the German territories now under Polish rule and from the Sudeten areas of Czechoslovakia. Young and old were driven out with only the possessions they could carry. The Russians, Poles and Czechs, after the way they had been treated under Nazi occupation, were now indifferent to the suffering of the Germans. Retribution fell on guilty and innocent alike and many Germans perished from the ardours of migration. When at Potsdam the Allies recorded their agreement that the 'transfer' of Germans from Poland, Czechoslovakia and Hungary should be carried out 'in an orderly and humane manner', the West was therefore doing no more than expressing a pious hope largely after the event.

A central issue at Potsdam was the need to reach agreement on the treatment of Germany. The idea of dividing Germany into a number of separate states was finally abandoned. But the principles on which control of Germany were based were contradictory from the start: the Allies sought to treat Germany as one while at the same time partitioning her into zones of occupation. The Allied Control Council was supposed to oversee Germany as a whole, but each of the commanders-in-chief in his own zone had complete authority as well. The plan to establish 'central German administrative departments, headed by State Secretaries . . . in the fields of finance, transport, communications, foreign trade and industry', but under the direction of the Control Council, proved impossible to carry through as long as each occupation zone fell under the separate control of one of the four Allies. There was to be 'for the time being' no central German government, but local self-government and democratic parties were encouraged. On the one hand, the Allies agreed that during the occupation 'the German economy shall be treated as a single economic unit'; on the other, reparations were a matter for each occupying power to settle in her own zone.

The immediate consequence of all these decisions in practice was to move towards the division of Germany into four separate zones. Four years later, the three Western zones would combine and create a democratic Western central government, and a communist regime would be imposed on the Soviet Eastern zone. There were some areas of agreement, however; the trial of war criminals, the destruction of Nazi ideology, the complete disarmament of Germany, and control of such German industry as could be used for war led to no real differences at Potsdam. But already the West and the Russians were compromising these principles. German scientists were too valuable a 'war booty' to be punished as Nazi war criminals. Rocket scientists who had perfected the V-1 and V-2 in Peenemünde were, despite their past, seized by the Americans and bribed to contribute their know-how to Western military technology. Many who should have been convicted of war crimes prospered instead in the West and worked for the United States in the space race. Other German rocket scientists were captured by the Russians and assisted in Soviet missile development. In the Cold War, ex-Nazis with expertise in military intelligence were recruited by both sides. Former Wehrmacht officers served both NATO and the Warsaw Pact armies. Only recently has the veil been lifted from some of the darker aspects of what happened in the aftermath of the victory over Germany.

Austria was separated once more from Germany and was fortunate to escape reparations. Austrian guards in concentration camps had not behaved with any less bestiality in the SS than their German counterparts, nor can a distinction be drawn between Austrian and German members of the Wehrmacht. Austria was allowed to establish a central government but was occupied like Germany and divided into four zones, American, British, French and Soviet, with Vienna under joint control.

The Potsdam Conference established a Council of Foreign Ministers, which it was expected would normally meet in London. Its main task was the preparation of peace treaties with Italy, Romania, Bulgaria, Hungary and Finland. A peace settlement with Germany was also mentioned, but it seemed a distant prospect in 1945 since it required the prior establishment of a German government with the consent of the Allies. Only those countries which were signatories to the terms of surrender of each state would be allowed to participate, with the exception of France, which was admitted to discuss peace terms with Italy. During the eighteen months of its existence and after much acrimony, peace treaties with all these states except Germany were agreed. The Council, which still represented the wartime alliance, came to grief over the German question, and the Cold War began (pages 378–9).

Potsdam marked the beginning of the end of any

hope that the wartime alliance would outlast the defeat of Germany, Italy, Japan and the minor Axis allies and, as Roosevelt had hoped, continue to safeguard the peace. It had achieved victory over the most powerful and barbaric threat ever faced by Russia and the Western democracies in modern times. Nineteen-forty-five marks a division in world history. This side of it the West once more perceived the Soviet Union as its most dangerous enemy. But this division should not obscure what lies on the other side, what the civilised world owes to the sacrifices made by the Soviet Union, by China, by Britain and by the United States, the great powers of their day which saw the struggle through together.

No one expected that the Japanese would be forced to surrender within three months of the Allied victory in Europe. In fighting as savage as any in the Second World War, the United States Navy, the marines and the army, under the command of Admiral Nimitz, had pushed the Japanese back from one tropical island base to the next. By the summer of 1943 the Japanese had been forced on to the defensive. A year later the Americans were closing in on Japan, capturing Saipan, Tinian and Guam. Meanwhile a Japanese offensive from Burma into India was halted by British and Dominion troops. In October 1944 General MacArthur began the attack on the Philippines. There ensued the last great naval battle of the Second World War – the battle of Leyte Gulf. The Japanese navy had planned a counterblow to destroy MacArthur's supply line and then his army. With the defeat of the Japanese navy in Leyte Gulf the United States had won command of the sea in Japan's home waters.

In the central Pacific, Nimitz advanced from Saipan to the island of Iwojima and then in the fiercest fighting of the war, lasting from April to June 1945, attacked and captured Okinawa, an island in the Ryukyu group just 500 miles from Japan. Japan's cities were being systematically reduced to rubble by the fires caused by constant air attacks. In south-east Asia, Admiral Lord Louis Mountbatten commanded the Allied forces which between December 1944 and May 1945 recaptured Burma from the retreating Japanese. But skilfully as this campaign was conducted, it was secondary in its impact on the war. The Americans in the Pacific were thrusting at the heart of the Japanese Empire.

In 1944 the Japanese military and naval leaders knew the war could not be won. Yet even as late

*Okinawa, 1945. The Americans begin the process of revitalizing Japan – leading her through the minefield of authoritarianism to the haven of democracy, much as this military policeman here steers a child clear of an unexploded shell.*

as May 1945 they hoped that the evidence of Japan's fanatical defence at Okinawa and elsewhere would deter the Allies from invading Japan herself, where the Allies, for the first time, would have to come to grips with large Japanese armies. Rather than lose tens of thousands of men, might not the Allies be prepared to offer reasonable terms?

Those advisers of the Emperor who were in favour of an immediate peace were not strong enough to assert themselves openly against the military and naval leaderships. But war supplies, especially oil, were rapidly running out and Japan's situation was deteriorating fast. By July 1945 even the military accepted that it was worth taking the initiative to explore what kind of peace terms the Allies might put forward. Approaches were made to the Soviet Union to act as mediators. The Soviets refused brusquely to help Japan to a negotiated peace. With the prize of Manchuria promised at Yalta, Stalin had his own reasons for wishing to prolong the war long enough to enable the Red Army to advance into Manchuria. Nevertheless, Stalin did inform Churchill of Japanese overtures when they assembled with Truman at the Potsdam Conference in July 1945, urging that the Allies should insist on 'unconditional' surrender.

But Churchill pressed moderation on Truman to save American and British lives. The upshot was that Truman and Churchill on 26 July issued an 'ultimatum' to Japan setting out basic conditions of peace. They called for the 'unconditional surrender' of the Japanese military forces. The influence of the military and all those who had wished Japan into the path of aggression would be removed. War criminals would be punished and reparations required. Japan would have to give up all her imperial conquests. Finally, Japan would be occupied. But, beyond this, the declaration went out of its way to promise Japan a future: 'We do not intend that the Japanese shall be enslaved as a race nor destroyed as a nation . . .' Japan's industries would be preserved, her soldiers allowed to return home, and democracy and justice would be established under the guidance of the occupation. Once this was securely rooted in Japan, and a freely elected Japanese government could safely be given responsibility, the occupation forces would withdraw. In short, imperial Japan with her divine emperor would be transformed into a Western-type democratic state. What was not clear, and it was a critical point for the Japanese, was whether the Emperor would be permitted to remain on the throne.

Japan's eighty-year-old prime minister, Admiral Suzuki, responded to the ultimatum with a non-committal statement. He was temporising in the face of the powerful military opposition; mistranslation unfortunately made his reply sound contemptuous. But was it really necessary to drop the atomic bomb or would a few more days have given the upper hand to the peace party in any case? The evidence suggests that only after Hiroshima – realising what terrible havoc would result from more such bombs – did the Emperor Hirohito conclude that he could no longer merely accept the decision of his leading ministers and the military, but that he would have to assert himself and overrule the military who still were inclined to continue the war. Ironically it was the last act of the Emperor's divine authority, soon to be destroyed, that saved countless American and Japanese lives. President Truman was probably therefore right in believing that only the atomic bombs could shock Japan into *immediate* surrender.

On 6 August an American plane dropped just one small bomb on a Japanese city still untouched by war. 'Hiroshima' henceforth has become a byword for a nuclear holocaust, for a threatened new world. There was instant recognition that the

**Europe after 1945**

ATLANTIC

OCEAN

NORTH
SEA

Dublin

London

BELGIUM

Paris

LUX.

FRANCE

Seine

Rhône

PORTUGAL

ANDORRA

Madrid

SPAIN

Tangier    GIBRALTAR

Algiers

NORWAY

SWEDEN

Oslo

Stockholm

FINLAND

Helsinki

DENMARK

NETHER-
LANDS

Copenhagen

SOVIET UNION

POLAND

FEDERAL
GERMAN
REPUBLIC

DDR

Berlin

Warsaw

Elbe

CZECHOSLO-
VAKIA

Curzon line
1919–20

Lvov

Vienna

SWITZ.

AUSTRIA

HUNGARY

ROMANIA

ITALY

Free Territory of
Trieste 1947–54

YUGOSLAVIA

Belgrade

Bucharest

BULGARIA

Sofia

CORSICA

Rome

ALBANIA

SARDINIA

MEDITERRANEAN    SEA

GREECE

Athens

TURKEY

SICILY

CRETE

Tripoli

–·–·–·–·–  Former German territory

——————  Post-1945 frontiers

0                              1000 miles

0                    1000 km

nature of war had been transformed. Scientists had harnessed the innermost forces of nature to a weapon of destruction that had hitherto been unimaginable. In one blinding flash the humans who were instantly vaporised were perhaps the more fortunate; 66,000 men, women and children were killed immediately or succumbed soon after the atom bomb had struck. Another 69,000 were horribly injured – they were found to suffer from a new illness, radiation sickness, and many died later in agony. Even future unborn generations were affected, deformed by the mutation of genes in the sick. The suffering has continued for decades. Four square miles of the city were totally destroyed on that terrible day. Three days later Nagasaki was the second and mercifully last city to suffer the effects of an atomic attack. It was not the end, however, of the development of even more destructive nuclear weapons of annihilation. The single Hiroshima bomb possessed the explosive power of 20,000 tons of TNT. Later hydrogen bombs were tested in the 1950s with a power 250 times greater than the bomb dropped on Hiroshima. There was and is no effective system of defence in existence that can stop the missile delivery of a destructive power that can wipe out civilised life on whole continents. The Japanese were the first victims and the last, if the world is to survive.

Ever since the horror of Hiroshima the debate has raged whether a weapon so indiscriminate in its mass destruction of human life should have been used. It has been argued that the main reason why it was dropped was to warn the Soviet Union of the new invincible power of the United States. No doubt the possession of the atomic bomb made it possible for the United States to feel that she was safe to demobilise even in the face of the superior weight of the Soviet armed forces. But the bomb would have been dropped even had the Soviet Union not existed. The investment in the construction of the two nuclear bombs available for use in 1945 had been huge. It was thought that using them would prove decisive in ending the war without more fighting and the expected further losses of hundreds of thousands of Allied lives from storming the Japanese home islands against fierce resistance. Okinawa and Iwojima would come to seem a picnic by comparison. The killing of enemy civilians in order to shorten the war was seen as entirely justified after so much death and destruction. No one thought in terms of drawing up a balance sheet of losses of enemy men, women and children as against the lives of Allied soldiers. That is shown by the devastating raids on German and Japanese cities with conventional weapons. Loss of civilian lives was greater in Tokyo and Dresden than in Hiroshima and Nagasaki, and no moral issue appeared involved whether this was the result of one bomb or 5000. So Truman had no hesitation.

The Soviet Union's declaration of war on Japan on 8 August and her invasion of China were fresh disasters but not decisive factors in forcing Tokyo's leader to make a decision. Messages sent by the Allies and received in Tokyo on 13 August 1945 indicating that the Emperor would not be removed from the throne were more important in the final deliberations. On 14 August the Emperor broadcast Japan's surrender. Over the radio he spoke for the first time to the Japanese people, saying that the unendurable had to be endured. The Second World War was over.

# PART VI

*Post-war Europe, 1945–1947*

# CHAPTER 30

# Zero Hour: The Allies and the Germans

In May 1945 a world seemed to have come to an end in Germany. So cataclysmic was the change that the Germans coined the phrase 'zero hour'. Their country was occupied and at the mercy of foreigners, who now took over the government. The victors' ideologies and values were imposed on the new Germany for good or ill; but nothing could be worse than what had gone before.

In the Western zones of Germany, constituting two-thirds of the former Reich, the social basis did not radically alter. Factory owners, managers of industry, and the professional classes, despite their involvement with Hitler's Germany, adjusted themselves to the new circumstances. Only the best-known collaborators like Alfried Krupp were arrested and tried. Expertise and efficiency does not have to coincide with morality. Defeated Germany thus did not lose the skills of her managers, engineers and workers, who thus made possible the later economic miracle of the 1950s. During the early years of the occupation from 1945 to 1949 their first task was to try to resist or circumvent and soften the draconian economic directives of occupiers bent on deindustrialising Germany.

In 1945, the Allies were amazed to discover how much of Germany's industrial strength had survived the war. The lost production of the steel industry did not exceed 10 per cent, and no key industry had suffered more than 20 per cent losses. Industrially, then, 1945 was not the zero hour, despite the huge problems of restoring some sort of normality.

The physical appearance of the German cities belied their underlying strength. Corpses still lay under huge mounds of rubble, and many were to remain permanently entombed there. The new Germany would have to be built on top of streets turned into cemeteries. Parts of Berlin, Cologne and Hamburg were totally flattened. In Hamburg, one district had even been walled in. No one had been permitted to enter it for fear that disease would spread from the corpses left there. Only the most rudimentary shelter could be made available for those civilians who had not already fled to the countryside.

The last weeks of the war, although it was lost for certain, had added to the needless destruction of life. The Germans had fought on, obeying orders. Some even believed that the Führer had a wonder-weapon which would rescue them or that the Americans and British would join them to fight the Russians 'to save civilisation'. There was also a good reason for holding on as long as possible in the east. The surviving German navy made it a last mission to evacuate the refugees stranded on the coast of East Prussia and now cut off from the rest of Germany by the Soviet advance. Tens of thousands were ferried to Hamburg and other ports in west Germany. German losses during the war had been horrendous. As best as can be established more than 3 million German soldiers had been killed or were missing, millions more were wounded and disabled; the Western Allied camps were filled with prisoners of war. Those in Soviet captivity who survived would not return home for ten years. More

*In a devastated Dresden* (above) *the war is over and life must go on. Elsewhere in rural Germany* (below), *it was possible to think that there had been no war at all.*

than half a million civilians killed were victims of the Allied bombing offensive.

Allied soldiers commandeered the more habitable buildings; military headquarters were set up; local administrative offices were supervised by Russian, British, French or American army officers. The war had displaced millions. German soldiers and civilians were trying to find their way home. Poles and Russians brought to Germany as slave labour were now stranded; there were also tens of thousands of Russians who had changed sides and had sought to escape death by helping the Germans. Some Ukrainians and Latvians, Lithuanians and Estonians had participated with the SS in terrible atrocities. Victims and murderers were now all intermingled. The concentration-camp survivors were released. Millions of 'foreigners' were on German soil; many were sick and unable to work – what was to happen to them? What was to be done with the pitiful remnants of the European Jews? A new and prosaic term was found for this flotsam of humanity, 'displaced persons'. They were put in camps again, in simple huts, and were fed by relief workers. It was to take years to sort them all out and settle them – not always in the country of their choice.

More than 20 million were on the move in Europe in the early summer of 1945, escaping something, going from somewhere to somewhere else. The roads were crammed with people on foot, on bicycles and with bundles of possessions. Some arrived crowded into or clinging to the outside of the few trains that were still running. The sheer scale of the forced migration during the war and in 1945, continuing for another two and three years, almost defies the imagination. From mid-1944 Germans and their allies were fleeing from the advancing Red Army in the east, where the Wehrmacht tried to hold a front line even during the last days of the war to enable millions more to reach the West. The loss of life probably exceeded 2 million, as the fighting at times overran the fleeing civilian columns. Nazi Germans who had lorded it over the Poles might have deserved their fate but not the children. Tragedy overtook both the guilty and the innocent.

When the war was over, under the terms of the Potsdam Agreement the Poles drove out most of the Germans who had settled in Poland during the war, as well as the ethnic Germans who had lived in Poland long before it became a sovereign state again; millions more were driven from the newly occupied German territories east of the Oder–

*German refugees sit, awaiting direction, on the streets of Cologne.*

*The last major German naval operation of the Second World War: rural Germans fleeing from the Russian armies sweeping through East Prussia are evacuated by ship.*

Neisse, which to all intents and purposes became part of the Polish state. From Czechoslovakia, the Sudeten ethnic Germans were likewise expelled. It was supposed to be done humanely, but pent-up hatreds often got the better of humanity. Atrocities were committed by both Poles and Czechs. In all, as many as 10 million Germans and ethnic Germans reached the Western zones of Germany without much more than the clothes they stood up in. At least they were 'home' with their own people, though not always welcomed by the local residents. They were not displaced persons (DPs for short) in the same sense as the 1.5 million Russians, the million Frenchmen, the 600,000 Poles and the hundreds of thousands from every country the Germans had conquered, whose people had been forced to work in German factories. Some of these DPs, like the Western nationals, had a home to go to; others, including many Russians, did not want to return – they knew what fate awaited them for collaborating with the Germans. The British, in accordance with agreements made with the Russians and Yugoslavs, forced thousands back at the point of the bayonet. Among the most pathetic DPs, who sought their home but were prevented from going there, were the Jews, the survivors of the death camps, who longed to enter British-controlled Palestine.

Rations for the Germans were very short, sufficient only to maintain life. Coal was lacking for heating and for industry. Hardly a tree that could provide fuel for a fire was left standing in the towns. The lovely Berlin park, the Tiergarten, was soon denuded of its trees. The destruction of the transport system made it even harder to provide basic needs for an estimated 25 million homeless and rootless people, as well as for the rest of the population. Many families had lost their breadwinner at the front, 'fallen for Führer and country'; many more men, women and children were crippled by war wounds. The immediate challenge in 1945 was mere survival. Curfews and the lack of postal and telephone systems cut off one community from another during the early weeks of peace; in Kassel the population did not know what was happening in Frankfurt. Only German farmers, in the countryside, were still relatively well off. They had their houses, their land, and flour, milk, vegetables and meat which they could exchange for a Persian carpet or jewellery brought to them by hungry city-dwellers. There was little fellow feeling in misfortune. Allied soldiers too swapped necessities

and cigarettes for expensive cameras and watches. Cigarettes became a currency.

That mass starvation and epidemics did not sweep through Germany and central Europe in 1945 and 1946 is a remarkable tribute to the victors and to the relief workers. It was also due to the efficiency of new pesticides: there was no repeat of the influenza epidemic that claimed millions of victims after the First World War; lice, the main carriers of disease, were killed by DDT. Much of the management of these huge tasks was entrusted to young inexperienced Allied officers. But the Germans who acted under their direction and succeeded in bringing some semblance of order out of chaos also deserve credit.

Contemporary observers remarked on the apathy and listlessness of the German population. In the towns only the bare rations to keep people alive could be distributed, and the first winter of peace, one of the coldest on record, claimed many victims among the elderly and the sick in Berlin, Hamburg, Munich and other cities, where makeshift shelters had to serve as homes. Germany was completely defeated and at the mercy of the occupying armies. But would Allied disunity rescue the Germans from their plight, as the Russians, the Americans and the British vied to enlist German help?

The Allies distrusted the Germans: that was the one point, amid all the disputes, on which in 1945 they were agreed. But they still expected Germany to remain unified under their supervision. Soviet and Western leaders shared what turned out to be an accurate perception of the capacity of the German people for recovery; but they also feared that the Germans, unless controlled, would be capable of rebuilding not only their shattered industry and their cities, but also their destructive military potential. In their hearts, the Allies thought the German people had not changed and were only temporarily submissive in the face of overwhelming defeat. They saw the great majority of Germans as incorrigibly militaristic and as a threat to a peaceful Europe. The German people, so history appeared to prove, were ready to subordinate individual ethical values to the good of the state, whose leaders then ruthlessly exploited Germany's strength at the expense of her neighbours. A new and terrible dimension of barbarism had been added by Hitler's German nation in arms. German victories from 1939 to 1942 were accompanied by destruction throughout continental Europe and by suffering and the killing

*On liberation by the Allies, the concentration camps in Germany were overflowing with survivors of the death marches that had brought Jews and other prisoners from the eastern extermination camps as the Russians continued to advance through Nazi territory (above and left). Thousands died of the diseases that swept the camps before they were liberated – among them a young Jewish girl called Anne Frank. Despite intensive medical efforts thousands more could not be saved even after being restored to freedom (top right). One such camp, with the idyllic name Buchenwald (Birchforest) (right), was situated close to Germany's cultural shrine, Weimar.*

of millions of men, women and children. By the end of the war, virtually every German was suspected of having been in league with the evil-doers. These Allied attitudes cannot be understood today without seeing again the newsreels of the liberated concentration camps shown in all the cinemas, especially (by Allied command) German ones, immediately after the end of the war, with their piles of naked corpses, the skeletal appearance of the survivors. For the first time, ordinary people in the West came face to face with the full evil of National Socialist Germany. In Russia and Poland newsreels were not necessary. The inhabitants had actually experienced on their own bodies the cruel and ruthless occupation.

Allied planning was based on the belief that, since Europe and the world had to go on living with some 70 million Germans, they represented a threat for the future unless they could be led to change fundamentally. The Russians, as well as the British, French and Americans, meant to impose these changes from above – though they had very different conceptions of what needed to be done. They were agreed, however, on the wholesale removal of the Nazi political leadership as a prerequisite.

The expediency of demanding the unconditional surrender of the German state has been much debated by historians, but to no purpose. Britain, Russia and the United States, together with France and the other Allied nations, had fought Germany in an all-out war for survival. How could they be expected to negotiate with the military successors of Hitler, on the basis of any terms that left Germany intact and her armies short of defeat? Germany had to be taught a lesson in defeat that would allow no false sense of military honour to survive. Germany's neighbours would not be able to live in peace unless control over Germany was taken away from the Germans – as had conspicuously not been done in 1919. That meant occupation and Allied rule over a completely powerless Germany (some spoke of this lasting twenty-five, even forty, years). On this interpretation of 'unconditional surrender' at least, Stalin, Churchill and Roosevelt were agreed in 1944 and 1945.

The first solutions suggested during the war to this problem of containing Germany proposed to render her harmless by standing down her armed forces and eliminating the general staffs, supposedly imbued with Prussian military traditions. In its original form, the Morgenthau Plan of 1944 allowed

Germany no heavy industry to manufacture cars and no machine tools; instead light industries could make furniture and tin-openers. Germany would thus become a 'pastoral' country; the industrial region of the Ruhr would be no more. The standard of living of the Germans would be at subsistence levels, no higher than that of the poorest of the countries in the east which Germany had occupied. There was, of course, a strong punitive element in these plans, felt to be justified by Germany's barbaric behaviour during the war. The large labour force, which would not be able to find employment in Germany, would provide reparations as forced labour working for the Allies to make good some of the damage done. But the plan was too unreal to survive. Seventy million Germans could not live without export industries. Europe could not manage without Ruhr coal and steel. Short-term reparations would not make up for the cost the Allies would have to bear to keep the Germans alive. The plan's shortcomings were realised immediately, but its opponents could not eliminate it altogether; they could do no more than introduce some changes.

After the war was won, US occupation aims were embodied in the order of the Joint Chiefs of Staff (US) JCS 1067, dated 26 April 1945, Germany; British policies did not differ from it significantly, though they embodied a more constructive view of the future rehabilitation of Germany. Sweeping deindustrialisation and the dismantling for reparations of German factories were mandatory. The German people would be allowed only the lowest standard of living that avoided death and disease. Yet they could not be condemned to mass starvation: $700 million annually were needed to pay for food imports to keep the Germans in the British and American zones alive. For Britain especially, with her desperate dollar shortage, this was an unacceptable drain. The Germans should be made to pay for what they needed themselves, but could do so only if they were allowed to manufacture goods again for export. This stimulated a revision of thinking about limitations placed on industrial production from the early draconian four-power decision of March 1946, to reduce it to 50 per cent of that in 1938. The economic occupation policies from 1945 to 1949 were a mass of contradictions: continuing to dismantle factories as reparations, desiring to break Germany's industrial potential for war, and removing possibly successful commercial rivals from world markets, such as the pharmaceutical industry. Patents became war booty. At the same time there was growing acceptance that Western Germany had to be rebuilt, that her prosperity was an essential support of West German and European democracy, threatened by the Cold War. Not until 1952 were all attempts to limit Germany's basic heavy industry, steel, abandoned.

Through the hardships of the early years, the Germans had survived better than anyone would have thought possible in 1945. They accepted certain limitations – for example, not to manufacture nuclear weapons or poison gas. For the rest, Allied efforts to restructure German industry, break up the powerful cartels and loosen the hold of the banks were soon reversed.

At the start of the occupation there was a haphazard mass internment of those deemed to have served the Third Reich in an important capacity. German prisoners of war in Allied hands and labouring abroad, on British farms for instance, were not sent home at the end of the war. The Western Allies only agreed to return them by the end of 1948. But most of the millions taken prisoner in Germany itself during the last stages of the war were released after a short time. From Soviet captivity hundreds of thousands never returned. German women had to undertake the heaviest manual labour, clearing the rubble. Where were strong men? Three and a quarter million were missing or dead, millions were crippled, and millions had been taken prisoner. Shortly before his death Roosevelt wrote, 'The German people are not going to be enslaved. . . . But it will be necessary for them to earn their way back into the fellowship of peace-loving and law-abiding nations.' They would never be entrusted again to bear arms. The captains of industry and the National Socialist leaders would be tried and treated as criminals. What was left of industry would be supervised and ceilings of production imposed.

The Germans were told they had been liberated, but Allied soldiers were strictly ordered not to 'fraternise' with them – to avoid all social contact. Shunned and struggling to survive hunger and cold,

*Guilty of perpetrating crimes against humanity: from left to right, Göring, Hess, Ribbentrop and Keitel in the front row of the defendants' box at the Nuremberg trials.*

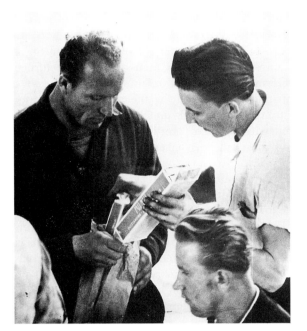

*Scenes from Occupied Germany. Many Russian soldiers had even fewer possessions than the defeated enemy (top right). Money became worthless and cigarettes, originally from the fabled US Army stores, were the currency in most frequent use (top left); while young Germans were being 're-educated' (left), the Fraüleins looked to simpler pleasures (right). To the GIs they did not look much like the enemy: the order against fraternization was readily disobeyed.*

the German people were obliged to submit to 're-education', the attempt to change their hearts and minds. Punishment and 'denazification' was one side of the coin, the inculcation of virtue and democracy the other. Control of the media and the re-establishment in schools of sound teaching of the right values were priorities. Gradually, decentralised political life was encouraged. The adoption of punitive measures, it was quickly realised, ran counter to the attempt to reform the German people. If they were to be treated as pariahs, how could they be convinced at the same time of the blessings of liberty?

Within occupied Germany, despite many absurdities and contradictions, denazification and re-education made a positive contribution. The Nuremberg trials of the leaders of Hitler's state, which began in November 1945, culminated in the death sentence on twelve of the accused eleven months later, and revealed the barbaric nature of the occupation in the east. This evidence confronted the ordinary German people with unpleasant truths which many of them had known about but could not face, and only the totally incorrigible still insisted that the gas ovens of Auschwitz were propaganda. No respect was felt for Hitler's lieutenants, who had led Germany into destruction and suffering, though some satisfaction was felt that Göring had outwitted his jailers by committing suicide before he could be hanged. The SS was condemned wholesale by the Allies as a criminal organisation.

Rough justice was meted out to the lesser supporters. All Germans were required to fill out a questionnaire, the famous *Fragebogen*, which served as a basis for denazification. Many millions of Germans had been National Socialists out of conviction, many opportunistically in hope of gain, some only under pressure; most had joined the party or one of its organisations. But only a minority, some 209,000 out of a population of 44.5 million, were actually prosecuted in the special courts set up in the British, American and French zones (more were tried in the American than in the British zone). In the Soviet sector, with a population of 17 million, the figure given for those tried is also small, just over 17,000. This did not imply that the Russians were more forgiving; they simply did not trouble with court procedures. Tens of thousands were put in former Nazi concentration camps and thousands lost their lives, not only Nazi criminals but also opponents of communism. When categorised, of

those charged with being Nazis only 1667 were regarded as chief perpetrators of crimes, 23,060 as partially guilty (*belastet*), 150,425 as less guilty and just over 1 million as 'fellow travellers'. Over 5 million suspects were not prosecuted in any way. Even the Allies came to realise how unsatisfactory the process was. Minor offenders were not infrequently treated more harshly than men with far more on their conscience, including the Gauleiter of Hamburg, who after imprisonment and a quiet period, prospered again in post-war West Germany. Justice proved too subjective, too haphazard, and punishment too arbitrary; there was no clean sweep of all those involved in the crimes of the Third Reich. The judges, with few exceptions, continued to sit in judgement, as they had in the Nazi years; the majority of civil servants now served their new masters and the files they kept frequently show no break around May 1945! There were simply too many National Socialists; the task of punishment had to be abandoned for all but the worst criminals.

Nevertheless, the great majority of Germans did change after the war. Allied re-education contributed to this but it was not the only or even the main reason for it. Correct as Allied assumptions were about Germany's capacity to recover from defeat, so they were wrong in believing that, given half a chance, the German people would once again turn to another Hitler with a policy of expansion and conquest. Henry Morgenthau even wrote a book about it in 1945 entitled *Germany Is Our Problem*, describing how some still unknown corporal was very likely plotting secretly that very moment how to rebuild Germany in order to prepare for a war of revenge. After more than four decades of peace, Morgenthau has been proven to have been wrong. The total military collapse and its immediate consequences did in fact convince the German people (except for a small extremist fringe) that in Hitler they had followed a false prophet. To the surprise of the Allies the expected Nazi underground movements, such as the Werewolves, came to nothing. The German people soon showed themselves anxious to learn from their victors, who had after all proved themselves stronger and more successful. Defeat of all things German had proved a radical cure for the mentality of *Deutschland über Alles*. British representative institutions now became the model, and the American way of life an aspiration – at least that part portrayed in Hollywood films and by the comparative illusion of wealth now sustained by the occupying GIs in their smart uniforms. From the Russians the benefits were less obvious and no one in Germany, except hardened communists, wished to emulate their style of life and lower standards of living. There is no doubt that the year 1945, unlike 1918, thus marks a decisive breach in German history. The lure of conquest and physical expansion, of lording it as the supposed *Herrenvolk*, had ended in evident ruin.

That is not to say that there was an immediate moral renaissance in Germany. Many Germans had fanatically believed in Hitler and in Germany's survival to the end; those who felt genuine shame and regret for the crimes of the regime were probably a minority. Most were sorry they had lost the war; fortunately some did recognise that they had been 'liberated' by the Allies – they would form a small nucleus for creating a better society.

Living conditions proved desperate during the first two years of occupation, and its rule by Russian, American, British and French soldiers and administrators brought home to every German the totality of the defeat. They were now faced with the practical task of material survival amid the ruins of their cities. Feelings of guilt did not in the circumstances spring first to mind; there were more immediate needs to attend to. Many of the older generation of Germans did not repudiate the Nazi past, but Hitler was dead and new masters had to be served, new political realities to be faced. It was different for the young. They increasingly questioned the values of their parents and could find no pride in German history or indeed in being Germans at all. They saw a way ahead in showing themselves to be good Europeans. And so the two Germanies became the first modern nations whose citizens consciously turned their backs on the past, some concentrating on rebuilding a new life and giving little thought to moral questions, others genuinely feeling shame for the past. The Western Allies were not confronted with a task they had thought would take at least a generation to complete. Instead, within two years of the German surrender, the East–West confrontation of the Cold War hastened Soviet and Anglo-American readiness publicly to accept at face value the 'new' reformed Germany, though in private there were still strong reservations about the trustworthiness of Germans. This residual suspicion of the dangers of too strong a Germany remained alive after almost half a century when German unity once more became a reality.

Stalin was just as anxious to 're-educate' the German people in the Soviet zone his way. His own life's experiences in the USSR may well have made him more optimistic about the prospects than the West was. The German people had shown an enviable readiness to follow strong leadership. For some it was only a question of exchanging a brown for a red shirt. It was particularly easy to form new red youth brigades. The Russians and their German nominees would now provide that leadership. As the victors they would carry away from Germany all the reparations they could, but Stalin saw no reason why he should wait before undertaking political re-education and the transformation of German society. Confident that sufficient power at the top could ensure the loyalty of those below, he was ready to use as instruments not only the Moscow-trained communists, but even leaders of the Wehrmacht, taken prisoners of war, who as early as 1943 had been formed into the Free Germany Committee. Former supporters of Hitler, provided they were useful enough, could now rehabilitate themselves by promising unswerving loyalty to Moscow. Others were simply set to work, like the scientists and rocket specialists. The Western Allies in this respect acted no differently. For Stalin the struggle in Germany would be between 'capitalism' and 'socialism', and the only safe Germany would be a country whose previous political and social patterns had been transformed. Given Stalin's ideological assumptions he was bound to be extremely apprehensive about developments in the Western zones of occupation, where the majority of Germans lived. In such fears the blossoming of the Cold War can be traced.

In their relations with the Allies the Germans were not entirely supine. A nucleus of post-war German political leaders, unsullied by the Nazi years, resurfaced, hardened and toughened. They had a vision of a new Germany and a better future. It was difficult for the communist leaders Wilhelm Pieck and Walter Ulbricht, returning from Moscow in 1945, to be anything but cynical after Stalin's terror years, which had claimed so many of their German comrades as victims, and after Stalin's sacrifice of the German Communist Party to the Nazis. But there were also idealistic communists, survivors of the concentration camps and returning exiles, who preserved their illusions of Stalin's Russia and now were ready to work for an 'anti-fascist' Germany.

It was the Soviet authorities in their zone of occupation in June 1945 who first announced the revival of the democratic political process by permitting the setting up of political parties – the Communist Party of Germany (KPD), of course, but also the German Social Democratic Party (SPD), the new conservative Christian Democratic Union (CDU) and the Liberal Democratic Party, better known in the West as the Free Democratic Party (FDP). One-party rule, the cornerstone of the Soviet political system founded by Lenin, was refined into Stalin's totalitarian state, in which no dissenting group was permitted any voice or even the right to exist. In Germany, then, Stalin was ready, according to his own lights, to make enormous concessions and to provide communist predominance with a more acceptable face for the local population and for the Western Allies.

When the Austrian communists in genuinely free elections in November 1945 secured only 5 per cent of the vote, Stalin knew that more would be required in Germany than just to let the parties compete freely. The Soviet authorities cajoled and pressurised the Social Democratic Party, led by Otto Grotewohl in their zone, to fuse with the Communist Party and so form the Socialist Unity Party (SED). In provincial elections in the autumn of 1946, the SED, despite Soviet help, failed to win outright majorities over the competing CDU and Liberals, so the SED had to resort to anti-fascist popular-front tactics to gain control in the *Länder* assemblies. Berlin, although it fell within the Soviet zone, had been placed under the joint authority of all the four powers, so its political parties could not be manipulated by Moscow like those in the Soviet zone. For that reason, moves to fuse the Socialist and Communist Parties in Berlin were comprehensively defeated.

This result marked a decisive split in Germany. Given the freedom to choose, the country's emerging political leaders rejected totalitarianism. Instead, the two most outstanding political figures of the immediate post-war German years, Kurt Schumacher (SPD) and Konrad Adenauer (CDU), laid the foundations of a party political system on which could be based the stable parliamentary democracy of the two-thirds of Germany that formed the Western zones, which together with West Berlin later became the Federal Republic of Germany. It is to the lasting credit of Schumacher as well as of Adenauer that German democracy was

not stifled at birth. In the Soviet zone, on the other hand, the German people were not to be given a free choice until forty-five years later. It should also be conceded that the Germans in the Western zones did not have a completely free choice: after all, the Western Allies would not have permitted their zones to be turned into a totalitarian communist state. The more important point, however, is that the Allies' aim to create a democratic society reflected the wishes of the majority of Germans.

The contrast between the two West German leaders, Kurt Schumacher and Konrad Adenauer, was striking. Schumacher's health but not his spirit had been broken after long years of incarceration in a concentration camp, an experience which had inspired him with a hatred of all forms of totalitarianism. He now looked to the British Labour Party as an example of a democratic socialist party supporting a parliamentary form of government. Schumacher was uncompromising on any issue he believed involved principle: it was a lack of firm principles that had driven the Germans into the abyss. He intended to lead a strong independent party committed to democracy, socialism and the recovery of dignity, and eventually sovereignty for a reunited Germany. The victorious Allies would once again be compelled to respect such a re-emerging German nation.

Adenauer was in an altogether different position. No political party except the SPD had emerged with credit during the Hitler years. They had either played Hitler's game before January 1933 or had compromised immediately after to hand him dictatorial powers. (The rank-and-file communists had no choice: they had to change allegiance or face persecution.) So Adenauer had to create an entirely new party, the CDU and its Bavarian ally, the CSU. This called for flexibility, adroitness and a high degree of political skill. Party political aims would need to be limited to essentials. A staunch Catholic and a Rhinelander, Adenauer enjoyed the better things in life, and, although he had courageously defied the Nazis as mayor of Cologne in 1933, thereafter he had played no active role in Germany's opposition. He had lived a comfortable retired life, storing up his energies for a better future. It was only during the last six months of the war that he was arrested and imprisoned by the Gestapo in the wake of the Hitler bomb plot of 20 July 1944, in which likewise he had played no part.

Unexpectedly, it was Adenauer in his seventies,

and not Schumacher, who dominated post-war German politics. Adenauer's re-entry into politics was not at first auspicious. Reinstated by the Americans as mayor of Cologne, his gritty personality and the scheming of political opponents led to his dismissal after the British took over control of the city. He re-emerged to challenge the support for Schumacher and the SPD. A third party, smaller than the other two, was the Liberal Free Democratic Party (FDP), which at times exercised a disproportionate influence because it held the balance between the two major parties.

In the summer of 1946 regional states (*Länder*) were created in the British, French and US zones, and local and regional elected assemblies reintroduced two-thirds of the German people to the democratic parliamentary process. Political party organisations were revived. The Social Democratic Party, led by Schumacher, competed with the Christian Democratic Union, which was opposed to socialism and to centralised state power at the expense of individual rights, and emphasised Christian ethical values as the foundation of the state.

Each of the *Länder* was headed by a minister–president answerable to a parliamentary assembly democratically elected. It was in the *Länder* that Germany's leading post-war political leaders first came to prominence – men like Reinhold Maier, Minister-President of Württemberg-Baden, Theodor Heuss, Heinrich Lübke and Professor Ludwig Erhard. The Western Allies, who had vetted and approved them (though not all had been active opponents of the Nazi regime) had chosen this leadership group wisely; in this they made a crucial contribution to Germany's post-war democratic development. Political life recovered. Its progress, however, depended on Allied willingness to transfer responsibilities to the Germans, to obtain their co-operation rather than their mere acquiescence. The process was accelerated by Western suspicions of the Soviet Union and the onset of the Cold War.

Political leadership is one thing, but how would the majority of Germans behave when asked to participate again in a democratic process after twelve years of dictatorship? How many politically active Germans were there who had been compromised? The majority of those whose hands were clean belonged to the left. They felt that their sufferings in concentration camps, their exclusion from the German state or their years in exile now gave them

a moral right to lead the new Germany. Business, big and small, had formed a part of the National Socialist state. German businessmen and farmers had accepted the help of 'slaves' from the east, had frequently exploited their forced labour and had only rarely treated them with humanity and consideration. The majority of Germans were saddled with the guilt of not having cared sufficiently for foreigners and for their own German Jewish neighbours. There were thus millions of Germans who wished to lie low. Survival might depend on not drawing attention to one's self unnecessarily by prominence in politics.

The more educated, the professional leaders of the state, civil servants, judges and lawyers, the better off and propertied, the doctors, many of whom had been implicated with Nazi measures, all those who had lived well and comfortably through the Hitler years and had provided expertise and leadership, were most heavily compromised and could least afford to play an active role in post-war politics. The workers, the poor, the conscripts in the army could more easily claim that they had been misled and were themselves the exploited, even though such a simple social division of those who supported and those who opposed National Socialism does not correspond to the facts. In the immediate months after the collapse, even the Western occupying forces looked with more favour on the communist resistance than on Germans with an uncertain political past. Gradually, the Western Allies sifted out a small elite group of political leaders in the *Länder*. It seemed likely at first that the left would dominate post-war German politics; adherents to the centre and the right of the political spectrum were willing to share power with the left for two or three years, ostensibly for the sake of national reconstruction, but in truth because they were too obviously compromised to assert their residual electoral strength more forcibly.

In the ill-fated Weimar Republic, there had been a disastrous political backlash from the extremists once Germany had regained most of her independence. That did not happen after 1945. The political leaders who convinced the Western Allies that democracy was safe in their hands and who complied with their terms were subsequently endorsed and won power through free elections. Most Germans had been cured of aggressive nationalism by their total defeat and the disastrous consequences. A new Germany was born of prosperity.

# CHAPTER 31

# The Soviet Union: The Price of Victory and the Expanding Empire

Victory over Nazi Germany and her allies came as an immense relief to the Soviet Union. No victorious power had suffered more. The war had devastated European Russia, 25 million were homeless, factories were destroyed, railways disrupted, mechanised farm machinery virtually non-existent. Of the population of 194 million before the war, between 20 and 24 million had lost their lives; more than one in four Russians had been killed or wounded. Stalin did not expect much help from the capitalist United States once the defeat of the common enemies was accomplished. Supplies had been shipped to Russia under the wartime Lend–Lease programme, but this was severely curtailed after the victory over Germany, and was ended altogether in August 1945 after Japan's defeat for all countries. But crucial Western food supplies still reached the Soviet Union in 1946 under the United Nations Relief and Rehabilitation Administration (UNRRA), mainly financed by the United States. This programme saved devastated regions from famine.

The Soviet Union tried to obtain immediate assistance by taking away from the former enemy countries everything that was movable: rails, factory machines and all kinds of equipment. It was an inefficient operation and probably only a small proportion could be used again when it reached the Soviet Union. The rest rusted away in railway sidings. Joint Soviet and Eastern European companies were formed on terms dictated by the Russians; special trade agreements were reached with former allies, generally favouring the Soviet Union. Another important source of help came from reparations exacted, not only from the Soviet zones of Germany and Austria, but for a short time, with Anglo-American co-operation, from the Western occupation zones as agreed at Potsdam. Destruction in the Soviet Union was on a scale almost unimaginable, and during the war the Germans had treated the Russians worse than animals. This helps to explain the Soviet insistence on huge reparations from the production of west German industry. But Soviet demands soon ran counter to Western occupation policies. The Western Allies realised that it was they who would in the end have to make good these losses or continue to support the Germans in the Western zones with their own subsidies for years to come (page 330). The inter-Allied conflict on the reparations issue became one of the causes of the Cold War.

There were desultory negotiations for a US loan after the war which never came to anything. In the last resort, Stalin had to rely on the sweat of the Russian people. There was work for the millions demobilised from the Red Army. During the war there had been some ideological relaxation. Now there was a return to orthodoxy. Stalin had not mellowed in old age: coercion resumed and an army of forced labour was herded into the Gulag Archipelago, the vast network of labour camps east of Moscow. Hundreds of thousands labelled as traitors were transported from the Baltic states, which had been annexed in 1940; many more from all over the Russian empire were also deported to virtual slavery. The Communist Party was allowed to re-emerge as Stalin's instrument of control over Soviet society. There was rigid ideological censorship of science and all forms of culture, even of composers. The party exploited to the maximum the labour of the peasants and the workers. Military heroes were relegated to the status of ordinary citizens.

The last decade of Stalin's rule was stifling. Terror returned. Stalin's Soviet Union was a country of immense hardship. Nascent internal nationalism was savagely crushed but could never be entirely suppressed. Jewish national feelings, especially after the foundation of Israel, drew world attention to another aspect of Soviet persecution. Rights, taken for granted in the West, did not exist in Stalin's Russia.

A new five-year plan was inaugurated in 1946. Enormous difficulties had to be overcome. Soviet statistics need to be treated with caution, but expert Western evaluation confirms that there was a remarkable recovery of Soviet heavy industry, coal, iron and steel, cement, oil, electricity and transport. As in the 1930s, Stalin's economic plans gave precedence to heavy industry at the expense of consumer goods, so the standard of living recovered only to a rudimentary level. Draconian labour laws deprived workers of all freedom and exposed them to punishment for lateness or drunkenness. Heavy burdens were laid particularly on the peasantry: the collectives were more tightly regulated and controlled; the productive private plots of the peasantry were taken away; in 1947 collectivisation was extended to the former Baltic states of Estonia, Latvia and Lithuania. But agricultural production, unlike industrial activity, hardly recovered from the wartime lows. Food was forcibly taken from the peasantry for ridiculously low prices. There was widespread famine in the Ukraine in 1946–7. By 1952 the grain and potato harvests had still not reached the 1940 pre-war level. The failure of 'socialist' agriculture has remained a permanent feature of the Soviet economy.

Stalin's emphasis on heavy industry was conditioned by his fear of Western industrial superiority. He took for granted the implacable hostility of the capitalist West to the Soviet Union. His grip over Eastern Europe and the maintenance of a large peacetime Red Army were to compensate for Russia's economic inferiority. Every effort was also made to catch up in the field of nuclear weapons. But Stalin clearly wished to avoid a war with the West. In 1946 he cautiously withdrew demands made earlier on Turkey, and later pulled the Red Army out of northern Iran and Manchuria. Yet the Soviet position in the post-war world would depend in the first instance on the Red Army. Globally the Soviet Union stood on her own, exhausted and deeply wounded by war.

Stalin feared that the Red Army, as it advanced westwards, would become aware of the much higher standard of living enjoyed by the 'fascists' and capitalists. The success of Soviet propaganda depended on keeping the Russian peoples from Western contact. Fraternisation with local populations was therefore severely limited where it was allowed to occur at all. Within the Soviet Union, rigid censorship about the world outside continued and a distorted picture of Western hostility and hate was propagated. 'Bourgeois culture' was condemned as decadent and everything Soviet praised as superior. The party and Stalin's leadership were glorified for winning the war.

Stalin's post-war revenge was indiscriminate. The victims of Yalta, those Russians who were forcibly repatriated by the British and Americans after the war from the zones of occupation, were lucky if they ended up in the Gulag Archipelago. Others were simply shot. But these thousands of men, women and children were just the tip of the iceberg. Whole national groups, such as the Muslim Tatars and Kalmycks, were deported with great brutality from the Caucasus when it was reoccupied by Soviet armies in 1943 and 1944. Possibly more than 1 million people were collectively punished and deported. Stalin's ferocity exposed his fanatical determination to wipe out any danger to 'Russian' communist power and Soviet unity from within. The years from 1945 to Stalin's death in 1953 were as repressive as the terrible 1930s had been. Stalin ruled by coercion and terror; he was omnipresent yet totally remote, never meeting the Russian people face to face. His character was, in Khrushchev's words, capricious and despotic, brutal tendencies that only increased as his faculties weakened in old age. But he never lacked henchmen and supporters for his policies, policies that no one man could have carried through alone. Coercion and terror formed one essential element; the other was compliance. To this end, Stalin's immediate helpers received material benefits; for the rest of the population, socialist idealism was perverted by propaganda. A slave army of millions of Russians, arrested for one reason or another, arbitrarily or not, and housed in the Gulag Archipelago, provided the forced labour to assist Soviet recovery.

The Western Allies had little inkling of Stalin's paranoid fear for his continued unchallenged rule at home and little understanding of his determination that no national group within the Soviet Union should be able to challenge Russian dominance. Stalin, a Georgian by birth, was convinced by their conduct in the war of the superiority of the Russian people. This did not inhibit him from condemning nationalism at home or abroad according to Marxist–Leninist doctrine as a phase belonging to bourgeois societies. To the Soviet Union nationalism posed a threat in two ways: 'bourgeois' and 'nationalist'. Wherever nationalist consciousness manifested itself, especially in communist states, such as Yugoslavia, its advocates were fiercely denounced.

In the communist states the leadership exercised its will through the one (communist) party that was allowed to function. The party's control was usually in the hands of one man, sometimes a small group, whose wills then became ultimate law. The party apparatus was essential as a means of government, providing the link between policy decisions and their execution. Only one party could be tolerated in the classic communist state as it existed until 1989, or the whole execution of policy would fall into confusion. After 1948, the nations which the Soviet Union dominated had to conform in leadership and party organisation to the Soviet model, even down to the details of the 'personality cult' and the theatrical plaudits for the leader. Their alliance with the Soviet Union was not a question of free choice: loyalty to this alliance was the price exacted for freedom from direct Soviet military control.

Between 1940 and 1945 Stalin expanded Soviet rule over new territories, though he was well aware of the difficulties such absorption of hostile ethnic groups could create for the Soviet empire. Where possible, he reasserted the historic rights of pre-1917 tsarist Russia. Poland was a special and most difficult case if only because there were so many Poles – some 30 million in 1939, but reduced to 24 million in 1945. In re-establishing the 1941 Soviet frontier, a mixed population of Belorussians and Ukrainians in the countryside and Poles in the towns was brought within the Soviet Union, and this was only mitigated by population exchanges of Poles, Ukrainians and White Russians. The frontier between Poland and the USSR had some historical justification, since it basically followed the demarcation proposed at the Paris Peace Conference by Lord Curzon in 1919. Finland too lost territory but retained more of her independence. Stalin shrank from incorporating the fiercely independent and nationalist Finns. Instead, he made sure that they understood that as Russia's neighbour, and located as they were far from possible Western help, they would have to follow a policy friendly to the USSR as the price of their comparative freedom.

In 1945 Stalin shamelessly retained, without Allied approval, the territories of the once independent Baltic states of Lithuania, Latvia and Estonia, which it had been agreed in the Stalin–Hitler pact of August 1939 should fall within the Soviet sphere. The Red Army occupied them in 1940 and set up puppet assemblies, which promptly abandoned their countries' independence and acceded to the USSR. Also in 1945, but this time in agreement with the Allies, the northern third of pre-war East Prussia was 'administered' by the Soviet Union – in practice incorporated into it. In the Balkans, Stalin wanted Bessarabia (Moldavia). It had been Russian until 1918. After the First World War ethnic Romanians of Moldavia had declared for union with Romania. In 1940, with the acquiescence of Hitler, Russia forced Romania to cede the territory back to her. Finally, to gain a direct link and common frontier with Hungary, Stalin pressured the Czechs to cede a part of their territory, Ruthenia, to the USSR. In this way he accomplished large acquisitions of land all around the periphery of the Soviet Union from the Baltic through central Europe to the Balkans in the south. But, even beyond these annexations, the Soviet Union desired further influence and control, to destroy the pre-war block of hostile states, the cordon sanitaire, with which the West had tried before 1939 to surround and contain communist Russia.

During the years from 1945 to 1948 Stalin brought Eastern and central European politics and societies under Soviet control. He was obsessed by the fear that eventually the capitalist powers would take advantage of their superiority to attack the Soviet Union, which therefore had only a few years in which to prepare. In Asia, he was reticent and pacific. He had little time for that continent. The real danger, he believed, would develop in Europe. To avoid the danger of too vehement a Western reaction, central and Eastern Europe was only gradually integrated into the Soviet system. One-party communist states tied to the Soviet party remained the goal. To reach it, Stalin had to overcome the obstacle not only of Western opposition but more seriously of the intense nationalism of the ethnic groups living in this region of Europe. It proved impossible to extinguish the loyalties to their own countries of Yugoslavs, Hungarians, Poles and Romanians. Their acceptance of the communist embrace, despite some genuine gratitude for their liberation, fell far short of seeing in the Soviet Union a desirable overlord. Polish history had consisted of the struggle for freedom from Russia; the powerful Catholic Churches in both Poland and Hungary identified themselves with their countries' national feelings. Added to such opposition was the resistance to the social and economic revolution demanded by the communists. The relationship between the Soviet Union and her allies in the socialist camp thus moved uneasily between attempts at rigid party and Soviet control and relaxation of that control to the extent of limited independence.

The central and East European states through which in 1944 and 1945 the Red Army marched on its way to Vienna and Berlin can be divided into two groups: the Allied nations, Poland, Yugoslavia, Czechoslovakia and technically Albania too; and the former enemies, Bulgaria, Romania and Hungary. The ability of Britain and the United States to intercede effectively for allies was paradoxically smaller than the ability to secure some say in the future of the enemies. In the case of allies, the only option was to withhold recognition of the government installed by the Russians in 1945. This was done, only for recognition to be granted two years later.

Over the future Czechoslovakia Allied influence was especially weak. President Beneš had decided long before 1945 that Czechoslovakia's post-war future left no choice but to accept Soviet 'friendship', which meant acquiescing in whatever limits Stalin chose to place on her independence. Beneš was rewarded by being the only Allied head of state to return to his own country by way of Moscow. As for Yugoslavia, the royal government in exile could not conceivably be re-established without the

support of a large Allied army, for Tito and his communist partisans had assumed control of the country, moreover without direct Soviet help.

The position of the enemies, of Hungary, Romania and Bulgaria, was different, although each was under Red Army occupation. Their governments and frontiers could not be regularised without peace treaties involving the consent of Britain and the United States. The Allies kept up a constant stream of protest at the undemocratic conduct of these regimes set up by the Soviet Union and withheld their recognition and their signature to the peace treaties until 1947.

In Poland, which he recognised as the most vulnerable country under Soviet control, Stalin kept the tightest grip, making few concessions. Poland remained under the thinly veiled direct military occupation of the Red Army. The Polish army which had accompanied the Red Army was largely officered by reliable Soviet officers. In the new communist-dominated government, the only politician with a considerable following was Stanislav Mikolajczyk, a non-communist and leader of the Peasant Party who had joined the Lublin government from London and now served as a deputy prime minister. The communist secretary of the Polish Workers' Party, Wladyslaw Gomulka, was the real power in Poland. The communists adopted their usual tactics of attempting to secure the agreement of the Peasant Party and the non-communist coalition partners to elections on a 'single list'; this meant the voters would be presented not with a choice of parties, but with one agreed list of candidates, of which the Peasant Party and others would be allowed only a minority. Stalin had promised the Western Allies early free elections. But, because the communists could not guarantee the results in 1945 despite holding key internal ministries and controlling the police, the army and much of the administration, they simply postponed the elections for two years. During these years there was open violence and armed struggle.

The Home Army, operating in Poland but loyal to the London government in exile, was dissolved in July 1945. Embittered by their experiences, some desperate units went underground again and with a few thousand members of the Ukrainian Independence Army began terrorist attacks on administrative officials of the Communist Workers' Party.

In parts of the countryside fighting escalated into civil war. Civilian administrators and police were attacked and killed. Jewish survivors once more became the murder victims. Not until 1948 could this violence be broken. Until then, the terrorist attacks served the interests of the communists, for they made the postponement of elections plausible.

By fair means and foul the communists did all they could to undermine support for their political opponents, who happened also to be their coalition partners in government. Nevertheless, the road to socialism was to be Polish and not Soviet. The economic plans were publicly declared to be based on the coexistence of a private, a co-operative and a public state sector. All the same, there was not much left but the state sector of industry by 1947. All industrial undertakings employing more than fifty workers per shift were nationalised, which effectively brought 91 per cent of industry and banking under state control. The land question was the most immediately important. In 'old' Poland all the large farms and estates were broken up and distributed to the peasantry. In the 'new lands', vacated by the Germans, peasant settlers were encouraged to join collective farms. This largesse politically neutralised the peasantry. Few lamented that the pre-war gentry and wealthy industrialists would not be allowed back their possessions. Intimidation of political opponents did the rest. Despite the appalling conditions, huge efforts were made to rebuild the devastated economy and the towns and villages of Poland, especially Warsaw.

In the election, finally held in January 1947, the communists won and almost eliminated their principal rivals the Peasant Party, many of whose candidates had been intimidated or imprisoned. The Catholic Church remained intact, however, sustaining its links with the majority of the Polish people. Gomulka tried to reconcile the Poles to communist rule, but his efforts were to be negated by the need to abandon the Polish road to socialism. During the barren harshness of Stalin's last years the Communist Party was disrupted by purges and Gomulka was disgraced in January 1949.

Soviet policies in Romania exemplified a different, gradualist approach determined by internal events and by the military situation. At first, Stalin may well have planned a ruthless and simple takeover, with communist-trained Romanians such as Anna Pauker setting up an administration in the wake of the Red Army's conquest. But the unexpected happened. In August 1944, King Michael led a coup which overthrew the fascist government and then changed sides, from Hitler's Germany to that of the Allies. This threw the country open to the Red Army, which with Romanian troops chased the Wehrmacht into Hungary. Romania again lost Bessarabia to the Soviet Union, but was rewarded by the return of Transylvania, which in 1940 had been transferred to Hungary by Hitler. Meanwhile a Romanian government, including pre-war Romanian communists, was established, though these 'native' communists were not trusted by Stalin. At Moscow's behest, the popular-front-type governments, which included non-communist parties, were reshuffled in December 1944 and March 1945 to provide the communists with greater though still incomplete power.

Soviet army intervention in local administration eroded popular support for the non-communist parties. Joint Soviet–Romanian companies were founded, landed estates were broken up, communists and fellow travellers were labelled 'democratic' and other parties showing any signs of independence were stigmatised as 'fascist'. So-called 'free elections' were held in November 1946. There was intimidation, and the results may well have been doctored, but the communists had won for themselves a sufficient power base to make their overwhelming electoral victory acceptable to the Romanian people. In any case the people had little choice beyond acceptance since Western protests would be limited to words. Britain and the United States had already recognised the communist-controlled government *before* the elections. Despite the unsatisfactory elections and the Anglo-American detestation of communist regimes, Romania had been written off as inevitably forming part of the Soviet camp, and a peace treaty was signed in February 1947 which recognised this. King Michael was forced into exile and Romania became a 'people's democracy', the beginning of four terrible decades.

Although Bulgaria was not at war with the Soviet Union, Churchill had made it clear to Stalin in 1944 that she would be allowed to fall within the Soviet sphere. War having been hastily declared on her, Soviet troops entered and overran the country in September 1944, without real Anglo-American opposition. Unlike its Romanian equivalent, the Bulgarian Communist Party had had a substantial popular following before the war and in Georgi Dimitrov a leader of international reputation following his acquittal in Nazi Germany for complicity in the Reichstag Fire. Although he became an influential figure in Moscow as general secretary of the Comintern in the 1930s, Dimitrov was not at first allowed to return to Bulgaria in the wake of the Soviet invasion. Instead Bulgarian communists were installed in 1944 in another popular-front government, the Fatherland Front, and to begin with the opposition was not ruthlessly suppressed. But the respite was only temporary. With the Red Army stationed in the country and Stalin determined to consolidate Soviet power, and with no effective Western counter-measures forthcoming, the fate of the Social Democratic and Agrarian Peasant opposition and its party leader Petkov was sealed. Dimitrov was now allowed to return to Bulgaria to strengthen the communists.

Despite the muzzling of the press, the elections held in October 1946 saw a striking success for the non-communist opposition. For a few months 101 deputies elected by over a million votes were able to act as a parliamentary opposition to the communist regime. But in August 1947 Petkov was arrested, tried and sentenced to death on trumped-up charges of working for 'Anglo-American Imperialism'. He was shot the following month. Britain and the United States had made public protests before his execution, but Dimitrov only reinforced the impression of judicial murder by declaring that Petkov might have been spared but for the Anglo-American protests. Of course, the execution could not have taken place without Stalin's acquiescence. To Britain and the United States events in Eastern Europe showed the extent to which Stalin was prepared ruthlessly to ignore his international obligations. Like their Romanian counterparts, the Bulgarian communists turned their country into a particularly brutal and repressive 'people's democracy'.

The Hungarians had been ruled from 1919 until 1944 by anti-communist regimes under the Regent Admiral Horthy. It was his fatal error to throw in his lot with the German invaders of the Soviet Union in 1941. When events revealed his error, he tried to disengage and achieve a peace with the Soviet Union, but it was too late. It was the Germans instead who first occupied his country. In pre-war Hungary army support for the authoritarian structure had been decisive, and the need for social reform had gone unsatisfied. The dominant aspiration of successive Hungarian governments was the recovery of territory lost principally to Romania (Transylvania) by the Peace Treaty of Trianon in 1920. It was this aspiration which drove Hungary into the arms of Germany and even to declare war on Russia in 1941. By then Hungary had already been rewarded, in 1940, by the transfer of northern Transylvania from Romania, as well as of portions of Czechoslovakia. Defeat in 1945 entailed the loss once more of all these gains as Stalin redistributed the territories, Britain and the United States again raising no objections.

Stalin's opportunism is well illustrated by the first anti-German Hungarian government set up by the Red Army in the part of Hungary they had liberated. Soviet military requirements at this time made it expedient to include many former supporters of Horthy, as well as communists and members of other parties. As circumstances changed, so would the composition of the government. The leading Hungarian communist was Mátyás Rákosi, who had lived in Moscow since 1940; he now returned to participate in coalition governments. He began with patriotic appeals in 1944 promising democracy and peaceful progress, yet within four years Hungary was transformed into one of the most ruthless of the Stalinist 'people's democracies'. Rákosi's approach corresponded to Stalin's own: cautious opportunism ruthlessly pursued. Hungarians, not Russians, would be allowed to transform politics and society and would guarantee national loyalty to the Soviet Union. Three parties besides the communists were allowed to organise and participate in national politics.

The Catholic Church too played an important role, acting as a bulwark against atheistic communism. Stalin proceeded in Hungary with caution, permitting free elections in November 1945. The communists lost badly. Stalin was not going to repeat such an error.

Still, Rákosi, with Soviet backing, retained the key to power through his control of the Interior Ministry and the secret police. He skilfully exploited differences between the government coalition parties, cynically commenting later that he had sliced them away like salami until only the communists were left. First the Smallholders' Party was eliminated, then the Social Democrats. In the 1947 elections, communist victory was no longer left to the whim of the voters. Within a few months, Rákosi and his lieutenants had taken over the country, and a new 'constitution' in 1949 turned Hungary into a Moscow-style 'people's democracy'.

There were few indications in 1945 that Yugoslavia would differ in any significant way from the other states in Eastern Europe liberated from the Nazis with the help of the Soviet Union. If anything. Yugoslavia was more obviously communist, controlled from the start by Marshal Broz Tito as undisputed leader organising a one-party state, ideologically bound to Marxism–Leninism. The military victory of the partisans who had been fighting the Germans left little alternative but to accept Tito's terms for the post-war reconstruction of Yugoslavia. Only a military occupation, Soviet or Allied, could have altered that. Interestingly, in 1944 Stalin had encouraged the idea of an Allied landing in Yugoslavia, evidently already seeing in Tito's Yugoslav communism a dangerous national deviation. A closer study of Yugoslavia shows both similarities with and important differences from the general pattern of the communist takeover of the central and East European states. None of the communist resistance forces was strong enough to defeat the Wehrmacht without the victories of the Red Army. This was no less true of Yugoslavia, although there the partisans actually liberated the country from German occupation.

Tito was well aware that the partisan victory would be dependent upon the victory of the Soviet Union. He also followed Lenin's precept of a tightly disciplined party as indispensable for maintaining communist power. During the war the German and Italian occupation had destroyed the pre-war social and political order. Yugoslav communists and the royalists fought each other for predominance at the same time as they fought the Germans. This triangular struggle was complex, the two Yugoslav sides accusing each other of helping the Germans to eliminate the internal enemy. Initially Tito drew his support overwhelmingly from Serb peasants attracted by promises of greater social justice and by appeals to their patriotism. The Serbs were the largest national group and Tito succeeded in winning over far more to his side than the royalist Chetniks did. But from the first he was also aware that Yugoslav unity required the support of all the major national groups – Croats, Macedonians, Montenegrins and Slovenes. He created people's committees in villages, towns and provinces, prom-

ising full national rights to the major nationalities in a post-war federal Yugoslavia.

Milovan Djilas, Tito's friend and supporter until 1954, has described Tito vividly as a man born a rebel, who combined a distinctive zeal for communism with a personal zest for power; like some Eastern potentate Tito, once the hardened partisan leader, built villas and palaces after the war for his exclusive pleasure, even though he could spent little time in any one of them. The dictatorship of the proletariat became in practice personal power wielded by an autocratic leader. Tito created a new party hierarchy, himself at the pinnacle and the secret police as the instrument for securing compliance by dealing ruthlessly with his opponents. In 1946 a constitution on the Soviet model was established, which guaranteed the cultural and administrative rights of all the nationalities in a federal Yugoslav state; this went some way towards solving the nationality conflicts of pre-1945 Yugoslavia, at least for a time. Tito's second achievement was his resolute defence of Yugoslavia's own road to socialism in 1948 in the face of Stalin's onslaught, and the assertion of Yugoslavia's independence from Moscow's control. The monolithic Soviet empire was cracked for all the world to see.

The road to total communist power was different again in Czechoslovakia. Edvard Beneš, the President of the Czech government in exile in London, had signed a formal alliance and friendship treaty with the Soviet Union in December 1943 by which the Russians undertook not to interfere in Czechoslovakia's internal affairs. But Stalin had already established a communist émigré group in Moscow, led by Klement Gottwald. The experience of Munich in 1938, when Britain and France had forced the Czechs to give in to Hitler's territorial demands, had convinced Beneš that he should stay on good terms with the Russians, because Western protection could not be relied upon. He hoped that by demonstrating the Czechs' genuine friendship he would be allowed to maintain democracy and Western values. He saw Czechoslovakia's role as forming a bridge between East and West. As if to emphasise Czech reliance on the Soviet Union, Beneš returned to Czechoslovakia via Moscow in the spring of 1945. Ominously he now had to agree to new terms which further limited his freedom of action. The government in exile would be replaced by a new National Front government for liberated Czechoslovakia in which only the parties of the left would participate, and key ministries for the internal control of the country would be in communist hands. In return Beneš received Stalin's empty promise that the Soviet leader would deal with any communists who gave him trouble. Beneš had also to agree to a social and economic transformation (designed to pave the way to communism) and to the expulsion of the Sudeten Germans. Real democracy through representative government was not re-established in 1945, only its appearance. Czechoslovakia was bound to follow the Soviet Union in any policy Stalin regarded as important, even before the communist takeover in 1948; the Czech recantation of participation in the Marshall Aid programme in 1947, on Moscow's insistence, was a good illustration of this.

The Czech communist leader, Klement Gottwald, was told by Moscow to content himself with a gradual path to absolute power. During the war the communists had organised a resistance movement against the Germans; after it they not only held the key ministries and dominated the trade unions, but established their national committees in villages, towns and provinces. Economic transformation began with the nationalisation of large industries and businesses even before the provisional parliament met in October 1945. But later that month the American forces and the Red Army, who had jointly liberated the country, agreed to withdraw, giving hope to the democrats, although the country was split between the communists and the democratic parties of the left. Elections were held in May 1946, but they were not absolutely free since only the parties comprising the National Front were allowed to participate. Furthermore, many Czechs feared that, if the communists failed to win, the Red Army would return. Given all their preparatory work and control, it is hardly surprising that the communists polled 37 per cent of the votes. But, even with their fellow travellers among the Social Democratic Party, this did not give them absolute control. Nonetheless the democratic opposition, stronger in Slovakia than Bohemia and Moravia, was weakened by being split among three parties.

In the new government, formed after the elections, Klement Gottwald became prime minister; the two Czechoslovaks best known abroad retained their former positions, Beneš as president and Jan Masaryk as foreign minister. But soon the communists inside and outside the government started to behave high-handedly, and mass arrests of their opponents were ordered. Clashes in parliament and between government ministers became increasingly heated and the supporters of the democratic parties were considering whether they would not have to resist violations of justice if democracy was to survive. But to the outside world the presence of Beneš and Masaryk appeared to guarantee the preservation of civil rights; that illusion was shattered early in 1948 (pages 386–7).

A survey of Eastern and central Europe shows a considerable variation of national experience and of the role played by the communists. Not everything that happened could be controlled by Moscow. Indeed one of the major headaches for the Eastern European communist leaders was the difficulty of discovering what Stalin really wanted. At lower levels, Russian advice and influence were at times confusing or contradictory. Gottwald, a loyal communist, believed in 1947, for example, that Stalin would not object if Czechoslovakia participated in the Marshall Aid programme; as we have seen, he was rapidly obliged to recant. But whenever Stalin made his views known the communists made speed to fall into line.

A façade of representative institutions would placate the West; meanwhile the United States was pulling all her armed forces out of Europe. Firm communist bases in Czechoslovakia, Romania, Hungary, Bulgaria, Poland and the Soviet zone of Germany were established. Everywhere communists were strongly entrenched and dominant in coalition National Front governments. The political activities of other parties were controlled, and those labelled 'fascist' were banned. The influence of the landowners was removed by dividing up their estates, and for the time being the peasantry benefited from the redistribution of land: for this, the communists gained the credit. Large industries were nationalised, and progressively the smaller ones as well. The economic base of the dominant wealthy pre-war social groups was destroyed; in Poland it had already been destroyed by the Germans, who had also killed many members of the professional classes. Everywhere, in local committees established in every community down to the smallest village, the communists entrenched their influence to prepare for ultimate control. Communism could move only one way – into a position of dominance – and would do so as soon as the Kremlin judged the time right.

In each country there were differences too. The Catholic Church was powerful enough in Poland and Hungary to form an opposing force. Social and economic conditions also differed, Poland having suffered more grievously during the Second World War than any other Eastern European state apart from the Soviet Union. The strength of the anti-communist opposition varied from country to country too, as did the tactics adopted by the communist leaders. In Czechoslovakia, the communists were sufficiently strong to seek control by semi-legal means; in Yugoslavia, the communists took control from the start. But all the countries in the Soviet orbit had this in common: the dynamics of the social and political changes introduced after 1944–5 were bound to end in a communist victory.

Communist domination after 1948 did not mean the end of political strife. This was now transferred to struggles within the party, between the groups which had the ear of Moscow and those which were denounced as the enemies of the Soviet Union. The Moscow-trained communist leaders turned on the 'native' communists in great purges during the closing years of Stalin's rule. The revolution began to eat its own children. Moscow's was a savage dominance over a turbulent region.

# CHAPTER 32

## *Britain and the World: A Legacy Too Heavy to Bear*

Victorious British armies had shared with the Americans the reconquest of Italy, France and Germany in arduous campaigns from the beachheads of Salerno and Normandy to the Elbe. What the British now feared was that the Americans would depart from Europe and simply return to pre-war isolationism and so leave Britain facing the Soviet Union alone.

The British people rejoiced on VE (Victory in Europe) Day and saw it as proving the powers of endurance and the superiority of the British; Churchill's government knew better and recognised the serious problems that lay ahead. The war in Asia against Japan had still to be won. Hidden from general public recognition were other facts: the bleak position of Britain's financial resources, her foreign assets decimated by the purchase of war supplies; the extent to which the United States had provided essential foods, raw materials and weapons under the wartime 'lend–lease' arrangement which meant postponing payment, not avoiding it altogether. Without US help, the British economy – geared until mid-1945 to the war effort – was not able to provide the British people even with the standard of living possible during the war. And now in addition came the cost of maintaining the minimum living standards of the former enemy in the British zone of occupation. The food imported into Germany had to be paid for by Britain from her small dollar reserves.

If continental Western Europe was to be prevented from sliding into chaos and protected from Soviet expansion or subversion, the active support of the United States was essential. Yet there were considerable and persisting Anglo-American differences. In the United States there was still a widespread belief that Britain remained an unrepentant imperialist power and a potentially formidable trading rival. British policies in Palestine restricting Jewish immigration caused bitterness on both sides of the Atlantic (pages 455–6). Finally, despite his robust language, President Harry S. Truman thought that the United States and the Soviet Union could reach an accommodation and that it was Britain, bent on defending her worldwide colonial interests, which might provoke the Soviet Union into conflict.

Until the United States was ready to recognise her new responsibilities in regions of the world which she had hitherto not regarded as falling within spheres essential to her own security, Britain had to fill the vacuum. Meanwhile, there was uncertainty about America's long-term commitment to Western Europe, and about her readiness to defend Western interests in Asia, the Middle East and the Mediterranean. So, until March 1947, it was Britain which financially as well as militarily took up the burden of supporting the anti-communist government in Greece.

With resources so overstretched, there was an urgent need to limit Britain's more costly responsibilities. India had been promised her independence, and after the end of the war it could no longer be delayed. The Labour government grasped this nettle: Lord Mountbatten arrived in Delhi as the last viceroy to India on 22 March 1947. On 14 and 15 August India and Pakistan gained their independence. Partition had proved unavoidable, and the tragedy of communal violence and murders marred Britain's wise decision to give up willingly the 'jewel' of her empire (see Chapter 40).

In the summer of 1945 there were among government ministers no illusions about Britain's own economic weakness and the need for American help. Even so, there seemed no reason to doubt that, after a transition period of five or six years, Britain would recover.

The first important post-war decision to be taken was a political one – who was to govern Britain? The election in July 1945 took place while the war was still continuing in the Pacific. British troops were fighting in Burma and the Japanese were fanatically resisting the advance of the Americans on the island approaches to their homeland. The war was expected to last many more months, until the atomic bomb revealed its awesome power and unexpectedly ended the fighting. But in the weeks following Germany's surrender all this was momentarily put aside. Churchill had contributed to a carefree post-war mood by ensuring the celebration of VE Day. There were parties in every street. Burma was far away except for those with relatives still fighting there or whose next of kin were starving in Japanese prisoner-of-war camps. The great majority of people in Britain were now hopefully anticipating the rewards of peace. Churchill wanted the coalition with Labour to continue until the defeat of Japan; when the Labour ministers in his government rejected this proposal, he fought the election in July on the appeal that he should be given the mandate to 'finish the job'. But he had unwittingly undermined his own election chances by helping to create the feeling that the war was already over.

Outside Britain it seemed incredible that the British people, who owed so much to Churchill, should now with apparent ingratitude turn him out of office. Even in his own constituency the Labour candidate attracted substantial support. But the election was not about the conduct of the war. Indeed, Churchill's electoral tour was a personal triumph, with ordinary people everywhere mobbing him to express their gratitude and genuine affection. The Labour leader Clement Attlee appeared a

colourless little man by comparison. Yet it was Attlee not Churchill who entered 10 Downing Street after the biggest landslide since the election of 1906, which had given the Liberals victory. However much the British 'first past the post' electoral system might exaggerate the disparity of the parties' fortunes, it was a striking turnaround from the last election, held in 1935, when the Conservatives and their supporters had returned 432 members and the opposition parties could muster only 180.

**Parliamentary Election, 1945**

|              | Seats | Votes      |
|--------------|-------|------------|
| Labour       | 393   | 11,995,152 |
| Conservative | 213   | 9,988,306  |
| Liberal      | 12    | 2,248,226  |
| Communist    | 2     | 102,780    |

Why was the swing of votes to Labour so large, especially among the servicemen? Churchill himself, as the electoral asset on which the Tory Party managers were banking, proved insufficient to turn the tide. Conservative promises of a new deal based on the Beveridge Report of 1942 were not so very different from those of the Labour Party, but the electorate doubted whether the Conservative heart was really in reform. It is also true that Churchill mishandled the electoral campaign by overdoing his condemnation of 'socialism' as embodied in the Labour Party's programme. He denounced Labour as setting out on a path to totalitarian rule which would lead to a British Gestapo. Did Churchill really persuade himself of this nonsense? His judgement proved equally fallible when he derided Attlee as a 'sheep in wolf's clothing'. It was impossible to persuade a sophisticated British electorate that Attlee, Bevin and Morrison were now not to be trusted despite their outstanding accomplishments as ministers in Churchill's all-party War Cabinet. The Gestapo jibe badly misfired.

But probably none of this explained the magnitude of the Conservative defeat. There was one factor more powerful than any other: the memories of the bitter hardship of unemployment during the 1930s, of slums, of ill-health and of a society that had failed to provide fair opportunities to the majority of the British people. In July 1945 millions of troops faced imminent demobilisation. Were the Conservatives likely to have their interests at heart? Would the government ensure that worthwhile work was found for everyone or would the employers be allowed to pick and choose, to depress wages in free-market style, careless of the poverty of the masses? It was this deep distrust of the Conservative Party, regarded by Labour supporters as the party of the well-to-do, that induced a larger proportion of working people and soldiers than ever before, together with traditional Labour supporters, to put their faith in a socialist government and in a prime minister, Clement Attlee, who had previously been overshadowed by Churchill. Ernest Bevin and Herbert Morrison had had a far greater impact during the pre-war and war years. Yet Attlee proved a most effective and even wily leader; with his pipe, his baggy trousers and his mousey moustache, his mild-mannered image was in sharp contrast to the larger-than-life Churchill.

The transfer from military service to peacetime employment was managed by the Labour government with considerable skill, an effective example of good planning. But the women who had manned the factory benches now frequently had to give up their jobs to the men. This time soldiers, unlike after the First World War, were demobilised in an orderly and fair fashion and only as fast as they could be reabsorbed in civilian work. This meant Britain still had more than 900,000 men in the forces in 1948. The free 'utility' civilian clothes supplied to everyone on leaving the army were just the first sign that the future had been thought out. Retraining facilities and vacancies in industry became available as wartime production was switched to that of peacetime. There was great demand for goods and a need for new housing and public works.

A most important feature of the celebrated Beveridge Report of 1942 agreed by all three parties at the time, Conservative, Labour and Liberal, was a commitment that the government's running of the nation's economy would ensure full employment. Never again should the hungry 1930s, with the hated means test, be allowed to return. Labour and Conservative governments were able to fulfil that pledge for a generation, unemployment rarely rising above 2 per cent or half a million. The other promises of the Beveridge plan, more whole-heartedly supported by Labour and the Liberals

than by Conservatives, were to provide insurance for the whole of the population for the basic needs of life, and on death a grant for their burial. The state would take care of its citizens from the 'cradle to the grave'. A health service would provide medical treatment for the whole family regardless of who was working and who was not. Together, these measures laid the intellectual foundations of the post-war welfare state. They represented a tremendous advance in working people's standards of living, an indirect 'social wage' provided by the Exchequer from the differential contributions and taxes of the whole population. The Conservatives were committed to similar provisions of state aid but would have proceeded differently and possibly at a slower pace. They doubted from the start whether the state could afford to make such far-reaching promises entailing vast expenditure. There were reforming Tories in the wartime coalition too, but by 1945 they had passed only one important measure through parliament, R. A. Butler's Education Act of 1944, which when implemented raised the school-leaving age to fifteen and reorganised the educational system so that better opportunities would be opened to all. The Labour government translated theoretical welfarism into practical measures. The Insurance Act of 1946 and – after a struggle between Aneurin Bevan, the fiery Welsh Minister of Health, and the doctors which ended in a compromise over the continuation of private medicine – the National Health Service Act of the same year were the two most important measures of the new government, which carried out and extended the Beveridge plan.

The commitment to socialism, however, remained largely a matter of theory. In practice the Attlee administration's approach was pragmatic, aiming at the gradual transformation of the British economy. This reflected the electorate's mood accurately enough. The majority of the people were interested, not in theories of socialism, but rather in gaining a better standard of living, a fairer share of the nation's production, more equal opportunity – in short, 'social justice'. The continued rationing of food was one way of sharing out what was essentially in short supply. Basic foods were subsidised, so even the poorest people could afford to buy their rations. State ownership was extended only where it seemed most obviously necessary. The Bank of England was nationalised, but not the commercial banks or the insurance companies. The coal mines, civil aviation, the railways, and gas and electricity production were also brought under state control by the close of 1947, with the employers and shareholders receiving compensation. But although now 'owned by the people', the workers did not play a new and significant role in running state industries. The government appointed a management team, who were frequently none other than the former managers, and the workers at best exchanged one set of employers for another. Consequently nationalisation had little impact on good industrial relations.

More important in this respect was the Trade Disputes and Trade Union Act 1946, which repealed the restrictions placed on trade union power after the General Strike of 1926. A generation later new efforts would be made by both Labour and Conservative governments to restrict trade unions once again in the actions they could take without incurring legal penalties. By then, the majority of the electorate had come to feel that the balance of power had swung too far in favour of the trade unions and against the national interest.

The ability to feed Britain during the immediate post-war years, to pay for raw material and to revive industry was dependent not only on following sound policies, which Labour did, nor on the mobilisation of Britain's depleted capital resources, but also on American help. By themselves, the British could not earn enough dollars to pay for the imports necessary for Britain and the German zone of occupation. There were no illusions about the country's plight in this respect. Yet, as we have noted, it was expected that, given help during the early post-war years, a reconstructed British industry would thereafter be able to cope. The problem thus appeared to be a transitional one.

The Roosevelt administration had made it clear that it was prepared to help in post-war reconstruction and that it would not return to isolationism. It was obvious that the United States would emerge from the war as the world's economic superpower, unscarred and unscathed by the ravages of fighting at home. In this task of reconstruction, Britain was America's principal partner, and Anglo-American economic plans for the post-war world had been prepared in continuous rounds of discussion since 1942. They took concrete form at a conference held under the aegis of the United Nations in a Washington suburb at Bretton Woods.

\*

In their planning of the world economic future the British and American administrations knew they were dealing with crucial problems that went far beyond technical details. If the mistakes after the First World War, which led to international economic warfare, mass unemployment and the great depression, were not simply to be repeated, a sensible method of achieving economic co-operation and mutual support would need to be worked out. The United States would, for a time at least, have to provide massive assistance. On this the Americans and the British were agreed. It corresponded to American custom that the form of this co-operation should be institutionalised. At Bretton Woods the foundations were soundly laid, even though solutions were not found for every international economic problem likely to arise in the post-war world.

The details of the Bretton Woods agreements are complex, but the essential points can be simplified and understood without expertise in high finance. The key was US concern about discrimination in worldwide trade. Individual countries in the 1930s had rigidly attempted to control their foreign imports. One important mechanism which national governments could most effectively use to this end was exchange control: the imposition of restrictions on the exchange of their own currency for those of other countries. Sterling was a currency used in world transactions; if its exchange into dollars were restricted, then Britain, the Commonwealth (except Canada) and many other countries trading in sterling would not be able to buy from the United States, and worldwide there would be a barrier to trade. An important part of the Bretton Woods agreements was an undertaking to make all currencies freely convertible after a transitional period of five years; exchange rates between currencies, including the dollar, would be fixed and regulated by a new international institution, the International Monetary Fund (IMF). It was intended that exchange rates should be stable and that they should be changed only with the consent of the IMF. The resources of the Fund were to be made up of contributions from each member country in gold and currencies in proportion to the strength of her economy. The United States supplied by far the biggest single contribution. Each country could draw on the Fund to make up a shortfall in foreign currency if its trade was not in balance; but if it drew on the Fund beyond a certain limit the IMF could prescribe conditions for its loan and demand that measures it thought necessary should be adopted to correct the trade imbalances. The decision-making apparatus of the IMF was a crucial feature. Members did not each have an equal vote with decisions by majority on important issues. It was intended that rates of exchange, for instance, could be changed only by a four-fifths majority of the Fund's board of directors. Each member country appointed one director, but his vote was weighted in accordance with his country's share in the IMF. This gave the United States a preponderant influence, and the IMF is appropriately located in Washington. In return for the large US contribution to the resources of the IMF, conditions were agreed which were aimed at preventing discrimination in world trade, and thus discrimination against the United States for lack of dollars. A twin to the IMF is the World Bank, which provides development loans, but it has played a much less important role than the IMF in post-war international trade and the world economy. But the hopes placed in these institutions for facilitating the free flow of world trade and the free convertibility of currencies were only partially realised after 1945.

It is curious that, in the pursuit of freer trade, import duties or tariffs did not play a more important role in American thinking. The United States retained her own high tariffs against imports and thought only in terms of their gradual international reduction by international agreement. The bargaining for reductions of tariffs began in April 1947 when twenty-three countries met in Geneva; in October that year they concluded the General Agreement on Tariffs and Trade (GATT). What the United States particularly wanted to achieve was the elimination of large trading blocks which traded among themselves preferentially, erecting higher tariffs against outsiders. The British Commonwealth had set up such a system in 1932 by the Ottawa Agreement, which established imperial preference. The American negotiators offered large reductions in US tariffs, but Britain – faced with myriad financial difficulties – clung to imperial preferences until obliged to eliminate most of them when joining the European Economic Community in 1973. Further rounds of trade bargaining continued under the auspices of GATT without resulting in the freeing of all trade barriers as originally envisaged. Nonetheless GATT has made a

valuable contribution over the years to the increase in the volume of world trade.

The arrangements worked out at Bretton Woods did not, however, solve Britain's or Western Europe's immediate problems. With the United States alone able to supply what Britain and the Western European nations needed for their reconstruction, and with inadequate recovery in Europe producing insufficient exports to the United States, not enough dollar funds were available to make the necessary purchases in America. This was called the 'dollar gap'.

In fighting Nazi Germany, Britain had subordinated all her economic policies to just one aim, to maximise the war effort. As a result her export trade had dwindled to a third of the pre-war level; not enough was produced at home to match wages, so inflation resulted; Britain's dollar and gold reserves and her large overseas assets had been used to finance the war; Britain had also accumulated large sterling debts as a result of wartime expenditure; the national debt had tripled and Britain's industry, adapted to produce armaments, now had to be transferred to peacetime manufacture for the domestic and export markets. The dislocation was enormous, in Britain as elsewhere. Millions were still in the services and could only gradually be demobilised. The dilemma for Britain was that she had to import food and raw materials to supply her people and industry, and to pay for them she needed to export manufactured goods as well as to earn returns from the City of London's financial and insurance services (invisible earnings). It was impossible to achieve such a turnaround from wartime production instantly. During the war itself, Britain's essential needs had been met by American Lend–Lease. Then came the crunch. In August 1945, with the President's economic advisers judging that the special circumstances of war were now over, and with Congress unlikely to agree to fund the arrangement in peacetime, Truman abruptly ended Lend–Lease.

Something had to be done about the yawning dollar gap that was immediately in prospect. Britain's most distinguished economist, John Maynard Keynes, was despatched to Washington to negotiate a loan to tide Britain over. The Lend–Lease debts now had to be settled. This seemed especially unjust in British eyes since the money had been spent fighting the common enemy:

furthermore Lend–Lease had been made available only in 1942 when Britain had been at war for three years. By then Britain had already spent most of her foreign reserves and assets. The Lend–Lease debts were settled with a loan, not cancelled. A loan of $3750 million at 2 per cent interest was granted to Britain to overcome her dollar shortage. Repayments were to begin in 1951 in fifty equal annual instalments. The loan was not as much as Britain had hoped for but the Canadians helped with an additional $1287 million. The total was sufficient to cover Britain's own immediate needs, including those of the British zone in Germany, though not those of the whole sterling area. The problems that arose related to some of the conditions the Americans had attached to the loan.

There was also the serious problem of the 'sterling balances'. (If all the sterling-area countries sought to convert their holdings of sterling at the same time, Britain could not have paid and would therefore have defaulted.) At Bretton Woods, Britain had reserved to herself the way she would settle the large sterling balances with her creditors during the transitional period, rather than accepting American help and making a joint Anglo-American approach to her creditors. Britain, with some justice, was suspicious of US anti-imperialist attitudes and did not wish the Americans to be able to meddle in Britain's Commonwealth and colonial relationships. Nevertheless these sterling balances were a Damocles sword overhanging the British economy because they were so large at $3,355 million. The United States in loan negotiations concluded in December 1945 made it a condition that within one year of drawing on the loan (that is, early in 1947) all *current* transactions by all the sterling-area countries should be freely convertible. As for the huge credits, the parties could do no more than reach an agreement in principle, without figures attached: some small part of these balances were to be immediately convertible to dollars; another tranche would become convertible in 1951; and as regards the rest Britain would seek agreement to write them off. Without figures this was a pretty meaningless arrangement, except that, in some magical way which no one could really envisage, the sterling balances would be made to disappear. There was much opposition to these American conditions in Britain, but there was little choice. They were accepted.

In February 1947 Britain honoured the loan agreement and made sterling convertible. The result was a disaster. The British Treasury could not control all the countries which now converted sterling into badly needed dollars. Not only current transactions as provided for in the loan agreement but some sterling balances held by other countries were converted as well. In August 1947, with the dollar reserves near exhaustion, Britain was forced to suspend convertibility. Her recovery was not far enough advanced to stand the strain. Exchange control was reintroduced and thus one important plank of Bretton Woods was abandoned. The Americans had misjudged the situation and had forced the issue of free convertibility too soon. By the 1950s sterling became partially convertible and in December 1958, almost thirteen years from the time of the first dollar loan, it became fully convertible. By then West European exports had recovered, the European dollar gap had disappeared and American overseas trade and expenditures were beginning to move into deficit. Other planks of Bretton Woods, however, continued to function for three decades. Fixed exchange rates were adjusted from time to time until they were abandoned in the early 1970s, to be reintroduced in the European Community in 1979 and in Britain in 1990 (to be abandoned by her in 1992).

Back in 1947, for Britain and Europe the situation would have become serious, with a new dollar gap in prospect once more, had not Marshall Aid come to the rescue the following year.

The effect of these abstract financial matters on the lives of ordinary people in Britain was very damaging. The manmade financial crisis came on top of an act of God, a terrible winter of heavy snowfall and ice. Coal was running out, unemployment temporarily soared, and now in the summer the government announced an austerity programme to cut imports. Rationing became more severe. Sir Stafford Cripps, gaunt and ascetic, symbolised the new era of austerity when he took charge of the Treasury as Chancellor of the Exchequer in November 1947. Food rations were small, though the population judged as a whole was in better health than before the war. Wages were low, and modest increases kept them low. Working people were asked to produce more without more pay – a theme to become familiar in the post-war era. Britain was probably one of the few countries in the world where a sense of fair play and discipline could make rationing work year after year without a large black market developing. Output in 1948 was already 36 per cent higher than before the war, and this production was being directed to support an export drive. Given the difficult conditions with which the government was faced, it could take credit for its achievements so far. 'Better times' for the people were nevertheless still a long way off. Full employment was taken for granted, so Labour would run into difficulties when people tired of the unending prospect of austerity.

Britain's dire financial plight forced the Cabinet to sort out British priorities in the rest of the world; Hugh Dalton, when at the Treasury (1945–7), constantly urged Ernest Bevin at the Foreign Office to cut back on Britain's overseas responsibilities. The Foreign Office, which rapidly came to admire him, had never known a Foreign Secretary like the tough, blunt and ebullient Bevin, proud of his working-class background and his long experience as leader of the largest trade union, the Transport and General Workers' Union; he had also been an effective Minister of Labour in Churchill's wartime coalition. Deeply committed to the democratic left, he was just as determined as Churchill not to allow communism any power base in Britain or in any region abroad where vital British interests were involved. Nor did he lag behind Churchill when it came to safeguarding Britain's empire. Thus he supported Churchill's policy of suppressing the communist-dominated front (EAM) in Greece (pages 380–1), despite vociferous protest from the British left, because, as he put it, 'the British Empire cannot abandon the position in the Mediterranean'. In Europe, Bevin in 1945 still regarded resurgent Germany as a greater danger than the Soviet Union. He shared Roosevelt's vision rather than Churchill's realism, however, in his belief that war could be avoided by a strong world organisation, the United Nations, with the United States, Britain and the Soviet Union guaranteeing the peace each in her own global region. Bevin was at first more ready than the Americans to accept the place of the Soviet Union in this scheme as having special interests and security concerns in Eastern and central Europe; he believed business could be done with Stalin. In the conduct of that business, Bevin's lifelong experience as a negotiator helped him to appreciate when to be tactically aggressive and when to be emollient. He did not wish to see the wartime Allies split into Eastern and Western blocs, and he was in any case

suspicious of US policies. In speaking to Stalin in December 1945, he made it clear that Britain's intentions were peaceful, but that 'there was a limit beyond which we could not tolerate continued Soviet infiltration and undermining of our position'.

The hostility of Soviet propaganda until the summer of 1946 was directed mainly against Britain, with threats to Turkey and Iran and complaints about Allied policies in Germany souring British relations with the Soviet Union. In March 1946, at Fulton, Missouri, Churchill delivered his famous 'Iron Curtain' speech. He saw Britain in the front line of halting communist expansion and subversion beyond the Soviet Union's own acceptable sphere of power in Eastern Europe. He was now trying to get the Americans to take these threats seriously. Bevin also saw the Soviet threat but he had not yet given up trying to persuade Stalin to work out problems co-operatively while remaining firm towards him. A Western alliance directed against the Soviet Union would only provoke her, and Bevin regarded public condemnations such as Churchill had delivered as counter-productive. Patient firmness was Bevin's policy until 1948; meanwhile his suspicions of the Germans continued to play a considerable part in his European outlook.

Bevin's main worry was that the United States would carry out her stated intention of completely withdrawing her military forces from Europe. He therefore encouraged the French to play a role in Germany as Britain's ally, but the Anglo-French relationship was not an easy one. After much difficulty, particularly over the French desire to detach the Ruhr from Germany, something Britain opposed, the Dunkirk Treaty of alliance was concluded with the French on 4 March 1947. Its terms were designed to meet the danger of renewed German aggression, but it was also intended to serve as the nucleus of a Western European grouping of nations without causing offence to the Soviet Union and so ruining any chance of future agreement and co-operation. The grouping would strengthen social democracy internally in Western Europe – after all, the communist parties were strong in both France and Italy. In following this policy Britain provided the important lead that two years later became the sheet anchor of Western security, the North Atlantic Treaty Organisation.

In 1947, Bevin was faced with two difficult problem areas on opposite shores of the Mediterranean – Palestine and Greece. The intractable problem of Palestine did more than anything else to cast a shadow over his reputation and indeed over the morality of the whole of Britain's attitude to the persecuted Jews since before the war, when the British government had restricted the entry to Palestine of the Jews wishing to escape from Hitler's Germany to no more than 75,000 over a period of five years. As a result fanatical Zionists accused Britain of acting as an accomplice to the Holocaust, though other countries, especially the United States, were even more reluctant to accept Jewish refugees. During the war British warships had patrolled the Palestine coast and prevented escaping Jews from landing (the Jews were not inhumanely sent back, however, but were interned in Mauritius). This set the secret Jewish militia, the Haganah, against the British. More extreme groups, such as the Irgun Zwai Leumi (National Military Organisation) and a small terrorist group, the Fighters for the Freedom of Israel (known as the Stern Gang in Britain after their leader), began attacking British policemen and installations in 1943. In November 1944 the Stern Gang assassinated Lord Moyne, the British Resident Minister in Cairo. Nonetheless, the majority of Jews in Palestine and those who lived in Allied countries fought with Britain against the common enemy.

While the great majority of Zionists condemned terrorism, British sympathies for the Jews after the horrors they had suffered during the Second World War were tempered by the effect which terrorism against British soldiers had on British opinion. One of the worst incidents was the blowing up on 22 July 1946 of the King David Hotel in Jerusalem, which housed the British Army Headquarters. Ninety-one people were killed – forty-one Arabs, twenty-eight British, seventeen Jews and five of other nationalities. Another outrage which caused the deepest revulsion was the hanging of two British sergeants in 'reprisal' for the execution of two Irgun terrorists. In all, some 300 people lost their lives as a result of terrorism between August 1945 and September 1947, almost half of them British.

After the war, the British government was pilloried for continuing to prevent large-scale immigration of Jewish survivors interned in Europe. Truman pressed for 100,000 entry permits, a plea which Bevin condemned as cynical political pandering to American-Jewish voters. The newsreels meanwhile were showing film of the Royal Navy intercepting ramshackle boats overloaded with refugees and forcibly detaining the ragged passengers. The most famous of these interceptions concerned the *Exodus*. There was an outcry when the Jews were returned to Germany, of all places (page 453).

Britain's policy was far from heroic but she should not be saddled with all the blame for what happened. The search for a peaceful settlement between Arabs and Zionists had been going on since before the war. It always ran into the same blind alley. The Jews were not willing to live in an Arab state; they wished to create their own state in Palestine and to allow unrestricted access to all Jews who wanted to come. This meant some form of partition, which the Zionists would accept. But the Arabs rejected the partition of Palestine, so if partition was the only solution, it would have to be imposed on the Arabs by military force. Yet Britain was not willing to use her troops to fight the Arabs, given her widespread interests in the Arab Middle East. In any case, why should Britain alone be made responsible for the creation of a Jewish state in Palestine? It was an international obligation. Even that leaves open the question whether partition corresponded to justice for the Arabs.

There was thus a certain logic when Britain in April 1947 decided to end her thankless responsibilities and to hand them back to the United Nations, the successor of the international organisation which had conferred the Mandate on Britain. Britain gave the UN until 15 May 1948 to find a solution. But Bevin's last hope that the terminal date of British rule in Palestine might, as in India, force the contending parties to the conference table proved a vain one. Meanwhile Palestine gradually descended into civil war. It was not so much Britain that seemed to abandon the Jews to the apparently superior might of the Arabs surrounding them as the nations at the UN, which duly voted for partition but, just as Britain had done, then left the Arabs and Jews to fight out the consequences (pages 455–6). For the time being at least the British had safeguarded their own interests in the Middle East, and the Americans had done the same. That need to safeguard British interests, in the Mediterranean as well as the Middle East, also lay behind the support for the royal Greek Government against the communists.

It was largely due to British intervention that Greece was not taken over by the communists after German forces withdrew in October 1944. The Greeks had fought the invading Italians and Germans courageously in 1940–1, and had gone to defeat despite the spirited intervention of British troops. In December 1944 British troops returned, for Greece, with Turkey, occupied a vital strategic position in the eastern Mediterranean. Stalin had accepted Western predominance in Greece and did not challenge the British directly, but communist Albanian, Bulgarian and Yugoslav partisans provided aid to the communist-led Greek National Liberation Front (EAM), with its military wing, ELAS. EAM had earned the admiration of the Greek people by their resistance to the Germans during the occupation. George II, the Greek king, was in exile with his government in Cairo. The majority of the Greek people did not wish to return to pre-war political and social conditions, with the result that EAM received wide support among non-communists. Opposed to EAM and ELAS was another, much smaller republican resistance group, EDES. Fighting broke out in Athens in December 1944. With the assistance of the British, EAM was prevented from taking over the country. A truce

was patched up in January 1945, but it was to provide no more than a pause in the mounting tension (with atrocities committed by both sides) that led to the outbreak of civil war in May 1946. Britain insisted on elections in March 1946, but these were boycotted by the left, so a right-wing government came to power and, with a plebiscite in his favour in September 1946, the King returned to Athens. British troops continued their support, but EAM retained strongholds in the devastated countryside.

By the time of the King's return the civil war had begun. For a country that had already suffered so much from foreign occupation and starvation during the war, this was the crowning tragedy. With the help of communist neighbours Bulgaria, Albania and Yugoslavia, EAM was able to continue the civil war for three years until October 1949. The great majority of the Greek people may have been in favour of change and moderate left policies, but the country was being destroyed by extremists.

The civil war in Greece played a major role in the post-war relations of the Second World War Allies. The communist insurrection, it was assumed,

*A plebiscite in Greece in September 1946 decides in favour of the monarchists. Unrest grows on the eve of full-blown civil war.*

was being masterminded from Moscow. As with later crises producing great international tensions, the 'domino theory' was brought into play. It was suggested in London and Washington that if Greece fell to communism the whole Near East and part of North Africa as well were certain to pass under Soviet influence. Bevin was in a dilemma. He had no sympathy for the corrupt royal Greek government and sensed that what the Greek people really wanted was social and political change. But his paramount motivation lay in his anti-communism. He was also constantly pressed by his colleagues not to squander Britain's limited financial resources in propping up the Greek regime with taxpayers' money. The Foreign Secretary decided on a bold stroke to help rivet US attention on the Soviet threat in the Mediterranean and at the same time relieve the financial burden on Britain. On 21 February 1947 he sent a message to Washington that British economic aid to Greece would have to be terminated by the end of March. Militarily the British actually continued to support the royalist government until the communists were defeated in 1949. The United States stood in the financial breach. This took the dramatic form of the Truman Doctrine announced on 12 March 1947, which pledged American help to defend the cause of the 'free peoples' (page 382).

The Truman Doctrine was followed in June 1947 by the offer of Marshall Aid. Bevin promptly responded by concerting with the French a positive Western European response. Stalin, on the other hand, ordered the Eastern satellite nations to pull out of the conference in Paris which met from July to September 1947 to discuss the details of Marshall Aid. The division of the East and West was becoming ever clearer, as was America's support for Western Europe. But this support still fell short of a firm military commitment, let alone an alliance. Thus in 1947, despite her weakened state, Britain was still the only major power which could be relied upon to defend Western Europe.

The breakdown in December 1947 of the London Foreign Ministers' Conference on the question of the future of Germany had finally convinced a reluctant Bevin that priority would have to be given to strengthening Western Europe economically and militarily. The communist coup in Czechoslovakia in February 1948 (pages 386–7) was interpreted in the West as signalling a new phase of Soviet aggression. Bevin was not willing to place total reliance on an American readiness to defend Western Europe and Western interests in the Middle East and Asia. It was true that Britain and Western Europe were shielded by the umbrella of the US monopoly of nuclear weapons, but America had only a small stockpile of atomic bombs and not until the Berlin crisis of 1948 were US bombers sent to Britain to act as deterrent to the Soviet Union. So Western Europe had to grasp the nettle of providing for its own defence. Bevin tackled this energetically. The outcome of his diplomatic efforts was the conclusion of the Brussels Treaty in March 1948, an alliance between Britain, Belgium, the Netherlands, Luxembourg and France. Its aims were not only to promote economic collaboration in Western Europe; Article IV provided for military assistance to any member of the alliance who became 'the object of an armed attack in Europe'. Although the preamble of the treaty referred only to Germany as a potential enemy, the defensive alliance applied to any aggressor in Europe – and the aggressor warned off in March 1948 was the Soviet Union. Britain had now joined a Western bloc and Bevin was its principal architect.

The Labour government's vision of acting as a peacemaker and mediator without exclusive alliances with any one group of nations, a vision which corresponded to a long tradition in British foreign policy, had been abandoned by Bevin and the Attlee Cabinet as the post-war dangers inherent in the Cold War became ever more apparent in 1948. But it was only a partial abandonment. Neither the Conservatives nor Labour intended to join a united Western Europe, a supra-national Europe. Britain's alliances with her continental neighbours were not exclusive: she valued her worldwide Commonwealth ties too highly. Bevin also believed that Western Europe was not strong enough to defend itself. For him, the Brussels Treaty was a stepping stone to a wider transatlantic alliance to be constructed when the United States was ready for it. In the event, that was not to be until 1949, when NATO was created. Thus in a significant sense the British Foreign Secretary was a principal architect of the most important Western alliance from 1949 to 1990. Bevin's desire that Western Europe should strengthen itself to avoid becoming a mere appendage of the United States was also sound. For many years, however, the power of the United States was dominant within the Western alliance.

# CHAPTER 33

# France: A Veil Over the Past

The Nazi victories in Europe cast a long shadow over all the countries the Germans occupied. For none is this more true than France. Hitler had allowed a French government to continue to function, and this Vichy regime under Marshal Henri Philippe Pétain enjoyed the support of the great majority of Frenchmen in 1940: for them the war was over. Vichy represented adjustment to the new realities and reconstructions, for the 'old France' had demonstrated her rottenness in defeat. There appeared to be no real alternative to 'honest collaboration', carrying out the terms the Germans had imposed. But where did honour end? Vichy militia and police helped the Germans to arrest other Frenchmen to be handed over to Gestapo torturers. Then the Jews were rounded up to be sent to their deaths in the east, not only the foreign refugees admitted before the outbreak of war, but French men, women and children. The war produced great heroes in France: men and women risking their lives for the persecuted, and for the Allied cause. But there were tens of thousands of Frenchmen who served Vichy France, some in important roles, others in minor capacities, from Pierre Laval, the Prime Minister to the lowliest policeman or civil servant. They made their living serving the state, and the great majority were able to continue their careers after the war, with no apparent stain on their character.

In France the situation changed only gradually in de Gaulle's favour, gaining added impetus after the German invasion of the Soviet Union in June 1941. The strong French Communist Party now reversed its policy of collaboration, and the resistance, until then scattered and weak, now with the adhesion of the communists developed into a strong movement. As the chances of German victory receded with defeats in Russia and North Africa, and as the Nazis more and more ruthlessly exploited the human resources of French labour, forcing many Frenchmen to work in German factories, so support for Vichy dwindled. In 1943 the various resistance groups agreed to combine, and, looking to de Gaulle in London for leadership, formed a National Council of Resistance with the help of a Gaullist emissary parachuted to France from England. Of course, this did not mean that all rival political ambitions had ended. While the communists fixed their eyes not only on liberation, but on a post-war communist transformation of France, de Gaulle skilfully laid his plans for frustrating them and for placing himself at the head of a national government. This meant controlling the resistance movement and subordinating it to his own administration. With liberation in 1944, the unity based on fighting the Germans came to an end, and France's political future stood shrouded in uncertainty. Would the communists take power? Would de Gaulle be able to do so? Or would there be a civil war and an Anglo-American occupation?

In the event, millions of ordinary people were now only too happy to identify with a French hero and to rally around a new saviour to replace the discredited eighty-year-old Marshal Pétain. With the help of the BBC, de Gaulle had projected the myth of an unconquerable France, and he himself fitted the desired image. It was an extraordinary feat, as he imbued the people with an inflexible faith in France and in the recovery of her rightful place as a world power, thereby relegating 1940 to no more than one defeat in battle that could not alter France's destiny. A gift for oratory enabled de Gaulle to do for France what Churchill had accomplished during the darkest hours of the war for Britain. Politicians in France, of all shades of belief, accepted de Gaulle as indispensable in the months immediately following the expulsion of the Germans. On 26 August 1944, in scenes preserved by the newsreel cameras, de Gaulle strode through liberated Paris, with snipers still firing from the rooftops. Even so, largely because of American reluctance, the Allies waited until October before granting full recognition to de Gaulle's provisional government.

In the resistance movement, the communists were the largest and most disciplined element. The socialists, as in Italy later, were divided on the issue of whether or not to collaborate with the Marxist communists in a broad-left front. The president of the Resistance Council was Georges Bidault, an anti-Marxist who identified with progressive Catholic aims; he headed a new party, the Mouvement Républicain Populaire (MRP), which after the communists and socialists formed the third and smallest group in the Resistance. But de Gaulle deliberately stood aloof from party politics in 1944 and 1945, refusing to lead any party of his own; he claimed to speak for France above parties. Yet, by stating as the aims of his policy the restoration of national greatness and the political, social and economic renovation of France, he appealed to popular feelings on the left: liberation from the Germans would go hand in hand with reform. Big business, which had collaborated with the Germans, and the conservative supporters of Vichy, as well as all those who had done well under German occupation, had to lie low politically. Until the eve of liberation, supporters of de Gaulle represented only a minority of Frenchmen; after liberation they were able to lay claim to the government without opposition.

How did this come about? The communists were on the spot, well armed and well organised. They had worked with the non-communist resistance under de Gaulle's aegis, but would they now capi-

talise on their strong position in the country to seize power? Again, as in Italy, the communists made no such bid to challenge de Gaulle directly. Their leader, Maurice Thorez, returned from Moscow in November 1944 and gave his public approval to communist co-operation with the other parties and their participation in a provisional government headed by de Gaulle. The French communists, like the Italian, had probably received their instructions from Moscow. The Germans were not yet defeated and it was in Russia's interest to maintain Allied unity. An open attempt by communists to take power in a Western country might alienate Britain and the United States. Stalin even thought that such an event could open the way to a change of alliances, the Western Allies siding with Germany against Russia – his ultimate fear. De Gaulle succeeded therefore more easily than anyone expected. The provisional government was able to establish its authority over the whole country, with the communists securing only the less important ministerial posts. The independent local committees and militia were dissolved without resistance. For two years, from 1944 to 1946, the communists participated in governments with the socialists and the MRP. Despite their strength, the communists could not dominate French politics in succeeding years and were excluded from government. De Gaulle's first period of office was short and ended in 1946, but he had already made a permanent impact on French politics.

During the first year de Gaulle had acted cautiously at home. The obligatory trials of prominent Vichy collaborators had taken place. The Vichy Prime Minister Pierre Laval was sentenced to death and executed, though Pétain's death sentence was commuted to life imprisonment. Newsreels showed pictures of girls with heads shaven for consorting with Germans. Wild summary 'justice' was meted out by the forces of Liberation; this gave opportunities, too, for the simple settling of old scores. The best estimate is that nearly 10,000 Frenchmen were killed. Regularly constituted law courts passed 7037 sentences of death, but most received the presidential pardon and only 767 executions were actually carried out. Of the just over 167,000 tried, almost half were acquitted and 27,000 received jail sentences. So the prisons were filled with collaborators. Even so, not all the French citizens who saw in Vichy a legitimate government which they actively supported could be tried. After 1950, less than

5000 remained in prison. The trials ceased. They had been intended to cleanse France from the Vichy taint. In fact the only practical policy was to draw a veil over the Vichy years, to conciliate and to unite the nation. It was left to a few ardent individuals to continue to the present day to uncover those responsible for Vichy crimes, much to the embarrassment of some of the older generation of Frenchmen. Somehow sleeping dogs will not lie; the whole war generation will have to pass away first.

The provisional government after Liberation was faced with daunting problems of restoring the dislocated and shattered French economy. There were grave shortages of food and fuel. The infrastructure of transport, bridges and railways had to be rebuilt. State intervention and the takeover of ailing industries were seen as necessary to enable the nation to recover rather than as policies in conformity with socialist ideology. The provisional government in 1945 responded to the demands of the resistance and nationalised the big banks, insurance, gas, electricity and coal as well as companies that, like Renault, had collaborated with the Germans. This created the large state sector of industry which has been characteristic of post-war France. Joint committees were set up in firms employing more than fifty workers to give employees a role and a stake in the success of the company. But hopes for 'industrial democracy' were unfulfilled, because employers continued to take the critical financial decisions. Employees did, however, gain from the increase of family benefits and the introduction of compulsory insurance. But this did little to relieve the grim economic situation. Workers' standards of living were under constant pressure from inflation. During the Vichy years (1940–4) retail prices had risen more than three times but hourly wages had only doubled. At the end of the war, with too much paper money chasing too few goods, prices shot up. There was much industrial unrest, made politically more dangerous because the largest union, the Confédération Générale du Travail (CGT), was controlled by the Communist Party. De Gaulle rejected the restrictive monetary policy necessary to reduce the flood of paper money held by the population and so defeat inflation and restore the value of the currency. Instead, to maintain his popularity, he decreed salary increases and simply postponed tackling France's economic problems.

Nevertheless, de Gaulle's greatest achievement must be recognised. He stopped France from sliding into a civil war between the active supporters of Vichy, including the police and militia, on the one side and the resistance on the other. Amid the chaos he used his enormous prestige as the embodiment of France to impose a centralised, unified state on the warring factions.

De Gaulle knew that, once the emergency was past and the war was over, the provisional government would need to be transformed into a democratically elected one, and the provisional state into a stable republic. Following a national referendum held in October 1945, the French people voted overwhelmingly for a new constitution to be framed and for a constituent assembly to be elected and given the task of drafting the constitution. In the unique post-war circumstances the left gained more seats in the Assembly than its usual electoral strength warranted, given that half the electorate tended to be conservative: the communists benefited most with 160 seats, and the socialists won 142. The new progressive Catholic Party, the MRP, also did surprisingly well, gaining 152 seats. The socialists and communists thus achieved an absolute majority in the Assembly of 586 deputies.

A deep rift soon opened up between de Gaulle and the majority in the Assembly on the question of the future constitution. De Gaulle was clear about the essentials: France must not relapse into the political instability of the Third Republic. He therefore insisted on a strong executive headed by the president, and on an assembly that would have a share in government but should not be able to exercise sovereign power. Meanwhile, in the Constituent Assembly the communists attempted to gain the agreement of the socialists to a common programme that would exclude the MRP, but the socialists, who held the key and had no wish to be swallowed up by the communists, insisted on a three-party (communist, socialist, MRP) alignment. The communists chose to bide their time, all parties agreeing to offer de Gaulle the presidency. In the complicated political manoeuvrings that followed, de Gaulle refused to give the communists any of the key ministries they claimed – War. Interior or Foreign Affairs – and threatened to resign. The socialists and MRP supported him, and the communists, faced with a choice of exclusion or participation, gave in. So the first round, with the critical help of the socialists and MRP, went to de Gaulle. The political crisis of November 1945 provoked by the communist demands was thus resolved and a government, headed by de Gaulle and comprising ministers drawn from all the major parties, was formed.

But the fundamental issue remained to be settled: despite deep divisions between the socialists and communists in the Assembly, it became clear that these two parties would reject de Gaulle's concept of a strong, independent presidency and executive in favour of leaving controlling powers with a parliamentary assembly. In many ways the Assembly was already asserting the right to make judgements on the policies that de Gaulle wished to adopt. On the constitutional question de Gaulle could count only on the support of the MRP, and he reacted with bitterness to the prospect of defeat in the Assembly. He believed that he could rely on the support of the mass of the French people. The politicians in the Assembly, he was convinced, were combining against him to safeguard their own selfish interests rather than those of France. Feeling nothing but contempt for the parliamentarians, he decided to force their hand. He confided to one of his ministers at this time,

I don't feel that I am made for this kind of fight. I don't want to be attacked, criticised, challenged every day by men who have no other distinction than the fact that they got themselves elected in some little place in France. . . . I can't resign myself to enduring criticisms of parties and irresponsible men, to seeing my decisions challenged, my ministers criticised, myself attacked, my prestige diminished. Since I cannot govern as I wish, that is to say fully, rather than see my power dismembered, I'm going!

That conversation took place shortly before de Gaulle dropped his bombshell on 20 January 1946 and resigned.

His frustration and anger were genuine. All his policies abroad, in Germany, Indo-China and the Middle East, had experienced setbacks as well. But there was calculation too. He did not believe the nation would be able to manage without him. It was a tactical retreat and he expected to be recalled on conditions he himself would set. Several years later he acknowledged his miscalculation: 'I have made at least one political mistake in my life: my departure in January 1946. I thought the French would recall

me quickly. Because they didn't do so, France wasted several years.'

After de Gaulle's resignation, the French people – influenced by his opposition – rejected the draft constitution in a referendum held in May 1946. Then a second constituent assembly was elected to draft an amended constitution. This gave women the vote, adopted proportional representation and created a second chamber but left the real political power in the lower chamber, the National Assembly, which also elected the president. The constitution resembled in most important respects that of the Third Republic and was to create the same governmental instability. But despite de Gaulle's strong opposition the new constitution was narrowly approved in a referendum in October 1946, nearly 8 million dissenting and just over 9 million in favour, with almost a third of the electorate not bothering to vote at all. It was an inauspicious start for the Fourth Republic.

Nineteen-forty-seven was a particularly bad year for France. Food became still scarcer in the cities, and coal production fell. Prices doubled. Workers whose real wages were rapidly diminishing came out on strike, needing little encouragement from the communist-controlled CGT. The Communist Party found itself in the spring of 1947 faced with a choice between remaining in the three-party government (with the MRP and the socialists), which opposed the strikes, and supporting the workers in their strike demands. Moreover, France's harsh policy of re-establishing her authority over the colonies, and the developing Cold War, made it increasingly difficult for the communists to collaborate with their coalition partners. The socialist Prime Minister solved the problem for them by dismissing the communist ministers. Despite their hold over the trade unions and their support among the electors, the communists could henceforth play only an oppositional role in French politics and society. They were not to regain a share of power in government for thirty-four years.

The stability of the Republic was also threatened from the right. Admirers of de Gaulle were secretly plotting to found a party as a vehicle for the General's early return. De Gaulle himself was thinking along the same lines and began recruiting supporters in the autumn of 1946 to set up a national movement drawing support from all Frenchmen to 'save France'. In April 1947, boosted by the wave of strikes, he went public in a speech in Strasbourg. He denounced the communists and proclaimed his new movement, a kind of anti-party party, calling for the 'Rally of the French People' under the banner of his leadership, the Rassemblement du Peuple Français (or RPF).

The question remained: if it was not a party, how would de Gaulle regain power under the constitution? The answer was far from clear, except that de Gaulle had no dictatorial intentions and would accept the presidency only if offered it constitutionally. But the movement still looked dangerously authoritarian, certainly unparliamentary, given de Gaulle's contempt for 'rigid parties' and his call for an 'orderly, concentrated state'. He promised that the movement would act within the framework of the law, but 'over and above differences of opinion', so that 'the great effort of common salvation and the profound reform of the state may be successfully undertaken'. It looked for a time as if de Gaulle would succeed, as millions of Frenchmen were ready to support him during that difficult year. In the local elections in October 40 per cent of the electorate gave their vote to candidates of the Rassemblement. But just four years later, in the elections for the new National Assembly in 1951, de Gaulle's support had nearly halved. The 'Gaullists' had become just another, albeit strong, parliamentary group. The game was up for the time being and two years later de Gaulle withdrew to the village of Colombey-les-Deux-Églises.

The economy of the Fourth Republic was recovering. A landmark in that recovery was the adoption in January 1947 by the National Assembly of what became known as the Monnet Plan. De Gaulle had appointed Jean Monnet after the Liberation to head a committee to prepare a plan for the reconstruction and modernisation of the French economy. Monnet's roots were deeply embedded in traditional France: he was born in 1888 in Cognac into a family of brandy distillers. But he learnt to combine his understanding of conservative France with the international experience he gained as a salesman for the cognac concern. In particular he was able to observe at first hand the drive, flexibility and efficiency of twentieth-century America. His international perceptions and idealistic belief in the betterment of society through co-operation were heightened by service for the League of Nations and the French government before the outbreak of war in 1939. Monnet joined the Free French and

came to Britain after the débâcle of 1940; it was he who suggested to Churchill the idea of an Anglo-French union. In 1943 he became a member of the French Committee of National Liberation, for which he organised a group of experts. The work of his committee bore fruit in the plan he proposed in 1947. Monnet was to exert a lasting influence, not only on French economic planning, but on the co-ordination of the West European economies and the establishment of the Common Market. Drawing on his practical experience he passionately believed that collective action, nationally and internationally, was necessary to solve the problems confronting France and Europe.

The plans produced by his Commission, the Commissariat Général du Plan, were not directives, but targets and guides showing how the different elements of the economy could best be co-ordinated in order to achieve the proposed increases in production. Monnet had no intention of controlling industry as was done in communist countries. Much depended on his personal influence. The nationalised industries provided a good starting point because they were more amenable to government planning, and Monnet's Plan dealt primarily with improving supplies of fuel and energy, as well as with oil refineries, transport, steel, cement and tractors to increase agricultural productivity. The aim of the Plan was to raise industrial and agricultural output by 25 per cent over 1929 within three years. This would make possible a substantial rise in the standard of living. It was presented as an emergency plan of action. Instead it was to become a much more permanent institution with a series of five-year plans. The remarkable success of continuous economic planning based on long-term objectives contrasted with what appeared to be the hopelessly inefficient political scenario so characteristic of France. This political instability led many to underrate her fundamental strength.

In world affairs, France had not won an equal place with Britain in 1945. France's German policy of attempting to detach the Rhineland and the Ruhr achieved no success. The United States and Britain were co-ordinating and centralising western Germany, isolating France in her German occupation zone. De Gaulle's cherished hope of establishing France as a third force and as a bridge between the Anglo-Saxons and the Russians, which had led him to Moscow and to the conclusion of a new treaty between France and the Soviet Union in 1944, was an idle dream. Stalin had no intention of using de Gaulle as an intermediary, and the realities of the Cold War destroyed any notions of French bridge-building. In reasserting French colonial rights by the use of force in Madagascar, the Middle East, Algeria and Indo-China, France enmeshed herself in Third World struggles for independence which for more than two decades caused many deaths, bled her of resources and weakened her at home and abroad, only to end in failure. Finally, 1947 was a year of economic crisis and industrial unrest. Yet in retrospect, it was those very failures and difficulties which turned French thoughts in new directions.

French economic recovery was not possible without German economic recovery and Franco-German co-operation. De Gaulle was the first French statesman to offer the German people reconciliation but it was on condition that they became junior partners and accepted a weakened German state deprived not only of the Saar but also of the Rhineland and Ruhr, which would be internationalised and formed into a separate 'European' state. But such aims were as much opposed by the United States and Britain as they were by Germany. As conflicts with the Soviet Union deepened, so earlier anxieties receded. Germany was likely to remain divided between the West and the Soviet Union; control over armaments and the Ruhr would continue in any case. But west German support would have to be won: this meant concessions and no further amputations of German territory.

For the governments of the French Fourth Republic it was, therefore, not so much a perceived *direct* Russian threat, the fear that Soviet tanks would cross the Elbe and head for France, that provided the impetus for a change of policy; it was rather the realisation that French aims in continental Europe – dominance over Germany, bridge-building to the East and maintenance of French independence in the face of the Atlantic Anglo-Saxon powers – were doomed to failure as an indirect consequence of the Cold War. France herself was now threatened with isolation as Britain and the United States chose to start building up west Germany. France might, nevertheless, have taken her time to change course had it not been for her dire economic condition, which obliged the government to rely on American aid.

Internally and externally in 1947 pressures were thus mounting for a reorientation of French policies. There was soon tangible evidence that a new course was being followed. An Anglo-French treaty of alliance was concluded in March 1947 (the Treaty of Dunkirk) to reassure France as Germany revived, and as a first step towards closer economic and political collaboration in Western Europe. In June 1947, General George Marshall, the American Secretary of State, delivered his famous address at Harvard (page 382) promising American aid on condition that the European nations co-ordinated their planning. His proposal was welcomed in France, and Anglo-French agreement on how to proceed followed speedily. On the initiative of the French and British foreign ministers, Bidault and Bevin, the European nations were invited to a conference in Paris with the purpose of formulating their responses to Marshall's offer. West Germany was included in Marshall's plan for European economic co-operation (theoretically the German Eastern zone, all the nations under Soviet control and the Soviet Union were likewise included, but they were expected to reject the conditions of aid). Acceptance of Marshall Aid was as essential for France as it was for the other Western nations if recovery was to be accelerated. The Plan also held out the hope that Western Europe might one day be better able to maintain its independence from United States influence. De Gaulle realised this as quickly as anyone and the Gaullists called for a European union based on a federation of states. Although their motivation and aims of policy were by no means identical, the United States, Britain and France found their policies converging in 1947. Britain still saw herself as separate from continental Europe but also favoured a strengthening of the Western continental states through collaboration.

Thus, despite earlier differences, perhaps the most significant outcome of the early post-war years was not only the recovery of France, but the drawing together of Western Europe under Anglo-French leadership with firm United States support. The shape of the future Western Europe and the broad Atlantic economic partnership had begun to emerge in 1947. The shocks of the crisis years 1947 and 1948, the coup in Czechoslovakia and the Berlin blockade, created a sense of common danger which reinforced these ties, but Britain, having first provided a strong impetus, was to draw back from closer economic co-operation with the beginnings of West European integration in the 1950s.

# CHAPTER 34

## *Italy: The Enemy Forgiven*

Nazi Germany's principal ally during the Second World War was Benito Mussolini's fascist Italy. There had been much destruction, particularly of housing, as the Allied armies pushed up the Italian peninsula after their landings in the south, but the country's industrial north-east region, where the Germans surrendered without severe fighting taking place, would allow Italian industry to recover quickly. Agriculture too could be brought back to normal within one or, at most, two seasons. The immediate dislocation caused by the war was, nevertheless, enormous. Even though most Italian cities, unlike Germany's, had not been turned into rubble heaps, the standard of living of most Italians had dropped to subsistence level and below. Communications and infrastructure had to be rebuilt. Relief from abroad was essential if the poorest Italian families were not to starve, and it came principally from the United States. In 1945 Italy was producing less than half of what had been her Gross National Product in 1938, yet three years after the end of the war the Italian economy had already caught up with pre-war levels.

In many respects the Italians were in a more fortunate position than the Germans at the end of the war. Italy was not divided; it was occupied and in reality under the control of the Western Allies alone. The Allied perception of Italians, reinforced by the way the war came to an end in Italy, was far more favourable than their perception of the Germans. At about the same time in the autumn of 1944 as the Morgenthau Plan of pastoralisation

and minimal living standards was being regarded as appropriate treatment for the Germans, Britain and the United States promised to help Italy recover from the wounds of war. Why the great difference? Mussolini had presided over a vicious puppet regime in northern Italy while the Allies in 1944 were slowly battling up the Italian peninsula. But the fighting had not been left to the Allies alone. A powerful anti-fascist partisan movement had attacked and harried the German troops and the Italian fascist militia. In this way the Italians had actively assisted in the liberation of their country. The Germans had fought for Hitler's Germany to the end.

The Allies had looked upon the fascists with contempt rather than hatred during the war. The Italian fascists, moreover, had not committed atrocities on the terrible scale of the Germans. Although Mussolini's regime was increasingly ready to accept German dictation, the Italian Army High Command during the Second World War had not become as depraved as much of the Wehrmacht leadership became; Italian generals had even shown resistance to criminal orders. The Italian people had tired of the war and genuinely welcomed the British and American troops as liberators. The cause of Italy was also assisted by the presence in the United States of a large Italian-American community whose members had not lost their love for their homeland: Roosevelt wanted to secure their support in the presidential election of 1944. Most importantly, the Italians themselves had overthrown Mussolini when the Fascist Grand Council and the King had dismissed him. The Allies were prepared to deal with his successor, Marshal Pietro Badoglio, even though he was the brutal conqueror of Abyssinia; what mattered most to them was that he was prepared to take Italy out of the war. The Italians were thus allowed by the Western Allies to change sides and become 'co-belligerents' – not exactly allies, but not enemies either.

Italy had achieved something remarkable. Without a revolution the old fascist establishment and the monarchy had transformed their fascist rule to one acceptable to the Allies. To all intents and purposes they had escaped the consequences of the Allied demand for 'unconditional surrender'. As far as Italy was concerned, the needs of war overrode other considerations in Allied counsels. For Churchill and the British, Badoglio and the monarchy represented the best bulwark against communism; the liberal politicians of the pre-fascist era had failed once and were not to be trusted again.

The southern half of Italy had always been predominantly conservative and royalist. With the Allied armies in the south and the Germans in the north, Italy was, in 1944, more physically split than ever. In central and northern Italy a coalition of anti-fascist parties was formed in September 1944 embracing all anti-fascists from the Liberals to Catholic Christian Democrats and from the socialists to the communists. Calling themselves the Committee of National Liberation, they demanded war against the German occupiers. By contrast, the King and his government, who had earned the contempt of many Italians by fleeing south to safety behind the Allied lines, seemed paralysed and hesitant. The Committee of National Liberation filled the vacuum and acted decisively, despite the German occupation of central and northern Italy. For this reason it became the effective political authority in Italy in 1945.

With 250,000 armed partisans, a fierce war was fought in the north against the well-armed German divisions. The partisans suffered heavy casualties in 1944 and 1945 but succeeded in liberating Milan and Italy's other northern cities even before Allied troops advancing from the south could reach them. Mussolini's puppet regime in the north collapsed and he tried to flee. He was captured by partisans and executed together with his mistress. Their bodies were then exposed to the savagery of public

vengeance. The newsreels which showed these horrible scenes, though they shocked many in the West, provided a glimpse of the passions the war had aroused.

Why then did the communists not seek to exploit their organisational strength among the partisans of the centre and north and their military success in sweeping through the Po Valley during the spring of 1945, 'the wind from the north', to try to hold on to effective power? Palmiro Togliatti, the communist leader, a cool and calculating politician, had left Moscow and reached southern Italy a year earlier, in March 1944. He had immediately declared that the communists would collaborate with the royal government and anti-fascist parties and he did not waver from this course at the moment of victory in 1945. It is probable that the strategy had been co-ordinated in Moscow. The similarity with the attitude of the French communists is striking. Stalin was anxious to maintain Allied unity until the war was won, and indeed after; he had pressed for spheres of influence in the Europe overrun by the Allied armies and he now tried to demonstrate to the Western Allies that the communists in the sphere he accepted as Western would not be allowed to cause any trouble. Realism, so Stalin believed, dictated that the Western Allies, whose armies would conquer the whole of Italy, would also decide future politics in Italy. The Soviet recognition of Badoglio's royal government in the south in March 1944 sent this signal clearly. Stalin, of course, was also anxious as an obvious *quid pro quo* to have the Western Allies accept Soviet dominance in Eastern and central Europe. Moscow, therefore, urged the communist parties of the West to follow popular-front tactics, to bide their time and to gain strength by working constitutionally within the system.

Togliatti too was committed to a policy of caution. An insurrection now would only have been crushed by the Allies; the path of legality, on the other hand, guaranteed the survival of the Communist Party, particularly when it was combined with the call that all Italians should unite to defeat fascism and the Germans. Togliatti's aims were long-term, to rally the Italian masses to an Italian Marxist line *after* the war, to establish what he enigmatically called 'progressive democracy'. The inevitable drawback of his policies was that by supporting the royal government he also strengthened the anti-communist forces, which, as it turned out, have dominated Italian politics ever since 1945.

The party in greatest difficulty after the war was the 'other party' of the left, the socialists. Should it be ready now to unite the left, to gain a majority in the country and to collaborate with the communists? It was led by Pietro Nenni, a warm and popular 'man of the people' who believed that it was the disunity of the working class which had allowed Mussolini and the fascists to gain and retain power. Hence his decision after 1945 to urge close collaboration with the Communist Party. This policy eventually split the party in 1947, a majority following Nenni; a minority under Giuseppe Saragat distrusted Moscow and the communists, left the party on this issue and formed their own party, the Social Democrats.

The Christian Democrats were to play the decisive role in post-war Italian politics. The principal aim of the party was to re-establish the constitutional parliamentary state of the pre-fascist era. Fervour for reform varied among party members, those on the left being the keenest. But the Christian Democrats enjoyed one large electoral advantage: the full backing of the Vatican. The leader of the party, who dominated Italian politics in the immediate post-war years was Alcide De Gasperi, a practising Catholic. Although not solely a Catholic party, the Christian Democrats depended on the support of the Church for their electoral success. Yet De Gasperi was no mere captive of the Church. Despite Vatican disapproval he was ready to work with the communists in the National Liberation Council during the war and he encouraged communist participation in the post-war coalition governments until 1947. It served the interests of the governments he led after December 1945 not to drive the communists immediately into opposition.

In post-war Italy the Church resumed its enormous influence over the lives of believers, the Vatican and priests backing from their pulpits the Christian Democrats against the godless communists. The Christian Democrats succeeded in attracting by far the largest support of any one party. However, the alliance of Togliatti's communists and of Nenni's Socialist Party, both strongly based in industrial northern and in central Italy, obtained as much support as the Christian Democrats, but, with the Allies occupying Italy until the peace treaty was signed in 1947, they had to content themselves with the position of coalition partners in govern-

ments led by the Christian Democrat De Gasperi. The communists and their socialist allies were in any case anxious to prove their good behaviour as a non-revolutionary political grouping. Dominating the reborn trade unions, the communists urged restraint on the workers in the north, and at the end of the war ensured that the partisans gave up their arms, so ending any possibility of revolution. Were these tactics a betrayal of the working class and the revolution, as extreme-left theoreticians later claimed? Revolution in the circumstances prevailing in Italy was unlikely to have succeeded. Stalin would have given no support. The overwhelming strength of the Anglo-American armies, the fact that the partisans were not all communists and their need for Allied supplies against the Germans made the notion of a seizure of power in 1944 and 1945 quite unrealistic.

Despite the support the Church gave to the monarchy Italy became a republic in 1946, in response to a national referendum. The majority for the republic had been slender, reflecting the small preponderance of the left. A constituent assembly was elected at the same time, with three parties gaining most of the votes: the Christian Democrats secured 35 per cent, the socialists nearly 21 and the communists just under 19. The revived extreme right, quasi-fascists, managed to obtain 5.3 per cent. On crucial issues, communists and socialists behaved moderately, so that a constitution setting up a parliamentary form of government was agreed on in 1947. It left many issues ambiguous and would allow the shift to the right to continue.

All three government parties collaborated on the urgent task of post-war reconstruction; unemployment, rampant inflation and shortages of food created enormous difficulties for the government and people of Italy. Flour was brought in by the United Nations Relief and Rehabilitation Administration (UNRRA), largely financed by the United States. American emergency loans further emphasised Italy's dependence on the United States. Reconstruction, it was held, must precede socialisation. The fascist economic controls over industry were dismantled and private enterprise was favoured over state-run industry by the orthodox economists who dominated the Treasury. They had little faith in Keynesian interference in the economy, after years of a corporate fascist state. The trade unions won some relief for the workers against rising prices, but distress remained widespread, even though production picked up and the yield of the 1946 harvest was better than that of 1945. As elsewhere in Western Europe, the hard winter of 1946/7 caused a grave crisis in Italy. The first two years after the war were a period of great hardship for the Italian people, with 1 million unemployed in industry alone. It was followed by an extraordinary upswing of production, which cannot simply be attributed to Marshall Aid. It was dubbed an economic miracle, but its foundations had been laid in the hard years after the war. Confidence in the currency was restored. The danger of a communist political and economic takeover receded. De Gasperi underlined the waning need for communist and socialist support when he excluded those parties from his new government in the spring of 1947. With their departure the last vestiges of the wartime Committee of National Liberation vanished. The politics of war, of possible revolutionary change, were over and Italy was returning to a kind of normality. Thus in little more than two years a certain political stability had been attained, and vital issues such as the future control of industry, the monarch and the role of the Catholic Church had all been defined.

No former enemy was quite so rapidly forgiven nor so speedily embraced as a new ally as was Italy. In February 1947, unlike Germany, Italy secured a peace treaty. The loss of her colonies appeared a heavy blow at the time, but later it was to spare Italy the trauma of decolonisation suffered by the victors. The Western Allies demanded no reparations, and those paid to the injured victims in the Balkans and the USSR were kept to a modest level, funded by grants and loans supplied by the United States. Yet the Italians did not escape entirely unscathed. Besides losing their colonial territories, Italy also had to give up Albania and her wartime Balkan gains. The most bitterly disputed territory was the province of Venezia Giulia, until 1918 part of the Austro-Hungarian Empire, its port of Trieste populated predominantly by Italians. Italy had had little to show for her heavy losses in the First World War, and her 1918 gains had enormous emotional significance. But the Yugoslavs, who had suffered so much from German and Italian occupation, were in 1954 granted most of the territory by the wartime Allies, the Italians regaining control only of the city of Trieste itself, which was made a free territory.

Of great economic, as well as national and emotional, importance was another former Habsburg territory, the South Tyrol, its predominantly German-speaking population antagonised by Italian rule. The Italians had gained this territory with the blood of more than 1 million war dead in the Great War. They would not now lightly give up the Brenner Pass frontier or the hydroelectric power they had developed in this region. Hitler had recognised Italian sensitivities and had assured Mussolini that he harboured no designs on the Tyrol. The Allies in 1946 rejected Austrian claims, not to mention the wishes of the majority of the population. The Austrians, who had helped the Germans, were after all easier to deny than the Yugoslavs, who had fought with the Allies. Even so, the Italians were far from satisfied with the peace terms. They claimed that, having changed sides in 1943, they should have been better treated. No war or peace since the Risorgimento had ever fulfilled all Italian aspirations. But today Italy has overcome the evils of nationalism and only an occasional bomb in the South Tyrol serves as a reminder of past injustices in the new era of West European co-operation.

The Russians consented to the peace treaty, which might appear surprising in the Cold War climate of 1947. But the treaty also marked the logical outcome of the Yalta Agreements. The occupying powers' decisions were not to be challenged in the spheres of influence recognised by the Soviets. In return for agreeing to the Italian terms, the satellite regimes in Soviet-controlled Bulgaria, Romania and Hungary received recognition and peace treaties at the same time, as also did Finland. Their gains and territorial adjustments as allies of Germany were reversed, but the Soviet Union retained Bessarabia (Moldavia) and northern Bukovina, which they had first occupied in 1940. Finland had to confirm the cession of territory made to the USSR in 1940, and the Soviet Union in addition secured a fifty-year lease of the Porkkala naval base. Unlike the Balkan states, Finland never became a satellite and was allowed complete independence while following a policy friendly to the USSR. Relations proved so satisfactory that the Soviets returned the naval base in 1955.

From the start Italy was not treated as Germany was. Even under American occupation from 1945 to 1947, the military supervisory government dropped the word 'Control' from its title of Allied Commission. Fascism was suppressed, but political life never came to a standstill. After the peace treaty, Italy participated on the same terms as France and Britain in the Marshall Plan (though receiving much less) and could take her place in the United Nations. Italy had been treated generously, and harboured no grudges against the nations that had defeated her. Italians escaped too the heavy burden of guilt that would continue to haunt the German people for more than a generation.

# PART VII

*The United States and the Beginning of the Cold War, 1945–1948*

# CHAPTER 35

*The United States: Problems Enough at Home*

As seen from Europe during the first post-war years, the United States was a land of plenty. The GIs, when they came to London or Paris, looked remarkably well fed and groomed, quite different to Europeans in their fourth year of war. The fabled US Army stores, the PXs, were filled with candy, cigarettes, lighters, watches, pens – everything that was in such short supply for the Europeans was available to the US troops in abundance. The image of wealth was reinforced by the dream kitchens and cars shown in Hollywood films. But these were false impressions. The life of John Doe did not match the celluloid representation.

At home Americans faced shortages, too, and industrial dislocation as the country after 1945 turned from the needs of war to those of peace. Worst off were the 20 million black citizens. They had already experienced discrimination in the army while fighting the 'crusade for freedom'. Now they were not willing to accept the conditions of ghetto housing or the prejudices and discrimination of the Deep South, where they were deprived of basic civil rights and prevented from voting by such subterfuges as the notorious 'literacy tests'. Southern juries, moreover, were overwhelmingly selected from white citizens; indeed, the chance of securing genuine equality before the law was not easy for non-whites to attain in the United States in 1945. Segregation was common in restaurants and diners, and on transportation. In education, black children in Southern states attended inferior black schools. Even occasional lynchings were still

occurring in the Deep South. Black citizens could well ask themselves, 'What were we fighting for?'

But there were both black and white citizens who wanted to right these wrongs. The long-established National Association for the Advancement of Colored People began to win some significant legal battles. But the struggle for civil rights proved long and hard. President Harry S. Truman, at first cautiously, then more boldly, took his stand on the issue. His motives were both altruistic and practical. The black vote was increasingly important as blacks became more involved in politics and their support was moving from the Democrats to the Republicans. Truman had to destroy the impression that on civil rights his party was dominated by the Southern Democratic wing. Yet he could not persuade Congress to pass civil rights legislation. The evidence of his concern was the setting up of a Committee on Civil Rights.

Not all white Americans were well-to-do either, as the European GI brides discovered when their husbands took off their uniforms. But the war had brought full employment to the United States. The GI Bill of Rights provided federal grants which gave to ordinary Americans opportunities to advance themselves in education and to acquire new skills. Army gratuities enabled many a new small business to be started or a home to be built. The average American was better off than ever before. But would the boom be as short-lived as that which followed the First World War? Would Roosevelt's New Deal and its network of benefits for those in need survive the death of its begetter? There was strong Republican resistance to the New Deal and to federal interference in industrial relations and social welfare. The New Deal, Republican Senator Taft claimed, was taking away independence and enterprise from the American people and substituting government paternalism. Up and down the country he preached, 'We have got to break with the corrupting idea that we can legislate prosperity, equality, and opportunity. All of these good things came in the past from free Americans freely working out their destiny. . . .' Roosevelt and what he stood for were denounced by conservative Americans with a vehemence that approached hatred.

Which way would America now turn? The answer was by no means clear and Truman, Roosevelt's successor, seemed to hesitate and fumble, overwhelmed by the size of the task that had unexpectedly fallen on his shoulders. The immediate problem facing the United States, as everywhere else, was to convert the economy to peacetime conditions. Should wartime controls of prices and wages continue? Inflation was gathering pace, too much money was chasing too few goods. Workers demanded wage increases to keep up with price rises. By inclination Truman was a New Dealer, believing that some federal intervention was essential to protect the vast majority of less well-off Americans, yet he also thought that government controls as established in wartime should be reduced, especially the many regulations holding down prices. Throughout 1945 and 1946, price controls were progressively relaxed. One consequence was that organised labour demanded an end to wage controls. The crunch came when the powerful United Automobile Union went on strike against General Motors to gain wage rises that would maintain the workers' standard of living. Then in April 1946 the redoubtable John L. Lewis led 400,000 coal miners on strike. The following month the Locomotive Engineers were ready to bring the railway system to a halt. Truman reacted as if this was a declaration of war, threatening as commander-in-chief to draft into the army all workers 'who are on strike against their government'. The rail strike was called off. Nevertheless, wages were inevitably rising fast as the controls proved to be increasingly leaky. But Truman had demonstrated that he was prepared to use the presidency and federal powers against any group which in his judgement was acting against the national interest.

In the making of policy much depends on the degree of collaboration achieved between the president and Congress. In September 1945, Truman enjoyed in the seventy-ninth Congress a Democratic majority in both the House and the Senate. But the Democratic Party lacked cohesion more than the Republicans did, the Southern Democrats aligning themselves with the conservative Republicans on many domestic issues. There was thus a majority of anti-New Dealers in Congress. Truman drew on his experience in the Senate to cultivate good relations with Capitol Hill. In his first message to Congress, outlining the twenty-one points of his administration's programme, he steered a moderate course, but he included some New Deal policy proposals for unemployment compensation supplementation, a commitment to full employment and assistance for blacks and other minorities. Truman was only partially successful. On civil rights issues, the alliance of Southern Democrats and conservative Republicans proved a virtually insuperable obstacle.

Truman's single biggest failure was his inability to check inflation. Wartime controls had been abandoned too quickly to stop the spiral of price rises and wage demands backed by crippling strikes. Congress blamed Truman, and Truman blamed Congress. The decline of Truman's popularity made itself felt during the elections in November 1946 for the eightieth Congress. The Democrats lost heavily, and the Republicans now gained majorities in both the Senate and the House. A Democratic president and a Republican Congress could easily lead to recrimination and paralysis in government, bad for the United States and bad for a Western world looking for American help and leadership. On domestic questions, Congress and the President found themselves at loggerheads. Taft and the conservatives dominated the eightieth Congress, and their nominees chairing the crucial Senate committees set out to push back the frontiers of the New Deal. Income tax was redistributed to favour the better off; proposals for more federal help for farmers, for public housing, for education and for additional social security were rejected. Taft set his sights on 'straightening out domestic affairs'. The most important measure of 1947 was probably the Taft-Hartley Act, which limited union power. The strike record of the unions and the disruption they had caused made this acceptable outside the circles of organised labour, and Truman's veto of the bill was overridden by Congress.

Yet, despite undoubted problems, the United States economy passed successfully from war to peace. The post-war depression that many Americans feared, repeating the historical experience after 1919, did not occur. There was a clamour for houses, furniture, consumer goods and cars. In Europe, unable to produce what it needed, there was a great demand for American exports. Some unemployment persisted in the US but the great majority of the millions demobilised from the armed services found work. American industry took up the slack left by the fall-off of wartime production, and during the post-war years from 1945 to 1949 Americans enjoyed growing prosperity.

It was perhaps natural that the American people should now wish to get on with their lives at home. Most of them felt that they had settled the world's problems. They were aware of great hardships suffered in Europe and as individuals responded generously, despatching food parcels through organisations set up to care for the needy. But to pay taxes and then have Congress vote huge sums as gifts to the rest of the world while there were still plenty of urban slums at home and much real poverty was a different matter. Should charity not begin at home? Something akin to the sacrificial spirit of wartime would be needed to alter these attitudes. The spectre of communism eventually provided the motivation, but not in 1945, when the Russians were still regarded by most of the American people as valiant allies. Congress too reflected a desire to get back to normal times as fast as possible and to reduce America's huge wartime commitments. With the end of the war against Japan, the administration suddenly cancelled the Lend–Lease arrangements. Special measures were justified in war but not in peace. Yet financial experts in Washington were perfectly aware that interim measures would be necessary to smooth the passage from war to peace. A blueprint for post-war international finance and trade had been worked out at Bretton Woods from 1944 (pages 349–50) based on freeing trade and currencies from restrictions. But how to get there, given the imbalance

between the American and European economies?

The United States in 1946 exported twice as much as she imported; her exports were now three times as large as in 1939. The exports of France and the rest of Europe combined amounted to less than half the imports to these countries from the United States. Italy, Germany and Japan had been crushed by the war, and their import needs, to maintain even the lowest standards of living, exceeded their exporting capacity. There was clearly a huge trade imbalance. Western Europe faced penury, and hopes of a better life depended on the United States. Eastern Europe also received relief through UNRRA until 1946, but then East and West parted company, and the Soviet Union and the nations under her control faced the daunting task of recovery without American assistance. The gap between progress in the two halves of Europe widened in 1945 and communist mismanagement continued to increase the differences in the era from 1945 to the 1990s.

Only the United States now had the financial capacity to become the world's banker and to recycle through loans and gifts the huge surpluses her favourable balance of trade earned her. The war had greatly increased her productive capacity, and to a lesser extent that of Canada; the needs of Americans at home and worldwide shortages provided the market for them. American financial policy responded with enlightened self-interest. New loans were negotiated on generous financial terms so that goods being shipped from the United States could be paid for. But the United States wished to return to normal commercial practice as soon as possible. American financial advisers were no doubt too optimistic about the timetable of West European recovery and thought special assistance would be needed for only two or three years. In their desire to move quickly towards conditions of freer trade and unimpeded currency exchanges in order to avoid a repetition of the 1930s, the Americans attached conditions to their loans which the West European economies were unable to meet when called upon to do so in 1947. Far more help would then be needed.

CHAPTER 36

# A Reluctant World Power and the Cold War

The void left by Roosevelt's death was felt even more deeply when it came to chart the course the United States should pursue in world affairs than it was in domestic affairs. Roosevelt had followed what at first glance appeared to be contradictory aims. The strong support the United States gave to the setting up of the United Nations and the freeing of international trade involved a global commitment to a peaceful world. The inevitable conflicts would be handled and resolved peacefully in the world forum of the UN. Simultaneously Roosevelt strove to maintain the wartime alliance of the Big Four, the Soviet Union, the United States, Britain and China. Each of the Big Four would be responsible for peace and security in her own part of the world. Roosevelt set great store by personal diplomacy, developing friendly relations with Stalin and Churchill. He was ready to deal with Stalin directly, to the discomfort of his British ally; but when there was a need to check Stalin he would acknowledge and emphasise the 'special relationship' that existed between Britain and the United States. He was opposed to colonialism and he looked forward to a gradual transformation of the European colonial rule in Asia, the Middle East and Africa with his country's benevolent encouragement, but these were ideals that could not easily be put into practice without losing the confidence and support of the West European states. The problem of what to do about China already loomed large in 1945, with the Nationalists under Chiang Kai-shek facing the well-entrenched

Communists led by Mao Zedong in a struggle for the control of China. Roosevelt's aim was to unite the two hostile sides against the Japanese invaders by persuading the communists to subordinate themselves to the Nationalists – a hopelessly impractical endeavour.

Roosevelt had deliberately avoided any coherent detailed masterplan to guide American policy in the post-war world. He was a pragmatist. Events would decide the degree of emphasis to be placed on one tactic or another so that they might complement each other in a workable way. The handling of the various policy threads would thus require a virtuoso in the White House, constantly adjusting a policy here while trying out new initiatives somewhere else. Whether Roosevelt could have handled the problems as successfully as he supposed must be doubted.

But the clash did not seem inevitable in 1945 or 1946. An early 'hot' war was not expected either in Moscow or in Washington. No thought was as yet given to building up rival armies or alliances to meet such an eventuality. The United States after victory on the battlefields wished to bring her troops home from Europe and Asia as quickly as possible. The army, navy and air force were massively demobilised; aircraft, warships and tanks when not actually broken up were mothballed or left rusting in fields and creeks. Roosevelt and Truman felt it safe to rely on America's nuclear monopoly. The American people wanted to return without undue delay to normality. They were not prepared to pay higher taxes for large armed forces in peacetime, and Truman for reasons of domestic policies wanted to balance the budget. Occupation troops in Germany and Japan were kept at the lowest level consistent with internal security. Assistance to former allies was limited to economic aid, to loans and goods, and, in the case of Nationalist China, to weapons. Truman talked tough and gave an outraged Soviet Foreign Minister Molotov a dressing down in April 1945. But, in what became the Soviet 'sphere' in Eastern and central Europe, the United States and Western Europe had neither the means nor the will to interfere effectively; all they could do was to refrain for a short time from recognising the Soviet-created governments.

Truman's experience of world affairs was limited. On the complex questions confronting the United States in the spring and summer of 1945, he tried to follow through Roosevelt's policies. But the counsels of his principal advisers were divided. The most important issue was whether to confront Russia or to try to arrive at some working arrangement with Stalin over disputed issues such as the future of Germany, agreements that would allow East and West to accept each other's differences and yet be able to live side by side. The future of Poland, and Stalin's determination to secure a 'friendly' neighbour here on his own terms, soured relations from the start. But if the United Nations could be set up, a world forum for resolving conflicts might settle current and future problems of this kind.

The conference called to draft the UN Charter met at San Francisco in April 1945. Vital differences still remained. The United Nations might yet founder. The United States was the keenest proponent of setting up the world organisation and that this was accomplished by the end of June 1945 was the most important diplomatic success of the early months of the Truman administration.

It was of course clear that the United Nations would not be a 'world government'. Its members remained sovereign nations. The decision-making procedure, however, would be based on the Western democratic process of the majority vote, which would place the Soviet Union and her associates in a minority. Therefore the nub of the problem became how far any nation would have to accept a decision by majority vote. Clearly nations were not equal in size or power, nor did they share the same ideals of government. The inequality of states had to be recognised by giving to what were then regarded as the most important nations – the Soviet Union, the United States, China, Britain and, sentimentally, France – a special status; they were to be the permanent members of the Security Council; a number of smaller states, six in 1945, were then elected by the General Assembly of the UN to the Security Council to join the five permanent members for a fixed period. All the founding member nations, fifty-one in 1945, were also members of the General Assembly.

But this division of General Assembly and Security Council did not solve the problem. The Soviet Union in particular wished to restrict the UN's powers to interfere in case her vital interests were affected, and it was clear that in voting strength in both the General Assembly and the Security Council the United States and the West could be certain of majorities. Nevertheless the United States and Britain did share one interest with the Soviet Union and that was to give themselves a special status; the five permanent members were therefore each given the right of a veto. The wrangling at San Francisco, where Molotov earned a reputation for dour negativeness, concerned how far this right of veto should extend – whether it should extend to practically everything or only to proposals to enforce decisions of the United Nations. Molotov wished to be able to veto even mere discussion of problems. A complicated formula, full of ambiguities, was eventually evolved to determine when a veto could or could not be exercised by a permanent member. There was no doubt, however, that any one of the permanent members of the Security Council could stop military action or any other form of sanction by the exercise of a veto.

Perhaps the limitations placed on UN powers in the end saved the organisation, for how otherwise could nations in conflict have continued to belong to it? The confidence reposed in the UN early on, by public fervour in the West, expressing the faith that it could solve the world's problems by diplomacy and debate, was misplaced. The Russians were more realistic in their assessment of what a United Nations based in New York meant from their point of view. It was therefore remarkable that they agreed at all and that the Charter of the UN was unanimously adopted on 25 June 1945. The United Nations over the years did prove itself a significant tool for the settling of problems, negotiations being conducted as often in the corridors and coffee bars as in public debate. The United Nations thus served as an important adjunct to the channels of international diplomacy. Sometimes in disputes countries have indeed used the UN as the principal forum of negotiation, but at other times they have bypassed it altogether.

Truman's UN policy was as successful as the West could have hoped. But American expectations were not fulfilled in China. During the Second World War, the Chinese people and their leader Generalissimo Chiang Kai-shek were built up as heroic allies. Pro-Chinese sentiments had been strong in the United States for decades as long as the Chinese people remained in China and did not emigrate to the United States. Something of a special relationship had developed. China became the principal preoccupation of American missionaries, who maintained an influential lobby in Washington. As for American business relations with China, they were as old as the American Republic herself. Thus China loomed large in America's consciousness.

Truman continued Roosevelt's policy of mediation between the Nationalists and communists but not on the basis of equality for both sides. The Americans tried to persuade the communists to be satisfied with a junior participating role in a Nationalist Chinese government, subordinating the communist army divisions to a Nationalist supreme command. At the same time, despite the corruption of Chiang's rule and that of his party, the Kuomintang, the United States backed Chiang with weapons and logistical support. In Washington it was thought that civil war might still be avoided. The true strength of the communists was underestimated in Washington during 1945 and 1946. The Soviet Union, too, wished to prevent an open conflict breaking out in China in 1945 and so was ready to recognise and co-operate with the Nationalist regime. Nevertheless, this did not inhibit the Soviets, when they evacuated northern China and Manchuria, from giving the local communists assistance in the expectation that they would take their place. The United States meanwhile provided massive support for Chiang Kai-shek's forces. At the end of the war the Americans transported nearly half a million Nationalist troops by air and sea to the north to put them in place in the regions vacated by the Japanese before the communists could get there. There was also a direct military intervention by the US when 53,000 marines were landed to occupy key areas in northern China. Confrontation in northern China became inevitable as the Nationalists increasingly clashed with communist forces, who had the advantage of fighting close to their bases whereas the Nationalists were hundreds of miles from theirs.

From 1945 to 1949 the United States shipped large quantities of arms to China's Nationalist forces to help them gain control of the whole of China. But, to begin with, US policy aims were finely tuned. Chiang was not to receive so much military support that he should feel confident about discarding his American advisers and American mediation efforts and so start an all-out civil war, yet he was to be given sufficient arms to bring Mao to the conference table. In this way the Americans wished to induce the communists to merge with Chiang's government.

General George Marshall, America's most distinguished soldier of the Second World War, was sent out by Truman to mediate in January 1946. He spent a fruitless year in China. He succeeded in bringing Chiang and Mao Zedong to the negotiating table, and to all appearances they even came close to agreement. But appearances hid the realities. Neither Chiang nor Mao was ready to compromise his position; both sought total control of China. Mao did not think American hostility was inevitable; both leaders wished to be able to persuade Washington that the failure of mediation was due to the intransigence of the other side.

Mao's faith in ultimate victory was remarkable. Although in 1945, 100 million Chinese lived under Communist Party leadership, the communists were still numerically far weaker than the Nationalists, whose army outnumbered theirs by four to one. If it came to war, the United States expected Chiang Kai-shek's Nationalist forces to beat the communists in the long run, but more damage would be inflicted on China. The Americans urged Chiang to reform the corrupt Kuomintang regime and to make his government more acceptable to the people of China. But in the summer of 1946 full-scale fighting broke out for control of north-eastern China in the wake of the Soviet withdrawal. Advice and military aid was showered on Chiang but simultaneously the Americans disengaged themselves from direct involvement. The American marines were withdrawn, and the Truman administration concluded that if Chiang's regime could not be saved by aid, the alternative of a massive US military commitment in China was simply out of the question. The rival Chinese forces would have to be left to decide the fate of China. This was a sensible view, showing that the Truman administration had a sense of the limitations of American power in the world. If at the same time in Washington a more balanced view had been taken of the Chinese communists, if it had been understood that the communists too were nationalists and that relations between Moscow and Beijing were full of ambiguities, then a more realistic China policy might have emerged.

The restoration of a friendly China as a great power – one of the Big Four – a China linked to the West, had been an essential cornerstone of Roosevelt's cherished concept of an orderly and peaceful post-war world. China, so he intended, would help the United States to maintain peace in Asia and the Pacific and hold Japan in check. Inevitably, Japan would one day recover and, against that day, it was to be China's role to prevent another round of Japanese aggression. The Chinese people, in contrast to the Japanese, were broadly perceived as humane and civilised, worthy allies in the cause of freedom. But during the 'decisive years' (1945–50) quite a different post-war world in Asia took shape. Communist China became the enemy, and Japan the indispensable base in Asia of the free world.

During the war Japanese behaviour was judged by Allied governments and peoples to have been even worse than that of the German National Socialists. In one important respect, as far as the Western Allied nations were concerned, the Americans, the British and the Dutch, this was true: the Japanese had treated captured prisoners of war with barbarity, many thousands perishing from starvation and overwork. In China, Japanese cruelty inflicted horrors indiscriminately on civilians and soldiers which had shocked the civilised world when the China war began in 1937, at a time when the rest of the world – except for Spain – was then still at peace and still shockable. These anti-Japanese perceptions were reinforced by long-held Western attitudes of racial superiority. The Japanese people, like the German people, would be made to submit totally, and could not be trusted. Henry Morgenthau's Treasury had drawn up a punitive plan for the post-war treatment not only of Germany but also of Japan. It was at first expected that Japan would need to be occupied and the Japanese ruled for a long time, not so much

for their own good, but to safeguard the world from their aggressive and barbarous impulses.

Despite unconditional surrender, the trial of war criminals and the purging of thousands from positions of influence in Germany and Japan, the history of the occupation in the two countries nevertheless developed differently in one important respect. Although Japan was stripped of all her overseas conquests acquired since her war with China in 1894, the Japanese homeland was not divided into separate Allied zones of occupation but remained a whole nation. Above all, the entry of the Soviet Union into the war only a few days before Japan's surrender and the fact that no Soviet military forces set foot on the main islands of Japan, meant that West–East disputes about the post-war treatment of Japan were contained on the purely diplomatic level. The Russians were represented on the Far Eastern Commission in Washington, and a Russian general was sent to the impotent Allied Council in Tokyo, but all real power remained in American hands, and American troops supplied the bulk of the occupation forces. In Tokyo that power was exercised by one man, a war hero who was already a legend in his lifetime, General Douglas MacArthur, Supreme Commander for the Allied Powers for the Occupation and Control of Japan, SCAP for short. MacArthur was pretty well able to do what he wished. In the immediate post-war years the problem regions of the world that commanded the anxious attention of Washington, London and Moscow were Europe and China. It was in these regions that the well-publicised crises were occurring, the European ones appearing even more urgent and menacing than the cataclysmic changes in China. Japan had seemingly become a backwater. General MacArthur's high-handedness in settling occupation policies without paying much attention to his superiors in Washington or to the other Allied governments caused irritation, but, as long as Japan did not become an added problem, matters were left in his hands. It would certainly have been hazardous to tangle with a living legend, who, although he did not regard himself as semi-divine, thus usurping the former divinity of the Emperor Hirohito, did see himself as the benevolent guide of the Japanese people, on whose shoulders the shaping of their destiny had fallen. He was determined to break up the pre-war feudal structure of Japanese society, to deprive the military–aristocratic and business elite that had run Japan before

1945 of all power, to ban notions of future military conquests from Japanese minds and to democratise Japan by order from above.

General MacArthur's supreme command, which ended with his dismissal in 1951, has remained in many respects a controversial period of Japanese history. Was his impact as great as he assumed or did the Japanese continue to control their own development more than is supposed? Would many changes have occurred just the same without the autocratic MacArthur? Was Americanisation just skin-deep, a matter of outward form, while the essence of the Japanese spirit remained intact? Such questions stimulate thought, but the reality is not so polarised. Of course, Japanese institutions and Japanese attitudes persisted, but defeat by the West had made an enormous impact.

Japan was the first nation to experience the horrors of atomic devastation, and the long-term suffering of the victims who were not killed outright served as a constant reminder that war could now destroy a whole people and deform babies born years after their parents' exposure to radiation. Article 9 of the Japanese constitution of 1946, largely written by MacArthur and his staff, is unique in its declaration that 'the Japanese people forever renounce war as a sovereign right of the nation. . . . Land, sea and air forces, as well as other war potential, will never be maintained.' It later proved an embarrassment to the Americans, who wanted Japan to be in a position to defend herself against China. So quickly do world perspectives change. But was it just MacArthur and his constitution-making that turned the Japanese away from military adventure? Clearly the Japanese experience had demonstrated the futility of war and went on to nurture a strong peace movement.

Many reforms introduced by the Americans during the occupation years fitted in with earlier Japanese traditions and were in practice adapted by the Japanese to suit their needs. Thus the associations which they were encouraged to form in rural and urban communities for social, political or cultural purposes were nothing new; the same was true of agricultural and fishing co-operatives. In the 1930s many such organisations had existed; they were not democratic but they were controlled and tightly supervised by the government, for which they were a useful means of communication. The occupation also introduced new legal freedoms to limit direction by the central government and to provide a basis for democracy. But they did not, as it turned out, inhibit 'guidance' from the national government – which was generally followed. The Japanese people were accustomed to act in a group and to look to authority for leadership. Nor did the American encouragement that they form trade unions to check the powers of industrialists lead to the results experienced in the United States. Japanese trade unions tended to be rather different. They were organised on the basis of each enterprise, that is all the permanent employees in one company would form a union to negotiate with management, rather than workers of particular trades organising themselves nationally. The family and the company became the dominant groupings of post-war Japan. Decentralisation of education, equal political rights for women and social welfare were among other notable innovations of the occupation dictated to the Japanese people from above. A constitution designed to make the elected parliamentary assembly sovereign, and reducing the Emperor to symbolic status, provided the political framework of post-1945 Japan. Until the Cold War in 1947 began to cast shadows, free political activity was permitted. From Japan's prisons communists and socialists emerged and they set out to radicalise the trade unions and politics. MacArthur, anything but a socialist, regarded such freedom as necessary. He was determined to teach the Japanese the meaning of democracy.

The single most remarkable difference between the occupation of Japan and that of Germany was the continuity of institutions that was maintained in Japan. While making it clear that he was the ultimate authority, MacArthur ruled indirectly through a Japanese government and Diet. He remained an austere and aloof figure, very much in the tradition of the Japanese *genro*, the elder statesmen, who had 'advised' the Emperor and who behind the scenes had once exercised much real authority. MacArthur observed oriental courtesies and, except in pursuit of those accused of war crimes, was benign. An extraordinary relationship developed between him, the occupying forces and the Japanese people. MacArthur issued no orders against fraternisation such as proved so ineffective in Germany: the Japanese people were not to be treated as enemies or outcasts. It was not pleasant for them to be under foreign occupation but in the first few months there were advantages too. The occupying forces brought in food to save the

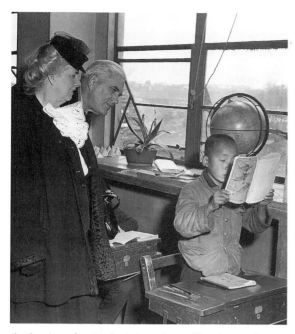

*An American educational mission to Japan. The educationalists keenly study Japanese education problems, but do they know exactly what the boy is studying?*

Japanese people from starvation and helped to rebuild the infrastructure of the Japanese economy.

The wholesale introduction of Western, especially American, models and their imposition on Japan, as if Japan were a blank sheet in 1945, did not always work. For example, MacArthur condemned the big business corporations like Mitsui and Mitsubishi – the *zaibatsu* which had dominated Japanese industry and which had been closely bound up with the ruling political oligarchies before 1945 – as bearing with the military the responsibility for the wars Japan had launched. He set out to break them up. Yet they were to recover dramatically after the occupation had come to an end in a new, more efficient form of co-operation of 'business groupings', the *keiretsu*. The close relationship between government and business in planning industrial development and economic policies was revived. The *keiretsu* became the pace-setters in the astonishing rise of Japanese industry in the 1950s and 1960s.

The land reforms instituted by MacArthur expropriated the large landowners and favoured the small tenant farmers. But holdings were insubstantial and relatively unproductive; with the industrial boom of the 1950s labour moved to the towns, so agricultural productivity had to be raised. This required mech-

anisation and investment; co-operatives were thus developed which pooled resources, attracted finance and took advantage of the economies of scale, although many small farmers had to supplement their income with other work. Politically and socially, the land reforms made an important impact in depriving absentee landlords and aristocrats of their wealth and with it their potential for special influence, while raising the living standards of the farmers, who formed a declining proportion of Japan's population.

For the conservative elite in government and business, 1947 proved a turning point. MacArthur and his headquarters staff during that year reversed their earlier democratic encouragement of industrial relations when a general strike was called by the unions in February 1947. Though in its aftermath a socialist coalition government was elected (May 1947 to October 1948) it could not cope with Japan's economic problems, the mass unemployment and hyperinflation. An entirely new wind too was blowing from Washington, that of containing communism. This reordering of Washington's priorities in Europe and Asia benefited Japan, which was to be allowed to revive so that communism would lose its attractions. With the outbreak of the Korean War in 1950, these attitudes were reinforced. In Japan, communists and left-wing sympathisers were suppressed. Once the conservative parties had come together into the Liberal Democratic Party in the mid-1950s, the political growth of the left was halted for more than three decades, during which the conservatives and business elites dominated Japan. Japan became America's principal ally in eastern Asia and a global economic giant. At the same time a uniquely Japanese way of government survived defeat and occupation. It was a Japan nevertheless, that had been transformed by the experiences of the Pacific War, by defeat and by close contact with the United States.

MacArthur found it best to assert the authority of his headquarters indirectly through a Japanese government. A remarkable Japanese statesman, Shigeru Yoshida, served during most of the occupation years and after (1946 to 1947 and 1948 to 1954) as Japan's prime minister. A subtle pro-Western diplomat, Yoshida created good personal relations with MacArthur but was determined at the same time to maintain what he saw as sound conservative Japanese government, free from any new military adventurism. The Japanese people were in desperate straits at the end of the war, relying on American food to save them from starvation. Yoshida was less concerned with a democratic transformation than with recovery, and he regarded with deepest misgivings MacArthur's new labour laws favouring militant unionism in the early years of severe shortages, as well as the upsurge of the left. The bureaucracy he recreated and the businessmen working closely with government bodies, which from the earliest days were masterminding Japan's recovery, were the same men who had efficiently overseen Japan's mobilisation for war in the 1930s. Now they were mobilising Japan's resources for peace and subtly avoiding SCAP's directives, relating for example to the dismantling of factories or to reparations, which would impede the recovery. As in Western-occupied Germany, managers, despite their early associations with the totalitarian regime, were the only ones available to bring about the economic revival on which alone a secure political structure offering individual rights and freedoms could be based – a strange irony.

Nineteen-forty-seven was a year of major foreign-policy reassessments in the United States after the failure to reach a settlement with the Soviet Union. It was the year when George Kennan was instructed by Secretary of State Marshall to set up the Policy Planning Department in the State Department, the year of the Truman Doctrine, intended to stop Soviet subversion in the eastern Mediterranean and Turkey, and the year of the Marshall Plan, designed to speed up the economic recovery of free Europe and thereby block the Soviet Union from spreading communism. In eastern Asia too some new defensive line had to be considered. The growing disillusionment with Nationalist China led to thoughts, by the end of that year, that US interests did not necessarily require an ally on the mainland of Asia. American security in the Pacific could be based on the islands of Japan and the Philippines. Japan would have to be sufficiently built up economically and militarily on land, on the sea and in the air to be able to defend herself. Since she was supposed to have no armed forces at all a National Police Reserve was recruited which eventually (after 1960) became the well-equipped and formidable National Defence Force with warships, an air force and tanks. MacArthur's call for a peace treaty in 1947 and his suggestion that the Japanese be left

to themselves was shelved when Russia and China rejected the initiative. Meanwhile the American occupation changed course. Conservative supporters of the pre-1945 Japan, purged in their hundreds of thousands, were quietly allowed to regain their civic rights; the liberal trade union laws were hedged about and this time it was the communists and the radical left who were purged. Having survived a period of political uncertainty, the conservative Japanese politicians gained a virtually permanent hold on power.

Japan's rapid recovery should be attributed principally to the hard work and skill of the Japanese people. Nevertheless, the United States during MacArthur's 'viceroyalty' had made, on balance, an important, positive contribution. In allowing the Japanese to retain their institutions in modified form, in ruling through the Japanese government with the full support of Emperor Hirohito, in rebuilding Japanese self-esteem, in providing humanitarian assistance and stimulating necessary reforms, the occupation was relatively benign. And this despite the injuries inflicted by the Japanese on the United States and her Allies during the war. The United States became not only Japan's most important export market, but also a model for the consumer's paradise which hard work would allow the Japanese to enter. The bitterness of the war years was expunged, and while American–Japanese relations have not always run smoothly since, a firm basis for the attachment of Japan to the West had been laid during these years of overwhelming American influence.

The confrontation that built up between the United States and the Soviet Union reflected each side's strong ideological preconceptions. The West believed it faced a relentless communist drive in Europe, Asia and the oil-rich Middle East, while the Soviet Union felt exposed to the hostility of the capitalist West. In Europe in 1945, neither the Soviet Union nor the Western powers were certain where the 'frontier' would finally run between them. Only in conquered Germany was the division becoming clear.

In Germany overwhelmingly large numbers of Red Army divisions and far fewer American and British troops faced each other across zonal occupation lines which were rapidly hardening into an armed border. Neither politically nor economically was Germany being treated as one unit, as had been agreed at Potsdam in 1945. Mutual recriminations grew. West and East were each piling up grievances against the other.

For the Americans, the problems of Europe after the defeat of Germany were seen more in economic and political terms than military. The agreements reached at Potsdam were difficult to carry out. The Soviet Union was proving an awkward 'ally'. But in 1945 and 1946, despite growing tension with the Soviet Union, American forces were leaving Europe to be demobilised at home. The divisions that remained were intended not as a defence against Russia, but as the minimum necessary to control the Germans. The main aim of US policy was to ensure that basic living standards were maintained and that money was made available for relief supplies. Each occupying power in Germany – the USSR, Britain, France and the US – went her own way. For the British, themselves weak economically, the task of maintaining food supplies in their zone was a heavy burden, using up the dollars loaned from the United States.

General Lucius Clay was the man appointed to oversee the US zone. Accusing the Soviet occupation authorities of not fulfilling agreements reached, in May 1946 he cut off German reparations to the East. As tensions grew, the United States continued to feel safe in the knowledge that she was the only nation to possess the atomic bomb. It was unrealistic to expect her to share her secrets with the Russians, any more than the Russians were willing to share their armaments secrets with the Americans. But the atomic weapon was something different. One day the Soviet Union would be able to make her own nuclear weapons – sooner than anyone expected – and other nations too. The United States could use her advantageous position to reach an international agreement which would eventually control production, perhaps eliminate the weapon altogether, so avoiding a nuclear arms race. The Americans did evolve a plan (the Baruch Plan) in June 1946 which entailed, as it was bound to, control and inspection in stages over raw materials and atomic plants through the establishment of a UN International Atomic Energy Authority. But the United States insisted she would retain her atom bombs until all the stages of control and supervision had been satisfactorily completed. Thus the Russians would have to reveal all their secret nuclear research while the United States alone would hold viable atomic weapons. The Russians countered

with a plan to ban the production of atomic weapons, to be followed by the destruction of existing (US) weapons, and at the UN they vetoed the American proposals. Without trust between the Soviet Union and the United States, neither plan would work. The Russians were determined to catch up with the Americans and the Americans understandably were not going to throw away their advantage and fall behind. Would an act of faith on America's part have persuaded the Soviet Union to be more amenable to Western demands over Germany or Eastern Europe? It seems unlikely.

For Washington the most urgent need was to assess Stalin's future intentions. There was a consensus that the Soviets were concerned for their own security and that Stalin was isolating the Soviet Union while continuing to build up her industrial might and thus her military potential at the expense of her people's standard of living. But in ensuring her security how aggressive would the Soviet Union prove to be? How many countries on her borders not yet within her full grasp would she seek to dominate? The degree of destruction the Soviet Union had suffered during the war, the paramount need for reconstruction which constrained Soviet leaders from risking war with the West, Stalin's own preoccupation with consolidating his power at home and Soviet power in Eastern and central Europe, his innate caution – all these factors were given insufficient weight. They were certainly underrated by George Kennan, an American diplomat serving in the Embassy in Moscow who did more than anyone else to provide on the Western side the intellectual Cold War rationale. In February 1946 he sent an 8000-word telegram to Washington with his psychological assessment of the Soviet leadership's outlook on world affairs. In it Kennan explained that he did not accept that the comparative weakness of the Soviet Union would force the Soviet leadership to pursue limited goals. But whatever utopias of distant future world conversion Marxist communism held out to its believers, it was current realism that would dictate Soviet policies. Kennan advised that Soviet behaviour in world affairs was not the result of any objective analysis of the situation beyond her borders but was shaped by a traditional and instinctive sense of Russian insecurity. Soviet leaders reacted to this insecurity by taking the offensive 'in a patient but deadly struggle for total destruction of rival power, never in compacts and compromises with it'. Therefore, coexistence between the West and the Soviet Union was not possible. The Soviets sought complete control; to secure Soviet power, the international influence of the United States therefore had to be destroyed. The Soviet Union was impervious to reason, Kennan warned, and responded only to force. She will withdraw, and usually does, he added, when strong resistance is encountered at any point. Soviet aims were revolutionary, unlimited and global.

Was the West not then facing a situation similar to the 1930s, when Hitler had aimed at domination while lulling his neighbours with talk of peace and limited aims? Munich and the folly and danger of appeasement provided a vivid lesson of history about which no one needed to be reminded a decade later. The opposite to appeasement was the new doctrine of 'containment'. The Soviet Union would not be allowed to expand further by direct aggression or indirect subversion. The provision of military equipment and economic assistance to the countries bordering on the Soviet sphere was intended to create the 'strong resistance' at every point which Kennan's 'long telegram' (as it came to be called) had advocated. Soviet intransigence in diplomacy over the German question and at the United Nations appeared to confirm Kennan's analysis, as did the Soviet refusal to withdraw from northern Iran. Soon after the arrival in Washington of Kennan's cable, which was much admired and widely distributed, the crisis in Iran broke.

Iran during the Second World War had provided a vital supply route for Western aid to the Soviet Union. But the Shah's inclinations had been pro-German, so in 1941 the Russians in the north and the British in the south had jointly occupied the country. The Shah had been forced to abdicate in favour of his son, with whom Britain and the Soviet Union had then signed a treaty undertaking to leave Iran six months after the end of the war. The Russians after the war promised to withdraw in March 1946. Meanwhile in the provinces they had occupied they were encouraging autonomy, promoting an independence movement and refusing the Iranian troops entry. As the price for withdrawing her troops, the Soviet Union demanded oil concessions and autonomy for the province. At the UN Security Council there were sharp debates. The American Secretary of State, James F. Byrnes, who until then had taken a conciliatory line towards

the Soviet Union, now strongly backed Iran. In May 1946 the Russians withdrew from Iran without gaining any of their aims.

The crisis was important for the lessons that were read into it. Firmness in resisting Soviet expansion had paid off. The Russians had been warned off. The United States had joined Britain in a region traditionally within Britain's predominant sphere. The United States judged her national interests to have been affected by events in a country on Russia's borders, thousands of miles from her own. This was an important psychological step to have taken. The new assumption, expressed in the policy of containment, was that after the great expansion of the Soviet sphere of control in central and Eastern Europe, further expansion must be resisted in regions on her borders to which Soviet control had not yet expanded – Turkey, Afghanistan and, lying in between, Iran. American motives were not entirely altruistic. Oil had become a vital issue. Oil reserves in the United States were no longer judged sufficient for her future needs and she was seeking, in commercial rivalry with the British, to expand her oil interests in the Middle East. American oil companies were accordingly receiving strong backing from Washington.

When the Russians that summer of 1946 delivered a strong note which made demands on Turkey, it seemed in the West, so soon after the Iranian crisis, to be part of a well-planned Soviet tactic to probe for the West's weak points. In fact Soviet desires for a revision of the Straits had been raised by Stalin during the wartime Allied conferences. The Turks had secured in 1936 complete sovereign rights over the Straits, and the Russians indicated their wish to reverse this, reverting to a degree of international control. At the time Roosevelt and Churchill told Stalin that they thought Russia's aims reasonable and just. But by August 1946 the wartime comradeship in arms had given way to deep distrust. The Soviet Union did not persist in her pressure on Turkey, and the tension eased.

By the winter of 1946/7 communist forces were also threatening the stability of Turkey's neighbour Greece, which was in the throes of a civil war, with Britain assisting the royal Greek government financially and militarily. By this time a consensus was emerging in Washington that the West was facing a tenacious and persistent Moscow-led communist offensive designed to expand Soviet control and to undermine the cohesion of the West through subversion or through local communist parties wherever points of weakness could be exploited. What was probably true up to a point became exaggerated in Washington into a belief that there was a masterplan in existence in Moscow and that everything that was happening was in accordance with such a plan. No doubt schemes were being devised in the Kremlin, argued about and constantly changed when the unfolding of events did not correspond to the scientific precepts of Marxism–Leninism. Nor were communists outside the Soviet Union entirely free from primitive nationalist deviations, as Yugoslavia was so soon to demonstrate to the world. In 1947, Moscow's communist empire was by no means secure and the devastated Soviet Union was far behind the West in economic strength. Stalin would not hesitate to take advantage of Western embarrassments where he could, and in the longer term would hope to benefit from social revolutions in the West. But the Soviet Union was in no condition to risk war.

The Greek communist guerrillas had received help from their communist neighbours, and it was believed in Washington and London that the Russians were really behind the conflict. The Greek communists on the contrary felt let down by Stalin. The most likely explanation is that Stalin kept to his undertaking not to help the Greek communists directly. The help they did receive from Yugoslavia, Albania, Bulgaria and Romania branded them in the eyes of many Greeks as traitors to the national cause, especially as this assistance was being offered by former enemies. The American administration was no partisan of the corrupt and inefficient royalist government but the need to check the Soviet Union, which stood to gain from a communist victory in Greece, overshadowed other considerations. When Foreign Secretary Bevin's telegram arrived in February 1947 announcing that Britain could no longer sustain the financial burden of supporting the anti-communist Greek government (page 355), Washington was ready to respond. Kennan's long telegram and the discussions in Washington during the course of 1946 and 1947 prepared the way for a spectacular American reaction to the 'Soviet communist threat'. The response would be global, not piecemeal, and so would mirror the perceived global communist threat. Greece was the catalyst, not the cause.

Secretary of State General George Marshall was helped in his new task by the experienced Dean Acheson, under secretary in the State Department and a strong supporter of Soviet containment. A difficulty to be overcome, however, was Congress, which would have to vote the funds, and the Senate was controlled by the Republicans, who were in no mood for high federal expenditures and had already blocked much of Truman's domestic programme. If bipartisan support could not be secured, Truman knew that his world policies would be wrecked just as surely as Wilson's had been after the First World War. So he carefully cultivated the Senate and was extraordinarily fortunate in that the leading Republican on the Senate Foreign Relations Committee was Arthur Vandenberg from Michigan. Once an isolationist, he had been converted by Pearl Harbor to a global view of America's national and security interests. On 27 February 1947 Truman met Congressional leaders, including Senator Vandenberg, in the White House and put forward the case for aid to Greece. Yet something more striking than Greek difficulties was needed

*US President Harry S. Truman addresses Congress on 12 March 1947. He asks for $400 million in aid for Greece and Turkey to implement what becomes known as the 'Truman Doctrine'.*

to persuade Congress, and Dean Acheson supplied it. Aid to Greece was placed in the context of combating the designs of a communist assault on the free world. Kennan and Marshall thought that Truman's celebrated message to Congress, which was to go down in history as the Truman Doctrine, was rather too sweeping, indeed an overstatement of the case, especially as Turkey was now included.

But on 12 March 1947 Truman went ahead regardless and delivered the message in person to Congress. The Soviet Union was not mentioned by name, but no one doubted which enemy he had in mind. 'I believe it must be the policy of the United States to support free peoples who are resisting attempted subjugation by armed minorities or by outside pressure,' he declared. 'In helping free and independent nations to maintain their freedom, the United States will be giving effect to the principles of the Charter of the United Nations.' Truman then asked for financial aid for Turkey and Greece and authority for American military and civil personnel to assist their governments. Voices were raised in opposition, but the great majority of both Houses of Congress approved. As far as American and world opinion was concerned, the Truman Doctrine was regarded as a dramatic turning point in US policy. On close examination it can be seen to have been steadily evolving during the first two years of the Truman administration. But it still left many questions unanswered. Was the United States committed to aid every government, however corrupt, provided it was faced with internal or external communist pressure? The world after all was not simply divided between communist tyranny and free nations. The Truman Doctrine did not provide a guide that could be uncritically and automatically applied regardless of all other considerations.

The Truman Doctrine set the stage for its natural complement, the Marshall Plan, publicly unveiled in a speech delivered by Secretary of State George Marshall at Harvard on 5 June 1947. He appealed to American altruism and generosity to help check hunger and destitution in Europe, but he made no references to combating communism, although that was the Plan's principal aim. On the contrary all of Europe, as well as the Soviet Union, was included in its scope. In 1945 the United States had extended economic aid on no more than a short-term basis in the belief that Western Europe would speedily recover. The problem at that time seemed to be one

of international financial mechanisms, a temporary dollar shortage, to be solved by pressurising the European recipients of American loans to accept the new international financial order worked out at Bretton Woods. In 1947 the Truman administration recognised that West European recovery was desperately slow and without further American aid would be slower still. Severe food shortages continued and Western Europe could not pay with its exports what it needed to import from North America. Without American aid, the Western European peoples would experience not only great hardship but possible internal disruption. Distress was the seedbed on which communism flourished. Occupied western Germany, Italy and France were believed in Washington to be most directly threatened.

In extending massive economic help to Western Europe, however, the Truman administration faced several problems. How to ensure that the enormous funds required would be properly used? The Americans intended to run the programme, yet a way of doing this without injuring European national susceptibilities had to be found. Which countries were to be offered aid? The Americans rightly believed that it was essential for the recovery of Western Europe that the west German occupation zones should be included, yet the recovery of west Germany would create difficulties with France.

It was clearly not America's aim to extend economic aid to the Soviet Union, yet Marshall did not wish to be accused of dividing Europe, so he avoided excluding any European nation by name·from his proposals.

Marshall and his advisers, above all Dean Acheson, solved these problems with subtlety. In his speech announcing the Plan, Marshall said that the offer of aid was directed not against any country but against hunger, desperation and chaos; assistance, he continued, should not be piecemeal, or a mere palliative, but should provide a cure. The gist of Marshall's proposal was that the European countries should first reach agreement among themselves on what they could do and what help was needed from the United States. The United States would not formulate a programme – that was the business of the Europeans, from whom the initiative must come. 'The programme should be a joint one, agreed to by a number of, if not all, European nations. The role of this country should consist of friendly aid in the drafting of a European

*The Reconstruction of Europe. The conferment of an honorary Harvard degree on US Secretary of State George Marshall provided the platform for a momentous speech, on 5 June 1947 (left); his announcement of a huge package of US aid to be given to Europe was warmly welcomed: British Foreign Secretary Ernest Bevin signed the Marshall Aid agreement barely a month later (below). Meanwhile, in the Soviet zone, American aid was roundly rejected. A poster at the 1948 Leipzig Fair (right) proclaims the DDR's own 'production plan' to be the alternative to 'enslavement' by the Marshall Plan.*

programme and of later support of such a programme so far as it may be practical for us to do so.' A week later, Marshall affirmed that the Soviet Union was included in the offer.

The American chosen to run the show was Paul Hoffman, president of the Studebaker automobile corporation. But it was now up to the European nations to respond. In London, Bevin recognised at once the significance of the ideas set in motion by Marshall's speech; it meant not only the involvement of the United States in the economic recovery of Western Europe, but American readiness to participate in its defence against communism. What mattered was to secure an immediate favourable response from the French. On his own initiative Bevin paid the French the compliment of flying to Paris in June to consult Foreign Minister Bidault and other members of his government. The French insisted that the Russians should be invited and be given an opportunity to join.

Molotov duly came to Paris on 27 June 1947 to join the Paris conference on the Marshall Plan. Had he remained and dragged out the negotiations, the chances of the US Congress voting large sums to aid the Russians were nil. But Molotov played no sophisticated game; he denounced the Marshall Plan and forced the East European states to boycott the offer. The Czechs, who had already accepted an invitation to attend, were forced to recant. The West went ahead. Ministers of sixteen European nations met in September 1947 together with the three military governors representing the western German occupation zones. They agreed on the outlines of a four-year European recovery programme. By the following April 1948, a permanent Organisation for European Economic Co-operation, the OEEC, had been set up. This in turn worked out the individual programmes of the participating countries (the German Federal Republic, formed from the western occupation zones, became a full member in October 1949). Congress meanwhile had established an American counterpart in 1948, the United States Economic Co-operation Administration. Through it, $12,992 million of aid between 1948 and 1952, as well as technical assistance, more than 90 per cent of which was not repayable, was channelled to the Western European nations. In the event little Western European economic integration, one of Marshall's aims, was achieved; but the aid was a significant accelerator of the recovery already under way before 1948.

The need the US perceived to reconstruct Western European societies was not entirely altruistic of course. Americans saw such reconstruction as the necessary condition of preventing the spread of communism. What did converge, however, were American policy aims and the greater prosperity and happiness of the peoples of Western Europe. It has been argued that a desire for American export markets was one of the motives behind Marshall's offer; in fact exports to Europe constituted only a small fraction of US trade. More notable is the American insistence on European economic co-operation. What most concerned the Truman administration was not any narrow United States economic advantage – indeed some of the policies Americans now urged ran counter to their immediate economic interests – but the strengthening of Western Europe. American policy in this respect coincided with the hopes and aims of the West European governments.

Relations with the Soviet Union deteriorated to a new low point in the wake of the Truman Doctrine, the Marshall Plan and the evident determination of Britain and the United States to move towards a separate west German state. The agreements reached at Potsdam to treat Germany as a whole were for all practical purposes dead by the spring of 1948. Would it be possible to maintain the Potsdam arrangements for the four-power occupation of Berlin? The Kremlin was to test the West's resolve. In the summer of 1948, the Soviet blockade of Berlin created the most serious crisis of the immediate post-war era.

# CHAPTER 37

# *1948: Crisis in Europe – Prague and Berlin*

From the Kremlin's point of view towards the end of 1947, things were not going well. The West was disputing Soviet dominance in Eastern and central Europe with the Truman Doctrine and the Marshall Plan. Was not the Soviet Union entitled for her own security to an extension of influence over her neighbours? Twenty million had died to achieve it. The Soviet Union had to safeguard herself against the eventual onslaught of the capitalist West, the great struggle which could be postponed but, according to historical determinism, could not be evaded. After the early and genuine welcome for the liberating Red Army among quite large numbers of Poles, Bulgarians and Czechs, communist support was eroding and nationalism was reasserting itself.

The Soviet response to US intervention in Europe was, nevertheless, one of uncertainty. In September 1947 the Cominform was established to try to bring all the communist parties into ideological conformity as prescribed by Moscow (page 340). The Soviet Union's principal ideologue, Andrei Zhdanov, laid down the doctrine that the world was now divided into imperialist, anti-democratic forces on one side, and the democratic, anti-imperialist camp on the other and that the United States was building up foreign bases and was expansionist in her aims. It was a clear message to all comrades that Moscow's interpretation should be accepted as correct. In Poland, Wladyslaw Gomulka stoutly insisted on following Poland's road to socialism; this did not include, for example, collectivisation of

Poland's farmers. Gomulka was allowed to remain in power for less than a year. In Czechoslovakia the parliamentary constitutional framework, political parties and a coalition National Front government had not moved forward yet to complete communist domination. Preparations for tighter communist control in Eastern Europe were no doubt initiated after the Cominform conference, but it was in Stalin's interests to postpone an open crisis as there still appeared to be some possibility of blocking Anglo-American plans for the consolidation of the west German zones of occupation into an eventual separate Western-orientated state.

After the failure in December 1947 of the London Foreign Ministers' Conference to reach any settlement over Germany, the Russians proved surprisingly accommodating over Austria and on a number of other East–West questions. The signal from Moscow was that progress could still be made, that the West should be patient. However, Anglo-American patience had run out and on 23 February 1948, another London conference was convened to discuss the future of Germany. This time it was attended only by the ambassadors of Germany's western neighbours, the Netherlands, Belgium, Luxembourg and France, plus Britain and the United States. Agreement was reached on ending the stalemate over Germany, with all its harmful consequences for west German and West European recovery. It was accepted that the new arrangements planned for the western zones of Germany would lead to a breach with the Soviet Union. Tension was expected but not the crisis of 1948. That this occurred was the fortuitous coming together of the Western plans for Germany and the communist coup in Czechoslovakia.

From Moscow's point of view the Czech coup could not have been worse timed. The government crisis in Prague lasted from 20 to 27 February 1948, at the very time when the Western foreign ministers were meeting in London. Communism was showing its most unacceptable face. Moscow seemed, so it was thought in the West, bent on ruthless expansion and the suppression of freedom. The end of Czech democracy was bloodily marked by Jan Masaryk's fall to his death from his study window. Whether the popular Czech Foreign Minister had been pushed, or whether he had deliberately chosen this dramatic suicide as a gesture to the world, will never be known. A few months later, the other monument of free Czechoslovakia, President Eduard Beneš, also died. All he had striven for lay in ruins.

Historians are still confused about the events in Prague that February. Was there really a planned communist coup or had the opponents of the communists miscalculated? Were they in fact responsible for what happened? In one sense they were. The Czech government was a broad coalition which included some communists, not least the Prime Minister, Klement Gottwald. But the February crisis was neither ordered by Moscow nor initiated by Gottwald. The ministers opposed to the communists had resigned and Gottwald replaced them with communists. With a general election due in the summer of 1948, it appeared that the communist opposition had committed political suicide and that there had been no coup as was claimed in the West at the time. But appearances are misleading. Let us examine the events more closely.

During the winter of 1947/8, both in the Cabinet and in parliament tension between the communists and their opponents had led to increasingly bitter conflict. The communist Minister of the Interior, protected by the communist Prime Minister, illegally extended his powers; the security apparatus and police were being transformed into instruments of the Communist Party, endangering basic civic freedoms. The non-communist ministers protested and insisted on bringing to book the offending communists in the government. But the communist ministers countered by threatening to use force and, in order to avoid defeat in parliament, mobilisēd

groups of their supporters in the country. The communist-dominated workers' factory councils met in Prague on 22 February 1948. It was intended that their well-orchestrated demands should provide the pretext for forcing out the non-communist government supporters. But twelve non-communist ministers chose to anticipate Gottwald's manoeuvre. When, on 20 February, the communist Interior Minister refused to reinstate eight non-communist senior police officers despite a majority vote of the Cabinet in favour of doing so, they resigned. The normal constitutional procedure would have been for them to continue in a caretaker government. President Beneš was expected to, and at first did, insist that no new government could be formed which did not include ministers representing the parties that were not communist. If Beneš had held to this line, Gottwald's communist ministers would not then have been able to form a government; the only non-violent way out of the deadlock for them would have been either to give way to the non-communists or to risk defeat in a general election which would have had to be brought forward. That would not have given the communists enough time to rig the elections. The opponents of the communists calculated that early elections were the best guarantee of preserving democracy in Czechoslovakia; the longer they waited, the less possible it would be for the non-communist parties to campaign freely, since the Interior Minister was subverting the impartiality of the police and placing communists in key positions. Thus it was in the interests of the supporters of democracy to bring the crisis to a head quickly. Admittedly it was a desperate throw and the democrats lost.

Gottwald proved to be tough and utterly ruthless. He resorted to a show of violence in Prague. Armed militia and the police took over Prague; communist demonstrations were mounted; an anti-communist student demonstration was broken up. 'Action committees' were organised throughout the country to carry through a purge of opponents of communism. The ministries of the non-communist ministers were occupied, civil servants dismissed and the ministers prevented from entering their own ministries. The army was confined to barracks and did not interfere. The show of force proved sufficient. Some dissidents in the democratic parties agreed, unfortunately, to work with the communists, giving Gottwald's list of new ministers a spurious National Front appearance. Beneš was old and

*President Eduard Beneš of Czechoslovakia, after the Communist coup of 1948, addresses Klement Gottwald and his new government.*

weak; he held out no longer. He believed that the country might be plunged into civil war and he thought that even Soviet intervention was possible if he did not give in to Gottwald's demands. He therefore agreed to a new communist-dominated Cabinet without holding immediate elections. On 27 February 1948, the new government was sworn in. Democracy was finished.

A party that in the last free elections had secured just over a third of the electorate's votes, and probably did not command even that support in 1948, could not have gained control of the government and of the country without threatening violence and undermining the democratic institutions and the loyalty of the police beforehand. It is true that the non-communists had chosen the time for the inevitable showdown, but it was bound to happen anyway. They may have been ill advised in their tactics, but it made no real difference. The communists were determined to gain control and they knew they could not do so in free elections only a few months away. A minority usurped the wishes of the majority. Gottwald had covered his coup with no more than a thin façade of constitutionality which did not fool the Czechoslovak people or the West

at the time, though it fooled a few historians later. The impact on Western governments and public opinion was enormous, strengthening their resolve. The majority of the US Congress was persuaded that America's own security required close co-operation with Western Europe against Soviet-led communism. The Prague coup finally discredited Soviet moves to prevent the formation of a west German state and accelerated the conclusion of a West European alliance, the Brussels Treaty, in March 1948 (page 355). It was self-evident in the West that it had been fear of Soviet intervention that had enabled the Czech communists to blackmail the whole nation. The Soviet threat would have to be met by measures of mutual security.

The formation of the Western alliance and the plans for ending the occupation of Germany were intimately linked. The French continued to fear a resurgence of Germany and fought a rearguard action to retain Allied control over the Ruhr. Bevin tried to calm their fears, stressing that France could rely on the Anglo-French Treaty of Dunkirk, concluded in March 1947, which promised immediate British military assistance if Germany

*A state funeral in Prague for Jan Masaryk, who had stayed on as Foreign Minister in Gottwald's Czechoslovak Communist government. The people were told that Masaryk had committed suicide by jumping out of his apartment window during the night of 9 March. It is far more likely that he was murdered and thrown out by thugs in the pay of the secret police.*

attacked her. By January 1948, Bevin had become more alarmed about Soviet intentions than about what the Germans might do at some future date. He called for a West European Union. What he was aiming for, however, was not a united Europe; the West European states were to preserve their sovereignty but should conclude treaties between them for their mutual defence. On 17 March 1948, Bevin, Bidault and their Belgian counterpart, Paul Henri Spaak, concluded the Brussels Treaty. This bound Britain, France and the Benelux countries (Belgium, the Netherlands and Luxembourg) to take whatever steps were necessary 'in the event of a renewal by Germany of a policy of aggression'; the signatories also promised to come to each other's defence if attacked by any aggressor in Europe. This article (IV) applied to the Soviet Union without specifically naming her. There was provision for other states to join. Although the Brussels Treaty was an essential preliminary to strengthening the

link between Western Europe and the United States, and was intended by Bevin as such, another year was to pass before the North Atlantic alliance (NATO) was concluded. The Brussels Treaty was in no way supranational. Neither Britain nor France intended to relinquish her sovereignty to any European council or parliament.

With the conclusion of the Brussels Treaty more rapid progress was made on the question of the future of west Germany. The Soviet response to all this was to protest and to withdraw from the Allied Control Council on 20 March 1948. As it turned out, that ended all formal four-power control of Germany. The Russians also put pressure on the Western Allies in the hope of deterring them from creating a separate west German state; they increasingly interfered with Allied land communications to Berlin, which ran, of course, through the Soviet zone.

Berlin, divided into four occupation zones, had

been placed at the end of the Second World War under separate four-power control. Access to Berlin was an obvious problem for the Western powers; this was not overlooked in 1945, as has often been asserted. The French, British and American commanders in Berlin had reached an agreement (29 June 1945) with the Soviet command guaranteeing to them the use of one main rail line, one main highway and two air corridors. Later a second rail line and a third air corridor were added. In January 1948, Soviet inspectors began to board American and British military trains demanding to check the papers of the German passengers. That was just the beginning; worse followed. Alleging technical difficulties and the need for repairs, two rail links were closed on 1 April and canal and road traffic was also interrupted. But the escalation of pressure did not deflect the Western states from their course of action in Germany. A joint conference held in London ended on 1 June with an agreement to set up a west German state. There was, therefore, no longer any reason to delay a separate currency reform in the west, thus ignoring the Russian objections. Without sound currency there could be no economic revival. By the end of June the currency reforms for western Germany were carried out and, after further unsuccessful negotiations with the Russians, introduced in the Western sectors of Berlin too. The Russians now, on 24 June, cut off all remaining land communications from the West by rail or road and three weeks later all barge traffic as well. The blockade of Berlin by land and canal was now complete.

The Soviet authorities justified the blockade by claiming that the three Western Allies had broken the four-power agreements on Germany; they cited the Western currency reforms in particular as being in breach of the agreement to treat Germany as an economic whole. The Western Allies protested and insisted on their rights of access. The one route left to the beleaguered city was by air – and the Russians had left the air corridors open, no doubt reluctant to launch an all-out challenge. One can surmise their calculations. The air corridors sufficed to supply the Allied garrisons and their dependants in the Western sectors of Berlin. It must have seemed inconceivable that 2.25 million blockaded West Berliners could receive supplies by air as well.

The blockade was intended as a 'tails you lose, head we win' gambit: the Allies would have to give up either Berlin or their German policy. After withdrawing they would be likely to pay more attention to Soviet interests. All this would be accomplished without real risk of war. The Allied position in Berlin was militarily hopeless. Was Western public opinion likely to start a third world war over a German city and over the fate of a people they had so recently done their best to destroy? Western military experts did in fact advise their governments that it was better to negotiate and to withdraw with honour than to be forced out a few weeks later. Even if the West were ready for war over Berlin, from a military point of view to fight a way through to the beleaguered city was not sensible strategy. General Lucius Clay's proposal of sending an armed convoy to Berlin was unrealistic.

The military 'realities' were, nevertheless, ignored. President Truman and Bevin rejected 'appeasement'. Despite Berlin, Allied plans for transforming Bizonia (created by the fusion of the British and American zones of occupation) into a west German state went ahead. A German Parliamentary Council convened in Bonn on 1 September 1948. Delegates from the eleven separate *Länder* parliaments and from West Berlin came to this historic assembly. The wily Konrad Adenauer was elected president of the Council. In May 1949 a Basic Law, a substitute constitution for the Federal Republic of Germany, was agreed, many differences and difficulties having been overcome. To all appearances it was a constitution for an independent sovereign state. But Britain, the United States and France still reserved to themselves ultimate authority. West Germany was not allowed to rearm, and the economy of the industrial Ruhr, though not separated from West Germany, was placed under inter-Allied control. Germans were not yet trusted; the new democratic institutions remained in probationary tutelage to the three Western military governors, renamed high commissioners. The new West German state and constitution laid claim to represent the wishes of the whole German people, whether living in the East or the West. The Russians could do little but respond in kind by turning their zone into a communist captive German Democratic Republic. It was ostracised by the West.

The changes in West Germany, with her temporary capital, Bonn, marked a giant step forward in the recovery of sovereignty. The Basic Law, West Germany's constitution, came into force on 24 May 1949. In August a general election was

*This time they came as friends. American DC3s form the aerial bridge to Berlin, during the Blockade of 1948.*

held and Adenauer and the CDU unexpectedly emerged the winners. In September, Theodor Heuss was chosen by parliament to become the first president and Adenauer was elected chancellor; so began his long years in office, which came to be known as the Adenauer era. On the 21st western military occupation ceased.

The Berlin blockade was the first great drama of the post-war years. It ended with a stunning diplomatic victory, a triumph for power and good sense. The air corridors between the West and the beleaguered city were crowded with a continuous stream of US and British transport planes carrying everything to the city to keep it alive, including coal. It was the Germans in Frankfurt, Hanover, Hamburg and Berlin-Tempelhof, loading and unloading the planes landing every few minutes, who were the unsung heroes of the day. Freddie Laker joined the fun and was later able, on the profits earned, to found an airline. The Soviets were careful too to avoid an ultimate showdown. Soviet air-control towers provided essential guid-

ance along the twenty-mile-wide corridors and some services located in the Eastern sectors of Berlin were kept functioning for the Western sectors. Before it was all over, 2.3 million tons of food and supplies had been flown to the city at a cost of $224 million. At the same time the hated Germans began to be transformed in Western eyes into steadfast, courageous, freedom-loving Berliners. In fact, whether in the East or West, the German people had little choice; but credit should not be denied to a number of sincere democratic leaders such as the charismatic socialist Mayor of Berlin, Ernst Reuter, whose moral authority symbolised the resistance of the democratic Western ideals against the brutal challenges of totalitarianism.

The Berlin crisis painfully demonstrated to Stalin the West's determination to contain the Soviet Union and to resist pressure. The Soviets had miscalculated. It was also the first crisis that could have turned the Cold War into a hot conflict. That it did not do so was due not to luck but to careful calculation and restraint on both sides. Berlin was the first example of an East–West confrontation taken to the new limits of post-war diplomacy, dangerously close to an armed clash but stopping just short of it. The defence of Quemoi and Matsu off the coast of China (page 515) and the Cuban missile crisis were others. The Soviets may have miscalculated in 1948, the West may have misinterpreted, but in Moscow, London and Washington care was taken from the first that a situation should not be created that was bound to lead to war. The American administration and the British Cabinet regarded the airlift as a way out, avoiding humiliation with minimum risk. It allowed the West to maintain its position in Berlin without use of force. The Russians also refrained from using force and let the airlift function without interruption. In January 1949, Stalin talked to an American journalist, and so gave the first hint that he was ready to negotiate and to lift the blockade. He tried hard to salvage something and to gain concessions from the United States and Britain on the German question, but without success. After secret negotiations in May 1949, the Russians lifted their blockade and the Western nations raised their counter-blockade of the Soviet Union and the eastern German zone, which had stopped valuable goods from going east.

The Cold War crisis of 1947 and 1948 hastened a fundamental reappraisal of American policies. The United States commitment to assist in the defence of Western Europe dramatically increased, but it still fell short of stationing large armed forces in Europe. American demobilisation after the war meant that there were still none to send anyway. Not until the outbreak of the Korean War in the summer of 1950 did the United States actually start to rearm on the scale necessary to back militarily her promise of global assistance. A year earlier, on 4 April 1949, the United States had taken a decisive step forward in forging an Atlantic–West European military partnership. The North Atlantic Treaty Organisation (NATO), although strictly speaking not an alliance like the Brussels Treaty, with provision for automatic military assistance, in practice, despite its careful wording, bound the United States to join with the West European allies in defence against the threat of Soviet aggression.

The conclusion of NATO and its ratification by the United States Senate marked a revolution in American attitudes to world problems. The defence of the United States was no longer seen in American hemispheric terms; the American defence frontier was now clearly delineated in Europe. It ran along the Elbe and through the Balkans. American security became global in scope; already deeply involved in eastern Asia, it would eventually spread to every part of the world. The US Policy Planning Staff, renamed the National Security Council, created in 1947, was given the brief of formulating 'the long-term programs for the achievement of US foreign policy objectives'. It sought to advise on priorities and the means to achieve them. George Kennan became its first chief. The National Security Council laid down the doctrine that the biggest threat was a Soviet advance and that priority should be given to the defence of Western Europe. Successive presidents accepted this advice. For Western Europe, the nightmare of abandonment by the United States was lifted. Bevin and Bidault, with Dean Acheson, Truman's Secretary of State after the retirement of the ailing Marshall in January 1949, were the principal architects of the North Atlantic Treaty. The Brussels Treaty had been the first essential step; now the new link was formed between the Brussels Treaty powers – Britain, France, Luxembourg, Belgium, the Netherlands – and the United States and Canada. On French insistence, Italy also became a founding member of NATO, and Iceland, Norway, Denmark and Portugal soon joined. 'North Atlantic' was thus something of a misnomer. The territory covered by NATO included French Algeria, and more importantly provided for the alliance to be activated if 'the occupation forces of any party in Europe' were attacked. In this way West Germany and the Western sectors of Berlin, the Western zones of Austria and Vienna were also included.

The heart of the alliance commitment was contained in Article 5, which stated that an attack on one member country would be regarded as an attack on all. Each member of the alliance would then assist the country under attack 'by taking forthwith, individually and in concert with other parties, such action as it deems necessary, including the use of armed force . . .'. The measures would then be reported to the UN Security Council and would cease when the Security Council had taken the necessary step to restore peace and security. The European partners would have preferred an automatic military commitment, but this was more than Dean Acheson could deliver. The great majority of US Senators, both Republicans and Democrats, had abandoned American isolation but not the constitutional powers of the Senate. That had been shown by the passage the previous year in June 1948 of Senator Arthur Vandenberg's Senate resolution by an overwhelming majority; this had advised that the United States should develop 'self-defense', 'regional and other collective arrangements' within the UN Charter, with other nations in case of an 'armed attack' threatening the security of the United States. The tortuous wording deliberately avoided the word 'alliance'. A significant addition was that such associations should be governed by 'constitutional process', which in plain words meant that the Senate would not abandon its rights to decide by majority vote on issues of war and peace. The resolution had paved the way for the North Atlantic Treaty, which was duly ratified by the Senate on 21 July 1949.

Not only the United States but Canada also came to the aid of Western Europe. During Britain's dollar crisis following the Second World War, Canada had provided $1250 million, a quarter of the total loan to Britain, with the United States supplying $3750 million in 1945. Under the premiership of the longest-serving prime minister in the Western world (1921–5, 1926–30 and 1935–48), the Liberal William L. Mackenzie King, Canada had made a remarkable economic recovery from the depression years of the 1930s and by the end of the war had become a major world commercial power. Her population sharply increased and immigration from Europe helped to fill gaps created by the sustained boom of the early 1950s and 1960s. American capital poured in and US–Canadian economic co-operation was most strikingly symbolised by the joint enterprise of the transportation–electric-power development of the deep-water route of the St Lawrence to the Great Lakes.

With a combination of political skill and ruthlessness, Mackenzie King mastered the formidable problems that faced any government in Canada: the multi-party system, which often resulted in government based on a minority of popular votes; the problems inherent in managing Dominion and provincial relationships; and the difficulty of handling the anglophone and francophone relationship with Liberal Party strength solidly based in Quebec. Mackenzie King's cautious policies fostered a Canadian sense of nationhood, emphasised the essential unity of the federal Dominion and strengthened the supremacy of Parliament and central federal government as far as provincial resistance would allow. The Liberals promoted progressive legislation in social security and housing, though Mackenzie King's own inclinations were conservative.

That politics was the art of the possible was Mackenzie King's abiding principle. In external affairs he reflected the isolationist attitude of the majority of the Canadians in the 1930s. Although Canada joined Britain in the war against Germany on 10 September 1939, his government promised that no conscription would be introduced. Nevertheless, Canadian volunteer forces distinguished themselves during the war and suffered heavy casualties on the Dieppe raid in 1942. They also participated in the Italian campaign and the Normandy landings. The conscription issue deeply divided French- and English-speaking Canada and cut across King's natural political base in Quebec. A plebiscite held in 1942 on the question whether conscription might be allowed when the government thought it essential had resulted in a 72 per cent 'no' vote in Quebec and an 80 per cent 'yes' vote in English-speaking Canada. Not until November 1944 were conscripts sent to fight overseas. In the elections of 1945 King nevertheless survived, beating both main opposition parties, the Co-operative Commonwealth Federation to the left and the Progressive Conservatives to the right. In 1948, suffering from ill health, he handed over the premiership to a French-Canadian Liberal Louis Stephen St Laurent, as firm a believer in maintaining Dominion power as Mackenzie King. The economic boom that continued and the success of the federal government held Quebec French

**Population** (*millions*)

| Canada | | United States | |
|---|---|---|---|
| 1931 | 10.4 | 1930 | 123.1 |
| 1951 | 14.0 | 1950 | 154.3 |
| 1961 | 18.2 | 1960 | 180.6 |
| 1979 | 23.7 | 1978 | 218.0 |
| 1989 | 26.2 | 1990 | 249.6 |

provincial nationalism in check until after St Laurent's retirement in 1957 following the victory of the Progressive Conservative Party in the June elections, after which John Diefenbaker became prime minister.

Like the United States, Canada turned her back on pre-war isolationism. Canadian perceptions of national defences had totally changed in the half-century since 1900. At the turn of the century the main threat was believed to be the possibility of an invasion from the United States, whose 'manifest destiny' might include plans to absorb her northern neighbour. There were even war plans drawn up by the British War Office which included British landings in New York and Boston in defence of the Dominion! In reality the US–Canadian frontier became the first undefended frontier between two great nations in the modern world, an example followed in Western Europe only since 1945. Canada and the United States have been indissolubly linked in the defence of the North American continent since the agreement reached at Ogdensburg in 1940. The relationship with the United States indicates both close co-operation on the one hand and the assertion of Canadian independence on the other. In Lester B. Pearson, External Affairs Secretary from 1948 to 1957,

Canada contributed a diplomat of world stature to international affairs. Lester Pearson played a prominent role in the UN and contributed to its peacekeeping activities. The award of the Nobel Peace Prize was fitting recognition for his skill in finding a diplomatic solution to the Suez crisis in 1956 (pages 471–2). He also took his country into the North Atlantic Treaty Organisation, Canada being one of the founding members. Thus the New World came to the rescue of the Old, completely reversing the imperial relationship.

NATO has formed the cornerstone of the West's defence in Europe. Greece and Turkey became members in 1952; but the role of West Germany remained a sensitive subject, since she could not yet be envisaged as a full ally of the West. Was it intended to rearm her and make her a partner in NATO? No, said the French Foreign Minister, Robert Schumann, to the French Assembly in July 1949; Germany 'has no arms and will have none. . . . It is inconceivable to France and her allies that Germany should be permitted to join the Atlantic Alliance as a nation capable of defending herself or of contributing to the defence of other nations.' But history was moving fast. The inconceivable became fact just five years later in 1954.

# PART VIII

---

*The Transformation of Asia,*
*1945–1955*

# CHAPTER 38

# The Struggle for Independence:
# The Philippines, Malaya and Indonesia

In 1945 to all appearances the Western nations once more dominated the world, including all of Asia. They had between them at their wartime conference mapped out the global distribution of power. They could display awesome military power on land, on sea and in the air and their technological superiority had been revealed at its most ruthless in Hiroshima and Nagasaki. The once invincible Japanese had been humbled and crushed and had become subject to American rule. So in 1945 why should the Europeans not regain their old colonies in Asia? Britain chose not to maintain her imperial role in the Indian subcontinent while resuming her control of Malaya and Hong Kong. The Dutch, with British help, intended to regain the Dutch East Indies, and the French to regain Indo-China. But the peoples of Asia were not simply waiting to welcome back their old masters. Everywhere there were political movements demanding independence and ready to fight for it, generally under leadership inspired by Marxist ideologies. The Europeans would have to use force to regain colonial mastery.

In 1945, the Cold War had not yet become the decisive influence on the shaping of Western policies. The Soviet Union was not then the most formidable opponent of British, French and Dutch colonial policies: at most, she gave ideological support to nationalist movements. It was the United States which opposed European colonialism.

Even before the First World War, Western rivalries and penetration of China had provoked nationalist Asian responses among the Chinese themselves and more awkwardly among the Japanese; by 1905, the Japanese had replaced tsarist Russia as the imperial power in Korea and northern China. The Second World War shattered the image of Western superiority in Asia. Within one decade from 1945 to 1955, nearly all the Western colonies and territorial empires were transformed. The Philippines gained independence in 1946, India in 1947, Ceylon and Burma the following year; in 1949 the Netherlands relinquished her 300-year-old rule over the Dutch East Indies; the French were defeated in Indo-China in 1954; and the British granted independence to Malaya in 1957. The most far-reaching transformation occurred on the mainland of eastern Asia, in China. The era of Chinese disintegration came to an end with the communist victory of 1949. During the four decades that followed, China successfully asserted her independence from Western controls. This pattern of enormous change emerged during the first four critical years following the Second World War. The first short phase lasted for just a few weeks, from the collapse of Japanese power until the British and American military commands were able to send troops, the Americans to the Philippines and Korea, the British to Malaya, to 'French' Indo-China and to the Dutch East Indies. During the brief interval before the troops arrived, the south-east Asian countries were still subject to the uncertain Japanese military. A variety of indigenous nationalist and socialist factions competed for power. Their aim was independence, but they had to decide what tactics to adopt towards the expected Western military reoccupation. The reoccupation, which opens a new phase, was nowhere seriously resisted at first. The hope that independence would be attained by agreement with the West was not fulfilled except on the Indian continent and later in Malaya.

The United States had never felt at ease as a colonial power, and Americans had a bad conscience about the forcible suppression of Filipino nationalism at the turn of the century. Strategic considerations had first taken the United States Navy to the Spanish Philippine Islands in 1898, which, with a naval base in Manila Bay, became America's most advanced outpost in the Pacific. For more than a century, the United States retained a strong presence in the Philippines for the same reason.

For the United States the economic benefits of colonial possession were never sufficient, except to special-interest groups, to dominate relationships. The Philippines, moreover, were too distant and the 'brown' Filipino population too numerous – 6 million in 1900, 48 million in 1980 – to consider their absorption in a racially conscious American

*Imelda, widow of the former Philippine dictator Ferdinand Marcos, is warmly received on her return from exile, despite the revelations of the Marcos' regime's corruption made while she was away.*

society. Self-government, and eventually some form of independence, was therefore seen early on as the only solution. As colonial rulers, the Americans were unique in virtually handing over the administration of the country to its indigenous population. By 1903, Filipinos held half the US colonial appointments; by the close of the 1920s, virtually the whole of the colonial government machinery in the Philippines was in the hands of Filipinos.

Forty years of American control and tutelage left an indelible mark on the Philippines. A Filipino political and economic elite had developed, whose fortunes as landowners, merchants, investors and industrialists were closely tied to the United States. Trade boomed with the opening of the US market to Philippine exports and with US investment in the islands themselves. From the American point of view during the depression years, economic preferential guarantees to the Philippines were proving disadvantageous. There were demands to restrict Philippine imports to the United States. The Philippines, not altogether willingly, were being pushed towards independence in the 1930s. The upper crust of Filipinos, who gained so much from the American connection, remained ambiguous about complete independence and sought a special American–Filipino relationship. Attempts to reconcile Filipino desire for independence and the economic interests of the Philippines and the United States eventually led to the promise in 1934 of independence after a twelve-year transitional period. But in 1942 the Japanese invasion brought the possibility of a transfer to a halt. The barbarous occupation strengthened American–Filipino bonds despite a Japanese proclamation of Philippine 'independence' and the existence of some Filipino collaborators. When General MacArthur returned, he was hailed with genuine enthusiasm by the great majority of Filipinos who hated the Japanese. The destruction caused by the war was enormous. One million lives were lost, the economy shattered, most of industry destroyed as well as agricultural production reduced to ruin and Manila devastated.

American reoccupation did not, however, usher in a tranquil period. The Americans upheld the existing social order of the landowners and the wealthy. The conservative post-1945 regime established in the Philippines clashed with the guerrillas, the Hukbalahap, or Huk for short. The Huk guerrillas had first fought the Japanese as well as their rivals. They retained their arms in 1945 and, to begin with, co-operated with MacArthur. They wished to change Philippine society radically, basing their power on the landless, debt-ridden peasants and urban poor. They were also nationalists who wanted to end the semi-colonial relationship with the United States. Their support in the country as a whole was not strong in 1945 and they declared they were ready to participate in elections and in the constitutional process. With their aims of social revolution, however, and their potential to engage in an armed struggle, they were regarded by the conservatives who held power in the government as a deadly danger to stability and order. The Huk's armed militia thus continued to pose a threat to the prosperous Filipino leadership. As early as 1945, members of the Huk militia were executed by the Filipino government.

In the 1946 elections the Communist Party of the Philippines took part, but the six elected deputies were disbarred from the Filipino Congress. One of them, Luis Taruc, left for the Huk centre in Luzon and organised a peasant rising. In 1946 drastic action was ordered against the continued Huk activities, with a military sweep to root out the Huk militia in central Luzon island. The Huk responded with an all-out armed rebellion in 1948, their supporters nearly 200,000 strong. In 1949 they were joined by the Philippine Communist Party and set up a provisional revolutionary government. The struggle went on for years, with the Huk holding in their grip inland Luzon, but by 1954 they were worn down and superior government forces crushed them. The government had also won some of the peasants away from supporting the rebels by offers of land and resettlement in protected villages.

In the United States by then the Huk were identified as forming part of the worldwide communist conspiracy of subversion in Asia, rather than as an extreme socialist–communist Filipino movement resorting to terrorist tactics and deriving their support from the economic condition of landless peasants. Communist international support was negligible. The chief victims of Huk recruitment and terrorism and of government reprisals were the peasants caught in the nutcracker of Huk guerrillas, the landlords and the government. In 1946 the United States granted formal independence to the Philippines, but it came with strings attached. The United States required that 100 locations should be reserved for US military bases and leased for ninety-nine years, though in 1959 this was reduced

to twenty-five. The United States constructed two great naval bases, an airbase and a rest camp, which formed a key to US security planning in the Pacific until the 1990s. The United States–Philippine defence agreement, their alliances and the presence of the bases with thousands of US personnel were regarded by Filipino nationalists as giving them a semi-colonial status. The United States did not hold herself aloof from internal politics either. Special economic rights for American businessmen were also secured, and all these conditions were linked to large-scale US aid and privileged access to the US market.

The Philippine government has introduced limited land reforms since 1954 but has rejected socialism. The landlord–tenant relationship was upheld, but the harshness of landlord exploitation was somewhat limited. With American support the Filipino ruling groups retained power. They, in turn, were not anxious to cut the connection with the Americans. The United States has suffered from being identified with the wealthy and corrupt ruling circles amid widespread poverty. Despite a large amount of US financial aid intended to restore the war-shattered Philippines and to help the peasants and the urban poor, little reconstruction was undertaken and the majority of the poor did not benefit: the wealthy Filipinos lined their own pockets. The continuation of distress among the peasantry provided the seedbed which nourished the Huk movement.

The diversity of American objectives in what had virtually been a colony could not be reconciled satisfactorily: to grant independence, to prevent a communist–socialist alliance from attaining power by the ballot box or arms, to ensure genuine basic economic reforms, to provide for the global security interests of the United States in Asia, and to find friendly and reliable partners among the Filipino political leadership. The United States, as a result, strengthened the few who exploited the weak and was blamed for their corruption. But US policy was overshadowed, especially after 1950, by one aim: to stem the advance of communism in Asia. This was seen primarily not as an internal Asian problem. The overriding objective was to create a defensive Asian block against the external enemy, the Soviet Union, and her ally, communist China. In pursuit of this aim, the United States felt her options were limited to supporting political leaders she would not otherwise have backed. It also led the United

States, despite her earlier disapproval, into a policy of backing the French, who sought to restore their colonial empire in Indo-China.

Of all the attempts by European nations to reclaim their former empires in south-east Asia, it looked as if Britain's return to the Malayan peninsula and Singapore would be the least troublesome. During the war the most active resistance to the Japanese had been mounted by the Chinese in Malaya, the majority of whom identified themselves with the communist leadership of the so-called Malay Communist Party; the party was, in fact, almost totally composed of Chinese immigrants to Malaya. The Allies had supported them during the war and, afterwards, had recognised their contribution. They alone among the three races in Malaya had actively fought against the Japanese, and for a good reason: the Japanese, during the early years of occupation from 1942 to 1943, oppressed the Chinese more savagely than the other two nationalities living in Malaya, the Indian immigrants and the indigenous Malays. Indeed, many Malays and Indians had collaborated with the Japanese and hoped to gain independence with Japanese consent. The Japanese later became more accommodating towards the anti-communist Chinese of the business community, whose help they needed. They might even have granted independence, at least nominally, had it not been for the sudden end of the war in August 1945.

The British returned to Malaya unopposed. The Chinese communists had decided to collaborate with them and to follow the constitutional path to independence. Chinese guerrilla groups came out of the forest where they had carried on the armed struggle and disbanded, hiding their weapons in the jungle as a precaution. The colonial administration hoped to re-establish peace and good order and to prepare for the electoral participation of all three races in Malaya on a basis of equality. These early plans envisaged that the peninsula of Malaya would be unified, the traditional Malay rulers deprived of most of their powers and a more democratic political regime introduced. Singapore, largely Chinese and a British colony, would be developed separately.

But the British solution satisfied no one. The leaders of the 3.5 million Malays, most of whom were peasants belonging to the poorest section of society, feared that by conceding equal rights to more than 2 million Chinese and 700,000 Indian immigrants they would lose control of their own country. They therefore opposed the reduction of the powers of the Malay rulers, who at least ensured that Malaya was ruled by Malays. The Chinese also objected. They were against the separation of Singapore from the rest of Malaya, as this would reduce their influence outside Singapore. In the end the British government had to withdraw these proposals. In the meantime, both the Chinese communists and the Malays soon realised that, while the British intended to rule benignly, their timetable for Malayan independence was long-term indeed. They had resumed imperial rule in Malaya, not for reasons of false national pride, but because Malayan rubber and Malayan tin were vital export earners for the shaky post-war British economy. When the standard of living of the British people was at stake, the Labour government which came to power in 1945 was as imperialist as the Conservatives.

In 1946, among the majority of the Malays, a non-militant party was formed, the United Malay National Organisation, to safeguard the rights of the Malayans and of the Malay rulers. The Chinese communists also became active in politics. They demanded that the British should leave Malaya and tried to make it unprofitable for them to stay, by infiltrating trade unions and calling strikes. When this had no effect they escalated their pressure by mounting terrorist attacks on the British rubber plantations and by murdering planters. Unable to make headway by constitutional means, the Chinese communists in 1948 resorted to an all-out armed struggle from jungle bases. But in Malaya they constituted less than half the population, and in the war – or Emergency, as the British called it – that followed they never enjoyed any support or sympathy from the Malays. With the help of some 100,000 Malay police, 10,000 British and Commonwealth troops, including Gurkhas, the British pursued the Chinese into the jungle. Although the Chinese guerrillas never amounted to more than 6000, to defeat them was an exceedingly difficult military operation. It involved the resettlement of some half a million Chinese peasants who had been eking out a living in the jungle and upon whom the Chinese guerrillas relied for food supplies. The Chinese kept up resistance for more than a decade, but by 1952 the real threat they posed had been removed.

In one significant respect, the communist insurrection simplified matters: those Chinese who did

*Malay special police forces patrol the jungle in which Communist guerrillas hid while attacking plantations during the insurrection which began in 1948.*

not support the communists now found common ground with the Malays. The future of Singapore remained a thorny problem, but the future of Malaya would now be settled in negotiation with the British; the Malays and anti-communist Chinese wanted neither an economic nor a social revolution, nor indeed an armed struggle for independence. The Malayans, skilfully led by the aristocratic Tunku Abdul Rahman, and the moderate Chinese under Tan Cheng Lock formed an Alliance Party calling for independence. It won overwhelming support in Malaya. The negotiations for independence were long and drawn out, but they reached a successful conclusion in 1957. The Federation of Malaya, independent but a member of the Commonwealth, was created. Singapore was to receive independence separately when it withdrew from the federation in 1965.

Nineteen fifty-seven marked the end of British rule and the peaceful transfer of power to the elected representatives of Malaya. The Chinese communist guerrillas could not now credibly claim that theirs was a struggle for independence from colonial servitude. Tunku Abdul Rahman and Tan Cheng Lock could no longer convincingly be pictured by the communists as mere stooges and puppets of the British. Their tough stand in negotiations and their subsequent success had earned them, in the eyes of the majority of Malayans, a reputation as genuine patriots who had created an independent nation. The British departed voluntarily, with the respect and friendship of the founders of the nation, leaving a Malaya, moreover, from which the menace of communist violence had been virtually eradicated. Britain's greatest imperial achievement, perhaps, was not the acquisition of her worldwide empire, but the manner in which she gave it up. Her more realistic and far-sighted attitude stood in dark contrast to those of France and the Netherlands.

The British, in the end, accommodated themselves to national aspirations in south-east Asia, despite their military superiority. The Dutch, by contrast, were militarily weak, but refused to give way to Indonesian nationalism until forced to yield. Yet it was the Dutch colonisers in the nineteenth century who had made a critical contribution to the emergence of an Indonesian sense of nationalism by bringing together for administrative convenience the cultures and ethnic groups of the many islands of their Dutch East Indies empire. The dominant group, 40 per cent of the whole, are the Javanese people, Muslims whose ruling class could look back on an ancient and splendid culture. Their social structure was subordinated rather than destroyed by the new Dutch masters.

The majority of Indonesia's large population, which had reached 60 million in 1930, lived on the overcrowded island of Java. Living standards were low, despite earnest efforts by the Dutch to improve the lot of the 'natives', and population increases – as elsewhere in the under-developed world – outstripped improvements and depressed living standards even further. Rice production in Java could no longer feed the people adequately, and the price of sugar, the principal export, collapsed in the blizzard of the world economic crisis of the 1930s. The outer islands, much less crowded, provided the important exports of oil and rubber. It was these commodities, essential to any war effort, that decided Japan to launch her 'southern drive' of conquest and so brought her into collision with the West.

In the Dutch East Indies, the Japanese invaders were generally welcomed as liberators in the spring of 1942, and the Dutch bureaucracy quickly collapsed unmourned. The mass of the people now turned against the traditional social structures, with the Javanese aristocracy at their apex, through which the Dutch had ruled the islands and imposed their policies. After years of Dutch repression, the nationalist movement – after a chequered history – surfaced more strongly than ever. Communism had failed to gain a hold, almost entirely due to the fierce repression of the Dutch colonial government of the 1920s, which resorted to internment and to the mass arrest of its leaders. The continuing resentment against the Dutch, however, enabled the two most outstanding nationalist leaders, the economist Mohammed Hatta and the engineer Achmed Sukarno, to rally the various nationalist movements and to win adherents among the educated elites. Their hour seemed to have struck when the Dutch were humiliated and defeated by the invading Japanese army. But for the Indonesians one system of repression was now replaced by another.

Although four centuries of European rule had at one stroke been destroyed, the new Asian 'liberators' gave no encouragement to social revolution or national experiments, let alone to thoughts of true independence. They left the traditional social structure and simply sought to work through it as the Dutch had done. All the same, there were now new opportunities for the Indonesian national leadership, who the Japanese judged could serve a useful role in mobilising Indonesians for the Japanese war effort. All that really mattered to the Japanese was to exploit the human and material resources of the islands. They forced the various national factions to patch up their differences and sent the Indonesian national leaders out to penetrate the far-flung regions of the archipelago. Since they did not regard the Dutch as their rightful masters and friends, these leaders had no qualms about collaborating with the Japanese. They also established links with the anti-Japanese underground movement. Their dream was Indonesian independence, and to achieve it the question of whether to work with or against outside powers, be they Dutch or Japanese, was a matter of tactics, not of loyalty to foreign rulers. Thus Sukarno had no hesitation in enjoying good relations with the Japanese military commander of Java, given their mutual interests and the reality of Japan's supreme power. Later, with the deterioration of their military prospects, the Japanese found it expedient to make concessions to Indonesian national feelings and to promise independence. Except briefly in Java in May 1945, and then only in outward appearance, it was nowhere achieved under Japanese rule, which collapsed too quickly for the changes of policy to take effect.

The Dutch and Japanese having been defeated in turn, at last it seemed that Indonesian independence would be achieved peacefully. Sukarno and Hatta nevertheless knew that they faced serious internal and external obstacles. Within the country, although the communists had not been able effectively to reorganise themselves after their suppression by the Dutch, a new, youthful generation of radical leaders working for social revolution had emerged during the Second World War. More seriously still, British and Indian troops under Mountbatten's supreme command landed in Indonesia in September 1945, not merely to disarm the Japanese but as it soon turned out to restore Indonesia to Dutch rule. The Indonesians had, however, made good use of the hiatus between the Japanese surrender and the arrival of Allied troops. In August, that is a month before the British landed, a constitution was agreed and an independent Indonesian Republic proclaimed. A sizeable armed militia of Indonesians, largely trained by the Japanese, whose arms they commandeered, controlled Java and were ready to defend the republic. Nevertheless after the British landings Sukarno decided not to resist by force and allowed the British to occupy Jakarta, the capital. But Sukarno's and Hatto's authority was not sufficient to prevent the development of Indonesian resistance and in October 1945, despite their efforts, the armed struggle became fiercer. In November the British General in command of the occupying force was killed by an Indonesian sniper and full-scale fighting broke out, culminating in a battle at Surabaya. No match for the British troops, some 15,000 Indonesians died in that tragic encounter. Bloodshed sanctified Indonesian nationalism, and the Battle of Surabaya is celebrated as Heroes Day in Indonesia.

Struggling to recover from the effects of the Second World War in Europe, successive Dutch governments tenaciously attempted to resume their colonial rule in south-east Asia. With British help, Dutch troops despatched from Europe were able to establish dominance over the principal cities, but the vast countryside was another matter. The suppression of Indonesian nationalism required far larger resources than the Netherlands could hope to command. Nor was international opinion in the United Nations or in Washington sympathetic to the Dutch. The pragmatic British saw the Dutch struggle as wasteful and ineffective, and after the failure of initial attempts at pacification concluded that the Dutch should take the same road as the British were travelling in India and Burma. More and more isolated, the Dutch hung on. Indonesia was of immense value with her oil and rubber, but the Dutch found themselves in a no-win position against the fifth most populated nation in the world the majority of whose citizens wished to get rid of the white colonial rulers. The Indonesians were not strong enough to force the Dutch army out, so Indonesian nationalists were forced into a series of compromises and trials of strength. The British government was glad to take advantage of a truce in November 1946 to withdraw completely and leave the islands to the Indonesians and the Dutch.

The Indonesian nationalists, despite making agreements with the Dutch authorities, did all they could to frustrate them. In 1947 the Dutch tried, as before the war, to crush nationalist opposition by a so-called police action. In 1948 they stepped up their military effort and attempted to impose a federal solution which denied Indonesia sovereignty, but the Indonesian political leaders simply would not co-operate with the Dutch. The Netherlands was therefore faced with an unending military commitment in Indonesia which she could not afford. Asian nationalism overcame military and economic superiority by sheer attrition in Indonesia, as later it did elsewhere in south-east Asia. This rather than the increasing pressure of the United Nations persuaded the Dutch to bow to the inevitable.

In December 1949 the Dutch conceded independence to Indonesia and in August the following year 85,000 Dutch troops and the colonial administration withdrew. With them went several thousand Indonesians who preferred to make the Netherlands their home and as a result turned the homogeneous Dutch into a multiracial society. But 1950 did not mark the end of conflict between Indonesia and the Netherlands. The Netherlands held on to Western New Guinea, which the Indonesians claimed, and she still hoped for some constitutional arrangement linking Indonesia and the Netherlands for another decade. A unitary Indonesian republic was not established until 1960, and not until two years later did the Dutch agree to hand over Western New Guinea (or West Irian, as the Indonesians called it). Decolonisation thus proved a painful and long-drawn-out process, damaging both to the Indonesians and to the Dutch. How recently European physical control of colonial empires was abandoned needs to be borne in mind, for the speed with which the bitterness abated between the former colonial subjects and the European nations is one of the most remarkable and surprising aspects of twentieth-century history.

Between 1945 and 1954 the international alignments of the world had been transformed. China became communist and Stalin's Russia had come to be seen by the West as a threat to world peace. The United States began a reappraisal of her policies in Asia in 1949 and 1950 in the wake of the communist victory in China and the Korean War. In the era of the Cold War, half-hearted support of the French colonial cause now turned into substantial backing for what France was now perceived to be doing: not reimposing colonialism but battling to halt the spread of communism in south-east Asia. From having been a region to which Americans had paid little attention, south-east Asia became the front line of the free world.

# CHAPTER 39

# The Origins of the Vietnam War and the End of French Colonialism

The French, as empire-builders in south-east Asia, were – like the Americans – late arrivals, conquering Indo-China in the mid-nineteenth century. They superimposed French rule on an ancient Vietnamese culture with a sense of national unity that did not diminish during the century of French occupation. The Vietnamese were brought by the French under one imperial umbrella with the Laotians and Cambodians to form the entity of French Indo-China. As elsewhere in the colonial world the amalgamation of Western ideas and the indigenous culture brought about rapid changes and created divided loyalties. The better-off, the landlords, the independent farmers and the traders, resisted far-reaching social change and, to this extent, identified themselves with the French administration. French education also nourished an intelligentsia, many of whom were inspired by Marxist ideals and committed themselves to an anti-colonial struggle.

The French took their civilising white man's mission seriously in the south of Vietnam (Cochin China), which they administered directly; central Vietnam was less affected; in the north, around Hanoi, some basic industrial development took place. The French built railways and roads, a university in Hanoi, schools and hospitals; they increased literacy and stamped out widespread diseases; mortality rates fell. There was less racial arrogance than in British colonies, and a greater promotion of education. Contact with France was also encouraged, and a small Vietnamese elite travelled there

in the 1930s, including Ho Chi-minh. On the debit side, economic development in Indo-China was dictated by the interests of metropolitan France. Industrialisation was slow. Over-population in the two most fertile regions, the Mekong River in the south and the Red River in the north, was a perennial problem. The great majority of the 16 million Vietnamese were poor peasants, hardest hit by the collection of rents and taxes. The depression of the 1930s, which saw steep declines in the price of rice and sugar, most affected those who could least afford it and led to waves of unrest. All peasant and student protest was met by the French with repression.

A small Vietnamese Communist Party inspired by the Russian Revolution had been formed in 1929 by Ho Chi-minh. In the social and political conditions of the 1930s its potential following was large, and it adopted the tactics of the popular front, softening its own revolutionary aims in the interests of unity to win the support of the revolutionary but non-Marxist Nationalist Party, which had been suppressed by the French. Vietnamese intellectuals were both attracted and alienated by French culture. Proud of their own civilisation, they discovered the hollowness of French revolutionary egalitarianism, which seemed to apply only to Frenchmen and not to colonial natives. Nonetheless, the overwhelming military strength of the French gave their colonial rule an appearance of stability and permanence. It was to prove illusory.

France's claim to superiority in Indo-China was

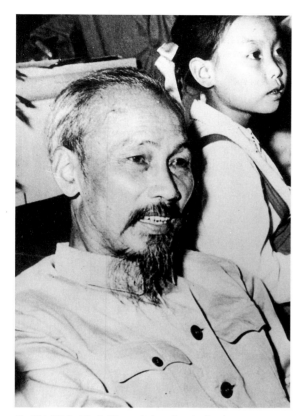

*Ho Chi Minh, North Vietnam's legendary leader, in 1955.*

hundreds daily pay their respects. Yet before 1945 no one in the outside world had heard of him. As a nationalist and communist conspirator he had used several pseudonyms in his lifetime and had travelled widely, working on boats, though between 1913 and 1917 he had been employed in the kitchen of the London Carlton Hotel. As a Vietnamese nationalist he became well known in socialist circles of Paris, and travelled to China and to Hong Kong, where he founded the Indo-Chinese Communist Party with a number of fellow conspirators in 1929. He visited Moscow in the 1920s and served as a delegate to various conferences, before disappearing from view from 1933 to 1941, when he reappeared in Moscow. He had probably spent the intervening years in Stalin's Russia. There can be no doubt that Ho Chi-minh had become a dedicated communist, but he was also a dedicated nationalist. In his own words:

> In the beginning, it was patriotism and communism which induced me to believe in Lenin and the Third International. But little by little combining theoretical studies of Marxism–Leninism with practical activities, I came to realise that socialism and communism alone are capable of emancipating workers and downtrodden people all over the world.

Tactically Ho Chi-minh was a chameleon, appearing to espouse many causes and roles. But the core of his beliefs was nationalism – Vietnam as one unified, independent nation – and Marxism. He was a man of intellectual brilliance and a complete personal incorruptibility rare in Asian leaders, modest in his needs, able to relate to the common people, yet utterly ruthless and inflexible in the pursuit of ultimate aims. No price was ultimately too high to create a united communist Vietnam, free from all outside interference.

When Vichy French power began to be destroyed in metropolitan France following the Allied invasion in the summer of 1944, Ho Chi-minh knew that the time for the power struggle in his country was drawing closer. The Japanese occupiers continued to tolerate the Vichy administration in Vietnam, which had collaborated with them under duress. But on 9 March 1945 the Japanese attempted to strengthen their position by making a bid for popular Vietnamese support. The French administrators were unceremoniously imprisoned and a Viet-

shattered by her defeat in Europe in June 1940. To the north, the Japanese were waging their relentless war against China and espousing a Japanese-dominated 'Greater East Asia co-prosperity sphere'. French weakness in September of that year brought the Japanese into Indo-China, pathway to the Dutch East Indies. The Vichy French authorities collaborated with the Japanese and suppressed nationalist guerrillas with French troops. A serious uprising in southern Vietnam was bloodily defeated and, in the process, the southern Vietnamese communist organisation was decimated. This was to be of crucial importance for the future, since the communists now remained strong only in the north. The anti-Japanese resistance, organised in the north by the Vietnamese nationalist League for the Independence of Vietnam, or Vietminh, was led by the charismatic Ho Chi-minh.

Ho Chi-minh became a cult figure in his own lifetime. Before his death in 1969 his photographic image was as widely reproduced as Castro's, Che Guevara's and Mao Zedong's. He lies buried in a glass cage within a mausoleum in Hanoi and

namese state independent from France was brought into existence by decree.

The Japanese needed a leader to give independence some credibility in the eyes of the people. They turned to Bao Dai, who had been crowned emperor in 1925 at the age of twelve. Although he had been groomed by the French for this role and educated in Paris, Bao Dai was no cypher and in the 1930s had attempted to win genuine independence for Vietnam, but without success. He could serve as a rallying point for unity and independence, so he was a leader of some importance in 1945. Realising this, the Japanese prevailed on him to head an 'independent' Vietnam in March 1945. Ho Chi-minh saw that Bao Dai's royal standing in the eyes of the peasantry made him a potential rival, but decided that it would be best to appear to recruit his authority to the Marxist cause. Bao Dai, with no army to protect him, had little choice after the surrender of the Japanese but to accept what Ho Chi-minh demanded of him. He abdicated, passed the Mandate of Heaven to Ho Chi-minh's emissaries and was appointed his Supreme Adviser.

August 1945 was a critical time. What authority would replace the Japanese after their surrender on 14 August and before the French could return? Ho Chi-minh played his cards well and quickly. He had neutralised Bao Dai and, with the help of organised peasant demonstrators and General Vo Nguyen Giap's small fighting force, he was soon in control of Hanoi, Saigon and Vietnam's other main population centres. On 2 September 1945 in Hanoi, in constitutional language borrowed from the American Declaration of Independence in 1776 and France's revolutionary Declaration of the Rights of Man in 1791, he proclaimed the Independent Democratic Republic of Vietnam with himself as president. He was looking for American support. Roosevelt before his death had been sympathetic to Ho Chi-minh's nationalist cause, and General Joseph Stilwell (commander of US forces in China, Burma and India) had supported his irregular troops. At that time Washington was more concerned with the evils of colonialism in Europe's former empires than with the global threat of communism. All that would change under Truman's administration with the onset of the Cold War. It was not the Americans, but the British and French in a determined effort who frustrated Ho Chi-minh's plans for a Marxist unified and independent Vietnam.

The country south of the 16th parallel, that is all of southern and much of central Vietnam, fell by earlier Allied agreement into Lord Louis Mountbatten's sphere of command. What followed is one of the most extraordinary episodes of the post-war period. If the south had been permitted to follow the north and the independence of the whole of Indo-China had been accepted by the British, the trauma of the longest war in Asia, which led to at least 2.5 million deaths and untold misery, might have been avoided. Mountbatten personally sympathised with the Asian peoples' desire for independence. But General Douglas Gracey, the British commander sent to southern Indo-China, took a different view. He was determined not to treat with local independence leaders in Saigon and to do all he could to restore French rule. There were no French troops at first in Indo-China and Gracey had only a few hundred Indian and British soldiers at his disposal. So he 'restored order' with the only available well-disciplined soldiers – the Japanese. Far from disarming them, he arranged for the Japanese divisions, with their own officers but under British command, to fight the local south Vietnamese during the summer and autumn of 1945 in a startling reversal of alliances. The Americans could do nothing. General MacArthur fumed, 'If there is anything that makes my blood boil it is to see our allies in Indo-China and Java deploying Japanese troops to reconquer the little people we promised to liberate.' By Christmas 1945, some 50,000 French troops had been brought to Indo-China to take over from the British and Indians, who were able to withdraw.

The British motivation is not difficult to understand. In London there was great suspicion of American intentions: if the French were to be deprived of their colonies in the name of liberation, what claims would the British have to the restoration of their colonies in southern Asia, especially Malaya? France, furthermore, was a vital future ally in Europe, the only potentially strong power to defend the continent against a resurgent Germany or a Soviet threat at a time when the Americans were withdrawing. But the French were not likely to act in Europe with Britain if Britain helped to deprive her of Indo-China. Yet these all proved short-term and wrong-headed calculations. For France, her return to Indo-China was to lead to defeat and humiliation; and the Americans, who eventually replaced the French, were ironically to suffer here

their only defeat in war and even greater humiliation. For the Vietnamese themselves the tragedy
was immense. Communist rule proved harsh and
destructive, but it came to that anyway.

War did not break out immediately between the
French and the Vietminh in the north. By the spring
of 1946, the French had taken control of the south
and had negotiated the withdrawal of the Chinese
from the north. Chiang Kai-shek complied, because
he needed his troops in China; Ho Chi-minh, who
was not ready at this juncture to start fighting,
agreed to allow a small French force to enter the
north in return for French recognition of the Vietnamese Republic he had proclaimed. The French
further stipulated that the Vietnamese Republic
should remain *within* the French Union. This was
a compromise that could never last. The French
had excluded the southernmost part of Vietnam
from their recognition of independence in the north,
which in any case was so circumscribed that it
would not have amounted to true independence.
Ho Chi-minh travelled to Paris, where negotiations
for a firm settlement broke down. He then returned
to Hanoi and claimed independence for a united
Vietnam. In November 1946 the French opened
hostilities, by shelling the northern port of Haiphong
and killing 6000 Vietnamese people. In December
full-scale fighting broke out.

. The French sent growing numbers of troops from
Europe to reinforce the southern Vietnamese levies.
Bao Dai had escaped from Ho Chi-minh's group
and took refuge first in Hong Kong, then on the
Côte d'Azur, where he enjoyed a life of luxury. In
March 1949 the President of France and Emperor
Bao Dai signed a treaty granting Vietnam independence though reserving all eventual rights to the
French, but Bao Dai's government was too obviously subordinated to France to gain respect in the
West. Nonetheless, the French appeared to be well
in control during the first five years of the conflict.
From 1946 to 1950, with Giap building up his
hopelessly outnumbered Vietminh in the Red River
valley of fertile rice fields in the north, there was
relatively little fighting. But the skill, discipline and
fighting spirit of his force, which by 1954 had grown
to 117,000, proved more than a match for the
100,000 French Foreign Legion soldiers supported
by 300,000 Vietnamese.

The victory of the Chinese Communists in 1949
transformed Giap's prospects, as large military
supplies including heavy artillery were soon

speeding south to support him. Mao's victory and
the outbreak of the Korean War also transformed
Washington's attitude: between 1950 and 1954 the
United States provided France with about $3 billion
to enable her to carry on the war. But, despite their
early successes, the French discovered they could
not crush the Vietminh. Their own casualties,
90,000 dead and wounded by the close of 1952,
were arousing increasing criticism at home. In
Vietnam the death of France's one brilliant tactician.
General Jean de Lattre de Tassigny, left her strategy
in the hands of generals who were not the equals
of General Giap, with little idea how to combat
peasants being politically indoctrinated and militarily trained to fight a revolutionary war. In 1953
Giap lured the French into defending Dien Bien
Phu. When his forces eventually outnumbered the
French garrison of 13,000 men by almost four
to one and his artillery commanded the heights
surrounding the French emplacement, Giap
destroyed the garrison and took Dien Bien Phu on
7 May 1954. Like the fall of Singapore to the
Japanese, this was a great Asian victory over a
European-led colonial army, and one that changed
history. The communist Vietnamese had won, not
only a tremendous battle, but the war against the
French – yet complete political victory was still
denied to them.

The news reached the Geneva Conference,
which had been in session since 26 April. The
United States would not fully participate. But Zhou
Enlai represented China, a China determined to
demonstrate reasonableness in the hope of
removing America's principal European allies,
Britain and France, from the Cold War in Asia.
Eden presided and to the bitter disappointment of
the Vietnamese – both the communist Democratic
Republic of Vietnam and the Republic of Vietnam
in the south – it suited China to maintain the
partition of Vietnam, thus keeping her too weak to
resume her traditional hostility to China. With the
communists sustained in the north, moreover, the
Americans, who had supported the French and the
Republic of Vietnam in the south, would be kept
at arm's length from China's southern frontier.
Elections were planned for the summer of 1956
which were intended to unify the country: Zhou
Enlai was shrewd enough to realise that, given the
hostility of the two Vietnam regimes towards each
other, they would never take place. The French
were satisfied at having found a way out of the

*Supplies for the beleaguered French garrison in Dien Bien Phu are parachuted in. The Vietnamese occupied the high ground.*

quagmire. The British could bask in the role of peacemakers on the world stage. But the Americans were hostile, rightly sceptical about communist promises, and warned against a resumption of fighting from the north. But they too had compromised in accepting a frontier drawn, not on the borders of China, but dividing Vietnam at the 17th parallel. Even so it seemed that another Korean situation had been created, with a clearly defined territorial limit on the extent of communist power.

That, however, proved an illusion. The two Vietnams were more realistic: the struggle for unity was not over. Both sides would have to prepare for it, Ho Chi-minh in the north, but who in the south? Bao Dai was too weak now that his French protectors had departed. The Americans wanted someone tougher and more single-minded. They backed Ngo

Dinh Diem, a tough nationalist and member of a leading Catholic family, who had already proved his patriotic credentials when opposing French interference in the 1930s. He had travelled, living in France and then ascetically in a Catholic seminary in the United States. In 1954 Bao Dai recalled him and made him prime minister. In 1955 he ousted Bao Dai and, in a rigged referendum, established the Vietnam Republic with himself as president. An implacable enemy of communism, autocratic and in time corrupt, Diem refused to accept the Geneva settlement as final. South Vietnam had not signed anything beyond a ceasefire. Ho Chi-minh too was biding his time before renewing the struggle for the unity of Vietnam under Marxist rule. Peace did not have a chance.

CHAPTER 40

# India: From the Raj to Independence, 1947

To any schoolboy who used to colour the Indian subcontinent red, its land-mass appeared to form nature's most natural unity. But, even under the glittering panoply of the Viceroy, that unity was never really achieved. India remained a patchwork; some regions came under direct British rule while more than 360 princely states, a few – like Hyderabad – large and others small, were allowed a substantial measure of internal self-government. The princes occupied a special place.

When aristocracy still mattered, the Indian maharajas – displaying their wealth ostentatiously and sending their sons to Eton and Harrow – became part of the British upper crust, or almost. So did the opposition to the Raj. The best-known Indian nationalists, Mohandas Karamchand Gandhi, Jawaharlal Nehru and Muhammad Ali Jinnah, were members of the English Bar. There was not only opposition to British rule but also Anglo-Indian co-operation. In the lower branches of administration, Indians and Anglo-Indians were providing efficient and loyal service. The best example of Indian unity was the Indian army. Racist yet loyal, it was for long exclusively officered by the British; not until the 1930s were Indians given commissions. Moreover, it incorporated all the divisive religious cultures of the Indian subcontinent: Nepalese Gurkhas, Sikhs, Muslims and Hindus were all imbued with a fierce loyalty to their regiments and to the Crown.

What would happen to the patchwork of British India once the unifying Crown and the institutions that supported it disappeared with independence? That was the crucial and immediate question facing the British and the Indians in the 1940s. Gandhi's vision was of an India where all her inhabitants would be brothers. It seemed only natural that British India should be replaced by the one Commonwealth of India. But during the century of British rule the deep divisions never healed – indeed, they grew deeper. Only by force and bloodshed was it possible to create two states in 1947, and nationalism continued to threaten the cohesion of these two successor nations, India and Pakistan. In 1971, the eastern region of Pakistan fought for and gained independence as Bangladesh; now the subcontinent had divided into three political units. Will this be the end? Will other groups, the Sikhs in the Punjab for instance, further split up the political map of India? It can be seen that the trend since 1947 has not been towards the unity and mutual toleration of India's many peoples.

Religion has been a prime cause of division. Hinduism is the religion of the majority of Indians, but there are many different kinds. Hinduism professes, but does not always practise, broad tolerance, and it can embrace many different religious practices; Hindus are opposed to the assertions of exclusive truth made by many other religions. But it is precisely these all-embracing Hindu claims that are seen as a threat to those religions which base their faith on providing a specific path to salvation. Muslims were the largest of these minorities, 120 million, a quarter of all the Indian population in 1947 of some 480 million. The next largest minority were 12 million Christians. Although the foundation of their religion in India dates as far back as the sixth century AD they were suspected of excessive susceptibility to Western missionary influence; the Christians of Kerala in southern India are poor and so have supported the Communist Party. The principal challenges to Indian unity in the 1990s, however, come from the militant Sikhs of northern India and the peoples of Kashmir. In 1947 the main enemy of the Sikhs was the Muslims, from whom they derive some of their religious practices. But since independence the 7.5 million Sikhs have asserted rights of independence from India's Hindus as well. The home of the Sikhs is the Punjab in northern India, while the majority of Muslims live in north-western India and in the east. They are divided by the large central Indian land-mass, which is predominantly Hindu. But minority communities of Hindus and Muslims are to be found throughout India and Pakistan. Bengal in the east had mixed Muslim and Hindu communities; the Punjab in the north is also mixed religiously between Muslims, Hindus and Sikhs. Some twenty major languages divide India, as well as the 3000 castes and subcastes of Hinduism; the landlord is divided from the peasant; the wealthy merchant and factory owner from the worker, and the bureaucracy and government have their own grades of influence. The hundreds of princes great and small contributed further to this fragmentation. It was Britain's imperial power which provided whatever unity India enjoyed before independence, but from 1909 to 1947 the British found no successful constitutional formula that would ensure her survival after their departure.

Racial prejudice marred British India before independence as it marred South Africa. It was condemned by the more enlightened Englishmen, among whom was Lord Salisbury, Prime Minister in 1900. Replying to the Governor of Bombay, he wrote, 'it interests me to find that you are struck with the damned nigger element in the British society at Bombay. It is bad enough in official and military circles here. I look upon it as not only offensive and unworthy but as representing what is now and will be ... a serious political danger!' A generation later, Nehru in his *Discovery of India*, which he wrote in 1943, expressed his own anger

at the racial discrimination of notices placed in railway carriages, on the walls of waiting rooms and even attached to park benches, with the insulting message 'For Europeans only'. Nehru comments,

the idea of a master race is inherent in imperialism. There was no subterfuge about it; it was proclaimed in unambiguous language by those in authority. . . . generation after generation, and year after year, India as a nation and Indians as individuals were subjected to insult, humiliation, and contemptuous treatment. . . . The memory of it hurts, and what hurts still more is the fact that we submitted for so long to this degradation.

Where did the balance lie between the harm done and the benefits brought by imperial rule? It cannot be calculated. Even economic arguments are finely balanced and what might have developed without British rule becomes a hypothetical judgement. Among the great benefits can be enumerated the creation of a common language of government throughout India, the establishment of law and order, the building of a railway network spanning the continent, the development of some industry and its protection after the First World War, the development of higher education, the training of a civil service and an army, vast irrigation schemes, the better control of famines when the vagaries of the weather decimated agricultural production, better health care and control of the killer diseases. But India was not a blank sheet which Britain 'modernised'. British rule was imposed on an ancient civilisation whose intellectual elite had produced philosophers, poets, historians, writers, artists and scientists of world renown, men such as Rabindranath Tagore (1861–1941), poet, philosopher and early advocate of international understanding based on respect and knowledge of the different cultures of the world, and the physicist C. V. Raman, awarded the Nobel Prize in 1930. One failure of British rule, by way of contrast, was the illiteracy of the masses.

That the resentment of British imperialism and the manipulation of India's economic development to suit British interests should create a nationalist reaction was inevitable given the growth of an Indian elite and middle class in the nineteenth and twentieth centuries. Nevertheless the British did not attempt to crush independent Indian political activities – on the whole they lacked the ruthlessness.

With all their arrogance and prejudice there was also a genuine desire for reform, for involving Indians increasingly in the governing of the country, while reserving to the British Crown, that is the Viceroy, only what were regarded as the powers necessary to preserve British rule. Parliamentary-type institutions and elections – at first confined to a small electorate and later widened – provided the basis for constitutional development after independence. The full scope of constitutional progress under British rule cannot be detailed here, but the salient measures were incorporated in the Indian Councils Act 1909, also known as the Morley–Minto reforms, which permitted Indians to be elected to the Viceroy's council and to provincial councils. Eight years later the growing demands of the Indian National Congress (founded in 1885) led Edwin Montague, Secretary of State for India, to promise to increase the association of Indians 'in every branch of the administration, [and to promote] the gradual development of self-governing institutions, with a view to the progressive realisation of responsible government in India as an integral part of the Empire'. It was not exactly independence, and self-government was gradual indeed – it was to take another thirty years before it became reality. Then came the Montague–Chelmsford report in 1918 which devolved more responsibilities upon the provincial assemblies when the reforms began to be implemented in 1921.

The 1920s and 1930s under British rule were paved with good intentions. India would be led to independence gradually by means designed to prevent the radical Congress Party with its democratic and socialist aspirations from gaining dominant power. The princes, Britain's loyal allies, would be given a prominent place and Muslim and Sikh fears of a Hindu majority would be appeased by the grant of considerable autonomy and separate electoral rolls. Long experience of imperial rule gave the British self-confidence in the exercise of their 'trusteeship'. But some of India's leaders wanted much more rapid progress to independence than Britain was disposed to grant, among them Gandhi. The British viceregal government in India and the Cabinet at home found it increasingly puzzling and difficult to know how best to deal with this small, skinny man in a loincloth, half saint, half shrewd politician, who moved the Indian masses as no one had done before, who defied the power of the Raj by encouraging civil disobedience to show

that Britain's rule lacked legitimacy, and who met the use of force by passive resistance.

Gandhi, once a dapper lawyer, had spent many years in South Africa, where racial discrimination had first aroused his anger and where he had evolved the new methods of harnessing 'people power' to overcome the apparently unassailable might of imperial white rule. British rule in India was met by this powerful non-violent defiance of the masses, inspired by Gandhi's example.

The viceroys, responsible for upholding the imperial law, for security and order, tried to avoid violence, preferring to govern through co-operation. Gandhi was not satisfied with the promised pace of British reforms, nor with the nationalism of the elitist Congress Party, which had little contact with the masses. He achieved the contact by arranging a protest against British laws designed to combat terrorism and to raise taxes (for it was the Indians themselves who had to pay for the administration and the soldiers of the Raj). In April 1919 a large crowd gathered in Amritsar in the Punjab. The demonstrators were not armed, but in an atmosphere in which revolution seemed possible the British commanding officer in Amritsar ordered his troops to fire on the crowd, killing more than 300 and wounding another thousand. For Gandhi this act of bloody violence changed his outlook: there could no longer be co-operation with the British Raj. By non-violent civil disobedience India would be made ungovernable. That was the plan of his campaign.

Gandhi was imprisoned for a time, the first of several arrests. In 1930 he led the famous salt march 240 miles to the coast in defiance of the government's salt tax. Picking up a handful of sand on the seashore, he boiled it to extract the salt. By this simple act he demonstrated that salt could be obtained from nature with no need to pay the British Raj for it. His defiance reverberated throughout India. He was arrested again, only to be released later and sympathetically received by the Viceroy. He created a sensation when attending in his loincloth a conference on reforms in London in 1931. A renewal of civil disobedience in India led to another spell in prison. The popular British press might derisively refer to Gandhi as the 'Indian fakir', but in official London and Delhi he was regarded with a mixture of irritation and admiration for the power he wielded by his simple example; the Indians called him Mahatma, 'great soul'.

*Gandhi and followers on a protest march, 1930. Non-violent civil disobedience proves a powerful weapon in the struggle for independence.*

In the 1930s Britain tried again to advance Indian representation. The Government of India Act was passed in 1935. The Raj, after the civil-disobedience campaigns of the 1920s and 1930s, had become convinced that preparation for Indian independence had to be taken seriously. The Act of 1935 set up eleven British Indian provinces with their own elected parliaments and limited control over their affairs. The religious communal groups would be placed on different electoral registers. A federal Indian state was the goal, with the princely states free to join or not. Meanwhile the Viceroy reserved crucial powers to himself and, at the centre, the nationalist Indian politicians would have only limited influence. It looked like a workable compromise from the British point of view, but to the leaders of the Indian National Congress the centre would be too weak, the Viceroy's powers negated the demand for Indian independence and the veto the conservative princes were to be allowed would condemn India to a patchwork of federated and independent states. Indian nationalists suspected that the British, acting on the age-old principle of 'divide and rule', were deliberately encouraging

religious and princely separation. Only the provincial assemblies were elected in 1937 and only that part of the Act came into force. This was nevertheless the start of the democratic parliamentary process in India and the restricted electorate of some 35 million voters overwhelmingly returned Congress members to the provincial assemblies; local administrations were then formed. But how little genuine power had been devolved soon became evident. When the Viceroy in 1939 simply declared India to be at war after Britain's own declaration of war on Germany, Indian national leaders were not even consulted. The provincial ministries resigned. But Congress had meanwhile grown in power, with a legitimate electoral base – and so had the Muslim League, of which Jinnah was president.

After the outbreak of war in 1939 the Viceroy of India had to revert to direct rule, since Congress led by Gandhi and Nehru had refused their co-operation and had brought the constitutional advances of the Government of India Act, which they hated, to an end. India's reaction to the outbreak of war in Europe and the Middle East, a fight for survival for the mother country, was split. On the one hand the nationalist politicians were uncooperative; on the other the Indian army fought with bravery and distinction under British and Indian officers far away from home, in the Middle East, in North Africa and later in Italy. Their loyalty was never in doubt.

With the sudden Japanese attack on Malaya in December 1941, British, Commonwealth and Indian troops fought together; tens of thousands were inhumanely treated in Japanese prison camps, beaten, starved and killed. For the Indian soldiers the Japanese offered an escape, to join an Indian liberation army sponsored by the Japanese. Even when the only major Indian nationalist who had thrown in his lot with Germany and Japan, Subhas Chandra Bose, attempted to win recruits, the majority of Indian prisoners preferred to share the appalling hardships with their British comrades, rather than gain their liberty and tolerable living conditions by reneging. It is remarkable evidence of the loyalty and pride which ordinary Indians felt for their regiment and flag. The Indian nationalist politicians reacted differently and saw an opportunity to push forward independence at a time when the British Empire was hard pressed.

Congress leaders had come to the conclusion

that the moment was ripe to force the British Raj to give up its control of India, but they had no intention of exchanging their British overlords for Japanese conquerors. If Japan attacked from Burma, Congress leaders would organise the resistance of free India with her allies in the United Nations military coalition, including of course the Commonwealth. It is not certain what would have happened, especially as the Japanese in Burma were content to remain on the defensive until 1944. Gandhi and Nehru and Congress were anxious to prevent a British transfer of power which would allow the conservative princes and the Muslim League separate powers. This would, they believed, only lead to a feudal, federal India in which religious fanaticism would open the way to communal strife and violence. Jinnah had already declared that the aim of the Muslim League was an independent Pakistan. The princes would attempt to hang on to their power and so frustrate Nehru's and Gandhi's vision of an India united, a progressive India socially reformed, caste discrimination gone, a secular India striving for religious harmony, a democratic India accepting elected representative forms of government.

With Japan at the gates, the British were deeply worried that Indian loyalty could not be counted on. In the spring of 1942 Sir Stafford Cripps was sent to offer India independence after the war was over, but to appease Islamic aspirations the Muslims would be given the option of secession if they wished. This condition made certain the rejection of the offer by the Congress leadership, who would in turn have had to promise support for the war. The Congress leaders were not to be cajoled into a government powerless under the Viceroy, thus indicating that they accepted imperial rule. For Congress another vital objection was that acceptance would encourage the Muslims after the war to divide India and set up their own state. They suspected that Britain wished to divide and rule. The British appeared to be more concerned with retaining the loyalty of the Muslims during the war. In August 1942 Congress launched the 'Quit India' campaign. The Viceroy then put an end to all debate. He decided that the only safe thing to do was to intern the political leaders of the Congress Party, including Gandhi, to prevent them from continuing to spread disaffection throughout India. The silencing of the Congress politicians enabled Jinnah's Muslim League greatly to strengthen its

position. The momentum for the partition of India and the creation of Pakistan was henceforth not to be halted.

By August 1945 with the defeat of both Germany and Japan, the curtain was about to fall on the final act. Churchill, who was reluctant to 'scuttle' out of empire, had been replaced by Attlee and a Labour government. Labour shared none of Churchill's historical sentimentality. The Viceroy, Viscount Wavell, was soon to discover this. During 1943 and 1944 his hands had been tied by London, who were afraid that talks with Indian nationalists would sow disaffection. After the war was won, all he could offer as the year 1946 came to a close were two options. The first was to strengthen the army and police, and to provide whatever resources were necessary to exercise imperial rule until all Indian parties had agreed to an independent government of India in which they would share power. It would be a major commitment – a paternalistic assertion that Britain would not relinquish her responsibilities until what in her view represented a just settlement had been reached. The alternative option was for Britain to withdraw from India province by province, disclaiming responsibility for the bloody consequences of communal strife which was bound to follow on her departure. This was truly Hobson's choice. What had led the Viceroy to such bleak conclusions? Wavell's attempts to arrive at compromises among Indian political leaders promised no early success, especially after the breakdown of talks between them at the Simla Conference of June 1945; a British Cabinet mission to India in March 1946 came no nearer to success. But this time it was not just a question of a conference of squabbling politicians in India. To show the strength of Muslim feelings and to protest at the tactics of Congress, Jinnah called for a Direct Action Day on 16 August. Fanatics stoked up communal violence and in Calcutta alone there were 20,000 casualties of the riots.

So ended the last prospects of a 'united India'; it was the end too of the Wavell plan as far as the Labour government was concerned. It was willing neither to earn the blame for leaving India in a state of chaos nor to pour the resources into India that were necessary if time for a solution was to be won. If Britain could no longer guarantee life and order from outbreaks of massive communal violence, something drastic had become necessary. In

February 1947 Wavell was recalled. He was replaced by a 'royal', a soldier of even greater fame, Viscount Mountbatten, until then the charismatic and successful supreme commander in south-east Asia; and, in an attempt to make the Indians accept responsibility for the consequences of their disputes, a definite date, June 1948, was fixed for the transfer of power.

The Mountbattens arrived in Delhi on 22 March 1947 with all the pomp due to a viceroy and consort. No viceroy's wife had ever made so deep an impression on Indians as Edwina Mountbatten, who threw herself into support for welfare and health programmes at a time of turbulence and misery for so many. Mountbatten began a weary process of talks with Pandit Nehru and the other leaders of Congress and with Mohammed Jinnah, representing the Muslim League. Gandhi was little involved. He used his remaining strength – he was now an old and frail man in his mid-seventies – to try to halt the mounting religious conflicts between Hindu and Muslims. The last two years of his life, devoted to humanity, were the most genuinely saintly.

Mountbatten got on well with the urbane and warm Nehru; Jinnah he found negative and forbidding. The Muslim leader fought for the underdog, the numerically weaker and dispersed 100 million Muslims outnumbered by Hindus three to one; and his intransigence would finally convince the British and the Congress leaders to abandon their cherished hopes for a united India and compel them to accept an independent Pakistan. Even then they would seek to weaken and confine a 'moth-eaten' Pakistan to such frontiers as would make her viability and continued independence highly questionable after the transfer of power. Jinnah reflected Muslim suspicions of the good intentions of the Hindu majority, influenced by bitter memories of discrimination culturally, politically and economically; a unified, centralised India, he feared, would simply perpetuate the tyranny of the majority over the minority. But an India without strong central authority accommodating autonomy for Muslim-dominant regions was anathema to Nehru and the Congress leaders, who believed it would be ungovernable.

Well aware of mounting tensions, Mountbatten calculated that the best chance of a peaceful transfer and agreement between the leaders lay in making them face a short deadline. He announced that the transfer would take place not in over a year, but in just six months on 15 August 1947. Nehru and Jinnah, Congress and the Muslim League would have to reach a practical solution for partition or they would be responsible for chaos on the date of transfer. Brought to the edge of catastrophe the Indian leaders were forced to accept the implications of Mountbatten's timetable and the plan he now put on the table. This involved partition but with the mixed Muslim–Hindu Punjab and Bengal provinces being allowed to choose which way they wished to go. They too voted for partition. A British jurist headed a commission which was given the task of demarcating the frontiers of India and Pakistan. The princes of the 562 states in 1947 were left to make the best terms they could with one or the other of the successor states to the British Raj.

Even if Muslim and Congress leaders had accepted the demarcation between the two states arrived at by the commission, immense practical problems would still have had to be overcome. The unified administration, police force, army and treasury would all need to be split up. Most of industry was located within those parts of India where Hindus were in a majority; the economy and communications would be dislocated. Would the break-up into two nations heighten tensions between Hindus and Muslims and lead to renewed violence and strife? It was clear from the outset that the creation of Pakistan was bound to entail the division of Bengal in the east and the Punjab in the north with one predominantly Muslim part being incorporated in Pakistan and the Hindu-majority districts going to India. Yet the populations of Muslim and Hindu were mixed throughout the subcontinent, with millions living on the 'wrong' side of any partition line that could be devised. The Punjab was a powder-keg of conflict, for here another minority of militant Sikhs saw an opportunity as a result of partition of becoming a majority and even gaining their own state of Khalistan. Communal suspicions, resentments and hatreds would not need much provocation to set the subcontinent alight. Bengal, the Punjab, Delhi and Calcutta were particular areas of danger at a time when the loyalty of the army and the police would be gravely weakened by the transfer of power. Gandhi could not permanently put out the flames of religious and ethnic hatred and himself fell victim to the bullets of a Hindu extremist, who shot him at a prayer meeting on 30 January 1948. Ethnic and religious

*Lord Mountbatten at the historic conference on 7 June 1947 discloses Britain's plan for partitioning India. On the right is Jinnah, and on the extreme left Nehru; next to him is Lord Ismay, the Viceroy's adviser.*

strife and bloodshed not only in India and Pakistan but throughout the world has proved the hardest to halt, the most resistant to the supposed progress of civilisation.

Bloody communal violence had also erupted in the Punjab. Jinnah, Nehru, Gandhi and the leaders of Congress had been aware of the dangers ahead and were determined to avoid them or at least to contain violence. Reports from the Punjab before partition clearly warned of the likelihood of conflict, and preventive plans were drawn up. A British-officered force (which included Gurkhas) of some 55,000 men was available to preserve law and order in the Punjab. But the scale of the violence that would follow on partition was not fully anticipated in Delhi and was to stain the transfer of power with the blood of many hundreds of thousands of innocent victims.

Independence Day in Pakistan on 14 August and in India on 15 August passed off with celebrations and praise for Mountbatten and the British. Jinnah publicly acknowledged that 'such voluntary and absolute transfer of power and rule by one nation over others is unknown in the whole history of the world'. He wished to live in amity with his neighbour. Yet the celebrations were hardly over before the tragedy of the transfer became manifest and

relations between India and Pakistan were deeply scarred and damaged for decades to come. The demarcation of the frontier had been announced on 16 August. The militant section of the Sikhs then set upon the Muslims, killing and raping and destroying their homes. How great the loss of life was has never been even roughly established, except that it was on a huge scale.

During August and September, between 200,000 and half a million Muslims fleeing the Indian half of east Punjab lost their lives. No mercy was shown to unarmed men, women and children. Even trains overcrowded with refugees were halted and the passengers murdered in cold blood. The local authorities either looked on or were powerless to stop the massacres. Pakistan never forgave. It was evident that the onslaught had been planned, the Pakistans believed with the foreknowledge of Delhi. Gandhi and Nehru, now India's prime minister, were horrified. There were killings too on the Pakistan side on a smaller scale. Certainly the Muslim League was also anxious to drive out the Sikhs and Hindus from what became Pakistan by organising riots. Millions of refugees crossed the frontier in opposite directions to India and Pakistan. Communal riots spread to Delhi, where more killings of the Muslim minority occurred. Gandhi hastened to Calcutta to stop the riots in Bengal. There he announced a fast to the death, and so great was his moral stature that large-scale killings did cease. But in the Punjab the Sikhs were deliberately expelling their Muslim neighbours so that they might at last gain power.

It is obvious that force and organised terror were required to drive people despairingly from their homes, their farms and their plots of land where they had lived for generations. They did not move willingly before the Independence Days. In West Pakistan only a small minority of Hindus remained; in East Pakistan (Bengal) a substantial number of the 30 million Hindus stayed. From India some 9 to 10 million Muslim refugees had crossed over to West or East Pakistan, yet millions of Muslims stayed, remaining the largest minority among 340 million Indians. Communal rioting and killings recurred in later years, but never again on the horrific scale of 1947. Nor did Sikhs and Hindus in the eastern Punjab peacefully coexist. While Sikh hatred of Pakistan secured the Indian frontier from any danger of internal subversion in any conflict with Pakistan, Sikh militants – because they constituted only a minority of some 10 million – have stridently and at times violently sought autonomy and independence. This stems from their fears of losing their identity, their way of life.

In an atmosphere of bitterness Pakistan and India only a few weeks after independence became embroiled in conflict over the future of a princely state bordering on both northern India and Pakistan – Kashmir and Jammu. The ruling Maharaja vacillated, refusing to opt for either Pakistan or India. He was a Hindu, though the majority of the population was Muslim. The key figure in Kashmir was not the Maharaja but Sheikh Mohammed Abdullah, the leader of a party not divided on religious lines and in agreement with the Congress leaders in India. Pakistan attempted to force the issue and encouraged Pathan tribesmen to invade Kashmir, which they almost succeeded in occupying. The Maharaja fled to India, where in return for a promise of Indian military assistance he agreed, without consulting his people or the political leaders, that his state should accede to India. Nehru sent in troops and promised to allow the people to choose their own future in a referendum. In Kashmir both Hindus and Muslims looking to Sheikh Abdullah resisted the Pathans and the idea of absorption by Pakistan, which claimed Kashmir on the ground that it had a Muslim majority. Abdullah was after all a close friend and admirer of Nehru, sharing with him the Indian ideal of a secular state in which Muslim and Hindu could live peaceably together. The Indians and Kashmiris now pushed the Pathans back, only for Pakistan to intervene with her own regular troops. Nehru, meanwhile, weakened his case by not implementing his promise to hold a plebiscite. With the two new states on the brink of war, the United Nations intervened, and on 1 January 1949 a truce line was established which left two-thirds of Kashmir in Indian hands and one-third with Pakistan. Nehru was deeply disappointed by this injustice. It was not the end of the Kashmir problem, nor did it settle Indian–Pakistan hostilities. Basic to these was the suspicion of the Pakistani leadership that India would one day seek to reunite the subcontinent and destroy Pakistan's hard-won independence.

# CHAPTER 41

# China: The End of Civil War and the Victory of the Communists

Will the victory of the Chinese communists in 1949 in the perspective of China's long history be no more than another episode in a succession of catastrophes and civil wars? Chinese Marxism, which has shaped the policies and development of China for more than four decades, was imposed on a quarter of the world's population. Its origin lay with a small circle of intellectuals and political activists who learnt the Western creed from Moscow and adapted it to Chinese conditions.

Once carried to power, the communists were able to establish effective rule over the mainland of China and end the warfare that had torn the country apart since the first decades of the twentieth century. Chinese sovereignty was soon extended to the offshore islands and in 1950 forcibly to Tibet. Only Formosa and a few other small islands remained outside the control of the new Chinese Republic. There Chiang Kai-shek, vowing anew each year to continue the civil war, established a separate state by occupying the islands with his fleeing army. Taiwan (Formosa), together with the Pescadores and the tiny islands of Quemoy and Matsu, continue to represent the other China. However, the possibility of renewing the civil war has long ago vanished. The People's Republic has ceased to be shunned by the West and her representative has taken his place as a permanent member of the United Nations Security Council. Even the brutal suppression of the movement, largely of students and young people, crushed so bloodily in Tiananmen Square in 1989, isolated the Chinese communist leadership from the West for only a short time.

The father of Chinese communism was Mao Zedong. The China he knew in his youth had been exploited and invaded in turn by foreign nations – Britain, France, Russia, Germany and Japan – in the nineteenth century and during the first half of the twentieth. The Chinese Republic founded and presided over by Sun Yat-sen was too weak to halt foreign depredation, and modernisation efforts failed in the face of the hugeness of China's problems, the backwardness of the overwhelmingly peasant population and the decades of incessant warfare.

This was the China Mao Zedong had known all his adult life. He was born in 1893, just two years before Japan's first victory over China in war had added to her humiliating record of defeats by the Europeans, defeat at the hands of her smaller Asian neighbour. His father, a poor debt-ridden peasant, through thrift and by means of lending his savings at usurious rates, amassed what was for a peasant modest wealth. Mao worked on his father's farm, collected his father's loans and, taught by a tutor, read widely. In the turbulent last years of the Manchu dynasty and during the revolution of 1911 that followed, Mao gained first-hand experience of the poverty and distress of the peasantry, and felt the stirrings of social revolt and patriotism of these years. For a short time he became a soldier in the service of the revolution. Like other Chinese progressives, he avidly read Western books to gain the new knowledge that the progressives believed would save China. But as Mao later remarked, 'Imperialist aggression shattered the fond dreams of the Chinese about learning from the West. It was very odd – why were the teachers always committing aggression against their pupil?'

The Russian Revolution then brought a new learning to China, Marxism–Leninism. Mao was an enthusiastic supporter of the May the Fourth Movement (1919), demonstrating and rising in protests against both the conservative society and foreign subjugation. His patriotic and radical views soon led him beyond the May the Fourth Movement to Marxism, and in 1921 he became a founding member of the Chinese Communist Party. For all his adaptations of this doctrine to Chinese conditions, Mao remained faithful to the basic tenets of Marxism–Leninism all his life. He would later claim that it was Russia after Stalin's death that was departing from the course prescribed by Marx, Lenin and the younger Stalin and that the mantle of the world leadership of the true faith had passed to China. But the sense of world mission did not exclude a strong feeling for China's unique national identity. The world would be transformed not by Chinese conquests but by the Chinese example and the successful struggle of the suppressed masses of other nations.

Through all the turmoil of fighting against his Chinese opponents from 1927 onwards and then against the Japanese too, Mao's vision was of a China that would be reborn 'powerful and prosperous', a 'people's republic worthy of the name'. Mao hated his enemies with passion, could act with bitter ruthlessness to destroy opponents but was also able with brilliant tactical good sense to persuade and cajole, to divide the opposition and so to emerge the strongest. For Mao, China's future required the mass mobilisation of the peasantry, the vast majority of Chinese citizens, and he believed that the application of Marxist–Leninist doctrines would transform their lives. The social classes which could not place the good of the community before their individualistic desire for gain might be reformed, but if that failed they would be destroyed. At the root of the social revolution, Mao observed, lay a revolution of the human spirit. This would occur not by itself, but only through unremitting class struggle and the teaching of the masses.

Mao repeatedly warned that perseverance was necessary to bring about the socialist economic revolution but that this would not be enough, that it was necessary also 'to carry on constant and arduous socialist revolutionary struggles and socialist education on the political and ideological fronts'. His ideology was fanatical; in his pursuit of it, millions would die and suffer. Marxism–Leninism provided Mao both with the means to be adopted and the ends which would thereby be achieved. The disciplined party – the party groups, the cadres, sent to convert the masses community by community – was the basic method used in the Soviet Union and later in China too. In China, Mao concentrated on the countryside, the poor peasantry, driven to increasing desperation by the combination of the natural and human depredations afflicting China in the 1920s, 1930s and 1940s. Village associations, youth movements, student federations, women's organisations and other societies had millions of members after 1949 and served as the means of linking the central authorities with the masses. But no mercy would be shown to those identified as the enemies of the people. The greater good would justify the destruction of hundreds of thousands if that should prove necessary. Violent death on a huge scale was nothing new to Chinese history.

The October Revolution in Russia had been spearheaded by the industrial proletariat. Mao's contribution to revolutionary theory, it is often claimed, is that he relied on the peasantry: to surround the towns with the countryside and then to conquer them – that was the model of the Chinese revolution. For Mao, however, this was a matter not of inventing a new doctrine but of practical necessity. He had to rely on safety in remoteness and on the peasantry for the recruits to his army and for its supplies. This led him to organise regions over which communist authority could be established as rural 'base areas' where the peasantry were to be won over by redistribution of land. Mao's revolutionary struggle thus also belongs to the tradition of the great peasant risings in China's history.

Mao's capacity for organisation had already showed itself in 1929 when he analysed the requirements of these communist base areas; he stressed the need for discipline, tight leadership and a ruthless, single-minded sense of purpose. The Chinese warlords were ruthless too, but the indiscipline and cruelty of their armies were wanton and indiscriminate. Mao's goal was political power, and the means to attain it was the Red Army. But this army was not to conform to the existing pattern of Chinese armies, to be encouraged by prospects of rape and booty or driven to fight by fear of punishment. Mao explained, 'The Red Army must not merely fight; besides fighting, it should also shoulder such important tasks as agitating among the masses, organising them, and helping them to set up political power.' His ideal was an army recruited from volunteers, a people's army, whose task it should be to teach and help the people of China in their daily tasks, to gain their support and to motivate them to communist victory. The Red Army was to be the instrument of the party, not its master; its ultimate objective was to make possible the revolution along the lines determined by the party. The army was to be a part of the masses, to be egalitarian and to win respect for its honesty and discipline. Theory and reality usually part company. The 'instrument of the party' tended to obey what the party's leaders believed was for the good of the people and not what people believed was good for themselves. It would be used whenever necessary to suppress popular discontent and to carry out orders against other Chinese groups which the leadership wished to exterminate.

Mao, just as Lenin did, saw that the fundamental problem in all societies was the relationship between the leadership and the mass of the people. If the commands were given by a small, all-powerful party group, how were they to be transmitted to the masses without an inefficient and corrupt bureaucracy filling the gap between the two? This was no mere theoretical problem. During the anti-Japanese-War phase of Chinese communism from 1937 to 1945, communist base areas had to be consolidated not only in Chiang's Chinese-controlled territory but also behind Japanese lines. The resources and production to maintain and expand the communist-controlled regions, which enabled the Red Army to carry on the fight against the Japanese, had to be developed within these areas.

Mao's response during those years was tactical flexibility, to which communist ideology, land reform and egalitarianism had at this stage to be subordinated. The peasants' aspirations had to be taken into account, the co-operation of the masses won as far as possible by persuasion and by material help. Mao's slogan was 'From the masses to the masses', and he developed a programme of contact with the masses which became known as the 'mass line'. It was a clever device for trying to win over the peasants. Trained communists, well indoctrinated, were sent in groups into the communities, where they said they had come to listen to the desires and ideas of the people. On their return, the party would then learn what measures would particularly appeal and would incorporate and adapt them to their own policies, which would be presented in turn to the people. The process was intended to be continuous and became a powerful tool of propaganda. By 1945 the communists had reached 100 million people and the mass line was now carried to the people by more than 1 million party members. The maintenance of party unity, the acceptance of common goals by the communists scattered over the vast regions of China, however, was a constant problem, and the mass line had to be matched by periodic attempts to tighten discipline and intensive periods of internal discussion and 'self-examination'. Over all this, Mao established in the 1940s his authority and leadership.

A large proportion of the trained Communist Party leadership did not come from poor peasant or worker backgrounds. Once in their own regions sympathies with relations and friends, even with their own social class, affected the way in which they accomplished their tasks. This became especially evident during the first two years after the communist takeover. A close study made of early communist rule in Canton shows that it took several years to bring under communist control the vast areas of central and southern China which had been militarily overwhelmed in a short space of time. Many administrative tasks had to be left still to Chiang's Kuomintang to provide the necessary expertise. The early transition from Kuomintang to communist rule was accomplished by example, by persuasion and by terror as 'enemies' were summarily executed.

From the first there were strong contrasts between the Russian and Chinese revolutions. While Marx, Lenin and Stalin provided models and inspiration, the Chinese were determined to develop a Chinese communism to suit the very different circumstances and needs of their country. Mao adapted dogmatic communist ideology to his experience in the years before victory in 1949. The leadership of Mao had been accepted by 1935. He never forgot the lessons of a decade earlier when the old Bolshevik leadership sought to spread revolution by first trying to capture the cities. It was in the rural regions that the communists built up their bases from which the cities and the rest of China were revolutionised. Revolution in China was not to be brought about within a short space of time, as it had been in Russia; indeed it took two decades to accomplish. The Chinese Revolution might never have been carried forward to a successful military conclusion but for the opportunities provided by the Japanese invasion of China. The barbarity of the Japanese turned the Chinese against them. They sought protection from the Japanese army's killings, lootings and spoliation and found it wherever the communists could establish their authority. Mao's call for resistance by all Chinese classes to the Japanese invaders, coupled with the programme for rural reform, attracted mass support. The composition of the Communist Party in 1949 provides striking evidence of this:

| | |
|---|---:|
| Poor and middle peasants | 3,240,000 |
| Rich peasants and urban middle class | 1,125,000 |
| Workers | 90,000 |
| *Total membership* | 4,455,000 |

Just as the war aided the growth of communism, so it revealed the corruption, incompetence and inefficiency of the Kuomintang and Chiang Kai-chek's leadership. The mistakes of the generals and the Generalissimo, a rank Chiang had accorded to himself, were accompanied by hyperinflation, which destroyed the economy in the rear. The arms supplied by the United States were frequently turned against the Nationalist armies as the Red Army captured them or as whole sections of the Nationalist forces deserted. The mass of the Chinese people had lost all confidence in the Kuomintang regime and longed for an end to famine, death, and the civil war.

Nineteen-forty-nine was the year of Mao's triumph. He now faced an entirely different problem – not only of organising a revolution against the state's authorities, but of managing the vast Chinese continent with the revolutionaries as the rulers. The greater part of China had fallen into communist hands only during the last months of the civil war, much more quickly than he had anticipated. Unlike the old liberated base areas where communist rule

*The last day in Shanghai before the Communists take power sees panic at the city's banks.*

had already functioned for years, more than half of China had recently been under Kuomintang government and control. There were simply not enough trained communist personnel to take over the running of thousands of villages, towns and cities. Faced with the alternatives of total disruption or of a more gradualist approach to the transformation of China, Mao chose to take time to win wide support.

The ideology and tactics of Mao and a few trusted advisers would determine the fate of millions of Chinese. But the Chinese people had won no more rights. Mao thought in terms of history and destiny, of the future of the quarter of humanity that was Chinese, of the fate of the world. In an almost godlike fashion he never doubted his mandate, and became impatient as he grew older. The sacrifice of millions of Chinese to promote the fulfilment of China's destiny counted for little in the scales of history as he saw them. Justifying the means by the end took on the most frightening aspects when applied to the lives of whole peoples by the twentieth-century ideological messiahs; they were tyrannical and ruthless in pursuit of their particular visions of a better world. Mao was one of these.

Mao was ready in the aftermath of military victory in 1949 to accept help from many quarters provided it would assist China in achieving the two main preliminary goals the communists had set: freedom from foreign control and the ending of 'feudalism'. Feudalism in this definition was a broad concept; it encompassed exploitation by the landlords and 'capitalists', so that in abolishing it China would undergo an economic and social revolution both in the countryside and in the cities. Mao was supremely confident that China's revolutionary role was as significant as Russia's. Although her revolution, like Russia's, would be based on the concepts of Marxism–Leninism, it was to remain distinct. In the early years Mao acknowledged Russia's leadership of revolution in the communist association of nations; but every nation, Mao believed, must remain the master of her own destiny, completely sovereign and independent. The corollary of this attitude was that revolution could not be imposed externally – it had to develop from within. Mao was at times ready to adapt policies opportunistically; at other times he imposed his own doctrinaire ideas. No particular interpretation of Marxism would block the path he wished to follow.

Among the most urgent tasks of 1949 was to work out a new relationship with the Soviet communist leaders. Mao could have had few illusions about Stalin or the Soviet Union. Stalin's chief concern appeared to be to avoid provoking the United States to war, and in his conservative view, as in Roosevelt's and Truman's, Asia took second place to Europe in the East–West confrontation. Stalin faced the task of reconstructing the Soviet Union, of building up her strength sufficiently to deter the capitalist West, of strengthening Soviet leverage in Eastern and central Europe; meanwhile he wanted Asia to remain relatively quiet. 'Reparations' were one obvious means of assisting the repair of Russia's devastated industries. As long as they could be moved, machinery and whole factories were transported to Russia from China. Half the capital equipment the Japanese had accumulated in Manchuria to develop industry there was carried off by the Russians with scant regard to China. Stalin, moreover, had completely miscalculated Chinese communist strength and had expected Chiang Kai-shek to stay in power and to have the capacity to crush the communists. Despite giving limited help to the communists in northern China, he had recognised Chiang Kai-shek and had allied with the Nationalist Kuomintang, thus backing the wrong horse. Mao therefore had little reason for gratitude to Stalin or to the Soviet Union. The Chinese had made their own revolution, despite the Russians. Nor did Mao regard a breach with the United States and the West as inevitable in 1949. Indeed, a very significant portion of China's export trade continued with the West after the communist victory.

Nevertheless in 1949 Mao counted on receiving Soviet help and on a reorientation of Soviet policy towards China. He wished to build up China's industrial potential, and China's communists had little expertise in bringing about the necessary changes in the urban economy and in urban societies. The Soviet Union, which had faced this task after 1917, could serve as a useful model. The communist cadres, Mao told his party followers in 1949, had to learn quickly the new task of administering cities. It was not out of love for Stalin or acceptance of Soviet leadership that Mao proclaimed early in 1949 that there was no middle way and that China must 'lean' to one side or the other and so against 'capitalist imperialism'. China was weak. The United States needed to be deterred from backing Chiang's cause further, indeed from protecting the Nationalist remnants on Formosa at all. The 'liberation' of the island was a priority in 1949, to complete the revolution territorially.

But there was a further reason for leaning to the Soviet Union. There was nowhere else the Chinese communists could go. Mao regarded himself as Marx's and Lenin's disciple and regarded the Soviet Union as the first successful revolutionary state. As he saw it, a broad ideological division existed in the world and China belonged to the Marxist–Socialist camp opposed to the imperialist aggressive nations. He also recognised the pre-eminent power of the Soviet Union in the communist alliance of nations and believed that this power was essential to safeguard the weaker socialist nations. What Mao would not accept was that this gave the Soviet Union a right to interfere with and dominate any of the smaller communist states, or that each nation should not be able to choose her own path of evolution based on Marxist–Leninist teaching but suited to her particular society and needs. There was thus, to use Mao's favourite tool of analysis, a 'contradiction' in the Sino-Soviet relationship. China, the weaker ally, needed the financial, technical and military support of the Soviet Union, so China would openly identify herself with the communist nations led by far the most powerful of them. But she rejected Moscow's leadership in determining the course of China's revolution. Mao's own strong sense of national and ideological independence here asserted itself.

After winning the civil war in China, Mao immediately turned to the Soviet Union, journeying to Moscow in December 1949. He was received by Stalin without much warmth. After all, not only was his victorious leadership in China living proof of Stalin's misjudgement, but Stalin recognised in Mao a leader of enormous strength of will and of an intellectual calibre approaching his own self-estimate. Then there were the more immediate material concerns of Soviet interests in China, which were now a problem. It had been possible for Stalin, with American and British backing, to impose Russia's terms on Chiang Kai-shek, who was trying to gain control of his country and to defeat the communists. It was going to be very much more difficult to justify these gains when face to face with a communist ally who was determined to rid China of all foreign 'imperialist' shackles. Two tough and ruthless men faced each other in Moscow during the winter of 1949. Mao and his entourage pursued their tasks with tenacity, remaining in the Soviet capital for an unprecedented eight weeks from December 1949 to February 1950.

A new alliance treaty was eventually concluded on 14 February 1950. Agreement was reached on the setting up of joint Sino-Soviet trading companies which would continue to give the Soviet Union a special position in Manchuria, though it was humiliating for Mao to concede this foreign 'colonial' incursion. In the treaty text Mao also had to confirm that China relinquished any claim to Outer Mongolia. But he won some major revisions of the 1945 alliance treaty Stalin had concluded with Chiang Kai-shek; he reasserted Chinese sovereignty over the Manchurian railways (the Chinese Eastern Railway), and Dairen and Port Arthur were to be handed back to China not later than 1952. Stalin promised to send technical advisers to assist the Chinese authorities especially in industrial and urban development, in which the Chinese communists lacked experience. He also promised financial aid. A meagre Soviet credit of the equivalent of US$300 million was granted. Finally, and perhaps most importantly from Mao's point of view, the Soviet Union and China bound themselves to a defensive alliance by which they agreed to come to each other's aid in the event of aggression by Japan or by any state allied with her: this referred to the United States, though she was not mentioned. Years later Mao recalled how difficult a struggle it had been to persuade Stalin to sign the treaty, not least because the Soviet leader wished to retain the option of mending fences with the United States; he had not wanted a victorious communist revolution in China in the first place and now that it had succeeded he was afraid that Mao might become another Tito in Asia. He did all he could to ensure communist China's subservience to and dependence on the Soviet Union through economic, military and ideological ties, and until his death China played internationally a secondary role – too weak and too reliant on Soviet help to do otherwise.

Mao, within China, followed his own course, and in his lifetime was to make several sudden changes. The policy laid down in the spring of 1949 by Mao and the Chinese Communist Party was to secure broad popular support and a wide coalition of political forces under the leadership of the party, excluding only the Kuomintang. Mao proclaimed this ideological line to suit the particular popular-front tactics he wished to follow as the 'people's democratic dictatorship'. All depended on Mao's definition. Thus the 'dictatorship' was designed to destroy the 'enemies' of the people, while the 'people' included not only poor peasants and the 'middle' peasants and workers, but also professional people, intellectuals, the propertied, merchants and those of limited wealth. The peasants would continue to own their land – even the better-off peasants were left in possession – and so were the landlords of the land they themselves farmed. The Agrarian Reform Law, which came into effect in the summer of 1950, reflected this moderation. The same gradualist approach in 1949 and 1950 can be seen in communist dealings with industry. The thinking behind it was not a belief in the merits of a mixed economy but rather the realisation that the production of the rich peasants and of industry in private hands was essential if the aims of socialism and the modernisation of the country were to be realised. But the communist administration also continued to provide itself with the means to exercise increasing control over all production in the many regions of China.

The early achievements of the takeover were impressive. There was far less disruption than would have ensued if a purist communist social revolution had been decreed from the start. The whole vast country of some 540 million people was pacified and brought under a unified control. The evil of rapid inflation was also mastered during the first two years of communist rule.

China's struggle to modernise had been dominated by the policies of the great European nations, which had carved the country into spheres of concessions, including ports which, like Hong Kong, became colonies or the scores of 'treaty ports' in which the foreigners enjoyed special rights. The impact of the foreigners had provided an impetus to modernisation in big cities like Shanghai, in the construction of railways and in the growth of the Japanese-controlled industry in Manchuria. But all this development was designed to benefit the foreigners rather than the Chinese.

In 1949 Mao and the communist leadership set out to change the fabric of Chinese society and to unite and strengthen the country. Modernisation as the West understood it – improving technology, increasing industrial and agricultural production, spreading education and literacy, developing communications, rejecting traditional philosophies – was necessary not only to lift the population from the trap of abject poverty and periodic famine but to enable a Chinese nation to survive at all. How else would it be possible to muster the strength to eject the foreigner and prevent his return on any but China's terms? Yet Mao tried to find a way to profit from Western culture without wholesale Westernisation, to assimilate it in an essentially Chinese way. The Soviet model could be followed, but like other Western models there would be no slavish imitation or subjugation. Mao was determined to wipe out the humiliation of the 'unequal treaties' exploiting China's resources which had been imposed by the Western powers, including Russia. For the time being Mao needed the protection of the Soviet Union, especially as he busied himself with expelling the Western 'capitalists'. While it was true that tens of thousands of Chinese had formed close ties with the West and that the Western presence – in missionary, educational and medical fields – was also humanitarian, most Chinese hated the foreigner for assuming a position of superiority in a land not his own. Many Western residents had already left the mainland by the time it fell under communist control. Those who remained were to be rapidly expelled in the wake of the Korean War.

The Korean War itself marked a watershed in the development of communist internal policies in China, in the relationships with Asia and in the triangular power alignments of the Soviet Union, China and the United States. The enormous impact of the Korean War was felt in Europe as well. The communist and anti-communist confrontation was seen in Washington, Moscow and London more and more in interrelated global terms. Global strategies were devised to meet the threat and the independent forces shaping the future of Asia came to be viewed by the nations of the First and Second Worlds, both communist and anti-communist, through the distorting mirror of their own ideological assumptions. One consequence of enormous significance for China was her isolation from the West.

# CHAPTER 42

# *1950: Crisis in Asia – War in Korea*

There are regions in the world where conflict is endemic. Between the latitudes of 35°N and 40°N and 125°SE and 130°E a mountainous, heavily forested peninsula extends southwards from Manchuria. Its lands border on China and Russia in the north and, across the Straits, with Japan in the south. The people call their country 'Choson', 'Land of the morning calm'. It expresses their longing rather than reality, for Korea's strategic importance and potential wealth have attracted covetous neighbours since the second century BC.

Korea became the pathway along which Chinese culture reached Japan, which in turn invaded Korea. The Korean peoples were usually too weak and divided to resist more powerful neighbours. But in the struggles ancient and modern against foreign invaders a sense of Korean identity was formed, as was pride in a Korean culture and tradition. Since ancient times too the fate of the Korean peoples was dependent on the development of their neighbours in Asia. Their country was repeatedly invaded, rent by factional struggles and her people oppressed. Paradoxically, for much of the nineteenth century the Koreans successfully resisted half-hearted Western attempts to open the country and were able to maintain their isolation. It was the Japanese once again who forced Korea to yield in the last quarter of the nineteenth century. But the Chinese too wished to reassert their ancient rights.

In modern times three wars of global significance were fought for control of Korea. The first, between China and Japan in 1894–5, ended in a Japanese victory. With the close of the nineteenth century Russia became a new contender for Korea. The second war was therefore between Japan and Russia; once more, in 1905, Japan was victorious, and for the next forty years she occupied and ruled Korea. But despite Japan's repression a strong movement for Korean independence developed. Both wars over Korea, especially the Russo-Japanese war and its outcome, had worldwide repercussions. Checked in Korea, tsarist Russia turned her attention back to the West, with the result that her concerns in the Balkans were to contribute to the outbreak of the First World War in Europe. Korean independence remained a dream. But that dream at last looked realisable to politically minded Koreans in 1945 with the defeat of Japan. The Allies (the United States, China and Britain) had promised at the Cairo Conference in 1943 that a unified, free and independent Korea would be established. But a period of trusteeship was envisaged, because Koreans were not thought to be capable of governing themselves. With Russia's entry into the war against Japan on 8 August 1945, an old contender for influence in Korea came back on the scene.

The suddenness of Japan's surrender left a large Japanese army still in effective occupation. The Russians were closest and were able to enter Korea from the north on 12 August. American troops could not be brought there for another three weeks. Working with Korean communist and nationalist resistance movements, the Soviets, who had promised to respect Korean independence, might well have been able to install a government of a united Korea sympathetic to them before the Americans could get there, even though their ostensible task was merely to disarm the Japanese and occupy the country north of the 38th parallel. The Korean People's Republic was proclaimed on 6 September 1945. To avoid a power vacuum in the south, meanwhile, the United States ordered the Japanese military command to maintain authority until US forces arrived, which they did on 8 September. The Americans were in fact doing exactly what the British had done in French Indo-China (page 406). The Korean People's Republic was opposed by the exiled Korean provisional government, which had been supported by the United States and by Kuomintang China. With the Russians north of the 38th parallel and the Americans to the south, the partition was supposed to be temporary. The stark fact was that the Korean people north and south were not to be given the complete democratic choice over the future of their country that they had been promised. Half a century later in the 1990s, Korea remains divided still.

There are parallels with occupied and divided Germany. In both Korea and Germany the military zonal frontiers became the frontiers of separate states. In both Germany and Korea, the Russians hoped that by building up a strong communist embryonic government they could attract the larger population in the rest of the country by pursuing popular-front tactics with the left dominating. The Americans in Korea were also following popular-front tactics, so to speak in reverse, in trying to bring together a coalition of the right, the moderates and the left under right-wing predominance. This coalition General John Hodge, the commanding US General in South Korea, hoped would attract the moderates of the North. The Soviet and American strategies therefore involved building a sound pro-Soviet or pro-Western political base in each of their zones prior to unifying Korea, which could then be expected to conform to their views. The Koreans, particularly in the far more populous South, proved not to be so amenable.

In the American-occupied South the rightist Dr Syngman Rhee emerged as the dominant Korean politician. He was not only violently anti-communist but also an ardent nationalist determined on the reality of an independent unified Korea. A tough

and formidable leader, he had spent most of his adult life from 1912 to 1945 in exile in the United States championing Korean independence. Now with Japan defeated, Rhee was in a hurry to get the Russians *and* the Americans out of his country and to defeat, if necessary by force, the communists in the North. He was suspicious of the bargaining of the Russians and the Americans over the future of Korea. Despite their concern over Rhee's extremism the Americans could not do without him since he clearly dominated the weaker moderate and left political groupings in the South.

It is an intriguing question whether Stalin achieved in North Korea exactly what he wanted. Russian aid between 1945 and 1950 built up a militarily powerful state which the weaker South could not hope to overrun. Strong guerrilla activity might then destabilise South Korea, and the partitioned country would be plunged into civil war, which the better prepared North would be expected to win. But Stalin took care to avoid any overt direct Russian involvement. Kim Il Sung, the autocratic, independent communist leader, was imposing his own brand of Marxist society on the Korean people; his thoughts were to have equal validity with those of the better-known Mao and Lenin. He was no mere puppet. Having built up the North the Russians withdrew in December 1948, leaving behind military advisers. This placed increasing pressure on the Americans to leave the South.

The Americans were eager enough to withdraw. The South had become a bed of nettles. But how to extricate themselves? When the US military advisers looked at the strategic situation they concluded that South Korea was not a suitable base for the defence of western Pacific interests. Japan and the Pacific islands, including the Philippines, formed the best defensive arc. A divided Korea, with the south looking to the West, was a perfectly acceptable solution. But there was the commitment to a unified Korea. The Russians and Chinese were willing to see a unified communist Korea come into being, the Americans a unified pro-Western, anti-communist Korea. No wonder the Russians and Americans could never agree at their joint meetings as trustees. Completely free elections throughout Korea would have put the communists into a minority, especially with the rightist South Koreans rigging the elections. So the Russians resisted that. Meanwhile in the part of the country under its control the American military government was being assailed on all sides to hand over to South Korean politicians. The Americans, at a time when they were championing the free world against communism, found the authoritarian Rhee an embarrassing ally.

This intractable problem was handed to the United Nations at the end of 1947. The UN was Western-dominated, so this involved no complete abandonment of South Korea. The UN was supposed to organise elections throughout Korea preparatory to unifying the country, but this was obviously a pipedream. No elections could be held in 1948 in the North, and in the South they were sufficiently corrupt with thousands of arrests to raise doubts whether the UN could accept the election as valid. The UN nevertheless did so and Syngman Rhee became the first president of the Republic of Korea, claiming to speak for all Korea. He was promptly recognised by the West. In June 1949 the Americans followed the Russians in pulling their troops out. In the North, the Democratic People's Republic under Kim Il Sung was recognised by China, the Soviet Union and the communist satellites. With the Russians and Americans no longer in direct control, civil war had come a step closer. The sparring, mainly verbal, continued until the summer of 1950.

Between 1948 and 1950 the East–West balance in Asia was radically altered. Communism in various national forms was spreading fast over the mainland. At the same time from 1948 to 1949 in Germany the United States and Britain were facing down the Russians over Berlin. The Russians and Americans each exercised sufficient restraint to avoid escalation into global war. Similar restraint was shown by the Americans, the Russians and the Chinese during the climax of the crisis in Asia from 1949 to 1950. Attention had focused on China before June 1950 rather than on Korea. American efforts on the Asian mainland had been limited, ambiguous and largely unsuccessful. Chiang Kai-shek had collapsed with his corrupt regime in China and the Americans had refused to make an all-out effort to save him; US help to the French in Indo-China had also been limited. American troops were not engaged in fighting anywhere, and it was to be hoped that the withdrawal of the Russians and Americans had reduced East–West tensions on the Asian mainland too.

The Truman administration had to decide early in 1950 what constituted the free world in Asia, how it could be defended and how, above all, any misunderstanding could be avoided that could turn the Cold War into a 'hot war'. The communists in China and the Soviet Union had to learn which vital Western interests the Americans would defend with their military might. An era of post-war uncertainty would then be ended. For both the Russians and the Americans the priority was Europe, where no further alterations in spheres of power and interest would be tolerated: there the frontiers were firmly set. Asia was too vast for America or Russia to control. The transformation from empire to independence, the rapid changes taking place in many societies and internal conflicts were all creating uncertainties about the future in a manner that was bad news for the West, which was identified with imperialism. In this respect, the West was at a disadvantage in the face of the 'liberating' claims of the various communist and socialist movements. The future of much of south-east Asia still seemed to hang in the balance, but American resources were not limitless, and Western Europe was still in a perilous condition. At least the Americans controlled the prize of Japan. The Truman administration's military advisers were reasonably consistent from 1947 to the summer of 1950: in eastern Asia the line of defence that could be, and would have to be, defended lay in the Pacific short of the Asian mainland.

Truman, more concerned with Europe, accepted their advice. But on one significant point he adopted the views of Secretary of State Dean Acheson rather than those of the Chiefs of Staff. Acheson thought that the Chinese communists could be encouraged to follow a line independent of Moscow's. They should therefore be conciliated now that Mao had proclaimed the Chinese People's Republic in October 1949. The sore point was the island of Taiwan (Formosa), to which Chiang Kai-shek had withdrawn with close on half a million still loyal troops. Although Mao claimed Taiwan as part of China, the United States continued to give aid to Chiang Kai-shek, though no American combat units were sent to support him. In a conciliatory speech on 5 January 1950 Truman publicly declared that the United States would not intervene in the Chinese civil war and that Taiwan was Chinese. If Mao had been strong enough to invade the island, the Americans would not have prevented it, but they knew that he was not. To emphasise that the United States was not about to embark on an appeasement policy, Dean Acheson delivered an important and trenchant speech a week later on 12 January, intended both for Moscow's ears and for public opinion at home. The United States would defend her vital interests in the Pacific, her essential line of defence running from the Aleutians to Japan, to the Ryukus and the Philippines; mainland China, Acheson pointed out, had been lost by Chiang's defeat, not by the Americans themselves, who could have done nothing to prevent Mao's victory.

It was notable that South Korea and Taiwan were both omitted from Dean Acheson's statement. The assumptions behind his and Truman's policies in 1949 and early 1950 were half right and half wrong. The view that the Chinese communists had national interests not identical with Russia's and should not be driven into Russia's arms was a sophisticated perception which was soon lost, not to be revived until the Nixon–Kissinger initiatives three decades later. Wrong was the belief that the speeches would bring about a reduction of tension. US support for the Kuomintang on Taiwan was too obvious for Mao not to be indignant that America was protecting his arch-enemy. The non-recognition of communist China by the US also denied to the People's Republic her rightful seat on the UN Security Council. To add insult to injury, the rump Chinese government in Taiwan continued as permanent member of the Security Council, with all the power accorded to this status, until 1971.

In the United States the signature of the Chinese –Soviet friendship treaty in February 1950 seemed to prove that Acheson was wrong, and pressure against the Truman administration, which was accused of having 'lost' China, overcame attempts to formulate more subtle policies. The decisive shift in America's Red China policy occurred on 25 June 1950, the day the North Koreans launched their invasion. In response to aggression by 'the communists', the Chinese being included in the general global conspiracy, Truman ordered the US Seventh Fleet to the Formosan Straits to prevent a communist Chinese invasion of Taiwan. In a show of ostensible even-handedness Truman declared that the US fleet would also prevent any attempt by Chiang (highly improbable) to invade the mainland again. In contravention of his earlier pronouncement, Truman had now intervened in the Chinese civil war. Communist Chinese and Americans were to remain frozen in mutual hostility. There were

no further US attempts to normalise relations with the new China, and the communist Chinese for their part now regarded the United States as their principal enemy. The formation of NATO, in 1949, though confined to Europe, led them to conclude that this Western alliance signified the coming of a global struggle between communism and imperialism.

It is against this background of the developing Cold War that the reactions of both the United States and China to the North Korean attack on South Korea on 25 June 1950 become intelligible. Acheson's omission of South Korea as vital to the defence of the United States encouraged Kim Il Sung. Had the North Korean leader also, while on a visit to Moscow shortly before, been given permission to invade the South? According to Khrushchev's memoirs the North Korean plan was known to both the Chinese and the Soviet leadership. Possibly only the precise date of the attack came as a surprise to Moscow. It certainly came as a total surprise to Washington, whose intelligence services had failed to provide any warning. The reaction of the Truman administration was nonetheless swift and decisive. Because of the world time difference, the news of the North Korean invasion reached Washington at 10 p.m. on the evening of Saturday, 24 June. The President had just finished a quiet family dinner hundreds of miles away at his home in Independence, Missouri, where he had gone for the weekend. There he received Acheson's urgent telephone call telling him about the invasion. The following day the President returned to Washington.

The earlier American policy of involving the United Nations in the search for a solution to Korean problems now provided the Truman administration with a card to play. The United States would not need to react alone to safeguard her Asian interests but could do so in the name of the UN Charter and at the request of the Security Council. This would have been impossible but for one fortuitous circumstance. A country's membership of the UN requires a two-thirds approval by the General Assembly on a Security Council recommendation, with a power of veto exercisable by any of the five permanent members. When communist China was not allowed to replace Chiang Kai-shek's regime on the Security Council, the Russians refused to attend the Security Council meetings. This proved a huge tactical blunder. Had

*US General Douglas MacArthur and President Syngman Rhee take the salute on 30 May 1950 as American forces are rushed to South Korea at the outset of the civil war.*

the Soviet Union been present and cast her veto, or had Mao's government been represented on the Security Council, the Security Council would have vetoed military action. The Soviet Union had thrown away the very safeguard – the veto – she had fought so hard to secure when the UN was founded.

Dean Acheson rapidly masterminded America's diplomatic reaction. The Security Council met on Sunday, 25 June and called on North Korea to halt the invasion and to pull back her forces to the 38th parallel. Truman independently authorised the use of the US Air Force in Korea south of the parallel to evacuate 2000 Americans, and General MacArthur was placed in command of operations in Korea. Truman also ordered equipment and arms to be sent from US bases in the Pacific to help the South Korean army. These unilateral American decisions anticipated a second, tougher resolution of the Security Council adopted on the night of Tuesday, 27 June and drafted by the US Ambassador to the UN. This called on members 'to render such assistance to the Republic of Korea as may be necessary to repel the armed attack and to restore international peace and security to the area'.

The first week of the Korean War brought another reversal of US policy. The headlong flight of the South Korean army made it essential to send reinforcements if they were to be saved from total defeat. Chiang Kai-shek's offer of soldiers was rejected but in his capacity as US commander-in-chief Truman ordered American ground troops to move into Korea. Militarily, the United States was unprepared, because Truman's 'economy budget' had slashed defence spending to the bone. And although the National Security Council in Washington had earlier that year drawn up plans for a massive increase of defence spending and a rapid expansion of the armed forces, they had not yet been acted on. But it was in the light of these plans that Truman announced during the first days of the Korean War that, to meet the threat of Asia, the United States would defend Korea and Taiwan and help the Philippine government and the French in their anti-communist campaigns. This was contrary to earlier strategic planning: on the assumption that Moscow was following a global strategy, US strategists had come up with the concept of regions of prime importance to be defended and those of less importance. Defence would not be diverted from prime regions by Moscow's attempts to distract the United States from her goals. This strategic thinking was overridden by Truman in the summer of 1950.

For Truman and Acheson the engagement in Korea was politically motivated. Communists must not be permitted to expand and overthrow independent nations anywhere. If not checked when they struck, wherever that might be, even in strategically unimportant Korea, then what faith would the allies in Europe have in America's readiness to resist aggression? For MacArthur, on the other hand, Asia came first – and now the hot war was actually being fought in Asia. As he saw it, the military objective was to defeat the enemy and to do so by any means necessary; this might even include the use of some form of nuclear weapons and, if China joined the war, the bombing of the Chinese Manchurian sanctuaries beyond the frontiers of North Korea.

The views of Truman's advisers on the political objectives to be achieved and the military means that could be used were different from MacArthur's from the beginning of the Korean War. Neither MacArthur nor Truman wished to provoke a Soviet or communist Chinese entry into the war. MacArthur, who saw himself uniquely able to interpret the oriental mind, did not believe that the Chinese would risk war against a victorious United States Army; a tough policy, he counselled, would be much more likely to deter them than attempts at appeasement. Truman, who was not so sure, vacillated, trying on the one hand to reassure communist China and on the other sanctioning a policy of crushing the North Koreans. But these differences between the commander in the field and Washington did not present an unbridgeable gulf until, in military adversity, MacArthur's conduct posed a challenge to the President's authority. As long as MacArthur was turning defeat into victory he had the backing of the country and the administration, even while there were nagging doubts in Washington that his mercurial temperament and self-esteem might divert US policy from the aim of restoring peace in Korea.

In Washington the concept of a 'limited war' was developed and first applied in Korea. The conflict was deliberately limited in two ways. It was fought as a localised war geographically: the Truman administration would not extend it to China, even when Chinese 'volunteers' poured into Korea, nor

would it take the risk of a Soviet entry and ensuing global war. It was also limited in that it was fought with conventional weapons: the use of nuclear arms was ruled out. All the wars fought since the Second World War have been limited wars. They have also all had one feature in common. None has been fought so far (1993) in which *both* protagonists possess nuclear weapons. The United States even preferred the option of defeat in Vietnam two decades later to making use of her nuclear power to destroy the North.

The reasons for Truman's decision to limit the war in Korea, a vital decision rightly taken, were neither understood nor approved by General MacArthur. He saw it as his duty to safeguard the lives of the men under his command and to fight for a complete and not a partial victory – yet the White House would not allow him to take up Chiang's offer of troops. MacArthur was also instructed that it was not part of UN aims to assist the Chinese Nationalists to retake the mainland of China. His immediate task was to stop the complete rout of the South Korean army. He brilliantly stabilised a short front in July and August 1950, covering the bridgehead of Pusan, a mere Korean toehold. The North Koreans had hesitated and missed the opportunity to occupy the whole of Korea.

With the best of North Korean troops concentrated on the tip of the Korean peninsula preparing to drive the growing American reinforcements into the sea, MacArthur executed one of the most audacious and successful counterstrokes in military history. In mid-September, he conducted an amphibious operation on the Korean west coast at Inchon, landing American troops with naval and air support far to the north of the Koreans fighting in the south, so cutting their supply lines. The North Korean army, in total disarray, was thrown into headlong retreat. For the American public it was a spectacular turnaround in the fortunes of war and confirmed the military genius of the seventy-one-year-old five-star General. MacArthur, never shy of self-praise, himself described the Inchon landing as a 'classic'. Unfortunately for the Americans and the Western cause it was not to be the last turning point of the war.

Rapidly advancing to the north, MacArthur reached the 38th parallel. From a small bridgehead, military control over the whole of South Korea had been wrested from the communists in just two weeks. The North Korean armies were incapable any longer of putting up effective resistance. On reaching the parallel MacArthur paused. Instead of ending the Korean War swiftly, the South Koreans, the Americans and their allies were to suffer another defeat, heavy casualties and almost three more years of war. This was solely the result of China's decision to devote substantial forces to the protection of North Korea. Historians have been inclined to blame MacArthur's insubordination in ignoring an important aspect of his military orders from Washington, not to push US troops close to the borders of China and the Soviet Union, but to use only South Korean troops in such operations. MacArthur regarded this as militarily impractical, so two American armies, facing little resistance, pushed north-west and north-east to the Manchurian frontier on the Yalu River and towards the Soviet frontier. First contact was made with Chinese troops towards the end of October; then the Chinese disappeared, and in a brilliant manoeuvre their commander Peng Dehuai struck at the advanced American divisions on Monday, 27 November (local date). The American troops reeled back and were extricated from the North only with the greatest difficulty. Seoul was soon lost again. In December General Ridgway took immediate command of the front line under MacArthur and in January 1951 stabilised a new front line some eighty miles south of the 38th parallel.

The blame for Chinese intervention needs to be attributed more to a divided administration in Washington than to MacArthur. The Yalu was a sensitive border, all the more so because a great dam and hydroelectric installation there supplied electricity both to Manchuria and to North Korea. MacArthur had been instructed to withdraw from contact if there were signs of Chinese or Soviet intervention in the north and to refer back for instructions to Washington. He had been ordered not to use US combat troops close to the borders. But he had also received clear instructions to cross the 38th parallel, so he began his advance on 7 October 1950. He was allowed much discretion, itself an indication of military irresolution in Washington and of the political weakness of Truman, who was under much pressure at home. He was reluctant to control MacArthur closely in the General's hour of victory. MacArthur's success would also convincingly answer the President's critics at home who were claiming that the administration did not have the necessary determination to

roll back communism in the world. The possibility of Chinese intervention was discounted despite clear signs to the contrary. Stalin's refusal to become involved was seen as far more important. The fighting capacities of the Chinese communists, regarded as mere Asiatics, were underestimated, and the readiness of the communist leaders to accept huge casualties was not anticipated. MacArthur did not believe they had a chance against the best-trained and best-equipped army in the world. Early newspaper reports, too, gave the impression that the Chinese offensive was being conducted by vast hordes of ill-disciplined primitives sounding their trumpets and striking cymbals. There was more than a touch of racial arrogance about all this. The Chinese victories, gained at heavy cost in lives and forcing the hazardous retreat of the US divisions, came as a shock to the Western world.

China's leaders had only reluctantly become embroiled in a war with the most powerful Western nation. Mao Zedong and Zhou Enlai sought a compromise: South Korean, not American, troops could cross the 38th parallel. The Soviet Union meanwhile threw out feelers for a negotiated settlement and the withdrawal of outside forces from Korea. In Washington this was interpreted as an attempt to save North Korea from total military defeat, without which there could be no permanent peace in Korea. Truman, after earlier virulent accusations that his administration had been soft on communism and had not provided sufficient support to Chiang Kai-shek, found it politically very difficult to resist MacArthur's wish to pursue a beaten communist enemy.

The day after US troops crossed the 38th parallel, Mao gave the order for Chinese intervention, thinly disguised as the action of Chinese 'volunteers'. He was determined at all costs to maintain North Korea as a buffer between China and the United States. After taking this decision for war, Mao discovered that China would have to rely on her own resources, for the Soviet Union provided no significant military supplies during the first year of fighting. The invasion of Taiwan had to be postponed and the reconstruction of China herself was delayed by the need to deploy resources for the war. For China, the Korean War, coming so soon after the civil war, was a serious setback, but her success in retaking most of North Korea, in following a policy independent of Moscow's and in holding a front against the

*War in Korea. After MacArthur's brilliant offensive at Inchon in September 1950 drove the North Koreans back across the 38th parallel, Seoul, or what was left of it at least, was recaptured (left). MacArthur's victorious march north, however, was soon halted when the Chinese intervened. The US Marines were caught by surprise and had to fend off numerous Chinese attacks while organizing their perilous retreat (right). Huge columns of refugees trailed south, too, all through the bitter winter of 1950/51, until the front could be stabilized once more (above).*

American and UN troops raised her international prestige. The Korean War made it clear to the world that China was now, along with the United States and the Soviet Union, a power to be reckoned with in Asia.

During the winter of 1950/1 the Truman administration had to take critical decisions. American prestige was suffering in inverse proportion to China's success. Truman now faced criticism from two opposite camps. There were those who blamed the administration for crossing the 38th parallel. And there was a vociferous minority, constantly encouraged by MacArthur himself, who called for a widening of the war and the defeat of China, at least in Korea. MacArthur sent back gloomy military reports to the effect that, unless the United States was prepared to give up fighting a limited war and was ready to bomb the Chinese sanctuaries in Manchuria, a total withdrawal from Korea would become necessary. Among the plans MacArthur advocated was to sow a 'defensive field of radioactive waste' across the supply lines leading to northern Korea. The military successes achieved by General Ridgway in pushing the North Koreans back across the 38th parallel did nothing to modify MacArthur's public criticisms of Truman's military and foreign policy of searching for a settlement with China. Despite repeated warnings, MacArthur continued his efforts to force a change of policy on the administration. The final straw was a letter MacArthur sent to a leading Republican congressman, which was released to undermine Truman's policies and in which MacArthur gave his backing to the use of Chiang's troops. The war in Korea, MacArthur wrote, had to be won: 'if we lose the war to Communism in Asia the fall of Europe is inevitable, win it and Europe most probably would avoid war and yet preserve freedom'. MacArthur regarded himself as above politics, as a wise guide to the free world in pointing to the dangers of the communist global conspiracy; he could not accept the change of policy in Washington, which expressed a readiness to end the war short of total victory by negotiating a compromise settlement with the aggressor. His enormous prestige and half a century of service, MacArthur had convinced himself, made him untouchable, beyond Washington's power to limit his freedom to speak his mind.

Truman, embattled at home, had no illusions about the storm that would break out if he dismissed MacArthur, nor about the use his Republican opponents on Capitol Hill would make of the differences between the civilian President and the great General on the issue of how to conduct a war. For Truman the great question had become a different one. Who was to control policy, the President or the General? Once Truman had made up his mind, he did not lack the courage to see things through. There could be no doubt that he would defend the presidency. In April 1951 he dismissed MacArthur with the concurrence of the Chiefs of Staff and in a radio broadcast explained to the American people that the US objectives in Korea were limited. In the short term, Truman's standing suffered. A Gallup poll showed that his popularity had dropped to an unprecedented low of 24 per cent. But it recovered. Reflection led to reappraisal, to a less emotional response and to the recognition of the dangers of getting into an all-out war with China. The Korean War, to be sure, was frustrating, as it dragged on with heavy casualties. Outright victory was preferred, of course, but not at the price of risking an even bigger war with still heavier casualties for a country few Americans took much interest in.

To conduct a limited war was the crucial decision the Truman administration had taken from the start. To stick to that decision in the face of a loss of American prestige in the winter of 1950/1 required courage and wisdom. There would be no extension of the Korean War. Perhaps Truman deserved better than have Beijing reject out of hand all attempts to settle Korea by negotiation at the UN. The chance of bringing the Korean War to an end was not all that was lost. Mao's radical turn in China prevented a new start being made in Sino-American relations with communist China taking her seat in the Security Council. Truman's decision to defend Taiwan set the United States on a course that opened an unbridgeable gulf in her relations with China for many years.

In the United States the Korean War had a major impact. Truman had sounded the alarm about the worldwide danger of communism since the early days of the administration. The Truman Doctrine, the Marshall Plan, support for West Berlin and NATO had all won the support of the majority of Congress and of the American people. But a new 'red scare' got out of hand. The revelation that a British atomic scientist, Klaus Fuchs, had passed secrets to the Russians, added to the setting off of first Soviet atomic bomb in August 1949, had raised fears about the dangers of communist internal subversion and had created an atmosphere bordering on hysteria. Congressional investigations into subversion by the House Committee on UnAmerican Activities had been on the increase since 1945. The sensational trials involving Alger Hiss, a State Department official, and Whittaker Chambers, who worked for *Time* magazine, increased American apprehensions about the red conspiracy to new heights and divided American society. Chambers, a former member of the Communist Party, accused Hiss of having worked for the communist cause in the 1930s and of having engaged in espionage. Hiss denied the accusations but was convicted in January 1950 after a second trial. The way was open now to link the 'loss of China' with the 'treacherous' activities of key State Department personnel and their active advisers. A quiet professor, Owen Lattimore, an expert on Outer Mongolia, was suddenly thrust into the limelight as a key figure in the 'conspiracy'. A young Republican senator from Wisconsin, Joseph McCarthy, grasped the opportunity to bring himself to national attention by making sensational and unsubstantiated accusations about communist infiltration of the US government, particularly the State Department. Dean Acheson, who refused to repudiate Hiss, was among the targets, but Truman stood up for him. Well-known actors and directors from Hollywood, trade unionists, teachers and many others were brought before the committee for questioning. Guilt by association was sufficient. Regarded as bad risks, their chances of employment were blighted for years. Immigration was tightened to exclude alleged subversives.

There was no McCarthy, fortunately, in Britain, where the excesses of the Senator were causing public concern about the lack of balance being shown by the country's principal ally. While McCarthy could uncover no spies in the State Department, apart from Hiss, there actually were three in the Foreign Office, two of them in Washington at that time transmitting information to Moscow via London. Kim Philby was First Secretary of the British Embassy in Washington; the Second Secretary was Guy Burgess; and the American Department at the Foreign Office in London was headed by another spy, Donald Maclean. Philby tipped off Burgess and Maclean that the Security Service, MI5, was on their trail

and they defected in May 1951. Philby maintained his cover until 1963 before he also escaped to Moscow. How much harm they did has remained a secret. In the depression years of the 1930s, and while the communists could claim in Spain and elsewhere that they were leading the fight against fascism, the Communist Party attracted many, including intellectuals, who were idealists and wanted to create a better world. Newspapers and books were at that time revealing the concentration camps and brutalities of Nazi Germany. The horrors of Stalin's Russia, the chain of forced-labour camps, the Gulag archipelago, were carefully hidden from view. The Soviet Union was shut off from the West – unlike Nazi Germany – and a few naive visitors, including the Dean of Canterbury, were shown only the country's happy face and then returned to the West to write ecstatic accounts of what they had seen. The admiration for the Red Army and the Soviet people, officially blessed by Allied propaganda during the Second World War, persuaded others into temporary support of communism.

For most of these Western communists, disillusionment set in steadily after 1945 with the growing evidence of the Soviet suppression of freedom in Eastern and central Europe. By the time of the crushing of the Hungarian rising in 1956 no illusions could remain. Many communists of the 1930s had left the party by then; substantial numbers had fallen for the propaganda of one of the communist front organisations only when young in student days. There were indeed thousands, and some had entered government service. McCarthy thus could build up fears on a basis of fact. But these men and women were not automatically disloyal to their country or subservient to foreign masters. The few who were frequently served Moscow for gain or out of twisted psychological motives. There will always be spies and traitors as long as nations are locked in hostile confrontation. The evil result of McCarthyism was to smear everyone with the same broad brush, whether there was good, flimsy or no evidence. The Senator appealed to low instincts of envy, of dislike for the intellectual establishment, and so struck a chord of meanness and worse. An atmosphere of fear began to prevail which eroded civil liberties.

Truman condemned McCarthy in forthright language. McCarthy, after MacArthur's dismissal, even called for Truman's impeachment; he next attacked General George Marshall, arguably America's architect of military victory during the Second World War and later Truman's Secretary of State, as part of 'a conspiracy so immense, an infamy so black, as to dwarf any in the history of man'. The Truman administration tried to meet public worries aroused by McCarthyism about communism by introducing loyalty checks on public employees. In the Senate opposition to McCarthy diminished as his power grew. It reached its zenith in 1954 during the Eisenhower administration. McCarthyism represented the exaggerated reaction of all those who hated the New Deal, Truman's Fair Deal and civil rights legislation. They believed that America was succumbing to creeping socialism and creating an all-embracing federal state hostile to the sturdy individualism on which (as they saw it) America had grown to prosperity and power. McCarthyism also provided an outlet for the frustration provoked by the realisation that the world could not be shaped in the image of the United States. Communism had made enormous advances and was a potent force for change: the United States had failed to halt its progress and had, in the McCarthyites' view, 'lost China'. They railed against the limitations of America's global policies and claimed that the limitations were self-imposed,

because the policies themselves had been inspired from within by communists. Setting aside the evils of the McCarthyite smear tactics, what many Americans found hard to accept was that the Second World War had not settled global problems, had not proved to be the war that ends all war.

Before the outbreak of the Korean War there had seemed to be a chance to deal with regional problems by paying careful attention to their local roots and not equating the situation in Asia with that in Europe. But in Moscow, Beijing and Washington after 1950 the world was seen to be dividing into three blocs, the communist and capitalist locked in confrontation, with a weak, neutralist Third World which might be drawn to one side or the other. This oversimplified global view of international relations in a rapidly changing world prevailed even when some conflicts clearly did not fit the pattern. The Korean War (see also pages 379–80) occupies a place of major significance globally. In terms of human suffering – with 4 million killed and wounded, most of them Koreans, though 1 million were Chinese – it has to be seen as a major war. The South eventually recovered. The North remained frozen in poverty under the iron hand of Comrade Kim Il Sung.

# PART IX

The Ending of European
Dominance in the Middle
East, 1919–1980

# CHAPTER 43

# Regional Conflict in the Middle East

Today the Middle East is ridden with strife. Arab nation is divided from Arab nation, fundamentalist Muslims from moderate Muslims who accept the secular state, Persians (Iranians) from Arabs, traditional monarchies from secular republics, the oil-rich from the poor nations. Why is there so much conflict? Is there one root cause? If the Zionists had not created Israel, would there have been peace? Were the Arabs set against each other by outside powers, by the Russians, by the British, by the Americans? Or do the present problems of the region derive from a backlash against the imposition of alien Western traditions on a traditional Islamic society? All these developments, and many others, have contributed to instability.

Central to the Middle East's geopolitical importance today is its oil, a commodity vital since 1945 to the prosperity of the oil states, the West and Japan. Before the Second World War Middle Eastern oil was less significant: the United States, Mexico and Venezuela were the major oil exporters, Venezuelan oil production alone in 1939 exceeding that of the entire Middle East. But during the war, Iraqi oil became vital to Britain, which occupied the country jointly with the Soviet Union. It was the dramatic expansion of oil consumption after the Second World War, the commodity's enormous potential, the industrial changeover from coal to oil and the expansion of motor and air travel that gave the Middle Eastern oil-producing nations so important a role in Western economies. The United States then ceased to be an exporter of oil and became an importer.

Between 1919 and 1939 the United States, Britain and the Netherlands had secured a virtual monopoly of Middle Eastern oil concessions and so came to dominate world marketing. Iran was the region's major oil producer, and Britain was able to keep out foreign competition, retaining control until the nationalisation dispute of 1951. The US oil giants, meanwhile, worried about oil reserves in the United States, with the backing of the American administration, gained a large share of the oil concessions, which were to prove the richest of the Middle East after the Second World War: Aramco, a consortium of US companies, secured oil rights in Saudi Arabia; Gulf Oil, a half-share of the oil resources of Kuwait; and the US also gained a share in Iraqi oil. Britain further agreed to share Iraqi oil with France, whose spheres of influence in the Middle East contained little oil. French-controlled Syria, and the Lebanon before 1945, earned additional royalties from the pipelines carrying oil from the Iraqi Kirkuk field to Tripoli; a 'British' line ran through Transjordan and Palestine to Haifa. Until the mid-1950s Britain remained not only the dominant political power in the Middle East but also the most important oil power.

The Middle East is one of the world's most unstable regions, with wars between Israelis and Arabs – the enmities between Arabs are less obvious. Westerners tend to see these societies of complex religious and ethnic diversity as much more homogeneously Arab and Islamic than they are. It is nonetheless true that, apart from Turks, Kurds,

Armenians, Jews and the Persians of Iran, the Middle East is predominantly Arab, and that the majority of Arabs are followers of Islam. This has created a sense of cultural unity: the Koran and the Arab spoken language help Arabs to feel that they belong to one civilisation, and hundreds of thousands of Egyptians, Palestinians and other Arab nations, mainly technicians, teachers and students, work and feel at home in Arab countries other than their own, principally in the oil-rich Gulf states. Although Islam is the dominant faith of the great majority of the peoples of the Middle East, not all Muslims of course are Arabs. The Turks, the Iranians and the Kurds are ethnically quite distinct from the Arabs, as are many converts to Islam. The ebb and flow of conquests is reflected in the diverse cultures and religions of the Middle East. This becomes clearer as one looks at the populations country by country.

Modern Turkey, shorn of her Arab empire in 1919, was the most homogeneous of the large Middle Eastern states. It was much less so by 1990, with a large minority of several million Kurds among its total population of 56.5 million. Syria's population was about 11.2 million in 1987, of whom more than 1 million belong to some eleven different Christian sects. Most Syrians are Sunni Muslims, but a minority, the Alawite Muslim sect, has built up a dominant military and political role in recent years, though the Druze is another Muslim sect of importance in Syrian political life. In Aleppo there is a large Christian minority.

Iran (Persia) had a mainly Shia Muslim population of 59 million in 1990. The division of Islam into Sunni and Shia occurred a generation after the death of the Prophet Mohammed in AD 632, following a dispute over the succession to the caliphate. Ali, Mohammed's first cousin, lost this contest, and his followers founded the Shia branch, whose members look to their spiritual leaders for divine guidance on the interpretation of the Koran. The Sunni are also known as orthodox Muslims. Differences between Shia and Sunni have important political implications, for the Shias are in a majority in Iran and in significant minorities in neighbouring Lebanon. Worldwide, the Shia branch comprises only one in ten Muslims. It should be remembered that there are also non-Arab Muslims such as the Sunni and Shia Kurds of Iran, Iraq and Turkey, who are fiercely independent and resist all attempts to subjugate them.

In Iraq the majority of the population of 19 million (1990) are Shia Muslims, while about a quarter of the Arab population is Sunni. There is also a large minority of Kurds in the north, divided between Sunni and Shia, and distinct from the Arab majority. In the region around Mosul there is an Assyrian Christian minority. In the capital, Baghdad, there was a large Jewish community until a mass exodus took place in 1950–1.

The most religiously and ethnically divided country is mountainous Lebanon, among whose population of 3 million today no one group has an overall majority. The Muslim population is divided between Shia, Sunni and the Druze; the Maronite Catholic Christians, who have their own patriarch but accept the Pope as head of the Church, are the largest single Christian group and, together with other Christian communities, once made up about half the total population. Today the Muslims form the majority. So sensitive an issue have precise population numbers been in the Lebanon that no official census of the communities has been taken for half a century. The breakdown in 1957 of a power-sharing agreement between Maronites and Sunni, the so-called National Pact, plus interference by neighbours, as well as by the militant Palestinian Liberation Organisation, plunged the Lebanon into bloody civil war.

The population of the territory under Jordanian control after the 1967 war with Israel was about 3.8 million in 1987. In the West Bank, assigned to Jordan (Transjordan) in 1949 after the first Arab –Israeli war, there were a further 800,000 Arab Palestinians under Israeli control. The relationship between Arab Jordanians and Arab Palestinians who are seeking their own independence has been a strained one. The Jordanians are Sunni Muslims; in the West Bank there is a minority of Christians.

In Israel proper some 900,000 of the total population of nearly 5 million (in 1991) are Arabs. Since the occupation of the West Bank and Gaza in 1967, Israel now controls just over 1.5 million Arabs. (For the Arab–Jewish population figures of Palestine before 1947 see pages 449–50.)

The Arabian peninsula's most important state is Saudi Arabia, unified by Ibn Saud and his zealous followers, the Wahhabi, after the defeat of his rival Hussain Sharif of Mecca in the 1920s and in 1990 having a population of about 14 million. Originally the poverty-stricken Bedouins of Saudi Arabia and their tribal chiefs were of political importance because they ruled over the holy cities of Mecca and Medina, and so, with British backing, could be set up as rival caliphs appealing to the Muslims of the Ottoman and Indian Empires against the Caliph Sultan of Turkey. This proved of some value to Britain in the First World War but her sponsorship proved insufficient to unite the Arabs. The tribes of the Arabian peninsula were among the poorest in the Middle East, and most of the peninsula, except for the pilgrimage routes and the coastline, was isolated from the rest of the world. Ibn Saud's new kingdom was backward and poor, his rule patriarchal. Patriarchal rule has continued to the present day, but the kingdom has become one of the richest in the world as a result of the post-war development of the huge oil discoveries made in the 1930s. Before then, there had been nothing to attract the British, who maintained friendly relations and did not interfere in Saudi Arabia's internal affairs. Desperate for revenue, Ibn Saud in 1933 granted concessions for oil-prospecting to American oil companies which were exploited after the war by the Arabian American Oil Company (Aramco).

Similarly, the discovery and development of oilwells along the Persian Gulf, in Kuwait and Bahrain, the United Arab Emirates (Trucial States) and Oman, transformed those regions of the Arabian peninsula into one of the wealthiest in the world. In contrast, Yemen, with a population estimated at 11 million in 1990, has few valuable resources and is very poor. But a number of companies, are continuing exploration for gas and oil and production is expanding. The Yemenites belong to a branch of the Shia Muslims – most Arabs are Sunni. Britain's interests in the Arabian peninsula, before the irruption of oil, were mainly strategic. To safeguard commercial routes and the oil supplies from Iraq and Iran, she held on to Aden and maintained protectorate relationships with the tribal sheikhs along the coastline of the Arabian Sea and Persian Gulf.

Egypt is among the largest Middle Eastern states but also one of the poorest. As elsewhere in the region, the population has increased very rapidly in the twentieth century and efforts to modernise, and especially to improve the lot of the peasants, can scarcely keep pace with the rate of population growth from some 18 million in 1947 to an estimated 52 million forty-five years later. The great majority of Egyptians are Sunni Muslims, but there is a large minority of about 4 million Arab-speaking Copts (Greek for Egyptian), who have followed Christianity under their own patriarchs. Most members of an ancient community of Jews were expelled after 1956.

The Sudan, to the south, which shares the life-giving Nile with Egypt, was nominally under Anglo-Egyptian rule from 1899 until independence in 1956 but she was, in reality, controlled by Britain. The main ethnic division is between the mixed, mainly Sunni Muslim peoples of the northern and central regions and the southern tribes, which tend to be either pagan or Christian converts. Some have been converted to Islam, others resist northern attempts at Islamisation. This division, which has often led to conflict and warfare, remains one of the most serious internal problems facing the modern Sudan's 24.5 million inhabitants (1989 figure), of whom just under a third belong to one of the black African peoples. The great majority of Libya's 4.6 million people in 1990 are Sunni Muslims; Arabic is the national language, though some Berber-speaking districts remain. Once one of the poorest Arab countries, comprised as it is largely of desert, the discovery of oil in the 1960s transformed the economy and the ambitions of the Libyan political leadership.

The Middle East is overwhelmingly Arab and Islamic. There are constant appeals to Arab unity and Islamic solidarity, as well as calls for the political organisation of an Arab League. Unions of different Arab nations are talked about and even established, though only for short periods. The State of Israel is seen as the common enemy, the intruder that has seized Arab lands and alienated most of Palestine from Arab rule. As we have seen, the sense of a common civilisation and language and the pride in Islam are shared by millions of Arabs, and the educated classes are conscious of these links across national frontiers. But nationalism is relatively new to the Arabs, except in Egypt, which was influenced by the Napoleonic invasion and Western ideas in the nineteenth century. Socialism, industrial development and attempts to introduce constitutional government are other signs of the Western impact on the Middle East of the nineteenth and twentieth centuries.

After the defeat of 1918 the Turks became a strongly nationalist country under Mustafa Kemal, known as Kemal Atatürk (Father of the Turks). Modern Turkey with a population in 1993 of 57

*Kemal Atatürk, who inspired Turkish national resistance, was elected president in 1920, and ruled the country until his death in 1938.*

million is based on the military success of Atatürk, who defied the Western Allies and by 1923 had re-established complete Turkish sovereignty over her territories, shorn of the Arab empire, by threatening to fight again for his country. The legacy was bitter rivalry with Greece, which had to abandon her own attempted expansion in Asia Minor. It is a rivalry that persists to the present day, with disputes in the Aegean and over the future of Cyprus. Mustafa Kemal broke with Ottoman and Muslim traditions and during the fifteen years of his rule as president forced Westernisation on the Turks, breaking the power of the clergy. The Atatürk tradition, under which the military became the guardian of the nation, lives on. In modelling institutions on the West in the 1930s, Atatürk combined a parliamentary system with his own virtual one-party rule and cult of personality. His protégé and successor was Ismet Inönü, who was president from 1938 to 1950 and then again from

1961 to 1965. But in the aftermath of the Second World War and in alliance with the United States, there was both external and internal pressure for more democratic rule. Strife-ridden civilian governments have been replaced intermittently by repressive military rule. The democratic tradition is weak.

Three peoples were denied the right to form their own independent nations in the carve-up of the Ottoman Empire: the Armenians, the Palestinian Arabs and the Kurds. The Armenians, with a history of independence and subjection going back to ancient times, seemed the most likely to gain independence after the collapse of the Ottoman Empire, under whose rule they had suffered genocidal atrocities. Britain and France hoped that the United States would accept a mandate over Armenia, still partitioned between Turks and Russians, but the US Senate rejected the notion. Nevertheless by the Treaty of Sèvres an independent Armenian Republic was recognised in 1920, but the West made no attempt to defend the new state when Turkey and Soviet Russia attacked and divided the Republic between them in December of that year.

The Kurds, who had struggled for independence when under Ottoman rule, took heart from Wilson's promise of self-determination and from the defeat of the Turks. The same Treaty of Sèvres recognised the creation of independent Kurdistan, but Kemal Atatürk tore up the treaty and forced the Allies to revise it by the Treaty of Lausanne in 1923; by then he had conquered Kurdistan. In the final disposition of the Ottoman Empire the Kurds found themselves minorities in five states. In 1991 it is estimated that some 500,000 lived in the USSR, 6.7 million in Iran, 4.9 million in Iraq, 1.4 million in Syria and 12–14 million in Turkey. They have rebelled sporadically, always to be savagely repressed. The tragedy of the Kurds in the aftermath of the Second Gulf War, when in March 1991 they rose against Saddam Hussein in Iraq, is that no nation wants to raise the issue of an independent Kurdistan. The United States wishes to build a 'stable peace' in the region through an alliance of Arab states, Iran, Turkey and the Soviet Union and these have a common interest in suppressing Kurdish nationalism in their own countries. The Palestinian diaspora also had its origins in the aftermath of the First World War (pages 447–50). For more than half a century the sense of national identity which characterises these three peoples has not been extinguished – nor as the twentieth century draws to its close, is it likely to be.

Radio and television can mobilise the masses in ways not dreamed of in the days of the Ottoman Empire. In addition, the movement of the rural population to the cities has been a phenomenon throughout much of the less developed world, including the Middle East. Some 6 million have crowded into Teheran, Iran's capital; Cairo's population exceeds 6 million; and even in the Lebanon, a country with a small population, three-quarters of a million live in Beirut. The explosive growth of urban living, the increase, especially in towns, of literacy, the frustrations and the thirst for activity among student groups, the restlessness of unemployed labour existing on the margins of subsistence, the abject poverty of most of the peoples of the Middle East, all these have added greatly to the volatility of the region and created a gulf between the urban and rural populations.

In the rural areas, despite some ambitious projects, high population growth has negated the advances in crop yields and agricultural methods, leaving the peasants no less backward and poor. In the oil-rich states – Saudi Arabia and those along the Persian Gulf – agriculture is of little importance. In Iran and Iraq, however, despite the revenues from oil, agriculture must absorb the labour and provide a subsistence living for up to half the population. So the possession of oil alone does not solve the economic problems of these states.

The purchasing power of the oil-rich states has turned them into vital elements in the Western world's economic advancement. Underdevelopment and backwardness rub shoulders with ambitious modern projects and international airports in the Middle Eastern states. In greatpower contests it remains a region of strategic importance. The continuities of cultures and religions provide links with the past, but there are also huge differences as a result of the transformation that has occurred in the twentieth century.

The resurgence of militant fundamentalism, especially after the overthrow of the Shah of Iran by the Ayatollah Khomeini in 1979, threatened to destabilise the whole region. It was not only a reaction against Western dominance, whether Russian, British or American, but also a reversal of the road to Western modernisation taken by Turkey under Mustafa Kemal after the First World War. Thus rival Islamic ideological conflicts were added to the Western ideological confrontations of 'socialism' and 'capitalism'.

Among the more powerful nations there is also a continuous struggle for regional predominance. In the 1980s there were several such national and international conflicts. A bloody war between Iraq and Iran was followed by Saddam Hussein's invasion of Kuwait in August 1990, which lined Syria, Egypt, Saudi Arabia and the Western powers up against him and led to the Second Gulf War in January 1991. As the twentieth century nears its end, the Middle East remains one of the most crisis-ridden regions in the world.

# CHAPTER 44

# The Middle East Between Two World Wars, 1919–1945

After the conclusion of the peace settlements following the First World War, Britain attempted, for a time successfully, to secure the benefits of empire in the Middle East while minimising the costs of control. Her time-honoured way of achieving this was to maintain old social structures and unreconstructed traditional rulers. Modernisation and democratisation was at best half-hearted, since mass nationalism would have threatened British dominance.

The Ottoman khedive of Egypt became a king under British supervision. The Hashemite amirs of Arabia were transformed into sovereign rulers. The Arab states were also provided with constitutions; assemblies were 'elected' and ministers were appointed who were supposedly responsible to the assemblies. British 'advisers' made sure that law and order were maintained and Britain's interests preserved. These arrangements proved unstable and, after the Second World War, progressively collapsed in Egypt, Iraq and the Sudan. Although not an Arab state, Iran (Persia) was subjected to a similar pattern of indirect rule after the war. This merely continued, in this region, the policy followed before the 1914 war. Britain was inventive in devising constitutional and international arrangements which gave her what was necessary to protect her imperial interests without saddling her with responsibility for the welfare of the indigenous peoples of the countries she controlled. An exception was Aden, which was annexed in the nineteenth century and became a colony ruled outright by Britain; her population, however, was small. A more ingenious solution was found for the Sudan, reconquered in 1898, which became half a colony, a so-called condominium, shared between Egypt and Britain in 1899; in reality, both Egypt and the Sudan were administered by Britain. Britain did not attempt to rule over the Arabs living in the sheikhdoms of the Indian Ocean or the Persian Gulf, or in the interior of Arabia. Instead, special treaties were signed and protectorates proclaimed excluding any foreign influence other than British. Iraq, Iran, Transjordan, Saudi Arabia and Egypt were ostensibly independent countries bound only to Britain by treaties of alliance 'freely concluded' against this general background of her imperial policy in the Middle East, the position of Palestine, a large, predominantly Arab land for which Britain assumed direct responsibility under the League Mandate, was different. From the first, Palestine proved a troublesome possession. Far from providing Britain with a friendly and secure base in the Middle East, increasing numbers of troops from Britain's small army had to be assigned to Palestine just to try to keep the peace.

Palestine was the most obvious trouble spot for Britain between the two world wars (pages 447–50). But in other parts of the Middle East British policy also ran into constant problems. It was already too late to extend imperial control by the mixture of force, efficient administration and paternalism which Britain had so successfully adopted in the heyday of imperialism. Taking on the heritage of the Ottoman rulers after the First World War turned out to be far more difficult than the British had expected. Not all the different ethnic and religious groups accepted the Arab rulers imposed on them. The largely desert regions of the former Ottoman lands which Britain had now acquired, with their stretches of irrigated territory along the coastlines and river banks, were divided into Palestine, Transjordan and Iraq. The 'royal' protégés whom Britain appointed to rule the Arab states were two sons of the Hashemite Sharif Husain of Mecca, Abdullah and Faisal. What territories they would actually rule remained uncertain, a detail not sufficiently worked out in 1919, especially as the French had their own ideas about how to govern Syria and Lebanon, the Arab territories that had been assigned to them. Abdullah had hoped to become King of Iraq with Faisal as King of Syria. Faisal actually established himself in Syria for a short time until he was driven out by the French. The British then decided to install Faisal as king of Iraq, which left his brother disappointed. Abdullah, at the head of a contingent of tribal forces, in turn threatened to avenge Faisal's unceremonious expulsion from French Syria, at the same time putting forward claims to rule over an Arab Palestine, claims that were totally unacceptable to the British government. Instead, the territories across the Jordan, Transjordan, were separated from Palestine and constituted into a separate state in 1921 with Amir Abdullah as ruler. This was intended as no more than a temporary arrangement until the French agreed to allow Abdullah to become king of Syria. But this the French never did. Syria thus nurses an historical grievance. The ruler of small, barren Transjordan hankered after Jerusalem but was totally dependent on Britain.

It is important to note that the creation of all these states was not based on any logical or natural divisions. It is hard to see how they could have been. Nor were they based on the Wilsonian principle of what the people wished, even supposing this could have been accurately discovered. Instead they derived from machinations of a few leaders and from the power-play of Britain and France. Ottoman dominion could be more easily destroyed than replaced.

The one country with clear national frontiers was Egypt. Britain's dominance was difficult to justify after the First World War. Egypt had received the benefits of continuous Western tutelage since the British occupation began, and an efficient adminis-

tration had been built up with outstanding and powerful British proconsuls, modestly named 'consul-generals' (because Turkish suzerainty was acknowledged until 1914). The Sudan too was under effective British control, as we have seen, though in theory it was shared with Egypt. During the war of 1914–18 Egypt was declared a British protectorate; a strong military base was established and all protest was suppressed. The war nevertheless brought about change. It created wealth among a minority of Egyptian merchants, and a small Egyptian elite evolved, whose members became determined to remove British control and govern the country in their own interests rather than Britain's. But they were split between the supporters of the monarchy and autocratic governments and supporters of a nationalist party, the Wafd, led by Sa'ad Zaghlul, who in 1918 made himself spokesman of the nationalist cause. How could Egypt be denied independence when it was promised to the backward Bedouin Arabs? After riots and demonstrations Egypt was offered limited independence. Zaghlul objected. He also demanded that Egypt should have a say in the Sudan, for control of the headwaters of the Nile was regarded as vital by the Egyptians, who were dependent upon its water. No one in Cairo would conclude a treaty on British terms, so Britain in 1922 unilaterally proclaimed a limited Egyptian independence but reserved all those rights considered essential to British interests.

So-called constitutional politics now revolved around the rivalry for power among the group of Wafdist politicians supported by wealthy landowners and the corrupt supporters of the King. Between Britain and an elected Egyptian Wafd government a *modus vivendi* was at long last achieved by the signature of an Anglo-Egyptian alliance in August 1936. British troops were withdrawn from Egypt's main towns but British air and land bases were maintained to guard the Suez Canal, and the Royal Navy had free use of the harbour of Alexandria. In the event of war or the imminent threat of it, the Egyptian government promised Britain its full support and unrestricted use of all Egyptian facilities and territory. Under the terms of the treaty the Egyptian army would also pass under British command in wartime. For a while all seemed peace and harmony and the Foreign Secretary, Anthony Eden, was even featured on Egyptian postage stamps. But within two years there was renewed bitterness about the continued presence of British troops in bases all over Egypt.

During the 1939–45 war King Farouk and the Egyptian government proved uncertain allies. Egypt did not declare war on Germany and Italy, but was nonetheless defended by the British Eighth Army against Rommel's Afrika Korps. Indeed, Farouk and his government were making secret overtures to Hitler in 1941, professing to welcome a German occupation. Hatred of Britain played a part, but there may also have been an element of reinsurance in case Rommel, as seemed likely, entered Cairo victorious. The British victory at El Alamein in 1942 settled Egypt's immediate future, since Britain's wartime needs overrode all notions of genuine Egyptian independence. To the Egyptians at the end of the war what stood out starkly was not that they had been defended against a German invasion but that, despite Britain's recognition of their independence in 1936, the British remained virtually an occupying power ten years later. By then an economically exhausted but still militarily dominant Britain faced a chorus of strident nationalist demands to revise the Anglo-Egyptian Treaty of 1936 and to hand complete independence over to Egypt's rival political leadership. As elsewhere in the Arab world, after 1945 Britain was faced in Egypt with the immensely difficult task of appeasing an Arab nationalism that was now stronger than ever.

Treaties and a special relationship also protected British interests in Iraq. In many ways Britain carried on where the Ottoman rulers had left off. The Arab governing elite in country after country was chosen from the same group, the Sunni Muslims, whether they were in a majority as in the Arabian peninsula or in a minority as in Iraq. Other minorities, communities of Christians and Jews, were left to the mercy of the Sunnis, as were some majority groups, such as the Shi'a Muslims of Iraq. The Iraqi Shi'ites were not reconciled to alien or Sunni rule and rose in revolt in 1920. The British helped to suppress the rising, the Royal Air Force brutally bombing the rebels into submission. The British then proceeded to install the Amir Faisal as king, but Iraq remained an unstable kingdom, with an ineffective and corrupt parliament. A few years later, in 1933, the Iraqi army carried out a horrifying massacre of Christian Assyrians. The British did not intervene; good relations with Iraq took priority.

The monarchy set up by the British did not prove a strong stabilising influence. After Faisal's death in 1933, his playboy son succeeded, only to kill himself six years later in one of his many sports cars. As in all the newly independent but politically under-developed states, the indigenous army played an increasingly important role. By the 1930s Iraqi independence was internationally recognised; Britain appeared to have fulfilled her task and preserved her interests in the form of a treaty signed in 1930 with a nominally independent Iraq. But internally Iraq remained as unstable as before, and in 1936 a successful coup saw the start of a series of military interventions in government.

At the start of the Second World War the German National Socialists seemed to many Iraqis to be natural allies; not only were they at war with the hated British, but they were enforcing a programme of anti-Jewish racial policies and were apparently ready to allow the Arabs their own way in Palestine. Germany's victories in 1940 and 1941 proved even more persuasive in turning Iraq away from the Allies. It now looked likely that Britain's dominance of the Middle East would be broken. Although Iraq was bound to Britain by special treaty, the country became a centre for anti-British Arab activity, and in the spring of 1941 a pro-German coup drove out the Regent and his government. For Britain the situation was very dangerous. With vital British interests, including the continued flow of oil from the Kirkuk wells, at stake, Churchill ordered the occupation of Iraq by British and Indian troops in May 1941. For the remainder of the war, and indeed for some years after, Britain was able to reassert her dominance, until it all collapsed in another bloody Iraqi coup in 1958.

Persia, during the First World War, was a partitioned country divided between Russia and Britain until the Russians departed after the Bolshevik Revolution. The end of the war in 1918 left the British in a dominant position with sole rights to the exploitation of Persian oil. As in Iraq, Britain in 1921 moved away from direct control to indirect influence. Among the leaders who seized power in Persia was the self-appointed commander of the Cossack Brigade, Reza Khan. He soon extended his military power over the whole country, crushing tribal revolts and political opposition, and dignifying his authoritarian rule with a constitutional façade. The Persian parliament, the Majlis, was dependent upon the rulers, not the other way round.

THE MIDDLE EAST BETWEEN TWO WORLD WARS, 1919-1945

THE MIDDLE EAST BETWEEN TWO WORLD WARS, 1919–1945

In 1925 Reza Khan had himself chosen as the new shah and declared the foundation of the Pahlavi dynasty, whose survival he sought to ensure by despotic rule and the murder of opponents. Britain did not intervene and even regarded it as in her best interests to deal with a strong ruler, allowing agreements to be made which would not be jeopardised by changes of leadership. What mattered was to maintain the Anglo-Persian oil concessions and the bulk of the profits. As oil production increased, the royalties paid to the Shah also grew; these he used to strengthen his army. Following the example of Kemal Atatürk, he forced Westernisation through. The emancipation of women and the spread of Western influences, especially education, began to change Iran, though more in the towns than in the countryside. Communications were improved and there was some industrial development. Centralised government, a growing bureaucracy and a new army represented the modern face of Persia, renamed Iran in 1935; but, for the masses of the poor, little was done. The Shah favoured the rich, the merchants and the landlords, over the majority, the poor peasants, from whom taxes and military service were exacted. To the poor's resentment against the rich was added a religious dimension: the peasants remained faithful to traditional Muslim teaching, while the middle and upper classes tended to Western secularism. The Shah's efforts to stimulate modernisation widened rather than narrowed the differences between the poor 90 per cent and the privileged few at the top of the social pyramid. The seeds of reaction were sown.

The Shah wished to throw off British influence and was attracted, when the Second World War began, to National Socialist Germany, as were other Middle Eastern leaders. In the midst of a devastating war Britain could not afford to jeopardise her oil supplies. The German invasion of the Soviet Union in June 1941 gave Iran an added importance as a vital Allied supply route to the Russians. With Britain and the Soviet Union now allies, joint action was speedily agreed. In August 1941 British and Russian troops invaded Iran and deposed the Shah. The twenty-one-year-old Mohammed Reza succeeded his father as shah. Under Allied supervision mass politics were encouraged, with the Russians, the Americans and the British seeking to broaden their support among the people. Thus the Russians promoted a pro-Soviet Tudeh Party with its base in the Soviet-occupied north. The British

supported tribal leaders in the south. The disruption the war brought to Iran compounded the problems from which the country was already suffering, but the national crises were postponed until the war's conclusion (pages 459–61).

France's power and role in the Middle East was once second only to Britain's. Despite her success in penetrating the eastern Mediterranean culturally and commercially – French became the language of the educated elite – French power was eroded by two world wars. The British succeeded in limiting her share of Ottoman spoils to the Lebanon and to a Syria much reduced in size. The Wilsonian rhetoric no longer allowed her to hold these as outright colonies, but until the mid-1930s France showed little interest in guiding her mandate to independence.

In 1920 the French made short shrift of Faisal's Syrian kingdom. They then proceeded to divide their mandate into five separate administrative nations and, when this proved unworkable, into two states (in 1925), the Lebanon and Syria. The mandatory governments were firmly controlled by the French military on the model of Morocco. Nationalist demonstrations and, all the more so, rebellions were harshly suppressed. Complete military control was the prior condition of France's civilising mission. In the aftermath of a serious Muslim revolt in Syria in 1925–6, the French decided it was expedient to grant more autonomy and proclaimed a Syrian republic in 1930 with a parliamentary constitution. Whereas Britain fostered Arab 'monarchies', the French promoted 'republics'. In 1936 a French–Syrian treaty, following the British example in Iraq, sought to lay the basis of a partnership between Syria and France in place of outright French domination. These were all genuine steps forward on the road to independence, but, as long as independence was not complete, Arab nationalism in Syria would not be satisfied. France had not abandoned her military predominance and so could, if her interests required it, reverse the whole process, as the British were to do in Iraq and Iran during the Second World War. The French military and bureaucracy maintained close supervisory control, their presence making it evident who the real rulers were.

In the Lebanon, with her large Catholic population balancing the Muslims, the French faced less opposition, and the constitution which they imposed sought carefully to distribute the offices and representation among the principal groups of inhabitants. But nationalist opposition to the French occupation developed among both the Christian Maronites and the Muslims. France's domination of the Levant became a vital symbol of her continued role as a great power, compensating her for the huge cost of maintaining a military establishment in the Lebanon and Syria, which more than counter-balanced any economic gains.

France took her cultural mission seriously and made sacrifices for it. Money and teachers were poured in to provide French education; hospitals were built and French judicial codes introduced. Communications improved, Beirut turned into one of the Middle East's best harbours, modern cities with fine public buildings and adequate utilities transformed the Ottoman towns and, most important of all, a genuine effort was made to improve the lot of the peasant, with impressive increases in agricultural productivity. France thus made a real and genuine contribution to the well-being of the peoples of Syria and the Lebanon, and left behind a valuable heritage. But it is in the nature of national fervour and religious fanaticism that even the good results are condemned if they follow from alien imposition.

In Europe, France suffered the humiliation of defeat in 1940. In Syria and the Lebanon, as well as North Africa, however, the French administration and army remained loyal to the government of Vichy France, and obeyed its orders. Although the generals on the spot wanted to fight on, suspicion of Britain's intentions also remained strong. Would she use this opportunity for her own purposes, perhaps purchase a Turkish alliance with the promise of handing to Turkey French mandatory territory? After the British attack on the French fleet at Mers el-Kebir on 3 July 1940 (page 266), there was little love for Britain, but the army was not pro-German either.

As long as Syria and the Lebanon did not become an enemy base, Britain, beset by enough difficulties already, was prepared to leave Vichy undisturbed in the Levant. But the Syrians, impressed by the German victories, became increasingly pro-Nazi. In neighbouring Iraq, in the spring of 1941, the pro-Axis coup threatened Britain's supply of oil and her strategic interests (page 296). The Iraqi uprising was enthusiastically welcomed throughout the Arab world, especially in neighbouring Syria. Had the

day dawned when the French and British would be thrown out of the Middle East and when, with German help, the Arabs would enter on their rightful heritage? Hitler sensed the opportunity of raising an Arab revolt against Britain.

Syria was the key. The Germans arranged to send military supplies to Iraq by way of neighbouring Vichy Syria. Vichy agreed to co-operate in return for substantial German concessions in France. Pétain's government also agreed to defend Syria against a British attack. So German planes landed on Syrian airfields with supplies for Iraq; but the effort was in vain. Churchill acted ruthlessly. If necessary the British would fight their former allies. Iraq was occupied before German supplies could get through and then, in June 1941, Britain, together with the Free French forces, invaded Syria and the Lebanon.

The Syrian and Lebanese campaigns signified a deep humiliation for France. The bulk of the French forces had refused to join the Free French troops and, though they capitulated, had been allowed to return to Vichy France. Despite the ceremonial return of Syria and the Lebanon to Free France, it was the British who were the clear masters of the situation. Capitalising on this, Britain demanded that the Free French proclaim, in order to appeal to Arab opinion throughout the Middle East, that the Lebanon and Syria would be free. De Gaulle had no choice but to comply. Deeply resentful, he accused Britain of driving France out of the Levant.

De Gaulle was more concerned to re-establish French authority than grant independence as Britain was demanding, but his efforts in that direction met with strong armed resistance from the Syrians. In May 1945 he ordered military action and a number of Syrian towns were shelled and bombed. But this was not 1920. Britain was in a position both of overwhelming military might and of decisive political influence in Europe and the Middle East. Supported by the United States, she forced the French out. It was a humiliating end to French rule, and de Gaulle neither forgot nor forgave.

The French were able to take comfort two years later when British rule in Palestine came to an end. Although Britain's Balfour Declaration had powerfully contributed to the creation of the State of Israel, there were in 1945 many Jews who no longer saw in Britain a benevolent friend. British policies had not won Arab friendship either. Was such failure inevitable? Could Jewish and Arab interests in the same land have been reconciled?

Biblical Palestine was a familiar concept in the West, but at the close of the First World War few people in Britain or elsewhere had more than the vaguest notion of its geographical extent; King David's and Solomon's empire had included much of today's Syria and Jordan, Egypt's Sinai as well as contemporary Israel. There was no simple guide to what the modern territorial frontiers should be since Palestine as a country had ceased to exist under the Ottoman Turks. It was the British who re-created Palestine within its post-1919 frontiers. To the north were Syria and Lebanon: how far should these countries extend? Agreement on the frontier was reached with the French government, then in 1922 the British decided to divide their sphere along the River Jordan, which thus formed the eastern frontier of Palestine. Beyond the river to the east a new country was born: the British Mandate of Transjordan.

The importance of the artificial frontiers arranged by the great powers shortly after the First World War is that they were never accepted as final by the peoples who lived within them. Syria could dream of being reunited with the Lebanon and of establishing a greater Syria by incorporating land belonging to present-day Israel. Jordan has claimed Palestinian lands west of the river, including Jerusalem. Israel claims the West Bank too – in biblical times Judaea and Samaria – which before 1947 was part of the Palestine Mandate. Possession has been decided by war and conquest and the Arab Palestinians, who wish to be subjects of neither Jordan nor Israel, have no country of their own. The Great War settlements did not bring peace to the Middle East: it was within the mandated territory of Palestine as geographically defined in 1922 that the Jews were to be permitted to build their National Home among the 650,000 Palestinian Arabs already living there.

As only 68,000 Jews inhabited Palestine in 1919 there could be no question of forming a Jewish state immediately. A National Home was a vaguer phrase; but there was no doubt about the end in view. Zionists, and also such powerful statesmen as Churchill, Smuts and Lloyd George, believed that a progressive Jewish state would, in future years, be re-created; the Balfour Declaration of 1917 was seen as providing a promise of assistance towards the goal of a pro-British Jewish state. How then

was the future viewed for the majority of the people who lived in Palestine? Until events proved otherwise, the Palestinian Arab population was regarded by the British as too sunk in poverty and backwardness to merit consideration. In some official papers they were contemptuously referred to as mixed 'Levantines'. The racial arrogance of an outmoded imperialist frame of mind was thus superimposed on the complicated Palestine issue. There was a significant silence about the political rights of the majority of the inhabitants of Palestine in the Balfour Declaration; they were given no more than an assurance that the 'civil and religious rights' of the 'non-Jewish population' would not be prejudiced. This language indicates that they were looked upon as if they were a minority rather than the overwhelming majority. Leading Zionists recognised that a Jewish state was a distant prospect and would require large-scale immigration of Jews; but that Jews in their masses would actually come was a matter of faith.

In 1919 the majority of Palestine's 68,000 Jews were settled in Jerusalem, most of them orthodox Jews who had lived there under Ottoman rule for four centuries in their own religious communities. These religious Jews were generally opposed to the aims of the 'new' late-nineteenth-century Jewish immigrants from Europe inspired by Zionist ideals of nationalism and statehood. It was persecution of Jews in the Russian Empire especially, and widespread anti-Semitism, which had led to the birth of Zionism before the First World War. Some 16,000 Zionist pioneers had settled in what had been part of the Ottoman Empire, mainly in agricultural colonies but also in towns. Working on the inhospitable land they had been inspired by the belief that they were laying the basis of a state for the Jewish people. Zionists rejected racialism, religious prejudice and anti-Semitism, and asserted, with Theodor Herzl, the father of modern Zionism, that the Jews were a people, dispersed in history, but one people wherever they now lived. One day they would return to Palestine, their historical country. The early Zionists saw themselves as colonisers reclaiming Jewish land, precursors of the Jewish nation. But the world was ruled by the great powers, so the Zionists would need the sympathy and protection of one of these if they were to set about building their own nation. Theodor Herzl had tried to enlist the help of the German Kaiser. The Zionist leader Dr Chaim Weizmann later turned to Britain.

The Jews bought land in Palestine and on this land built their kibbutzim, their own agricultural communities. The majority of the Arab population was seen by the Zionists and their Western supporters as benefiting rather than suffering from this economic development of the barren Palestine soil, which Jewish zeal and skill would turn into productive plantations. It was a vision wounding to the pride of the Arab elites, conscious of their own culture and resenting the label of backwardness, of being likened to the natives of Africa. From this followed the frequently heard Arab identification today of Zionism with 'Western imperialism'. There were also, it is true, educated, moderate Arabs who got on well with their Jewish neighbours, but the Jewish and Arab societies in Palestine were different from the beginning and the differences widened rather than narrowed. With the growing influx of Jewish immigrants, Jewish society became over-whelmingly European, democratic and socialist. Arab society, on the other hand, was traditional and patriarchal, and the few wealthy Arab landowners dominated the poor tenants scratching a living from the soil. Paradoxically, Arab landowners profited greatly from Zionism: because the Jews were eager to buy land, property values soared, and Arab wealth was hugely augmented. The growth of Jewish industry and commerce also introduced a new factor and transformed small Arab towns like Tel Aviv into modern Jewish cities. Development increased the gulf between the more prosperous urban and agricultural Jews and the mass of poor Arabs. The fundamental problem, however, was political: the question was whether Arab or Jew would ultimately control Palestine.

The rate of Jewish immigration and the related question of Jewish land purchases were, in the early years, at the heart of that problem. The Arabs did not, after all, turn out to be a negligible political factor. There was indeed a widespread Arab reaction against the Balfour Declaration. Arab nationalism and expectations had been aroused by Faisal's establishment of an Arab kingdom in Damascus in 1918 (see page 443). In October 1919 Curzon, who did not share his predecessor's Zionist sympathies, replaced Balfour in London as Foreign Secretary. British official views were hardening against the wider Zionist aspirations and moving towards a policy of even-handedness as between Arabs and Jews, which meant taking the Arab point of view into account. What the Arabs feared was

that, as soon as a large Jewish population was built up in Palestine, the Zionists would impose their own Jewish state on all the Palestinian people. Accordingly, they wished Jewish immigration to be restricted. By early 1920, tension between the Zionists and the Arabs had risen dangerously. The British responded by limiting Jewish immigration and imposing annual quotas, a policy that was anathema to the Zionists, who wished Jews to enter Palestine freely. Nevertheless, the British in 1920 imposed a quota of 16,500 for one year. This was, even so, more than the Arab political leadership could accept and they organised their followers to react with violence. In May 1921 Arabs attacked Jews and Jews retaliated. By the time the British could bring the violence under control, forty-eight Arabs and forty-seven Jews had been killed. It was the beginning of the tragic sequence of bloody Arab–Zionist conflicts.

The British now tried to allay Arab fears and to make further concessions to their views. First immigration was suspended, then it was announced that Jewish immigration would be strictly controlled, restricted to the economic absorptive capacity of the country. The Jews were not to take over the whole of Palestine: their National Home would be established in only a part of the country. But this reassurance had a boomerang effect, for Churchill, as Colonial Secretary, also explained that the Palestinian Arab majority could not expect to be set on the path to independence like the other Arab mandates, owing to the pledge of a National Home given to the Jews. The denial of independence to the Jews because of the Arabs, and to the Arabs because of the Jews, had all the makings of a bankrupt policy. Finally, the British undertook to take some account of local political attitudes; a legislative council, with more Arab members than Jewish, as well as British nominees, would be set up. The British hope was that the Jews and Arabs would work together in this forum, but the Arabs rejected the proposal out of hand. They also refused to form any representative Arab organisation in parallel with the existing Zionist organisation, later known as the Jewish Agency. The refusal of the Arabs to co-operate politically with the British, and to provide an elective Council of Palestinian Arabs, weakened their position. The Jewish Agency, mean-while, became the nucleus of an effective government for the Jews.

Yet the problem of the Jewish state and the

pressure of would-be Jewish settlers appeared to be easing in the 1920s. After an initial influx of Jews, immigration slackened. In 1927 more Jews actually left Palestine than entered, and in 1928 the net increase was only ten. However, Zionists and Arabs still wanted assurance about the future. The British Labour government elected in 1929, buffeted by Zionist demands for a coherently defined policy, did not follow a steady course: in 1930 promises were made to halt Jewish immigration altogether; then, in 1931, it was allowed to continue. This tendency to veer first one way and then the other only encouraged more violence in Palestine and increased the pressure on London from both sides in the struggle to influence British policy.

It was Hitler's persecution of the Jews in Germany, and the rest of the world's rejection of large-scale Jewish immigration, however, that more than anything transformed the Palestine question in the 1930s and after the Second World War. All of a sudden there were hundreds of thousands of Jews who wished to escape the Reich. The fate of the Jews of continental Europe appeared to prove the Zionist case that the Jews would always be maltreated and so had to possess a country of their own. Before 1933 only a minority of Jews had supported Zionism, though prominent men were among them. The great migratory wave of Jews from the late nineteenth century onwards moved out of Russia and Romania west to Germany, France, Britain and, above all, the United States. Hitler's violent persecution converted more Jews to Zionism in the 1930s than Herzl had done. But from 1936 onwards conversion to Zionism was less important a factor in the pressure to enter Palestine than the closing of the doors of the European countries and the United States to large-scale immigration of the increasingly desperate German and, later, Austrian and Czechoslovak Jews who had fallen under Nazi German rule. Their fellow Jews in Palestine were willing to provide refuge and to share their possessions; Jews in other countries were willing to provide financial aid to enable their persecuted co-religionists to emigrate; the Germans wanted to force them out of the expanding Reich, yet the British mandatory authority in Palestine, fearing Arab reactions, barred the way to any but controlled immigration. Nevertheless, between 1932 and 1936 the quotas were sufficiently large for the Jews who wished to leave Germany and to settle in Palestine

to be able to do so, encouraged by the National Socialists, who for a time agreed to the transfer of Jewish property. Emigration from Germany soared, reaching a peak of 62,000 in 1935 alone.

As we have seen, it was precisely Jewish immigration that lay at the root of Arab fears. If the Jews gained a majority in Palestine they would not be satisfied with a Jewish Home in Palestine, but would demand a sovereign Jewish state, to which the Arabs now in a majority would be subjected. In just two decades from 1919 to 1939, the Jewish population of Palestine had increased sevenfold, while the Arab population had not quite doubled. The trend was all too clear. With financial help from abroad, the Jews purchased land from absentee Arab landlords and found work for their co-religionists. Not surprisingly, the displaced Arab tenants and workers were easily aroused to religious fanaticism and hatred of the Jews by Arab politicians led by the Mufti of Jerusalem, Haj Amin. Haj Amin, a nationalist, was corrupt and totally unscrupulous in dealing with Arab opposition to his leadership, and the murder of Arab opponents and terror thus became an unstated part of his political programme. Yet he also enjoyed genuine large-scale backing from Palestinian Arabs fearful of the spectre of a Zionist-dominated Palestine.

### Population of Palestine, 1880–1939

|      | Jews    | Arabs     |
|------|---------|-----------|
| 1880 | 24,000  | 475,000   |
| 1919 | 60,000  | 640,000   |
| 1931 | 177,000 | 859,000   |
| 1939 | 429,000 | 1,010,000 |

The Arab nationalist movement was implacably hostile to any Jewish development or to Jewish–Arab collaboration. The Mufti mobilised the Arabs not only against the Jews but also against the British. In the spring of 1936 an Arab strike was called and violence broke out. Jews were once again the target and for a time the Arab political leadership presented an unaccustomed united front. But the British hit back, refusing to reduce Jewish immigration and imprisoning Arab terrorists. Palestine was on the verge of civil war. Determined to restore order and to find a solution, the British responded with massive troop reinforcements. A Royal Commission was sent to investigate and its conclusions were embodied in the important Peel Report, published in July 1937. The commissioners had realistically concluded that the Arab and Jewish communities were irreconcilable and recommended that Palestine should be partitioned between Arab and Jew. Partition of a small country was a bitter pill for both Zionists and Arabs to swallow. The Zionists, after careful deliberation, finally accepted partition as a solution which would give them a small state in northern Palestine. It was a starting point. But the Arabs rejected independence if it meant partitioning Palestine; no less unacceptable to the Palestinian Arabs was the loss of Jerusalem, which under the partition plan would have remained a permanent British mandate.

The British government accepted the report as the basis of policy in Palestine. But it was one thing to adopt a policy, quite a different matter to enforce it against strong opposition. The Palestinian Arabs were reacting with increasing violence, and in 1938 their revolt was renewed; there was fighting throughout Palestine, with Jewish settlements and British troops and police being attacked by militant Palestinian Arabs. The British reacted fiercely, executing convicted Arab terrorists and arming the Jews to defend their outlying settlements, which in turn strengthened the Haganah, the Jewish secret army. The Arab revolt continued into 1939. Despite Britain's firm response in Palestine, in London the government retreated from forcible partition against Arab wishes. Just when the need for Jews to leave Europe became most urgent, Britain further restricted immigration into Palestine. For five years Jewish immigration would be limited to 75,000 and thereafter would be permitted to continue only with Arab consent. The Zionists reacted with predictable anger: the new quota meant not only that the threatened Jews of central Europe could not be rescued, but that the Arabs would remain a large majority in an unpartitioned Palestine. Thus dreams of statehood, so recently endorsed by the British, were dashed again. British calculations were simple: the Arabs far outnumbered the Jews in the Middle East; in a war with Germany, Arab friendship was important and uncertain, while Jewish support could, it was thought, be counted on, because the war would be fought against the common German enemy.

In Palestine, British troops finally crushed the Arab revolt but the Palestinian Arab political leadership continued to protest that British policy was too favourable to the Jews and was denying Palestinians their independence. The Second World War and the mass murder of between 5 and 6 million European Jews by Hitler's executioners transformed the Palestine question. From this searing experience the State of Israel emerged, peopled by Jews ready to defend with their lives a country of their own. In their eyes the injustice to the Palestinian Arabs paled in significance when compared with the fate that had befallen 5 million European Jews under Nazi rule in a world that had even placed obstacles in the way of saving them and their brethren. Such murderous indifference created a new hardness and bitterness among Jews. The Arab cause, in the meantime, was not helped by the attitude of the Arab political leadership to the global contest. The Second World War found the Arab world on the sidelines, more hostile to its British 'protectors' than to the Nazi aggressors. In 1941 the Mufti became Hitler's ally and tool, the chosen Führer of the Arabs: a German victory, it is clear, would have meant the destruction of the Jews of Palestine and of the whole of Europe. But even while Jews all over the world wanted the Allies to win and fought in Allied armies, Zionists were preparing for the post-war period. Among them were extreme nationalists ready to fight not only the Arabs but also the British rulers if necessary to create a Jewish nation.

# CHAPTER 45

# Britain, Israel and the Arabs, 1945–1949

Military victory in 1945 sustained the illusion of Britain's imperial dominance a decade longer. But the rising tide of nationalism in Turkey, Egypt and throughout the Middle East since the 1920s should have served as a warning signal. Now after the Second World War popular British support for empire was rapidly ebbing away, especially now that it could be seen to involve sacrifice and to impose financial burdens.

Governments, both Labour and Conservative, faced a difficult task defending the remaining outposts for what were perceived as strategic or economic reasons. The two came together in Iraq, which had been occupied during the war by the Russians in the north and the British in the south. When the war ended, the Russians were reluctant to move out. Oil was now the lifeblood of the West, and Britain and the United States were determined to retain the Middle East as a Western preserve. In 1946 the Russians at last bowed to the pressure on them exerted through the United Nations and withdrew their troops.

The Russians did not threaten Palestine. But the future of this land, with its special significance to great cultures and religions, was once more heading towards bloody conflict. Here the Anglo-American alliance was most strained immediately after the war. Peace in Palestine had been maintained only by the overwhelming military strength of an occupying outsider, first the Turks and since 1919 the British. Both Arabs and Jews claimed it as their homeland. So at the end of the war Britain faced challenges throughout the Middle East. In Iran and Iraq nationalism focused on foreign control of oil resources; in Egypt it was Britain's military occupation of the country and her control of the Suez Canal. The ferment of the Middle East was due not only to struggles against foreign powers but also to the rivalries of the Middle Eastern nations among themselves and to the social conflict between the ruling elites, the emerging middle classes and the masses of poor. In the immediate aftermath of the war, Britain played a decisive role.

Ernest Bevin, the British Foreign Secretary in the Labour government of 1945, was clear about the choice facing his country. He resisted arguments that Britain's post-war weakness would force her to give up a dominant role in the Middle East. He knew perfectly well that Middle Eastern societies were backward and feudal and that social upheavals in the long run were inevitable. He was a socialist at home and an imperialist abroad. Britain's standard of living was dependent on Arab oil, and what mattered was the immediate future. Britain should not, therefore, withdraw. But there was a solution: imperial dominance might be made more palatable by creating a framework of Anglo-Arab partnerships. If this meant partnerships with feudal princes and kings, so be it; British interference in the internal affairs of Arab nations would otherwise only arouse the Arab cry of imperialism. Once the social upheavals had taken place, Britain could then establish good relations with the new leaders. Not everyone in the Cabinet agreed. The Prime Minister

Clement Attlee believed that imperialism, even when cloaked by Bevin's palliatives, would prove impossible to sustain. Would it not be better for Britain to retire with goodwill ahead of time, as she had agreed to do in India? The West faced a fundamental problem in the Middle East: how to ensure the future stability of the region, and how best to meet the needs and wishes of its peoples without jeopardising the West's vital strategic and economic interests.

In Iraq at least British interests appeared secure in 1945. In the Prime Minister, Nuri-es-Said, London believed it had a firm pro-Western friend. A new Anglo-Iraqi alliance treaty was concluded in January 1948 which established Iraqi control over British bases in Iraq in peacetime, but provided for military assistance in war which meant in effect that Britain could then reactivate the bases. It was ironic that British socialists should make a deal with politicians like Nuri, who represented the interests of the wealthy landowning class opposed to social reform. But Nuri had underestimated the anti-British feelings in Iraq, which were whipped up into a frenzy immediately after the conclusion of the alliance treaty. The treaty was now dead and Britain's influence became more precarious though it persisted for another decade.

Britain favoured agreement between the Arab states, which was to be further enhanced by a regional grouping. In March 1945, with Britain's blessing, the Arab League was founded. Despite the yearning for greater unity in the Arab world, however, the ruling elites were not able to provide it. Abdullah, the Hashemite ruler of Transjordan, despised the backward Egyptians and looked on them as degenerate Arabs. Nor was there any love lost between the Hashemites and the rival and victorious dynasty of Ibn Saud in Saudi Arabia. Other Arab nationalists looked down on poverty-stricken Transjordan as a client state in British pay. The Arabs were deeply split. Egypt and Iraq eyed each other with hostility, both laying claim to leadership of the Arab world.

The Arabs, including the Egyptians, had been largely hostile spectators during the Allied struggle against Germany. Although Egypt was nominally independent, the British troops swarming throughout Cairo and Alexandria, and guarding British bases along the Suez Canal during the war, gave every appearance of moving about in an occupied country. The end of the war did not essentially alter the situation. The Suez Canal and the Suez bases remained under foreign control. A better relationship could be built only on a revision of the 1936 treaty (page 443).

Meanwhile, Britain's post-war economic plight required that expenditure be avoided wherever possible. Thus Bevin was prepared to make extensive concessions to Egyptian national feelings, but insisted on ironclad treaty guarantees that the Suez Canal would never fall into hands hostile to Britain. In May 1946 the Attlee government accepted the principle of a complete military evacuation in times of peace. Eventually in October of that year a draft alliance treaty was agreed against a background of mounting Egyptian violence in the streets. Britain undertook to withdraw her forces by September 1949, but Egypt had to agree to invite the British back to their Suez bases and to co-operate with Britain if any conflict threatened 'against countries adjacent to Egypt'. Yet the new treaty was never concluded; what wrecked the negotiations was Egypt's claim to sovereignty over the Sudan, which Britain was not ready to accept. By then, attention was no longer focused on Egypt: Britain's difficulties there were overshadowed by the crisis in Palestine.

Both Arab and Jew in 1945 considered that British rule in Palestine was destined to end soon. The growth of both Arab and Zionist nationalism meant that foreign rule could be maintained only by an increasing use of force. But what form would a Palestine state take? During the years between the two world wars no clear indication emerged. Some sections of the Arab population of Palestine were ready to take up arms against the Zionists and the British to prevent an increase in the rate of Jewish immigration. They feared that the talk of a Jewish Home in Palestine only obscured the real objective of turning Palestine into a Jewish state. These fears proved stronger than the amicable relationships between many moderate Jewish and Arab leaders and between many ordinary Arabs and Jews.

The Nazi slaughter of between 5 and 6 million Jews during the Second World War, while the rest of the world looked on, entirely changed Jewish attitudes: noble words and mere promises to punish the perpetrators did not help the Jews murdered in the death camps. Yet many Arabs, in their hostility to British colonialism, had sympathised with the Nazi rather than the Allied cause during the war.

Support for Zionism and a Jewish state in 1945 became overwhelming among the Jews both of Palestine and in the rest of the world. Never again would mass murder be permitted; Jews were ready to fight to prevent it, to create their own nation, to guarantee the future survival of Jews everywhere. That the creation of Israel would involve injustice to the Arabs in Palestine was an inevitable consequence, because the territory of a viable Jewish state would contain almost as many Arabs as Jews. After Auschwitz, the chances of finding a solution in a federal nation with equal rights for Arab and Jews and with something less than full Jewish control had vanished. What followed between 1945 and 1949 was a bloody struggle between the Jews, the British and the Arabs.

The British despaired of finding any solution to which both Arabs and Jews could agree. Partition was the only practicable policy. In the last resort the Jews would have accepted it, but the Arabs were ready to resist it by force. Thus in the end military arms would decide the issue; to enforce partition Britain would have been drawn into fighting the Arabs. But her interests were overwhelmingly involved in maintaining goodwill with the Arab nations. Bevin solved the dilemma by handing responsibility over to the United Nations. Meanwhile, as long as Britain continued to station her troops in Palestine and to be responsible for law and order and for the administration, she was exposed to both Jewish and Arab hostility.

The position of the Jews in Palestine was precarious. They faced catastrophe if the British should depart before they could sufficiently mobilise to augment their own armed defence force, the Haganah. The Zionist leader David Ben Gurion tried to persuade the British to delay their departure, appealing to Bevin as late as February 1947. He offered to root out Jewish terrorism against the British, provided the British troops stayed. Bevin believed that the Ben Gurion offer was just a tactic to build up a Jewish majority under cover of the Mandate.

The acceptable face of Zionism was represented by Chaim Weizmann, who more than anyone had been responsible for securing the Balfour Declaration in 1917, and by David Ben Gurion; the Haganah was the tolerated armed wing of the Jewish Agency. The Irgun, led by Menachem Begin, who eventually became prime minister of Israel in 1977, belonged to the unacceptable face of Zionism, and

the Stern group was even more extreme. Begin and Stern were ready to fight the British, who were (in their eyes) accomplices of the Nazis in their failure to take all possible steps to rescue the Jews from the Holocaust. Begin was a Pole, a member of the East European Jewry whose homelands had become one great graveyard. In the struggle for Israel's survival, both the Irgun fighters and all Jews able to bear arms would be needed once the British had left, so the breach between Ben Gurion and Begin could never be total.

Jews of all political complexions in Palestine were ready to help outwit the British authorities to make it possible for the Jewish survivors, sailing in their ramshackle boats from the displaced-persons camps in Germany, to land secretly in the Holy Land. From the beaches, where men and women were waiting for them, they were smuggled into the Jewish agricultural settlements – the kibbutzim. In material terms these refugees were no great catch: penniless men, women and children, the sick and the old predominating over the able-bodied. For them Palestine was a haven – it was what the ideal of a Jewish state was all about. The 'illegal' immigration did not always succeed; the Royal Navy had the unenviable task of intercepting and boarding the boats and forcing the refugees to new camps in Cyprus. The seizure of one such ship, the *Exodus*, led to worldwide condemnation of Britain, especially when the refugees were shipped back to Hamburg, to the country responsible for the Holocaust. It was a gift for Zionist propaganda.

For Britain the option of remaining in Palestine became increasingly less attractive. The price that was being paid for the strategic base was too high: 100,000 British troops were being tied down in Palestine to try to keep the peace, which they increasingly failed to accomplish. The British administration, the army and the police were exposed to hostility and attack. British conscripts were being killed in raids carried out by the Irgun and its splinter groups, the Lehi. The Irgun's answer to a massive military and police action to round up suspects and disarm Jewish irregulars was to blow up the King David Hotel in Jerusalem, which housed the British Army and Secretariat Headquarters, on 22 July 1946. Menachem Begin later claimed that part of the plan had been to avoid loss of life and that sufficient warning had been given by telephone. But the time allowed between the telephone call and the explosion was far too

*The Promised Land. On 22 July 1946, the King David Hotel in Jerusalem is bombed (top). In September 1947, Jews in Germany seeking to embark for Israel are forcibly repatriated by British troops and sent to a Displaced Persons Camp at Lübeck (right). Under the watchful gaze of Zionist pioneer Theodor Herzl, David Ben Gurion proclaims the State of Israel at 4pm on 14 May 1948 to the strains of the Jewish Philharmonic Orchestra playing the national anthem.*

short; part of the hotel collapsed and ninety-one people were killed. An attempt was also made to plant a bomb in the Jerusalem railway station, but this was fortunately frustrated in time. In all, between August 1945 and September 1947, some 300 people lost their lives as a result of terrorist action, nearly half of them British; seven captured Jewish terrorists had been executed, two awaiting execution had committed suicide, and another thirty-seven were killed fighting. It was the manner of the loss of these lives as well as their actual number that caused such revulsion.

The decision to withdraw from the thankless task of governing Palestine had broad British public support. The British government was not prepared to enforce partition on the Arabs by military force. Nor, for all its criticisms of British policy, was the Truman administration willing to do so. The Jews were to be left to fight for their own national survival, a decision which came as no surprise to Jewish leaders like Begin. In February 1947, the British Cabinet decided to give notice to hand the Palestine problem to the United Nations by mid-May 1947. The last vain hope was that this deadline would bring Arabs and Jews to the conference table.

The United Nations appointed a Special Committee on Palestine, though it was boycotted by the Arab political leadership. In August 1947 the committee reported that Palestine should be partitioned into an Arab and a Jewish state, but that the economic unity of Palestine should be maintained; the committee also suggested that for another two years Britain should continue to administer Palestine under the auspices of the United Nations and that during this transitional period 150,000 Jews should be admitted. The possibility that the transitional period might be extended was also envisaged. Thus the UN committee had reached much the same conclusions as the British Peel Commission ten years earlier. Did it stand any better chance of winning acceptance in the face of Arab hostility? The United States and the Soviet Union, moreover, would both need to give the UN plan their backing if sufficient votes were to be cast to provide the necessary two-thirds majority in the General Assembly.

In the event, both the United States and the USSR, though the Cold War was at its height, voted in favour of the UN partition plan. Hitherto the Soviet Union had always opposed Zionism as an ideology likely to inflame Jewish Soviet citizens. One can only conjecture about the reasons for Russia's change of front. Possibly the Soviet leadership calculated that the creation of Israel would undermine Western relations with the Arab states and thus provide for the Soviet Union a means of entering the Middle East, or even that a socialist Israel was likely to become a natural ally. The American State Department and the British Foreign Office were well aware of these dangers and were doubly anxious now that Middle Eastern oil was becoming a crucial factor in Western industrial development. They wanted to avoid a policy that was bound to arouse Arab hostility.

At this critical stage President Truman's attitude was probably decisive. His sympathies for Zionism were deep and genuine; but the electoral advantage of appealing to the American-Jewish vote was at least a bonus in supporting a UN partition plan that would create a Jewish state. With the United States and the Soviet Union organising support at the UN, the required two-thirds majority in favour of partition was achieved when the vote was called in the General Assembly on 29 November 1947.

The intervening months were among the worst time for the dying British administration and the British troops. In a vain attempt to save Irgun terrorists from execution, two British sergeants were kidnapped by Irgun and found hanged on 31 July 1947. There was an outcry and revulsion in Britain.

The British Cabinet now concluded that Britain's total withdrawal had become inevitable.

The months between the end of November 1947 and 14 May 1948, when the last British soldier left and the State of Israel was proclaimed, were extraordinary. The British would not co-operate with the UN on the partition plan and when fighting between Arabs and Jews began in December 1947 they increasingly confined their authority to military camps and police stations. The Jewish Agency emerged as the effective Jewish government and made desperate preparations to fight for the Jewish state against the expected Arab assault.

The Grand Mufti of Jerusalem was also mobilising Palestinian Arabs, and sporadic fighting broke out between Jews and Arabs. Beyond Palestine the Arab League began planning to raise 'volunteer' armies against the day the British departed. Their mission was to overrun the Jewish state while it was still in its infancy. By April 1948, even before the British had left, the Arab threat to isolate Jerusalem completely, with its large Jewish population, as well as other Jewish settlements, had become very real indeed. The fighting spread. The Jewish leadership saw its only chance of salvation in declining to wait for the co-ordinated Arab attack. In April and May the Haganah seized the initiative and undertook a number of offensive operations. They succeeded in checking the Arabs.

The first Arab–Israeli War created a particular problem that was to fester and provoke unrest in the Middle East to the present day: the Palestinian refugees. In the territory assigned to Israel by the UN in 1947 lived some 510,000 Arabs and 499,000 Jews. The majority of these Arabs fled in fear of their lives, leaving their land and possessions to be taken over by the Israelis; half of them had already left before the British Mandate had ended. They had genuine cause for terror; many panicked, caught in a war between Jews and the Arab invaders. Arab villages presented a special threat to the Israelis; when they supported Arab military units they were attacked. The ordinary Arab, however, who had lived on the land for generations was caught in the crossfire of war, just like the Jews. Jew and Arab were exposed to the danger of falling victim to atrocity. Irgun's 2000 fanatical fighters joined in the struggle, cooperating with but not subordinating themselves to the Haganah. The most horrific of Israeli attacks, which was intended to intimidate and drive out the Arabs, undertaken during the night 9 and 10 April 1948 by the Irgun on a village close to Jerusalem called Deir Yassin. Two hundred and forty-five men, women and children were murdered. Though the Israeli government and the Haganah repudiated the Irgun's savagery, the memory of Deir Yassin stained the foundation of Israel. After Deir Yassin many tens of thousands of Palestinian Arabs fled from the territory under Israeli control into Arab-controlled Palestine on the West Bank, into Transjordan, Lebanon, Syria and the Egyptian Gaza Strip. Unable to return to Israel these unfortunate people became pawns in Middle Eastern politics and the seedbed for the recruitment of militant Palestinian political, military and terrorist organisations. The Arabs also retaliated with terror to Deir Yassin, killing seventy-seven Jewish doctors and nurses in a convoy on their way to Mount Scopus. It was a savage conflict.

The Jewish Agency, during the early weeks of conflict, was desperate for arms. Once more Soviet support was critical. The Czechs were encouraged to transport weapons and an airlift was begun which delivered them just in time. In a tricky operation in April 1948 the Haganah organised a convoy of supplies to the 30,000 beleaguered Jews in Jerusalem. Once the Haganah took the offensive, the disunited Arab war effort began to crumble. After David Ben Gurion had declared Israeli independence on 14 May 1948 renewed fighting between the various Arab forces and the Haganah and Irgun broke out all over the country.

The Jews astonished the world by winning the first round, despite their apparently hopeless position confronted by the Arab world. The Arab armies proved less formidable than their rhetoric. It was nevertheless a desperate struggle at all points of the compass against greater numbers. The Israelis possessed not a single warplane nor any heavy military equipment. But the Arab armies of five states, Iraq, Syria, Lebanon, Transjordan and Egypt, were totally uncoordinated. Abdullah, King of Transjordan, was far more concerned to seize the West Bank of the River Jordan and to add this, as well as Jerusalem, to his kingdom than he was to destroy Israel. He had no intention of creating an independent Arab Palestine state. The Egyptians and Syrians too were intent on serving their own national interests. Responding vigorously and daringly the Israelis halted the Lebanese and Syrian attack in the north, and the attack was not pressed. Much more serious was the advance of the Egyptian

army along the coast to Tel Aviv, which stopped short just a few miles from the city. The Egyptians had also advanced to the suburbs of Jerusalem, which was also invested by Transjordan's British-led and -trained Arab Legion, a first-rate fighting force. The struggle for Jerusalem was the most bitterly fought of the war. The Arab Legion captured the Old City; despite bombarding the New City and causing heavy civilian casualties (1400), they failed to take that from the Israelis. Arab forces also sat astride the main Jewish supply route, the road from Tel Aviv to Jerusalem. In one of the most celebrated episodes of the war, the Israelis managed to construct a new road to the beleaguered city. At least part of Jerusalem was saved for the new state.

At the United Nations, meanwhile, a resolution was approved which authorised the enforcement of a truce on the exhausted belligerents. The truce came into force on 11 June 1948. Both sides, using what turned out to be no more than a breathing space to strengthen their military positions, ignored the truce provisions. A renewal of fighting was regarded as certain. While the Arabs increased their regular troops to 45,000, the Czechs and French sent large quantities of arms to the Israelis, including fighter planes. On 8 July 1948 fighting resumed. The Israelis went on the offensive; a second UN truce on the 18th was soon broken. Count Bernadotte charged by the UN with brokering a permanent peace, was gunned down in Jerusalem in September, probably by a group of extremists. The Israeli government now proceeded to imprison members of the Stern Group (Lehi). Israel's lack of control over murderous extremists had become a serious handicap in her international relations at a time when she desperately needed friends.

In mid-October 1948 fighting was once more renewed between the Israelis and the Egyptians, who continued to hold parts of the Negev which had been assigned to Israel by the original UN partition plan. The fighting ended in the defeat of the Egyptians in January 1949. Egypt's Arab allies, far from helping, took advantage of the catastrophe. King Abdullah of Transjordan who had already stopped fighting on 1 December 1948 and arranged a ceasefire with the Israelis declared the union of Palestine and Transjordan, annexed the West Bank and henceforth called his kingdom Jordan. This wily Arab ruler, alone among the Arab leaders, had greatly profited as regards territorial expansion from the Arab–Israeli War and drew upon himself the especial hatred of the Egyptians. Under the auspices of the UN Israel in the spring of 1949 concluded armistice agreements with all her neighbours, Egypt, Jordan, Syria and the Lebanon, but not with Iraq. It was not peace, because the Arab nations would not accept a permanent peace treaty with Israel, and the Arab refugee question continued to fester as the refugees lived mainly in makeshift camps sustained by the UN Relief Organisation. In the aftermath of the war, over the next decade, the centuries-old tradition in some Muslim Middle Eastern nations of tolerating Jewish communities in their midst was broken. Almost half a million Jews were driven out but, unlike the Arab refugees, they had a new home waiting for them in Israel. The influx enormously strengthened Israel, which as a result of the war had already gained considerable territory in the north, part of the West Bank and land in the south. Her territory had become more integral, instead of being divided into three parts connected only by two narrow land bridges. The Arabs felt humiliated by the victory of the Jews, whom they saw as Western imperialist intruders, and the British as the once dominant Middle Eastern power were blamed for the débâcle. Some six hundred thousand Palestinian Arabs deprived of their farms and property became penniless refugees. Hopes for a Palestinian Arab state were thwarted, and the Palestinian Arabs nursed a burning sense of injustice. The Palestinian question and hatred of Israel and Zionism also became powerful and emotive weapons in the political struggles of the Arab states themselves.

The Arab–Israeli War also showed up as nothing had done before the rivalries of the Arab states and their competition for land, leadership and influence. In the war itself they were more intent on gaining their own objectives than on helping each other or the Palestinian Arabs. The rivalry and bitterness between them was never submerged for long. Their disunity, their general military backwardness and the traditions of their societies in which the poor were exploited for the benefit of the rich landowners left them no match for an Israeli state, ardent, nationalist, modern and progressive, in which all Jews felt they had a stake and whose continued strength and existence they felt was their only guarantee against a second Holocaust.

# CHAPTER 46

# 1956: Crisis in the Middle East – Suez

The victory of Israel in 1949 marked a watershed in the history of the Middle East. It laid cruelly bare the comparative weakness of the Arab nations and the growing strength of the new State of Israel. In the Arab nations the upheavals that followed brought new forces to prominence. They had been developing, however, long before the outbreak of the war. The foundation of Israel in the heat of war was not alone responsible. But, within a decade of those Arab defeats, Britain's bases of power in Egypt, Jordan and Iraq had been eliminated by a renewed wave of Arab nationalism. Yet, as it turned out, the United States was unable to take Britain's place. The Soviet Union, in the longer term, fared no better: attempting to take advantage of the conflicts, she made her own costly entry, only to gain unpredictable and troublesome 'allies'. Western influence declined during the Cold War for the paradoxical reason that the Arab nations knew that the Western powers would defend them from Soviet attack. The Middle East, with its vast resources of oil in the Gulf and Saudi Arabia, was vital for Western industry and for Japan, leaving aside the strategic importance of the region.

As the West became more dependent upon Arab goodwill, so Western influence over internal developments in the Middle Eastern states diminished. The monarchial Arab states did not become more Westernised, constitutional and liberal; indeed, there was a decisive turn to authoritarian rule by new elites, to internal suppression, police states and torture. There was also a new urgency to build up

military and economic strength against the twin threat of Israel and Western interference. Israel alone remained Westernised and democratic, heavily dependent upon Western, especially American, financial and military support. As the United States' only reliable anti-Soviet ally in the region, Israel was able to follow an independent Middle Eastern policy, frequently to the discomfiture of her Western allies.

The Palestine war in 1949 weakened the undisputed hold of the Arab ruling classes of landowners and politicians over the nations created under Western tutelage after the First World War. The old ruling elites were not overthrown simultaneously, but were steadily supplanted in a process that saw radical change in the ten years after 1949 and that still has not come to an end. A new, much more violent Arab nationalism now swept through the Middle East. Pan-Arab divisions between Iraq and Egypt deepened, the international conflict of the Cold War provided added tensions, as well as opportunities for the new Arab leadership to play off West against East to extract supplies of arms and development aid.

The appeal of the new leadership lay in its calls for a renewal of Arab national pride and for complete independence from the Western powers, whether Britain, France or, later, the United States, even while the Arabs benefited from the Western shield of security against the threat of Soviet territorial expansion. The new leaders promised an acceleration of social change and a concern for the welfare of the poor masses, with the state playing a planning role. A new radicalism and impatience with the corruption of the past and with the Western imperialist connection stirred Arab society. There was a search for fresh solutions and frequent conflict about the best course to adopt. Communists sought revolutionary change, but the new rulers feared that such a pace would sweep them away as well. Some groups, such as the powerful Muslim Brotherhood, insisted that the only road to Arab salvation was to reject Western secularism altogether and to return to an Islamic past which would allow religion to embrace the whole way of life and guide all aspects of social policy and statecraft. Others insisted that outside help, whether Western or Soviet, was essential for rapid progress and that Islamic fundamentalism was an obstacle to modernisation. The emerging leadership derived its authority not from the ballot box or from constitutional procedures, but from violent coups. In this way the military replaced the landowners as the backbone of the new regimes. When they came to power the officers frequently had no central strategy nor any detailed policies; the coherence of their programme depended on the quality of the leadership. Only on one issue was there consensus: no recognition could be accorded to that usurper of Arab lands, the State of Israel.

In Syria the repercussions of the lost war contributed to a military coup in March 1949. Three further military coups occurred during the next three years, but it was not until 1966 that the secular socialist Ba'athist Party, strong in the army, seized undisputed power, by staging yet another coup. Neighbouring Lebanon, with her delicate compromises, began to fall apart when, in 1958, the Christian President attempted to forestall pro-Nasser and anti-Western Arab nationalist movements (for Nasser, see below). The struggle between Christian and Muslim groups plunged the country into confusion, and the presence of Palestinian refugees had added a further destabilising element to the kaleidoscope of the Lebanese polity. The United States threw her weight behind the Christian President, landed marines and for a time an uneasy peace was maintained between the various armed factions loyal to their own leaders, Druze, Sunni, Shia and Christian Maronite falangist. The threat of civil war was not banished, only postponed.

In Jordan too the rise of Arab nationalism made

itself felt. The astute King Abdullah, who had wanted to live peacefully with the Jews provided they would accept his rule over Palestine, and who had then gone on to capture the West Bank and half of Jerusalem during the Palestinian war, was assassinated by a Palestinian Arab in July 1951. His successor in 1952, after a brief interlude, was the young King Hussein, who managed to retain his throne only by preserving the loyalty of the army and – despite Jordan's continued financial and military dependence on Britain – severing treaty ties with the British, so asserting Jordanian independence. Saudi Arabia, still feudal, still disciplined by a fundamentalist Islamic tradition and mercenary Pakistani troops, remains the only major Arab nation apart from Jordan where the monarchy has survived into the last quarter of the twentieth century.

In Iraq, King Faisal II and the most powerful politician in the country, Nuries-Said, seemed to guarantee a firmly pro-Western conservative government, but Arab nationalism in Iraq in 1948 already limited the conservatives' freedom of action. There was no open break with Britain, but even Nuries-Said could not afford to identify himself too closely with the West. The Arab League, of which Iraq was a leading member, also contained Egypt, which disputed with Iraq the leadership of the Arab peoples. Policies of reform and development were too slow in Iraq; the landowners and conservative politicians had no wish to promote radical change, so Nasser's Egyptian revolution proved a serious threat to the 'old gang' in Iraq. In 1958 the Iraqi army led a bloody revolution. It came as a shock to the West, not least because of the brutal murders of Faisal and Nuries-Said. The alliance with the West was discarded.

In neighbouring Iran, after the Second World War, a groundswell of discontent threatened to oust the Shah and the conservative politicians from power. The withdrawal of the Russians and the provision of US advice and aid had not solved the inherent problems of Iranian society. A widespread rejection of foreign influence, both American and British, was just one indication of the growth of nationalism. The technologically advanced Anglo-Iranian Oil Company was the most visible sign of foreign exploitation, and though it provided much of the state's revenue it employed only a very small proportion of the Iranian working population. Despite the development of the oil industry, Iran was still one of the most backward Middle Eastern

*The Anglo-Persian oil refinery at Abadan. The Iranians demanded a greater share of the profits.*

nations and the peasant masses were sunk in poverty. Yet revolutions are made not by the backward masses but by emerging, politically conscious groups. Urban development, especially the growth of Teheran, expanded the number of artisans and shopkeepers at the bottom of the social scale, who formed, with a burgeoning bureaucracy, a disparate lower-middle class. But it was students who became the spearhead of revolutionary and nationalist sentiment, aided by a backlash of Islamic fundamentalism against modern Western ways and their accompanying corruption and secularism.

In the spring of 1951 the Shah's political control was loosened when opposition pressure forced him to appoint as prime minister a veteran, radical politician called Mohammed Mossadeq. With the struggle focusing on foreign influence – of which the most potent symbol was the Anglo-Iranian Oil Company – Mossadeq put himself at the head of the nationalist movement. The importance of Middle Eastern oil had increased exponentially since the period before the Second World War (page 437), so control of oil supplies became the vital new factor in the region's politics after 1945. In the five years following the war the production of crude oil was doubled from 250 million tons to 500 million; by 1960 production reached 1000 million tons. The

West's demand for oil seemed insatiable, output reaching 2000 million tons in 1968. By far the largest producer was Saudi Arabia, which also had the largest reserves.

Britain's position in the Middle East seemed seriously threatened when in May 1951 the largest oil refinery in the world, at Abadan, and all other installations of the Anglo-Iranian Oil Company were peremptorily expropriated and nationalised by Mossadeq. Anti-British rioting heightened the tension. The British Labour government considered using force to protect the valuable British investment, but the Prime Minister, Clement Attlee, wisely chose to work with the Americans and the United Nations to achieve a peaceful settlement. A nation could not be prevented from taking charge of her resources; the oil companies, moreover, had not paid a fair and proper price for the oil which they had been extracting. Pressure to settle was put on the Iranians by Britain and the United States, with British technicians withdrawing from Abadan and bringing the refinery to a halt.

But the most important lesson learnt by the oil-producing countries was that possession of the resources and installations did not give them complete control. Since the oil-producers had to export the bulk of the oil to the West, the international companies continued, through their marketing facilities and outlets, to exert great influence. Thus in 1951 the Americans co-operated with Britain to block the sale of oil produced by the national Iranian oil company. Mossadeq's moves, at first applauded, plunged Iran into economic difficulties and his political supporters began to fight each other. In August 1953, the Shah staged a coup to recover the powers he had lost, with strong support from America's Central Intelligence Agency and Britain's intelligence services. In the following year, the oil dispute was settled. For the next twenty-five years, until 1979, the Shah's authoritarian rule, with American support, appeared to provide the West with a secure ally.

Far-reaching in its consequences for the whole of the Middle East was the Egyptian revolution of 1952, which produced the dominant Arab leader of the 1950s and 1960s, Gamal Abdel Nasser. Defeat in Palestine had not immediately brought about the fall of King Farouk: there were plenty of other fuses besides Palestine that led to revolution. The inequitable distribution of land, made worse by a rapidly increasing peasant population, meant that living standards for the mass of under-privileged Egyptians were falling, not rising. The luxury and corruption of the Palace came to be symbolised by the figure of the gross King Farouk. Worse, the politicians and the King had failed to remove the British troops from the Suez Canal Zone. The last Palestine war was seen as the latest indication of the inability of Egyptian rulers to stand up to foreign, imperialist influence. The Wafd Party had also, by this time, become identified with weakness and corruption. A Wafd government in 1951 tried to deprive the British of any right to remain in the Suez bases by unilaterally abrogating the Anglo-Egyptian Treaty of 1936. The British did not leave, so all that this gesture demonstrated was the continued helplessness of the Egyptians.

Guerrilla attacks were launched on the British in their bases and were answered by British counter-attacks which culminated in a British assault on the Egyptian police headquarters in Ismailia. Forty-one policemen were killed in the battle that followed, martyrs of the Egyptian nationalist cause. With nationalist feeling aroused to a frenzy, Cairo was burnt and looted by mobs of angry Egyptians. Within Egypt, the only force, other than the British, able to restore order was the Egyptian army. The politicians had lost control and the army leadership now held the key to the future of Egypt. Farouk had long since become a spent force.

Inside the army a nationalist group of middle-ranking and younger officers conspired to seize power to provide Egypt with new leadership. Calling themselves the Free Officers, they were led by Lieutenant-Colonel Gamal Abdel Nasser. To provide a figurehead among the generals, General Neguib was won over to the conspiracy, but most of the senior military commanders remained loyal to the King.

Farouk believed he could rely on the army and underestimated the conspirators. They seized power in a bloodless coup in July 1952. The old order had collapsed without a fight and with amazing rapidity. Farouk was allowed to depart on his luxury yacht into exile. It was a revolution from above without any really popular participation. But there was no lament over Farouk and the departed politicians either. They had made too many enemies among influential groups, including the powerful Muslim Brotherhood, to be able to offer any effective resistance. Nor did the British see any reason for defending Farouk, who had so recently turned violently on the British presence in Egypt. They adopted a wait-and-see approach. There was no rioting in Cairo and the people evidently accepted the transfer of power.

The revolutionary colonels purged the army of the senior officers who had remained loyal to Farouk. Beyond this the Free Officers had no constructive plans for a new society or state. They knew, however, what they wished to end: the monarchy and corruption, British imperialism and Egypt's military weakness. When General Neguib sought real power, Nasser ousted him in the spring of 1954 and became Egypt's sole authoritarian leader. The Muslim Brotherhood, however, and the Wafd, both of which could still command popular mass support, stood in his way. They had taken the side of Neguib, so Nasser now marked them down for suppression. His own support, he noted, had come from the army and from the poor. Socialism, with its promises, appealed to the masses, and Nasser realised that by espousing it he would strengthen his popular base. He had come to power with no ready-made ideology; the two characteristic features of his regime, socialism and Pan-Arabism, were only gradually developed and adopted. Fundamentally, however, it remained a military dictatorship which won mass support from the Egyptian people. It relied heavily on his personal charisma.

Was there a clear division in the mid-twentieth century between those countries which used force to get their way and those which accepted international standards and took their obligations under the Charter of the United Nations seriously? There was certainly supposed to be. The Suez Crisis and the Hungarian rising occurring at the same time in November 1956, should have demonstrated to the world that contrast in the international behaviour of the powerful when confronting the weak. But it did not, at least to begin with. Yet it was British scruples, the wish to appear to be acting with right on her side, that ensured the failure of the Anglo-French attack on Egypt. The figleaf of rectitude with which the ingenious French had attempted to cover the aggression proved too transparent. There was an outcry in Britain and the government lost the necessary backing of a deeply divided electorate at home. Without that backing a democratic country could not for long wage a distant war. In the end the free world did not behave as the Soviets were doing in Hungary, and for one reason: the most powerful democracy, the United States, compelled Britain and France to withdraw and to accept the will of the United Nations, whereas Soviet control over Hungary after the brutal repression was allowed to endure.

Suez was a watershed in the process of differentiating between superpowers and the old great powers like Britain and France, now in the second rank. They had to accept their dependence and adjust painfully to their inability any longer to pursue global imperial policies on their own. The impact on the Middle East, Africa and Asia was profound, as elites in former colonies struggled for the control and then the independence of their countries. For all these reasons it is worth uncovering the twists and turns, hesitations and secret goings-on of the Suez Crisis. None of the countries involved, Egypt, Israel, Britain, the United States, France and the other Arab nations, followed clear and consistent policies from the beginnings of negotiations in 1954 to the invasion in November 1956. That makes it hard sometimes to distinguish the wood from the trees and from the tangle of undergrowth.

For Nasser and the Egyptians the desire to end a semi-colonial status and subservience to Britain took first place. British troops stationed in the Suez Canal Zone were an army of occupation on Egyptian soil. The Canal Company, with its headquarters in Paris, was alien too. It managed and organised the passage of ships through the Canal thousands of miles distant. No wonder that in the mid-twentieth century Egyptians saw the Company and its protectors as the successors of the imperialists who had first occupied Egypt in the 1880s. The Egyptians were regarded as backward by Westerners, 'wogs' incapable of running the Canal effectively by themselves. All this was deeply humiliating to nationalists in Egypt. Moreover, Egypt was still smarting from her defeat by Israel. As most Israelis had come from Europe in recent times they too were regarded as Westerners and Zionism as another form of imperialism. They had displaced hundreds of thousands of Palestinian Arabs during the war for Israeli independence. Now these Arabs were refugees in their own part of the world. Not that Colonel Nasser or any of the Arab leaders were much bothered about Palestinian Arabs. But Nasser's credentials as a Pan-Arab leader depended on espousing the Arab cause and proclaiming his enmity to the Zionist intruders.

Nasser knew that Egypt was militarily weak but he did have some cards to play. The Suez Canal had been constructed by Ferdinand, Vicomte de Lesseps in the typical imperialist manner of the nineteenth century. Ruthless and brilliant, de Lesseps had set up the Suez Canal Company and had plundered the Egyptian Treasury, while the Egyptians had supplied 20,000 forced labourers. Construction began in 1859 and was completed in 1869. When the Khedive went bankrupt he sold the Egyptian shareholding in the Canal to Britain for a mere £4 million in the famous financial coup masterminded by the Rothschilds for Disraeli. The Canal Company, with its British and French shareholders, did not actually own the Canal; the territory through which the canal was constructed remained under Ottoman–Egyptian sovereignty. The Company had merely acquired a concession to operate the Canal for ninety-nine years after its opening. Thus it would end in November 1968. That gave Nasser not only a moral historical claim for Egypt to assume control but also a legal one, provided he was prepared to wait. Conversely, for France and Britain time was running out.

The Zone through which the Canal ran was effectively controlled by British troops. Under the

Constantinople Convention of 1888 the Canal was to be 'free and open in time of war as in peace'. The Anglo-Egyptian treaty of 1936 was supposed to give Egypt real independence and was indeed a step towards it. But Britain extracted as the price the right to continue to occupy the Canal Zone for twenty years and even to reoccupy the rest of Egypt if necessary in the event of war. Britain made use of this right during the Second World War.

The time for renegotiating the alliance, then, was rapidly approaching in the 1950s. And here was the quandary for the West; in the era of Cold War antagonism, to concede completely equal rights in the Suez Canal to all countries, as required by the Convention of 1888, could allow the Soviet Union to secure a foothold. That was unthinkable as far as London and Washington were concerned. There was a way out, the solution the West had found for that other crucial international 'canal', the Straits of Constantinople. There was one exception to the requirement for free passage of international canals. The sovereign power through which the canal ran could take any measures it felt necessary for its defence. By tying Turkey into the NATO alliance the Soviets could be kept out. So, if Egypt could be induced to continue the Western alliance, the Soviet Union would be denied any influence. The situation would of course be catastrophically reversed if Egypt concluded an alliance with the Soviet Union!

With all the later talk about the sanctity of international obligations, the Cold War and the fear of Soviet penetration of the Middle East provide the key to an understanding of Washington's and London's policies in the early negotiations with Nasser. Anthony Eden, Foreign Secretary in Churchill's government, worked hard to secure a friendly agreement with Nasser over the issues outstanding between Britain and Egypt, and he was backed by the US Secretary of State John Foster Dulles. There was an additional issue of the future of the Sudan, hitherto under dual Anglo-Egyptian authority. In February 1953 agreement was reached that the Sudanese should decide their own future. To Nasser's surprise they opted not for union with Egypt but for independence. The following year Nasser was more successful. In October 1954 a new Anglo-Egyptian treaty was concluded which provided for the complete evacuation of all British troops from the Suez bases within twenty months. The bases were to be mothballed. This compromise

formula would allow Britain to reactivate the bases should war break out in the region. The treaty was to run for seven years until 1961. The British Chiefs of Staff calculated they would not need a Suez base after 1961 anyway. Nonetheless, with the Suez Canal still foreign-owned and foreign-run, it was less than immediate complete freedom for Egypt. The Muslim Brotherhood denounced Nasser's agreement with Britain as treachery, while in London Eden was accused by right-wing Conservatives of 'scuttling from the Canal Zone'. Eden had made considerable concessions on Britain's behalf and had taken a risk with his popularity at home, which made him later all the more sensitive to the charge of appeasing the Egyptian dictatorship.

Britain, together with France and the United States, claimed the right to exercise a major role in ensuring that stability should be preserved throughout the Middle East. During the years immediately following the signature of the armistice between Egypt, Israel and the other Arab states in 1949 an uneasy peace prevailed. But the Arabs refused to accept that Palestine had disappeared, her territory partitioned between the new sovereign State of Israel and an enlarged Jordan. The armistice could not be turned into a permanent peace. To stop the outbreak of another war the United States, Britain and France, by their Tripartite Declaration on 25 May 1950, sought to regulate the arms supplied to Israel and her Arab neighbours; and they appointed themselves policemen in the Arab–Israeli conflict, stating that 'should they find that any of these States was preparing to violate frontiers or armistice lines, [the three powers] would, consistently with their obligations as members of the United Nations, immediately take action, both within and outside the United Nations, to prevent such violation'. The Arab states and Israel were not a party to this treaty nor was the Soviet Union invited to join it. Indeed, the fear that the Soviet Union would take advantage of the Middle Eastern conflicts was one of the motives behind this Western co-operation. But, by leaving out the Russians, the unregulated supply of arms from the Eastern bloc led to the very arms race the West had tried to prevent.

The Declaration, with its assumption of great-power overlordship, was more impressive on paper than in actuality. Britain, France and the United States were uneasy partners. The United States believed, not unjustly, that Britain had still not abandoned her old colonial attitudes, which would alienate the Arab nations. The British, for their part, resented the growth of American influence and the way in which the United States was diminishing Britain's commercial stake. Although France was to co-operate with Britain in the mid-1950s at the time of the Suez crisis, co-operation was based on considerations of *Realpolitik*. Had not the British ruthlessly destroyed France's empire in the Lebanon and Syria at the end of the Second World War? The purpose of France's continued involvement in the Middle East was at least to retain, and if possible to expand, her shrunken influence in North Africa after the military débâcle in Indo-China (page 407). The most critical struggle of all was being waged in Algeria, which the French declared to be an indivisible part of France. Nasser's propaganda supported the Algerian rebels, and the tension was raised still further because the French were overestimating the quantity of weapons Nasser was able to send to the Algerian nationalists.

The United States too faced a dilemma. Britain and France were her most important Western allies but she also wished to be regarded as the friend of independent Arab nations; she saw herself as being free from the colonialist taint and condemned the old British and French attitudes. How to side with Arab nationalism as well as with Britain and France? There was no reconciling such a contradiction six years later during the Suez crisis of 1956. In strengthening US economic power in the region through the oil giants her disinterested friendship had in any case carried little conviction. America's opposition to social revolution – any form of socialism being regarded as little different from communism – meant that US support was given to kings, princes and feudal minorities, the 'old gang', thus making anti-Americanism an appealing slogan with which the political opposition in the Middle Eastern states could arouse the masses. British governments, whether Labour or Conservative, took a similar line to the Americans and had done so for much longer, allying themselves with the feudal leaders of the Arab peoples and failing to change course after the Second World War. For these Arab monarchs and their ministers the West became an essential pillar of support against their own peoples in opposition. But it exposed them to accusations of betraying Arab independence for the sake of maintaining their corrupt regimes. That their

accusers could be just as corrupt did not lessen the power of their propaganda.

Still, in 1954 it seemed that Anglo-Egyptian relations, and so Western influence, had been reasonably secured. But the Middle East in the aftermath of the Arab–Israeli War was an unstable region. Regional conflicts and hostilities might yet undermine the West. To promote a general peace in the Middle East was therefore the other side of the coin to the Cold War objective of keeping the Russians out.

The Arab refusal to accept Israel meant that no peace treaties were concluded between her and her Arab neighbours. The Arab states continued publicly to declare that they would attack and destroy Israel. In reality Nasser was seeking a peaceful solution from 1952 until February 1955, and secret, high-level Israeli–Egyptian negotiations were held but they led to no settlement. Britain, France and the United States had meanwhile stepped in as guarantors of the frontiers.

Making friends with Nasser, though, was not going to be easy. There was another bone of contention. Nasser's bid for revolutionary Pan-Arab leadership was opposed by the feudal, oil-rich rulers of Saudi Arabia and the sheikhs of the Gulf states. They in turn had the backing of the United States and Britain. Nasser's ambitions were also opposed by the kingdom of Iraq, whose pro-Western government had just concluded the military Baghdad Pact as a Turkish–Arab–Western-backed barrier against Soviet penetration. The Arab world in the mid-1950s was thus rent by the bitter rivalry and antagonism between Egypt and Iraq. In trying to be friends with both sides, Britain was attempting to ride two horses at once.

The Anglo-American Middle Eastern peace project was a secret effort known by the codename Alpha. In the very month that the Baghdad Pact was signed between Iraq and Turkey, in February 1955, Eden flew to Cairo to meet Nasser. The Egyptian leader left him in no doubt about his hostility towards the Pact but appeared more moderate on the Palestine issue, even discussing the possibility of peace with Israel. This gave some hope for Alpha, had it not been for the militant Palestinians. The Palestinian guerrillas, known as the *fedayeen*, had in 1953 begun conducting raids into Israel from Egyptian-held Gaza and the Jordanian West Bank. The Israelis responded with massive reprisal raids which they hoped would deter the countries hosting Palestinian fighters from allowing incursions into Israel. One such Israeli reprisal in October 1953 had destroyed much of the Jordanian village of Qibya; more than fifty men, women and children lost their lives in the attack. There were further, though less savage, reprisals against Jordan in 1954. Why then did the Palestinians continue their attacks? Their leader, Yasser Arafat, calculated that provoking Israeli strikes inside Jordan and Egypt would prove counter-productive for the Israelis: Jordan might not be able to strike back but Egypt could. The Israelis fell into the trap. A Palestinian raid from the Gaza Strip led to an Israeli counter-blow on 28 February 1955 in which sixty-nine mainly Egyptian soldiers and Palestinians were killed or wounded. This brought to an end the direct contacts between Israel and Egypt in pursuit of a peaceful solution of their differences. Nasser could not accept such a humiliation. Egypt's priority now was to increase her military strength to enable her to confront Israel at least on equal terms in the future. Nasser wanted a huge quantity of arms. He would get them from the West if he could; if he could not, he would get them from the East.

The prospects for Alpha had been reduced, if not extinguished. There was further desultory talk of a settlement with Israel, but Nasser insisted that Jordan should be given the Israeli Negev and that the new frontier should run across to Gaza. Then Jordan and Egypt would share a common frontier − and Egypt, as the stronger country, would have dominated Jordan. Such a proposal had no chance of acceptance.

In April 1955 Churchill retired and Eden became prime minister. With a small inner Cabinet of ministers, Eden dominated the foreign policy of his administration. During the summer of 1955 he and Dulles were still hoping to woo Nasser. His request for arms, however, ran into difficulties in Washington. Khrushchev saw his chance to vault the Baghdad Pact barrier and trumped anything Nasser could hope to secure from the West with an offer of planes and tanks on terms the Egyptian would find hard to refuse. That October the arms deal with the Soviet Union was publicly confirmed.

The dismay in London and Washington was nothing compared to the alarm felt in Israel. In November Prime Minister Ben Gurion started to plan for war. Israel's geographical position made her extremely vulnerable; a mere fifteen-mile

advance by an enemy would have cut the country in half. What is more, the combined populations of her Arab neighbours dwarfed Israel's. Unlike those neighbours, Israel had to draw on all of her manpower to wage war, but she could not do so for long without facing ruin at home. This determined Israeli strategy. The war had to be carried deep into enemy territory and to maximise the chances of success the enemy had to be caught off-balance. In such a mortal combat the Israelis were not concerned with legalistic arguments over who had technically started the war. As Israel interpreted it, the huge build-up of Egyptian arms meant that an Arab attack was only a matter of time. But who could she rely on to help her? Western supplies of arms were controlled by the Tripartite Declaration of May 1950, yet the Soviet Union and Nasser had driven a coach and horses through it. In the winter of 1955, the French began supplying arms to Israel, including their superb Mystère IV fighters. It was the start of a more intimate relationship between Israel and France, left in the cold by Britain and the United States.

Eden and Dulles had not, however, given up hope that autumn and winter of pulling Nasser back from the Soviet orbit. Nasser's great ambition was to transform the economy of Egypt and he planned to do so by means of a huge new High Dam at Aswan which would supply electric power and irrigation for the Upper Nile. The finance needed was to be provided by the World Bank, on condition that the United States and Britain contributed as well. Eden urged Dulles to support the deal in order to avoid a Soviet−Egyptian financial arrangement. An offer by Britain and the United States to finance the first stage was actually made in December 1955. There was at this point no British alignment with France, let alone with Israel − support for Israel would have alienated the very friends Britain and the United States wanted to make among the Arab states.

Yet within a few months the situation had totally changed. Britain and the United States increasingly suspected each other's policies and their co-operation came to an end. Britain instead, with much hesitation, forged an alliance with France and Israel, and was drawn into a secret plan to defeat Egypt and topple Nasser. What had brought about such an extraordinary upheaval, above all in British aims?

By March 1956, Nasser was seen by Eden as a danger to British interests in the Middle East, an unreliable leader deeply committed to the Soviet

Union. Cairo's propaganda against Britain's Arab friends, especially against Britain's influence in Jordan, and Egypt's hostility to the inclusion of Jordan within the Baghdad Pact sparked off the breach. Jordan's King Hussein was too weak to resist the pro-Nasser sentiment that swept through his country. Bowing to pressure, on 1 March 1956 he dismissed the British officer, known as Glubb Pasha, who commanded Jordan's Arab Legion. Eden reacted angrily: it seemed to him that Nasser was intent upon undermining Britain in the Middle East. From then on Eden was determined by one means or another to rid the Middle East of Nasser.

In April 1956 Dulles and Eden agreed to let the Aswan loan negotiations languish. Nasser was now no longer seen as a possible supporter of the West. Britain's and America's withdrawal was formally announced by Dulles on 19 July 1956. That Congress would vote the necessary money to part-finance Nasser's dam with the World Bank was by now inconceivable. But the abrupt manner of the announcement unnecessarily and probably unintentionally increased the snub to Nasser, who could not meekly accept such a setback. His next move should not have come as such a surprise. On 26 July, in a dramatic speech in Alexandria, Nasser declared that Egypt had nationalised the Suez Canal Company, thus ending Western control twelve years ahead of the expiry date of the Suez concession. Overnight he became the hero of the Arab world. He was not acting unlawfully, however, as he offered to compensate the Company's shareholders. Nasser had turned the tables on Britain and the United States. At first this was not appreciated. With what was still a common Western arrogance, it was widely believed that the Egyptians would not be able to manage the Canal once the European pilots and technicians were withdrawn. It came as a shock therefore when the Egyptians, with some help from Eastern communist friends, demonstrated that ships would continue to pass through the Canal without difficulty.

For Eden, Nasser's behaviour, little more than a month after the last British troops had left the Canal in compliance with the 1954 Treaty, was a personal humiliation which exposed him to a renewed attack from the Conservative right. Moreover, with two-thirds of Western Europe's oil passing through the Canal, Eden believed that Nasser's control of it would give him a stranglehold on the economies of Britain and Western Europe, or as Eden graphically put it, the Egyptian dictator 'would have his hands on our windpipe'. If Nasser was allowed to get away with it, Eden concluded, there would be no stopping him from trampling over other British interests. Personal anguish, an exaggeration of the threat to Britain and ill-health all combined to drive Eden forward (albeit with Cabinet support) into an ill-considered international adventure.

The decision in London to prepare a military option had been taken by the British Cabinet on 27 July, a day after Nasser's speech nationalising the Suez Canal. There was agreement that, if all else failed, Egypt would be attacked and forced to accept an international agreement ensuring free passage of the Suez Canal not merely until the Suez Canal Company's concession ran out in November 1968, but in perpetuity. The Egyptians, it was assumed, were not capable of managing and running the Canal by themselves or of assuring that international agreements would be observed. The Cabinet accordingly instructed the British Chiefs of Staff to prepare a war plan. As yet there was no real thought given to co-ordinating military and diplomatic moves with France. That came later in mid-August. As for Israel, Eden insisted that she be kept out of the conflict so that Britain's Arab friends would not be antagonised. An inner Cabinet committee of six, including the Chancellor of the Exchequer Harold Macmillan, was set up to manage the crisis. The United States at this stage in late July was kept in touch. Eden cabled to President Eisenhower that Britain could not afford to let Nasser win. There was, he stressed, a need for a firm stand by all maritime countries because, if Nasser were not stopped, 'our influence throughout the Middle East will, we are convinced, be finally destroyed'. In the last resort Britain would use force, and he added, 'I have this morning instructed our Chiefs of Staff to prepare a military plan accordingly.' He asked for an American representative to come to London to help co-ordinate policy. While Eden expected to be working with the Americans, the French, who were even more determined to topple Nasser than the British, offered to place their forces under a British commander. Not only was the nationalisation of the predominantly French-owned Suez Canal Company an affront to France's international standing, but Nasser as the champion and hero of the Arab world was undermining the French hold over Algeria. Nasser's open support for the Front de Libération Nationale with propaganda and arms was rated so serious in its effect that it could swing the balance against France in the Algerian struggle (pages 548–5). The French worked hard to forge a military alliance with Britain, but feared that Eden might in the end continue to work with Dulles and adopt the American policy of seeking a negotiated settlement.

If Britain would not act with France to destroy Nasser, was there an alternative? The French chiefs thought so – a military alliance with Israel. But an alliance with Britain was preferable and they would have to be careful not to jeopardise that by premature discussions with Israel. So the French Prime Minister Guy Mollet and his Foreign Minister François Pineau had a difficult game to play. Discussions with the Israelis would have to be held secretly at arm's length from the joint military planning with Britain. The Israeli Prime Minister was deeply suspicious of Eden's pro-Arab policies and had little faith in British reliability. Thus Eden's opposition to any Israeli involvement was reciprocated by Israeli doubts about the wisdom of acting with Britain.

Before the French were ready to start military conversations with the Israelis, their priority was to co-ordinate Anglo-French military planning. This did not happen until mid-August 1956. Eden by then was following a two-track policy: military preparations would be pushed ahead at the same time as international negotiations between the maritime nations and Egypt.

It was the US Secretary of State John Foster Dulles who took the lead in the effort to diffuse the Canal crisis by conference diplomacy. He and President Eisenhower also found themselves in a difficult position. Britain was America's most important ally in the Cold War. But Eisenhower suspected Conservative-led Britain of lapsing into colonial attitudes. To make war on Egypt was legally and morally unjustified, would not be sanctioned by the UN and would, so Eisenhower believed, turn the whole Arab world against the West. The attempt to assure Britain of friendly support while also trying to restrain her produced much ambiguity in what the United States would or would not sanction. A conference was convened in London from 16 to 23 August 1956, with India and the Soviet Union participating. Nasser rejected the two proposals that were the outcome of the London Conference as infringing Egypt's sovereign rights. Nor did the

proposals made by a second conference convened in London on 21 September find any more favour in Cairo. Britain and France then took their dispute to the Security Council of the United Nations early in October. Nasser seemed to be playing for time, in the mistaken belief that the longer it took the less likely was any military aggression by Britain and France. Dulles and Eisenhower, however, continued to urge restraint and patience and to seek new solutions.

Military plans for Operation Musketeer, the assault on Egypt, were proceeding apace, but they had to be revised constantly for military and diplomatic reasons. It took time to marshal sufficient aircraft and paratroops in Cyprus and to assemble troops there and in Malta, who were to be ferried by the Mediterranean fleet to Port Said. During August and September the one clear development was that Eden learnt that the Americans would not actively support the use of force. So he switched to France. But, although Britain and France were in close partnership militarily, that did not extend to their diplomatic aims in the Middle East beyond Egypt. There they were almost on opposite sides: France was supporting Israel; Britain was supporting the Arab states, and she confirmed the full validity of her alliance with Jordan against Israel when Jordan became the victim of two Israeli reprisal raids in September 1956. One of the most extraordinary aspects of the Suez Crisis is how late British policy changed, only days before the attack on Egypt: Eden abruptly agreed to make use of Israel in a plan to legitimise the assault on Egypt. But until that change took place, the French had to keep the Israeli connection secret from their British ally.

During the latter part of September the French, with diplomatic finesse, began involving the Israelis and the British in a secret gameplan for war on Egypt. When Eden and his Foreign Secretary Selwyn Lloyd visited Paris for talks with Mollet and Pineau on 26 September it is possible that the French revealed that they were having contacts with the Israelis. The French aim was for the Canal to be threatened with closure because Israel had attacked Egypt and was advancing towards Suez – would not Britain and France then be justified, in the interests of keeping the Suez Canal open to international traffic, in acting as policemen, demanding that both sides withdraw from the Suez Canal and occupying it if either the Israelis or the

Egyptians rejected the demand? Given her fears of Egyptian rearmament, Israel might well make a pre-emptive attack on Egypt, and in that event the British and French could justify military intervention to keep the combatants apart and at a distance from the Canal.

An Israeli delegation led by the redoubtable Golda Meir arrived in Paris and went into secret talks on 30 September and 1 October. Mollet and Pineau outlined their scheme. For the Israelis a war with Egypt might determine their country's future existence, yet relations with Britain after the Israeli raids into Jordan had sunk to a new low. Indeed, since the days of the Mandate, Britain had not been held in high esteem in Israel nor regarded as trustworthy. What if Jordan joined in on the Egyptian–Israeli war? Golda Meir wanted to know on whose side Britain would then fight. Pineau did his best to persuade the Israelis that Britain's priority would be the defeat of Egypt but he went on to explain that the British government needed a pretext to attack Egypt.

The first two weeks of October were decisive. At the beginning of the month Eden was still undecided, the Chancellor of the Exchequer Harold Macmillan was a hawk and the Foreign Secretary Selwyn Lloyd a dove. Under the aegis of the United Nations, Selwyn Lloyd was in New York trying to negotiate a settlement of the Canal problem directly with Mahmoud Fawzi, the Egyptian Foreign Minister. Pineau, the French Foreign Minister, who was also involved, was far less keen on a peaceful outcome. On 12 October they finally reached an agreement based on 'six principles', and the UN Security Council endorsed them. Eden cabled Selwyn Lloyd at lunchtime on 14 October that he was ready to negotiate further with the Egyptians and those members of the Security Council anxious to see the issue peacefully resolved.

The possibility of joint Anglo-French military action seemed to have receded, though to maintain pressure on Egypt Eden reserved Britain's rights to use force if the Egyptians did not accept a settlement satisfactory to her. But later that afternoon Eden received two envoys from Paris. The French Prime Minister wanted to know what Britain would do if Israel attacked Egypt. The Tripartite Declaration of 1950 had promised US, British and French help to the victim of aggression, though the French pointed out that Nasser had recently repudiated its application to Egypt. The French then revealed the plan they had discussed with the Israelis on 30 September and 1 October: Israel would attack Egypt and, on the pretext of separating the combatants and safeguarding the Canal, a French and British force would invade Egypt and occupy the Canal Zone. Eden promised to reply by 16 October but was clearly attracted to the scheme.

Eden saw the French proposal as a possible escape from mounting difficulties. War was drawing closer in the Middle East and Britain would not be able to keep out of it. Jordan was in crisis. On 10 October, that is four days before these crucial Anglo-French conversations in London, in a massive reprisal raid on Qalquilya which marked the climax of Israeli–Jordanian clashes, over seventy Jordanians were killed. The Israelis were trying to foil an agreement between Iraq and Jordan, backed by Britain, to bring Iraqi troops to the help of the Jordanians. Where did Britain stand? Her credibility in the Arab Middle East and her strengthening of the Baghdad Pact now depended on her honouring the defensive alliance concluded with Jordan. Thus Britain looked like being dragged in *against* Israel and on the side of the Arab states if war broke out between Israel on the one hand and Jordan and Egypt on the other. This involvement in the general Arab enmity towards Israel now cut right across Britain's own conflict with Egypt. France, moreover, was backing Israel. No wonder Selwyn Lloyd thought that any outbreak of war would be a disaster for Britain.

While French and Israeli military staffs worked on plans to attack Egypt, Eden now made up his mind that the best way out was to accept the French plan of Anglo-French military action in collusion with Israel. As part of this plan he could ensure that Israel would *not* attack Jordan, and so save Britain from the dilemma of defending her. Time was now running out: military plans could not be for ever revised and postponed without demoralising British forces being readied for the attack. On 16 October Eden and Lloyd returned to Paris to consult further with Mollet and Pineau. The 'contingency' of an Israeli attack towards the Canal was discussed, as was the proposed response of an Anglo-French ultimatum requiring both sides to withdraw from the Canal. This would then be followed by an Anglo-French invasion of the Canal Zone, as the Egyptians were bound to reject the ultimatum. Eden fell in with this deception and, after the return of the Prime Minister and the

Foreign Secretary to London, the Cabinet endorsed it too.

Events now moved swiftly to their climax. As the Israelis were assigned the role of starting the war, they would need to be certain of the support of the British and French. A general understanding was not enough – there had to be a precise timetable too. It was one thing for Eden and Lloyd to say what Britain would do if, supposedly regrettably, the Israelis attacked Egypt and threatened the Canal. It was quite another to encourage and pre-plan with Israel an attack on Egypt to be followed by Anglo-French intervention. Israel's war objective was not the Suez Canal in any case, but the breaking of a naval blockade of the Tiran Straits dominated at its mouth by the Egyptian batteries at Sharm al-Sheikh. The military sideshow towards the Canal was intended only to provide Britain and France with the pretext they needed to join Israel in defeating Nasser. The Israelis would open hostilities as part of the general plan only if they secured watertight guarantees from the British. Prime Minister Ben Gurion, accompanied by General Dayan, flew to Paris at the invitation of the French to confer with them and the British. The crucial secret discussions were held in a villa in the suburb of Sèvres.

Mollet and Pineau and the Israelis were joined on 22 October 1956 by the Foreign Secretary, Selwyn Lloyd, who was uneasy about the whole scheme. On Eden's instructions the discussions were to be so secret that no official record was to be made of them. The Israelis nevertheless made notes. Selwyn Lloyd confirmed that if the Israelis decided to attack Egypt Britain and France would intervene to safeguard the Suez Canal. A timetable was discussed. The Israeli attack was to begin on 29 October. The Israelis had been promised the support of French pilots, planes and warships. At Sèvres there was discussion about how long after an Anglo-French ultimatum the bombing of Egyptian airfields would begin. Nothing had been definitely decided when Lloyd left to consult Eden and the Cabinet.

In fact the meeting had not gone well. Ben Gurion's mistrust of the British in general and Selwyn Lloyd and Eden in particular had not been lessened by the encounter. In London the following day, 23 October, the Cabinet received a report from Selwyn Lloyd about the secret Paris meeting which indicated that the Israelis would not launch a war on their own. One implication, therefore, was that

Israel would start a war allowing Britain and France to intervene only if a prior agreement with Britain and France had been reached. The Cabinet met again on 24 October. From a confusing discussion it was not evident to them that an agreement with Israel actually to launch a war was being contemplated. That same day, Foreign Office official Sir Patrick Dean was sent back to Paris after being instructed by Eden. He was authorised to reach an agreement with the Israelis on the military timetable.

The Paris discussions ended with a three-page typed statement in French embodying 'the results of the conversations which took place at Sèvres from 22–24 October 1956 between the representatives of the governments of the United Kingdom, of the State of Israel and of France'. The famous and much debated agreement, which still has not been officially published, provided, first, that the Israelis would launch a large-scale attack on Egyptian forces on 29 October and would thrust towards the Canal zone on the 30th; secondly, that on the 30th Britain and France would 'appeal' to the Egyptian and Israeli governments to halt acts of war, withdraw troops ten miles from the Canal (this left the Israelis in Egyptian territory) and accept the temporary occupation of key positions on the Canal by Anglo-French forces until a final settlement guaranteeing free passage to all nations could be reached. If Egypt or Israel did not agree within twelve hours, Anglo-French forces would intervene. Thirdly, if the Egyptians did not agree, Britain and France would launch military operations on 31 October; there was a provision that the Israeli forces would occupy the Egyptian western shore of the Gulf of Aqaba. Fourthly, Israel undertook not to attack Jordan unless Jordan attacked her; in that event the British would not come to the aid of Jordan. An article was added which stipulated that the agreement would be kept strictly secret. Finally, it was stated that the agreement would enter into force after the concurrence of the three governments.

On 26 October the Israelis received France's assurance in a letter from the Prime Minister. Britain's agreement was circuitous; it took the form of a letter to Mollet from Eden noting the conversations at Sèvres and confirming 'that in the situation there envisaged they [Britain] will take the action described'. Why such circumlocution? It was an attempt by Eden to lay the basis for a denial that there had been any secret treaty between the three countries to attack Egypt – Eden believed it could be presented merely as a contingency plan, setting down what Britain would do in certain circumstances. He would claim that he could not be certain the circumstances would arise. The difference unfortunately was rather less than paper-thin. Eden had all along wanted to avoid a treaty, any written and signed agreement. But the hapless Dean, not knowing this, had added his signature to Pineau's and Ben Gurion's copies and taken his copy back to London. Eden was upset when he learnt that there was now a written record. Of course, if it had all been entirely above board he would not have minded. Dean was sent back to Paris to retrieve all the copies so that they could be destroyed. He did not succeed. Ben Gurion, ever suspicious of the British, had carefully folded the document in his pocket and returned with it to Israel. Neither he nor Pineau would now give up their copies. The British request added a touch of humiliation to the subterfuges adopted to cover up the secret arrangements. The way was now clear for the military plans to go ahead.

If the collusion with Israel was not to be obvious, the Anglo-French invasion of the Canal Zone could only take place for logistical reasons six days after the Israelis began the campaign. The troops which would have to be conveyed to Port Said were assembled in Malta and Cyprus; it was expected to take eight days from the start of Israel's attack to ferry them to Egypt. Nor could the parachute brigade stationed in Cyprus be dropped immediately without land support, so they too would have to wait. But it was part of the secret tripartite agreement that Egyptian airfields would be bombed at dawn on 31 October, some thirty-six hours after the Israeli attack, so as to put the Soviet-supplied Egyptian bombers out of action. The French had also secretly agreed to station their fighters in Israel to protect her cities.

The final preparations were made with the Americans still being kept in the dark. The Hungarian rising was occupying the headlines of the world press. The presidential elections too were rapidly approaching, with voting on 6 November. A few ships were authorised to leave Valletta Harbour in Malta on Sunday night, 28 October, and the aircraft-carriers on the morning of the 29th, that is before the Israeli attack that same afternoon. All that weekend preparations had been actively under way in Malta and Cyprus. The Anglo-French and Israeli troop movements alerted Dulles and

Eisenhower in Washington. But from London to Washington there was a freeze on all communication about the impending Suez war. The majority of government ministers in London too were not fully briefed. The same was true of British ambassadors abroad, so great was the secrecy insisted upon by Eden.

At 5 p.m. on 29 October the Israelis began their attack as arranged. Their prime object was to reach the tip of the Sinai Peninsula, where the batteries at Sharm al-Sheikh were closing the Straits of Tiran to Israeli shipping. The batteries were taken on 5 November. A diversionary thrust towards the Canal also began on 29 October and was completed by 2 November, with Israeli parachutists, after suffering severe casualties, capturing the Mitla Pass some forty miles from the Canal. On 30 October Britain and France sent their ultimatum to Egypt and Israel to withdraw ten miles from the Canal, according to the Sèvres scheme. Egypt was given just twelve hours to reply.

In Washington the response was anger, heightened by the fact that the British–French–Israeli defiance of international law was distracting attention from the brutal Soviet repression of Hungary. Eisenhower made it clear that the United States would not back France and Britain. At home Hugh Gaitskell, the Leader of the Labour Party, warned Eden on 31 October that his party would not support the government in warlike actions against Egypt. Gaitskell received no answer when he demanded to know if Britain was at war. By the morning of the 31st, the ultimatum had expired but no shot had been fired by Britain or France. The Security Council was in session in New York that day. In Cairo, Nasser had not panicked, but was getting ready to defend Egypt from the threatened Anglo-French assault. The British Ambassador was still unmolested, occupying the Embassy in Cairo; to preserve secrecy he had not been recalled; nor were the British and French civilian employees of the Suez Canal Company evacuated in time – this put many civilian lives at risk. Then during the evening of 31 October RAF Canberras and Valiants started bombing Egyptian airfields. The Egyptian air force was grounded throughout the Suez War, thus removing Israel's principal concern.

The attack on Egypt in breach of the UN Charter deeply divided the British people. In the House of Commons the Conservative majority ensured the defeat of a motion of censure tabled by the Labour

*Nasser blockades the Suez Canal in November 1956 by sinking and scuttling ships.*

Party, and much popular opinion welcomed Britain's standing up to Nasser, though the more thoughtful condemned the aggression. But there was no doubt where the United States stood. Dulles nevertheless attempted to help Britain by delaying United Nations action. France and Britain were able, by using their veto power, to stymie the Security Council, but they could not prevent the General Assembly from acting under the United for Peace Resolution invoked six years earlier when the Korean War broke out. Even so, the interval between the air attack on Egypt on 31 October and the actual main landings of troops brought by sea was too long. On 3 November, unhappily for Britain, Dulles – who was trying to limit the damage – entered hospital for a cancer operation that put him out of action. On 4 November the General Assembly called on the Secretary-General to arrange a ceasefire.

The pressure on the three belligerents was now considerable. The Israelis promised to comply if the Egyptians also agreed to a ceasefire. Nasser, though, was naturally not intimidated, given the worldwide condemnation of Britain and France. He was ready to carry on a guerrilla struggle if Britain and France occupied the Canal Zone. Meanwhile differences were also opening up between Britain and France on how best to carry on military operations. After the UN ceasefire resolution, Eden was determined that the invasion should take place even

though he had accepted 'in principle' a UN peacekeeping force to take over from the British and French. The creation of a peacekeeping force was approved by the UN on 4 November; a day later French and British paratroops landed in the Canal Zone. The main landing from the sea followed on the 6th. The Anglo-French troops needed only three more days to advance south from Port Said and to complete the occupation of the Canal Zone. But politically time had run out.

Cynical nuclear threats uttered by the Soviet Union were not taken seriously; in any case, the Soviets were being condemned for their bloody repression of the Hungarian rising (pages 501–2). But US pressure on Israel, plus the capture of Sharm al-Sheikh, decided the Israelis to stop fighting. How could Britain and France now credibly continue, given that they had claimed that the purpose of the military action was to keep Egypt and Israel apart? The French were ready to defy the UN for a little longer, but Eden saw no alternative to accepting the ceasefire on 6 November. Harold Macmillan, the Chancellor of the Exchequer, forecast a financial catastrophe as foreigners were depleting their sterling holdings and the United States was refusing to help. There would anyway be the additional costs of bringing in oil now that the Egyptians had blocked the Canal by scuttling fifty ships.

What had been achieved? Eden's reputation for statesmanship had been tarnished just as ill-health forced him to rest. He left for Jamaica on 23 November, but it was the prelude to his retirement in January 1957, a tragic end to a long and distinguished career. UN troops began arriving in Port Said in late November 1956. Anglo-American relations reached their lowest ebb that autumn with the re-elected Eisenhower administration refusing either to ship oil from the Gulf of Mexico or to help stem the flight from the pound. Without dollar support Britain could not afford to pay for the oil from the Western hemisphere. But relations improved the moment the Anglo-French troops handed over to the UN peacekeeping force; the British and French finally left two days before Christmas. The French Prime Minister was then welcomed in Washington; ironically, it was Macmillan, originally a strong proponent of the Suez adventure, who succeeded Eden in January 1957 and was received by Eisenhower and Dulles the following March in Bermuda. The alliance was restored. On 24 April of that year the Egyptian Canal Authority opened the Canal to traffic again. Nasser had not fallen. The Zone and the Canal were the property of Egypt. The Americans, pronouncing the Eisenhower Doctrine in January 1957, attempted to fill the void left by the defeat of Britain and France in the Middle East (page 475).

Was Suez, then, misconceived and doomed to failure from the start? The question cannot be viewed in isolation; the conflicts of Suez were just a part of the continuing Middle Eastern crisis which the West failed to solve then or later, any more than it had imposed a peace settlement on the Middle East after the Second World War. When it came to armed conflict, neither Britain nor the United States had been prepared to jeopardise her relations with the oil-rich Middle East to create an independent Israel in Palestine. The Israelis had to achieve this by their own fortitude. The Tripartite Declaration of 1950 might then have served as a basis for a great-power imposition of peace, but the Cold War, the rise of Nasser and his challenge eventually to Israel, France and Britain sowed divisions in the West and shifted Britain, France and the United States away from the role of impartial peacekeepers. The Soviet Union took advantage of this to fuel Egyptian–Israeli tensions by her large arms deliveries to Nasser. The Anglo-French attack on Egypt in collusion with Israel appeared to serve the interests of all three nations threatened by Nasser's ambitions.

Eden only entered late, in mid-October 1956, into the plan. He knew that the United States did not believe during the summer and early autumn that diplomacy had been exhausted. It seemed, according to Washington's perceptions, that Egypt was showing readiness to compromise in order to reach a settlement over the Canal. The French from the start were far more ready to act independently; it was they who persuaded Eden to join in the Sèvres scenario and to work behind America's back. Eden and Mollet mistakenly believed that Eisenhower, faced with presidential elections on 6 November 1956, would not be able to act against Israel, Britain and France if they attacked Egypt before then. Finally the condition the Israelis made that they would launch an attack on the Egyptians, which was to provide the pretext of French and British intervention, only if the British and French neutralised the Egyptian air force by bombing their airbases within thirty-six hours of the Israeli attack was bound to reveal the collusion. In a vain attempt to preserve the fiction of the impartial policemen, the main combat forces were obviously not supposed to sail from their base in Malta until after the start of hostilities between Israel and Egypt. (They actually left a little earlier.) It was thought that they would need at least eight days, though they actually made it in six, reaching Port Said on 6 November. That had left a week for the international community at the UN to intervene. Had France and Britain been less concerned to maintain the fiction of not colluding with Israel they could have landed earlier and faced the United States and the UN with a *fait accompli* and occupied the Canal Zone; they could even have dispensed with Israeli co-operation altogether. But even a successful occupation of the Canal Zone would not have been the end of the affair. In the last resort it was not really a question of timing. It was not the Americans who doomed Suez to disaster, even though from his sickbed Dulles later confused the issue by asking Selwyn Lloyd, 'Why did you stop? Why didn't you go through with it and get Nasser down?' Arab nationalism was not the creation of a single man, nor could the conflicts of the Middle East have been resolved by his removal. Even the most powerful Western nations could no longer simply impose their will on the whole region without unacceptable costs to themselves.

# CHAPTER 47

## *The Struggle for Predominance in the Middle East*

One common bond between the Arab nations was hatred of Israel. Beyond this the rivalries between the Arab rulers, the old and the new, led to bewildering diplomatic manoeuvres, coups and changes of sides, some even secretly securing Israeli assistance. The outside powers and the Cold War further complicated what were rapidly changing alignments in the Middle East after 1956. International, regional and internal struggles for predominance have created there continuing war and conflict.

The Anglo-French débâcle at Suez raised Nasser's prestige enormously. But he was handicapped by Egypt's poverty and lack of valuable resources such as oil; indebted more and more to the Soviet Union to pay for new weapons, Egypt had to pledge her only important cash crop, cotton, in return. The rapid growth of the population meant that increased production hardly improved the lot of the peasants and the urban poor. Nor did the Aswan High Dam deliver the promised transformation of the Egyptian peasantry. But externally Egypt looked as if she might assume a powerful place in the Middle East. The Pan-Arab cause appeared to be in the ascendant when Syria in 1958 initiated steps to unite with Egypt to form the United Arab Republic. Other Arab nations were invited to join. But Syria was as poor as Egypt and the union was largely one of paper only. The only other state to join was the poorest of all the Arab states, Yemen. There was no geographical contiguity between these three nations. The union did not last long: in September 1961 the pro-Nasserites were overthrown in a military coup in Syria, which thereupon left the United Arab Republic. It was no serious loss, but the Yemen connection proved very costly for Egypt.

In 1963 civil war broke out in the Yemen Arab Republic. The hereditary rulers were backed by Saudi Arabia, and the officers who had rebelled looked to Moscow and Egypt for support. Egypt despatched some 70,000 troops eventually and the fighting dragged on, a costly drain on the Egyptian Treasury. The other Yemen, which comprised what had from 1956 to 1967 been Britain's Aden and hinterland, turned herself into the pro-Soviet People's Democratic Republic of Yemen. (Unification of the two Yemens was eventually proclaimed in May 1990. The new state was named the Republic of Yemen.) To complicate matters further, while Egypt and Saudi Arabia were sworn enemies and at war by proxy in the Yemen, Saudi Arabia supported Egypt in her conflict with Israel. But, until rearmed, Nasser could not contemplate another war with Israel. For ten years raids into Israel from Egyptian territory ceased. It was an armed peace. Nor was there any attempt to stop Israeli commerce from using the seaport of Eilat and passing down the Gulf of Aqaba through the Straits of Tiran. The passage was guaranteed by France, Britain and the United States. The Sinai had been handed back to Egypt after 1956; a United Nations force policed the border and was stationed in the Sinai Desert on the Egyptian side of the

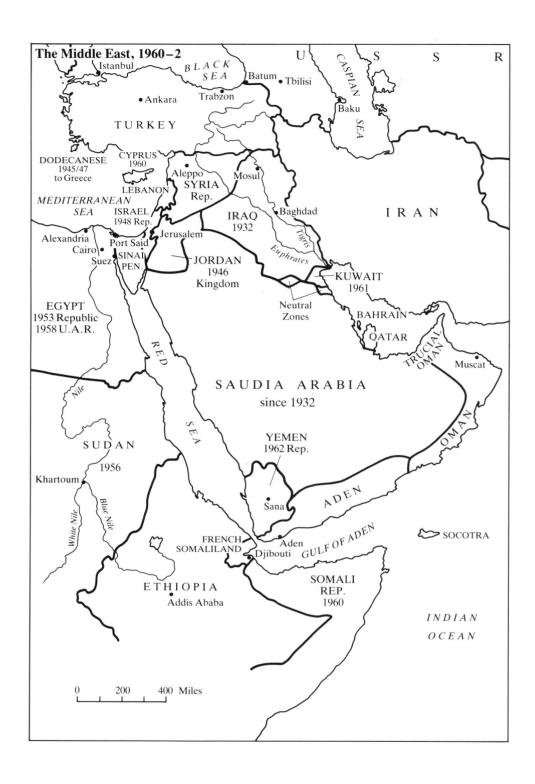

**The Middle East, 1960–2**

Istanbul
*BLACK SEA*
Batum • Tbilisi
•Ankara  Trabzon
Baku
*CASPIAN SEA*

U    S    S    R

TURKEY

DODECANESE
1945/47
to Greece
CYPRUS
1960
Aleppo  Mosul
SYRIA
Rep.
LEBANON
*MEDITERRANEAN SEA*
ISRAEL
1948 Rep.
IRAQ
1932  Baghdad

I R A N

Jerusalem
Alexandria
Cairo•
Port Said
SINAI
PEN.
Suez
JORDAN
1946
Kingdom
*Tigris*
*Euphrates*
KUWAIT
1961

Neutral
Zones
BAHRAIN
QATAR

EGYPT
1953 Republic
1958 U.A.R.

*Nile*

RED
SEA

SAUDIA ARABIA
since 1932

TRUCIAL
OMAN
•Muscat

OMAN

SUDAN
1956
Khartoum

*White Nile*
*Blue Nile*

YEMEN
1962 Rep.

Sana

ADEN

FRENCH
SOMALILAND
Aden
Djibouti
*GULF OF ADEN*

⌒ SOCOTRA

ETHIOPIA
Addis Ababa

SOMALI
REP.
1960

*INDIAN*

*OCEAN*

0    200    400  Miles

Egyptian–Israeli border.

In reality, Nasser's position after Suez was a weak one. There was no hiding the fact of his defeat by Israel. No one realised this more clearly than the astute King Hussein of Jordan. Before Suez he had been forced by powerful groups in his country to denounce the West and to embrace Egypt. After Nasser's defeat by Israel, Egypt was in no condition to interfere. In April 1957 Hussein foiled a coup and declared martial law, assuming personal power with the support of the army.

With Egypt and Syria already relying on Soviet support, the United States stepped into the vacuum left by the British after Suez. The so-called Eisenhower Doctrine, approved by Congress and signed by the President in March 1957, involved the United States more deeply in the Middle East. The US offered economic and military aid and empowered the President to use armed force to assist any nation in the Middle East requesting such help against armed aggression 'from any country controlled by international communism'. Since the Cold War was not the root cause of instability and conflict in the Middle East, the Doctrine did not contribute a great deal to peace.

For Arab leaders to embrace the United States openly as friend and protector in the 1960s and 1970s was made virtually impossible by American support for Israel. Only Lebanon, with a Christian non-Arab president, responded positively to Eisenhower. To counter the Soviet alignment with Egypt and Syria, Eisenhower ordered the US Sixth Fleet into the eastern Mediterranean and sent financial aid to Jordan. The United States also tried to destabilise the regime in Syria. This attempt failed. Worse still, the West's most reliable ally, Iraq, changed regimes and left the Baghdad Pact.

In July 1958 a bloody revolution broke out in Iraq, and the King and his chief pro-Western minister were brutally killed. General Abdel Kassem, with local communist help, seized power. In Jordan, King Hussein was greatly alarmed and, fearing for his throne, asked for British help. Britain sent troops and Hussein held shakily on to power. For a time too, in response to a call for assistance from the Lebanese President, US marines were landed from the Sixth Fleet. As it turned out, it was not these applications of the Eisenhower Doctrine which constrained the Soviets in the Middle East, but the rivalry of the Arab nations among themselves. Fundamental to inter-Arab conflict was the hostility between Iraq and Egypt. Nasser interpreted communist support for Iraq's General Kassem as an unfriendly act towards Egypt. By the spring of 1959 Kassem denounced Nasser, and Nasser denounced Kassem.

Ultimately neither the Soviet Union nor the United States could enlist the Middle Eastern nations in the Cold War. The leaders of these nations were primarily concerned with their internal and regional conflicts; they made use of Cold War antagonisms to further their own interests. The naval-base facilities which the Soviet navy acquired over the years in Egypt, Syria, Libya and the People's Democratic Republic of Yemen as well as on the Red Sea entailed great costs directly and indirectly. Foreign naval bases, moreover, are dependent on the changing attitudes and policies of the leaders in power in these unstable countries. The Soviet Union's expensive policy was singularly unsuccessful. In one respect, though, she was a major player in the Middle East and that was in her role of supplying arms to Israel's principal enemies, Egypt, Syria and Iraq. This in turn stimulated the United States and other Western nations partly for strategic reasons and also for profit to try to replace the Soviet Union as the provider of arms. The most modern weapons flooded into this region of rival states. Inevitably the Middle East became a danger to world peace.

Israel, despite her historic roots, is a new country whose development in the post-war world has been astonishing. The great majority of the people who built the nation had left a Europe whose soil had been soaked with Jewish blood. The young fighters and pioneers who had reached what was Palestine before 1947 had often lost their families in Hitler's Holocaust and in Poland, even after the war had come to an end. The diverse European Jews speaking no common language were forced into a nation sharing one purpose above all others: they would never again be defenceless. They are bound together by the common memory of the Holocaust when no nation cared enough to try to save millions of Jewish men, women and children from death by starvation, poison gas or the bullet. During the Second World War, these scattered Jews were powerless against the armed might of National Socialist Germany. Jews have been denigrated and persecuted for centuries in the Western world. A people whose religion is the ethical foundation of

Christianity were stigmatised since medieval times as the 'killers of the Son of God'. Massacres were blasphemously justified as the work and will of a Christian God. Only gradually granted the same rights and opportunities as their Christian neighbours in the nineteenth and twentieth centuries, Jews were seen as workshy, dishonest, reluctant to perform manual labour and military service, servile and cowardly. It is the essence of all prejudice to ascribe common negative characteristics to a whole group of people without regard to individual differences. The Second World War exemplified to what horrors prejudice and indifference can lead.

The immigrants to Palestine did not come to empty lands. The Jews settled in towns which then flourished and prospered. There was enough room for Arabs and Jews in Palestine. There were many who believed they could live well together, but instead the Jewish immigration ended in conflict and a struggle for predominance. The Arabs, displaced from their land, were filled with resentment and hatred for the new settlers from other parts of the world. There were many Jews who claimed the land as theirs by historical right, looking back to the kingdom of David and its capital city, Jerusalem, established a thousand years before Christ. But there had been no Jewish state for 2000 years since its extinction in Roman times. Jews had been dispersed (the diaspora) to live in the Christian and Islamic world. Their religion and culture survived and with them the belief that there would one day be a return to the Holy Land. An orthodox Jewish community had constituted the largest single religious group in Jerusalem since 1840. (The others were the Christians and Muslims.) It was persecution in the Russian Empire in the late nineteenth century and Nazi persecution and Soviet discrimination in the twentieth that created a mass migration of Jews from central and Eastern Europe. Until then Zionism had attracted only a small minority of European Jews; the majority were proud to be Germans, Poles and Hungarians. (The Jews of Britain, France and the United States are still proud citizens of their countries, even if they materially support Israel at the same time.)

The early pioneers from central and Eastern Europe have provided the great majority of Israel's political leaders up to the present day. Chaim Weizmann, the first President of Israel, and David Ben Gurion, her first Prime Minister and dominant political leader until 1963, were both born in Russian Poland. Golda Meir was born in Kiev, and after she and her parents had emigrated to the United States in 1906, she settled in 1921 at the age of eighteen in a kibbutz; prominent in politics and diplomacy she became prime minister in 1969 on the death of Levi Eshkol. Menachem Begin's family perished in Poland; he had headed the Irgun and uncompromisingly claimed the whole biblical land of Israel. The strong political influence of central and Eastern European Jews is not surprising. They formed the largest group of immigrants from 1903 to 1939, some 200,000. In the 1930s a new wave of immigrants from Germany, about 80,000, entered Palestine. The majority were professionals, doctors, lawyers, teachers, traders or the children of middle-class parents, whereas the majority of Eastern and central European Jews were skilled workers or farmers. It is perhaps surprising that the German-descended Israelis have not played a larger political role so far. After 1945 the survivors of the death camps who came to Palestine were again mainly Jews from Eastern Europe and the Balkans. The next large-scale migration after the war for independence came from the Middle East, the oriental Jews, of Morocco, Tunisia, Syria, Egypt and the Yemen. They were the least educated and as a group are economically and socially the least privileged. After three generations the gap between the European and oriental Jews remains wide and is only slowly narrowing, despite common service in the army, which is a great leveller. The biggest pool of potential immigrants are the Jews of the former Soviet Union. Indeed, they provided the largest group of immigrants in the 1970s and 1980s.

The population of Israel, excluding the territories conquered in the 1967 war, grew almost six times from 750,000 in 1948 to 2.8 million by 1968 and to 4.3 million by the end of the 1980s. Not all are Jews. In 1948–9 some 600,000 Palestinian Arabs fled to neighbouring Arab countries and became refugees in camps, but 150,000 remained in their homes in Israel; by 1987 they had grown to 650,000, two-thirds of them Muslim and the remainder Christian. Clinging to their land as peasant farmers and poor villagers, economically the great majority remained disadvantaged and from 1949 until the 1960s, their loyalty suspected, they were placed under many restrictions, curfews and military rule. Yet outwardly they were accorded the civic rights of all Israelis, including the right to vote for the Israeli parliament, the Knesset. Then in the 1960s a policy to integrate them was followed with some success. The Palestinian Arab Israelis have remained a separate community, sympathetic to the Palestinians denied self-determination in the occupied lands of the West Bank and Gaza (after the 1967 war), but they remain Israelis striving for equality, their economic well-being far higher now than that of the Palestinian Arabs outside the State of Israel.

Israel is the only democracy in the Middle East, with a multiplicity of parties already well established in Palestine before independence. The dominant party forming the core of all coalitions until 1977 was the Labour Party (Mapai), the Marxist Mapam never enjoying anywhere near the same support. The Herut belonged to the right-wing group of parties. The third minority group was composed of the religious parties, who wished to expand religious law in the Jewish state; their influence was often greater than their numbers in the Knesset would have justified because they could demand a price for agreeing to join the coalition governments formed after elections. The bargaining that preceded the coalition agreements – especially in the 1980s when the adherence of minor parties became crucial – added cynicism and disillusionment to the democratic process of Israeli politics.

The biggest challenge facing Israeli governments has been and remains how to absorb thousands of destitute immigrants. Israel is open to all Jews who wish to settle there. The costs are huge and, when added to the immense burdens of defence, present difficulties of budgetary management unique among the developed countries. The Labour Party, a pragmatic party quite willing to compromise socialist principles, followed policies encouraging capitalist investment. Economic growth has been one of the most rapid in the developed world, financed by loans, grants, gifts (especially from the United States) and German reparations payments. This has, however, burdened the economy with a huge external debt. It has also created an Israeli dependence on the goodwill of the United States, a relationship reinforced by a dependence on weapons from the West, with first France and then the United States supplying the tanks and the aircraft essential for Israel's security.

The brilliant military commanders of Israel's victories in war play an influential role in Israeli politics, readily exchanging active army service with Cabinet posts in government. Moshe Dayan was a successful leader in war and a hawk in peace from the creation of Israel to the Yom Kippur War in 1973; General Yitzhak Rabin took over as prime minister from Golda Meir after serving as chief of staff in the Six-Day War of 1967; General Yigal Allon, Dayan's rival as a military hero, served as foreign minister in the 1970s and General Ariel Sharon, the military hero of the 1973 war when his tanks crossed the Suez Canal and trapped the Egyptian Third Army in the Sinai, became a dominant member of Menachem Begin's Cabinet and masterminded the Israeli invasion of Lebanon in 1982.

Israel enjoyed a breathing space of ten years after the Suez–Sinai War of 1956. Neither Nasser nor Hussein wished to plunge his country into another war with Israel for the sake of the Palestinians. Indeed, the establishment of a Palestinian Arab state was not part of the programme of any of the Arab national leaders. But when Nasser's bid for Arab leadership and his efforts to export his revolution met with resolute opposition from the royal leaders of Jordan and Saudi Arabia, and with hostility in Syria and Iraq, the only Pan-Arab appeal left to him was to emphasise the common enemy – Israel. Radio Cairo broadcast hate campaigns against the Jewish state, and President Nasser himself proclaimed in a speech in Alexandria on 26 July 1959, 'I announce from here, on behalf of the United Arab Republic people, that this time we will exterminate Israel.' On 27 May 1967, nine days before the start of the Six-Day War, he declared, 'Our basic objective will be the destruction of Israel.' No less extreme was the President of Iraq on 31 May 1967: 'The existence of Israel is an error which must be rectified. This is our opportunity to wipe out the ignominy which has been with us since 1948. Our goal is clear – to wipe Israel off the map.' These bloodcurdling speeches can be dismissed as public rhetoric, since they are belied by the much more cautious attitudes otherwise displayed by Arab leaders. But for Israelis in Tel Aviv and Jerusalem it was clear that their very survival would be threatened if ever they should prove the weaker in the continuing conflict, for the Arab nations refused to make peace or to recognise Israel's right to exist.

Israel's response to Arab enmity is to place the whole nation in arms. A professional nucleus of officers and NCOs is supplemented by conscripts: every man and woman has to serve for two to three

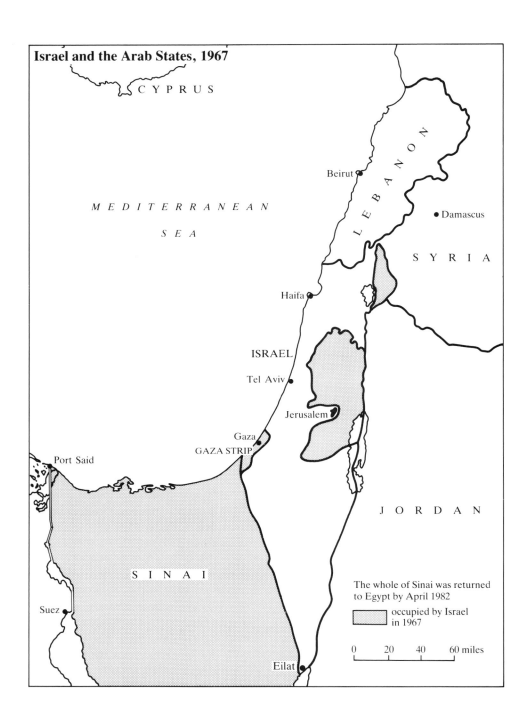

**Israel and the Arab States, 1967**

CYPRUS

MEDITERRANEAN
SEA

LEBANON

Beirut

• Damascus

SYRIA

Haifa

ISRAEL

Tel Aviv

Jerusalem

Gaza
GAZA STRIP

Port Said

JORDAN

SINAI

Suez

The whole of Sinai was returned
to Egypt by April 1982

occupied by Israel
in 1967

Eilat

0    20    40    60 miles

years; then follows a long period in the reserve (for men to the age of forty-nine) with annual battle training. The standing army of some 80,000 can in time of emergency be quickly mobilised into a force of 300,000. The army, the air force and the small navy, in a constant state of readiness for war, have always proved effective when put to the test. Arab Israelis are not conscripted but a minority have fought in the Israeli army.

While Nasser rebuilt and re-equipped the Egyptian army with Soviet help, Israel continued to strengthen her relations with France, a source of some of the best weapons and aircraft. The French also helped her to build up a nuclear potential with the construction of the Dimona reactor. The unsigned alliance with the United States, however, remained the sheet anchor of Israel's international security. After seven relatively peaceful years, in 1964 Israeli–Arab tensions once more began to grow. The Israelis completed a project to divert some of the waters of the Jordan and the Sea of Galilee, which sparked a belligerent Syrian response. Nasser felt obliged to fulfil the role of Pan-Arab leader and summoned a conference in Cairo in 1964. The Arab nations were not ready for war, but 1964 was notable for the endorsement given later in the year to Yasser Arafat and for the formation of the Palestine Liberation Organisation. Coupled with Arab non-recognition of Israel this was an ominous development. But Nasser had too many problems at home – attempting to advance the economy, fighting in the Yemen and losing US economic aid – to be thinking of any immediate resumption of war. The most extreme Arab regime was the Syrian.

Syria's politics consisted of unstable power-plays between rival groups. In 1966 the most radical wing of the Ba'ath seized power and sought to consolidate its grip by taking the lead in fighting for the liberation of Palestine. Syrian gunfire harassed Israeli settlements on the frontier, armed Palestinians belonging to Fatah (the PLO's largest fedayeen guerrilla group) and supported by Syria infiltrated Israel during the autumn and winter of 1966/7, raided settlements and set off explosives. The Israelis sent retaliatory raids into the territory of their Arab neighbours, sometimes to attack Palestinian bases, sometimes hitting innocent Arabs in Jordan and the Lebanon and causing many deaths. Israel, Syria, Jordan and Egypt were drifting into an all-out war. Nasser, albeit hesitantly, escalated

the crisis, unable as self-styled leader of the Arab world to appear to follow in Syria's militant footsteps. The Israeli government was also cautious, not believing that it really faced an imminent war. The Soviets, meanwhile, were stirring up the Egyptians with intelligence reports that Israel was readying for an all-out invasion of Syria, though the Israelis were probably only preparing another punitive strike against Syria for supporting Palestinian raids. Nasser moved army units into the Sinai in mid-May 1967, and terminated the right of UN observer troops to remain on the Sinai Egyptian frontiers with Israel. But his most decisive hostile challenge, on 22 May 1967, was to close the Gulf of Aqaba to Israeli shipping. Then on 30 May King Hussein placed his troops under Egyptian command. Washington tried to ease the tension, but in Israel the rubicon was crossed when on 1 June the moderate Prime Minister, Levi Eshkol, appointed General Dayan, who had been chief of staff in 1956, to be defence minister; Dayan insisted that Israel had to defend herself by war. On 4 June Iraq joined the Jordanian–Egyptian military pact.

Early in the morning on 5 June 1967, the Israelis struck. The Six-Day War astonished the world by its demonstration of the immense superiority of the Israeli armed forces. Within twenty-four hours the air forces of Egypt and her allies had been destroyed. The Egyptian pilots had not been sufficiently trained and the Soviet pilots stationed on their airbases stood aside. After six days it was all over. Israeli divisions had reached the Suez Canal and had raced down to the tip of the Sinai Peninsula, once again occupying Sharm al-Sheikh, which commanded the passage through the Straits of Tiran. Israeli forces also occupied the Gaza Strip, which was inhabited by Palestinians and under Egyptian sovereignty. Jordan joined in the war despite Israeli pleas to stay out. Israeli troops then fought house-to-house battles against Jordanian forces, suffering heavy casualties before capturing East Jerusalem and the West Bank. In the north, the Israelis broke through the Syrian defences and occupied the Golan Heights, from which Syrian artillery had shelled Israeli settlements. Israel's victories against Egypt, Syria and Jordan were complete and overwhelming. Everything had gone according to the Israeli military plan. A major portion of the highly professional and efficient Israeli force was composed of part-time soldiers who spent eleven out of twelve months as civilians. It was an astonishing achievement that left the Israelis elated and, with hindsight, over-confident. The 1967 victory changed Israel for a generation, creating opportunities and problems not solved to the present day.

King Hussein's decision to join Egypt cost him the territory of the West Bank, which Jordan had captured in 1948/9; before then it had formed a part of the British Palestine Mandate. Israel was now faced with deciding what to do with the 845,000 hostile Palestinian Arabs living there. When they had been Jordanian citizens they had been Jordan's problem and might have assimilated. Under Israeli occupation, they rediscovered their Palestinian identity and demanded separate nationhood. The possibility of a 'Jordanian solution' receded as Israel's capture of the Old City of Jerusalem and her determination to retain an undivided Jerusalem as her capital blocked any peaceful arrangement with Jordan. Adding the Palestinians living in the Gaza Strip, the Israelis had now assumed responsibility for more than 1 million Arab Palestinians. Unlike their predecessors in 1948/9, the Arabs had not fled, but neither could they be reconciled to living under foreign occupation. The Israelis at first regarded the occupied territories as bargaining counters to attain peace; security required that they retain a relatively small part; the rest would be returned in exchange for peace treaties. Then Israel would enjoy secure borders and peace. It did not work out that way, though. Years later, it is true, peace was secured on this basis with Egypt. But the longer Israel occupied Gaza, East Jerusalem and the West Bank, the stronger grew the voices of those who claimed the territories as her historic land.

The famous UN Resolution 242 passed by the Security Council on 22 November 1967, despite its ambiguities and the different Arab and Israeli interpretations, provided a framework for peace negotiations. It promised Israel secure frontiers, it required her to withdraw from the conquered territories and stated the need for a just solution for the Palestinian refugees. But it was only a framework. There was no timetable for implementation. Nasser had already in September 1967, at a conference of the Arab heads of state in Khartoum, made an uncompromising demand for complete withdrawal of the aggressive Israeli forces and insisted that there could be no peace with Israel or negotiations without proper recognition of 'the rights of the Palestinian people in their own country'. The Arab nations did not move from this stand until Egypt broke ranks in 1977 (pages 914-15). The Israelis in turn were not prepared to give up what they had gained without something in return. Their interpretation of Resolution 242 is that it assures Israel safe and secure frontiers and that consequently the extent of her withdrawal has first to be negotiated between her and the Arab nations involved; such negotiations must precede any withdrawal. The Israelis reject withdrawal prior to possible negotiations.

It would take another war before Egypt was ready to negotiate and conclude a separate peace with Israel. But in the intervening years the influence of the right in Israel grew, the influence of politicians like Begin who passionately argued against giving up the territories of the West Bank, biblical Israel ('Judaea' and 'Samaria'). Nasser proclaimed a war of attrition against Israel in 1968; Palestinian guerrilla raids and sporadic Egyptian attacks forced Israel to remain on constant alert; the two sides also shelled each other across the Suez Canal until a ceasefire was agreed in August 1970. This proved to provide only a breathing space.

In September 1970, Nasser died. His death was mourned by millions of Egyptians and Arabs throughout the Middle East. He was not a scheming dictator, the reincarnation of Hitler, as he was seen at the time by some in Britain and France. In contrast to leaders elsewhere in the Middle East in his time and later, in Syria, Iran and Iraq, he was not a tyrant, killing thousands of opponents. Nor, unlike his royal predecessors, was he corrupt. He genuinely wanted to raise the standard of living of the Egyptian masses, but his state socialism and police security brought only order, without prosperity. He was defeated in his aims by population growth and by the costly wars he fought against Israel and in the Yemen. He fought to restore Arab pride and, despite his defeat, was paradoxically triumphant in achieving this wider goal. In the West, the Egyptians and other Arabs had been regarded as a lesser species of humanity, servile and incompetent. All that changed in 1956 when Nasser nationalised the Suez Canal and humiliated Britain and France. He served notice on the feudal royals left in the Arab world that the time was coming to an end when they could rule without the participation of the people. All of this boosted Arab self-esteem, without which there can be no peace

*The two heroes of the Yom Kippur War, General Moshe Dayan and General Ariel Sharon, are pictured here in October 1973, having just crossed the Suez Canal into Egypt.*

between Israel and her neighbours in the Middle East. Nasser's attitude to the Cold War, too, can now be judged in a different perspective. He manipulated Moscow and Washington to supply him with arms and aid but supported the neutrality of the Third World, the poorer countries, which could only lose and not gain by becoming involved in the conflicts of the superpowers.

Egypt's new president Anwar Sadat, after the failure of the United States to bring the two sides together, believed he was faced either with accepting Israel's conditions of peace or with fighting once more. He chose the latter. On 6 October 1973, the Jewish Day of Atonement, Yom Kippur, Syrian and Egyptian forces attacked Israel. Until hours before the attack was launched, the Israelis had not expected an all-out war and their Cabinet had rejected another pre-emptive strike. Mobilisation of reserves was ordered too late. The initial attacks broke through the much smaller Israeli forces, and it was not until the civilians were mobilised that the Syrians could be halted in the north. The fighting against the Egyptians, whose tanks had successfully

crossed into the Sinai, proved far more difficult. Only when General Sharon daringly crossed to the Egyptian side of the Suez Canal with Israel's armour on 15 October and so cut off the 100,000-strong Egyptian Third Army in the Sinai were the Israelis able to take the offensive. But the Israelis, after suffering early losses of their fighters, brought down by Soviet-supplied missiles, had succeeded in turning the tables on Syria and Egypt only after receiving replacement fighters and large quantities of arms flown in from the United States. The unwritten Israeli–French alliance had ended after 1967, the French being now more concerned to achieve better terms with the Arab states; and neither Britain nor West Germany was prepared to supply the arms the Israelis desperately needed. This reticence did not help the Western Europeans much. The Arab oil states expressed their solidarity with Egypt and Syria by imposing an oil embargo on the United States and on all the other countries which did not support the Arab cause. Western Europe was hit by an oil shortage and large price rises.

Henry Kissinger, the Secretary of State, was masterminding United States policy. President Nixon was in the grip of the Watergate crisis (pages 812–13) but he gave his full backing to Kissinger's policy of working for a durable Arab–Israeli peace, ready to assist Israel only to the extent of enabling her to defend herself effectively but not so much as to produce an Israeli victory as overwhelming as that in 1967. In that respect the United States and the Soviet Union held the same views, and Brezhnev and Kissinger and Nixon co-operated well during the first few days of the Yom Kippur War to bring about a ceasefire. On 20 October, Kissinger flew to Moscow at Brezhnev's invitation. The two super-powers agreed to present a ceasefire resolution to the Security Council on the 22nd, which Syria, Egypt and Israel accepted after some Soviet and US arm-twisting. Yet two days later, during the night of 24–25 October, the United States placed her forces in readiness for war. After such fruitful co-operation with the Kremlin, how had events taken this turn? It seemed like the Cuban missile crisis over again (Chapter 60). Was the world on the brink of the Third World War?

The Israelis were the culprits initially, in that they failed to observe the truce completely and, in ·an attempt to improve their military position, tightened the noose around the Egyptian Third Army. Brezhnev responded with a proposal to the United States that a Soviet–American peacekeeping force be sent. Kissinger did not wish to see Soviet troops in the Middle East, but the forceful US reaction was to the latter part of Brezhnev's proposal, a threat that if the United States did not agree then 'we should be faced with the necessity urgently to consider taking appropriate steps unilaterally. Israel cannot be allowed to get away with the violations.' US intelligence at the same time detected evidence of Soviet military preparations. Kissinger responded with a tough rejection, and US forces around the world were placed on intermediate war alert. But on 25 October Kissinger sent an olive branch: if Brezhnev abandoned the idea of unilateral action, there would be no need for a confrontation at all. Brezhnev immediately climbed down and that same day joined with the United States in sponsoring another United Nations ceasefire resolution setting up a UN peacekeeping force which would exclude both US and Soviet contingents. In return the United States ensured that this time the Israelis would stop all hostilities.

The Third Egyptian Army was thus rescued, and Egypt and Syria saved from further humiliation.

The 1973 war was no walk-over for Israel. This time her losses in men and material were heavy: 5500 dead and wounded and 800 tanks destroyed. Egypt's and Syria's losses were greater in absolute terms but not in proportion to their larger populations. Yet out of the Yom Kippur War developed positive consequences. Egypt and Syria had to accept realistically that they could not hope to inflict a total defeat on Israel, but their early successes had restored Arab pride. For the Israelis a state of no peace imposed harsh burdens and grave risks. They were now more prepared to return Arab territory if they could thereby obtain peace. For the Americans, the Arab–Israeli conflict seemed only to provide opportunities for Soviet intrusion in the Middle East. From this matrix of interests, US diplomacy succeeded – with the signature of the Camp David accords in September 1978 – in bringing Egypt and Israel together to agree a peace treaty (page 815). It is the cornerstone on which a comprehensive peace still awaits to be built.

Amid the turmoil of inter-Arab conflicts and the Arab–Israeli tensions and wars, of Soviet interventions in the Middle East and Iraq's anti-Western policies, the West had one powerful, oil-rich and secure ally in Reza Pahlavi, the Shah of Iran.

Until Islamic Iran forced herself into the news in the 1980s, the peoples of the Western world had only the haziest notions about the country and her people. Iran lies between the Caspian Sea and the Persian Gulf, and has borders with no less than five countries: to the north the Soviet Union, to the west Turkey and Iraq and to the east Afghanistan and Pakistan. She occupies the eastern shore of the Persian Gulf; on the northern shore Iraq has an outlet along the estuary Shatt al-Arab; from the north down the western shore lies the oil-rich sheikhdom of Kuwait, the kingdom of Saudi Arabia and the sheikhdoms of Bahrain, Qatar, the United Arab Emirates and Oman. It is oil which gives this region its significance, supplying much of the needs of Western Europe and Japan, with additional exports to the United States, the Middle East and Africa. A glance at a map (page 474) reveals Iran's and Iraq's key positions. Iran is a vast country of 627,000 square miles, five times the land area of Britain, though half of it is desert. In the Middle East (not counting Pakistan or Turkey) only Egypt has as large a population.

Given Iran's size, her oil resources and population, the heritage of an ancient civilisation and the history of a once great Persian Empire, her rulers might understandably dream of making their country a great power once more. But Iran (known as Persia until she was renamed in 1935) had first to free herself from foreign domination. The oil and her strategic position on the path to India had encouraged Britain to dominate southern Persia and the Gulf, agreeing to a division of interests which left Russia dominant in the north. Never genuinely independent, the country was occupied once more in 1941 by British and Russian troops for fear that the Shah would throw in his lot with the Germans. He was forced to abdicate and his son succeeded him (page 446).

During the post-war years the nationalist movement led by Mossadeq tried to win true independence and to loosen the control of the British oil giants over the country's main resource. The British government resisted and there was new turmoil, which was brought to an end in 1953 with the help once more of foreign intervention. The Americans and British helped the Shah to oust Mossadeq and the nationalist politicians and to stage a coup (page 461). In the eyes of the nationalists the Shah now owed his authority to foreign intervention, thus further diminishing Iran's sovereignty and independence. In 1955 Iran joined the Western alliance – the Baghdad Pact (renamed the Central Treaty Organisation after Iraq's revolution in 1958 and her subsequent departure), characterising the Shah still more as a lackey of the Anglo-American 'imperialists'. Iranian nationalist fervour could never reconcile itself to the 'Western' Shah.

Yet the Shah, though he owed his assumption of real power at least in part to American and British assistance in 1953, had every intention of asserting Iran's independence and creating a military base for new greatness. As his rule grew increasingly dictatorial, he appointed Iran's parliament and imprisoned politicians if they showed any sign of opposition. He established the National Information and Security Organisation, better known as SAVAK, a security police which collected information on opponents, often imprisoning, torturing and even murdering them. American attempts to influence the Shah and to persuade him to introduce democratic reforms, using economic and military aid as levers, had little effect. The Shah made token gestures in response. Western diplomats were by no means ignorant of the Shah's misrule, or of the corruption of the court and its dependants, but in Washington and London no alternative policy to supporting the Shah was acceptable. If a revolution should topple the Shah's regime, the country's mass poverty would, so it was thought, lead to a seizure of power by radicals and communists. The disturbed state of the Middle East had already allowed the Soviet Union to establish bases in Syria and Yemen; Iraq was uncertain and Egypt unstable. So Iran was the bulwark protecting the West's vital interests in the Persian Gulf. What the West did not foresee was the Islamic revolution.

The public in the West was given a positive image of the Shah. The tabloid press dwelt on his marriages to beautiful brides and the apparent tragedy of his divorces when his wives failed to produce the desired male heir; better fortune attended his third marriage. The handsome ruler seated on his Peacock throne in beautiful uniforms looked every inch a royal and made it easy to forget that his father, a dashing cavalry officer, had seized power in 1921 to become the founder of the Pahlavi dynasty. The lack of blue blood was compensated for by pomp and circumstance, which reached the height of folly when in 1971 the Shah staged a sumptuous celebration attended by international dignitaries to mark the anniversary of two and a half millennia of the Persian Empire. The pageant, staged to impress the visitors at Persepolis, ancient capital of the Achaemenian kings of Persia, cost tens of millions of dollars and was televised worldwide. For once the Shah's pretensions and megalomania lay exposed. But more generally he was regarded as a firm friend of the West internationally and as a reformer at home who was dragging his people out of the darkness of ignorance and prejudice into the modern age.

As a reformer his record was deeply flawed. Authoritarian and careless of political and human rights, the Shah resorted to brutal repression to preserve his power. In the early 1960s when the Americans were pressing for reforms, the economy was running into trouble and the National Front politicians were growing in strength, the Shah responded by arresting the National Front leaders and in 1963 organised a national referendum on a comprehensive reform package. It included land reform, a new election law including women's suffrage, a national literacy corps, profit-sharing and the sale of factories to private industry. The reforms were supposed to establish the Shah as a popular leader and were presented as the Shah–People Revolution. The referendum was rigged.

The most formidable opposition now came from religious leaders and their followers, and for the first time the name of one of these, Ruhollah Khomeini, was heard. Students were killed when paratroopers attacked the religious school of Qom where he taught and preached. His rearrest in June 1963 sparked off an insurrection in Teheran and other towns. The Shah ordered troops and tanks to shoot on the demonstrators and declared martial law. The number killed has never been accurately established: the Shah's government claimed less than a hundred, but reliable witnesses speak of thousands. Thousands more were imprisoned. Ayatollah Khomeini was released, but after persisting with his opposition he was in 1964 at the age of sixty-two forced to leave Iran. It turned out to be the Shah's worst mistake. From his exile successively in Turkey, Iraq and Paris, Khomeini was able to send a stream of clandestine propaganda into Iran, uncompromisingly condemning the Shah as an American lackey and his efforts to modernise and Westernise the country as contrary to Islamic law. By the end of his fifteen years of exile Khomeini was recognised by the masses as the spiritual and political leader who was most effectively challenging the Shah's fitness to rule.

In Iran, the Shah kept a tight grip on the country, backed by the military forces on which he lavished money and by SAVAK. He spent a quarter of Iran's income on purchasing the latest weapons, tanks and planes from the United States, though the US administration and Congress were reluctant to gratify all his wishes. The huge increase in oil revenues, especially after the price rises of 1973, gave the Shah the dollars with which to purchase whatever caught his fancy. The West, meanwhile, was tempted to reduce the imbalance of trade caused by the high cost of oil by selling all it could to Iran and the Middle Eastern oil states – who placed arms high on their shopping lists.

Successive development plans imposed reforms from above. Land reform deprived absentee landlords of most of their land and more than doubled the number of peasant proprietors of smallholdings. Large agricultural co-operatives were formed, and

### Iran's Oil Output and Revenue, 1938–1974

| | Output (barrels per day) | Revenue (US$ millions) |
|---|---|---|
| 1938 | 203,900 | 17 |
| 1950 | 635,000 | 45 |
| 1960 | 1,020,000 | 285 |
| 1970 | 3,845,000 | 1,013 |
| 1974 | 6,021,000 | 18,523 |

tractors and fertilisers used. But, as in the Soviet Union, it proved exceedingly difficult to improve agricultural productivity, which continued to rise more slowly than the increase in population. The government official replaced the landlord as the peasant's boss. Industrial growth, from a low base, was more impressive. New factories, steel mills and assembly plants for motor vehicles were constructed. Education and health services also benefited from large investments, and many Iranian students were sent abroad to Western universities. The statistics reflect a remarkable economic development; what they do not reveal is the unevenness of the distribution of wealth and the social dislocation that these rapid changes produced. The Shah demanded far too rapid an expansion. The gulf between the privileged elites – higher army officers, administrators and leading merchants – and the masses of urban poor, farmers and labourers remained huge. In the northern parts of Teheran, the shops, hotels and offices catered to the rich and exuded wealth. To the south lay a different world of slums where most of the city's 4.5 million lived in abject conditions. Many peasants had migrated to Teheran and to other towns, where they turned to the mullahs and the mosques for spiritual guidance and self-respect. In the countryside the income of three-quarters of rural families was so low that malnutrition was widespread. Nor was the small but growing middle class reconciled to the Shah's authoritarian regime. For thousands of students no worthwhile prospects awaited them on graduation. So it can be seen that all sections of society had reasons to resent the Shah's rule. Yet the speedy weakening of his position, leading to his overthrow in January 1979, came as a surprise.

Despite criticisms of Iran's violations of the democratic process and of human rights, the United States still felt that the Shah's regime was the best guarantor of Western interests in the Persian Gulf. After the British withdrawal as protecting power of the Gulf sheikhdoms in 1971 (page 921), the Shah with his well-equipped army and air force of some 350,000 men came to be seen as the indispensable policeman of a potentially turbulent region. President Jimmy Carter, who entered the White House in January 1977, likewise shrank from criticising the regime publicly, despite the prominence he gave to human rights. In November 1977 when the Shah visited Washington, with tear gas wafting around the White House lawn from protest demonstrations beyond the gate, Carter fulsomely pledged US support. On his return visit to Teheran in December he praised the Shah in a New Year Toast. 'Iran', he declared, 'is an island of stability in one of the more troubled areas in the world. . . . This is a great tribute to you, Your Majesty, and to your leadership and to the respect, admiration and love which your people give to you.' The repressiveness of his regime had been well reported to Washington by then. Carter's support was to cost him dear when the Shah's opponents came to power (pages 815–16).

In the West few in authority could imagine how the Shah, at the head of armed forces which owed him everything, could fail to crush with his tanks any popular protests likely to arise. The Shah could also count on an upper echelon of society who derived their wealth from his economic development and his favours. Ignorance of the dynamics of Iranian society led Western analysts to underestimate the hold of the mullahs over the people and the unrelenting sense of mission of an exiled ayatollah in a Parisian suburb. When the television cameras paid attention to Ayatollah Khomeini, all they showed was an old religious leader in his seventies sitting cross-legged on a carpet. He commanded no army, no government in exile, yet he proved more powerful than the Shah.

How did the revolution come about? From the mid-1970s, the Iranian economy did not prosper, despite the large oil income. The oil-price rise of 1973–4 was causing recession in the West and a drop in demand. The consequence was inflation, of food prices particularly; these price rises were most severe for the poor, whose rents in Teheran soared at the same time. Carter had hardly left Teheran early in January 1978 before demonstrations on behalf of Khomeini began in the holy city of Qom. The Shah responded fiercely; police opened fire on the students, some of whom were killed, the first martyrs of the revolution. From then on protests escalated in other cities and in Teheran in March, May and August 1978. Moderates and radicals, the National Front politicians, clerics and merchants were coming together to bring the Shah's personal rule to an end. In September a large demonstration converged on Jaleh Square in Teheran. The Shah imposed martial law. When the crowds would not disperse, the army started firing indiscriminately. Estimates of the ensuing casualties varied between several hundreds and 2000. It was a turning point. Strikes spread throughout the country.

The revolution was an example of people power, the first of several, to be followed later in the 1980s in South Korea, in the Philippines and in Eastern Europe, where the mass of people prevailed over the firepower of the military and police. The majority of the Shah's soldiers were conscripts, sickened by the orders to shoot defenceless civilians; some even joined the protesters. Rallying around posters of Khomeini, the accepted leader of the masses, the people engaged in a righteous struggle against their oppressive ruler. The Shah, uncertain whether to send in more troops or to try to negotiate with the moderates, lost control.

By December 1978, when the US administration was urging the Shah to accept a constitutional monarchy, it was far too late. On 16 January 1979 the Shah left the country without formally abdicating, and his departure released an outpouring of joy on the streets of Teheran. In the aftermath, no matter who managed temporarily to gain power in Iran's government, there was only one leader who really counted and that was the Ayatollah Khomeini. On 1 February 1979 television screens around the world showed an old man slowly descending from an Air France plane to a delirious reception from the Teheran crowds.

The first few months of the revolution were grim. Khomeini, the undisputed leader, chose a layman, Mehdi Bazargan, to head the provisional Islamic government. Bazargan was an Islamic scholar and had been an opponent of the Shah's authoritarian rule. Power was divided. Revolutionary courts sentenced and executed generals of the Shah's army responsible for the repression. By mid-March sixty-

*Ayatollah Khomeini's return to Iran on 1 February 1979* (above) *begins a new era. He aroused a religious fervour, evident at his funeral in June 1989* (below), *that astonished the world.*

THE STRUGGLE FOR PREDOMINANCE IN THE MIDDLE EAST

eight leading supporters of the Shah had been executed. On 1 April Khomeini declared the establishment of the Islamic Republic, which had been endorsed by a referendum. Real power lay with the Islamic Revolutionary Council, which took its orders from Khomeini. To 'protect the revolution' Khomeini sanctioned the formation of a militia, the Islamic Republican Party. The army and civil service were purged of those who had supported the Shah's regime, and attempts by Kurdish and Arab minorities to take advantage of the turmoil in order to set out on their own path to independence were put down. Thus was the revolution made secure.

Khomeini blamed the Americans for all Iran's ills and for their support of the Shah's corrupt regime, and he aroused the masses to see in the United States the main danger to the revolution's success and Iran's independence. Washington's efforts to establish normal relations were rejected. Bowing to humanitarian pressures, President Carter permitted the mortally sick Shah to receive medical treatment in New York. The Iranian government demanded his extradition to face charges in Iran. Khomeini supported these demands, urging the Teheran students to widen their attacks against America and Israel. There followed in November 1979 the seizure of the American Embassy by a revolutionary student group and the taking of the American diplomats and secretaries as hostages. Prime Minister Bazargan resigned and the Islamic Revolutionary Council took charge of the government. The United States became the Great Satan and Carter the enemy. The revolution was radicalised and for fourteen months the hostages remained imprisoned. Carter's attempt in April 1980 to rescue them by sending a special task force secretly to Teheran misfired when three of the eight helicopters developed malfunctions; the raid was aborted but unfortunately two of the rescuing planes crashed on making ready to return killing eight men; the mission could not any longer be kept secret. The impact on Carter's electoral chances was devastating. But Khomeini had demonstrated that Iran could safely defy the United States. Not until the day Carter left the White House were the hostages released to fly home (page 816). By then Iran had already been at war for four months with her neighbour Iraq. It was the beginning of the devastating Gulf War that lasted for almost seven years and led to the death of a million young men on both sides, the bloodiest conflict of the Middle East in modern times.

# PART X

---

*The Cold War: Superpower
Confrontation, 1948–1964*

# CHAPTER 48

# The Rise of Khrushchev:
# The Soviet Union and the West

Stalin never trusted the West, though he did not anticipate any immediate Western aggression. The orthodoxy still persisted in his day that capitalism would never tolerate communism and that a clash between the two worlds was historically inevitable. The deplorable state of the Soviet Union after the Second World War, however, made a postponement of any new conflict the highest priority of Soviet policy. This meant avoiding extreme provocations of the West, maintaining as long as possible the co-operation of the wartime alliance. It involved resisting Western moves dangerous to the security of the Soviet Union, above all the reviving and rearming of Germany. It was equally essential, Stalin believed, that despite the need for reconstruction and the poverty of the Russian people the armed forces should be kept strong and that nuclear and missile developments should be continued so that the arsenals of the West could at least be matched. The Soviet Union had to avoid appearing vulnerable; and the Red Army had to maintain its strategic grip on Eastern and central Europe, where uncertain allies acted as buffers. Given this pessimistic global outlook the prospects of building up confidence and allaying Soviet suspicions were never very good. There seemed to be a glimmer of hope in 1945 and 1946 after the defeat of Nazi Germany, but Western demands that the Soviet Union pull back to her redrawn frontiers and permit the countries of central and Eastern Europe a free choice of government – demands justified from a Western

point of view by the agreements reached at Yalta, and by Western values – alarmed Stalin. Soviet security rested now, in his view, on Soviet military dominance in Eastern and central Europe: western demands, if fully acted on, would only recreate a line of hostile states along Soviet borders.

Stalin did attempt to compromise initially by holding a loose rein (according to Soviet, not Western, standards) in Poland, Czechoslovakia, Bulgaria and Romania, where he did not insist on the establishment of one-party communist governments and permitted freedoms unthinkable in the Soviet Union at the time. He kept out of the Greek civil war, and provided no encouragement to communist parties in Western Europe, though they were especially strong in Italy and France. According to Soviet perceptions, this moderation had not paid any dividends. The West showed no appreciation of Russia's losses and sacrifices during the Second World War, even going so far as to halt reparations from the western zones of Germany.

The reconstruction of the western zones of Germany was viewed by Stalin with the deepest suspicion. The failure of an East–West agreement over the future of Germany was a crucially important reason for the start of the Cold War. The nightmare of new German armies in a capitalist coalition haunted Stalin and his advisers. The Truman Doctrine and Marshall Aid were seen as further evidence of implacable Western hostility, of a grand design to revivify former enemies and to undermine the hold an economically weakened Soviet Union held over her satellites. Finally Britain and the United States would not share their nuclear secrets with the Russians except on terms which were totally unacceptable (page 379), and they maintained a stockpile of atomic bombs as a threat to the Soviet Union.

The Soviet perception, as expressed in press and broadcasts, ran along the lines just described. There is little other evidence. The Soviet archives have not yet been analysed by scholars, unlike the once secret American and British records, which now divulge the debates and ideas of more than thirty years ago. Western archives have revealed, for instance, that American and British secret services were indeed planning clandestinely to roll back the Soviet control of Eastern Europe. From 1949 until the early 1950s there was, for instance, a bizarre scheme to restore King Zog to the throne of Albania; this, it was hoped, might start a wave of hostility against pro-Russian governments in the Balkans. Albanian exiles were actually landed, but they were quickly rounded up and shot. Several operations were nevertheless conducted over a period of some years, but none had any chance of success. This was not surprising, since British spies in high places in the Foreign Office and the Secret Intelligence Services (MI6) were passing information about these operations to Moscow. They had been recruited by the KGB as far back as the 1930s for just such a role. In the Baltic too in the 1950s, there was guerrilla resistance in Estonia, Latvia and Lithuania, whose independence had been snuffed out by the Soviet Union in 1940. After the war, MI6 organised the return of Latvian and Lithuanian émigrés to encourage uprisings. They were betrayed, met by the KGB and executed or imprisoned. It was in any event unlikely that any nationalist uprisings, even if they could have been organised by these missions, would have provoked any other Soviet reaction but bloody suppression.

Stalin blundered when he tried to intimidate the West to give way in Germany during the Berlin crisis and the blockade in 1948 (page 384). His overall German policy, as well as Soviet harshness in Eastern Europe, was even more calamitously counter-productive, for it led to the formation of a firm Western alliance, NATO, and eventually to the rearmament of West Germany. If, and it is a big if, there had ever been any chance of establishing Soviet–Western relations on a fresh basis, it had certainly been lost by 1948.

From the Kremlin's point of view, Russia faced three overriding challenges in the post-war world. There was the perceived external threat from Western capitalist hostility to communism; there was the unwillingness of the majority of the people of Eastern and central Europe to accept, unless imposed by Soviet-backed force, the communist transformation of their society and economy; and finally there was the danger that a greater awareness of Western standards of life would create dissatisfaction among the Russian people, who had been conditioned into believing that they were building up a better and more just society. Stalin, moreover, realised that in the aftermath of the war the Soviet Union, with its western territories devastated, was in an appallingly weak state and that to provide for security and reconstruction would demand once more heavy sacrifices from the Russian people.

In Eastern and central Europe the Soviets imposed a communist minority on the majority, and this minority then faced strong popular opposition to its social and economic policies, as well as the opposition of the Catholic Church, which retained the adherence of the majority of Poles and Hungarians. To this opposition was added the fierce nationalism of these peoples – the one characteristic they shared, whether Poles, Yugoslavs or Albanians. Only the Yugoslavs and Albanians had escaped direct Soviet control. Elsewhere the leaders of the satellite communist regimes soon set up by Stalin, the 'little Stalins', were not only hated but were regarded by their own people as puppets of their Soviet masters. All this discontent within the Soviet sphere of power was a source of instability. It would need little to transform it into open revolt, even without Western assistance. The very existence of the West on the borders of the extended Soviet empire was a provocation, irrespective of Western policies.

The inherent problems of ruling over the Soviet Union herself presented the gravest problems to the isolated communist elite. The war against the Germans had revealed strong nationalist feelings in the Ukraine and elsewhere and much disaffection in the face of Stalinist rule. On the other hand, the horrors of German occupation and national fervour had also helped to unite the peoples of the USSR. Significantly, the war came to be known not as the great communist struggle against capitalism in its fascist manifestation, but as the Great Patriotic War, thus emphasising the nationalism and patriotism which transcended the revolution and the Soviet state. With the war over, how could the harshness of communist rule from above continue to be justified? The threat of a hostile world beyond Soviet frontiers was stressed and the West painted in the blackest colours.

While Stalin lived he ensured that no one else had a power base to rival his. Even so, the Soviet Union was not a monolithic society. Stalin could intervene arbitrarily, but control lower down the scale had to be left to others, to Beria's secret police and to the tens of thousands of functionaries in the police, party and governmental apparatus who administered the Soviet republics. By changing his top henchmen, killing suspects and those who showed any signs of independence, by filling the prison camps of the Gulag and by promoting for a time those he trusted, Stalin's hold remained unshakeable to his dying day. A bureaucracy ruled over the people and individual freedom was subject to the whims of authority. There could be some genuine debate about policies in the Kremlin, but generally only if Stalin permitted it.

As Stalin's health deteriorated after the war, political repression became more fierce and any independence of thought was stamped out. Newspapers and magazines parroted the party view. In science, drama, history, literature, art, even in music, the party line had to be followed. Stalin shortly before his death was probably preparing another great purge to safeguard his power and to maintain the system. The Doctor's Plot was unveiled in January 1953. It had strong (and popular) anti-Semitic overtones. The startling public announcement was made that nine doctors, all but two Jewish, who had looked after top Soviet leaders, had been arrested a few weeks earlier and had confessed to murdering Zhdanov and other members of the Soviet elite; they were accused of having acted on orders from Israeli Zionists and the American and British secret services. Jews in prominent positions were particular targets of the thousands of arrests that followed. How little decades of loyalty to Stalin counted was evidenced by the arrest of Foreign Minister Molotov's wife, who was Jewish. Fortunately for many, Stalin suffered a stroke and died in his dacha on 5 March 1953, the scared Politburo members tiptoeing to his room, when they heard, to make sure he was really dead.

The leader who had shaped Russia's destinies

for good and evil had unexpectedly gone. Despite his crimes, Stalin was widely admired as one of the Soviet Union's greatest men, second only to Lenin – Lenin's 'comrade-in-arms', 'the standard bearer of his genius and his cause', as the eulogies after his death declared. He had ruled the Soviet Union with an iron fist, responsible for the deaths of millions but also for gigantic material achievements. Men and women in their prime of life, indeed everyone under the age of forty-five, had known no adult life except under Stalin. The Soviet Union had become powerful and respected in the world and, during the great Patriotic War, which was the central event of their lives, Stalin had saved his country from defeat and had then presided over the victory of the Red Army and its final entry into Berlin. There followed an unprecedented expansion of Soviet power, and even a small but steady improvement in living standards from 1948 to his death. He dwarfed those Soviet political leaders who survived him. And even they, as Khrushchev recalls, dreaded what seemed an uncertain future without him, although the shadow of his terror was lifted from their lives.

The Russia Stalin had helped to shape and had now left behind was a state stifled by bureaucracy without the safeguards of civil liberties, where all apparatchiks, whether in politics or industry, uncritically obeyed the orders of superiors. The system made each individual play for safety, sheltering under the decision of the man above rather than risking personal initiative. What mattered was who would cover you, look after you and provide you with the advantages and bribes earned by performing a service for the system. Corruption was endemic. The command economy was firmly established with all its inefficiencies, which became glaringly obvious thirty years after Stalin's death. The Soviet Union was set on a course from which no divergence seemed possible without inviting chaos. Stalin shamelessly exploited the vested interests he had created. In the Kremlin those who served him had to pander to his whims and adapt to his erratic lifestyle of working into the small hours, drinking or watching his favourite films. His popular image was that of the benevolent father of his people, the fount of all wisdom, whose actions, like those of a demi-god, could not always be comprehended by ordinary mortals.

Stalin would never officially have designated a successor. In his lifetime he had to appear irreplaceable. In this respect, history seemed to be repeating itself. Lenin, the father of the Soviet Union, had had mixed feelings about his possible successor and appeared to leave an unfillable vacuum, but the leadership was nevertheless replaced by three Bolshevik leaders before Stalin emerged as dictator and eliminated his rivals. After Stalin's death a collective leadership again emerged; not one of these once loyal henchmen of Stalin's day was powerful enough to oust his rivals immediately. Power depended on the support of the other leading Bolsheviks, as well as on the backing of a constituency, the will not of the people of course, but of the government in terms of the administration and economic and industrial management of the state, or of the party which had once constituted the supreme constituency, or of the separately organised secret police, its armed units and prison regimes which controlled a labour force of several millions. Finally there existed the constituency of the Red Army command; though its broader political ambitions were carefully controlled by the party its support was important to any aspirant to power.

Stalin had dominated Russia without using any one channel of control exclusively, so that at the time of his death it was uncertain where power lay, or rather how it was distributed in the absence of an autocratic final arbiter. Georgi Malenkov had presented the main report to the party Congress in October 1952, which was possibly Stalin's way of indicating that he was his choice as successor. Beria, as secret police chief, had served Stalin faithfully and ruthlessly, too ruthlessly for the other claimants not to fear him. Molotov had seen long service since the revolution of 1917 and had held important offices, including that of an unsmiling unbending foreign minister. Finally Nikita Khrushchev had served Stalin loyally in the party during and after the war, accommodating himself to Stalin's purges. Malenkov was unable to establish himself as sole leader. But the struggle for power was hidden from the outside world, as so often since when a change of leadership has taken place. The premiership, or leadership of the government, was assumed by Malenkov. Khrushchev became secretary of the Central Committee of the party. Other leading communists gained control of the different ministries which their Stalinist experience appeared to entitle them to: Molotov foreign affairs, Bulganin defence and Beria interior and security. These three were members of the Politburo, which also included

Khrushchev, Kaganovich, Mikoyan, Voroshilov and two others, and was presided over by Malenkov. The first outcome of the power struggle was that Beria was isolated. Only a few weeks after being accorded an honoured place as a pallbearer of Stalin's coffin, Beria was secretly arrested, tried and shot. The first public awareness of his fall was his omission from a news report about leading communists attending a performance at the Bolshoi Theatre. This became the stuff on which a new foreign political science came to be built, Kremlinology. The inner workings of the Politburo remained shrouded in secrecy before the Gorbachev era, so Kremlinologists had to make do with more oblique indications of conflict and changes in the distribution of power: the line-up of leaders at the May Day parade, the priorities evident at receptions, disappearances from view, an absence due to a 'cold'.

It now seems that during the months that followed Stalin's death several important changes occurred. The party recovered step by step its former pre-eminence. Stalin's personal dictatorship, it was now claimed, had distorted the correct line laid down by Lenin. What was being affirmed was the eternal validity of communist ideology. The condemnation of Stalin's rule, by Khrushchev, did not indicate at this stage a loss of faith in communism itself.

In the spring and summer of 1953 the collective leadership's first priority was to maintain control. The army had been a powerful ally against Beria and, if the terror machine was not to be relied on to the same extent as before, control might better be established by concessions. A cautious beginning was made of releasing some of the tens of thousands who had been falsely imprisoned. Malenkov lowered prices and allowed more resources to be devoted to consumer goods. To ease food shortages, the peasants were promised a better deal, prices paid by the state for agricultural produce were increased and taxes reduced. Khrushchev took charge of the agricultural question – the key to better living standards – and launched the development of the 'virgin lands', a vast scheme to grow grain on lands in the remoter regions of the Soviet Union not previously cultivated because they were subject to droughts or other unfavourable conditions. It was a crash programme that produced spectacular results between 1953 and 1956. Later results proved disappointing.

As always the Soviet leadership faced the problem

of how to stretch inadequate resources to provide for policies each of which was highly desirable in itself: more investment in agriculture, a switch, even if a modest one, from heavy to consumer industries, and full support for the military establishment and defence. One conclusion reached was that an openly aggressive policy towards the United States and her allies, such as Stalin had followed in 1948 and 1949, would only cement the anti-Soviet alliances and lead to increased Western rearmament, so widening the gap between the West and the Soviet Union even if Soviet defence expenditure were greatly increased. Soviet relations with the rest of the world therefore followed a calmer course. But the question of balance always had to be carefully considered. It was essential that the West should not realise that the Soviet Union was acting from a position of weakness, above all in the field of nuclear weapons. Nor should the West be left with the impression that the opportunity now existed to undermine Soviet control of Eastern and central Europe, which was fundamental to the Soviet Union's perception of her continued security. So a tightrope had to be walked between concession and firmness. Of course there was debate among the hardliners and the reformers on each issue of policy, and personal political ambitions came into play. Nevertheless a surprisingly consistent line of policy emerged from 1953 until 1956.

In April 1953, only a month after Stalin's death, the Soviet Union began to use her influence to help bring the Korean War to a conclusion. Next, it was indicated that a peace treaty might be possible for Austria. But, to hold the balance, emphasis was placed on the continuity of Soviet policy: there would be no withdrawal from Eastern Europe. The point was underlined when Soviet tanks suppressed disorders in Berlin which threatened to turn into a general uprising against an unpopular Stalinist regime (page 534). But in the summer of 1953 further friendly signals were sent. An American journalist in Prague who had been imprisoned as a spy two years previously was released, and Malenkov delivered a speech in which he declared that there were no problems that could not be settled by negotiation. To satisfy the hardliners these 'new' views were interspersed with classic Stalinist declarations as well. Actions, however, indicated the new approach more clearly: the resumption of diplomatic relations with Greece, with Israel and even with Stalin's sworn enemy, Tito's Yugoslavia. Concili-

atory statements were made to improve relations in the Middle East with Turkey and Iran. In the spring of 1954, the Soviet Union and China participated with Britain and France in the Geneva Conference, which reached a settlement relating to the French Indo-China War. The largest and most unexpected concession the Russians made was to conclude the long-drawn-out negotiations over Austria by agreeing to withdraw from the Soviet zone and from Vienna, which they did tactfully to the strains of the Radetzky March. The Austrian Treaty was signed on 15 May 1955. A new epoch in East–West relations appeared to have been achieved two months later at a conference of the Big Four (the United States, the Soviet Union, Britain and France), also held in Geneva. Although far-reaching disarmament proposals by both sides got nowhere and no real progress was made on any substantive issue, the friendly human contact between the Soviet leaders – Khrushchev clearly emerging as Russia's decisive voice in foreign affairs – and President Eisenhower created an illusory feeling that a new era was about to start. The Cold War looked like being liquidated. Even so, Soviet policy failed in one of its main objectives: to prevent the rearming of Western Europe in general and of Western Germany in particular. Nor did the relaxation of tension sufficiently encourage the West to abandon NATO and to dissolve the Western European–North American military lifeline. Suspicions of the Soviet Union ran too deep, Soviet military power in Europe was too overwhelming to tempt France, Britain and the Federal Republic of Germany to exchange the American alliance for Soviet promises of peaceful coexistence and some form of German reunification.

The decision to withdraw from Austria coincided with the fall of Malenkov in February 1955. Foreign relations was one of the issues in the internal power struggle among the Soviet leadership in the Politburo (or rather in the Praesidium, as the Politburo was renamed from 1952 to 1966). Khrushchev was prepared to go further than Malenkov and Molotov in improving relations with the West, with China and with Yugoslavia. Malenkov also proved himself indecisive and slow-witted in the face of Khrushchev's ruthless and brilliant manoeuvring, especially on investment priorities and other domestic issues. Khrushchev had progressed since Stalin's death from being the most senior secretary to First Secretary of the party. Unlike Beria, who was executed,

Malenkov was bloodlessly demoted and remained a member of the Praesidium. Khrushchev nevertheless continued to be fettered by the collective leadership of the Praesidium, where hardliners like Molotov had only been temporarily eclipsed. On no one would Stalin's mantle of absolute power fall. Khrushchev was not yet strong enough to combine the position of head of the government with that of party chief, so Bulganin replaced Malenkov as premier.

But Khrushchev was riding high. A man of great energy, he displayed a down-to-earth bluffness, despising formality and protocol; what he lacked in consistency and steady application of carefully prepared policies, he made up for in boldness. He tried to cut through the stultifying dead weight of state bureaucracy by making a personal and human impact, quite unlike the aloofness and austerity of the Stalinist period, and by pragmatism, trying first one way and then another. He was convinced that the governing leadership had to win more popular consent, to persuade and cajole, and to minimise the use of state force. With Russia's backward agriculture lacking incentives, Khrushchev again raised prices of agricultural products, increased investments in farm machinery and fertilisers and extended the virgin lands. More state farms, run like industrial enterprises, were established as the virgin lands were opened up. An impressive rise in agricultural output was achieved, though at a high cost in resources, and agricultural productivity remained low by comparison with advanced countries like the United States, even if a more favourable comparison could be made with the less efficient small French or southern German farms. As in Soviet industry, over-centralisation of planning led to much waste and inefficiency.

Less hidebound by ideology in the narrow sense, Khrushchev was ready to try new remedies. He nevertheless held to the central tenet of Stalinist ideology that ultimately the Soviet Union had to be ruled from above not only politically but with regard to the determination of economic priorities and paths of development. The difference between the Stalinist and the post-Stalinist period lies in Khrushchev's genuine effort to make communism work for the people to give them a better quality of life. That was the purpose of economic and social reform: attempts were made to alleviate the extreme shortage of housing and to provide minimum wages; workers were free to change their jobs; at least some

basic legal rights for the ordinary citizen began to emerge; but the most remarkable change of all was the massive release of political prisoners from the Gulag, which began only after Malenkov's fall. This was the most visible indication of the ending of Stalin's mass terror regime, though the leadership would continue to protect the system against individuals who were thought to endanger it, by imposing sentences of imprisonment, exile or more subtly, in later years, detention in psychiatric hospitals. Rights were granted only to those ready to work within the system, not to those who were accused of actively propagating views against it. Thus censorship remained, though it was less stifling: criticisms of specific features of Soviet life were tolerated, writers and artists could breathe more freely, and foreign visitors to the Soviet Union were encouraged. But neither Khrushchev nor his communist successors ever granted anything like the freedoms ordinary people in the West enjoy.

A Soviet citizen could not leave the country without the most careful scrutiny of his past, even when visiting a fraternal communist Eastern-bloc state; visits to the West were generally permitted only to members of official delegations accompanied by a KGB minder; other members of the family had to stay behind as hostages, and wives were not allowed to join husbands. The fate of Soviet Jews who wished to emigrate to Israel was particularly harsh (page 477), given that it was forbidden to make a declaration of allegiance to anything but the Communist Party and Soviet state. Nationalism continued to be suppressed. The Orthodox Church was one symbol of national consciousness and was kept under rigid control. Zionism was treated as ideologically hostile to the state – mere Jewish descent officially was not – and the teaching of Hebrew and of Jewish culture was prohibited. Punishments were harsh. Attempts to stamp out the corruption widespread in the system involved the imposition of death sentences for large-scale fraud or transgression against economic laws.

Khrushchev's first move after forcing Malenkov's fall with the support of Bulganin and Voroshilov in February 1955 was to discredit his opponents in the Praesidium. In the winter of 1954/5 he had argued that in the dangerous international circumstances of the time Malenkov was wrong to espouse light consumer industries at the expense of the heavy industry needed for defence. Molotov could hardly dispute that. A few months later Khrushchev

*Marshal Tito brought stability to the peoples of Yugoslavia and established an independent Communist state that the Soviet Union could not easily bully.*

turned to attack Molotov's inflexible stance on foreign relations. Yugoslavia became the touchstone of Soviet policy and the key to the making of a complete break with Stalinism, a repudiation which Molotov resisted. Molotov had been ready to re-establish formal diplomatic relations with Yugoslavia as between two nations, but he was not prepared to accept that the party could agree to a reconciliation with a nationalist Yugoslav Communist Party. Khrushchev prevailed and headed a Soviet delegation which visited Belgrade in May 1955. This public Soviet acceptance of Tito's right to follow his own nationalist path to communism without having to accept Soviet leadership was like the mountain coming to Mohammed.

At the plenum of the Central Committee of the Communist Party in Moscow held in secret in July 1955, it came to a showdown between Khrushchev and Molotov. Khrushchev's arguments were powerful. The Soviet Union had to avoid a conflict with the West, but opportunities existed in the uncommitted under-developed countries, which could be won over to the socialist camp. Khrushchev thus recognised that there were independent nations which, while not willing to accept Soviet leadership, could be encouraged to follow policies friendly to the Soviet Union. At the same time, the splits in the Soviet bloc, with Yugoslavia and China, should be healed as far as possible. Molotov argued for the more traditional line of policy that to condone Tito's break away from the control of the Soviet party would only endanger the Soviet position in the other people's democracies such as Poland. But before this crucial meeting had ended, Molotov had to admit to errors – for the time being he could not resist Khrushchev's line of policy. But Khrushchev was not yet powerful enough to oust him, the most senior of Stalin's lieutenants still surviving in power.

Almost as sensational as Khrushchev's visit to Belgrade was West German Chancellor Konrad Adenauer's visit to Moscow in September 1955. Adenauer had taken the German Federal Republic into NATO and had refused to recognise the German Democratic Republic (East Germany) as sovereign, claiming to speak for the whole of Germany. The two issues he raised in Moscow were German reunification and the return of German prisoners of war, and as a result of his visit the surviving German prisoners of war returned home. Relations between the Federal Republic and the Soviet Union were normalised as between two sovereign nations. Only a few weeks later in November and December 1955 Khrushchev and Bulganin visited India, Burma and Afghanistan, to be met everywhere with enthusiasm. To Afghanistan, in dispute with Pakistan, massive Soviet military aid was sent, and economic assistance was given to India and Burma; only Pakistan could not be wooed but remained loyal to the Western Baghdad Pact (page 655). On their return to Moscow it was clear that Khrushchev's and Bulganin's prestige had risen as a result of their foreign travels. Khrushchev could claim that Soviet influence and security had been enhanced by the policies he had followed: a rapprochement with Yugoslavia and China, good relations with the countries of south-east Asia, a relaxation of tension with Western Europe and, after the Geneva summit of July 1955, with the United States as well. Soviet influence was on the increase in the neutral Third World, that is among the ex-colonies of Western European empires. Finally, the Soviet Union had leapt over the Baghdad Pact in arranging an arms deal with Egypt shortly after the Geneva summit. This showed that Khrushchev's policies were not purely defensive but were intended rather to create opportunities for the expansion of Soviet power and influence without risking war.

Khrushchev was riding high in the winter of 1955. At the Twentieth Party Congress, which assembled in February 1956, he now made his boldest bid for leadership, seeking the support of the Soviet party and government elite in his famous 'secret speech'. In it he launched what he believed were artfully and hardly concealed attacks on Molotov, Malenkov and Kaganovich, his rivals in the Praesidium. The most sensational part of his speech was his denunciation of Stalin's despotism, of the crimes Stalin and his close associates (by implication including Molotov and Malenkov) had committed, such as the murder in 1934 of Kirov, the First Secretary of the Leningrad party. Khrushchev graphically spoke of the tortures and purges that followed; he demythologised Stalin's image as all-wise, describing how he had miscalculated in June 1941 when the Germans attacked and how he had completely lost control for a time. He emphasised how loyal members of the party, the state and the armed forces had been wrongly arrested and shot. Stalin had usurped the party; it was not the system or the party which had been at fault, but Stalin's lust for power and his insane suspicions, which became murderously manifest in 1934. Khrushchev was careful not to attack the way the state had evolved as such after Lenin's death but placed all the blame on Stalin and his associates like Beria. The opposition to Khrushchev, led by Molotov, later dubbed the 'anti-party' group, nevertheless survived until June 1957, when its final concerted challenge failed.

In the same sensational speech Khrushchev also fundamentally redefined the Soviet Union's external relations. The world had changed since Lenin's day, he declared. War was no longer inevitable. The capitalist imperialists could now be restrained by powerful social and political forces, and aggression would receive a smashing rebuff. The capitalist West would not rapidly decay, though Khrushchev had no doubts about the ultimate triumph of communism in the world. Meanwhile there could be 'peaceful coexistence' between countries with different social systems. Khrushchev was anxious to win over the socialist Third World, especially India with her democratic constitution, asserting that the socialist transformation of society need not be achieved by violent revolutions but could also be brought about by parliamentary institutions. He even hoped to allay the hostility to communism of the socialist parties of Western Europe and to help create a united front of the working class. The Western European nations were encouraged to dissolve their links with the United States, whose only purpose was to exploit them.

To further these aims B and K, as they became popularly known, continued their travels, visiting Britain in April 1956. They stayed with their entourage incongruously at the most aristocratic of London hotels, Claridge's, and then laid a wreath on the tomb of Karl Marx. But the visit was not a success, either publicly or in ministerial meetings. The shadow of the Middle East hung over discussions with the Prime Minister, Anthony Eden, who blamed the Russians for encouraging Nasser and unbalancing the Middle East by supplying the Egyptians with arms via Czechoslovakia (page 465). Khrushchev's sensational denunciation of Stalin meanwhile was read with astonishment and avid interest; the Western world hoped that Soviet policy would now break with the past altogether.

In Soviet-dominated central and Eastern Europe the changes in Soviet policies since Stalin's death had spectacular repercussions. Khrushchev's efforts to make communism more acceptable to the people, to restrain the arbitrary abuse of power by the 'little Stalins' and by their subservient party machines, resulted in popular outbursts and demands for other freedoms the Kremlin would not lightly concede: more national independence and a loosening of the Soviet grip. Paradoxically, the communist leaders in East Germany, Bulgaria and Romania most disapproved of by Khrushchev for their rigid Stalinism were the ones best able to keep control against rising nationalism.

# CHAPTER 49

## *Eastern Europe and the Soviet Union: The Polish Challenge and the Hungarian Rising*

Stalin's Russia was determined to turn Poland into an obedient Soviet-controlled state; all vestiges of democratic influence were to be swept away. A Tito-like defiance could not be tolerated in Poland, which was strategically far more vital to the USSR than Yugoslavia. Fearful that the orthodox communist but nationally minded Polish First Secretary of the Communist Party, Wladyslaw Gomulka, could cause trouble, Stalin had him removed and imprisoned. Gomulka's rival for power, the President of Poland, Boleslaw Bierut, a former Comintern man, was placed in the crucial position of first secretary. To make doubly certain, a Soviet general, Marshal Konstanty Rokossowski, installed as deputy premier and minister of defence, ensured that Poland did not stray from the Soviet fold. Rokossowski could call on a Polish army of 400,000 men and on the Soviet divisions stationed in Poland, which was ruled by the party rigidly on the Stalinist model. Fears of West German demands for the recovery of Germany's 'lost' territories of Silesia and east Prussia could be used to make Poland the most important member besides the Soviet Union of the Warsaw Pact alliance, which the Russians had set up in 1955 to counter the formation of NATO in the West. Economically, too, Poland was closely linked to the Soviet Union through bilateral treaties. She was also a member of Comecon, the Soviet-dominated Council of Mutual Economic Assistance, set up in 1949. In its early years Comecon hardly bestowed 'mutual' benefits on its members but was largely inactive, a propaganda answer to Western co-operation and Marshall Aid.

Industry and small workshops were almost totally nationalised in Poland. The economy was directed by a central plan which gave greatest emphasis to heavy industry and armaments. The workers suffered from the exploitation of their labour, and independent trade unions had been crushed. To these privations, the easiest responses were absenteeism, petty theft and shoddy work. Thus the Polish socialist state in this command economy did not win the support of the class on which communism was supposed to be firmly built – the industrial workers. The party tried to push state agriculture too, imposing prices and exacting taxes. Stalinist collectivisation made only slow progress, however: less than 10 per cent of arable land had been collectivised by 1955. The rest remained in the hands of small farmers, but they were defenceless against rigid state controls and reacted by producing less and less.

The Catholic Church, traditional custodian of Polish culture, came to embody national independence and resistance to communism and Russification. Relations between state and Church rapidly got worse after 1949; the Church's privileges and possessions were curtailed and in 1952 bishops and priests were arrested and imprisoned. Then in 1953 the primate of Poland, Archbishop Stefan Wyszynski, was forced to retire to a monastery.

All these repressive measures failed to break the religious feelings of the majority of Poles. Farmers clung to their soil and workers could not be persuaded to build up a socialist Poland which offered them so little reward. The bureaucracy, the secret police and the party were 'them', to be suffered only as long as was necessary – and that meant, as Poles realised, as long as Soviet military force held Poland in its grip.

Stalin's death did not lead to any immediate thaw in Poland. Bierut held on to power, though on Moscow's insistence 'collective' leadership had to be adopted by splitting the positions of party secretary and premier. Soon a split developed, as it had in Moscow, between the Stalinist hardliners and the reformers, and Bierut was forced into concessions. Beria's fall in the Soviet Union had downgraded in the Soviet Union the previously all-powerful security apparatus and limited its murderous activities. Poland's regime had to follow suit. Communists unjustly imprisoned were rehabilitated and Gomulka was quietly released from prison. Discussion became more free and critical; even Western jazz could now be played. The Stalinist years had proved to be no more than a cloak as far as people's minds were concerned: a religious, patriotic and critical population remained very much alive in town and country and so showed up the isolation of the Polish communist leadership. Khrushchev's not so secret speech to the Twentieth Congress of the Communist Party in February 1956 denouncing Stalin was a heavy blow to Bierut and the hardliners in Poland. Indeed, it may have contributed to the heart attack and death of Bierut in Moscow a few weeks later.

Edward Ochab, formerly a Stalinist, now with the wind of change from Moscow a more flexible communist, succeeded as party secretary. He had turned reformer. Khrushchev's speech was read out at Communist Party meetings throughout Poland; a general amnesty released many political prisoners. Reforms eased the lot of farmers and workers, but the firm control of the party made people regard talk of 'democratisation' with cynicism, and the Russians remained ever present. Yet three years after Stalin's death popular pressure from below intensified in Eastern Europe, fuelled rather than appeased by half-hearted reforms, as it turned into open risings in Hungary in November 1956. But the most serious crisis appeared first to be occurring in Poland, when in June 1956 the Poznan steelworkers escalated a pay dispute into a disturbance of much wider significance. They now loudly demanded 'Bread and Freedom' and so challenged the whole Soviet-backed system, though only in peaceful demonstrations. The authorities reacted with brute force. Army units fired into the crowds, killing and wounding more than 300. Poles were killing Poles. In the aftermath of these events in Poznan the Politburo of the Polish Communist Party was thrown into confusion by the deep division between the Stalinists and the reformers. According to the Stalinists the Poznan disturbance was the work of 'enemy agents'; according to reformers it was an expression of legitimate grievances. Most worrying were demands of 'freedom', not just internal freedom, but freedom from the Soviet Union. This no Soviet leaders at the time would tolerate and the Poles knew that if Russia's position were seriously threatened Poland would be forcibly brought back into line. Nevertheless the Polish reformists gained the upper hand. 'Workers' councils' were established to bring a 'democratic' element into management. A reform programme was adopted and Gomulka emerged as its leading exponent on the Central Committee. In the struggle with the Stalinists he soon enjoyed extensive popular support in Warsaw and other cities. The crisis point was reached in mid-October 1956. The Soviet leadership became so alarmed that Khrushchev and a high-powered Soviet delegation arrived uninvited in Warsaw to halt the slide, which might end in a repudiation of Soviet control and of socialism. Soviet troop movements were set in motion. Poland was on the brink of bloody conflict. It is interesting to compare the situations in Poland and Hungary at this time and to ask why an armed conflict developed in Hungary but was averted in Poland.

It is clear that Khrushchev wanted to avoid a military showdown, whether in Poland or in Hungary, because he realised the immense setback it would mean for his reformist policies and for his own position in Moscow. From a Soviet point of view the danger Gomulka presented lay in his Polish nationalism – another Tito could not be tolerated. Then there was the even greater danger that a national popular uprising would occur and that the Polish leaders would lose control. Gomulka convinced Khrushchev that only he and the reformers could retain control, that while he wished to correct the Stalinist errors of the past he was a convinced communist, and that while Polish nationalism required that Poland assert the right to be treated as a sovereign nation Poland would remain loyal to the Soviet alliance. What was equally clear to Khrushchev was not only that Gomulka enjoyed immense popular support for his stand, but that the Polish army would be likely to side with the Polish leadership, however hopeless the struggle. Khrushchev had enough trouble on his hands without inviting more, but he returned home with misgivings. Before the end of the year the Stalinists were purged from the Polish party and the Russians agreed to abandon direct interference in Polish affairs. The way was open for 'national communism'. Gomulka also delivered his side of the bargain. Poland remained a communist state; she did not repudiate her membership of the Warsaw Pact and did not intervene on Hungary's side. The Polish leaders recognised the limits of Soviet tolerance. The Hungarians did not and paradoxically it was Hungarian support for Poland that radicalised the Hungarian unrest into a full-scale rebellion against Soviet domination.

Hungary had suffered particularly under the iron hand of the Stalinist First Secretary Mátyás Rákosi, having since the summer of 1949 been turned into a communist state on the Soviet model. Rákosi eliminated his communist rivals, even hanging Laszlo Rajk, a former minister of the interior. The peasantry was forced into collectivisation and industry was placed under central state control. The prisons filled and a vast and much hated secret police enormously extended its activities. To Khrushchev and the majority of the Kremlin leadership an unreformed Rákosi was a distinct liability. Rákosi in turn anxiously watched the destalinisation developments in Poland and was shaken by the apparent Yugoslav–Soviet reconciliation. His response to demands for economic reforms and for more freedoms within a communist system, which were being advocated by intellectuals and the more progressive communists around Imre Nagy, was to clamp down even more severely in the summer of 1956. In July, however, the Kremlin forced him to resign.

There was no strong and popular communist like Gomulka to replace him. The post of first secretary was given to another, hardly less hated Stalinist, Ernö Gerö. At least János Kádár, a cautious reformer, who later was to play a critical role in the revolution and the post-revolutionary history of Hungary, joined the Hungarian Politburo.

After July, the divided Hungarian leadership and the still overwhelmingly Stalinist party machine failed to provide any firm national communist direction to those such as the students, intellectuals and many urban Hungarians who were looking for change. Imre Nagy was potentially the only popular communist around whom the nation might have rallied, but like a good communist he refused to organise an opposition. Concessions by the Politburo were interpreted as signs of weakness. Opposition grew and took more and more challenging forms under the influence of the Polish October. On 23 October 1956 students spearheaded a mass demonstration of support for Poland in the Hungarian capital. A ban on the demonstration, which looked as if it would have been in vain, was lifted. At first everything proceeded peaceably. But during the evening the hated Hungarian security police, the AVO, started firing on demonstrators. The demonstrators were joined by huge crowds calling for Imre Nagy. Gerö then agreed to the intervention of Soviet troops to restore order. At this stage they behaved with restraint. On the following day, 24 October, the Hungarian Politburo, in the hope of containing the revolutionary situation, appointed Nagy premier but Gerö remained first secretary.

The party had lost the support of the people and, although the greater part of the Hungarian army did not join the rising, the Politburo felt too uncertain of the soldiers' loyalty to use them against their fellow countrymen. The rising was spreading through Hungary and was taking the form of a national rebellion. That same evening of 24 October two important emissaries arrived from Moscow, Mikhail Suslov, the party ideologist, and Anastas Mikoyan, the oldest member of the Politburo to have survived Stalin's purges, a man of negotiating skill and adaptability. They agreed with Nagy that Soviet intervention had been a mistake and consented to the dismissal of Gerö and his replacement by Kádár. The Kremlin saw a 'Polish solution' as the lesser evil, despite the danger of allowing the uprising to spread disaffection to Czechoslovakia, Romania and Bulgaria. That did not happen. Nor was there a Polish solution in Hungary.

Nagy was being swept along by the rising and the committees and organisations springing up all over Hungary. His success in securing the withdrawal of Soviet troops from Budapest only created the illusion that the mass protest of Hungarians against communist autocracy and foreign occupa-

*Budapest, November 1956. Astonished faces abound – could Soviet domination really be toppled so easily?*

tion had succeeded. A heady Hungarian nationalism asserted itself. Nagy tried to ride the revolutionary wave in order to direct it into less dangerous paths. On 29 October Suslov and Mikoyan were back again in Budapest. The following day Nagy announced that Hungary would return to a multi-party system, making a decisive breach with communist (though not necessarily socialist) rule. But when he gave way to the demand that Hungary should withdraw from the Warsaw Pact, the writing was on the wall. The Kremlin could not afford to lose total control or to take the risk of being replaced in Hungary by the West. Anglo-French preoccupation with Suez (pages 466–71) made the Russian decision to intervene easier; it was equally clear that the United States would restrict herself to diplomatic protests. What the Soviet leaders had to weigh was the effect of their decision whether or not to intervene on Eastern and central Europe. The Warsaw Pact and Russia's whole position was in jeopardy. The Chinese, Bulgarian, Romanian and Czechoslovak leaders were urging intervention; Poland was busy with her own affairs and Yugoslavia could not oppose the Soviet Union in Hungary.

So the Kremlin decided on the repression of the Hungarian rising.

The pretext for intervention was provided by Kádár. The First Secretary had left Budapest and had broken with Nagy, whose supporters he condemned as counter-revolutionaries. On 3 November 1956 Soviet tank divisions returned in force. The Hungarians, who had hastily armed themselves, were joined by only a few detachments from the Hungarian army. Civilians were resisting trained troops and the Russian suppression of Hungarians fighting for independence and democracy could be seen on Western television screens. The fight lasted long enough to influence Western opinion against the Russians. In the West it also opened the eyes of many communists and fellow travellers, who now left the party. Nagy and the Hungarian military commander Pal Maleter were arrested while negotiating (they were later tried and executed). Soviet tanks showed no restraint this time but pulverised any building from which rifle fire was heard. Thousands of Hungarian refugees fled to the West, and armed resistance in Hungary was soon crushed.

Kádár, carried to power on the back of Soviet tanks, now worked to restore some semblance of credible Hungarian independence. He accepted that the Kremlin would not permit any democratic multi-party government or Hungarian neutrality. Provided, however, that the Kremlin could be reassured on these two crucial points, then, as in Poland, the Kremlin would allow Hungary some degree of autonomy and freedom to choose her own path. That was Khrushchev's policy and, to the surprise of the West, Kádár at first very cautiously and then much more boldly charted the course of Hungarian autonomy within the Soviet alliance. In economic policies, Kádár followed a new course, less repressive, less rigidly centralised, allowing some scope for private enterprise and so eventually turned Hungary into the most liberal and for a time most prosperous communist state. Kádár's realistic nationalism and his country's growing prosperity in the end reconciled the Hungarians to his regime, which had saved them from the threat of another Soviet intervention.

# CHAPTER 50

# The Fall of Khrushchev:
# The Soviet Union and the Wider World

The Polish and Hungarian crises, following on Khrushchev's violent denunciation of Stalin and advocacy of reform, undermined the Soviet leader's position within the Kremlin. He had never been strong enough to oust the Stalinists in the Praesidium (Politburo), among them Molotov and Malenkov, who now attacked him on the easiest of targets – the economy, which under centralist control never lived up to expectations. The struggle took the form of disputing which were the right reforms to follow: reforms which sought to make the government ministries more efficient, a policy backed by Malenkov and Molotov, or reforms based on reconstituted party control over the economy regionally organised, as advocated by Khrushchev. The conflict came to a head in June 1957 when the Praesidium, by a majority of seven to four, voted against Khrushchev. That should have been the end. But Khrushchev turned the tables by appealing to the larger party body, the Central Committee, which he claimed alone could deprive him of the post of first secretary. With Marshal Zhukov's help, military aircraft flew the party representatives to Moscow from the outlying provinces. Khrushchev won the support he needed and dubbed his opponents on the Praesidium the 'anti-party' group. All these opponents now lost real power for good, but there was to be no return to Stalinist vengeance. They were sent far away; it was with a touch of humour that Khrushchev decided to send the dour Molotov as ambassador to Mongolia and Malenkov to manage a power station in Kazakhstan; only

Bulganin was allowed to remain at the centre, acting as titular premier until 1958.

From 1957 until his sudden deposition by the Praesidium in 1964, Khrushchev dominated the Soviet Union in her domestic and foreign relations, though not as Stalin had done. Opponents no longer had to fear death, but a displeased Khrushchev could end their careers and demote them or banish them. His enduring contribution was to dismantle the Stalinist terror regime and to discredit it. Indeed, discrediting it became a potent weapon with which to defeat his rivals, who had played subordinate roles in it. Khrushchev restored the party, with its hierarchy appointed by him, to primacy in the economic and political administration of the country. This meant that no far-reaching economic reforms would be possible: the Soviet Union remained a command economy. But she had become a more tolerant country; her leader was the son of a miner, robustly human, resilient, tough, with a sense of humour, unpolished in speech and manner, but someone with whom it was thought in the West it was possible to do business. Khrushchev announced that he believed in peaceful competition and that the Soviet Union would win; boastfully he added, 'We will bury you,' a remark which was taken too literally in the West. Khrushchev genuinely wanted to better the lot of the ordinary people in his own day, not to sacrifice them to some future goal. He comes across as a man who wanted to be liked, but also as one who wished to be acknowledged as leader without the danger of Stalin's cult of the personality re-emerging.

Despite Khrushchev's goals, which seemed to be not unlike those of the West, the apparent convergence of West and East was an illusion. Khrushchev had lived all his life within a state system which was ruled from above. He wished to correct its most gross errors, but believed that centralised planning was essential to communism. The Soviet Union would continue to be ruled from above; reforms would be introduced only as the necessity for them was perceived in the Kremlin. At the same time the people would be brought into more active participation. Khrushchev tried to reduce the dead weight of bureaucracy but was caught in the paradox that this could not be done unless decision-making was decentralised. The most maddening aspect of Khrushchev's period of power was its unpredictability, a reflection of Khrushchev's mercurial temperament; he delighted in springing surprises.

Typically writers and intellectuals could never be sure where they were. Thus in 1958 Boris Pasternak was persecuted and forbidden to collect the Nobel Prize, but Solzhenitsyn's novel about a day in Stalin's labour camp was allowed to be published because it was in line with Khrushchev's own denunciation. Censorship remained erratic, though more freedom was allowed to writers. But Khrushchev was far less tolerant of organised religion, and many churches and synagogues were closed.

Unrestrained by powerful rivals, Khrushchev's policies were frequently changed, which contributed to their lack of success. His various reorganisations of industrial and agricultural controls created confusion and waste. In the area most vital to Soviet living standards, agriculture, the improvements of the early years were not sustained after 1958. Bad weather and unsound farming methods reduced the contribution from the virgin lands. In industry, Khrushchev's decentralising reforms, removing one level of planning to the

regions, also caused severe disruption. The growth rate of Soviet industry slowed down and failed to fulfil his unrealistic plans.

Khrushchev understood the enormous changes the Soviet Union was undergoing as she developed from a mainly rural to an urbanised country with a population that was better educated and a large section of professional people demanding higher standards of living: more consumer goods, better housing, better health provision, more varied and more plentiful food and more opportunities for higher education. He launched special campaigns concentrating on one or other sector of supply, organised and reorganised the running of the economy and made promises and set ambitious targets which could not be fulfilled. In the decade from 1955 to 1965 growth was impressive but could not match expanding expectations. The failure of agriculture to make anything like the progress planned is illustrated by the following figures:

|  | Grain harvest (million tons) | Meat (million tons) |
|---|---|---|
| 1958 | 135 | 3.4 |
| Planned for 1965 | 164–80 | 6.1 |
| Actual in 1965 | 121 | 5.25 |

Khrushchev was not only ambitiously attempting to raise production, and nuclear-missile capacity, but simultaneously working to rejuvenate and make the party more effective. Neither he nor his successors could solve the basic problem of how to organise an increasingly sophisticated economy without relegating the party to a subordinate role in the state, a subordination which they feared would undermine the leadership and government of the USSR. Yet

## Growth in the Soviet Union, 1958–1965

|  | Workers (millions) | National income | Consumer goods | Steel (million tons) | Coal (million tons) | Oil (million tons) | Gas (million cu. m) | Electricity (million kwh) |
|---|---|---|---|---|---|---|---|---|
| 1958 | 56 | 100 (index) | 100 (index) | 55 | 493 | 113 | 28,085 | 235 |
| 1965 | 77 | 158 | 160 | 91 | 578 | 243 | 127,666 | 507 |

a centralised authoritarian party structure seeking to take the major decisions without reference to self-regulatory market forces is simply not equipped to manage the vast and complex industry of a modern state. In agriculture various communist efforts to stimulate production also proved wasteful of resources.

Khrushchev's erratic course was especially evident in his handling of the Soviet Union's external relations. He correctly foresaw the importance of nuclear weapons and ballistic missiles as the vital deterrent and measure of military power. 'Going nuclear', moreover, allowed a reduction in the size of the Red Army at a time of labour shortage due to the smaller wartime birthrate. The launching into space of Sputnik in October 1957 was a rare propaganda triumph – the Soviet Union appeared briefly to be technologically ahead of the United States. The reverse was true, and the Soviet Union paid dearly for this propaganda first. It helped to discredit Eisenhower's more restrained armaments policies and prompted John F. Kennedy to close

the 'missile gap' that never was. The nuclear arms race was significantly accelerated just as the Soviet Union was closing the real missile gap with the United States in the 1960s.

In the Middle East, Khrushchev took advantage of Western hostility to Egypt to establish bases in Egypt and in Syria and to assist in building the Aswan High Dam. But the benefits Russia gained were limited and her Arab allies proved uncertain friends more concerned to take advantage of Soviet aid than to offer much in return. But Soviet commitments, though costly, were likewise limited. Khrushchev threatened Britain and France during the Suez War in November 1956, but they were idle threats. The United States did not withdraw her fundamental support of Israel, and the Soviet Union would not risk a direct military confrontation with the Americans by involving Russian 'volunteers' and pilots in actual fighting in the Middle East. The Arab states did not want to introduce Soviet-style communism nor to be dominated by the Soviet Union as her East European allies were.

*Chinese Communist Party Chairman Mao Zedong despised Soviet Premier Khrushchev for his revisionist approach to the tenets of Marxism-Leninism. Khrushchev characterized Mao's revolutionary militancy as the ravings of a madman.*

Indeed, the identity of interests was a tenuous one. The shift from Stalin's European-centred policy to the post-Stalin global policies cost the USSR a great deal and yielded few dividends. The Horn of Africa, Afghanistan, Egypt, Cuba, Ghana, Indonesia, Ethiopia, Iraq, Angola and India all received Soviet aid at various times and were courted by the Soviet Union. But the Russians suffered setbacks in all these relationships, most spectacularly in China.

China had expected to be treated as an equal after Stalin's death, but although she had developed an independent world policy she still relied on Soviet aid. Divergences between the Chinese and Soviet viewpoints increased as the 1950s drew to a close. According to Mao, Khrushchev's emphasis on Soviet material advances sapped the true revolutionary spirit that should be impelling the communist camp forward in the world. The Russian leader's pursuit of detente with the United States after 1958 led the Chinese to conclude that the world was once again endangered by the national chauvinism of the two superpowers. This became even more evident to the Chinese when the Russians refused to help them to become a nuclear power. During Khrushchev's last two years of leadership the Sino-Soviet break became unbridgeable (pages 637–8).

Ironically, the Soviet–US detente did not last long, given the way Khrushchev handled it. The Paris summit in May 1960, intended to seek solutions to Berlin and the German question, was called off before it began, Khrushchev deciding against negotiating with Eisenhower in the terminal period of his presidency, and the U-2 incident provided the means to humiliate the American President (page 523). A meeting with President Kennedy in Vienna in June 1961 brought the Russians no nearer to their desired solution of the German problem. Meanwhile, Berlin remained the open door through which the citizens of East Germany poured to express their preference for the West. The construction of the Berlin Wall in August 1961 to block that exit became an open admission of the bankruptcy of Soviet policies and those of the East German regime. Neither conciliatory statements nor threats which succeeded on each other had much effect on the West except to accelerate the arms race. Khrushchev's most daring attempt to redress America's geographical advantage in her confrontation with the Soviet Union came to grief in the seas surrounding the island of Cuba. America's allies on the borders of the Soviet eastern empire provided bases from which missiles could hit Soviet cities; the Soviet Union at this time could threaten only America's European allies and had no reliable missiles with which to attack the United States.

Rebuffed by the United States in 1960, Castro had turned to Russia for aid, and agreements to provide credit to Cuba and to purchase her sugar crop were concluded in 1960. The failure of the CIA's Bay of Pigs landing of Cuban exiles to overthrow Castro in April 1961 convinced the Cuban leader that the United States was determined to subjugate his country and drove him deeper into Russia's arms. Khrushchev promised to defend the island and accused the United States of banditry. In the following year, 1962, Khrushchev decided to install nuclear missiles in Cuba and to build a Soviet base there. This daring Soviet move, which would bring the United States within range of many more Soviet missiles, was carried out secretly. The Cuban missile crisis which followed appeared to bring the Soviet Union and the United States to the brink of nuclear war. But Khrushchev was obliged to withdraw (Chapter 60). For the Soviet Union this perceived failure marked a great setback, less in her relations with the West, which soon improved again, than with her standing in the socialist camp. The Chinese took due note: the Soviet Union too had proved a paper tiger. Finally, any hope the Kremlin might have had of overawing the West in future negotiations over Berlin or Germany lay in ruins. But the world beyond the two superpowers could breathe again, relieved that sanity had prevailed and that ideological fanaticism had not this time as in 1939 plunged the world into unimaginable devastation.

Khrushchev's dynamism and experimentation alarmed the party bureaucracy. His lack of success, especially in agriculture, did nothing to compensate for the constant upsets he inflicted on the power establishment. He probably paid less and less attention to other members of the Praesidium, and in due course they decided to get rid of him, having had enough of his erratic policies or 'hare-brained schemes', to use their phrase. In October 1964, while he was holidaying on the Black Sea, his removal from the leadership was announced in Moscow. He was allowed to retire quietly and died in obscurity in 1971 – at least that had been the intention of the new Soviet leaders. They underlined their contempt by not honouring his remains with a state funeral or a burial place close to Lenin. But Khrushchev refused to become a nonentity and had one more surprise in store before his unceremonious end. He had recorded his memoirs on tape and shortly before his death saw their first publication in the West. Like his other breaches with the past, this was a first in Soviet history. In the decades between Stalin and Gorbachev, Khrushchev did more to change the Soviet Union than any other leader, albeit without finding remedies for the shortcomings of communist rule of the economy. Nor could communism be reconciled with basic freedoms. History will nevertheless accord him a more important place than the Soviet leadership was willing to acknowledge.

From the vantage point of the 1990s, Khrushchev's years of power are viewed in a different light inside and outside the Soviet Union. The Russian people look back on Khrushchev with gratitude for introducing the first breath of fresh air and freedom, although it was stifled again during the long interlude of the Brezhnev decades. Banished from Red Square, Khrushchev lies buried in the Novodevichy Convent grounds with other famous Russians, Chekhov, Scriabin and Gogol. The grave is not neglected, but is covered with flowers in memory of the man who first opened the gates of the vast prison complex of Stalin's Gulag.

CHAPTER 51

# The Eisenhower Years: Conservatism and Caution at Home

Dwight D. Eisenhower was a military hero before he became president. Immensely popular, with an infectious boyish grin, he represented, like Abraham Lincoln, an important aspect of the American tradition. His parents were neither influential nor wealthy. He grew up in Abilene, Kansas, a small farming community where his father managed a creamery. Through sheer force of intelligence and character, Ike (his nickname from boyhood) succeeded in passing the highly competitive entry tests to West Point military academy. Practically his whole adult life was spent in the army, his career reaching its peak when he was appointed Supreme Allied Commander of the D-Day invasion forces in 1944. He stayed in Germany for only a few weeks after accepting the surrender of the Nazi armed forces in May 1945 as American military governor. His European command was far more than a military one. He had to handle temperamental Allied generals as well as American, not to mention statesmen as varied as Churchill and General de Gaulle. He succeeded brilliantly, playing a decisive diplomatic and military role. After three years (1945–8) as US Army chief of staff, and an uncomfortable spell as president of Columbia University, he was appointed by Truman in 1951 to the overall command of the allied forces being organised in Europe under NATO.

His transition to the political arena, leading to his nomination as Republican presidential candidate in July 1952 at the Chicago Convention, was swift, having been organised behind the scenes by influen-

tial Republicans such as Senator Henry Cabot Lodge, Governor Dewey and the financier Paul Hoffman. Eisenhower allowed himself to be prevailed upon, despite his misgivings about the participation of the military in politics: American history provided the unhappy example of a military hero turned president – Ulysses S. Grant, whose administration was wracked by scandal. But there was another precedent – George Washington, the wise Founding Father. Eisenhower was persuaded to follow his Crusade in Europe with another crusade, to preserve the two-party system and democracy in the United States, to free Americans from excessive government and, above all, to ensure that the United States would lead the free world against the perils of atheistic communism. The Republican Party machine was dominated by the conservative wing led by Senator Robert Taft, who not only reflected a widely held belief that the Truman administration was soft on communism, but also rather perversely represented the revived isolationist 'America first' patriotism. Eisenhower viewed a return to isolationism and to the 'fortress America' mentality as a disastrous error. He saw it as his duty to meet this challenge, if his own popularity was all that could prevail over the Taft forces within the Republican party and over the Democratic candidate Adlai Stevenson in the United States at large. In a campaign marred by personal attacks by the foul-mouthed Wisconsin Senator McCarthy and by Republican charges against the failure of the Truman administration to defend the United States within and without from the communist enemy, Eisenhower appeared out of touch, unable to check the excesses of those Republicans he despised. He relied on his personal popularity, on the trust he inspired as a plain-speaking, honest man above partisan politics and on his final vote-winning promise that he would go to Korea to make peace. In this way he persuaded the voters that, as an experienced general-statesman, he was best equipped to end the long war, which had reached stalemate but was continuing to cause heavy US casualties. Eisenhower's running-mate in the 1952 election was the youthful Senator Richard M. Nixon, who during the campaign survived the accusation that he had accepted a slush fund for his political campaign. The growing importance of television in politics was demonstrated by the success of his emotional appeal for support flanked by his family and his pet dog.

Governor Adlai Stevenson, the Democratic candidate, possessed none of Eisenhower's charisma, which could be exploited on television in the nation's homes. He did not present himself as an 'image president' who, like Eisenhower, blurred issues and relied on projecting himself as a trustworthy father-figure. Instead he campaigned on real issues: civil rights, foreign policy and the domestic problems confronting Americans – 'Let's talk sense to the American people.' His speeches analysed problems with intellectual sharpness and wit. His opponents derided him as an 'egghead' and distributed buttons bearing the simple slogan 'I like Ike'. Stevenson lost, but not badly, with 27.3 million voting for him as against 33.8 million for Eisenhower. The Republicans also gained small majorities in the Senate and the House. In 1956 Eisenhower stood for a second term, once more against Stevenson, and won – increasing his own share of the vote but this time losing both Houses of Congress. It seemed that when it came to domestic issues, the American people trusted Eisenhower more than they trusted the Republican Party.

When Eisenhower entered the White House in January 1953, he brought with him a firm set of values without having formulated much in the way of specific policies. American prosperity was based on rugged individualism and self-reliance, on business enterprise and on minimising the weight of government on both citizen and industry. The United States was, in the view of Eisenhower and many other Republicans, suffering from creeping

socialism and from government waste, which drained resources from the nation's wealth-producing activities. Increased government spending, moreover, and budget deficits had led to inflation. Eisenhower's inner Cabinet was composed of successful and practical men, such as the Secretary of the Treasury, George Humphrey, who were intended to bring to government the effective management skills with which they had run their businesses and banks. Even his international expert, Secretary of State John Foster Dulles, a lawyer by training but with considerable experience of foreign affairs, had been closely connected with the corporate world. The spirit of the Eisenhower administration was perhaps encapsulated in the words of the Secretary of Defence, Charles E. Wilson, formerly president of General Motors: 'What was good for our country was good for General Motors, and vice versa.' Decades later, this may seem naive, and the identification of business interests with human welfare insensitive. But at the time Americans approved such sentiments; moreover, it is an undeniable precondition of better welfare that a country has first to produce more wealth.

In domestic affairs Eisenhower conveyed an impression of weakness and indecision, of a simple man more at home on the golf course than dealing with political infighting on Capitol Hill. He certainly wished to avoid confrontations, especially with the 'old guard' of the Republican Party; entrenched in Congress, these conservatives were led first by Senator Taft, and after his death by Senator William Knowland. Eisenhower believed in moderation and compromise. Despite the rhetoric uttered during the Republican campaign, he made no efforts to undo the welfare provisions for the poor – indeed he extended social-security payments to another 10.5 million people and raised benefits when unemployment increased under the impact of the recession in 1953 and 1954 that followed the end of the Korean War. He described himself as 'liberal on human issues, conservative on economic ones'. It is true that he was liberal on some issues, such as social welfare or immigration, but in general he cannot be described as progressive. In fiscal policy, although unable to cut the federal expenditure of the last two years of the Truman administration as much as he had hoped, Eisenhower and George Humphrey refused to consider the Keynesian

*'Ike' (US President Dwight D. Eisenhower) on the campaign trail in October 1956.*

solution of deficit-financed government spending to stimulate the economy.

Eisenhower's failure to combat Senator McCarthy until much damage had been done at home and to America's reputation abroad exposed a deficiency in the President's political skills. As the Senator's accusations grew wilder and bred a destructive atmosphere of suspicion and denunciation among tens of thousand of loyal American citizens, many appeals reached the White House demanding that the President speak out against McCarthy. Eisenhower's response was that it was the task of McCarthy's fellow senators to discipline one of their own; the presidency, he claimed, should not interfere in Congress. He loathed McCarthy's smear tactics and hated the man, but he to some extent also shared the belief that communist subversion of America's free society needed to be checked by loyalty oaths, by investigations and, where necessary, by other stern measures. His main reason for non-intervention was undoubtedly political: he wished to curry favour with the Republican conservatives even when he privately disagreed with them. He rationalised his lack of political courage in various ways. He would claim that even to mention McCarthy's name would increase the Senator's importance. A leader's job was to win goodwill; it followed, so Eisenhower explained, that the leader

should reserve all criticism to private discussion and in public should utter only favourable sentiments. But in the end McCarthy's continued attacks forced Eisenhower to defend some of the Senator's targets. Even so, McCarthy went on unchecked until the Senate in December 1954 at last censured him after he had overreached himself in levelling indiscriminate charges against the army and the administration. By then, McCarthyism had lost credibility and public support, and the Senator himself had become a political liability, his methods and behaviour condemned by a majority of senators, many of whom nevertheless still shared the exaggerated fear of the 'communist traitors' within. Although the Senator tried to continue his crusade, after December 1954 the media gave him less and less attention. By the time of his death only three years later in 1957, this once feared and powerful man had lost all his influence.

What is the significance of McCarthyism, which disfigured American politics for more than five years? It unjustly ruined many lives and many brilliant careers. The smear of 'guilt by association' cast the net so widely that thousands of innocents suffered. Against these thousands of loyal citizens, how many real traitors who meant harm to their country were really uncovered? It is right that a free society should defend itself. That national security has to be protected is equally incontestable, and it was perfectly reasonable to conclude that the Soviet Union posed a danger to the West that had to be guarded against. But in defending itself against dangers, a society should not destroy the very values it seeks to uphold. What was 'unAmerican' and counter to the ideals of American values was McCarthyism itself. McCarthyism also proved a temptation: it pandered to the resentment of the less well-off against the privileged, the so-called eastern establishment. McCarthy declared that the traitors were to be found not among the poor or the minority groups but among 'those who have had all the benefits'. Those who identified themselves with McCarthyism thereby automatically proclaimed their 'patriotism'. The pre-eminent significance of the McCarthy years, however, is that the Senator and his works were in the end rejected, that American institutions proved sufficiently strong to cleanse themselves after a period of weakness.

But there was another issue, of much longer standing, going back to America's colonial past, which starkly revealed the contrast between the constitutionally endorsed aspirations of a free and democratic people and the reality.

The issue of civil rights and equality came to dominate American political life in the 1950s and 1960s. About one in nine Americans was classified by the census as non-white, the great majority of these being black: in 1950 some 15 million, in 1960 18.9 million and in 1970 (out of a total US population of 203.2 million) 22.7 million. Blacks were denied civil rights not only in the South but also in the North, where they were increasingly crowded into city ghettos. They suffered more than their share of poverty; social deprivation as well as segregation and the prejudice of the majority whites meant that from one generation to the next opportunities for advancement were limited.

The shared experience of the Second World War began to shift attitudes. Black and white soldiers had died for the same cause. In particular they had fought against the 'master race' and all its crimes against those it held to be 'inferior races'. But black GIs stationed in the Nazi citadel of Nuremberg at the end of the war could not share their quarters with white GIs; and most of their officers were white. This of course reflected the superior and inferior racial attitudes which still prevailed in the United States. Not until the Vietnam War were black servicemen truly integrated in the armed services, yet at home black and white Americans did not mix socially and were segregated in schools, for housing, on transport and generally in worship. In a thousand and one ways a black American was made to feel separate and inferior. In the nation's

*Senator Joseph P. McCarthy, the orchestrator of a virulent campaign to 'flush out' all the Communists supposedly in positions of influence in America, at Congressional hearings in 1954 (left). Outside, sympathizers demonstrate their support (below).*

capital a black person could not enter a good restaurant and expect to be served. This became particularly embarrassing when black diplomats from the newly independent African nations were being sent to Washington. Segregation, moreover, was a gift the Soviet Union did not fail to exploit, for example by honouring the great black American singer Paul Robeson, who spoke up for black equality and expressed his admiration for the USSR.

During the 1950s and 1960s agitation in the South by blacks and by whites, many of the latter college students from the east, made headlines. Police truncheoning defenceless civilians, bombings and riots presented the dark side of American civilisation. But more and more whites supported black protests against injustice, and those with faith in the American people and institutions believed they would overcome the entrenched prejudice. The success of the civil-rights movement in changing laws and procedures – making itself felt slowly, despite many setbacks, in the 1950s before gathering force in the 1960s – provided striking evidence that in the contemporary world traditional discrimination had to yield to reform. Arguments in favour of inherent racial superiority became unacceptable in the second half of the twentieth century. The bastions of 'Jim Crow', discriminatory anti-black practices in the South, began falling one by one.

The United States shares with many other countries the problems caused by racial or religious intolerance. But few could have foretold the changes in attitudes that have taken place in the US within just one generation. Black Americans now wield significant political power. Even so, practical as opposed to legal discrimination in education, job opportunities and housing remains to be overcome at the end of the twentieth century. In conditions of unemployment and recession blacks continue to suffer far more severely than their fellow citizens.

The landmarks of black protest in the 1950s and 1960s are clearly delineated. Lawyers of the National Association for the Advancement of Colored People won a Supreme Court ruling in 1954 that swept away the segregationist subterfuge of 'separate but equal' in public schooling. There would no longer be any justification for separating children solely on account of their race, a principle already applicable to higher education. But a ruling, no matter how valuable, is one thing, its enforcement – in a country where state rights and community control over local services is strong – quite another. Integration was fiercely resisted everywhere; racial prejudice, of course, played a large part, but resistance was also sparked by social and educational tensions as better-off families found themselves being forced to share their facilities with the deprived. The bussing of children between the more affluent parts of a city and the worse off aroused fierce resentment, for example, when it proved more difficult to maintain the educational standards of mixed social groups. The real test came in the South on the issue of whether local communities could defy Supreme Court rulings when blacks were courageous enough to insist on the rights accorded by them. The struggle could not just be left to lawyers. In 1956 a black girl was prevented by force and intimidation from entering the University of Alabama. In the following year there was a dramatic confrontation between federal authorities and the State of Arkansas when school officials at Little Rock demanded that nine black girls be prevented from entering the Central High School. Governor Orval Faubus backed the school officials, and only when Eisenhower reluctantly met the challenge by ordering federal troops to ensure the black children's safety in entering the school did the state authorities back off. The crisis as far as the children were concerned festered on for many months, as the troops remained to protect their rights: sensational conflicts reached the newspapers and other media, but thousands of less newsworthy incidents across the United States did their damage in obscurity.

The change in attitudes was brought about by black leadership, championed by ardent groups of white Americans and backed by mass black support. Federal authorities, the presidency and Congress were slow to act. Eisenhower, more cautious on the issue than Truman had been, claimed that it was a question of changing hearts and minds, which could not be accomplished by law or by force. So, before they could receive justice, the blacks would have to wait for the gradual reformation of their fellow citizens. Eisenhower had his eyes fixed on the political repercussions in the South of forcing the issue and so provided little leadership, except where federal authority was directly challenged, as it had been at Little Rock. In the 1960s the Kennedy brothers and President Johnson were to take a much more positive attitude to the demands of the emerging black leaders (pages 604–8).

The Reverend Martin Luther King, a Baptist minister, rose to prominence in organising a black boycott of buses in Montgomery, Alabama, in 1955, after Rosa Parks, a courageous black seamstress, had refused to give up her seat to a white man and move to the back of the bus. The black boycott hit the pockets of the bus company, until a year later the Supreme Court ruled that segregation of transport, state as well as interstate, was unconstitutional. Blacks were flexing their economic muscles and soon other businesses were similarly placed under pressure. All aspects of segregation, in schools, restaurants, housing and political rights, became the targets of the organised protest movement in the decade that followed.

# CHAPTER 52

# The Eisenhower Years: Waging the Cold War

The 1950s was the decade of the Cold War, when for the first time the world lived under the shadow of two countries, now called 'superpowers', both possessing nuclear weapons. In August 1949 the Soviet Union tested an atomic bomb and by the mid-1950s had perfected the hydrogen bomb. The testing of these weapons by the nuclear countries was poisoning the environment, though at the time few were aware of the additional cancers that were being caused. Research and testing of the necessary intercontinental missiles to deliver destruction progressed equally fast. The Soviet Union was catching up with the United States, though not as rapidly in missiles as the Americans supposed.

Nineteen-fifty was a crucial year in the history of the Cold War. The United States administration reached the conclusion that economic and military aid alone were no longer enough to defend the West. American strategy made its priority the containment of communism within the Asian mainland. Troops were sent to Korea, the only territory on the mainland defended by US troops, in order to prove that communist aggression did not pay. In September 1950 the decision was taken in Washington to send US combat troops to Europe as well, to form part of the military defence of NATO; three months later Dwight D. Eisenhower was appointed the alliance's supreme commander. This marked a radical new commitment. So, by the time Eisenhower was inaugurated as president on 20 January 1953, the Cold War in Europe and the hot war in

Korea faced the United States with global challenges and the prospect of huge military expenditures. Now that the United States had a president who was a general of great experience, perhaps the Cold War would be waged not emotionally but with careful military planning. Eisenhower was a cautious man, fully aware of the immense dangers of war, but also conscious of the dangers inherent in constantly preparing for a war.

The ending of the Korean War, wasteful of both lives and resources, became an obvious priority. Eisenhower had become convinced that it was military folly to allow the American forces to remain bogged down in the face of the Chinese and North Koreans. Armistice negotiations had dragged on at Kaesong and Panmunjon since the summer of 1951. The issue of 22,000 North Korean and Chinese prisoners of war in UN camps who did not wish to return home deadlocked all negotiations, which India, as honest broker, attempted to facilitate. Eventually on 27 July 1953, following more than three years of war, after bitter wrangling and despite the resistance of Syngman Rhee, who did not want to end the war short of unification on South Korea's terms, a truce was concluded. The fighting stopped and Korea was effectively partitioned.

The Eisenhower administration on 10 October signed another security treaty, with the Republic of Korea (South Korea), to provide a guarantee of joint defence if an attack was renewed from the north. The United States also promised economic aid to restore the south. But the truce did not prove a preliminary step towards unification, despite endless negotiations. South Korean 'democracy', moreover, was a mockery during Syngman Rhee's eight years of rule and even after he was driven from power in 1960. The link with the West and the United States in particular, however, provided the basis for South Korea's economic miracle of the succeeding three decades.

Until his death in May 1959, Secretary of State John Foster Dulles exerted a commanding influence over US foreign policy during the two Eisenhower administrations, especially over its style and tone. A Presbyterian layman, a lawyer with experience of international affairs, he represented a tradition in US foreign policy of asserting that morality and principle must underlie all America's dealings in the world. He criticised Truman's policy of containment of communism, insisting that it was no more than a negative reaction to an evil. The communists should be made to give up what they had illegally seized; the Soviet Union's sphere of influence should be rolled back in Eastern and central Europe; there could be no accommodation with Russia. Nor did Dulles shrink from threatening the use of nuclear weapons in defence of the free world. He condemned neutralism in the Third World – as he saw it, the choice was between two kinds of societies, the good and the evil. In meeting the communist challenge Dulles came to be regarded as a 'Cold War warrior', as his rhetoric and deliberate brinkmanship in threatening war proved to be thoroughly alarming. It was verbal deterrence to back up nuclear deterrence. Dulles was skilful, tough and predictable. In a world of upheaval and uncertainty the policies he advocated – the creation of defensive alliances in Asia and Europe – contributed to the stabilisation of the *status quo*, except in Indo-China. For all the talk of rolling back communism, caution prevailed when unrest spread through the Soviet satellites of East Germany, Poland and Hungary; Dulles, though, must share some blame for encouraging revolt and then denying all material assistance. Eisenhower presented the more conciliatory side of American diplomacy. Their partnership was formidable and on the whole successful.

Reducing American armed forces in Korea fitted in with Eisenhower's and Dulles's perception of how best to meet the threat of world communism. While they recognised that there were national differences within the communist alliance which might be advantageously exploited, they also subscribed to the view that communism was a coherent and dangerous ideology, and that the Kremlin was co-ordinating a policy of global thrusts wherever the West was weak. That co-ordination might not be complete, but Eisenhower and Dulles believed that all the Kremlin's policies were purposeful and could be seen at work in what appeared to be unrelated events: the Korean invasion, the Huk activities in the Philippines, the determined effort to overrun Vietnam, the attempted subversion of Laos, Cambodia and Burma, the well-nigh successful attempt to take over Iran, the exploitation of the trouble spot of Trieste, and the penetration attempted in Guatemala.

Dulles concluded that the communist leaders knew that their system could not survive side by side with the free world; consequently they had no alternative but to try to destroy freedom in the world. The death of Stalin in March 1953, he thought, had only made Soviet policies towards the rest of the world more subtle, without altering their essential goal. Dulles urged that a policy of maximum pressure on Russia's allies was more likely to move them away from the Soviet Union than a competition for their favour. Communist China in particular was recognised as a potentially unstable Soviet ally.

America's China policy was one of unrelenting hostility. In his first State of the Union message to Congress, Eisenhower declared that the Seventh Fleet 'would no longer be employed to shield communist China'. This was, however, pure verbal hostility, since the prospect of the aged Chiang Kai-shek successfully reconquering the mainland from his Taiwanese base was no longer credible. The following December an American–Nationalist Chinese defence alliance was concluded, and in January 1955 Eisenhower even secured the passing of a joint resolution of Congress declaring that American forces would be deployed, if necessary, to protect from invasion two small islands, Matsu and Quemoy, lying just off the Chinese mainland and garrisoned by Chiang Kai-shek's troops. Warfare between the Nationalists and the communist Chinese was now confined to ineffectual ritual shelling between the two islands and the mainland. It seems extraordinary now that Eisenhower and Dulles seriously considered war, even nuclear war, with China in defence of the two small islands, but for the Americans they were of enormous significance. The containment barrier of Red China must be drawn in the Pacific, restraining her from adventures beyond her mainland coastline, otherwise she could extend her attacks not only to Taiwan but to Japan and even the Philippines. Communist China became such a bogey that even Eisenhower's cautious judgement was affected. Dulles came to regard the successful defence of Quemoy and Matsu as his greatest triumph and believed that brinkmanship had here saved the peace.

Eisenhower was following a broad spectrum of policies to meet what he saw as the communist global threat. As an experienced military commander he was ready to employ all the weapons and means at his disposal and rejected as naive the view that spying or covert operations should be avoided by the West on moral grounds, even though the communist nations, unconstrained by Western morality, made full use of them. He recognised as well as anyone that a nuclear war between the Soviet Union and the United States could not be won and would spell the end of Western civilisation. That, however, was precisely why he was prepared to 'wage peace' as he had waged war, using every available method at his disposal.

The Central Intelligence Agency under Allen Dulles, the brother of Foster Dulles, was now given a much expanded secret role which could not be publicly admitted. Even today not all the measures then contemplated have been identified, nor is it clear to what extent they included assassination. Certainly subversion of foreign countries became a part of the CIA's task even while the State Department conducted normal diplomacy with them. Eisenhower authorised the overthrow of the Mossadeq regime, which he believed was opening Iran and her vital oil to Soviet penetration. Although he avoided leaving behind official evidence which could link him as president with the covert operation (codenamed Ajax) to restore the young pro-Western Shah to power, the President authorised and ultimately controlled it. In carrying out Ajax, the CIA acted in concert with the Iranian army, which arrested Mossadeq and restored the Shah in August 1953 (pages 460–1).

That same year Eisenhower and Dulles became concerned about reports that Guatemala was 'succumbing to communist infiltration'. Central America was nearer home than Iran, and the domino theory, though not enunciated by Eisenhower until April 1954, was very much in his mind. If Guatemala

was allowed to fall to the communists, then communism would spread to her neighbours and perhaps even eventually to Mexico and the borders of the United States. This cataclysmic picture drove Eisenhower into action. Colonel Jacobo Arbenz, President of Guatemala since 1950, had embarked on a policy of economic nationalism, taking over uncultivated land and transport and docking facilities belonging to American corporations, of which the most powerful was the United Fruit Company of Boston. Business interests were implacably opposed to economic reform and, for the implementation of his measures, Arbenz increasingly relied on communists within the trade unions and government departments who were certainly not interested in seeking compromises with the United States. The Soviet Union saw an opportunity to fish in troubled water. Eisenhower and Dulles concluded that the international communist movement, by subverting Guatemala's political and economic structure, posed a threat to the hemisphere. Unable to persuade the Latin American states to take collective action against Guatemala, the President called in the CIA to organise the overthrow of Arbenz. Exiles were armed in Honduras and with American air support drove Arbenz into exile, the population remaining passive and the Guatemalan army staying on the sidelines. In this way, with the use of relatively little force, the political structure was wholly changed.

Guatemala now fell under the control of a right-wing military dictatorship. The mass of the country's poor were the principal losers in these power struggles. Governed by corrupt military regimes, Guatemala cried out for political, social and economic reform. The Eisenhower administration, meanwhile, was accused of having acted in the interests of the United Fruit Company, which grew the bananas that constituted Guatemala's principal export. Yet that was untrue. Eisenhower had acted because he believed that Guatemala was falling under communist control and because he assumed that the strings were being pulled by Moscow. As he saw it, he had in 1954 successfully defended the Monroe Doctrine. But the inherent weakness of American policy in Guatemala and elsewhere in Latin America lay in the contempt felt by the right-wing militarists helped to power by the United States for Western democratic values and their opposition to economic and social reforms. They were prepared to protect United States corporations, however, as part of the bargain to gain American support. In this expectation they were not disappointed. American aid poured into Guatemala after the coup. The strategy of combating global communism, and so ensuring that those in power professed friendship with America, overshadowed in administration policy the need of the great majority of Guatemalans for basic reforms.

As long as pro-American governments retained power in the Latin American republics, however corrupt or dictatorial, the Eisenhower administration turned a blind eye and ignored the fundamental problems besetting the continent. Latin American radicals were equally unrealistic in blaming the mass poverty and repressive dictatorships entirely on the United States.

In Iran and Guatemala the CIA had successfully accomplished its mission. When it began to adopt the same technique in Cuba, however, it experienced humiliating failure and thereby damaged the interests and prestige of the United States. Cuba was ruled by another corrupt and brutal dictator, Fulgencio Batista. Her economy was dominated by sugar cane, whose growth and production were owned and controlled by American companies. Here also land reform and the raising of the living standard of the poor peasantry could not be accomplished without clashing with the interests of American corporations. Even so, the Eisenhower administration once again was motivated not by a desire to support the American owners but rather by dread of communism and of its control from the Kremlin.

Since the 1890s American administrations had feared that the conflicts in Cuba could allow a powerful European nation a base a mere ninety miles from the coast of Florida. US interests determined official attitudes to Cuban leaders and as long as they safeguarded those interests even brutal dictators enjoyed American support. But there was also public sympathy in the United States for Fidel Castro's revolutionary fight against Batista, a sympathy which was combined with a growing recognition that the United States should support popular and democratic regimes. The CIA, on the other hand, warned the President of communist infiltration of Castro's guerrilla movement. On 1 January 1959 Castro overthrew Batista and took control of the government in Havana. The executions of his opponents which followed produced a revulsion of feeling in the United States.

*A victorious Fidel Castro making one of his lengthy speeches, in Santa Clara, Cuba, 1959.*

The Cuban Communist Party was legalised, two prominent communist associates of Castro, Che Guevara and Antonia Jiménez, were brought into the government and Castro, in the Latin American tradition, made himself the leader of the country. Clearly a leader of charisma with genuine popular support, he promised radical reform to the poor masses and proceeded to expropriate large estates and factories, many of which were American-owned. The earlier American support for Batista, moreover, had provoked strong anti-American feelings in Cuba. The United States responded to her perception of the pro-communist and anti-American sentiments of Castro's rule with a trade embargo against Cuban sugar. But this policy of economic sanctions badly misfired because it offered Russia the opening to step into the breach by giving aid to Cuba and buying her sugar. It also drove Castro to seek closer relations with the Soviet Union. There was an obvious alternative for the United States which had been frequently resorted to: intervention. Eisenhower turned once more to the CIA. Cuban exiles were trained in what was now friendly Guatemala to support a Cuban challenger to Castro. But the Guatemalan operation could not be repeated, for there was no exiled Cuban leader of sufficient stature and popularity available to rally anti-Castro political groups. Eisenhower therefore withheld his approval of military intervention. Castro's defiance of 'Yankee imperialism' meanwhile was gaining much popular support throughout Latin America. But the fuse that led to the Bay of Pigs in 1961 had been laid (page 589).

During the two Eisenhower administrations the credibility gap widened between the publicly professed policy aims and the actual policies adopted in dealing with the world's problems. This eroded one of Eisenhower's main personal assets, his reputation for honesty. The impact was greater on American public perceptions and on America's allies than on the Soviet Union, whose leaders had no high regard for capitalist moral protestations: even without this credibility gap the Russians were not willing to respond to Eisenhower's various disarmament proposals as long as the Soviet Union lagged behind in nuclear capability. But by making the CIA the secret arm of United States policies and greatly extending its role, Eisenhower left a dangerous legacy to his successors.

To deter communist expansion, Eisenhower increasingly relied on allies in Asia and Europe to help shoulder the burdens of fighting on the ground as well as on America's growing nuclear armoury. By raising the possibility that the nuclear threshold would quickly be crossed he sought to prevent even local wars in Asia and Europe. Nuclear weapons were stockpiled in Western Europe, though they remained under American control. Britain possessed her own nuclear deterrent and France was developing an independent nuclear striking force as well. It was part of Eisenhower's and Dulles's psychological deterrent to keep the Soviet Union, China and the North Koreans guessing at what stage of conflict nuclear weapons would be used. The President was fully aware of the serious consequences that would follow battlefield nuclear exchanges and therefore regarded the maintenance of local conventional forces as indispensable. But he hoped to build up West European, South Korean and Nationalist Chinese forces to obviate so far as possible reliance on American conventional forces. These he reduced to strengthen the American

economy, while promoting alliances in Asia and in Europe and providing military and economic aid. In the last resort the United States would counter communist aggression with her own nuclear capabilities.

The United States and the Soviet Union would survive if nuclear weapons were used on battlefields beyond their territories. But densely populated Germany, France and Britain, Taiwan, South Korea and Japan, where the Western bases were located and the armed forces assembled, would be destroyed. So the administration had to provide an alternative strategic plan, however implausible. This Dulles did in his famous speech to the Council of Foreign Relations on 12 January 1954, declaring that 'local defence had to be reinforced by the further deterrent of massive retaliatory power'. That last phrase, which became shortened to 'massive retaliation', when coupled with other statements that nuclear strikes would be made against targets of American choosing, was clearly intended to warn Moscow and Beijing that war might not be confined to the regions which the communists decided to subvert or attack. Thus the United States implied that a communist attack on one of her allies in Asia or Europe would lead to an American counterstrike against China or Russia. In due course the Soviet Union threatened the reverse. An attack from a European base on the Soviet Union would lead to Soviet retaliatory attack on the United States. Thus ran the logic of nuclear diplomacy.

Tough anti-communist speeches, Dulles's rhetoric about American readiness to go to the brink of war and talk of rolling back communism were part of the psychological dimension of the Eisenhower administrations' foreign policy. But these robust verbal stands also had a domestic political purpose. Despite the cuts in the defence budget Eisenhower wished to convince Congress and the country that this did not mean that his administration was soft on communism. In particular, he wished to reconcile an isolationist 'old guard' of conservative Republicans in his own party who repudiated Yalta and Roosevelt's policy as a sell-out to Russia and blamed Truman, Acheson and their 'red' advisers for the 'loss' of China.

But these policies also had negative repercussions abroad. Dulles was misread as being 'trigger happy', a man who might through miscalculation plunge the world over the precipice into a nuclear holocaust. In 1954, as secret British Cabinet minutes reveal, one senior Minister in Churchill's government thought that Dulles was a greater danger to world peace than the Russians. It was a sentiment shared throughout the world. Furthermore, the Soviet leaders were made to feel Russia's technological inferiority, especially in the nuclear field. Was this wise? With a national economy far weaker than America's, the Russian leaders redoubled their efforts to convince the United States that her economic superiority did not mean that the Soviet Union was bound to remain militarily the weaker. The Soviet Union and the United States began to stockpile nuclear weapons in such quantities that they would be able to destroy each other's population centres several times over.

Though the USSR in the 1950s had fewer nuclear weapons than the United States, she switched successfully from aircraft to rockets. She tested the first intercontinental missiles (ICBM) in 1957 but serious problems remained to be overcome and they were not deployed until the 1960s. The Soviet Union concentrated on Western Europe first, where her more reliable intermediate ballistic missiles were targeted in ever increasing numbers from 1959. The Russians had scored a psychological victory when on 5 October 1957 they had sent the first earth satellite, Sputnik, through space. After early failures an American satellite was successfully launched from Cape Canaveral three months later in January 1958. But the Soviet scientific first gave a rude jolt to American confidence and created the myth that the United States was lagging behind and that Eisenhower had allowed a 'missile gap' to develop. In this way propaganda and achievement stimulated the nuclear arms race from the 1950s onwards.

The impression America gave of ruthlessness, even recklessness, in being prepared to escalate every local conflict between communist and non-communist nations to all-out nuclear conflict was in fact a false one. Both the Soviet Union and the United States clung to the need for the ultimate deterrent, but Eisenhower and Malenkov (and his successor Khrushchev) were agreed that nuclear war offered no hope of victory to either side. A first surprise strike would not eliminate all the nuclear capabilities of the other side, so sufficient nuclear weapons would remain to inflict a catastrophic retaliatory strike on the attacker. By the mid-1950s a new era in superpower relations and so in world history had thus been reached. It is graphically summed up by three letters: MAD, or mutual assured destruction. The fact that a nuclear exchange would destroy both countries thereafter dominated Soviet–American relations. Their awesome nuclear capabilities make direct war between them inconceivable. Unhappily, however, wars were not banished between smaller nations.

What Eisenhower and Dulles achieved during the years from January 1953 to the end of the Eisenhower presidency in January 1961 was to end American involvement in the Korean War and to keep the United States out of further conflict. The contrast between bellicose rhetoric and the actual record became evident as early as the first year of the administration when on Stalin's death the first cracks in Soviet control became visible in East Germany.

There was not even a hint that military action would be taken by the US on behalf of Soviet satellites which rebelled. On 16 and 17 June 1953 Berlin workers rose in revolt against their communist regime. Throughout Eastern Germany other industrial towns followed. If its rhetoric meant anything, this was the moment for the West, led by the United States, to respond to appeals for help. There was a short, chaotic interlude while the East Germany regime showed itself quite unable to suppress the rising. Then the Russians, who had large troop concentrations on the spot, intervened and quickly quelled the revolt. Apart from offering pious declarations of moral support, the United States did nothing. It was a tacit admission that an acceptance of the divisions agreed at Yalta was the basis of continuing peace, and that great-power intervention in the sphere assigned to the other side carried with it the risk of nuclear war. In reality there could be no rolling back of frontiers by force. But Radio Free Europe, financed almost entirely by the CIA, nevertheless kept up the barrage of propaganda directed towards Eastern Europe.

While Europe was seen as the primary scene of action in the Cold War, America's Western allies were fighting communism in Asia: Britain in Malaya, and France in Indo-China (as Vietnam, Laos and Cambodia were then known). Eisenhower shared the traditional American antipathy towards colonialism, which was seen as a sin confined mainly to the old European empires. The granting of independence, the President believed, would undermine the support the communists were receiving in their fight against the French. On the other hand, he also agreed with Foster Dulles that the national communist struggles in that part of Asia were controlled by the Kremlin, which could call them off if it wished. The Soviet purpose, they believed, was to weaken the West. Eisenhower concluded that the United States would be playing the Kremlin's game if she allowed her armed forces to become embroiled in the endless land-mass of Asia. Instead, the US would provide finance, arms and advice to European and Asian allies to fight their own wars against communist expansion. The question left unanswered was what should be done if America's allies proved too weak or too unwilling to resist. American perceptions also over-simplified the problems confronting Beijing and Moscow, whose control over events in their spheres of influence was not nearly so complete as the US believed.

The French struggle in Vietnam went from bad to worse. The greater the effort the French devoted militarily in Vietnam, moreover, the less would be their capacity to play their part in the defence of Western Europe against the Soviet Union. Military logic suggested that they should pull out. Yet the defence of Vietnam too seemed vital. Dulles and Eisenhower subscribed to the domino theory, that if Vietnam fell to the communists then the rest of south Asia would be lost. But increased American aid to France was not turning the tide. By 1954 the French wanted not only US bombers but also the personnel to keep them flying. And so in response Eisenhower, despite his misgivings, sent the first American servicemen to Vietnam. He was still determined, however, to keep America out of any large-scale involvement: his military judgement was against it and furthermore he did not wish to identify the United States with a colonialist cause. The key struggle in the spring of 1954 was taking place around the fortified French position at Dien Bien Phu, invested by the Vietminh.

In March and April 1954 the French requested the direct intervention of American armed forces, but Eisenhower procrastinated. There was even talk of using atomic bombs: this he rejected decisively. Dien Bien Phu surrendered on 7 May 1954. Eisenhower now accepted the inevitability of a compromise peace, a partition of Vietnam that would draw a new line against communist expansion. He had made peace in Korea; he would not start a new war in Vietnam, with the United States taking over the role of France.

By the time of Dien Bien Phu's fall the Geneva Conference (attended by France, Britain, the Soviet Union, the People's Republic of China and both Vietnams) had already been in session for some days (page 407). Realising that the United States was not going to provide the military help needed to win the war against the Vietminh, the French decided to make the best bargain they could with the Vietnamese communists. While negotiations dragged on in Geneva the French and Americans thought they faced the danger that Ho Chi-minh would order his victorious forces to drive the French out of the whole of Vietnam. In Washington, in May 1954, a real war-scare ballooned. The National Security Council came to the drastic conclusion that US power should not be used in defence of south-east Asia but should be directed against 'the source of the peril', China, 'and that in this connection atomic weapons should be used'. Dulles appeared to agree, saying that any Chinese intervention in Vietnam would be the 'equivalent of a declaration of war against the United States'. In the supercharged Washington atmosphere, Eisenhower now proved that he was his own man. At this fateful moment in world history it was fortunate that the President was a man of great military prestige. An all-out nuclear war, Eisenhower told the Joint Chiefs of Staff, would have to be fought not only against China but also against her ally, Russia. He brought his advisers back to reality with a rhetorical question: 'If Russia were destroyed, what would be the result of such a victory?' From the Elbe to Vladivostock there would be starvation and disaster, no government or communications. 'I ask you,' Eisenhower challenged his military chiefs, 'what would the civilised world do about it?' He then supplied the answer, 'I repeat, there is no victory except through our imaginations.' In charge of policy at this critical time for the world, the President firmly rejected the use of atomic weapons in Asia and refused to consider wild notions of launching a pre-emptive nuclear war against Russia or China.

The superiority the United States enjoyed in stockpiles of nuclear weapons in the 1950s could be employed only in defence of the West's most vital interests, not to attack weaker opponents. Eisenhower would have used them if the Red Army had attempted to overrun Western Europe or if China had invaded Taiwan or improbably had attacked Japan. But for Eisenhower their real value lay in their deterrent effect – he was not trigger happy and prayed they would never be used. Yet he did not believe peace in Asia could be restored by peaceful negotiation and compromise. That, in the President's judgement, was the appeasement policy of Munich. When in July 1954 an armistice was finally concluded at Geneva between the North Vietnamese and the French, and Vietnam was partitioned close to the 17th parallel, the United States would not participate in the settlement because it left the future of the whole of Vietnam to be settled by elections in 1956.

In 1954 Eisenhower's and Dulles's main effort was directed to bringing to life an Asian defensive alliance similar to NATO in Europe. By September the South-East Asian Collective Defence Treaty (SEATO) was concluded and signed in Manila by the United States, Britain, France, Australia, New Zealand, Pakistan, Thailand and the Philippines. It promised self-help and mutual aid to develop the signatories' individual and collective capacity to resist armed attack or subversion; an attack on one was held to be a threat to all, and the allies undertook to act to meet the common danger. Cambodia, Laos and South Vietnam were included in the region to be defended. But SEATO never achieved the credibility of NATO. There was no automatic provision of military aid and Britain and France withdrew from providing any military support.

The contrast between Europe and Asia in the 1950s and after is striking. NATO became an effective alliance; SEATO did not, but relied for its teeth on the United States. In Europe policy decisions had to be shared with allies where questions of European defence were concerned. In Asia, the United States took her own decisions in the face of lukewarm support from Western European allies. US policy fulfilled most of its aims in western Europe. For example, it was largely American pressure and Adenauer's unequivocal decision to side with the Western powers that restored the Federal Republic to full sovereignty and brought her to membership of NATO in 1955. And, despite threats and diplomatic confrontations, there was no war between communist states and the West in Europe. The Asian peoples, by contrast, suffered turmoil and wars. America, after Eisenhower left the presidency, became increasingly involved in the renewed Vietnamese civil war.

In 1956 the hollowness of the political rhetoric of 'freeing the enslaved nations' from communist control was so forcibly exposed that it was not seriously employed again. The Soviet Union proved herself strong enough to impose her will on the central and Eastern European nations. In October of that year the Poles defied the Russians, and this encouraged the Hungarians, who took the notion of independence from Soviet control much further. During the last week of that month fighting broke out between Soviet troops and the Hungarians. Unbelievably, the Russians withdrew from Budapest only to return in force on Sunday, 3 November 1956 (page 502). Eisenhower, with Dulles in hospital after his first operation for cancer, was dealing simultaneously with the problems of the British–French–Israeli war against Egypt (page 471), with the Hungarian revolution and with his approaching re-election (6 November). Increasingly desperate Hungarian appeals for American help were rejected by Eisenhower, although the CIA were eager to supply air drops of arms. Eisenhower acknowledged that Hungary lay within the Soviet orbit and that the Soviet Union might well prefer to fight rather than accept the disintegration of the Warsaw Pact. The United States thus confined herself to resolutions which would be vetoed by the Russians in the UN, and to accepting some of the Hungarian refugees fleeing across the Austrian frontier.

Eisenhower's and Dulles's Middle Eastern policies were less successful. America's overriding concern was to keep the Soviet Union out of this vital region with its huge oil reserves, though she also wished to be regarded as the friend of the Arabs, sympathetic to their strivings to free themselves from a semi-colonial status, above all in relation to Britain. But the unstinting support the United States gave to Israel aroused Arab suspicion and hostility. Moreover, Britain was America's most important ally in Europe. The United States could not escape the inconsistencies in her position. Nonetheless, each policy sought to preserve the peace and the post-1949 *status quo* in the region. These aims served the interests of Britain too, and the two countries worked together to this end until their co-operation became undone in the aftermath of Suez.

Eisenhower and Dulles had co-ordinated their policy with Eden to combat Nasser, who was leaning to Moscow. They agreed in the spring of 1956 to withdraw their financial backing for the Aswan High Dam, making this public in July, and when Nasser

522 THE COLD WAR: SUPERPOWER CONFRONTATION, 1948–1964

nationalised the Suez Canal Dulles exerted what pressure he could to co-ordinate the international reaction. Eisenhower and Dulles wanted to get rid of Nasser, but not at the price of arousing the whole Arab world against the West. They were, therefore, unenthused by British suggestions that military action could become necessary. They urged caution and delay. But Britain and France in collusion with Israel went ahead on 31 October with the bombing of Egypt and kept Washington in the dark about their precise military plans (Chapter 46).

Suez represented a serious crisis in the United States' relationship with her principal European allies. After some initial hesitation Eisenhower decided that he had to try to end the British–French–Israeli invasion of Egypt and so backed a UN call for a ceasefire in November 1956. He exploited Britain's financial weakness to force the Eden Cabinet to accept the UN resolution. The Israelis and the French bowed to the inevitable. The US managed to mend fences with Britain the following year, but there was no disguising that in dealing with Nasser's Egypt American diplomacy had been inconsistent.

After Suez, despite her efforts to persuade the invaders to withdraw, the United States did not gain many plaudits from the Arab world. US policy in the Middle East continued to be hampered by the question of how support for Israel could be reconciled with Arab friendship. Then in 1958 the US landed troops in the Lebanon, at the same time pronouncing the Eisenhower Doctrine, which committed the Americans to providing help to Middle Eastern states threatened by communist aggression or subversion. As this did not reflect the reality of the conflicts within the Middle East, the doctrine was ineffectual. But uncertainty about how best to handle the Middle East in the light of America's conflicting interests was not unique to the Eisenhower administrations and continued long after.

During his two terms (1953–7 and 1957–61) as president, Eisenhower, skilfully supported by Dulles, was generally able to establish clear US policies for the rest of the decade and beyond. There could be no military intervention in the regions of the world under effective Soviet and Chinese military control, even when rebellion broke out within the Soviet camp. In Europe, the United States was committed to the defence of the NATO alliance countries. In Asia, the defensive line had been

drawn close to the Chinese mainland, protecting the islands of Quemoy and Matsu as well as Taiwan. In August and September 1958 a new crisis broke out with mainland China over the offshore islands, which Chiang Kai-shek, who still believed that internal disruption would allow him to reconquer China, had heavily reinforced. When the Chinese communists blockaded and shelled the islands, he saw an opportunity of embroiling the United States in a war with China. Eisenhower ordered the Seventh Fleet to sail in support of the Nationalist Chinese, but once again he scotched the advice of the Joint Chiefs of Staff to use atomic weapons against mainland China. Mao Zedong and Zhou Enlai abandoned their assault on the islands, thus ending all question of a war with China. But Eisenhower continued Truman's policy of refusing to recognise the communist republic as the legitimate state of China. With American support, Chiang Kai-shek's Taiwan continued to occupy China's seat on the Security Council of the United Nations. Meanwhile, in south-east Asia, SEATO defined the limits of Chinese and communist expansion, and in the Middle East the Baghdad Pact created a military barrier along the frontiers between Turkey, Iran and the Soviet Union supported by Iraq and Pakistan.

The future of Germany was a critical problem for both the East and the West, as well as for the Germans. Was there any real possibility of disengagement and agreement, of German unification on conditions of neutrality? Soviet leaders from Stalin to Khrushchev strove to achieve this objective as long as the Soviet regime in East Germany was preserved. The Soviet Union above all attempted to prevent West German rearmament and integration in NATO. To this end Khrushchev worked hard to relax tension in Europe. Eisenhower asked for proof of Soviet sincerity, for example the conclusion of an Austrian peace treaty, which had been fruitlessly discussed for years. A few weeks later, to the West's astonishment, Khrushchev agreed and the Austrian Treaty was signed in May 1955. But the subsequent Geneva Conference in July of that year made no real progress on the more important German question. Eisenhower rejected the principle, insisted on by Khrushchev, that a unified Germany could not join NATO. Khrushchev in turn refused to accept Eisenhower's 'open skies' proposal, under which the Americans could inspect Soviet military sites and vice versa. Nor was the nuclear arms race halted. But Khrushchev and Eisenhower did agree to conduct relations in a conciliatory spirit – the so-called 'spirit of Geneva'. The first stage of detente had begun. But it did not last long: there were warlike exchanges during the Suez crisis of 1956; relations were strained by the Eisenhower Doctrine in the Middle East (page 475); and new tensions arose when in November 1958 the mercurial Soviet leader threatened that the Soviet Union would conclude a peace treaty with East Germany and end Western rights in Berlin. But Khrushchev remained personally friendly, inviting Eisenhower to visit the Soviet Union. Eisenhower responded by indicating to Khrushchev that, provided Western interests were preserved, he was ready to negotiate over Berlin and German unification and over an atomic test-ban treaty. Test-ban negotiations were accordingly started in Geneva, and Khrushchev postponed the unilateral alteration of Berlin's status. Eisenhower wanted to crown his presidency as it drew to its close by establishing a firm basis for world peace. John Foster Dulles's last illness had reduced his influence, though he was careful to warn Eisenhower against adopting any policy that smacked of appeasement. In May 1959 Dulles died and was replaced as secretary of state by Christian Herter.

Detente seemed assured when Khrushchev accepted Eisenhower's invitation to visit the United States in September 1959. It was an unprecedented event for a Kremlin leader to come to see for himself the country perceived by the Soviet Union as the leader of the anti-communist capitalist bloc of powers. The visit was a success, though Khrushchev tried not to show that he was impressed by the achievements of capitalism. He and Eisenhower agreed to hold a summit meeting in Paris the following May, after which Eisenhower and his family were to visit the Soviet Union.

Eisenhower's hopes were soon to be dashed by Khrushchev. The United States had since 1955 been sending spy planes over the Soviet Union at such high altitudes that the Russians could not bring them down. But just before the Paris summit was to take place in May 1960 they at last succeeded in shooting one down with a missile. Believing the pilot dead and the plane destroyed, the US administration impaled itself on the falsehood that the plane – the U-2 – was a weather-research plane that had strayed off course. The Russians then triumphantly displayed the captured pilot together with incontrovertible evidence that the plane was spying. Khrushchev, who had arrived by this time for the conference in Paris, demanded an apology and a statement from Eisenhower that the spying missions had been conducted without the President's knowledge. They had not. But the President was not to be caught in a lie, nor trapped in a position where he had to admit publicly that he did not know what was going on. So, unable to humiliate Eisenhower, Khrushchev broke off the summit meeting before it had got properly started. Not that the U-2 issue was a new one: the Russians had known about these missions for three years. In any case, satellites from both sides would soon be able to pass unimpeded over any region they chose. Possibly Khrushchev had simply decided that there was no point in dealing with a president in the last months of his administration, and that it would be necessary to postpone serious negotiations.

Eisenhower had dominated the Western side in global international relations for eight years. His greatest achievement was a negative one: to have resisted all temptation to use atomic weapons and to start a war against China, as some of his advisers had urged. Nor had he panicked his country into seeking excessive nuclear-weapons leadership over the USSR. And although he wanted genuine disarmament, it is difficult to see how he could have halted the arms race, given the circumstances and the fears prevailing at the time. In his memorable 'farewell' address he alerted his countrymen to the power of the industrial–military establishment, which had grown up as a result of the Cold War, and warned of the 'potential for the disastrous rise of misplaced power', which should never be allowed to 'endanger our liberties or democratic processes'. Both the armaments industry and the military, he believed, would always demand more than was necessary.

The 1950s were a dangerous decade. For all Eisenhower's and Dulles's ideological simplifications about the 'international communist world', their narrowly conceived interventions in the Third World, in Iran, in Guatemala and in Vietnam, it was fortunate for the world that a president of unchallengeable military prestige was in a position to control a military establishment prone to advocating at times of crisis policies which might have endangered the peace of the world in the nuclear age.

# PART XI

---

*The Recovery of Western Europe in the 1950s and 1960s*

# CHAPTER 53

# West Germany: Economic Growth and Political Stability

No one could have foreseen the remarkable transformation undergone by a defeated Germany in just one decade. Two Germanies had emerged by the 1950s, military allies of their former enemies, Russia, Britain, the United States and France. Germans in the West were no longer treated with contempt and condescension but were admired for the discipline and hard work that had restored their prosperity. Not that both halves of Germany prospered equally. The free-market economy in the Western part proved itself to be far more efficient in the production of wealth than the state-planned economy of the Eastern third. The Democratic Republic was a truncated state: the former German agricultural and industrial territories east of the Oder–Neisse had been lost to Poland and the Soviet Union. In 1945 some 17 million Germans lived in the Soviet zone, the later Democratic Republic, and nearly 44 million in the Western zones. Twenty years later, together with their respective parts of Berlin, the preponderance of West Germany over East had become even greater; almost 60 million were living in the Federal Republic and West Berlin, and 17 million in the DDR including East Berlin. The two Germanies provided something like a test of the relative efficiency of the Western economies and the command economies of the East, given that both of these new states were starting from much the same base in 1945.

The results were little short of astonishing. Progress was certainly made in the East, but the disparity in wealth, let alone liberty and quality of life, between the countries grew with every passing year. Just how backward the DDR had become was hidden from the West until the collapse of the East German state in 1990.

Before the Berlin Wall was built in 1961 millions had walked to the freedom of the West. They tended to be young, more active and more enterprising. With barbed wire, control towers and orders to shoot, the East German regime survived almost another three decades. It is possible that without the fortified barrier between East and West the DDR would have collapsed many years before from a haemorrhage of its active population seeking a better life in the West.

The transition to parliamentary democracy in the West seemed smooth, the path almost too easy. But the widespread feeling that the German people as a whole were guilty of allowing the Nazi excesses, reinforced by punitive re-education and denaz-ification, did not provide firm foundations on which to win hearts and minds for democracy and civil liberty. In the early years of occupation the Allied authorities still had much suspicion of German grass-roots revanchism. At least one generation had to pass before support for the democratic institutions of the Federal Republic became something more than opportunism for the majority and turned into a conviction that democratic values were worth defending, if necessary at personal cost. The concerns of the adult population in the immediate post-war years were necessarily materialistic: to put together the bare necessities for family life and after that to gain a share of the good things – a home, furniture, enough to eat, a refrigerator, a car.

The Germans were also asked in the 1950s to help defend the West. The sudden change in Allied attitudes on the issue of German rearmament was not universally popular, since only a few years before German militarism had been condemned as the root of all evil. But the Second World War had brought about a great change in German thinking: if a third world war broke out, it would be fought in Germany, and everyone understood that it would totally destroy the country. Militarism was dead. Indeed, in the 1950s, a strong extra-parliamentary movement opposed to rearmament made itself felt – the first post-war stirrings of grass-roots political involvement on an important issue.

The weaknesses and failures of the Weimar Republic, which had paved the way for National Socialism and the end of liberty, served as lessons which were well absorbed in the drafting of a new constitution. The Federal German Republic in any case had a better start than Weimar, because its birth in May 1949 did not coincide with the hour of defeat, as had that of the Weimar Republic. Instead, it was the Allies and their occupation policies that were blamed for the hardship of the early years. The evolution of a fully sovereign parliamentary democratic state was a gradual one that was not completed until six years later in 1955. Political parties, assemblies and administrations had been set up in ten Länder (regional territories), though West Berlin was not included in the Federal Republic. In the spring of 1948, France, Britain and the United States had agreed to the formation of a central German government for the Western zones, but ultimate powers still remained in the hands of the three Allied governments. The minister-presidents of the Länder were invited to call a constituent assembly to draft a constitution. But the minister-presidents, fearing that this would make the division of Germany permanent, would agree only to call a 'council' and to draft a 'basic law', thus emphasising the transitional nature of what they were doing: Germany would not have a constitution until it was reunited. The two major parties, the SPD and the CDU/CSU, sent the same number of delegates to the parliamentary council; Adenauer by astute management secured the presidency, so establishing an ascendancy in German politics that was to last for fifteen years.

Given the bitter personal relations and conflicts between the SPD and the CDU/CSU, not to mention the deep divisions within the parties themselves over the extent of federal powers, over regional self-government, over voting procedures and over a host of other practical questions, the framing of an agreed basic law was a remarkable achievement. Behind all these questions always lay assessments of how eventually complete sovereignty could be achieved and how reunification could be brought about. Reunification was still the goal; it appeared unthinkable then that Germany would remain divided for long.

The Basic Law, or West German constitution, stood the test of time and by the 1980s had lost its provisional appearance just when it indeed turned out to be provisional. The weaknesses of Weimar were consciously avoided: voting was by a combination of proportional representation (with candidates drawn from party lists in each of the Länder) and constituency representation by simple majority; a barrier was created on the Länder list, so that no party with less than 5 per cent of the vote in the Federal Republic could win a seat in the parliament, the Bundestag (although, if three seats were won in direct constituency elections in one Land, the 5 per cent rule was set aside). Presidential powers were less extensive than those held by the presidents of the Weimar Republic. The Chancellor became the most powerful member of the executive; he and his government could gain office only if he enjoyed the support of a parliamentary majority. But a vote against him by a majority would bring about his fall only if the Bundestag could agree by majority on a successor. The rationale for this 'constructive vote of no confidence' was to prevent a repetition of the extinction of Weimar, brought about by the combination of two anti-democratic parties, the National Socialists and the communists. The constitution could be changed only by a two-thirds majority and was buttressed by nineteen articles defining inviolable fundamental rights; a constitutional court was set up to decide claims that the constitution was not being observed. Legislation by the elected Bundestag could be delayed by the Bundesrat, a second chamber to which the Länder sent representatives and whose purpose is to scrutinise legislation which affects particularly the Länder.

The constitution is a long and complex document and only its salient features are here described. As a written constitution embodying individual rights and a constitutional court to enforce them, it provides safeguards against their abuse by simple party majorities in the parliamentary assembly. The strong element of proportional representation allows a voice for the views of those who do not wish to choose between the two mass parties. The 5 per cent rule prevents the proliferation of small parties which destabilised Weimar and has undermined governments in Italy; on the other hand, proportional representation can allow too much influence to a minority. In most years since 1949, the two major parties could gain a majority only with the help of a third party, the Free Democratic Party, which could bargain with either in order to gain its objectives and switch support accordingly.

No constitution is perfect; its success depends on the politicians and the parties who bring it to life, and on the attitude of the electorate towards the government and the institutions established under it. The Federal Republic has enjoyed great stability in good times and, more importantly, in bad. The constitution or Basic Law has served it well. But, if democracy is to become an integral part of a nation's life, it requires more than just the right institutions: there has to be a sense of fairness and propriety among opposing parties and among opposing individuals, a recognition of a greater whole. The dangers posed by a revival of racism are better understood in Germany than elsewhere.

The German socialist party (SPD) was the most coherent and best-organised mass party to put itself before the electorate when the first Bundestag elections were held in 1949. Despite a tendency to strong central leadership, local and district organisations during the subsequent four decades acted as ginger groups and at times stood well to the left of the party leadership. This became especially true of the young socialists after the revolt of youth in the 1960s. A serious handicap for the party was the separation from the Federal Republic of Berlin and the Soviet zone, which had traditionally been the stronghold of the Social Democratic Party. Their leader in 1949 was Kurt Schumacher, passionate and autocratic in style, but his suffering in concentration camps had undermined his health, and he died in August 1952, only three years after the elections. He stood for a clear, uncompromising policy in both domestic and international affairs. His opposition to communism was total and he

ensured that the Western SPD would have no truck with the communists. Schumacher's socialism had its basis in ethics: his appeal was a moral one, for the betterment of the majority, of the poorer sections of society, for an end to the exploitation by capital of labour, of working people. But the party stressed that socialism without democracy would only lead back to the dark years of Hitler's totalitarianism or to Soviet tyranny. The British Labour Party had demonstrated since 1945 that state control of leading industries, especially coal and steel, and the breaking up of large estates were not incompatible with democracy and a respect for civil liberty. Two other planks in the party programme were important: a strong anti-clericalism, which condemned interference by the Church in politics and education, and an insistence on the recovery of national independence for all of Germany, not just for the Western zones. The Social Democrats did not want to be identified with the 'November criminals' who had been accused in 1919 of acting as the stooges of the victorious Allies. This time the SPD would be seen as the patriotic party. This stance led to the most bitter clashes with the governing Christian Democrats.

The Christian Democrats were less coherent than the Social Democrats, even to the extent of avoiding the label 'party' and calling themselves a 'movement' (union). They too set out to learn the lessons of the Hitler years. Politics should be anchored in ethical values, not vaguely but specifically in Christian ethics. Yet the Christian Democrats would not become a narrow Catholic party. From its foundation Protestants participated with Catholics in its organisation. Christian Democrats also championed parliamentary democracy and saw in communism the principal threat to civil liberties in the West. They were fiercely anti-Marxist, vociferous in their opposition to class warfare and state ownership of production. The Rhineland CDU, with its strong industrial Ruhr base, was overwhelmingly Catholic and led successful efforts to align the party with policies limiting the exclusion of workers from the exercise of power and its concentration in the hands of industrialists. Worker participation in industrial management became one of the planks of the CDU in the 1950s and so attracted support from sections of the trade unions. Capitalism was to be modified and restricted: industrial policies would be based on free enterprise, but the social good would be taken into account. The CDU's sister party, the Bavarian CSU, has traditionally represented more conservative views. Adenauer, more conservative than the Rhinelanders he led, skilfully reconciled the different elements, moving the party to the centre-right in doing so. Until his last few years *der Alte* (the Old One, a term of affectionate respect) stood head and shoulders above his party colleagues; he succeeded in putting his stamp on a broad pragmatic party that could attract progressive liberals, trade unionists, farmers and conservatives.

Adenauer had lived through the agony of the last years of Weimar, when the splintering of parties had been one factor in bringing Hitler to power in 1933. He had no high opinion of the democratic instincts of his fellow Germans. Their tendency to form religious, political and interest groups, which zealously pursued their aims without regard to the destructive effects on the polity as a whole, had left Adenauer with the conviction that strong leadership was necessary. He knew his people, their strengths and weaknesses, and so was determined that the CDU/CSU should draw its support from a broad cross-section of conservatives and liberals and of all classes and religions. This would isolate the irreconcilables, even if they breached the 5 per cent electoral barrier. Better some former National Socialists inside the CDU, where they could be controlled, than outside forming an opposition. The CDU/CSU faced a harder task in this respect than the SPD, which to begin with could count on a traditional following. That the danger of apathy towards democracy was real is shown by the millions of Germans who opted out of democratic political participation altogether.

To the left of the CDU, but opposed to socialism, stood the Free Democratic (Liberal) Party (the FDP), whose programmes were a different mix of compromises to those of the CDU: they agreed with the SPD in wishing to exclude clerical influence but concurred with the CDU in supporting an ethical or social-market economy. Other parties gaining more than 5 per cent have come and generally gone. Despite many internal divisions, the Green Party, emphasising the dangers of relentless industrial exploitation of the environment, especially from nuclear power plants, and advocating a more anarchic, grass-roots democracy, have survived as a party of protest longer than many political commentators prophesied when they were first formed in 1980.

### Bundestag Elections (excluding West Berlin), 1949 and 1953

|  | 1949 | | 1953 | |
| --- | --- | --- | --- | --- |
|  | % | Seats | % | Seats |
| CDU/CSU | 31.0 | 139 | 45.2 | 243 |
| SPD | 29.2 | 131 | 28.8 | 151 |
| FDP | 11.9 | 52 | 9.5 | 48 |
| Communist | 5.7 | 15 | 2.2 | – |
| Others | 22.2 | 65 | 14.3 | 44 |

The first elections for the Bundestag in August 1949 confounded the expectation of pollsters and others that amid general hardship the Social Democrats would win and that Kurt Schumacher would form the first government as chancellor. Schumacher had fought a strident campaign, denigrating the policies of the CDU and the big bosses, and asserting Germany's right to self-determination and self-respect. Now, he declared, was the German people's chance to break decisively with the social structures, the politics, the economic policies and the interfering clerics that had brought a Hitler to power. These policies attracted 6,935,000 votes, not only from the poor and the working classes. But the broad coalition represented by the CDU/CSU gained 2 per cent more votes. Why had the SPD lost? Schumacher had attacked the opposition on too many fronts and had alienated voters, among them a number of the Catholic workers of the Ruhr. The result was very close, but it proved a decisive turning point. Had Adenauer listened to a chorus of advice that with so small a majority a 'general coalition' of CDU and SPD should be formed, parliamentary democracy might have been strangled at birth. Many politicians did not understand this, and such coalitions existed in the *Länder*, forcing the small remaining opposition into impotence. Instead Adenauer was determined to follow policies which would be in clear contrast to those of the opposition, the 'socialists'.

The CDU/CSU had emerged as the largest party thanks to its broad approach and its compromises with capitalism, mainly worked out by Professor Ludwig Erhard, who called his system a 'social-market economy'. Free enterprise and competition

*Konrad Adenauer campaigning in Bamberg for the West German general election. The German people preferred Adenauer's Christian Democrats to the Social Democrats, but the Free Democrats were to hold the balance of power, as they so often did in post-war West Germany.*

on the American model would create national wealth, but working people would be protected by wide-ranging social-security measures guaranteed by the state. The Nazi economy, and the economic management by the occupying powers had been rigidly planned and controlled. As far as the Allies would allow, Erhard (though no more than an adviser) had daringly made a bonfire of controls and set the Germans free to choose. The currency reform of 1948 was another key aspect, substituting for the worthless old Marks a small circulation of sound Deutsch Marks. Overnight the shop windows filled up with goods, confidence in the currency returned, and after an early period of inflation prices stabilised by the time of the elections. Erhard's policies and the injection of Marshall Aid were beginning to lift the economy. Living conditions were still harsh but they were getting better.

Given that for social and political reasons both parties could count on a bedrock of a third of the electorate, the floating voters decided the outcome of elections. As long as the SPD remained restricted by its socialist doctrines (which it was until 1959), it could achieve no more than 40 per cent of the vote; on the other hand, CDU/CSU was strong enough only in 1957 to govern without the coalition support of other parties; its main partner was the FDP. This allowed the FDP a role in German politics far greater than the electoral support it could muster, which reached at best about 10 per cent. The communists barely passed the 5 per cent barrier in 1949; in 1953 they could not manage even that and so lost their representation in the Bundestag; banned until 1969 on the ground that the party did not support the democratic state, its support (less than 1 per cent) thereafter remained too small to regain representation in the Bundestag.

Adenauer so dominated German politics from 1949 to 1963 that the period is often referred to as the Adenauer era. These years irrevocably determined the course of German history, which changes of government and international conditions could only modify before 1990. Adenauer was no doubt lucky that elections had not been held in 1947 or 1948; appointed chancellor, he followed a clear course, exhibiting an unblinkered view of the morality and behaviour of the majority of the electorate and the particular needs of the new West German state.

The most immediate need was to extricate the Federal Republic from its leading strings: the Ruhr, with its steel and coal production, had been placed under an international authority; the Saar had voted to remain in close association with France; the Federal Republic itself was not permitted to follow an independent foreign policy. It was still bound to the Allies by the Occupation Statute (10 April 1949), which reserved supreme power to the USA, France and Great Britain, acting through their high commissioners. The Federal Republic was not truly sovereign in September 1949, but was on probation.

Adenauer made concessions and obtained some in return. He realised that he must win the total trust of the Western Allies as a precondition for regaining complete sovereignty. For all his rhetoric about German unity, he did not seriously believe it possible that the Soviet Union would withdraw and grant genuine freedom of choice to the German people living in the Soviet zone. After twelve years of Nazi totalitarian rule, the German people in the Federal Republic would have to learn and experience the blessings of democracy and civil liberty for some years and resist any temptation to compromise with the Soviet Union or to enter partnership with communists as the price of unity. In the world of the 1950s, Adenauer saw a choice that had to be unequivocally made: between falling into the grip of the communist-dominated East and forming the closest possible association with the Western states prepared to defend their freedom. There was no neutral road. Moreover, Adenauer reflected in his memoirs, 'It was my conviction that the only way for our country and people to regain their freedom lay in close agreement and co-operation with the high commissioners.' But the Germans were not necessarily prostrate, nor completely dependent on Allied goodwill. With Cold War tensions reaching a climax, the United States was not about to leave West Europe, as she had intended to do in 1944 and 1945; Adenauer understood that in such conditions it was in America's own vital interests to create a strong Western Europe, and for this, as he wrote in his memoirs, Germany was indispensable: 'A country in shackles is not a real, full partner. I therefore thought that our fetters would gradually fall away.' In time the Federal Republic would

become a full partner but he recognised that 'the most important prerequisite for partnership is trust'.

With tenacity and skill Adenauer exploited the logic of his country's position. This meant he had to work simultaneously on many fronts: to assure the Americans of his anti-communist commitment, to point out to the three Western Allies that the dismantling of German industry must stop and that growing German prosperity was essential to their own well-being; to stress that they, especially the French, need never fear a revival of German nationalism and aggression; and to demonstrate that Germany would contribute to Western European unity and defence and would work for the common good. At the same time the German people would have to be convinced of the benefits, above all the material ones, that would be conferred by these policies. Adenauer needed to be flexible, adroit, sometimes tough, sometimes ready to agree to disadvantageous bargains, able to assess correctly the feelings of his neighbours, while proceeding step by step to fulfil his major objectives. Meanwhile from the opposition benches he was assailed by Schumacher – sounding a strident nationalist note and rejecting conciliation with France – as the 'Chancellor of the Allies'. But Adenauer could show results. In 1950 West Germany became a member of the Council of Europe; the dismantling of German industry was first slowed down, then halted. Then in May 1950 the Chancellor responded with warmth to the French proposals known as the Schuman Plan to place the French and German production of coal and steel under a joint high authority and to invite other states to join. Jean Monnet had put forward the idea as a practical means to bring Western Europe into a federation of states and to remove forever French and German fears of aggression since neither country could build up armaments against the other without national control of her heavy industries (pages 543–4). The problem of the Ruhr as a source of French anxiety was thereby imaginatively solved. Italy, Belgium, the Netherlands and Luxembourg participated in the Paris negotiations. These were completed in April 1951 and Adenauer paid his first visit to Paris to sign the momentous European Coal and Steel Community treaty; it was the first step towards the formation in 1958 of the European Economic Community of the six. In Paris, Adenauer was the first official representative of the new German state to be received as a friend. He had moved steadily forward despite hostile French moves in 1950 designed to ensure that the Saar would become French. Patience was rewarded: the Saarlanders were given the opportunity to vote to rejoin West Germany; just as material interests had first turned them towards France, they now, in 1957, voted to join the Federal Republic as the tenth of the *Länder*.

Two years earlier, on 5 May 1955, the Federal Republic had regained her sovereignty, and the occupation was ended – though of course it persisted in the Soviet-controlled DDR and in divided Berlin. A treaty had in fact been concluded on 26 May 1952 to hand back sovereignty. But it was dependent on a second treaty signed in Paris a day later, providing for a German military contribution to Western defence; this treaty required ratification by the parliaments of the participating countries including the French Assembly. What had transformed the situation so dramatically since 1949 and what had then delayed the actual consummation of a changed relationship with West Germany? The process, as we have seen, was closely related to the growing tensions of the Cold War as a result of the Berlin crisis and the Korean War. The costs of West European defence had become so high that both the French and British came to regard German help in some form as indispensable. So far, the armies of the North Atlantic Treaty Organisation, which had been founded in April 1949 (page 391) had borne the burden alone. Recognising the sensitivity internationally of the question of German rearmament, Adenauer showed no unbecoming keenness but suggested that only if hard-pressed by the Allies would his countrymen consider a West German contingent within the framework of a European army. In discussing Germany's possible readiness with the high commissioners in August 1950, Adenauer astutely linked the issue to the recovery of sovereignty. The offer was now on the table. The Americans urged that it should be taken up. The French were more than hesitant but nevertheless in October 1950 the Prime Minister René Pleven found a way to still the popular fear of a revived Wehrmacht. Why not create something similar to the economic federation of the Schuman Plan in the military sphere? Pleven proposed what became known as the Pleven Plan – a European army with only small German contingents under European command (page 543). The procrastination over ratifying the treaty to set up a European Defence Community signed on 27 May 1952 and

the refusal of the French Assembly in August 1954 to ratify delayed acceptance of the Federal Republic as an equal, but it was only a delay. The die had been cast. A West German army was needed by the NATO allies.

The path to German sovereignty was complex. A nine-power conference was called in London in September 1954 consisting of the five original European Allies – Britain, France, Belgium, Luxembourg and the Netherlands (the Brussels Treaty powers) – together with the NATO allies Italy, Canada and the US; to this conference the Federal Republic was invited. It then transferred to Paris, where a number of interdependent treaties, the Paris Agreements, were concluded on 23 October 1954. The Federal Republic was now integrated into the Western alliances – the European alliance (to be known as the West European Union) and NATO. But limits were placed on West German rearmament, the most important of which was to forbid the manufacture of nuclear weapons. The occupation regime was ended, except for the Allied rights in Berlin, whose integrity and survival rested on Allied agreements made with the Russians in 1945. Adenauer gained the right for the Federal Republic to speak for all of Germany. The Federal Republic for her part bound herself not to attempt to change her frontiers nor to attempt to reunify Germany by force. Thus the Federal Republic made clear that she would act only in her own defence with her new allies – NATO was a defensive alliance. This reflected Adenauer's own beliefs. In this respect the foundation for the new policy towards West Germany's Eastern neighbours in the Chancellor Brandt years of the 1970s (pages 845–7) was already laid in the 1950s. Finally, France and the Federal Republic agreed on the new Saar plebiscite. It was a comprehensive clearing up of problems.

Schumacher's opposition was in part an opposition to Adenauer personally and to what he believed he stood for, the gradual reintroduction to the leadership of German society of all those who had served and flourished under Hitler. Schumacher wanted to bring about a thoroughgoing reform. He was bitterly opposed to communism and ready to see Germany align with the West, and he too championed West European integration. But he demanded the full recovery of German sovereignty first, the regaining of respect, before the Federal

Republic could, as a free agent, ally with the West. What he condemned was the kind of bargaining – a West German military contribution as the price of sovereignty – in which Adenauer was willing to engage in the spirit of *Realpolitik*. But Schumacher's nationalist tone and his demands for reunification had an air of unreality. His terms, that the Germans in the Soviet zone were to be allowed to choose freely and the Russians were to withdraw, were unacceptable to the Soviet leaders despite their blandishing of West German opinion by holding out the prospect of reunification provided Germany remained neutral and unarmed. Such a condition was as unacceptable to Schumacher, to Erich Ollenhauer (who succeeded to the party leadership after Schumacher's death in 1952) and to the majority of the SPD leadership as it was to Adenauer. The SPD was also united in opposing all the practical measures for rearmament Adenauer had negotiated, on the ground that West Germany had negotiated from an inferior position. But on the issue of rearmament itself the party was deeply divided. As an opposition, without ultimate responsibility for policies, they could more easily afford to take their principled stand.

Adenauer's approach to rearmament and sovereighty won majority support in the Bundestag. The former enemy was now accepted and welcomed as an ally. Adenauer's closely linked foreign and rearmament policies had also overcome the most bitter division at home and had resisted the attacks unleashed on them by the SPD. Among young Germans, who now faced conscription, there was understandable opposition; the 're-educated' Germans could hardly fathom such a turnaround, and then there were those genuinely convinced by the experiences of the war that Germans should not bear arms again. On the right, among ex-soldiers' organisations, arose the demand that the besmirched honour of Hitler's Wehrmacht must first be restored. Schumacher's arguments in the Bundestag were powerful: the linking of rearmament with political concessions to German sovereignty, he thundered, was a cynical bargaining that marked the end of democracy. But Adenauer secured ratification of the Paris treaties by the Bundestag in March 1953, and, after his great electoral victory in September of that year, a bill introducing conscription was passed in February 1954. The debate was not over. Echoing Dr Goebbels, the mass-circulation weekly *Der Spiegel* asked

rhetorically, 'Do you want total war?' What, in other words, would happen to Germany if a nuclear war broke out? Popular opposition to the stationing of nuclear warheads and missiles in Germany was to remain a powerful rallying cry in demonstrations outside parliamentary debate until 1969 and was to revive in the 1980s.

Adenauer's foreign and rearmament policies did not win universal support, but the acceptance of their chancellor as a respected equal in the capitals of Western Europe, and even in Moscow in September 1955, restored the buffeted sense of German pride. Yet, more than anything, the evident success of Erhard's economic policies and the marked improvement in standards of living, the visible recovery of West Germany with the rebuilding of her cities, assured Adenauer and the coalitions he led of seemingly inevitable victories in elections. The CDU/CSU was further helped in 1953 by the June risings in Berlin and the Soviet zone, in 1957 by the continuing fear of Soviet aggression. In both these years, Adenauer easily won an overall majority. By the next election in the summer of 1961, confidence in *der Alte* was slipping. His dithering reaction to the Berlin Wall crisis (page 506) and his age (he was now eighty-five), combined with his reluctance to step down to make way for Erhard, the heir apparent, cost the CDU/CSU its absolute majority. His last two years in office were unhappy. The Cabinet squabbled; the FDP partners made difficulties; then the Defence Minister, the ebullient Franz Josef Strauss, unwittingly resurrected memories of the totalitarian past. *Der Spiegel* had published an article on defence matters in October 1961. Believing that confidential information had been leaked, Strauss ordered police to search the magazine's offices and an editor was arrested; meanwhile Adenauer absurdly referred to *Der Spiegel* as 'a hotbed of treason'. But it all ended with a government rout: democracy had passed a test in the face of arbitrary government. Two years later, in October 1963, Adenauer at last made way for Erhard.

Adenauer had never doubted the path West Germany had to follow. Unerringly he anchored the Federal Republic to the community of Western European nations and to NATO. He rejected all Soviet blandishments and hints that a neutral, disarmed Germany might be reunified. Was there ever a real possibility that West Germany could

**Bundestag Elections, 1957–1965**

|            | 1957 | | 1961 | | 1965 | |
|------------|------|------|------|------|------|------|
|            | %    | Seats | %   | Seats | %   | Seats |
| CDU/CSU    | 50.2 | 270  | 45.3 | 242  | 47.6 | 245  |
| SPD        | 31.8 | 169  | 36.2 | 190  | 39.3 | 202  |
| FDP        | 7.7  | 41   | 12.8 | 67   | 9.5  | 49   |
| Others     | 10.3 | 17   | 5.7  | 0    | 3.3  | 0    |

have chosen the 'Austrian' solution? The ifs in history cannot be answered with certainty. It is unlikely that the world would have been a safer place with a neutral Germany or that such a Germany would have been given the opportunity to prosper, as the Federal Republic has done as a founding member of the European Economic Community.

Adenauer regarded as the centrepiece of his achievement the Franco-German reconciliation, and the creation between them of an 'unarmed frontier' as existed between the USA and Canada. The Franco-German friendship treaty of January 1963 symbolised the special relationship that had been established between the two countries. Adenauer did not have to create tension with the Soviet Union to drive his countrymen into the arms of the Western alliance. The repression of freedoms in the Soviet zone, the harsh Ulbricht regime in the German Democratic Republic which led to the building of the Berlin Wall in 1961 to prevent even more millions of Germans leaving their people's republic, the periodic Soviet threats to West Berlin, the preponderance of Soviet troops and tanks, not at a safe distance but just across the border, their use in East Berlin in 1953 and in Budapest in 1956 were all sufficient to convince the majority that safety lay in close alliance with Germany's NATO partners.

In the Adenauer period there was little opportunity to improve relations with the Soviet Union and the GDR. Adenauer's claim that his government could speak for all Germans until free elections were held in what was in Western eyes still the Soviet zone took up the moral high ground, even if the claim was looking increasingly unreal. The Federal Republic broke off diplomatic relations with

any country which recognised the sovereignty of the GDR and exchanged ambassadors (the Hallstein doctrine). On his visit to Moscow in 1955, however, Adenauer had to breach this line and agree to an exchange of ambassadors with the Soviet Union, as part of a bargain to release German prisoners of war still languishing in the USSR. The Soviet Union in the post-Stalin decades was realistic too and accepted the Federal Republic as an independent and powerful nation whose loyalty to the Western alliance could not be shaken. Responding immediately to the Schuman Plan (page 544), Adenauer had also helped to lay the foundations of the European Economic Community (pages 545–6), accepting that in her relations with France, Germany would for a time have to show deference to de Gaulle's visions of grandeur. In changed circumstances, his successors were able to modify the policies adopted towards the Soviet Union and the DDR, but in all its essentials Adenauer had set the fundamental course to be followed by the Federal Republic in her relations with her neighbours and the rest of the world. He possessed that rare gift of the statesman, the ability to distinguish the important from the secondary, and steadfastly to pursue the main objectives of his policy without being led astray by subsidiary considerations.

In his policies at home Adenauer was less successful. Autocratic in his Cabinet, he manipulated colleagues and felt little loyalty towards them. His views of the past and present were clear to the point of cynicism. Above reproach in his own behaviour during the Nazi years, he knew that the same could not be said of the majority of his countrymen. But the nation could not simply discard all former adherents of National Socialism – who would have been left to run the country and to rebuild it? Everyone would need to pull together, whatever their past, except for a few members of the Nazi elite. There would be no witch-hunts. The administration that had run the country before 1945 ran it again in the 1950s. Owners, managers and workers pulled together to achieve better living standards. The watchword was *Wiedergutmachung*, restitution. Pensions to those who had helped Hitler were honoured; refugees from the East received capital to start again; those who had survived the war with property intact were taxed to pay for this. Jewish victims received compensation and, for those millions who had been murdered during the war, the new State of Israel received a global sum which by 1980 amounted to nearly 3.5 billion DM. But despite the large sums paid they could not match all the looted wealth or compensate for millions of murders – though this was not the view taken by many Germans at the time. Nonetheless, Adenauer persistently backed *Wiedergutmachung* as morally necessary, and essential for the good name of the new Germany. At the same time he defended the employment of former high officials of the Nazi state, even employing in his own office Hans Globke, the civil servant who had helped to draft the Nuremberg anti-Semitic laws in 1935. It was a new beginning in the sense that the past was past and new loyalties were allowed to replace old ones. But this philosophy had a negative side: the general failure to face the past with frankness and honesty.

To one man in his Cabinet Adenauer owed more than to any other. Ludwig Erhard, Minister of Economic Affairs, symbolised the new-found German prosperity: jovial and rotund, he was never seen in public without a fat cigar. A vote for the CDU/CSU was as much a vote for Erhard and his concept of the socially responsible market economy as it was for Adenauer, the father-figure, the 'helmsman'. How did the economic transformation come about? Erhard could only provide the right conditions for workers and management to create the export-led boom. It was the quality and reliability of German manufacture, machine tools, products of heavy engineering and cars that brought success. It was also the willingness of the trade union leaders to give up class warfare and for two decades to restrain wage demands. Abroad and at home there was an almost insatiable appetite for capital goods and cars. The cities had to be rebuilt. The 'American dream' propagated by Hollywood created desires and expectations which only hard work could fulfil. The change for the better from the low point of 1945 to 1947 was so dramatic by the mid-1950s that people spoke of an 'economic miracle'. Economists can explain everything – at least afterwards. Possibly the term 'economic miracle' is no longer acceptable to academics, but it describes what it felt like for Germans at the time. Confidence in a better future was rekindled.

The statistics in the accompanying tables reveal the steady growth with unemployment falling to negligible proportions in 1971, though inflation increased from 1 per cent to 5 per cent in the

### West German Industrial Production Indices, 1945/6–1959 (*1913 = 100*)

|        | Coal | Iron | Steel | Chemicals | Cars    |
|--------|------|------|-------|-----------|---------|
| 1945/6 | 18.7 | 10.9 | 14.6  | –         | –       |
| 1950   | 58.3 | 49.1 | 69.1  | 240.6     | 936.6   |
| 1955   | 68.8 | 85.4 | 121.4 | 439.8     | 2,656.0 |
| 1959   | 66.1 | 95.3 | 147.3 | 630.9     | 4,266.0 |

### West German Unemployment and Production, 1950–1970/1

|        | Unemployment | | Index of Growth of Industrial Production |
|--------|--------------|-----|------------------------------------------|
|        | Number       | %   |                                          |
| 1950   | 1,870,000    | 8.0 | 100                                      |
| 1960   | 270,000      | 1.0 | 248                                      |
| 1970/1 | 185,000      | 0.7 | 435                                      |

1960s. Unemployment was a particularly sensitive issue in Germany. High unemployment in 1932–3 was widely credited with having made possible the rise of Hitler. Could the democracy of the Federal Republic survive high unemployment? Progress was not smooth: between 1954 and 1958 unemployment reached 7 per cent and fell no lower than 4 per cent, which alarmed the electorate; but thereafter until 1973 it never exceeded 3 per cent, and for the whole period 1961–6 it stayed below 1 per cent. The shortage of workers was first filled by the steady influx of refugees from the Soviet zone of Germany and then increasingly from the pool of unemployed in the Mediterranean countries, especially Italy and Turkey. By 1973 there were 2.6 million *Gastarbeiter* (guestworkers) in the Federal Republic. This availability of labour was one reason for West Germany's rapid industrial expansion. Periodic boosts were given by Marshall Aid, by the boom that followed the outbreak of the Korean War in 1950 and by the establishment of the Common Market in 1958. Management and trade unions were prepared to work together, investment provided up-to-date production methods and German goods gained a reputation for quality in

*The People's Car. The Volkswagen retained its pre-war name, but went on to conquer the roads of the world.*

a widening world market hungry for goods. The over-valuation of the German currency during the 1950s and beyond acted as a spur to efficiency and productivity. Ultimately it was the skill and will of management and workers that created the 'miracle' of recovery based on export-led growth. The Germans had come to expect improvements in their standard of living and low inflation; a sound economy was regarded as the natural state of affairs.

By 1963 Erhard no longer received the credit for Germany's prosperity as he had before. The heir apparent had been kept too long in the wings. Now as federal chancellor he lacked lustre and soon ran into difficulties with his FDP partners and particularly with the ambitious Franz Josef Strauss. There were Cabinet squabbles over Erhard's preference for America to de Gaulle's France, over the support price for grain which caused a deep Franco-German rift and over the supply of arms to Israel. The electorate in the 1960s, however, was more concerned with continuing the economic poli-

cies that had served them so well and were not about to entrust government to the Social Democratic opposition. Despite Erhard's declining prestige, the CDU/CSU won another resounding electoral victory in 1965. Just a year later, the FDP ministers resigned; the economic climate had worsened temporarily, and between 1965 and 1967 the Gross National Product grew by less than 2 per cent. Haunted by fears of inflation – another trauma of the 1920s the Germans could not shake off – government expenditure was cut back and unemployment averaged 3 per cent. To German perceptions it appeared as if a grave crisis was at hand. What in fact had occurred was no more than a swing in the business cycle. As the economy developed the Federal Republic could not sustain the rates of growth of earlier years. But Erhard had lost the confidence of his own party, the CDU, and Strauss and other leading politicians were ready to fight for the succession; in the event, Kurt Georg Kiesinger emerged as his successor and leader of the CDU/CSU.

The outcome of all the political intrigues and negotiations was an astonishing one. The FDP became the opposition party, and the CDU/CSU and SPD led by the charismatic former Mayor of West Berlin, Willy Brandt, formed a Grand Coalition in December 1966 under Chancellor Kiesinger, with Brandt as his deputy and Foreign Minister. The coalition had been possible only because the SPD had formally abandoned its Marxist doctrines in 1959 at the Gotha party conference. To win the opportunity of becoming the party of government, the SPD moved to the political centre. Like the CDU, the SPD now turned itself into an umbrella party appealing to a wide spectrum, from the still socialist left, who had nowhere else to go, to the liberal centre. This became its source of electoral strength, but also brought with it an internal weakness as the left wing came into conflict with its right wing. The years of the Grand Coalition also saw a kind of midlife crisis for the Federal Republic. A new, young post-war electorate, bored with bourgeois values and prosperity, made its presence violently felt in 1967. Traditional society in the Federal Republic and elsewhere in Europe and the United States was on the eve of fundamental changes.

# CHAPTER 54

# *The French Fourth Republic:*
# *Economic Growth and Political Instability*

The post-war history of France is full of contradictions. To outward appearances her Fourth Republic was plagued by a degree of political instability that promised to repeat the weaknesses and follies of the Third, which had ended with Vichy's disgrace. The individualistic French, divided on so many issues and by so many parties and groupings, seemed ill-suited to a parliamentary democracy. De Gaulle certainly believed this when he withdrew from government in January 1946 and then, a little less than a year later in 1947, launched his movement grandly called the *Rassemblement du Peuple Français*, offering his leadership above party in place of the squabbling, weak politicians who by their jostling for power were reducing the National Assembly to ridicule. But the constitution of the Fourth Republic had vested power in the National Assembly rather than in the president and the executive. De Gaulle had to wait in the wings for eleven years.

The spectacle of twenty-two governments from December 1946 to May 1958, the shortest lasting four days and the longest a little over a year, seemed to justify the behaviour of those groups who treated parliamentary democracy with scorn. The French Communist Party, which still looked to Stalin's Russia for guidance and was excluded from any share in responsible government after May 1947, attacked each government successively, and felt no sense of commitment to the institutions of the Republic. Its domination of the trade unions through the communist-led Confédération Général

du Travail (CGT), whose membership was larger than that of the MRP–Catholic Union and the Socialist Union (Force Ouvrière 1947) combined, enabled it to harass the governments of the Fourth Republic. During the years of acute inflation and shortages (1945–8), when wholesale prices tripled but wages lagged behind, there was plenty to fuel discontent. Split ideologically and frequently calling strikes that were politically motivated, organised labour was limited in the constructive role it could play to help reform and modernise the economy. French working people did not feel that their standard of living had significantly improved during the twelve years of the Fourth Republic or that disparities of wealth had decreased. Apart from a short period of comparative price stability from 1952 to 1955, inflation had become endemic.

The difficult conditions of working people's lives help to explain why, despite the Cold War, the French Communist Party was able to retain the electoral support of one in every four voters, polling the largest percentage of the votes in every election from November 1946 to January 1956. But its split with the fiercely anti-communist socialists deprived the left of a commanding parliamentary role. Support for the socialists was not as strong as that for the communists and fell away from the end-of-war peak of 23 per cent to 15 per cent in 1956. The Fourth Republic was also threatened by the re-emergence and recovery of the right and by the tactics of de Gaulle, who had re-entered active politics in 1947. Those on the right discontented with the workings of the Fourth Republic, from de Gaulle's Rassemblement to various conservative groupings, polled 26 per cent in 1951, and later with the popular Poujadists in the 1956 elections gained 32 per cent. Thus coalition governments were threatened by the prospect of disagreement among the partners.

If we add to this political instability the conservative structure of the greater part of French industry, dominated by small enterprises and widely dispersed – in 1956 there were still 499,000 industrial plants, each employing an average of eleven workers – a backward agriculture, much of it split into uneconomic small farms, as well as a much higher rate of inflation than that of her industrial rivals, the total picture is bleak.

Armed resistance to the threatened loss of empire after 1945 greatly increased France's burdens in the first difficult post-war decade. De Gaulle was not the first French leader to attempt to compensate for the humiliation of defeat by reasserting France's grandeur overseas. Even the French communist leader Maurice Thorez supported the French army against the communist Vietnamese independence movement, declaring that he 'did not intend to liquidate the French position in Indo-China'. Their unsuccessful war in Indo-China from its start in December 1946 until the armistice agreed in Geneva in July 1954, debilitated the French, costing them more than they had received in Marshall Aid; 10 per cent of the national budget had been swallowed up by it and 75,000 officers and men had lost their lives. Meanwhile, in North Africa, the French were facing serious conflict in their protectorates of Tunisia and Morocco. Here too they had refused to bow to nationalist demands until terrorism and resistance wore down their will to maintain their rule. Independence was granted to Morocco and Tunisia in 1956. The withdrawals from these two North African countries had another cause. A French presence there was regarded as secondary to continued French rule in Algeria: for Algeria was not a protectorate, it was 'France'. The savage conflict, which began in 1954 and was to last for eight years, finally broke the Fourth Republic and brought back de Gaulle. In the summer of 1958 France came close to civil strife and the politicians, in despair, gave way to de Gaulle's Fifth Republic.

This catalogue of disasters and burdens is, however, only one side of the history of the Fourth

*Jean Monnet, one of the architects of French recovery, and instrumental in putting a European economic community on the agenda.*

Republic. Behind the unstable political façade, the Fourth Republic inaugurated an industrial revolution by a remarkable combination of state encouragement, central planning and private enterprise. From 1944 to 1947 the state had acquired considerable economic power, having brought into public ownership and control the Renault motor works, Air France, the Bank of France and the larger private banks, insurance, gas, electricity and the coal-mining industry. Although the departure of the communists from government and the decline of the socialists halted the expansion of state ownership, there was no denationalisation, and what had been nationalised was vigorously developed. The results of the modernisation of agriculture were patchy and less spectacular; nevertheless over a decade and a half some real progress was achieved. The new concept of modernisation was typified by Jean Monnet, one of France's most distinguished public servants (page 360).

Monnet had persuaded de Gaulle after the war to allow him to organise a group of experts to prepare a plan for the recovery and modernisation of France. The first Five-Year Plan was approved in January 1947. It placed Monnet at the head of a small secretariat in the modest offices of the Commissariat du Plan de Modernisation et d'Équipement charged with promoting the realisation of its objectives. The Plan indicated growth targets for specific sectors of the economy; modernisation commissions were set up for each sector at which the details of how this growth could be achieved were worked out with industrialists, civil servants and the unions, with the assistance of members of Monnet's secretariat. Monnet's Plan bears little resemblance to Soviet five-year plans, with their detailed targets and directives. In place of the stifling bureaucracy and rigid, inefficient central planning of the USSR, cajolery, incentives and more subtle means of persuasion were employed. This method of proceeding was greatly aided by a closely knit French establishment.

A peculiarity of the French establishment was the interrelationship of government, regional administration, senior civil servants, politicians, industrial management and higher education. The French leadership was recruited from elitist educational establishments. Young men would be selected on academic merit for entry to the École Polytechnique or the École Nationale d'Administration, and then recruited into one of the Grands Corps, where the career ladder reaches to the top posts in the ministries or the prefectoral administration. This elitist group of graduates also runs the state industries and is to be found in the private sector too. The close old-boy network gets things done and counterbalances the rigid administrative divisions of the state. The expertise developed by groups of brilliant technocrats in engineering, in administration and in business skills, together with their dedication to the state, which rewarded them handsomely with high salaries, created a powerful elite that, in the unstable political conditions of the Fourth Republic, spearheaded the drive for modernisation in industry and agriculture.

Such a high degree of institutionalised elitism has its weaknesses and its dangers too. It is fundamentally undemocratic. It is possible for those of poor background through sheer talent to enter one of the Écoles, but it is very much easier for the children of the better-off Parisian families who can afford the best education in preparation for the competitive entrance examinations. Of course, France is not unique in this respect. The same is true in Britain of Oxbridge entry or entry to Yale and Harvard in the United States. The French system has differed in not providing equal opportunities to those who in their youth missed the highest

academic achievement to rise to the most senior positions 'through the ranks'. The system tends to stifle talent and initiative lower down; it also encourages patronage and allows excessive influence to a small number. On the other hand, it has provided France with an able corps of innovators and administrators in key positions, and so counteracted the disruptive political and industrial conflicts which plagued the Fourth Republic.

Monnet's First Plan (1947–1952/4) concentrated on key sectors fundamental to a general modernisation programme: coal, electricity, steel, cement, the mechanisation of agriculture, fertilisers and transportation. But the most immediate needs of the workers for better housing and consumer goods were largely sacrificed, with the exception of food, to provide for a better future. Nor were financial controls exerted, so the currency rapidly lost value, which in turn created industrial instability for most of the years of the Fourth Republic. All efforts were directed to improving the productivity of industry and agriculture. The result was not an overall advance across the board, but the creation of some modern, efficient and technologically progressive industries and farms alongside the small, backward nineteenth-century enterprises and peasant holdings. It was too much to expect the First and Second Plans (1947–57) to transform the whole French economy; much of agriculture remained backward and traditional attitudes prevailed throughout France. Indeed, the difficulties facing modernisers in France were great. There was no large increase in the labour force, as there was in West Germany. From 1929 to 1945 industrial production had fallen steeply to less than a third of the 1929 level; the waging of colonial wars, an inefficient system of indirect taxation and high inflation were all serious handicaps. But during these hard times, which largely contributed to the return of de Gaulle in 1958, the foundations were laid for the expansion of the 1960s and later. The modernising of key sectors enabled France to compete successfully with West Germany. They also provided 2 million more jobs, compared with before the war, and productivity significantly increased. From 1947 until the early 1960s, successive plans had an important influence. As they became more sophisticated after 1966 so French administrations also turned less interventionist. Plans had to be 'adapted' in any case to reflect economic realities such as the unexpected oil shocks of the 1970s.

**French Industrial Output**

|  | 1929 | 1946 | 1952 | 1957 |
|---|---|---|---|---|
| Coal (*million tons*) | 55.0 | 49.3 | 57.4 | 59.1 |
| Crude steel (*million tons*) | 9.7 | 4.4 | 10.9 | 14.1 |
| Cement (*million tons*) | 6.2 | 3.4 | 8.6 | 12.5 |
| Petroleum (*million tons*) | 0.7 (1938) | 0.28 | 0.3 | 1.4 |
| Electricity (*billion kwh*) | 15.6 | 23.0 | 40.8 | 57.5 |
| Tractors (*1000 units*) | 1.0 | 1.9 | 25.3 | |
| Fertiliser (*1000 tons*) | 73.0 | 127.0 | 285.0 | |
| Meat (*1000 tons*) | | | 2,065.0 | 2,500.0 |
| Wheat (*million quintals*) | | | 84.2 | 110.0 |
| Housing (*units completed*) | | | 74,920.0 | 270,000.0 |

**Growth Rates of Gross Domestic Product and Labour Productivity**
(*average annual percentages, 1949–59*)

|  | Gross Domestic Product | Labour productivity |
|---|---|---|
| France | 4.5 | 4.3 |
| Italy | 5.9 | 4.8 |
| West Germany | 7.4 | 5.7 |
| United Kingdom | 2.4 | 1.8 |
| United States | 3.3 | 2.0 |

But for the majority of French workers and small farmers the gradual transformation of France, with islands of highly advanced technology, did not mean rising standards of living in accordance with their expectations. France continued to be a divided society of great inequalities between the rich and the poor, between the privileged technocrats of the École Polytechnique and small businessmen and traditional peasant farmers who vented their frustrations in supporting populist movements.

\*

It was a curious paradox of the Fourth Republic that so much solid progress in changing the fundamental economic and industrial structure of France could be taking place in parallel with the political and social strife reminiscent of the 1930s and the Third Republic. Proportional representation and the French electoral system permitted a multiplicity of parties. The so-called 'Third Force', standing between Gaullism and communism, played musical chairs in successive government coalitions, the exclusion of communists and Gaullists from government being the one point of agreement among the other parties from left to right. From 1947 to 1951 coalitions were built around three parties; the Mouvement Républicain Populaire (MRP), the Socialists and the Radicals. At the election of 1951, the Conservatives and Gaullists increased their strength and the MRP was weakened, but the Socialists decided to leave the government and return to opposition in a bid to rebuild their support. From 1951 to 1954 governments were based on centre–right coalitions. From 1954 to 1958 the Socialists once more returned to government in coalitions with the centre. On specific policy issues the coalition parties held strongly opposing views, and there were endless rounds of compromise, accommodation, rupture, and back to compromise.

The MRP, that is to say the French Christian Democrats, managed to remain partners in all these coalition governments. It was not a narrowly Catholic party, though it reconciled its majority of Catholic supporters to the Republic. It inclined to the Conservatives in believing in a market economy and private property, but was progressive in seeking to overcome traditional industrial conflict by collaboration between employer and employee. On issues of social and welfare policies it sided with the Socialists, but differed from them and the Radicals in seeking to retain independent Catholic education with state aid. But on policies relating to Western European co-operation, generally favoured by the MRP and the Socialists, they were aligned against the conservative right. The parties in the National Assembly were prepared to make compromises only on a short-term basis. The instability which so discredited the Fourth Republic was an inevitable outcome. Nonetheless, there was greater continuity than might at first be supposed, since a number of able ministers, for instance the Socialist Jules Moch, were appointed to several of the governments. The Foreign Ministry remained from 1944 to 1954 in the hands of the MRP, alternately in the charge of Georges Bidault and Robert Schuman.

Against the disasters of the colonial wars have to be set the success of the Fourth Republic's West European policies, and the conciliation and practical co-operation of France and the Benelux countries with their former enemies, the Federal Republic of Germany and Italy. During the years of the Fourth Republic, the Christian Social Democratic leaders of West Germany, Italy and France, Adenauer, de Gasperi and Schuman, laid the foundations for the new economic and political relations of the principal Western Europe nations, which proved so powerful a force in promoting their mutual economic growth and prosperity, and settled their historic and territorial enmities.

The French recognised that the imbalance in Europe had only been temporarily solved by Germany's defeat. German vitality would lead, so the French feared, to a resurgence of power and a renewed threat of aggression. De Gaulle at first followed past traditions in maintaining the 'French thesis' that even after the East–West division of Germany, West Germany would need to be curbed further and permanently. In the wider European context he saw the continued need for an eastern link with Russia. In the treatment of occupied Germany the French stubbornly resisted the Anglo-American efforts to bring the Western occupation zones together and to centralise their adminis-

tration. What is more, the French demanded the economic detachment of the Ruhr and the Saar from West Germany, and some form of internationalisation of the industrial Ruhr. The Cold War, and the resulting American and British military presence on the continent of Europe, shattered de Gaulle's vision, shared for a time by many French ministers after his withdrawal in 1946, that France could be the dominant continental West European state, acting as arbiter between East and West. Instead, the French risked total isolation. They therefore went along with Anglo-American plans put forward at the London Conference in 1948 on the future of Germany. A West German state would be created with a federal constitution; safeguards would remain, especially Allied supervision of heavy industry, coal, iron and steel in the industrial Ruhr complex. But the United States and Britain, for whom the occupation was proving a costly strain, were determined to help West Germany to recover economically and to stabilise her politically and socially. With the continued threat from the Soviet Union, a chaotic and dissatisfied West Germany could be dangerous. The French accepted the need for change.

In September 1949 the federal West German state came into being, its government, however, still subject to some Allied supervision and controls (pages 532–3). The occupation of the French zone came to an end. France would have to find a new way of living with her powerful neighbour.

France's foreign policy adjusted to the changed international conditions of the Cold War and the revival of West Germany with difficulty and only after fierce debates in the National Assembly, which had to ratify the treaties embodying the shift in France's position. In 1949 France agreed to become a founding member of the North Atlantic Treaty Organisation, but the spectre of Germany was what most concerned Frenchmen. Would Germany be built up militarily by the Americans and also become a member of NATO, eventually overshadowing France? Despite Schuman's robust rejection of such a possibility 'even in the future', and his insistence that Germany would remain disarmed, others saw the writing on the wall. The debates in the National Assembly show how far France was from reconciliation with Germany.

There was also another current at work, the call for a federation of Europe – a cause strongly espoused by Winston Churchill. The ideal of a united Europe was appealing, especially to a younger generation seeking an escape from the recent past. The high point of the European movement was reached at The Hague Congress in May 1948, but practical results were few.

In May 1949 ten West European governments agreed to set up the Council of Europe, the purpose of which was to achieve a greater unity between its members. There was to be no pooling of sovereignty, however. The Council's work was largely confined in the 1950s to cultural spheres. The signature of a Convention of Human Rights in 1950 was nevertheless a notable and lasting achievement. The European movement had come to a dead end by then, as far as the political integration of Western Europe was concerned. Neither France nor Britain, nor any of the other members, was ready for a real United States of Europe. But the public support generated for the idea of Europe played a part in preparing the way for the more hard-headed approach of piecemeal economic integration followed in the 1950s.

For France the fundamental problem of the overwhelming strength of Germany, even a divided Germany, remained to be faced. The outbreak of the Korean War and the likely continuation of the Cold War made it obvious that the Americans and the British would insist on West German recovery. Wartime policies pursuing the demilitarisation and industrial dismantling of West Germany were ended, and the French came under great pressure from Washington to permit West German rearmament and a German contribution to defence. France had to make the best of it: she could not be defended without the alliance of Britain and the United States. The French Prime Minister, René Pleven, therefore took the initiative in October 1950 to call for a European army subject to a European Defence Community (EDC), which would avoid the danger of creating a separate West German army. Under the Pleven Plan, German combat units would be kept small and thus incapable of independent action. In May 1952 the Occupation Statute was repealed and the Federal Republic of Germany took a further step towards the restoration of full sovereignty (page 533); simultaneously the European Defence Community Treaty was concluded between France, the Federal Republic of Germany, Italy and the Benelux countries (Belgium, the Netherlands and Luxembourg). Britain was not a member. The

Anglo-Saxon separation from continental Europe had, from the first, worried the French as they faced a resurgent Germany, for memories of Britain's lack of support in the inter-war years were still fresh. To reassure the French, the British Conservative government concluded a mutual defence treaty with the EDC. The French had, however, to concede that the national army units would be 12,000–13,000 men strong, rather than the 1000–2000 they had envisaged, and that West Germany would contribute half a million men.

The signature of the treaty was not enough to secure its adoption. It had to be ratified by the signatories' national parliaments as well, including the French National Assembly. No issue since the Dreyfus case divided France more deeply than the EDC and its consequential endorsement of German rearmament. Successive French governments, uncertain of ratification, procrastinated until in August 1954 the National Assembly, when the treaty was finally submitted, rejected it. The opponents of EDC initially refused to see that France could not veto the creation of a new German army in the long run since the other West European nations and the United States were insisting that the Federal Republic be accepted as a full ally. By December of the same year, enough members of the National Assembly had shifted their views for the restoration of sovereignty to the Federal Republic and her membership of NATO to be accepted. Policy had thus run full circle, from Pleven's attempt to create a European army that would have avoided a new German national force, to an acceptance of German rearmament and the creation of the Bundeswehr. Pleven's plan to counterbalance German strength by playing the card of 'European integration' had been aborted at the military level.

German industrial power had been closely linked with German aggression – for example, the alliance of the Krupps with the Hohenzollerns before 1914 and with Hitler after 1933. European integration could break these links. Accordingly the French developed dynamic European policies which were to change the economic and political face of Western Europe. But what form should European integration take? By 1950 it was clear that the hopes for a 'federalist' solution to create a United States of Europe, by which a member state's interests would be subordinated to a federal European government, were not going to be realised. The Council of Europe could not be developed further along integrationist lines, but there was another way. Prussia's *Zollverein* in the nineteenth century had shown how common economic interests could bind states together; the way to proceed was not at the top, at national level, but rather 'functionally', where collaboration could be shown to benefit all concerned. Belgium, the Netherlands and Luxembourg had shown the way. During the war they had agreed to form a customs union which came into operation in 1948. The Belgian statesman, Paul Henri Spaak, was an ardent Europeanist; he had been elected to the presidency of the Council of Europe and was later to play an important role in the creation of the Common Market.

The Americans also sought to further West European integration. Marshall Aid had been offered on condition that the Europeans themselves should co-operate and work out a co-ordinated plan for reconstruction. This led to the setting up of the Organisation for European Economic Co-operation (OEEC) in April 1948. The carrot of US aid spurred sixteen Western European nations (in October 1949 the Federal Republic of Germany joined and, in 1949, Spain) to agree on how to share the aid. The Council of the OEEC was composed of representatives of the member states, but it could not impose its decisions on individual nations. It was not a supranational body, but its expert committees developed the practice of discussing economic co-operation. Their most important and difficult task was to agree on the division of dollars which the US was making available.

European integration policies became, as far as their leading proponents were concerned, a question not just of idealism but also of hard-headed realism. For the French a comprehensive arrangement with the German iron, coal and steel complexes made good economic sense in safeguarding French heavy industry; at the same time supranational control would remove any possibility of undetected or uncontrolled German rearmament. French determination to secure access to the coal mines of the Saar, without the bad blood a separation of the Saar from West Germany would cause, was an additional incentive. The outcome of all these considerations was the famous plan proposed in May 1950 by the Foreign Minister, Robert Schuman.

The Schuman Plan, largely Jean Monnet's brainchild, put forward the bold scheme of pooling French and German production of coal, iron and steel – it would be open to other West European countries to join if they wished. A crucial aspect of the Plan was the setting up of a supranational 'high authority' which would make decisions not on a national level, but in the overall interests of the integrated industries. Adenauer saw the advantages of the Plan and promptly accepted it. West Germany would be treated as an equal, and the European solution allowed relationships of trust to be re-established which would facilitate the recovery of full sovereignty for the Federal Republic. This was finally attained only five years later in May 1955 (page 533).

The European Coal and Steel Community played the key role in taking its six West European member states (France, West Germany, Italy and Benelux) forward at last along the road of economic and political co-ordination. By this means the 'German problem' became manageable, and, more than that, West European economic co-operation made all of the participating states rapidly more prosperous. The success of the original ECSC was due, in the first place, to the fact that its aims were strictly limited.

As with the Monnet Plan for French modernisation, a practical start had been made in just one crucial sector of industry; the creation from the start of a comprehensive European political and economic union was recognised as impossible. Secondly, institutions were created which downgraded national sovereignty – an important reason why Britain would not join – and transferred decision-making to the supranational High Authority. Working with it were a Council of Ministers, a Common Assembly and a Court of Justice. Thus an embryonic European executive, Parliament and Court were set up, which worked with government representatives in the Council of Ministers – but most decisions did not require the separate consent of national governments. Jean Monnet was the choice for the first president of the ECSC.

The ECSC overcame an early period of difficulty and haggling between rival national interests to prove in the mid-1950s the benefit to all the participants of having established a common market in coal and steel. Business interests in France and Germany, and the other four countries, now advocated extending the common market in coal and steel to the rest of their economies.

Thus pressure was building up in a realistic way

for more ambitious integration. This is not to under-rate the continued enthusiasm for the idea of 'Europe'. The European Movement, founded at The Hague in 1948, was still active and had won important adherents in the political world of the six nations. 'Europe' offered a road forward and away from the guilt-ridden past, especially for a new generation of young Germans; it also offered the best means of reconciliation after two destructive world wars. The foundation of such reconciliation rested on the new relationship developing between France and West Germany, carried forward by many political and social groups in both countries. Meetings organised between politicians, journalists, educators, Chambers of Commerce, town partner-ships, cultural exchanges, school exchanges and textbook revisions to remove national bias are just some examples of this many-faceted effort to bring about a fundamental change of attitudes. It worked because it reflected a massive desire for change by millions of ordinary people.

The ideas – inculcated through propaganda and schooling – that national patriotism automatically involves hostility to a neighbour, that national fron-tiers should be fought over so that one country may expand her territory at the expense of another, and that enmities between nations were a law of nature have all vanished in Western Europe. A perceived common threat, from the Soviet Union, also led to alliances and military co-operation. But the collab-oration of Western Europe encompasses more than the kind of alliances which have been formed for common purposes throughout modern history. That such a fundamental change in national relations can be brought about in a region of the world which was torn with strife is a momentous achievement in the history of the twentieth century.

The three Benelux foreign ministers – the Dutchman Johan Beyen, the Belgian Paul Henri Spaak and Joseph Bech of Luxembourg – took the initiative in the spring of 1955 at governmental level to provide new momentum for European inte-gration: an example of statesmen of small nations who have exerted a disproportionate influence. Their proposal for a large extension of economic collaboration received the backing of the European Coal and Steel Community. The failure of military integration after the French rejection of the Euro-pean Defence Community the previous year had been seen as a setback but not as an end to inte-gration in other spheres. In May and June 1955 the

foreign ministers of the Six met in Messina, Sicily. Their agreements paved the way for further inter-governmental conferences and negotiations which took place during the following two years. Britain was not excluded, but her co-operation was half-hearted and she withdrew without making a serious effort to overcome the problems of her association. The Six had difficult problems to iron out and did not wish to be impeded by Britain, though they were able to resolve their differences far more speedily than the British had expected. They signed the treaty setting up the European Economic Community (and Euratom) in Rome in March 1957; these treaties were ratified in the succeeding months of that year. The majority of the French Assembly in July voted for European collaboration and thus dispelled the fears that the spectre of defeat aroused by the EDC failure would be repeated. That same month, the Bundesrat in West Germany completed the process of German ratification. The treaties entered into force on 1 January 1958.

All the members of the European Economic Community had had to make concessions and compromises. Obstacles to trade between the Six were to be removed eventually. Those of most immediate importance were the duties levied on industrial goods in order to protect the importing country's home industry. The French and Italians especially feared competition from the more efficient West Germans. A transitional period of twelve to fifteen years was therefore agreed, though in the event the abolition of duties was speeded up and completed by July 1968. Free trade required many other aspects of economic management to be harmonised as well, and complex arrangements were agreed over the years: for example, common rules of competition, free movement of workers, of capital and of services, harmonisation of taxation and of quality standards, and a system of managing currency exchange rates. An essential feature of the EEC, beyond the removal of internal barriers of trade between the Six, was the erection of a common tariff which non-member states had to pay when exporting industrial and agricultural goods to the Common Market. This provided protection where it was most needed by the Six. Together with payments from its members it provided the funds of the common budget of the EEC which could be used to support economic and educational activities within the Six and to pay for the administration of the Common Market. But it also led to much tension with the United States, whose agricultural exports particularly were discriminated against.

The most controversial aspect of the Community has proved to be the support given to farmers by the Common Agricultural Policy (CAP). Intervention prices are fixed annually by the Council of Ministers for each kind of agricultural produce and the farmers are guaranteed these prices. What they cannot sell in the Common Market, that is the surpluses, are bought by the Community; exports to non-Community members are subsidised so that the farmer secures the intervention price. The farm costs are met by the EEC budget, which has had to devote to them the greater part of its funds. The CAP benefits the countries with most farmers – France, Eire and Denmark – and is unfavourable to countries like Britain, a member since 1973, which imports food, because world prices frequently are below those fixed by the Common Market to support its farmers. If not corrected by other mechanisms, this would result in Britain and Germany paying disproportionate contributions to the common budget. A second undesirable feature is the high prices which have to be paid by the consumers of the member countries and the stimulus to agricultural production which was to lead to costly cereal, meat and butter mountains maintained by the EEC as it bought up what cannot be sold at the set prices. The funds required by the CAP became larger as each year passed, but member governments found it difficult to deny their farmers, who form an important political constituency. Not until the later 1980s was any serious reform attempted.

As France braced herself for the full impact of German industrial competition in her markets, her politicians could boast that they had secured benefits for the large agricultural sector. But the Common Market proved an immediate success, greatly surpassing the hopes of those who had negotiated its establishment. French industry was stimulated by competition and by the new export opportunities. Industrial production between 1958 and 1962, far from declining, grew by almost a quarter; the West Germans did even better, increasing industrial production by more than a third. West Germany's and France's trade with the rest of the Six doubled and trade between France and West Germany tripled in the same period. The continued economic success of the Common Market won it the support of the peoples of the Six as they gained in prosperity from economic collaboration, but hopes that it would lead to closer political union were frustrated, especially after the return of General de Gaulle in 1958.

The Commission is the body that runs the EEC, two commissioners being appointed by each of the member states. In practice, on important issues it can only put forward plans and proposals. Decisions are reached by the Council of Ministers, which represents the viewpoints of national governments. Here again, escape clauses allow individual countries to opt out of joint decisions if they believe their vital interests to be affected; what is more, it later turned out that individual countries could exercise a veto. Even so, the degree of integration actually achieved went much further than Britain and her European Free Trade Area partners were at that time willing to accept. The European Parliament of the Six was also given only limited supervisory powers. The most important controlling body to emerge was, therefore, the Council of Ministers. That has remained the case to the present day.

Two of the most important achievements of the Fourth Republic were the French contribution to the creation of the European Common Market and Franco-German reconciliation. Yet, little more than a year after the signature of the Treaty of Rome, the Fourth Republic came to an ignominious end as General de Gaulle returned to power on his own terms. The General had no time for Monnet's visions of supranationalism. The European institutions were not to be permitted to override national decision-making; they were, in de Gaulle's view, to act as no more than forums where national differences could be discussed and negotiated.

By 1958 the majority of Frenchmen perceived that the rivalries of the political parties in the National Assembly had made active government on many of the crucial problems facing France virtually impossible. The achievements – the Common Market, reconciliation with West Germany, security through NATO – were easily overlooked as their benefits became apparent only later. It was de Gaulle who was to be credited with the rising prosperity and modernisation of France. High inflation from 1947 to 1951, when retail prices more than doubled, followed by three years of greater stability (1952 to 1956) and a resumption of inflation proved very unsettling, even though wages and salaries kept abreast. The harsh economic measures introduced in the autumn of 1957, higher taxes and devaluation to reduce inflation, once again hit the pockets of French families. Constant strikes, some for the most trivial reasons, were one symptom of the discontent and general malaise. But the final blow was the government's inability to deal with the crisis in Algeria, where a military takeover raised a near panic in Paris at the prospect that the whole country might fall victim to a military dictatorship.

# CHAPTER 55

# The War of Algerian Independence:
## The Fifth Republic and the Return of de Gaulle

The defence of her empire in Indo-China and North Africa proved a crushing burden for post-war France. The fall of Dien Bien Phu in May 1954 brought down another French government, but the new Prime Minister, Pierre Mendès-France, was a politician in a different mould. He was, like Léon Blum, a Jew, tough, intellectual and at last ready to face realities – at least some of the realities. He fulfilled his undertaking to bring France out of the disastrous dirty war in Indo-China in July 1954 by agreeing to the peace terms of the Geneva Conference, and he negotiated Tunisian autonomy, but, ostensibly over weakness in dealing with North Africa, he was brought down in February 1955. The determination of the Gaullist right to maintain France's colonial rule led to more falls of government until, in 1956, independence was conceded to both Tunisia and Morocco. But Algeria was different. Politicians of all parties – communists, socialists and conservatives – regarded Algeria, governed through the French Ministry of the Interior, as part of France. One million French settlers, the *pieds noirs*, from the wealthy to the hard-working fisherman or carpenter, who had lived in Algeria for a generation or more, saw themselves as the French of Algeria, not as Frenchmen living in a colony of France. All the French political leaders echoed Mendès-France when he declared, 'France without Algeria would be no France.'

Yet all the talk about Algeria being a part of France was paradoxical and hypocritical, as was the rhetoric in the constitution of the Fourth Republic,

whose preamble promised equality without distinction of race or religion. Racism was as rampant in Algeria as it was in the worst of European colonies overseas. How could Algeria be France if the majority of its inhabitants, the 9 million Muslim Arabs, were not Frenchmen with equal rights? There was no place for the Algerian in the higher administration of the country; the economy was dominated by the wealthy European settlers; the plight of the land-hungry poor Muslim Algerian was aggravated by a high birthrate; meanwhile, the larger, more mechanised settler farms no longer required large numbers of peasant labourers. The Fourth Republic instituted some reforms but, on the key issue of political rights, only a measure of ostensible power-sharing was introduced. An Algerian-elected assembly was created, chosen by two electoral colleges, one composed of the European French citizens, plus a few meritorious Muslims, some 500,000 electors, who chose sixty members of the Assembly; the rest of the Muslim population chose the other sixty members. Even this was not enough for the European settlers: electoral corruption made doubly sure that the European minority would continue its domination.

The tragedy of Algeria was that violence and atrocities, involving great loss of innocent lives, marked the path to nationhood. That was not how the majority of moderate Muslims wished to achieve their rights. A lack of vision and of generosity and the resolution of the *pieds noirs*, actuated by fear and material self-interest, to deny the Muslim Algerians genuinely equal rights and self-determination left the outcome of the struggle to be decided by the extremists. The settlers believed that their power, backed by the army of all France, could always overwhelm such guerrilla units as the FLN (Front de Libération Nationale) could muster. But their confidence misled them. In the end, the French were sickened by the bloody excesses and the slaughter of civilians, which spilled over into metropolitan France. The majority that ultimately counted was not that of the *pieds noirs* in Algeria, but the majority of voters in France. To them the price of retaining Algeria and defending the European settlers proved too high. De Gaulle ended the Algerian conflict on the only terms that could be secured: those demanded by the FLN leadership.

The twisted road from the close of the Second World War to Algerian independence in 1962 was punctuated by waves of violence, abortive negotiations and constitutional crises. The liberation of Europe in May 1945 had raised the expectation of colonial peoples that a new era had dawned for them. In Sétif, a small Algerian market town, these expectations led to a bloody clash, the first of many. Extremist Muslims carrying nationalist flags turned on European settlers that May, murdering and raping more than a hundred. The French response was to 'pacify' the region in typical colonial fashion, killing thousands of Muslims. The indelible impression of racist conflict and bloodshed overshadowed all political speeches. De Gaulle had promised a new deal to the French colonial peoples: they would be led *eventually* to self-government, but the time and manner would be decided by the French. Thus the initial stance of the Europeans was that violence would not wrest that decision of decolonisation from them. French military power was so overwhelming that proposals put forward by the more moderate Algerian nationalist leaders, such as Ferhat Abbas, for a compromise solution were not entertained (Abbas had proposed an independent Algeria federated to France). The movement for independence, therefore, became more radical, and new leaders, such as Ahmed Ben Bella and Belkacem Krim, were ready to use violence. With just a few hundred armed men, Belkacem Krim started an open revolt on 1 November 1954. Throughout the country a proclamation was distributed addressed 'To the Algerian people' and announcing the formation of the Front de Libération Nationale, whose objective was to gain Algerian independence.

But the FLN also promised that French settlers and French interests would be dealt with fairly: the *pieds noirs* could even opt for Algerian nationality. For more than seven years the FLN fought, without deviating from their objectives. But the implacable hostility of the settlers made it impossible for any agreement to be reached which might have safeguarded their future. In 1954 the Fourth Republic rejected as unthinkable the very idea of Algerian independence. The prime minister at that time. Pierre Mendès-France, and his socialist minister of the interior, François Mitterrand, were ready to abandon colonialism in Indo-China, Morocco and Tunisia, but not in Algeria – for, as they repeatedly proclaimed, 'Algeria is France.' Their solution was military repression, which was to be combined with economic reform to reduce unemployment. But Reform had no chance. The FLN answered repression with terrorism.

Ten years after Sétif, in August 1955, indiscriminate terrorism was repeated at Philippeville. The murder of Europeans and their Muslim allies by an FLN-instigated mob led in turn to the killing of more than a thousand Muslims in reprisals. Such violence could only play into the hands of the FLN, who regarded as their enemy, not only France, but those moderate Muslims who were prepared to accept French rule. The FLN killings were directed as much against these 'traitorous' Muslims as against the French. Indeed the Muslim Algerians who had placed their trust in France were to become the most tragic victims of the war. The FLN resorted to bombing cafés and dance halls in Algeria, causing bloodshed wherever Europeans came together in large numbers. The French army responded with equal ferocity, torturing FLN suspects to gain information. French military power, however, could not crush the terrorists. All that could be achieved were temporary victories over the FLN, as in what became known as the Battle of Algiers.

Meanwhile, the *pieds noirs* became suspicious of the intentions of the government in Paris. Would they negotiate with the FLN above their heads? The FLN was gaining respectability internationally at the United Nations, receiving support from Tunisia, while Nasser's Egypt – recently victorious over the French – broadcast pro-Algerian propaganda from Cairo. Practical help, however, was not so readily forthcoming.

In the spring of 1958 the paths of the European

settlers and the recalcitrant generals in Algiers, on the one hand, and the politicians of the Fourth Republic, on the other, fatefully crossed. From 15 April until 13 May 1958 Paris was politically paralysed: no government could be formed. The way was opened for the return of de Gaulle at the end of May. This spelt the collapse of the Fourth Republic and, after another four years of confusing politics, military repression and bloodshed, of French Algeria as well.

De Gaulle, in 1947, had miscalculated and as a result of his resignation spent a long decade in the political wilderness, preparing for his return. He wished to end the Fourth Republic and what he regarded as its fatally flawed parliamentary constitution, which he believed had brought back the errors of the Third Republic. But he would not seize power unconstitutionally. The Fourth Republic must turn to him and ask him to save France from chaos. This did not mean that he was reluctant to exploit the feelings of those groups of Frenchmen in France and Algeria who were ready to conspire against the Fourth Republic. His refusal to condemn disloyalty to the Fourth Republic or those ready to defy the government in Paris before he came to power was sufficient to encourage the belief that his Algerian policy would be resolutely French. A master of lofty rhetoric, de Gaulle could be all things to all men. When, three weeks after the fall of the government on 15 April 1958, President René Coty had found no politician able to form a new government, he consulted de Gaulle. But on 13 May, it was Pierre Pfimlin, a man who was anathema to the army in Algeria, to whom he turned.

In Algiers, 13 May 1958 was the decisive day. Brigadier-General Jacques Massu and Commander-in-Chief General Raoul Salan, with their associates, were practically in open revolt against Paris. Although Pfimlin received the backing of the National Assembly to form the next government, the conspiracy on both sides of the Mediterranean was in full swing. De Gaulle had to make his move. Although it was the insurrection of the army in Algiers and the threat of civil war that was forcing the hands of the President and legitimate government of the Fourth Republic, de Gaulle had to give the appearance of total independence and personal disinterest in anything except the cause of saving France. In a crucial public statement of 15 May de Gaulle avoided mentioning the insurrection in Algiers beyond referring to 'disturbance in the fighting forces'; he condemned the 'regime of the parties', which he said could not solve France's problems, and harking back to his mission in 1940 concluded, 'Not so long ago the country, in its hour of peril, trusted me to lead it ... to its salvation. Today with the trials that face it once again, it should know that I am ready to assume the powers of the Republic.' By placing himself at the 'disposal' of the French people over the head of the President, the government and National Assembly de Gaulle undermined whatever authority they might have been able to exert. The French people would not have taken kindly to a usurpation of power led by the army, which would have provoked protests, riots and widespread civil disturbances.

There were still formidable obstacles in the way of a *legal* transition of power. After all a government under Pierre Pfimlin was functioning and there was no real danger of an insurrection in metropolitan France other than by armed units from Algeria. General Massu knew he would need to camouflage any use of force. He planned a coup in Paris code-named Resurrection: mass demonstrations would be organised, *backed up* by paratroopers airlifted from Algiers and the south-west region of France who would occupy strategic government buildings. The crisis reached fever pitch on 28 and 29 May. De Gaulle's relationship with Resurrection is one of the most hotly argued controversies among historians. Had the General himself given the order to set the coup in motion or was it Gaullist supporters in Paris who gave the green light to the army generals in Algiers? What seems likely is that de Gaulle had expressed himself in an ambiguous way, yet had given clear indication that if he failed to gain power by legal process, which he preferred, he would have taken advantage of the Algiers plot.

The airlift actually began when six Dakotas took off early in the afternoon of 28 May. That evening in Paris President Coty called in de Gaulle and invited him to form a 'government of national safety' since France was on the verge of civil war. Coty also had to accept de Gaulle's demand that he would take over only if he could prepare plans for a new constitution; meanwhile he would govern without the National Assembly. De Gaulle then agreed that he would be granted special powers for only six months and would first need to appear before the National Assembly for confirmation as head of government and to receive authority to plan and submit a new constitution. When they received this news, the generals postponed Resurrection. The National Assembly on 1 June 1958 by a majority voted its approval of de Gaulle as head of government with special powers, but a sizeable minority voted against him, 224 members out of 553. The following day he received the necessary three-fifths majority for submitting a new constitution to the French people by referendum. So de Gaulle, at the age of sixty-seven, had become head of the government again, but Coty remained president, an arrangement which conferred legality and continuity on the interim period that marked the last months of the Fourth Republic.

De Gaulle had achieved a constitutional transfer of power just this side of legality – but he could not have done it without the military threat from Algeria. His immediate problem was now not metropolitan France but Algeria, where settlers and generals, together with French Gaullist politicians back home, would look upon any retreat from 'l'Algérie Française' as rank treachery, which would absolve them from owing loyalty to any government guilty of it. But what did de Gaulle really think?

It is a question not easy to answer. In letters and private conversations he seems to have tried out ideas, using those he addressed as a sounding board. But he was clearly pragmatic. The conflict would be brought to an end and de Gaulle did not believe that that could be achieved by continuing to discriminate against the Muslim majority or by employing military force and the torture of opponents. He relied on his own immense prestige among the settlers and the millions of Algerian Muslims, to whom he proposed a new deal. To the fighting men of the FLN he offered an olive branch by praising their courage. He was under no illusions that one day Algeria would be independent, but that independence would be best achieved gradually and in harmony with France and in some form of association with her.

For all his rhetoric and grandeur, de Gaulle was far from sure of his ability to impose a policy opposed to the wishes of the French settlers and the army generals, who were congratulating themselves on their destruction of the Fourth Republic. Nor did the killings in Algeria cease with de Gaulle's return. Indeed, the savagery was worse than ever during the next four years, while the General

Left: *Muslims rally to de Gaulle as he arrives in Bone, Algeria, on 7 June 1958.* Right: *Algerian nationalists' growing confidence is on display as a girl flaunts her rebel flag on the eve of de Gaulle's national referendum, of 8 January 1961, to approve plans to grant Algeria the right to self-determination.*

seemed to procrastinate, switching from concessionary overtures to the FLN to renewed efforts to achieve 'pacification', and the toll of death, maiming and torture mounted. If de Gaulle really represented, as he claimed, the greatness of France, is he not to be condemned for vainly attempting to save France's position in Algeria? The ambiguity of his policies was to be revealed on his first visit to Algeria, only three days after his investiture. To Algerian Muslims and the French settler crowds, he proclaimed on different occasions the delphic utterance, 'I have understood you'; however, in all but one of his speeches he carefully avoided uttering the *pieds noirs*' slogan, 'l'Algérie Française'.

De Gaulle's impact on the population in France and in Algeria was enormous. The great majority of Frenchmen and of Muslim Algerians were prepared to place their trust in him and to be led to new relations and a better future. He was the best guarantee that France would not be plunged into civil war. The trouble was that the trusting French settlers and military expected a completely different outcome from that expected by the trusting Muslim Algerians. Even so, the referendum on the new constitution, held in France, in the French Commonwealth and in Algeria, was a personal triumph for de Gaulle. In metropolitan France over 80 per cent voted for him. In Algeria, where the Muslim Algerians could vote with the Europeans on equal terms for the first time, army intimidation cannot account for the large majority of 76.4 per cent, achieved in the face of FLN threats. So why was there no prompt settlement in accordance with the wishes of the great majority of Muslim Algerians, who were clearly ready to accept some form of association with France? After all, de Gaulle himself was deliberately using the weapon of democracy, of the majority, as the best means of finding a settlement.

It was not majorities which decided the issue in Algeria but the organised force of settlers, the French army and the minority of militant Algerians who made up the FLN. The FLN would not lay down their arms for anything less than complete independence. They survived as a guerrilla force in the country and in urban areas despite 'successful' French military actions, attacking the French settlers and their Muslim Algerian supporters. De Gaulle's attempts to negotiate with them, even at moments of their greatest military weakness, came to nothing. Moreover, the extremists among the

*pieds noirs* soon recognised that, whatever his personal preferences, de Gaulle would in the end settle with the Muslim Algerians and abandon the settlers if need be. These extremist settlers mounted some thirty assassination attempts against de Gaulle, and one revenge shooting in August 1962 riddled his car with fourteen bullets and nearly succeeded in killing him and his wife. In February 1961 they had formed the Organisation Armée Secrète in Algeria, soon known throughout the world as the OAS. They declared that they would act as ferociously as the FLN and take their terror tactics to Paris if de Gaulle and metropolitan France tried to abandon 'l'Algérie Française'.

On 30 March 1961 de Gaulle announced that peace talks with the FLN would begin shortly at Evian. This was the signal for an open rebellion carried out in April by OAS plotters with the assistance of four retired army generals in Algeria. But the French army in Algeria was split. Once more de Gaulle's appeals averted the danger of civil war. During the long-drawn-out negotiations at Evian, the OAS did their worst, but they were unable to prevent agreement being conceded practically on FLN's terms on 18 March 1962. On 1 July that year Algerian independence was granted after a referendum in France and Algeria. The previous month the OAS gave up the hopeless struggle in Algeria. The extremists had ensured that there could be no future for the French Algerian settlers, most of whom now migrated to metropolitan France.

Was it an honourable peace? The French could not protect all the Algerians who had been loyal to them and were now condemned as traitors by the FLN. Muslim Algerians who had served in the French army had numbered 210,000. Only a minority took refuge in France, and it is not known how many of those who remained behind were executed or murdered. Estimates vary between 30,000 and 150,000. The leaders of the new Algeria later admitted that there had been 'blunders'. Whole families, even children, were massacred. Many Third World countries have passed through the suffering of colonial repression and then through the wars of national liberation, which involved not only the fight against the 'occupier' but also the savagery of fratricidal civil war. Algeria was one of the worst examples of this process. De Gaulle's military training helped him to face this inescapable consequence. Certainly the blame cannot be placed solely on him.

Whatever failings are attributed to de Gaulle in handling the crises in Algeria from 1958 to 1962, only his enormous prestige in the army and among the people of France saved Algeria from seizure by a rebellious army backed by the settlers and France from a confrontation that might have led to a neo-fascist regime in Paris. The ending of the war was greeted with enormous relief by the great majority of Frenchmen, and by none more than the half-million conscripts sent to Algeria. The verdict on de Gaulle offered by the historian Alistair Horne seems eminently just: 'the way he extricated France from Algeria may not have been done well – but certainly no one else could have done it better'.

De Gaulle succeeded in 1958 in re-establishing the constitutional authority of France over the recalcitrant army and rightist extremists. Not his least important weapons were his impressive personal television appearances in which he addressed the nation. Even opponents were bound to admire the authoritative style of the *grand Charles*, dressed in the uniform of a brigadier-general, during these early years of turbulence. He had been given just six months of rule without parliament to reshape the institutions of government. He lost no time. Invested with special powers in June 1958, de Gaulle created a consultative committee (which he chaired) to draft the new constitution. It was approved by an overwhelming majority in a referendum on 28 September.

The constitution of the Fifth Republic, which came into force in January 1959, enormously increased the powers of the presidency. Under article 16 it permitted the president in case of grave national crisis to take 'whatever measures are required by the circumstances'. Until the 1958 constitution was amended in 1962 by a further referendum, the president was not directly elected by the people but chosen by an electoral college consisting of all members of the Assembly and other 'notables': de Gaulle was proceeding cautiously. On paper the prime minister shared executive power with the president, but the president chose the prime minister, and other ministers on the recommendation of the prime minister. On paper, Parliament retained considerable powers. Governments were responsible to it and were required to resign if the National Assembly censored them or rejected their programme. The prime minister (article 20) was charged with determining and

conducting the policy of the nation and was given responsibility for national defence as well as the power to appoint top officials; moreover, his counter-signature was required for treaties. Responsible for negotiating treaties and empowered to initiate new laws, the president is commander-in-chief and presides over the Council of Ministers. For the constitution to work, the government would have to act as the junior partner of the president, thus eliminating the overlapping powers and potential sources of conflict. De Gaulle interpreted his powers widely and was able in practice to make decisions in all areas which he regarded as important, at home as well as abroad. In fact he treated the prime minister and the ministers of the government like civil servants. The government was little more than the means by which the executive presidential will was carried out. Prime ministers Michel Debré (1959–62), Georges Pompidou (1962–8) and Maurice Couve de Murville (1968–9) were the President's men, and many ministers were technocrats rather than party leaders. Their divorce from the political parties of the National Assembly was emphasised by the provision that members of the government could not hold seats in the Assembly. This was to distance them from the political manoeuvring among ministers that had caused so much instability to the Third and Fourth Republics. With the support of the Gaullists and their allies in the National Assembly, which following the elections of November 1958 and November 1962 formed the largest group, de Gaulle was able to override such powers as the constitution of 1958 had on paper awarded to the prime minister, government and parliament. He established overwhelmingly presidential rule for the period of office to which he was democratically elected, but was mindful of the individual liberties and civil rights of Frenchmen. This starkly differentiates de Gaulle from the dictatorships in Spain, Portugal and much of Latin America. The President's position was further strengthened in 1962, as we have seen, when an amendment to the 1958 constitution replaced indirect election with direct election by the people for a term of seven years.

De Gaulle led France effectively, and by making use of the special provisions for referendums could bypass parliament and seek approval for his policies by popular mandates. He was clearly the choice of a large majority of Frenchmen until at least 1968–9, even though there were many who disapproved of his highhandedness and regarded his treatment of governments and parliament and his political monopolisation of radio and television as a threat to democracy. But there seemed no other choice, no man of equal stature, who could provide the political stability France so badly needed. De Gaulle had become both intolerable and indispensable.

The economic transformation of France, both industrial and agricultural, had been rapid since 1949 and accelerated further during de Gaulle's eleven years from 1958 to 1969. Her progress was achieved by a mixed economy, with state intervention, planning incentives and government encouragement. Key sectors of French industry were modernised. De Gaulle adhered to the Treaty of Rome and the economic competition it opened up among the Six signatories. There was no turning back to France's traditional protectionist policies, and the free circulation of goods in the EEC was achieved on 1 July 1968 after the agreed ten transitional years allowed to France: her trade now had to reorientate towards the new European markets, which were expanding fast. France excelled in many branches of the new high-technology industries – chemicals, aeronautics, oil, precision engineering and automobiles – while cheap power, based first on oil and then, increasingly, on nuclear energy, helped to make her more competitive. Between 1949 and 1969 French economic growth increased by an annual average of 4.6 per cent in the 1950s and 5.8 per cent in the 1960s, so that, having lagged behind her West European neighbours, France overtook Britain in the 1960s. Her industrial production index moved as follows:

| | |
|------|-----|
| 1937 | 100 |
| 1949 | 112 |
| 1959 | 193 |
| 1969 | 341 |

French agriculture was also rapidly modernised. The number of farms decreased by a third between 1955 and 1970, with the numbers of farmers and farm wage-earners declining still more steeply, while output increased. Agriculture, which has declined in importance within the French economy, by the close of the 1960s employed only 16 per cent of the working population, as against more than a quarter just after the war.

The most obvious negative feature of France's economic growth was inflation, which had been rapid during the Fourth Republic. On coming to power, de Gaulle and Antoine Pinay, the Finance Minister, made a determined effort to create a stable currency. First, the franc was devalued, then a new franc was introduced. Confidence in the currency soon returned, and inflation was reduced. Strikes in 1963 were followed by another austerity package by the new finance minister, Valéry Giscard d'Estaing. Economic expansion was aided by the sudden increase in the labour force when nearly a million *pieds noirs* from Algeria emigrated to metropolitan France; further cheap labour was attracted, especially from Italy, North Africa and Spain. In the 1960s the West European consumer market for cars, refrigerators and television sets seemed to be insatiable, and French industry grasped the opportunities provided by this enlarged market. Full employment was maintained until 1968–9, and even then, with less than 1 million unemployed (though the figure alarmed contemporaries), unemployment amounted to no more than 4 per cent of the working population.

As old traditional structures were adapted to modern conditions, there were many Frenchmen who deplored and resisted these painful changes. The French peasantry repeatedly and sometimes violently gave vent to their grievances. Artisans and small shopkeepers protested, while frequent strikes expressed the frustration of industrial workers. The increased national wealth, moreover, was unevenly distributed. The industrial wage-earners did better than the non-industrial; skill was rewarded; and management considerably improved its standards of living. But a society as stratified as France's was exposed to growing tensions which were suddenly to boil over in May 1968 (pages 556–7).

De Gaulle did not share the enthusiasm for a united Europe displayed by Monnet and his followers and had been critical of the establishment of the European Economic Community with its supranational Commission. Would the EEC be launched at all on 1 January 1959, requiring as it did France to begin dismantling her protectionist industrial tariffs? France was in deep financial crisis, but de Gaulle did not attempt to abort the birth of the Common Market. For him it was not the economic aspects of the Treaty of Rome that mattered most, but the political. He now discovered important positive aspects and calculated that through leadership of the European Economic Community France could regain influence in the world and wrest Europe away from economic and military dependence on the Anglo-Saxon nations. The recovery of France's international position was foremost in de Gaulle's mind. An alliance with the United States would remain essential to counter the Soviet threat, but that need not mean subservience or a European junior partnership. In a Western Europe still looking to the United States for its defence and advanced technology, de Gaulle's was a bold vision of the future.

When de Gaulle returned to power in 1958 one major obstacle to his ambitions was the so-called 'special relationship' between the United States and Great Britain. Britain was not willing to make a choice 'for Europe' if this entailed weakening her links with the United States and the Commonwealth; and so, although British policy favoured the creation of an industrial free-trade area in Western Europe, the common external tariff, which would operate against all non-European members as required by the Treaty of Rome, was unacceptable. But without Britain in the Common Market, and with West Germany within it and anxious not to appear assertive, France would be the unchallenged leader of Western Europe. As far as the wider world was concerned, de Gaulle in September 1958 proposed to President Eisenhower and Prime Minister Harold Macmillan that it should be directed by the United States, Great Britain and France. This policy would have gravely offended America's other NATO allies, Italy and the Federal Republic of Germany, and rejection was a foregone conclusion. De Gaulle simultaneously sought a special relationship with the West German Chancellor, Adenauer, who was invited to de Gaulle's home at Colombey-les-Deux-Églises. The terms he offered to Adenauer were that Germany should abandon any idea of a nuclear partnership with France, that an agricultural common market should be added to the industrial common market of the EEC, and that France and the Federal Republic should press ahead with the Common Market of the Six in preference to Britain's larger Free Trade Association. Adenauer assented. De Gaulle, who had come to power with a free hand, had by the close of 1958 already achieved much for France and had enhanced her international position. The historic enmity between France and Germany had

been buried and replaced by a new and special intimacy, which was sealed by the Treaty of Friendship in January 1963. The French role would be crucial to the EEC's further development. Britain had been excluded and could continue to be excluded as long as de Gaulle chose to make use of France's veto. But he wished to shape the Common Market into a close alliance of sovereign states and opposed the transfer of powers to Brussels, the new headquarters of the European Commission.

De Gaulle's priority was to reassert France's position in the world. She had been excluded from the wartime settlements and from the nuclear club. Without her own nuclear weapons France would not be given a place at the table of the great powers. In September 1959 de Gaulle announced that France would build up her nuclear strike force. But was there any point? France could never hope to match the Soviet or American arsenals. De Gaulle of course realised this but what he feared and suspected was that the United States might not defend Western Europe with her nuclear weapons if it meant destruction of the United States. France needed her own strike force to be independent of others. The new American doctrine of 'flexible response' (pages 600–1) only increased de Gaulle's fears that a nuclear war between the Soviet Union and the United States might be confined between the Elbe and the Atlantic. The Americans, moreover, were changing their strategic plans fundamentally without first consulting their European allies. In February 1960 French scientists exploded France's first atom bomb. Then France went thermonuclear with repeated tests in the Pacific.

Signals were also sent to the United States that France regarded NATO as an unequal alliance and required change as the price of continued membership. In April 1959 de Gaulle forbade the presence of American nuclear weapons on bases in France; but increasing French pressure for changes to NATO which would give France a larger voice failed to impress the Americans or the British. And, however much the Germans wished to maintain good relations with France, no German chancellor would run the risk of alienating the United States, on whose support the defence of the Federal Republic against the Soviet Union principally depended. In July 1966, after years of growing non-cooperation, de Gaulle therefore took the dramatic step of withdrawing France from NATO's integrated military command structure altogether. But he was careful to maintain her political alliance with NATO. Indeed, de Gaulle was conspicuous in supporting the United States and the NATO allies in every confrontation with the Russians, over successive Berlin crises, the building of the Wall in 1961 and the Cuban missile crisis in 1962.

By 1966, de Gaulle appeared to be overplaying his hand and his policies carried less conviction. His stately visits to the Third World, Latin America and Canada earned him personal applause but no tangible benefits for France, which was seen as dangerously anti-American. Adenauer's successors, Erhard and Kiesinger, were less inclined to accept French tutelage as Germany recovered not only her economic strength but her confidence too. De Gaulle irritated his EEC partners in 1965 by boycotting the Common Market when its members tried to move towards majority voting at the Council of Ministers. After several months, the French in 1966 won the so-called Luxembourg Compromise which, in effect, allowed each member to oppose a majority vote when it considered its vital interests were at stake. De Gaulle had halted the move toward supranationalism. This stance accorded with the views of the British government (which had applied to join the club) and ironically made possible the later accession of Britain, which de Gaulle had vetoed in January 1963 and November 1967. France's five partners, too, were now anxious to bring in Britain to check France and did not take kindly to his Olympian despatch of Britain's applications.

Elected for a second term as president in December 1965 on, admittedly, a reduced majority, de Gaulle at the age of seventy-five was still seen as indispensable to the maintenance of stability. But Mitterrand, the candidate of the united left, had also impressed and with 32 per cent of the vote was only 11 per cent behind the General. Internationally, de Gaulle had succeeded in winning back an independent role for France. The question which now arose was what he would do with it, how he would exploit France's position to break the superpower deadlock. A visit to the Soviet Union in the summer of 1966 led to agreement on Franco-Soviet consultations, but de Gaulle could make no headway in achieving his real aim of freeing Europe from Soviet and American military dominance. The time was not yet ripe for de Gaulle's vision.

In world affairs de Gaulle took up positions diametrically opposed to American policy. He advised the Americans to leave Vietnam and during the 1967 Six-Day War reversed France's traditional policy of support for Israel against the Arabs (page 479). Visiting Canada that summer, his behaviour seemed downright quixotic when he encouraged separatism in French Canada by declaring in Montreal, 'Vive le Québec Libre'. This was blatant interference in Canadian affairs, though French influence had been lost for good in that country two centuries earlier. Visiting Poland, de Gaulle openly encouraged Polish nationalism. Not only did de Gaulle surprise the world with his policies and pronouncements, but the personal exercise of power began to cause misgivings in France too. By the close of the 1960s, a great swing of the pendulum was in the making. French society was no longer uniformly ready to trust and follow its remote and grand leader. The divisions made themselves felt in the explosion of May 1968, which almost removed de Gaulle; he mastered the crisis but his prestige was irreparably damaged.

The May outburst had several causes, some of them loosely connected. It was followed by an apparently overwhelming Gaullist electoral victory, some belated reforms and a rapid return to calm and stability. Was it just a brief period of turbulence of no great significance? With hindsight, the events of 1968 look different, the dramatising of a change in Western society that had been slow in the making. It was a revolt in the first place against authority: in the professions, and especially among would-be professionals in the universities, it marked a rejection of preordained patterns, of subservience and patronage, and of the concomitant corruption. It was a revolt of youth against an older generation that it held responsible for the mismanagement of the past. With the security provided by the welfare state, relatively full employment and student grants, students no longer had to concentrate on providing their daily needs but could aspire to something better. The success of the assault on the bastions of privilege and archaic structures in education and the professions was uneven, but a recognition of the need for change, a loosening of rigid hierarchies and the granting of a larger role and greater freedom to the younger members of society have been among the positive results of 1968. It reflected a movement evident throughout Western society during the 1960s and 1970s.

The May crisis in France revealed the frustrations of an active minority section of the population, no longer confident that change could be effected through the existing channels of bureaucracy and government. Thousands took to the streets, giving the upheaval its particular character: half revolution, half carnival, shaking off the strait-laced conformist stupor identified with Gaullist France. The crisis was easily mastered because, outside certain parts of Paris, France remained profoundly conservative in attitude, a conservatism affecting all parties from left to right, as politicians of all shades preferred to lead the masses rather than to have them take control into their own hands. The efforts of the small group of extremist students, such as the Marxist Danny Cohn-Bendit, who were working for revolutionary change, were doomed to failure, though for a short while they drew the limelight on themselves. The red flags and non-stop speeches by students in Nanterre and the Sorbonne were not the real stuff of which revolutions are made, but the increase in student numbers to more than half a million nationally since 1958 had made them a significant force. The repressive police actions in response might have become a more serious cause of revolution, because they were met by counter-violence in the streets of Paris, reinforced by barricades and burning cars.

One reason why revolution did not break out was that workers did not make common cause with the intellectuals and students, and this was so even though the workers had their own grievances. The growth of their real wages had been hit by an austerity economic programme, and unemployment, though small, was rising. Trade unions, receiving no co-operation from management, called a strike, and workers throughout France spontaneously occupied factories. But the unions, the communist one included, were seeking better conditions, not revolution. De Gaulle, incredulous at the sudden storm, left crisis management to Prime Minister Pompidou. At the height of the crisis, on 29 May, he secretly withdrew and, near breaking point, flew to a French military base in Baden-Baden, West Germany, intending to depart permanently from office and from France, but General Massu persuaded him not to give up and the following day he returned to Paris. Pompidou, left to himself, had in the meantime bought off the unions with large concessions. By the time de Gaulle reappeared to broadcast a plea for massive support and for a counter-demonstration to the previous left-wing march on the Champs Élysées, the response was immediate and impressive. In June disturbances were practically over. Students went on their vacations and the workers returned to work. The National Assembly, with its slender Gaullist majority in 1967, was dissolved in June 1968 and France gave her verdict at the polls: the opposition was severely weakened and the Gaullists secured an overwhelming majority. But this was not quite the positive vote for de Gaulle that it appeared to be. It was a fearful reaction against the left, and a display of support for Pompidou, whose moderation had brought success. De Gaulle knew this and promptly dropped Pompidou, appointing Couve de Murville as his successor. Fresh economic problems were countered with another austerity programme in the autumn in preference to devaluation. By the spring of 1969 de Gaulle had decided to put his leadership to the test by another referendum on the issues of regional devolution and the reform of the upper house of parliament. His call for support for French people to choose between him and 'upheaval' rang hollow. On 27 April 52 per cent voted against and de Gaulle promptly resigned. French society was now sufficiently stable and mature to benefit from a less authoritarian style and from new leaders who did not claim to embody the mystic spirit of France. Yet it is difficult to escape the conclusion that de Gaulle had been necessary and that Gaullism, with all its drawbacks, had provided a bridge between the old government and the new.

# CHAPTER 56

# Britain: Better Times and Retreat from Empire

The war had been won by the British people acting in rare unison. Traditional class differences were softened by the wartime experience of common danger and loss. But in all essentials the class structure survived and was to impede Britain's post-war progress. It survived above all in education, so denying equal opportunities to talented children from the lower classes. Social mobility improved, but far too slowly. The first post-war Labour government, though not revolutionary, did move the country in new directions, taking a gradualist road to impose more state control and planning on private industry, and to provide through social legislation a society which would care for the basic needs of all. Labour's social policies were more successful than its industrial ones. Britain's wealth was more equitably shared but it was created at a slower rate than the more successful European economies achieved after the war. The Labour government of 1945–50 enacted the measures which laid the basis of the post-war welfare state (pages 348–9). It also set up the National Health Service and nationalised the coal and steel industries and the railways. The enactment of such a large and radical legislative programme required many compromises, and these, together with the deliberate avoidance of direct state control, ensured that Britain did not experience the kind of socialist revolution imposed on the communist states of Eastern Europe.

The first post-war Labour government presided with considerable success over the transition from peace to war. The miseries of the 1920s and the 1930s haunted Labour politicians and the working people alike. Careful planning and staggered demobilisation of the millions serving in the armed forces ensured that jobs were waiting for the returning men – and that they would not be temporary jobs, as many of them had been after the First World War. Strict rationing was continued, low wages and subsidised food prices kept the cost of living down, while the provision of health care and social security was spreading a safety net for the lowest income groups. In comparison with devastated continental Europe, Britain in the post-war 1940s was relatively well off. There was a market for all she could produce and as yet little serious competition. The immediate problem was the balance of payments: Britain did not export enough to earn the dollars to pay for imports from the United States, to continue high defence expenditure abroad and to assist the British occupied zone of Germany, whose people would otherwise have starved. Yet she still saw herself as a world power, the number three behind only the United States and the Soviet Union, and, though recognising that the American alliance remained the indispensable first condition of West European security, was determined to maintain an independent capacity to defend herself in Europe and her still far-flung imperial interests. In 1945 it would have been unwise to have counted on any long-term US commitment to Western Europe. In any case, British and American interests overseas frequently clashed, as for example in the Middle East.

The Labour government showed itself at least as passionately attached to parliamentary democracy, civil liberties and the independence of the law as any previous administration. But it also showed a much greater concern for social justice. No doubt the early post-war years were an 'age of austerity' for the few millions who before the war had enjoyed higher standards of living, more varied food and cheap domestic servants, but it was also an age during which the much more numerous poor for the first time were freed from the fear of unemployment, the workhouse, sickness, hunger and even a pauper's burial. As a nation the British people had never enjoyed such good health, subsisting on adequate rations that kept the people lean. It is characteristic of the period that the word 'utility' was widely stamped on furniture and clothing to denote good standard quality without any frills.

By pre-war standards, Britain made sound progress as her factories switched to peacetime production. A major problem was how to earn enough dollars from exports to pay for all the imports Britain needed to feed her population, to provide tobacco and to get industry moving. That Labour recovered from the crisis year of 1947 (page 451) was due less to Attlee, who provided little leadership, than to Stafford Cripps, who as Chancellor of the Exchequer emerged as the strong man. His strict economic policy, wage restraint and cuts in spending put Britain back on course. But despite Marshall Aid, Britain ran into renewed crises and devalued the pound in 1949 from its pre-war rate of $4.03 to $2.80. Bread was rationed for the first time from 1946 to 1948. When Labour finally fell from power in 1951, after winning the 1950 election by so narrow a margin of seats that Attlee decided to call another election, Britain was still enjoying a higher standard of living than her continental neighbours. There was a small drift of support from Labour to Conservative, 3 per cent in 1950 and a further 1 per cent in 1951. It was just sufficient to end the first Labour era of post-war Britain.

The elections brought a Churchill-led government back to power, the Conservatives holding 321 seats and Labour 295. The swing was not remarkable given Labour's six years in office and that the socialist leaders were becoming old and sick. Sir Stafford Cripps retired in October 1950 suffering from cancer, Bevin died in April 1951

and Attlee also fell ill. A split within the Labour movement also became publicly known and weakened the party. The left-wingers led by Aneurin Bevan were outraged by the introduction of a charge for spectacles and false teeth, which destroyed the principle of a completely free National Health Service. Bevan and Harold Wilson, a rising young star, thereupon resigned from the government. But the majority of Labour supporters did not wish to go further on the road to socialism, and extending nationalisation was not popular. Also, Labour's reforming zeal had weakened in the face of the practical constraints of the slowly recovering economy.

While Labour declined, the Conservative Party struck a note which appealed to the voters of 'grey' Britain, promising to rid the country (which was tiring of uniformity and the continuation of wartime rationing) of unnecessary restrictions and regulations – but they also undertook to maintain the new welfare state created by Labour. The most important of their assurances was that they would maintain full employment: the new Conservatism was laying the ghosts of the 1930s. For all these reasons – and a redistribution of constituency boundaries had also aided the Conservatives – they won power in 1951 and held on to it without interruption for thirteen years until 1964.

Churchill was back at Number 10. Seventy-seven years of age, he was still a statesman of world stature who could speak on equal terms with Truman and Stalin. There were no other such statesmen. This obscured a little the fact that Britain had ceased to be a world power when measured in terms of economic strength. With R. A. Butler, who fully accepted all the Beveridge Report stood for, at the Exchequer, the country was assured there would be no return to pre-war Toryism. Churchill's Cabinet contained ministers who wished to reshape Conservative ideology to encompass more concern for the poor; they believed in the healing power of consensus politics, in the acceptance of the welfare state and in the application of Keynesian economics to counter the effects of cyclical depression. Butler, the most senior member of the government after Churchill, represented this now dominant wing of the party, though its most radical exponent was Harold Macmillan. Macmillan was entrusted with redeeming Tory pledges to build 300,000 houses a year, and he succeeded brilliantly. Lord Woolton was another popular minister; responsible for food, his success was inexorably linked to the rising meat content of the British sausage. Anthony Eden at the Foreign Office enjoyed a national prestige, in part based on his resignation before the Munich settlement and in part on his close association with Churchill during the war.

The last Churchill administration set the guidelines for successive Conservative governments for more than a decade. In overseas relations and foreign affairs British policy followed what were intended to be five complementary aims: to strengthen as far as possible the alliance with the United States; to maintain an independent military capacity as a great power by joining the nuclear superpowers, the USSR and the USA, in building atomic weapons; to defend what were regarded as Britain's essential worldwide economic and strategic interests in eastern Asia and the Middle East; to promote co-operation among the Commonwealth countries and to adjust to a new relationship; and finally to assist as an ally West European defence without becoming embroiled in continental moves for closer collaboration. This combination of policies, reflecting what were then the perceived national interests, was based on a mixture of foresight and rather more hindsight. It delayed Britain's decline in influence in world affairs only to hasten it later, as the attempt to play a more independent role revealed Britain's growing inability to sustain it. At home these efforts overseas diverted resources which were badly needed to renew the industrial base. But the retreat from power is probably more difficult to manage successfully than mastering the problems of expansion.

In fostering the American alliance, Britain hoped to counterbalance her declining strength by emphasising the historic special relationship that has often been said to bind together the two English-speaking countries. British statesmen could also emphasise their country's long experience of world affairs and saw themselves as able to provide wise counsel to their 'inexperienced' American cousins. In the real world most of these assumptions were illusory. Despite her nuclear capacity, Britain ceased in the 1950s to be regarded as the third world power. Anglo-American interests in the post-war world coincided on some questions, especially the defence of Western Europe against Soviet threats, but they could also diverge, especially in the Middle East. That was to be demonstrated starkly over Suez in 1956, after Anthony Eden had taken over the

premiership (pages 465–72). The American alliance, and America's continued commitment to European defence, which could not be taken for granted in 1945 or 1946, has remained the cornerstone of British foreign policy, but since the 1950s Anglo-American co-operation could not truly be said to amount to an exclusive or a special relationship.

Britain's choice of the nuclear option did not give her the added weight in world affairs her leaders expected from it, nor did her role at the head of the too-disparate Commonwealth. For a time, Britain was the only nuclear power besides the Soviet Union and the United States. In 1946 the Americans had repudiated agreements to share with Britain the secrets of the bomb, so Attlee decided to develop an independent bomb. Research and development in Britain, however, reached fruition only in 1952, a year after the Conservatives had returned to power. Even then the full lethal consequences of radiation were not understood; Britain's chief scientists had recommended that the atomic tests be conducted off the coast of Scotland. In the event, Monte Bello Island off the coast of Australia was chosen and, in consequence, Australian rather than British lives were unknowingly jeopardised. Only a month after Britain's first successful test in 1952 the ante was raised when the United States demonstrated the much more destructive thermonuclear bomb, the H-bomb. Churchill was determined to keep pace with the United States and the Soviet Union: Britain would not surrender the option of pursuing independent policies. Five years later, in May 1957, Britain carried out her own successful H-bomb test. By then Harold Macmillan had taken over the premiership from Eden after the 1956 Suez fiasco (page 466). A strong adherent of both traditional British independence and the American alliance, Macmillan was able to restore some glow to the special relationship by persuading Eisenhower to resume Anglo-American nuclear co-operation. In one respect this was fortunate, for time was running out for Britain's ability to remain completely independent in nuclear weaponry.

Britain failed to develop her own missiles to carry the nuclear warheads and so was obliged to buy them from the United States. In December 1962 Macmillan met President Kennedy in the Bahamas and successfully negotiated the Nassau Agreement, under which the United States undertook to supply Polaris missiles to be fitted to British-built atomic

*Mutually Assured Destruction.* Top left: *by 1957 this was an all too familiar image. This nuclear H-bomb cloud rises over Christmas Island during British tests in May 1957.* Top right: *in protest at the selfsame tests, Japanese students pitch a tent in front of the British Embassy in Tokyo.* Left above: *the women of Greenham Common, Britain, outside the US air-base in 1982, provided an impressively dogged focus for resistance.* Right: *the increase in deployment of nuclear weapons in Europe in the early 1980s reactivated the Campaign for Nuclear Disarmament.*

submarines. This Anglo-American deal was to have profound implications for Anglo-French relations and so for Britain's attempts to join the Common Market in the 1960s (pages 569–70), because de Gaulle interpreted it as evidence of a British decision to opt for the United States rather than Western Europe and of a British desire to relegate France to a second-class status. As a result, in 1963 the General turned down Britain's application to join the Common Market. Although eventually Britain and the United States sought to pacify their non-nuclear NATO allies by setting up in 1966 joint nuclear defence committees which would share nuclear planning rather than weapons, the French – who by now had their own nuclear missiles – maintained their refusal to participate in NATO's integrated nuclear structure and went their own way, testing their weapons in the South Pacific.

The continuous nuclear debate highlights the significance of these decisions at home and internationally. At home the horror aroused by a weapon of indiscriminate mass destruction prompted in 1958 the largest popular protest movement of postwar Britain, the Campaign for Nuclear Disarmament (CND). Originally its moral appeal cut across traditional party and class lines. CND became a powerful radical movement led by middle-class left-wingers, who sought to persuade the Labour Party to abandon the bomb unilaterally and so give a moral lead to the world. Within the Labour Party, demands for unilateral disarmament became a serious embarrassment for its leaders from Gaitskell to Neil Kinnock in the 1980s.

Britain's fivefold policy aims as outlined on page 560 looked fine on paper, but the essence of a successful and coherent strategy is that all its elements should harmonise and that its priorities should be ordered correctly. Britain was handicapped by her success in the Second World War and by her unbroken historical tradition. It would have been difficult to foresee in the 1950s the rapidity of Western Europe's recovery from the war. Towards her European neighbours Britain followed her traditional policy of seeking a balance of power. This involved encouraging the collaboration of the Western European states, the Federal German Republic, France, Italy and the Benelux countries, without embroiling Britain too closely in their emerging political and economic arrangements. Britain saw her role as a powerful ally – supporting, together

with the United States, the strengthening of Western Europe rather than trying to lead it. This was partly because considerable importance was still attached economically and politically to Britain's ties with the Commonwealth, the independent Dominions – Canada, Australia, New Zealand and South Africa – which were joined by India and Pakistan and later by many former colonies as they gained independence.

In colonial and imperial affairs Britain continued to adjust gradually to the new realities, but not without difficulty. Even if she had wished simply to abandon her colonial possessions quickly, it could not be done without ensuing conflict. There were always rivals ready to take Britain's place, who even before her departure tried to make good their claims by fighting for them. British troops, and often their families too, were exposed to terrorism. Palestine was thus only the first of many quagmires.

Cyprus, an important British base, flared into violence in 1955 after the British, Greek and Turkish foreign ministers, meeting in conference, failed to agree a solution to the problem of the island's self-government. The leader of the Greek Cypriots, Archbishop Makarios, representing some 80 per cent of the inhabitants, wanted union with Greece, *enosis*, which was anathema to the Cypriot Turks. Britain wanted to retain a secure base, which became all the more important after the Suez débâcle in 1956. A terror campaign was launched on the island by EOKA (the National Organisation of Cypriot Struggle), headed by a former Greek colonel, Georgios Grivas. Greece was backing the Greek Cypriots, and Turkey followed suit, backing the Turkish Cypriots with still greater militancy. Only in 1959 was there sufficient agreement between Britain, Greece and Turkey to allow the setting up of an independent republic of Cyprus, whose Turkish minority population was granted special safeguards, with both Greece and Turkey promising to respect Cypriot sovereignty. Britain secured two sovereign bases. It was a solution imposed from outside by the three powers, one which denied the majority of the islanders the right of union with Greece. Cyprus enjoyed an uneasy peace under Makarios, interspersed with serious conflict between the Greek and Turkish communities, until the final breakdown, the Turkish invasion and the effective division of the island into separate Turkish and Greek halves in 1974. The problem remains no less insoluble today, but it has ceased to be Britain's responsibility, having been handed over to the UN, like so many other lost international causes.

In Malaya, Britain was more successful. A determined military campaign was waged against a communist revolt started in 1948 with the objective of seizing power from the British. There were some 4000 of these communist guerrillas, fighting fanatically from bases deep in the jungles. But the insurgency was defeated by 1954 and Britain granted independence to the Federation of Malaya three years later. Singapore was made self-governing under the terms of this settlement, but became completely independent two years later.

In the same year in which Malaya was granted independence, Britain began her retreat from colonial dominance in West Africa; the Gold Coast attained independence as Ghana in 1957 (pages 751–3), Nigeria in 1960 (pages 754–5), Sierra Leone in 1961 and Gambia in 1965. The Commonwealth had become multiracial, a force (it was hoped) for racial harmony in the world. Britain appeared to be shedding her responsibilities and burdens with grace and little hardship. Macmillan, in a speech before the United Nations, reflected the false optimism of the time when he declared in 1960, 'Who dares to say that this is anything but a story of steady and liberal progress?' Yet the 1960s were soon to witness the breakdown of British-style parliamentary rule in the West African states, and Nigeria was plunged into civil war.

Britain's withdrawal from her East and Central African colonies proved far more difficult than withdrawal from the West. Here the white settlers, who claimed the land as their own and who possessed disproportionate wealth and held dominant power over the black majority, foresaw that majority rule and independence would mean the end of their pre-eminence. Nevertheless the Conservative government succeeded in 1961 in reaching a satisfactory settlement in Tanganyika, which with Zanzibar soon after became the state of Tanzania. In contrast, the relinquishment of control in and the granting of independence to Uganda in 1962 started the country on a path of tribal rivalry and bloodshed. In Kenya, the 30,000 white settlers and Europeans wielded more influence than those in Tanganyika, so the path to independence here was more violent. As in Malaya, Britain faced a major uprising in the 1950s organised by the Mau Mau, a militant secret society comprised mainly of Kikuyu.

Britain reacted to this revolt by banning black political activity and using military force. Military action, as in Malaya, was successful, but, unlike in Malaya, the black independence leaders were not on the British side – they were all in prison. Macmillan, proclaiming the 'wind of change' in a celebrated speech in South Africa in 1960, pressed on with the decolonisation policies, which placed Kenya under black majority rule and gave her independence in 1963. But, from the British point of view, the policy of 'steady and liberal progress', pursued with a mixture of military force, flexibility and diplomacy and intended to transfer power gradually to black political leaders, came seriously unstuck in Central Africa. Nyasaland and Northern Rhodesia, which became the independent states of Malawi and Zambia in 1964, had been federated with Southern Rhodesia. Here a white minority of settlers held all political power, but their demands for independence could not be accepted in the progressive climate of the 1960s. The position had changed radically in the half-century since the white South Africans had obtained all political power and had been entrusted with the future of the country. Now the Commonwealth was multiracial, with Asian and black member states. South Africa was forced to leave it in 1961.

Talks intended to lead to a settlement in Southern Rhodesia broke down in 1965 and the white Rhodesians declared their unilateral independence in November. The new Prime Minister Harold Wilson sought a solution by negotiating with the Rhodesian Premier Ian Smith, a former Battle of Britain pilot, who enjoyed considerable public support in Britain, not least because what was happening in the Congo and Uganda was a bad advertisement for black rule. The British government had neither the will nor the backing to use force to topple Smith and impose majority rule. Instead, economic sanctions were adopted, but they proved leaky, with oil and other supplies reaching Rhodesia through South Africa and Portuguese Mozambique. Smith was able to hold out until 1979: the issue was decided in Africa and not in London. Britain, once at the centre of imperial power, had moved to the sidelines. (For a more detailed discussion, see Chapter 76.)

What is perhaps surprising to foreign observers is the equanimity with which the majority of the British people accepted the loss of empire. To the serving

British soldier direct experience of the squalor and poverty of what became known as the Third World was a reality which replaced the romantic simple patriotism of a bygone age. Only a minority who had directly benefited mourned the passing of the Raj. Realistic Conservatives did not reverse Labour policies after 1951, as might have been expected if Churchill had been taken seriously, but extended and hastened the process of granting independence. To the man in the street setting former colonials free did not solve the problem: they emigrated to Britain, making use of their rights as subjects of the Crown to settle in the home country, though only a tiny proportion of the population of the empire did so.

There was nothing new in the experience of accepting immigrants – Russian and later German Jews, and during the Second World War foreign allies from many nations had settled in Britain. Large numbers of Poles, some 157,000, who had fought with the British refused after the war to return to their country, now dominated by the Soviet Union. The Polish miners of Mansfield with their own social club, the German refugees in Swiss Cottage, and other nationals elsewhere in Britain exhibiting different cultures were accepted with tolerance and good humour. Their British-educated children were soon indistinguishable from the rest. Although immigration aroused some contemporary argument, the assimilation of more than 300,000 immigrants presented no long-term problems, and their early concentration within certain areas gave way within a generation or two to their spreading out and absorption throughout the British Isles. These were the white immigrants.

The problem of coloured immigration from the former colonies and the new Commonwealth countries proved very different. Immigration of West Indians and Asians did not begin in the 1940s and 1950s – in London, and in seaports such as Cardiff and Liverpool, sizeable black communities had already settled, attracted by the prospect of work. The essential features of the problem revealed themselves from the start. There is a natural tendency among all immigrants to concentrate in particular towns among their own peoples with similar cultural backgrounds. Here they are more protected and can expect some assistance. Discrimination by whites meant that coloured immigrants, especially blacks, obtained only labouring jobs, and not even those when employment became scarce.

Moreover, the whites' assumption of racial superiority and their acts of prejudice drove an increasingly impoverished black community back in on itself. Violence in what became virtually coloured ghetto areas fed on discrimination and resentment. In 1919 there occurred serious riots in Cardiff, Newport and London. In Liverpool blacks were attacked by a white mob.

The assimilation of the coloured immigrants has not proceeded as quickly and smoothly as that of the whites. Both Asian and black communities take pride in their own culture and distinctiveness, frequently reinforced by their own religious observances. West Indians, the blacks from the colonies and Indians had all been welcomed as fighting men during the war, and after 1945 West Indian labour was encouraged to come to Britain to fill jobs for which there were not sufficient whites. London Transport, for instance, recruited 4000 workers in the Caribbean, and the National Health Service could not have functioned without cleaners and nurses from overseas. Need reduced prejudice. Increasingly doctors from India and the Commonwealth entered the Health Service too, thus draining the Third World of the educated and skilled personnel it could spare least of all. It has been estimated that by 1973 more than a quarter of the doctors in the National Health Service had not been born in the British Isles.

**Coloured Immigrants living in Britain before the 1962 Commonwealth Immigrants Act**

|      | Pakistanis | Indians | West Indians | East Asians | West Africans |
|------|-----------|---------|--------------|-------------|---------------|
| 1951 | 5,000     | 38,800  | 15,300       | 12,000      | 5,600         |
| 1961 | 24,900    | 81,400  | 171,800      | 29,600      | 19,800        |

When immigrants wishing to escape the poverty of their homeland could no longer be absorbed by a growing British demand for their labour, pressure for control of immigration grew stronger. Now arguments were added explaining why the 'New' Commonwealth citizens were no longer welcome in Britain. The 1962 Commonwealth Immigrants Act ended unrestricted immigration, and the exclusion of immigrants later became still more rigorous. But the entry of new groups, such as some 100,000 East African and Ugandan Asians holding

British passports, driven out in the late 1960s and 1970s by racial and economic resentment and by greed for their wealth, the arrival of dependants of existing immigrants, the small number of new immigrants, and above all the second-generation children born to the original immigrants, all enlarged the coloured communities in Britain from 392,000 in 1962 to 1.85 million in 1976, out of a total population in Britain of 55 million.

But of what significance is origin anyway? Will there be a serious 'racial problem', as the former Conservative Minister Enoch Powell prophesied, with peoples of alien culture affecting the 'British way of life'? Will extremism, white and black, poison relationships? The signs today are ambiguous. Discrimination, especially in employment, alienates the British-born, second-generation West Indian. The blacks have also been the worst sufferers in times of depression. Much, then, will depend on the future direction of Britain's economy.

There is also a more positive side. Britain has come a long way since American black airmen (of the USAAF) landed in 1944 in a Norfolk village whose inhabitants had never seen a black man before. Britain is now a multi-ethnic society and a new generation has been born into it. Racial differences are commonplace, accepted as part of life in Britain today, while intermarriage is more frequent. Just as the rigid barriers between Jews and Christians have broken down and anti-Semitism has greatly diminished, so racial prejudices have lessened. The significance of the immigrants' contribution to the wealth of Britain still needs to be fully emphasised and set against the problems. Even these are not simply racial. In times of depression and high unemployment the deprived inner cities have vented their anger and frustration against the forces of the establishment, whose most visible manifestation is the police. The evils of unemployment have increased criminality and the maintenance of law and order has been perceived by the deprived as tinged with racism. Yet the spectacular riots of the 1970s and 1980s are the exception and not the rule; the violence of the few attracts more attention than the patience of the many.

There was a broad consensus among the British people from the 1950s to the 1970s about the kind of society they wanted: gross poverty and misfortune, whether through ill-health or old age, to be banished by the state's provisions of welfare and medical care; decent standards of housing and education for the population as a whole; a growing supply of consumer goods, the pleasures of a car for every family and summer holidays away from home; an expanding economy to bestow these benefits; greater personal freedom of choice in lifestyles and the shrinking of the frontiers of legal sanction on questions of morality; a move away from authoritarian 'Victorian' standards; and finally a decent livelihood for all, with full employment. The maintenance of law and order was taken for granted, respect for the law and the police was almost universal, violence the exception. In seeking the good things in life, there was an expectation that they could be attained without too much effort, by a kind of natural progression, though interrupted from time to time by brief setbacks.

CND was an overwhelmingly peaceful movement whose respectable leaders, with Canon Collins of the Church of England at their head, were accompanied by a few policemen on their ritual Easter march to Aldermaston. The Teddy boys, the Mods and the Rockers provided more entertainment than serious teenage challenge, to be tolerated good-humouredly. At the same time the more cerebral

*Bertrand Russell addresses CND supporters in Trafalgar Square on 21 February 1961.*

Angry Young Men confined their rebellion against the prevailing materialistic mood of complacency and optimism to novels and the theatre. Harold Macmillan caught the prevailing mood in his often quoted phrase 'Most of our people have never had it so good.' But class divisions remained, with great inequalities of wealth, an educational system that despite widening opportunities did not provide anything like equal opportunities. Discrimination for senior positions was based on unconscious assumptions in favour of their 'own kind'. Preference for Oxbridge graduates in the foreign service, in the City and elsewhere persisted. Of course there were always exceptions, but exceptions they remained.

Throughout these three decades, both major parties, Labour and Conservative, could count on a bedrock of class support. Elections were decided by the floating voters. To 'float' was not a difficult ideological feat since there was so much common ground between the two parties on foreign affairs, defence and the welfare state. Judgements by the floaters were based on which party could provide the more competent prime minister, and which party's policies promised to deliver that steady advance of the economy which had eluded the party in power; the floating voter was frequently voicing the need for a change, a vote against the party in power, rather than expressing ideological convictions. Labour in power was not intent on extending socialism but was willing to work with the mixed economy. Conservatives were ready to accept the social legislation of their Labour predecessors.

From 1950 to 1970 there appear to have been only relatively small shifts in voting patterns, the biggest swing towards or away from Labour was less than 5 per cent. Only Labour and the Conservatives secured sufficient support to be considered credible government parties, the Liberal Party being unable to break the two-party mould. In fact, the traditional Labour working-class base was shrinking and British politics was moving towards a radical reshaping in the 1970s (pages 863–71).

Churchill's 1951–5 administration will be remembered for the old wartime giant whose now rare speeches could still inspire. But few outside the inner circle of politicians knew how physically impaired the Prime Minister had become, partly as the result of two strokes. His well-tried ministerial colleagues performed well enough, except for R. A. Butler at the Exchequer, who gave the economy

### Parliamentary Elections, 1945–1970
(*percentage of vote*)

| Elections | Labour | Conservative | Liberal |
|-----------|--------|--------------|---------|
| 1945 | 47.8 | 39.8 | 9.0 |
| 1950 | 46.1 | 43.5 | 9.1 |
| 1951 | 48.8 | 48.0 | 2.5 |
| 1955 | 46.4 | 49.7 | 2.7 |
| 1959 | 43.8 | 49.4 | 5.9 |
| 1964 | 43.4 | 44.1 | 11.2 |
| 1966 | 48.0 | 41.9 | 8.5 |
| 1970 | 43.0 | 46.4 | 7.5 |

too great a boost just before the election by lowering income tax, only to have to raise it immediately after it was won. Macmillan's success at housing did more than any other single policy of Churchill's administration to restore faith in the efficiency of private enterprise and the free market. The hybrid policy of encouraging private enterprise while maintaining the main features of the welfare state, a harmonisation of Labour and Conservative economic and social policies, became known as 'Butskellism' (Hugh Gaitskell had been Labour's Chancellor of the Exchequer).

Churchill kept Eden, his unchallenged heir, waiting too long. Eden had first entered government twenty-six years earlier as a junior minister. He had spent a lifetime in diplomacy, emerging unscathed from the condemnation of 1930s appeasement thanks to his break with Neville Chamberlain in 1938. As Churchill's lieutenant in foreign affairs he had served the country throughout the Second World War. He again demonstrated his diplomatic skill as foreign secretary after 1951. The future of Western Europe was still uncertain in 1951. Could former enemies, especially West Germany, be trusted? The thorniest problem was whether, and under what controls, to permit German rearmament as part of the joint defence effort of the North Atlantic Treaty Organisation (page 533). The Americans pressed for West German rearmament, while the French, looking back on their historical experience, felt grave misgivings. The attempt to overcome these difficulties by creating a West European Defence Community (the Pleven Plan) finally failed when the French Assembly rejected ratification in August 1954 (page 543). Britain had been willing to join not as a full member but only as an ally, thus indicating again her unwillingness to give up her status as the third great power and to combine with her continental allies as an equal European. Eden was the principal architect of the compromises which created the framework for West European defence at a nine-power conference over which he presided in London in the autumn of 1954. This was followed by the formal treaty signatures, the Paris Agreements, in October. With the admission of Italy and the Federal Republic of Germany, the Brussels Treaty Organisation was superseded by a Council of West European Union. That winter West Germany was admitted as a member of NATO. The Federal Republic of Germany had been restored to full sovereignty, but had agreed to certain restrictions, the most important of which was not to manufacture nuclear weapons. Berlin alone retained its status as an occupied city, since any Western alteration of the agreements reached with the Soviet Union would have opened the way for the Russians to declare them void. Eden had demonstrated full British support for a restored West Germany and for the military defence of Western Europe in alliance with the United States and Canada. Thus West European Union and NATO were closely linked. But the British policy of keeping her distance from continental Europe was also confirmed.

Eden's second triumph was to preside over and bring to a successful conclusion the Geneva Conference in 1954, which extricated France from Indo-China. Unfortunately in the longer term this proved to be only another act in the tragedy of Vietnam (pages 407–8). In the same year as these diplomatic successes Eden began to negotiate the treaties intended to place Anglo-Egyptian relations on an entirely new and friendly basis; they provided for the withdrawal of the British from Suez, but allowed the retention of the military base in emergencies. A group of Conservative MPs responded by accusing him of weakness. Eden was hypersensitive to charges of appeasement, and the shadow of Munich was to overwhelm his good judgement. The fuse was laid for the Suez Crisis two years later. Churchill finally accepted retirement in April 1955, the unavoidable consequence of his age and ill-health. Eden called an election in May and won comfortably.

The new Prime Minister entered 10 Downing Street with the broad support of the party and Conservative voters behind him. Yet the impression soon grew that he lacked the leadership qualities required of a prime minister. The economy was not going well either. Eden's health was suspect and the constant disparagement unsettled him, by nature impatient of criticism. The Suez invasion had widespread support from a public which saw this drastic action as a signal to the rest of the world that Britain could not be pushed about. But a more considered view, highly critical of Eden, was expressed among both Conservative and Labour members of Parliament. Gaitskell (who had replaced Attlee as leader of the Labour Party in December 1955) was particularly vehement in his attacks on the Prime Minister. When the Suez expedition failed, Eden's health completely broke down and he left London to recuperate in the West Indies. During his absence Butler acted as *de facto* prime minister.

When Eden resigned in January 1957, the premiership did not pass to Butler, as had been widely expected. Since the Conservative Party had no leader, the Queen sought the advice of senior Conservatives, among them Churchill and Lord Salisbury. Soundings were also taken among ministers. The shadow of Munich and appeasement still clung to Butler, and the preferred candidate was Harold Macmillan. His record seemed to be one of brilliant achievement. As Churchill's representative in the Mediterranean from 1943 to 1945, he had mastered the complex political problems of rival French, American and British interests in North Africa and later in Italy. Shrewd, ambitious, tough and ruthless when the need arose, Macmillan politically dominated the decade from the mid-1950s until ill-health and fatigue loosened his grip. Although he had occupied the senior offices of state during the short space of 1951–7 – Housing, Defence, the Foreign Office and the Exchequer – Macmillan had been the outsider among Conservatives in the 1930s, accepting the new economic theories of John Maynard Keynes and castigating the policies which he blamed for the unemployment of that decade. Intensely patriotic, he wished to rebuild Conservatism to embody the vision of 'one nation', the creation of harmony between the classes. By promoting social mobility, the Conservatives would loosen adherence to the Labour cause. The large university expansion of the 1960s helped to serve this end among others. The working people of Britain were not the enemies to be kept at bay, in Macmillan's philosophy, but the 'sturdy men' who had defeated the Kaiser's and Hitler's armies. They would respond to a policy of fairness which gave them a share in growing prosperity. Unemployment was an evil and not an option of policy. The majority of his countrymen, Macmillan believed, would respond to an emphasis on traditional British values and to a paternalistic aristocratic style of leadership. It was a cleverly packaged update of Disraeli's Tory vision.

Macmillan was the first British politician to master the new television medium. He presented himself as the disinterested statesman–gentleman who would lead the country to reform without tears, the antithesis of the puritan ethic which preaches that only what hurts can be truly beneficial. His style of government was conciliatory rather than confrontational, both at home and abroad. After the shock of Suez a more careful alignment of policy to match British resources in the world had become necessary. Indeed the Conservatives were at a low ebb when Macmillan took over. Yet less than three years later Supermac (as a cartoonist christened him) had restored the party's morale and increased its share of the vote in the October 1959 election sufficiently to win an overall majority of a hundred seats in the House of Commons. The Labour Party, it is true, was not well placed to fight that election, its rank and file divided between unilateral disarmers and Gaitskell's majority in favour of retaining the bomb, and between those who wished to extend nationalisation and Gaitskellites who believed that nationalisation was not only irrelevant but an electoral handicap. The Liberal vote had more than doubled, but in the absence of proportional representation the party was left with exactly the same number of MPs as before – a mere six.

How had Macmillan brought about the recovery? What had the Conservatives achieved? In foreign affairs, the deleterious effects of Suez were overcome and good relations with the United States restored. Macmillan also played the role of world statesman with relish, attending summits with Eisenhower in Bermuda and Khrushchev in Moscow before the abortive Geneva Conference in 1960. He had the sang-froid to react coolly to Soviet threats over Berlin and the vision to press on with independence for former African colonies (page 753). And he was astute enough to recognise that a world role could place unacceptable burdens

on the British economy and frustrate the goal of greater prosperity. Britain still kept 700,000 men under arms and maintained conscription, devoting a larger share of her Gross National Product to defence than her continental neighbours. The far-reaching Defence White Paper of 1957 saw the solution in relying on a nuclear deterrent, reducing the armed forces to 400,000 and abandoning conscription in favour of professional forces. Meanwhile, almost unnoticed in Britain, the European Economic Community had been created by the Rome Treaties of 1957. Britain had rejected the opportunity to become a founder member on the ground that she did not wish to weaken her Commonwealth ties (page 545). Macmillan still saw Britain as playing a world role, not as just another European nation like the Federal Republic of Germany, France or Italy. But rather than be isolated, Britain formed the European Free Trade Association with Austria, Denmark, Norway, Sweden and Switzerland. These nations undertook to eliminate tariffs between each other, but they did not adopt a *common* tariff. This was one essential difference between them and the EEC, which levied a common tariff against external agricultural imports in order to protect the less efficient French and German farmers. Britain remained free to import cheap agricultural produce from New Zealand, Australia, Canada and elsewhere in the world. The Treaty of Rome appeared to be contrary to Britain's economic interests and its supranational aspects were distasteful to her government and Parliament, which wished to retain undiminished sovereignty.

In a few years the Six would outstrip Britain in economic growth and prosperity. It is in retrospect curious that Supermac's electoral success was in no small measure due to the feeling that Britain was on the right course and that standards of living would rise uninterruptedly in an era of full employment. This optimistic view was buttressed by the people's insularity and their ingrained belief that Britain did all things best. The economic stagnation of 1957 and 1958 were quickly forgotten and expansive government budgetary measures produced a boom in 1959 and 1960. Macmillan had timed the election well.

Macmillan's second administration (1959–63) did not fulfil the promise of the first. The economy was soon thrown into reverse as Britain yet again faced economic crisis, with each crisis more serious than the last. Ensuring full employment was an

*The 'Special Relationship'. At a meeting in Bermuda in December 1962, US President Kennedy and British Prime Minister Macmillan confirm that Britain is to retain her independent nuclear deterrent.*

undertaking that might no longer be possible to honour as unemployment reached 800,000 during the winter of 1962. The nuclear option turned out to be neither nationally independent – because it had to rely on United States missiles – nor cheaper than conventional forces. The 'remedy' of a new boom engineered by the last of Macmillan's series of chancellors of the exchequer proved no remedy at all, whether for the economy or for the Conservatives' chances of re-election in 1964. Macmillan meanwhile sought the limelight in the role of statesman, asserting British influence on the basis of her great experience as a world power. In reality his part in bringing about the American–Soviet detente that followed on the Cuban missile crisis in October 1962 (Chapter 60) was marginal. But the Nuclear Test Ban Treaty of 1963, which sought to prevent the spread of nuclear weapons, undoubtedly owed much to Macmillan's persistent diplomacy and he took justifiable pride in his achievement. On the negative side, it reinforced Britain's illusions that she had retained her great-power status as a member, along with the

superpowers, of the exclusive nuclear club.

As Britain's weak economic performance became evident, Macmillan turned towards the Six, whose progress and growing influence threatened to leave Britain on the sidelines. Britain now, in August 1961, made a belated bid to join them, but characteristically she did not come as a supplicant – she was offering her political experience and her own internal market as bait, and in return expected special terms which would allow preferential entry into Britain of Commonwealth food and raw material exports and also permit Britain to meet her new obligations to fellow EFTA partners. Britain might have realised her essential aims had she been a founding member in 1957; now, four years later, the difficult bargains struck between the Six, and especially France's success in protecting her backward agricultural sector, had created a successful going concern. Each of the six member states believed that her national interest was best served by the maintenance of the EEC, and were not prepared to jeopardise it, even though the less powerful Benelux countries and Italy would have welcomed a counterbalance to the Franco-German axis of Adenauer and de Gaulle. Public opinion in Britain was deeply divided, with many people suspicious of foreign entanglements. Negotiations for a package deal nevertheless seemed to be making reasonable progress when de Gaulle in January 1963 brought them to a halt, declaring that Britain's Commonwealth ties and Atlantic interests prevented her from becoming a fully committed European partner. It was a body-blow to Macmillan's aura of success.

Supermac's second administration proved a disappointment to the electorate, not least because the brakes had been applied to the economy immediately after the election of 1959. The new Chancellor Selwyn Lloyd attempted to introduce a 'pay pause' in 1961, but lack of agreement with the trade unions doomed it to failure, and its application to the wages controlled by government led to strikes by railwaymen, postmen and nurses. In 1962 Macmillan replaced Selwyn Lloyd by Reginald Maudling, who exuded confidence and optimism, qualities much needed in the face of growing unemployment, particularly in the north, which reached 800,000 in the winter of 1962/3. Maudling went for an expansionary policy and planned to break out of the dreary 'stop–go' cycle of deflation and boost and achieve sustained growth by accepting a substantial once-and-for-all deficit on the balance of payment. The problems this caused were inherited by Harold Wilson's Labour government in 1964.

Macmillan appeared to have lost his magic touch. With the economy in difficulties, Britain's attempt to join the European Economic Community vetoed by de Gaulle, the 'independent' nuclear deterrent dependent on American missiles, the only relative success was the continued disengagement from colonial responsibilities: in Africa, Nigeria, Sierra Leone, Tanganyika, Uganda, Kenya, Zambia and Zanzibar all gained their independence between 1961 and 1964, as did Cyprus, Malta, Trinidad and Jamaica, and the Queen gained many new titles as former colonies became sovereign members of the Commonwealth. But independence did not solve all problems at a stroke. Nigeria was to be rent by a terrible civil war (page 755), and Uganda suffered grave misfortunes at the hands of her own rulers. Neither in Uganda nor Cyprus have internal conflicts been resolved. The problems of Rhodesia were to plague successive Conservative and Labour governments for more than a decade. But the most serious problem facing not only Britain and the Commonwealth but the Western world as a whole was the denial of equal rights to the non-white majority in South Africa. By 1961 South Africa had recognised that it had become impossible for her to remain in the new Commonwealth, the majority of whose members were now Asian and African countries. But Britain retained close and friendly relations with her, particularly in trade, while at the same time rejecting the policy of apartheid. Opposition, however, was confined to rhetoric and, later, sporting contacts, Macmillan in one of his more memorable speeches admonishing his white South African audiences in 1960 that he had been struck by the strength of African national consciousness: the 'wind of change is blowing through the continent'.

Macmillan was later to feel the 'wind of change' much more immediately at home. Conservative voters, disillusioned with the government, seemed to be switching to the Liberals in droves. Macmillan took drastic action, reshuffling his Cabinet in 1962 by sacking an unprecedented number of Cabinet ministers simultaneously, a display of ruthlessness which became known as the Night of the Long Knives. Then security scandals began to haunt the government and to throw doubt on Macmillan's grip on affairs. The most dramatic concerned John Profumo, the Secretary of State for War, who had shared an attractive mistress with a Soviet military attaché. There was no breach of security in bed but the Secretary of State, having earlier denied the association in the House of Commons, later admitted to it and resigned. A sexual scandal in high political places was, of course, a great media event. Macmillan was described as gullible and failing. In the House of Commons Labour's brilliant young leader, Harold Wilson, made the most of the government's discomfiture. But Macmillan, perhaps the most astute and skilful politician of the post-war era, might still have recovered had not serious illness incapacitated him in October 1963. He was rushed from Downing Street to hospital and there resigned the premiership.

# CHAPTER 57

# The Tribulations and Successes of Italian Democracy

Italy remains the most underrated major country of Western Europe, and persistently self-effacing in international affairs. The Italian people have with relief turned their back on the 'glorious' years of the bombastic Duce. Two decades of fascist rule and two bloody European wars brought Italy to a point in her history in 1945 where she seemed unlikely again to exert a major influence, even if she was a country of great beauty to which at least the tourists would return. In many other respects (except the economic) the outside world has neglected Italy, paying scant attention to her language and culture.

The continued neglect is all the more surprising as Italy has emerged with Britain, France and the Federal Republic of Germany as one of the big four democracies in Western Europe, with a population comparable in size and a large economy to match, which in 1987 generated about one-fifth of the Gross National Product of the European Community. The Italians have concentrated their talents on their own welfare. The post-war years were in many respects decades of achievement and success, of rising standards of living, though they were also years beset by problems.

The fortunes of war decided Italy's future in the first place. It was the Allied armies of the West which liberated the Italian peninsula in 1944 and 1945. Italy thus found herself on the Western 'free nation' side of the great post-war divide of Europe. This determined not only her international position

**Population** (*millions*)

|  | 1946 | 1962 | 1979 |
|---|---|---|---|
| Italy | 44.99 | 50.17 | 56.80 |
| Great Britain | 49.18 | 53.44 | 55.93 |
| West Germany | 43.29 | 56.9 | 61.0 |
| East Germany | 18.6 | 17.1 | 16.8 |
| France | 40.60 | 46.99 | 53.38 |

after the conclusion of the peace treaty on 10 February 1947 (page 365), but also her internal politics and social developments. Her relations with the east (and her markets there) were cut off; economically her future lay in close relations with the West. Liberal economics, the abandonment of fascist autarchy or self-sufficiency, the Italian version of a more socially responsible capitalism, all set Italy on a fundamentally Western path of political and economic development. The politics of post-war Italy were dominated by the Christian Democratic Party, firmly committed to a parliamentary system. In the post-war world Italy moreover occupied a crucial strategic position in the Mediterranean and Adriatic, and was seen as a bulwark against communist south-east Europe.

Yet impoverished Italy in the early post-war years, in the aftermath of the destruction and dislocation of the war, facing dire poverty in many regions and with an industrial proletariat in the north, did not appear secure against a communist takeover from within. The resistance had attracted the working masses to communism, especially in the north. The Italian Communist Party now numbered 2 million, the largest in the Western world. According to Cold War ideology, a communist anywhere had but one purpose, to subvert democracy and to seize power violently when the moment was ripe, following the successful model Lenin had created in 1917; it was believed, moreover, that all communists were totally subservient to Stalin and followed the dictates of the Kremlin. In 1945 the partisans in the north of Italy were strong and there were many communists among them who believed that the hour of revolution had indeed struck, but, disciplined and obedient to their leadership, they took care to avoid any direct challenge to the anti-communist Anglo-American forces.

The Italian Communist Party after 1945 behaved in a way which was contrary to communist tradition, deliberately seeking general acceptance by shedding its violent revolutionary image. The party was led by the astute veteran Palmiro Togliatti, who had returned from Moscow as recently as 1944. The communists would prevail, he believed, only by following a democratic course, winning mass support among the Italian people first and then dominating society from this position of strength. It would take time. This was a rejection of Lenin's revolutionary line and Togliatti had to assert himself against the more ardent traditional communists. Stalin probably approved this strategy for communist parties in Western Europe, where the 'Anglo-Saxons' had taken firm control, because he hoped to be left in peace to consolidate Soviet power in central and Eastern Europe. Togliatti's avowal of the constitutional, non-violent path to socialism prepared the way for a close electoral alliance, virtually a fusion, with the Socialist Party, which was led by another veteran and Togliatti's companion in arms during the Spanish Civil War, Pietro Nenni.

One pivotal question for the future would be whether a democratic left, including the communists but not necessarily dominated by them, would emerge in post-war Italy. Nineteen-forty-seven was a crucial year for the future of Italian politics. The United States and Britain had identified a critical Soviet challenge in Europe: Turkey was under pressure and in Greece civil war was raging – they

were, in Truman's words, 'still free countries being challenged by communist threats both from within and without' – while in Poland and the rest of Eastern Europe the Soviet Union and the indigenous communists were tightening their grip. Truman's response was to offer the democratic Western European states US support – diplomatic, economic and military. The outcome was the Truman Doctrine, the Marshall Plan and the North Atlantic Treaty Organisation. The effect of this support on Italian politics was that the Christian Democratic leader Alcide De Gasperi, after a visit to Washington, forced his communist–Socialist partners out of the governing coalition in May 1947.

The heightening tensions of the Cold War also created enormous strains within the communist–Socialist pact. Could the communists continue to be trusted? A minority among the Socialists led by Giuseppe Saragat demanded that their party break off their close relationship with the communists; when they failed to persuade their colleagues, they left the party in 1947 and eventually formed the Italian Social Democratic Party (PSDI). By giving up the struggle within the party and splitting the socialists, the PSDI left the communists in a position from which they were able for the next three decades to dominate the left. Thus the communists opposed the Marshall Plan, though earlier the communist–Socialist alignment had accepted American economic aid. But the communist and Nenni Socialists were never strong enough to form an alternative government on their own, nor could they find any other small parties to join them to provide a majority in parliament. Domestically the Communist Party tried to make itself acceptable by espousing democracy and a multi-party system, an Italian road to socialism. But the autocratic organisation and leadership principle which the Communist Party itself strictly adhered to undermined confidence in the authenticity of their democratic avowals. Their unwavering support of Moscow in international affairs had a similar effect: they defended the Soviet invasion of Czechoslovakia in February 1948, opposed Italy's membership of NATO and military links with the United States, were against Italy's membership of the European Economic Community and failed to denounce the Soviet invasion of Hungary in 1956.

Not until nearly two decades later did Italian communism openly take a lead in the formation of what became known as Eurocommunism, a policy of independence from Moscow and the United States, and the declared pursuit of national interests. In fact Togliatti had been critical of Moscow long before this, and a change of attitude had been evident, for example, with the acceptance by the communists of membership of the European Economic Community in 1962. But it was the Soviet invasion of Czechoslovakia in 1968, the brutal assertion of Soviet dominance over a supposedly sovereign country, albeit a Soviet ally, that provoked the broad Eurocommunist movement of Western Europe. By the mid-1970s, the Italian communists were even sanctioning NATO.

The acceptable face of communism, with its enhanced appeal to the electorate, caused even more apprehension in Washington than did traditional communism. In this respect little had changed in Washington's assessment over forty years. In the immediate post-war years, communism was believed to be deriving its support mainly from conditions of poverty and misery, and there were plenty of those in Italy and Europe. Opponents of communism were given financial aid and sustained by whatever means were possible. But, since former enemies were being taught the arts of democracy, interference could not be too obvious. To safeguard the Western alliance from a communist takeover in Italy, a very secret organisation called Operation Gladio, named after the double-edged Roman sword, was set up. It was to play a sinister and corrupt role in Italian politics, though its existence was not uncovered until a judicial investigation in 1990.

The threat of communism had a beneficial effect for Western Europe and Italy too. Extensive, predominantly American, aid was sent to Italy through the United Nations Relief and Rehabilitation Administration (UNRRA), then the US provided direct economic aid, because (in the sombre words of a State Department Policy Planning Staff report) the margin of safety politically and economically in Western Europe had become extremely thin. These stop-gap forms of aid were followed after 1948 by the planned approach of Marshall Aid.

Between 1948 and 1952, Italy received more than $1400 million in US grants and loans. So once the Italian economy had taken off in the 1950s, state, private and foreign capital ensured an investment rate in industry which fuelled rapid expansion (pages 000–00). The millions of Italian immigrants who lived in the USA made this largesse easier to justify. But in general it was appeals to America's own self-interest and above all the need to contain communism that persuaded Congress and the American public to provide such a huge transfer of resources to Italy and Western Europe.

One of the more important objectives of the Marshall Plan was to bring the non-communist European nations into closer collaboration. The means was the European recovery programme, which was to be planned jointly by the European participants. In April 1948, sixteen countries signed a treaty which for this purpose set up the Organisation for European Economic Co-operation (OEEC) with headquarters in Paris. The sixteen countries were Austria, Belgium, Denmark, France, Britain, Greece, Iceland, the Irish Republic, Italy, Luxembourg, the Netherlands, Norway, Portugal, Sweden, Switzerland and Turkey, together with the three Western zones of Germany. Italy was one of the full members, but her adherence to this block of non-communist nations still seemed problematical to Washington, even after the resounding victory of the Christian Democratic Party in the elections of 1948. Contrary to the experience in the Western zones of Germany, the Cold War had not discredited the Italian Communist Party in the eyes of the Italian electorate. American hopes that Marshall Aid would weaken the communist left remained unfulfilled.

In her relations with other countries, Italy has not sought a leading role. In the aftermath of the war, the dispute over the Trieste territory created some agitation until it was resolved in the mid-1950s. An agreement with Austria in 1969 settled the only other problem affecting her own territory, the Alto Adige region or South Tyrol, with its predominantly German-speaking population, though irredentist terrorism still upsets internal law and order in this region from time to time. Post-war Italy has not aggressively sought any special areas of influence in the Mediterranean. In a revulsion against wartime experience and imperial vainglory, the Italian people wish to be left in peace and to leave others in peace. Italy's policy has been to maintain good relations with all her neighbours and to keep out of conflicts in the region, whether in the Middle East or over Cyprus. There is indeed a strong neutralist tendency noticeable in the attitudes of the major political parties. But successive Christian Democratic-led coalitions have remained firm in the Atlantic orientation, the alliance with the United States, the membership of NATO and the European Economic Community. For four decades Italian foreign policy has been strikingly consistent.

Consistent would not be so appropriate a description of Italy's policies at home. Italian democracy's unique feature is that government has not alternated between a party in power and a party in opposition. The communists and their allies, the Nenni Socialists, polled between 31 and 36 per cent of the votes at general elections. Even after the Socialists had broken away from the communists in 1963, the communists polled more than 30 per cent of the vote on their own. Only the Christian Democrats could also claim to be a mass party, attracting some 38 per cent of the votes. None of the many other parties even reached 10 per cent.

Since neither the Christian Democrats nor the various small parties from the centre to the fascist right would accept communists in the national government, the communists formed a virtually continuous opposition, while the Christian Democrats remained permanently in power, forming various opportunistic alliances with smaller parties in order to carry the necessary vote of confidence in parliament. But there were constant conflicts between the coalition partners, as frequently over personal differences as over questions of policy, the distribution of ministerial posts being an especially rich source of animosity. Party discipline hardly exists outside the Communist Party; indeed, because voting in parliament is secret, party members can vote with impunity against their own ministers in office. Personal ambition became a major cause of instability. Between 1944 and 1988 forty-seven Italian governments came and went. After a short-lived period of stability from 1983 to 1986, the pattern of frequent change resumed. Another important feature of Italian politics is the strength of grass-roots organisations and dependent interest groups. Decades of uninterrupted power have enabled the Christian Democrats to look after their clients through patronage, from high civil service appointments to postmasterships.

Italian Christian Democracy, which contains elements of both left and right, has no distinct ideology of its own and represents no single interest group. It is not the party of industry and big business, but industry and big business have no other mass party to turn to. Moderate conservatives also support the Christian Democrats. At the same time, state intervention in industry has been a consistent feature of Christian Democratic government, coexisting with private enterprise and of course private property in the mixed Italian economy. In its early years particularly, the party had the advantage of the support of the Vatican. Through the parish priests, especially in the south, the support of the peasants was won for Christian Democracy, to set against the support of the urban workers for the communist–Socialist alliance. But the conservative landlord also votes Christian Democrat. Yet Christian Democracy, though avowedly dedicated to Catholic values, is not simply a confessional party. Its unifying spirit is a virulent anti-communism, and since the 1950s it has sedulously contrasted communist policies with its own pro-Western European and Atlantic ties.

Alcide De Gasperi, Prime Minister from December 1947 to August 1953, headed eight successive governments. His anti-fascist credentials were impeccable. One of the founders of the People's Party, a newspaper editor and a member of parliament in 1921, he opposed Mussolini and was imprisoned for his pains. On the intervention of the Pope, he was released in 1929 and spent the next few years quietly employed in the Vatican as a librarian, stealthily making contact with Catholic anti-fascists in Milan, Florence and Rome. Already in his sixties, he joined the active resistance and earned wide respect, though he lacked the charisma of a really popular leader. A practising Catholic, his relations with the Vatican remained close, but during the last years of his political life he was careful not to let the Church dominate the Christian Democratic Party. After leading governments of national unity until May 1947 he thereafter headed coalitions with small centrist parties, though the 1948 elections had given the Christian Democrats – as it turned out for the only time – an absolute majority. By the time of De Gasperi's sudden death from a heart attack in 1954 (he had resigned the premiership a year earlier) Italy was set on a course embodying moderate, conservative policies and featuring an economic boom, increasing integration with the Western alliance and West European economic union.

For four decades the Italian electorate has shown extraordinary stability in its political preferences. This seems to indicate that the associations and

*Democracy in post-war Italy: Prime Minister Alcide de Gaspieri campaigns in Milan in April 1948.*

## Chamber of Deputies Elections, 1946–1968 Percentage of votes

|                              | 1946  | 1948  | 1953  | 1963  | 1968  |
|------------------------------|-------|-------|-------|-------|-------|
| Communists (PCI)             | 18.96 |       | 22.46 | 25.31 | 26.96 |
|                              |       | 31.03 |       |       |       |
| Socialists (PSD)             | 20.72 |       | 12.73 | 13.87 |       |
|                              |       |       |       |       | 14.51 |
| Democratic Socialists (PSDI) | –     | 7.09  | 4.52  | 6.11  |       |
| Christian Democrats (DC)     | 35.18 | 48.48 | 40.08 | 38.27 | 39.09 |
| Liberal Party (PLI)          | 6.79  | 3.38  | 3.02  | 6.99  | 5.83  |
| Monarchists                  | 2.70  | 2.78  | 6.86  | 1.77  | 1.31  |
| Neo-Fascists (MSI)           | 5.30  | 2.01  | 5.85  | 5.11  | 4.46  |

benefits the party could confer on individuals were at least as important as considerations of national policy. Shifts in voting patterns were small, though sometimes crucial when it came to bargaining to secure parliamentary majorities for legislation.

De Gasperi resisted Vatican pressures to ally with the right; instead the Christian Democrats established centrist coalitions with a reforming programme. In the south, land reform divided up large estates and gave land to the peasants to farm. The government also wanted to lessen the divisions between the poorest regions and the industrial north. The Southern Italy Fund was created to finance the building of infrastructures, roads, aqueducts and irrigation schemes. The hope was that tax concessions and various inducements would tempt private industry south. Later in the 1950s the government established factories in the south, but few succeeded. The results of all these reforming efforts fell far short of their aims.

The Christian Democratic share of the votes declined after the high point of 1948 throughout the 1950s and early 1960s and with this loss the centrist coalitions became increasingly vulnerable, finding themselves in a minority in overall parliamentary votes. This, together with the tensions within Christian Democracy as the reformists looked left and the conservatives sought to move to the right, was the main cause of government unsteadiness. The Christian Democrats attempted to bolster their parliamentary position by copying a fascist device: they changed the electoral law so that an electoral alliance gaining just over half of the popular vote would obtain an almost two-thirds majority of the seats in parliament. The communist and Socialists bitterly attacked the 'swindle law'.

But the new electoral law did not help the Christian Democrat centrist coalition in the elections of June 1953, because they just failed to gain 50 per cent of the popular vote. Since they therefore had to rely on the votes of the right, the governments from 1953 to 1958 had difficulty in maintaining their reforming policies, though some progress was made, particularly the adoption of a ten-year development plan designed to reduce unemployment in the more backward regions of Italy through increasing investment. But for most of the decade the centrist coalitions were locked in a domestic stalemate, concerned with keeping their clients happy. Thus the Christian Democrats in the south

worked with the Mafia and the landlords and also tried to assist the peasants; while in the north-east, the Christian Democrats appealed to workers and industrial leaders. The main political principle was not to represent a cohesive ideology but to amass as much support as possible from whatever source.

There was movement politically on the left too. The communist and Nenni Socialist alliance fell slowly apart under the impact of events in the Soviet empire following Stalin's death in 1953. Khrushchev's denunciation of Stalin's crimes in February 1956 shocked the socialists, but the invasion of Hungary in November of the same year was even worse for the image of communism. Though Togliatti declared the Italian Communist Party independent of the Kremlin leadership, he could not hold the socialists, who now accepted NATO, as well as the need for a multi-party state as a necessary safeguard against dictatorships of the Stalin variety. The Nenni Socialists nevertheless moved slowly; not until January 1959 did the Socialist Party Congress formally approve the break with the communists. Meanwhile, Amintore Fanfani, who was the dominant politician of the Christian Democrats in the late 1950s and 1960s, led the party away from the right–centre support which could no longer command a majority in parliament. The political crisis reached its climax in 1960, when for months no government capable of winning acceptance by the Chamber of Deputies could be formed. The choice for the Christian Democrats was between the fascists and the Socialists, the latter alignment bitterly opposed by the Vatican and the right wing of the Christian Democratic Party itself. But the Vatican's Italian politics were also changing under the influence of a reforming pope, John XXIII. Even so, not until December 1963, after further government crises, did Aldo Moro, Fanfani's successor, manage to form a coalition government which included Nenni's socialists.

The change to a Christian Democratic alignment with the small Socialist Party did not, however, lead to any lasting stability. The relationship was an uneasy one in the 1960s. The socialists feared that they would lose votes to parties standing to their left, especially the communists, if socialism was watered down too far and the new coalition did not pursue vigorous reform and economic planning. Fanfani had nationalised the electricity industry in 1962, as the price for socialist co-operation, but as far as planning and social reforms were concerned,

Moro, his successor, was cautious. He had in his own party, after all, a suspicious right wing to contend with. The key feature of the political landscape was the health of the economy. The extraordinary period of economic expansion had not come to an end, but it was certainly decelerating, just at a time when trade unions and workers had become far more strident in pressing their demands. During the previous fifteen years the industrial north had been transformed, and contributing to this transformation was the low cost of labour, the Italian worker having failed to gain any but small rises.

The Italian economy from 1945 to 1963 had been built on the back of low wages. The profits made by successful industrial expansion tended to be ploughed back, rather than distributed to shareholders or to the workers. This was made possible by two features of the Italian economy: there was a large labour pool from the south, which kept unemployment high and so weakened trade union bargaining power, though it is true that between 1946 and 1973 there was a net migration loss of 3 million people (7.1 million emigrated, 4.1 million immigrated); and there was no large group of shareholders to satisfy. Since the fascist years, the Italian state had indirectly controlled a large variety of industries through the IRI, a holding company for industrial reconstruction dating from the depression. The IRI controlled the banks, which in turn owned large holdings in engineering, steel, shipyards and armaments. After 1945, it also inaugurated public works programmes in the south, but its most important contribution between 1945 and 1955 was the modernisation of the steel industry, basic to the success of private industry, which was complemented and supported by the public sector. After a period of great inflation up to 1947, the Italian governments' fiscal policies produced price stability until the 1960s, which helped to create

*The Cinquecento rolls off Fiat's production line in Turin.*

the right conditions for industrial growth. State investment in housebuilding, transport, railways and motorways, television and telephones and agriculture fuelled that growth in the 1950s. Through another holding company the state also developed the huge gasfield in the Po valley, and a petrochemical industry grew up. Entry into the Common Market in 1957 as a founding member was good for exports, Italy's most efficient industrial sectors in private hands having been poised to take full advantage of the removal of tariffs. The most successful of Italy's industrial giants was Fiat. Other Italian manufacturers became household names throughout Western Europe: Olivetti, Pirelli, Snia Viscosa and, in chemicals, Montecatini; their dynamic managers made Italian cars, office machines, domestic appliances, rubber products, textiles and chemicals fully competitive with those of the rest of the world. The increase in Italian

**Italy's GNP Growth and Unemployment, 1951–1974** (*percentages*)

|  | 1951–8 | 1959–63 | 1964–5 | 1966–70 | 1972–5 |
|---|---|---|---|---|---|
| Growth of GNP | 5.0 | 6.3 | 3.2 | 6.0 | 1.6 |
| Unemployment | 7.0 | 5.0 | 3.0 | 5.6 | Northern Italy 2.5 (1972–6) Southern Italy 5.0 (1972–6) |

production from 1958 to 1963 reached a peak which came to be called the 'economic miracle'. But the growing prosperity of the north contrasted with continued stagnation in the south. The gulf of wealth and poverty between Italy's regions widened.

Industry's easy years of expansion, profits and high investments based on low wages came to an end in 1963. For the ordinary people, however, living standards continued rising in the 1960s; with low unemployment rates the unions recovered in strength. Wage rises now regularly outstripped productivity and the country began to suffer again from a high rate of inflation. Economic growth became erratic, the kind of stop–go policies familiar in Britain as balance-of-payment difficulties forced successive governments to tighten the economic reins in the mid-1960s. Nevertheless, the 1960s, when judged as a whole, still showed outstanding economic growth when compared with the rest of Western Europe. Italy held her own in the Common Market and in world competition, with substantial exports of cars, washing machines, refrigerators, typewriters, textiles, chemicals and consumer goods. A flair for design, good marketing and managerial skills kept the best of Italian industries abreast with the best in Europe. Where Italy began to lose out was in the new, less labour-intensive technological industries of the third industrial revolution. Italians were in danger of being overtaken unless a programme of modernisation was instituted. Like Britain, Italy fell behind the world competition in the 1970s. The south remained backward, with

employment and wages much worse than in the north, although successive governments made large-scale investments. Public development funds and regional reforms consistently failed to produce the hoped-for results.

The years 1968 and 1969 mark a watershed between two decades of stability and steady growth and a period of social, economic and political impasse, conflicts and crises. Nineteen-sixty-eight was the year of student revolt, when youth challenged attitudes and authority all over Western Europe. The new generation in their twenties and thirties were no longer content with what had been achieved since the end of the war: their standard of comparison was not with the depression of the 1930s or the miseries of war and defeat. They had grown up during the steady but not stirring days of reconstruction, when for the ordinary people life was unexciting. Their expectations went far beyond what was being provided. The political leadership from left to right had followed the road of compromise and bargain, while the young activists had utopian visions of social revolution and regeneration. The shining example of democracy and prosperity, the United States, was cast in the role of barbaric aggressor in Vietnam. The disillusionment was as exaggerated as the earlier admiration had been, and riots broke out in the cities. While the froth on the surface of these exciting events soon blew away, in Italy 1968 had a long-term impact on industrial relations and economic growth (Chapter 83).

# PART XII

*Who Will Liberate the Third World? 1954–1968*

# CHAPTER 58

# Who Will Liberate the Third World? Laos and Vietnam 1954–1961

The fragile stability achieved after the Korean War armistice (1953) and the Geneva settlements of the Indo-Chinese question (1954) did not last long. With the rise of Khrushchev, the Soviet Union was pursuing a much more dynamic and aggressive policy in regions from which her influence had previously been almost wholly excluded. She had backed Nasser's Egypt in the Middle East; she had sought to offset American economic pressure by purchasing Cuba's principal export, sugar; in civil war in the recently independent Belgian Congo (now Zaire) she supported the left-wing leader Lumumba (and so began meddling in Africa); in Europe relations were uncertain still over the issue of divided Germany and in particular over the future of Berlin. In south-east Asia after the defeat of the French by Ho Chi-minh and General Giap in the summer of 1954, there appeared to be a chance of a negotiated solution. The Geneva Conference of that year had resulted in a number of agreements and compromises. The fighting was ended, and Vietnam was divided close to the 17th parallel, with the North Vietnamese controlling what became the Democratic Republic of Vietnam, recognised by the communist states; in the south arose the anti-communist Republic of Vietnam. Vietnam, it was proposed, would be unified again following elections in July 1956. In Laos, which was not divided, the communist Pathet Lao had made far less progress, though they were granted *de facto* control of the two northern provinces. The French undertook to withdraw their

forces from Laos and Vietnam, and no foreign troops were to enter those countries or to establish bases there; excluded from this provision were a specified number of military advisers – thus a small French mission continued for a time in South Vietnam and Laos.

The two crucial features of the Geneva Accords were thus that Vietnam and Laos were to remain unitary states whose future would be decided by elections, and that no foreign troops were permitted to assist North or South Vietnam. But from the start the prohibition against the introduction of foreign 'arms and munitions' (Article 4) was a dead letter. Eisenhower and Secretary of State Dulles regarded the Geneva Accords as appeasement of communism and a defeat for the free world. They dissociated themselves from the agreements but promised not to overturn them by force provided there was no aggression from the North. They also expressed doubts about the all-Vietnamese elections and insisted that they be held under the auspices of the United Nations. The South Vietnamese government, headed by the Catholic Ngo Dinh Diem, refused to sign any of the treaties but carried out the military truce conditions.

Eisenhower's conduct in 1954 marked another turning point in the tragic history of Vietnam – and of the United States' involvement in that tragedy, which led to extensive sacrifices in men, material and, a decade later, social cohesion. What Eisenhower and Dulles refused to accept was that no firm line had been drawn against further communist expansion, further erosion of the Western position in south-east Asia, though they had no wish for the United States to replace colonial France or to exploit South Vietnam. A halt had been called in Europe and in Korea: now it appeared that the communists were poised to move south. Although eventually tragic in their consequences, the Eisenhower–Dulles reactions should not be judged as inhumane or dominated by simplistic ideology. Indeed, it was the communists who deserved their reputation for cruelty. In 1955 and 1956, thousands of Vietnamese 'traitors', French sympathisers and 'landlords', including many peasants, were killed by the communists in the North. The entire populations of Catholic villages fled from the North, and altogether nearly a million refugees headed south when the North Vietnamese state was established.

Not that Diem and his brother Ngo Dinh Nhu were paragons of democratic virtue in the South. They imprisoned opposition leaders, rejected any real land reforms to aid the peasantry and allowed corruption to run riot; even so their authoritarian rule did not compare with North Vietnamese atrocities during the first years after the new states' foundation. Uncertain of their outcome, Diem refused to participate in the Vietnamese elections scheduled for July 1956 under the Geneva Agreements. He knew that the North would be coerced to vote solidly in favour of the communists and that the opposition parties in the South would join them to form what might prove to be a majority. It was an election which would not be free whoever supervised it. Diem's control of voting in the South would be far less effective than the communist control in the North. That view was shared by Dulles and Eisenhower. It was Diem who refused to hold the elections, but he knew that the American administration was no keener to see them take place in 1956 and had advised on 'postponement' to soften the breach with Geneva.

Eisenhower and Dulles were prepared to accept the 17th parallel as marking the new boundary of the communist advance in south-east Asia. They did not encourage Diem to reconquer the North or even envisage such a conquest; equally they were not prepared to tolerate any communist encroachment on the territory of South Vietnam. They were also obliged to accept Diem's rule – there seemed no one else who could hold the country together. At first Diem appeared to be mastering the situation. The year 1956 passed and surprisingly, despite

North Vietnamese protests, there was no renewal of conflict between the North and the South. For this there were good reasons. Ho Chi-minh was ruthlessly consolidating communist power in the face of 'traitors', 'landlords' and peasants, while 'land reform' was accompanied by thousands of executions. In the south Diem likewise moved mercilessly against remnants of the North Vietnamese Vietminh, who had been left behind as a nucleus around whom a communist insurrection might be constructed. The South Vietnamese communists, the Vietcong, began organising in the countryside in 1957, planning the assassinations of Diem's village headmen and officials. But Ho Chi-minh was still holding back. Diem's authoritarian rule, his ruthlessness and his corruption aroused opposition not only among peasants but among all those groups excluded from power and from a share in the loot. The Vietcong assassinations soon made themselves felt, exciting deep unease throughout the country. Murder of government officials increased from 1200 in 1959 to 4000 a year by 1961. Diem's response was to drive the peasants into fortified hamlets, but this proved both ineffective and counter-productive, alienating the peasantry, who objected to being placed under military commanders and were anyway caught between Diem's reprisals during the day and the Vietcong at night. The US administration failed to appreciate that the Vietcong were not lackeys of the communists in the North but were an expanding and powerfully organised army of southern communists engaged in a guerrilla civil war. Clearly South Vietnamese stability was deteriorating, though Diem was still in control of the cities and much of the countryside of South Vietnam.

The position in neighbouring Laos by the close of the Eisenhower administration (January 1961) was more immediately critical. Ostensibly a kingdom whose unity was confirmed by the Geneva Agreements of 1954, Laos was torn by regional, tribal and factional strife. The communist Pathet Lao (Lao National Movement) were growing stronger in the north. Another army faction, which was anti-communist, was backed by the Americans. A third group, the so-called neutralists, tried to maintain at least the semblance of unity by constructing a coalition of all parties and factions, which would each be left in *de facto* control of the regions they held. That was most unwelcome to the Americans, since the communist regions of the country bordered on North and South Vietnam and so acted as a passage for supplies and men along the maze of jungle trails known as the Ho Chi-minh trail, by which it took two months to reach the South from the North. The Pathet Lao were also threatening to expand their influence into the strategic central Plain of Jars, controlling routes between the capital Vientiane, the royal palace at Luang Prabang and North Vietnam. This sparsely populated country of some 2.5 million bordered not only on North and South Vietnam, but also on China, Burma, Thailand and Cambodia, and so was a potential cockpit of struggle between more powerful neighbours.

In Washington, Laos appeared to hold the key to the defence of non-communist south-east Asia. The Eisenhower administration was therefore determined to maintain a Laotian government in power untrammelled by communist or neutralist coalition partners. In neighbouring Cambodia, Prince Sihanouk sustained a skilful balancing act between rival factions and no less adroitly maintained a precarious neutrality and unity from 1954 to 1970. That was also the aim of the most durable of the Laotian leaders, Prince Souvanna Phouma, who tried to establish a neutralist coalition with his brother, the red Prince Souphanouvong, who represented the Pathet Lao, and with the American-supported General Phoumi Nosavan. He succeeded for a time, but the US backing for Phoumi and for the Royal Laotian Army ruined any chances of a neutralist solution. As American penetration increased, so did North Vietnamese support for the Pathet Lao. But by 1961 the ineffectualness and weakness of General Phoumi had become painfully evident. With Soviet and North Vietnamese support, the communists threatened to take over the whole of Laos. Eisenhower's and Kennedy's hostility to the neutralist Souvanna Phouma had removed the one Laotian leader who, if only for a time, might have held the Pathet Lao in check.

SEATO, the south-east Asian collective defence treaty, organised by Dulles in September 1954, unlike NATO had no standing armies, nor had its signatories promised military support to each other. So, although it was extended to cover the defence of Cambodia and South Vietnam, it provided no guarantees of help and proved of limited value when the United States did appeal for military assistance. The Eisenhower administration also sent military advisers to South Vietnam and to Laos, yet the Laotian Royal Army never became an effective fighting force capable of dealing with the guerrilla tactics of the Pathet Lao. The influx of Americans and dollars, moreover, corrupted and undermined the South Vietnamese and the Laotians. American advisers, in any case, suffered from one disability they could not overcome: they were foreigners, white outsiders. The Pathet Lao and the Vietcong, for all the violence and disorder they brought to their fellow countrymen, were their own people. An enormous amount of financial aid was poured into south-east Asia; most of it went to the military or lined the pockets of corrupt officials. What the pattern of military aid reveals are the priorities of the United States in south-east Asia from the mid-1950s to the mid-1960s. By far the largest amount of aid as calculated per head of population was sent to Laos and South Vietnam during the decade from 1955 to 1963. About half that amount per head went to Cambodia and the Philippines. Thailand also received substantial aid whereas in comparison, Indonesia, Burma and Malaysia were granted very little assistance.

Eisenhower was committing technical, financial and military aid to enable the anti-communist forces in south-east Asia to defend themselves against the communists. But he was opposed to using US military forces on the Asian mainland (except in South Korea). The mighty US Seventh Fleet with its nuclear weapons was close by. What if the nuclear threat did not deter the Pathet Lao or the Vietminh, while supplies continued to reach them from China and the Soviet Union? What if, despite US aid, the anti-communist groups were too weak to resist effectively? That dilemma Eisenhower bequeathed to his successors.

# CHAPTER 59

---

## *America's Mission in the World: The Kennedy Years*

In November 1960 the Democratic Senator from Massachusetts won the US presidential election, defeating the Republican contender Vice-President Richard Nixon by the narrowest of margins. Despite fourteen years in Congress, John F. Kennedy had no detailed grasp of the international situation, only general attitudes to world problems: the futility of European colonialism, the need to stand up to communism and to the Soviet Union, the attractions of issuing a call to the American people to inspire them for the noble mission of leading the free world. Kennedy's electoral theme, that if elected he would get American moving again, was clothed in stirring rhetoric reminiscent of Roosevelt's early New Deal days. His own theme was the 'New Frontier'. But detail and concrete undertakings on the serious issues facing the United States, especially at home, were lacking. That such vagueness overtook the presidential campaign was hardly surprising if Kennedy was to have any chance of beating Nixon. Issues of civil rights and social reform did not divide Republicans from Democrats, but cut across party lines. Those Republicans who supported civil rights voted in significant numbers for the Democratic ticket; the majority of the white Democrats in the Southern states, on the other hand, would not all support Kennedy. But many Southern Democrats regarded the vice-presidential candidate, the Texan Lyndon Johnson, as a conservative, and this helped Kennedy to retain the Southern Democratic vote in eight crucial states, including Texas. The margins were narrow; indeed, without Texas and Illinois, where the legendary political boss Mayor Richard Daley of Chicago was able to marshal the multi-ethnic vote – black, Polish and German – Kennedy would have lost.

The Democrats had to court the votes of minorities: African-Americans, Jews and the disadvantaged of all ethnic origins. Kennedy also had to overcome the widespread prejudice against a Catholic president. So there was not one constituency of Democratic voters, but many separate groups. Apart from seeking to awaken in the country an appetite for progress after the mild recession and the Eisenhower years of slow reform, Kennedy turned to the political safety and easy appeal of outdoing Eisenhower and Nixon as guardian of the free world. He attacked their record over Cuba; he would be tougher. And he discovered an issue which threw the Republicans on to the defensive, the supposed 'missile gap' between the Russians and the Americans. That the notion of such a gap, greatly boosted by Khrushchev's boasts, turned out to be a myth in no way lessened its potency in 1960. In the famous television debates watched by some 70 million Americans, Nixon and Kennedy confronted each other. Kennedy looked fresh and youthful, Nixon sardonic, cynical, even shifty, his dark jowl insufficiently concealed by make-up. Nixon attempted to contrast his own long experience in government with Kennedy's inexperience, but his defence of the Eisenhower record did not sound very inspiring and Kennedy edged ahead to victory.

Kennedy personified in looks and vigour the youthful drive of a new generation, and he and his wife Jacqueline brought a new eloquence and easy-going manners to Washington. The handicaps arising out of the injury to his back sustained when the torpedo boat he commanded was sunk in the Second World War were played down. He needed constant painkilling injections and daily doses of cortisone to restore him to something approaching normal health, although he continued to suffer from the progressive anaemia of Addison's disease. Nevertheless he was a prodigiously hard-working president who aroused the loyalty and affection of his close supporters and advisers in the White House. More importantly, the Washington press corps was largely on his side. This was just as well, because Kennedy had another characteristic he wanted hushed up – his promiscuity.

Middle America before the permissiveness endemic later in the 1960s, would have been shocked by Kennedy's insatiable appetite for new sexual partners, in and out of the White House. His marriage was inevitably placed under extreme strain, and his liaisons with beautiful women even brought him into contact with the underworld. After his death, many women claimed to have been his mistress, but, as one of his genuine lovers commented, if all who said that Jack Kennedy had made love to them had been telling the truth, he would not have had the strength to lift a cup of tea.

In his domestic policies Kennedy was hardly audacious. He appointed Keynesians as his economic aides, but also invited a conservative financier, Douglas Dillon, to be secretary of the treasury. Kennedy was aware that his majority in the country was small and that Congress was in no mood to pass extensive measures involving large public expenditure. Federal aid was provided in selected depressed regions where unemployment was especially high. Increased government expenditure on defence and a liberalisation of social security benefits provided a stimulus to the economy, but it was anyway on a cyclical upswing in the summer of 1961. In 1962 there followed a Trade Expansion Act to reduce tariffs, but Congress – with which he had an unhappy relationship – severely cut Kennedy's proposed public works programme. Nor were his relations with big business helped when he put pressure on the United States Steel Corporation to rescind a price increase. This provoked a

severe collapse of share prices on the Stock Exchange. In 1962 Kennedy pressed forward with more resolution on issues of social reform. He wanted 'Medicare' to be granted to retired workers over sixty-five, funded by social security, but the powerful medical lobby, objecting to 'socialised medicine', and a Congress worried about the likely cost defeated the measure.

In 1963 with employment remaining high (5.5 per cent) by the standards of that period of full employment, Kennedy boldly proposed a substantial cut in income tax, only for Congress to hold the measure up. Before the tragically premature end of his presidency, Kennedy had achieved little in the way of giving assistance to the more deprived sections of American society, but his focus on housing aid, education and medical provision pointed to a future when all these programmes would be enacted. The one glaring omission was civil rights legislation. But on this explosive question Kennedy could not postpone decisive action by instituting modest and well-intentioned changes by presidential executive orders. The battle for black equality was reaching a pitch so intense that all America became involved (pages 511–13).

Kennedy felt more drawn to global issues, the great questions of war and peace and America's relations with the rest of the world. In the struggle with communism, the free world seemed to be entering a new and dangerous phase. Berlin, Cuba and Indo-China lay at the heart of the 'unfinished business' left over from the Eisenhower administration, and all three issues came to the boil within the first six months of 1961. A speech by Khrushchev on 6 January 1961, declaring that the Soviet Union would support what he called 'national liberation movements' in the under-developed countries, turned Kennedy's attention to Third World issues. The ideological subtleties of Khrushchev's phrase, which aroused bitter debate among communists about what exactly he meant, were not fully grasped in Washington, though the growing rift between the USSR and China was no secret.

In the White House, Khrushchev's statement was interpreted as a challenge: that the communist world would back insurgency in countries which so far had resisted communist takeovers. It was a paradox that, though the West appreciated the significance of nationalism and those other elements which determined international and domestic conflicts, communism was still viewed as a monolithic and undifferentiated threat to the free world.

Kennedy surrounded himself at the White House with some of the best brains in the country, charged with helping him to formulate an effective counter to the threat of a continuing advance by communism, especially in the Third World. He decided that the United States did not have to balance her budget slavishly, as Eisenhower had tried to do, and that a boost to public expenditure in the spirit of Keynesian orthodoxy would help to get the sluggish economy moving, cut unemployment and expand trade, profits and incomes, so generating more money for the administration to spend. Kennedy, though cautious about creating large budget deficits, believed that the United States did not lack the necessary resources to undertake all that was necessary for her security and for her position as the leader of the free world. The military budget was immediately increased. The Secretary of Defence, Robert McNamara, with his experience of running the giant Ford Motor Company, was to apply the latest business techniques to ensure the most effective application of funds, both in respect of procurement and to identify the right policies to be pursued. Another adviser was Walt Rostow, an economics professor who had studied the stages of economic growth of particular importance to under-developed countries. Dean Rusk was Secretary of State, and for personal military advice

Kennedy turned to General Maxwell Taylor. Returning from a fact-finding mission to South Vietnam, Rusk and Taylor both advocated increasing the American commitment there. For Kennedy, the crucial question was how much. The military situation had not yet deteriorated to the point where a massive infusion of American troops seemed to be essential. Nevertheless it was already under discussion.

April 1961 was a critical month for the White House. Cuba, Vietnam and Laos simultaneously became the focus of crisis management. On 19 April the invasion by American-backed Cuban exiles of their homeland had ignominiously failed in the Bay of Pigs (page 590); the following day Kennedy ordered a review of what military, political and economic action – overt and covert – it would be necessary for the United States to undertake to prevent the communist domination of South Vietnam. On the 26th the American position in neighbouring Laos seemed on the brink of disaster. There was wild talk by the military of air strikes against North Vietnam and southern China. On 29 April US troop deployments to Thailand and South Vietnam were discussed within the administration. Kennedy kept his nerve. Alerts went out to American bases, a modest 100-man increase in the nearly 700-strong American advisory mission in South Vietnam was approved and, early in May, approval for the despatch of a further 400 Special

*Back to South-East Asia.* Left: *captured Vietcong soldiers are led to an uncertain fate.* Right: *who will liberate the Third World? Kennedy faces the press, 1961.*

Forces troops was given. Extra military resources were provided, enabling the Vietnamese army to be expanded from 150,000 to 170,000 troops. Finally US troops were stationed in Thailand.

Later that same May the panic in the White House over Laos subsided. America's threatening posture seemed to have been effective in restraining the Chinese and North Vietnamese. Khrushchev, too, had been alarmed and wanted to quieten things down. The White House's primary concern was once again Vietnam.

Doubts had surfaced about the strong man of South Vietnam, Ngo Dinh Diem. He and his brother Ngo Dinh Nhu, and his formidable sister-in-law Madame Nhu, were heading a government pervaded by corruption, and internal opposition was growing; the lack of morale among the South Vietnamese army was also only too evident. Might not American training, advice and leadership be the best way to stiffen their resolve? But this would entail a considerable increase to the US military presence in South Vietnam. By the autumn of 1961 General Taylor had recommended to the President the despatch of 8000 US combat soldiers; in a memorandum the Joint Chiefs of Staff had estimated that 40,000 US troops would 'clean up the Vietcong threat' and that if the North Vietnamese and Chinese intervened another 128,000 would be sufficient to repel them. The idea of punishing North Vietnamese intervention and discouraging further incursions by bombing North Vietnam had also been raised. All these were proposals to Americanise the conflict in Vietnam. Vice-President Johnson had already provided the justification for this after returning from a fact-finding mission the previous spring: he had advised the President that the battle against communism had to be taken up in south-east Asia or the United States would lose the Pacific and have to defend her own shores. But, even faced with such exaggerated catastrophe scenarios, Kennedy resisted sending substantial numbers of US servicemen. He was sceptical whether a few thousand US troops would make the crucial difference to the military situation. Nevertheless, by October 1963, shortly before his assassination, his administration had already sent more than 16,000 men to South Vietnam. The Geneva Agreements (page 407) were dead, as the United States responded militarily to increasing Vietcong activity in the South.

More important than the numbers, which were

*Ngo Dinh Diem, President of South Vietnam.*

small compared with Johnson's eventual decision to fight an all-out war employing almost half a million US combat troops, was the commitment the US made to South Vietnam during the Kennedy presidency and the decisions that were taken about the basic strategy needed to prevent South Vietnam from falling to the communists. Kennedy had expressed doubts at times about the intrinsic importance of Vietnam; on other occasions he subscribed to the notion that her loss would entail the loss of southern Asia.

Although Kennedy frequently showed a better sense of proportion than some of his advisers about the dangers of escalation following the despatch of US troops, he never departed from his policy of increasing the US commitment as much as he judged necessary to defeat the Vietcong. His reasoning was political and global: political because after agreeing to the neutralising of Laos (page 590) and the Cuban Bay of Pigs disaster, he could not afford to seem in retreat again; global because he accepted what he interpreted as the communist challenge to the free world, which had now shifted to a struggle for the Third World. He ignored the advice he received from General de Gaulle in the summer of 1961 not to get bogged down in an interminable war in Indo-China as the French had been and he was undeterred by the refusal of his principal ally, Britain, to join the US military effort, as she had once done to halt communist aggression in Korea. Vietnam became America's fight, with relatively little help from America's Pacific allies, Thailand, South Korea, Australia and the Philippines. It was the kind of struggle, moreover, for which the Eisenhower military doctrine of meeting any communist aggression with massive nuclear retaliation against Moscow or Beijing was extraordinarily ill suited, as Eisenhower had already discovered in Laos.

The new military concept suitable for Third World struggles with communism was worked out mainly by Rostow, General Taylor and McNamara. At the heart of it was the notion of flexible response. Insurgency and guerrilla tactics would be met by counter-insurgency and specially trained units – the Green Berets. The Vietcong would be sought out and destroyed in their hideouts in the countryside and jungles. Combat troops would meet the enemy troops in just sufficient strength to defeat them. This would enable the United States to resist force by counter-force in situations and over conflicts which in themselves could not possibly be regarded as important enough to risk the destruction of the United States in a nuclear exchange with the Soviet Union. Only in defence of Western Europe and over the question of Berlin did the United States threaten to use nuclear missiles. But even this determination was doubted by de Gaulle, who developed France's own nuclear missile capacity, and by the British, who though they later decided to rely on American missiles sold to Britain, also maintained their own national deterrent.

In Vietnam, Kennedy's acceptance of the doctrine of flexible response meant that the United States would be drawn into an ever increasing commitment. This was foreseen by intelligence reports reaching Washington which pointed out that neither bombing the North nor increasing the level of American combat troops in Vietnam would dissuade the North from matching every increase. The United States would be setting out on a war of attrition without any foreseeable end. Or rather it would be ended first by the United States, when the American people and Congress came to say no to

any further resources, any further loss of American lives.

Kennedy himself at one time asked what was so important about Vietnam, and Secretary of State Dean Rusk, more of a hawk than a dove, wondered how the Americans could win a war in South Vietnam which the South Vietnamese themselves were mishandling and even losing. For Kennedy the struggle was not about Vietnam alone but about American leadership, about the perception of America's determination to defend the free world, whatever the cost. This was America's mission in the world. In his election campaign, in his inaugural and subsequent addresses to the American people, Kennedy exhorted America to live up to her ideals. But this exhortation to play a world role had its dangers. In his televised debate with Nixon, Kennedy declaimed, 'In the election of 1860, Abraham Lincoln said the question was whether this nation could exist half slave or half free. In the election of 1960 ... the question is whether the world will exist half slave or half free,' rhetoric which raised American expectations to such a pitch and so over-emphasised US power that withdrawal or defeat anywhere in the world ceased to be acceptable. The US presidency thus became the victim of its own projection of America invincible, of America the righter of moral wrongs anywhere in the world (provided they were perpetrated by communists). If Americans could reach the moon, they would surely be able to defeat a second-class, Third World country. The prospective disillusionment of the American people should it turn out that they had been misled, and that defeat in war had to be accepted, haunted successive presidents. Indeed, the gap between expectation and reality was to shatter the next three presidents: Johnson over Vietnam, Nixon over Watergate and Carter over the American hostages in Iran.

Kennedy was fortunate that he did not have to face the consequences of America's early involvement in Vietnam. While brilliant men and their theories pushed him forward, his own steadier judgement held him back. He was inclined to ambivalence, first going along with the advice of experts, but then cautiously scaling their recommendations down. The application of this ambivalence to his dealings with Cuba led to a humiliating defeat, an early personal disaster puncturing his electoral rhetoric.

*

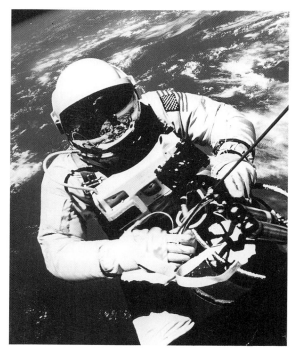

*The New Frontier. US astronaut Edward White taking mankind's first space walk, June 1956.*

The Eisenhower administration had bequeathed the 'unfinished business' of Cuba to the incoming President and his advisers. Not only had Castro nationalised American businesses and taken over the US oil refineries but his country's links with the Soviet Union were becoming closer. By 1962 he had turned Cuba into a one-party communist state. But, even as he accepted Soviet help, Castro was at heart a Latin American nationalist, unwilling simply to become a Russian pawn in the Cold War.

The problem Kennedy faced was whether to tolerate the continued presence of Castro or to follow through plans initiated by Eisenhower to use Cuban exiles trained in Guatemala for an invasion of the island to overthrow its leader. Kennedy was urged by some advisers to go ahead with the invasion and to provide it with air support. He was told that many Cubans on the island were only waiting to be rallied against Castro. Others, including the sagacious Senator Fulbright, warned the President against foreign adventures. Kennedy struck a hopeless middle course, permitting the invasion of Cuba to proceed while trying to disguise American involvement. He accordingly limited the air support

*Not the way these Cuban exiles expected to return – after the Bay of Pigs crisis, April 1961.*

to exiled pilots flying American-procured planes and refused to sanction any direct US participation in the air or on land.

The Bay of Pigs landing, launched on 17 April 1961 by the Cuban exiles, became for the administration and for the President personally a humiliating fiasco. At least Kennedy kept his head when on 18 and 19 April 1961 the exiles were pinned down by Castro's troops on the beach. By then it was becoming clear that the invasion was failing and that only US intervention could retrieve it. Khrushchev, to rub salt into the wound, declared that the Soviet Union would defend Cuba, but Kennedy did not raise the ante further. The Cuban exiles were left to their fate; more than a thousand survivors were rounded up and imprisoned by Castro.

Kennedy did not try to evade personal responsibility. He tried all the harder now to retrieve America's good name by pushing ahead with the Alliance for Progress, which he had already proclaimed in March 1961. This represented the positive side of US policy, an effort to transform Latin America, to solve its serious social and political problems, eradicating destitution over the next decade and so heading off communist revolutions. Covert action against Cuba meanwhile took dark and bizarre forms, with the Central Intelligence Agency hatching various plots to assassinate Castro by such ingenious devices as a poisoned cigar or dropping pills into his drink. In October 1962 Cuba would be in the news again in the most serious Cold War crisis since the Berlin blockade of 1948–9.

The Alliance for Progress was the positive aspect of America's world mission. It promised $20 billion of US aid for development, which was to be matched by $80 billion from Latin American sources over the next decade. The lever of US partnership and of financial and technical assistance was intended not only to develop Latin American trade and production so that the growth of wealth would outpace the growth of population, but also to bring about basic political and democratic constitutional change and desperately necessary agrarian reform. Latin America would be turned from the path of revolution to one of evolution and human betterment. The threatened advance of authoritarian socialism provided the spur, as it had done in Europe, where it had prompted Marshall Aid, yet the presence of a genuinely humanitarian motivation should not be overlooked. Although the Alliance

created some spectacular developments, it failed in its basic purpose of transforming Latin America socially and politically. It worsened rather than narrowed the gap between the rich and poor, as funds were channelled to large enterprises already owned by foreign corporations or by wealthy indigenous elites. Authoritarian rulers further misappropriated large amounts of money. Vested interests naturally resisted any transfer of their wealth and power to the poor, and when faced with a choice of supporting them or allowing them to fall in the face of radical socialist revolutions, the United States provided them with military aid. This strengthened military leaders and so weakened further the prospects for democracy. Raised expectations came up against corruption and repression. Latin America was thus heading for further instability and violent revolution, and not for the 'peaceful revolution' Kennedy had envisaged (Part XIV).

Kennedy's failure in Cuba did not seem to diminish his appeal at home. A Gallup poll taken soon after the Bay of Pigs showed his popularity soaring to an unprecedented 83 per cent approval rating. The American people rallied to their president, but this support even in the face of a fiasco showed something more significant: that they trusted their administration and were looking for strong leadership, for government to get things done and to solve the nation's manifold problems.

Kennedy was not at ease when he met Khrushchev in Vienna during the summer of 1961. It was to be a low-key meeting, each leader gauging the mettle of the other. Kennedy had Laos on his mind. Khrushchev wanted to restrain the North Vietnamese and Chinese in order not to provoke strong US reactions. For reasons of their own the Chinese were also ready to take a longer-term view and this made possible the convening of a second Geneva Conference in May 1961, which after fourteen months of tedious negotiations agreed in July 1962 to 'neutralise' Laos, with a coalition of all parties in a royal government presided over by Prince Souvanna Phouma. It was papering over the cracks. None of the parties concerned in Laos or outside had actually abandoned their ambitions to dominate the country.

Another crisis loomed over the status of West Berlin. The West's determination to maintain its position in the city deep in the Soviet orbit had become a powerful symbol of resistance to any attempted Russian encroachments by force or diplomacy. Khrushchev's threat to sign a peace treaty with the German Democratic Republic the Soviets had created, thus handing over control of access to a communist regime which the West refused to recognise, was an unacceptable solution as far as the NATO powers, including the United States, were concerned. But Khrushchev could create such a crisis by ostensibly giving up Soviet responsibility for the air and land routes and handing these to the DDR. At their Vienna meeting on 3 and 4 June 1961, Kennedy made it clear that the West would resist by all means at its disposal any unilateral Soviet moves and warned Khrushchev against 'miscalculation'. The two leaders also clashed on the issue of the Third World.

Unknown to the West, Khrushchev had his own problems with his Kremlin colleagues in the Praesidium. No Soviet leader after Stalin's death had enjoyed the old dictator's undisputed power. For the time being Khrushchev was accepted as *primus inter pares*, but Soviet leadership was ultimately a collective affair. There were hardliners dissatisfied with Khrushchev's efforts to achieve detente. Others criticised his erratic course and his oppor-

tunism. The ideologues wanted to pursue a 'pure' Marxism–Leninism believing that the revolutionary cause could be led only by the proletariat. Khrushchev was more of a realist, ready to take advantage of developments that weakened the West and which in the longer term would further the Soviet Union's global interests. In the Stalin era Third World communist parties had been instructed to take up the revolutionary struggle not only against the colonial imperialists, but also against the 'national-bourgeois lackeys'. But the anti-colonial struggle in the Third World was fiercely nationalist, led and supported by an indigenous, educated middle class, rather than by peasants or workers. While Third World radicals included active groups who believed in the need for socialist or even communist transformations of society and in centrally planned economies to break existing feudal elites, they were not in favour of exchanging a dependency on the West for a dependency on the East. The nationalists were in any case broad coalitions united only by a wish to get rid of their country's colonial status. In Egypt, they were led by army officers; elsewhere they were led by civilian revolutionaries.

Khrushchev had thrown Russian support behind President Nasser of Egypt in 1955. The Soviet

*Kennedy, Khrushchev and Soviet Foreign Minister Andrei Gromyko. This meeting in Vienna in June 1961 led Khrushchev to underestimate the US President.*

Union began to dispense her own financial and military aid programme to win friends and influence nations. It was on a smaller scale than the American programme, but was carefully applied where it seemed to serve Russian interests best. Egypt and India received most aid; regionally, the Middle East was given priority, relatively little going to Latin America; the sums devoted to military aid were more than twice as large as those earmarked for economic credits. Despite the views of the purists, Khrushchev was prepared to back anti-colonial movements, even if they included bourgeois elements. This is what he meant when he offered to help 'national liberation movements'.

At Vienna, Khrushchev reaffirmed his support for 'national liberation' struggles, accusing the United States of representing the *status quo* and of intervening to support it. Kennedy countered with the argument that the balance of power between the communist and non-communist worlds should be preserved. There was thus no meeting of minds. Kennedy returned to the United States and in July that year increased the defence budget and the strength of the armed forces.

Khrushchev chose another method of breaking the Berlin deadlock, which was also an infraction of treaty agreements, but did not threaten Western rights in West Berlin. Walter Ulbricht, the East German communist leader, had been pressing for effective action to stop the ever increasing flow of East German citizens across the open Berlin frontier to the West. The flow of refugees had reached such proportions that the stability of the East German state was endangered. On 13 August 1961, barbed wire was erected along the frontier right across Berlin, later replaced by the Wall, complete with armed guard towers. East Berlin and the German Democratic Republic were turned into a gigantic prison. The West protested but did not attempt to remove the Wall by force. It was another compromise, but one that was regarded as ending the Berlin crisis. As the eventful year of 1961 drew to its close,

*In a bizarre tug-of-war, a 77-year-old East Berliner is the prize for which two East German policemen and a West German youth are competing, in 1961.*

the conclusion of a Soviet peace treaty with the DDR was once more postponed; no date was now set for its conclusion.

Khrushchev's world policies had brought the Soviet Union few concrete benefits. The dispute with China was growing; over Berlin, Khrushchev had had to abandon his stand; and even the success of Soviet missile development was clearly being overtaken by the dynamic policies of the Kennedy administration. Khrushchev badly needed a dramatic coup, or at least the appearance of one. That need probably inspired the bold Soviet initiative that was to lead to the Cuban missile crisis.

# CHAPTER 60

# On the Brink of a Nuclear Holocaust: The Cuban Missile Crisis, October 1962

On Wednesday, 24 October 1962, some 500 miles from the shores of Cuba, two Soviet merchant vessels, the *Gagarin* and *Komiles*, escorted by Soviet submarines, were heading for the Caribbean island. At 10.15 a.m. precisely they encountered patrolling US warships. The *Essex* had orders to sink the Soviet submarine escorts if they should refuse to surface when challenged. Two days earlier President Kennedy had proclaimed a naval blockade of Cuba after the discovery of Soviet missile sites on the island. On the United States mainland, aircraft armed with nuclear weapons were on maximum alert. Special strike forces were readied for an invasion of Cuba. The world held its breath. Was civilised life on the brink of destruction, on the threshold of a nuclear holocaust? What if the White House or the Kremlin in this dreadful trial of strength miscalculated?

That Wednesday morning the Soviet ships halted. At 10.15 the news was flashed to the White House. Secretary of State Dean Rusk, with evident relief, drew his own conclusion: 'We're eyeball to eyeball, and I think the other fellow just blinked.' People all over the world, anxiously watching their television sets, were no less relieved: the dramatic crisis was over. Actually it was not. The really serious danger of conflict occurred three days later. On Saturday, 27 October Kennedy only just drew back from ordering an air strike on the Cuban missile sites, to be followed by an invasion of the island. But when on Sunday morning, 28 October, the White House received the news from Moscow that Khrushchev had agreed to withdraw the missiles, the crisis really was over.

The nuclear confrontation of the two super-powers had been genuine enough. But how close had the world really come to the brink of a third world war? Kennedy and his advisers in the White House and Khrushchev in the Kremlin acted in the knowledge that one false step could lead to a nuclear exchange and the end of civilisation. The strains on the two men were enormous. The drama was intense but appearances did not always reflect realities. The conflict was not exactly what the public thought it was about. By placing intermediate and intercontinental missiles with nuclear warheads just ninety miles off the coast of Florida, the Soviet Union would have given the impression that the military threat to the United States had significantly increased. It was actually more a question of propaganda and prestige, of positioning in the global Cold War. The conflict turned on the Russian claim to an equal place in the world, to the right to compete with the United States for influence anywhere in the Third World, in regions of Asia not under communist control, and in Latin America. The mere existence of Castro's Cuba was, from an American point of view, a breach of the Monroe Doctrine. After the humiliation of the Bay of Pigs in the previous year, to accept tacitly the establishment of a Soviet military base on the island was unthinkable. It would raise doubts whether the United States, when faced with an ultimate show-down, would have the toughness to meet resolutely and effectively such a communist challenge. If the United States failed on her own doorstep, what reliance could there be placed on American readiness to defend Western interests in Europe or the Middle East or Asia? That is how the thinking ran in Washington during the autumn of 1962.

Yet in the political and international sense, the confrontation certainly was for real. For Kennedy, another defeat over Cuba would have been calamitous domestically to his standing as president. His opponents would have gone to town, charging him with being soft on communism. The stakes were high and Kennedy was fully aware of the implications.

From a purely military point of view Kennedy agreed with his Secretary of Defence Robert McNamara that missiles placed in Cuba did *not* significantly add to a Soviet threat. Just a few months earlier, in March 1962, he had concluded that there was not much difference between missiles stationed in the American hemisphere and those positioned 5000 miles away. During the October crisis later that year McNamara applied cold logic in analysing what the effect of having missiles in Cuba would be. Should the Soviets fire their limited number of Cuban missiles first, they would reach the United States *before* any missiles from the Soviet Union and so act as a warning, leading to massive retaliation by the United States, with her 1685 nuclear warheads obliterating much of the Soviet Union. The injury to the USSR would be megatimes greater than the injury that forty-two Cuban-based nuclear weapons could inflict on the United States. What McNamara did not know was that only a handful of Soviet intercontinental missiles were operational, so that forty-odd Cuban-based missiles would more than double Russia's still puny (compared to the US) nuclear capacity. Nonetheless, Kennedy's and McNamara's analysis would have held true for the future. In October 1962 Kennedy played on the anxieties of the American people about this 'new' nuclear threat to win their support for his initial strong response to Khrushchev's opening gambit.

Kennedy had not been too greatly alarmed by Soviet support for Castro before September 1962. This did not mean he was soft on communism or prepared to tolerate a communist state in the Western hemisphere. In fact, the overthrow of Castro became an obsession. The ill-advised and in the end ineffectual policies pursued before and after the Cuban missile crisis were revealed only

when Central Intelligence Agency documents were published in 1975 by the US Senate under the title *Alleged Assassination Plots Involving Foreign Leaders.* A counter-insurgency expert, General Edward Lansdale, had been instructed by Kennedy to recommend actions which would lead to Castro's overthrow. In December 1961 with the backing of the President and his brother Robert Kennedy, the Attorney-General, Operation Mongoose was launched. The orders read, 'No time, money, effort – or manpower is to be spared. We are at war with Cuba.' With assassination seen as a legitimate option, the CIA hatched plots to 'knock off Castro'. Every effort was made to isolate Cuba politically and economically; sabotage teams infiltrated the island early in 1962 to destroy strategic targets, including bridges and vital communications, oil refineries and sugar mills; there was even a plan to poison turkeys. Another crazy scheme, never carried out, was to 'incapacitate' with poisonous chemicals the farmers collecting the sugar harvest, or alternatively to poison the sugar being sent to Russia in order to provoke a breach between the Soviet Union and Cuba. Intelligence was collected.

The objective of all this was to create havoc and dissatisfaction in Cuba and so to incite a popular uprising. Consideration was given to the possibility that a revolt could then be supported by American armed forces, to avoid another Bay of Pigs fiasco. The results of so much activity were disappointing. Early in October 1962, a few days before the missile crisis, Robert Kennedy passed on new instructions from the President to escalate Mongoose, to increase the number of sabotage missions – results had to be achieved. That Castro should in the face of so much hostility have become paranoid himself is, therefore, understandable. He appealed to Moscow for help, believing an American invasion to be imminent. Khrushchev responded by supplying arms and missiles. Publicly he declared that the Monroe Doctrine had 'died a natural death'.

Little thought had been given in Washington to the likely reaction in the Kremlin to the threats against Cuba. Khrushchev was a curious mixture of dreamer and realist, cunning, trusting in his own abilities and his superior gamesmanship, ready to gamble on the inferior capacity of his opponent to respond. The United States, he had concluded in the spring of 1962, was becoming too self-confident and arrogant, and needed to be checked. Robert McNamara and other members of the administration had been openly boasting of America's growing superiority in nuclear strength and her ability to deliver it and crush the Soviet Union. Even worse, President Kennedy, in an interview reported in the *Saturday Evening Post* in March 1962, had referred to the possibility that circumstances could arise which might lead to a US first strike against the Soviet Union. Khrushchev knew that the Soviet Union was indeed hopelessly inferior in nuclear missile strength, that she was ringed by nuclear bases from Turkey to Western Europe and that American superiority placed him in a poor bargaining position over Berlin and other areas of conflict. Bluff was his answer. The Soviet Union would act like a superpower until she could catch up. Khrushchev had boasted that the march of communism in the world could not be stopped. Cuba was a test. The Soviet Union must be seen to stand by her only ally in the Americas. 'Coexistence' did not mean softness, as Mao was claiming.

During April and May 1962 Khrushchev conceived of a 'brilliant' counter-move. He would move missiles into Cuba. They would act as a deterrent, protect Cuba from invasion and help to even up the balance of power. Khrushchev rejected the misgivings of Foreign Minister Gromyko and the wily old Armenian Bolshevik Mikoyan and went ahead with the plan. He was playing for high stakes, at home and internationally.

Liberalisation in Moscow and the open access to US archives make it possible to reconstruct what went on in the White House and the Kremlin during the crisis. That the Soviet Union in 1962 was engaged in arming Cuba was no secret. The ships carrying missiles in their holds and under tarpaulins could not be made invisible on the high seas. The high-flying U-2 planes were able to spy on the island and photograph with great accuracy and detail what was going on. On 29 August a spy plane took pictures of Soviet technicians constructing a SAM (surface-to-air missile) launching pad. Four days later, Washington being a leaky place, a Republican Senator raised the possibility that the Soviets might be stationing in Cuba short-range and intermediate missiles with a maximum range of 2500 miles. That would enable them to reach Washington, New York and other US cities. Both Houses of Congress now passed resolutions authorising military intervention should that prove necessary. Kennedy had to do something, even though SAM missiles were clearly defensive, but he did not wish to provoke a crisis

needlessly. He and most of his advisers did not think it at all likely that Khrushchev would be foolhardy enough to introduce offensive nuclear missiles. Still, public apprehension and the demand for action required a weighty pronouncement. It came on 12 September. Kennedy held a news conference and declared that the United States would do 'whatever must be done' to protect her security and that of her allies if any offensive base was established by the Soviet Union in the Western hemisphere.

A crisis now became inevitable. How far Kennedy had changed his mind about the military significance of Soviet missiles in Cuba is not clear. What is certain is that the political fallout in the United States would have been devastating had the administration just tacitly accepted a Soviet missile base in Cuba. Kennedy's mistake had been to trust Khrushchev. Now the warning came too late. Khrushchev had already sent the missiles. There seemed to be no way out. Khrushchev, in his ignorance of the US political climate, had grossly miscalculated the likely reaction of the President. With the presidential elections looming, Khrushchev thought that Kennedy would hide the fact that missile bases were being constructed in Cuba if he found out about them. Such a cover-up was possible in the Soviet Union but not in the United States, where political opponents and a free press could not be silenced.

Kennedy could not afford another defeat over Cuba. He had allowed the Russians to send large quantities of military equipment to Cuba after the Bay of Pigs and could do little to counter Khrushchev's boast of defending Cuba. But he could not allow his position to be publicly undermined any further. He could not, of course, reveal his own secret plans to get rid of Castro; Operation Mongoose would have given the lie to assertions that he was soft on communism, but public knowledge would have caused an international outcry.

During the crisis itself credit must go to Kennedy for keeping options open and for not reacting in haste. He received much conflicting advice. Even his brother Robert Kennedy, the Attorney-General, had swung from hawkish to dovish moods during the crisis days. Most of the military advice was for getting on with the job and striking at Cuba; the military were chafing at the bit. Perhaps in the end there was one good thing that came out of the previous year's Bay of Pigs disaster: Kennedy was not going to be pushed again and his innate

CHERRY PICKER

LAUNCH PAD WITH ERECTOR

LAUNCH PAD WITH ERECTOR

MISSILE READY BLDGS

OXIDIZER VEHICLES

FUELING VEHICLES

*Superpower Conflict Looms.* Above: *an American reconnaissance photo of a Cuban ballistic missile-base taken from a U2 spy-plane.* Below: *the US destroyer* Vesole *intercepts a Russian freighter which is leaving Cuba, carrying missiles, November 1962.*

conservatism and caution prevailed. After the crisis was past, he showed commendable restraint in not trying to exult over his worsting of the Russians.

The drama of the days of crisis and confrontation can now be briefly told. On 14 October 1962, a U-2 spy plane took photographs of possible missile construction sites. Interpretation of these photographs was not easy, but assistance was received from an unlikely source, from Oleg Penkovsky, a Soviet spy then in Moscow, who was passing information to Western intelligence services. (He was later caught and executed by the Russians.) The President was first shown the photographs the following day, on the morning of 15 October. They provided incontrovertible evidence, he was told, that the Russians were constructing offensive missile bases. That was the start of the emergency; the White House, where suspicions had been aroused, was nevertheless surprised by the incontrovertible facts. Taken unawares were the US experts on the USSR on whose advice Kennedy had relied. Indeed before September, Washington's worries had been focused on Soviet threats against West Berlin rather than Cuba; in the previous year Washington had even feared it might be faced with having to abandon Berlin to the Russians or go to war.

The thirteen days of crisis which followed the discovery of the sites were punctuated by intense debates among the inner circle of advisers. They were constituted as the Executive Committee of the National Security Council, or Ex. Comm. for short. From the first meeting on 16 October until the end of the crisis the assumption was that the United States would get the missiles out of Cuba by diplomacy or force, whatever the risk. Throughout those tense days there were continuing rounds of freewheeling discussion: all possible options were examined. These ranged from what was referred to as a 'surgical air strike' against the missile sites to proposals for a naval blockade, an air strike on the missile bases and an all-out invasion of Cuba. The military favoured an air strike on the missile bases. Robert Kennedy, who also at first had suggested creating a pretext for attacking Cuba, later opposed this option; he then likened such a surprise raid to the sneak Japanese attack on Pearl Harbor in 1941.

Yet Kennedy and his advisers felt themselves to be under inexorable pressure of time. A decision would have to be reached. If allowed to continue undisturbed, US intelligence calculated, the Russians would complete the installation of the missiles and be able to arm them with nuclear warheads in fourteen days. In the end a majority of Ex. Comm. favoured the naval blockade as a first step. The final decision could be made only by the President. On 21 October Kennedy came down in favour of the blockade option. Up to this point the proof of the installation of missiles had been kept a secret in Washington, as had the discussions in the White House about how best to deal with it. The missiles would soon be ready for firing: decisions had to be reached. No one in Washington knew whether they were equipped with nuclear warheads, but it was thought safer to presume that some warheads had already reached Cuba. In fact, Soviet archives later revealed that some twenty nuclear warheads were on the island but under exclusive Soviet control. Khrushchev did not allow Castro to have his finger on the trigger.

On the next day, 22 October, the President delivered a sombre television broadcast to the American people at 7 p.m. He announced his decision to impose a blockade around Cuba as an *initial* step and coupled it with the demand that the missiles had to be removed. He also explicitly warned the Russians not to attempt a counter-move against West Berlin. The broadcast was very dramatic. He warned that Soviet nuclear missiles and bombers based on Cuba were 'an explicit threat to the peace and security of all the Americas', and added that the Soviet Union had no need of missile sites outside the Soviet Union. Finally, he accused the Soviet leaders of deliberate lying when they had assured him that no offensive weapons would be based on Cuba. That they had been lying was true. The missile threat, however, was exaggerated. No wonder the American people felt threatened when maps appeared with arcs showing that missiles launched in Cuba could reach most of the United States. The Soviet gamble was presented as pointing a dagger to the heart of America. It was a time for everyone to rally to the President. Kennedy's first counter-move was the naval blockade. This less aggressive option was in line with the advice given by the British Ambassador in Washington, David Ormsby-Gore, a close friend of the Kennedys. Ormsby-Gore, moreover, contributed the suggestion that the line of blockade be set up not 800 miles, but 500 miles from Cuba, so as to give the Kremlin more time for reflection. Thus the die was cast. US forces, including B-52 bombers armed with nuclear weapons, were put on alert. How would the Russians react now?

On 24 October, as has already been related, two Soviet ships reached the blockade and halted. During the next five days, oil tankers and 'inoffensive' Soviet vessels were allowed through. The crisis, however, was far from over. The missile sites in Cuba were still being feverishly prepared. Kennedy insisted that they should be dismantled. A new crisis loomed. Soviet intentions were dangerously unclear in Washington.

The missiles had been placed in Cuba according to the classic deterrent theory: they would deter and not lead to actual combat. Khrushchev's determination to defend Cuba was real; like Castro, he expected the Americans to invade unless effectively deterred. But in the last resort deterrence was bluff. The missiles would not have been fired. The defence of Cuba was not worth the destruction of the USSR. According to the recollections of former Soviet officers, Khrushchev had been so hard-pressed by the military at the time that in the end he had consented to allow the Soviet commander in Cuba to use the missiles against an invading US force. But such claims are not very reliable.

On 25 October at the United Nations Adlai Stevenson worsted the Soviet delegate with dramatic proof of Russia's deception, and television pictures of the UN confrontation were shown all over the Western world. The following day, the possibility of a deal was first suggested by the Soviet side. Alexander Fomin, counsellor at the Soviet Embassy but, according to US intelligence resources, in reality a KGB colonel, asked John Scali, a journalist, to lunch with him at the Occidental, a restaurant close to the White House whose well-known advertisement ran, 'where statesmen dine'. The agent outlined the deal: if the United States undertook not to invade Cuba now or later, then the Russian missiles would be removed. When Secretary of State Rusk was told, he accompanied Scali to the White House to inform the President. That same afternoon a long rambling letter from Khrushchev, confused but friendly in tone, reached the White House. The most important passages suggested that the Soviet Union would not carry arms to Cuba if the President would give an assurance that the United States would not attack Cuba. It was much vaguer than Fomin's proposal, but it likewise seemed to indicate the beginnings of a deal. Scali was instructed to meet Fomin again and to

assure him that the United States saw possibilities in the deal but that there was little time left. To the present day we do not know whether Fomin was acting on his own initiative, but in Washington his proposal was regarded as emanating from the Kremlin. It lent more substance to Khrushchev's own vague proposals.

The following day, Saturday, 27 October, another letter was received from Khrushchev, sharper and more definite. This time he undertook to remove the offensive missiles from Cuba, but he added that to emphasise equality he required the removal of American missiles from Turkey. It was a face-saving device and nothing illustrates the military unreality better than the fact that the US regarded the old Jupiter missiles in Turkey as useless anyway and had wanted to remove them in 1961. But now they could not openly agree without appearing to give Khrushchev a justification for sending missiles to Cuba.

As Kennedy and his advisers were debating how to react to Khrushchev's two letters, the news reached the White House that a U-2 plane over Cuba had been shot down by a surface-to-air missile, killing the pilot. The atmosphere entirely changed. It was mistakenly assumed that this was a deliberate Soviet escalation. In fact, the Soviet commanders in Cuba had acted on their own initiative and were severely reprimanded. The US Chiefs of Staff, who had been urging stronger action than a naval blockade, now pressed for an air strike and the launching of an invasion. Kennedy too asked how U-2 planes could any longer be sent to observe what was going on if the pilots' lives were thereby exposed to danger. 'We are now in an entirely new ball game.'

The final escalation of the crisis appears to have been prompted by the kind of accident Kennedy had always feared could lead to fatal miscalculation. Another U-2 plane had accidentally strayed into Soviet airspace over Siberia and had been damaged by a missile (it made it back to its base in the United States). But the next 'accident' might prove more serious and the chances of it happening would increase the longer the crisis lasted.

It is significant that Khrushchev avoided making any obvious military preparations in the Soviet Union, though no doubt the Soviet Defence Ministry took secret precautions. Khrushchev was anxious not to raise the temperature further. The news that the American U-2 plane had been shot down over Cuba had as big an impact in the Kremlin as in the White House. Khrushchev rightly feared that the confrontation could slip out of his and Kennedy's control. It was probably at this point that Khrushchev decided that the crisis was now too dangerous and made the decision to withdraw the missile threat if he could secure a *quid pro quo*, the defence of Cuba.

In the White House, meanwhile, Kennedy only just pulled back from ordering immediate armed action against Cuba and the Soviet installations. Everything was to be thought through again and another message conveyed to the Kremlin. Kennedy was rightly convinced that the Russians did not want to fight any more than the Americans. The President asked his brother to arrange an immediate meeting with the Soviet Ambassador, Anatoly Dobrynin. Dobrynin hastened to the Justice Department within half an hour of receiving the telephone call. Though Robert Kennedy later denied it, the message he gave the Ambassador was practically an ultimatum. He told Dobrynin that by the following day, Sunday, the Soviet Union would have to agree to remove the bases and missiles or the United States would remove them. That was the stick. The carrot was that the Jupiter missiles would be removed from Turkey later, but not under Soviet threat. On the suggestion of McGeorge Bundy, national security adviser, no reply was sent to Khrushchev's second message; it was simply ignored. Instead the proposal contained in the first was accepted: if the Soviets removed their missiles, the United States would undertake not to invade Cuba. These represented the maximum concessions the President was willing to make.

That same Saturday evening, after Robert Kennedy returned to the White House, there was considerable gloom. Would Khrushchev yield? The President ordered the military to be ready to invade Cuba. The decision about an air strike was to be reviewed on Sunday. As everyone dispersed that Saturday night they wondered whether they would wake to a peaceful morning. In Moscow Khrushchev was spending Saturday night in his dacha. Kennedy's reply reached him there on Sunday morning, 28 October. He summoned the Praesidium, which agreed to issue a positive response to the broadcast immediately, since every minute's delay was considered to be dangerous. Later that morning, the State Department received the message over Radio Moscow that Khrushchev had

accepted the US proposals. The 'offensive' missiles would be removed under UN supervision in exchange for the American undertaking not to invade Cuba – to which Khrushchev had added: nor any other nation of the western hemisphere.

Kennedy's response was conciliatory. He praised the Soviet leader's 'statesmanlike decision', but would not help him to save face by making public the US promise to remove the American missiles from Turkey. The missile crisis was over. But tension lingered on for some weeks. The Americans were also demanding the removal of Soviet bombers. The Russians gave way on that issue only late in November. Castro, who had not been consulted, was in a rage. Feeling that he had been used, a pawn in the American–Soviet confrontation, he called Khrushchev a son of a bitch, Mao Zedong stepped in to increase his rancour. Castro refused to co-operate with the detailed procedures for removing the missiles, but the Russians honoured their undertaking to remove them. Kennedy then lifted the quarantine of Cuba and, exploiting Castro's lack of co-operation, watered down the United States commitment not to invade Cuba by writing to Khrushchev, 'there need be no fear of any invasion of Cuba *while matters take their present favourable course*; (italics added). No treaty was ever concluded between the Soviet Union and the United States formally setting out what had been agreed, but both countries have for the last three decades acted as if there had been one.

What then was the significance of the Cuban missile crisis? What were the lessons drawn from it by contemporaries and what assessment can be made with hindsight? The memoir literature of participants and the outpouring of academic work reveal a wide variety of views. Broadly speaking, the almost wholly favourable view of Kennedy's handling was popularised by his brother in his book *Thirteen Days*, the theme of which is that Kennedy's flexible responses and careful handling won for the United States all her essential interests, forcing the Russians to pull back from challenging the United States in the western hemisphere, and convincing them that the United States had the courage to stand up to nuclear blackmail. This positive assessment has been challenged by Republicans and revisionist historians. Nixon in 1964 blamed Kennedy for having 'pulled defeat out of the jaws of victory'. In other words, Kennedy had the opportunity to call the Soviet bluff and to overthrow

Castro; instead, Castro became secure. Kennedy had in fact appeased. At the other end of the spectrum a number of historians have criticised the unnecessary escalation of the crisis, because the missile threat had not really been heightened by missiles or Soviet bombers in Cuba.

The romantic Camelot representation of Kennedy was not sustained in later years. There is much that can be criticised in the handling by the United States of relations with Cuba. Operation Mongoose was misconceived and a failure. But to Kennedy's credit a close analysis of the crisis itself does not support the charge that he tried to enhance his macho image. The evidence indicates a cautious president weighing up all the possible consequences of every move. What would have happened had Cuba been invaded? In the nuclear age to take a step that carries even a small risk of indescribable destruction is unacceptable. And what would the consequences of an invasion have been for the United States? US intelligence reports had greatly underestimated the strength of the Cuban forces and of their Soviet allies. Casualties would have been heavy and guerrilla resistance could have been continued for years. The times were past when a US-backed Cuban government could have functioned without trouble. Instead Kennedy had avoided driving Khrushchev into a corner from which there was no escape, and the world was able to breathe a sigh of relief that the leaders in the Kremlin had proved, not fanatical ideologues, but rational pragmatists.

Had Khrushchev's move succeeded in 1962, the nuclear balance would not, in the short term, have shifted significantly in Russia's favour. The United States in the 1960s remained in a position of overwhelming nuclear superiority. But the creation of a Soviet base with nuclear-armed missiles and bombers close to the United States would have been seen as a Soviet advance into the western hemisphere and would have supported Khrushchev's boast that the Monroe Doctrine was dead. Although there was much criticism among NATO allies of America's failure to consult adequately during the crisis, had she hesitated to accept so direct a challenge to what she regarded as her own vital interests (even though there were many who criticised the current US interpretation of the Monroe Doctrine), doubts would have been raised about her readiness to defend Western Europe in the face of a Russian threat with nuclear weapons out of fear that this could have led to a nuclear attack on the United States.

As we now know, Kennedy did not always retain his cool judgement during the crisis, and his nerves were at times stretched taut, but he always regained his balance in time. He did not jump to hasty conclusions, did not surround himself with men who would tell him only what he wanted to hear. On the contrary he encouraged free discussion of all the different points of view, an exploration of every option, while reserving to himself the final decision. His handling of his colleagues was skilful, as he took care to extract every piece of information that might be important in his decision-making. He did not allow himself to be rushed into over-reaction. While it is true that the roots of the crisis must be attributed to Washington's handling of Castro from 1959, the immediate cause was Khrushchev's decision to challenge US dominance in the Caribbean. Had he succeeded in that challenge, what would he have tried next? He would certainly have been encouraged to 'rectify' Soviet weaknesses elsewhere, for instance in Berlin.

The crisis was followed by a reassessment of nuclear-war theories. McNamara became a convert to the view that nuclear weapons could not be used in limited war; indeed they were not weapons that could be used at all except as a deterrent to starting a war; and so the doctrine of mutual assured destruction (MAD) was developed. According to this theory, peace between the Western and Eastern alliances could be preserved provided each side knew that it could not knock out the arsenal of an opponent's nuclear missiles in a first strike; in other words, a sufficient number of missiles would survive a hostile first strike and would be used in a counter-attack to destroy the opponent's country. An important lesson learnt from the crisis was that the 'game' approach to handling international relations was far too dangerous in the nuclear age.

There clearly was an enormous risk in allowing any crisis to escalate to the point the Cuban missile crisis had reached. Such confrontations had to be dealt with and resolved at a much earlier stage. Rusk's 'they blinked first' conclusion is more appropriate to the era of the Hollywood western than to a nuclear showdown. One significant result of the crisis was the establishment of a 'hot line' between the Kremlin and the White House in 1963 in an effort to avoid any future possibility of miscalculation. It was not

*Kennedy signs the Test Ban Treaty in Washington on 5 August 1963.*

actually a telephone link but a simple teleprinter. This was later improved and by 1983 maps and other data could be rapidly transmitted.

The two superpowers had discovered common interests. The most important was that 'surprises' were exceedingly dangerous in the nuclear age. There was also an urgent need to prevent more and more nations from acquiring the capacity to make their own nuclear weapons: control should be retained in the hands of the superpowers. Two agreements were concluded in the next five years, designed to inhibit development by other nations. In August 1963 the 'limited' Test Ban Treaty was signed. This forbade testing in the atmosphere, in outer space and underwater; but, because the Soviet Union and the United States wanted to develop *their* weapons further, testing underground was permitted. That was one serious flaw; another was that no nation could be forced to join. France and China continued to test their weapons in the atmosphere. The second treaty which was expected to be more significant, was the agreement on the non-proliferation of nuclear weapons, signed on 1 July 1968. This bound its signatories not to

transfer their nuclear weapons to non-nuclear nations nor to help them to manufacture their own weapons. The Soviet Union had already recognised its common interests with the United States by withdrawing all assistance from China.

Just as important as the bombs were the missiles that delivered them. Britain was a third signatory to these treaties of the 'nuclear club'; she made her own hydrogen bombs but needed US missiles to deliver them. When Prime Minister Harold Macmillan and Kennedy met at Nassau in the Bahamas in December 1962, the Anglo-American special relationship was sufficiently intact for the US President, who held the avuncular Macmillan in high regard, to promise to provide the Polaris missile for British submarines. The Soviet Union and the United States, with Britain as a junior partner, thus tried to provide a lead, performing a policeman's role, in preventing the spread of nuclear weapons, though at the same time they themselves were updating and increasing their own arsenals. The efforts to limit the spread of nuclear weapons in the world were doomed to failure.

The 1960s and 1970s ushered in an unprecedented nuclear-arms race between the Soviet Union and the United States. They trusted each other no more than before, despite their shared interest in making the world a less dangerous place by not placing control of nuclear weapons in the hands of other states. This did not prevent the Kremlin from stationing nuclear warheads and missiles under Soviet control in Poland and East Germany, any more than it prevented the United States and Britain from doing the same in West Germany and Italy. The US–Soviet detente of the 1960s and 1970s coincided not only with huge military expenditure but also with acute rivalry in the Third World.

The most uncomfortable truth learnt from the Cuban missile crisis was that the decision to inflict or not to inflict radiation poisoning on much of the world lay in the hands of potentially unpredictable leaders in Moscow and Washington. In both the democratic and the communist states, the crucial decision-making depended on a handful of men, on their judgement, stability and good sense as they operated behind closed doors. The US President informed the Western allies, even conferred with them, but in the end he made his own decision. The Kremlin is unlikely even to have consulted allies. It was comforting, however, that the West was evidently not dealing with fanatics of Hitler's kind. For the Kremlin leadership the mercurial temperament of Khrushchev posed too great a danger, and the risks he took during the missile crisis contributed to his fall in 1964.

Turning to United States policy in the hemisphere, her efforts to line up all Latin America against Cuba after the 'Bay of Pigs' fiasco had not been an unqualified success. Cuba was expelled from the Organisation of American States in February 1962, but the countries of Latin America refused to follow the United States in imposing a general trade embargo. Nor was the United States able to stop trade between her NATO allies and Cuba. Canada, for example, became an important exporter to and importer from Cuba. The loss of the US market for Cuba's sugar, her main export earner, threatened enormous dislocation until the Soviet Union filled the breach. Up to the 1990s, Castro became dependent on Soviet largesse to bolster Cuba's failing economy as well as on ill-advised loans from Western banks, which are unlikely to get their money back. Sabotage efforts directed from the US against vital Cuban targets, such as sugar mills, electric power stations and communications centres, continued until President Johnson ended them in April 1964. American policies deeply injured Cuba, but the objective of getting rid of Castro and his communist regime, at first through military and economic means and later by economic and diplomatic isolation, demonstrably failed. For the first time since 1898, Cuba's powerful neighbour no longer controlled the island's destiny.

Cuban national pride is one reason why Castro survived more than three decades. The redistribution of income in favour of the poor and from the cities to the agricultural regions gained him solid support among the peasantry. Better health care and education were genuine achievements of the revolution. The poor, during the early years, became ardent adherents of the revolution. But Cuba has suffered from the inefficiencies of her socialist policies and command economy. With the collapse of the Soviet Union, the future for the people of Cuba is grim. Castro controls the military and police, but how much longer will the ageing leader be able to maintain his authority? When change comes in Cuba, however, it will be brought about not by a Yankee invasion but by her own army and her own discontented masses.

\*

Once the immediate crisis was over in 1962, the rest of the world debated a new question: was it really safe to rely on the Soviet Union and the United States in relation to questions vital to the superpowers' own security and well-being? Indeed, would the United States and the Soviet Union, whatever they said, really risk a holocaust of their own peoples for the defence of others? Two nations, China and France, openly defied the superpowers and built up their own nuclear-missile forces. Neither accepted the policeman role of the USSR and the United States in the world; Mao sought to develop independent Asian policies, and de Gaulle to construct a European role while he denounced US dominance. Britain was punished for her pretensions and her 'subservience' to the United States by de Gaulle's veto of her application to join the European Common Market. But successive British governments have essentially followed de Gaulle's nuclear policy by insisting on the preservation of an independent nuclear-strike capacity, even though it has relied on US missiles. There was much national posturing, but NATO continued to be regarded as essential for Western defence.

In fact, only the Soviet Union was able to block nuclear proliferation – among her own Warsaw Pact allies. West Germany and Japan did not attempt to join the race. The spread of knowledge could not be prevented and the profit motive ensured that 'peaceful' nuclear reactors were exported from the advanced nations to the Second and Third World. Plutonium for weapons could be made by these reactors, as India demonstrated when she exploded a bomb in May 1974. West Germany has supplied reactors to Brazil, the US has supplied them to Egypt and Israel, France to South Africa, Iran, South Korea and Libya, Canada to the Argentine.

There is no certainty exactly how many countries, besides the core nuclear-weapon nations – the US, the USSR, Britain, France and China – are able to make their own weapons. Other nations include India, Pakistan, South Africa, Argentina, Brazil, Israel and, until the Gulf War, Iraq. Nuclear non-proliferation has proved a vain hope, and there are many fingers on the nuclear trigger now. The certainty that these terrible weapons cannot be used without risk of self-destruction has so far preserved the world. The shadow of a nuclear war set off by the US and the Soviet Union which dominated four decades was lifted as the twentieth century drew to a close.

# CHAPTER 61

# The Limits of Power:
# The United States during the 1960s

The 1960s were one of the most turbulent decades in American history. The United States fought a seemingly unwinnable war in Vietnam thousands of miles from home with young men in a largely conscripted army. Protests against war increased as ultimately more than half a million men were sent to Indo-China and as the brutality of the fighting became clear to Americans at home. It was furthermore a decade of unprecedented black protest and of an unusually violent backlash against political leaders, black and white. Three assassinations were especially shocking: of President Kennedy in 1963, of his brother Robert, a presidential contender, in 1968 and, shortly before, of Martin Luther King, the leading non-violent voice in the civil rights movement. The murders of the two Kennedy brothers were shown on television, reaching into practically every American home. Was the United States still governable?

In Dallas on 22 November 1963 a tragedy unfolded before the nation's eyes. The smiling President, his radiant wife beside him, was riding in a slow motorcade, waving to the crowds. When his car reached a point opposite a dreary office building, the Texas School Book Depository, shots rang out from an upstairs window. The President fell backwards; a bullet had passed through his head and throat.

Lee Harvey Oswald, an unbalanced twenty-four-year-old ex-marine attracted to communist causes and to the defence of Cuba, recently returned form the Soviet Union and with a Russian-born wife, had assassinated President Kennedy. The right in America accused the communists of an assassination plot; others from the left claimed that irreconcilable conservatives had plotted the murder of a popular and liberal president. There appeared to be awkward facts that did not sit with the conclusion that Lee Harvey Oswald had acted alone. In a bizarre scene, captured by the television cameras a few days later, Oswald was in turn slain by a nightclub owner before he could give evidence at his trial. Violence was again seen to be a strong undercurrent in American society. The Vice-President, Lyndon Johnson, who had been completely overshadowed by Kennedy, now stood in the limelight. Unelected to the office, he would have to see out the remaining fourteen months of the presidency.

Lyndon Johnson was the eldest son of a small farmer married to the daughter of a prosperous lawyer. He had climbed the political ladder the hard way, with much careful calculation, entering Washington politics in 1937 as a congressman who fervently admired Roosevelt. By the time he came to serve in the Senate, eventually becoming Senate Majority Leader in 1955, he had become much more conservative, reflecting the majority of his Texan electorate. His skill in managing the Senate, applying his persuasive powers to individual senators in what became known as the Johnson Treatment, earned him a reputation for effectiveness among Washington insiders. Johnson might

*Dallas, 22 November 1963, moments after Kennedy's assassination. People cried on the street.*

have echoed the words of Robert Louis Stevenson and declared that his politics were 'to change what we can, to better what we can . . .'. This meant reconciling reformers and those opposed to social change, persuading the more liberal legislators that half a loaf was better than none, and those who were more conservative that acceptance of some reform would avert the danger of more fundamental and undesirable change. But, as vice-president, Johnson had made little impact nationally; that all changed as he stood grim-faced next to Jackie Kennedy aboard Air Force One as he was sworn in as president.

Appearances proved deceptive. The Kennedy image and dynamism seemed to have died with the assassinated President as the older man, who had already suffered one heart attack, started his term of office with the words, 'Let us continue.' Johnson proved much more successful than Kennedy in gaining Congressional approval for the moderate measures already sent to Capitol Hill, where they had lain logjammed by the opposition of Congress. Bills for foreign aid, for wider access to college and university education, and for tax reductions to stimulate the economy all passed into law. Among the most significant legislative leftovers from the Kennedy administration but enacted under its successor was a bill concerning civil rights.

'Civil rights' meant, in effect, legislation to remove the discrimination and disabilities suffered by non-white Americans, the great majority of whom were black. Between 1950 and 1980 the total population of the United States increased from 152.3 million to 227.7 million. The majority of those Americans classified as 'non-white' were 'black', that is 15 million in 1950 and 26.6 million in 1980. The Hispanics from Puerto Rico (US citizens) and Latin America are the second-largest ethnic minority, numbering 14.6 million in 1980. The population from Asia also increased rapidly; joining the Chinese and Japanese immigrants of the late nineteenth century, there now came a large influx of Filipinos, Koreans and Vietnamese. But it was the blacks who led the civil rights protests with a success that influenced other ethnic minority movements.

*In the 1960s, the time for asserting the civil rights of black US citizens more forcibly had come. Above: the 'freedom riders' braved injury in 1961 to protest against segregation in the Deep South. Top: in Martin Luther King Jr, all Americans – regardless of colour – had a charismatic leader and a spokesman for humanity and justice. He is shown here in Baltimore, shortly after becoming the first black man to win the Nobel Peace Prize. Left: the impressive culmination for the campaign for civil rights was the march on Washington DC that took place on 28 August 1963. The demonstrators sought to persuade Congress to pass the civil rights legislation. From the steps of the Lincoln Memorial, Martin Luther King addressed the 200,000 present. His powerful oration – 'I have a dream . . . ' – and vision of racial equality inspired a nation.*

The decade from the early 1960s to the early 1970s became one of stark contrasts, the federal administration, Congress and the Supreme Court playing a leading role in supporting civil rights and intervening against the attempts by the Southern states to apply state laws to suppress black protest and demonstrations. At the same time the federal government sought to banish poverty through an expansion of social security entitlements and payments. It was thus a decade of reform not witnessed since Roosevelt's New Deal. But there was an important difference: unlike in the 1930s, in the 1960s the United States was riding an economic boom that seemed self-generating provided administrations just kept spending. The 1960s also saw a loosening of customary restraints, as a new generation made news by rejecting sexual furtiveness and taboos. But the liberal hope of integrating society, the blacks and the whites and the other ethnic minorities, of lessening the gulf between rich and poor, of establishing a consensus on America's mission to lead the free world, ended instead in bitter conflict and deep disillusionment.

At the close of the period a president facing impeachment left the White House in disgrace, Richard Nixon becoming the first president to resign his office. Officers of the respected Federal Bureau of Investigation, the incorruptible 'Untouchables' who had broken the gangsters of the 1930s, were now revealed as having infringed, under the leadership of J. Edgar Hoover, the civil liberties of American citizens. The Central Intelligence Agency had likewise become virtually a law unto itself, and the seamy side of Washington politics caused widespread disillusionment with the whole process of government.

Ten years earlier, in the South, the black protest movement of the 1960s gathered such force that it overwhelmed the efforts of Democrats, enjoying widespread support from their fellow whites, to 'keep the niggers in their place'. The enforced segregation of the black citizens and the humiliations to which they were daily exposed to remind them that they were 'inferior' racially – a system which was called apartheid in South Africa – was very much alive and well in the United States in the 1960s, and not only in the South. In the nation's capital, Washington, discrimination would prove a serious handicap to America's claims to lead the free world in newly independent Africa and elsewhere. 'Whites only' signs could still be seen prominently

posted in many eating places in the South. But thousands of black Americans would no longer accept this state of affairs.

Martin Luther King, a Baptist minister, had risen to prominence as one of the leaders of the mass protests in Montgomery, Alabama during the 1950s. The black churches were the one place blacks could gather in large numbers without being harassed by state laws used against demonstrations and black meetings. The blacks in Montgomery, inspired by King's doctrine of non-violent militant protest and unafraid of arrest and imprisonment, achieved two things by asserting their rights. The black protest movement gained self-confidence and a sense of its own strength; it also brought black protest in the South to national attention. In a decade when the new magic of television could carry pictures of police setting their dogs on unarmed protesters and could convey the determined mood of black people and their leaders into millions of American homes, it prompted localised black protests and brought sympathy and support from all over the country. The violence perpetrated by white Southerners on unarmed civil rights supporters shocked most Americans. Seeing and not just reading about it made a considerable difference.

In 1960 four young black students sat down at an 'all white' luncheon counter in a Woolworths in Greensboro, North Carolina. They were not served. Soon sit-ins spread everywhere. What was new was that the blacks were taking the initiative and not just waiting on Congress, the courts or the federal government to assert and protect their rights. Black and white segregation on buses travelling from state to state was already illegal; yet even this right had to be asserted, because many laws which in theory safeguarded blacks from discrimination were not being enforced. In 1961, northern blacks supported by whites attempted to travel through the Southern states by bus. These Freedom Riders, as they came to be called, many of them students, were set upon and brutally attacked in the South, and their buses were burnt. They were deliberately challenging the Kennedy administration to protect their rights. Robert Kennedy, the Attorney-General, eventually provided federal protection from mob violence but not from illegal arrest. He was hoping to reach acceptable compromises in the South when the time for such compromises was long past. The efforts of the administration were concentrated on civil rights legislation, above all to prevent the debarring of black votes by intimidation and by spurious literacy requirements in the Southern states. It was held up in Congress. In August 1963 Martin Luther King and other black leaders organised a great March on Washington of 200,000 blacks and whites, warning of a 'whirlwind of revolt' if racial injustices were not remedied. But the Kennedy administration had drawn the sting of this protest by identifying itself with the protesters.

Kennedy was undoubtedly persuaded of the moral rightness of the black cause, but, though he hated violence, he resented having the administration's hand forced by black militancy. He felt he could not act too far ahead of Congress or of white opinion in the South. The process of education was a gradual one – too gradual for the blacks. Kennedy's modest civil rights proposals were still held up in Congress on the day of his death. Johnson then speedily pushed them through with the help of Robert Kennedy, who carried on as Attorney-General. But violence continued against the blacks and the volunteers from the north who were exercising their rights to meet and protest. In Mississippi three black and two white civil rights workers were beaten to death.

The frustration of the blacks was aroused not merely by the hostility that prevented them from exercising their voting rights but by a whole range of discriminatory practices. Unemployment among blacks was three times as high as among whites; black schools were inferior to those of whites in the more prosperous suburbs. And they were not only black – they were also poor. Few blacks had overcome their disadvantages to rise to the middle class; few possessed the necessary education to better themselves. Equal opportunity, even where it existed in federal employment, was of little use to the majority of blacks without an improvement in their basic living conditions. In the slums of the big cities blacks lived in overcrowded, rat-infested ghettos. Crime was rife, the people demoralised. The high-minded oratory of love and passive resistance uttered by leaders such as Martin Luther King inspired many blacks to join in the stirring freedom-song 'We shall overcome'.

But other, more radical black leaders also won an increasing following. They did not call for brotherly love and integration with white society, a sharing of Christian values and materialist aspirations. The blacks were gaining their national freedom and their self-respect in Africa – why not in America too?

The appeal of these black leaders was to a sense of self-identification, 'black is beautiful', and a rejection of white values, among them the 'capitalist system' of oppression. In the north Malcolm X was preaching a heady mixture of protest, revolt and separate black nationhood. 'I see America through the eyes of the victim. I don't see any American dream – I see an American nightmare,' he declared. Then in February 1965 he was assassinated. Elijah Muhammad led a black religious movement, turning blacks from mainstream American religions to the Muslim faith, which had won many converts in Africa. To emphasise their separate identity his followers changed their names; the best known was the unbeaten world heavyweight boxing champion who adopted the name of Muhammad Ali. There were now many blacks for whom passive resistance was not enough. The Black Panthers armed themselves, ready to defend blacks with the gun. By the close of the 1960s, when federal laws had brought little change in the living conditions of the majority in the ghettos, the doctrine of separateness and violent protest – Black Power – had won over many new adherents.

The violence which exploded in New York's Harlem in 1964 was spontaneous rather than organised, but it spread through the ghettos from coast to coast in the next few years. The presence of white police, the symbol of white authority, could now spark a whole area of a city into an orgy of destruction. One of the worst city riots erupted in the black Watts community of Los Angeles in the summer of 1965. Indeed, summer after summer, when the heat made the overcrowded ghettos least bearable, violence would break out in cities all over America. In 1967 parts of Detroit and Newark were set alight; after the assassination of Martin Luther King in Memphis, Tennessee on 4 April 1968, there were riots in hundreds of towns across America. King's funeral brought white and black leaders briefly together in a show of unity and revulsion against the racist fanaticism which endangered the lives of all prominent blacks. But fundamental obstacles to racial reconciliation could not be suddenly removed. They exist still.

Desegregation made slow progress in education and job opportunities. With successive civil rights measures and increasing federal enforcement of these laws, spectacular progress was made, however, in one area – black voting rights. A cynic might observe that the blacks tended to vote Democrat, and it was Johnson's Democratic administration which had taken action. Nonetheless, the hold of the racist white politicians was broken. In 1952 only one in five of the Southern blacks had been able to register for the vote; by 1968 it was three out of five, the same proportion as white voters.

Blacks began to hold important city offices too. By 1977 seventy-six American cities had elected black mayors. Where the majority of blacks failed to make substantial inroads was in health-care, housing, income and economic power. The ghettos persisted. Almost three decades of protest and violence have not much changed the economic disadvantages of the majority of blacks in employment, especially of teenagers. By the end of the 1970s one in three blacks had incomes below the poverty line, and the position of young blacks and black women was made worse by the higher incidence of family breakdowns as many mothers with young children became dependent on welfare. But educational opportunities have given a minority of blacks middle-class incomes and status, perhaps as many as a third. The effect of this rise of a black middle class has been to divide black society. It has not made the ghettos less violent or better places to live in; indeed, some areas of New York City, with their burnt-down and dilapidated housing, began to look like the bombed cities of Europe in 1945.

But in the mid-1960s, violence at home was mirrored by violence abroad in far-off south-east Asia.

In 1964 the human and material costs of the war in Vietnam were still insignificant for Americans. Johnson saw no reason why the nation's growing wealth should not be simultaneously applied to assist South Vietnam abroad and to fund programmes at home ensuring the welfare of all of America's citizens. In November 1964 he won the presidential election by a landslide over a right-wing Republican, Barry Goldwater. But a significant conservative backlash had developed against the Democratic notions of reform through federal-led action. These 'radical conservatives' wanted a return to American self-reliance, less government and a much tougher war on communism. Their time was to come with the election of Ronald Reagan two decades later.

During his short first term in office Johnson had already established an outstanding record as a reformer who got things done; a tax-reduction bill and a civil rights bill had been approved by

Congress. In his first State of the Union message Johnson declared 'unconditional war' on the greatest national blemish – the poverty and destitution amid plenty of a large segment of American society. Between 1964 and 1967 the Johnson administration spent just over $6 billion on anti-poverty programmes, food stamps, job training, small business loans and community-action programmes to motivate the poor to help themselves. Even this huge sum proved to be too little, and federal aid did not always help the most needy. Certainly, poverty was not eradicated. That large enough tax revenues could be generated to help all the poor and that a huge state-directed programme would work without large sums being squandered or lining the wrong pockets turned out to be illusions.

Of course the aid was not all wasted. State education and college education received extensive support and improved both in quality and in the number of students benefiting. In its provision of a welfare and medical 'safety net' for the poor and elderly, the United States was far behind what was being provided in most West European countries, and had been since 1945. Even so, interest groups such as the American Medical Association protested against 'socialised medicine'. In 1965 Johnson secured the passage of the Medicare legislation; financed through tax and administered by the social security system, it provides for hospital and nursing-home care for the elderly. Medicaid made federal funds available to help the needy. Unfortunately medical costs through the years soon proved an almost bottomless pit. Between 1964 and 1968 Johnson, supported by a compliant Congress, provided the leadership that passed into law these Great Society programmes, which included the federal funding of urban renewal.

It is fashionable now to decry these social programmes and to label them as failures. The problems of poverty, of the lack of equal opportunities and so on were too deep and extensive to be eradicated by Johnson's Great Society programmes. But millions of Americans were helped, not least the elderly, and new educational opportunities have provided a ladder for social advancement. Nonetheless, the US government was only providing what was regarded as a matter of course in France and Britain in the 1960s and 1970s, and its state paternalism did not compare with that of prosperous Sweden. As entitlements to aid expanded over the next two decades in the United States, the total cost threatened to make social security insolvent. In the 1980s the Reagan administration began cutting back the Great Society programmes while increasing defence expenditure, so running up the largest budget deficits of any American administration (page 834).

During the early years of his presidency Johnson judged that American economic growth could fund the Great Society programmes without the need to increase taxation, which would have been politically unpopular. But in the course of 1966 opinion polls showed that support for him had dropped from 63 to 44 per cent. Why? The reasons are not far to seek: the black riots in the cities exposing the shortcomings of the Great Society, the tribulations of an economy beset by rising inflation, the shadow of the escalating war in Vietnam, and the President's apparent loss of interest in social reform as he grew more absorbed in his efforts to bring the war to a victorious conclusion. The 'silent majority' no doubt still regarded as unthinkable the possibility that the United States might not win a war, but the revolt against American involvement in Vietnam began to encourage an increasingly vociferous opposition, exasperated by the hollowness of repeated claims that victory was around the corner.

Meanwhile the brutality of the war in Vietnam was vividly portrayed on millions of television screens: the attacks on poor peasants, the burning of their huts, the heartlessness of combatants. Civil rights and Vietnam protests linked up – was this a black man's war? In 1967 Martin Luther King spoke out against Vietnam: 'This madness must cease.' How the Johnson administration came to lose all sense of proportion and direction has been minutely chronicled in published documents, such as the leaked Pentagon Papers. In September 1964, before any substantial US commitment had been made, Johnson had asked his advisers whether 'Vietnam was worth all this effort'. His scepticism was met with the unanimous response that the loss of South Vietnam would be followed in time by the loss of all south-east Asia. Johnson's error was his failure to question that false 'expert' judgement; by 'loss' in this context was meant the communist domination not only of South Vietnam but also of Malaya, Thailand, Laos, Cambodia and Indonesia, possibly even of the Philippines. Exactly how this could actually occur was never explained; it was just assumed. So South Vietnam became the Cold War

front-line state of Asia, as West Germany was in Europe – though the analogy was a false one. The whole of south-east Asia did not turn communist and the communists in Vietnam, Laos and Cambodia were later to be locked in struggles among themselves with rival communist Soviet and Chinese backing. None of this nationalist, inter-communist rivalry was anticipated in Washington.

In August 1964, in a controversial incident North Vietnamese torpedo boats attacked an American destroyer in the Gulf of Tonkin; despite US claims, it is not certain that the destroyer did not itself initiate or provoke hostilities. Two days later there was allegedly a second attack, though later there was doubt whether it occurred at all. But the significance of these incidents was the strong reaction in the United States. With the Gulf of Tonkin Resolution Congress granted Johnson the widest discretion to repel armed attack on US forces and 'to prevent further aggression'; furthermore the President was empowered to take all 'necessary steps, including the use of armed force' to assist any nation covered by the SEATO treaty that asked for assistance 'in defence of its freedom'. That blanket authorisation applied to South Vietnam. It meant the President could practically go to war in Vietnam without formally declaring war or seeking Congressional support for war. At the time Congress did not anticipate the consequences of the resolution, nor was American public opinion much excited by it. Nor indeed did Johnson in 1964 anticipate a large-scale US war effort. The Tonkin Resolution was simply intended to give him the discretion to punish the North Vietnamese, but it was nonetheless regarded as essential to bring stability to an independent and non-communist South Vietnam in order to counter Khrushchev's claim to have the right to support 'wars of national liberation'. Secretary McNamara had by now raised the 'domino theory' in justification for US involvement in Vietnam. Yet in August 1964 Vietnam was still seen by the public as no more than a minor problem: the United States would need only to flex her muscles for the communists to back down.

Seven months later, in the early spring of 1965, the punishment of the North Vietnamese was stepped up as US bombing raids against carefully defined military targets began. This was Operation Rolling Thunder, which was expected to bring victory without costly US losses. Airfields in South Vietnam which served as bases for these raids soon came under communist land attack. Inevitably escalation followed: in March 1965 US marines were sent to defend the US airbases; before long they came to be used not only in defence but in wider-ranging combat missions.

A consensus was reached by Johnson's advisers. The Vietcong could be defeated, and the North Vietnamese would be forced to negotiate once they realised they could not win. It was assumed that the pattern seen during the Korean War could be repeated and that the Vietcong without North Vietnamese backing amounted to no real threat. Robert McNamara's 'military option' was approved by everyone, not least by the Congressional leaders consulted. But approval was not quite universal: one man warned that, by increasing the numbers of US combat troops and the frequency of bombing raids, the United States still would not achieve her aim of stabilising a non-communist South Vietnam. The Under Secretary of State George Ball advised the President against military escalation. Johnson too was sceptical at first, asking if the North Vietnamese would not be able to match any American escalation. But in the end he was persuaded that America's standing throughout the world would suffer disastrously if the United States 'abdicated leadership' and showed irresolution; the communists would only continue their aggression. The fatal consequences of such appeasement had been demonstrated by Chamberlain at Munich in 1938. One general spoke of the need for 500,000 men and a conflict that would last five years. The President concluded that a combination of increasing military pressure on the ground and punishment from the air, provided it was coupled with peace offers, would force the North Vietnamese to call off the conflict and accept the existing division of Vietnam. The South would be saved for the free world.

The momentous decision to plan for a major war was taken in the White House in July 1965, after extensive discussion by the President and his closest advisers. There was no recognition that the South Vietnamese were fighting among themselves and that the North Vietnamese were also Vietnamese. Worst of all, by painting such a catastrophic scenario it seemed justifiable to avert it by virtually any means. From some 175,000 combat troops, American involvement by the end of 1967 had risen to 525,000. The North Vietnamese and Vietcong matched and outpaced the US build-up. The impact of this on Vietnam is described elsewhere (page 407), but victory over the communists proved as elusive as ever. General William Westmoreland, commanding US forces in South Vietnam, then called for further large reinforcements. But how much more would American public opinion take, with American casualties mounting daily? Throughout 1967 the assessment made by the military and intelligence services on the ground war was optimistic: American troops and their South Vietnamese allies were grinding down the enemy. This was the reassuring message given to the American people – with steadfast determination the war would be won.

Then followed a rude awakening. During the Vietnamese Tet holidays, on 31 January 1968, the Vietcong mounted a huge offensive, penetrating several towns in an attempt to destroy the morale of the South Vietnamese and Americans, who believed that their power was confined to the countryside. In the end the communists were bloodily repulsed, but the terrible scenes of fighting shown on American television screens convinced most Americans that US soldiers should be brought home. The ability of the communists to penetrate and even to hold their positions in a number of South Vietnamese towns hitherto believed to be firmly in South Vietnamese and American hands succeeded in undermining American morale in their longest and most unsuccessful war. The President's assurances that the Tet offensive was the most disastrous Vietcong defeat of the war were perfectly true, but they carried little conviction.

Nothing was coming right. The dropping of 1.2 million tons of bombs a year had not broken the determination nor destroyed the fighting capability of the North Vietnamese. All diplomatic efforts to bring them to the conference table through a carrot-and-stick approach of alternately halting and resuming the bombing had also so far proved fruitless. Nineteen-sixty-seven was supposed to have been the year of victory. But early in 1968, after the Tet offensive, Washington was forced to the awful conclusion that the United States could no longer win the war. Robert McNamara, one of the chief architects of the military response, had lost faith in the prospect of victory and on 1 March 1968 was replaced as Secretary of Defence by Clark Clifford. But the President was still resolute. The issue: should another 206,000 troops be sent to Vietnam, bringing numbers there to almost three-quarters of a million? Clifford and the President's advisers rejected the increase. The only hope now was that a continued war of attrition would break North Vietnam's will before American public opinion, shaken by the Tet casualties and the diminishing hopes for success, demanded withdrawal.

Demonstrations against the war grew apace in 1965. The young of the more privileged and better-educated social groups of the 1960s felt a new sense of liberation, a fresh vitality demanding that they challenge the assumptions of their elders. Protests and demonstrations erupted. In April 1965, 25,000 marched to the White House. In October a National Committee to end the war in Vietnam was formed. Early in the following year the highly respected Senator J. William Fulbright began public hearings to find out whether any national interest was served by the war. The contrast with public attitudes to the defeat of Japan and Germany in the Second World War or even to the Korean War could not have been greater. America was deeply split. Johnson still enjoyed the support of the majority, but a powerful opposition was forming. The most affected were the young men called up to register for the draft with the possibility of being sent to Vietnam. Before the war ended for American servicemen in 1974, 110,000 had burnt their draftcards and 40,000 young men had evaded call-up by leaving for neighbouring Canada and for Europe.

It was clear to Johnson by the spring of 1968 that the Americanisation of the war, the sending of more than half a million combat troops to Vietnam, had become insupportable. His political position at home had been severely eroded by the war. He was challenged by a 'peace candidate', Senator Eugene McCarthy, and also by Robert Kennedy, both seeking the Democratic nomination to run for the presidency in November that year. On 31 March 1968 Johnson announced his decision not to seek re-election; he also indicated that there would be a measure of disengagement from the war, reflecting the new consensus among his advisers, including former hawks. That at least freed his hands from the inevitable political infighting as the election loomed nearer and enabled him to concentrate on finding a viable alternative strategy in Vietnam. This took the form of rejecting any further build-up of US forces, and placing greater reliance on assisting the South Vietnamese army to bear more of the fighting.

That same March, Johnson announced a partial bombing halt and invited the North Vietnamese to begin peace talks. The response from Hanoi early in April was surprisingly positive. But hopes of an early peace quickly faded as the almost interminable negotiations in Paris followed a tortuous path from their commencement in May 1968 to their conclusion almost five years later in January 1973. Nevertheless March 1968 marks the time when the United States took the first step to disengage from Vietnam. It was left to Kissinger and Nixon to complete the process, to try somehow to save South Vietnam and bring the war to an 'honourable' end.

The presidential election of 1968 was overshadowed by tragedy. In the run-up on 5 June, while celebrating his victory in the Californian primary, the almost certain Democratic contender Robert Kennedy was assassinated in full view of the television cameras. Personalities do matter in history. With Eugene McCarthy now eliminated, the choice for Democratic candidate fell on an old liberal, the Vice-President Hubert Humphrey, whose association with Johnson's Vietnam policies had discredited him among many liberal supporters. In Chicago there were large demonstrations against his candidature, brutally dispersed by police. All this boded ill for Democratic prospects in November. The durable Republican candidate Richard Nixon won by a large majority of states, though the popular vote was only narrowly in his favour, 31.7 million to 31.2 million. What if Robert Kennedy had been the candidate instead? Nixon might well have lost to a Democratic candidate with the glamour of the Kennedy name. There would have been no Nixon era, with its startling international successes (such as the opening to China) and its spectacular domestic failure, the discrediting of the office of president by the Watergate scandal.

The 1970s proved for many Americans a troubled decade at home and a humiliating decade in the wider world. Johnson's dream of a new society and American leadership of the free world had been shattered by the experience of the Vietnam War, which comprehensively overshadowed the administration's achievements. What had led the American people and their leaders into an enterprise that turned out to be tragic for both Indo-China and the United States?

First and foremost it was ignorance, a failure to understand the true nature of the conflict in Vietnam, reducing it to the simple formula that it was part of the worldwide struggle between the free and the communists. But it was not a war arising simply out of communist aggression from North Vietnam. The Vietcong were a South Vietnamese force, the expression of a political opposition and disaffection with the rulers of South Vietnam. It was this misreading of the situation that underlay the US decision to intervene on a massive scale. The belief that superior technology, the bombardment from the air, could break the will and capacity to fight of the North Vietnamese and Vietcong caused heavy loss of life and terrible destruction, but in the end was ineffective. Nor could the ground forces defeat an enemy prepared to answer escalation with escalation. The military experts were wrong in their optimistic assessments, and once President Johnson had engaged American prestige he found it impossible to pull out and to admit defeat. But meanwhile the war had been Americanised and, after Tet, the propping up of an unviable South Vietnamese government became increasingly problematical. The United States had been sucked into a civil war and faced a determined and ruthless enemy. Attrition in the end broke the American will to continue fighting in a country thousands of miles away and for a cause that could not be won.

# PART XIII

*Two Faces of Asia: After 1949*

# CHAPTER 62

# Turmoil, War and Bloodshed in South-east Asia

During the colonial era the armed strength of the European nations had by and large subdued factional and national struggles in south-east Asia. The British tried to leave Asia in an orderly way. Even so the partition of India was accompanied by internal upheaval and great bloodshed, and the legacy of partition was two more wars between independent India and Pakistan. Seen in terms only of British interests, the Labour government had acted wisely in disentangling Britain from direct responsibility for the conflicts of southern Asia. The Dutch attempted to hold on too long to their empire. Even after they left in December 1949, they retained West New Guinea, to which Indonesia laid claim, though its mainly Stone Age peoples were not Indonesian. After years of conflict the Dutch gave way and the renamed West Irian was transferred to Indonesia by the United Nations in 1963. The French also tried to turn the clock back and to re-establish their pre-war colonial domination, fighting a bitter war with Indo-China until 1954. It is ironic that Britain, a victorious great power, was willing to reduce her imperial commitments, while the European nations defeated in the Second World War attempted to reassert their colonial power.

Tragically for the 330 million peoples (1989 figure) of south-east Asia, the departure of the Europeans did not produce a more peaceful era. In what had been French Indo-China, that is Laos, Cambodia and Vietnam, fighting continued for another twenty years and in the early 1990s Cambodia was painfully trying to find a peaceful compromise. The devastation and impoverishment of this potentially fertile region of south-east Asia, with a population in 1989 of some 75 million, identifies the post-1945 period as the most destructive in its modern history. To the west lies the independent kingdom of Thailand, a sometimes uncertain American ally which provided bases for the United States during the Vietnam War and on her borders with Laos. Thailand accepted 400,000 Khmer Rouge refugees after 1975. To the south, Malaysia, Singapore and Indonesia kept out of any involvement in Indo-China, not least because during 1963–6 they were locked in confrontation with each other. Indonesia, the largest and most populous of south-east Asian states with 178.2 million inhabitants in 1989, followed ambitious plans for expansion until the fall of Achmed Sukarno from power in 1967. Burma pursued a policy of non-alignment and, under the military rule of General Ne Win from 1962 to 1988, remained largely in isolation. Finally the Philippines, independent but still closely allied to the United States and dependent on American assistance, made available to the US two bases, a naval base at Subic Bay and Clark Air Base for the defence of the western Pacific; the American presence and influence is resented by a large proportion of the population as an infringement of sovereignty. In the decades since independence profound changes have occurred in each of the individual nations.

In the countries which fell under Japanese occupation from 1941 to 1945 – Indonesia, Malaya, Burma and Indo-China – indigenous resistance and independence movements, which continued the struggle for independence after 1945, created new balances of power. Whenever independence was achieved by armed struggle, as in Indo-China and Indonesia, the army tended to become an important factor in the subsequent power struggles, either forming an alliance with one of the political elites or taking over control itself. South-east Asian countries have had to cope with severe development problems – just feeding a rapidly growing population was an immense challenge. Within the newly independent countries the power struggles between communists and non-communists produced strife and civil war. Arbitrary national frontiers inherited from the colonial era were defended by those nations whose interests they served and denounced by neighbours who rejected the post-colonial settlement.

The great majority of the people of south-east Asia are still poor peasants. Although degrees of state planning are common to the whole region, it is remarkable that with the exception of the former French Indo-China, with its population of 75 million (1989), no radical agrarian reforms were introduced anywhere in the region. Only the communists in Vietnam adopted ruthless collectivisation of the farms, a programme which had disastrous consequences. In the non-communist countries of south-east Asia, the largely feudal system of landlords, peasant-owned farms and landless peasants continues. Famine and under-nourishment have afflicted the region, aggravated by its high birthrate. But better methods of cultivation (introduced in 1960 and known as the 'green revolution') and the increasing use of pesticides and fertilisers have enabled food to be produced faster than the population has grown. But extremes of inequality and climatic calamities have still left millions starving or near starvation.

Many landless peasants have moved in desperation to the towns, with large numbers of young girls turning to prostitution. The growth of these destitute populations in the shanty towns of Third World cities has been one of the most tragic features of development. In the years after independence, Jakarta, the capital of Indonesia, grew from less than 1.5 million inhabitants to over 4.5 million, Calcutta to more than 7 million, the population of Delhi doubled to over 3 million and that of the

capital of Pakistan, Karachi, rose from 1 million to over 3. Amid this waste of Asian urban poverty, two contrasting exceptions stand out. One is prosperous Singapore, an island republic whose population is concentrated in the city of Singapore itself, which has grown from 1 million to over 2 million; the other is Phnom Penh, the capital of Cambodia, whose population was barbarously driven out of the city into the countryside, where the majority perished when Pol Pot's Khmer Rouge forces captured the city in 1975 (pages 624–5). Under the ten-year Vietnamese occupation Phnom Penh slowly recovered, achieving an estimated population in 1988 of 600,000.

As if the conflict over national borders, between rival political elites and over the distribution of resources was not enough to cause bloodshed, this vast region's ethnic and religious conflicts added to the general turmoil. Chinese and Indians have settled throughout south-east Asia. In Singapore the Chinese form the majority. In Malaysia, a Chinese communist insurrection was suppressed before independence was gained in 1963 (pages 400–1). The Tamils in Sri Lanka continue in armed rebellion against the Sinhalese majority, Indian intervention in 1987–8 to force the Tamils to surrender having failed. India herself faces severe problems in the Punjab, where extremist Sikhs demand their own state. In Burma a number of minorities turned to insurgency. The traditional rivalry between China and Vietnam has led to the Vietnamese treating their Chinese minority harshly. In the Philippines a Muslim separatist movement has grown into a major rebellion. Almost every independent south-east Asian nation has not one but several minority problems. For half a century, these conflicts have continued unabated and are getting worse, often exacerbated by outside intervention.

Cold War competition between the Soviet Union, China and the United States turned regional conflicts into devastating warfare in Vietnam, Cambodia and Laos. China and the Soviet Union sought to advance their influence as well as to keep each other and the Americans out, providing weapons to rival groups of Laotian, Cambodian, North Vietnamese and South Vietnamese. The Americans alone among the major powers joined in the wars of Vietnam with combat troops. Cold War rivalries were thus superimposed on the already existing internal and intra-regional struggles of south-east Asia.

**South-East Asia, 1960**

The majority of the nations in south-east Asia in the early 1990s were ruled by authoritarian systems of government. The very nature of Dutch and French colonialism, aggravated by the interlude of Japanese military occupation, meant that democracy and constitutional government, regular elections, an independent judiciary and basic civil freedoms, including free expression and a free press, had shallow roots. The British Empire in Asia, on the other hand, with the exception of Malaya and Burma, was spared the Japanese occupation. British colonial rule was the most enlightened, introducing some of the essential features of constitutional government. The Republic of India is the largest nation in southern Asia to have survived internal strife as a democracy; Malaysia and Singapore have done likewise. But Sri Lanka, despite a parliamentary system, is rent by civil war. Burma, Pakistan and Bangladesh fell under authoritarian rule, and the whole of former French Indo-China after nearly thirty years of war had succumbed to communism.

Despite widespread poverty and its manifold problems, it is remarkable that the greater part of south-east Asia has not proved fertile ground for the Chinese or Soviet communists models. For this there are good reasons. Tradition still has a firm hold in the region, which is pervaded by especially strong religious beliefs opposed to atheistic communism. And the nationalism of south-east Asian countries had to assert itself first against the Europeans, then against the Japanese and finally against the Europeans again. Another disadvantage for communism was that for a time after 1949 the only Asian great power remaining was Red China. The newly independent states did not want to fall into the hands of a new Chinese empire, a threat made all the more real by large minorities of 'overseas Chinese' who might act as an internally disruptive force. In the continuous internal struggles for power, furthermore, the leaders of coups were reluctant to alienate the most influential sectors of society – the middle classes and the propertied. Fundamental redistribution of wealth and agrarian reform, let alone moves towards full-blown communism, would have stirred up a hornet's nest of opposition. In this respect, as well as in many others, Burma was something of an exception.

No sooner had independence come to Burma in January 1948 than internal disruption threatened to plunge the country into chaos. The British had left behind a democratic constitution modelled on Westminster, which proved unsuitable for a country so under-developed and so disorganised. At the time of independence, Burma was led by U Nu, an outstanding politician who managed to maintain constitutional democracy intact for ten years until 1958. It had barely survived the first four years, during which ethnic minorities and two communist groups, the Red Flags and the White Flags, collaborated and took control of central and most of southern Burma, nearly capturing Rangoon. U Nu and constitutional government were saved by the army and General Ne Win, and by the disunity of the insurgent groups, who hated each other as much as the system they were trying to overthrow. To this day, no government has achieved effective control over all the remote areas of Burma.

In the wider world Burma was almost unknown except for two circumstances: U Thant, the Burmese educator and diplomat (U is an honorific title meaning 'honourable sir'), was twice elected United Nations secretary-general, in 1962 and 1966, and served ably until 1971, during a period of severe conflict in the Third World. Burma's more negative contribution has been the illicit traffic of opium out of the 'golden triangle', a tongue of remote territory spanning Burma, Laos and Cambodia.

The Burmese military was at first prepared to support the constitutional government of U Nu, who was carefully edging Burma away from the West to a neutralist position. Burma had either to secure India's firm backing or to establish good relations with her most powerful neighbour China, with which she shared a long frontier. It was the latter policy which in the end proved the only feasible one, unless Burma were to be caught up in the Cold War. Potentially a rich country, with resources of rice which had once made her Asia's biggest exporter of the grain, not to mention timber and minerals, Burma's development nevertheless languished under U Nu's regime. One reason continues to be the protracted ethnic conflict; another was the failure of over-ambitious development plans recommended by American advisers. In 1958 the state of the country had become so serious that U Nu handed over power to his supporter, General Ne Win. Two years later Ne Win organised a general election from which U Nu emerged victorious, and Ne Win restored him to power. But having tasted supreme power, and seeing the unity of the country once more threatened, Ne Win in 1962 overthrew U Nu in a bloodless coup and abolished the constitution, convinced that only authoritarian socialism could save his country. He ruled Burma for the next twenty-six years, introducing a communist-style one-party (Burma Socialist Programme Party) authoritarian regime. Keen to find a Burmese way to socialism opposed to both communist insurgency and U Nu's liberalism, Ne Win claimed to be following a middle way in the true Buddhist fashion. In fact the military junta under his leadership isolated Burma, forcing her to turn her back on Western traditions. Industry and banking were nationalised, but the economy performed disastrously. In an attempt to get it moving Ne Win secured large development funds from abroad and the Burmese overseas debt soared from $231 million in 1973 to $3.8 billion in 1988.

The standard of living, however, remained one of the lowest in Asia. The rice grown is hardly sufficient to feed her own population of 38 million.

The patient people of Burma, who had suffered for twenty-five years from the Burmese road to socialism, began to give vent to their frustration in largely student-led riots in Rangoon in September 1987. The seventy-seven-year-old General Ne Win decided to move to the sidelines and resigned in the summer of 1988 amid signs of military disaffection. Reforms were promised. For a brief period with a civilian as her leader, detainees released and free elections promised, it looked as if Burma would move out of her self-imposed isolation and darkness. But just a month later, in September 1988, the military took over and General Saw Maung emerged at the head of a junta. The 'restoration of law and order' marked the beginnings of a repression against students and dissidents, brutal even by Burmese standards. As many as 3000 pro-democracy demonstrators are believed to have been massacred.

In 1989 the name of Burma was changed to Myanmar, a transliteration of the English 'Burma'

into Burmese. Surprisingly the new military leaders promised that new political parties could register and that there would be free elections in May 1990. But they then, in the summer of 1989, placed under house arrest the most likely leaders of any opposition, including Aung San Suu Kyi, the daughter of Aung San (who played a crucial role at the birth of Burmese independence) and wife of an English lecturer at Oxford. Suu Kyi had returned to her native land to lead a new party, the National League for Democracy. It was her criticisms of Ne Win and her call for justice and democracy that led to her arrest. But to the chagrin of the junta, which had fielded its own front party, the National Unity Party, the National League for Democracy gained a clear and outright victory at the 1990 election, winning a huge majority in the Assembly. The military junta had no intention of bowing to this verdict. In 1992 Aung San Suu Kyi remained under house arrest. The military declared that they would release her only if she leaves the country, which she has refused to do. For her courage and her adherence to her principles she was awarded the Nobel Peace Prize in 1991. There were no signs

*The courageous Burmese opposition leader, Aung San Suu Kyi, did not enjoy the freedom to campaign publicly as here for long, she was placed under house arrest in Rangoon on 20 July 1989. She was awarded the Nobel Peace Prize in 1991 while still in captivity.*

at the end of 1992 that the junta planned to hand power over to a democratic majority. Instead, its oppressive rule continued, and campaigners against ethnic minorities, students and rebellious tribes on the north-west and north-east borders of Burma were fiercely pursued. A new campaign against Muslim groups in the south-west led to a flood of refugees escaping to Bangladesh. But, despite its appalling human rights records, Burma was not shunned by the international community, which valued her resources and her market. Oil companies were prospecting and concluding joint production agreements, and the country was being opened increasingly to foreign investment. Trade with Thailand grew with particular rapidity.

*Two leaders of the 'non-aligned' nations. Nasser of Egypt (right) greets Sukarno of Indonesia (saluting) in May 1955, a month after the Bandung Conference.*

**Burma, Indonesia, Malaysia, Singapore and Thailand, 1987**

|  | Population (*millions*) | Gross National Product per head (*US$*) |
| --- | --- | --- |
| Burma | 39.3 | 200 |
| Indonesia | 171.4 | 450 |
| Malaysia | 16.5 | 1,810 |
| Singapore | 2.6 | 7,940 |
| Thailand | 55.6 (1989) | 1,038 (1988) |

Indonesia is the largest country in south-east Asia, with more inhabitants than Britain and united Germany combined. Yet the only one of her 3600 islands, extending over 3000 miles of ocean from east to west, that has captured the popular imagination is Bali. The great majority of the people are Muslims, but there are many ethnic groups, and the unity of this far-flung nation of islands is based on centuries of Dutch empire-building rather than on the homogeneity of the people or on common attitudes. Two men held continuous power from independence in 1949 to the mid-1980s, Achmed Sukarno and General Suharto. Following independence, constitutional government lasted only until 1958. At least outwardly it had been based on Western parliamentary models, but Sukarno, the first president, chafed under its restrictions and used the army to undermine parliamentary and political development. Parliamentary-style govern-

ment had not worked well. None of the then existing four parties, including the Communist Party, the largest in south-east Asia, had been able to establish a commanding lead. Uneasy coalition governments regularly fell apart. The loyalties of the population were in any case regional and local. Sukarno had to cope with a series of rebellions in the outer islands, and in 1958 with a military insurgency in Sumatra. Political rivalry and widespread corruption did nothing to foster national pride.

Sukarno attempted to fashion a national image, an Indonesian identity which increasingly rejected the West. The constitutional façade had at least served the purpose of encouraging Western development aid, as in 1952 when Indonesia participated in the Commonwealth Colombo Plan. Sukarno accepted Western aid and in 1960 Soviet assistance as well. Championing a Third World approach to global problems, he hosted in 1955 the Afro-Asian Bandung Conference, attended by Nehru and Zhou Enlai, but it was regarded with great suspicion in Washington, where a stance of non-alignment was interpreted as anti-Western and pro-communist. Sukarno's rule was supported by both the Communist Party and the anti-communist army. Although Khrushchev saw an opportunity to extend Soviet influence, neither Moscow nor Washington knew how to assess Sukarno's Indonesia, as he cleverly played the Cold War game, benefiting from both sides.

In 1958 Sukarno moved to an authoritarian form

of government, within a short time stifling the influence of constitutional safeguards such as the elected parliament, the political parties, the independent judiciary and the press. He became the supreme leader of his 'guided democracy'. Meanwhile, two powerful factions watched each other warily, the communists and the military. Most of the military approved of Sukarno's coup. Then, in October 1965, in what was the most violent convulsion in Indonesian politics, the communists murdered six generals. What really occurred has never been properly clarified. Was it really the beginning of an attempted communist coup? The army reacted with savagery and staged its own coup against Sukarno. General Suharto, one of those not on the assassination list, emerged as Indonesia's strong man. Over the next few months communist supporters were killed in a bloodbath that may have seen more than half a million dead. Suharto effectively took control, though Sukarno remained president until replaced by Suharto.

In world affairs Sukarno had emerged as a charismatic Third World leader, loud in his denunciation of Western imperialism and strident in promoting Indonesian nationalism. This impeded economic development as he tried to run Indonesia without Dutch technical assistance. Later efforts to encourage Dutch and international investment foundered in the face of his conflict with the Dutch over the future of the western part of New Guinea, West Irian, which the Dutch did not cede until 1963.

In south-east Asia Sukarno pursued expansionist policies, in particular adopting a stance of confrontation with Malaysia. He denounced the Malaysian Federation as a Western colonial outpost. For a time in 1963 and 1964, with Indonesia promoting armed incidents, there seemed to be a real threat of war between the two countries. Hastily assembled Commonwealth troops, British, Australian, New Zealand and Malaysian, set up an effective defence force which deterred Sukarno from further provocation. Suharto's military coup of 1965 was nonetheless greeted with relief by the West.

General Suharto and the military had virulently opposed the communists long before they massacred hundreds of thousands of them on taking control of the country in October 1965. Reflecting

*Indonesian President Sukarno* (left) *was succeeded as head of state by Suharto* (right).

this opposition internationally, Suharto dropped Sukarno's friendships with China and the Soviet Union and reorientated to the West. With fears prompted by the Vietnam conflict of a communist takeover of the whole of south-east Asia, the United States supplanted the Soviet Union as the arms supplier and provider of foreign aid to Indonesia. The country was opened to Western enterprise, but, despite her plentiful resources and even though in the 1970s she became the largest oil producer in Asia, corruption and inefficiency marred her economic development, so that she remained a poor Third World country. State planning largely failed to remedy the gross disparity between the wealth of a minority and the poverty of the majority; loans were not properly applied; and Indonesia's foreign debt rose enormously, swallowing up nearly a third of all export earnings in 1991, despite considerable expansion of oil and gas exports in the 1980s. In the late 1980s the regime began a policy of liberalisation from state control.

In external affairs, Indonesia's relations with her Malaysian neighbours and with Singapore were generally easier than they had been during Sukarno's era. Indonesia is a member of the Association of South-East Asian Nations, which, although not a well-functioning organisation, has done something to promote trade and peace. At the end of the 1980s Indonesia also played a more positive role internationally in helping to broker the peace agreement finally reached in Cambodia. But General Suharto did not abandon Indonesian expansionism. Among the worst atrocities in south-east Asian history was Indonesia's invasion in 1976 of East Timor, which the Portuguese had left in 1975. The invaders crushed the movement for an independent East Timor with such brutality that a fifth of the population of some 700,000 were either killed or disappeared. Nonetheless, independence as an ideal was not abandoned by the politically active in East Timor. Attention was once more focused on Indonesia's military when a peaceful demonstration on 28 October 1991 led to the killing of many demonstrators, amid worldwide condemnation. Within Indonesia, insurgencies on some of the islands were no less brutally suppressed, with the tacit support of the majority, who preferred military rule to continual strife and bloodshed provoked by the minority insurgents.

Suharto's military rule allowed no opposition or constitutional development, nor did his modification of Sukarno's 'guided democracy' liberalise the authoritarian government of the country. All effective power was concentrated in his hands, and even the discarding of his uniform could not disguise the truth that his rule was based on military force. Periodically 're-elected' as president by a carefully controlled and largely ceremonial parliament, he brought a certain stability after the hectic Sukarno years. But the increasing wealth of a small middle class and the rising discontent of students occasioned a questioning of authoritarian rule. Here, as in the rest of Asia, the wind of change was blowing, albeit very gently.

Stability and national unity were the watchwords of the junta, repression the means of achieving them, whether combating communism, (non-Indonesian) nationalism or the demands of fundamental Muslim groups. That strategy left little scope for the development of civilian democratic rule. The stability provided by an authoritarian military regime also encouraged the developed world to invest in Indonesia. In the early 1990s President Suharto and the army attempted to present a more liberal image to the outside world by allowing some political activity and trying to appease more moderate Muslims after years of preventing Islam from playing any role in state politics. These were but small beginnings.

Without British and Commonwealth support Malaysia, with her relatively small population, could not have stood up to Indonesian pressure in the early 1960s, though her resources of rubber, tin and timber make her one of the wealthiest countries of south-east Asia. Like some other former British colonies, she followed a constitutional, democratic path after attaining independence in 1957, but she faced severe problems of national unity from the start. The feudal Malay princes were jealous of their ceremonial powers. Worse still, the country was divided into three distinct ethnic groups: the Malays formed the majority, but the Chinese, who were almost as numerous, were the wealthiest and most dynamic group; there was, thirdly, a relatively small group of ethnic Indians. The solution was to share power between all three in an Alliance Party. It was dominated by the most distinguished statesman Malaya had produced, Tunku Abdul Rahman, the father of independence.

A conservative but tolerant prime minister from 1957 to 1970, Abdul Rahman upheld democratic

*Lee Kuan Yew, leader of the People's Action Party, pictured in 1959 at the beginning of his long reign as Prime Minister of Singapore, which ended in 1990.*

and constitutional government and supported an independent judiciary and a free press. Nevertheless, the tension between the Malays and the Chinese could not always be contained. The policies designed to compensate the Malays for their disadvantaged position bred resentment among the Chinese. Communal riots forced on the country two brief emergencies when democratic rights were suspended. But, even with renewed communist insurgencies after the communist victories in Vietnam in 1975, there was always a return to constitutional government and free elections.

The differences between the Chinese and Malays also led to the break-up of an expanded Federation of Malaysia, which included the two north Bornean colonies and Singapore. The Chinese predominated in Singapore, and the party working for independence, the People's Action Party, was led by Lee Kuan Yew, who originally suggested to Abdul Rahman the plan for the federation of the territories. It came into being in 1963, and Britain transferred to it control of Singapore and the two north Bornean territories. The Philippines protested and put forward their own claims to North Borneo. More serious was the confrontation with Indonesia. Between 1964 and 1965 fighting sporadically broke out as the federation moved to defend her territories.

In 1965 Lee Kuan Yew withdrew Singapore from the Malaysian Federation to form an independent republic within the Commonwealth. Thereafter he won every election until his retirement in 1990. His authoritarian paternalism significantly interfered with constitutional government, while his puritanism kept Singapore singularly free from crime, drugs and sexual licence, which he regarded as decadent features of the Western way of life. Without natural resources, except fish, Singapore has been transformed into the financial and industrial centre of south-east Asia, her population of 2.5 million enjoying the highest standard of living in the region (with the exception of the fortunate people of Brunei, whose wealth comes not from their work but from oil). In these respects she compares with Hong Kong. Singapore demonstrates the astonishing rise from poverty that has transformed the countries of the Pacific rim since 1945 – Singapore, Taiwan, Japan (the economic superpower) and South Korea.

Malaysian wealth depends more on the world prices of her natural resources. With her fine educational system and well-trained, British-oriented judiciary, the roots of democratic government seemed to have struck more deeply here than elsewhere in the region. With the Alliance Party in disarray, Mahathir Mohamad, prime minister since 1981, claimed that the communist and Chinese threat in the early 1990s required increasing vigilance. In 1987 he invoked a security act to imprison many opponents. More ominously, he harassed and weakened the judiciary and so placed a question mark over Malaysia's democratic constitutional future. By 1993 repression had not resulted in a serious Chinese backlash; but, even if there were one, the great majority of Chinese Malays would not support the Chinese or Viet-namese communists in the north.

Siam, renamed Thailand in 1949, is one of the five relatively prosperous states of south-east Asia, the others being Singapore, Malaysia, the Philippines and Sri Lanka. With a population of over 50 million in the 1980s, Thailand possesses rich resources, principally tin, wolfram, rubber and rice. In the capital, Bangkok, a downtown commercial centre and some factories stand cheek by jowl along its hundred of canals with shanty dwellings lacking sanitation. In the West and in Japan, Thailand achieved notoriety for encouraging tourists attracted by the unrestricted nature of her prostitution, which catered for all varieties of Western and Eastern tastes. Aids is now rampant in the sex bazaars, threatening the lucrative tourism and, worse, the country's population. Every new ruler and govern-ment promised to clean up Thailand, referring not to this specialised tourism, but to widespread admin-istrative corruption. Thailand is a monarchy, but power is exercised by a group of generals who periodically engage in coups against each other. By 1993 there had been six such successful coups since 1945 and numerous unsuccessful attempts. On three occasions the military handed the government back to civilian control, but never for very long. Consequently, parliamentary democracy had little opportunity to develop.

Thailand and Japan were the only Asian countries to escape colonisation by one of the European powers, but Thailand lost some of her territory in the nineteenth century to Laos and Cambodia, then French Indo-China. Her geographical position poses particular problems for her foreign policy, for she cannot afford too many enemies simultaneously. She has borders with five countries. To the north and west lies Burma, with which she cultivates good relations. To the south-west is Malaysia, with which she shares anti-communist interests and a desire to avoid being drawn into war. Thailand's problems emerge on her north-eastern borders with Laos and her south-eastern borders with Cambodia, both of which countries were threatened with communist insurgencies in the 1960s. A communist (Pathet Lao) takeover of Laos with North Vietnamese support was a particular danger, as there are about three times as many Laotian-speaking inhabitants within Thailand (more than 8 million) as in Laos itself. Thailand provided support and bases for US troops in the Vietnam War during the 1960s, but was critical of America's reluctance to fight commu-nism in Laos with determination. She viewed the international agreement to neutralise Laos in 1962 as merely a step in the direction of a complete communist takeover.

Thailand's worst fears were realised in 1973 when the United States pulled out of the war in Vietnam; two years later communism was victorious in Vietnam, Cambodia and Laos. But in the 1980s civil wars continued to be fought in neighbouring Cambodia, with most of the country occupied until 1989 by Vietnam. In the early 1990s Thailand found herself the unenthusiastic host of some 400,000 refugees who had crossed her eastern borders, though her borders remained secure. The United States in SEATO (1955) and subsequent declar-ations pledged herself to defend Thailand, but in 1976 as part of a general withdrawal from south-east Asia gave up her Thai bases. A leading member of ASEAN, the Association of South-East Asian Nations, founded in 1967, Thailand hoped with her four partners, Malaysia, Singapore, Indonesia and the Philippines, to maintain the existing peace. But her best protection was an unexpected one: the disunity, confusion and latterly collapse in the communist world.

Of all countries involved in civil wars, bloodshed and great-power conflicts, no country, not even Vietnam, suffered as much as Cambodia. Under Japanese control from 1941 to 1945 the country came into being on the eve of Japan's defeat in March 1945, when King Norodom Sihanouk proclaimed Cambodia's independence. After the French had returned, Sihanouk placed himself at the head of the national movement and succeeded in extracting full French independence for his small kingdom (5 million inhabitants in 1954). By then the King had to contend with communist rivals supported by the North Vietnamese.

Sihanouk attempted to rescue the country by creating a neutralist coalition, which might also help prevent internal rivalries from wrenching the country apart. From 1945 to 1970 he was the most respected Cambodian politician, and in order to play an effective part in politics he took the unusual step of giving up his throne to his father. He then (1955) presented himself as humble Mr Sihanouk, though he continued to be known as 'Prince'.

Realising early on that North Vietnam and the Pathet Lao were likely to prove the stronger in the war, he abandoned America and the West to seek the friendship of China in the 1960s. He was powerless to prevent the North Vietnamese from using the Ho Chi-minh Trail in Cambodian border territories for moving troops and supplies from the communist North to South Vietnam. But his pro-Chinese, pro-communist stance was unwelcome to the United States, and while in Beijing in 1970 he was overthrown; with American support, Lon Nol took control of the royal government in Cambodia's capital, Phnom Penh. This marked the end of any hope that Cambodia might achieve neutrality: she was invaded by American and South Vietnamese troops intent on destroying the Vietnamese communist bases and supply lines on the borders, which were also bombed. In Beijing, Sihanouk now threw in his lot with the Khmer Rouge communist opposition. American policy in Cambodia proved a disastrous failure, and after the US withdrawal from Vietnam in 1973 there was no possibility that Congress would have accepted a new military commitment in Cambodia. Deprived of US combat support, the Lon Nol regime could not survive the onslaught of communist forces, so when the Americans finally left, the Khmer Rouge easily captured Phnom Penh in April 1975 and took over the whole country.

Had the Americans not turned against Sihanouk, one of the cleverest and wiliest of south-east Asian leaders, Cambodia might have been spared the almost unbelievable horrors that followed. Sihanouk was now practically a prisoner in Khmer Rouge hands; for a short while he served as a useful figurehead, but the infamous Khmer Rouge leader, known as Pol Pot, wielded total power. He forced the inhabitants of Phnom Penh to march into the countryside, where most of the helpless urban population perished. A campaign of genocide was directed against all intellectuals and educated Cambodians who might have resisted his fanatical communist regime. No one knows exactly how many hundreds of thousands perished in the notorious killing fields, now preserved as national shrines. Possibly it was as many as 2 million, but up to one-third of the population has disappeared; Cambodia's population declined from some 7.5 to 5.5 million.

To satisfy their own ambitions the communist Vietnamese put an end to Pol Pot's bloodthirsty regime by invading Cambodia, which had been renamed Kampuchea, in December 1979 and setting up a government under their control. A large Vietnamese army occupied most of the country until 1989, when the invaders at last withdrew. It had proved a costly intervention, and the puppet regime had never been recognised by the West. It was true that the Vietnamese could not but be an immense improvement on Pol Pot's murderers, but south-east Asia's non-communist countries fear a powerful Vietnam far more than they fear the Khmer Rouge. Extraordinarily, the Khmer Rouge, part of the Khmer People's National Liberation Front, were for a long time recognised as representing Kampuchea at the United Nations.

The search for a peaceful settlement in Kampuchea was long and arduous. The opportunity arose only with the ending of the Cold War. It was now also in China's and Russia's interests to liquidate the civil war in Kampuchea. In January 1990 an Australian peace plan was accepted as a basis for a settlement by the five permanent members of the UN Security Council, including of course the former Cold War contestants, the United States, China and the Soviet Union. A peace accord between the Kampuchean factions brokered by the United Nations was subsequently signed in Paris on 23 October 1991. It would allow the genocidal Khmer Rouge to participate in a transitional administration called the Supreme National Council. Some 400,000 refugees on the Thai–Kampuchean border were to return home, and they would swell the support the Khmer Rouge could claim.

*Victims of Pol Pot in Phnom Pen, Cambodia – survivors of 'the killing fields'.*

In 1991 Prince Sihanouk returned to his palace in Phnom Penh and an advance party of UN officials arrived. The United Nations took on a supervisory role as 'transitional authority' to run the main ministries, enforce an arms embargo and ensure the demobilisation of the rival armies – the 35,000 Khmer Rouge guerrillas, the 18,000-strong Sihanouk National Army and 8000 troops of the anti-communist National Liberation Front, who together formed the 'national resistance coalition'. The UN held elections in 1993 but the Khmer Rouge refused to participate. A huge international peace effort which required funding by the wealthier nations to the tune of over $2 billion, 16,000 UN troops and 5000 civilians was undertaken under

### Laos, Kampuchea and Vietnam, 1989

|  | Population (*millions*) | Gross National Product per head (*US$*) |
|---|---|---|
| Laos | 3.9 | 156 |
| Kampuchea (Cambodia) | 6.8 | Less than 100 (no estimate available) |
| Vietnam | 65.0 | 100 (1984) |

the auspices of a UN 'transitional authority'. In 1993 violence had not ended and a peaceful outcome remained in doubt.

# CHAPTER 63

# The Vietnam War and After

Nowhere was human suffering greater in Asia than during the 1960s and 1970s in the lands of Vietnam, Cambodia and Laos. The Vietnam War was a fratricidal conflict between the Vietnamese people. It also marked the climax of the Cold War in Asia, which immeasurably increased the suffering of the indigenous peoples. Because American leaders believed that far more was at stake than just the future of South Vietnam, that the security of the non-communist world was being tested here in the jungles and rice-swamps of Asia, they first supplied money and arms and eventually half a million combat troops in an attempt to help one side in the Vietnamese civil war defeat the other. But America's Western allies saw it differently, so there was never the unity displayed during the Korean War. France and Britain gave advice but sent no troops. In Asia, Australia was the most enthusiastic supporter and, with New Zealand, despatched several thousand men; other small token allies which sent some troops were Thailand and the Philippines. The Russians and Chinese gave aid and arms to the communists to support their fight but were careful to keep out of combat themselves. The Chinese communists did not want America on their southern frontier; they had already fought in North Korea to keep the enemy from their northern Manchurian border. It suited the Russians, on the other hand, to see America quagmired in south-east Asia, far away from regions bordering on the Soviet Union.

The ordinary people, mostly peasants in Vietnam, followed their leaders either through conviction or because they had no choice, conscripted and coerced into rival armies or units of irregular combatants. In Vietnam resistance was punished by death. Only in a Western democracy was public protest possible. Most young Americans accepted their call-up, but there were tens of thousands who did not view the Vietnam conflict as necessary or just and avoided the draft. In the United States the war became increasingly unacceptable after 1968, with its heavy losses of American life. With the progressive US disengagement on land, the Vietnamese were left to fight to the finish in an orgy of destruction. The communist forces were the stronger, and they would have won sooner in the war between the Vietnamese had the US not intervened. Whether the Chinese and Russians would have supplied arms so lavishly had the Americans not joined in as combatants remains an open question. The Soviet Union and China had supported the Vietminh against the French, and in Cold War logic the increasing supply of arms to both sides as fighting escalated was an inescapable consequence. It was tragic that the Johnson administration had failed to grasp the true nature of the conflict it was facing.

The Vietnam War was also a tragedy for the United States, for the parents of the 57,000 men killed, for the wives who saw husbands returned in bodybags, for the more than 300,000 wounded servicemen whose scars were not only physical. It was a war fought by nineteen-year-old American conscripts in rice-fields and jungles. The enemy was everywhere and not necessarily recognisable by his uniform. There was nothing to distinguish the Vietcong fighter from unarmed peasants, men, women and even children. In fear of their own lives, the US troops shot first, at anyone who ran away from them or who even looked suspicious; atrocities were committed, villages burnt, innocent and guilty killed. The Americans' South Vietnamese allies had even less regard for the lives of those of their fellow countrymen who were assisting the Vietcong and Vietminh. It was a most brutal, brutalising war even by the standards of the twentieth century.

The losses the Americans suffered were small in comparison with those of the Vietnamese people. The scale of death, crippling injury and destruction in Vietnam was so great it is difficult for Westerners to grasp how any people could have tenaciously gone on fighting. That was the prime error made by the American generals, who with superior weapons thought they were fighting a war of attrition. Since America's goal was not to win a total victory but 'only' to force the North Vietnamese communists to abandon their efforts to occupy the central and southern regions of Vietnam, it seemed to any Westerner that a point would be reached when the leaders of the Democratic Republic of Vietnam would accept that the price of extending their rule over the centre and south was too high in human lives and material destruction.

The cruelties of the Vietnam conflict plumbed the depths of human conduct – prisoners were tortured by both sides, and in practice the Geneva Convention on warfare counted for nothing. The communist atrocities were largely hidden from Western eyes. The freedom of the press in the West, however, ensured that some idea of the barbarities committed by the South Vietnamese army and of the effects of American warfare reached every sitting room. Two images especially etched themselves on the public eye: the execution of a Vietcong suspect, shot in the head by the chief of police in a street in Hue; and the spectacle of a naked Vietnamese girl, burnt by napalm and running screaming towards the camera.

The land war in the southern and central regions of Vietnam that formed the Republic of Vietnam was fought in rice-fields and jungle. The Americans 'punished' North Vietnam by starting in March 1965 a bombing offensive, codenamed Rolling Thunder, intended to batter her population into the Stone Age. More bombs were dropped on North Vietnam than the Americans had dropped during the whole of the Second World War. The continuation of a war against such odds, it was believed in Washington, made no rational sense. Vietnam was pitted with bomb craters; large areas of jungle were defoliated by a chemical, 'agent orange', in an attempt to reveal communist hide-outs. The land was poisoned and so were its people.

Rational? Ho Chi-minh and his North Vietnamese Politburo was not 'rational' when measured by Western moral standards. Ho Chi-minh and General Vo Nguyen Giap were ready to press into the fight as many hundreds of thousands of Vietnamese as might be needed to overwhelm the Americans and the South Vietnamese army. 'Body counts' of Vietnamese did not matter to them. Vietnamese fertility was high. The only 'body counts' that mattered were those of the Americans, who sooner or later would have to abandon a war being fought in a far-away country, a war whose outcome was no possible threat to US security. Whether the war lasted ten years or forty, Ho Chi-minh knew that the Americans would not fight for ever. The communists did not have to defeat US forces in the field. This they could not do. But, provided they continued to inflict casualties and just prevented the Americans and their South Vietnamese allies from winning, the United States would in the end leave Vietnam. It was a war of attrition. The American people's threshold of acceptable losses, in an Asian war fought on ideological grounds, was much lower than their enemy's. For the Vietminh it was a fight to the end to free the south from American imperialism. The death of Ho Chi-minh in September 1969 altered nothing – his policies continued to be ruthlessly pursued by his comrades in arms.

The price in blood the Vietnamese paid for their victory was terrible. No accurate figures are available. It has been estimated that 900,000 North Vietnamese combatants were killed and 2 million wounded. To appreciate the scale of these casualties they should be seen against the total North Vietnamese population of some 18–20 million. It is as if 10 million Americans had been killed and 20 million wounded in war. In addition at least another 1 million civilians were killed throughout Vietnam. The ARVN – the army of the southern Republic of Vietnam – suffered a quarter of a million deaths and 600,000 wounded. Thus total losses of life throughout Vietnam reached at least 2.5 million and those wounded several millions more.

The so-called lessons of history are often at their most dangerous when they are used to justify the adoption of specific policies. The failure of the attempts to appease Hitler in the 1930s was resurrected in circumstances after 1945 that were very different. The assumption was made that all dictators behave in exactly the same way, that their ambitions are always limitless and that concessions feed their appetites. There was no need, therefore, to differentiate or even to study the situation in the area of conflict. It did not matter whether the crisis was occurring in Europe, for instance in divided Berlin, or in Asia in divided Vietnam. The Cold War wonderfully simplified everything in what was perceived as a global struggle against expanding communism. From Washington's standpoint, the real enemy was in Beijing and Moscow. Here the strings were supposed to be pulled, with the smaller communist countries as mere puppets with no will of their own. There can be no denying Russia's and China's influence in Vietnam, but it was not always decisive. The critical decisions were taken in Hanoi. Moreover, the United States could not carry the war to China or Russia without the danger of nuclear exchange. So there was no choice but to fight conventional wars against smaller communist states which were apparently being pushed forward into aggression against the free world.

Ho Chi-minh transformed North Vietnam into a rigid communist state by stages. Until the fighting with the French began, from 1946 to 1949 he played down communism under the slogan 'Fatherland all'. Having secured much of the countryside by 1950, a new phase began under a fresh slogan, 'the anti-imperialist fight and the anti-feudal fight are of equal importance'. The 'land reform' from 1953 to 1956 was modelled on Mao's example and ruthlessly eliminated the landlord class, anyone connected with them and all 'reactionary elements'. The wave of terror took many lives, and after the 1954 Geneva Conference there was a mass exodus of hundreds of thousands of refugees from the North to the South.

Some of the Vietnamese people were motivated by powerful ideological or religious beliefs. But the majority of the poor peasants would not have chosen to be ruled harshly by the Communist Party in the North or by the succession of corrupt governments in the South. As for the minority – the professionals, the well-off, the army officers, the politicians – they

looked after their own interests or supported what they regarded as the lesser evil. Vietnam in contemporary history is the product not of what the mass of its people have chosen, but of half a century of power struggles among the Vietnamese leadership elites within a Cold War framework.

The Geneva accord had divided Vietnam at the 17th parallel. In the southern Republic of Vietnam, Ngo Dinh Diem established an increasingly autocratic and nepotistic regime, distributing posts to his brothers and relations. He was supported by the large landowners, which necessarily limited the scope of agrarian reforms. His regime uprooted millions of peasants and forced them into 'strategic hamlets' to cut their ties with the Vietcong. The peasants, who wanted only to get on with their own hard lives, were terrorised in turn by Vietcong guerrillas and Ngo Dinh Diem's security forces. Some were attracted by the communist promise to distribute land to the peasants, but most were just afraid for their lives if they did not comply with whomever was able to exert the greater pressure at any one time. The peasants did not feel any loyalty towards the Diem regime. Internal demands for reform were stifled, coup attempts suppressed. When Buddhists set fire to themselves to attract attention to their grievances, the world was aghast, but Diem remained confident that the United States had no alternative but to support his anti-communist government.

For all Diem's military efforts and those of the American advisers to 'pacify' the countryside, the Vietcong remained a powerful insurgent force in the jungles and rice-paddies, despite their heavy losses, concentrating on the killing of South Vietnamese government officials. In 1960, Ho Chi-minh had formed a National Liberation Front, to co-ordinate the fight in the North and the South and to try to control the Vietcong, but although they needed the supplies from the North which were passing through the jungle down the Ho Chi-minh trail just inside the border, the Vietcong maintained a separate political identity.

In Washington the creation of the National Liberation Front confirmed the mistaken belief that the conflict was in reality with communist North Vietnam, that there was no separate, internal South Vietnamese struggle. But, faced with Diem's embarrassing autocracy and corruption, disenchantment had set in. Attacks on Buddhist temples organised by Diem's brothers and protest riots in the streets in August 1963 were the last straw, and Washington withdrew its support from Diem and his family coterie. A coup by disgruntled generals was in the making. Henry Cabot Lodge, recently arrived as US ambassador in Saigon, had foreknowledge of it, and his contacts with the generals encouraged them in the belief that Diem's overthrow would be welcome in Washington. On 1 November 1963 the officers went into action and ousted Diem, who fled from the presidential palace. What the Americans had not anticipated was Diem's murder the following day. The junta of feuding army and air force officers governed South Vietnam incompetently. American pressure ensured that some sort of elections were held, but in the war-torn conditions of the republic the military ensured that they retained control.

The Vietcong and Vietminh were getting stronger and gaining support among the peasants by means of terror, indoctrination and persuasion. Confidence in the corrupt South Vietnamese regime was waning. In the summer of 1965 the Americanisation of the war began. Within three years more than half a million young American combatants were fighting in Vietnam, and thousands had died. American generals more or less took over the war. In 1967, by counting all the communists they killed in hundreds of skirmishes in rice-fields and forests and in attacks on villages by day which supplied the Vietcong by night, they thought they were surely winning the war. But these missions to seek out and kill the enemy did not bring the conflict to an end. American tactics proved of no avail in the jungles of Vietnam, Cambodia and Laos. A helicopter gunship was not as effective as tens of thousands of Vietcong and Vietminh, each armed with a rifle and able to live on a daily bowl of rice. It was impossible to kill them all. Casualties would be replaced with new recruits, increases in American combat troops with increased numbers of Vietminh. The Vietcong controlled much of the southern countryside.

After a decade of these tactics the communists planned a devastating blow. The Tet offensive, launched in January 1968 by the Vietcong and Vietminh against the towns of South Vietnam, was designed as an all-out effort to impress on the Americans that the Vietcong were far stronger than they had supposed. It caught the Americans and the South Vietnamese completely by surprise, because Tet was the national New Year holiday period, during which a truce had always been observed, and because the towns of South Vietnam had hitherto been thought secure against the largely rural Vietcong. In preparation for Tet, the North Vietnamese had endeavoured to draw US troops from the towns by a diversionary attack on a northern US base at Khesan. Then, on 31 January, scores of Vietnamese towns were assaulted by some 70,000 Vietcong and Vietminh, who created widespread destruction and even penetrated the heavily fortified US Embassy compound in Saigon. The carnage was worst in the ancient city of Hue in central Vietnam: there the Vietcong overwhelmed the South Vietnamese garrison and during their three-week occupation massacred 3000 people and buried them in hastily dug mass graves.

Before American and South Vietnamese troops regained control, the Tet offensive had caused them 6000 combat deaths. Thousands more Vietnamese civilians died, caught up in the fighting. For the Vietcong, the casualties amounted to a devastating 50,000. As a fighting force they never recovered. The weakening of the Vietcong was not unwelcome in Hanoi. Indeed, in a sense Tet was a double victory for the North Vietnamese: it undermined American confidence that the war would ever be won and it prevented the independent communists in the South from being able to challenge the northern communist regime. The Vietminh henceforth played the major military role and so gained the upper hand in determining the future of Vietnam.

The North Vietnamese were certainly encouraged by the growing protest movement against the war in the United States and by their success in undermining the authority of the South Vietnamese regime. They calculated that an American withdrawal would be hastened if they showed a readiness to talk peace while continuing to inflict heavy casualties on Americans in Vietnam: a point would be reached when American public opinion would force the administration to accept the communist peace terms in all essentials. Nixon's policy of Vietnamisation played into their hands as they negotiated interminably in Paris. Their prime aim was to reach an agreement which would get the United States out but would leave them able to continue the war within the country until final victory. So they resolutely rejected any proposal put forward by Henry Kissinger, America's chief negotiator in Paris, which required both North Vietnamese forces and the Americans to withdraw from the South.

American bombing caused grievous losses, but, making use of widely dispersed factories and with supplies of arms from China and Russia, the communist leadership in Hanoi was prepared to continue waging war for years to come.

In January 1973 a ceasefire was finally agreed. The Americans would withdraw from Vietnam within sixty days and the settlement would be left to the Vietnamese. But the ceasefire was not a prelude to peace. The North Vietnamese soon resumed the conflict and, despite massive supplies of American arms, the badly led South Vietnamese army crumbled completely. The Watergate scandal had removed Nixon in August 1974, and his successor President Ford knew only too well that the American people would not sanction a renewed US involvement in the war. As the North Vietnamese army thrust south, millions of refugees fled in terror towards Saigon, but the capital itself fell on 30 April 1975 as the last Americans and accom-

Left: *South Vietnamese refugees are slung into the hold of a cargo ship as they anxiously strive to flee the advancing Vietcong.*

Below: *Humiliation: 29 April 1975. A US helicopter evacuates Americans and a few lucky Vietnamese to the safety of a nearby US warship a day before the fall of Saigon.*

panying Vietnamese were lifted from the American Embassy in a frenzied evacuation, seventy helicopters carrying 1000 people to safety on the US warships lying offshore. But hundreds of thousands of Vietnamese officers and civil servants who had been loyal to the American-backed South Vietnamese regime were left behind to face the rigours of 're-education' by their new masters. They were taken to camps, where some spent months and others years, a Vietnamese Gulag.

The communists now applied their Marxist, centrally directed economic policies in the south and imposed a one-party state. They set out to abolish capitalism and collectivise land, with disastrous results. The people suffered once again from the corruption of officials and the incompetence of the administration. During the 1980s more market-oriented economic policies were introduced, permitting entrepreneurs, especially in the south, to run small factories and services for profit. Within the top echelon of the party there was a constant struggle between the reformers, the pragmatists who wanted to follow China's example, and the party ideologues, who believed that these experiments weakened Marxism–Leninism. The conflict was principally about the correct economic policies in order to raise Vietnam's low standards of living, which in bad years led to widespread malnutrition. But there was no thought of turning the one-party state into a multi-party democracy. Economic liberalisation won the upper hand in the second half of the 1980s, but bad state management of the economy led to hyperinflation checked periodically by austerity measures. Attempts to attract foreign investment had little success. With the outbreak of revolution in Eastern Europe and Soviet *perestroika*, Vietnam's political control tightened once more in 1989 and 1990. Vietnam remains one of the poorest countries in the world, barely able to feed her rapidly expanding population, which reached 66 million in 1989.

One major reason for Vietnam's poverty besides communist mismanagement is the great amount still spent on defence. Her army is over 1 million strong. Since 1975, Vietnam has lived in regional isolation. Only the Soviet Union provided aid, which rapidly decreased after 1985 (Russia gave no aid in the early 1990s). The United States maintained a trade embargo. The failure to account for US servicemen missing during the war is one stumbling-block to improved relations with the United States, though some American aid has been given. Relations with her northern neighbour reached their nadir when Vietnam invaded and occupied most of Kampuchea in December 1978 and expelled the Chinese-backed Pol Pot regime. The Vietnamese-installed government was ostracised by the international community and Vietnam was condemned. The Chinese mounted an armed attack across the Vietnamese border in February 1979, but withdrew three weeks later in March having, as Beijing put it, 'taught' the Vietnamese a 'lesson'. Thereafter in the 1980s the Chinese maintained a threatening posture on Vietnam's northern border with occasional armed clashes, but relations have become much less tense since Vietnam withdrew from Kampuchea in 1989. The constant stream of refugees from south Vietnam by sea (the 'boat people') and overland to Thailand, Malaya and Hong Kong also aggravated Vietnam's neighbours. The United States accepted hundreds of thousands of Vietnamese and, more recently, numbers of 'Amerasians', the mixed children of US servicemen and Vietnamese.

Vietnam remained isolated until the early 1990s, and no large-scale international aid or capital investment had reached her. The potential of the hardworking and adaptable Vietnamese continues to be unexploited. A people who had suffered so much deserved a better fate, and there were increasing signs that the United States felt she had a moral responsibility to help.

# CHAPTER 64

# Continuous Revolution: Mao's China

There was one aspect of Chinese life that did not change after the communist victory in 1949: China continued to be ruled autocratically by an all-powerful leader who used terror to keep the people under control. Mao Zedong manipulated a tight group of supporters in the central party apparatus, ridding himself of 'enemies'. During the twenty-seven years from 1949 to his death in 1976, his was the guiding spirit. He made clever use of the Politburo members to represent a variety of policies, from the radical and revolutionary socialist to the more pragmatic reformists, who believed that modernising China as rapidly as possible and increasing the wealth of the people who were among the poorest in the world, was more important than revolutionary socialism. Mao would back one group against another according to what suited his immediate purpose; he felt no personal loyalties. This way of operating allowed him every option, and a change of policy would discredit yesterday's men rather than the Chairman. Mao believed in driving the revolution forward by appeals to the masses, but just as important was the exercise of control through coercion. The great surges of revolutionary fervour were masterminded by Mao himself, though at crisis-points he expediently accepted pauses, even temporary reversals. Thus the revolutionary drives were interspersed with periods of retrenchment during which economic recovery was permitted to take precedence over revolution. But Mao feared that too long a soft period would weaken mass revolutionary ardour and lead China back on to the capitalist road to 'bourgeois values', instead of advancing her towards a communist utopia.

Continuous revolution, faith in the power of the masses and in his ability to compel them to follow his lead, self-help if foreign aid was not available without unacceptable strings, the need to propel China irrevocably towards her communist goal – these remained Mao's consistent guidelines even when abrupt changes of direction bewildered the outside world. Those who opposed him were ruthlessly eliminated. The picture of the benign, fatherly Mao was as much a product of propaganda as that of 'Uncle Joe'.

Soon after Mao's death in 1976, the concepts of 'revolution' and 'socialism' were replaced by new ideas about modernisation; class conflict was dropped from the official vocabulary; even capitalist experiments were encouraged. Much of Mao's revolutionary Marxism was now condemned. Yet in one crucial respect there was no change. The all-powerful inner group of party leaders could alone decide on the proper course China should follow; the Chinese people had no choice. As none of Mao's successors could hope to achieve his prestige, the struggles within the party leadership assumed a new significance. Neither Mao nor his heirs could set China on a consistent course.

Mobilising the masses involved the use of terror against those designated as the enemy. Whole families were made to suffer for the alleged delinquency or opposition of any one of its members.

Revolutions require enemies and after 1949 these enemies were 'uncovered' not only outside the continental confines of China but also within. The first target was the hated landlord class, who were delivered up to peasant vengeance. During the first four years of communist rule some three-quarters of a million enemies, principally landowners, were summarily executed. Four-fifths of China's population lived in the countryside, so Mao was making sure that they would view the revolution favourably: this was the first step towards their mass indoctrination. To this end Mao even allowed the landlords' holdings to be divided up among the peasants – a step backwards from his ideal of a socialised peasantry. Possibly he had learnt from Stalin's disastrous attempt at rapid collectivisation in 1929–31. For a time the Chinese peasant was allowed to own his land.

The redistribution of land after 1950 gave the peasants what they most hungered after. Their tiny holdings, although still meagre, were on average doubled or trebled in size. The richer peasants, the so-called 'middle peasants', benefited the most. The extortion of taxes was abolished and a more just system introduced. Before the road to communism could be taken, China's industrial strength had to be built up and greater yields obtained from the land. The Chinese head of state, Liu Shaoqui, declared these to be the country's basic policy aims; Mao, chairman of the party and the undisputed overall leader of China, was prepared until the mid-1950s to bide his time before driving the revolution on. From 1949 to 1955 the party preached harmony (except for its hostility towards feudal landlords and agents of Chiang Kai-shek). In the cities private enterprise and ownership were allowed to persist in a mixed economy, while in the vast rural areas socialist schemes were brought in gradually and were always voluntary. The peasant owned his land, but 'mutual aid teams' introduced shared labour and shared use of animals and equipment, and a number of co-operatives were formed. The most urgent task in 1949 was reconstruction. For this the professionals, the engineers, the businessmen and the owners of factories in the newly liberated areas were for the time being indispensable, and they were provided with the class label of 'national bourgeoisie'.

Mao's China in 1949 proclaimed not a communist republic but the People's Democratic Dictatorship. Democratic did not mean that the proletariat would be supreme in the state; rather it meant that the four classes of peasants, workers, petty bourgeoisie and the national bourgeoisie would work together under the leadership of the party to bring about China's recovery. How long this apparent harmony would be allowed to continue only Mao knew. While he presided over an apparently cohesive central party committee, allowing his principal lieutenants wide-ranging debate over different policy options and acting as a genuine chairman, receiving advice from different quarters, his deeper purpose was revealed by his incessant discovery of new contradictions, his stirring up of new conflicts. In 1951 he launched a campaign against the 'three evils' of corruption, waste and bureaucracy among the local communist cadres, its purpose being to increase central control and keep local party officials on their toes. The following year was added a campaign against the 'five evils'; this time the masses were aroused against the 'bourgeoisie' in a struggle to eradicate bribery of government officials, tax evasion, theft of state property, cheating on government contracts and speculation. In this way private industrial and commercial enterprises were constantly threatened. Mao's revolution fed on fear, intimidation and denunciation – three genuine evils of the system that were never admitted.

Nevertheless the first years of communist rule also brought about genuine improvements for most of the Chinese people. The cessation of fighting and destruction was the greatest and most immediate. There was also a measure of genuine mass idealism, as the people acted together to improve conditions. This was most noticeable in the cities, where neighbourhood groups organised by party officials tackled the sanitation systems and spread poison to get rid of the rats, carriers of disease. Life on the land and in the factories was made more congenial. One measure of success was a dramatic fall in the mortality rate. After the ruinous inflation of the Kuomintang years, prices had become stable. Living standards, especially of the poorest peasants, had risen. In the cities unemployment was halved, attendance at school and college nearly doubled; cholera and plagues had been brought under control. The gross output of industry was one and a half times greater in 1952 than it had been in 1949; agricultural output, on which the country depended, was up by half. Roads and railway lines were constructed. These were the considerable accomplishments of the New Democracy.

In 1952 Mao set out the general line of policy to be followed. China was in a period of transition, from the foundation of what was now called the People's Republic to the socialist transformation of agriculture, industry and handicrafts, to be accomplished 'step by step over a fairly long period of time'. The priorities were to increase production, to raise standards of living, and to strengthen China's defences. Liu Shaoqui announced at the Eighth Party Congress in 1956 that the transition to socialism had been largely accomplished and would be completed over the next decade.

During the early years of Mao's rule China conducted herself aggressively on the international stage. In 1950-1, she claimed sovereignty over Tibet, overcoming local resistance with great brutality, though the Tibetans under the Dalai Lama were promised internal autonomy. The United States developed an implacable hostility to China and maintained her support for Chiang Kai-shek in Taiwan. The outbreak of the Korean War opened another front, when Mao, overriding his more cautious advisers, decided on China's intervention in November 1950 (pages 430-2). Isolated from the West, China had no alternative but to align herself with the Soviet Union. The Korean War imposed huge strains and sacrifices on China, and until the armistice was signed at Panmunjon in July 1953, Mao had to restrain his revolutionary drive.

When planning began in 1953 to increase China's industrial base, the Soviet model was adopted. The Russians provided considerable assistance and sent 10,000 engineers to work with the Chinese while three times that number of Chinese were accepted for training in the Soviet Union. Plants, machinery and technical designs all came from Russia. The emphasis was on the expansion of energy supplies and heavy industry – iron and steel mills, electricity power stations, machine-tool factories. In all, 156 projects were sponsored by the Soviet Union. Without this help China's modernisation of industry would have been far slower. America's Marshall Aid to Europe likewise accelerated the recovery and prosperity of Western Europe, but it came in the form of loans and grants which enabled the Europeans to import from the United States what they needed. Soviet aid came in the form of people, training and technology, but the Chinese had to pay for them. The Soviet Union needed capital for

her own reconstruction and her loans to China were small. But the joint Soviet–Chinese companies which had been established were not a success. Mao insisted on complete Chinese sovereignty and they were amicably dissolved in 1954 after Stalin's death.

Just as the First Five-Year Plan was getting under way, Mao bypassed the central party leadership and in 1955 began his long campaign to transform China's independent landowning peasantry into collectivised socialist workers on the land. Despite vicissitudes, Mao never abandoned that aim and had substantially achieved it by the time of his death. But the cost to China was huge. The famines that followed alone caused some 20 million deaths.

Mao's plans for collectivisation differed from Stalin's and are a good illustration of his determination to build socialism with Chinese characteristics. The peasant continued to own his home and, in less radical phases, small plots – but the rest of the land and all the labour were collectivised in three tiers. The bottom tier was called the production team, perhaps a village of thirty or forty families. Everything was pooled and the earnings of the team shared out between them. A larger collectivised unit was the production brigade, made up of several production teams. Production brigades together formed the collectives. Whether earnings would be accounted for and distributed at the production team, brigade or collective level depended on Mao's decree and varied with different phases of more or less radical policies.

In 1955 Mao launched a campaign to form socialist co-operatives: labour and resources would be pooled, though small plots would remain. But the better-off 'middle peasants' were reluctant to co-operate with the poorer, and the production of rice and soya beans, staple Chinese foods, scarcely kept pace with the country's growing population. For a short period the party blamed the poor results not on Mao but on the over-hasty setting up of the large co-operatives. And following the Soviet model, the party leaders concluded, had led to a lopsided development of heavy industry at the expense of light industry and agriculture. From 1956 until early 1957 was a period of relaxation and consolidation. The emphasis at the Eighth Congress of the Communist Party in September 1956 was shifted from building socialism, which it was claimed had been more or less accomplished, to increasing productivity and correcting the agricultural backwardness. This new line, which was intended to help China catch up with the West, required more individual enterprise, encouraged in part by the provision of incentives. Students and intellectuals, cowed by previous campaigns against them, were now wooed. Deng Xiaoping, one of Mao's rising lieutenants, advocated more worker participation in management as one way of increasing productivity. This, in the Chinese definition, was greater participation – always subject, though, to the leadership of the party.

In February 1957 Mao delivered a speech 'On the Correct Handling of Contradictions among People'. One passage in particular received widespread publicity for its apparent espousal of freedom of ideas among the scientific and intellectual community – 'letting a hundred flowers blossom and a hundred schools of thought contend'. But what seemed to the West to be a move towards tolerance and plurality was no more than a tactical device, a means to an end, the perceived precondition for what became known as the Great Leap Forward. It encouraged China's intellectuals and was meant to act as a restraint on party bureaucracy at the local level. Freedom of thought would not, however, be allowed to challenge central control and leadership.

During the winter of 1957 and into the spring of 1958 60 million peasants were put to work on water-conservancy constructions to aid agriculture. Mass human power was to be used in place of more advanced technology to achieve quick results. At the same time as plans for the Great Leap Forward were implemented, a purge of intellectuals was begun in a bewildering reversal of the previous year. The pendulum had thus swung once more. Mao intervened to pronounce a new line after watching the turmoil of destalinisation in Poland and Hungary in 1956; this was called the Anti-Rightist campaign. The 'hundred flowers' had blossomed for little more than one season. In every factory 5 per cent of the workers had to be denounced as 'rightists' and subjected to a witch-hunt. Up to 700,000 'intellectuals', or educated Chinese, were thrown out of their positions and professions and sent to the countryside for so-called labour reform. The contempt for the intellectuals, the need to control and subjugate them, now took precedence over China's desperate need for their skills. It was easy to treat them harshly as they were isolated from China's masses of peasants and workers. Denunci-

ation by family, friends, colleagues and fellow workers, which inevitably sowed distrust, was one of the party's most effective means of control. Abroad, China's softer line co-operating with a neutral Third World, exemplified by the Bandung Conference in 1955 (page 620) and the stance of 'peaceful coexistence', was followed by increased militancy and self-assertion. In 1958 China's relations with Taiwan reached a new crisis-point, and on India's border in 1959 there were armed clashes.

Mao's faith that the ideologically motivated peasants and workers could overcome all obstacles, that the grassroot masses were what mattered, not the professionals and intellectuals, found practical expression in what party propaganda described as the Great Leap Forward – actually two leaps, in 1958 and 1959–60. They proved an unmitigated disaster for the Chinese economy and people.

In the countryside the people's co-operatives were merged into huge communes under ideological local party leadership. They now comprised not only agriculture but also grassroots industrial units. Unrealistic production targets were set. Now not only would steel be smelted in the efficient new modern mills, but iron would be produced in small peasant furnaces. Chaos ensued: industrial production declined and agricultural output dropped by a quarter. A renewed 'leap' in 1959 and 1960 resulted in further disastrous agricultural and industrial losses. In the first quarter of 1961 alone output of twenty-five key industrial products dropped by between 30 and 40 per cent. There was a chronic grain shortage as China's population increased, and famine became widespread. An estimated 19 million people died.

After the failure of the Great Leap Forward, Mao permitted a reformist party leadership to follow policies at variance with his longer-term objectives, because priority had to be given to increase food supplies and resume industrial growth – in other words, to repair the ravages of the Great Leap Forward. Thus from 1960 to 1963 the party returned to more rational planning. China's professionals were appeased and told that they were part of the working people. Private plots and handicraft enterprise were again permitted. The peasantry were allowed to sell their produce in a free market provided they fulfilled their state quotas. To feed China's growing population – it increased by 80 million between 1957 to 1965 – incentives were necessary to raise production. Even so, agriculture barely recovered to its 1957 level and the shortfall had to be made good by grain imports.

All these policies of the so-called reformists were opposed by an ultra-left group which placed the revolutionary class struggle first. The reformers were led by the nominal head of state, Liu Shaoqui, and Deng Xiaoping; the Defence Minister Lin Biao, who in 1959 had replaced Peng Dehuai, dismissed for openly criticising Mao's Great Leap Forward, was a sycophantic supporter of Mao's most extreme policies; Mao's wife, the former actress Jiang Quing, was another uncompromising extremist. Then there were various groupings between the two; Premier Zhou Enlai was the most enduring and able, manoeuvring cleverly so that he never lost Mao's approval. Mao waited until he judged the time right before resuming the revolutionary lead.

Unquestionably there was serious inner-party strife at the top level of the Politburo from 1958 to 1966. Mao permitted the different groupings to coexist, acting only if there were any outright criticisms of the Chairman himself, such as those voiced by the disgraced Peng. The inner workings of Chinese party politics permit more than one interpretation. It is possible that Mao genuinely had to struggle against opponents in the party to reassert his authority. Much more likely, Mao deliberately chose to withdraw from time to time to study and reflect, and to dissociate himself from 'rectification' policies which he would later attack and condemn.

This explains certain simultaneous but contradictory currents in Chinese politics. In the autumn of 1962 Mao indicated a return to a more radical course with a campaign against writers and the resurfacing of bourgeois and capitalist tendencies. He turned to a new generation: 'youth must be educated so that our nation will remain revolutionary and incorruptible for generations and forever'. In the spring of 1963 he claimed that landlords and rich peasants were regaining their influence, corrupting and manipulating local party officials, and 'developing counter-revolutionary organisations'. Meanwhile, Deng Xiaoping, now the party's general-secretary, was giving priority to economic recovery, above all to repair the ravages in agriculture. Deng had expressed this view uncompromisingly: 'As long as we increase production, we can revert to individual enterprise; it hardly matters whether a good cat is black or white – as long as it catches mice . . .' This did not mean that

Deng was a liberal in the Western sense, that he envisaged abandoning communism or authoritarian control from the centre. He was adopting a pragmatic approach to China's immediate economic problems – any incentives offered to private enterprise would be determined by the party. The party would continue to control China.

By 1963, Mao was preparing to move against Deng and the policies he advocated, but 'self-criticism' saved him in 1966. Liu Shaoqui was not so fortunate; dismissed from all his posts in 1968, he died in prison a year later. With the help of Lin Biao, Mao embarked on an intensive campaign to radicalise the young army recruits with 'the thoughts of Chairman Mao'.

The famous Little Red Book was written to indoctrinate them. 'Study Chairman Mao's writings, follow his teachings and act according to his instructions,' ordered Lin Biao. Mao's quotations can indeed be cited in justification of all the changes of policy resorted to and cover every possible condition. They are taken from his writings and speeches from the 1920s to the 1950s. By grouping them in thirty-three thematic chapters under headings such as 'Self-Reliance and Arduous Struggle', 'Serving the People' and so on, but then jumbling up any chronological sequence within each section, they can be used to support many different arguments by selective citation. They thus convey a sense of infallibility despite their contradictions. The Little Red Book became the holy writ of the student youth revolt of 1966 – that is, of the Red Guards.

China's difficulties were compounded by her international isolation. Khrushchev's destalinisation in the Soviet Union led to a breach with Mao, who accused him of revisionism and of leading the Soviet Union back on to the capitalist road. He condemned him for betraying the revolution while exhibiting great-power chauvinism by suppressing nationalism in Eastern Europe. Mao vehemently rejected the Soviet leader's attempts to use the assistance given to China to control her policies. In 1959 Khrushchev first withdrew Soviet help from the programme to build China's own atomic weapons. Faced with America's nuclear threat, China would have to construct nuclear weapons by herself, and she succeeded in doing so. In 1960 Khrushchev dealt a heavy blow to the Chinese economy, stopping all aid and recalling some 30,000 Soviet engineers and technicians from China. Mao discerned ominous signs of Soviet–American collusion after the Soviet failure in Cuba (page 599), and the Test Ban Treaty in 1963 was a clear indication to him that the United States and the Soviet Union were joining one great-power camp.

Mao placed China in opposition to this supposed collusion, calling on the Third World countries in Asia, Africa and Latin America not to be afraid but to struggle for their independence: 'People of the world, unite and defeat US aggressors and their running dogs ... Monsters of all kinds shall be destroyed.' Nuclear weapons need not strike fear in the hearts of peoples struggling against imperialism, Mao declared, using a colourful metaphor, for the nuclear powers were just 'paper tigers'. But when in 1962 he conceived the fear that America would back a Chiang Kai-shek invasion, he allowed himself to be reassured by a hastily arranged contact between the Chinese and American embassies in Warsaw.

Mao took care not to involve China again directly in any fighting against a stronger enemy. His diatribes against the Soviet Union and the United States remained rhetorical. He was opposed to any military confrontation with the United States, even when he was urged to intervene in Vietnam, where the Americans were stepping up their support for the anti-communist southern republic. The case of India was different. Earlier good relations with Nehru deteriorated when the Indians expressed their sympathy for the subjugated Tibetans and welcomed the Dalai Lama and Tibetan refugees after the revolt of 1959. When the Indians occupied some Chinese border posts on the ill-defined Sino-Indian frontier, Mao reacted forcefully. Launching a major military offensive in October 1962, he routed the inferior Indian forces. But, having taught India a painful lesson, he declared a unilateral cease-fire in November and withdrew to a rectified frontier line which India later accepted. Thus the early 1960s were years of danger and crisis as perceived by Mao; his response to the United States, the Soviet Union and Taiwan was not appeasement but independence, a determination to defend China. But he was also cautious, avoiding direct military engagement except on the Indian frontier, where it was strictly limited.

As Mao contemplated Khrushchev's errors in the 1960s, he feared that leading party members in China might well be tempted to emulate him and take the capitalist road. So his condemnation of Khrushchev was intended also to serve as a warning at home to the party. One of the roots of the Great Proletarian Cultural Revolution was certainly Mao's concern that the revolution was being betrayed by the 'bourgeois' ideas of Deng and Liu.

Mao sought to revive the revolutionary spirit by unleashing a conflict between the masses on the one hand and the party functionaries, the bureaucracy and all those who had a stake in preserving the *status quo* in China on the other. To Westerners one of the most curious features of Chinese politics is the oblique way a new policy is signalled by a development that might seem quite trivial. Mao preferred this approach. He began his assault in 1965 by criticising the writer Wu Han, one of whose plays some years earlier he had interpreted as an attack on himself. This seemed innocuous. But Wu was the protégé of Deng Xiaoping, the party general secretary. Mao then left the capital and manoeuvred to gain support among the various factions within the widespread Chinese power structure. In February 1966, with his wife Jiang Quing now playing a prominent role, he declared his intention to launch the Great Proletarian Cultural Revolution.

A distinguished Chinese economic historian, Xue Mugiao, director of China's Economic Research Centre, in the 1980s condemned the Cultural Revolution as initiated by a leader labouring under a misapprehension and capitalised on by counter-revolutionary cliques; it led to domestic turmoil and brought catastrophe to the party, the state and the whole people. Such criticism of Mao became possible only in the reformist 1980s. At the time party members attempted to defend themselves while sycophantically declaring their loyalty and obedience to the Chairman. Liu was not so lucky.

The convulsion of the Cultural Revolution wrecked millions of lives. From 1966 to 1968 the struggles assumed the proportions of a civil war, with fierce fighting and brigandage in many parts of the country. Mao had aroused the people to denounce each other. In the process he raised his teaching to an unprecedented personality cult. The revolution began with the dissident students and disgruntled teachers, who organised themselves spontaneously into 'Red Guards' to carry out Mao's will. The Cultural Revolution was unique among student revolts of the late 1960s in that it was encouraged from the very top against the more

privileged elders. The students proceeded physically to assault the 'monsters and demons and all counter-revolutionary revisionists of the Khrushchev type' and to ransack their homes; they vowed that they would carry Mao's socialist revolution through to its end. Their instruments were terror and humiliation. On 18 August 1966, Mao appeared on the gallery of the Tiananmen Gate of Heavenly Peace, to be adulated by huge crowds of Red Guards, who packed the square before him all day. Eventually he descended into the square itself to be among them; more than a million Red Guards had come from outside Beijing to join those in the capital already. They were ordered to 'spread disorder', to attack the party bureaucrats, to root out Chinese tradition and bourgeois revisionism – indeed to eliminate all the elements that had infiltrated the party and were taking the false capitalist road.

The student Red Guards fanned out throughout

*At a mass demonstration at the height of China's Cultural Revolution, Red miners recite in unison from Chairman Mao's* Little Red Book.

*At a rally in Beijing in 1966, half a million young Communists turn out to cheer Mao and his chosen successor Lin Piao, who stands to the right of his mentor. Only five years later, Lin was to die in a mysterious plane crash and be denounced as a traitor.*

the country to radicalise the masses in the cities; the vast countryside of China remained less affected. In factories they enlisted workers. It was a movement that became anarchic and violent; teachers, professionals, anyone in authority could become the target of their attacks. The Red Guards were rendering China's urban centres virtually ungovernable, as local party structures were paralysed by their onslaught. Much destruction was inflicted on Mao's orders, but the Red Guards were incapable of putting a new orderly structure in place of those that had ceased to function.

After a few months Mao had to call a temporary halt. The People's Liberation Army was the one force able to restrain Red Guard rampages, and had already intervened in places. But it was not a proper instrument for furthering revolution; it was more suitable for repressing disorder of whatever ideological nuance. By the spring of 1967 the army had become a dominant force in the country and was gradually restoring order, fighting the radicals, replacing the party, moving into factories and controlling the extremists. It was not the outcome of the revolution Mao had planned. Cities were destroyed, and hundreds of thousands of lives were lost.

Mao now unleashed the second phase of the revolution, attempting to curb the army. Red Guards went back on the rampage. Throughout China different factions were locked in confrontation. Mao could influence events but even he could not control their outcome. Among the most strident voices encouraging the Red Guards to persevere was that of Mao's wife, Jiang Quing. Violence reached new heights in August 1967. The revolutionary committees which had replaced the local party machines now battled against more extremist youths. Trains carrying weapons destined for Vietnam were looted. Peasants in rival factions, army units, Red Guard groups all fought each other. In Wukan military groups refused to obey directives from Beijing. The army itself became divided. In Beijing, Liu Shaoqui, nominal head of state, still remained as a symbol of party opposition to Mao, although he had been made to 'confess his crimes'. But the control Mao and his supporters could exercise over the central apparatus could do nothing to restore China to order and sanity.

By September 1967 Mao was ready to accept that the most important task now was to stop China from disintegrating further. Only the professional

army could restore order; blame for excesses could now be shifted on to Mao's advisers and the Red Guards, who had exceeded their functions. The betrayal of his most fervent supporters meant nothing to Mao. The myth of his detached infallibility of judgement had to be preserved, although he was the author of China's woes. His wife indirectly admitted to mistakes and now sided with the army against the Red Guards, who were exhorted to practise self-criticism. Mao had to admit that they had proved incapable of providing leadership and impetus to revolutionary China. Only strife and chaos had followed in their path. Behind the scenes Prime Minister Zhou Enlai and Lin Piao, the Defence Minister, were taking charge. The distinction between a Red Guard and a criminal became blurred. Many were executed. The restoration of order was an enormous task, only gradually achieved, and social ferment and the killings by radical factions continued sporadically even as late as 1968. The army was now praised for imposing revolutionary discipline and for defending the 'dictatorship of the proletariat'. The Red Guards,

## China, 1949–1968

| | | Indices of gross industrial and agricultural output value at constant prices (*1952 = 100*) | | | |
|---|---|---|---|---|---|
| | | Agriculture | Light industry | Heavy industry | Population (*millions*) |
| 1 | 1949 | 67.4 | 46.6 | 30.3 | 542 |
| 2 | 1953 | 103.1 | 126.7 | 136.9 | 588 |
| 3 | 1958 | 127.8 | 245.1 | 555.5 | 660 |
| 4 | 1960 | 96.4 | 269.7 | 1,035.8 | 662 |
| | 1961 | 94.1 | 211.4 | 554.2 | 659 |
| | 1962 | 99.9 | 193.6 | 429.0 | 673 |
| | 1965 | 137.1 | 344.7 | 651.0 | 725 |
| 5 | 1966 | 149.0 | 394.7 | 830.0 | 745 |
| | 1968 | 147.5 | 348.7 | 630.1 | 785 |

*Key:*

1 Reconstruction (1949–52)
2 First Five-Year Plan (1953–8)
3 Great Leap Forward (1958–60)
4 Gradual Recovery and Conflict with Soviet Union (1960–5)
5 Great Proletarian Cultural Revolution (1966–8)

*Source*: Liu Suinian and Wu Qungan, *China's Socialist Economy, 1949–1984* (Beijing, 1986), pp. 477, 479.

yesterday in the vanguard of socialist progress, had become 'leftist opportunists', 'anarchists' and 'class enemies'. Mao's army 'Thought Teams' were sent in to take charge of universities and colleges.

Mao now initiated a new movement which won the approval of both the army and the Beijing moderates. The cities and universities were cleared of students and intellectuals and rowdy youths; they were overpopulated anyway. Some 20 million Chinese were forced into the countryside in 1968 and 1969 to learn to labour as peasants. The 'young intellectuals' were undergoing re-education. In October Liu Shaoqui's disgrace was complete. Only Mao emerged intact. Lin Piao at the Ninth National Congress of the Chinese Communist Party in April 1969 absolved Mao of all blame and buried the Cultural Revolution, describing its demise as a 'great victory'. The cost in lives, in blighted careers, was enormous and was to set China back by a decade even after the immediate losses of production in 1967 and 1968 had been made good.

During the last years of his life Mao became more remote, removed from the day-to-day running of the state. Now virtually deified he continued to symbolise for China the communist victory and China's emergence as a world power. And herein lies the final contradiction: Mao's benign reputation was not deserved; terror and violence were the result of the ideological utopias he had pursued. He had ruined millions of lives in the Great Leap Forward, the Cultural Revolution and the wholesale forced migrations. Mao had attempted to ensure that as his life drew to a close the revolutionary fire would not be extinguished with him. The excesses of the Cultural Revolution, however, taught some of the Chinese leadership a bitter lesson in the dangers of Mao's line of thought and action. By the time he died in September 1976, in the context of economic planning there would only be a revolutionary flicker of his radical ideas left. But the heritage of a repressive political one-party state remained very much intact.

The Chinese revolution had created its own gulag, a network of Forced Job Placement and Labour camps. Millions of prisoners were condemned to forced labour, sometimes for decades, without trial. During the frequent famines, like that after Mao's disastrous experiment in 1958, life was reduced to searching for scraps of food. We know from surviving witnesses that in such camps the obsession with food replaced all feelings and other desires. Those suspected of 'wrong thinking', the 'rightists' and other dissidents fared the worst and had to submit to sessions of re-education to crush their independent spirit. How many hundreds of thousands did not survive can still not be estimated. It is only recently that the dissidents who reached the West have enabled the world to gain fuller knowledge of the penal and camp system of 're-education' and forced labour. There were variations between conditions in different camps depending on the camp commanders, the work to be performed and the prevailing political mood. One truth emerges from all this horror: the resilience and courage of the survivors show that the human spirit knows no boundaries of nationality or race.

CHAPTER 65

# *The Last Years of Mao and His Heirs:*
# *The Revolution Changes Course*

Even in the aftermath of the Tiananmen Square killings in 1989, the Chinese communist leaders acted like a caste of high priests. They alone could delineate the right path to be followed by a billion of their fellow Chinese. Yet since 1949 Chinese history had been marked by abrupt changes. The correct line at any one moment was determined by the ascendant group among the elite. After Mao's death in 1976, no one carried enough prestige to assume his mantle, though Deng Xiaoping managed for a decade to exert overriding influence. When there was a change of policy, the leader turned on his erstwhile supporters, who were now revealed as deviationists, enemies or counter-revolutionaries – exposed by the vigilance of the victorious faction. The rest of China, from the regional cadres to the humble peasant, was coerced into following the new line. The imprisonment and even execution of opponents was commonplace, as was the execution of criminals. Consistency was found only in the ruthless exercise of centralised power, the maintenance of a one-party state with the support of the military, the police and the secret services.

This structure, however, in no way inhibited power struggles among China's leadership, which occurred right through to the 1990s. But the tensions and conflicts within the Politburo could only be guessed at until the disgrace of one group at the hands of another brought them out into the open. The contradictions in society, which provided the basic Marxist explanation of historical develop-

ment, furnished both the weapons used against opponents and the justifications adopted for the new policies. The party could 'reform' only from the top down. Reform from below or outside the party – that is, democracy – would undermine this self-perpetuating system. So any radical change in the way China was ruled had to be effected by the leadership itself, as in the latter part of the 1980s in the Soviet Union, or by a successful revolt made possible by the disaffection of the army. For any Chinese leader control of the army was thus as vital as control of the Politburo. The chairmanship of the Military Affairs Commission was a key position of great power; its occupant ensured that posts held under him, such as the deputy director, the Chief of Staff and the director of the political department, were filled by his supporters.

Until his death in 1976, Mao continued to dominate China whenever he chose to set the line of policy to be followed. The violent changes from 1949 to 1976 reflected his perversion of the Confucian doctrine of the Golden Mean – a radical move would be followed by consolidation and relaxation only to be succeeded by the next step forward. The demise of the Red Guards in 1968, however, was succeeded not so much by consolidation and relaxation as by a change in the direction of the revolution. The student Red Guards had experienced real and heady power; in the name of Mao they had taken the law into their own hands, believing that they should lead Chinese society through revolution to communist utopia. They had ventured forth with Mao's blessing, causing mayhem and attacking not only the local officials, as Mao had instructed in his Big Character Poster of 5 August 1966, 'Bombard the Headquarters', but also anyone belonging to the traditional establishment. Their bitterness and disillusionment when Mao and the party leadership suppressed them and forced them to labour in the countryside were fierce indeed. Paradoxically the Cultural Revolution also gave rise to the Democracy Movement, whose ideals of individual rights and liberties were the exact opposite of the Red Guards' cry of submission to Mao's doctrines and vision.

During the last years of his life Mao acted more and more autocratically. He found it useful to maintain in power a Politburo in which the extreme left group (Gang of Four), which included Jiang Quing, his actress wife since 1938, was balanced by the reformists, led by Deng Xiaoping, who returned to the central stage in 1973 as one of the vice-premiers. Premier Zhou Enlai, who had weathered all the turns of policy, moving just sufficiently in whatever direction the wind blew, was a moderating influence. His unqualified loyalty to Mao and his flexibility help to explain how he alone among China's political elite had remained at the centre. The attempts by the Gang of Four to undermine his position only earned them Mao's reproof, but they too retained considerable influence until the Chairman's death. It was Mao's way of balancing rival forces. Nonetheless, a victim had to be found who could be blamed for the excesses of the Red Guards. From the highest ranks of the Politburo, Mao chose his intended successor, Lin Biao, Minister of Defence since 1960. Accused of plotting to assassinate Mao, Lin Biao was never brought to trial, and died conveniently in an aircrash in 1971, allegedly while trying to escape.

In 1975 Zhou Enlai fell seriously ill. Mao, who recognised Deng's abilities, delegated to him the running of the state, despite the hostility of the Gang of Four. Zhou Enlai died the following year, in April 1976, but Deng's ascendancy was short-lived. Thousands of people demonstrated in Beijing's Tiananmen Square, ostensibly to mourn the death of Zhou Enlai but in reality protesting against the repression of the ultra-left. There were scuffles with police and the square was cleared by force, an uneasy precedent for what was to happen there thirteen years later.

Between 1970 and 1974 the economic recovery was proceeding in fits and starts. This did not deflect the party leadership from making grand plans for the future. At the Fourth National People's Congress in January 1975 Zhou Enlai proclaimed that the country's objective now was to catch up with the developed world by the end of the century by concentrating on the 'four moderns': the modernisation of agriculture, of industry, of national defence and of science and technology. But within the constraints of Mao's ideology such results could not be attained. It would be left to Mao's heirs to try new ways of achieving the necessary growth.

What has subsequently been called the second phase of the Cultural Revolution continued to disrupt China. Some 12 million students, professionals and intellectuals had been sent into the countryside to be educated in the realities of Chinese peasant life. Many unjust imprisonments were upheld. Education and science was disrupted; schools and universities only gradually reopened in the 1970s. The see-saw policies of Mao's hierarchy inflicted untold hardship and suffering on millions of Chinese. They would remember the decade from 1966 to 1976 as the years of great turmoil.

Yet there were also, at least in principle, some beneficial aspects. The relocation of industrial activity throughout China, away from the manufacturing cities of the southern China coast spurred a more even development and mitigated the Third World phenomenon of developing mega-cities unable to cope with the population influx. Had there been more rational planning, with transport and communications keeping pace and with the older urban centres being maintained and renewed as necessary instead of suffering from neglect, China's economic development would have suffered less from Mao's Cultural Revolution. As it was Mao's faith in the power of ideology created a fatal impediment. He did not think through his plans, and that is one explanation for their spectacular failure.

It is remarkable that one branch of technology nevertheless held its own during the decade when intellectuals were most fiercely persecuted: that was the missile and atomic-bomb sector. After Russia's withdrawal from the nuclear programme, Chinese scientists went ahead on their own, and in October 1964 China exploded her own atomic bomb, becoming the fifth nuclear power in the world. Two years later guided missiles provided a delivery system. By 1967 China had built the even more terrible hydrogen bomb. Three years later she sent up her first satellite and in 1975 launched a retrievable model. Chinese missiles are among the most reliable and can place commercial payloads into space more cheaply than either the American missiles or Europe's Ariadne missile.

One of the most startling developments of Mao's last years was the reorientation of China's foreign policy. Relations with the Soviet Union had gone from bad to worse after Khrushchev's fall, and in March 1969 there was actually hand-to-hand fighting over an insignificant island in the middle of the Ussuri river claimed by both the Russians and the Chinese. But the border dispute on the Soviet Pacific along the Amur and Ussuri rivers was less a cause than a symptom of Sino-Soviet hostility, with Brezhnev in the 1970s stationing some of Russia's best divisions on the border, complete with nuclear-missile installations. The Chinese anyway knew that they were no match for the Russians. Mao interpreted Soviet foreign policy as entering a new imperialist era, and he could cite as evidence the Brezhnev Doctrine (page 798), which was used to justify the invasion of Czechoslovakia in 1968. The United States by contrast had in Mao's view become overstretched and in the early 1970s was looking for a way out of Vietnam. Mao saw in the American–Soviet rivalry a contradiction which China might exploit: he was now prepared to seek agreement with the country which had hitherto been China's main antagonist – the United States. In Washington, President Nixon and

Henry Kissinger also saw a chance to create a better balance of power against the Soviet Union by playing the China card.

It began in a characteristically Chinese fashion with an agreement early in 1971 for a United States table-tennis team to visit China. This was the first direct link between the two countries. The United States still recognised Chiang Kai-shek's regime in Taiwan as the legitimate Republic of China, and its representatives occupied China's place on the UN Security Council. In July, Kissinger, President Nixon's national security adviser, journeyed secretly to Beijing. This paved the way for one of the most momentous U-turns in the history of international relations.

President Nixon, Mrs Nixon, William Rogers, the Secretary of State, and Kissinger flew to Beijing for discussions and negotiations with Mao and Zhou Enlai in February 1972. The outcome was incorporated in a joint US–Chinese communiqué published in Shanghai on 28 February in which the American and Chinese signatories declared that they wished to normalise relations between the two countries. They reviewed the world situation, and the Americans and Chinese each issued a statement of their own. Despite different ideologies, the US document declared, no country was infallible. The US stressed her commitment to freedom and to support for South Vietnam and South Korea. The Chinese countered that oppression bred resistance, that strong nations should not bully the weak: 'China will never be a superpower and it opposes hegemony and power politics of any kind.' The Chinese

*President Nixon's momentous visit to Beijing in February 1972 publicly announced the change in US global strategy. Secretary of State Henry Kissinger sits at Nixon's right hand.*

expressed their firm support for the peoples of Laos, Vietnam and Cambodia (here the Chinese took the opposite side to the United States), but both declared they wished to reduce the danger of international conflict and did not seek hegemony. The touchiest and most crucial difference was over the future of Taiwan, so long allied to the United States. The Chinese uncompromisingly declared Taiwan to be an internal question and insisted that Taiwan as a province of China should return to the motherland. They also demanded that US forces be withdrawn from the island. The Americans agreed that there was but one China – a point, they added tartly, which Taiwan and Beijing had in common. The US wanted to see a peaceful settlement and gave a momentous if somewhat vague undertaking: 'it affirms the ultimate objective of the withdrawal of all US forces and military installations from Taiwan'.

In December 1978 full diplomatic relations were resumed between Beijing and Washington. America's trade embargo had long ended and China had taken her place fully in the international community, replacing Taiwan's representative as a permanent member of the UN Security Council. Relations with the West were normalised, a process which began with the Soviet Union only in the late 1980s. Thus the opening to the West had begun under Mao's auspices in the 1970s. It was to reach a high point in the 1980s, with many thousands of Chinese students being sent abroad – most to the capitalist United States, where over 20,000 were sent to study advanced technology and management. Deng's younger son studied for his doctorate at Rochester University. It was an ironic reversal: in the 1950s it had been the Soviet Union which had provided the education.

Mao's immediate successor, chosen as chairman by the geriatric Politburo, was an orthodox Maoist, Hua Guofeng. His most significant contribution was to drive the Gang of Four, that is the extreme left, from the most powerful positions. We can only guess at the struggles within the Politburo which led to Deng's recall to his former posts in 1977. Natural disasters which struck the countryside in 1977 and 1978 slowed down the economic recovery then under way and probably helped the reformist section of the Politburo. A distinguished Chinese historian has called the third plenary session of the Eleventh Party Central Committee held in December 1978 'a turning point of far-reaching significance'. Hua was dismissed from his position as party chairman in 1978, accused of persisting in the 'two whatevers' – that is, of wanting to uphold whatever policy decisions Mao had made and whatever directives Mao had sent down.

A main plank of Marxist strategy was now abandoned with the dropping of the 'class struggle' as the key to development and the shift to 'socialist modernisation'. What this meant in reality, despite lipservice to Maoist thinking, was a break with Mao's revolutionary drives, founded on the belief that the creation of communist man must come first through education and the organisation of the peasantry in collectives and workers into state-managed enterprises. The benefits of well-being and economic progress were supposed to follow automatically. It was now thought that the prime task was to modernise China, to do whatever was necessary to increase production on the land and in industry as rapidly as possible so as to raise within a generation the Chinese standard of living from one of the lowest in the world to rank with that of the West. The new line (which had to be sloganised to conform to political practice) was called 'Seeking truth from facts'. Where Marxist ideology proved a hindrance it would be jettisoned. The party, whose standing had reached rock-bottom during the Cultural Revolution, was to be restored to pre-eminence, to ensure that the reforms decided by the leadership would be carried through; and the People's Liberation Army was cosseted to ensure that it would remain the loyal instrument of power and preserve order, unity and obedience to the party leadership. Democracy in the Western sense of pluralism and of a leadership chosen by the people played no part in this programme – indeed, demands for such things were seen as jeopardising the aims of modernisation, as destroying the essential unity of purpose.

Deng Xiaoping, the man who represented the new line and who had already played a significant role in attempting to make China more modern economically, belonged to that elderly group of revolutionaries who had been active in the 1950s. The open distancing from Mao's supposed infallibility was signalled by subjecting the Gang of Four to a televised trial in 1980 in order to expose the wrongdoings of the Cultural Revolution. Jiang Quing, Mao's widow, alone offered a spirited defence, refusing to admit any guilt: 'You can't have

*China's Gang of Four stand trial. Mao's widow Jiang Quing defied her accusers, but was given a death sentence that was later commuted to life imprisonment.*

peaceful coexistence in this area of ideology,' she spat out. '*You* coexist, and *they'll* corrupt you.' She was sentenced to death, but this was later commuted to life imprisonment. As a symbol of the Cultural Revolution she became the most hated woman in China. Meanwhile, a younger generation of politicians had been placed in the top positions: Hu Yaobang became party leader and Zhao Ziyang the head of government, both of them reformist followers of Deng. Deng himself eschewed Mao's personality cult, though as a member of the Politburo in charge of the army he was careful to counter the 'old guard' of conservatives, who remained powerful and strong, ready to make a comeback should his reforms fail or loosen party control or threaten China's unity. So it can be seen that Deng's position could not be compared to Mao's. When public protests became too strong, Deng himself was ready to back a more conservative line.

Deng's reforms of the political structure were never intended to create a Western-style democracy, which he condemned as 'bourgeois liberalism'. But without some reforms of the existing structures his economic programme would fail. For years he

manipulated the factions in China with the skill of a poker player. Just so much criticism had to be encouraged to galvanise corrupt or inefficient party bureaucrats and the patronage system which placed a premium on who you knew. Between 1982 and 1985 slow but steady progress was made in weeding out those who had become too old or were too incompetent, usually by offering generous retirement terms. At a special national party conference in September 1985, half the Politburo was retired and a fifth of the Central Committee. Deng Xiaoping, Hu Yaobang and Zhao Ziyang now had a majority vote in the Politburo. At this point Deng had probably reached the height of his influence and power.

Deng could also look back on a remarkably successful start to his programme of economic reform in education and technological progress, but most especially in agriculture. Socialism was gradually modified and the peasant was given the incentive of growing some of his crops for profit and of engaging in handicraft industry. The people's communes were replaced between 1979 and 1984 by a new system which in practice returned the land to the peasantry under a contract, called a lease, hardly distinguishable from private ownership. The contract had been used before for short periods to revive agricultural output, but now it became the system adopted in place of the collectives. Contracts were made with individual households: taxes had to be paid and an agreed amount of grain had to be sold to the state, but beyond this the household (or groups of peasants) could keep whatever they could earn. Efficient households soon became quasi-landlords, employing sometimes as many as a hundred peasant labourers.

Prices were raised. There was a boom in some regions of China as the successful farmers built themselves large houses and bought consumer goods never before seen in the countryside – colour television sets and refrigerators. Rural enterprises and factories also developed and some owners became rich. What mattered most to the state, however, was the increase in agricultural production, which in the years after 1979 was spectacular, starting as it did from the low base of the collectives. By 1984 Deng's agricultural reforms appeared to have vindicated his approach.

The reform of state factories and urban enterprises took off later, in the mid-1980s, Deng having given priority to the agricultural reforms. The reformers now turned to free industry from state shackles and to devolve responsibility to the factory manager; here too the profit motive was designed to provide incentives. Small, privately owned enterprises were encouraged. By 1987 20 million one-family undertakings had been started. But the most startling reform was the development of what were called Special Economic Zones – capitalist enclaves within socialist China.

Though the West had exploited China in the nineteenth and early twentieth century, establishing Western enclaves in China, the treaty ports and concessions, these had also been a channel by which Western management and technology were transferred to China. The most successful of these international concessions had existed in Shanghai, whose trading and commercial pre-eminence in China was entirely due to the presence of the Westerner. But the communists had reasserted Chinese sovereignty and driven out the West from all the enclaves. For a decade the Soviet Union had filled the gap as educator, but then she also withdrew. Under the communists, the Parker factory established in Shanghai continued to manufacture for export cheap imitations of the Parker 51 pen without innovation or change for three decades. Deng and the reformers wanted to bring Western knowledge and capital back to China. That was the purpose of the Special Enterprise Zones. One such, Shenzhen, was placed strategically across the frontiers of Hong Kong, the prime example of what a combination of Chinese skill and the capitalist system could achieve. Favourable conditions and the availability of cheap Chinese labour attracted large-scale investment from Hong Kong. No doubt Deng was trying to kill two birds with one stone. By showing that capitalism and socialism could exist side by side he furthered the reunification of all of China – the British colony of Hong Kong, the Portuguese enclave of Macao and hostile Taiwan. Most of Hong Kong would revert to China when the British lease ended. In 1984 the British and Chinese governments concluded an agreement that embodied Deng's formula 'one country, two systems'. After the British lease ended in 1997 Hong Kong would be allowed to maintain her capitalist system and her freedoms for fifty years as a Special Administrative Region of the People's Republic.

While it seemed that Deng and the reformers were transforming China, opening the country to the West, attracting tourists and foreign capital, developing new joint enterprises and placing orders for machines and whole factories with the United States, Britain, West Germany and other countries, problems were emerging which in 1989 were to place question marks over Deng's decade of reform.

Free-enterprise agriculture was concentrating on the production of more profitable crops than grain, such as jute and tobacco. In 1985 grain production fell as China's population, despite intensive birth-control campaigns enforcing 'one couple, one child', inexorably grew. Greater productivity on the land meant less need for labour. China's urban population almost doubled between 1980 and 1986 – another 180 million mouths to feed in the cities. There was under-employment and unemployment in the cities; housing shortages grew more severe. The mixed state and free market encouraged corruption. Favouritism and bribery became widespread. Price rises unsettled the population, more used to the stability of stagnation. Economic development has been uneven, fastest in the last 1980s in the coastal cities. Agricultural output from what are predominantly small farms has little scope to increase and so match China's population growth. With an economy in which prices are not yet market-oriented there is confusion and dislocation. Worse still, China is still overburdened with a vast bureaucracy, whose planning functions continue to shrink. Vested interests damaged by these changes did their best to slow up or undermine Deng's reforms.

The biggest problem was Deng's recognition of the need to transform the attitudes of the individual Chinese, to make them more independent-thinking, responsible and enterprising. To the extent that he succeeded he also raised expectations beyond what the party could fulfil. Educational reform created a larger professional class and more idealistic students, who demanded new freedoms and 'democracy'. This set Deng's reformers and the party leadership on a collision course with a vociferous, educated, urban minority which wanted political reforms on the Western model. The West had come to expect more from the Chinese leadership as China's economic and diplomatic involvement with the rest of the world had grown. Tourists visited China and found her people generous and friendly; Beijing even allowed some discreet nightclubs to open, offering the services of hostesses. It looked as if China would adopt the Western way of life, importing not only Western capital and goods but also some of the West's values. But in 1989 the Chinese leadership showed an unexpected and different face. The West recoiled with horror.

In the China of the twentieth century there is a tradition of student and intellectual protest. The calendar is marked by events such as the anti-foreigner demonstrations of 4 May 1919, which became the focus for new demonstrations in the 1980s. Student idealism and frustrations were manipulated from time to time by the aged party leadership against their rivals, not least by Mao himself, with the launch of the Red Guards in 1966. It was a dangerous tactic and those who used student protest for their own purposes then had to contain what they had helped to arouse. Deng and his chosen successor, the man he had placed in the position of party leader, Hu Yaobang, together with the head of the government Zhao Ziyang, decided to allow much freer expression of views. Deng, however, kept his lines open to the more conservative aged Politburo in deploring decadent Western 'bourgeois' influences.

It was not surprising that China's students were in the forefront of protest and demonstrations. They lived in atrocious conditions and were rigidly controlled by their elders. Their future usually lay in the hands of the state or party machine, which would assign them to a job somewhere in China – possibly in the wildest, most remote regions. Added to the instinctive desire of youth to be free of the restrictions imposed by an older generation, to find new solutions to long-lasting problems, was a growing impatience with party politicising, with corruption and with repression. The old certainties enshrined within Mao's infallibility had been replaced by a jumble of ideas. The rapid pace of economic change and contact with foreigners, with foreign literature and with some of their teachers, who bravely spoke their minds, all created a ferment of unrest. In the winter of 1986 the students took to the streets and gathered in Tiananmen Square. Economic reforms were not enough – they wanted control over their own lives. The demand was for 'democracy', symbolised on their banners by the Statue of Liberty. It was a spontaneous expression of feeling; but the students had no notion of how a transition to democracy might be managed in the prevailing conditions of China. They were brave and impetuous, and rejected Deng's cautious approach to greater freedoms and prosperity which was then producing more dislocation than progress. The student protest was contained and dispersed without undue violence. The hardliners in the Politburo may well have regarded this as misplaced tolerance.

Deng's economic reforms, which encouraged more choice and freedom in the lives of the Chinese, were blamed for these dangerous demands for political freedoms, which challenged the role of the party and its leaders. Deng could not stop halfway on the road of economic reform, but he agreed with the conservatives that liberty of expression could not be allowed at this critical stage to affect the leadership's firm control of policy decisions. The man he was thought to have chosen as his successor, the pragmatic reformist Hu Yaobang, was removed from the leadership of the party but not from the Politburo. In the course of 1987 Deng managed to readjust the balance between reformers and conservatives while pressing ahead with economic modernisation and encouraging Western capitalism to invest in China. Hu Yaobang's position was taken by Zhao Ziyang, whose administrative skills were intended to help reform the party and to rid it of corruption. A younger Politburo member, Li Peng, a rather colourless Moscow-educated technocrat, was placed at the head of the state administration. In a wily masterstroke Deng retired from his posts and thereby persuaded many of the ageing conservative members of the Politburo to retire with him. But a secret party agreement acknowledged that he would continue to take major party decisions.

Rapid change caused increasing economic problems in 1988 and 1989. Price inflation reached 30 per cent; with the new economic freedoms, some did well, but the army, the hundreds of thousands of party and state officials and all who derived their income from state salaries were left behind. The disadvantaged began to see Chinese society as increasingly unjust; food queues in Beijing were painful evidence of agricultural shortfalls and corruption. It was probably the example of Gorbachev's bold policy of *glasnost* and his impending visit to Beijing that enthused the students in the spring of 1989 to demonstrate and to demand political reform. Countless banners in Tiananmen Square celebrated the 'Pioneer of *Glasnost*' and hailed the

Soviet leader as an 'Emissary of Democracy'. Gorbachev's arrival in May was in itself a turning point in China's international relations. At the end of a chaotic four-day visit, Deng and Gorbachev announced that after thirty years of hostility the relations between China and the Soviet Union had been normalised. But no very specific evidence of collaboration emerged. The visit was in any case overshadowed by the dramatic events outside the Great Hall of the People in Tiananmen Square. Such turmoil had not been seen in China since the Cultural Revolution twenty years earlier.

The students, who had been demonstrating since April, occupied the square throughout May and attracted growing attention. China's advances in technology – television and satellite links – vividly conveyed this mass protest, with its demand for democracy and an end to the exclusive role of the corrupt party, to the whole world. It all seemed good-natured, even when students peacefully reinforced their demands by going on hunger-strike. For seven weeks the Chinese leadership tolerated the students' occupation of the square –

*Student demonstrations in Tiananmen Square, Beijing, on 19 May 1989 on the eve of the killings.*

in strong contrast to 1976, when a previous student protest in Tiananmen Square had been forcibly and bloodily dispersed. On that last occasion Deng had fallen from power; now he was in charge. China seemed truly to have changed.

Inside the Great Hall of the People a power struggle was evidently going on between the party leader Zhao Ziyang and the more hardline premier Li Peng. The proclamation of martial law on 20 May and the recall to the Politburo of four octogenarian revolutionaries all indicated that Deng was ready to act forcefully and was not prepared to tolerate for much longer mass protests in defiance of the party. He must have been aware of the immense damage a bloody crackdown would do to the image of a reforming China, just when with her economic troubles mounting he needed Western help more than ever. Might the army prove unreliable, even though he was head of the Military Commission? An early attempt to use troops stationed in Beijing failed. More ominously workers went on strike and the students began to secure mass support. In a

final show of defiance they erected in the square a plaster Goddess of Liberty, which looked much like the American Statue of Liberty. Deng ordered thousands of troops from outlying parts of China to Beijing. These young recruits had no idea what was really at issue; still less had they any idea who they were being ordered to suppress as dangerous revolutionaries. The students massing in the square could not believe that the People's Liberation Army could be prepared to harm their fellow Chinese, young men and women the same age as they. In a dramatic last bid Zhao Ziyang tearfully tried to placate the students.

During the early hours of Sunday, 4 June 1989 the army with tanks and guns fired on the unarmed students. The massacre that followed, in which hundreds were killed, was witnessed by the whole world as courageous television crews and reporters provided live coverage of the scenes of bloodshed, of students rushing corpses and the wounded on their improvised bicycle ambulances to Beijing's hospitals. The hospitals, unable to cope, simply

*One Chinese student attempts to defy the tanks in Tiananmen Square, Beijing, 5 June 1989. His sort of courage proved insufficient to sway the Communist authorities.*

stacked the corpses in the corridors. All Sunday the soldiers fired indiscriminately, killing men, women and children, often bystanders unconnected to the demonstration. For days Beijing was at the mercy of the military. The striking workers were threatened and made to return to work. In the Politburo the students were condemned as revolutionaries, and a conspiracy manipulated by outside forces hostile to China was 'uncovered'. The massacre was simply denied and the demonstrators were accused of killing the soldiers – it was true that in their fury the crowds had savagely burnt some trucks and killed the few occupants they could lay their hands on. The troubles had spread to other cities as well. In Shanghai there were massive demonstrations, but there heavy bloodshed was avoided.

In the immediate aftermath student leaders and demonstrators were arrested. The universities emptied as students and staff dispersed, their future uncertain. A number of public trials were televised and sentences of execution pronounced. A hunt for student leaders and supporters of the democracy movement, now branded revolutionaries, began. Zhao Ziyang was ousted as party chief and placed under house arrest. Li Peng became the spokesman for the hardliners. But the power struggle was not over even as China outwardly returned to normality. Deng, as an octogenarian, could not be expected to retain power for much longer. With the population still growing despite birth-control campaigns – it was likely to have increased from 540 million in 1949 to a probable 1300 million by the year 2000 – the need to increase production through modernisation was indispensable. China was poised between free enterprise and socialist planning, between some fragile individual freedoms and party control, governed by a small band of political leaders locked in strife with each other. Despite the progress made since 1949, she still faced a very difficult future. Thousands of the best-educated Chinese had been alienated into secret opposition, yet they were the very young men and women most needed to make modernisation possible. The brutal use of the People's Army against the people had opened up a breach that would take a long time to heal.

The issue of whether economic reform and modernisation had to precede fundamental political change, as Deng believed, or whether economic reforms had reached the state where they could be carried no further without political reform, had been decided. What China's leaders believed was that to

have given way to demands for 'democracy' would have plunged China into chaos and disruption, and quite probably bloodshed on a large scale. Control and discipline would be needed as the precondition of material progress. They saw no reason why, for the immediate future, one-party control could not sit comfortably with the expansion of what has come to be called the socialist market economy. The economic progress achieved since 1989 has proved many a pessimistic Western theorist wrong. Politically, the events of 1989 dispelled much facile optimism in the West about China's future. For some months the West cut off relations with China. In Hong Kong there was greater anxiety about what the Anglo-Chinese settlement held in store. But China was too important, her vote on the Security Council too crucial, for the West to maintain the ostracism. So despite everything realism demanded a gradual normalisation of Western dealings with

### China, 1968–1984

| | Indices of gross industrial and agricultural output value at constant prices (*1952 = 100*) | | | |
|---|---|---|---|---|
| | Agriculture | Light industry | Heavy industry | Population (*millions*) |
| 1968 | 147.5 | 348.7 | 630.1 | 785 |
| 1976 | 207.1 | 766.4 | 2,104.3 | 937 |
| 1978 | 229.6 | 970.6 | 2,780.4 | 963 |
| 1980 | 259.1 | 1,259.5 | 3,036.4 | 987 |
| 1980 | 259.1 | 1,259.5 | 3,036.4 | 987 |
| 1984 | 393.7 | 1,880.7 | 4,078.4 | 1,035 |

*Source*: Liu Suinian and Wu Qungan, *China's Socialist Economy, 1949–1984* (Beijing, 1986), pp. 477, 479.

China in 1990. The Chinese were careful to avoid further offence and tried to demonstrate goodwill towards the West by backing the Security Council resolutions against Iraq after the August 1990 invasion of Kuwait. In the early 1990s the Chinese leadership had managed to insulate their country from the revolution that had swept communist Eastern Europe and brought enormous changes to the Soviet Union. In China the pace of reform is set from above.

In China's vast interior, trials of dissidents, sentences of execution and incarceration were meted out as a harsh lesson after June 1989. Obedience to party and leadership were not to be challenged. China would continue to be ruled politically by the Communist party and its leaders as before. The leaders would decide on the limits of debate and intellectual freedom. There has been some liberalisation in the 1990s; visitors were welcomed and students continue to study abroad. The intellectual ferment in China settled down surprisingly quickly. Dissent is kept under wraps.

One explanation is the booming economy and rising standards of living, faster in the 1990s in the cities than in the countryside. The senior leader, Deng Xiaoping, observed with satisfaction that he had chosen the right course. Political liberalisation, *perestroika*, in the Soviet Union had accompanied economic reform, and made commercial modernisation infinitely more difficult and led to conflict and the disintegration of the Soviet state. The Chinese people would be less concerned with notions of western style democracy if the party could deliver higher standards of living, and a plentiful supply of enticing consumer goods. Beijing has been transformed, with its modern hotels, department stores, foreign goods, Benetton sweaters and monied inhabitants. China's immense landmass is divided between some wealthy regions and impoverished lands. The Fourteenth Communist Party Congress which met in October 1992 confirmed the policy the 89 year-old Deng had tenaciously followed for fifteen years: the transition to a market economy, called for appearance's sake 'the socialist market economy', presided over by a communist party with a monopoly of political power. China was going her own way yet again.

CHAPTER 66

# *Freedom and Conflict in the Indian Subcontinent: India, Pakistan and Bangladesh*

In the end it was a peaceful revolution that brought freedom from colonial rule to one-fifth of mankind. The massed bands of the Indian army and the Scottish Highlanders on parade side by side first played 'God Save the King' and then when the saffron, green and white flag of free India was raised, with Gandhi's spinning-wheel at its centre, the bands together struck up the Indian national anthem. It was symbolic of the new relationship. Prime Minister Nehru asked Lord Mountbatten to stay as independent India's first governor-general. But independence solved only one problem, the relationship with imperial Britain. Daunting tasks faced the new rulers; they had to maintain law and order when the cauldron of ethnic and religious animosities turned to murderous violence; they had to define and to secure the new national frontiers in the vacuum of power left by the British which had not been completely filled by the agreements reached at independence; and they had to find ways of raising the standard of living of the hundreds of millions surviving at subsistence level in rural India and in her teeming cities. All these things had to be tackled simultaneously. Ever since independence, the combination of poverty, the fervour of ethnic–religious minorities and the manipulation of politics by the wealthier elites has resulted in a cycle of violence and repression that has continued for half a century. Gandhi's vision of an India where all her inhabitants would be brothers was not to be realised.

Before 1947 it seemed only natural to suppose that British India would be replaced by the one Commonwealth of India. But the deep divisions, never healed during the century of British rule, proved stronger. Only by force and bloodshed was it possible to create two states in 1947. Ethnic conflict and nationalism continued to threaten the cohesion of the two successor nations, India and Pakistan. In 1971, Bengal, the eastern region of Pakistan, rose in rebellion and, with India's help, gained independence from West Pakistan. The new state was called Bangladesh. The Indian subcontinent had thus divided into three nations. Will other groups, the Sikhs in the Punjab or the Kashmiris, further split the political map of the Indian subcontinent?

The Republic of India and the Islamic Republic of Pakistan, though facing many similar problems of poverty and of ethnic conflicts within their states and though inheriting the same British imperial traditions and institutions, have developed very differently. With hardly a break since independence, Pakistan has been ruled by a bureaucratic–military alliance under an authoritarian military ruler, while India has preserved a democratic framework of government. In India the politicians have allied with the civil service to exclude the military from decision-making. The commander-in-chief of the Indian army is not a member of the Cabinet, is subject to the orders of the prime minister and defence minister, and, to make doubly certain that he can build up no personal power in the army, is replaced every two years. The Indian army has no tradition of mounting coups against the civilian government. Instead of authoritarian military rulers, the Nehru family – down to and including Rajiv Gandhi – acted for most of India's history as a 'dynasty' able to win the necessary electoral support to maintain itself in power except for short periods. India's leaders have made it a fundamental objective of nation-building that the republic is secular and that the majority Hindu and minority Muslim populations enjoy equal civil rights. No 'nationalism' based on religious foundations is tolerated.

In recent years, Pakistan has been identified as an Islamic state; indeed, her official title since the constitution of 1962 has been the Islamic Republic of Pakistan. But appearances are misleading. Certain aspects of Islam, for example the enforcing of the *sharia* law with amputations and floggings, were introduced by General Zia-ul-Haq, who seized power in 1977 and cloaked his military dictatorship with an Islamic façade of respectability. His death in August 1988 in a plane crash, probably the result of sabotage, removed a tyrant who had ordered more than 4000 floggings of criminals and political opponents during his decade in power. But under Zia the religious leaders, the *ulema*, had no controlling influence, unlike those in Khomeini's Islamic Iran. The exclusion of the *ulema* from the management of the nation's political affairs has been determinedly maintained by all Pakistan's leaders since independence.

In 1947, Mohammed Ali Jinnah, the leader of India's Muslim League, was determined to establish an independent secular Muslim state if he could not get a loosely structured, unified India with circumscribed power at the centre – something which Nehru and the Congress Party leaders would not agree to. The independent alternative, Pakistan, then became the only other means of protecting Muslim lives and property in the Indian subcontinent (pages 414–15). But a separate Pakistan could be justified only on ethnic and religious grounds. The Muslim League thus had to emphasise religion as a ground for demanding independence and as a basis for its appeal to the Muslims spread throughout India. There was one Muslim to every four non-Muslims (most of whom were Hindus), and the appeal of the Muslim League was particularly successful in central India, where the Muslims faced the hostility and discrimination of Hindu majorities. An independent Muslim nation would not only free Muslims within its confines from fear but also promised economic and social improvement for the repressed Muslim poor. The incitement of religious feelings was, however, bound to be dangerous; it led to the fanaticism and massacres that followed partition – consequences which the Muslim League had desperately wished to avoid but which were beyond their control.

Jinnah's secular Muslim state thus from the very beginning implied ambiguities. The *ulema* were nevertheless powerful in the independent state and could stir up the masses against the ruling elite, so constitution-making proved a long-drawn-out affair. Jinnah, the father of the nation, lived for only one year after independence, and during the decade from 1948 until 1958, when the military first seized power, political development in Pakistan was stunted by the failure of the Muslim League to develop as a mass party – a decade characterised by the factionalism and corruption of the politicians.

Nation-building was in any case going to be difficult, and there was no one of Jinnah's stature to take his place. Pakistan was divided into two parts, separated by a thousand miles of the Indian land-mass. In Eastern Pakistan, where the majority (54 per cent) of Pakistanis lived, the Muslims were ethnically homogeneous Bengalis. In Western Pakistan, there was ethnic diversity among Punjabis, Sindhis, Pathans and Baluchis. The central Pakistan government, situated in the western half, set itself the task of dominating the divided West and sought also to dominate the East. In the West, more than half the population lives in the Punjab, the remainder in four provinces and in the capital, Islamabad. The army and the higher civil service were predominantly Punjabi, and the political leadership of the Muslim League had strong roots in the refugees who had fled from India, where they had been in a minority. The building up of a mass democratic base would have ousted the Punjabi–Muslim refugee elite from power and handed it over to the far more united Bengali East. But the desire to hold on to power meant that the Punjabi–Muslim refugee elite would continue to rule with the assistance of the army and the higher civil service, suppressing ethnic nationalism and securing their predominance over the more populous eastern half. Here in a nutshell lies the reason for the catastrophic development of Pakistan's politics – its undemocratic features, the army's subversion of civilian government without a broad popular mass base, and ultimately the rebellion of disadvantaged and resentful East Pakistan in 1971.

To manipulate the constitution to their advantage, Pakistan's rulers forcibly amalgamated the provinces in the West into one West Pakistan region which was then given an equal voice to the more numerous East Pakistan. But the constitution of 1956 caused much dissatisfaction among the steam-rollered participants east and west. The Muslim League politicians meanwhile could not establish a stable civilian government based on a parliamentary assembly. Between 1948 and 1954 the Constituent Assembly had been less than a hundred days in session and one prime minister had been assassinated.

The constitution of 1956 provided for elections in February 1959. Provincial elections in East Pakistan in 1954 had already shown that one political party there, the United Front, would carry all before it; the Muslim League had come last, gaining only ten of the 309 seats. In West Pakistan, with its fourfold ethnic rivalry, no single party could hope to equal the performance of the United Party. The United Party and East Pakistan would thus take control of the whole country. The rulers were not prepared to accept this. In 1958, General Ayub Khan extinguished parliament, first in East Pakistan, where he had been sent as military governor, and then in West Pakistan, when in the same year he became head of state. It was a military coup, but few regretted the passing of the self-serving politicians.

President Ayub Khan invented an ingenious constitutional device, the indirect referendum: an electoral college of 'basic democrats' was formed, which then overwhelmingly confirmed him in office. Although power was concentrated in the President's hands, he relied for day-to-day government on the civil service. There was no room for political parties under the constitution he drew up in 1962; the members of the National Assembly were chosen on 'personal merit' as judged by the President and his advisers. The judiciary and press were fettered, and subordinated to presidential rule. Provincial autonomy, to the extent it had survived, was brought completely under central control. East Pakistan, deprived even of the rights of the 1956 constitution, erupted in riots. The political opposition there formed the Awami League under Sheikh Mujibur Rahman, whose proposals for a two-nation federation landed him in jail. In the unfavoured provinces in West Pakistan, resentment against the Punjabi–

Muslim refugee elite which, with the army, continued to control policy and patronage under the Ayub presidency also produced growing unrest. Ayub's most capable opponent was Zulfikar Ali Bhutto, whose Pakistan People's Party gathered the support in the provinces of both rural and urban groups disadvantaged by the changes brought about by industrialisation.

Ayub Kahn also had to face the problems of Pakistan's national security. Relations with India went from bad to worse after independence. Pakistan had taken advantage of the Cold War tensions to redress the balance as against a larger and stronger India by tying herself to the US-backed anti-communist line-up of nations in Asia, joining the South-East Asia Treaty Organisation in 1954 and the Baghdad Pact the following year. As expected, Pakistan thereupon received substantial American military and financial aid.

For Pakistan and India, however, it was not the Cold War that primarily concerned them but relations with each other. At the heart of their conflict lay the problem of Kashmir. All attempts by Pakistan to negotiate directly with India came to nothing; nor could the United Nations find a peaceful way to mediate. Every attempt was blocked by Nehru, who refused to hold the plebiscite he had earlier promised. The possibility that the majority of Kashmir's people might opt for Pakistan because they were Muslims struck at the heart of India's nationhood as conceived by Nehru and the other Congress leaders: India was a secular state in which both Muslims and Hindus should find their rightful place. The secession of Muslim Kashmir might prompt demands by Muslims elsewhere in India for a plebiscite and ultimately for the right of secession, thus undermining Indian unity. India was the stronger and could afford to sit tight, in control of most of Kashmir. Inside Kashmir the Indians suppressed all opposition and stifled a growing demand for independence. Sheikh Abdullah, Nehru's friend, was arrested and imprisoned in 1953 for declaring that he found integration of Kashmir into India an unacceptable solution. He was not released until 1964.

Nehru's India was treated with suspicion by the United States and the West. He followed a non-aligned policy in the Cold War and was one of the architects of the non-aligned Bandung meeting in April 1955 (page 620). He also enjoyed the support of Khrushchev over Kashmir when the Soviet leader visited Delhi in December 1955, and sought good relations with communist China. China's claim of sovereignty over Tibet caused India anxiety, but this was dispelled by the Indian–Chinese 'peaceful coexistence' agreement in 1954. When the Chinese army invaded Tibet to put down a revolt in 1959 and the Dalai Lama fled to India, relations between India and China deteriorated to the point of armed conflict. To ensure better control of Tibet, China had occupied an area of Kashmir, the Asai Chin, and had constructed a road through it from China to Tibet. When China next attacked the ill-defined Chinese–Kashmir and Indian frontier in October 1962, the Indian army was woefully unprepared and was defeated. Nehru had to ask for Western help, and since the opponent was now communist China received military aid from the United States, Britain and the Soviet Union. In a show of strength China thereupon invaded the frontier region of India but unilaterally withdrew after securing the frontier she wanted. A ceasefire in December 1962 in effect settled the issue in China's favour. Pakistan did not take advantage of India's military plight.

In need of Western aid, Nehru was now pressurised by the West to reach a settlement over Kashmir. The West was anxious to ensure peace on Pakistan's eastern Indian frontier so that she could concentrate on her western alliance against communism. But *realpolitik* dictated otherwise. In May 1964, Nehru died. Pakistan was now convinced that only by war would it prove possible to resolve the Kashmir issue and the frontier disputes with India. The rearrest of Sheikh Abdullah by the Indians made the conflict more certain. In December 1964, India declared that Kashmir's accession to 'the Union was final and irrevocable', a move which greatly angered Pakistan.

Western policies dictated by Cold War consideration had been particularly uncertain on the Indian subcontinent, veering from support for Pakistan to supporting India after 1962 and arming both sides. The Soviet Union also sought to play an influential role by supporting India with arms and aid during Khrushchev's ambitious period of world politics. India, meanwhile, always regarded Pakistan as her principal enemy. As the West after 1962 massively increased the armed forces of India, Pakistan normalised relations with the Soviet Union and drew closer to China again.

The poor performance of the Indian army against the Chinese encouraged Pakistan to believe she could now capture Kashmir. At the end of August 1965 Pakistani troops struck across the UN cease-fire line in Kashmir. On 6 September the Indian army replied with an all-out war against Pakistan. Two countries of the British Commonwealth were now at war with each other. Despite India's military superiority, Pakistan forces resisted effectively. For the second time the Soviet Union and the United States were agreed that a war should be ended (the first time was over Suez – pages 471–2). Both were anxious to keep China in check. The United States did not help her ally, Pakistan, and the Soviet Union did not help her 'ally', India. After only seventeen days, on 23 September, fighting ceased in accordance with a Security Council resolution sponsored jointly by the United States and the Soviet Union, with Britain's full support. Alexei Kosygin, the Soviet Prime Minister, achieved a diplomatic coup in bringing Nehru's successor, Lal Bahadur Shastri, and Pakistan's President Ayub Khan, to a peace conference at Tashkent in January 1966. In effect, the Kashmir question was put on ice and India and Pakistan agreed to withdraw their forces behind the frontiers as they had existed before the outbreak of the war. So ended the short Pakistani–Indian war. It had achieved nothing but casualties for both sides, but the Soviet Union's posture in Asia as a peacemaker was enhanced.

In one respect, Pakistan's development appeared to contrast favourably with India's: the growth of her economy in the Ayub Khan military era. Political stability, even of the repressive kind, is seen by investors as a positive factor. In both agriculture and industry Pakistan's wealth and production grew rapidly in the 1960s. The magic formula was to encourage a capitalist, market-oriented economy and to loosen the bureaucratic regulations imposed in the 1950s. Ayub Khan was following with seeming success the development prescriptions of theoretical economists. One of the consequences they anticipated during the phase of rapid development in what was a Third World country was the unrestrained urge for profits among the owners of the few existing large-scale enterprises. The resulting inequalities of wealth were truly staggering. Just twenty-two families owned the greater part of industry, banking and insurance – or, to be more precise, two-thirds of industry, four-fifths of banking and almost the whole of insurance. Their wealth was fabulous. The senior military and civil service prospered as well, together with a small middle class. In the countryside agriculture benefited from what was called the 'green revolution', the creation of new plant breeds bearing much heavier crops. This necessitated shorter stems, which would not bend over when carrying more grain.

Agricultural research was given high priority in India and Pakistan. A rapidly growing population needed to be fed. The uneven rainfall, the monsoon period followed by drought for nine months of the year, was the main problem on the Indian subcontinent. The seeds which produced the new 'green revolution' plants of rice, wheat, maize, sorghum and millet seeds were imported from the Philippines, Taiwan and Mexico. Farmers had to be taught better techniques of husbandry and the correct use of fertilisers. In India, the government, with the assistance of the Ford Foundation, promoted an all-round programme. In Pakistan, education and research were undertaken by the universities. Mexico also assisted by training many agricultural scientists. In Pakistan it was the farmers of the larger farms in the Punjab who benefited rather than the peasants and small farmers and those in the east, in Bengal.

The price paid for an economic development in Pakistan that made the well-to-do richer and the poor poorer, despite the rapid growth as measured nationally, was a heavy one. The low living standards of industrial workers and of peasants fell even further. Development was also lopsided regionally – West Pakistan did much better than the eastern half of the country. The tensions were heightened until there was an explosion that ended in civil war and swept the military rulers from power, if only for a time.

In 1969 there was massive unrest, labour strikes and student demonstrations coupled with demands for the restoration of parliamentary rule. Ayub Khan promised to hold elections; he had no desire to rule the country any longer under some form of military repression, which was the only alternative. Unlike Zia, he was no ruthless dictator. He handed over power to another general, Yahya Khan, who also honestly attempted to preside over a transition to civilian rule with the army in the background as a check on unbridled political conflict, which might otherwise lead to chaos. In December 1970 genuinely free elections were held. The results and the

behaviour of the politicians led to civil conflict and the Indian–Pakistani war twelve months later.

The elections split the country politically in two, corresponding to the geographical division. No major party gained a seat in both East and West Pakistan. In East Pakistan the powerful political grouping known as the Awami League, still led by Sheikh Mujibur Rahman and on a platform advocating wide-ranging autonomy and only a loose federal linking with the West, carried all before it, gaining 151 seats and losing only 2. In West Pakistan eleven parties competed, and none reached double figures except Zulfikar Ali Bhutto's Pakistan's People's Party with 81 seats. Bhutto was a charismatic, populist leader from a wealthy landowning family in the province of Sind. His power base in that province was a somewhat opportunistic alignment of opposition to the capitalist–military rule: socialists in Sind and the Punjab, resentful urban workers, liberal reformers and feudal landlords in Sind looking for more favourable regional treatment supported the PPP and turned it into a mass party.

Sections of the army, discontented with the outcome of the brief Pakistani–India war in 1965, also backed Bhutto. The elections over, the National Assembly should have met shortly after. It did not. The Awami League would have been the governing group in it and the President, General Yahya, first wanted an assurance that the League's policy would not in effect create a two-nation state. In taking this step, he was reinforced by the strident West Pakistani nationalism of Bhutto. Talks between Mujibur, Yahya and Bhutto failed, and Mujibur was arrested. Bhutto and elements in the army sought by violent threats to prevent the convening of the National Assembly; shortly before it was due to meet in March 1971, Yahya postponed it indefinitely.

The scene was now set for the tragic events that followed: the attempt by the army to subdue East Pakistan by force. Bengal, suffering another natural catastrophe in cyclones and floods, had felt neglected by the lack of effective Western relief. Now her right to democratic representation was being denied by West Pakistan. The result of all these cumulative failures was war in East Pakistan. Ten million Hindu refugees flooded across the frontier into India, prompting the Indian army to intervene in East Pakistan, and also to attack in Kashmir. It was all over in two weeks. The Pakistani army in the East became prisoners of war. India and Pakistan concluded a peace settlement at Simla in December 1971 and the independent state of Bangladesh was born.

Independence did not much help the Bangladeshi people. Theirs is one of the poorest countries in the world, her population exposed to periodic cataclysms of cyclone and floods. Here, too, the army for most of its history has been the controlling element in repressive government. In 1975 Mujibur was assassinated in an army coup. Powerless parliamentary assemblies and army strongmen have ruled this country, beset by huge economic problems and a rapidly growing population. General Ershad seized power in 1982, retaining it until overthrown by a wave of popular protest in 1990 which ended years of corruption, only to start a new period of turmoil. Meanwhile, in little more than a decade, the population had grown from 84.6 million to over 110 million.

In West Pakistan the lost war decided the army to take a back seat, and Yahya transferred power to Bhutto and his PPP. Would Bhutto now usher in the long-delayed social and political reforms, heralding a new era of parliamentary democratic government? In this respect, the Bhutto years from 1972 to 1977, that is until his own violent overthrow by another army coup, were a disappointment. The 1973 constitution was indeed intended to transform Pakistan into a parliamentary democracy; but only a year later it was amended. Bhutto's political corruption undermined the development of democratic political parties, as he likewise violently repressed political opponents. Civil liberties were severely limited and in the provinces autonomy was crushed. His socialist zeal soon flagged after some early and limited measures of nationalisation. Funds for the promised free education and for the provision of health care for the poor failed to materialise, leaving unfilled the huge gap in the basic social services. Economic growth slowed. But there were some reforms which particularly benefited the factory workers and urban poor – a revision of labour laws and the raising of wages. Bhutto consequently continued to enjoy, even after his fall in 1977, the mass support of millions of Pakistanis, who remembered him for caring for the poor.

Crucial to his political survival were Bhutto's relations with the army. He sought to appease the military by increasing defence expenditure. He appointed as his loyal army chief of staff a young officer who had foiled an army coup in 1972.

Bhutto's fatal error was to chose the wrong man – the ambitious, clever and utterly ruthless Zia-ul-Haq. Zia waited for Bhutto to run into political crisis. This occurred after the elections of March 1977, which Bhutto had so blatantly rigged that the opposition parties would not accept the results. Fearing military intervention to quell the ensuing turmoil, Bhutto agreed to the holding of new elections, but before they could be held, on 5 July 1977, Zia staged his military coup. He claimed that Pakistan was on the verge of civil war and that he would hold elections within ninety days, whereupon he would hand power back to the elected civilian government. It was the first of his many broken promises. To rid himself of Bhutto, meanwhile, the fallen Prime Minister was tried and then, despite worldwide protest, hanged in 1979. After that, Zia made little pretence of ruling other than dictatorially.

Zia's excuse for exercising arbitrary power was the need to wage a moral crusade to create an Islamic state. He devoted himself to arresting, imprisoning and executing his political opponents and army rivals. Martial law was declared, and the remnants of civil liberties and political parties were destroyed. Yet this tyrant won the support of the West. Once more the Cold War had distorted Western perceptions of priorities. The decisive event was the Soviet Union's invasion of Afghanistan in December 1979. Pakistan became the base from which the Afghan mujahideen were supplied. Moreover, since the Soviet invasion was interpreted as a threat to the oil-rich Persian Gulf, Pakistan once more was seen as a crucial military bulwark of the West. An earlier US arms embargo was reversed into massive US military and economic aid.

By 1983 it appeared to Zia expedient, both for internal reasons and to improve his image in the West, to incorporate some civilian ministers and a controlled electoral body into the governing structure of the country. The assemblies so elected were to be Islamic rather than parliamentary, and were not to feature competing political parties. The National Assembly elected in 1985 nevertheless showed signs that it saw its own creation as only the first step in the transfer of power from the military. There was a strong revival of political activity. Miss Benazir Bhutto, the daughter of the Prime Minister hanged by Zia, was allowed to return to Pakistan in 1986 and attracted large crowds at her rallies. The Prime Minister and his government,

Above: *Zulfikar Ali Bhutto, Prime Minister of Pakistan. He was hanged in 1979 after being deposed in a 1977 coup orchestrated by General Zia.* Below: *Benazir Bhutto, Zulfikar's daughter and leader of Pakistan's People's Party, campaigns in the Punjab prior to the elections of December 1988, which saw her become Prime Minister. She was dismissed from that post in August 1990.*

appointed by Zia, showed an unwelcome desire for real power. It was no surprise when, in May 1988, the Prime Minister was dismissed and the Assembly was dissolved. But a return to further authoritarian military rule was avoided by an accident, the death of Zia in a plane crash in August 1988. The promised new elections were held in November and Miss Benazir Bhutto emerged as the winner with the PPP gaining the largest number of seats of any party. It was a startling result for a Muslim country – the first woman prime minister.

The West, especially the United States administration, heaved a sigh of relief at being rid of the blemish of association with Zia. Prime Minister Benazir Bhutto promised to continue the pro-Western Afghan policy of her predecessor but the lessening of Soviet–US hostility as the Cold War came to an end made the military establishment less important in American eyes. Benazir Bhutto's hold on power was fragile, dependent on maintaining a coalition partnership with an unreliable ethnic party. The government could make little headway in solving the country's economic problems, in easing regional tensions with the provinces or in improving its international position. The Afghan civil war continued even after the departure of Soviet troops in December 1989, and millions of refugees remained across the border in Pakistan. With democracy restored, Pakistan was welcomed back into the Commonwealth, but the most serious problem – the perennial conflict over the future of Kashmir – was brought no nearer to a solution. In 1990 Benazir Bhutto was dismissed, accused of leading a corrupt government. After fresh elections her fall from power was confirmed by the voters. In the early 1990s the army continued to abide by its undertaking not to intervene. Parliamentary democracy, however, remained a fragile plant in Pakistan.

India's democracy is embodied in her constitution, which, enacted by the Constituent Assembly in November 1949, came into force in January 1950. In its form of government the Republic of India leans heavily on British constitutional theory. The president has a similar role to that of the sovereign; the power of government is exercised by the prime minister, who chooses his Cabinet colleagues and is dependent on the majority support of a political party competing regularly at general elections. The Indian constitution departs from its unwritten

British model by incorporating a Bill of Rights; another novel feature is the inclusion of 'Directive Principles' of state policy, intended in a positive way to remedy particular Indian conditions of exploitation and discrimination such as exist in the caste system of Untouchables. India was proclaimed a secular state. Except for one period of authoritarian rule under Indira Gandhi's Emergency (1975–7), democracy – with general elections by adult suffrage, freedom of speech and of the press, the toleration of non-violent political opposition, an independent judiciary and freedom from arbitrary arrest – has prevailed since independence. This reflects a harmonisation of British tradition and post-independence Indian political will. But, in practice, Indian democracy is peculiarly Indian, and no mere copy of that in Britain or in the United States.

Political parties do not function as in most Western parliaments. The prime minister's role became pre-eminent not only in comparison with the president's, but – under Nehru – in relation to the Assembly as well. This was one consequence of Nehru's complete dominance of politics for the eighteen consecutive years he served as prime minister. He was not even formally chosen as their leader by the Congress Party, but the mantle of Gandhi's heir unquestionably fell on his shoulders. He enjoyed support throughout the country and enjoyed touring and addressing mass rallies. He carried the Congress Party with him at every general election, in 1952, 1957 and 1962. In the Assembly, the Lok Sabha, Congress was by far the strongest party with never less than 45 per cent of the total vote; the other parties were fragmented and drew support only from largely regional bases. So India looked like becoming a one-party democracy. There are parallels with Italy here. This had its effect on the Congress Party itself. It lacked any common ideology or policies; it was just the 'winning party', split into factions, with supporters of the right and supporters of socialism. Various interests believed themselves best protected by being on the government side. This was hardly a healthy basis for the development of a parliamentary democracy.

Power corrupts, or it nearly always does so. Nehru's claim to statesmanship and greatness is that power did not corrupt *him*. He had the means to become authoritarian and follow the example of other charismatic Third World leaders who, once elected, became dictators, but he set himself the task

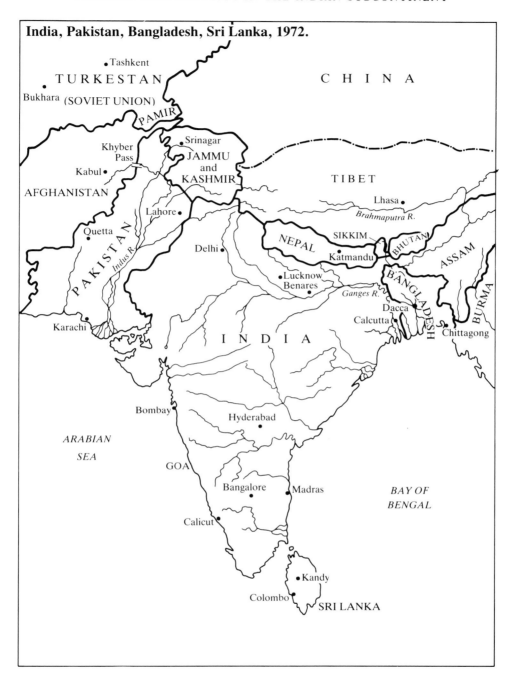

India, Pakistan, Bangladesh, Sri Lanka, 1972.

of making a success of the democratic experiment in this huge country where the majority were poor or destitute and unable to read. He toured the country, educating the people to use their precious right to exercise the vote. He was prepared to listen, to discuss and debate with his ministerial colleagues and with the leaders of the Congress Party. Some were opposed to one or other of his policies, such as his insistence on a secular state, his pragmatic socialism, his opposition to caste discrimination and his relations with the states of the Union. In his dealings with those who opposed him, he was humorous, patient and tolerant. He distrusted theory, rigid thinking and doctrinaire solutions. Consequently, clear-cut and consistent policies were not a mark of his years in office.

*Prime Minister Nehru of India celebrates his birthday amongst his public supporters on 14 November 1955.*

encies. His handling of Kashmir was one of these. To allow religion to decide allegiance could plunge India into chaos. For similar reasons he also sent the Indian army to suppress the independence movements of the tribal peoples in the extreme north-east of India.

With the hundreds of princes and their states, Nehru had less trouble, apart from Kashmir and Jammu. He left it to his able lieutenant, Sardar Patel, to negotiate the abandonment of their rights and the integration of their states in return for pensions. The princes, large and small, were in a hopeless position confronted with the Indian army. The Muslim Nizam of Hyderabad nevertheless postponed a decision: his people were Hindu and his large territory was entirely surrounded by India, but he was not left a free choice whether to accede to Pakistan or to India – in fact, he dreamt of independence. An Indian army police action in September 1948 put an end to his prevarication and the integration process was completed in 1950, the year in which Patel, India's most able political leader after Nehru, died. There was no room for the princes in modern India.

Nehru showed more forbearance when confronted by another problem that threatened to fragment India. This was the vexed question of the 'official' language to be spoken by all Indians. English was the only common language, but it was confined to a tiny percentage of the educated. Of the more than thirty major languages, the language of northern India, Hindi, was spoken by the largest single group but not by a majority of all Indians; large minorities of between 20 and 45 million (in 1971) spoke Urdu, Telugu, Bengali, Marathi, Tamil, Gujarati and so on – some fourteen major languages. Urdu is the language of the largest minority, the Muslims: in its spoken form it is Hindi, but it uses a different script. Because it involved the Muslim minority it was therefore especially important to Nehru to find an acceptable solution. The sensitivity of the language issue is that it can move beyond ethnic and cultural identity to assertions of national independence. Nehru wisely compromised, allowing many languages to coexist with English and Hindi and postponing the introduction of Hindi as the national language for fifteen years – whereupon it was postponed again. Nehru's readiness to envisage a multi-cultural India took the heat out of the divisive language issue. But when language was being used as part of an independence

Nehru could irritate the West by preaching peace; it accused him of hypocrisy, of underrating the menace of communism, and pointed to inconsistencies in his tolerance and pacifism, especially in his denial of self-determination to the people of Kashmir and his readiness to use force to defeat secessionist movements in the 1950s and 1960s. He was also ready to use force against foreign nations. Portuguese Goa represented the last vestige of European colonialism in India. After long and fruitless negotiations Nehru marched Indian troops into Goa in December 1961 and the Portuguese surrendered.

Nehru set himself a number of clear objectives for the future of India. With these he would not compromise. The first was to preserve the physical unity of the state. The second was to ensure the rights of all India's inhabitants, whatever their religion or ethnic cultural background. This meant that India must be a secular democratic country. The third was to raise standards of living, to develop India into a great modern state. The fourth objective was to ensure Indian security. This involved freeing India from economic dependence on other countries. She would also need a powerful army, but that army would be subject to civilian control. Nehru's aims help to explain his apparent inconsist-

claim, as in the extreme north-east of India, Nehru used force to suppress such movements.

Nehru laid down the fundamental principle that religion and politics should be separated and that India was a secular state, all of whose citizens, of whatever religion, enjoyed equal civil rights. This necessarily represented a step away from the spirituality that lay at the heart of Gandhi's mission. Muslims, who constitute about 11 per cent of India's population, had traditionally been supporters of the Congress and continued to be elected to the Assembly and to serve in India's governments. Nehru and his successors worked hard to remove any discrimination against the Muslims, but the improving Muslim–Hindi relationship was threatened in the second half of the 1980s by the rise of a group of Hindu fundamentalists. They began to stir up religious animosities by attempting to reclaim former Hindu sites on which mosques now stood. So some fanatical Hindi groups were acting against a tradition renowned for its tolerance towards other religions.

Nehru was the privileged son of a wealthy family. He nevertheless regarded democratic, humane socialism not only as the best means to secure Indian economic development, but also as the best weapon to break down the evil of India's discriminatory class and caste society. Before and after independence, he linked socialism in India, which he believed would free her peasant and urban poor from dependence and indignity, to liberating the oppressed in Asia and Africa from the dependence imposed by Western imperialism. He was optimistic that reason, law and democracy would overcome tradition and prejudice. His was a noble vision which diverged significantly from reality both in his lifetime and after. But his democracy of the poor did not deliver the results he hoped for. The democratic structure became distorted by the power and influence of family connection and of caste, by the landowning class and the wealthy elite. A huge conservative bureaucracy clogs and frustrates fair and efficient government. India did not make the progress Nehru expected by adopting scientific socialism and Western liberal values, but that does not mean that the fundamental principles of his policy were wrong. Indians, in developing their country, did not suffer the harsh fate which befell millions of Stalin's subjects and Mao Zedong's peasants.

India's economic development from independence to the 1990s only just kept ahead of her population growth. In successive five-year plans Nehru accepted the premise of the Soviet experience, that to come of age as an independent state India would need to give priority to becoming a modern industrial and military power, with her own heavy industries. The public sector would enter into contracts with the key industries, and central planners would control the commanding heights of the economy. As in Britain, communism and doctrinaire socialism were rejected in favour of a mixed economy. Not until the 1980s did the emphasis revert back to greater reliance on the private sector. Despite the establishment of a modern industrial core – steel, oil, chemicals, power and transport – India's economic development mainly benefited a growing urban middle class, which demanded all the consumer luxuries of the West. That development left behind the urban poor and the destitute, living in shacks and on pavements in the cities – cities which in this respect resembled the Third World urban sprawls, with their contrasts between rich and poor.

The increase in agricultural production was also disappointing compared with that attained by other Asian countries, such as South Korea. The 'green revolution', which achieved a tripling of cereal production in India, proved far less successful in raising the output of her staple food, rice. Again, agricultural production kept only narrowly ahead of population growth. The emphasis on industrial development delayed the investment necessary to accelerate the growth of farming. By world standards, Indian yields were low, though that at least left scope for spectacular improvement. But such improvements would not occur without social change and without greater resources being devoted to the education of India's numerous peasantry. The states of India whose influence predominated on questions of land reform were controlled by the very landowners who had little interest in bringing it about. Consequently, reforms such as land distribution to the landless or to those peasants without viable holdings were not implemented to any great extent. Mass poverty persisted in India in the 1990s.

Nehru died in 1964. His death left a political vacuum. Would so flawed a party democracy survive after so many years of stability under Nehru's leadership? The Congress leaders had to choose between the pro-Western conservative Morarji Desai, a former finance minister, Lal Bahadur Shastri, an elderly follower of Gandhi, or, on the left, Nehru's daughter, Mrs Indira Gandhi. Their choice fell on Shastri. He held the premiership only briefly, incongruously a period notable for the war with Pakistan (page 656), before dying suddenly in 1966 while at Tashkent seeking to make peace. Indira Gandhi succeeded to the premiership. In the Congress Party, Mrs Gandhi defeated her rival Morarji Desai and went on to win the elections of 1967; the reverence accorded to her father was an enormous asset, though the Congress Party lost seats. But Mrs Gandhi's opponents in the Congress Party, especially the party bosses in the states, had not given up the struggle against her. In 1969 the party split. Indira Gandhi was expelled but carried the majority of the party in the Assembly with her, which became known eventually as the Congress (I) Party. She called another general election in March 1971 and completely defeated her opponents in the rival Congress Party. Her intervention in Bengal when civil war broke out in Pakistan in 1971, the ensuing defeat of Pakistan by India and the creation of Bangladesh made her a popular national leader and enabled her to win state elections too in 1972.

Indira Gandhi, lacking the moderation and restraint of her father, established a strong, central-ised and personal style of ruling. She sought to dominate state politics completely by appointing her own nominees to the chief posts. Was her motive personal power alone? The old bosses had certainly blocked all radical land reform and Indira Gandhi tried to help the peasants. But her new policies promoting the 'green revolution' and the anti-poverty programmes had only limited success. She soon ran into trouble. There were food shortages, outbreaks of violence in some states and country-wide protests, until a court ruling in June 1975 declared her 1971 election to be invalid owing to corruption. She was ordered to be suspended from holding office, but she put a sudden end to oppo-sition moves to discredit her by requesting the President to declare an emergency.

Indira Gandhi now put in question her father's work and the future of Indian democracy as civil rights were suspended, press censorship imposed, thousands of opponents imprisoned and the elec-tions due in 1976 postponed. Particularly resented was her arrogant son Sanjay, not least for his laud-able but insensitive campaign to limit population growth by persuading peasants in the villages to submit to sterilisation. Disaffection against the various arbitrary measures of the government grew.

Mrs Gandhi, out of touch with the true feelings of the country, called an election in December 1977 and was defeated by a coalition of opposition parties known as Janata. In a perverse way, she had now produced a functioning democracy with the first defeat of the governing party. But Janata was simply a coalition of convenience to oust Mrs Gandhi. Led by the venerable Morarji Desai it restored normal government but in 1979 fell apart, allowing Mrs Gandhi to return to power after the General Elec-tion of January 1980.

She relied increasingly on her son Sanjay, until his death in an accident as well as and on other members of her family and loyal retainers. She retained power because the opposition was too divided to defeat her.

The most notable crisis of Indira Gandhi's rule occurred in the Punjab. Here, the Sikhs had organ-ised their own political party, the Akali Dal. Even after partition religious and communal antagonisms in the Punjab were a cause of conflict between Hindu and Sikh. Although Sikhs in the Indian army have been conspicuously loyal, in the 1980s extremist groups demanded the creation of an inde-pendent Sikh state, Khalistan. Moreover, a religious fanaticism was growing among the Sikhs in the 1980s. Indira Gandhi made matters worse by attempting to play off the more moderate Sikhs against the terrorists in her efforts to secure central domination over the state. In the end, in 1984, the killing of innocent Hindus forced her to crack down on the extremists, who withdrew with their armed bands to a Sikh holy place, the Golden Temple in Amritsar. In June she ordered the assault of the Golden Temple and, with the loss of hundreds of lives, it was bloodily cleared. The assault provoked outrage among the Sikh community and cost Indira Gandhi her life: two of her Sikh bodyguards assas-sinated her in November 1984. A wave of violence and murders followed, directed against innocent Sikhs in Delhi and other Indian cities. It was all a far cry from the days of Nehru, who had sought to conciliate and to reduce communal strife and bloodshed.

On a wave of sympathy and Hindu solidarity, Rajiv Gandhi succeeded his mother to the premier-ship and won a landslide victory in the general election held in December 1984. But his govern-ment found no solution to India's perennial problems, prominent among them ethnic–

nationalist stirrings in some of India's troubled states. Terrorist attacks in the Punjab eventually caused hundreds of deaths and brought about the imposition of emergency rule. And, despite meeting Benazir Bhutto, Rajiv Gandhi was unable to bridge the gap between Pakistan and India over the Kashmir dispute. His boldest move, to assist the Sri Lankan government to suppress the Tamil Tigers by sending an Indian army to the island in 1987, ended in failure when his forces withdrew in the summer of 1989. Sri Lanka continues to be torn by civil war. Rajiv Gandhi and his ministers were accused of corruption, of accepting bribes when concluding a 1986 agreement with the Swedish arms manufacturer Bofors. His Congress (I) Party, meanwhile, was as heavily divided as ever, so it came as no surprise when it decisively lost the

*Right: Militant Sikhs demonstrate in the precincts of the Golden Temple at Amritsar in 1984.*

*Below: Prime Minister Indira Ghandi of India is cremated on 3 November 1984, having been assassinated by her Sikh bodyguards. Her son Rajiv (second from left in photo) was to suffer the same fate – he was killed by a bomb presented to him hidden in a bouquet in Tamil Nadu – within six years.*

general election held in November 1989.

A coalition of opposition parties assumed control of the government under Prime Minister Vishwanath Pratap Singh. Central and state government relations dominated the new government. Kashmir erupted in what was more or less rebellion and in 1990 suffered fierce and bloody repression from the Indian army occupying it. This increased tension between Pakistan and India, now both capable of fighting with nuclear weapons. In the south, the government has cracked down on India's Tamil state, which was aiding the Tamils in Sri Lanka. At home Pratap Singh's efforts to assist the lower Hindu castes through positive discrimination in government jobs led to violent protests in 1990 by the better-educated, higher-caste Indians, and young men set fire to themselves. Singh's uneasy and feuding coalition partners in government could not provide the consistent and stable development policies India desperately needed.

Since the assassination of Rajiv Ghandi, India's party divisions have made it difficult to create governments based on stable parliamentary majorities. The emergence of the Hindu-nationalist Bharatiya Janata Party (BJP) has even threatened the cohesion of the state. Ambitious Hindu leaders inflamed religious passions condemning concessions to minority Muslims as a means to power in an attempt to replace the Congress (I) party as the largest party in parliament. They succeeded only two well in 1992 in stirring up sectarian feeling. The flashpoint occurred in December 1992 when a fanatical mob of tens of thousands of Hindus tore down the sixteenth-century Muslim mosque at Ayodhya. Militant BJP leaders accused the Muslims of having desecrated an earlier temple on the site dedicated to the Hindu god Ram. The riots between Hindus and Muslims and bloodshed that followed were reminiscent of confrontations of earlier years. Had civilized India made no progress? Even Bombay, where Muslims and Hindus were devoted to making money and had lived together for decades, erupted in violence in early 1993 with tombs and riots leaving hundreds dead. Yet quietly India's seventy-two-year-old Prime Minister, appointed in June 1991 as a 'stop

### The Indian Subcontinent and Sri Lanka, 1990

|  | Population (*millions*) | Gross National Product per head (*US$*) |
|---|---|---|
| India | 815.0 | 360 |
| Pakistan | 111.0 | 400 |
| Bangladesh | 113.0 | 170 |
| Sri Lanka | 17.0 | 440 |

gap', with the able support of the Finance Minister Manmohan Singh, set in motion a programme of reform, lowering taxes, and liberalising trade which has led to foreign investment and lower inflation. The BJP's influence has weakened and prospects for stability and development in 1994 began to look better. Violence has nevertheless a way of erupting unpredictably in India.

The history of the Indian subcontinent from independence in 1947 up to the 1990s was marred by continuing regional, ethnic and community strife. Only in India was a secular democracy, albeit flawed in many ways, established – a considerable achievement. The explosion of religious violence and bloodshed, the weakness of the Congress (I) party, the corruption of local politicians and the rise of the Hindu-nationalist BJP party as the major opposition severely tests the unity of the democratic secular state of independent India's envisioned by founding fathers. Despite these deep divisions and nationalist separatist regional movements India has overcome crises before and may do so again. Hopefully in the 1990s the passions will die down once more. Other fundamental problems that have afflicted the subcontinent for decades will, however, remain. Under-development, the failure to check population growth, and the obstacles in the way of land reform and education continue to condemn the majority of the continent's peoples to abject poverty.

CHAPTER 67

# The Prosperous Pacific Rim: Japan, Taiwan, Hong Kong, Singapore and South Korea

The impact of the American occupation years on Japan was momentous. The victor was admired and America's national sport, baseball, and clothes and manners were widely copied, especially by the young. The occupiers found it hard to believe that this was the enemy that only recently had fought so fiercely and cruelly. To all outward appearances Japan was adapting quickly to a new image of 'Made in America'. A brand-new constitution in 1947 introduced 'democracy' and was based on the finest ideals of the West, a mixture of Jefferson and Montesquieu. It provided for a parliament with an upper and a lower house elected by universal suffrage, political parties, a prime minister and Cabinet dependent on a majority in the lower house, and an independent judiciary. The Emperor became a mortal, a national symbol rather than a divinity. The changes were for real, but this Western model of democratic institutions had a very traditional Japanese orientation. Western and Japanese attitudes fused to create something different from the constitutional governments of the West but also from the autocratic military-dominated regime of pre-war Nippon.

The traditions survived of a hierarchical society which placed great emphasis on personal relations between the leader and the led, each knowing his place. Japanese society tends to be organised in groups, each with its own charismatic leader – the 'parent' groups begetting 'child' groups, thus building up powerful 'families'. Policies are decided by the manoeuvres of the leading groups. Group thought prevails. Democracy, with its emphasis on the individual, does not sit very easily with such an ethos. Another weakness of Japanese democracy was that one party dominated Japanese politics for nearly half a century after the Second World War; patronage and corruption became so widespread, they were practically institutionalised. In this respect Japan is not unique – there are similarities here with Italy.

An important feature of Japanese government is the role of the bureaucracy, of the leading personalities who guide the ministries and work in close association with business. They are not civil servants in the Western sense, simply carrying out the instructions of politicians, their elected masters; rather, Japanese mandarins built up an independent network, providing constant guidance and exchange of information with the business elites. This role is not laid down in the constitution, but conforms to Japanese traditions. The prime minister and ministers rely on the bureaucracy not only for carrying out policies but frequently for initiating them. So the bureaucrats are in practice legislators themselves, and the proceedings of the Diet, or Assembly, no more than a formality. In relations with the citizen they also provide *gyosei shido*, or 'administrative guidance', which does not have the character of legislation, and they enjoy a close relationship with members of the ruling Liberal Democratic Party. It takes prime ministers of exceptional strength and ability to impose their wills on the bureaucracy, and of these there have been

*Japanese Emperor Hirohito in a role to which he was unaccustomed – the mortal.*

relatively few. The careers of bureaucrat and politician were not mutually exclusive, and it helps to understand their close relationship when the careers of ministers between 1955 and 1980 are examined. Former bureaucrats held the office of prime minister for no less than twenty out of these twenty-five years.

In dealings with business elites and with financial policy the bureaucrats of a number of financial institutions have played a leading role, pre-eminent among them the Japan Development Bank and the Export–Import Bank, working with the Ministry of Finance and the Ministry of International Trade and Industry – MITI. Numerous other agencies play a part, including the Science and Technology Agency. Rivalry between these institutions is endemic, which makes co-ordination difficult. Japanese government is not therefore, as it is frequently believed to be, an efficient, well-oiled machine. Errors are made – for example, the neglect until recently of the environmental consequences of industrial growth – and it can take a long time before decisions are reached. Despite these draw-

backs, the Japanese political, bureaucratic and business elites have since the war contained enough men of outstanding vision and ability to propel Japan's phenomenal economic growth.

Business is well organised. The Federation of Economic Organisations (Keidanren) was founded in 1946 at the nadir of Japan's industrial fortunes and rapidly developed wide national and international interests, maintaining close contacts with bureaucrats and the ruling party. The Japan Federation of Employers deals with employer–employee relations, when necessary taking a leading role in fighting labour demands. Another influential body, which is independent but works closely with the bureaucracy, is the Japan Chamber of Commerce and Industry. All these trade organisations publicise their views on national policy and exert great influence on the political process. This is not unconnected with the huge financial contributions which they make to the Liberal Democratic Party, to groups and even to individuals within the party. The other smaller, non-communist parties have benefited to a lesser degree from business contributions. Nor are bureaucrats immune from more subtle forms of business 'patronage'. What businessmen want from government is to be able to conduct their operations as profitably as possible at home and abroad with the minimum of interference – in other words, capitalist enterprise with government providing incentives, information, tax breaks and so on, restricting imports and leaving the door open for exports. Government, in other words, is required to create an environment in which businesses may flourish.

During the first decade after the war, a number of parties competed for power, most of them conservative, though there were also Socialist and communist parties. The Socialists, in coalition with conservatives, actually held power for a few months in 1947 and 1948. The threat that, with a more united left, the Japanese Socialist Party might return to power overcame the differences among the various conservative parties and drove them to form in November 1955 the Liberal Democratic Party (LDP). But the left split again, and from 1955 to 1990 was unable to mount an effective challenge or to offer a credible alternative administration to the LDP. This enabled the LDP to form the government on its own or with minor allies following the twelve elections held between 1958 and 1990. Only twice, in 1976 and 1979, did the LDP fail to win an absolute majority in the House of Representatives and then only just; the opposition was far too split to form an alternative coalition government. The Japanese Socialist Party, at its strongest in the decade 1958 to 1967, could never muster enough votes to gain more than 166 out of 467 seats (1958) and continued to grow weaker in the 1980s despite a temporary upsurge in 1989. For more than three decades the LDP was the 'eternal' ruling party.

Nonetheless, there was plenty of political infighting within the umbrella Liberal Democratic Party. The various groups within the party all follow their own leader, whose views they then unanimously back. Membership of a group is a matter not of political attitude but of personal attachment and loyalty. The 'boss' determines the power of the group or faction, which rises or falls or splits according to its success in influencing the overall leadership. Thus strong men dominate the party, and bargains and alliances are struck between the six or seven most powerful groups. Cabinet posts, ministerial portfolios, party executive positions comprise the patronage which the president of the

party is able to bestow once he has obtained the support of enough factions to take over the leadership. The 'leadership factions', having backed the right horse, enjoy enhanced power; the 'non-leadership factions' now work for change so that they can be on the winning side next time. So 'democracy' works after a fashion, not *between* parties but within the Liberal Democratic Party. The emphasis is less on policies than on the power struggles among the factions. The president of the party automatically becomes the prime minister of the country. That was how all the prime ministers of Japan were chosen from the 1950s on.

The Japanese in-groups in politics, business and the bureaucracy know the rules and know how to play by them so as to make their influence felt. As individuals they have to conform to the wishes of the leadership of their particular interest group. From the interplay between these groups, consensus policies eventually emerge. But what about the sizeable minority who are not part of the in-group – the politicians of the left, the more militant trade unionists, citizens who do not share the views of the Liberal Democratic Party? What about the generation gap, those young people who rebel against the elders' practice of trying to determine every facet of their later life? And what about the small band of traditionalists or nationalists who reject imported American culture and Western-style politics? There is no safety valve for their views. They are condemned to be permanent outsiders, and their lack of influence through the established channels leads to pent-up frustrations which periodically explode into violence – as happened at the massive demonstrations against the ratification of the US–Japanese Mutual Security Treaty in April and May 1960.

Just as it did in the West, student protest boiled over in 1968 and 1969 in Tokyo, over the need for university reform. In 1968 large-scale demonstrations demanded the return of Okinawa, the US-occupied island in the Pacific, and clamoured for the removal of American bases. There were also street battles between police and students over the government's decision to build another international airport outside Tokyo on farmland. The clashes continued into the 1970s. This was 'direct democracy', given that other constitutional means of voicing dissent were blocked. But protest was never strong enough seriously to imperil the Japanese way of government or of conducting business. Economic progress and the promise of material benefit encouraged the majority of the people to compete for the best opportunities and to conform.

The dominant political leader during the occupation years and immediately after was Shigeru Yoshida, who was out of sympathy with General MacArthur's liberal and democratic views. He welcomed the 'reverse course' which was adopted as soon as Washington became primarily concerned with the containment of communism. Yoshida headed the government five times from May 1946 to May 1947 and then from October 1948 to December 1954. A former career diplomat, he became prime minister only because Ichiro Hatoyama, who was president of the Liberal Party, had chosen him as his successor. Hatoyama had had to leave politics for a time because he was unacceptable to the Americans: like many early leaders, including Yoshida, he had shared the ideology of Japan's 'co-prosperity sphere' in Asia before 1945. Yoshida rehabilitated himself in the eyes of the Americans by courageously pressing for peace when the war was all but lost; moreover, he blamed the military for their adventurist readiness to go to war with the West in 1941. In 1946 he recognised that Japan's recovery depended on being trusted again by the United States. This meant winning over MacArthur and accepting the directives of his headquarters, SCAP, when they could not safely be circumvented. He thus played a similar role to Adenauer in West Germany. The escalation of the Cold War in Asia, Washington's loss of China as an ally and the outbreak of the Korean War in 1950 hastened Japan's rehabilitation.

Yoshida exploited with great skill the American–Communist confrontation. MacArthur had long been persuaded that his prescriptions had turned Japan into a democracy. In June 1950 Secretary of State John Foster Dulles came to Japan, to win the Japanese as allies in Asia. He wanted the famous Article 9 of MacArthur's constitution to be set aside so that Japan could rearm. Yoshida rejected rearmament, stressing all the negative results it would have on the Japanese and on Japan's neighbours. Dulles was 'flabbergasted', but MacArthur sided with Yoshida. Japan should build up her industrial potential and in that way help the free world. Soon after the outbreak of the war in Korea, American orders for arms came pouring in and gave

*Japan turns to peace and recovery. Prime Minister Shigeru Yoshida declares Japan's acceptance of the 'fair and generous' terms of the Peace Treaty at the Conference in San Francisco in September 1951.*

the Japanese economy a much needed boost.

Eventually the Japanese, under American pressure, did create a Self-Defence Force, initially of only 75,000 men. It expanded to 165,000 by 1954 and 250,000 by 1980. The army, navy and air force came to be equipped with the most modern weapons, but in relation to Japan's size and wealth it was a small force. The Japanese expended no more than 1.3 per cent of their GNP on the military. The 'saving' as against the expenditures of the Cold War countries was enormous and was available for investment in industry. But the Japanese elite was less niggardly in building up a powerful paramilitary police force of 250,000 to guarantee internal order.

The negotiations leading to the peace treaty and the end of the American occupation were long and arduous. Yoshida made as few concessions as possible. Japan would not rearm heavily; she would not herself participate in international disputes; she would rely on the United States and her nuclear umbrella for security. Japan would be the reliable but passive ally of the United States, which she would provide with bases, and she undertook to grant no bases to other countries without American consent. The Americans retained Okinawa for military use only, and the Japanese had to give up all the conquests they had made since 1895. Yoshida also had to concede that, if requested by the Japanese government, the United States would provide assistance 'to put down large-scale internal riots and disturbances in Japan . . .' American rights inside Japan certainly reminded the Japanese of the special rights which foreigners had enjoyed in Japan until their abolition at the close of the nineteenth century. It was humiliating. Nevertheless these terms, embodied in the US–Japanese Security Treaty, were signed in San Francisco on the same day, 8 September 1951, as the Treaty of Peace with the Allied powers. Australia and New Zealand were reluctant signatories, since they feared a Japanese military revival, but they were reassured by a defensive treaty, ANZUS, with the United States; the US–Pacific alliance structure was completed by US treaties with the Philippines (1951), with South Korea (1952) and with Taiwan (1954), and by SEATO (1954). Thus Japan was tied to the anti-communist containment policy of the United States and thereby limited in her ability to adopt an independent foreign policy.

Japan had to follow the US lead in recognising Chiang Kai-shek on Taiwan as representing China, and she was thus prevented from normalising her relationship with the People's Republic. Not surprisingly the Soviet Union refused to sign any peace treaty with Japan, and a Japanese–Soviet agreement formally ending hostilities was not reached until 1986 and territorial disputes still stood in the way of a definitive peace treaty.

The US–Japanese Mutual Security Treaty of 1951 became a burning issue in Japanese politics. The possibility that there might be nuclear weapons on US warships became a particular problem; the left identified this treaty as a form of US hegemony, which also keeps the conservatives in power. Public hostility to it proved so strong, with widespread demonstrations against it, that Washington agreed to revise it in 1960. The changes were cosmetic, though they allowed Japan a more equal voice; the Japanese stressed their country's residual sovereignty in the islands still militarily occupied by the United States. The revised treaty then came up for ratification by the Diet. In April and May 1960

there were unprecedented demonstrations and street battles between the police and students and other demonstrators. After unseemly scenes in the Diet itself, the Liberal Democratic Party forced ratification through. President Eisenhower was so incensed by these strong anti-American feelings that he called off an intended visit to Japan.

In 1970 the treaty was renewed again indefinitely, subject to either country giving a year's notice to terminate it. The following year a problem was solved that closely touched Japanese pride. The Ryukyu Islands, including Okinawa, were returned to the Japanese in the spring of 1972, though US bases were allowed to remain by agreement. But the territorial claim to four islands of the southernmost part of the Kuril island chain occupied by the Russians continued to prevent good relations with the Russian Republic. Thus after 1951 the American alliance, despite all the difficulties it caused in internal Japanese politics, remained the sheet anchor of Japan's international position and defence.

It was Yoshida who had set Japan on that course. The close relationship with the United States has enabled Japan to eschew extensive military pretensions, which could be seen as a threat to her Asian neighbours and endanger political stability at home; but the relationship is also based on a recognition that the United States is indispensable to Japanese prosperity, mainly by providing the enormous single market on which that prosperity is based. The Japanese have on a few occasions followed a more independent line from Washington when their interests seemed to demand it. The most notable instance has been in Japanese dealings with the Arab oil states in the Middle East. After suffering from the effects of the Arab oil embargo in 1973 (page 484), Japan made it clear to the Arab states that she did not share Washington's views on Arab–Israeli issues and indeed supported the Arab cause. In this way she bought the goodwill of the Arab states, who continued the oil supply vital to Japanese industry. During the Iran–Iraq war in the 1980s the Japanese attempted to stay on good terms with both sides, despite America's estrangement from Iran, especially following the seizure of the American Embassy hostages (page 487). In 1990–1 during the Gulf crisis, Japan again displayed no enthusiasm for the US position. The Americans have at times shown little sensitivity for Japanese feelings – for example, Nixon's sudden opening to China and the dropping of the Nationalists in Taiwan in the 1970s were undertaken without consulting Japan, which had faithfully followed the Washington line in refusing to recognise communist China. But despite strains, especially in matters of Japanese–US trade, the alliance has held and what later became known as the 'Yoshida Doctrine' continued to chart the course of Japanese policy, with only minor modifications.

What then was the essence of that doctrine? Yoshida believed he would satisfy America's demands on Japan as an ally by offering facilities and bases and by restricting Japan's own military build-up. The Japanese forces were to be purely defensive, forbidden to act except in defence of the home islands, and Japan should forswear development of nuclear weapons. In international disputes her profile should be low. She had finally turned her back on achieving greatness through military conquest; all her energies were to be concentrated on economic rehabilitation and growth. For her own security, Japan had no choice but to rely on her American 'ally', which was also Japan's most important trading partner. The Yoshida strategy for Japan's recovery was accepted by the Liberal Democratic Party consensus as the basis for Japan's national policy and long outlived Yoshida's relinquishment of the premiership in 1954. The doctrine was elaborated and put into practice by Yoshida's disciples and protégés, for example Hayato Ikeda, who became prime minister 1960–4, and Eisaku Sato, prime minister 1964–72, and on into the 1970s and 1980s. Yoshida's vision helped to make Japan into an industrial and financial superpower, second only to the United States, during the second half of the twentieth century.

The inner workings of a society are often obscured by outward appearances. This is certainly true of Japan. Her industrial successes and her recovery from the low of war's end might at first sight be ascribed to purposeful governments setting planned targets and, with the help of the bureaucrats in the relevant ministries, especially the Ministry of Finance, the Ministry of International Trade and Industry (the famous MITI) and the Economic Planning Agency, achieving them unfailingly. From the mid-1950s onwards, plan after plan, some ten of them in thirty years, were produced, often interrupted, amended or discarded before they could run their five- or ten-year terms. There is no doubt that in the early post-war years the influence of

governmental–bureaucratic measures was considerable. At first, priority was given to coal and steel, to provide the basic energy and material for manufacture; then other sectors were successfully developed – chemical fertilisers, shipbuilding, cars, machine tools, transistor radios, cameras, television sets, video-recorders and microchips. MITI encouraged the formation of the *keiretsu*, the pre-war *zaibatsus*. Mitsubishi and Mitsui were back in business and huge new conglomerates came into being, such as the electronic innovator Sony and car manufacturers Toyota and Nissan.

Government–bureaucracy assisted during the early years in various ways, most importantly by managing the nation's finances and investments through controlling revenue and banks and by making cheap loans to targeted industries through the Reconstruction Finance Bank, the Export–Import Bank and the Japan Development Bank. Industry expanded fast, fed by enormous investments. Governmental–bureaucratic rules and legislation in the 1960s and 1970s meanwhile protected the emerging home industries, employing many devices to prevent foreign imports from being competitive – where they could not be kept out altogether. This was to lead to tension with the United States and Western Europe, which were threatened with a flood of Japanese exports. Japanese trade unions became steadily more co-operative after the more turbulent 1950s; continual conservative government and rising prosperity undermined union militancy and membership.

Undeniably, then, the government–bureaucracy has played an important role in Japan's rapid economic growth. But the notion that she has developed anything like a command economy is very misleading. Since 1945, command economies have failed all over the world. It would be strange if Japan were the one exception. In fact Japanese government planning had far more in common with the approach of Jean Monnet in France (pages 539–41), that is indicative planning, than with Stalinist forms of control over production, investment, distribution and pricing. Japan's economy was and remains thoroughly capitalist, with a profit-oriented outlook, fiercely competitive at home and abroad. The role of MITI declined after the early 1960s; it remains a source of supplementary assistance to industry but it has long since ceased to be decisive.

Business leadership, however, was certainly

decisive. But neither government–bureaucracy nor business could have generated the colossal investment in technology necessary for the economies of scale achieved as huge industrial conglomerates were built up but for the availability of funds. These came not from abroad but from the Japanese man in the street, who lived frugally and saved a fifth of his income year after year. The rewards of this frugality were not large in the short term. The return from interest and the growth of pensions was kept very low so that companies could borrow money cheaply. In the longer term, however, the Japanese did benefit from industry's prosperity. Meanwhile, government expenditure for non-industrial purposes was also held down – welfare payments, housing, the infrastructure were all neglected. The contrast between an automated industry employing the largest number of robots in the world, on the one hand, and the inadequate sewerage system in many large cities, the overcrowded roads and extensive pollution, on the other, was the price paid for the single-minded pursuit of industrial growth.

At the start of the 1960s, the new prime minister, Ikeda Hayato, promised to double everyone's income in ten years. Business met this target with extraordinary rapidity, more than quadrupling exports of ships, textiles, cars and electronic goods during the 1960s. The effects of this expansion percolated far beyond the Japanese islands – to Australia, where the ore was mined to provide Japan with steel, to the Middle East, which supplied much of her oil, to south-east Asia, especially Indonesia and Malaya, from which she imported oil and raw materials. The rest of the world took note and tried to gain access to Japan's market for industrial goods. The Japanese government lifted restrictions and made genuine efforts in the 1980s to open the home market more freely, to head off international hostility, especially from America. But the bureaucracy and business have used administrative obstacles to make it as difficult as possible for foreign goods to penetrate the Japanese market. If Japanese business, however, had not been able to take advantage of the protected home market as a base from which to expand, protection in the end would have made home industry less efficient, which is what usually happens to featherbedded home industries. Why instead did it become more efficient?

The leaders of the big corporations were simply not satisfied with easy profits as a measure of

success. Their particular industry had to become the best in the world, for the greater glory of the company and Japan. Toyota and Nissan began making cars before the war, copying British and American designs. In 1950 Japanese motor manufacturers produced less than 2000 cars. To take on the American giants, Ford and Chrysler, or the British Austin and Morris seemed a futile ambition. Initially they made agreements with Western car manufacturers to use their designs and technology, and they studied American factories. In 1970 Japan produced 5 million cars, providing Western customers with what they wanted at a lower price than similar Western cars. By 1990 Japanese car manufacturers were making reverse agreements to transfer their technology to the ailing British car plants, such as Rover in Birmingham, which forged a link with Honda. To overcome foreign resentment and pre-empt the exclusion of Japanese exports, the Japanese electronic firm Sony and the Japanese car giants have set up factories in the United States and Europe. In industry after industry, the Japanese improved technically on the Western product, whether cameras or machine tools. Then, exploiting heavy investment, the hard work of a skilled labour force, the economies that come from large-scale production, a more or less closed home market and a worldwide export market, they raised productivity sharply so that better goods could be produced much more cheaply. There is a constant battle for improvement, for keeping ahead in research, design and methods of production. The new generation of computers in the coming information age is the latest industry to be targeted by Japan to become a world-beater. There will be few industries of the twenty-first century in which the Japanese will not excel; one of these, in the 1990s still dominated by the United States, is the aircraft industry. After a

**Japan, 1950–1990**

|  | Population (*millions*) | Gross National Product per head (*US$*) |
| --- | --- | --- |
| 1950 | 83.0 | 200 (in 1955) |
| 1978 | 115.2 | 7,300 |
| 1987 | 122.1 | 15,800 |
| 1990 | 124.0 | 27,000 |

phenomenal growth rate in the GNP of 10 per cent a year in the 1960s, annual growth in Japan has slowed in the 1970s and 1980s to an average nearer 6 per cent, but that has the effect of nearly doubling output in a decade.

Japan is governed by career politicians, by leaders of factions and local 'favourite sons' returned to the Diet. Allegiance is less to mass parties, more to individuals. Politicians play a considerable role in the communities which elect them, attending hundreds of events, including weddings, funerals and festive occasions, at which they are expected to distribute largesse. Their resulting need for money breeds corruption. They do favours for their supporters, using their influence as members of the Diet with ministries. In return they receive cash donations. For example, the country farmers enjoying farm subsidies support the LDP. The opposition support comes from the newer urban areas, which are discriminated against in that each of their electoral districts contains a much larger number of voters than those in the countryside. This suits the LDP. When he gets to Tokyo, the young LDP politician has to join one of the factions; thereafter he will gradually rise in the hierarchy of national politics, increasingly able to bestow favours.

The Yoshida faction and followers dominated Japanese politics from 1946 through to the 1980s. A rival was Hatoyama, who had earlier stepped down and passed the presidency to Yoshida, whom he expected to make way for him later. From 1956 to 1960 two protégés of Hatoyama became successively president of the party and prime minister. But the second of these, Nobusuke Kishi, fell from power in 1960. Kishi's anti-unionist and anti-socialist stance earned him the hatred of a wide grouping among the opposition. The renewal of the US–Japanese Security Treaty in 1960 became the catalyst which brought the opposition on to the streets in April and May 1960. The polarisation, the violence of demonstrators and police, and the intemperate scenes in the Diet itself presented the ugly face of Japanese politics. These spectacles and the manoeuvring of the factions within the LDP forced Kishi to step down. Hayato Ikeda took his place, representing the Yoshida line, as did his own successor Eisaku Sato (1964–72). Eisaku Sato's selection was probably effected by a deal between Ikeda and Kishi; he had the advantage of being

Kishi's brother, and he proved himself a very adept politician.

Sato's eight years in office were notable for the estrangement between Japan and the United States arising out of the Nixon administration's demands that Japanese textile exports to the US should be restricted. Nonetheless, the renewal of the US–Japanese Security Treaty in June 1970 prompted Nixon, after much Japanese agitation, to promise to return Okinawa, and an agreement to that effect was concluded in June 1971. A month later relations were soured again by Nixon's announcement that he would visit China; his failure to inform Japan of this reversal of US policy towards Nationalist China on Taiwan, which the Japanese had hitherto supported, greatly angered the Japanese, who did not relish being treated as very much a junior partner in Asia. The second 'Nixon shock', in August 1971, was a devaluation of the dollar – in effect making Japanese exports more expensive – and the imposition of a temporary import surcharge. The Japanese interpreted America's defensive economic moves as unfriendly to themselves. These foreign-policy difficulties and internal LDP manoeuvres ended Sato's premiership. In July 1972, after bitter internal feuding between Sato's two principal lieutenants, the younger, more ambitious Kakuei Tanaka defeated Takeo Fukuda to win the presidency and become prime minister.

Tanaka was unusually active in foreign affairs. He visited Beijing, following in Nixon's footsteps, and toured south-east Asia, where memories of the Japanese occupation were still too recent to ensure a good reception. In Indonesia, the Philippines and Thailand, demonstrators carried placards demanding 'Tanaka Go Home'. His premiership was anyway a stormy one. In 1973 the Arab–Israeli War produced the shock of the quadrupling in the price of oil. This hit Japan particularly badly, as she depended overwhelmingly for oil on the Middle East, and there was widespread panic. Tanaka now called in his arch-rival Takeo Fukuda, a financial expert, to take charge of the Ministry of Finance. Fukuda imposed drastic measures to squeeze the economy. It worked. By 1975 the Japanese economy was expanding once more by a healthy 6 per cent, which it continued to do for the rest of the decade. Tanaka's ambitious plans to develop the Japanese regions had been put into cold storage and were only gradually revived after 1975. More significantly, Japan took effective steps to reduce her reliance for power on Middle Eastern oil by securing alternative sources and developing nuclear power stations.

Even among Japanese political leaders, Tanaka was exceptional in the power and money he commanded. Institutionalised corruption had reached new heights. In the end publicity about his financial misdeeds in Japan and in the foreign press undermined his standing. The LDP factions agreed to replace him with a minor figure, Takeo Miki, to restore an image of propriety. But Miki proved rather too energetic in trying to reform the LDP, especially when he had Tanaka arrested in 1976 for accepting bribes in the Lockheed aircraft-purchase scandal. Lockheed had handed over $12 million in bribes to Japanese bureaucrats and politicians, including Tanaka, to ensure that the aircraft order went to them. Tanaka spent only a short time in jail and was then let out on bail, still a power-broker behind the scenes among the LDP factions. The close of the 1970s was a turbulent time in internal LDP politics, and from 1978 to 1982 further tame successors were found.

In November 1982 the LDP factions of Tanaka and Suzuki chose Yasuhiro Nakasone for the presidency and premiership. He turned out to be much more decisive and more of his own man than Tanaka or Suzuki liked. His success in winning the general election of 1986 enabled him to stay a further year in office, although LDP rules would normally have required him to hand over the presidency that year.

Nakasone wanted to break away from Japan's outdated traditions, to remove the heavy hand of centralised control with its myriad regulations, and so prepare the way for a new phase of economic growth. He asserted Japan's claim to respect from the world's powers, a claim that entailed her losing her pygmy international status and her dependency on the United States. In 1986 he hosted the annual summit of leading industrial nations in Tokyo and that same year visited Beijing. War guilt was now part of history. He would lead Japan, backed by popular approval, in the American presidential style.

Nakasone's self-confidence and his promise of a more active Japanese foreign policy were welcomed by Western leaders. Visiting Washington in 1983, Nakasone promised President Reagan Japan's active assistance in the containment of the Soviet Union. He toured south-east Asia and indicated that he was ready to expand Japan's military capacity. But his attempt to revise the constitution for this purpose

*Robots do the work of many men at this Nissan car plant at Yokahama, Japan.*

so alarmed the Japanese that he promised not to go ahead during his first term of office. Nakasone engaged in high diplomacy with a relish, but government efforts to open the domestic market to foreign goods, as the rest of the world was demanding, were constantly frustrated by bureaucracy and business. Every year Japan amassed huge balance-of-payments surpluses, while the United States had to cope with the largest debt in the world. The deficit was in part managed by Japan recycling her surplus into the purchase of US Treasury bonds. But the Japanese also bought many physical assets abroad – real estate in California, the Rockefeller Center in New York, factories in America and Europe. Japan's financial and manufacturing power globally seemed to be on an ever continuing upward trajectory. When Nakasone finally left office in November 1987, his reputation internationally and at home was at its peak. He had achieved a great deal during his five years in office, aligning Japan more closely with the West and freeing her from her shackles of tradition. But Japanese politics were about to take a surprising turn.

Nakasone's successor, after much factional struggle, was Noboru Takeshita, who enjoyed Nakasone's support. Takeshita continued Nakasone's foreign travels, exhibiting thereby a more independent Japanese foreign policy, though the American alliance remained the bedrock, despite growing trade tensions. Progress towards closer relations with China, however, was temporarily upset by the Chinese leadership's brutality in the massacre of Tiananmen Square (page 650). Takeshita's efforts at home were concentrated on reducing direct taxation and increasing indirect taxation through a sales tax, which was especially unpopular with the poorer Japanese families. But the most sensational event of the Takeshita premiership was the uncovering of yet more corruption in what became known as the 'Recruit scandal'. The Recruit group operated in publishing, real estate and other areas, and it needed favourable decisions from the government and bureaucrats if it was to expand and start making large profits. To gain favours, the group not only lavished legal donations on the political parties but also made illegal payments to politicians and officials. As usual, money had been needed in the leadership race between the factions in 1986, and huge profits were made by Nakasone's ministers in illicit share-dealings. The scandal broke in 1988 and its investigation continued into the following year. Even Prime Minister Takeshita had received political donations and was forced to resign. Many suspected Nakasone too, but he was not formally charged. Nonetheless, the standing of LDP politicians reached a low point in public esteem, and for the first time it looked as if the party might lose power. Sousuke Uno, the new president and prime minister, did not last long when a sex scandal arose to titillate the public. Next, Toshiki Kaifu became prime minister and leader of the LDP; he pulled the party together and promised to rid it of corrupt politicians.

It was enough. In 1990 the LDP was securely back in absolute power after a landslide victory. The dream that a charismatic female politician, Takako Doi, who led the Japan Socialist Party, might effect a decisive change in Japanese politics on two counts – forcing the LDP into opposition and advancing the cause of what was very much the second sex in Japan – quickly faded again. The majority preferred to stick with the party that had presided over Japan's growing prosperity.

But the Japanese miracle began to fade in 1990. Financial scandals continued to undermine the standing of ministers and leading members of the LDP. Some of the most renowned names among securities companies had manipulated stock market prices by agreeing to compensate some favoured clients against losses. Production plummeted, loans based on inflated house and land prices turned into bad debts, the Stock Exchange registered huge losses and the whole financial fabric appeared threatened.

Kaifu was regarded as a weak prime minister by the barons of the LDP factions, a good stopgap while scandals still hung in the air. During his two years in office Kaifu nevertheless was very popular among the Japanese people as a clean politician. This mattered little to the LDP and in October 1991 Shin Kanemaru, the most powerful of the barons and chairman of the Takeshita faction, forged the necessary alliances in the corridors of power so that the premiership should fall to Kiichi Miyazawa. Miyazawa had been minister of finance at the time of the Recruit financial scandal and had resigned in December 1988. His return to politics was intended to mark the end of any recriminations. Cabinet posts were distributed among the factions. Miyazawa faced new challenges. The trade surplus with the United States was the cause of considerable tension while America remained bogged down in recession, and President Bush's visit to Tokyo in January 1992 did little to repair the image of the United States, unable to compete with Japan in manufactures such as automobiles where she was once the world leader.

Miyazawa, who abandoned most of Kaifu's reform programme, was saddled in 1992 with a new investigation of a financial scandal that promised to be bigger even than the Recruit affair. Known as Sagawa, it concerned the handouts made to some hundred politicians, mainly LDP, including two cabinet ministers. Sagawa Kyubin was a parcel-delivery firm that went into bankruptcy with huge debts. It was one scandal too many. The political power-broker Shin Kanemaru was forced to resign in October 1992. A breakaway faction of the LDP formed the Renewal party. Elections in July 1993 resulted in a political upheaval. The LDP fell from power. Morihiro Hosokawa headed a new seven-party coalition government committed to reform until his fall in April 1994.

The contrast between Japanese politics – faction-ridden, endemically prone to scandal – and Japan's success as an economic superpower subverts the claim that in all regions of the world democracy is essential for prosperity. Indeed prosperity has undermined the growth of a healthy democracy in Japan and in the more prosperous nations of Asia – Taiwan, Singapore and Thailand, not to mention Hong Kong. There is a parallel here with China, where Deng too believed that the great majority of the people would accept the communist political system as long as it delivered rising standards of living; conversely, democracy would be in danger where standards fell. Will Japan break this cycle and combine democracy and prosperity? Change may yet occur in Japan before the twentieth century has run its course, as a younger, well-educated generation takes over.

Unlike the inhabitants of many countries in the world, the Japanese enjoy civil liberties, and their government is neither dictatorial nor authoritarian. If it were, the politicians would not have to distribute so much largesse and favours to ensure their reselection. They have to keep on the right side of the people. Politics is marginal to the ordinary Japanese, except for necessary favours, his own job prospects, education and the outlook for his children. Material progress and security are what matter. For those who won places in the right schools, universities and companies, there were jobs for life. The company took care of you, and you owed it absolute loyalty. It was good for those who were 'in' – once they survived the fearsome competition. There is a place, too, for those who are 'out', but there is also much frustration and crime.

The development of modern Japan has been called an economic miracle, but there is nothing miraculous about it. Superb management, a workforce better educated than any other in the world, the pride that goes with striving for the best, single-mindedness of purpose and favourable world conditions provide a large part of the explanation. Furthermore, what Japan has achieved is already being replicated elsewhere in Asia, albeit on a smaller scale. But prospects dimmed in the early nineties; growth stalled, industrial and banking profits plunged. The last decade of the century is bringing changes and challenging old customs.

The 'other' China, the Republic of China on Taiwan, was founded when the remnants of Chiang Kai-shek's army withdrew to the island in 1949.

Some 20,000 Taiwanese who resisted Kuomintang rule were killed that year and martial law was imposed. Under American protection and with American forces stationed in Taiwan, Chiang Kai-shek and the ageing Kuomintang party and military leaders were able to rebuild a formidable military force of half a million men, ruling over the native Taiwanese with only the façade of a constitutional process. Security police ensured that no opposition could make itself felt for long. Despite American influence, civil liberties and democracy were given no real opportunity to take root. Politically, Taiwan was an ally, and as such the Kuomintang acted internally as it thought best. Taiwan was poor, but even under the Kuomintang economic progress was achieved in the production of textiles and simple electronic goods such as transistor radios. Chiang Kai-shek died in 1975, and after an interval was succeeded by his eldest son, Chiang Ching-kuo, in 1978.

The rapprochement of the United States and the People's Republic of China gradually led to the withdrawal of US troops (in 1979) and of US diplomatic recognition. Chiang Ching-kuo had to readjust Taiwan's international stance. He cautiously improved relations with the People's Republic, and trade and other links expanded. The leaders in Beijing, meanwhile, had no intention any longer of attempting to unify China by force. At home Chiang Ching-kuo likewise gradually followed a reforming policy, having to carry with him the gerontocracy of Chiang Kai-shek's former political and military companions. He finally lifted martial law in 1987 and permitted a multi-party system to evolve. On his death, Vice-President Lee Teng-hui, the first Taiwanese to head the Kuomintang, became president and continued the reforms of the fragile democratic process. Taiwan's human rights record had previously been lamentable; in contrast her economic growth was another of the so-called economic miracles, giving her an income per head twenty times greater than mainland China's.

President Lee skilfully set about enhancing Taiwan's international standing in Asia and normalising relations with Beijing. Although he rejected the Beijing formula of 'one country, two systems', he encouraged economic links and family visits to increase contacts. Taiwan's formula was not reunification but 'one country, two regions', code for separate governments. The state of war

*Chinese President Chiang Kai-Shek and his wife take the crowd's salute on National Day in Taiwan, 29 October 1968. He had left the mainland nineteen years previously, but still claimed he would return.*

between the two Chinas was concluded. Beijing in 1990 agreed to renounce using force against Taiwan and on 1 May 1991 Taiwan declared the forty-two-year-old 'communist rebellion' at an end, code for recognising the communist government of mainland China. Thus Taiwan's flexible diplomacy became more pragmatic after the end of the Cold War. Even so, the idea of a totally independent state of Taiwan was acceptable as a solution neither to the government of Taiwan nor to the rulers in Beijing: both persisted in seeing just 'one country'.

At home President Lee introduced political reforms, and opposition parties were legitimised. In the elections held in December 1991 for Taiwan's Assembly, the Democratic Progressive Party was able to win some parliamentary seats against the Kuomintang, which remained the ruling party.

Another Chinese 'miracle' is Hong Kong, which has no resources except the ingenuity of her merchants and the enterprise of her Chinese population. Capitalist Hong Kong adjoins the communist mainland of China, on which she is dependent for water and food imports. Her geographical position makes her in practical terms indefensible. Hong

Kong island was seized by Britain in 1841, and more territory was forcibly secured in 1860. Then in 1898 the Chinese were made to lease the so-called New Territories for ninety-nine years, in what then looked like becoming a 'scramble for China'. The lease thus expires in 1997, and the prosperous colony of Hong Kong must then inexorably rejoin the rest of China.

Margaret Thatcher's Conservative government tried to make the best of this predicament by negotiating conditions for the return of the Crown colony, at a time (the mid-1980s) when the presence in office of a reform-minded Chinese leadership seemed to promise a liberal future. In the Sino-British Joint Declaration negotiated in 1984, China pronounced that the government of Hong Kong would be composed of local people and that what would be known as the Hong Kong Special Administrative Region would enjoy a high degree of autonomy. Britain, afraid to offend Beijing, declined to pre-empt the choice of a system of representation by creating a wholly elected legislature before the Chinese takeover. The Declaration promised that the 'current social and economic systems in Hong Kong will remain unchanged, and so will the lifestyle. Rights and freedoms, including those of the person, of speech, of the press, of assembly . . . of travel . . . [as well as] Private property [and] . . . foreign investment will be protected by law.' But Beijing's Basic Law for Hong Kong, published in April 1988, raised fears that Hong Kong's freedoms and autonomy would not be respected after 1 July 1997 and would make meaningless Beijing's doctrine of 'one country, two systems'. In June 1989 the Tiananmen Square massacre of the student demonstrators not only aroused passionate sympathy in Hong Kong, but further undermined confidence in a Chinese takeover.

For the first time in her history elections were held in Hong Kong in September 1991. But the Legislative Council was still dominated by nominees, just over two-thirds chosen by the Governor and just over one-third by professional bodies, leaving only eighteen of sixty seats to be contested. China's shadow loomed over Hong Kong's development. The attempts belatedly to broaden representative government before the take-over as proposed in 1993 by the British governor was sharply condemned in Beijing. Democracy is anathema to Beijing. Only 50,000 favoured Hong Kong British passport holders will be allowed to come to Britain. The future of the more than 3.5 million people of prosperous Hong Kong lies with China.

The Chinese of Singapore are much more fortunate in having their own independent island state to which no one else lays claim. Singapore, which has been independent since she seceded from the Federation of Malaysia in 1965, is a well-ordered state with a democratic constitution, although one party, the People's Action Party, has ruled since 1959. Prime Minister Lee Kuan Yew, who headed the government for thirty-one years until he stepped down in 1990, was notable for his authoritarian tendency, his incorruptibility and his almost puritanical zeal for law and order, which extended to requiring long-haired youths to cut their hair short. In common with Thailand and some other Asian countries, Singapore combated the drug menace with draconian laws, including the death penalty. She was at best half a democracy. Opposition politicians and parties were allowed, but the Internal Security Act passed in 1963 permitted the authorities to detain suspects without trial, and the power of the courts to review administrative decisions was

severely restricted. Repressive politically, Singapore was economically free – enterprise was encouraged and since the island, like Hong Kong, was without resources except fish, manufacture and trade flourished.

Lee kept a watchful eye on his chosen successor, Goh Chok Tong, remaining in the government as 'senior minister' and staying as general secretary of the Action Party. Democratic progress of sorts was made in Singapore in the general election held in August 1991, when the opposition quadrupled its representation, from one to four members, albeit swamped by the ruling Action Party's seventy-seven. Singapore remained an economic power-house in Asia in the 1990s, robustly tied to the West – the government welcoming the US fleet, which was offered facilities in Singapore after the Americans lost their Philippine bases.

### Taiwan, Hong Kong and Singapore, 1990–1991

|  | Population (*millions*) | Gross National Product per head (*US$*) |
|---|---|---|
| Taiwan | 20.0 | 8,970 |
| Hong Kong | 5.7 (1988) | 9,600 (1988) |
| Singapore | 2.7 | 14,300 |

After the terrible devastation of war Korea was still a partitioned country in the early 1990s. Sporadic talk of bringing the two Koreas together, of uniting families again, had made little progress. No personality cult anywhere equalled the excesses of worship bestowed on Comrade Kim Il Sung, in 1992 the longest-ruling communist dictator in the world. He had presided over the 'democratic' Korean Republic since 1948 and was already a veteran communist then. There was no freedom in North Korea, with her showpiece capital Pyongyang, her huge and costly military establishment and all the trappings of an oppressive one-party state. Living standards were appallingly low in consequence and did not compare with those in the South.

The history of South Korea can be told in two quite different ways. When the world came to Seoul in 1988 and the XXIV Olympic Games were televised, a fine modern city came into view with well-dressed people in the streets. The economic recovery and industrial growth of South Korea,

*The Olympic Games, Seoul, South Korea, 1988.*

line state of the free world, and the credentials of the South Korean rulers as implacable opponents of communism were never in doubt.

South Korea's first president, Syngman Rhee, lasted until 1960. By then the old autocrat had lost his grip and was forced to bow out after student-led riots in April of that year, protesting against corruption and election fraud. There was a brief hope that the politicians might create at least the semblance of civilian, democratic government. After some months of turmoil, in May 1961 the military stepped in and a junta led by Major-General Park Chung Hee took control. His repressive military-police regime allowed just enough leeway in the 1970s for political activity to function sporadically. But, whenever such activities threatened to become too assertive or violent, Park reimposed rigid control by emergency decree, arresting opposition politicians and suspending civil rights. Suppression would be followed by a measure of liberalisation, as long as it did not threaten military power. Korea's Chief of Intelligence assassinated him in October 1979. A civilian president was tolerated for nine months but the military remained the real power in the land.

In 1980 a new general took over, General Chun Doo-Hwan, who was no less determined to keep the opposition under firm control than Park. The 1980s, like the 1970s, were plagued by periodic demonstrations and riots answered by police truncheons, firearms and torture. The killings in the riotous town of Kwangju in May 1980, when hundreds lost their lives, were just the worst of these. But Korea's rapid industrial development made it desirable to create a better image in the West. The opposition was again allowed a degree of activity, political prisoners were released, and the most prominent opposition leaders, Kim Dae-Jung and Kim Young, were from time to time freed from house arrest and allowed to campaign. In 1987, on the eve of the Olympics, a relatively free presidential election was held. The General's nominee, Roh Tae-Woo, won, but the opposition would have succeeded instead had they been able to close ranks behind a single candidate. Without full democracy it is difficult, if not impossible, for political parties and institutions to develop which are necessary for democracy to function. So South Korean politics were caught in a vicious circle. Roh Tae-Woo was prepared to allow a wider margin of political freedom than his predecessors. In May 1990 the opposition was strengthened and gained a majority

which accelerated after the 1970s, now place her in Asia's club of rich nations. The other side of South Korea's history, however, has to recount the violence and brutality of her politics. For most of the years since the early 1950s the military ruled Korea oppressively, violent student and popular protest were put down with force and bloodshed. Aligned with the West, especially with the United States, South Korea had to make some show of a democratic process with a national assembly and elections. But the military made sure that they held on to power, ruling under martial law, imprisoning opposition leaders and resorting to torture and bloodshed to suppress demonstrators who, in their frustration, frequently turned to violence. The ruling cliques were identified by those who opposed them with the United States, so anti-American and anti-military agitation often merged. For the Americans such authoritarian regimes were an embarrassment, but pressure to democratise took second place before 1990 to the global aim of containing communism. South Korea was a front-

**Asia, 1991**

in the National Assembly when two opposition parties combined. The well known dissident Kim Young Sam, leader of the Liberal Democratic Party, was elected president in December 1992. He took office in February 1993, the first civilian president in 32 years.

The dichotomy between political backwardness and economic modernisation had been a characteristic since 1962. For the ordinary Korean, politics took second place to material welfare, which so rapidly increased for the majority of the people. Opposition politics and violent demonstrations were for the young and for the minority of political activists, not for the majority. For those who did not actively oppose, there was not only far greater prosperity but also greater freedom in the South. The influence of the generals receded, and the president tackled corruption; in the 1990s democratisation looks set to make some headway. In the North, nothing much was likely to change until the death of Kim Il Sung, who was eighty years old in 1992. His son was being groomed as his successor.

By the 1990s the reunification of Korea had for long been one of the demands of the radical opposition. All politicians in the South were in favour of it; it was the official policy, and visits of government delegations from the North and the South were exchanged in 1990 and in 1991. In December 1991 the communist North and the capitalist South at their fifth meeting signed a non-aggression pact. The meetings continued in 1992. North Korea was working towards the manufacture of nuclear weapons. The Americans withdrew their army from the South, so President Roh's prime interest was to stop the North from making her own bomb. The whole of Korea, according to the wishes of the South, of Japan and of the US, should be free of nuclear weapons. But, alarmingly, North Korea became the first country ever to withdraw its recognition of the nuclear non-proliferation treaty in the spring of 1993. South Korean enthusiasm for merger with the North was at its height when Germany reunified in 1989, but it waned in the light of German experience. The population of the North with her low standard of living is far greater proportionate to the South's than East Germany's was to her well-off Western

cousins. The Korean statistics bring out this contrast very sharply.

**North and South Korea, 1990**

|  | Population (*millions*) | Gross National Product per head (*US$*) | Foreign trade (*US$ billions*) | |
|---|---|---|---|---|
|  |  |  | Exports | Imports |
| South Korea | 42.8 | 5,569 | 65.0 | 69.8 |
| North Korea | 21.7 | 1,064 | 2.0 | 2.6 |

If the West Germans had to make sacrifices to absorb the East Germans and to modernise the east, the impact on South Korea of unifying with the North would be much greater, imposing a drop in the standard of living of as much as a quarter or a third. National fervour was tempered by material self-interest. Some kind of federal solution was, therefore, more attractive for the South in the 1990s. Yet by 1994 North Korea's nuclear programme had raised fears and tensions between North and South and the South's ally, the US, to new heights. Japan also felt threatened by the situation's volatility. Reductions in the large armies and numerous weapons, a tremendous burden especially to the North, a lessening of tension and more intercourse between North and South nevertheless brought their own tangible benefits to a people who had suffered so much in the twentieth century.

# CHAPTER 68

# The Prosperous Pacific Rim:
## Australia and New Zealand

Of the inhabited continents of the world, Australasia is the least developed and the most empty of people. The Aborigines had been building their lives and culture for millennia when in the late eighteenth century settlement from Britain began and progressively dispossessed them of their lands. Regarded as little more than savages, exploited and treated at best like children, they lived an existence that was marginalised until the third quarter of the twentieth century. Gough Whitlam, the Labor Prime Minister, in 1972 condemned Australian racism: 'Australia's treatment of her Aboriginal people will be the thing upon which the rest of the world will judge Australia and Australians – not just now but in the greater perspective of history.' But the Aborigine voice of protest is not strong enough to have made much impression on the world.

Before the European came there were, according to rough estimates, between 300,000 and 400,000 Aborigines; by 1961 it was estimated that only 40,000 had survived. No one could judge their precise numbers because they were not included in the census before 1967. They posed no threat to white Australia. The menace Australians felt came from outside the continent.

The geographical position of Australia at the 'edge' of Asia did much to shape the outlook of Australians during the twentieth century. Asia, with its poverty-stricken teeming millions loomed menacingly over its southern neighbour, with her tiny and comparatively prosperous white population of some

7 million in all in 1945, largely of British stock, few of whom inhabited the northern half. Could Australia survive as a 'white' outpost of civilisation? That was the burning question. For Australians a civilised culture was a Western culture, the preferred 'race' people of British descent.

In the nineteenth century there had been some Chinese immigration and labour had been brought in from the Pacific islands. The number of these workers, however, remained small, and they mostly remained aliens with little defence against deportation. In 1901 immediately after Australia had ceased to be a colony and become a self-governing federal commonwealth, significantly the issue of paramount concern was immigration. The Immigration Act of that year was enacted to keep out 'undesirables'; that included all 'non-Europeans', as the official phrase went, though the immigration programme is better known as the 'white Australia' policy. Even after large-scale immigration from Britain and Ireland, from 1909 to 1913 and from 1921 to 1925, the population of Australia during the Second World War had reached only 7 million.

Before the Second World War Australia was still closely tied to Britain, and not only by common bonds of origin. As a member of the empire and Commonwealth, Australia's trade in wool and other rural products enjoyed their main market in Britain. British industry supplied most of her imports. For her defence, Australia looked to Britain too. When Britain went to war in 1914 and 1939, Australian volunteer divisions fought side by side with the

British in Europe and the Middle East. These were distant wars in defence of the mother country. But the threat of Japan hung over the Pacific. In June 1940 after the fall of France a cable from London to the Australian and New Zealand governments warned them that they would need to look for protection to the United States. When Japan did enter the war in December 1941, the British nevertheless undertook to defend the key Singapore naval base. The unexpected and rapid victories of the Japanese came as a tremendous shock to Australians. The British and Dutch failed to contain the Japanese advance, and three days after Pearl Harbor, on 10 December 1941, two of Britain's modern battleships, the *Repulse* and the *Prince of Wales*, sent to defend Malaya, were sunk from the air. Worse followed. In February 1942, the great defence bastion, the Singapore naval base, surrendered to the Japanese. Fifteen thousand Australian troops were taken prisoner. Next the Japanese speedily captured the Dutch East Indies (Indonesia). They were now close to the northern shores of Australia. Darwin was bombed. Queensland and the Northern Territories lay open to invasion.

In Australia a mood close to panic ensued. Three seasoned divisions were fighting overseas in Libya. Two were withdrawn. Plans were made to abandon central and northern Australia, up to the 'Brisbane line'. Now what London had foreshadowed came to pass. Australia and New Zealand were dependent on American protection. The arrival of General Douglas MacArthur and a contingent of United States troops, with headquarters in Melbourne, steadied nerves. Black American GIs were another shock, of a different kind, but they had to be tolerated while the war lasted. Not Britain now but the United States had become the principal Australian ally. Australians made a major military contribution. While one division continued to fight under Montgomery's command, the main effort was directed to the war in the Pacific. By the time the war came to an end 863,000 Australian troops had been mobilised.

The experience of war heightened Australian fears of the Asian menace from the north. Empty Australia must be filled with migrants or Asians would move in. Immigration had now become a matter of survival. These fears also reinforced the 'white Australia' immigration policy, which was racist at heart. The Labor government, in power since 1941, shaped these racist preconceptions.

Prime Minister Chifley had appointed Arthur Calwell to head a new department of immigration. A propaganda campaign was launched to overcome Australian fears that substantial immigration would only increase unemployment. The government played on Australian fears that in the absence of such migration Asians might overrun the continent. In Europe, Australia was presented as a country of sun and freedom where families could build a new life and prosperity in a society not riven by class consciousness and prejudice. Passage for ex-servicemen and their families was free; others paid a nominal £10. The assisted migrants found life hard, especially during the first two years, during which they were housed in camps and put to work on such huge schemes as the Snowy Mountain hydroelectric dams.

The post-war boom fortunately created labour shortages in Australia. Britain and Ireland were regarded as the right reservoir for immigrants, and immigration officers were sent secret instructions to reject applicants of non-European origin; a Jamaican grandparent in Cardiff would exclude a whole family. The immigration officers were left to form a judgement based on the colour of the skin or such 'tell-tale signs' as an oriental slant of the eyes. Some unfortunate British applicants were even rejected when they arrived sunburnt from a Mediterranean holiday. Jews too were virtually excluded; only a few hundred were allowed in from displaced-person camps in an attempt to obscure the policy. But there simply were not enough pale white Britons to satisfy the enormous demand for migrants. Calwell flew to Europe to widen the net. Light-skinned Balts were favoured next. Until the mid-1950s immigration officers were instructed to ensure that migrants were of pure 'Aryan' descent, a throwback to Nazi ideology which the Australian government had some difficulty explaining away when news of it was leaked. But the efforts to increase the rate of immigration were a great success. When the supply of pale northern Europeans proved insufficient, the government encouraged, at first discreetly, immigration from the Mediterranean countries – Italy, Greece, Yugoslavia, later on Turkey and the Lebanon – and simply braved the continued prejudice in the 1950s and 1960s of the majority of the Australian people. Asians, except in small numbers, were rigidly excluded, and some of those who had settled were even deported.

With the changing generation came a change in attitudes. Australia could not escape her proximity to Asia. From the late 1960s onwards, Asian immigration was liberalised. Refugees from Vietnam were accepted in the early 1970s. A third of all immigrants now came from Asia. An obsession with assimilating all 'new Australians' to Australian culture and the English language was replaced by an acceptance of a multicultural approach. Australia's population would have increased only slowly but for mass immigration from Europe and Asia. By 1967 her population had reached 12 million and by 1990 17 million, a rate of increase exceeded only by Israel. The successful absorption of so many millions, the weakening of blinkered racial attitudes and greater tolerance are among the most important achievements of recent Australian history. Australia, despite recession, enjoys in the 1990s the second-highest Gross National Product per head of population in Asia (GNP per capita in 1989 was $14,360), beaten only by Japan.

The expansion of the Australian economy was made possible by the migration, which brought young families and people of working age to man the factories and the mines and to help build the country's infrastructure. The demand for housing, furniture, cars and other goods is largely met by Australia's own manufacturing industry, which together with mining and services absorbs most of her labour, housed in big-city conurbations. Australian society is obviously no longer pastoral, but the rest of the world is not so aware that Australia has fundamentally changed since the Second World War. Nevertheless, her export trade is still heavily dependent on primary products – wool, wheat, minerals, coal, iron and steel – and on their price fluctuations.

Wool no longer held first place as an export earner during the last quarter of the century; coal and iron ore brought in more dollars. Australia's prosperity was always dependent on her external trade. Britain had traditionally been the best market and supplier of capital and manufactured goods, but long before she joined the Common Market on 1 January 1973 the trend for Australian exports to go to Asia, the United States and the wider world had been well established. Exports to the United States and Canada in 1967 began to exceed those to Britain, while exports to the rest of the European Community almost equalled exports to Britain. But the most startling change was exports to Japan, which exceeded in value exports to any other country. A new trading pattern was being established. Australia aggressively sought new markets in the Pacific. Wheat exports went to China, beef to the United States. The south-east Asian nations and Japan accounted for more than 40 per cent of her exports.

The economic miracle in Japan, which began its take-off in the 1960s, had a huge impact on Australia. Initially short of coal, iron ore and minerals, her mining industry rapidly expanded; vast new reserves of iron ore were discovered in the Pilbara region of Western Australia. The industrial development of south-east Asia added to the demand. During the last quarter of the century prosperous Western Europe has remained an important market, but Australia's most important trading partners are the nations of the Pacific basin.

When Emperor Hirohito died in 1988 flags on official buildings in Canberra flew at half-mast. This token of respect symbolises just one facet of the transformation of Australia's relations with the rest of the world. She is still an important member of the British Commonwealth, the Queen of Britain was still Queen of Australia in 1992. Australia owes her constitution and legal system to Britain, as also her commitment to democracy. Test matches between the two countries are followed avidly by cricket enthusiasts throughout the Commonwealth. Thousands of Australians visit London. Family ties persist. But Australia's future lies in the Pacific. Fear of Japan has been replaced by economic interdependence. Japanese investment, businessmen and technologists are welcome in Australia. Australians can no longer look to Britain to safeguard her security in Asia but most rely on her own relations with post-colonial Asian nations, and on her alliance with the United States.

For more than two decades after the Second World War the United States and Britain were Australia's most important allies. Together with New Zealand, Australia concluded the defensive ANZUS alliance with the United States in July 1951. The United States was only reluctantly willing to extend her commitments to the southern Pacific to meet Australian fears of a resurgent Japan, with whom the United States was then wishing to conclude a peace treaty. Britain, although abandoning her imperial role in India, was still the military shield of her own and Australian interests in the region, vigorously defending Malaya during the communist insurrection in the 1950s. During that decade aggressive communism was perceived in Australia as posing as great a threat as Japan had done in the past.

The Cold War, which began in Asia in 1949–50, came to dominate relations in south-east Asia and Australian foreign policy. The communist victory in China in 1949 revived fears of millions of poor Asians expanding south by direct aggression and subversion. China might repeat Japan's thrust south – prosperous and under-populated Australia would be a tasty morsel. But it was in the north Pacific, in Korea, that war actually broke out in 1950 (page 427). Australia sent troops to South Korea to help American and United Nations forces to halt aggression. Still closer to Australia lay Indonesia. Australian leaders after the war had sought to establish friendly relations with the newly independent states. Indonesia, after India and Pakistan, was one of the earliest objects of this policy, as Australia mediated between the Indonesians and the Dutch.

But Indonesian expansion was a worry. Britain in the 1950s and for much of the 1960s was still the dominant military power in this region. In the early 1960s after the formation of Malaysia, Australia joined Britain in the confrontation with Indonesia (page 621), though she wanted to live on good terms with the former Dutch colony, whose population dwarfed her own. In 1962 Indonesia and Australia became neighbours in New Guinea when Indonesia absorbed West Irian. Until 1968 when Britain progressively withdrew from her military role 'east of Suez', Australia maintained links with a British and Commonwealth alliance. But the events of the Second World War had shown that for Australia's and New Zealand's security in Asia the alliance of the United States had become more important, indeed essential.

The defeat of France in northern Indo-China in 1954 and the Geneva settlement did not bring peace to the region (page 407). Australia became a founding member of the South-East Asian Defence Treaty (SEATO), which under US leadership attempted to provide collective security. Britain and France were members too, yet refused to send military help for the defence of South Vietnam. But successive Australian governments accepted the validity of the domino theory – that communist China was fighting proxy wars to advance communism and that unless she was halted one state after another would fall like a row of dominoes. So it was in Australia's own security interests to provide military help to South Vietnam. It was no less important to demonstrate to the United States that Australia could be relied on as an ally. But sending conscripts to Vietnam proved controversial at home. From the 1950s to the 1990s the American alliance has remained the cornerstone of Australia's foreign relations, as the ties that bound Australia to Britain weakened. Fear of Japan has long since been replaced by co-operation. The prosperity of the region has been hugely promoted by Japan's economy and overseas investment in the non-communist nations of south-east Asia. In the 1990s Japan has emerged not just as the most important bulwark against communism, but her successful example is undermining the ideology of central planners in the remaining Asian communist nations.

Australian politics at home revolved around three parties, the Australian Labor Party, the Country Party and the Liberal Party, but in practice a two-party system operated, with the Country and Liberal Parties forming coalition administrations. Each party itself represented various interests and views. The Labor Party, founded by trade unionists, fought to improve conditions for the poorer section of the population by means of legislation, but in practice it was not a Marxist–socialist party and supported a privately owned, free-enterprise economy with a minimum of state financial controls. At state and federal level the differences between the parties was more a matter of personalities, emphasis and attitudes than anything profoundly ideological. Labor's long period in opposition from 1949 to 1972 increased factional tensions within the party, but it achieved a sustained period in office from 1972 to 1975 and after 1983. The Country Party has its base in the rural areas and represents the farmers and their special interests. Vehemently anti-socialist, it is a minority party but as coalition partner of the Liberal Party its influence has been greater than its numbers. The Liberal Party too is largely conservative, reluctant to extend welfare and keen to prevent the trade unions from exerting too much influence. A small Communist Party has its strongest support among some trade unionists. On the whole, Australian politics revolves less around ideologies than around the appeal of individual politicians and special-interest groups.

As prime minister John Curtin led a Labor government which earned Australia's gratitude for the successful prosecution of the Second World War. Welfare provisions were modestly extended and Canberra's federal muscle in policymaking was greatly strengthened in 1942 by taking over from the states the sole right of imposing income tax. The states remained jealous of their constitutional rights and the tug of war between them and the federal government continued as a recurring feature of post-war Australian politics.

As early as December 1942 Curtin's government made plans for a better post-war Australia, setting up a department of post-war reconstruction. The guiding inspiration was more Roosevelt's New Deal and Keynes than socialist doctrine. Able young economists worked on a masterplan under Ben Chifley, the minister responsible. It was Chifley who on Curtin's death in 1945 became prime minister. What haunted Australians, as it haunted the rest of the Western world, was the prospect of a return to the 1930s and mass unemployment. So planning was undertaken in relation to housing, farming, industry and training. Australians were to be assured that they would have work and adequate housing for the family. The extension of welfare provision was more modest: pensions for widows were granted, but persistent efforts to extend state cover against illness, even the minimal proposals for free medicines, fell foul of the powerful medical lobby, which fought tooth and nail against any form of 'socialised medicine' and which especially abhorred the model of Britain's National Health Service, the most important achievement of Britain's post-war Labour government.

Ben Chifley's attempts to extend welfare benefits and to maintain in peacetime the federal powers Canberra had secured in war were challenged by the states, whose claims were generally supported by a conservative High Court. The most important of Chifley's reforms was to secure government control over monetary policy by nationalising Australia's central bank, the Commonwealth Bank, in 1945, though an unpopular and unnecessary attempt to extend control over all private banks was eventually struck down by the High Court. Conditions were favourable for the Australian economy in the post-war years, there being a high demand for her wool, meat and wheat, which ensured good prices, growing prosperity and labour shortages. Chifley's sound financial management and limited federal engagement in industry left the bulk of the Australian economy in private hands. Unlike the British Labour Party, the Australian Labor Party was ready to work with and profit from private enterprise, attempting only to regulate the market and rejecting nationalisation.

Chifley's Labor Government would have no truck either with militant trade unionism, which was now recovering after the hardship and exploitation of working men before the war. Strikes were blamed on the communists, and the opposition tried to tar Chifley's cautious and pragmatic administration with this brush. But the Prime Minister continued to insist that settlement of trade union demands should be reached through the Arbitration Court, which he refused to dismantle. The Arbitration Court was conservative, as was clearly shown for instance in its rejection of equal pay for women in 1950, but granted basic wage demands and the forty-hour week which the trade unions had fought for. Chifley did not hesitate to take tough measures against unions which went on strike. The most serious of these stoppages was the miners' strike in the summer of 1949. With the country threatened with paralysis, troops were sent in to reopen the coal mines and the miners were forced back, winning only some of their claims. The general influence of communists in the trade union movement receded, though it was strongest among the miners after the unsuccessful 1949 strike, but obsession with a non-existent communist threat remained a feature of Australian politics for years to come.

In December 1949 Australians felt secure enough to vote the Labor government out of office. Robert Menzies, who had led the Liberal–Country Party opposition, promised prosperity and a better life free of bureaucratic control. Like the Conservatives in Britain in 1945, where the tactic had misfired (page 347), he now warned against totalitarian socialism. There was no such danger of course, but the electorate was ready for a swing of the pendulum. Menzies, who soon became one of the best-known politicians on the world stage, had founded the Liberal Party and rebuilt the opposition during the war. He was a moderate conservative, appealing for consensus, an Australian version perhaps of Stanley Baldwin, a middle-of-the-roader with a common touch, standing for decency and family values and fulminating against communism and trade unions, especially when they went on strike. Later his staunch support of British royalty and his deference to and affection for the young Queen Elizabeth II appeared to reinforce the old traditional Britishness and dependence of Australia. But behind the avuncular image lurked a shrewd politician.

His government made no great changes from Labor's previous policies. Some welfare provisions were improved; more was done to pay for health care, in the teeth of the suspicious medical profession. Although Australia was in no danger of being subverted by communism, Menzies attempted to stir up feelings against the small Communist Party and in 1950 legislated to outlaw it and seize its assets. It is to the credit of the Australian High Court's sense of democratic values that it struck this measure down by a majority decision; the Australian people themselves rejected it, but only by a tiny margin, when in 1951 Menzies campaigned to outlaw the party in a national referendum.

Menzies dominated Australian politics in the 1950s and 1960s. These were the golden years of expansion and continuous improvement in the standard of living. More than 2 million immigrants were successfully absorbed. The black spot was the continued neglect of Aborigine interests. They had little share in Australia's boom. As far as white Australia was concerned there seemed no need to take risks by turning to Labor, whose policies were no more hostile to the capitalist basis of the Australian economy than the Menzies-led government. The Liberal–Country Party coalition was therefore able to stay in office for most of the three decades up to the 1980s. Prosperity had eroded working-class support. Condemned to almost virtual opposition Labor became factionalised. Can parliamentary democracy really survive in such conditions? Reassuringly it did. Labor did win power in a number of state governments. In 1966 Menzies retired after serving continuously as prime minister for sixteen years. His one enduring domestic achievement, apart from presiding pragmatically over Australia's years of prosperity, was the giving of government support for school and university education, which greatly expanded. The timing of his departure was well judged, as more difficult economic times lay ahead, and a new generation of Australians prepared to face them.

Most Australians remained resolutely anti-communist, but the challenge from the younger generation which swept the Western world in the mid-1960s did not entirely pass Australia by. The Vietnam War gave the discontent a focus. Demonstrations were mounted against the support which successive governments gave to the United States from 1966 to 1971 under Harold Holt, John Gorton and William McMahon, the three prime ministers who followed Menzies. They were precursors of a shift in Australian political loyalties after twenty-three years of Liberal–Country Party domination. Industrial disputes became more frequent. The Labor Party drew new hope from these conditions, which many Australians blamed on the Liberal–Country Party's political elite, just at a time when Labor had at last found a resourceful new leader with national appeal and charisma in Gough Whitlam.

In December 1972 a majority of Australians voted Labor to power and Gough Whitlam became Australia's first Labor prime minister since 1949. That vote for Labor was a signal for a fresh start, for new faces, but not for socialism. Australia would remain an economy of free enterprise where the few could amass large fortunes. Whitlam had not risen from the ranks of the working man. University educated, a lawyer by training, a politician by profession, he relished power and did not go out of his way to avoid confrontations and antagonism. He regarded Labor's victory as a mandate for social change and promised to bring it about with an immediate burst of activity, as Franklin D. Roosevelt had done in the early weeks of the New Deal. God had taken seven days to create the world; Whitlam reshaped Australian politics in fourteen. The list of decisions taken and promises given was startling: Aborigines were promised better treatment, Papua New Guinea was given independence, national service was ended, Vietnam draft defaulters were pardoned, a stand was taken against racism in the Commonwealth, communist China was recognised, and plans were drawn up for closer supervision of manufacturing industry.

During the first two years the Labor government's main goal was to reduce the inequalities of opportunity suffered by the less well-off Australian – migrant, worker or professional, white, brown or black. The great leveller was education, and better schools for the disadvantaged and universities open to students on merit were among Labor's achievements. Another was the legislation creating a universal insurance-based health service. Labor's concern for the poor was also reflected in the expansion of the social services. It all cost money, and inflation could not forever delay the day of reckoning. Labor's fortunes declined in 1974. The economy had been hit by the world economic crisis which followed the ending of the Vietnam War and the oil-price rise. Inflation and unemployment were rising. The measures taken to curb inflation were bound to be unpopular. Financial ineptitude and scandals, and unemployment reaching 5 per cent, cast Labor's management of the economy in a bad light. The anti-Labor press made the most of these difficulties.

The Labor government came to a dramatic end in November 1975. The leader of the opposition, Malcolm Fraser, assembled enough votes to deny passage of the Budget, justifying this by accusing the government of financial mismanagement. At the height of the constitutional crisis, the Governor-General Sir John Kerr, who as representative of the Queen held a ceremonial appointment with theoretical powers, chose actually to use them and, acting insensitively and high-handedly, dismissed Whitlam from the premiership. Whitlam accepted his dismissal and gave Fraser the task of forming a caretaker government until new elections to be held

in December should decide the issue. When Australia voted there was less concern for the constitutionality of the dismissal than for the country's economic prospects, which were grim. It seemed safer to a majority of Australians to return to power the Liberal–National (formerly Country) Party. Labor had been unlucky to hold power during what had been difficult years throughout the Western world. Whichever party had been in office would probably have been voted out. But, for all its mistakes, the Labor government's aims of greater social justice and racial harmony foreshadowed a return to these aspirations when Labor regained power in 1983 and this time stayed in government for more than a decade.

The Liberal–National coalition headed by Malcolm Fraser took up the reins of the administration again after the short and eventful Labor intermission. There was nothing startling about the next seven years of moderate conservative government. Where Whitlam had stood somewhat left of centre, Fraser was not too far to the right of centre. The trade unions were conveniently blamed for economic ills. When the world recession eased, Australian exports, which were so dependent on

*A day after Australian Prime Minister Gough Whitlam was dismissed by the British Governor-General, he addresses a protest rally outside Parliament House, 12 November 1975.*

international economic health, recovered. Fraser was more conciliatory than his predecessor had been towards state rights and their relations with the federal government in Canberra.

Australian society had steadily become more polarised. Many Australians, particularly the professional classes, enjoyed a high standard of living. But working people during the 1970s had made less progress and more than one Australian in every six was classified early in that decade as living in poverty or close to it. Fraser's economic policy was orthodox. Despite increasing unemployment, social benefit expenditure did not rise. A backward step was the dismantling of Whitlam's health-care provision, Medibank, and its abolition in 1981; free medical provision was restricted to the poor, who qualified by a means test or as old-age pensioners. In March 1983 Fraser's Liberal–National coalition lost the general election and a Labor government was once more returned to power.

Robert Hawke, who dominated Australian politics as Labor's dynamic and colourful leader for the remainder of the 1980s, was academically well qualified and had won his spurs in Australian politics as a research officer for the Australian Council of Trade Unions (ACTU) thirty years earlier. Bob Hawke had been an active and skilful advocate on behalf of ACTU, and eventually its president. He entered the House of Representatives in 1980, determined to gain the leadership of the Labor Party.

Hawke's period in office was marked by conciliation with the business community on the one hand and trade union moderation on the other. He wanted all sides of industry to work together, with the federal government playing the role of benevolent third party. This time Labor was lucky in the timing of its victory. The mid-1980s were years of unprecedented world economic boom. Australia did well out of it. There was nothing radical or socialist about Hawke. He used to good advantage his trade union experience of negotiating and balancing opposing sides, in this way holding the Labor Party together and resisting its tendency to split into left and right wings. Nor was there any great move to benefit the poorest section of Australians by extending and increasing social benefits, except in the area of health care. A national health scheme providing universal benefit had become something of a political football in Australia, with the Australian

Medical Association fighting a fierce rearguard action over the decades. Hawke's administration resurrected Whitlam's Medibank, now called Medicare, and Australia's doctors acquiesced. But the Labor government did not engage in a spending spree or impose high taxation policies, and in this Hawke was loyally and ably supported by his ministerial colleague Paul Keating. But the private sector and state governments were running up large debts. Most political excitement during these years was caused by Hawke's efforts to rid Australian politics of corruption. Australians approved of his undoctrinaire approach, his friendly relations with business and the apparent stability of the economy, which was expanding with the influx of foreign capital. The price was paid later in recession and spectacular business failures. Hawke won the two elections of 1984 and 1987, his expansive personality and self-confident espousal of an Australian identity making him for a time the most popular prime minister in the country's history. He presided over the bicentenary in 1988, a fitting celebration of an Australia reaching maturity.

But the festivities also became a reminder that one group of Australians, its oldest settlers, the Aborigines, had not shared equally in that wealth, and that their grievances had not yet been adequately addressed. The early settlers of the late eighteenth century had been instructed to deal with the Aborigines as a whole, leaving them 'in the full enjoyment of their possessions'. But the benevolent intentions of the sovereign's government in London thousands of miles away did not make much impression on pioneers engaged in the hard task of making a living out of what appeared to them to be empty lands. State governments' efforts in Australia and missionary endeavours could do little to alleviate the disastrous impact of Western lifestyles on the culture and way of life of the exploited Aborigines. After the Second World War the Aborigines began to organise themselves, demanding citizens' rights and better wages. In 1957 the Northern Territory admitted mixed-race Aborigines and full Aborigines who could look after themselves to citizenship. Aborigines were regarded as civilised if they assimilated to white Australian culture – assimilation was the welfare aim. The 'white Australian' policy in practice had the effect of demoralising them.

Only slowly, beginning in the 1960s, did Aborigines win equal rights. An Aborigine leadership emerged able to organise effective protest move-

*Aborigines live between two cultures in the Australian outback.*

ments and focus demands on wage issues, discrimination and land rights. Gough Whitlam, when he came to power in December 1972, broke with tradition by paying attention to the needs of the Aborigines, promising schools for them and the protection of their land rights against mining companies which wished to exploit the mineral wealth below. The companies' desire to extend exploration in this way pitted profit, national production and wealth against the rights of the Aborigines. The following year another well-intentioned effort led to the establishment of a National Aboriginal Consultative Committee. The improvement in Aborigine welfare has brought abuses into even sharper relief.

Discrimination remained rife in Australia in the early 1990s. The Aborigines, denied good health care, housing and education, were trapped; high unemployment added to their misery, to the problems of crime and alcohol abuse. Australians were shocked by a report that more than a hundred Aborigines had died locked up in police cells since 1980. As recently as 1992 one of the commissioners investigating these deaths found it necessary to say, 'We as a community have to change our attitude toward Aborigines. We have to recognise them as a distinct people who were dispossessed of this continent and deal with them with respect.' Racism could not be obliterated overnight. But white Australia was not alone in confronting what in the

1990s was now one of the major causes of war and bloodshed elsewhere in the world. The task of raising the standards of a minority who had for decades lived in or close to destitution was a formidable one. The Australian Labor government in 1992 unveiled another scheme to improve the educational, housing and health provisions for Aborigines and above all to ensure better treatment by the police and courts. White Australians would be obliged to consult with representatives of Aborigine groups about measures and actions which affect them.

The boom of the 1980s began to overheat in 1988. But despite economic worries Bob Hawke led Labor to a fourth successive victory in federal elections in 1990. Labor had been following a market-economy philosophy, reducing protection for Australia's industries, raising interest rates and striving to keep money supply under control. Hit by a recession that showed no sign of lifting, and faced with another election in 1993, the Labor Party changed its leader in December 1991. Bob Hawke was dropped and his long-time Treasurer (finance minister) and political rival Paul Keating became prime minister. Far from changing direction, Keating announced the government would move with even greater determination to make industry more efficient, abolish tariffs and help business with tax breaks, while keeping government expenditure under tight control.

In the early 1990s Australia suffered badly from the recession in the West, with an unemployment rate of 10 per cent. The growth of the south-east Asian economies of Indonesia, Thailand and Malaysia did not provide an immediate cure to unemployment as Australian business increasingly relocated industry where the markets were and where labour was cheap. In March 1993 Keating narrowly won another term for Labor against the expectation of many observers that the severe recession would cripple his chances of re-election.

By the 1990s Australia was a sophisticated cosmopolitan culture. With more than 30,000 millionaires it was hardly classless, but 'class' had hitherto been based on the wealth of the self-made man, not on birth to high station. But that would change as wealth was inherited. The Australians were conscious of great changes to come. Industry and industrial exports would have to play an ever increasing role in the economy. The traditional export markets of Europe and the United States retained their importance but the new, rapidly expanding markets lay in Asia, where nearly half of Australia's exports now went. Australia could no longer afford to 'fight against the reality of its own geography', to quote Gareth Evans, Australia's dynamic Foreign Minister. Japan was the model for effective, advanced industrial organisation. Yet Australia is not an Asian country: the majority of her people are of European origin, and her majority culture and way of life and her democratic form of government are Western. In the 1990s she was being inexorably drawn closer into Asia yet remained apart. Although she abandoned the 'white Australia' immigration policy in the mid-1970s, Asian resentment of Australian racism had not disappeared. Nor has the multiracial Australia universally accepted by Australians. No wonder that the national identity and future of Australia were hotly debated.

Not Sweden, but a small and remote British colony in the South Pacific, New Zealand, can make a good claim to be the precursor of the welfare state. Since its foundations in the 1890s when a Liberal government came to power and passed welfare legislation, benevolent intervention by the state to protect the poorer and weaker in the community was a persistent feature of politics, whichever party was in power, at least until the early 1990s, through both good times and bad.

The Liberals, in power for twenty-one years (1891–1912), were radical reformers. Compulsory arbitration of labour disputes introduced in 1894 protected what were at that time weak trade unions. A year earlier women had been enfranchised. In 1898 New Zealand pioneered the old-age pension. The Liberals believed in democracy and what in later times would be called 'social justice'. They accepted capitalism, that is private ownership and the market, and had no socialist aspirations, but wished to use the power of the state to curb the exploitation of the weak. Their ideal was a more egalitarian society. But in the process the national government also greatly increased its own power. Early in the century some of the main lines of political development were set.

The Liberals aimed at a harmonious national consensus, between country and town, worker and employer, farmer and businessman. They succeeded for a long period but sectional interests in the end destroyed the aim though not the reforms the Liberals had enacted. The increase in the number of urban workers stimulated the formation of a distinct Labour Party more narrowly identified with their interests, and the trade unions grew more militant. Largely based on the dairy farmers, a more conservative opposition, the Reform Party, evolved. Between 1912 and 1935 no one of the three parties had a clear lead over the others. The 1920s were a period of general depression, with falling prices for New Zealand's farm produce. The depression of the early 1930s was even worse. New Zealand was utterly dependent on world prices for her exports, and Britain, her main market, was deeply depressed. Even so the early Labour Party's socialist programme could not hope to find sufficient support to make Labour the governing party. The great majority of New Zealanders had no truck with Marxist socialism or the abolition of property rights. On the contrary they aspired to a higher standard of living and to owning their own land and home. The New Zealand Labour Party therefore accepted socialism in theory but not in practice. These were the politics of the white New Zealand settlers. But what of the original indigenous New Zealanders, the Maoris?

The early impact of the European was catastrophic, as it was on the indigenous peoples of the Americas. The new settlers sometimes acquired land by fair means but more usually they did so by foul. As their numbers increased so did the pressure on Maori land. European settlers disrupted traditional societies. Worst of all, they introduced new diseases against which the indigenous people had no defence. When the Europeans first settled it is estimated that there were about 200,000 Maoris in New Zealand, mostly inhabiting North Island, which was divided by warring tribes. Possession of land by the tribe was the most important indication of status – and it belonged to the community as a whole and not to individuals. In the nineteenth century dispute over land led to violent conflict with the settlers, the Maori wars. Some 2000 Maoris lost their lives. The rapid decline of the Maori population to 42,000 by the turn of the century was, however, due more to disease and the disruption of their traditional culture and lives than to war.

Far away in distant London the intention of governments towards indigenous peoples had been benevolent. Unlike the Aborigines of Australia, the Maoris had even received guarantees by treaty intended to preserve their rights. That compact was the Treaty of Waitangi in 1840, by which Maori chiefs ceded New Zealand to the British Crown and in return were guaranteed possession of their lands, forests and fisheries and granted the rights and privileges of British subjects. This gave the Maoris a solid legal basis for demanding the righting of wrongful seizures, which has persisted to the present day. In the relations between the white settlers and their descendants and the Maori people this treaty is a crucial contract, though its interpretation in contemporary conditions is certainly complex. The Maoris thus attained rights in the nineteenth century not enjoyed by the Aborigines until late in the twentieth century. They were also granted separate electorates and four members of parliament in 1867. Later in the twentieth century, to preserve their sense of identity, Maoris as well as descendants of mixed race who wished to be identified as Maori could be entered on the Maori electoral roll on request.

The Maoris began to recover only in the twentieth century after they had lost or sold most of their lands. A leadership educated in an Anglican school for Maoris began to emerge early in the century and a modest measure of local self-government was granted before the First World War. The Maori population recovered slowly. By 1921 it numbered 56,000. Their cultural identity was now greatly strengthened by the establishment of a distinct Maori religious cult, the Ratana Church, founded by Tahupotiki Wiremu Ratana, who had had a vision in 1918. Ratana disciples captured all the Maori political seats in parliament and formed an alliance with Labour. When Labour came to power in 1935 it began a programme of Maori welfare campaigns in education, social entitlements and land settlement.

By 1946, the Maori population had increased to about 100,000 and it had doubled a generation later (1966) to over 200,000; by then about half the Maoris lived in urban areas. White New Zealand no longer aimed to assimilate them. New Zealand had become a multicultural society. Racial discrimination lessened and was replaced by a renaissance of interest in Maori culture. Maori achievements in battle during the Second World War and on the rugby field became a matter of pride for all New Zealanders. Discrimination remains, however – not on grounds of colour but because of the lower educational attainments of the Maori people. This places Maoris at a severe disadvantage and their unemployment in times of recession is much higher than that of white New Zealanders.

From 1935 to 1949 New Zealand politics regained stability with the Labour Party in power. The party had shed much of its theoretical socialism and now appealed to sections of the middle classes as well as to working people; it also guaranteed prices for farm produce. Labour wished to protect the farmers and manufacturers by insulating New Zealand from her dependence on world price fluctuations through greater state control of marketing and distribution. It also followed the earlier humanitarian tradition of the Liberals in extending welfare safeguards for the poor. The Labour government led by Michael Joseph Savage was an able one and was lucky to come to power as world economic conditions began to improve. It created the modern welfare state. Workers were safeguarded by a minimum wage, but trade union power was limited by the reintroduction of compulsory arbitration for industrial disputes; public works programmes on the model of the New Deal were implemented; unemployment was reduced; pensions were increased. The Social Security Act of 1938 was also notable for starting a national health service with virtually free treatment and medicines a decade before Britain did so. In 1945–6 a second burst of legislative energy provided child benefits without a means test for every family. New Zealand thus created an integrated and comprehensive social-security system which abolished fears of extreme poverty and included white New Zealanders and Maoris alike. The contrast between New Zealand's social policies and Australia's treatment of the Aborigines at the time and Australia's bitter battles over health services is striking. But social provisions had to be paid for by a relatively high level of taxation. New Zealanders could afford their welfare state during the post-war decades because there was great demand for their farm products – beef, lamb and dairy produce.

The opposition, the Reform Party and the old Liberal Party, combined to form the National Party. Like Labour it accepted the welfare-state provisions – indeed, in outlook it no longer differed markedly from Labour, except insofar as it emphasised reduced state intervention and the importance of individual enterprise. New Zealand's most distinguished historian, Keith Sinclair, described both the Labour and National Parties post-war as 'conservative'. This remained true for Labour in the 1980s.

In the 1949 general election the National Party won power, promising to end unnecessary socialist controls and to follow policies more in New Zealand's interests than the internationalism of Labour had been. Sidney George Holland became prime minister. By this time, Cold War hysteria had spread to New Zealand. The government defeated the more militant unions, which were accused of fomenting unrest in Russia's cause. The National Party won election after election. New Zealanders were well satisfied, prospering from the post-war economic boom. Sid Holland anticipated British conservative politics in enabling tenants to purchase on favourable terms their publicly owned (state) houses. But control over the marketing was retained to ensure more stable prices. In 1957 Holland was replaced by Keith Holyoake. The general election gave Labour a narrow victory, only for the party to preside over three difficult economic years, 1957–60. In consequence the government had to raise taxes and was punished by defeat at the next election. Keith Holyoake, returned to power, led a government determined to carry on the reforming tradition: capital punishment was abolished; an ombudsman was appointed who could adjudicate where aggrieved citizens had complaints against government departments; compensation for accidents and equal pay for men and women were introduced.

Another Labour administration in 1972 had to cope with the worry about New Zealand's future exports now that Britain was joining the European Economic Community, though transitional arrangements cushioned the blow. Meat and butter were still the major exports. Diversification of markets and the development of non-primary products became ever more urgent. By the mid-1970s markets had diversified and the Japanese imported from New Zealand almost as much in value as Britain. While only a minority of the workforce was needed for farming, and industry had greatly expanded in petroleum products, paper, wood, plastics, chemicals, iron and steel and machinery, New Zealand was still dependent on exports of meat and dairy products to pay for her imports. This made her rely on her earnings from farming and on the low cost of imports. But the former dropped and the latter rose, plunging New Zealand into severe economic difficulties in the 1970s, especially after the rise in the cost of oil. The golden years of affluence were over.

The electorate was fairly evenly divided between National and Labour during the unsettled 1970s. In 1975 Robert Muldoon became prime minister when the National Party won the general election and he and his party just managed to gain more seats in parliament for him to retain the premiership after elections in 1978 and 1981. Elections were decided by the state of the economy and by promises to lead New Zealand back to prosperity. Muldoon was a robust political leader, inclined to berate the opposition. But in the one area of government dear to all New Zealanders, social welfare, he legislated the most generous retirement provisions in his country's history. The economic condition of New Zealand was grim in the 1980s, with unemployment and inflation rising.

New Zealand is divided from Australia by 1300 miles of sea, but by the 1990s relations between the two former British dependencies had become increasingly close. No other Western developed country may be reached after a few hours' air travel. In their white pioneering phase, both countries had faced similar problems. Yet their development has been distinctive in the twentieth century, and the New Zealander takes pride in the differences.

Economically New Zealand's mineral and petroleum resources were of limited significance. Unlike Australia, she was overwhelmingly dependent on agriculture for exports. But in one respect the two countries confronted a common concern in the twentieth century. They were countries with small populations in relation to the millions of Asians to the north. To safeguard their security both countries felt the need for a powerful ally. As part of the empire and Commonwealth it was Britain on whom they could rely. As long as Britain still ruled the waves, they would be safe. Reciprocal feeling of kinship and support played a part, and New Zealanders (no less than Australians) fought with Britain in both world wars in Europe and in the Middle East.

After the fall of Singapore in 1942, New Zealand did not bring the bulk of her troops home from Europe and the Middle East. The threat of Japan now loomed large, but Britain could spare no forces. It was a portent for the future when a US marine division of 20,000 men was stationed in New Zealand. The United States was seen to be protecting the Dominion.

In 1944, New Zealand and Australia formed their own regional mutual security alliance, the Canberra Pact, since they could no longer rely on the defence link provided by Britain before the war. When the war was over, the United States became New Zealand's principal ally, as she was of Australia. But the Americans had been willing to extend their commitment to the South Pacific only after the Cold War had broken out in Asia. The United States resolved to rebuild Japan and concluded the tripartite ANZUS defence treaty in September 1951 to allay Australian and New Zealand fears of a Japanese resurgence and of Asian communism. Excluded from ANZUS, Britain – with New Zealand – joined SEATO. New Zealand sent forces to defend Malaysia in the confrontation with Indonesia, and a token force in the 1960s to Vietnam. New Zealand was showing loyalty to both allies, the United States and Britain. But there was little doubt which was the more important. From 1966 to 1976 Britain progressively withdrew from her responsibilities 'east of Suez'. ANZUS remained the sheet anchor of New Zealand's and Australia's defence policies. In New Zealand this was to change dramatically only in the mid-1980s.

The Labour government which came to power after the landslide victory of 1984 set to with a will to cure New Zealand's economic problems with Thatcherite fervour. The identification of Labour in New Zealand with politics of the left is quite inappropriate. The consensus over welfare legislation remained intact, as it did in Conservative-governed Britain. What Labour set out to do was to make New Zealand more competitive – deregulating, removing subsidies and tariffs, turning state enterprises into corporations and raising new taxes. At the same time a tight monetary policy was followed. Unemployment increased and the standard of living began to drop. But the electorate trusted the government's harsh remedies, believing there was no other way. Labour was re-elected in 1987, despite the hardship the restructuring was causing to many New Zealanders.

Prime Minister David Lange's forceful conduct of New Zealand's relations with powerful nations gained popularity and compensated to some extent for problems at home. New Zealand would not be pushed around. Lange rightly discerned that the old Cold War mentality was outdated. Nuclear testing in the Pacific by the French had been widely condemned. Labour had made an election pledge in 1984 to ban nuclear-powered warships. Lange's government saw no future in a nuclear defence of New Zealand which would destroy the Dominion. But in American eyes the nuclear deterrent was the only credible means of defence. The temperature of the nuclear controversy was raised to fever pitch in New Zealand when in July 1985 French secret agents sank Greenpeace's ship *Rainbow Warrior* in Auckland harbour just as it was preparing to set sail for the French nuclear testing site; one crewman was killed, and two French agents were captured. Later a US nuclear warship was refused permission to visit New Zealand. For Washington this was a test case. When the Lange government would not relent, the United States responded by declaring that she no longer felt bound by the ANZUS commitment to defend New Zealand. Fortunately, with the world changes taking place, the need to defend New Zealand from any hostile nation became ever more remote.

In the 1990s New Zealand's future was bound up with her foreign relations and trade in the Pacific basin. The European Community, including Britain, remained an important market for her agricultural produce, but her largest trading partners were Australia, Japan and the United States. The Pacific now accounted for three-quarters of her trade. Although the economic remedies were not lifting New Zealand out of recession, the govern-

*New Zealand, one of the more environmentally conscious countries of the world, played host to Greenpeace's ship* Rainbow Warrior, *only to see it blown up in dock. The ship was about to sail for Mururoa to protest at continued French nuclear testing in the South Pacific; it was later discovered that the French secret services had orchestrated the bombing.*

ment did not alter the main thrust of its policies. In 1989 David Lange gave up the premiership, but this did nothing to aid Labour's popularity. The electorate had suffered enough pain, and no benefits were in sight. During the election of 1990, many people supported third parties in their disillusionment. This allowed Jim Bolger to lead a National government.

Bolger's main policy was to continue deregulation. In an attempt to alleviate unemployment, his government repealed those measures which protected wages and trade union rights. The consensus over welfare support was broken. Universal family benefits were abolished and cuts in other welfare programmes were made. The government succeeded in reducing inflation in 1991 to just over 2 per cent. The cost – over 10 per cent unemployment – was high. The rich had got richer and the poor were poorer, with the Maoris, lacking the whites' standards of education, now at the bottom of the unemployment heap. The ideal of an egalitarian society had long ago vanished. The government responded to the country's economic ills by slashing welfare further. But the New Zealand economy in the early 1990s failed to respond to these drastic changes. In conditions of prolonged depression the real danger lay in the electorate despairing of their politicians altogether.

New Zealanders are pioneers. They pioneered the welfare state. In the early 1990s they were pioneering the most radical U-turn away from the welfare state, with the intention as the government saw it of weaning the people off the expectation of automatic handouts. Trade union power was weakened by the ending of the closed shop and centralised wage bargaining; trade union protest in 1992 was faced down by Bolger's government. Publicly owned industries were privatised or turned into corporations, and the financial sector was deregulated. Protected markets of farmers and manufacturers were opened to the winds of competition. State spending was slashed. The break with an almost century-old tradition of state regulation and welfare was a radical one. Instead of progressive taxation, which transfers income from the rich to the poor, high rates of income tax, typical of the welfare state, were slashed. The shortfall in revenue was made up by an indirect tax on services and on everything sold, even food, which hit the poor hardest.

What endured were the democratic parliamentary traditions and the legal framework of the state, with her ideal of equal justice for all her inhabitants of whatever race, religion or ethnic background. New Zealand had grown from a population of less than 1 million at the turn of the century to close on 3.5 million in 1992, and enjoyed one of the highest standards of living in Asia.

# PART XIV

*Latin America after 1945:*
*Problems Unresolved*

# CHAPTER 69

## *The World of Latin America: Colombia, Peru and Chile*

The population of Latin America and the Caribbean reached 455 million people in 1990; by the year 2000 it was likely to exceed 600 million. Yet in twentieth-century world history Latin America was usually marginalised, perhaps because it did not in the first half of the century play a major role in the global conflicts of this century, which had their epicentres in Europe and Asia. Latin American history was thus relegated to the specialist. Perspectives began to change only in the 1950s – not because of a belated recognition that millions of the world's population deserved better, but because of the Cold War. Before then only Argentina's flirtation with fascism had aroused wider interest. After the Second World War the spread of Marxism and the influence of the Soviet Union aroused Western concern, especially that of the United States. Attention focused on Arbenz's Guatemala, on Che Guevara's efforts to spread communism from Cuba to the mainland, on Allende's Chile, on the Sandanistas in Nicaragua and on the civil wars in El Salvador, Guatemala and Peru.

With the launching of President Kennedy's Alliance for Progress in 1961 the United States made an attempt to address the social, economic and political injustices of Latin America. But as the fear of Marxist revolution grew in the 1970s and 1980s, positive policies took second place to ensuring the military defeat of revolutionary movements. Then, as the 1980s drew to a close, two new issues attracted world attention to South America. One

was the dangers besetting the global environment. Life on earth is dependent on careful balances, on a shield in space enveloping the world. The ruthless destruction of Brazil's huge rainforest could have incalculable consequences for the world's climate. Attention was thus drawn to the plight of the Indians in Brazil and to the devastation of large forest areas.

The second problem was drugs – cocaine, heroin and marijuana. Heroin was transshipped mainly from Asia, where the poppies grew, and also from Mexico. Marijuana was cultivated in Mexico, Colombia and Jamaica. The greatest demand, especially in the United States, came to be for cocaine and its derivative, crack. Drugs posed an immediate threat to the well-being and lives of mankind. It was estimated that in 1990 there were 14.5 million addicts in the United States alone, spending a hundred billion dollars annually. The drug scourge had a particular hold on the deprived and unemployed, so it was rife in the poor black ghettos. But it was by no means confined to the poor: crack was used by the jaded and hedonistic of all social classes. Yet the illegal drug trade was associated with crime and violence on a hitherto unprecedented scale.

For many peasants in Latin America in the last decades of the twentieth century the growing of the coca leaf was their only source of income. They were paid little for it. Most of the leaves were grown in Peru and Bolivia, but Colombia, with her illegal refineries, was the drug centre of Latin America; here cartels and drug barons reap colossal rewards.

**The Americas, 1990**

GREENLAND

ALASKA
Anchorage

C A N A D A

HUDSON
BAY

Edmonton
Regina
Vancouver

Quebec
Ottawa
Detroit   Toronto
Chicago
New York
Washington

ATLANTIC
OCEAN

U N I T E D
S T A T E S

San Francisco
Los Angeles
Houston

Monterrey
MEXICO  Mexico

BAHAMA ISLANDS
WEST INDIES
CUBA          HAITI
              DOMINICAN REPUBLIC
              PUERTO RICO
JAMAICA

BELIZE
GUATEMALA
EL SALVADOR
HONDURAS
NICARAGUA
COSTA RICA
PANAMA

CARIBBEAN SEA

VENEZUELA
GUYANA
SURINAM
FRENCH GUIANA

Caracas
Bogota

Quito
EQUADOR

COLUMBIA

PERU

BRAZIL

Lima

Salvador

PACIFIC

OCEAN

La Paz

BOLIVIA

Brasilia
PARAGUAY

Rio de
Janeiro
São Paulo

Asunción

Santiago  Buenos
          Aires
CHILE

URUGUAY
Montevideo

ARGENTINA

0     1000    2000 miles

## Colombia, Peru, Bolivia and Paraguay, 1987

|  | Population (*millions*) | Gross National Product per head (*US$*) |
| --- | --- | --- |
| Colombia | 32.3 | 1,240 |
| Peru | 21.3 | 1,010 |
| Bolivia | 7.1 | 620 |
| Paraguay | 4.2 | 1,090 |

The economic problems of these debt-ridden countries gave the United States some leverage in her battle against the drug scourge. In return for aid and trade concessions, President Bush hoped to co-operate with the governments of the three Andean nations, Colombia, Bolivia and Peru. Peru was in bad shape economically and politically. She was beset by a hardline active Maoist guerrilla movement, the Sendero Luminoso or Shining Path, which specialised in killing supporters of the government. Peru also had a large foreign debt equivalent to half her Gross National Product. Neighbouring Bolivia was one of the poorest countries of Latin America, with a crushing foreign-debt burden. The armed forces of these countries, with US help, destroyed some of the plantations of coca in almost impenetrable jungle clearings, but the growing of coca leaves continued in many others. Medellín, the drug capital of Colombia, became the centre of violence too, with determined government efforts to strike against the drug barons being answered by bombs and assassinations. In Paraguay, where the dictator General Alfredo Stroessner ruled for thirty-four years supported by the military, government enjoyed a cosy relationship with the drug barons. A military coup finally overthrew him in 1989. It was uncertain whether his successors would end the corruption and curb the trade in drugs. Drug trafficking involved the whole of Latin America in shipments to North America and Peru from the Atlantic ports as well as those of the Pacific. As long as so profitable a market existed in the West, the chances of suppressing it at its source were slim.

With the end of the Cold War and the demise of the Soviet Union, the problems of Latin America were viewed in less ideological terms. It was an important world trading partner and its debts were a significant factor impeding trade and development; to default on them would present a serious problem to Western banking. Latin America was also a vital source of raw materials, not least Venezuelan oil. In Latin America, the Third World and the Western world lived side by side. But the enormous economic growth since the 1960s did not improve social justice; democracy remained weak, the military strong; the rich became richer, the poor benefited little, if at all. Latin America presents a rich palette of cultures; there is racial injustice but also much intermarriage and blending of races. As the twentieth century neared its end, a demographic time-bomb was ticking away: could the rapid population growth be slowed to a manageable increase? The problems of the continent were enormous, and it was vital to find solutions for them. Latin America was not likely to disappear from the agenda of world history again.

In the nineteenth century, investment in Latin America became a profitable destination for the venture capitalists of Western Europe and the United States. Britain built railways and became the principal investor before the First World War, and the United States invested particularly in Cuba and Central America, buying up many great plantations. While coffee-growing remained largely in Central American hands, American investment and political influence at its height was epitomised by the United Fruit Company, which monopolised the banana plantations and trade, owning its own shipping line and much else besides by the close of the nineteenth century.

Despite this large influx of foreign money, the masses of Latin America remained poor and the disparity of wealth and poverty extreme. During the first half of the twentieth century, moreover, there was only a small manufacturing industry throughout South America. Essentially there existed an alliance between the Latin American elites – the cattle-raisers of the Argentine, the owners of the coffee plantations of Brazil and local merchants – and foreign-owned enterprises, from which both drew immense profits in good times, to the exclusion of the subsistence masses. For the consumption of manufactured goods and luxuries the Latin American market remained small, since 90 per cent of the population did not earn enough to buy them. This has been one of the principal impediments to the continent's industrial diversification. Without an adequate domestic base the difficulties of establishing manufactures which can be profitable at home and competitive abroad are immense.

**Accumulated Foreign Debt and Accumulated Flight of Capital Abroad as of 1988** (*US$ billions*)

|  | Foreign debt | Capital flight |
|---|---|---|
| Brazil | 120.0 | 31.2 |
| Mexico | 107.4 | 83.8 |
| Argentina | 59.6 | 45.9 |
| Venezuela | 35.0 | 55.9 |
| Chile | 20.8 | 2.8 |
| Peru | 19.0 | 2.1 |
| Colombia | 17.2 | 7.1 |

Latin American governments are also characterised by instability, which has discouraged investment in the past – the local elites simply sent their money abroad to safer havens. It is instructive to compare the heavy indebtedness of Latin American nations with the estimated flight of capital abroad from 1982 to 1988. Nevertheless, state sponsorship and foreign investment since 1945 are gradually transforming Latin America, and large-scale industries have been established in all the major Latin American nations, Mexico, Brazil, the Argentine and Chile. As in industrial Europe, there has been a shift from agricultural pursuits to manufacture, from rural society to urban. But the forced pace of rapid industrial development has left many Latin American states burdened with huge debts to the West which most have no prospects of repaying at high interest rates. The expectation that with modernisation, with the expansion of a professional middle class, with the growth of an urban skilled workforce, their standard of living rising, and with increasing education and literacy Latin American authoritarian politics would give way to Western-style democracies is not yet being fulfilled. In Latin America, as in other developing regions, there is no such automatic and inevitable link between economic progress and democracy.

In many Latin American states in the 1980s, the military handed government back to democratic civilian rule. But frequently this represented an improvement only on the surface. Amnesty International publishes an annual survey of human-rights violations. It makes salutary reading. Torture and killings are still widespread in the exercise of political power against opposing groups. During the 1970s and early 1980s this barbarism probably reached heights not witnessed before in modern Latin American history and, one hopes, not to be reached again. At least 90,000 people simply 'disappeared'; no one knows for certain how many were picked up from their homes or in the street, never to be heard of again. At the trial of the Argentinian junta chiefs in 1985, it was estimated that 9000 had disappeared during the six years of military rule from 1976 to 1982; in Guatemala, Chile, Haiti and El Salvador, torture and executions without trial by 'security forces' or death squads were widespread.

In the 1960s a powerful new voice of protest against oppression made itself heard. The Catholic Church, which for centuries had been a pillar of conservative society, ceased to give unconditional support to the ruling elites. But the Vatican and Pope John Paul watched with consternation any Marxist leanings of bishops, priests and nuns amid the social tensions and political struggles of Latin America. In its most extreme form, 'liberation theology' looked to Marxism for an explanation of poverty and oppression but rejects atheism. But mostly the Church was simply speaking out against the extreme inequalities of wealth and against the unjustified and indiscriminate use of force.

This became clear to the rest of the world in 1968 when the bishops of Latin America met at Medellín in Colombia in the presence of Pope Paul VI and published a most remarkable declaration which read in part:

> Latin America still appears to live under the tragic sign of under-development ... Despite all the efforts that are made, we are faced with hunger and poverty, widespread disease and infant mortality, illiteracy and marginalism, profound inequalities of income, and tensions between the social classes, outbreaks of violence and a scanty participation of the people in the management of the common good – Complaints that the hierarchy, the clergy, the religious are rich and allied with the rich also come to us ...

The Church dedicated itself to becoming the Church of the poor and oppressed. In 1978 the Latin American bishops met again in Puebla, Mexico, and the majority progressives pressed on with the new liberation action. 'Between Medellín and Puebla, ten years have gone by,' the bishops declared. 'If we focus our gaze on our Latin American region, what do we see? No deep scrutiny is necessary. The truth is that there is an ever increasing distance between the many who have little and the few who have much ... we discover that this poverty is not a passing phase, instead it is the product of economic, social and political situations and structures ...' What was needed, the progressive Church leaders urged, was 'personal conversion and profound structural changes that will meet the legitimate aspirations of the people for authentic social justice'.

In Latin America the leading members of the Church hierarchy knew that if the Church failed to take the side of the poor the masses in their desperation would turn for their salvation away from the Church to a godless Marxism. The Church soon discovered the inevitable political implications of its new role. It spoke out against the 'disappearance' of people in Argentina and Chile and against the death squads of El Salvador during the 1970s; it defended the rights of labour unions and spoke up for the Indians excluded from the mainstream of development in Bolivia and Peru.

The most far-reaching change in the attitude of sections of the Catholic Church took the form of a campaign to reach out to the ordinary people, to give practical help, to communicate and to organise by creating thousands of grassroots community groups. These Christian communities in Latin America sought to 'liberate' the people through exercise of the faith and through stress on the value and dignity of human life. They were based on self-help through discussion and common action concerned with the practical issues of life and politics. Priests, nuns and Catholic laity provided leadership and teaching. But, unlike a left-wing party under rigid hierarchical control, the groups which sprang up relied on their own initiative. In Brazil, where the communities were developed to their greatest extent, tens of thousands of such groups had been formed in the countryside and in the shanty towns by the early 1990s, and as many as half a million of the disadvantaged poor had been brought together. A community might consist of twenty or thirty people meeting in a simple building. They would celebrate mass with a priest, and then discuss their immediate problems and concerns. They would decide on action: to demonstrate, to

petition, to demand basic services for their community, such as electricity and housing or perhaps a health centre. They acquired a sense of self-worth and confidence in acting together against corrupt local authorities. Devoted priests, nuns and laity served them. They taught respect for Christian values, as well as basic democracy and non-violent methods of action to improve their lives. In Brazil, the hierarchy spoke strongly in support of this community movement and accepted the strained relations thereby created with the state.

Repressive governments understood the risk nationally and internationally of taking any drastic steps against such a strongly united Church. Nevertheless, there were many martyrs when the military, no longer confining themselves to accusations of communist infiltration, resorted to harassment and murder. One such incident which attracted worldwide attention in 1980 was the murder of Archbishop Oscar Romero, an outspoken critic of the regime in El Salvador, who was shot dead while administering mass in a hospital chapel. Where military regimes suppressed opposition, the Church became the sole national voice of freedom. It was itself deeply divided in some Latin American states, where the hierarchy might be more ready to support the fight against communism than criticise authoritarian governments. In others, as in Brazil and El Salvador, the Church was more united in opposition. On the whole the Church was not revolutionary in action, but where it took a clear spiritual stand against injustice and economic exploitation it became a force that weakened the standing of repressive authoritarian regimes and tore aside the veil of secrecy with which these regimes attempted to hide their crimes. In the longer term the Church functioned as an opposition, which because of the international respect it enjoyed undermined Western, especially American, support for regimes whose human-rights records had become indefensible. Other organisations, such as Amnesty, trade unions and resistance groups, also highlighted the practices of torture and murder, but the majority of the churchmen when they spoke out enjoyed the inestimable advantage of not being identified as part of the left of politics, despite the attempts by regimes seeking to silence them to slander and misinterpret their motives.

In the early 1990s the Church was still making great efforts to improve the lot of the poor masses. But on the crucial issue of population control Pope

John Paul's pronouncements were uncompromising. The only means of birth control permitted
by the Church, the rhythm method, was too unreliable and was anyway not effectively practised.
Millions of women suffered the dangers and misery
of repeated abortions. But high rates of infant
mortality and poverty were also responsible for the
poor desiring large families. So there were multiple
reasons for high birthrates. Whatever its cause, the
galloping population growth undermined progress.
It is characteristic of regions with high birthrates
for the young to predominate, and boys and girls
from the shanty towns surrounding many of Latin
America's major cities turned to begging, stealing
and prostitution. Young lives became cheap, for
instance in Rio de Janeiro, where vagrant children
and petty criminals were found shot dead by vigil-
ante groups. Moreover, millions of peasants and
urban poor in Latin America were malnourished.
Much of the increase achieved in agricultural
production, including coffee, was sent for export –
it did not feed the peasants, who were landless or
eking out a living on the small areas of arable land
divided between them. Most of the land was allotted
to the larger estates. Only two Latin American
countries had low rates of birth in the early 1990s
and these were the two with predominantly European populations, Argentina and Uruguay. Without
population control, modernisation would do little
to help the urban poor or the peasants.

With an average annual rate of increase of 3.4
per cent, the population doubled every twenty-one
years. Population growth in different countries
varied enormously. Cuba under Marxist policies cut
its increase to just 1 per cent; the highest rates,
above 3 per cent, were to be found in Central
America and Mexico. More than half the population
of the continent lived in two countries, Brazil and
Mexico, with a growth rate above 2 per cent in
Brazil and 3.5 per cent in Mexico.

Generalisations about Latin America tend to
require many qualifications. For instance, it is true
that only two languages predominate, Portuguese
in Brazil and Spanish in the remainder of Latin
America (except for French in Haiti), but numerous
Indian languages are still spoken, such as Quechua
and Aymará, derived from the Incas and Maya and
Guarani. Cultural traditions originate not only from
the indigenous Indians but from the waves of immigrants through the centuries: Spanish, Portuguese,

*Wealth and poverty are in stark contrast in Latin America.* Top: *Brazil's poor compete with vultures in foraging for food and anything of value.* Above left: *in La Paz, Bolivia's capital, a child beggar is a common sight.* Left: *municipal services are hopelessly inadequate in Brazil's favelas.* Above: *but, for the idle on Copacabana Beach, Rio de Janeiro, life is sweet.*

**Population** (*millions*)

|        | 1880 | 1947 | 1962 | 1980  | 1989  |
|--------|------|------|------|-------|-------|
| Brazil | 30.6 | 46.4 | 75.3 | 126.4 | 147.3 |
| Mexico | 14.2 | 22.8 | 37.2 | 70.0  | 84.6  |

Dutch, British, French, slaves from Africa and in the nineteenth and twentieth century labourers from Italy, Germany, North America and Asia.

Colombia is ostensibly a democracy on the United States model with a directly elected president and an elected Congress, but the conservative elite continued to ensure its retention of power. Between 1910 and 1930 literacy qualifications for the franchise excluded 90 per cent of the people. The landowners dominated Colombia in the first half of the twentieth century. Coffee became her principal export, while bananas were cultivated by the ubiquitous United Fruit Company. Modest reforms inaugurated by the Liberals in the 1930s made only a small impact. The major consequence of such attempts was to galvanise right-wing reaction supported by the hierarchy of the Church, the wealthy landowners and industrialists. Their declared enemy was one of the leaders of the Liberal left, Jorge Eliécer Gaitán, whose radical proposals in the 1940s of land reform and state intervention in industry were anathema to Colombia's elite of so-called liberals and conservatives, who shared power. It was this coalition of interests which controlled Colombian politics for a decade after the Second World War.

The discontented masses of workers and landless peasants looked to Gaitán for leadership and change. The government responded with repression. In 1948 Gaitán was assassinated, an event which prompted one of the grimmest chapters in Colombia's violent history. Workers in Bogotá and peasants in the countryside rose against the government, occupying factories and seizing land. Order was restored by the army at the cost of thousands of lives.

After an election had been held in 1950, the conservatives ruled dictatorially alone. Colombian politics now exhibited two characteristics: violent repression and liberal economics. But repression never solved the problem. The geography of the country, with poor communications, mountains, valleys and plateaux isolated from each other, was

ideal for Marxist guerrilla groups to operate in. Police terror and anarchy, guerrilla warfare and banditry swept through the countryside. By the mid-1960s more than 200,000 Colombian peasants had been killed.

Violence remained endemic in Colombia in the 1990s. Reforms have been too few and too ineffective to help the million landless peasants. In the cities the harsh economic climate of the 1970s the world over was a further blow to industrial workers. Coffee prices fluctuated but were generally low. The isolated peasantry now turned to a new crop, the growing of coca leaves. As the 1980s drew to a close, guerrillas and drug barons perpetrated a culture of violence unparalleled elsewhere in Latin America. In the early 1990s the Colombian government tried to end the violence by reaching agreements with the drug barons and the guerrillas, and a new more democratic constitution was framed. The 1990s would, it was to be hoped, see a turn for the better in Colombian politics and society.

The vast Andes mountain range divides the coastal strip of western South America from the rest of the continent. The highlands of the western coast from Ecuador to Peru and Chile are populated mainly by Indians, whose way of life has changed little over the centuries. In complete contrast, in the cities on the coast, Santiago, Valparaiso and Lima, Western traditions and a twentieth-century way of life prevail.

The masses of Peru suffered during the course of the twentieth century from a kaleidoscopic variety of more or less oligarchic governments, none of which succeeded in bringing about the fundamental economic and social reforms the country needed. Despite opportunistic political parties proclaiming high ideas of reform, periods of government by Congress and presidency with a semblance of democracy were punctuated by spells of authoritarian rule. Peru was unable to develop her industries, oil extraction or mining from her own capital resources. Loans and foreign investment were encouraged in one decade only to arouse a nationalist reaction against foreign dependency in another. The economy swung from expansion to bust, depending on world prices for the commodities Peru exported, and later in the century the crushing foreign debt added its burden. But the pattern of her economic development did not fundamentally differ from that of her neighbours.

The effect of bad times on the poor was all the more catastrophic as the disparity in wealth between the top 7 per cent and the bottom 40 per cent was extreme, even in the 1990s. Almost all the Indian population, comprising about a third of the total, was wretchedly poor, the children malnourished. Alcoholism and ill-health flourished and in the early 1990s cholera from polluted water supplies reappeared.

The splendid buildings in Lima dating from the Spanish colonial period present a bitter contrast to contemporary misery. In the sixteenth and seventeenth century this was Spain's most prized possession, from which silver was transported to the Old World. Lima was called the City of Kings. Then the precious metal ran out; the country won her independence early in the nineteenth century and was ruled by a succession of military men. Not until the mid-nineteenth century was there any recovery, when bird droppings were discovered to be rich in nitrogen. Peru suffered once again in the last quarter of the nineteenth century from the bloody War of the Pacific (1879–84). The birds continued to do their duty, but the Chileans, who had been victorious in the war, annexed the coastal strip where they nested. In the first half of the twentieth century, with the help of foreign investment, sugar, cotton, wool, copper, oil (for a time) and fish meal became Peru's major exports. Foreign companies had a major share in developing these goods for foreign markets. The first three decades after the Second World War saw demand expand. The rise and fall of governments mirrored the changing fortunes of the economy.

A society so deeply divided was bound to be a society in conflict. Those who ruled Peru variously tried reform and repression, sometimes both at the same time. The landless Indians in the highlands hungered after land reform, migration of Indians to Lima created unsanitary shanty suburbs, and local industries produced an urban working class. It was fertile territory for communism in the 1920s. One of Peru's best-known political leaders, Víctor Raúl Haya de la Torre, responded with a socialist programme of anti-imperialism, state control, nationalisation and the protection of freedom and human rights. He founded in 1924 the Alianza Popular Revolucionaria Americana, APRA for short. APRA was still a political party in the 1990s and still had a strong following. It soon shed its Marxist intentions when it came to practical politics,

since it could attain power and the presidency only with the support of the middle class. It never effectively tackled the Indian problem, which could not be solved without radical land reform.

In the 1960s Belaúnde, of the Popular Action party, was elected as a reforming president. But when the 300,000 Indian peasants rose in revolt in 1965, the army was sent in to crush them. The history of Peru does not always follow what is regarded as a Latin American pattern. The army staged a coup in October 1968 at the height of another economic slump. The junta was headed by General Juan Velasco Alvarado, a man with sympathy for the oppressed Indians and the poor (the Peruvian military has not always been a reactionary force). Alvarado declared that the junta would reform the 'unjust social and economic order' and end subordination to foreign economic interests. A revolution was attempted from above. The large coastal sugar estates were expropriated and turned into co-operatives. The landowners on the coast and in the highlands were destroyed as an elite with political power. About 40 per cent of land had been transferred by 1975. The three-quarters of a million squatters in the shanty towns were given rights to the land and a sense of community was encouraged. Worker co-ownership in factories and management was designed to establish 'industrial communities' in parallel to the rural communities. Foreign-owned companies, mainly American, were nationalised. General Velasco's aim was to establish a distinctive Peruvian socialism.

The economic flaws soon made themselves felt. While some workers and Indians were helped, overall the reforms did not bring the full benefit that had been expected. Artificially low food prices, designed to help the urban poor, hit the peasantry. The world economic recession of the mid-1970s led to a fall in copper prices and those of other commodities at a time of heavy Peruvian indebtedness to foreign investors. The discredited military junta handed the country back to the civilian politicians.

In 1980 Belaúnde was elected president again. He dismantled the kind of corporate state the junta had wanted to set up. Orthodox financial management, especially policies designed to reduce the foreign debt, inevitably resulted in hardship, unemployment and protest. There were many strikes in Lima. In the remote highlands opposition was being organised by a new guerrilla group, the

Sendero Luminoso, known in the West as the Shining Path. Inspired by Maoist doctrines, the Shining Path was ruthless in waging war on the class enemies. Despite sweeps by the army, it has kept up a civil war ever since. A separate insurgency was mounted by the Tupac Amaru Revolutionary Movement.

In 1985, Peru's new hope for recovery was the election of the leader of the Alianza Popular Revolucionaria Americana (APRA), Alán García. Young and dynamic he instituted an economic reform plan which attempted to promote Peruvian industry. He was no socialist, preferring to leave industry in private hands, and his refusal to pay all the interest due to foreign investors made him popular. Thus began a long tussle between foreign governments and banks, with the Latin American debtors no longer prepared to impoverish their people in order to honour their financial obligations. Initial American reactions were hostile especially as García also took a stoutly independent line in foreign policy. By the 1990s, with the United States now taking the lead, it was accepted that Latin America's debt burden was too heavy, and that it was better for bankers to accept a reduction than repudiation and a breakdown in trade relations. By the time it came to elections again in 1990, the economy was in a dreadful state, crime and drugs were rampant and Shining Path was carrying the bloody struggle from the interior to the shanty towns around Lima, murdering fifty mayors in the countryside, as well as missionaries, priests and peasants. In just one year, 1989, insurgents and the government death squads between them killed over 3000 people. The people's disillusionment with their politicians was vividly demonstrated during the contest for the presidency in June 1990 when the son of a Japanese immigrant Alberto Fujimoro, a university academic promising reform but virtually unknown before, won by a convincing majority.

Fujimoro was determined to crush the Shining Path. In return for protection of the coca growers and drug barons, Shining Path was financed by the drug traffic. The president introduced emergency powers in 1991 and the conflict was stepped up by both sides. Fujimoro also launched an economic austerity programme, at the same time liberalising the economy and denationalising state enterprises. The immediate result was huge unemployment. In April 1992, backed by the military, Fujimoro seized dictatorial powers, dissolving Congress and

*Abimael Guzmán, the captured leader of Peru's guerrilla movement, Sendero Luminoso (Shining Path), is displayed to the world's press in his cell, 25 September 1992.*

arresting some of the political leaders.

Fujimoro claimed that he required executive powers to carry out his programme of deregulating the economy, cutting subsidies and privatising, as well as to fight the Shining Path more effectively. His first success was to capture the guerrilla group's leader after an intelligence operation in a flat in Lima in September 1992. But that was not likely to end the struggle with the Shining Path or the drug growers and merchants. For the Indians the growing of coca leaves had become an essential part of their survival economy. Great hardship was suffered by the people of Peru, and economic reforms – if they succeeded – would take several years during the 1990s to raise the low standards of living.

The Chilean people are predominantly homogeneous, descended from the Spaniards and the indigenous population and later European immigrants. Among Chile's population, intermarriage has created a society European in outlook and relatively free from racial prejudice. There are few pure Indians left, perhaps 300,000, among them the Araucanian Indians of the south, who have tried to preserve their way of life against the encroachments of modernisation.

Chile's riches in metals and minerals made her by the 1990s one of the most developed and urbanised nations in Latin America. In the course of the twentieth century the towns absorbed most of the population. Agriculture played a significant but decreasing role in the economy, with the traditional structures of large estates in the fertile valleys of central Chile worked by a poor landless peasantry surviving into recent times. The close ties between wealthy landholders and wealthy industrial magnates enabled these conservative groups to wield political power far in excess of their numerical strength. Industrialisation and urbanisation in the twentieth century created a relatively large working class, born in Chile and playing an important role in Chilean politics. The authoritarian Pinochet regime that ruled for two decades (1973–90) concealed what had been one of the distinguishing features of Chilean politics in Latin America, its traditional constitutional and parliamentary system, with the military accepting their subordinate though highly respected position. Escalating political conflict, the result of violent clashes of economic and social interests in the 1970s, a national economy in deep trouble as a result of failed socialist measures and of a denial of assistance from the West, especially the United States, led in 1973 to a military coup and, as few had expected, to a prolonged, ruthless dictatorship.

The Chilean economy was dependent on the world price of a single commodity, nitrates, before the 1920s, and it has been copper since then. Prices fluctuated violently and so impeded consistent internal development. Politics, too, were volatile. It is all the more remarkable that from 1891, after the end of a short but bloody civil war, until 1973, with the exception of a short period (1927–31) of suspended civic liberties and military rule, the parliamentary system survived, with regular national elections and peaceful transfers of power from one ruling political coalition to another. Throughout these years political fortunes were heavily dependent on the economic health of the state, which in turn was dependent on the economies of the industrialised West. What made Chilean progress even more problematical was that its prime export-earner, copper, was owned by foreigners. US companies transferred the bulk of the profits home and did not invest them in the less favourable conditions of Chile. The one issue on which all political parties were agreed was resentment of the United States, and when the copper companies were eventually nationalised in 1971 by Salvador Allende, the measure uniquely received unanimous support in the Chilean Congress.

Characteristic of the period of politics in Chile from 1891 to 1927 was the emerging alliance between the conservative landowner–merchant elite and a middle class alarmed at the rising demands of trade unions whose members were struggling in the inflation-ridden economy to maintain their living standards. The government response was more often repression and imprisonment of union leaders than concession and legalisation of union activities. At the same time efforts were made to reduce workers' militancy by means of welfare legislation. The military took over in 1927, but the impact of the depression made government a thankless task and the generals handed control back to the civilian politicians and Congress in 1931. Copper prices, which had fallen precipitously, recovered very gradually after 1932; the economy was so managed that Chile escaped the scourge of the 1930s, mass unemployment, at the cost of low wages and inflation. As the decade drew to a close, Chilean politics had become polarised. Working-class politics and union strength had greatly increased and a popular front was formed, a coalition that was no more than mildly socialist in its policies, and inherently unstable when in office. At no time did it pose a threat to the Chilean tradition of parliamentary government.

The coalition of the left was exposed to the hostility of the United States as the Cold War developed. In 1948 the Communist Party was outlawed (though not for long). During the next twenty-five years, Chilean politics remained deeply divided, elections fiercely contested. The left could not muster majority support and was kept out of power by a coalition of the centre–right. Unemployment was still held in check but the economy was stagnating and inflation a constant problem. The benefits of a substantial rise in copper prices from 1945 to 1955 were counterbalanced by an equally large fall in production. In the 1960s Chile's economic and social problems multiplied and would have been even worse without the support of Kennedy's Alliance for Progress (page 590). The problems of the rural poor had not been effectively tackled; their influx into the cities created massive new demands for housing, education and employment, a common experience in the under-developed regions of the world. The small population (11.2 million in 1980) and its weak buying power could not sustain large-scale home industries except in the most basic goods, which poor people can afford to buy.

No Chilean government in the twentieth century had so far found a solution to social and economic problems: to the confrontation of political parties and to the opposing interests of the poor, the middle classes and the wealthy elite. Any bold policy which attempted to breach the *status quo* was immediately stymied by the opposition in the Chilean Congress. Yet, for just one decade from 1964 to 1973, Chile's political leaders did try to break out of this cycle, and their failure had tragic consequences.

As the presidential elections of 1964 approached, the communist–socialist alliance, led by a veteran Marxist politician Salvador Allende, looked like polling the most votes, though he would not win an absolute majority; the parties of the right were second in strength, and third was a new Christian Democrat Party, pledged to implement thorough reforms and led by Eduardo Frei. To prevent the left coming to power, the parties of the right decided to back Eduardo Frei. Allende called for a socialist revolution and Frei for a 'revolution in liberty', which would not endanger civic rights or rights to property. The Johnson administration in Washington was determined to do what it could to keep Allende from winning. There must be only one 'Cuba' in the hemisphere. The CIA channelled substantial funds to Frei's campaign, and he won easily. Nevertheless, Allende, who had nearly won in 1958 in a three-cornered contest, made a strong showing.

Frei's policies were boldly reformist and he was helped by a large influx of US aid amounting to $327 million from 1964 to 1967. One long-standing problem concerned the US copper concerns. Frei did not nationalise them, but bought a state share as part of a Chileanisation programme. The state took an interventionist role in planning the economy. Local industry was diversified; with the country rich in timber, a paper industry was established, and petrochemicals were developed. Joining the Andean Pact with Peru, Bolivia, Ecuador and Colombia created a larger market. But the emphasis was on nationalism and independence from foreign economic domination. A more determined attempt at rural reform was made and the break-up of the large estates was begun. Between 1964 and 1967

copper prices rose steeply, as did production. Then copper prices fell again and inflation soared. There were large-scale strikes met by violent repression. As the 1970 presidential elections approached, all classes of society, for different reasons, were becoming disenchanted with Frei's economic reforms. With the conservative right now putting up their own candidate and the constitution preventing Frei from standing again, it was clear that this was Allende's opportunity.

President Nixon and his National Security Adviser, Henry Kissinger, regarded an Allende victory as totally unacceptable to the United States. It would end Cuba's isolation and they believed mark the beginning of an advance of Marxism in South America. They therefore sought to prevent Allende's election. Subsequent US Congressional investigations have revealed the extent of US intervention. The Chilean military were encouraged by the CIA, on instructions from Washington, to stage a coup to prevent Allende assuming the presidency. But the Chilean army Commander-in-Chief, General René Schneider, stood by the constitutional process and blocked the plot. The conspirators thereupon decided to remove him: he was shot and killed, possibly accidentally, when a third attempt was made to abduct him. This brutal intervention outraged the Chilean generals and the planned military coup did not materialise; another constitutionally minded commander-in-chief replaced the murdered man. When the election results were announced, Allende had won the largest number of votes, 36.3 per cent, but his rightist rival came a close second with 34.9 per cent and the Christian Democrat had secured 27.8 per cent. Allende could rightfully claim the presidency and was duly inaugurated by Congress, but he could not assert that he had won a national mandate to undertake a socialist revolution. For that, in any case, he would need majorities in Congress, which would be able to veto any Marxist transformation.

The three years of Allende's presidency in Chile are one of the most bitterly disputed periods in Latin American history. To some Allende became a martyr; his supporters accused the United States of repressing the righteous struggle of a Marxist for the betterment of the people. In fact, he achieved more by his death at the hands of the military than he had accomplished during his presidency; the barbarity of what followed brought out the contrast between the humane president and his successor,

General Augusto Pinochet. 'Allende' became the rallying cry of the left and of the many demanding justice and change in Chile.

The economic fundamentals were not favourable to Allende, and the price of copper was turning down from a peak in the late 1960s. Although Frei had made progress, it was not enough; and high inflation, which Frei had attempted to check with austerity measures, had returned. Allende restored and improved the living standards of the workers by a large increase in wages while controlling prices. The benefit was short-lived: a boom was followed by higher inflation. Allende's left coalition was committed to a transition to socialism, which meant state control of the economy to a much greater extent than his predecessor had thought possible or desirable. On the issue of foreign companies operating in Chile, nationalism and resentment of their economic role united all parties when in 1971 Congress approved the nationalisation of the US copper companies. Compensation was denied on the ground that their excess profits over the years had exceeded any compensation due. Other US companies, powerful in the United States, such as Ford and ITT, were taken over too; but when it came to nationalising the big banks and the largest concerns in Chile, there was an outcry from the industrial elites. Vigorous land reform enacted by Frei but until then hardly implemented added the landowners to the implacable opposition. The middle classes were alarmed by the expansion of state control, from which only the smallest enterprises appeared to be exempt; it was easy to frighten those small shopkeepers by suggesting that their private ownership would not last long either. Meanwhile, the expectations of many workers ran high. Through occupation of factories they tried to force the hand of the government, and sometimes they succeeded in doing so, though Allende tried to retain control of policy.

A number of key questions now arise. Was Allende leading Chile to a fully Soviet-style state, as his opponents maintained? Allende was an experienced politician who had participated in Chile's constitutional politics for many years. He now headed a coalition of the left, which extended from moderate socialists to the communists, who were themselves more moderate than their East European counterparts; but the coalition also embraced extreme radical groups who wanted to hasten the creation of a socialist state. Would Allende be able to

control the coalition, or would the extreme elements take over? By 1973 Allende had boxed himself in; he could rid himself of the extremists only if he could secure the support of the reformist Christian Democrats. That he tried to make an opening to the centre shows that his intention was not only to maintain himself in power but to moderate the course of change. He was not a mouthpiece of Moscow but a socialist seeking a Latin American solution to Chile's economic and social problems.

Nor was Allende following in Castro's path, though the Cuban leader was enthusiastically received when he visited Chile in 1971. Allende did not forcibly dissolve Congress, abolish the opposition parties or rule by making use of repression, terror, censorship or the suspension of civic liberties. There may have been supporters for such a course among his coalition partners, but the army's loyalty was to the constitutional process and if Allende had tried to establish an authoritarian Marxist regime he would have plunged Chile into civil war.

The path to socialism was blocked by Congress, where the opposition had a majority. Allende resorted to undemocratic means to bypass Congress and to continue expropriations, making use of his presidential powers. He proposed a constitutional amendment, replacing Congress with a People's Assembly and submitting this to a plebiscite. Congress predictably rejected this device in 1972. The proposal marked the high point of Allende's attempts to create a Marxist state. Allende did not pursue this extra-legal course; instead with the economy in chaos he moved towards Frei's Christian Democrats. Their support would have provided the coalition with a firm majority in the country while neutralising the extremists in the coalition. The negotiations came to nothing and the appalling state of the economy in 1973 was creating widespread unrest. The inflation rate had reached 150 per cent, inexperienced bureaucrats were running the state sectors of industry, private industry was demoralised and factory owners were not inclined to co-operate with a socialist government. A black economy flourished. Foreign credit was exhausted. And the sorry state of the economy was primarily the result of Allende's policies, though the Nixon administration remained implacably hostile and helped to undermine Allende. The principal US weapon was to deny aid and loans, which totalled only $18 million for the three years from 1971 to

*President Allende's Last Day. He died inside the palace being guarded here the very next day – during the military coup that brought General Pinochet to power in Chile.*

1973, as against $156 million from 1968 to 1970. Since mid-1970 Nixon had blocked the Chilean economy, and private investment dried up.

For a year, from the summer of 1972 onwards, there were increasing numbers of strikes, boycotts and mass street demonstrations of the pro- and anti-Allende masses. The opposition encouraged this public confrontation and the Marxist coalition called out its supporters. In the Congressional elections in the spring of 1973, which were free and democratic, Allende's Unidad Popular not only held on to its support but increased it (compared with the presidential election) to 43 per cent, though this was still less than the combined opposition figure of 55 per cent. The weakness of Allende's 'transition to socialism' was that it never won the support of the lower-middle class – the shopkeepers and small traders, those with some stake in a free-enterprise economy. By the summer of 1973 terrorist incidents were added to large-scale strikes and demonstrations. After negotiations with the Christian Democrats had failed, Allende sought the support of the army and brought in a moderate general as Minister of Defence. On this general's resignation, Allende turned to another who was believed to share the army's traditional consti-

tutional outlook – Augusto Pinochet. But the military were plotting a coup. On 10 September 1973, they struck. Allende hurried the following morning from his private residence to the presidential palace, rejecting offers of safe conduct and exile in the Latin American tradition. By this courageous decision he ensured that the coup would be condemned as unconstitutional. An attack by fighter planes set fire to the palace and Allende died there resisting the assault on his authority, an outrage in the long constitutional history of Chile.

The military junta's campaign of repression against civilian supporters of the former Allende government also had no parallels in Chilean history. Certainly nothing as bloody had occurred since the civil war almost a century earlier. 'Suspects' were rounded up in the football stadium. Thousands of likely opponents were imprisoned; thousands were murdered, perhaps 5000, possibly three times that number, during the early days after the seizure of power. The hope of the urban poor and peasants for a new deal was buried under bayonets. The military ruled, Allende was gone and Washington heaved a sigh of relief. But it was one thing to get rid of a Marxist leader, another to replace him with a reformist, democratic, free-enterprise government respecting human rights. This is what the United States wanted, as did the majority of the Chilean people. General Pinochet, who emerged as the caudillo, the strongman of the junta, broke with Chilean military tradition and did not hand back power to the civilian politicians. His regime 'suspended' all political activity, sent Congress packing and drove political parties underground. The democratic representative constitution was set aside and an emergency 'state of siege' declared which effectively abolished freedom and civil rights. These were not short-term measures. The 'state of siege' was only lifted fifteen years later in the summer of 1988 as Pinochet was seeking to improve the image of his repressive regime on the eve of a referendum designed to confirm him in power; even Chilean exiles were now invited to return.

But Pinochet's first task in 1973 was to ensure the security of his military regime. This he did during the next fifteen years by waging a ruthless campaign to eliminate any opposition; people were picked up in the street or in their homes and just 'disappeared', without trial; their relatives were told that nothing was known about them. All social classes were affected, and all shades of political opinion, though the main target was the left wing. A regime of terror was inaugurated. Women as well as men were imprisoned, tortured and killed; others languished in prisons and camps. The 'disappeared ones' became one of the most horrifying features of recent Latin American history. In Chile (a rough estimate) 3000 are missing, in Argentina 30,000, in Guatemala 35,000, in El Salvador 9000, in Haiti 15,000; children were orphaned, their identities obliterated, and they have been adopted by politically 'safe' parents. These flagrant violations of human rights aroused only sporadic protest in the West, but Pinochet was safe from any effective international interference. The attitude of the United States was of particular importance.

The Nixon–Ford administrations wanted in Chile a stable government, preferably one that was reasonably democratic and supported a free-enterprise economy, with a decent human-rights record. But the United States also saw in Marxism a cancer spreading out from Cuba; it had to be contained in Cuba; should it break out of this isolation, given the severe problems of Latin America, it would not halt in any one country, but would spread to the neighbours of the United States and present a threat to her in her own hemisphere.

The fight against communism had therefore to be given priority. Large-scale aid once more flowed to Chile: loans to assist economic recovery, aid under the Food for Peace programme (eight times larger than what was given during the Allende years) and funds to purchase arms. In all these measures the Nixon–Ford administrations expressed their support for Pinochet. It is true that their purpose was to defeat communism, not to underpin the Chilean regime's brutalities, but they could not escape the dilemma: the two were linked – they were making, as they saw it, the choice that best served US interests. As Kissinger explained, the United States should not become involved in 'temptations to crusade'. But Senator Edward Kennedy and other members of Congress embarrassed the Republican administrations with their opposition and their attempts to restrict aid to Chile by linking it to human rights. The administrations' task thereby became more difficult, but ways were found to continue giving aid from 1973 to 1976, the most repressive years of the Pinochet regime, during which the opposition was decimated. For them, by the time the new Democratic President Jimmy Carter made human rights a key plank of US policy, with particular reference to Latin America, it was too late. Aid to Chile and other repressive regimes was drastically cut, without noticeable effect on the brutality of these regimes. The United States could not bring about their fall by economic means, nor was economic aid sufficient to maintain them. That is why US policy in Chile is such an instructive example of the difficulties and frustrations that appeared to face Washington's policymakers.

It was in Chile, too, that Western academic economists and technocrats were allowed a decisive influence in policymaking to cure the economic chaos that was prevailing at the end of Allende's presidency. The Chilean generals did not understand economics, but, opposed as they were to socialism, backed free-market remedies being advocated by Professor Milton Friedman's Chicago School. At its most basic, the theory was that the free-market system should be allowed to function and that all artificial restraints, such as protection of economic sectors that were otherwise not competitive, trade unions bidding up wages beyond their market value, state-run industries not dependent on commercial profits, should be removed. Inflation would be cured, and market forces would achieve a balance between supply and demand, provided the government balanced its own budget and kept the supply of printed money in check. Ideologically the father of this economics was Friedrich Hayek, who saw in socialism and its central controls the modern road to slavery. The attitudes and expectations of workers and employees could best be changed by the sharp shock of changing the protectionist system quickly. Paradoxically, it was a nation that had fallen under a vicious dictatorship, the kind of state Hayek most abhorred, which now provided the laboratory.

In Chile the technocrats did not have to worry about the immediate practical consequences: workers would be cowed and trade unions would not be allowed to interfere. In a less authoritarian regime, the severity of Chile's inflation (it had reached 500 per cent in 1973) would have ensured that the remedies were applied with more circumspection. Looked at in the short term, the economic policies adopted in Chile were successful. People even talked of a 'Chilean miracle'; inflation was down within a few years to less than 10 per cent; the growth rate in the 1970s was healthy. But the price paid in terms of distress experienced by the poorest was equally spectacular; there was large-scale urban unemployment and mounting debts. The bankers had miscalculated in their belief that good profits could be earned from Latin America's most repressive regimes which had a record of keeping their countries stable and which repaid their foreign loans punctually. Then the decline in commodity prices in the early 1980s hit Chile hard, dependent as she still is on exports of copper; servicing the foreign loans places an increasing drain on an economy.

The Pinochet regime also came under mounting pressure, not only from opposition at home expressed in massive strikes, but from the Reagan administration, which in 1986 sponsored a UN resolution criticising Chile's human-rights record. Even his fellow generals opposed Pinochet when he declared he would stay in office until 1997. In September 1986 he narrowly survived an assassination attempt; this he countered with another bout of severe repression, which included arresting

leaders of the opposition. The left-wing guerrilla group, the Patriotic Front, planted bombs. The papal visit of John Paul II in 1987 brought more criticism on Pinochet's head and the generals were openly calling for a hand-over to a civilian president. Violent street demonstrations accompanied Pinochet's 1988 campaign for the plebiscite designed to confirm him in the presidency until 1997, but the General was sufficiently confident to lift the state of emergency and to allow the opposition to campaign against him. In the event the Chileans rejected Pinochet by the surprisingly small majority of 463,833 votes out of a total of just over 5 million. No doubt the improved economic situation, with substantial growth from 1985 to 1988, and memories of the chaos Allende had left behind him had persuaded nearly half the voters to back Pinochet – better the devil you know. But the result was decisive enough. In December 1989 Patricio Aylwin Azócur, a seventy-one-year-old lawyer, won the presidential elections and was inaugurated in March 1990. Pinochet did not retire but confined himself to the role of commander-in-chief. In November 1990 he celebrated his seventy-fifth birthday – too old, one might hope, to turn the constitutional clock back again, but it remained to be seen whether the army would resume its former role of respecting representative constitutional government. Although the price paid in human terms was considerable, the Pinochet years transformed the national economy.

In the aftermath of the military regime, the country learnt the grisly truth about the years of dictatorship. Nearly 2300 had died, many by shooting and torture, and nearly a thousand had simply disappeared (at least one unmarked mass grave was uncovered). One of the hardest tasks confronting Chile in the 1990s was to come to terms with her past, and to keep the military in check. She also faced the challenge of reforming her social and economic structures – including health provision, education and housing – while at the same time ensuring employment and maintaining a free-market economy.

# CHAPTER 70

# The World of Latin America:
# Argentina, Uruguay, Brazil and Venezuela

Like Chile, Argentina was ruled by an authoritarian military junta during the 1970s which paid no respect to human rights. Unlike Chile, however, Argentina had never developed a broadly based parliamentary tradition. The second largest country in Latin America after Brazil, Argentina covers an area greater than Western Europe, but the countryside is sparsely populated, since grain-production and cattle-ranching, the agricultural backbone of Argentina's export economy, require relatively few labourers. She trades profitably, exporting wheat and refrigerated beef and importing manufactured goods. Before the Second World War, Britain had the largest foreign stake, having invested in railways and some industries. Argentina's population is concentrated in the towns and grew rapidly from less than 2 million in the mid-nineteenth century to 8 million by 1914, and to 31.1 million in 1987. This growth derived mainly from massive immigration from Italy and Spain during a period of rapid expansion from the 1880s until the onset of the depression in 1929. Argentina thus became the most Europeanised of Latin American nations, but these Western traditions were more those of southern Europe, where representative government and democracy had not flourished in what was still then a largely under-developed region. Government in Argentina was nominally representative and democratic, but in reality it was manipulated by a wealthy oligarchy whose power was based on their ranches and related agricultural industries and, of course, on the support of the army. The oligarchy had nothing to fear from peasants in the countryside, as there were practically none; nor were there indigenous Indians in significant numbers: they had been decimated in the last of the Indian wars towards the close of the nineteenth century when the military took away their lands to the south and south-west of Buenos Aires.

Political, social and economic tensions arose from a different quarter as Argentina developed – from the urban workers, the small shopkeepers, the low ranks of trade, industry and the professions, excluded from influence and from a fair share of the country's growing wealth. They did not, however, organise themselves to participate in the electoral process. Trade unions, which followed the anarchist and syndicalist traditions of Spain, were severely repressed and their leaders imprisoned.

More successful was another new group of outsiders, the recently prosperous and the middle classes, who had gained their share of economic but not political power. They formed the Radical Party and finally came to power in 1916. In the strikes following the First World War, their earlier, more sympathetic attitude to the urban workers turned to repression. In socialism, syndicalism and anarchism they identified the enemy within. During the 1920s the urban workers' wages rose but expectations grew even faster. The Radicals had made many enemies on the left as well as among the ousted conservative oligarchy, and a limited democracy functioned only until a military coup in 1930.

The conservative–military alliance, contemptuous of democracy – though manipulated elections were held – saw much to admire in the Nazi Germany of the 1930s and only entered the war against the Axis at practically the last possible moment to avoid exclusion from the Allied United Nations in 1945.

By then the military had tired of the vestiges of representative government, with its party system and the disproportionate power the conservative oligarchy enjoyed. In 1943 the officers organised a coup; the rising star among them was Colonel Juan Perón. While the corporate state in Europe faced defeat, it survived in Franco's Spain and was to survive in Perón's Argentina. Perón and his mistress and later wife, Evita, created a new power base, an alliance of the army with the hitherto politically powerless masses of urban workers. The workers remained powerless but they gained the illusion of power by supporting the charismatic caudillo. Franco in Spain, Salazar in Portugal and Perón in Argentina were apparent anachronisms in the Western world, which had fought for freedom and democracy, but they survived and flourished. Perón could also claim legitimacy after he won elections in 1946 with a strong showing of 54 per cent. One reason for his success was the introduction of a host of social welfare schemes, higher wages, minimum wages and pensions. Evita used state funds to finance her foundation which showered benefits on orphans and the poor. When she died in 1952, still young and beautiful, the national mourning was unprecedented. The myth of Evita supported Perón's rule, which under its glossy populist surface used the repressive tactics of a fascist regime. A state economic plan and state intervention, with a drive to industrialise, were designed to build a new Argentina. The workers prospered.

The economic downturn after 1949, however, soon brought old tensions to the surface. More orthodox economic management lowered standards of living and political theatre and the support of the Peronist masses alarmed the Church and the oligarchic and military elite. In September 1955 the military engineered another coup and Perón quietly departed into exile. An independent elected civilian president was allowed to rule for just four years from 1958 to 1962, before the military deposed him and seized power again: they were always ready to mount coups when the outcome of the electoral process displeased them. The president elected in 1963 lasted only another three years before a further

*'Evita' Perón, the idol of the Argentinian people, in Buenos Aires in October 1950. Her death, two years later, considerably weakened her husband Juan's grip on power.*

military coup. But throughout the decades the appeal of Peronism, despite the efforts of the military to suppress it, did not lose its glamour among the urban masses.

Argentina depended on world markets for her exports and imports, but in general the terms of trade during the 1950s and 1960s moved against primary producers, though there were brief periods of prosperity, not least because she presented a home market large enough for considerable expansion of the industrial sector. Argentina was plagued by wild swings of economic policy between boom and slump, and she was saddled with the ever increasing burden of foreign loans. Despite her 'European face', in her economic development and the strength of her military Argentina was also very much a Latin American country.

Amid mounting political violence, Perón returned in 1973 and was elected president, but it was too late for him to achieve a political rerun of his former success. Nine months after his election he died. His third wife briefly assumed the presidency, but she was quite unable to master the deteriorating economic and political situation. In March 1976 a military junta staged yet another coup and took over power for the next six years.

This junta turned out to be the most bloody and repressive in the modern history of Argentina. The world media was able to draw attention to its brutality thanks to the courage of the women, the 'grandmothers', who every week demonstrated silently before the presidential palace, holding placards and pictures of members of their family who had 'disappeared'. Their disappearance was the consequence of the 'dirty war' the junta waged indiscriminately against the opposition; not only were guerrillas arrested and killed but anyone regarded as subversive could suffer the same fate. For the military there were no constraints imposed by a rule of law. Mass graves were subsequently discovered, but no one can be sure how many died during the years of terror – perhaps 30,000. And in managing the economy the generals were no more successful than their predecessors. Early improvements in response to stricter monetary controls gave way to inflation and recession in the 1980s.

In a bid to divert popular discontent the junta, then headed by General Leopoldo Galtieri, decided on a surprise invasion of the British Falkland Islands, claimed by Argentina as Las Islas Malvinas. The Falklands had come under British occupation in 1833, and the sparse population of some 2000 overwhelmingly wished to remain British. Under international law, the Argentinians had a doubtful case, but successive British governments would still have preferred a solution that satisfied Argentinian national pride. The main obstacle to a settlement proved to be the British Parliament which understandably would not hear of any diplomatic solution that might hand British citizens over to an authoritarian Argentinian regime. There was no chance of any peaceful outcome once the Argentinians launched an invasion of the islands on 2 April 1982. The British Governor and his guard of a few soldiers could offer only token resistance. The United Nations and other intermediaries, including General Alexander Haig, the US Secretary of State, attempted to find a peaceful solution before the British military and naval task force being assembled 8000 miles away could reach the Falklands. One of the most controversial events in the war was the sinking by a British submarine of the Argentinian cruiser, the *Belgrano*, on 2 May with great loss of life, at a time when the Argentinian navy was on its way back home. Prime Minister Margaret Thatcher was accused at the time of having deliberately torpedoed a promising peace plan which had only just been proposed. It is more than doubtful that

the generals would have withdrawn the force from the Falklands, which was the minimum British requirement. In a short conflict the untrained Argentinian conscripts were no match for the British professionals, but the Argentinian air force, with its modern fighters and up-to-date weapons, inflicted severe casualties on the task force. On 14 June 1982 Port Stanley was recaptured and the Argentinian commander surrendered.

In Britain there was no feeling of enmity or hatred for the young Argentinians caught up in the conflict. At the 'victory' church service in St Paul's Cathedral, prayers were said for both the British and the Argentinian dead. It was the most unnecessary war of modern times, and could perhaps have been prevented had the British government listened in time to warnings of an impending invasion. Instead, inadvertently, the wrong signals were sent to Buenos Aires. The invasion itself had been greeted in the Argentinian capital with wild enthusiasm, though the British colony was not in any way molested – to that extent, at least, it was a civilised conflict. A deep chord in Argentinian nationalism had been touched, and the generals were heroes. The let-down of defeat was bound to be traumatic. The one good result was that the military junta could not hope to stay in power much longer. The military made way for civilian rule in October 1983. Raul Alfonsín and the Radical Party won the subsequent election.

Alfonsín inherited appalling economic problems exacerbated by his inability to end the state of conflict on the basis of accepting British sovereignty over the Falklands. After the casualties the British had suffered, a compromise of that principle, possible perhaps before the invasion, had now become unthinkable. The Argentinian economy did not recover, which made Alfonsín increasingly unpopular at home, but the President, a lawyer by profession, restored the rule of law, and human-rights violations ceased. This earned him international recognition and goodwill. Those in the military responsible for torture and murders during the 'dirty war' were brought to trial, a development unprecedented in Latin American history. A handful of the military, as well as the leaders of the junta, were sentenced to various terms of imprisonment in 1985. But Alfonsín was not really strong enough to come to grips with the many criminals in the army, which remains a potential power in the state. The most serious and immediate threat to democratic institutions in Argentina, however, has been the perennial problem of the economy. When Raul Alfonsín became president in December 1983, the inflation rate had reached 2000 per cent, and foreign capital had fled from the shattered economy. Alfonsín's conservative economic measures and his wage and price controls stabilised the economy only for a time, and did so at the expense of the workers' standard of living.

In 1986 the Peronist General Confederation of Labour called strikes against the economic programme and in the following year the Peronist opposition provided good evidence of their reviving strength when in elections for provincial governors they won most of them while Alfonsín's Radical Party only just retained a majority in the Chamber of Deputies. The economy continued to deteriorate, and the army was growing restless, though attempted coups by rebellious elements of the military were easily defeated by loyal commanders. Inflation was close to 200 per cent in 1988 and reached 600 per cent in 1989; the hardships this caused were a gift to the Peronists. Their choice for presidential candidate in May 1989 was an unusual one, the charismatic fifty-nine-year-old Carlos Saúl Menem. Alfonsín had lost the will to govern and transferred the presidency to Menem (who had won the election) prematurely in July.

Menem began with a drastic austerity programme, but by the end of the year Argentina was suffering even worse inflation. The President attempted in a Peronist spirit to build agreements between state employers and trade unionists, with the blessing of the Church. Amnesties granted to those members of the military convicted of human-rights offences, including three of the imprisoned junta, were also intended to reconcile the army. The breakdown of Menem's marital relations, his wife claiming she had been locked out of the presidential palace, added an element of colour to Argentina's chaotic domestic situation.

In October 1990 Menem issued decrees curbing the right of the Peronist-dominated trade unions to strike, a move which created a split among his supporters. Two months later, the restiveness of the military led to an attempted coup, and to pacify the armed forces Menem pardoned the high-ranking officers responsible for torture and murder during the 'dirty war'. His reputation ultimately, though, would depend not only on whether he could dismantle the Peronist corporate state, with

its featherbedding, its swollen bureaucracy and its uncompetitive state enterprises, but also on whether inflation could be kept under control in the long term. He made a determined start in 1991 to privatise state industries and turn Argentina into a deregulated market economy.

A contrast to a large and powerful country is the small state of Uruguay. Uruguay had for a long time enjoyed a tradition of comparatively free and representative civilian government. She was a progressive and prosperous country exporting meat, cereals and wood and her population of less than 2 million in the 1950s, with large-scale European immigration, was relatively homogeneous. Uruguay also enjoyed the distinction of having introduced the first welfare state in the Western hemisphere. It was not coincidental that tiny Uruguay was chosen to launch the Alliance for Progress in Latin America (page 509). But the strength of these traditions did not save Uruguay from a military coup in 1973. The excuse was the need to suppress the left-wing Tupamaros guerrillas. The first three years of military rule witnessed torture and killing of victims as horrifying as any in Latin America. One US Congressman referred to Uruguay as a 'cesspool'. With a cowed opposition, the ferocity of the onslaught lessened; the refusal of the United States Congress and the Carter administration to grant military aid as well as the humanitarian pressures from such organisations as Amnesty International also persuaded the military rulers to act with restraint.

As elsewhere in much of Latin America, mounting economic problems returned the soldiers to barracks in 1984. The military leaders handed over to a civilian government the task of clearing up the mess and assuming responsibility for the unpopular austerity measures that would be required. The civilian President in turn attempted to amnesty the military who had been involved in human-rights abuses but angry demonstrations and the Uruguayan Congress frustrated his efforts until 1989. Austerity measures provoked strikes and general dissatisfaction. One positive development was that the Tupamaros guerrillas ended their fight and entered politics; another that free presidential elections could be held in November 1989, which gave victory to the candidate of the opposition. Democracy, which is closely bound up with the state of the economy, remains shallow-rooted.

*

Uruguay's north-eastern neighbour is Brazil, the largest and most powerful country on the South American continent. Although Brazil is the neighbour of all but two South American nations (Chile and Ecuador on the west coast), geography and the Portuguese roots in her history have tended to isolate her from the rest of the continent. Yet there are common Latin American features too, such as the question of the fate of the indigenous Indians; in Brazil, intermarriage has practically submerged them in the multiracial society of European and African origins. In the least approachable recesses of the Amazonian jungle Indian tribes are precariously surviving, threatened by progress, exploitation and the cutting down of the rainforests. There are probably only about 220,000 Indians still inhabiting the frontier regions, who supposedly enjoy government protection.

Until the end of the empire in 1889, Brazil, despite her rich mineral resources, was a comparatively backward country relying mainly on the export of coffee. To provide labourers for the coffee plantations, Africans were sold into slavery and transported to Brazil, where slavery was not abolished until 1888. Republican Brazil continued to rely mainly on exporting coffee and importing manufactured and luxury goods to satisfy the small urban middle class and the wealthy plantation owners and merchants. By the 1920s only a small industrial sector had developed, and the coffee oligarchy dominated politics until the revolution of 1930. The first strong push for industrialisation occurred during the years from 1930 to 1945 when the country was ruled by the authoritarian regime of Brazil's first outstanding political leader of modern times, Getúlio Vargas.

Vargas, brought to power by the army in 1930 against a background of economic crisis, introduced a new authoritarian constitution in 1937 which established what was called the *estado novo*. The state became supreme in politics, industrial relations and economic management. No parallel social revolution was attempted. Vargas had to maintain the support of a coalition of interests: merchants, industrialists, the landed oligarchy of plantation owners with their ill-paid dependent rural workers, a subsistence peasantry, and urban workers preserved their unequal shares of the national wealth. Strict labour laws controlled the growing numbers of industrial workers. The state nationalised the banks and basic industries, and an iron and steel industry

was started. Although by the close of the Second World War Brazil still relied mainly on the export of coffee, the basis for her later industrial growth was laid during the Vargas dictatorship.

That dictatorship came to an end in October 1945, when the army forced him into exile. In the conditions prevailing after the war, with the victory of the Western free world over Nazi tyranny – although Vargas had shrewdly joined the Allied cause in 1942 – Vargas's authoritarian state was regarded by the army as an embarrassment. The United States was now all powerful in the Western hemisphere. An election was held in December 1945, though only half the electorate was enfranchised; two generals competed for the presidency. The outcome was the formation of a conservative government ardently hostile to communism. In 1950 Vargas entered the next electoral contest and won, but his attempt to create a power base by gaining the support of the workers with wage rises and sympathetic labour legislation soon revealed the limits of Brazil's constitutional system. He did not last out his term. The right-wing military charged Vargas's administration with corruption and communist penetration. Driven from office for a second time in 1954, Vargas ended his contest for leadership by committing suicide.

The presidential election of 1955 was won by Juscelino Kubitschek with the popular João Goulart, Vargas's minister of labour, as running mate. Kubitschek campaigned for the defence of democracy and fast economic growth. The army watched to make sure that he did not stray too far to the left, but mounted no military coup, as some urged it to do. In a limited sense it could, therefore, be credited with safeguarding parliamentary government. The military saw it as their patriotic duty to stabilise a guided democracy with a preference for civilian rule. A decade later Goulart, by then the elected president, attempted to reform the country's archaic land and tax structures. He also wanted to extend the franchise to the illiterate peasantry to check the power of the rural oligarchies. Such fundamental changes were designed to move Brazil forward socially and to create a new dynamism in the economy. Frustrated by Congress, Goulart's policy initiatives grew more radical as he appealed to the left for support, and not only to the industrial workers but to the peasants as well. He now added land expropriation and the legislation of the Communist Party to his reform package. This brought the wrath of the army and opposition down on him.

A conspiracy had been taking shape in 1964 among right-wing army officers and conservative politicians, with urban middle-class support, to stage a coup. It was assured in advance of United States goodwill. On 1 April 1964 Goulart was overthrown virtually without a struggle and fled to Uruguay. The military took over. This time they did not hand power back to civilian politicians.

During the early years of the generals' rule, repression had not yet taken its more extreme forms. A façade of parliamentary government was maintained. Then a new constitution in 1967, which curtailed political rights, prompted left-wing urban and rural guerrillas to resort to arms, but they never secured a mass following. Their only spectacular success was the kidnapping of the United States Ambassador in 1969. From 1968 to 1973 the military junta reacted with ferocity. The torture and murder of opponents became common and widespread, and the repressive security apparatus survived the defeat of the guerrillas. The various attempts made by the generals to enlist broader support and a more acceptable constitutional image all failed. Internal opposition, strikes and, particularly, the condemnation of the most radical Catholic Church in Latin America wore down the generals' desire to accept the responsibility of ruling Brazil. They handed the government back to civilian rule in 1985. It was no coincidence that this was done at a time of severe and prolonged economic crisis. And the military in the 1990s had not abandoned their role of intervening when they judged it to be necessary.

The Brazilian economy had expanded spectacularly since the Second World War, transforming the country into a modern industrial giant. Coffee no longer dominates and amounts to only about 10 per cent of total exports. By 1981 Petrobas, the huge oil and chemical state industrial complex, was the largest corporation in Brazil by far. Modern technology is represented in the armaments and aircraft industries, which export to the rest of the world. The multinational oil companies have established themselves, while Ford, General Motors and Volkswagen have developed an efficient motor industry. Foreign industry and private investment, and the large bank loans required, were attracted by the availability of cheap and plentiful local labour, which

showed itself eminently capable of being trained; no less attractive were the repression of labour and the comparative freedom from strikes, as well as the political stability which the generals' police state seemed to guarantee. Thus the unhappy link was established between capitalism, foreign penetration and repression which so powerfully fuels anti-Western, particularly anti-North American, sentiment among the masses.

The Brazilian economy achieved rapid growth but it also had to weather periods of austerity and retrenchment when forced development produced high inflation and severe balance-of-payments crises. After the Vargas period, the next phase of spectacular growth was kickstarted by the ambitious economic plan masterminded by President Juscelino Kubitschek in the 1950s. It was he who decided to construct the brand-new capital of Brasília as an expression of the country's unity, confidence and ultra-modernity, but his boom based on attracting foreign investment had to be followed by another period of austerity. Under the generals a new boom began in 1968. It was checked but not stopped by the tripling of oil prices in 1973–4. Foreign bankers, flush with Middle Eastern oil money, poured it into Brazil, which accordingly accumulated the largest foreign debt in the world. In the early 1990s it was unlikely ever to be repaid in full with interest. The bankers' miscalculation in Latin America had cost them dear – the United States, Germany, Japan and Switzerland were especially heavily exposed.

Brazil had already become predominantly urban before the 1950s, but the urban workers did not share in their country's growth. Their real wages, which had been rising in the 1950s, fell again after 1960; many workers received no more than the minimum wage, which during these two decades almost halved. This in turn provided the profits for an industrial and technical elite and allowed Brazil to enjoy spectacular growth rates. By 1981 the cycle of growth had come to a full stop. The economy in the 1980s was overshadowed by the need to service the foreign debts and, despite a successful industrial sector, the Brazilian government could not devote to social and welfare programmes the resources so desperately needed by the poor. The crippling constraints which this imposed on the Brazilian economy created that vicious circle of social deprivation and political instability characteristic of so much of the South American continent.

As elsewhere in Latin America, the civilian

administration of President José Sarney in 1986 introduced a harsh austerity programme; inflation was halted for a time, but the plan collapsed and inflation was back at 800 per cent in 1987. Apart from the state of the economy, the burning question was whether Brazil would become some sort of democracy by virtue of the new constitution. When this was promulgated in October 1988, the president was allowed wide-ranging powers and the armed forces were given the ambiguous responsibility of maintaining 'constitutional order'. In other respects the repressive rule of the previous military dictators was repudiated. The new constitution guaranteed basic civil rights, including the right of workers to strike as well as freedom of speech and the freedom of the press. Another restructuring plan for the economy to beat rampant inflation was launched in January 1989. President Sarney's obvious failures led to his defeat in the presidential elections that November. A more positive aspect of his administration was that it took the first steps towards protecting the Amazon rainforests, whose despoliation had aroused international concern.

In March 1990 the new President, Fernando Collor de Mello, was inaugurated. Collor promised to transform Brazil's economic chaos. A stylish forty-year-old, he vowed to help the underdogs, the 'skirtless ones', and to end the mismanagement and corruption of the years of the generals and President Sarney.

Collor began his presidency with the most radical austerity measures of any Latin American reformer by freezing 80 per cent of all but the smallest financial assets for eighteen months. He slimmed down the large bureaucracy and vowed to move towards a free-market economy, dismantling Brazil's high tariffs and exposing the featherbedded state industries. The result in his first few months was unemployment and recession. By the summer of 1990 he had to ease up on some of his draconian measures and inflation began to rise once more. The economic future also depended on a favourable settlement with foreign creditors to ease the payments on her huge debt. A preliminary agreement was reached in 1991. Collor's determination to stop the despoliation of the Amazon and to protect the few Indian peoples still left won world approval. Brazil was also chosen for the Earth Summit, a conference intended to protect the environment but which achieved little. As the economy deteriorated again, Collor lost much of his credibility. Once

again, hopes had been dashed. In 1992 Collor was charged with corruption, impeached and forced from office.

Venezuela is able to generate a large proportion of her wealth not from manufacture but by extracting oil from among the most productive oilfields in the world. Oil contributed 90 per cent of her export earnings in the 1980s and nearly a third of her Gross National Product. Agriculture plays only a small role in the economy. In the 1960s she overtook Argentina as the wealthiest country in Latin America. In 1987 her population of 18.3 million was estimated to have a gross per-capita income of US$3230. The two oil-price explosions in 1973–4 and 1979–80 brought enormous new wealth and enabled her to diversify industrially into petrochemicals, iron, steel, paper, and the aluminium industry. Western bankers fell over themselves to provide credit. Caracas acquired the skyscrapers of a twentieth-century city. And yet by the close of the 1980s Venezuela too was beset by the severe problems common to the rest of the continent. Oil prices stagnated and fell back, and Venezuela was unable to meet the scheduled payments to service her large debt. Her economy was over-extended. The bonanza of 'black gold' did not benefit everybody.

Caracas in the 1990s was surrounded by some of the worst slum townships in Latin America, and there was a high birthrate among the poor. Despite the best system of roads in Latin America, the countryside was cut off and the number of Venezuelans making their living from it dropped rapidly from 40 per cent in 1950 to 18 per cent in 1980. The peasantry, largely landless, survived in conditions not much better than servitude; three-quarters of the land were held in large estates, despite land reforms introduced in the 1960s. Although from the 1920s until the Second World War Venezuela was the largest oil exporter, and in the early 1990s still ranked among the top producers, comparative wealth and economic development did not go hand in hand with enlightened politics and social policies.

Until 1958, Venezuela was renowned for being a country under the control of military caudillos. By shrewd manipulation a prosperous cattle raiser and coffee grower Juan Vicente Gómez had managed to make himself one of Latin America's longest-surviving dictators, remaining in office from the time he seized power in 1908 until his death in

1935. This was a remarkable effort, accompanied by corruption and self-aggrandisement. By the time of his death Gómez had acquired land equivalent in extent to Denmark and the Netherlands put together. Venezuela's development based on the oil industry, however, allowed a new professional and middle class to emerge, who were excluded from power by the landed elite and the military. They turned for support to the peasant masses and formed the Acción Democrática Party under the leadership of Rómulo Betancourt. In 1945, with the appearance of democratic government very much the fashion, Betancourt and his Acción Democrática seized power with the help of disgruntled members of the military. Reforms were attempted – land reform for the peasantry and an extension of the franchise in the constitution of 1947. Elections followed. But the military and landed elites threw out the newly elected President Rómulo Gallegos in November 1948 and for ten years Venezuela was ruled by the military. Under Pérez Jiménez (1953–8) the opposition was suppressed. 'Stability' suited the foreign, especially US, oil interests in Venezuela, and foreign technocrats developed the industry under Jiménez's benevolent eye.

In 1958 Jiménez and his corrupt government were overthrown in a military coup which for once had popular support, and Betancourt returned from exile. Vice-President Nixon arrived in Caracas on a Latin American goodwill mission to a rough reception from a stone-throwing crowd which identified the United States as the principal supporter of the former dictator Jiménez. The elections held in 1959 were won by the Acción Democrática Party, and Betancourt became the first president to complete his term of office, surviving many assassination attempts. The democratic process was at last striking firm roots, with peaceful transfers of presidential powers in subsequent elections. As far as land reform was concerned, however, the drive had gone out of the Acción Democrática, and the more conservative Christian Democratic Party, with which it alternated in power, blocked reform anyway. But in both health care and education,

Venezuela made significant progress during the Betancourt years.

The man who made the biggest impact on domestic politics was Carlos Andrés Pérez, who became president in 1974 and nationalised the iron and steel industry and the foreign-owned, mainly US, oil companies. Venezuela was distancing herself from US economic and political hegemony. Her joining with Mexico, Colombia and Panama in the 'Contadora' peace initiative to bring peace to Nicaragua and the other Central American states rent by guerrilla wars was another attempt to organise Latin American affairs without United States intervention.

From the mid-1980s Venezuela faced grave problems economically, with the fall in oil prices and the burgeoning foreign debt. Carlos Andrés Pérez returned as president after winning the election in 1988, but his introduction of an austerity programme in 1989 led to rioting in Caracas that left 300 dead. He had won the election on his promise to ease Venezuela's debt repayments. The oil-price rises of 1990 lightened the burden, but as long as Latin American states remained heavily dependent on the unpredictable price fluctuations of one or two commodities, while carrying large debts from earlier profligate development plans, their economies would remain precarious. The hardship caused by economic reform and austerity programmes repeatedly threatened the democracies with social unrest. The unequal distribution of wealth aggravated the problem. Despite a spurt of growth again in Venezuela in 1991, profits failed to trickle down to the poor. Early in the following year, Pérez's popularity had sunk very low and disaffected elements in the army, hit by declining wages, attempted a coup. Pérez was attempting to reform the democratic process shot through with corruption. Narcotics became a major export besides oil. In hard times the people became disillusioned with their unprincipled democracy. Democracy in Latin America has few friends when the people are made to suffer from the economic measures implemented by their elected presidents.

# CHAPTER 71

# Central America in Revolution: Costa Rica, Nicaragua, Honduras, El Salvador, Guatemala, Panama and Mexico

In the 1980s, revolution, civil war and the anti-communist drive of the United States in the Western hemisphere turned world attention to Central America. The year 1990 marked a turning point in these bloody Central American conflicts. The civil war in Nicaragua ended. After a fair election the Marxist Sandinista regime stepped down and handed the government peacefully over to the opposition.

There are six states wholly in Central America: Costa Rica, Nicaragua, Honduras, El Salvador, Panama and Guatemala. Their combined population was only about 26 million in 1989, though population growth had been very high in the region, as it had been throughout Latin America.

Indeed, population growth in the early 1990s threatened to prevent any increase in the standard of living and to condemn the masses to deprivation and poverty. In addition, the resources that were available were not shared fairly. The continuing inequalities were most marked in the unjust distribution of the available land. The wildly fluctuating prices for the agricultural exports of coffee, bananas and cotton, on which these nations were still dependent, created a severe economic crisis, because the prices of manufactured imports did not move in unison, while the cost of oil imports reached dizzying heights before falling back and rising again in 1990.

An attempt was made in the 1970s to create more balanced economies which would rely less on manufactured imports and develop import-substituting industries. Ten years later this only added to the general economic calamities of the majority of Latin American nations. In common with the rest of Latin America the Central American states borrowed heavily from bankers flush with Middle Eastern oil money. The result was that a crushing debt burden, getting ever larger with high interest rates, turned the apparently temporary difficulties of the 1970s into permanent crises. Of course, the difficulties never were just temporary. Political and social reforms, including a redistribution of land, were indispensable preconditions of better economic and social health. The causes of Central America's problems required radical remedies, regional as well as international. Nothing short of a massive effort could stabilise the region – an effort of will on the part of the developed world to cease protecting its own markets and to pay higher prices for Central America's agricultural exports, as well as to guarantee these prices against

**Population** (*millions*)

|  | 1920 | 1940 | 1960 | 1980 | 1989 |
|---|---|---|---|---|---|
| Costa Rica | 0.42 | 0.62 | 1.25 | 2.2 | 2.7 |
| Nicaragua | 0.64 | 0.83 | 1.41 | 2.6 | 3.7 |
| Honduras | 0.72 | 1.15 | 1.95 | 3.7 | 5.0 |
| El Salvador | 1.17 | 1.63 | 2.45 | 4.75 | 5.1 |
| Guatemala | 1.23 | 2.2 | 3.8 | 7.3 | 8.9 |

wild fluctuations. International bankers would also need to write down their investments realistically, while wealthy Latin Americans would have to invest in their own economies instead of sending their money abroad.

In 1961 hopes and expectations had been raised by President Kennedy when he launched the Alliance for Progress. His aim was to transform Latin America's economic and social ills by peaceful means. This was to be the free world's democratic answer to the Marxist revolutionary challenge. But enough aid to meet the enormous economic problems was not forthcoming; much of what was given was diverted to military security against social revolution in the 1960s. Social revolution and a more equitable distribution of wealth and land was condemned by the powerful elites in Latin America, who claimed these measures would open the way for communism. Just as fearful of far-reaching reforms were the Latin American middle classes. Thus there was no will for political and social change among the ruling and influential groups. Yet this lay at the very heart of what the Alliance for Progress was supposed to be about. Consequently, no real partnership or alliance could develop between the United States and the Latin American oligarchies. It was more a marriage of convenience. With the death of Kennedy and Johnson's growing preoccupation with Vietnam, the Alliance petered out as more democratic and socially responsible regimes failed to evolve. The Alliance for Progress did not achieve for Latin America what the Marshall Plan had done for Europe. The cycle of violence, deprivation and revolution was not broken in the 1960s, 1970s and 1980s; the answer given to Marxist revolution was military suppression.

However, in some of the Central American states a certain amount of progress was achieved, especially in Costa Rica and Honduras; but even here it was too little; in the others – Nicaragua, El Salvador and Guatemala – repression and the murder of peasants and of the urban opposition goaded into armed terrorist resistance created a thirty-year cycle of bloodshed and violence. Despite Washington's good intentions in pushing for democratic and economic improvements and for an end to the abuse of the most fundamental human rights, the image of the United States was marred, especially during the two Reagan administrations (1981–9) by the priority given to security and to efforts to halt the spread of Marxism in the Caribbean and South and Central America. The misery and destruction borne by the people through the years of revolution, civil wars and conflict were a terrible price to pay.

Costa Rica is the most fortunate of the Central American states, free from civil war (except for a brief period in 1948), with a GNP per capita in 1987 of $1610 with the highest income per head of population and one more equitably distributed than elsewhere in Latin America. It is also the only Latin American nation with something approaching an established democratic parliamentary system. Abuses of human rights are not totally absent, as Amnesty International reports reveal; but their scale is small compared to those of the other states. Yet Costa Rica did not escape the economic crises of debt and unbalanced development brought to a head by the quadrupling of oil prices in 1979–80.

Costa Rica had established a constitutional liberal state in the 1920s with free and fair elections. The collapse of coffee prices, on which she depended, had a devastating effect throughout Central America. The more liberal oligarchic parliamentary governments in the region gave way to the strongmen, the caudillos, who would preserve the interests of landowners and merchants and meet the threat of labour and social unrest. Only in Costa Rica, with her strong constitutional tradition, was the *caudillismo* somewhat softened in the 1930s and 1940s by regular presidential elections. José Figueres was the outstanding political leader to emerge in the post-1945 period. Reformist Costa Rica enjoys an extensive social-welfare programme, and José Figueres's revolutionary junta (1948–9) strengthened the parliamentary tradition. Women were enfranchised and after losing the elections Figueres stood down. Perhaps the junta's most unusual action, given the Latin American context, was to abolish the army. Still, by Western standards, Costa Rican constitutionalism had decided defects. Organised labour was harshly repressed, reforms would be granted from above rather than negotiated with workers and peasant organisations from below. Figueres was elected president in 1953 and extended his reforms to welfare, health and education. As in most of Latin America, standards of living in the early 1990s remained tied to agricultural prices and the cost of manufactured imports. Despite diversification of the economy, coffee and bananas were still the backbone of exports. The problems of the 1970s and 1980s burdened Costa Rica with a huge foreign debt.

Meanwhile internationally, Costa Rica, which aided the Sandinistas in the overthrow of the Somoza dictatorship in neighbouring Nicaragua, was drawn into the struggle between the Nicaraguan Marxist regime and the United States. She became the far from enthusiastic host to the Contra bases along her borders. Her President, Oscar Arias Sánchez, was a leading proponent of attempts to mediate peace in the region (page 729). The end of the civil war in Nicaragua and the electoral defeat of the Marxist regime in 1990 lessened tension and promised a better future as the presidency changed hands and Arias Sánchez left office.

Honduras, in contrast to Costa Rica, is by far the poorest of Central American states, and its high birthrate impedes efforts to raise living standards substantially. The income per head of population in 1987 was only $810. Look up Honduras in the index of a Latin American history and the first subheading is 'bananas', yet the miserable returns from the foreign-dominated banana plantations kept the country poor and under-developed. Honduras is the most apt example of a 'banana republic', practically speaking under US economic control because Americans own most of the agricultural sector and much else besides. US administrations wanted to see progress towards constitutional democratic government and rising living standards, especially during the years of the Kennedy Alliance for Progress, but this would have necessitated agrarian reform, the raising of agricultural wages, and the acceptance of some of the demands made by labour organisations, which in turn would have damaged the interests of American investors. Official Washington had its own set of priorities. Foremost among them was a wish to halt the growth of the left. Although the United States wished to promote democracy and human rights, the authoritarian military rulers were regarded as safer allies, as well as providing a better guarantee of security for investors.

The policies adopted by Washington from Kennedy to Reagan varied, but ideological and security concerns in the last resort predominated. In 1954, a successful strike by the banana workers against the United Fruit Company ushered in a period of unexpected change in this most backward of republics. After a period of political turmoil

Villeda Morales became president and attempted, like Arbenz in Guatemala and Figueres in Costa Rica, to reform Honduras's rigid social structure and to transform society from above. But when land reforms threatened to hurt the interests of the United Fruit Company, Washington forced a retreat. In 1963 a vicious and bloody military coup overthrew Morales. Although Honduras gradually returned to civilian rule in 1981, the army with its American-trained officers remains, behind the constitutional façade, the real power in the nation. The economy cannot free itself from foreign domination, and progress has been slow, while corruption is rife. In the conflict with Nicaragua, however, Honduras was the most important ally of the United States and was host to the principal Contra bases. Even after the end of the Nicaraguan conflict, she remained politically unstable.

The problems besetting Guatemala are those of a nation half of whose population, the 4 million Mayan Indians, do not share any sense of identity with the other, white Spanish-American half. The gross income per head of population in 1987 was only $870. Power resided with the army and the coffee-growing elite. For a century, from the mid-nineteenth to the mid-twentieth, four caudillos ruled the country. The first hope for the poor and illiterate majority came in 1944 with a small middle-class revolution supported by sections of the army. Free elections brought to power Juan José Arévalo (1945–50) and Colonel Jacobo Arbenz Guzmán (1951–4). Forced labour was abolished, social reforms were initiated and extended to the Indians, a labour code and land reforms were started. Arévalo had opened government to the left and Arbenz accelerated the process, thereby thoroughly alarming the land-owning aristocracy and Washington, which believed that communism was gaining the upper hand. US-owned companies and land belonging to the United Fruit Company were nationalised, and more nationalisation was threatened. The Communist Party was legalised,

With the help of the CIA, Arbenz was overthrown in 1954 (page 516). The clock was turned back; the old oligarchy and the United Fruit Company regained their influence, with the army now again the real power in the land. There were thousands of killings and the Marxist labour movement was wiped out. Corrupt and inefficient military-run regimes became the despair of the American advisers, who could see no alternative other than the communists. In 1960, Guatemala became the staging post for the invasion of Cuba. After another military coup in 1963, the military remained in control of Guatemala until 1982. The repression of guerrillas and leftist opponents was particularly bloody – the civil war killed 120,000. The sheer extent of the abuse of human rights was unequalled in degree even by the low standards of Central America. Labour leaders, university teachers and political opponents just 'disappeared'; 40,000 are estimated to have died in this way. By the early 1980s the army chiefs fought each other for the spoils of office – and this was the army which had received substantial US military aid. Amnesty in 1982 accused the Guatemalan government of mass-acring 2600 people, and that was an underestimate.

Guatemalan politics are subject to a cycle of hope and disillusionment. In 1986 Vinicio Cerezo Arévalo was inaugurated as a popular reforming president. The hope was that he would end the brutal excesses of the generals who had dominated Guatemala for three decades and under whose authority the security forces had murdered an estimated 65,000 civilians. But the reforms did not last. The military soon began to exert their power again. Death squads resumed their murderous missions, killing student leaders, trade unionists and human-rights advocates. Guatemala became a profitable transit point for Colombian cocaine on its way to the cities of the United States. Almost half the population was unemployed and inflation was high; civilian government in 1990 was losing control and making little effort to check violence, crime or corruption. In January 1991 Jorge Serrano Elías became president and assumed the burdens of trying to end violence and restore the economy.

El Salvador's descent into civil war and bloody conflict was equally tragic. It is the smallest and most densely populated Central American republic. Some forty families owned most of the coffee plantations and dominated banking and the mercantile sector. The distribution of wealth is grossly unequal and the per-capita income of $860 in 1987 was almost as low as that of Honduras.

The history of peasant uprisings and protests is a grisly one. A communist-inspired peasant revolt ended in 1932 in wholesale slaughter, a precedent for contemporary times. Here too US attitudes after the Second World War were shaped by the fear of communist penetration. Alliances between the wealthy oligarchy and the military were regarded as the only viable alternative and the United States has supported them, thereby impeding reform and change. In 1969, El Salvador briefly went to war with Honduras and the resulting victory further enhanced the prestige of the military. But the military and oligarchy began to be challenged by the rise of an urban middle sector. José Napoleon Duarte led a rapidly expanding Christian Democratic Party. By the 1970s there appeared to be a possibility of more representative government. It was a false hope. In 1972, the army frustrated the election that would have brought Duarte to power and he barely escaped with his life. But repression in El Salvador did not bring stability. The economic deterioration following on the oil-price rise in 1973–4 led to increased guerrilla activities as more and more Salvadorans became desperate. It also led to another 'dirty war'. Brief efforts at reform were superseded by military regimes which paid no regard to human rights. Worldwide attention was directed to the methods of the hated regime when Archbishop Oscar Romero, an outspoken critic of these abuses, was murdered in 1980. Right-wing death squads set about murdering whomever earned their disapproval. In 1980 alone there were close to 10,000 political murders. The civil war rages on and the United States has aided and trained the Salvadoran army to crush the guerrillas, who terrorise the countryside. Under pressure from the Reagan administration internationally supervised elections were held in 1982, but the guerrillas refused to lay down their arms and participate. The extreme right won, but in 1984 the more moderate Christian Democrat José Duarte was finally elected president.

Under heavy US pressure, civilian rule and regular elections appeared to change El Salvador's politics for the better. But the government was hardly in control: guerrillas dominated regions of the countryside, and the army remained a law unto itself. The activities of right-wing death squads lessened – the United States could claim an improvement in the human-rights position – but so many thousands had fallen victim that the urban population was cowed. The Reagan administration in the 1980s gave $6 billion in aid and by lobbying for land reform hoped to undercut support for the guerrillas and to promote democracy. But Duarte did not solve the political or economic problems of

El Salvador and the Marxist-led guerrillas provided evidence of their ability to strike by knocking out nearly all the electricity supplies on the eve of the Congressional elections in 1988. People who bothered to vote turned to the right. The small country was ravaged by civil war which by the early 1990s had claimed at least 70,000 lives and by left-wing and right-wing terror. Almost half the population was unemployed. Duarte, on whom Washington's hopes rested, was terminally ill from cancer and his influence weakened. He was replaced in the election of June 1989 by Alfredo Cristiani, the candidate of the extreme right-wing party. Guerrilla terrorism and right-wing death squads continued to abuse human rights. Despite substantial US economic and military aid, the future for El Salvador remained as uncertain as ever, though the outgoing UN Secretary General Javier Pérez de Cuellar brokered a peace plan in December 1991. On 1 February 1992 a peace agreement was concluded, which promised reforms and UN-supervised elections in 1994.

In Nicaragua Washington saw the greatest challenge to United States interests in the 1980s and to Latin American progress towards constitutional democratic governments. The Marxist state which emerged after 1979, which was hostile to private enterprise and nationalised foreign-owned interests, also faced severe economic problems. They were in part due to the economic embargoes of the United States, which could not be fully compensated for by trade with Europe or loans from sources not under the control of the United States; they were also due to the inefficiency of planned socialist economies as evidenced for example in Cuba.

Nicaragua is the most thinly populated state in Central America, with the lowest per-capita income after Honduras, at $830 in 1987. Here too can be found the link between the dominance of coffee and bananas as Nicaragua's principal exports, until disease in the 1930s devastated the crop, and the gross disparity of wealth between the few plantation owners and merchants and a landless peasantry, the largest in Central America. Diversification into beef, cotton and sugar in the 1960s could not compensate for the low income from agricultural exports and the declining terms of trade (commodity export prices rising more slowly or falling, as against rising costs of manufactured imports and in the 1970s the rising cost of oil). On such a social and economic basis,

democracy could not be built up; on the contrary, deprivation and extremes of wealth and poverty provided the soil for revolt and savage repression.

Nicaragua has traditionally been an area of US concern. When disorder and foreign financial claims threatened her in 1912, US marines moved in and did not finally leave until January 1933. By then they had had to cope with a nationalist backlash. Augusto César Sandino led a guerrilla campaign against them and against the Nicaraguan government they were supporting. He was tricked into taking part in negotiations by the Nicaraguan leaders whom the marines had left behind in power, and in 1934 he was murdered by the Nicaraguan National Guard. Sandino was a liberal reformist and patriot, and now he became a martyr, a powerful symbol whose name and mantle the Marxist Sandinistas appropriated in their struggles during the 1970s against the rule of the Somoza family.

The Somozas had established a dynasty in Nicaragua. In the 1930s power in the country was wielded by the National Guard, which had been organised by the United States to maintain internal security. At its head was General Anastasio Somoza Garcia. The constitutional institutions were a façade behind which the National Guard operated. In 1937 Somoza made himself president and ruled the country for the next nineteen years, until he was assassinated in 1956. His authoritarian rule became notorious for corruption, nepotism and repression. This was not a turn of events Washington had anticipated when creating the supposedly non-political National Guard, but defence of constitutional proprieties was not high on Washington's list of priorities, as long as US interests were safeguarded. Somoza's National Guard was preferable to having to send in US marines. Somoza took care not to offend US interests and aligned Nicaragua as a dependent and reliable US ally. He was also adept at manipulating the political and landed interests at home. In the division of spoils, the National Guard were pampered, and plantation owners and merchants were allowed to reap unhindered the profits of their enterprises. This left the vast majority of the population in wretched poverty, illiterate and with no hope for the future. On Somoza's assassination his eldest son Luis took over the presidency and the younger son, Anastasio Jr, assumed command of the National Guard. The 1950s and 1960s were relatively peaceful in Nicaragua, a period of diversification into cotton and other crops; a small but growing middle class began to emerge with the help of Alliance dollars, and some economic progress was achieved. But for the peasants the expansion of cotton-growing meant displacement from the land.

Luis was the 'weakest' of the Somozas, and in 1967 Anastasio assumed the presidency. Nicaragua's most bloody and repressive decade now began. Anastasio made no pretence of ruling as a politician. He used the naked power of the National Guard, employing murder and torture to crush the growing opposition. When a devastating earthquake in 1972 all but destroyed Managua, Nixon sent large-scale aid. It did not reach the victims; only half of it could be accounted for by the Nicaraguan Treasury. Corruption was rife, and for a time the National Guard could keep order only with US help. Reconstruction after the earthquake benefited mainly Somoza's supporters, not the poor. The guerrilla war flared up and National Guard atrocities perpetrated in repressing the guerrillas outraged the Church. Human-rights abuses were now affecting American support. There was growing opposition in the United States to providing dollars in support of ruthless dictators, yet even under President Carter military aid continued to be granted to Somoza, since the alternative of a Marxist-led Nicaragua was regarded as totally unacceptable. But the abuses of Somoza and his National Guard, worldwide condemnation and the evident crumbling of Somoza's power left the Carter administration little alternative but to abandon all support for the regime by the spring of 1979. A few weeks later, in July, Somoza was overthrown by the broad opposition coalition of guerrillas, the Sandinista National Liberation Front (FSLN).

The abuses of the Somoza family, their amassing of enormous wealth and the general corruption had made them many enemies, especially among those who had not shared the spoils. These groups ranged from the right, conservatives opposed to any genuine democratic reform, through to the professional and mercantile middle sectors, and to the socialists and Marxists. It was an alliance of the left that formed the first guerrilla groups of the 1960s, recruiting support from peasants and students. The corruption and repression following on the Managuan earthquake of 1972 broadened the opposition. After the assassination in 1978 of the respected editor of the leading newspaper in Nicaragua, *La Prensa*, the middle class and conservatives were ready to support armed opposition against Somoza. FSLN forces with Cuban help were now well organised and, in a series of attacks, demoralised the National Guard and seized power on 19 July 1979. Somoza fled the country.

The revolutionary junta was dominated by the Marxist–Leninist leadership from the start. Decision-making was collective. FSLN's most influential figures were the hardline Tomás Borge Martinez and the two brothers Humberto Ortega and Daniel Ortega. The junta was more pragmatic than most communist regimes, permitting some degree of political plurality and private ownership. But it was equally determined on the Leninist Soviet model to retain real power and build a socialist society. The National Assembly reflected the firm control the junta exercised over the country through the revolutionary party, the army and the state security services. Until its closure in 1986, *La Prensa* remained a lone voice in opposition. Throughout the country there was censorship and control of the domestic media. During the 1980s, splits began to occur among the junta. The more moderate coalition partners of the original Council of State went into exile, leaving the country under the domination of the FSLN. In exile also were remnants of Somoza's National Guard and dissidents from FSLN's regime. Together they formed disparate guerrilla bands on Nicaragua's borders, the so-called Contras, who, with the help of supplies from the United States, waged a guerrilla war against the Sandinistas.

Within Nicaragua the junta did not honour its commitment in 1979 to establish a democracy, but postponed elections until its power was consolidated in 1984. Daniel Ortega became president. By adopting a programme of reforms from above, and by mobilising nationalist feelings against the United States and her support for the Contras, the junta was able to dominate Nicaragua for a decade, backed by the powerful party and security apparatus. The main opposition refused to participate in elections before 1990. In health-care, housing and particularly education, the Sandinistas nevertheless achieved progress. State planning and land reforms were instituted more gradually. But the combination of the effects of the civil war, the huge resources devoted to building up a large army to fight the US-backed Contras and US economic embargoes devastated the Nicaraguan economy. Only the limited Soviet and European assistance enabled the

*Guerrillas under the command of Eden Pastora prepare to overthrow the Somoza regime in Nicaragua, November 1978.*

Sandinistas to survive. But Moscow's own economic troubles led to a cut in aid, and the Soviet–US rapprochement forced Daniel Ortega and the Sandinista leadership to modify their policies and invite a more genuine popular mandate through free elections. The Contras, at the same time, despite Reagan's strong support, were being denied essential war supplies by the US Congress's refusal to supply the funds.

These conditions provided an opportunity for the long-drawn-out peace negotiations sponsored by Colombia, Mexico, Panama and Venezuela, whose presidents met on the island of Contadora in the early 1980s, and then by Costa Rica's President. Arias Sánchez's peace plan was signed by the presidents of Costa Rica, El Salvador, Guatemala, Honduras and Nicaragua in August 1987 and earned Arias Sánchez the Nobel Peace Prize. It called for regional ceasefires in all the guerrilla wars, democratic reforms and the ending of foreign support for the rebels. It marked an attempt by the Central American leaders to solve their own problems without outside interference. In Washington, the Reagan administration greeted the peace plan with scepticism and suspicion. It was difficult to believe that the Sandinista leadership had any other motive but to persuade the US Congress that

the US administration's support for the Contras was an obstacle to peace; then, with Contra pressure removed, the Sandinistas would be able to rule with impunity. As it turned out, Arias Sánchez's optimism, despite many setbacks, proved at least partially justified. Daniel Ortega had changed: he was no longer the Marxist–Leninist revolutionary leader determined to build a socialist Nicaragua at all costs. The failures in Nicaragua were all too obvious. Daniel Ortega now took the lead in following the *perestroika* line. In April 1990, free elections were held in Nicaragua and the opposition won, to the surprise of the Sandinistas. Ortega handed over power peacefully to Violeta Chamorro. Violeta Chamorro in turn followed a policy of reconciliation acceptable first of all to the Sandinistas, who were allowed to retain command of the army, and acceptable in the end to the Contras as well, who abandoned the armed struggle. At least for war-shattered Nicaragua the future began to look a little more hopeful as the guerrillas gave up the armed struggle. But the economy remained in dire straits, with almost half the population unemployed.

Latin America after the early 1960s experienced accelerating economic and social change. Its traditional power structures adapted by increasing reliance on military force and repression, or they shared power with other sectors of society but still placed reliance on the military to check organised peasant and urban labour groups, as happened in Brazil. Socialist alternatives were never able to retain power; the hostility of the United States ensured support for anti-socialist opposition forces in Guatemala (1954), the Dominican Republic (1965), Chile (1973), Grenada (1983) and finally Nicaragua. The Soviet Union was in no position to challenge the United States effectively in the Western hemisphere.

During the 1980s, Latin American political developments came to seem more in conformity with Western hopes and American intentions. Military regimes receded in Ecuador, Peru, Bolivia, Uruguay and Brazil. Colombia, Venezuela and Costa Rica were already ruled by civilian governments. Indirectly the United States helped to bring about the fall of the military junta in Argentina. By providing intelligence to London, crucial assistance was given to Britain's recapture of the Falklands in 1982, a blow the junta could not survive. In the Caribbean, the worst of the dictators, Duvalier, had been forced from Haiti into exile (1986); the leftist regime in Grenada, which had lapsed into murderous infighting, was eliminated by a US invasion in 1983, to the evident relief of the local population. What had led the Reagan administration to intervene was its determination to halt the spread of Cuban influence. After a long struggle and despite many setbacks, US policies also succeeded in making authoritarian Marxist rule by the Sandinistas untenable. US policies in Central America and the Caribbean (see Chapter 72) in the 1980s were an update of the Monroe Doctrine, which was justified by the need to exclude great powers from beyond the hemisphere – Britain and Germany before 1914, the Soviet Union after the Second World War.

The United States has continued since the Spanish-American War of 1898 to occupy the Guátanamo naval base in Cuba. And ever since Alfred Thayer Mahan highlighted the crucial strategic importance of a transisthmian canal in the 1890s, the United States was determined to assure herself of predominant influence in Panama and to exercise sovereign control over any canal that might be constructed.

In 1903, ardent Panamanian nationalism against Colombian rule provided the opportunity. The United States helped the Panamanian revolution but exacted a price: control of the future canal. Herein lies the crux of Panamanian history in the twentieth century. Ostensibly independent and sovereign, Panama was little more than a US colony for six decades. Panamanian nationalism was inflamed by the country's lack of sovereignty in the canal zone and by the extensive rights the United States exercised over her economy and her foreign policy. She was ruled by a wealthy and corrupt oligarchy of the kind common in Latin America, but one which was also required to accept a client relationship with the United States. If popular riots occurred, US troops intervened to suppress them. In Panama too, the United Fruit Company enjoyed extensive land and rights. Payments made by the United States for use of the canal zone were an important prop for the economy, at times providing a third of Panama's national income (bananas and sugar are other important resources). President Roosevelt's attempts to construct a 'good neighbour' policy could not convincingly reconcile Panamanian nationalism, resurgent in the 1930s, and US interests. The 1936 Canal Treaty was wonderfully ambiguous. 'The Canal zone', it stated, 'is territory of the Republic of Panama under the jurisdiction of the United States.' In the 1950s and 1960s popular resentment against the United States grew, and 1964 saw widespread riots.

After 1968 the political oligarchs lost power to Panama's National Guard. Any pretence at even a corrupt democratic constitutional process was abandoned and General Omar Torrijos emerged as the undisputed authoritarian leader. He inaugurated harsh labour laws but also a radical programme of land reform with a populist promise that he would help the poor. He also gained support by adopting a stridently nationalist stance on the issue of the US-controlled canal and canal zone. After thirteen years of negotiating with successive US administrations, carefully controlling the pressure of mass nationalism and anti-American feeling, Torrijos in 1977 concluded a new canal treaty with the Carter administration, which was ratified by the US Senate in the following year only with considerable difficulty and the addition of reservations. In stages the canal is to pass under the control of Panama by the year 2000. Yet the United States is guaranteed passage of the canal in perpetuity for her merchant ships and warships, and she is entitled to use force to protect these rights after the year 2000 if Panamanian troops fail to do so. Panama secured something less than total sovereignty.

The 1980s saw the nadir of Panamanian–US relations. Torrijos died in an aircrash in 1981, which may have been arranged. General Manuel Noriega, an unscrupulous and brutal soldier, soon took his place. He had been recruited by the CIA, which was anxious to make use of his contacts to uncover the drug trade passing from Colombia to Panama and on to the United States. Embarrassingly, Noriega drew huge profits from the drug trade himself; indeed, in corruption and brutality no previous Panamanian dictator compared. He transformed the National Guard into the Panama Defence Forces, with new powers, to act as his tool of repression. Even so, GNP per capita (the population was 2.3 million) rose to $2240 in 1987. The elections of 1984, which allowed his nominee to become president, were a farce. The United States now tried to rid Panama of the General. In 1988, Noriega was indicted for drug trafficking in the US. He countered by beating the anti-American nationalist drum. President Reagan's pressure and economic sanctions were not enough to topple him, nor two attempted military coups which enjoyed US goodwill. In May 1989 Noriega held elections again, but when the leader of the opposition, Guillermo Endara, gathered most votes despite intimidation from Noriega's thugs, the results were falsified. On 20 December 1989, President Bush cut the Gordian knot and 24,000 US troops descended on Panama City to arrest and overthrow Noriega. He fled to the Embassy of the Vatican but gave himself up in January 1990. He was tried and sent to prison. Guillermo Endara was installed as president of Panama. It is the end of a chapter but not of a book. Panamanian–US relations were unlikely to run smoothly for the rest of the century.

The hemispheric role of the United States was also deeply resented in Mexico. Yet no country was more dependent on the United States economically. Within the Organisation of American States, Marxist Cuba and Nicaragua had in Mexico their only supporter. She made her own revolution in 1911, the first large Third World country to declare her independence from Western colonial and economic domination. In 1848 she had lost nearly half of her territory, from Texas to California, to the United States, only to suffer occupation by the

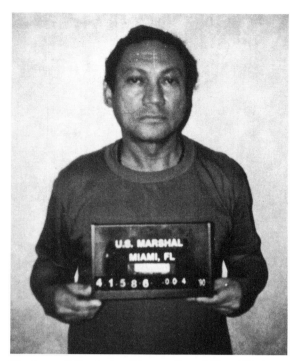

*The drug-trafficking leader of Panama, General Manuel Noriega, is captured and arraigned in Miami, Florida.*

French (1863–7); stability finally came to Mexico when General Porfirio Díaz seized power in 1876 and maintained it for thirty-five years until 1911. Economic progress was spectacular; a wealthy Creole upper class saw in Europe the civilisation to follow, but the masses of Indian peasants were landless labourers, working on the haciendas of the large landowners. The Catholic Church and the military were the two pillars on whose support Díaz relied. In the towns, Mexican labourers were employed in sweat-shops and textile mills at low wages.

The Mexican Revolution began in 1910 with a split among the ruling oligarchy. Díaz was toppled with surprising ease in 1911 and new elections brought a more liberal-minded president to power. But the fall of Díaz began an avalanche. The great hero of the Mexican revolution was Emiliano Zapata, who on his white charger became the romantic martyr of the revolution. In 1913 Mexico was plunged into civil war. Zapata led a peasant army, and a flamboyant ex-cattle rustler, Pancho Villa, fashioned a small but effective mercenary force against the repressive dictator, General Victoriano Huerta, who now occupied the presidential palace. In 1914 Huerta faced a third enemy.

*Emiliano Zapata, 1911.*

Woodrow Wilson sent in the marines and Huerta fled. The outcome of the Mexican revolution remained in doubt until 1923. By then both Villa and Zapata had been killed by government forces.

Despite the socialist rhetoric of the Mexican constitution, reform would be instituted from above – peasants and workers were not to become the arbiters of power. There were to be no revolutionary social upheavals. The secularisation of the state and the expropriation of Church wealth were important outcomes of the revolution. An alliance between the military, the wealthy and the middle class consolidated the powers of the presidents, and their followers were rewarded by the spoils of office. But the difference between Mexico and other Latin American countries is that an effective party organisation, renamed several times and since 1945 called the Partido Revolucionario Institucional (PRI), controls the country and embraces workers and peasants as well as the rising middle-income groups. Lázaro Cárdenas, president from 1934 to 1940, developed a corporate state in which each section

of the population, workers, peasants, the military, the middle class, was placed under the party umbrella as groups rather than as individuals. Through large-scale land distribution Cárdenas carried forward one of the principal aims of the revolution, breaking up the haciendas and granting the land as private plots or joint peasant farms; another aim was to take control of Mexico's major resources, the most important of which was oil. Cárdenas nationalised the largely US-owned oil companies. Dissatisfied with the compensation received, but even more disturbed that other countries might follow Mexico's example, the international oil companies boycotted her oil and inhibited development of the state oil company until uncertainties in the Middle East after the Second World War made Mexican oil too valuable a Western resource not to be utilised.

Westerners regarded Mexico as a truly revolutionary country for a number of reasons: the attack on the Church, the official government espousal of atheism, nationalisation, reforms which hurt the wealthy landowners, the propagation of the myth of a peasants' and workers' revolution and admiration for Marx and Lenin, the assertion of a Mexican identity and pride in her Indian roots, immortalised by the political–historical murals of Mexico's most famous artist, Diego Rivera, and the granting of asylum to Leon Trotsky. In fact Mexico conformed far more closely to Latin American patterns than to the Soviet model. In any case the authoritarian state was not exclusive to the Soviet Union but was common among the fascist nations of Europe in the 1930s. Private property in the early 1990s remained the source of great wealth in Mexico for a minority, while poverty was the lot of the peasants and the urban masses, the high birthrate undermining efforts to raise living standards. Mexico too had seen extensive migration from country to city. In ten years, from 1970 to 1980, Mexico City increased its population by 7 million to 15 million, with a huge marginalised population living in shanty slums. The population of the country as a whole grew from 25.8 million in 1950 to 34.9 million in 1960, to 84.6 million in 1989 (by which year the gross per-capita income was US $2010).

The Mexican state is a conglomeration of elements of socialism, state planning and a constitutional electoral process. Mexico enjoys a surfeit of elections for mayors, governors, assemblies and the president; some opposition parties are tolerated and compete. Presidential elections have occurred every six years, and the presidency has always changed hands peacefully, so the spoils are regularly redistributed. But only one party, the PRI, dominates and has decided the outcome of national and presidential elections. Miguel de la Madrid Hurtado, candidate of the PRI, was elected president in 1982 with a vote of over 74 per cent.

Distribution of land to the *campesinos*, the peasant owners of smallholdings, and revolutionary rhetoric have kept the majority of peasants quiet as the 1990s began, engaged in trying to make a subsistence living. The seasonal and illegal exodus across the 2000-mile border into the United States provided a safety valve for tens of thousands of the poor. Even so, in urban areas where most Mexicans live there was massive unemployment. The well-to-do were surrounded by mass poverty. The middle classes enjoyed the high standard of living which the growth and diversification of the Mexican economy had made possible, while the spoils of office were used to ensure a faithful following for the incumbent president and the dominant PRI party. There was more freedom in Mexico than in many Latin American states, but it was carefully controlled. Most sections of the population tended to accept their lack of political influence. In any case the state had a special security police which, according to Amnesty reports, in the early 1990s continued to employ torture and murder against anyone considered to disturb Mexico's political order. In Mexico too, hundreds 'disappeared', but repression was not on the same vast scale as Argentina or Chile experienced. Mexican stability rested for four decades on a revolutionary myth and authoritarian conservative control.

Below the surface, the rapid economic changes caused dissatisfaction with the authoritarian style of government to grow. During the Olympic Games in 1968, widespread student protest led to the killings of hundreds in Mexico City and attracted worldwide attention. In the early 1970s guerrilla bands appeared but were suppressed by the security services. With the enormous increases in oil prices engineered by OPEC (of which Mexico was not a member) and new oil discoveries, export earnings after 1975 increased ten times to US$20 billion. But lavish expenditure and ambitious development resulted in high inflation. The end of the oil boom in the 1980s and worldwide economic stagnation burst the Mexican bubble. Heavy foreign borrowing

and austerity programmes drastically reduced standards of living, while the birthrate, if it continued unabated, would double the population every twenty years; and half the population was under sixteen years of age. Mexico was saddled with one of the largest foreign debts in the world, whose payment had to be periodically rescheduled; the bankers demanded austerity and Mexico found herself caught between trying to satisfy international financiers by making economies, while trying to prevent internal unrest as a result of policies imposed externally. The inability of the regime to cope effectively with the catastrophic earthquake which hit Mexico City in September 1985 added to a loss of credibility, which was compounded by Mexico's economic crises. The stability maintained by the political system began to look increasingly fragile. The right-wing opposition Partido de Acción Nacional (PAN) claimed massive electoral fraud, but the ruling PRI made few concessions. Despite misgivings about the undemocratic nature of Mexican politics, Washington saw a greater danger in further destabilising Mexico and provided financial support. In the 1988 presidential elections the PRI candidate, Carlos Salinas de Gortari, claimed to have won. There was fraud on a colossal scale, but the PRI monopoly of power had been broken in the Mexican Congress. Nevertheless, the PRI President remained firmly in power and an economic austerity programme was instituted. But for the first time in many decades there were indications of future political changes.

In 1961, Kennedy's Alliance for Progress was to have been the starting point for the transformation of Latin America. The cycle of deprivation, economic and social injustice was to have been broken and Latin American societies were to have started on the road to political democratic reform. Over thirty years later the problems of the continent were still daunting. Population growth outstripped development. The danger of Marxist revolution had been contained, but terrorism and repression continued. The root causes of instability had not been removed. The immigration from the countryside had swollen the shanty towns that surrounded the fashionable streets of the wealthy. Everywhere there were thousands of children begging, stealing or offering themselves for prostitution. Mexico City served as but one example of their plight. The *pependores*, or rubbish pickers (10,000 of them), made the City's three huge rubbish dumps their home. Even here they were exploited by 'bosses' who made their money out of the refuse that could be recycled.

By turning to a market economy, privatising and liberalising trade with the expected coming into operation of a free-trade region comprising herself, the United States and Canada, Mexico hoped in the 1990s to create her own economic miracle. Many companies were privatised and in 1990/1 a good growth rate was achieved, while inflation, which in 1987 ran at 160 per cent, was slashed in 1992 to 12 per cent. Foreign debts were reduced and foreign investment began to return. Salinas toured the country and won support among the peasantry. He used proceeds from the sale of state-owned companies to build schools, to link rural communities with the electricity network and to ensure that clean drinking water was available. More than 1200 health clinics were opened in 1991 to serve the Indian peoples. Huge problems remained. Carlos Salinas de Gortari declared that his aim during his six-year term of office as president from 1988 to 1994 was to take Mexico from Third World to First World status. During the first years of his presidency he made a dynamic start.

There were at last some hopeful indications of change in Latin America in the 1990s. A number of countries are determinedly trying to turn the economic corner and make a start on raising the standard of living of the most deprived.

The enormous level of Latin American debt, which had risen from $68 billion in 1975 to $410 billion in 1987, threatened to cripple efforts towards further investment and development. But, unable to recover all of it, the West agreed to write a portion of it off. Western institutions such as the International Monetary Fund insisted on the medicine of austerity and better economic management,

which Mexico had to accept in order to attract new funds. Among left-wing guerrilla movements there was a collapse of morale following the demise of the Soviet Union. All but Marxist fanatics were ready to end the fighting and to exchange the rifle for the ballot box. Civilian elected governments and multi-party parliaments became the norm. It was not democracy, but it was progress, a move away from tyrannical and authoritarian regimes.

Even so, there was no guarantee that democratic representative institutions could long survive economic mismanagement, as the example of Peru showed in 1992. Democracy cannot be divorced from social and economic progress. It can not take firm root unless the needs of the poor are also met. When elected officials accept that their power derives from the people and not just from the nation's elite, true democracy can be established.

Widespread corruption still plagued Latin America in the last decade of the twentieth century. Birthrates still tended to be too high, though they were dropping in Argentina, Chile, Brazil and Mexico. High birthrates meant that even countries on the path of economic reform would be faced with increasing poverty. The distribution of wealth, or rather lack of it, to the poor majority scarcely diminished the gap between rich and the poor. The statistics for income per head of population obscure this because they are averages: the poor were much worse off than the average. Simply absorbing the young and providing some employment for them when nearly half the population was aged under twenty was a formidable problem. Urbanisation and the growth of mega-million cities magnified the problem. The power base of the energetic political leaders of Latin America was fragile and their austerity policies to cure inflation were deeply unpopular. The leaders themselves were all too often tempted by the fruits of office.

# CHAPTER 72

# The Nations of the Caribbean

Stretching in an arc 2500 miles long from the southern coast of Florida to the northern coast of Venezuela lie a string of Caribbean islands. They were once the oldest colonial possessions of the empires of Western Europe, dating from Christopher Columbus's discovery of the New World. Their original inhabitants died out centuries ago, by exploitation, disease and intermarriage with the peoples who settled in the islands as planters or merchants or slaves brought from Africa or indentured labour from Asia. The colonies were highly prized for the sugar cane that was grown there, until the production of beet in Europe deprived sugar of its status as a luxury by the end of the nineteenth century.

The islands were isolated from each other before the Age of Discovery. Five centuries under foreign domination kept them divided. Martinique had closer contact with France than with Cuba, while Jamaica's dealings with Britain thousands of miles away were more extensive and more frequent than those with Curaçao – a vivid illustration of the impact of global history.

Diverse languages – English, Spanish, French and Dutch – and a political status different in each of the islands of the Caribbean reflect their long colonial history. The British possessions were Jamaica, the Leeward and Windward Islands, including Grenada and Trinidad and Tobago; the French islands are Martinique and Guadeloupe; and the most important of the Dutch islands is Curaçao. The United States captured Puerto Rico from the Spaniards in 1898, and she has retained the Guantanamo naval base in Cuba; she also purchased the Virgin Islands from the Danes in 1917. On the Atlantic coast of South America lie the three Guianas, one British, one French and one Dutch (Surinam). All these former colonies have plantation and mining economies in common, supplying raw materials to Europe and the United States, principally sugar, bananas, bauxite and later oil. The cultural and racial composition of their peoples is also derived from the colonial economies, which required the influx of African slaves and indentured labour. Their colonial status, which tied them to different countries in Europe, has divided the region politically. This fragmentation impeded the West Indies' efforts after independence to create common regional organisations. No less important is the apparent paradox that those islands which had not gained independence by the early 1990s enjoyed the highest standards of living.

France's policy after the Second World War was not to grant independence to former colonies but to associate them more closely with the mother country. Thus the French Caribbean Islands in 1946 became full overseas *départements*, integral parts of the French Republic and members of the French Community. The advantages for the peoples of those islands was considerable: the social benefits enjoyed in metropolitan France were gradually extended to the French Caribbean inhabitants – indeed social expenditure per head of population in the 1980s was more than twice as much in

Martinique as in Paris. There was free movement still in the early 1990s: the people on the islands were full citizens of France and they could migrate to the mother country, a valuable right because unemployment on the islands was high. Moreover, France had provided schools, hospitals and housing of a high standard. On the downside the planter elite had survived and controlled much of the commerce. Industrial growth had been slow and agricultural production and employment had failed to increase to match population growth and needs. There was criticism of the French state, but the demand for independence was weak: the benefit of being French was too self-evident.

While the French wished to retain the islands as integral parts of France, the Dutch after the bitter and unsuccessful struggle in Indonesia in the 1940s would have preferred to lead their dependencies in the Caribbean and South America to full independence and thereby divest themselves of responsibility for them. An arrangement made in 1954, whereby they became autonomous partners in the Kingdom of the Netherlands, was intended as a halfway stage. Surinam in 1975 did become independent, induced by generous financial terms, but the islands of the Dutch Caribbean, despite urgings from The Hague, refused to follow suit. As full Dutch citizens the island peoples enjoyed the right of free movement to the Netherlands as well as full social benefits. One-fifth of the population in fact did migrate. Independence would have closed this opportunity and most likely reduced the large amount of development aid the Dutch spent on the Netherlands Antilles. Not surprisingly an overwhelming proportion of the population of the islands remained opposed to independence in the 1990s.

There are parallels here too with Puerto Rico. Not independence but greater integration with the United States as one of the states of the Union was what most Puerto Ricans desired in the last decade of the twentieth century. Instead, what they enjoyed was US citizenship, granted in 1917. Whatever criticisms might justly be made of the government of Puerto Rico, which in the past had resorted to imprisonment of political opponents, Puerto Ricans were well aware that they were much better off than some of their Spanish-speaking neighbours suffering at the hands of venal dictators. Even so, hundreds of thousands escaped unemployment and poverty in Puerto Rico by migrating to New York

and elsewhere in the United States. As full US citizens they were entitled to all the social services and welfare provisions available in America. There were many Spanish-speaking inhabitants of certain independent nations of the Caribbean who ardently desired to escape from them.

The most wretched independent nation in the region and one of the poorest, Haiti, was also the first (in 1804) to declare her independence from her European coloniser, France. In her long and dismal history, one of Haiti's worst periods was the rule of François Duvalier, a black physician who became known and feared as 'Papa Doc', terrorising his opponents with a band of personal thugs, the Tontons Macoutes or Bogeymen, instantly recognisable by their dress and the sunglasses they always wore. Torture became routine. On Duvalier's death in 1971, his son Jean-Claude Duvalier, 'Baby Doc', succeeded to his position and continued his dictatorial rule until he fell from power in a violent upheaval in 1986. Washington had attempted, without much success, to link aid to human rights reforms. The eventual cutting off of US aid altogether had driven Duvalier into exile but political conditions in Haiti did not improve. The election of a former priest, Father Jean-Bertrand Aristide, in December 1990 raised hopes for democratic change. He did not last a year before being ousted by a violent army coup in September 1991. Drugs, corruption, disease, malnutrition and illiteracy oppress the islanders. Not surprisingly Haiti is one of the two poorest countries in the Western hemisphere.

Haiti's neighbour is the Dominican Republic, whose independence dates from 1844. Her history in the twentieth century was dominated by the dictatorial rule of General Rafael Trujillo, who gained the presidency in 1930 and was assassinated in 1961. Corrupt and violent, he suppressed all opposition. Although not as poor as Haiti, the Dominican Republic is one of the poorest states in the Western hemisphere.

Powerful Western Countries, especially the United States, did not simply ignore these two independent Caribbean nations. In Haiti, the Dominican Republic, Puerto Rico and Cuba, Americans invested in plantations and factories, making use of the cheap labour available there. The business instinct to maximise profits might lack ethical foundations, but investment brought economic benefits

*A sugar cane plantation in the Dominican Republic.*

**Haiti and the Dominican Republic, 1989**

|  | Population (*millions*) | Gross National Product per head (*US$*) |
|---|---|---|
| Haiti | 6.4 | 360 |
| Dominican Republic | 7.0 | 790 |

to local populations, even when rates of pay were only a fraction of labour costs in the United States. The shifting of such investments to Asia and elsewhere after the 1960s was a further blow to the Caribbean nations.

Why did governments which had systematically abused human rights survive so long? Business interests favoured stability, even the stability of dictators. For the lack of reforming zeal shown by the United States, when the twentieth century is considered as a whole, there was another more important reason. Washington regarded the Caribbean as the region where US security could be most directly threatened by powerful foreign enemies. After 1945, the most important criterion for gaining US support was unqualified opposition to communism. Earlier in the century the United States had feared that European imperialism would spread aggressively in the New World.

The United States knew she had nothing to fear

from Spain, which ruled the colony of Cuba in the nineteenth century. The US did not at first intervene in the Cuban War of Independence waged by Cuban insurgents from 1868 to 1878. When the war was resumed in 1895, however, the international situation had changed. Germany was thirsty for more colonies. To have the Queen of Spain as a neighbour was one thing; the Kaiser was a very different prospect. In 1898 the United States went to war with Spain, ostensibly to achieve Cuban independence. After winning the Spanish–American War, the United States made sure that she would be the only nation able to dominate the island, even after Cuban independence. The twentieth-century history of Cuba became one of dependency on the United States, until 1959 and Castro's revolution (pages 517–18).

By the early twentieth century the United States had replaced Britain as the dominant power in the Caribbean, and she intended to maintain that position. In 1903 President Theodore Roosevelt manoeuvred to acquire control over the Panama Canal. Washington also found it necessary now to pre-empt the ever present danger that the mismanagement and corruption of the Caribbean governments might lead to European intervention to collect debts or to avenge the maltreatment of European citizens. Such 'chronic wrongdoing' or 'impotence', Theodore Roosevelt declared in 1904 in a new definition of the Monroe Doctrine, required 'intervention by some civilised nation'. He invoked the Monroe Doctrine to justify the United States' assumption of the role of 'an international police power'. This was no mere rhetoric. Haiti was occupied from 1915 to 1934 and the Dominican Republic from 1916 to 1924. If these occupations, like the colonial impact of France, the Netherlands and Britain, had led to great improvements in the government of these states, there would be little to criticise in retrospect. This was patently not the case, however. Those 'independent' states where the United States was able to intervene without clashing with a powerful European country have the worst records in standards of living and human rights.

After the Second World War it was once more Washington's strategic calculations that dominated policy, above all calculations relating to the Cold War. Corrupt dictators denying civil and human rights were an evil, but an even greater evil was perceived in the spread of Marxism and, with it,

Soviet influence in the Western hemisphere. In Cuba's case, after Castro's revolution of 1959, the United States was unsuccessful. The Soviet link with Castro's Cuba could not be broken from the 1960s to the 1980s (see Chapter 60). In the Dominican Republic the assassination of Trujillo had created the opportunity for change. The first free election for the presidency was held in December 1962 and was won by Juan Bosch, the candidate of the left. But a military coup ousted him in September 1963, and soon the country was rent by civil war, with the supporters of Bosch attempting to reinstate him. The United States landed troops in October 1965 to prevent this outcome and, having succeeded, they left the following year.

The Cold War during the 1980s was responsible for indirect US intervention in Central America, and also for direct intervention when US marines invaded the small island of Grenada (population 95,000) in October 1983 during the Reagan administration. This greatly embarrassed Margaret Thatcher's government in London, because Grenada was a member of the British Commonwealth yet Britain had received no prior warning. The US justified her action as necessary for the safety of American citizens and added that Grenada had become 'the victim of Cuban and Soviet "internationalism"'. Grenada was riven by internal strife, revolution and bloodshed, and her leading revolutionary party, the New Jewel Movement, was Marxist–Leninist. A military coup and the murder of the left-wing Prime Minister – much deplored by Cuba, which had supported his revolutionary government – were the immediate causes of the breakdown of law and order. The Soviet Union had been reticent. The small island would not have served as a Soviet base and could hardly have mounted any threat to US security, however unpalatable her governing ideology was to Washington.

On the positive side the United States' aid initiatives provided assistance, but not on a scale to make a major impact on the economic and social conditions of the poorest nations in the Caribbean. With the ending of the Cold War the perceived global threat of communism as feared by Washington receded in the Caribbean in the 1990s and tension in the region considerably lessened.

Life in the Bahamas presents an enormous contrast to life on the poorest islands of the region. These small islands to the north of Cuba (they are actually in the Atlantic, not the Caribbean) supported a small population of 254,000 in 1990, living mainly on tourism, though in the recession of the early 1990s that source of income suffered a setback. In the past, large quantities of drugs also passed through the Bahamas from Central America. The GNP per head – it was $11,300 in 1989 – is the highest in the region. The majority of the members of the Bahamas parliament, twenty-five out of forty-nine in 1990, were millionaires. The islands are thus very untypical of the region's economies.

The Bahamas were part of the former British colonial possessions of the West Indies. Fragmentation is also a feature of what were formerly the British West Indies, which persists as a heritage from colonial times. Their social make-up is complex, with descendants of white settlers, of African slaves brought over to work on the plantations and of migrants from India. The advance to self-rule and the type of representative institutions were different in each of the fifteen colonies. Barbados had the oldest system of local representative partnership in the form of a governor's executive committee. Jamaica had a constitution which allowed elected members to participate in ruling the island, and there were different arrangements for indigenous consultation in Trinidad and the other islands. But real control until well after the Second World War rested with the Colonial Office in London. The West Indian colonies were simply not judged to be capable of self-government. The depression of the 1930s had hit them particularly hard and there were riots, outbreaks of violence and an upsurge of radical political and trade union activity. In Jamaica, Marcus Garvey, Norman Manley and Alexander Bustamente created disciplined political and trade union movements.

In London the government on the eve of the Second World War recognised that the time had come for change. A royal commission, set up in 1938, recommended that economic help was more urgent than constitutional reform. A beginning was then made to provide additional welfare and development funds during the Second World War, and universal adult suffrage was promised.

Despite discontent with the conditions prevailing in the islands many West Indians when the war broke out still looked upon Britain as the mother country. There was no conscription: the West Indians, more than 10,000 of them, who came to

*The US Marines land in Grenada in October 1983. The opposition they encounter is less than formidable.*

Britain after 1939 to join the army, navy and air force did so as volunteers. West Indian airmen participated in the Battle of Britain. They were the first sizeable influx of black servicemen to reach Britain, arriving long before American blacks. They suffered from racial prejudice, especially once the war was over, and their contribution, usually overlooked in histories of the Second World War, deserves to be honoured and recorded with that of other volunteers in the struggle against Hitler's Germany.

After the war, adult suffrage was extended from Jamaica, the largest and most populous island, where it had been introduced in 1944, to Trinidad and Tobago, Barbados and (by 1953) to British Guiana on the Latin American mainland, the largest of Britain's Caribbean colonies. The goal now accepted in London was Dominion status for the West Indies. But it did not seem feasible unless the various islands could be brought together to form a larger federal unit, which even then would have had a total population of only 3 million. But, apart from a famous cricketing side, there was very little contact between the islands, each with her own distinctive institutions, and there was hardly any inter-island trade. The indigenous politicians in the 1950s, moreover, wanted independence quickly for their own islands and had already made some progress by having attained what was called 'responsible government'. The Colonial Office in London took the initiative which led to the creation from above of the Federation of the West Indies in 1958, to which it was hoped power could be transferred as a new Dominion in the British Commonwealth. It lasted only four years. The Jamaicans were the first to leave. Full local independence took precedence over an artificial federation whose members had little in common. The island states became independent – Jamaica and Trinidad in 1962. Ethnic strife delayed independence for British Guiana (which became known as Guyana) until 1966, and in the same year Barbados gained her independence. With the smaller islands, a 'free and voluntary association' with full internal self-government was agreed in 1967. Britain's entry into the Common Market then produced a coming together of most of the independent West Indian nations in a Caribbean Common Market in 1973.

Aid and special trade agreements for the export of sugar and bananas were negotiated with the European Economic Community. Economic growth in the West Indies through the 1980s was good by international standards but the extremes of income distribution mean that a large majority of the population continues to live in poverty.

After independence the nations of the West Indies searched in vain for solutions to their fundamental problems of poverty and dependence on what the rest of the world would pay for their primary products and on what it would charge for the essential imports they need. The trade balance was generally heavily weighted against these Third World countries through to the 1990s and, despite aid, development was difficult. Guyana had to overcome not only poverty but racial violence. Her government encouraged the formation of co-operatives and took control during the 1970s of the greater part of the economy, nationalising domestic and foreign-owned industries. The economic effects proved ruinous. Politically too the people of Guyana suffered under Linden Forbes Burnham from 1964 until his death in 1985. The People's National Congress Party won every election, opponents were intimidated and elections rigged. Forbes Burnham governed Guyana after independence in 1966 at first with more moderation than could have been expected of the rival communist People's Progressive Party led by Cheddi Jagan, but he soon created an authoritarian one-party state. His successor Desmond Hoyte continued his policies and the country decayed further in the second half of the 1980s, rivalling Haiti as the poorest Caribbean nation. With the country in deep political and economic crisis, Hoyte in 1990 initiated the first steps towards reform, assisted by the International Monetary Fund, but the elections due to be held in 1991 were postponed until 1992. There was, however, some progress in the running of the economy with Western help. This was an example of how the collapse of communist autocracies in Eastern Europe had significant repercussions far away, as countries like Guyana could now turn only to the West for help.

Jamaica is a parliamentary democracy. The dominant politician during the 1970s was Michael Manley, who headed the People's National Party. Manley was a Fabian socialist opposed to authoritarian Marxism, and sought to improve the standard of living of the great majority of his country's poor, partly by raising additional taxes on foreign-owned companies. His friendly relations with Cuba aroused United States hostility in the Cold War era. Forced to turn to the IMF to help the country's deteriorating economy, the conditions attached to the loan worsened the immediate plight of Jamaicans and in 1980 Manley lost the election to the more conservative Jamaica Labour Party. The new prime minister Edward Seaga remained in power until 1989. The IMF imposed further severe conditions to rectify a burgeoning deficit, but, despite substantial aid from Western countries, the growth of tourism and profits from the bauxite (aluminium) industry, the people continued to suffer severe hardship. Free-market policies gradually increased Jamaica's earnings and when in 1989 Michael Manley returned to power he did not revert to his previous socialist policies but continued those of his predecessor. Jamaica remained heavily in debt. The state of the economy and popular discontent with the harsh conditions would have threatened political stability were it not for the strong tradition of parliamentary democratic government.

In general the West Indian nations tried to adopt development policies different from those attempted previously by their colonial rulers. A variety of forms of socialism were introduced which failed to provide solutions for their economic plight, and by the early 1990s the free-market approach was widely adopted.

### Guyana, Jamaica and Trinidad and Tobago, 1989

|  | Population | Gross National Product per head (US$) |
|---|---|---|
| Guyana | 796,000 | 340 |
| Jamaica | 2,400,000 | 1,260 |
| Trinidad and Tobago | 1,300,000 | 3,230 |

# PART XV

---

*Africa after 1945:*
*Conflict and the Threat of*
*Famine*

# CHAPTER 73

## The Ending of White Rule in West Africa

For a British university graduate in the early 1950s, the Colonial Service offered a fine opportunity for a fulfilling and worthwhile career. After a brief apprenticeship, in his late twenties or early thirties, he could expect to become a district commissioner in the Fiji Islands or an African colony and to be given responsibility for thousands of 'natives' as the ultimate magistrate and authority on the spot. Such opportunities for young men to exercise paternalistic power did not exist in the Western world. The only drawback of colonial service was the question of marriage, or more accurately the problem of how a single white male might find a suitable wife to take to the bush. Marrying locally was impractical; there were few, if any unattached white girls, and an interracial marriage was unthinkable. Fulfilment of this basic human need therefore had to be arranged rather rapidly on a spell of leave back home; the DC's wife thereafter fulfilled an important role in the white colonial society, which had its strict pecking order from the governor and his wife downwards. On the surface, little had changed for half a century in the customs and mores of colonial government and the same held true for the French. A career in the colonies was a career for life. But then, little more than ten years later, it all came suddenly to an end. District commissioners are no more. Black Africa asserted its political independence in country after country.

The story of the demise of the colonial civil servant, a mere microcosm of history, has a wider bearing; it illustrates a phenomenon historians can repeatedly observe. Major upheavals often occur abruptly, surprising contemporaries with their speed and dynamism. It is historians – themselves actually no better than anyone else at anticipating the future – who later analyse how changes have been gradually in the making over a period of decades.

As empires go, European rule over most of the African continent was of relatively short duration; apart from forts and territories on the coast, political empire began much later than in Asia and the Americas and ended sooner. Economic empire was, however, older. Europe's interest in Africa was predominantly economic long before partition in the latter part of the nineteenth century. The Europeans replaced the Arabs in linking Africa's produce with the rest of the world. Until the nineteenth century the most important African product was human beings – slaves. Other resources were harnessed to serve Western needs in the world economy. From an African perspective the dominant theme is white exploitation. But eventual Western political control also led to the imposition of a new order, the creation of embryonic nations. These took the form of European colonies with internationally agreed frontiers, and they were opened to the influx of Western ideas of government, which included the doctrine of self-determination. The supplanting of the African means of exchange by European money and the introduction of market economies, roads and infrastructures and capital investment transformed traditional African societies. Over the course of

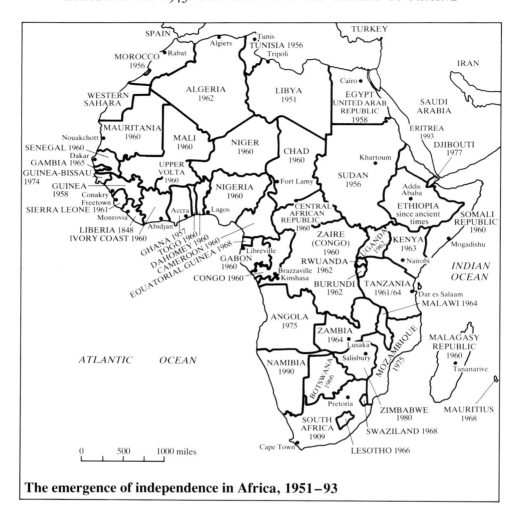

**The emergence of independence in Africa, 1951–93**

three generations the continent evolved into numerous independent nation states. Within them tribal and cultural divisions continue to cause tension and conflict; colonial national boundaries were not everywhere willingly accepted in the post-colonial era. In Nigeria and the Congo there was civil war in the 1960s and in the Horn of Africa – Eritrea, Somalia and Ethiopia – devastating fighting continued for decades. Nevertheless the pre- and post-independence maps of divided Africa have remained remarkably similar.

The boundaries drawn by the British, French, Belgians, Germans, Spaniards and Portuguese in the late nineteenth and early twentieth centuries reflected penetration by missionaries and traders, the strategic and political interests of governments in Europe or of enterprising colonialists in Africa and the outcome of their rivalries. They did not coincide with any natural geographical, ethnic or tribal divisions.

The diversity of the fifty-odd countries so created is extraordinary, ranging from the immense to the tiny, from those rich in resources to the desperately poor. The great religious divide between Islam in the north and north-west and Christianity further south splits Nigeria, the Sudan and Ethiopia. The new African countries were also divided ideologically, between Marxist Mozambique, for example, and the feudal kingdom of Ethiopia. It is remarkable how little fighting there has been over the many colonial frontiers between the new African nations. Plans for a powerful 'Pan-Africa', such as was urged by the charismatic Kwame Nkrumah, Ghana's (the Gold Coast's) first leader after independence, proved completely unrealistic. The transfers of power created new ruling groups and leaders who wished to exercise authority in their own countries and were with few exceptions unwilling to contemplate fusing with others.

The voice of independent Africa as a whole is a regional international organisation made up of sovereign nations, the Organisation of African Unity (OAU), created in 1963 and modelled on the United Nations. The divisiveness of independent Africa has not made it an influential or effective body. Its main effort was to work for the completion of liberation, the decolonisation of those parts of Africa still under European rule, and to defend black rights where they were being denied, as in South Africa. It provided a means of mediation in inter-African disputes but accepted the principle of non-interference in the internal affairs of the sovereign states. The inherited colonial frontiers were specifically recognised by the OAU at its second meeting in Cairo in 1964. Could they have acted otherwise?

Given the artificiality of the colonial African frontiers, to have attempted to redraw them would have invited chaos. Nor, as in the Balkans, could viable nations based simply on tribal identities be formed without subdividing the continent into hundreds of parcels. The principle of self-determination thus took second place in fashioning the political shape of independent Africa. The colonial era created 'facts' – the clock could no longer be turned back. Even Nkrumah had to accept this. The conflicts in Africa thus became internal, civil conflicts within existing states, an ethnic group fighting for independence, such as the Ibo revolt in Nigeria or the long Eritrean struggle against the Ethiopian state, or straightforward civil war, as in Mozambique and Angola, former Portuguese colonies, where the strife was for decades prolonged by outside interference. Independent African countries also aided the black population in what was Rhodesia to gain majority rule. And Black Africa supported the black majority in South Africa in its struggle for equal rights. By the early 1990s Africa had not yet found a continent-wide peace.

The timing of independence was not primarily determined by the readiness of the colonies, by the stage of economic, social and political development they had reached. The political complexion of the governments in Europe, the perception of their leaders, economic considerations as they affected the mother country – all played a greater role. Crucial too was the differentiation between colonies with unhealthy climates as in West Africa and those with temperate zones on the southern coast or along the highland ridge running north from South Africa to what was Southern Rhodesia (Zimbabwe) or those where mineral wealth had attracted European immigration.

The white farming settler families, some of whom have been in Africa for generations, or the Dutch, English and Indian immigrants who had built up a modern industrial society as in South Africa, the majority of them born in Africa, regard Africa as their homeland too. The whites and Asians in South Africa constitute a large minority (whites about one in five, Asian rather less than one in twenty-five, and of mixed race, the so-called coloureds, one in ten). There and in the Belgian Congo (as formerly in Southern Rhodesia), the whites owned most of the useful land and wealth. A transfer of power, enabling the black majority to rule the country, threatened the white Africans not only with a loss of political power but also with social and economic revolution. White resistance, with their control of the armed forces, especially if they were backed by the colonial power, as the French settlers were in Algeria, was an enormous obstacle to independence with majority rule. The large increase of white settlers after the Second World War, soaring in British Rhodesia from 55,400 to 160,000, in Northern Rhodesia from 9900 to 50,000, in Kenya from 18,000 to 42,000, in Portuguese Angola from 30,000 to 80,000, in Mozambique from 10,000 to 50,000 and in the Belgian Congo from 18,600 to 77,000, created interest groups not easily set aside. Not surprisingly, the white settler colonies were the last to gain independence – Mozambique (1975), Angola (1975), Zimbabwe (1980), Namibia (1989) – while majority rule in South Africa in 1992 had not yet been established.

In the colonies where the whites were most numerous the black majority resorted to arms. In Algeria, Rhodesia, Angola and Mozambique there was no bloodless transfer of power, and the future of South Africa still hangs in the balance. The history of European colonialism in the various African countries and their emergence to independence has some common features but is also distinctive for each region and country.

How can a balance sheet of European colonialism in Africa be set out? The question is unanswerable. The link between Africa and the rest of the industrialised world in the twentieth century was bound to bring about a transformation of African society,

African economic development and indeed every aspect of African life. The question might better be posed thus: how far did the colonial era facilitate the transformation to the benefit of the African peoples? Education and technical training were one key aspect and both were woefully inadequate, yet a base was created that generally made rapid expansion possible after independence. Medical advances and the control or eradication of diseases were an obvious benefit derived from colonial administration. But undeniably the main purpose of colonial rule was to profit from the links with Africa and to enhance the European nation's own wealth and power. Missionaries and others too acted out of a sense of genuine paternalism but in the last resort the lives of the African peoples were shaped by the economic needs of the colonial power and by the political, administrative, economic and social conditions created by the interplay of European governments, colonial bureaucracies, trading companies, merchants, white farming settlers, skilled white professionals and workers. In this process, the rivalries of the European nations and their respective strengths decided the geographical colonial entity, not ethnic affinities or the vestiges of former African empires. These were obliterated. The Africans were not a homogeneous group either, but themselves varied in beliefs and in their roles in society.

When the Europeans expanded all over Africa in the nineteenth century, African textiles, pottery, and weapons comparable to artefacts from preindustrial societies were mismatched with European market needs. Some were carried off to London, Paris and Brussels as artistic curios and housed in museums. Africa's 'export trade' had early on consisted of minerals, above all gold, and agricultural produce, tobacco, salt, spices, cotton and later palm oil from the Niger delta. Not all agricultural produce was indigenous to Africa. Cacao was introduced by missionaries in the 1860s and in the twentieth century became the Gold Coast's principal export. Manufacturing industries in Europe found markets in the colonies for their goods, but except in South Africa no substantial manufacturing industries developed in the European colonies despite the abundance of cheap black labour. The Europeans gained virtual monopolies of trade; inland, with territorial occupation, they replaced the African merchants who had previously controlled trade to the coast. The African capitalists who did

emerge were few and were dependent on Europeans in powerful trading-company monopolies. European capital abroad was more profitably invested in the booming white industrial societies of Europe and the Americas, which were already technologically advanced. Investment in Africa flowed into rapidly expanding mineral and plantation resources which required a large unskilled labour input and relatively little skilled labour. Ideology and racism played a role in this too. Black Africans, with few exceptions, were simply not considered capable of learning technological skills: Europeans tended to regard them as more like children.

But, in the last resort, neither prejudice nor government policies dictated African economic development as decisively as the workings of a global capitalist economy in the twentieth century. The dependence of the African economies on the West for their monetary system, credit and development and for the nurturing of African resources and trade was so well set by the time of independence in the 1950s and 1960s that fundamental changes would have been difficult to bring about. Black Africa in the 1990s remained chiefly in the role of primary producer; attempts to create self-sustaining growth through industrial production, as in the West or in parts of Asia, had ended in failure. But manufacture was increasing and beginning to substitute manufactured imports. The primary products were restricted to two or three in each country, so that African wealth continued to be largely dependent on the world prices of these commodities, whether of oil as in Nigeria and the Gabon or of phosphates and cacao in Togo or of diamonds and coffee in the Central African Republic. Meanwhile food production in Africa had not kept pace with population growth; in the 1980s and 1990s Ethiopia suffered from terrible famines. Looking to the future the spread of Aids was yet another devastating problem faced by black Africa, whose own resources were inadequate to cope with the crisis.

The imperialist European nations were parsimonious when it came to colonial expenditures. The British, French and Portuguese relied on private finance, the great chartered companies such as the Niger Company and the British South Africa Company, which in return for subjugating and administrating stretches of Africa received trade and land concessions in the conquered territories. The opening of Africa was accomplished by force and by African manual labour. Nowhere was this human exploitation conducted with greater systematic cruelty than in King Leopold's personal fief in the Congo. Here the creation of an administration, of an infrastructure of roads and of a labour force to collect rubber resulted in torture and genocide. Even white Europe, used to regarding blacks as racially inferior, was shocked when this state of affairs was revealed shortly before the First World War.

But this was not an isolated instance. In the process of developing Africa's resources, the European was not prepared to undertake the unskilled manual work necessary to harvest plantations, extract ores from mines or construct the roads and railways to the coast. A conscripted force of black people, in conditions at times worse than slavery, created the foundations of modern Africa. Feudal conditions of forced native service persisted in French West Africa as late as 1946. In South Africa, cash taxes could be paid by blacks only if they earned cash in the mines. Men were recruited on contracts, running for a year or other specified periods, and immigrant labour became a feature of African economic life. The continent's human reservoir was also used beyond its shores. Africans were no longer sent across the Atlantic to develop other continents; they were used in the twentieth century to develop Africa and so created the profit necessary for further development. But the financial investment came from outside Africa; the technological skills were also almost entirely confined to the white man, which left black Africa dependent and weak. Moreover, during two world wars Africans supplied soldiers in the internecine conflict of Europe.

How then did the colonial powers view Africa's future, how did they see the relationship between the Africans and their conquerors? Would it forever remain one of master and servant? The European Enlightenment had expounded the notion of human progress. Africans could not be entirely excluded; they were after all a part of the human family. But crude racialism divided this family and its state of civilisation by 'colour' from white to black, with 'brown' Indians at an intermediate stage. In the British Empire the white people were regarded as fit to rule themselves; Indian independence was accepted before 1914 as inevitable at some distant date; but, for black people, the time when they could be considered ready was not even envisaged.

After the First World War the German colonies of German East Africa, South-West Africa, the Kamerun and Togoland were divided as spoils between Britain (German East Africa, renamed Tanganyika), South Africa (German South-West Africa, later Namibia), France (most of Togo and the Cameroons) and Belgium (Ruanda and Urundi, formerly part of German East Africa, and later the independent countries of Rwanda and Burundi). But these territories were not supposed to be regarded simply as colonies; they were placed under the guardianship of the League of Nations and 'mandated' to Britain, South Africa, France and Belgium, who were to act as 'trustees' for the advancement of their inhabitants. Their special status did not, however, help them to advance to independence sooner. Indeed one of the mandated territories, Namibia, was among the last to gain independence in 1989.

A small number of Europeans controlled Africa. They could only do so by leaving to Africans – under European supervision, administration and command – the task of managing their fellow Africans. This was the model of 'indirect rule'. As the first task was pacification, European officers and black soldiers played a large role in Africa. Later, Africans filled the lower administrative positions in all the colonies; there were simply not enough Europeans for the task. In the British Gold Coast colony for example, less than 850 European officials in the 1930s filled the senior administrative, military, police and technical posts in a country of 4 million African inhabitants. This meant that Africans had to be educated to fill clerkships and lower supervisory roles. Schools were established, but even so in the 1930s less than two out of a hundred Africans received formal education and very few had the opportunity of university training. Yet the Gold Coast was more advanced in African education than the rest of Africa. The situation improved in the 1950s, but primary and even more so secondary education was open to only a small minority of Africans.

The lack of African technical and professional training before independence undermined any chance of fast development afterwards and created a small group of African politicians and soldiers in whose hands real power lay. This was not the kind of society where democracy could strike roots. The neglect by the colonisers of the Africans was the consequence of a policy which was economically exploitive and which provided government on the cheap for the European colonial powers. Though they recognised African needs after the Second World War, European governments were slow to effect fundamental improvements in the decade or two before independence. In any case there would have been more catching up to accomplish than there was time for. Their ideas about the future of their colonies also differed.

The French had established a hierarchical, highly centralised and authoritarian form of administration with African chiefs acting as executives, overseen by provincial commissioners and a governor-general who in turn was responsible to the Colonial Ministry in Paris. The French followed the doctrine that black Africans could be elevated to equality with white Frenchmen through education and acceptance of French civilisation, French beliefs and French attitudes. In short, their ultimate aspiration was to become indistinguishable from Frenchmen except by the colour of their skin. They then acquired all the rights and obligations of French citizens, including being able to vote and to hold ministerial office. On the face of it this was an enlightened ideology, but it had nothing to do with guiding African colonies to their own independence. The capital of French Africa was Paris. The number of Africans who qualified for equal rights was kept very small and the idea was that they would be grateful enough to defend the virtue of a system so beneficial for them as to distinguish them from the poor African masses. The objective then was 'assimilation' not 'independence'. When at the famous Brazzaville Conference of French African governors in January 1944 the 'free French' discussed the future of French colonial Africa, there were proposals for economic reforms, but not for independence. De Gaulle afterwards spoke of a future in which each of the peoples would develop and administer themselves and later even govern themselves – 'later' meant 'much later'. There was talk of some form of association and federation with France; it was all very vague, and no African was invited to attend.

The impact of the Second World War and the emergence of an educated and well-to-do African leadership protesting against economic disadvantages and voicing African grievances began to bring about change. In the Ivory Coast Félix Houphouët-Boigny founded an African Democratic Party in 1946 which won widespread support, in large part fired by the continuing system of forced labour and low wages – that is, grievances directly affecting African life. Meanwhile, French governments were ready to abandon the more blatant forms of centralised colonial control, to introduce reforms in their colonial administration and to allow more representation in the French Assembly. The idea being propagated was internal autonomy in a French Union freely supported by the African peoples. In fact, the Union was intended to maintain and indeed strengthen economic and political links between metropolitan France and French Africa, and indeed with the whole French empire, now so unfashionable. The vision was one of partnership in a common cause in the service of a French Republic restored to greatness as a world power. It was never intended as an equal partnership. It proved an illusion which led France and her former empire in Indo-China and North Africa to much grief and bloodshed. Independence was conceded only after bitter conflict. In black West Africa, however, unlike Algeria, armed conflict was avoided, except in the Cameroon. The transfer of power from the mid-1950s was peaceful and inevitable. But the setting up of territorial assemblies with elected African deputies, increased representation in the French Assembly in Paris, and the establishment of a federal Grand Conseil for French West Africa to assist the governor-generals, now renamed high commissioners, were no more than palliatives. Black Africans remained second-class citizens. After Ghana had become independent in 1957, with the struggle in Algeria still at a crucial stage, de Gaulle marked his return to power in 1958 with an elaborate initiative: he devised a new constitutional settlement. The French Union would now become the French Community; its members would continue to receive French economic and technical aid; the former French colonial territories would receive internal autonomy and titular independence but would still be tied to Paris. The French Community was submitted to a referendum in the French colonial territories in November 1958. As economic aid was still indispensable, all but one West African state, Guinea, voted to approve the Community and to remain within it. But during 1959 and 1960 the African governing elites all demanded complete independence, and Paris had to accept that its efforts to maintain imperial political control in ever more ingenious guises had failed: the remaining black African nations of former French West and

Equatorial Africa were granted independence in 1960.

The Ivory Coast, the most populous of the former French territories, was economically better off in the early 1990s as an independent country, though she was still impoverished by Western standards. In the 1930s agricultural development had been rapid, and cacao, coffee and palm oil became the chief export crops. As the 1990s began, the Ivory Coast was a one-party state and had been ruled since independence in 1960 by French-educated Félix Houphouët-Boigny, formerly a minister in Paris and a member of the Assembly who had abandoned his early adherence to communism. Economically the Ivory Coast advanced and diversified as the pragmatic Houphouët-Boigny welcomed Western capital and French aid and associated the country closely with France. Eighty-seven years old in 1992, he no longer enjoyed reverential respect. The fall of the prices of cocoa and coffee had had an adverse effect on the economy, and servicing the foreign debt swallowed up a sizeable proportion of export earnings. Economic conditions rapidly deteriorated. A new generation of students, teachers, professionals and trade unionists was no longer prepared to accept meekly the rule of the 'fathers of the nation', the corruption and one-party states. The West became dominant on the continent following the collapse of the Soviet Union, and Houphouët-Boigny had to make the gesture of allowing for the first time in October 1990 a contested presidential election. His control of the levers of powers ensured an easy victory, but that did not end demands for a transition to a broader sharing of power and spoils.

Like Nkrumah, Houphouët-Boigny spent millions on imposing architecture in his poor country. The capital boasts the famous basilica modelled on St Peter's in Rome with space for 18,000 people. It was (reluctantly) consecrated by Pope John Paul II in 1990.

Guinea was also a one-party state until the military took over in 1984. But, in contrast to the Ivory Coast, she began independence by cutting her ties with France in 1958. The strong man of Guinea and its leader for decades was Sékou Touré, who had built up his support through the trade union movement. He erected an authoritarian state and adopted an African Marxism, though rejecting the basic tenet of the class struggle. What he took from communism was the highly organised one-party state, and his harsh regime drove hordes of refugees into neighbouring countries, estimated at between 1 and 2 million. At one time it looked as if Guinea would fall into the Soviet orbit, but Sékou Touré was a passionate African nationalist, ready to accept aid from all sides and adjusting his relationships with West and East to suit his perception of Guinea's national interests. Potentially rich in mineral deposits, especially of bauxite for aluminium, Guinea by the 1990s had earned too little from their export. The Russians, who developed the extraction of bauxite, paid a low price and Guinea remained at the mercy of a few foreign buyers.

With Sékou Touré's death in 1984 the repressive control his party had exercised ended. There was to be no opening to civilian party rule, however. The armed forces seized power in a bloodless coup led by a new strong man, Colonel Lansana Conté, who denounced Sékou Touré's bloody and ruthless dictatorship. The economy was in a terrible state after twenty years of Marxism, and the new leader turned to the West. With nowhere else to go for economic aid, he ended the policy of isolation. France, the World Bank and the International Monetary Fund offered assistance with aid and in liberalising the economy. Opposition to military rule mounted and the military procured a five-year programme in 1988 for a transition to civilian rule, with elections for a parliament in 1992 and a presidential election in 1993.

One-party states and authoritarian leadership became the norm for the newly independent French African territories in Benin, Niger, Cameroon, Togo, Burkina Faso and Mauritania. The same was essentially true of Senegal, although her leader, Léopold Senghor, was an impressively educated man in the Christian humanist tradition, a Catholic and a professor at the Sorbonne who expounded 'negritude', the identification with African culture; Senghor's very French education led him to seek the value of black culture and to set limits to assimilation, yet he also adopted the socialist Western model of a dominant one-party state.

With the collapse of the people's republics of Eastern Europe in 1989 and the economic failures of communist economic state management, which became so evident as the 1980s drew to a close, the authoritarian rulers sought to change their image. A further cause of change was the perilous economic condition of developing Africa. African states overspent lavishly in the 1970s, only to suffer economically from the upheavals of the mid-1970s and from falling commodity prices in the 1980s. Most African states became saddled with heavy foreign debts. To gain access to essential new funds from the World Bank and the International Monetary Fund, their leaders had to accept a painful restructuring of their economies and their politics. But the impoverished masses ceased to be docile; workers, teachers and civil servants went on strike to halt the steep falls in their standards of living. Corruption became the most obvious target for their anger. As a result, the style of African government began to change: African leaders at least had to appear accountable to the people. The President of Benin in 1990 renounced failed Marxism and introduced a multi-party system. The presidential election in 1991 marked a first in continental Africa. It was free and an incumbent president lost it, accepting

**Fourteen French-Speaking African States, 1987**

| | Population (*millions*) | Annual income per head (*US$*) |
|---|---|---|
| Mauritania | 1.86 | 440 |
| Mali | 7.77 | 210 |
| Niger | 6.78 | 260 |
| Chad | 5.26 | 150 |
| Central African Republic | 2.72 | 330 |
| Congo | 2.01 | 870 |
| Gabon | 1.05 | 2,700 |
| Cameroon | 10.86 | 970 |
| Benin (Dahomey) | 4.31 | 310 |
| Togo | 3.24 | 290 |
| Burkino Faso (Upper Volta) | 8.31 | 190 |
| Ivory Coast | 11.12 | 740 |
| Guinea | 6.5 | 320 |
| Senegal | 6.95 | 520 |

*Note*: Formerly part of French West and Equatorial Africa. All gained independence in 1960, except Guinea (1958).

defeat and bowing to the democratic process. The military gave way to civilian rule. In Gabon, where President Omar Bongo ruled uninterruptedly for more than twenty years, the one-party system ended in 1990. Bongo survived the transition and retained power. But the old problems of under-development, lack of mass education (though there were remarkable improvements), ethnic conflicts and past political traditions did not augur well for the establishment of deeply rooted, democratically based representative governments in the 1990s.

The British colonies followed another path to independence which differed from the French; retention of imperial control, or – in the case of the white settlers – of the settlers' control, was after all the common objective in both French and British African territories until the 1950s. British governments allowed more initiative to the men on the spot, allowing a colonial administration that was less rigidly centralised than the French. British territories were ruled by a mixture of direct and indirect control. There were so few Europeans that what became known as 'indirect rule' was almost inevitable; agreements were made with indigenous African chiefs and potentates, who accepted British suzerainty but were left to rule their fiefs under ultimate British supervision. Administration by indirect rule is particularly associated with Frederick Lugard, who conquered northern Nigeria (1900–6) and then combined it with southern Nigeria into one large colony. But northern Nigeria, with 10 million inhabitants, could not be directly governed by a handful of Europeans, so Muslim Fulani emirs were left with a semblance of their old authority to maintain order and undertake the administration.

The significant point about British rule over tropical Africa is that what began as expediency became a general doctrine of 'indirect rule', a means of British–African co-operation in the development of colonies. Thus, so it was believed, African society – shorn of its worst features, such as slavery – would be preserved for an eventual African future. But indirect rule generally functioned only in the least developed regions of Africa; on the West African coast direct rule had long replaced the older African society. Where significant numbers of white settlers were claiming the territories as their African birthright, as they were in southern Rhodesia, Kenya or South Africa, or where large-scale mining of copper had given rise to important industrial enterprises, as in northern Rhodesia or South Africa, traditional African structures were subservient to white needs and exploitation.

In West African colonies educated Africans were emerging as an elite group, participating in the administration. The great majority of such Africans hoped to play a role in the colonial hierarchy and to profit from the status thereby achieved: European control was far too tight to give Africans any realistic hopes of African 'independence' before the Second World War. Africans collaborating with the colonial government could thereby exercise some influence in defence of African rights but could not challenge overall colonial dependency. But it was possible for Africans to combine together to protect their interests, a move which at the same time served to identify and strengthen an African identity and solidarity. Examples ranged from the association of prosperous African cocoa farmers on the Gold Coast to organised strikes in Sierra Leone, Nigeria and Senegal in the 1920s. African political stirrings in the 1920s and 1930s are significant only insofar as they represent the roots of African politics after the Second World War, when movements at last began to achieve a mass following. But the depression of the 1930s and the Second World War itself were fundamentally to change the face of Africa and undermine the pillars of European colonial control.

The British bestowed on Africa all the trappings of parliamentary democracy – the Speaker's mace, the judges' wigs and legislative institutions. The French superimposed the accoutrements of their democratic civilisation. But this panoply of democracy did not correspond to the realities of colonial rule. Judged positively, Britain and France had begun to guide Africa along the road to democracy, but that road was intended to be a long one indeed. Governments in London and Paris after the end of the Second World War believed that Africans would only be capable of complete self-rule after one or even two generations. In the event, independence was conceded much sooner, little more than a decade later. Representative constitutions were conferred on peoples who lacked technological skills, who were poorer than most of the other peoples of the Third World and of whom the great majority were illiterate. The strongest groups and individuals gained power and held on to it as long as they could, repressing any opposition, which was

treated as sedition. Thus black Africa was ruled for decades by strong leaders or, if the political leadership did not prove powerful enough, the soldiers would rebel and clear out the corrupt politicians until government corrupted them too. Post-independence, many African countries have a bad record. Some, such as Uganda, have suffered more through internal conflict and tyrannical rule since colonial rule was ended than they ever did before independence. But this too is one of the legacies of the era of colonialism and under-development.

The Gold Coast was the most developed and prosperous of Britain's African colonies. The Western-educated elite of teachers, administrators, lawyers and businessmen became increasingly frustrated by the continuing dominance of British interests in the management of the colony after the Second World War. But though Britain now had a Labour government, which felt greater sympathy for the African people, her own interests, especially given the parlous state of sterling, ruled out independence: the Gold Coast's cocoa was too valuable an earner of dollars. India was granted independence speedily for fear of serious political unrest, but none was expected in the African colonies, which would be permitted to govern themselves step by step through a long period of partnership, with Britain controlling the pace. That pace was too slow for the Gold Coast African elite, and Dr Danquah, a prominent lawyer, in 1947 formed a moderate political party, the United Gold Coast Convention, to hasten constitutional reform. The fiery young Kwame Nkrumah was appointed its secretary. In February 1948 there were riots in protest against economic restrictions and European businesses which led to widespread destruction after a British police officer had fired on demonstrating ex-servicemen and killed two; twenty-nine more died in the violence. The Labour government in London reacted positively, hoping to win over the moderate nationalist leaders. Danquah was invited, together with other moderates, to advise on a new constitution which would allow more African representation. It was established in 1951.

Nkrumah, who was far more radical than the African establishment, opposed this development, which he regarded as a sell-out to the British. He passionately believed in African power, in Pan-Africanism. Although inspired by Lenin's writings on anti-imperialism, he was to be no tool of Moscow

*Scenes From Equatorial Africa.* Above right: *the modern and the traditional in Accra, Ghana.* Top left: *drought expands the Sahel desert, a belt of semi-arid land 200–800 miles wide that extends across the African continent from Mauritania to Chad, leaving the people of nine countries impoverished in its wake. In Tiguent, Mauritania, a family tries to revive a small, life-giving patch.* Above left: *others have given up the desert for the city, and its overcrowded hovels.* Top right: *a classroom in Mali.* Left: *the Paris-Dakar rally reaches Gao – Western culture speeds through in a day, leaving behind it only some cast-off merchandizing.*

or slavish follower of communism. His prime objective was Africa for the Africans. In the Gold Coast he discovered his talent for oratory and organisation. Objecting to the elitism of the United Gold Coast Convention, he resigned as secretary – the Convention leaders were probably ready to remove him anyway – and organised his own mass base in June 1949, the Convention People's Party, adroitly choosing the platform 'self-government now' – not total independence. He challenged the 1951 constitution, and government efforts to suppress his movement prompted him to respond with 'positive action' and a general strike. The British Governor arrested and imprisoned him and other leaders of his party, but – not for the first time in colonial history – this coercion simply rebounded to create a national hero. Nkrumah's party won nearly all the seats in the Legislative Assembly when elections were held in 1951.

Britain now showed a characteristic sense of realism, without the least regard for saving face. Nkrumah was released from prison and almost at once invited with his colleagues to assume ministerial office. From 1951 to 1957, the Gold Coast administration was Africanised, with Nkrumah as prime minister, and yet another election and constitution in 1954 became the last step but one to complete independence. If the British hoped that a strong rival would emerge with the help of an alliance of parties led by Dr Kofi Busia, whose strongest backing came from the Asante region, they were disappointed. Nkrumah's party once more enjoyed a clear majority in the 1956 election, and on 5 March 1957 the peaceful transfer of power was ceremonially enacted; the Gold Coast became Ghana and its red, green and gold flag replaced the Union Jack.

As an African leader taking his country to independence, Nkrumah has a well-deserved place in history. But, as the first political leader of Ghana, he exhibited some of the worst features of post-independence rulers. Political freedoms were speedily curtailed and abolished. Danquah and other political opponents were imprisoned without trial. Nkrumah went on to destroy the parliamentary and independent legal institutions the British had left behind. Power corrupted him. His megalomania found outlets in wasteful public buildings and a personality cult, and – made redundant by his dictatorial presidency – his party withered away. His grandeur impressed the masses, but his inconsistent

economic policies, which passed from capitalist enterprise to state socialism and massive public spending, speeded the economy on a downward path. There was hardship and Nkrumah was deservedly blamed, but a root cause was the decline in the world price of cocoa; between 1954 and independence in 1957 it had almost halved, and then between 1957 and 1965 it nearly halved again. A military coup in 1966, while Nkrumah was abroad, ended his rule and he died in African exile.

The subsequent political history of Ghana is one of military coups interspersed by periods of civilian rule. The military, whose officers were frequently trained by the West, proved more powerful in many independent African states than the politicians, who also derived their training and models from Western or Eastern Europe. Without secure party bases and electoral legitimacy, power has been too often concentrated in the hands of one leader. When he is removed in a coup it becomes relatively easy to change the power elite and its beneficiaries. The masses accept the change because they have to, or they may welcome it optimistically, hoping for better times. Reliance on one or two commodities has resulted in violent swings in the fortunes of African countries. The people suffer when prices are low and blame the rulers then in power, whose corruption becomes even more provoking.

General Ankrah led the first Ghanaian military coup in 1966, but he had little success in solving the complex economic problems, and his policies tended to benefit the military. Ankrah did, however, intend to return Ghana to civilian government, and Nkrumah's political opponents were released. But charges of bribery and corruption forced Ankrah to resign in 1969. In the subsequent election, Busia's party won a majority. A not altogether happy period of civilian rule, during which Dr Busia in turn exhibited authoritarian inclinations, was ended after only three years when a new military coup in 1972 created another National Redemption Council. At first, a rise in cacao prices favoured the military regime, but then in 1973–4 it had to face the huge rise in the oil price and its disastrous consequences for the Ghanaian economy. Another military coup in 1978 was short-lived. The fourth coup in May 1979 brought into the limelight a charismatic leader who promised to rid Ghana of corruption and to return the government to civilians. Flight-Lieutenant Jerry Rawlings was of mixed Ghanaian and Scottish parentage and enjoyed widespread popularity. After a grisly period of punishment and a bloodbath of executions of prominent Ghanaians, including three former heads of state, Rawlings did hand over to civilian government in September 1979, but this lasted only until December 1981, when Rawlings once more seized power.

Rawlings ruled Ghana throughout the 1980s, a decade of great economic difficulty for the people. In 1984 he declared his intention of working towards a representative system of government, but he insisted that in the meantime the failures of economic development would have to be remedied. The economy improved slowly, but hardly any progress towards representative government was made in the 1980s at all. The reality was a country ruled by a military regime, whose political opponents were arrested and detained. Rawlings increasingly associated civilians with the government, while making sure that he retained control, but the lack of accountability inevitably bred corruption. By the close of the decade the demands for democracy were growing louder, even though opposition leaders had been detained. Internationally, there was more confidence in the economic policies of the regime than there was in its claim to be leading the country back to representative democratic government. But in 1991 there was at last some progress. Opposition groups combined and Rawlings called on a constituent assembly to draft a new constitution. He promised to lift the bans on political parties and to hold national and presidential elections in 1992.

Ghanaian history illustrates how in what was formerly British West Africa neither the civilian politicians nor the military were able to solve fundamental problems. When the military could no longer cope they handed over to civilians, and when they in turn proved incompetent and corrupt the military would engineer a coup and return to power.

The same unstable military–political rivalry for power is evident in the history of Nigeria, by far the most populous of African nations. It reached independence in 1960, soon after Ghana. In addition to the problems of under-development common to the rest of British West Africa, Nigeria presented a post-colonial dilemma rooted in her territorial conquest and administration under the British. In the Muslim north, the ethnic Hausa-Fulani ruled indirectly through their own emirs, while the Yoruba inhabited the western region and

the Ibo the eastern. Each region overwhelmingly supported its own political leader and party. In the 1950s and 1960s Nigeria produced some outstanding political leaders, who transcended tribal and regional outlooks even though their electoral bases were largely regional and ethnic.

Among the earliest Nigerians to fight colonial status was the American-educated Dr Nnamdi Azikiwe, who started a chain of newspapers, the first in 1937, to spread his ideas about racial injustice, opposition to British rule and the need for positive action. His papers clashed with the British authorities when in 1945 they backed strikes by workers in government service. Azikiwe's electoral power base was in the eastern, Ibo-dominated region, which supported the party he had founded in 1944, the National Council of Nigeria and Cameroons (NCNC). The Yoruba, in the western region, supported the party led by Chief Obafemi Awolowo. But together the peoples of the western and eastern regions constituted no more than half of Nigeria's total population. The Muslim-dominated north of the Hausa-Fulani created its own party, the Northern People's Congress, whose most impressive politician was the deputy leader Abubakar Tafawa Balewa. The early misfortunes of Nigerian independence stemmed from the fact that the cultural and regional clashes and the militancy of regional groups proved more powerful than the urge to create a united Nigerian nation which would allow each region some measure of autonomy. The parliamentary system which Britain had created before independence gave no regional party the majority, though the north was allowed a representation larger than the west and east combined.

Immediately after independence in 1960, power was exercised by a coalition of the north and east, Ibo and Hausa, who had nothing in common except the desire to gain patronage. Azikiwe became head of state and Tafawa Balewa federal prime minister, and Awolowo headed the opposition until imprisoned in 1962. Electoral rigging and corruption created intense bitterness, and there were serious disturbances. In January 1966 Ibo officers of the federal army led a mutiny and assassinated prominent politicians, including the federal Prime Minister Abubakar Balewa. The officers all came from the south; their objective was to overthrow the north's political domination.

Major-General Aguiyi Ironsi re-established

control and assumed power, the military taking over from the failed politicians. Ironsi, adopting a policy of unifying Nigeria and abolishing the federation, favoured Ibo advisers and so aroused the apprehensions of the conservative north. The Ibos who had migrated to the north to take up posts in the railways and banks and who had established themselves as enterprising traders formed a better-off elite deeply resented by the Hausa. Ironsi's military coup was soon interpreted in the north as an Ibo plot to dominate the country. When the false rumour was spread that the many Ibo officers in the north planned to kill their fellow officers, the northern junior officers and NCOs in July 1966 organised a second coup which began by mass killings of Ibo officers. Among the victims was General Ironsi. His chief of staff, Colonel Yakubu Gowon, a Christian from a Muslim region without ethnic prejudice, was chosen by the coup leaders as the new military ruler.

Gowon, who had so accidentally come to power, was to play a major role in Nigeria's history. But during the following months, despite conciliatory efforts, he was unable to master the growing fanaticism in the north and east. In the north, the unrest culminated in the massacre of thousands of Ibos. Hausas who lived in the east were driven out and retaliatory killings took place. Two million panic-stricken refugees, mainly Ibo from the north, tried to get back to their own people. Nigeria was threatened with anarchy, each region going its own way.

The biggest tragedy was yet to come – civil war. The military commander of the eastern Ibo region, Odumegwu Ojukwu, on 30 May 1967 declared the region's independence as the new state of Biafra. Fighting on the ground began in July as Gowon, despairing of a peaceful resolution, determined to maintain Nigerian unity. The civil war lasted nearly three years, until January 1970. The Biafrans, with the main oil reserves and the refinery at Port Harcourt in their region, had for a time the resources to secure weapons and help from abroad, especially from France, Portugal and South Africa. Their secession was soon recognised by a number of African states. Although the Ibos fought fiercely, they faced an overwhelmingly larger federal army, and when a blockade was imposed, food supplies to the civilian population dwindled. Famine killed hundreds of thousands, many more than died in the fighting. Pitiful television pictures and newspaper reports reached the West and aroused widespread

*Victims of the Nigerian civil war, 1967.*

sympathy for the cause of Biafra, but Britain refused to intervene. Gowon made it clear that the federal government and army were not engaged in genocide.

Gowon's statesmanship was proven when Biafra surrendered. There was no revenge such as the Ibos had feared, for Gowon wanted to heal the wounds. Ojukwu fled into exile. A few Biafran ‘officers were imprisoned for a short time, but many Ibos were reinstated in federal jobs. Unfortunately Gowon proved to be indecisive and incompetent as a peacetime leader. Despite the oil boom which followed the price rise of 1973–4 and huge increases in export earnings, the development plans of the 1970s and 1980s did not bring greater prosperity to the majority of the people. Money was made by a business elite; industry, transport and social services expanded; but agricultural growth could not keep pace with a rapidly increasing population.

In 1975 General Gowon was overthrown by another military coup, and the anti-corruption drive that followed led to the dismissal of some 10,000 bureaucrats. During an army mutiny in 1976 the head of state was murdered and another general succeeded. By then the oil boom was over and the Nigerian economy fell into deficit. Economic development was hindered by political instability. In 1979 the military handed the government back to the civilians, but this Second Republic lasted only until 1983, when another coup restored the military to power with promises to hand the country back to civilian rule, when the corrupt politicians of the First and Second Republic would be barred from office. Although Nigeria's oil earnings reached a peak in 1982 following the 1979–80 price rise, a flood of imports created a huge foreign debt in less than a decade. After General Ibrahim Babangida became the head of state in 1985, efforts were made to correct the mistakes of the oil-boom years, to increase agricultural production and exports and to diversify industry. Nigeria passed from economic reform in 1986 to mismanagement and corruption under its military rulers. Whether there would be an improvement in government stability in the 1990s also remained an open question. Local and state elections took place in 1990 and 1991 and the prospects for a transition to representative civilian rule began to look more promising until frustrated in June 1993. In November the military seized power.

Conflict and turbulence since independence are not just consequences of European colonial rule in the nineteenth and twentieth centuries. This is shown by the history of Liberia and her wartorn condition in the early 1990s. Liberia was the only part of West Africa to avoid outright European colonisation. She is unique in Africa in another way: the overseas settlers who imposed their rule on the indigenous African peoples were not white but black. Early in the nineteenth century the philanthropic American Colonisation Society had the romantic notion of undoing some of the harm done by the slave trade by resettling freed slaves in Africa and so returning them to an African way of life. The Society induced indigenous African chieftains to allow a settlement on the coast of what became Liberia. The first freed slaves landed in 1822. But it was a white American, Jehudi Ashmun, who during his stay in the territory (1822–8) organised the government of the black settlers and so became the real founder of Liberia. The dependence on Anglo-Saxon Americans was to be characteristic of the next 150 years of Liberia's history. Her independence was recognised by the European nations in the mid-nineteenth century, but she remained under American protection, though the United States was actually the last major nation to recognise her independence, in 1862.

A constitution modelled on that of the United States was adopted and the capital was named Monrovia in honour of the American President. But only the 'civilised' had the vote, and that meant the descendants of the American freed slaves known as Americo-Liberians. The hinterland, where the great majority of the population lived, was administered by indirect rule through chieftains. The majority of the population was thus colonised as in white settler colonies. In 1919 part of this hinterland which the Americo-Liberians could not control was simply ceded to France. A worse scandal came to light in the 1920s when a League of Nations investigation uncovered forced labour and the shipment of virtual slaves to the Spanish plantations in Fernando Po. Greed for profit knows no colour bars.

Liberia was ruled by one party, the True Whig Party, which monopolised power and patronage for more than a hundred years. The majority living in the hinterland only gradually became associated as citizens of Liberia after the Second World War. During the era when William Tubman was president from 1944 to 1971 (he was always re-elected!), a minority representation was achieved by the majority of the people. Tubman, conservative and always ready to welcome Western economic penetration, died in office. His successor, Vice-president Tolbert, inaugurated a more liberal regime and was sworn in wearing an open-necked shirt. He followed a policy of moderate reforms and closer integration with the peoples of the hinterland.

The world economic problems of the mid-1970s and the growth of opposition groups undermined Tolbert. Corruption remained endemic. In 1980 Master-Sergeant Samuel Doe organised a military revolt, and a new generation of soldiers seized control from the political elite. Former ministers were publicly executed by firing squad, Doe ordering the executions to be filmed. His bloody coup ended the reign of the True Whig Party and the Americo-Liberians. The new military People's Reception Council confiscated the assets of the former political leaders and raised wages. But Liberia remained poor and under-developed, and government deteriorated once more into corruption.

Liberia's ties with the United States, and Western loans and aid, failed to lift the population out of poverty. To the outside world the Liberian economy became synonymous with the Firestone Rubber Company, which introduced rubber plantations in the 1870s. Rubber became Liberia's most important export and was invaluable after the fall of Malaya during the Second World War. After the 1950s the mining of iron ore replaced it as the principal export, and together iron and rubber contributed 90 per cent in value to Liberia's export trade. Industry remained very small, so that her economy is typical of Third World countries in depending on world trade conditions and the prices of a few basic commodities. But a description of Liberia would not be complete without noting one more peculiarity. She possesses nominally the largest merchant fleet in the world. These are, of course, not Liberian but foreign ships registered under the Liberian flag, notorious for lax regulations and low registration fees, and so widely favoured by shipowners.

President Doe ruled the country tyrannically for ten years. In 1989 Liberia erupted in civil war between rival ethnic groups. The savagery of that conflict, with ill-disciplined rebel forces shooting and pillaging, has wrecked the country. Doe grimly held on to dwindling power in his palace in Monrovia, refusing American offers to escort him to safety. In the summer of 1990 an African peacekeeping force entered Liberia and in September one of the rival forces captured Doe and killed him. The state was bankrupt, and administration collapsed as rival factions spread terror throughout the country. Black African intervention with troops and through mediation succeeded in establishing a ceasefire and an agreement on an interim president, but Liberia's uneasy settlement proved fragile. Civil war and political chaos thrived in 1993, despite the presence of a peacekeeping force from neighbouring West African states. Here too, human tragedy unfolds as the innocent fall victim to the indiscriminate fighting.

# CHAPTER 74

# Freedom and After in Central and East Africa

European colonial rule, based on over-whelming military power, established common patterns of control. Resistance to authority was harshly suppressed, and equal rights and opportunities were withheld from the African majority. British, Belgian, French and Portuguese colonial government each had its distinctive features and the European nations hoped that these would form the basis of government in independent Africa. The influence of the colonial period was never obliterated, but each newly independent African nation developed along her own path. Much depended on the dominant African leadership, on the accident of the personality and outlook of the most powerful man or group, on whether his or their prestige survived the struggle for independence or whether new groups and leaders seized control in a separate struggle for power. Africa abounds with examples of the influence of the individual on history. This at least in part accounts for the very different evolution of Tanzania, Kenya and Uganda after Britain relinquished colonial power.

The Belgian Congo in Central Africa could not remain isolated from the new nationalism sweeping through British and French West Africa. But it was a latecomer as far as black nationalism was concerned. When it came to 1960 the transfer of power was sudden, and the least successful. For years afterwards this huge country was rent by internal conflict; to make matters worse it became the focus of international Cold War rivalry. Yet in one sense the Belgians had been among the more

enlightened colonial administrators in Africa, once the Belgian Parliament had taken responsibility for the country in 1908. This paradox requires some explanation.

The Congo's real capital was Brussels. The colony was governed from Europe in a highly centralised way by Belgian administrators, with no African participation. The 100,000 or more Belgians in the Congo, unlike the whites in the British settler colonies, had no local political rights. For this there was no one simple reason; before 1957 there was no elective body or legislature in existence in the Congo. The idea was that, until the Africans were judged capable of exercising the vote, no one should have it, thus hopefully avoiding white-settler domination. In 1949 the Belgian Parliament approved a ten-year plan for the econ-omic and social development of the Congo and for raising African living standards. Primary education was the best in Africa and literacy the highest. This was largely due to the missionaries and to Belgian official encouragement. But there was practically no advanced schooling. The very first African graduated at a Belgian university only in 1956, nor was there a single black officer in the Congolese police or in the military or in the Force Publique, responsible for public order. Independence was a distant prospect.

The most important economic developments in the Congo were concentrated in the province of Katanga on the borders of Rhodesia and Tangan-yika. From there rich deposits of copper, cobalt and other valuable minerals were exported. To the north-west, the province of Kasai provided in 1959 most of the world's industrial diamonds. This mineral wealth was in the hands of Belgian trusts, the most important being the Société Générale and the Union Minière. Although most of the profit flowed out of the country, as in other colonies, the Belgians were at least more enlightened than the South African mineowners in encouraging Africans to acquire technical expertise in their mines. The other regions of the Congo were very poor, and here agriculture provided the means of livelihood and the source of exports.

When nationalism developed late in the mid-1950s it was strongly ethnic, regional and divisive. The main parties were four: the Abako, led by Joseph Kasavubu; the Parti Solidaire Africaine, led by Antoine Gizenga; the Katangan association, Conakat for short, led by Moise Tschombe; and the Mouvement National Congolais, whose fiery and controversial leader was Patrice Lumumba.

In the 1950s the Belgians belatedly decided that some African representation in the administration of the Congo had become necessary. They accordingly organised municipal elections in 1959 by manhood suffrage, one man one vote. This in turn stimulated agitation: in 1959 there was rioting and looting in Léopoldville. The pace now quickened. The Belgians, at first so slow to accept Africanisation, now seemingly could not get out fast enough. They wanted to abandon the increasingly burdensome task of keeping order in the country but to retain their industrial interests. After all, the Congolese would not be able to run the mines and market the metals without them. The fact that the Congolese were not prepared to run their government administration nor their army and police did not deter the Belgians. The Congolese, they reasoned, could always ask for their assistance. So elections were arranged in May 1960 and the independent Congo handed over to a cobbled-together coalition of political rivals, with Kasavubu as president and Lumumba as prime minister.

Independence day was 30 June 1960. Not a week later violence erupted. The frustration of the Congolese NCOs and soldiers in the Force Publique boiled over; they were angered by the fact that only Belgian officers gave commands. Mutinying soldiers murdered their officers and went on the rampage, killing and raping whites and looting. The Belgian troops still in the Congo left their

bases to protect and evacuate their nationals. But Kasavubu and Lumumba suspected the Belgians of harbouring sinister designs, especially when Tschombe declared the richest mining province of Katanga independent. The world was horrified by the anarchy and the televised pictures of bloated corpses floating downriver. To check the atrocities and safeguard the Europeans, Lumumba had no reliable force apart from the Belgian troops, but he wanted the Belgians out. Wishing also to recover control of Katanga, he appealed to the United Nations. The UN responded with promises to help restore law and order; but it declared that the secession of Katanga was not its concern.

During July, the UN peacekeeping force began to arrive and the Belgian soldiers left. But paramilitary troops and mercenaries from Europe, Rhodesia and South Africa were ready to defend Katanga and the European mining interests. Lumumba now made the error of turning for help to the Soviet Union, asking the Russians to equip a still largely unreliable Congolese army to occupy Katanga and crush the secession. Lumumba's refusal to rely on UN forces and his determination to maintain the ill-disciplined Congolese soldiers under arms ensured that the disorders and the attacks on white missionaries and Europeans would continue. Then, in August, his troubles multiplied when the province of Kasai also seceded. Without the two mineral-rich provinces, a Congo state would become one of the poorest in Africa. In response to Lumumba's appeal, Moscow saw a chance to gain influence in the strategically important country. Soviet aid arrived by air, and Kasai was retaken for a time. But Kasavubu and the African Chief of Staff Mobutu Sese Seko decided to rid themselves of the radical Lumumba and to rely instead on Western help. Lumumba was dismissed, and then arrested when Mobutu took power. In December 1960 the pro-Lumumba region rebelled and set up a rival government. Mobutu thereupon planned to silence Lumumba, who, despite UN protection, was transported to Katanga by Mobutu's soldiers. There, in January 1961, he was killed 'while trying to escape'. Nothing can excuse what was in all probability a murder; but a myth was in the making.

The dead Patrice Lumumba was celebrated in Moscow as the anti-colonialist hero of African independence, true patriot and Marxist. Had Lumumba lived it is unlikely that he would have acquired such an exalted reputation. As a politician he had lacked adroitness and good judgement, and this had contributed to his fall from power. He was indeed an African patriot, but an unrealistic one, and his brand of socialism, common among Africans struggling against colonialism, had little in common with Soviet communism.

The year 1961 saw no lessening of the chaos in the Congo. Tschombe, installed in Katanga and effectively separated from the rest of the Congo, though supported by the Belgian mining interests, talked and talked, claiming that he was ready to negotiate with the UN, but gave up nothing of substance. In the Congo a new parliament assembled under UN protection and a weak new civilian regime was installed. Katanga meanwhile continued to maintain her independence, in practice helped by the Belgians' decision to pay the mining royalties to Tschombe and not to the central government. But Tschombe had not reckoned with a determined and ambitious UN secretary-general. Dag Hammarskjöld wanted to crown this first major UN peacekeeping effort with success. It cost him his life. In rather mysterious circumstances his plane crashed in September 1961, while he was engaged in negotiations with Tschombe. This hardened the attitude of the UN towards Katanga. Fighting had

broken out between UN troops and Tschombe's forces in Elisabethville, the capital of Katanga. With the central Congolese government now pro-Western in orientation, the situation had changed. The UN ordered the forcible occupation of Katanga, and in January 1963 the province at last fell to an international force.

Tschombe had left Katanga only to return in July 1964 as prime minister of a united Congo. But he did not last long in office. In October 1965 Mobuto, exercising the real power in the Congo with his army command, organised a coup and once more took over the country. The Belgian colonial pact was expunged. The major towns were renamed, Léopoldville becoming Kinshasa, and the Congo became Zaire.

The immediate post-colonial turmoil in the Congo, the atrocities and the savagery and the hiring of white mercenaries, all seemed to justify the cynical view that black Africa was unfit to govern itself. What was really shown in the Congo and elsewhere in black Africa, however, was the weakness of democracy and elected national parliaments; parliaments whose members were tribally divided could not maintain unity in countries as under-developed as Zaire, where in many rural areas there

*During the Congo Crisis in 1961, the United Nations' Secretary-General Dag Hammarskjöld greets Moise Tshombe, who had proclaimed the independence of Katanga.*

was little education. Loyalties were tribal and ethnic in such conditions. Pent-up resentments against the better-off of other races, whether European or Asian, could and did explode into violence. If unity and order were to be maintained, the country needed a strong man with an obedient party or a soldier who could count on an obedient army.

For the first thirteen years of his rule Mobutu was occupied in putting down rebellions with European aid. For the next twelve years he ruthlessly eliminated all political dissent. But the collapse of the communist regimes in eastern Europe and the Soviet Union seemed to convince Mobutu that one-party authoritarian rule had become even less acceptable to the outside world on which Zaire relies for aid and trade. In 1990 he promised to introduce multi-party government. Mobutu explained that his version of a multi-party state envisaged himself as above politics, the final arbiter and guarantor of national unity. Unrest and dissenters were ruthlessly put down, and at the university in Lubumbashi large numbers of students were massacred on their campus. In 1991, 130 political parties combined for a time against the President. More seriously the army rioted when it was not paid. In the following year more units of the army mutinied and the Belgians evacuated thousands of their citizens. The country was economically in ruins, despite her rich resources. The West cut off aid to register its displeasure but was determined not to become involved in rescuing Zaire from misrule which in 1992 continued in internal disarray.

The history of independent Uganda is scarcely happier than Zaire's. This once fertile and rich country suffered decades of conflict and destruction. The path to independence also involved overcoming difficulties special to Uganda. It was not the white settler who impeded the granting of independence. There were less than 10,000 of them, and Asian settlers – although 70,000 lived in Uganda – were hardly considered. The path to independence was bedevilled by old colonial agreements which had preserved traditional local monarchies; the most important was that of Buganda, ruled by the kabaka. This arrangement was a matter of colonial expediency, a form of indirect rule as was later developed in northern Nigeria. The kabaka and the Bugandans still wanted to preserve their autonomy and customs, which

by then were in conflict with the rise of African nationalism in the rest of Uganda. Even so, the usual process towards self-rule was followed: first African representation on the Legislative Council was increased in the 1950s, then in 1961 parliamentary elections were held. Milton Obote, leader of the Uganda People's Congress, which sought early independence, followed a tactic adopted by politicians in other divided African countries of forming temporary political alliances in order to persuade the colonial power to grant independence. Irreconcilable conflicts were papered over. Britain was only too anxious to accept at face value that the African politicians had indeed formed the consensus necessary to make independence viable. And so in October 1962 Uganda gained independence with the kabaka as titular president; in 1963 Dr Obote became the chief minister. Obote attempted to overcome the internal conflict by authoritarian rule and reliance on the army. In 1966 Obote set aside the special rights enjoyed by the Buganda tribe in the Kingdom of Buganda and the kabaka was driven into exile. A short insurrection in May of that year by Bugandans was suppressed by force.

The tragedy of Uganda was her so-called army, an undisciplined force which for years wreaked destruction on the country. In 1971 it seized control of the government under its infamous chief of staff Idi Amin, who even before independence had murders on his conscience. A soldier of great physical strength, with minimal education but an outwardly jovial presence, Amin was ostensibly a Muslim, although in fact he was a barbarian. He had been one of the few blacks promoted to officer rank in colonial times – the Ugandan army, like the Congolese, had lacked black officers – and so he became a colonel almost immediately after independence. Ugandans, who were at first glad to be rid of Obote, soon began to suffer even more under Amin, who as a Muslim had the support of President Gaddafi of oil-rich Libya. Amin gave the army free rein to massacre the inhabitants of this small country of less than 10 million; possibly as many as 300,000 disappeared or were murdered. The exact number of victims was never established. Opponents 'disappeared' and met violent deaths. Amin ruled by terror. Cabinet ministers, a courageous chief justice and the Anglican Archbishop were all killed. During Amin's years of misrule human rights were utterly disregarded. Yet the civilised world, including the UN, recognised him as president

*The mark of respectability: President Idi Amin addresses the United Nations on 2 October 1975 wielding a field-marshal's baton and sporting the medals he had bestowed on himself.*

and received him with honour. Most African states behaved no better. The Organisation of African Unity paid him the compliment of meeting in Kampala and elected him president. It was politic to ignore his part in the murder of hundreds of thousands of his own people. This was the *Realpolitik* of the 1970s. It was Nyerere of Tanzania who finally toppled Amin from power in 1979 after the Ugandan leader had invaded Tanzania to settle by force the disputed frontier between them.

Amin was never brought to justice for his crimes; instead he was given shelter by Gaddafi in Libyan exile. Obote thereupon sought a new mandate in rigged elections and assumed the presidency. But unhappy Uganda was rent by civil wars and tribal conflicts, until in 1986 the National Resistance Army led by Yoweri Musevani captured Kampala. The task then was to rebuild Uganda. This would not be easy after the policy of Africanisation which on Amin's orders had in the mid-1970s driven tens of thousands of industrious Asians out of the country. Their enterprise instead benefited Britain, despite the reluctance with which they were allowed entry.

President Yoweri Museveni and his ministers made valiant efforts to bring about a reconciliation of warring factions, with some success. The economy, dependent on coffee exports, was badly hit when the world price of coffee fell again in 1992. Foreign economic aid helped to support efforts to reform the economy. In 1991 it became evident that a new catastrophe threatened Uganda – Aids. The Ugandan government was more open than most in facing the scourge which kills the young and leaves behind the old. In 1991 1.2 million were estimated to be HIV-infected and the numbers increased daily thereafter. Yet perversely the Africa of the early 1990s was still threatened by over-population and famine.

Murderous and corrupt rule was unfortunately not confined to Uganda alone. Human-rights abuses were common in the one-party African states, and democracy was quickly discarded as part of the colonial past. Some African states were notorious for their leader's savagery, not least Benin in the 1970s, whose president was executed for genocide after a coup in 1979. The height of absurdity was reached in one of Africa's poorest countries, the Central African Republic, where Colonel Jean-Bedel Bokassa seized power in

*The glittering career of an African despot: beginning as a humble sergeant, Jean Bedel Bokassa rose to occupy the throne of the Central African Empire. His Napoleonic 'coronation' is reputed to have cost $20 million.*

December 1965 and, not satisfied with becoming president, had himself crowned emperor. He invited over 3000 dignitaries from all over the world to his ruinously expensive coronation. He curried favour with France, calling de Gaulle his 'adoptive father' and presenting diamonds to those whose favours he wished to win. The murder of a group of children in 1979 proved his undoing; he was beyond protection now and with the help of French troops he was ousted later that year. Like Amin he was not brought to account for his crimes, but was allowed a comfortable exile in the Ivory Coast.

A horrifying example of the world's selective conscience – no intervention as long as blacks are slaughtering blacks (or Asians, Asians) – were the massacres that occurred in two small independent African countries, Rwanda and Burundi. Here the

Tutsi minority ruled over the majority Hutu. Tribal wars began in 1959 and thousands of Tutsi fled. In 1963, in fear of a Tutsi invasion from neighbouring Burundi, the Hutu massacred thousands of Tutsi. In Burundi, after an uprising of the Hutu in 1972, at least 100,000 of them were slaughtered. The tribal warfare did not end there. The Burundi army next killed thousands of Tutsi in 1988. The world confined itself to relief work by the UN High Commission for Refugees. Rwanda and Burundi remain cauldrons of tribal hatreds. Independence suited Belgium, the former colonial power in the two countries, which were not prepared for independence nor given adequate assistance.

It took television cameras and a pop singer, Bob Geldof, to rouse the world's conscience for the victims of famine in northern Ethiopia. Live Aid concerts watched by 1.5 billion worldwide raised £503 million for famine relief in 1985 and Sport Aid the following year raised £8.2 million. Official government reactions were slow and followed rather than led public opinion in the developed world. Animals in the West were better fed than millions in Africa. In the famines of 1984 and 1985 nearly 1 million died. In the early 1990s drought and famine in sub-Saharan Africa threatened millions of lives again. Famine and starvation had become the rule rather than the exception.

Tanzania, unlike Uganda, was not beset by serious ethnic conflict. It is the largest of the East African countries and by far the poorest. No tribe is powerful enough to dominate the others, and the Swahili language forms a common bond. Here too African nomination to the colonial Legislative Council had to wait until the end of the Second World War. By 1960 a nationwide election was held in preparation for independence from Britain. Dr Julius Nyerere and his Tanganyikan African National Union (formed in 1954) swept the board. The firm unity evident in the country facilitated rapid independence, which was achieved in December 1961. A new election in 1962 followed, and Nyerere became president. Nyerere stood for African Democratic Socialism, which in practice meant a one-party state and a radical form of socialism particularly suitable, so Nyerere believed, for a people who would have to pull themselves up by their bootstraps.

The neighbouring island of Zanzibar with her feudal sultan and mixed Arab–African people of Muslim faith was granted her own independence by Britain in December 1963. A month later a coup by Africans overthrew the Sultan's government and put in its place a revolutionary council which in April announced union with Tanganyika, now renamed Tanzania. Africans had constituted four-fifths of the population of Zanzibar, and many Arabs and Asians now fled. On the mainland in the same year Nyerere faced his own troubles when the army mutinied for higher pay and better promotion, but with the help of British troops he defeated the challenge.

For twenty-eight years from 1962 Nyerere was the undisputed father and 'teacher' of the nation, until he retired in 1990 of his own free will. His was an authoritarian paternalism which owed much to Mao, whom he admired. Like Mao, Nyerere was a scholar–leader, writing tracts to explain his own socialist ideology to the people. His authoritarian rule was motivated by a humane utopian vision, which so often can lead to coercion and control over the mass of the people who need 'improving'. He justified the one-party state as necessary to overcome class and ethnic division so that everyone could strive together to overcome ignorance, hunger and disease. 'War' on these evils together with African self-reliance were what Nyerere propounded in his Arusha Declaration of 1967. Economic development would focus on basics – on agriculture rather than on grandiose industrial projects. Tanzania would not make herself dependent on foreign investment. Following communist models, land was collectivised and peasant families were brought together into Africa 'family villages', often at some distance from their land. When voluntary exhortation proved inadequate, millions of peasant families were relocated. The concentration on agricultural development and illiteracy was sound enough, but everywhere in the world peasants fail to produce when the land they cultivate is no longer their own. Nyerere's new society did not raise standards of living. His major success was the spread of elementary education and literacy; another great plus was that his country was not marred by political executions or massacres.

Authoritarian and visionary, Nyerere in retirement was held in respect and affection. His successor President Ali Hassan Mwinyi, however, began to move away from the ideology of the one-party state. The United States, indirectly the chief provider of finance through the World Bank and the International Monetary Fund, made her hostility to

one-party states felt. In the early 1980s the corruption of the one-party state and socialist planning were ruining the economy, including agriculture, which employed 90 per cent of the population and earned 80 per cent of foreign exchange. Julius Nyerere, in a fashion typical of black independence leaders imposing their ideology, voluntarily stepped down from the presidency but declared that he would continue to guide the country as chairman of the ruling party. In 1990 he gave up the chairmanship as well. Under her new president, Ali Hassan Mwinyi, Tanzania began to move away from her ruinous socialist experiments and turned to the West, to the International Monetary Fund in Washington for loans, and after 1986 had to accept the remedies prescribed. Nyerere disapproved, but Mwinyi became increasingly his own man and was re-elected for a five-year term as president in 1990. In 1991 cautious steps were taken to explore whether Tanzania should liberalise politically as well as economically.

Kenya's road to independence was very different from Tanzania's peaceful progress. Kenya was the one East African colony where a widespread and bloodily suppressed insurrection preceded independence. But this was not the only difference. Kenya also had a significant white settler population which increased in size after 1945. With a population at the time of independence of nearly 10 million Africans, the 45,000 Europeans were, of course, significant not in numbers but in political clout. There were far more Muslim Arabs (35,000) and Indians (188,000), originally brought in to build the Ugandan railway, but Asians and Arabs were not significant in Whitehall in the way the politically powerful white settlers were.

The foundations of colonial government were undeniably racist. But the white settlers could claim that they had worked hard to make their farms productive and had invested their lives and those of their families in becoming White Africans: Africa was now their homeland. On the other hand, only one-third of Kenya was fertile, and the highland plateau, the best of the land, was until 1960 the exclusive preserve of the white settlers. With the approach of independence the settlers expected to preserve their privileges and to retain influence far beyond what their numbers could justify.

The oldest of African political leaders came from Kenya. Jomo Kenyatta had been involved in early

African nationalist policies in the 1920s and, when these were forbidden in the 1930s, came to study and live in Britain, where politics could not be proscribed. In 1947, by then already an elder statesman, he returned to Kenya to lead the Kenya African National Union. His aim was to win African majority rule constitutionally step by step, beginning with an increase in the number of Africans on the Legislative Council. But a more radical wing of the party – the Forty Group – determined to drive the British out by force. Kenya's political parties were largely ethnically based and the two most powerful groups were the Kikuyu and the Luo. The Kenya African National Union, which was predominantly Kikuyu, organised a rising in 1952. The Kikuyu had plenty of grievances, in particular a desperate shortage of land. But there was also anger about discrimination and the colour-bar; ex-servicemen had already experienced a different world of comradeship with white Europeans. Kikuyu nationalism was strong too, and the oaths administered to the Land Freedom Army deliberately harked back to Kikuyu traditions. At the height of the rebellion there were some 25,000 fighters in the forests. The British ruthlessly suppressed the rebellion. The picture presented in Britain depicted the valiant farmer, with a rifle across his knees, protecting his family and homestead from savages crazed by the blood oaths of the secret Mau Mau society to hack the whites to pieces with their *pangas*. In reality during the four years of the rising less than seventy whites lost their lives.

The main victims were the Africans. Some 90,000 Kikuyu men between the ages of sixteen and thirty-five were herded by the authorities into detention camps. One of these, the Hola camp, became notorious for beating and even murders. African soldiers officered by the British meanwhile defeated the guerrilla army. Black casualties on both sides came to some 18,000 and many black African civilians died from malnutrition in the forests. The Governor, who had proclaimed an emergency, also arrested Kenyatta and the principal leaders of the Kenya African National Union, accusing them of having organised the Mau Mau. Kenyatta was tried and sentenced in 1954 to hard labour. It was a typical knee-jerk reaction. Once the rising had been put down and the emergency ended in 1956, wiser counsels prevailed. The constructive work of preparing Kenya for independence proceeded.

In 1961 Kenyatta was released. In Britain Harold Macmillan was now prime minister. Always a realist and a progressive conservative, Macmillan recognised the futility of attempting to perpetuate the privileges of a few thousand white settlers at great cost to the British taxpayer. In 1960 at the end of a tour of Africa he delivered his famous 'wind of change' speech in Cape Town. The practical implications were soon enough evident. The Kenyan highlands were opened to African settlement, and restrictions on what the Kikuyu could cultivate, like coffee, were lifted. Kenyatta resumed leadership of the Kenya African National Union. Ethnic political rivalries impeded progress for a time, but when Kenyatta's KANU in May 1963 won a majority, complicated plans for a federal structure were abandoned and Kenyatta was honoured as prime minister. This was the last staging post on the road to independence, which was duly accorded in December 1963.

During the Mau Mau struggle rival politicians, Oginga Odinga (a Luo) and Tom Mboya, had come to the fore, but Kenyatta's personality and reputation dominated the country. Ethnic politics continued for some years to create disturbance, which Kenyatta countered by setting up a one-party state. By the close of the 1960s his two principal rivals had been eliminated: Tom Mboya had been assassinated and Odinga detained.

Kenyatta encouraged foreign investment and capitalism, but this was capitalism with the African difference that it was state-dominated. The state played a guiding role in agriculture too, and formulated national plans. Kenya at the time of independence was the most commercially advanced of the three East African nations. Agriculture provided the main source of exports, especially coffee, tea and dairy produce. With Kenyatta placing national interests above the desire for revenge, the Europeans were encouraged to stay and to help the new African country with their knowledge and expertise. Not so the Asians, who played a leading role in trade; confronted by Kenya's efforts to Africanise, they were driven out and many thousands holding British passports settled in Britain. Kenyatta encouraged private investment, and foreigners were attracted to invest in this one black country which was politically stable, aligned with the West and opposed to communism.

The mixed free and state economy overall did well until the mid-1970s, although agricultural and industrial progress was uneven. But with one of the

*President Jomo Kenyatta celebrates Kenyan independence in 1963.*

fastest-growing populations in Africa the loss of Asian enterprise was a serious setback. Worse still was the growing corruption of those in power during the Kenyatta years from 1963 to 1978, an inevitable consequence of one-party rule.

On Kenyatta's death in 1978, Daniel arap Moi, the Vice-President, came to power, and maintained the one-party rule of the Kenya African National Union. Economic growth after 1984 was one of the best in black Africa and at 5 per cent kept ahead of the annual population growth of 3.5 per cent. But Moi developed his own style of authoritarian rule and cowed all opposition. Even by African standards his one-party regime was particularly repressive. There occurred the murder of the respected Foreign Minister, Robert Ouko, in 1990 after he had attacked government corruption – the results of an investigation were not made public and a government cover-up was suspected. Pressure on Moi increased in Kenya and abroad. In

December 1991 he allowed the constitution to be changed to allow the establishment of other political parties. It was not clear whether genuine political reform would develop from these reluctant beginnings. Stifling bureaucracy and widespread corruption were making Kenya less attractive to foreign investors. Moi attributed Kenya's better economic performance to the one-party state and continued to resist Western pressure to introduce democratic reforms.

Before independence these three East African states under colonial rule benefited from common economic structures, a common market and a common currency. The British hoped by establishing the East African High Commission (1948) and the East African Common Services Organisation (1961) that on independence the three nations would unify or federate into one large viable nation, which would have had a population in 1990 of 70 million. Nyerere of Tanzania favoured this idea too and was prepared to delay Tanganyika's independence. But local ambitions, the very different conditions in each country and Kenya's separate road to independence nullified these hopes. Nor did the later East African Economic Community (1967) prove successful. African nationalism proved stronger than regional co-operation. A strong united African voice in the world had no more emerged by the 1990s than a single Arab, Asian, American or European one had.

### Central and East Africa, 1987

|  | Population (*millions*) | Gross National Product per head (*US$*) |
|---|---|---|
| Uganda | 15.7 | 260 |
| Rwanda | 6.4 | 300 |
| Burundi | 5.0 | 250 |
| Tanzania | 23.1 | 180 |
| Kenya | 21.1 | 330 |
| Zaire | 32.6 | 150 |

# CHAPTER 75

# War and Famine in the Horn of Africa

Of all the regions of independent Africa the peoples in the Horn of Africa have probably fared the worst. Much of the land is desert, and rainfall is uncertain, so that surviving even at subsistence level is difficult. Famine has stalked the region and claimed more than a million lives. Five million remained in danger in the early 1990s. Only Libya has reaped untold riches from below this desert, in the form of oil, but she fell under the maverick rule of Colonel Gaddafi, who properly used a part of these riches to benefit the Libyans but also fanned conflict among his neighbours and elsewhere in the world. Gaddafi remained unpredictable. Libya's wealth did not help the whole region; indeed, her neighbours Chad and Somalia are among the poorest in Africa. Authoritarian regimes in Ethiopia and Somalia, characterised by corruption and economic mismanagement, added to the misery. But it was above all the tribal and civil wars of the region which were responsible for the sufferings of millions of helpless people. Precious resources and aid were used to pay for weapons to fight these wars. The West and East, when their priorities were dictated by the Cold War, supplied them. Yet these were the countries 'liberated' by the United Nations from European colonial rule, their independence intended to signal a new era for the suppressed peoples of the world. What went so dreadfully wrong?

The first African nation rescued from colonial dependency was Ethiopia (then called Abyssinia), thanks to the internecine Second World War between the European colonial powers. In 1941 she was liberated from Italian occupation, which had begun in 1936, and Haile Selassie was restored as feudal emperor. Ethiopia alone had successfully resisted by force of arms European colonial partition in the nineteenth century as the Italian army, advancing inland from the colony of Eritrea on the Red Sea, was defeated in 1896. When Haile Selassie returned in 1941 he benefited from the modernisation and centralisation of the Italian occupation and launched an Ethiopian drive to try to bring his backward kingdom into the twentieth century. Progress was impressive in education, and a small start was made in setting up some factories and in industrialising. With the assistance of the United States a properly equipped and trained army was created. These developments, however, undermined the old structures of the monarchial state. By the early 1970s new shocks resulted in government and society falling apart.

Nineteen-seventy-three proved a disastrous year. The rise in oil prices hit the poorest countries especially hard. This coincided with a calamitous drought. There was famine in the Tigre province and the royal army was defeated by Eritrean freedom fighters. The rising, which turned into revolution, began in the spring of 1974. Behind it was a group of officers, army mutineers, who were joined by students and teachers in the capital, Addis Ababa. Gradually the revolution became more radical. The eighty-three-year-old emperor was deposed in September 1974 and imprisoned; later he and his family were murdered. Strife within the military and among the radical groups followed until in February 1977 Colonel Haile Mengistu eventually emerged as the victor and unleashed a reign of terror; opponents were rounded up and summarily executed. Assuming the red star and the trappings of a Marxist people's republic, he wielded absolute power over the political and economic life of the country and crushed his opponents as enemies of the revolution.

The Soviet Union saw here an opportunity to advance her influence in a region of Africa bordering on the Red Sea, which was of obvious strategic significance. Moscow cynically hailed Mengistu's seizure of power as a truly 'Bolshevik' revolution and provided arms and aid. Meanwhile the internal divisions in the country and Mengistu's dictatorship had one other result: the resumption of fierce fighting between the central Politburo in Addis Ababa and outlying Eritrea, a province attached to Ethiopia after the Second World War. Faced with Eritreans in the north and with Somalis in the south-east, Mengistu depended on Soviet weapons and military training. The demands of the military, the devastation of the endless warfare over a disputed frontier with Somalia, and the Eritrean war of liberation condemned the Ethiopian people to one of the lowest standards of living in Africa. Periodic famines killed hundreds of thousands and threatened the lives of millions more. Television cameras revealed the terrible scenes of hunger to the horrified West in 1984 and 1985. But spectacular public responses, such as Band Aid organised by a pop singer, to provide cash for the starving could not attack the roots of the problem – the corruption and mismanagement of Mengistu's dictatorial regime added to the continuous warfare in the Tigray and with Eritrea and Somalia.

It was already too late when on 5 March 1990 Mengistu declared that the state would abandon Marxism–Leninism. In May of the following year, the game was up: the rebel forces were closing in. The coalition led by the People's Revolutionary Democratic Front captured Addis Ababa. By that time Mengistu had fled to safety in Zimbabwe. The guerrillas had overcome a 350,000-strong, seemingly modern army and air force equipped with weapons supplied formerly by the Soviet Union. The old ally had deserted Mengistu and the army was demoralised. After seventeen years Mengistu had lost all credibility.

Threatened by the turmoil were a group of black Ethiopians professing as their religion a form of ancient Judaism. The Ethiopians called them 'strangers', Falashas. Some 140,000 – that is, most of those who had remained after the first airlift in 1984 – were now rescued, plucked out of Africa and brought to Israel. The Israelis had once more demonstrated to the world that they would protect their own, regardless of all other considerations – economic, international, political and social. Black Jews would be integrated into Israel like Jews from all other continents, races and ethnic groups. Service in the army and education of a new generation would do their work.

The new leaders in Ethiopia faced a daunting task in their attempts to revive a devastated country. At least they were no longer at war with Eritrea, whose independence was in sight. As if her own problems were not enough to cope with, Ethiopia was also attempting to feed hundreds of thousands of refugees fleeing from southern Sudan.

Eritrea had a population in the early 1990s of 3.5 million. The country had been forcibly colonised by Abyssinians, by Turks and finally in 1889 by the Italians. Italian colonies were run mainly for the benefit of Italy, so local nationalist feelings were suppressed. 'Liberated' by the British in 1941, Eritrea was not granted independence, despite wartime promises. In fact, there were long wrangles after the war between the victors about what to do with the former Italian colonies. The British and the French could not simply take them over as new colonies, as spoils of war. The climate prevailing at the United Nations would not have permitted such blatant colonialism. There was only one thing on which the Western victors were agreed and that was to keep the Soviet Union out. Eventually, in 1951, the former Italian colony of Libya was granted independence.

The Eritreans fared the worst. By a UN resolution, they were to be assured respect for 'their institutions, traditions, religions, and languages, as well as the widest possible measure of self-government'. Instead they were federated with Ethiopia, so that Ethiopia might have access to the sea. The dominant West at the United Nations believed it had a secure ally in Haile Selassie, and the Red Sea was too important strategically to allow a small Eritrean state independence and so decisive influence. The Eritrean Liberation Movement was soon formed, only to be brutally suppressed, and

*The Falashas of Ethiopia fled famine, and in March 1985 a few hundred were secretly airlifted to the Promised Land, where they became Israeli citizens, and one racial group amongst many; more followed their brethren in 1990 as Ethiopia collapsed into chaos.*

in 1962 Haile Selassie annexed Eritrea. With the assistance of Arab neighbours, the newly founded Eritrean Liberation Front took up the armed struggle against Ethiopia in the 1960s and, despite splits and intrigues, fought the longest war in Africa until Mengistu's overthrow in 1991. South of Eritrea lies northern Ethiopia, inhabited by the Tigray peoples, some 5 million strong. They too waged a liberation struggle against Mengistu's rule. Droughts and fighting devastated subsistence agriculture, so that famines decimated the Tigreans. At the same time, the Ethiopians were fighting the Republic of Somalia over the territory known as the Ogaden. The new rulers of Ethiopia brought peace to the country. The regions enjoyed some autonomy; when a referendum was held, Eritrea overwhelmingly chose independence in 1993. All this gave a chance for famine relief to reach starving peoples and for recovery to take place in the 1990s.

The Republic of Somalia was created in 1960 from the Italian and British colonies of Somaliland. Somalians share language, culture and Islam, and

nationalism is a strong force, able to survive the colonial partitions by Italy, Britain and France. The Ogaden had been conquered by the Abyssinians in the 1890s, and after the Second World War it was once more handed back to Ethiopia. Conflict between the two countries arose soon after the establishment of Somali independence. In 1969 there was a military revolution in Somalia, which received Soviet support, but when Somalia and Ethiopia went to war again in 1977 the Soviet Union – forced to choose between two of her clients – eventually backed the stronger Mengistu. The Somali army was defeated in the Ogaden in 1978. The United States meanwhile replaced the USSR in Somalia.

Thus internal strife in the strategically important Horn of Africa led to a Cold War game of musical chairs. Nothing illustrates better the hollowness of the pretensions of these African military regimes when they claim they are following 'democratic free world' principles of government or modelling themselves on the Marxist people's republics. The politics of Africa reflect African realities: the first

*Famine in Ethiopia, 1984. Pictures such as these made a difference when televised in the West – money flowed in to aid the needy.*

requirement of leadership is to stay in power and to maintain the cohesion of the new nation. The Somali Democratic Republic was ruled by a Supreme Revolutionary Council under its president, General Mohammed Barre, until his downfall in 1991. Warfare and internal strife had reduced this poorest of African countries dependent on subsistence agriculture to near starvation. The country in 1990 descended into chaos, with Barre trying ruthlessly to hold it together by using his elite guards.

In January 1991 Barre was driven from power. Even worse was in store for the people of Somalia than Barre's brutal rule. Although the 6 million Somalis are almost unique in Africa in forming one nation, all speaking one language and following the same religion, a Sunni branch of Islam, clans had fought each other for centuries over ownership of pastures, and Barre's rule – far from eradicating the clan rivalries – had only suppressed them. Now, like a release of steam from a pressure cooker, clans, local warlords and gangs erupted in an orgy of civil conflict. The country was awash in weapons.

The rest of the world was horrified by the television reports sent from the capital, Mogadishu, a ruined city in which over a million were seeking some sort of shelter. The UN and relief agencies sent in food aid to the starving population, but a few hundred 'blue berets' – UN troops – were totally inadequate to guard the supplies and to see that emergency supplies reached the people. For hundreds of thousands who had starved to death, it was already too late. Despite repeated UN intervention, Somalia remains fractured by its multiplicity of warring clans.

Somalia presents the most pitiable face of contemporary Africa. Independence led to dictatorial rule, corruption and the lavishing of scarce resources on armaments. The end of dictatorship was followed not by a transition to democracy but by chaos, anarchy and ruin. A more determined international effort which got under way in the autumn of 1992 endeavoured to save some 2 million Somalis from starvation.

Bordering the Red Sea to the north-west of Ethiopia lies the Sudan, where starving peoples from the Tigray and Eritrea found refuge. In one of the

## The Horn of Africa, 1987

|  | Population (*millions*) | Gross National Product per head (*US$*) |
|---|---|---|
| Ethiopia | 44.8 | 130 |
| Somalia | 5.7 | 290 |
| Sudan | 23.1 | 330 |
| Libya | 4.1 | 5,460 |

most extraordinary migrations thousands of Ethiopian Jews, the Falashas, also crossed into the Sudan (1983–4) on their secret journey to Israel. The Sudan provides the main route through which aid can be channelled to Eritrea and Tigray, but she is not herself a stable country politically or ethnically. The south is African and vehemently opposes the spread of the Muslim religion and law, which the Arab north of the country seeks to impose. When the Sudan gained independence from Britain in January 1956, paramount British consideration had been to prevent Nasser's Egypt from dominating her, but it was left to the Sudanese to decide the issue. A rebellion in the south in the summer of 1955, motivated by the fear that all power would in practice be transferred to the north, was repressed and did not delay independence. Britain was in a hurry and failed to insist on safeguards for the south. British Middle Eastern policy required strong unified nations, not weak political divisions which might be exploited by the Soviet Union.

After a short period of multi-party government in the Sudan, the military seized power in 1958 and ruled for the next six years. General Abboud's regime followed a harsh policy of Arabisation, established Koranic schools in the south and expelled Christian missionaries. Nineteen-sixty-two saw the beginnings of a civil war that was to cause destruction and great loss of life among the southern people. After a second brief civilian interlude, another military coup in 1969 brought Colonel Jaafar al-Nimeiri to power. His more conciliatory approach enabled the fighting in the south to be brought to an end in 1972. But a renewed attempt in 1983 to force Muslim law and custom on the south led to a fresh outbreak of fighting. The endemic north–south conflict in the Sudan and her unstable political conditions have added to the immense problems of a country whose vagaries of climate hinder agricultural production, while a rapidly expanding population requires more not less food. Devastating floods in August 1988 made 2 million homeless.

In June 1989, after months of turmoil, a military coup overturned the government and General Omar Hasan Ahmed al-Bashir became head of state and commander-in-chief at the head of a Revolutionary Council of National Salvation. Political parties were dissolved and many politicians and professional people were detained. The regime was ruthless in dealing with its opponents and potential enemies. Attempted coups in 1990 and 1991 led to the execution of the army officers involved, but protests continued. Behind the army stood the National Islamic Front of fundamentalist Muslims led by Hasgan Turabi. Islamic criminal law, the *sharia*, was applied again. Khartoum became filled with some 1.8 million refugees, possessing practically nothing, and half a million more were forcibly settled outside the city. The civil war between north and south continued. The non-Muslim south, African, Christian and Animist (a religion which holds that both living and inanimate objects have souls) was in a desperate condition with widespread famine added to the civil war and preventing relief agencies from reaching the starving. With fighting continuing in the south, prospects remain bleak.

The Sudan is one of the poorest countries in Africa. Libya is the richest. In 1951 she became the first African state to exchange colonial status for independence. This was not because it was advanced in any way. During the Second World War, the Italian colonial territories of Tripolitania and Cyrenaica were conquered by the British Eighth Army. Britain's main concern was to ensure that the Russians would not secure a foothold by claiming a share in the trusteeship of the Italian colonies. So the provinces were combined on independence with French-administered Fezzan to form Libya, and the head of the most powerful Cyrenaican family, Emir Mohammed Idris, whose conservatism could be trusted, was elevated to become King Idris. It was not an ideal solution from a Western point of view. Britain and Italy would have preferred a long period of trusteeship, but at the UN the Arabs and their allies were able to push independence through. Idris fulfilled Western expectations and permitted the construction of a huge NATO airbase on the outskirts of Tripoli. No one dreamt of the wealth the discovery of oil would bring to the desert kingdom or the trouble it would later cause the West.

Libya began exporting oil in 1961. By then Nasser had changed the politics of the Middle East and, after Suez, British and French imperialism was on the retreat. These transformations affected the students and junior officers of Libya, who were drawn to socialist ideas and to a revival of Muslim values, at the same time as they felt increasing antipathy towards Western, especially American, military and commercial domination. In September 1969, a twenty-nine-year-old officer, Major Muammar Gaddafi, overthrew the regime of King Idris. He had long planned the coup as a necessary step to freeing Libya from foreign exploitation and raising the Arab peoples to live their lives according to the teachings of the Koran. All the peoples of Libya, those of the oases as well as those of the towns, should share in Libya's prosperity. Gaddafi expounded his ideology in his Green Book. His 'Third Universal Theory' rejected the Western ideologies of capitalism and communism, as well as the concept of the 'state'. The masses should rule through local people's committees, and life should be conducted according to Muslim law. In practice Gaddafi was the supreme ruler, though fellow officers in the General People's Committee may from time to time have exerted some influence on policy.

In developing Libya economically, Gaddafi was shrewd. In 1971 he led the oil-rich states in a policy of forcing the Western consumers to pay vastly more for the oil they had hitherto obtained so cheaply. The riches this bestowed on Libya were used for agricultural development and industrial diversification. They also enabled Gaddafi to create an Arab welfare state. Thus the oil income brought considerable benefit to the people.

Gaddafi's relations with the rest of the world were warped by an uncompromising revolutionary zeal. Foreign bases were closed down and the Western military presence expelled. In the 1970s and 1980s Gaddafi intervened in the ethnic civil war in Chad, backing the northerners against the southerners and occupying part of northern Chad. The government in the south was saved only by

*The United States strikes at Libya on 26 March 1986 in retaliation for its sponsorship of terrorist activities, and sinks a boat armed with missiles.*

French intervention. But Gaddafi's notoriety in the West mainly derived from his support for terrorist groups, ranging from factions of the Palestine Liberation Organisation to the IRA. A terrorist attack on a Berlin nightclub which left American servicemen dead was followed in April 1986 by an American attempt to silence Gaddafi for good by bombing his living quarters and military targets. They missed Gaddafi but caused civilian casualties. The intended 'surgical' air strikes, using British bases, were widely condemned, but Gaddafi's support for terrorism became less overt.

Libya will continue to play a large role in oil politics, in the Horn of Africa and in the Middle East, her power arising not from her population size, but from her enormous wealth. Gaddafi was prevented from manufacturing poison gas – his factory was destroyed – and from making a nuclear bomb. But in future decades the greatest danger to world stability and peace may well arise from leaders such as Gaddafi securing nuclear and biological weapons.

# CHAPTER 76

# Southern Africa: Vanishing White Supremacy

In African countries with substantial minorities of white settlers, resistance to African majority rule led to savage conflicts and wars. By the early 1990s the white settlers had lost power in all but one country; the future of South Africa still hung in the balance as turmoil threatened. Two decades earlier another powerful group of ruling white settlers in Rhodesia had fought to resist an early end to their dominance. Despite their overwhelming military resources, they had to accept defeat in the end. Southern Rhodesia became Zimbabwe, Nyasaland was renamed Malawi and Northern Rhodesia, Zambia.

Cecil Rhodes had first conquered these territories towards the close of the nineteenth century for the British South Africa Company. White settlers soon came to the healthy highlands of Southern and Northern Rhodesia. Nyasaland, administered directly by the Colonial Office in London, attracted fewer settlers. Northern Rhodesia, which in 1924 likewise fell to direct administration by the Colonial Office, had a single rich resource to exploit – the Copperbelt, whose mines produced the second-largest quantity of copper in the world. At the time, with only 4000 whites among 1 million Africans, there could be no question of handing over power to the settlers. In 1929 a British colonial secretary declared that in Northern Rhodesia, as in the East African territories, the interests of the Africans were paramount. In practice this meant little. The land distribution favoured the white minority at the expense of the

expanding African population. But the white settlers in Northern Rhodesia wanted to make their position more secure. That was the logic behind their desire to create a union between Northern and Southern Rhodesia, with her larger white-settler community.

The conquest of Rhodesia in the 1890s had been brutal. As the railway moved further inland, settlers followed. There was some gold, but agriculture gradually became far more important. The assumption always was that when the white settlers were ready to govern the country they would take over from the Chartered British South Africa Company. The decisive year was 1923, when the 34,000 settlers of Southern Rhodesia rejected union with South Africa and were granted full internal self-government, which meant ruling over 900,000 Africans. Constitutionally, Southern Rhodesia became a Crown colony with the imperial government reserving to itself the right to veto legislation affecting the African majority.

During the next three decades London allowed the Southern Rhodesian whites to run the country as they thought fit. The African majority had to accept white rule and subservience to unjust laws. The best lands went to the white settlers, a social system which effectively amounted to apartheid was enacted. The Land Apportionment Act in 1931 forbade Africans to occupy land in white areas; 50,000 whites were to receive 49 million acres and 1 million Africans were to receive 29 million acres. Pass laws, taxes, control of Africans in towns and the Masters and Servants Act all ensured black subservience. A ban on blacks forming trade unions, separate schools, hospitals, clubs and swimming pools for blacks were all just part of an extensive structure of discrimination. Black Africans were in practice deprived of the vote as the settlers made sure that the blacks would not be able to meet the franchise qualification.

But Southern Rhodesia appeared to be prosperous and orderly. There were a few strikes but they were easily dealt with. With the army and air force under white command, the position of the settlers seemed impregnable in the 1950s. White immigrants poured in, attracted by the new life in the beautiful highlands away from overcrowded Europe. Southern Rhodesia seemed to have advanced to the stage of gaining independent Dominion status. The prospects were enhanced when the white settlers persuaded the British government to permit all three territories, Northern Rhodesia, Southern Rhodesia and Nyasaland, to form a federation in 1953, with a federal government in Salisbury. The African majority were granted a few parliamentary seats in the new federal parliament, some civil service posts, even a black minister to make the transfer to independence more acceptable. There was some genuine but limited progress, such as a multiracial university in Salisbury where blacks could qualify as doctors, their degrees being authenticated by the University of Birmingham in England. These gestures to the blacks merely revealed the confidence which the white settlers felt that they would continue to rule the country for at least another hundred years. It went about as far as the white settlers were ready to go. Few at the time foresaw how rapidly the tide was turning. Indeed black majority rule would have come much sooner than the twenty-seven years it took to achieve. It was delayed after 1963 because of the armed resistance of the white settlers.

Black political stirrings had come relatively late, so powerfully entrenched did the white position appear to be to black Africans. The first black nationalist target was the Federation, with its offer of an unequal partnership. Joshua Nkomo was the elder statesman among black African politicians, although only forty-five years old. As general secretary of the Railway Workers' Association he had become known as an African leader. He was also a Methodist lay preacher who did not believe in violence and worked for compromise and gradual reform. Nkomo led the Southern Rhodesian African

National Congress. It won support from the African masses deprived of land and a fair share of the country's wealth. The reaction of the Rhodesian government was repression. In 1954 several hundred black Africans were arrested. The African National Congress was banned and harsh laws against 'subversion' were enacted. In the hope of reducing support for radical black policies the discrimination laws were modified. Would this be sufficient to satisfy the blacks and persuade Britain to give up her suzerain right, which included protection of the blacks? London had done little to help black Rhodesians anyway. Black West Africa was being granted independence; it surely could not now be denied to white Rhodesia. But times had changed, passing most white Rhodesians by. In London black nationalist views were no longer ignored: 1960 was the year of Harold Macmillan's famous 'wind of change' speech.

In Southern Rhodesia a new black political party was formed, the National Democratic Party, led by Ndabaningi Sithole, Robert Mugabe and Herbert Chitepo. Joshua Nkomo acted first as the NDP's spokesman in London, and later as its president. With black West Africa and East Africa either independent or on the road to independence on the constitutional basis of one man one vote, black African nationalist leaders saw no just reason why the same principle should not apply to the three territories of the Federation. Since the white-settler population in Nyasaland of 72,000 in 1960 was much smaller than the white population in Southern Rhodesia black nationalists calculated that progress towards majority black rule would be easier to achieve in the north. In the federal parliament, with its overwhelming white Southern Rhodesian influence black nationalism would find the struggle harder. They therefore launched a campaign to break up the Central African Federation as a necessary step towards gaining the independence of Nyasaland and Northern Rhodesia under black majority rule.

The Federation had been imposed on the Africans in 1953, but there was a promise to review its workings after ten years. The nationalist movement in Northern Rhodesia was led by Harry Nkumbula and Kenneth Kaunda, and that in Nyasaland by Dr Hastings Banda. In London the Prime Minister Harold Macmillan was determined to settle what could be settled. Britain already had enough trouble on her hands with Kenya and the Mau Mau rising (page 765). It had required a major and costly British effort to suppress it. Southern Rhodesia presented severe problems with her many white settlers, but the position was different in Nyasaland and Northern Rhodesia. A few thousand white settlers in those two countries would not be allowed to stand in the way of a settlement with African nationalism there. A British fact-finding commission was sent to the two territories and found the majority of Africans opposed to the Central African Federation. In December 1963 the Federation was dissolved. In July 1964 Nyasaland, later called Malawi, was granted independence and in October of the same year so too was Northern Rhodesia, renamed Zambia by the African leadership.

This left the intractable problem of Southern Rhodesia. The federal armed forces now fell under the command of Southern Rhodesia, and, although small, they were formidable, equipped with Hunter jets, Vampire and Canberra bombers, artillery, armoured cars and helicopters. The army consisted of 3500 men of whom 1000 were black Africans. It is one of the worst features of white supremacy that it pitted the indigenous peoples against each other, blacks against blacks. This force could maintain white rule for years. The struggle for supremacy in Rhodesia was waged in the 1960s and 1970s between black nationalists (who were themselves split but were aided by black African neighbours) and the white settlers. Britain's imperial role was invidious. London could deny Rhodesia formal independence but no government, whether Conservative or Labour, was in a position to use military force against the Rhodesian authorities. British public opinion would not have tolerated fighting white Rhodesians, the men who during the Second World War had rallied to Britain's side. However racist this attitude may now be judged, it was an inexorable fact facing successive prime ministers – Macmillan, Home, Wilson, Heath, Callaghan and Thatcher. The next best thing was to try and mediate a general constitutional settlement which the settlers and the black Africans could be persuaded to accept. The only pressure which could be exerted from outside was economic sanctions through the United Nations and the Commonwealth.

From 1961 to 1971, repeated efforts were made by British governments to grant Southern Rhodesia independence on terms acceptable to a black majority and the Rhodesian whites. Ian Smith, an ex-RAF fighter pilot, was the tough settler leader of the Rhodesian Front Party. A settlement acceptable to him would have to fall short of equal votes for all Rhodesians and immediate black majority rule. Would the African nationalists accept less? Nkomo made the mistake of doing just that at a constitutional conference held in 1961 under British auspices. The proposed constitution that emerged would have delayed African majority rule for many decades, perhaps for ever. But the British government seized this opportunity to give up practically all its reserve powers, except for the final acceptance of Rhodesian independence. The African nationalists, who had organised themselves into a new party – the National Democratic Party – repudiated the agreement and Nkomo was forced to accept this reverse. One man one vote now became the unyielding demand of the black nationalists. When the Smith administration then banned the National Democratic Party, this simply led to the creation of a new African grouping, the Zimbabwe African People's Union (ZAPU). In 1963 distrust of Nkomo's leadership caused a split – Ndabaningi Sithole formed a more radical Zimbabwe African National Union (ZANU). The split gravely weakened African political influence during the struggle for independence. In 1965 Smith decided to cut the Gordian knot and declared Rhodesia unilaterally independent (UDI). It appeared intolerable to the white settlers that their two neighbours should have been granted independence in 1964 as Zambia and Malawi but not their own country.

The British government and Ian Smith might have been able to reach a fudged agreement even after UDI, which was denied British and international recognition. Negotiations were resumed on the basis of 'five principles': unimpeded progress to majority rule; guarantees against retrogressive amendments to the constitution; immediate improvement in the political status of the African population; progress towards ending racial discrimination; British satisfaction that proposals for independence agreed upon by Britain and the white settlers were acceptable to the people of Rhodesia as a whole. But how many years would have to elapse before the black Africans gained majority rule? Smith declared in 1968 after meeting Wilson, 'There will be no majority rule in my lifetime – or in my children's.' That clearly was totally unacceptable to black nationalist leaders. In 1969, Smith's

Rhodesia Becomes Zimbabwe Top left: *Prime Minister Harold Wilson and Premier Ian Smith trying in vain to reach an Anglo-Rhodesian settlement in October 1965.* Above: *White Rhodesians give a warm reception to their champion on his return from London talks.* Left: *the races shop in uneasy harmony in Salisbury.* Below: *supporters of Prime Minister Robert Mugabe celebrate the anniversary of Zimbabwe's independence, which was achieved in June 1980.*

Rhodesian parliament imposed a constitution which allowed greater African participation and promised eventual 'parity', but 'eventual' in the light of Smith's time-scale was a prospect beyond the horizon. Smith simply condemned black nationalists as communists and criminals, many of whom had been safely detained. He argued that to allow black majority rule would be a catastrophe for the country, as it had already turned out to be in the Congo and Uganda. Smith's Rhodesia at this time, he claimed, was a country of law and order, of economic development despite sanctions, thanks to the help of South Africa and Portugal. The blacks, too, would benefit more from progress under white rule than from chaos under black.

In 1971 Smith's tenacity appeared to have paid off. The Conservative government now in power made a new attempt to reach a settlement with him. After lengthy negotiations, the five principles – somewhat watered down – became the basis of an agreement between the rebellious Rhodesian government and Britain. On the crucial issue of majority rule, the time-scale was to be left to the white Rhodesians. There were objections to this from Nkomo, Sithole and other nationalist Africans who were still being detained. London and Salisbury nevertheless proceeded to test black opinion. In 1972 a British commission was sent out. Their findings shattered illusions in both Britain and Rhodesia. The commission unequivocally concluded that the 'people of Rhodesia as a whole' rejected the proposed settlement.

The two outlawed African nationalist parties ZANU and ZAPU were faced with liberating black Rhodesia by force, since the British government seemed powerless. With a few hundred guerrillas from bases in Mozambique and Zambia the task looked hopeless. ZAPU looked to Moscow, and ZANU guerrillas received their training and arms in Algeria, Ghana, China and Czechoslovakia – assistance which enabled Smith to denounce them as communists. The black peasants in the north-east of the country became victims of the brutal warfare between the guerrillas and the security forces. Not until the mid-1970s did the guerrillas make any progress. And by 1974, Ian Smith was more ready for compromise with the African leadership inside and outside Rhodesia than he had been in the 1960s. The coup in Lisbon that year had undermined Portuguese determination to remain in Mozambique; South Africa began to be anxious to

dissociate herself from Rhodesia, whose actions had been condemned by the United Nations. Sanctions too were taking their toll. So Smith negotiated with Kaunda of Zambia and released the black leadership, including Nkomo, Sithole and Mugabe. But new negotiations failed. Mugabe joined the guerrillas.

Sanctions and the settlers' fears for the future were now sapping settler morale. ZAPU and ZANU increased the pressure by temporarily burying their differences and forming the Patriotic Front. Though the Rhodesian forces could still inflict terrible damage on the guerrillas and pursued them to their bases, resistance could not be extinguished. Smith again tried to reach a settlement by negotiation with the black nationalists. He was prepared to make major concessions. In March 1978, a power-sharing 'internal agreement' was actually reached between Ian Smith and two black nationalist leaders, Bishop Muzorewa and Sithole. There would be a black prime minister and a black parliamentary majority, with the white minority retaining a veto. Ten years earlier this solution might have been sufficient. Now it was too late. The Patriotic Front of Mugabe and Nkomo rejected the settlement. Nevertheless, there were elections and Muzorewa won them. Smith hoped he had split the African opposition and won over the majority of blacks who were longing for peace. But the guerrilla war waged by the loosely aligned Patriotic Front only intensified.

In an effort to contain the guerrillas, who now numbered several thousand, the Smith–Muzorewa regime herded villagers into so-called 'protected villages', which in fact were usually unsanitary compounds with totally inadequate facilities. The Rhodesian armed forces, meanwhile, attacked the guerrilla base camps across the borders in Zambia and Mozambique, killing combatants, women and children indiscriminately. Unexpectedly, the fighting was nearly over.

Under Mrs Thatcher's new Conservative government the transfer of power to black majority rule was finally arranged at a conference called at Lancaster House and presided over by Lord Carrington, the Foreign Secretary. Starting in September the Lancaster House Conference did not end until just before Christmas 1979. Carrington, Commonwealth leaders and the President of Mozambique played a positive role in bringing all the African leaders, Muzorewa, Mugabe and Nkomo together.

Mugabe was the most reluctant to accept compromise, especially the stipulation that one-fifth of the seats of the parliament of the independent state should be reserved for whites. The armed conflict continued even while the negotiations were taking place around the conference table. A ceasefire, it was agreed, would come into force only after a settlement had been reached in London. Then elections would be held in Rhodesia–Zimbabwe. Meanwhile, an interim government would function under a British governor until an elected government could be installed in Salisbury. Almost to the end Mugabe refused his consent, but on 21 December agreement was reached and a week later a ceasefire came into force. The settlement guaranteed the whites twenty seats in a multi-party parliament and gave undertakings that their property could not be expropriated without full compensation and that the constitution could not be changed without a two-thirds majority in parliament which would give the *united* white MPs a veto.

The transition in January and February of 1980 was truly remarkable. Britain and the Commonwealth played a crucial supervisory and policing role: 122,000 guerrillas assembled in some eighteen areas and were reassured by the presence of the Commonwealth Observer Group. The election, too, was hazardous. Supervised by British observers and 500 British policemen, the election was held in February 1980 amid recriminations and accusations of intimidation. The outcome gave an overwhelming majority not to Bishop Muzorewa but to Robert Mugabe and the ZANU wing of the Patriotic Front. Nkomo's ZAPU, which had borne far less of the fighting, lost out to Mugabe. Muzorewa, who had shared power with Smith, was humiliatingly defeated. The independence of Rhodesia–Zimbabwe, now renamed simply Zimbabwe, was internationally recognised in April 1980.

After all the bloodshed and conflict, and faced with what at the time seemed to be insuperable difficulties, the transfer to black majority rule and a reasonably stable state was a remarkable event in modern history.

The dominant personality of Zimbabwe's early years of independence was Robert Mugabe. He deserved much credit. His leadership turned out very differently to what might have been expected after he returned to Rhodesia in January 1980 to participate in the election, after sixteen years spent in detention or exile. The white settlers had good

grounds to fear the coming to power of this most uncompromising of the guerrilla nationalist leaders. Mugabe had made his admiration for Marxism clear during the struggle against the settlers, whom he had condemned as 'white exploiters'. Ian Smith, in Mugabe's view, was no more than a criminal who deserved to be shot. His consent to the Lancaster House agreement had been the most difficult to secure. Unless restrained by more moderate black nationalists, there seemed little prospect that he would actually honour for long the concessions and guarantees the white settlers had secured. Mugabe's moderate tone during the election campaign which followed the Lancaster House agreement seemed to be belied by the violence and intimidation practised by his followers.

The results of the election and Mugabe's success were announced on 4 March 1980. They came as a shock to the settlers. But Mugabe's first address on television that evening was almost as much of a surprise. He was conciliatory, called for reconciliation and unity, and promised to uphold the law and private property. Deeds followed words, when the white general Peter Walls, in charge of Rhodesia's security forces, was confirmed as the commander of the country's new army, into which would be integrated the guerrilla fighters. Ministers were appointed to Mugabe's government who supported Nkomo; white ministers were also appointed. Ian Smith was able to lead a white settler party in parliament and to enjoy freedom and comfort. There was no retribution. Mugabe did not abandon his vision of a socialist, one-party state, but he was not going to drive out the white settlers and businessmen on whom the country's economy depended or risk plunging the country into new conflict.

Mugabe's leadership of Zimbabwe was statesmanlike from the outset. His pragmatic handling of Zimbabwe's politics gradually won him the confidence of the majority of the white settlers, whose lifestyle did not have to change much after independence. From the first, the chief political problem of the new state was the old rivalry of Nkomo's ZAPU, with its tribal base among the Ndebele in Matabeleland, and Mugabe's ZANU, whose members were Shona. The Shona bitterly resented the lack of military support received from Nkomo's ZAPU during the fight for freedom. The Patriotic Front had never been more than a marriage of convenience. Nkomo, the cautious, weaker and vacillating older man, lost the contest to the younger Mugabe, who had clear goals: progress towards a one-party state and the abolition of the separate (and 'racist') reserved white seats in parliament. Mugabe bullied and cajoled Nkomo. Unrest in Matabeleland was suppressed in the mid-1980s by harsh repression. The Mugabe government continued to arrest and detain opponents without trial under the Emergency Powers legislation first introduced by Ian Smith in 1965. In 1987 Mugabe came close to achieving two of his aims. With the necessary two-thirds majority assured, which included support from white settlers, the reserved white seats were abolished and Nkomo agreed to a union of ZANU with ZAPU, ending the rivalry of the previous twenty years. Nkomo entered the government as vice-president. But events in the Soviet Union and Eastern Europe led Mugabe in 1990 to abandon the progression to a one-party state. He also jettisoned some economic planks of Marxism. Once more cool pragmatism and the need for Western aid won over ideological commitment.

The economy was from the start the Achilles heel of Mugabe's regime. While denouncing South Africa's apartheid racism, Zimbabwe was neverthe-less dependent on her neighbour for much of her imports and exports. The principal exports, which did reasonably well during the decade, were tobacco and cotton. Agriculture was dependent on the vagaries of the weather and Zimbabwe suffered from some long droughts. She was also dependent on world prices, and the rise in the cost of oil had a bad effect here as elsewhere. The mining sector did less well, and state planning and high taxation impeded economic growth. A number of financial scandals implicated Mugabe's ministers, and there was some financial mismanagement. The bureauc-racy was also inefficient. Mugabe's political skills did not extend to the handling of the economy.

But this did not affect the judgement of the electorate that he remained indispensable as presi-dent. In 1990 the ZAPU–ZANU party won a landslide victory and Mugabe was overwhelmingly endorsed as president. He could feel secure. He underlined his non-racist approach by appointing a white lawyer to the position of chief justice and, after twenty-five years, ended the state of emer-gency.

After 1990 Zimbabwe tried to follow the market prescription of Western institutions, causing severe economic difficulties in the short term. The drought

in 1992 had a disastrous effect, with over a million people in the countryside having to rely on aid for survival until the rains allowed a new harvest to be brought in. However, the government was able to cope better than elsewhere in central Africa. For this there was one reason: there was no civil war or conflict in Zimbabwe. That was one of Mugabe's most notable achievements.

Dr Hastings Banda became president of Zimbabwe's neighbour Malawi when independence was granted to Nyasaland in 1964. In appearance there was nothing traditionally African about Dr Banda, who dressed in neat three-piece dark suits and a Homburg hat. A local touch, however, were the *mbumbas*, dancing girls in colourful dress who surrounded and accompanied him on public appear-ances, singing his praises. Dr Banda had practised as a doctor in Britain and was a pillar of the Church of Scotland. The struggle to force the break-up of the Central African Federation, which bound Nyasaland to Southern and Northern Rhodesia, propelled him to power. He mobilised opinion against the Federation, was imprisoned for a time, headed the Malawi Congress Party and became prime minister in 1963. The British government was persuaded by Banda's arguments to dissolve the Federation and to allow Nyasaland indepen-dence and separate nationhood the following year.

On gaining independence, Dr Banda ousted rival political leaders, turned Malawi into a republic and became its first president. After the early turbulent years, he was soon able to consolidate his position in the state. His official birthdate is given as 'about 1906'; he was thought in fact to be as old as the century, his grip on power likely to be relinquished only on death. Malawi's reputation for stability over a quarter of a century rested on his longevity and hold on the 'life-presidency'.

Banda's Malawi was much admired by the West. He cultivated a close political and economic relationship with Britain. With black African leaders he frequently quarrelled, especially with Zambia and Tanzania. He condemned criticism of South Africa as 'hypocritical and dishonest', urging greater realism, and he pursued no policies of retribution against white settlers in Malawi. They continued to live a privileged lifestyle, undisturbed. White farmers and white civil servants had nothing to fear. His admirable tolerance did not extend to black opposition. Strict censorship and the security services suppressed dissent. He kept Malawi out of involvement in the black independence struggle of neighbouring Southern Rhodesia in the 1970s. Nor did Banda attempt to stop the South African-supported resistance to the Marxist government in Mozambique from launching incursions into Mozambique from Malawi bases on the border. His policies were regarded by black Africa as a betrayal, but his main concern was to keep Malawi free from the bloody struggles and civil wars of Africa. His greatest achievement was undoubtedly the maintenance of peace in his country. Remarkable too was Malawi's humanitarian response to the civil war in Mozambique. By 1991, 1 million refugees had crossed into Malawi and had been accepted and looked after by this small and poor country, a response more civilised than that witnessed in the early 1990s in some countries of Western Europe.

Malawi's domestic peace, however, was a peace based on repression. By the 1990s, fired by examples of the overthrow of dictatorship elsewhere in the world, an internal opposition had grown ever more determined to be granted a voice and to criticise Banda. The disastrous state of the economy added fuel to discontent. Long one-party and one-man rule bred corruption, while state-run enterprises were inefficient and uncompetitive. Malawi's exports of tea, coffee and tobacco and her imports were badly disrupted by the civil war in Mozambique, which practically closed the railway line to the port of Beira. Bowing to international and internal pressure, Banda conceded a referendum in 1993 which voted in favour of multi-party rule. Malawi has some good farming land, but mismanagement has led to widespread malnutrition.

The contrast between Malawi and Zimbabwe's northern neighbour, Zambia, is a stark one. Zambia was dominated for twenty-seven years after independence in 1964 by the nation's founding father, Kenneth Kaunda, until he was voted out of office. Until Kaunda's departure, Zambia was virtually a one-party state but of a rather unusual kind: Kaunda, who espoused his own ideology of 'humanism', did not resort to repression or the imprisonment of opponents, and no politician had to flee into exile. His own personal influence overcame the serious tribal and regional conflicts during the early years of independence. On the issue of the black struggles for equal rights he took a principled stand in support. The African National Congress

found shelter and assistance in Zambia, though it was periodically attacked by incursions of special forces from South Africa.

The economy suffered badly, virtually a hostage to South Africa, through which most of Zambia's exports and imports have to pass. Zambia relies on copper for 90 per cent of her export earnings, and the metal's price plummeted for much of the 1980s. Under the guidance of the International Monetary Fund and assisted by aid, reform was attempted, especially in the field of agricultural production, whose low prices needed to be raised. This, in turn, led to riots in the Copperbelt, where production and real income were falling while basic foods were costing more. Lack of investment in modern mining equipment and exhaustion began to show up in the copper mines. When the price of copper did rise, production could not be expanded. Although Kaunda had broken off relations with the International Monetary Fund in 1988, he could not halt the continuing depression, even in the short term. Unrest and opposition, strikes and disruption in the Copperbelt, undermined his popularity. Unemployment escalated and standards of living fell rapidly. The mismanaged one-party political system was doomed.

In October 1991 Kaunda accepted the demand for multi-party elections. His United National Independence Party was defeated by the newly formed Multi-Party Democracy, whose leader, Frederick Chiluba, was duly installed as Zambia's second president. Kaunda bowed to the democratic will and retired.

### Zimbabwe, Zambia and Malawi, 1989

|          | Population (millions) | Gross National Product per head (US$) |
|----------|-----------------------|---------------------------------------|
| Zimbabwe | 9.5                   | 650                                   |
| Zambia   | 7.8                   | 390                                   |
| Malawi   | 8.2                   | 180                                   |

The demise of white power in Rhodesia could have been interpreted at the time as sealing the fate of white rule in southern Africa. Indeed, only ten years after the collapse of white rule in Rhodesia, the white South African government began negotiations which it hoped would lead to a power-sharing constitution. The African National Congress, the major but not the only black participant in the negotiations, demanded majority rule. The gap between these two positions was a wide one, but that there should be negotiations at all in the 1990s in South Africa had been unthinkable only a few years ago. There are some parallels with Rhodesia. The application of international sanctions, the isolation of South Africa and the increasingly severe economic pressure as the flow of foreign investment was reversed finally convinced the government and the majority of white South Africans that a solution had to be found to the white–black conflict.

Nevertheless, there are important differences between South Africa in the early 1990s and Rhodesia then. Although the whites form a minority both in Rhodesia–Zimbabwe and in South Africa, their positions in the two countries in other respects are not at all comparable. In the first place the white population of South Africa forms a much larger minority than that in Rhodesia. They are not a few hundred thousand whites among millions of blacks, but 4 million. Nor are South Africa's whites comparatively recent immigrants; the great majority are South African-born, and their families have lived in Africa for generations. The Afrikaners can look to historical roots as far back as the seventeenth century, when their ancestors settled on the Cape only some seventy years after the first establishment of English colonies in North America. Their motherland is no longer in Europe but in Africa. But unlike the settlers in North America they did not grow and develop to outnumber by many times the indigenous peoples. Despite substantial English immigration they remained a minority. It is crucial to an understanding of contemporary South Africa that the disparity between whites and blacks, coloureds and Asians is widening and will continue to widen. Twenty-eight out of one hundred people were white in 1911; by 1980 this had fallen to twenty out of a hundred; projections to the year 2000 suggest the proportion would drop further to fourteen or less out of a hundred.

Yet the minority of whites in 1993 still claimed rights to most of the available land and, through ownership of the gold and diamond mines and industry, dominate South Africa's economy. The earnings from mining exports allowed South Africa to take off on a rapid industrial revolution from the 1940s onwards on a Western model. Industrial manufacture increased several times over, making

**Population of South Africa** (*millions*)

|  | 1911 | 1951 | 1970 | 1980 | 1992 |
|---|---|---|---|---|---|
| Blacks | 4.0 | 8.6 | 15.1 | 19.0 | 29.1 |
| Whites | 1.3 | 2.6 | 3.8 | 4.5 | 5.0 |
| Coloureds | 0.5 | 1.1 | 2.0 | 2.6 | 3.3 |
| Asian (mainly Indian) | 0.2 | 0.4 | 0.6 | 0.8 | 1.0 |
| *Total* | 6.0 | 12.7 | 21.5 | 26.9 | 38.4 |

South Africa self-sufficient in many manufactures and bringing to the white population a prosperity comparable to that enjoyed by Western nations. Although the black and coloured peoples earned only a fraction of white incomes, they also shared in the growing prosperity. As the South African government never tired of pointing out, the country's blacks had incomes comparable to the highest of any black in Africa.

This economic transformation had important social and international repercussions. Afrikaners were no longer poor farmers, and the division between them and the 'English' lessened. Blacks, coloureds and Asians were needed both in skilled labour, in trade and in the professions, because there were not enough whites to run a modern industrial country and serve her economic needs. The better-educated and better-organised of the non-whites, with higher aspirations, were able to compare their quality of life with that of the whites, a comparison that created bitterness and conflict. It made their exclusion from trade union and political rights increasingly impossible to justify. Internationally, too, a modern economy interacts with the world economy, making it impossible for a state to ignore world opinion or the economic pressures exerted by sanctions. More important even than sanctions was the judgement of foreign businessmen that a politically unstable South Africa, possibly heading towards revolution and bloodshed, was not a good country to invest in.

Nevertheless, the white South African government was able to hold up progress towards equal black political rights for so long thanks to its own armed strength, economic power and independent status. Unlike in Rhodesia, Britain had retained no reserve sovereign powers. At the turn of the century (1899–1902), she had fought the two Boer Republics, the Orange Free State and the Transvaal, to affirm imperial paramountcy; it was a war of supremacy between whites. To the Liberals in Britain the Boers had been wronged and they wished to make amends when they came to power. The Union of South Africa was formed in 1910, granting the whites independence as a Dominion within the British Empire. But bitter memories of the camps into which Boer families had been forced during the war, many dying from disease, continued to affect relations between the more nationalist Afrikaners and the English until the middle of the century. As for the blacks, the Boer War did not help them. Their enfranchisement was dependent on the white majority. Deprived of adequate land, Zulus rebelled in 1906, only to be bloodily suppressed. Protest and the expression of independent black opinion found a focus, just as in the Southern states of America, in black churches. They have played an important role during the twentieth century, and as religious institutions enjoy some protection. The Asian, mainly Indian, community, meanwhile, had found a brilliant spokesman and organiser in a young lawyer, M. K. Gandhi (page 411).

When in 1910 the existing self-governing colonies, the Cape, Natal, the Orange Free State and the Transvaal, formed the Union of South Africa, they did not federate, but became provinces of a central union. No non-whites could be elected to Parliament, and the franchise was left as it had been before the Union; this allowed some voice to the coloureds and blacks in the Cape, but none elsewhere. In London, a black and coloured delegation, which had raised objections to the political colour-bar, was listened to with sympathy, but the constitution of the Union was seen as a question to be decided by South African whites. There were some prominent white South African politicians who opposed the colour-bar in politics; indeed throughout twentieth-century South African history there have been a number of distinguished whites, from Walter Stanford early in the century to Mrs Helen Suzman in our own time, who have spoken for the rights of the other races in Parliament, but they have been a small minority. The only safeguards London had provided for black people when the Union was formed was to retain British protectorates over Basutoland, Bechuanaland and Swaziland, which were to continue unless their black inhabitants consented to incorporation in the Union. This the populations did not want and Britain rejected South African attempts to incorporate them. They eventually became independent – Basutoland as Lesotho and Bechuanaland as Botswana in 1966, and Swaziland in 1968 – though all three countries are nevertheless wholly dependent on the South African economy. The limited voting rights (they entitled blacks to white representation only) which blacks and coloureds enjoyed in the Cape province, as confirmed by the Act of Union, were abolished for blacks in 1936 and for the coloureds in practice in 1955.

Whatever differences existed between the white political parties in other matters, in their attitudes to non-whites they were broadly similar. They abhorred intermarriage between the races; they were determined to maintain white domination and government; the black African was to be denied equal political and economic rights; his role was to serve the white state.

The policy followed was called 'segregation', a forerunner of apartheid. Early in the history of the Union, legislation was enacted which made it clear that the path of South African development would not be towards common goals for all its peoples without regard to colour. The 1913 Native Land Act made it illegal for blacks to buy or lease land outside the overcrowded designated African reserve areas. In the greater part of South Africa they were thus deprived of a fundamental right of all citizens of a country, ownership of land. The Act was not rigidly applied, except in the Orange Free State, but the principle of such discrimination was here clearly enshrined in law. The Native Urban Area Act ten years later segregated the black from the white population in towns. It had been prompted by the unsanitary conditions of black housing and the fear that disease would spread to whites. But, in laying down the government's right not only to segregate but to control the numbers of black people allowed to live in towns, it formed the basis, together with the Land Acts of 1913 and 1936, of the whole post-1948 apartheid structure.

The year 1948 marked a turning point in African politics. Before the Second World War, from 1933 to 1939, the radical and the more moderate wings of Afrikaner politics had come together to create the United Party, which formed a government. The Prime Minister was General Hertzog, and the statesman General Jan Smuts was a deputy prime minister. Not all Afrikaners accepted the fusion. A small group led by F. Malan formed a 'purified' National Party in 1934, to which the racist ideology of Hitler's National Socialism particularly appealed. Afrikaner nationalism was strengthened by the Second World War. Hertzog split the United Party in 1939, because he wanted to opt for neutrality, while Jan Smuts narrowly carried Parliament into entering the war with the other Commonwealth countries. The war itself obscured the strength of Afrikaner nationalism. Some extreme pro-German Afrikaners were interned, but the majority of South Africans, Afrikaner and English, fought against the Nazis. Smuts seemed completely dominant. Yet Malan, with considerable skill, nurtured a small reunified National Party. Once the war was over, the unambiguous race policy of the Afrikaner National Party – the policy of apartheid – confronted the liberalising sentiments of Smuts's United Party and gave the Malan party a bare majority in the 1948 election, despite Smuts's enormous prestige. Smuts died in 1950 and the United Party fell into a decline. The Nationalist Party's majority increased with every election until the 1980s. After 1948, the political, social and economic development of South Africa was (until 1990) based on apartheid, which had the support of a large majority of the white population but was opposed with increasing vehemence by blacks.

For sixteen years Dr Henrik Verwoerd was the architect of the apartheid structure, first as minister of native affairs from 1950 to 1958 and then as prime minister until 1966. He elaborated and adjusted to modern conditions the laws underpinning the maintenance of white supremacy in a society that was segregated with increasing strictness. He in turn, after his assassination by a crazed white, was succeeded by B. J. Vorster, who remained prime minister until 1978. Proponents of apartheid even claimed that the system was supported by the law of God, according to the teachings of the Dutch Reformed Church. Each race should be kept pure and allowed to develop its own national existence. But the assumption behind all this was that the different races were not of equal worth. The White Afrikaner belonged to a *Herrenvolk*. What made apartheid so offensive and unacceptable to world opinion were the lessons learnt from the actions of that other prophet of a master race, Adolf Hitler. His master race had murdered and enslaved millions belonging to 'inferior' races. It would not be fair to claim exact parallels between the policies followed by the governments of South Africa and Nazi Germany. Nevertheless, after the events of the Second World War no ideology of unequal races could win respect. UN membership is composed largely of non-white nations, as is the British Commonwealth. Paradoxically, by insisting on separate black and white development, apartheid stimulated black nationalism and encouraged the development of a separate black power base. When in 1990 the white political leadership recognised this danger and opened the National Party to black membership, it was too late to undo the harm done by the decades of racially divided political power.

The doctrine of apartheid went far beyond political segregation, of course. Blood laws very similar to the notorious Nazi Nuremberg laws of 1935 were passed in 1949 and 1950, forbidding mixed marriages and sexual relations (outside already existing marriages) between whites and non-whites. In parallel, the Population Registration Act of 1949 classified each individual into his or her racial group – white, black, coloured or Asian. The Nazis, to distinguish Jews from Aryans, focused on the religion of the four grandparents. But since the blacks were as Christian as the whites the South African Nationalist Party could make judgements only according to appearance: the curl of the hair, the colour of the skin. Some 'doubtful' cases slipped into a 'better' category, and every year there were appeals for 'regradings'. One reason for this categorisation in 1949 was that such 'slippage' could be controlled once everyone had been duly classified according to race. The pass laws were also tightened in 1952. Every non-white was obliged to carry a pass indicating his or her race and where he or she was authorised to work and live. Blacks were not allowed to live in white towns unless born there or unless they had worked there for a number of years already. Illegal squatters in town and country could be forcibly removed. In 1953 the Bantu Education Act separated black education and prescribed a schooling suitable for the lowly positions blacks could occupy in South African society. Many of the segregationist laws also applied to Indians and coloureds. To enforce all the apartheid laws, large and small, the government needed to control the population and crush opposition. By the Suppression of Communism Act 1950, the government virtually turned South Africa into a police state. The label 'communism' could be stretched almost infinitely to encompass opposition to government policies. For instance, it enabled the government to move against multiracial trade unions even before they were banned in 1957.

Blacks, coloureds and Asians had been organising themselves into protest movements since early in the twentieth century. In 1912 the African National Congress (or ANC – so named in 1923) was founded by Pixly Ka Izaka Seme, a Zulu lawyer educated at Columbia and Oxford Universities and the Middle Temple. His voice was one of moderation and reason, not seeking confrontation but confident that the franchise would be extended to the relatively small number of 'civilised' blacks. It was not. During the depression between the wars the ANC backed black strikes and launched protest movements against the pass laws. But the government was too strong and was able to emasculate the ANC by mass arrests. There were also congresses of unity between the non-white organisations; tragically there has also been much tension and conflict between blacks and Indians. In 1942, a section of the ANC – the Youth League – adopted a more militant outlook. In the early 1950s, Indians and blacks once more co-operated in defiance of the unjust laws. But the government always had the political strength to put down strikes and. mass protests by using force and arresting and trying

thousands. This simply increased militancy. While the ANC continued to co-operate with Indians and communists and socialist whites, a split occurred in 1958 and a rival black organisation was founded, the Pan-Africanist Congress, which objected to such links.

Early in 1960 both the ANC and the PAC launched a mass campaign against the pass laws. On 21 March 1960, in the small town of Sharpeville, whose name was to reverberate around the world, a large crowd assembled outside the police station. Although the people were not violent, the police panicked and opened fire, killing sixty-nine blacks and injuring another 180. In most, though not all, towns black demonstrations were dispersed without deaths. Pictures of what became known as the Sharpeville massacre were flashed around South Africa and out to a shocked world. Blacks began to stay at home, away from work. The government came down as usual with great severity and declared the ANC and PAC illegal organisations. Thousands were detained and later sentenced to prison. Prime Minister Verwoerd also declared a state of emergency. Not long after, a mentally disturbed white man shot the Prime Minister in the head, badly injuring him and heightening the crisis atmosphere.

That autumn white voters approved a proposal

*The Sharpeville Massacre, 21 March 1960.*

to turn South Africa into a republic, thus cutting the last link with Britain. In 1961, South Africa left the Commonwealth, anticipating the refusal of the Commonwealth prime ministers to allow her to remain a member.

In the aftermath of Sharpeville, the black protest movement formed a new National Action Council to work non-violently against apartheid, and in 1961 it chose a young black lawyer named Nelson Mandela as its leader. A strike was called. More was needed than peaceful protests to persuade white South Africa to grant rights to the blacks. Mandela went underground and organised an active militant wing of the ANC – the Spear of the Nation. Its intention was to sabotage installations without causing injury to people. Meanwhile, the banned ANC established its headquarters outside South Africa in Zambia. Mandela was caught in August 1962 and in 1964 was sentenced to life imprisonment with other militant ANC leaders. His political trial earned him worldwide admiration. The South African authorities attempted to smear him as a communist working for Russia. That became the line adopted to condemn all black efforts to defeat injustice. Yet Mandela's words at his trial had expressed a different ideal; he spoke of a 'democratic and free society in which all persons live together in harmony and with equal opportunities . . . It is an ideal which I hope to live for and to achieve, but if need be, an ideal for which I am prepared to die.' Mandela became an inspiration for black Africans, though he was completely shut off from them for twenty-eight years, twenty of them in the harsh conditions of Robben Island.

The white leaders of the independent South African Republic from 1960 onwards tried to promote a more positive image of their policies. 'Apartheid' was dropped in favour of what was called 'separate development'. The new policy was to develop the black reserves into 'homelands' and eventually into 'independent' black nations, which of course would remain totally dependent for their livelihood on South Africa. Then the whites would be able to claim that they were 'democratic' and no longer denying blacks political rights, for these they would enjoy in their own nations. The homelands, or bantustans, were fragmented regions of land quite incapable of accommodating or sustaining the majority of South African blacks. Yet, by making every black a citizen of a bantustan whether he lived there or in the Republic, the black majority in the

Republic would be turned into migrants who were not entitled to political rights there. In the 1960s and 1970s this policy was pushed vigorously ahead. Self-government and later 'independence' were bestowed on Transkei in 1976, on Bophutatswana in 1977, on Venda in 1979 and on Ciskei in 1981. The international community has refused to recognise their independence. Six other states have been granted self-government but not independence. The most important is KwaZulu; its chief minister Mangosuthu Buthelezi wishes to maintain regional autonomy in a South Africa with majority black rule. He has worked within the law to assert black rights. He rejects the socialist ideology of the ANC and is determined to maintain Zulu separateness in increasingly bitter struggles with the ANC.

Some attempt was made in the 1960s and 1970s to improve conditions in the homelands by increasing government spending. Although there is a certain amount of industry and trade to provide a livelihood for the blacks, most of them must find employment in the Republic, either as immigrant workers from the bantustans or as permitted residents in townships. The migrant worker is often separated from his family for long periods but the earnings he remits home constituted in the mid-1980s nearly half the income of the so-called black nations. Continuous repression by the police has seen the forcible removal of some 3.5 million blacks to their bantustans.

Bantustans and the banning of the ANC did not solve South Africa's problem, even though police repression and the military power of white Africa made a black seizure of power impossible. Black leaders continued to organise movements against the whole system. One of these, a non-white student movement led by Steve Biko, had much success, advocating black consciousness and non-cooperation with whites. Biko was arrested by police in 1977 and his death in custody, after brutal police interrogation, further damaged the Republic's reputation. From their exile, the fragmented black militant opposition, the ANC and the PAC, were able to perform some acts of sabotage; as guerrillas they were ineffective, but they kept the whole question of black political and economic rights on the agenda of South African politics.

Unrest which broke out among blacks in the overcrowded townships, such as Soweto outside Johannesburg, owed less to black political organisa-

*No anatomical difference exists, but, under the laws of apartheid, whites are not allowed in the toilets for blacks, and vice versa, in Johannesburg, South Africa.*

tion than to black resentments. Like the rest of the world, the South African economy suffered from the recession of the mid-1970s. Recession always hits the blacks hardest and in 1973 there were massive black strikes. After Sharpeville, Soweto came to stand for the worst aspects of white repression. In 1976, in Soweto, schoolchildren began demonstrating against being forced to use Afrikaans as the medium of instruction. On 16 June, 15,000 black schoolchildren and youths gathered together. The police fired on them to disperse them, killing twenty-five and wounding many more. A wave of black protest swept the country. It was crushed, but not eliminated – only driven underground. The blacks could not be pacified, however many thousands were imprisoned.

The 1980s were dominated by the imperious President P. W. Botha, who became more authoritarian as he grew older and earned the less than flattering epithet, *Die Groot Krokodil*. The doctrine of a purist apartheid was being discarded by the majority of the white population as impractical and unenforceable in a South Africa which required millions of blacks to work with whites in the modern economy. Even Botha, on becoming president in 1979, had accepted that the whites would have to adapt. In foreign policy this meant trying to establish workable relationships with South Africa's black neighbours – a policy already initiated by the arch-racist Dr Verwoerd in the mid-1960s and greatly eased by the economic dependence of the six so-called 'frontline states' – Angola, Zambia, Botswana, Zimbabwe, Mozambique, Malawi and Tanzania. (The coup in Lisbon in 1974 had led in the following year to the independence of the two Portuguese colonies, Angola and Mozambique, which were to cause South Africa serious problems (pages 790–2).) But this policy of doing business with each other went hand in hand with opposition – the black nations (except Malawi) condemning apartheid and South Africa sending troops in to raid the bases of guerrillas operating against the Republic. Another aspect of South Africa's defiance of the black nations and the United Nations was her continued occupation of Namibia (page 791).

Inside South Africa during the Botha years of the 1980s, a policy of relaxing some of the aspects of apartheid went hand in hand with military and police repression against black political organisations in forceful displays of white supremacy. Police beat up demonstrators with sticks and whips, and occasionally shot them. The years 1985 and 1986 were filled with protests, violence and thousands of arrests. Botha introduced a state of emergency. Violence in the black townships could not be controlled by any responsible black political organisations, because the security services had ensured that they could not operate coherently inside the Republic with most of their leaders in prison and some 20,000 blacks, many of them children, detained for months in 1987. Protest organisations were fragmented and blacks also killed blacks, accusing them of collaborating or just because they belonged to a different group. When law and order break down, genuine protest and the struggle for freedom become inextricably mixed up with arson, crime and gang warfare. This allowed the government to claim that the black movement was both criminal and communist.

As Botha carried through a ruthless policy of repression, he also began to amend some of the 200-odd apartheid laws and regulations. In 1979, blacks were allowed for the first time to join official trade unions; the entry of blacks into towns and their right to take up new jobs were made easier by the abolition of the pass books in 1986. But these moves did not touch the fundamental pillars on which white supremacy rested, of which the most crucial was political power. The complex new constitution introduced by Botha in 1984 established separate Asian, coloured and white parliamentary assemblies while leaving ultimate power in white hands, but it satisfied no one, least of all the majority of the blacks, who were not represented at all. International business unease and some tightening of international sanctions in 1986 also increased pressure. More importantly in the course of the 1980s the majority of whites came to recognise that some fundamental changes had to come, however much they were disliked by the majority.

The old white–black relationship, which had frequently involved caring bonds between black nannies and white children or between paternalistic employers and their workmen, was at best an unequal master–servant tie based on the distinction of race. It was as out of place in modern South Africa as the master–servant relations between

rich and poor in Victorian England. The black population was no longer composed of semi-literate unskilled workers. There was a growing number, albeit still small, of skilled, professional and middle-class blacks, many of them driving BMWs. The Anglican Archbishop Desmond Tutu was black. The total exclusion of blacks from the government system became increasingly impossible to justify.

It was these doubts growing throughout the 1980s among a majority of the white community about apartheid, rather than the opposition from the small white minority that for many years had fought for black rights, that cracked a system which could otherwise have been upheld by the military force the whites commanded. The outside world had helped, but these internal changes of attitude were more vital. The Dutch Reformed Church no longer supported apartheid but condemned it as irreconcilable with Christian ethics. White South Africans in the early 1990s tended to feel apprehensive about a future that would be very different from the past once the black majority had gained power, but most were resigned to it. The task, as they saw it, was to make the best of it, to entrench some white rights and to guard the Republic against a black backlash and radical socialist experiments.

South Africa was at the crossroads. In 1989, it found in two remarkable men the leadership to help guide the country out of its impasse of violence and bloodshed. In September 1989 F. W. de Klerk was inaugurated as president in succession to Botha. He had a reputation for caution and was thought to be in tune with Botha's approach of dealing with South Africa's problems by a mixture of reform and repression. As education minister he had introduced the requirement of Afrikaans instruction in black schools, which led to the Soweto outbreak and the school boycott in 1976. The Nationalist Party which elected him could regard him as a safe choice. But in only a short time de Klerk charted a new course of reform and serious negotiations with black leaders. In February 1990 he lifted the bans on the ANC and on the PAC, prohibited since Sharpeville in 1960; to general astonishment he also repealed the even older prohibition on the South African Communist Party, which was working with the ANC. President de Klerk's partner in the forthcoming negotiations was Nelson Mandela, unconditionally released, to a rapturous welcome, on 11 February 1990 after twenty-seven years in prison. Soon afterwards, in May, substantive negoti-

*Chief Buthelezi and the Zulu warriors of the Inkatha Freedom Party – the only black organization equipped to challenge the supremacy of the African National Congress.*

ations between Mandela, the ANC leadership and de Klerk began. Early progress was rapid and in August the ANC announced that they were suspending the 'armed struggle'.

Neither de Klerk nor Mandela, of course, had a free hand. In the first place Mandela had to work with the collective leadership of the ANC. Nor could he claim to speak for all blacks. Chief Buthelezi, representing mainly Zulus and his Inkatha movement, had followed a separate approach to African rights within Africa for many years. A black leadership power struggle, looking beyond the end of white majority rule, led to bloodshed between Inkatha and the ANC. Buthelezi with 1.5 million followers was not prepared to be pushed aside. The smaller Pan-African Congress was also suspicious of the ANC and its left-wing outlook and was less prepared to compromise with white South Africa, but it could count only on minority support among black Africans. The black so-called homelands, with 'governments' and administrators of their own, backed up by the administration in Pretoria, had created self-interested groups in favour of maintaining the *status quo*. In any settlement they knew

they would vanish. Differences of wealth as much as tribal differences also divided black interests. World attention was fixed on Mandela, whose dignified leadership, free from rancour against his former white jailers, had earned him worldwide admiration. In any settlements, other non-white leaders would also play a part, including those of the coloureds and the Indians. The ANC, the largest African political organisation, however, could claim to speak for the majority of black Africans.

De Klerk's first hurdle was that not only had he to reach a settlement with black leaders but he had to carry his own National Party and the white community with him. Rather more than a quarter of former supporters opposed him, ranging from militant white racialists with neo-Nazi emblems to Afrikaners who claimed they were ready to trek again to establish a pure Afrikaner republic in one of the distant corners of the Union. The business community was fearful of the ANC's communist alliance. The threat of confiscation of white property and of nationalisation of South Africa's industries, mines and financial institutions lessened after 1990 with the collapse of Soviet-style command economies. Even so, a black majority government would wish to improve black standards of living and conditions of work as rapidly as possible. Such an aim suggested an active, interventionist government, rather than one following free-market, laissez-faire policies.

The upsurge of black violence, though directed against other blacks, was also fuelled by rogue elements in the South African police and intelligence services; it raised the awful spectre of a complete breakdown of law and order. If black aspirations could not be satisfied, would blacks turn on the better-off whites? How were white minority rights to be safeguarded against a black majority? The difficult task of reaching political settlement had to address these concerns and others. There were sections of the white population determined to derail the negotiations. Some sinister elements in the South African security services and police exploited the hostility between the ANC and Inkatha and themselves fomented violence. In the past, moreover, Inkatha had received financial support from government sources. There is white as well as black violence. The ANC accused de Klerk of double dealing, of not doing enough to stop the violence. If de Klerk was sincere in his efforts, and it was difficult to doubt this seriously, then clearly he had enormous difficulty in controlling all that was done in the name of the government.

De Klerk began by dismantling minor apartheid laws which prevented blacks mixing with whites socially on beaches and elsewhere. The ANC and PAC were recognised as political organisations and were no longer defined as terrorists. Their leaders were released from prison. Over a period of three years, by the middle of 1992, the whole legal system of apartheid was repealed. But the social and economic effects of the system did not thereby disappear overnight. Discrimination of more than a century had left the great majority of blacks in a depressed and severely disadvantaged position in housing, in training and education, in the provision of social services, in employment, in health, in income – in every aspect of life.

Violent clashes in the early 1990s between Inkatha and ANC supporters and in the homelands resulted in several thousand deaths and threatened to undermine further progress towards a settlement and transitional government. President de Klerk, who was blamed for the violence by the ANC, succeeded in calling a 'peace conference' in

September 1991, which was attended by the Inkatha Freedom Party, the ANC and the National Party. But, despite a 'national peace accord' which set up procedures to contain violence, the bloody clashes continued. Nevertheless, the negotiating sessions, periodically broken off by the ANC in protest at the violence, had made solid progress.

In December 1991 representatives of nineteen political groups of all races created a Convention for a Democratic South Africa, CODESA for short, which began work on establishing how an interim government of national unity might be formed and a parliament or assembly called whose task it would be to agree a constitution. The gap between the ANC's demand for majority rule and de Klerk's desire for a more decentralised state founded on the power-sharing principle, no majority being able to override a minority, remained the major obstacle to a settlement. In economic policy Mandela had reassured whites that there was no plan to nationalise everything. A significant step forward was taken in March 1992 when in a nationwide referendum of white South Africans de Klerk gained a large majority in favour of his policy of reform and of sharing power with blacks. CODESA was the best hope of resolving existing differences about how to create a new constitutional South Africa. To put more pressure on the government, the ANC launched 'mass action' to end white rule. The protest campaign led to more bloodshed, lawlessness and violence. White South Africa was in 1992 in the throes of recession, with at least a third of the blacks unemployed; the potential for an ever escalating violence undermining the process towards a negotiated peaceful settlement was great. But the majority of blacks had accepted the leadership of Mandela, who was striving for a just settlement with de Klerk. They also knew that de Klerk was the one white political leader who could deliver it and carry white South Africa with him.

The deal was struck in the spring of 1993. De Klerk abandoned the principle of power sharing and Mandela agreed to the postponement of undiluted one man one vote majority rule until 1999. A new constitution will be drafted meanwhile by a constituent assembly and an interim national unity government will be set up. Many problems remained ahead: the hostility of Butheleze and the fears of Inkatha, a white backlash and remaining differences between the ANC and the National party. Violence continues. But having travelled so far towards a

*Nelson Mandela is released from prison on 15 January 1990 after 27 years' incarceration – ready to lead black and white South Africa.*

peaceful settlement, the Rubicon has been crossed. Who could have foretold all this but a few years ago?

Mandela is the one African leader likely to be able to gain the backing of the majority of the South African people for any power-sharing compromise negotiated between black and white and black and black. The prospects for peaceful change in South Africa hinge on the health and stamina of an elder statesman, a man in his mid-seventies. However, de Klerk too deserves credit for setting out on course for democratic reform with resolution. South Africa's daunting task is to contain violence – White and Black – and to fulfill the expectations of the 28 million Blacks enfranchised in 1994.

As the 1990s began the south-western region of the African continent had been the scene of continuous bloodshed and of international involvement since the 1960s. In Angola the Cold War and the post-independence conflicts between rival black movements, which had fought the Portuguese before independence in November 1975, inflicted devastation on the country. South Africa became heavily involved in the civil war for ideological and racial reasons and in order to retain her grip on Namibia. It was a devilish brew. Parts of the inter-

locking conflicts were finally resolved when Namibia gained her independence in 1990 and South Africa withdrew. International intervention, spearheaded by the United Nations, had led to a measure of success in the pacification of this region of Africa.

In Angola the three independence movements – the National Liberation Front (FNLA), the National Union for Independence (UNITA) and the Popular Movement for Liberation (MPLA) – started fighting each other soon after independence was gained in 1975. It was a power conflict with strong ethnic influences. The MPLA was a Marxist organisation which tried to appeal across tribal divisions; the FNLA in the north-west of Angola drew support from the Bakongo tribe; while the most formidable resistance against the MPLA was organised from southern Angola by Dr Jonas Savimbi's UNITA, his support founded on the largest tribe, the Ovimbundu. The FNLA and Savimbi courted South Africa and the West for support against communism. Troops from outside the African continent were sent in 1976 to help the MPLA to defeat Unita and the FNLA. By arrangement with Moscow, Cuban troops began to

*Since achieving independence from Portugal in 1975, Angola has schooled its children ceaselessly in war.*

arrive and at the close of the 1980s were 50,000 strong. Thus the Cold War was extended to exacerbate the bloody conflict in the region. After continuous fighting the Angolans and Cubans were unable to overcome the South African-backed Unita; South Africa's support for the FNLA and Unita was bound up with her occupation of Namibia. But after 1989 South Africa became increasingly anxious to disengage from Angola. In May 1991 a peace accord was finally signed in Lisbon. The Portuguese, the United Nations, the Organisation of African Unity, the United States and the Soviet Union had all acted as mediators. It would take many years to rebuild the devastated country if peace could only be maintained.

In September 1992, as part of the peace accord, general elections were held, monitored by the UN. José Eduardo's Popular Movement for the Liberation of Angola (MPLA) won 58 per cent of the congressional seats. Savimbi and his supporters (UNITA) refused to accept the result. His well-armed guerrillas resumed the civil war. The Cold War sponsors have withdrawn their support from the respective warring sides, but neither this, nor the destitution of the people and the destruction

of the country, seems likely to guarantee a peaceful compromise. For some 3 million Ovimbundus UNITA remains their cause and the MPLA an implacable foe. The people will continue to suffer as the rest of the world stands helplessly by.

Namibia had been the German colony of South-West Africa until the close of the First World War, when it was handed over to South Africa under a League of Nations mandate. In 1966 the United Nations revoked the mandate, and in 1969 the Security Council again called on South Africa to withdraw. The Western powers were not prepared to force South Africa out – her gold mines and economy, her strategic importance and her anti-communist stance ensured that her survival was vital to the West, more vital than Namibia. Britain in particular was lukewarm about sanctions and about any other undue pressure, even while condemning apartheid. A resistance movement, the South-West Africa People's Organisation (SWAPO), began guerrilla operations against South Africa in 1966, backed by Angola's MPLA after 1975. South Africa mounted offensives into southern Angola in a vain effort to destroy SWAPO.

The stalemate gradually wore down the will of

the contestants. The United Nations headed a peace mission which in December 1988 reached a settlement over the future of Namibia. South Africa agreed to withdraw her troops and to give up Namibia, provided the Cuban troops withdrew from Angola. The Cold War had been removed from the contest. SWAPO won the general election held under UN supervision in November 1989, and the SWAPO leader Sam Nujoma formed a government when Namibia gained her independence in 1990. Namibia is largely composed of desert but she has valuable resources of uranium and diamonds. The SWAPO-led government followed a policy of moderation: members of other parties were included in the administration, and the 70,000 whites were not dispossessed. Moreover, South Africa left behind a good infrastructure, so Namibia had a promising future if internal peace continued to prevail. But no solution had been found to the problem of settling the landless former SWAPO fighters who returned to the country from Angola.

In Portugal's other former colony, Mozambique, there was little prospect for a better future; until 1990, no major international peace-keeping effort had been made, partly because the Cold War did not impinge with the same intensity as it did in Angola, and partly because Mozambique has no important resources like Angola's oil. The Soviet Union and China sent aid and technical assistance, but no troops from the Eastern bloc were introduced. Although the post-independence government of the victorious liberation movement, Frelimo, was Marxist, there was always a tussle between the hardliners and the pragmatists. The flamboyant first president, Samora Machel, who was killed in an aircrash in 1986, was succeeded by the more moderate Joaquim Chissano, who enjoyed much Western sympathy. Mozambique has been subject to the depredations of the Mozambique National Resistance (MNR), set up in 1976 by the Rhodesian intelligence service. In 1980, the MNR moved its bases to South Africa. As in Angola, South African intervention has been racial in motivation, to maintain white South African supremacy and to restrict the activities of the African National Congress. Although the ANC had no military bases in Mozambique but trained in Angola and Tanzania, Mozambique was the transit route used for guerrilla incursions into South Africa. South Africa retaliated by supporting the MNR. In 1984 President Machel tried to win South African

support by refusing the ANC transit. But this treaty of 'non-aggression and good neighbourliness' had little impact on conditions in Mozambique.

The civil war raged on, with brutalities and atrocities perpetrated against the civilians caught up in it. One million refugees fled to Mali, a quarter of a million camped beside the two railway lines running from Zimbabwe to the sea. Famine threatening half the 16 million people in Mozambique added to the huge death toll. In 1990 the efforts of mediators from Kenya and Zimbabwe and the international community succeeded in bringing the Frelimo government and the MNR to the negotiating table, Frelimo having abandoned Marxism–Leninism. In 1993 the situation looked more hopeful than in Angola; a ceasefire and UN-supervised elections offered some hope of peace.

Africa in the early 1990s was in crisis. Independence had not brought the hoped-for benefits in the longer term. Political freedom had not altered economic fundamentals. Dependent on world prices for their primary export products – coffee, cotton, cocoa, palm oil and minerals such as copper – Africans remained poor during the last quarter of the twentieth century, though there were a few good years. During the good years the West lent money for development, but after modest advances in the 1960s the huge rises in oil prices in the 1970s contributed to stagnation and decline as the nations struggled with mountains of debt and falling earnings from what they produce. During the 1980s African development went into reverse. But this was not solely due to world economic conditions.

Africa's nations have airlines and some splendid public buildings but these are mere symbols of nationhood. Since their borders were based on European colonial partitions, tribal, cultural and religious differences run like fault-lines through many of the forty-seven African nations – fault-lines which, at their most extreme, have caused civil war, as they have in Nigeria. As the 1990s began, civil war raged seemingly without end in the Sudan, as it had since independence. At best, tribal conflicts made it difficult to create functioning states founded on representative government – this was true of Zimbabwe. In South Africa the fighting between the Inkatha Zulu-based black movement and the ANC was just one of the more serious obstacles to creating a non-racist nation.

The widening gulf between the few who were rich

and the poor masses made any genuine democracy difficult to achieve. Survival rather than representative government was the people's first concern. Survival in the conditions prevailing in Africa required ingenuity, breaking laws when necessary, taking advantage of patronage and deals, engaging in bribes in return for favours.

India has proved that democratic institutions can be built on a largely poor peasant society, but her middle and professional classes and her infrastructure were more advanced than black Africa's. What chances did the Belgian Congo have in comparison?

To overcome the divisiveness within the African nations, strong men with their own tribal base and with military backing became a common post-colonial feature, only to exacerbate that very divisiveness. A few authoritarian rulers, after almost three decades, survived into the 1990s: Mobutu in the Congo, Houphouët-Boigny in the Ivory Coast and Hastings Banda in Malawi, but old age and political change had removed the fathers of other nations. President Kaunda of Zambia, twenty-seven years in power after independence in 1964, allowed himself in 1991 to be elected out of office – a rare occurrence in Africa. President Nyerere made a dignified voluntary exit, unlike President Barre of Somalia, who was overthrown by rebels. Many years of unchallengeable and uninterrupted power inevitably bred corruption and the patronage of a favoured tribe. Bureaucracies on state payrolls became swollen, though soldiers' pay tends to have priority – when it runs out, as it did in the Congo, anarchy threatens. Western loans did little to promote sound development, and much of the money was wasted. Now Black Africa is saddled with a debt mountain. Meanwhile, some African leaders enriched themselves, living in luxury and misappropriating their country's earnings, to be secreted in bank accounts abroad.

African nations also embarked on unsuitable economic policies which in the end were disastrous. Central planning and state ownership caused a deterioration in what had previously been more efficiently managed in private hands. Nor did the dash for growth through industrialisation result in products which could compete internationally. Agriculture was neglected and prices of farm produce kept artificially low. The authorities' emphasis on cash crops for exports meant that food for the people was neglected. Economic growth in the 1980s was among the lowest of the world's under-developed nations.

In sub-Saharan Africa food production actually fell by a fifth in the two decades after 1970, but the population was increasing annually by more than 3 per cent and by the 1990s had reached 530 million. Drought, famine and wars had created millions of refugees; those who survived ended up in camps dependent on Western charitable aid. Yet, despite man-made disasters, Aids and the calamities of nature, the population of Africa would continue to increase rapidly.

The end of the Cold War also had an enormous impact, for both good and bad. The superpower antagonists no longer jockeyed for influence in Africa or bribed leaders with their favourite imports – weapons. They no longer backed opposing sides in civil wars, thereby engaging in power struggles by proxy. The conclusion of the Cold War also meant that less interest was now shown in propping up nations or ending ruinous civil conflicts: economic reforms and restructuring were insisted on before more aid was granted. In countries with living standards as low as those in Africa, what was right in textbook theory could be politically disastrous and lead to mass unrest when subsidised food became too dear.

Transition from authoritarian rule to democracy is not a smooth process anywhere. Africa, where old tribal rivalries and political conflicts have long been suppressed, is no exception. When the strong man or the one-party state backed by ruthless security forces is toppled, new conflicts – even anarchy – may follow.

There was a positive side as the twentieth century moved into its last decade: some civil wars, such as that in Namibia, ended. There emerged black leaders of wisdom and humanity like Nelson Mandela, who is striving to assure South Africa of a better future. The hope was that the lessons of past mistakes were being learnt. Half a century after the struggles for independence, Africa faced as great a challenge again to alleviate the consequences of civil wars, to prevent new conflicts from breaking out, to end those still in progress, to feed the people and to match the growth of population with development best suited to Africa's needs. That is the hope – even as the wars and famines of the 1990s still deface the continent.

# PART XVI

The United States and
the Soviet Bloc after *1963*:
The Great Transformation

# CHAPTER 77

## *The Soviet Union and the Wider World: Crushing the Prague Spring*

During the Brezhnev years, the Soviet Union's relationship with the outside world began to change significantly. The Kremlin now accepted that an armed clash with the West was unlikely, provided the Soviet Union was strong enough to ensure that war would prove suicidal for both sides. It was paradoxically also an era of rapid growth in nuclear-missile armaments.

Latitude was permitted to the Warsaw Pact allies to develop their economies on less rigidly state-planned lines. In János Kádár's Hungary limited private enterprise, various incentives and Western loans turned a stagnant economy into what was, for a time, a flourishing one, by the previous standards of the people's republics. But Kádár knew where to draw the line and accepted the *diktat* imposed by Soviet intervention in 1956. The Polish economy, despite large Western loans, failed to make much progress. The general detente between East and West in the 1970s and the recognition of Poland's existing frontiers at the Helsinki Conference in 1975 eased relations, but popular criticism of the Communist Party's failure to improve living conditions led to recurrent crises. Nationalism was strong in Eastern Europe, and anti-Russian feeling was kept barely below the surface.

Communism appeared safest in the rigid hands of the orthodox leadership of the German Democratic Republic: the Protestant Church was the only organisation left capable of any opposition, but it raised its voice mildly, while expressing loyalty to the state. Romania, equally orthodox under the Stalinist rule of Nicolae Ceauşescu, followed an uncomfortably nationalistic and independent course. The Soviet Union did not discourage the people's republics from seeking Western economic assistance or trade; their development also assisted the Soviet Union, which delivered oil at advantageous prices in return for more advanced technological manufactures, for example computer chips from the DDR. The US and Western embargo on the sale of goods such as advanced computers made this technical support especially valuable. But Soviet troops were still stationed in Eastern Europe as members of the Warsaw Pact and as ultimate guarantors of Soviet dominance.

There were limitations to sovereignty. The Soviet leadership imposed two conditions on the Eastern European states within her security sphere: that each should adhere to the Warsaw Pact alliance and that the Communist Party should exercise sole political power. The coalition partners, the other small political parties to be found in Poland and the German Democratic Republic, were mere satellites, agreeing with whatever course the Communist Party decided to follow. Their real influence was non-existent. The Communist Party with its *nomenklatura* – the network of appointees occupying all key posts in administration, industry and party – took its instructions from the Politburo and derived its privileges and income from the system. All this was in accordance with Lenin's principle that there could be discussion within the party but that there could be no anti-party: only one party was allowed.

The Hungarians had broken both conditions in 1956. A decade later, in 1968, the Czech leadership of Alexander Dubček appeared to the Kremlin to be following the same dangerous course. Dubček's 'Prague Spring', granting greater freedom to press and radio, and promising economic reform, was intended to modernise socialism, to create 'socialism with a human face', turning it into an attractive system of government rather than a repressive one to be feared. But Dubček's reforms appeared to be heading towards the forbidden shores of 'democracy', a multi-party system which would reduce the power of the Communist Party machine. The reforms were immensely popular, and started the process of replacing control from above by support and consent from below. Was Czechoslovakia only a step away from abandoning the Soviet alliance for the West? The Kremlin's fears were exaggerated; with the experiences of Hungary before them, the Czech leadership understood that they could not afford to denounce the fraternal Soviet alliance. Despite the international outrage that would ensue, Brezhnev and the Politburo, after repeated altercations with the Czech leadership and debate among themselves, opted for armed intervention. The Prague Spring was crushed by Soviet tanks on 20 August 1968. It was a clear indication of the Kremlin's continued paranoia about safeguarding the frontiers of the USSR. The figleaf of intervention by all the Warsaw Pact allies – Romania alone refusing – only made a bad situation worse when East German troops entered Prague thirty years after Hitler's Wehrmacht had crossed the frontiers of a democratic and sovereign Czechoslovakia.

The Soviet justification was embodied in the so-called Brezhnev Doctrine, which held that socialist states (that is, communist) had the right to intervene if a neighbouring ally threatened to revert to capitalism. That, it was claimed, represented a danger to all; by Soviet definition this unnatural course could only be the result of internal and external Western subversion.

Little more than a decade after the Prague Spring and the reimposition of one-party communist rule in Czechoslovakia, the Politburo faced what looked like a similar challenge to the Brezhnev Doctrine in Poland.

The economic failure of the Polish communist regime in the 1970s became evident when the dash for modernisation based on heavy industries and

*Tearful crowds holding flowers congregate in Prague to confront the Russian invaders who seek to terminate the 'Prague Spring' in August 1968.*

Western technology landed the regime deeply in debt. Agriculture, though largely in the hands of small peasant farmers, lacked the investment necessary to make it productive. To provide food at prices the urban population could afford on their low wages required heavy state subsidies. The huge rise in oil prices in 1973–4 added to the country's woes. When the government attempted to improve its economic management by cutting food subsidies, workers marched in protest at the ensuing price rises. From 1976 onwards, despite arrests and repression, the Polish masses could no longer be totally subdued by the regime. Intellectuals led by Jacek Kuroń set up a Workers' Defence Committee, demanded the release of arrested workers, and insisted on truth instead of lies, the reality of justice in place of rhetoric and propaganda. Polish nationalism was further encouraged by the visit of the Polish Pope John Paul II in 1979. An alliance formed with the workers by Catholics, intellectuals and other opponents presented a powerful challenge to the regime. Another rise in food prices in the summer of 1980 sparked off strikes and a nationwide political confrontation.

It began in the Lenin Shipyard at Gdańsk. An electrician, Lech Wałęsa, emerged to become a national hero. The striking workers at Gdańsk proved more determined than the communist

*Lech Wałęsa at a church service by the gates of the Lenin Shipyard in Gdańsk, 31 August 1980.*

leadership. The Gierek regime, forced into negotiations, effected a tactical retreat, promising to allow the setting up of free trade unions, the right to strike, freedom of the press, and the right of religious organisations to propagate their faith. The new free trade union was called Solidarity and soon attracted 9 million members, presenting as it did an alternative organisation to the Communist Party and to communist satellite organisations. Though it had in theory accepted the 'leading role of the Communist Party' and claimed not to be a political party, it nonetheless represented a political challenge to the communist state. The Polish Communist Party was losing its grip. It is likely that the alarmed Kremlin signalled the need for a Polish (rather than Soviet) crackdown, especially as the Soviet Union had become embroiled in the civil war in Afghanistan (pages 800–1). Even so, in Poland there was much talk of a possible Soviet intervention. General Jaruzelski, austere and colourless, pre-empted any such move by declaring martial law in December 1981 and by establishing a communist military regime. The army proved reliable and, even though the Communist Party lost so much credibility that it could never recover, Jaruzelski imposed a martial

peace. Solidarity leaders were arrested or driven underground. But the Jaruzelski decade could not solve Poland's fundamental problems nor cow the spirit of Solidarity. In central Europe Soviet dominance was upheld with difficulty. Cracks were showing – but no one expected that the whole system would disintegrate before the 1980s had ended.

Brezhnev was anxious to present a peaceful image of Soviet intentions. The missile and space programmes were costly but only by catching up could the Soviet Union treat with the United States as an equal partner and perhaps limit this huge drain on resources. Anything that extended the capabilities of conventional warfare or that raised tensions would not only impede the attempts to halt the continued increase of nuclear armament expenditure, but provoke an inexorable rise in the cost of conventional weapons as NATO increased its own military preparedness. Thus Brezhnev welcomed West Germany's readiness to promote relaxed relations with the East German regime and to reassure Poland that her new western frontier, which enclosed within Poland former German territories, would never be changed by force. West Germany became an essential trading partner of East Germany. That was incentive enough for the communist regime. But the easing of movement between the two Germanies and an effective settlement of confrontation in Berlin by four-power treaties in 1971 and 1972 (which reaffirmed Western rights in the city) made a real contribution to a more peaceful international atmosphere. The Federal Republic also recognised the DDR.

This reluctance to become directly involved in other countries' affairs during the 1970s was particularly marked in Asia, until the invasion of Afghanistan in December 1979. The development of friendly relations between the Soviet Union and India in the 1970s and 1980s is one of the few success stories of Soviet foreign policy. But it did not come cheaply. The Soviet Union supplied substantial military and economic aid. And good relations with India meant, almost inevitably, bad relations with Pakistan. These were exacerbated by Brezhnev's decision – there were rumours in Moscow that he was drunk at the time – to invade Afghanistan in December 1979. That invasion was, however, a logical extension of the Brezhnev Doctrine to a neighbouring state whose communist regime had to be maintained against the revolt of Muslim fundamentalists, even though they enjoyed wide popular support.

A successful coup to place an efficient Afghan communist puppet in power supported by a brief intervention was what the Kremlin had anticipated. Instead the Soviet armed forces had to be reinforced until they exceeded 100,000. The mujahideen in their mountain strongholds could not be wiped out by helicopter rocket attacks. The communist Afghan army and Soviet troops controlled the cities and the main lines of communication, but in the rugged countryside and mountains the mujahideen, fortified by American weapons and by rear bases in Pakistan, proved unbeatable. Non-combatants streamed into refugee camps in Pakistan, thus relieving the fighting units of their care. For Brezhnev the long war was a treble disaster. For the privates conscripted to fight in Afghanistan and for their families, the endless struggle (which was to bring 60,000 casualties) against largely hidden enemies far away from home was a heavy and unpopular burden. For the Red Army generals the war was an opportunity to try out tactics and weapons and to demand more and better tanks,

guns and planes. These could not be denied them, and Brezhnev had to find and divert resources to meet new military needs. Finally, Washington's failure to understand Soviet motivation put paid – at least for a time – to detente, and impeded – in critical areas, halted – Western technological assistance so badly needed in the USSR.

Apart from Afghanistan, the Soviet Union's policy in Asia was cautious. She supplied only limited help to the North in the Vietnamese civil war, and took care not to respond in kind to American intervention on the ground. The most serious problem in Asia was the hostility of China.

The Sino-Soviet split, which had opened up in the days of Khrushchev, deepened with Mao's radicalisation in the 1970s. Mao condemned Soviet relaxation of repression as counter-revolutionary. The Chinese also criticised the invasion of Czechoslovakia and saw themselves as the only true centre of the world communist movement. This did not stop them from improving relations with the United States in the 1970s: in Chinese eyes, the arch-enemy now was not Western imperialism but Soviet 'hegemony'. In 1969 serious armed clashes occurred in places along the Sino-Soviet border, the longest frontier in the world. The USSR had stationed crack divisions armed with nuclear missiles to defend her territory. A paranoia akin to that provoked by the 'yellow peril' at the turn of the century began to take a grip on the Kremlin. The sheer size of China, with a population five times greater than that of the Soviet Union, and with a radical and xenophobic leadership, presented an increasingly nightmarish threat to Moscow. From the 1960s until the early 1980s periods of vituperative exchanges alternated with Soviet efforts to place relations with Beijing on a better footing. But everywhere in Asia, for example in India and Vietnam, Soviet diplomacy and aid were countered by Chinese diplomacy and aid, as in Kampuchea and Pakistan.

The Soviet Union's ambitions to extend her influence to the Third World and the Middle East in the 1960s and 1970s brought little reward and created obstacles in the path of detente. In Africa, poverty, ethnic and racial conflicts and the fierce new nationalism provided fertile ground for the proselytising of the authoritarian socialist system as the only way out of the continent's cycle of devastation and deprivation. The Eastern bloc gave support to movements struggling to overthrow the

*The Soviet army in Afghanistan. Sophisticated weapons did not deliver the expected victory.*

last vestiges of white supremacy in Portuguese Africa, Rhodesia and South Africa. The global East–West struggle was thus extended to Africa. But Moscow's new clients were fickle.

When Nasser's successor Anwar Sadat could not get what he wanted from Moscow he showed no gratitude for the huge amount of civil and military aid (including training in modern weapons technology) which Egypt had received – the largest amount of aid the Soviet Union had supplied to any single country during the two decades from 1955 to 1976: $4750 million. In 1972, Sadat ordered Soviet personnel to leave the country and took over the installations and weapons they had to leave behind. It was a valuable lesson: whatever the complexity of the indigenous government, socialist or not, its authoritarian leaders sought only to exploit superpower rivalry in pursuit of their own interests. Other African countries accepted Soviet aid and tutelage only to break with the Soviet Union and expel Russian advisers. The list is long: Algeria, Ghana, Mali, Sudan, Somalia and Equatorial Guinea. More enduring was Soviet influence in Ethiopia, Angola and Mozambique. Colonel Gaddafi, the Libyan leader, proved more of an embarrassment, since his support of terrorist groups and his territorial ambitions in Chad have been strong destabilising factors.

In the Middle East, Syria was Russia's most reliable ally. After the fall of the Shah of Iran in 1979, Iraq too became the recipient of Soviet arms as Moscow sought to check Khomeini's Muslim fundamentalists, who cursed not only the American devil but also atheistic Russia. With millions of Soviet Muslims susceptible to an Islamic resurgence, Khomeini's ideology posed a new threat to Soviet stability.

In Latin America in the 1960s and 1970s the Soviet Union had gained her first communist ally in Cuba. Castro was no easy bedfellow and the promise to purchase Cuba's sugar crop, previously exported to the United States, in order to keep the Cuban economy afloat cost the USSR thousands of dollars annually in the 1980s. The Soviet Union's client states in Africa, the Middle East and Asia were a further enormous drain on resources which were so badly needed to modernise the Soviet Union herself and raise the living standards of the Russian people. World aid was unpopular in the Soviet Union, whose citizens point to the saying that charity should begin at home.

Central to Soviet foreign policy was detente with the United States, which in the 1970s and 1980s could by itself enhance overall security and reduce the military budget. The exorbitant expense of developing modern weapons and of attempting to frustrate the US Strategic Defence Initiative, or 'Star Wars', became a Soviet nightmare (page 836). The much greater industrial and technological capacity of the United States and the West meant that it was essential to the Soviet Union to set limits on the development and deployment of nuclear weapons. In a non-nuclear war, moreover, the outcome would be determined by the sophistication of conventional weapons. American cruise missiles without nuclear warheads could still cause havoc, destroying command centres; superior aircraft and anti-radar devices could penetrate Soviet airspace. So military budgets had simultaneously to carry the burden of conventional-weapons development. But to have provided all the armaments which the military were clamouring for would have crippled any attempt to improve living standards for the ordinary Soviet citizen, when it was in any case becoming increasingly difficult in the second half of the 1970s to raise national production. Worst of all, the failure to give the Soviet people some sense of material progress would undermine morale, arouse nationalist rivalries between the constituent republics and so threaten the stability of the whole Soviet system.

Brezhnev and his successors responded to this dire predicament by launching peace offensives. Brezhnev and Andropov repeatedly declared that the nuclear arsenals of the superpowers were more than sufficient to serve deterrent purposes and that no nuclear war was 'winnable'. As Andropov put it, 'One has to be blind to the realities of our time not to see that, wherever and however a nuclear whirlwind arises, it will inevitably go out of control and cause a worldwide catastrophe.' The Soviet Union and the United States, however suspicious they might be of each other, also shared common interests. One of the most important was to prevent the spread of nuclear weapons. Accordingly they concluded on 1 July 1968 a treaty on the non-proliferation of nuclear weapons, which bound them to refrain from assisting non-nuclear nations to obtain or make nuclear weapons. Although the treaty has been signed by more than a hundred countries, nuclear-weapon capability continues to spread; the supposed safeguard of inspection by the International Atomic Energy Agency is proving ineffective in such countries as Israel and Iraq.

During the 1970s there was a rational dialogue between the Soviet Union and the United States about how a nuclear war between them, which would destroy both countries, could best be guaranteed never to take place. The answer they found seems perverse. They concluded that it could best be prevented by ensuring that both countries would indeed perish. This could be effected by a treaty severely limiting the defences that could be set up to destroy incoming nuclear missiles. The Treaty on the Limitation of Anti-ballistic Missile Systems, known as the ABM Treaty, was signed on 26 May 1972 during a visit to Moscow by President Nixon. On the same day an Interim Agreement on Limitation of Strategic Offensive Arms, known as SALT I, was also concluded. The United States already had more than enough nuclear missiles to destroy the Soviet Union.

MAD, mutual assured destruction, was the name given to this doctrine that was designed to ensure peace. Then the impetus for further disarmament came to a halt. SALT II, negotiated by President Carter and Brezhnev, and apparently sealed when the Russian leader kissed the US President on the cheek in Vienna on 18 June 1979, was refused ratification by the US Senate. It had sought to reduce the nuclear weaponry on each side, but it was a dead letter after the Soviet invasion of Afghanistan in December 1979; there now appeared to be no prospect for negotiation towards SALT III to reduce offensive weapons on both sides. But during the Brezhnev period meaningful Soviet–US negotiations had begun to find a way out of the blind alley of piling on more and more weapons of mass destruction. After an interval of nearly a decade, Gorbachev and Reagan in the second half of the 1980s resumed this sequence of mutual accommodation in the interests of the Soviet Union and the United States, and indeed of the whole world.

# CHAPTER 78

# The Brezhnev Years and After:
# The Failure of Reform from Within

The seventeen Brezhnev years, together with a brief postscript, marked the final phase of authoritarian, monolithic communist rule, a military superpower with economic feet of clay, an empire of nationalities held together by force. Not until well after Brezhnev's death in 1982 did the West, to its own astonishment, recognise how weakened the Soviet Union had become. It has been another example of how the undercurrents of change in history accumulate slowly, until there is a sudden disintegration of stability evident to everyone.

The Soviet Union was losing the race with the West, unable to present a viable and attractive alternative to market capitalism and democracy. These were the years when the communist leadership tried to reform and to make their system work better. The results in the early years were mixed; the exploitation of Russia's rich oil and mining resources at a time of high energy prices in the 1970s provided a boost. But the lack of investment had dire consequences as factories were not renewed and the infrastructure, roads and means of communication, was neglected. Vast sums were diverted to the military. Maximum exploitation without thought for pollution prepared the way for ecological disasters. A vast bureaucratic machine, which could only stifle initiative, had to be paid for. With increasingly outdated technology and lacking incentives, the Soviet worker became hopelessly unproductive. In the end, though 'reform communism' did produce changes and some improvements,

they were not enough to save the system.

Twenty years earlier, the first attempt to give the communist state a new face had ended with the fall of Khrushchev. The Politburo for a time preferred not to trust any one successor after that. In 1964, three leading members were assigned the principal offices of state: Nicolai Podgorny became president, Leonid Brezhnev party leader and Alexei Kosygin chairman of the Council of Ministers. Kosygin was an able technocrat who was well aware of the shortcomings of the Soviet economic performance. In place of Khrushchev's sudden changes, Kosygin, very much in harmony with the thinking of his two colleagues, attempted a more consistent and gradual approach.

The task the Soviet leaders set themselves was to improve standards of living, to keep the KGB under control, to catch up technologically and quantitatively in the military sector, whose backwardness America's missile superiority had so cruelly exposed during the Cuban crisis, and to do all this without creating new tensions in Soviet–American relations. The course set was one of reform and ambitious development, but the political system and central control were not to be weakened, let alone endangered. Brezhnev was to become the leading exponent of this policy of trying to please everyone, particularly the three main pillars of the communist system, the party hierarchy, the bureaucrats and the army. The anti-religious course followed by Khrushchev was also dampened down. Given these priorities, the room for change and development was severely circumscribed. Progress between 1964 and 1984 was very uneven. After a spurt from 1961 to 1975, which owed something to the economic reforms introduced by Kosygin, there was stagnation.

But the changes achieved in the Soviet Union were not fundamental: prices of input materials and output product were still fixed by the central planners; the 'profit' incentive introduced into the pricing structure could therefore be arbitrarily adjusted. Nevertheless the new incentive provided a stimulus to industrial managers and to workers, who welcomed bonus payments for higher productivity. During the decade from 1970 to 1980, 1 million workers were redeployed in the more efficient sectors of industry, thus reducing chronic overmanning and increasing productivity. But the central planners, Gosplan and the ministries continued to set prices, fix production targets and control supplies.

The approach to economic reform was piecemeal, and good results were achieved in only a few sectors of the economy, which were held back from making faster progress by the backward sectors, the lack of communications, poor roads, widespread corruption, mismanagement and an overall lack of co-ordination, each ministry seeking to achieve the best results statistically in its own sphere without regard to the whole. This 'sectional' approach rarely brought any benefits to the consumer, unless a particularly efficient section actually produced what consumers required. Sometimes this had bizarre consequences. The strategic rocket forces began to produce the best refrigerator, and the Ministry of Aviation manufactured an excellent vacuum cleaner.

The army had backed the overthrow of Khrushchev and had benefited from the increasing defence expenditure necessary to achieve parity with the United States in nuclear and missile weaponry and to remedy Russia's inferiority on the high seas. The strengthening of the armed forces from 1964 to 1974 was dramatic and absorbed a disproportionate part of the Soviet budget. But Brezhnev also wanted to preside over a consumer boom, and the armed forces and their ministries saw a chance for profit. They began by providing goods for their own military and civilian personnel – vegetables, prams and so on – then their products became more widely available. The problem of how to relate consumers and producers in a centrally directed economy

without a market mechanism, in a system where prices and costs are arbitrarily fixed, was neither tackled nor solved. Could such an economy be reformed and adjusted to meet Soviet requirements, and yet retain its socialist character? That was the basic question which confronted reformers from the 1960s to the 1980s.

With the relaxation of repression and increasing contact with the West, the Soviet citizen, especially in the major cities, became more sophisticated. Complaints and criticisms were articulated. One of the few success stories of the Soviet Union is the spread of education. Though loyalty to the Soviet state remained a basic requirement, education was provided on merit. This created a large educated class. Critical discussion began in the 1960s and 1970s among enquiring groups of university students, to one of which Mikhail Gorbachev belonged; it encompassed professional circles of a whole new post-war generation but had to be conducted discreetly and privately. The thaw which had begun with Khrushchev could no longer be reversed in the Brezhnev era. But strict limits were set and exemplary punishment imposed on the most prominent dissidents, who courageously continued to speak out publicly – outstanding men such as Andrei Sakharov and the writers Andrei Sinyavsky and Yali Daniel. Some of the most prominent dissidents were Jewish. Anti-Semitism increased, and Zionism was equated with treachery. Jews who applied to leave the Soviet Union would lose their jobs, though some were eventually permitted to emigrate. But the restrained repression of a 'reformed' KGB, placed under the control of Yuri Andropov, could only contain, not eradicate, the by now widespread dissident movement. Duplicating machines acted as an underground press, whose *samizdat* editions passed through hundreds of hands. That dissent flourished is evidence of the courage of a section of the intelligentsia; years of communist propaganda could not obliterate independent thought.

Now that world opinion was concerning itself with the fate of the dissidents, the Soviet authorities could no longer behave as they had in Stalin's time. Moreover, the Soviet Union had officially adhered to the Helsinki Agreement of 1975, promising to respect basic human rights; this provided the protesters with some legal standing, at least internationally. The denial to Soviet Jews of permission to emigrate was countered by American

Congressional pressure which linked credit and trade concessions to the USSR to Soviet liberality in allowing Jews to leave (Senator Jackson's amendment) at a time when American imports were of particular value to the Russians. Moscow reacted angrily to what it regarded as unwarranted Western interference in Soviet affairs. Over the longer term, however, the growing links with the West made mass repression of dissenting opinion impossible. In the 1970s the 'prisoners of conscience' in the Soviet Union, suffering hardship from house arrest to exile, from hard labour to forced detention in psychiatric institutions, were numbered in thousands, rather than the millions of Stalin's day, and executions ceased.

For the mass of Soviet peoples the awareness of poor living conditions coincided with the improvements made during the Brezhnev years. Grain production from 1964 to 1969 averaged 156 million tonnes a year, but varied in a particular year from a low of 121 million (1965) to a high of 171 million (1966). The average only just covered basic Soviet needs – there were no longer any famines or shortages of bread. But the people wanted more variety, more milk, more meat and more vegetables. Agricultural production, though higher, could not keep pace with what was required.

Increased use of fertilisers, higher payments to farmers, the introduction of a number of incentives, including licences for larger private plots and allowing sales on a free market once production quotas were reached, all these reforms of the Brezhnev years failed to satisfy the growing demand. The deficit had to be covered by grain imports, above all from the plenitude of American over-production, until the invasion of Afghanistan in 1979 and the resulting US grain embargo forced a switch to other suppliers. More meat was made available; between 1970 and 1985, the average consumption rose by half. But grain production continued to vary widely from year to year. About 210 million tonnes was the normal annual requirement. A bumper harvest in 1978 produced 237 million tonnes, which covered all the grain requirements of the Soviet Union; but the following year the figure dropped to 180 million tonnes; in 1980 it rose to 189 million tonnes, only to drop again in 1981 to a catastrophic 160 million tonnes, requiring the importation of 46 million tonnes of grain from abroad, which used up valuable foreign currency reserves. Incentives and reforms and high invest-ment were producing far from satisfactory results during the closing years of the Brezhnev era.

With more money earned, the average monthly wage almost doubling, farmers, transport and construction workers doing even better and miners trebling their income, the ordinary Russian was living better and standing longer in queues chasing the subsidised goods in state shops or buying goods at high prices in the free and semi-black markets. Vodka consumption and alcoholism became an ever growing problem. The available goods, other than those satisfying the basic needs of shelter and food, were inordinately expensive by Western standards and were generally of poor quality. But it needs to be borne in mind that a much smaller proportion of the wage packet had to be spent on housing and the basics, whose costs were fixed arbitrarily low. The high prices for other consumer goods acted as a form of indirect tax to mop up excess money.

Even so, the available consumer goods could not absorb the wages and millions of roubles piled up in savings accounts. The miner could not buy better housing despite his savings; he was rouble-rich but continued to live primitively. The most prized possession of newly weds was privacy and a home of their own. But young marrieds had to live for years with in-laws until a modest home could be allocated. The next most prized possession was a car. The mass production of Fiat-designed cars also started in the Brezhnev years and, though by Western standards the proportion of car owners was low, by Soviet standards it was remarkable that one in seven families possessed a car, almost every household had a television set, a third of them in colour, a refrigerator and a washing machine. Leaving aside the chronic lack of space and the large number of extended family households that ensued, in terms of domestic labour-saving devices the average Soviet household had catapulted from pre-revolutionary conditions to the modern age in less than two decades. But if other indicators are considered, such as telephones and personal computers, the differential between the West and the Soviet Union remained huge. The economy as a whole was grossly inefficient in use of resources and burdened by out-of-date factories. Even more trouble was in store as machines wore out, and pipes, valves and pumps in the oil industry leaked and rusted. The Soviet Union could not even take advantage of her rich resources, her grain rotting for lack of transport and proper storage capacity.

She was heading for a complete breakdown.

The negative aspects of the Soviet command economy and the one-party state hierarchy were very evident. The burden of a stifling bureaucracy, the almost universal need for bribery, without which little got done, and the irrational division between rival authorities, ministries and party organisations were hindrances enough. In addition, the privileges enjoyed by the *nomenklatura*, their special shops, hospitals and holiday resorts, attracted jealousy and resentment. The residual heavy-handedness of the security services persisted during the Brezhnev years. Long hours of work were the norm for the average Soviet citizen. The protection of the law was never certain, especially as it was almost impossible to live strictly within it. The possession of a car, for instance, necessitated resource to the black market for spare parts and services. Thus disregard for the law, petty bribery and corruption were endemic. Higher up the administrative elite, corruption was practised on a grandiose scale during the Brezhnev years. Brezhnev himself provided a prominent example of high living, owning vast estates and a fleet of luxury cars.

Promotion for men and women of ability still required the patronage of someone higher up in the party or a ministry. Corruption was not confined to the Kremlin but was widespread in the Soviet republics, indeed had become legendary in Georgia, where huge bribery allowed enterprising businessmen to build up private empires. Members of the *nomenklatura* lived in a style reminiscent of American tycoons. For the privileged few the products of the West were easily available: Mercedes cars, hi-fi equipment and Russian luxuries like caviar. Andropov's clean-up campaign while he was head of the KGB could scratch only the surface, though it reached all the way to Brezhnev's family: his daughter, with her diamonds, was a conspicuous consumer, while his son Yuri, though often drunk, lived a charmed life. The Western lifestyles of many of the children of the elite were bitterly resented by the average Russian.

Brezhnev's deliberate consumer boom had nevertheless made many hitherto scarce goods more readily available, though they were often of poor quality. One of the most intractable problems of Soviet central planning was that the demands that had to be satisfied were those of the relevant ministries, not those of the consumer for whom the goods were intended. The consumer represented a mere abstract unit; the ministries decided what the consumer needed. Of course, the citizen's wishes are not paramount in a command economy. It can hardly be otherwise, since no computer can be adequately programmed to take account of the complexities of consumer demand – the nationwide supply of shoes of different qualities and prices, sizes and fashions which would match consumer's wishes, to give just one example – and in any case powerful computers were in short supply in the Soviet Union. Another bane of the system was the notorious 'gross output' indicator as a measurement of the fulfilment of plans. The distortions this created are illustrated by a factory that produced nails. Its target was set in terms of weight. The manager accordingly arranged for the manufacture of only very large and heavy nails. When the ministry discovered this and set the target in the form of quantity, the manager switched to very small nails. The story is probably apocryphal but it provides a good illustration of the shortcomings inherent in central planning. Where the consumer can set the requirements, as happened for instance in the supply of weapons for the armed services, the Soviet Union did better. The Soviet space enterprise, another example, caught up with the West and was perhaps even more reliable than America's NASA.

The record of the Brezhnev era was uneven. A start was made in economic reforms, though without questioning fundamentals. The exploitation of the Soviet Union's vast mineral resources – the oil and gas and gold in Siberia and east of the Urals – and the limited introduction of Western technology raised output, but the greater part of industry was not renewed. The restraints placed on the KGB and the better life enjoyed by the Soviet people were positive aspects, but the Soviet authoritarian system was not democratised in any essential. Brezhnev's determination to stabilise the power base of the Soviet political structure entailed a policy of live and let live at the top: secure party fiefs and party cadres ensured stability, while corruption and privileges bought their support. The ordinary people, however, had few rights and had to do as they were told. This did not preclude the emergence of able and incorruptible party functionaries such as Eduard Shevardnadze, who as party chief in Georgia carried through a wholesale purge of the system erected by his corrupt predecessor. Yuri Andropov, as head of the KGB, was of a similar caste, and tried to rid the party of corruption.

*The USSR invested all its hopes in its ambitious space-exploration programme. Here Soyuz astronauts are honoured at the Kremlin in October 1969.*

Although something like a cult of personality was fostered around Brezhnev, his power was not absolute. During his last years of ill-health much of the work had to be carried out by deputies. The growth of general public irreverence towards the leader was perhaps best shown by the many jokes circulating about him during those latter years. Much had changed. No one would have dared to joke about Stalin's decline thirty years earlier. But Brezhnev was perceived as a benevolent and increasingly easy-going leader. Although living conditions varied enormously from region to region, while in the countryside housing continued to be neglected and primitive living conditions persisted, life became better in the cities and overall. The new freedom of movement allowed to the peasants increased the drift to the cities so typical of countries in the under-developed world.

Yuri Andropov seemed just the right choice to take over after Brezhnev's death in November 1982. His lifestyle was in complete contrast to Brezhnev's. He lived very modestly and had built his reputation on his shrewd handling of the KGB, bringing that secret organisation under control while maintaining its secrecy. He was a reformer, but by no means a liberal in the Western sense. Reform for Andropov meant control by the party leadership, reform of

the communist state to achieve a more effective communist system, striking a careful balance between extra-legal repression of dissidence to maintain the communist order and avoiding unnecessary excess and personal abuse of power. Exile and detention in psychiatric hospitals were no longer the result of personal whims but were carefully calculated to deter dissent. The Western attitude to justice and legality was not acceptable, despite Helsinki (page 804), and the dissident Russian human-rights group which made it its task to monitor the observance of the Helsinki accords was under constant threat of persecution.

Andropov reacted with a subtle mixture of tolerance and concessions; nearly 300,000 Jews were allowed to leave the USSR, after they had been deprived of jobs and privileges, some of them imprisoned on trumped-up charges and most kept waiting, often for many years. Russia's most celebrated dissident writer, the Nobel laureate Alexander Solzhenitsyn, was also allowed to leave for the West. The redoubtable physicist and dissident Dr Andrei Sakharov rejected such a course and for years suffered exile and deprivation with his wife. Western media attention eventually led to their release after Gorbachev came to power in 1985. Executions were reserved for serious corruption and could reach high in the party ranks. As

KGB chief, Andropov had built his reputation on his fearless attack on high party bosses in a series of anti-corruption drives during the 1970s.

The Politburo had chosen Andropov without hesitation. To them his merit was that he was ready to get the USSR moving again economically without endangering ideological orthodoxy. He was thus a reformer of the right kind, in the opinion of the majority of the Politburo. The succession did not fall, as expected, to Konstantin Chernenko, who was too closely identified with Brezhnev's declining years. But Andropov himself was ill, and under his ailing leadership his principal ally Gorbachev in 1983 took charge of a special task force in a vain effort to stimulate economic reform. An attempt was also made to change the composition of party leadership in the regions and districts throughout the Soviet Union. Andropov's health declined too rapidly for these initiatives to bear much fruit; he spent his last few months confined to hospital with renal failure and died in February 1984.

Gorbachev at this time was regarded as too young and too impetuous to be entrusted with the leadership and the post of general secretary of the party. But it was evident that the course set by Andropov was not to be abandoned. The septuagenarian Chernenko took over, but the powerful Politburo determined policy, with Gorbachev in charge of the economy and one of the longest-serving members, Andrei Gromyko, remaining in charge of foreign affairs. Chernenko's health likewise rapidly deteriorated; he was allowed to carry on until his death (he died of the progressive lung disease, emphysema) in March 1985. The deaths of three elderly leaders in the space of two and a half years, far from projecting an image of reform and change, created in the Soviet Union and the wider world the perception of a country that had become rigid in its ways and was presided over by a gerontocracy. That was about to change dramatically.

# CHAPTER 79

# The United States: From Great Aspirations to Disillusion

The 1960s and early 1970s were a distinctive and decisive period in American history. They were years of rapidly growing prosperity, but they were also the years of the Vietnam War, disillusionment and protest.

The post-war economic boom passed all expectations. The standard of living of most Americans increased nearly every year. Was this not a vindication of American free enterprise? Americans had become citizens of an affluent society – at least most of them had – and had discovered the wonders of credit. Millions moved to a better life in the Sunbelt from Texas to California. Florida became a haven for an older generation. But in 1962 one in four Americans, over 42 million, were still living in dire poverty. That included nearly half the Afro-American population, single parents and children, the old and sick, and the poor, who lacked education and skills. From poverty-stricken Mexico, immigrants entered California and Texas illegally to work for low wages which Americans would not accept. From Puerto Rico and Latin America the poor, seeking a better life, finished up in the deprived housing of the inner cities. Here they joined the native Americans, who had left their own barren reservations. But the lot of the poor improved dramatically.

President Johnson in his first State of the Union address in 1964 declared 'unconditional war on poverty'. The federal government pumped billions of dollars into welfare and ambitious anti-poverty projects. Johnson's Great Society programmes worked. By 1973, the number of poor had more than halved to 11 per cent. The anti-liberal Nixon, though faced with increasing federal deficits when he became president in 1969, did not retrench seriously on welfare. Positive anti-poverty measures taken by his administration included increased social security benefits and greater expenditure on education; federal housing subsidies were also continued.

Nevertheless, the United States was still a deeply divided society; the liberal 1960s of welfare, of protest, of student revolt and anti-Vietnam draft boycotts was creating a backlash by construction workers and outraged Middle America, which attributed the rising crime rates and the disrespect shown by youth to excessive licence and softness. The Americans who turned to Nixon saw in him a president who would uphold America's traditional virtues.

After his narrow defeat by Kennedy in 1960 and, two years later, his devastating drubbing in the contest for governor of California, Nixon's controversial political career seemed to have ended. At what he thought would be his last press conference, he hit back at the newsmen, who he felt had never treated him fairly: 'You won't have Nixon to kick around any more . . .' A few days later, ABC Television broadcast a special, *The Political Obituary of Richard Nixon*. Nixon left his California base and joined a law firm in New York, though in 1964 he supported the presidential campaign of Barry Goldwater, who was well to the right of mainstream

Republicans. In 1966 and 1967 he rebuilt his political support as the man best able to unite Republicans. By the time of the party's Convention in 1968, he was once more the obvious candidate to contest the next presidential election.

Driving ambition and sheer hard work rather than privilege and a silver spoon got Nixon to the White House. He saw himself as the underdog who had had to make his own way. As president he retained a sense that he faced danger from many unscrupulous enemies and from an ill-disposed establishment. Determined to defeat them, he responded with conspiratorial ruthlessness. There was a loneliness about his White House years, with his reliance on a small team of White House political staff, from whom he demanded absolute loyalty. For Nixon, safety would be guaranteed only if he could gain control over those he believed wished to discredit him and his policies. It all ended with the Watergate fiasco and his resignation to avoid impeachment. But his performance as president during his first administration won him the trust and confidence of a far greater majority of American voters in the 1972 election than in the lacklustre election of 1968.

Nixon's passion was to devise for America a new global strategy that would extricate her from the rigidities of the Cold War. He appointed William P. Rogers, a former attorney-general under Eisenhower, Secretary of State. But in shaping a new foreign policy he called on the help of a Harvard professor, Henry A. Kissinger, to act as national security adviser. Kissinger replaced Rogers as Secretary of State when Rogers resigned in the autumn of 1973. Kissinger proved a brilliant strategist in tackling contemporary international problems. The most pressing need was to extricate the United States from fighting an endless war in Vietnam.

Vietnam had divided the nation. During his election campaign Nixon promised that he had a plan to end the war. The plan was to roll the film backwards, to the point before massive numbers of US combat troops had been sent to Vietnam, and the hope continued to be that the American-equipped South Vietnamese army plus punitive bombing by the United States would force the North Vietnamese to give up the struggle. Kissinger was as tough-minded as Nixon about the war, determined that it should not end in a humiliating defeat. The US position he put forward at the Paris peace negotiations – these had begun during Johnson's

presidency in May 1968 – was that all foreign forces should leave South Vietnam, which should then be left to decide her future in free elections. This was unacceptable to the North Vietnamese; they knew that whichever side organised the free elections would be sure to win them. They demanded a coalition government in South Vietnam, to include the communist South Vietnamese National Liberation Front, which they easily dominated after the Tet offensive had inflicted terrible losses on the Vietcong (page 630).

The Nixon plan was to Vietnamise the war on land and to bring US combat troops home in stages. The Americans suffered heavy casualties in 1969 and were increasingly demoralised, many soldiers resorting to cheap drugs. In 1968 US forces had reached their maximum of 536,100 men; in 1969 they were reduced to 475,200; by 1971 their number had dropped to 157,800 and when the armistice was signed in January 1973 only 23,500 were still left in Vietnam. But while US troop reductions took place the air war was secretly extended to Cambodia along the North Vietnamese supply routes, the Ho Chi-minh trail. In April 1970 American and South Vietnamese troops actually invaded Cambodia, to the dismay of American public opinion, which wanted to get out of the war and not into a new one. On the ground the North Vietnamese and Vietcong were showing no signs of weakening. Nixon's only response was to step up again the bombing of North Vietnam. Kissinger meanwhile had made secret contact with the North Vietnamese negotiator in Paris, Le Duc Tho, in February 1970. Not until the Americans were prepared to abandon their insistence that the North Vietnamese forces in the South should withdraw at the same time as the Americans could a deal be struck. It was bitterly opposed by the President of South Vietnam, General Nguyen Van Thieu. If the Americans left, the South Vietnamese would have to face the full weight of the Vietminh in the South alone. There were hitches in the final negotiations in Paris when the North Vietnamese resisted amendments to the peace agreement. To persuade them, Nixon ordered the heavy Christmas bombing of Hanoi in December 1972. On 27 January 1973 the communist negotiators accepted a ceasefire and concluded a comprehensive agreement to end the Vietnam war; the South Vietnamese were left no alternative but to join, since they were totally dependent on US support.

The last long-drawn-out stages from 1970 to 1973 of what had become the most unpopular war in US history continued to be accompanied by protests at home. Nixon's own reactions tended to polarise the conflict between 'conservatives' and 'liberals'. In May 1970 National Guardsmen fired into a crowd of student demonstrators at Kent State University; four students were killed and several wounded, which shocked even the conservatives. Protest swept American university campuses. The war was still not over in November 1972 when Nixon again presented himself to the electors.

That Nixon won the presidential election by a landslide, with more than 60 per cent of the popular vote, reveals the change in public feeling. Nixon personally, shy, aloof and not entirely trusted, was not popular; 'Would you buy a second-hand car from him?' it was asked. But he also appeared moderate and competent at home. He and Kissinger capitalised on the conservative backlash that was demanding law and order and a return to health of the American economy, and was disillusioned with the costly Great Society and the exaggerated aspirations of the Johnson years. The boys were coming home from Vietnam and few now remained. Kissinger's skilful handling (though he was not the secretary of state) of foreign affairs, the evidence of relaxation of tension with the Soviet Union, the Nuclear Non-Proliferation Treaty and the arms-limitation talks with Russia all helped to enhance the administration's image. The greatest Nixon–Kissinger coup and the most surprising was the establishment of friendly relations with Mao's China. Their secret diplomacy began to show results when the Chinese in April 1971 invited an American table-tennis team to China. This was followed by Kissinger's own secret trip to Beijing to prepare the way for Nixon's spectacular visit in February 1972. The reorientation of US policy strengthened the hand of US diplomacy the world over. In May 1972 Nixon was in Moscow signing an arms-limitation agreement; detente was in full swing.

That Nixon's posture as a successful world statesman restoring US prestige after the frustrations of Vietnam helped him to win a second term in the presidency there can be no doubt. But his electoral victory was also aided by the weakness of a divided opposition. The Democratic candidate, Senator George McGovern, did not prove a strong vote-winner. Edward Kennedy, the last of the Kennedy brothers, might have done, but his chances of selection had disappeared three years earlier in the shallow waters at Chappaquiddick, where, in an accident when the car he was driving plunged off a bridge, his lady companion was drowned. The Senator's subsequent behaviour in failing to raise the alarm sooner led to controversy and blighted his presidential ambitions.

Within the space of less than two years Nixon fell from triumph to disgrace. But the world did not entirely revolve around Watergate. The 'Agreement to end the Vietnam war' in January 1973 and the accompanying international declaration of support for it signed by twelve nations in the presence of the Secretary-General of the United Nations was, despite its solemn promises, bound to fail in its main purpose: the achievement of peace. It left the opposing communist and anti-communist forces in control of their own areas and regions of South Vietnam. The advantage lay with the North Vietnamese forces, which did not have to withdraw north of the 17th parallel. Nor was Vietnam any closer to a political solution. The South Vietnamese government felt it had been sold down the river, as the remaining US forces progressively withdrew, the last departing in March 1973. It was not quite like that. The Americans handed over their installations to the South Vietnamese and supplied enormous quantities of equipment, until South Vietnam possessed the fourth-largest air force in the world. It was up to the South Vietnamese government to win the war, if it could.

Neither the Vietcong nor the North Vietnamese nor the South Vietnamese had any intention of honouring the armistice – though the communists were also on their own, both the Chinese and the Russians having refused to help them further. If the communists broke the agreement, as they did, Nixon could have ordered new air strikes, but they would have been unlikely to restrain them. By the autumn of 1973, when fighting resumed, Nixon was weakened by Watergate. The fighting continued until April 1975, when the communists took Saigon. The end came switfly. For the United States the indescribable scenes as South Vietnamese men and women, allies of the United States, crowded on the US Embassy roof, mostly in vain, desperately trying to join the helicopter evacuation of the American Embassy staff, marked a graphic and humiliating end to America's efforts to save South Vietnam from communism. The men who had died in the war and those who had returned – the Vietnam veterans – received little honour or thanks. Americans wanted to forget the war. In the words of Nixon's successor President Gerald Ford, 'Today, Americans can regain the sense of pride that existed before Vietnam.' He rightly insisted that the tragic events 'portend neither the end of the world nor of America's leadership in the world'. But this was wisdom after the events. If only it had existed when Johnson massively involved the United States between July 1965 and March 1966.

At home during his second administration Nixon had to grapple with inflation and the deteriorating financial situation. He began by cutting back on some of the Great Society social programmes. He devalued the dollar, and for a time his administration imposed wage and price controls. With the huge rise in Arab oil prices all Western economies were in trouble in 1973 and 1974. In the United States, unemployment and inflation were rising while production was falling, a state of affairs that prevailed in most Western countries. According to Keynesian economics, inflation should have led to a growth in production and falls in unemployment. Now the economic world was topsy-turvy. A new term was coined to describe what was afflicting the West – 'stagflation', stagnation plus inflation.

In the political world, however, the Watergate scandal soon overshadowed all else. America's allies were puzzled by the way US newspapers and media hounded a president who had arguably showed himself more successful in securing American and Western interests, more far-sighted, than any other president in the twentieth century. Domestically too the Nixon presidency seemed to be following moderate and sensible policies. But American politics are rough, and dirty tricks are nothing new. Illegal telephone-tapping, bribery and misuse of funds have been practised by some of America's most eminent leaders. The press did not expose discreditable information about all politicians or even all presidents. J. F. Kennedy's love-life was kept quiet; Martin Luther King was bugged. The CIA and the FBI were engaged in activities beyond anything that had been sanctioned. Nixon believed he had many enemies determined to get at him. The knives were certainly out for him, but he had himself contributed to this beleaguered atmosphere. The White House staff were becoming a second secret administration. They plotted how to strengthen the President and how best to lay low

his enemies. Nixon was no outsider to these secret discussions. They proved not to be so secret in the end because he had them all taped.

The Watergate story really began a year before the famous break-in with Nixon's determination to get at the opponents of his policies in Vietnam and at home – at those, especially, who from inside the civil service were leaking secret documents to the press. The White House set up the Special Investigations Unit in the pursuit of their undercover investigations. The Unit's staff became known as the Plumbers. It was they who organised the break-in at the Democratic Party campaign headquarters in the Watergate Building in Washington in June 1972; the purpose was to steal information to help Nixon and discredit the Democrats during the presidential election campaign. The burglars were caught. Nixon had not known about the burglary beforehand, nor had he authorised the break-in, but some of his principal aides were implicated. The White House managed to keep the scandal from affecting the elections in November 1972, which Nixon won with a landslide majority, but the Watergate fuse had been lit, to detonate early in 1973 as the culprits were tried and threatened with severe sentences. Some broke down and implicated the President's staff.

Criminal charges against senior White House staff were nothing new in the 1970s, so why did it touch the President himself? The judicial investigations dragged on for months, with the President defending himself with ever less conviction. The administration lost even more credibility when Vice-President Spiro Agnew resigned after a tax investigation unconnected with Watergate. When Nixon was forced by the Supreme Court finally to hand over the White House tapes it became irrefutably clear that early on the President had with his advisers tried to obstruct justice, desperately trying to distance the White House from Watergate and other dirty tricks. The cover-up proved Nixon's undoing. To liberals, Nixon and the White House conspiracies had become a real danger to American civil liberties and constitutional government. With impeachment imminent, Nixon was the first president to resign. On 9 August 1974 he took off in a helicopter from the White House lawn, waving goodbye to a small, tearful party. Outside the United States, where Nixon's prestige stood high, the assessment was more cynical – Nixon's mistake had been to get caught. He

*President Richard Nixon resigns, 8 August 1974.*

continued to be received with respect in China and elsewhere after his fall; his advice and help in international affairs has also been sought by succeeding presidents. The good that emerged from Watergate was that it acted as a warning to subsequent administrations; the 'fourth estate', the press, with its extensive rights of investigation and freedom to publish and uncover scandals, is a deterrent, at least to some degree.

The Vice-President, Gerald Ford, was sworn in and saw Nixon's term out. He began with an unpopular move, granting a pardon to Nixon. He gave the impression of a decent man, a clean politician, but one who did not inspire and who simply did not seem up to the job of running the presidency. He frequently stumbled, sometimes literally. His relations with Congress were poor and American economic prospects worsened in 1974 and 1975. In foreign affairs detente made a little dubious progress but this was overshadowed by sweeping communist victories in Vietnam and Cambodia. To be sure, the blame for these cannot be placed at Ford's door; they were the results of a situation he had inherited.

Kissinger, appointed secretary of state, was the star of the administration as he established new records for 'shuttle diplomacy'. During the Middle Eastern crisis between Israel and the Arabs (1973–5), world television showed the tireless

Secretary of State stepping out of his personal plane in Arab and Israeli airports at a dizzying speed. He accomplished a provisional disengagement and an end of hostilities between Egypt and Israel in September 1975 (page 482). The achievement was all the more remarkable in that he won acceptance by all sides concerned as a mediator of goodwill, although he had entered the United States in the 1930s as a Jewish refugee from Nazi German persecution.

Gerald Ford has probably been underrated. His calm and reassuring manner helped to re-establish the integrity of the presidency. He provided a transition from one of the lowest periods of American self-confidence, a period of violence and assassinations at home, of Watergate and Vietnam. Middle America was learning to appreciate less dynamic, less obviously ambitious politicians. They recognised that Gerald Ford was an American like millions of others. The Democratic candidate for the presidency, James Earl Carter, was another seemingly ordinary American with whom millions could identify. In November 1976 the US electorate had a choice between two contenders ready to lead the world, neither of whom some two years earlier had been heard of outside their immediate constituencies. Ford had been catapulted from obscurity by Agnew's resignation and the demise of Nixon. Carter, former navy officer and, after the death of his father, successful peanut farmer, had risen to become governor of Georgia – a reforming and successful governor. By a narrow margin, Carter beat Ford and thereby ended eight years of Republican power in the White House. But the economic fortunes of the United States had changed since the last Democratic president, Johnson, had launched his Great Society with the grand vision of abolishing poverty in America. Carter did not have an easy time before him.

Carter was the first president since the Civil War to come from the South. He was also a Washington outsider, and owed his electoral victory partly to this fact. The credibility of government had fallen, and the American people were looking for a change from the old gang. Ford was intelligent and his integrity was above reproach, but the pardon he gave to Nixon had damaged him badly, though seen in longer perspective it was both in the national interest and a courageous step in the face of public feeling at the time. Ford lacked charisma, though, and a good tele-image. Carter also lacked a commanding presence, but his warm, folksy manner and broad grin won him friends. He was patently honest, untouched by sordid Washington politics or past scandals. Even so, the margin of electoral votes that carried him to the White House was small; his strength in the South and North-east carried the day, but he was weak in the West and so lacked a broad national base of support.

Carter was determined to emphasise that his presidency would represent a break with the past, especially with Nixon's 'imperial presidency'. He would be the people's president, a trustee for their needs, concerned with the wider national interest. This implied not a weak presidency but strong leadership, 'doing what's right, not what's political'. He saw himself as above party politics, acting differently from Congress, whose Senators and Representatives were actuated by political considerations, having to bear in mind the special interests of their constituents and their financial backers, and having to keep a constant eye on re-election. Although Carter had comfortable majorities in both Houses, this did not mean automatic support for all that he wished to accomplish. He avoided any distinctive label: he was liberal in some aspects of policy and conservative in others.

After so much turmoil and change, Carter saw a need for consolidation at home, efficiency and honesty in government, a pruning of wasteful welfare programmes, a reduction in government interference and a lightening of the regulations imposed on business and industry. American politics do not neatly divide between one party right of centre in its outlook and the other to the liberal left of centre. Rather the more conservative and the more liberal social policies cut through each party. Trusteeship for Carter meant a careful husbandry of the money demanded in taxation. Sound government finance required the balancing of the budget, not spending more than the money in the coffers. Carter hoped to reduce armaments and military expenditure. But he was also sensitive to immediate needs, especially the scourge of unemployment. To stimulate the economy and reduce unemployment he adopted a Keynesian approach, sending to Congress a moderate tax-cutting bill and making federal grants to create jobs. Congress changed the proposals in detail but approved of the general thrust.

During the later years of his presidency, Carter became more cautious, avoiding any costly reshaping of welfare as he became more concerned about inflation and a rising federal deficit. The 1970s, after the shock of the oil-price rise of 1973–4, were a difficult period of economic management throughout the Western world, and of course throughout the Third World. Governments are lucky or unlucky when it comes to world economic conditions and the business cycle, over which they have very little control. But they get the blame when unemployment rises and living standards fall. Carter in 1978 fell back on the old remedies of regulation, limiting the salary increases of federal employees and setting voluntary – and ineffective – guidelines on wages and prices. The classic remedy for inflation of raising interest rates was also employed. There was a coal strike and Carter invoked the anti-union Taft–Hartley Act. Other federal regulatory measures were passed that protected the environment in Alaska and limited the damage done to the land by strip-mining.

Carter did not achieve anything like all the reforms he had hoped for during his presidency. He would have had better relations with Congress had he employed a less high moral tone and more flexibility. His White House staff, also Georgian outsiders, lacked the necessary experience to handle Congress more skilfully. They were surprised by how long it took for the legislative process to be completed; they sent many measures to Congress without having established a clear idea of their priorities. A centrepiece of Carter's endeavours in the wake of the oil-price rise of 1973–4 was to cut down on the extravagantly wasteful use of energy in the United States. But his energy plan ran into opposition from many interest groups. For the average American, freedom is a car and cheap gasoline. After more than a year of wrangling, a watered-down National Energy Act became law in the autumn of 1978.

In the relations of the United States with the rest of world, Carter was determined to strike a new note. He wanted to reduce tensions, especially with the Soviet Union, but he was also determined to stand up for human rights, 'the soul of our foreign policy'. He promised to be positive, to give as much attention to relations with the poor Third World as to East–West relations. In June 1979, SALT II was concluded with the USSR, by which the superpowers accepted a balance of nuclear missile capacity between them. Although bitterly criticised, it left each side with far more warheads and missiles than would be needed to turn any nuclear war into a holocaust. MAD (mutual assured destruction) remained intact as the doctrine of the day. This required that some US missiles should survive any first strike. In pursuit of this doctrine, a number of crazy schemes were devised, but in the end none was adopted. At the heart of the administration, there was a conflict between the policies advocated by Carter's aggressive national Security Adviser Zbigniew Brzezinski and the more conciliatory Secretary of State Cyrus Vance, with the State Department supported by the military.

In Latin America the perceived need to combat communism led to a drift of policy (pages 730–1), but the Panama Canal Treaty of 1977, by which the US agreed the eventual transfer of sovereignty over the canal zone to Panama, was one of the clear successes of the Carter foreign policy. But uncertainty was evident in the administration's dealings with the revolution in Nicaragua.

The Soviet invasion of Afghanistan in December 1979 reinvigorated the Cold War. The Carter administration was particularly alarmed by the strategic threat now presented to the Gulf and its oil and warned the Soviet Union off in forthright terms,

Carter declaring that an 'attempt by any outside force to gain control of the Persian Gulf region will be regarded as an assault on the vital interests of the United States of America, and such an assault will be repelled by any means necessary, including military force'. What made the situation doubly worse were the upheavals in Iran.

The conduct of US policy in the Middle East earned for Carter both the biggest praise and the most severe condemnation. For thirteen days he tirelessly laboured at Camp David in September 1978, and the accords reached there between Menachem Begin and Anwar Sadat had laid a firm basis for peace between Israel and Egypt.

In Iran, Carter had continued the US policy of unconditional support for the Shah despite his human-rights abuses. Until late in 1979, given the support of the army he had modernised, the Shah was believed safe, the ally of the United States and policeman of the Gulf. But it appears that the administration was badly served by the advice it received from intelligence sources and diplomats. Assessment of the Shah's chances of survival was not made until the autumn of 1978. In January 1979 he fled the country. The fanatical new rulers of Iran, who gained power the following month,

*Israeli Prime Minister Begin embraces Egyptian President Sadat in front of US President Carter after the signature of the Camp David Accord.*

*Freedom at last in January 1980 for the 52 American hostages held in their Teheran Embassy for 444 days.*

condemned the United States as the 'Great Satan', and the moderates lost control. When the terminally sick Shah was admitted to the United States for medical treatment in October 1979, the radicals in Teheran used it as a pretext to escalate their attacks on the United States. Demanding that the Shah be returned to stand trial, they seized the US Embassy that same month and took hostage the sixty-three Americans they found there. The hostage crisis overshadowed Carter's last year in the White House. He opposed using force, fearing that the hostages' lives would be in danger. Instead he imposed economic sanctions, froze all Iranian assets in the United States and broke off diplomatic relations in April 1980. Later that same month he approved a mission to rescue the hostages by aircraft and a specially trained task force. It went tragically wrong. Eight men of the rescue mission were left dead in the desert for the Iranians to gloat over. It was a profound humiliation and contributed to Carter's loss of the presidential election in November, although the hostages' release was negotiated later by the administration. Spitefully, they were not allowed to leave by air from Iran until half

an hour after the inauguration of Ronald Reagan on 20 January 1981.

The Carter administration had ended with a period of inflation and economic troubles in the wake of the second oil-price rise in 1979–80. Carter looked like a perpetual loser. The energy crisis was only temporary, but somehow the President became fixated on it. Congress was proving recalcitrant, so Carter addressed the American people on nation-wide television in July 1979, claiming that 'energy will be the immediate test of our ability to unite this nation . . .' It was an extraordinary exaggeration. In what became known as the 'crisis of confidence' speech, he attacked Congress and painted a dire picture of the future. The problems of America, he claimed, had their origins in a 'crisis of confidence'. Ronald Reagan, by contrast, was upbeat and optimistic. He promised a new beginning, an America that would 'stand tall'; he appealed for a renewal of patriotism, a new beginning. Many Americans did not bother to vote in the presidential election in November 1980, but those who did gave Reagan a decisive majority over the luckless Carter.

# CHAPTER 80

# Gorbachev, Reform and Crisis: The Break-up of the Soviet Union

The changes which took place in the Soviet Union after Mikhail Gorbachev succeeded to the position of general secretary of the Communist Party and to the leadership of the country in 1985 astonished the world. Gorbachev set a new agenda for relations with the Warsaw Pact allies and allowed Poland, Czechoslovakia, Bulgaria, Romania and Hungary to choose their own internal and external relations. It was the end of communist one party states, so jealously defended by Big Brother for four decades. Even more astonishingly Gorbachev laid the ghost of a revanchist Germany and allowed the East Germans to choose unification with the West. His policies went a long way to dispelling Western fears of the Soviet Union. Disarmament lay at the heart of the Kremlin's new policies. 'Gorby' was welcomed and applauded in the streets of Bonn and amid the skyscrapers of New York. People in the West pressured their governments to respond more quickly and warmly to the Soviet leader's offer of disarmament and peace, and Gorbachev's genuine desire to end the Cold War finally overcame Western suspicions. The Warsaw Pact was dissolved and a united Germany joined NATO. The Cold War ended in 1991 and the Soviet Union and the United States began working towards common aims in the Middle East, Asia and Europe.

Gorbachev outlined his ideas for radical change in his book *Perestroika*, published in 1987 as a paperback all over the world, its subtitle *New Thinking for Our Country and the World*. In it, Gorba-chev explains his aims to 'restructure' and reform Soviet society, to rekindle the initiative and personal responsibility of every Soviet citizen. Corruption and inefficiency would be ended, the falsehood which cloaked the oppression of the people – who were 'guaranteed' constitutional freedoms that existed only on paper – would be purged. The twin of *perestroika* or 'restructuring' was *glasnost* or 'openness'. 'Restructuring' and 'openness' were mild words for Gorbachev's objectives, which in the context of Soviet history were truly revolutionary. The people would be granted genuine legal freedoms and the right to criticise, to express their views, to choose on merit (by exercising their votes) between rival candidates for important political functions. Did Gorbachev indeed intend finally to rid the Soviet Union of the ideology of the Russian Revolution and all its works?

A careful reading of *Perestroika* reveals the schism in Gorbachev's thinking which was there from the start. He was not a democrat in the Western sense or a convert to the view that capitalism would rescue the Soviet Union from her economic backwardness. He was a socialist reformer, inspired by beliefs that were in line with Western idealism, that is beliefs in individual civic rights and freedoms, and he exerted all his power and employed all his talents to allow the Soviet people to gain them for the first time in Soviet history. The distinguished dissidents Anatoly Sharansky and Andrei Sakharov were released respectively from prison and from exile in 1986. But he also rejected capitalism. 'Capitalism', he declared in a speech in February 1986, 'regarded the birth of socialism as an error of history which had to be corrected at any cost by any means . . .' *Perestroika*, he wrote, did not signify a 'disenchantment with socialism', and was not motivated by a 'crisis for its ideals and ultimate goals. Nothing could be further from the truth than such interpretations . . .'

In the Soviet Union's internal and external policies much needed to be changed and improved. But Gorbachev was not about to lead the Soviet Union on the path which Czechoslovakia or Poland were following. The Czechs and Poles saw as their model the Western parliamentary multi-party system, together with a market economy dominated by private ownership of land and industry. Gorbachev rejected 'bourgeois capitalism'. The Soviet Union's socialist ideals were not to be called into question, nor was the essential cohesion of the USSR. For all his radicalism, Gorbachev intended to place limits on 'new political thinking'.

But was the Soviet economy reformable if it clung to what Gorbachev regarded as unchallengeable – socialism? Zbigniew Brzezinski, once President Carter's national security adviser, wrote a remarkable book just before the revolutionary upheavals in central and Eastern Europe entitled *The Grand Failure: The Birth and Death of Communism in the Twentieth Century* in which he forecast the end of communism. Gorbachev agreed with Brzezinski on the wasted years, on the lack of productivity of Soviet labour and on the inefficient use of resources, but for Gorbachev these spelt not the death of Communism but the need for renewal, for *perestroika* and *glasnost* as the engines of change. Communism had simply not reached its full potential. This faith prevented Gorbachev from seeking to reform the Soviet economy and its politics as fundamentally as he transformed the Soviet Union's external relationships. Internally, his policies revealed hesitations and ambiguities as the economy shuddered from bad to worse.

In the towns, queues for essential foodstuffs and goods lengthened, the black market and 'free market' flourished, and it became difficult to distinguish between the two. The reform of the party and its corrupt bosses had the side-effect of loosening discipline; *glasnost* had gone beyond healthy criticism to challenge the fundamentals of the Soviet state. Each of the republics became determined to do what was best for herself, and ethnic strife undermined the cohesion of the union. Better economic conditions and a clearer policy that delivered results might have held the Soviet people together in the absence of repressive force. But worsening conditions fuelled strife, and nationalism is such a primitive and powerful force that its repression for decades had left it ready to explode.

In 1985 as Gorbachev began his enormous task of radically changing the Soviet Union he was supported by a reformist minority in the party, but he also faced a majority in key positions who, though persuaded of the need for some change, were not ready for a revolution entailing the loss of their powers and privileges. Gorbachev therefore had to work against the prevailing sentiment of the majority. He improvised with dexterity until the juggling came to grief. He outmanoeuvred his opponents and displayed dazzling political skills as he altered party and state structures, changed their names and their functions, introduced new electoral procedures and created new bodies. All in all, it was a virtuoso performance. It left the Soviet people breathless but in the end disillusioned as standards of living dropped precipitously after 1987. To underline the extent of his accomplishment, it may be helpful briefly to examine the structures of state and party inherited by Gorbachev.

Though the different party bodies were supposed to be chosen democratically from the grass roots upwards, the reverse was true; they were appointed from the top down, except for the leading position of the general secretary of the Communist Party of the Soviet Union, who was chosen from among the Politburo members, though formally the Politburo recommended and the Central Committee approved. Gorbachev was 'approved' on 11 March 1985. The Politburo consisted of ten full and six candidate members who in theory were 'elected' by the Central Committee of 319 full and 151 candidate members meeting normally every six months. The Central Committee also 'elected' the Secretariat, whose head was the second secretary, deputy to the general secretary. The Secretariat of eleven members controlled twenty departments which supervised 109 government ministries. A network of republican, regional, city, town and district committees spanned the Soviet Union, dependent on the Central Committee's Secretariat bureaucracy of some 3000 employees.

It is important to note that until 1985 the party

supervised the ministries, which were also responsible to a prime minister and government ministers. Thus there was dual control of ministries by the government and the party, supposedly co-ordinated by the general secretary. The general secretary was also chairman of the USSR parliament, the USSR Supreme Soviet, which was little more than a ceremonial body, listening annually to the general secretary and dutifully applauding all he said. Carbon-copy supreme soviets and soviets fanned out in republics, cities, towns and districts.

This structure was supplemented by other bodies. At irregular occasions a conference of the Communist Party of the Soviet Union could be called; the eighteenth such conference had been convened in 1941; Gorbachev used the nineteenth called in 1988 to make far-reaching changes to party structures. Finally, it was also possible to call a congress of the CPSU, which also met irregularly when the general secretary wished to call one. Gorbachev used two such congresses, the twenty-seventh in 1986 and the twenty-eighth in 1990, as springboards for his reforms.

During his first years of power, Gorbachev encouraged pressure from below to win support for his reforms and to overcome party inertia and opposition. But here he trod a thin line between the imperatives of keeping popular protest under control and of reassuring the party leadership that he was not dismantling the Soviet communist system. Economic change necessitated a reform of the party itself, a reform of the old power structures, the KGB, the army and the *nomenklatura* – the *nomenklatura* being the means by which the party elite controlled the key positions in the administration, the judiciary, industry, agriculture and education.

Gorbachev's major effort at 'democratic' reform was to inject some grass-roots participation in the filling of the lower *nomenklatura* vacancies. This is what he meant by the democratisation of the Soviet state. But from the start it was questionable whether the party could ever regain the respect of the people, having for decades been a virtually autonomous self-appointed group within the state whose senior functionaries enjoyed many privileges denied to the rest.

During Gorbachev's first five years a plethora of meetings, conferences and congresses took place, their open debates televised for the Russian people in an unprecedented attempt to mobilise and educate public opinion. Gorbachev set the pace in speeches which were widely reported in 1985. In the Central Committee, which had endorsed him as general secretary, he had to move cautiously: it was crucial for him to build up support there and in the Politburo. In his first year he replaced two-thirds of the key leaders at the top and continued to make changes in later years. But this did not remove all opposition to his views, as the dramatic events of August 1991 were to show. At the April 1985 meeting of the Central Committee, the blueprint of *perestroika* was agreed and some practical reforms undertaken. In an attempt to make the central ministries more efficient, rival departments were eliminated: in agriculture six separate ministries were combined into one super-ministry with 20,000 staff cuts; two other super-ministries were created in the key areas of machine-building and computers. Unfortunately the ministries themselves were equipped with computers whose input and output remained flawed – they could not cope with the complexities of the economy.

On 25 February 1986, the Twenty-Seventh Congress of the Communist Party opened in Moscow. The streets were festooned with slogans, 'The Party and the People Are One', which was certainly not true. After its ten-day session the Congress accepted Gorbachev's blueprint for half-hearted reform of the socialist economy, but concrete reforms of the party were largely blocked. Another failure was an attempt to revive Khrushchev's rule that no party official could serve more than fifteen years and that one-third of the members on all committees had to change every five years. This meant that the majority of the long-serving party officials of the Brezhnev era would remain in place, but their privileges were reduced over the next three years, they became more accountable above and below, and corrupt practices became more dangerous. Millions of party workers thus felt nothing for Gorbachev's reforms but resentment and had little personal interest in lifting a finger to further them.

In April 1986, soon after the Twenty-Seventh Congress, disaster struck the Soviet Union: an explosion took place within the nuclear reactor at Chernobyl. The Ukraine was severely affected by radiation: hundreds were killed, the health of thousands more was affected for years to come, and the rich farming land was severely polluted. Moreover, the damage was a major setback for the Soviet

*Poisoned Earth.* Above: *thousands in the Ukraine and Belorussia are stricken by radiation-related illnesses, by cancer, or give birth to defective babies – the enduring legacy of the nuclear disaster at the Chernobyl reactor on 29 April 1986.* Left: *whole regions should have been evacuated, but the authorities only declared a small area 'dangerous' in the aftermath of the explosion.*

economy. Where was *glasnost* then, as Gorbachev and the Kremlin hesitated for days before revealing the truth about the nuclear fall-out spreading through Scandinavia to Western Europe? The successor republics of the Soviet Union have many nuclear reactors built to the same design which they cannot do without. They remain potential time-bombs.

Yet Gorbachev showed himself to be a very different leader from his predecessors. There was a new openness and humanity, and an air of excitement about changes to come, but little was actually achieved in 1985 and 1986 to improve the life of the average Soviet citizen. The Gorbachev media image promised much but there was a danger that expectations would soon outrun performance. Even so, there were real signs of change. *Glasnost* was ending the persecution of human-rights activists, most notably of Sakharov, released from his Siberian exile in December 1986. A new foreign minister, Eduard Shevardnadze, was appointed in

July 1985, when the old Cold War warrior Andrei Gromyko was replaced and kicked upstairs into a ceremonial presidency. In October 1986 the General Secretary met Reagan at the Reykjavik summit and proposed complete nuclear disarmament; this breathtaking suggestion came to nothing because Reagan would not accept Gorbachev's condition of confining the US 'Star Wars' Strategic Defence Initiative to the laboratory. Yet it proved not the end of detente but the beginning.

As Gorbachev was breaking new ground at home and abroad, he also faced fierce resistance from two, opposed, sides. Yegor Ligachev, the powerful Second Secretary of the party, voiced misgivings about the direction of reform. For Boris Yeltsin, Moscow's active party chief and a member of the Politburo, Gorbachev's economic and political reforms were far too hesitant. Yeltsin (a former Ligachev protégé before being taken up by Gorbachev) and Ligachev clashed bitterly in the Politburo. Ligachev was determined to destroy the political influence of the now radical Moscow leader, who had been denouncing party privileges, corruption and even what he called the new personality cult of the General Secretary. In the Central Committee Yeltsin forced a showdown, announcing at its meeting in October 1987 his intention to resign from the Politburo. Gorbachev was furious. The outward appearance of unity of the Central Committee had been broken on the eve of the annual November celebration of the Russian Revolution. Yeltsin, a sick man at the time, probably suffering from heart trouble, was obliged to go into hospital. The streak of ruthlessness in Gorbachev is revealed by what happened next. Yeltsin was forced to leave hospital to attend a meeting of the Moscow party committee; he was humiliated and sacked. It was Ligachev's revenge and triumph. But Yeltsin's disgrace also marks the beginning of the bitter rivalry, personal and political, that set Yeltsin against Gorbachev. For the time being Yeltsin was cast into the political wilderness. His re-emergence was to change the course of Soviet history.

In 1987 Gorbachev felt secure enough to begin to push through startling political and structural changes to the party and the state. In January, he proposed to the Central Committee that deputies should not simply be appointed to local regional and republican soviets by the party *apparat* – the people should participate and should be allowed a genuine choice of candidates. What was more, the deputies need not be party hacks but could be professionals, and they should be chosen by the people in a secret ballot. It was not democracy yet, for the candidates would all be vetted and had to be approved by an official selection committee, but for the Soviet Union it was a vital break with the past. Similar elections were to be held in factories to select managers. Gorbachev also proposed the holding of another, the nineteenth, national party conference.

The year 1987 also witnessed cautious initiatives in the field of economic reform. Gorbachev contemplated some form of leasehold of agricultural land. Small private businesses were allowed to start; a few individuals became wealthy. The free-enterprise co-operative movement grew from small beginnings to 133,000 concerns in 1989, employing 3 million people, but they were constrained from developing fully. The state, directly or indirectly, was still the employer of the overwhelming mass of the Soviet peoples, and it was still the most important customer. Attempts to make the state sector of the economy more efficient by such measures as the Law of State Enterprises in June 1987, which removed the detailed control of central planners, ended in disaster. Reform was slow and halfhearted. Prices were not set by the market and the consumer but by the state planners. Genuine cost accounting was lacking. This, coupled with less draconian party control, threatened the economy with the worst of both worlds: it was no longer comprehensively planned nor was it a market economy.

The government continued to print money to ease workers' discontent and so, with too many roubles chasing too few goods, produced sky-high prices on the black and free markets; meanwhile, deliveries at state prices were diminishing, as the goods were illegally diverted to the more profitable free market. Resistance to more fundamental and rapid reform was strong. The radical reformers and economists such as Yeltsin were locked in battle with the conservatives and reactionaries. Gorbachev now inclined to caution.

Another serious problem was surfacing in 1987 – nationalist and ethnic unrest in the republics. In August that year there were large-scale demonstrations in the Baltic republics, Lithuania, Latvia and Estonia, which had been annexed by the Soviet Union in 1940 after a pact concluded with Hitler. In the following year the demand for autonomy grew stronger. The Estonian parliament claimed the right to veto laws passed by the Supreme Soviet on national issues. In the Caucasus the Christian Armenians of Nagorno-Karabakh became embroiled in internecine conflict with Muslim Azerbaijan, in whose republic they formed an enclave; demonstrations followed and blood was shed. The troubles spread to the republic of Armenia, and Moscow ceased to be fully in control. The ethnic conflicts presented a serious threat to Gorbachev's reforms because they were likely to provoke a conservative backlash against the greater freedom from central party control which lay at the heart of his *perestroika*; he told the Armenians they were stabbing him in the back. He also recognised that to reopen now the question of frontiers between the republics threatened unstoppable conflict. He was therefore unsympathetic to the nationalist agitation, whether it arose in the Caucasus or in the Baltic.

Gorbachev achieved a major international success in 1987. After the Reykjavik failure, negotiations between Washington and Moscow continued. By the close of the year agreement was reached on getting rid of two whole classes of nuclear missiles, those of intermediate and short range. A treaty recording their agreement in principle was signed in Washington by Reagan and Gorbachev. It was an important moment: confidence was being built up.

The Nineteenth Party Conference, summoned by Gorbachev, brought on 28 June 1988 to Moscow from all over the country 5000 party members, most of them conservatives. Despite all the efforts of the Communist Party organisation, a minority of radicals had made it too. Among them was Boris Yeltsin, who secured his election in Karelia. Nor had the elections of delegates everywhere been the tame preordained affairs of the past. There were public demonstrations in a number of cities against the party's tactics – that in Moscow's Pushkin Square attracted worldwide attention. Radicals within the party had formed the Democratic Union, whose objective was to create a multi-party democratic parliamentary system. Many of these were among the 2000 people who had gathered in Pushkin Square. Heavy-handed police attempts to remove the most militant demonstrators were caught by the television cameras, as was the crowd's courageous insistence on what were supposed to be guaranteed legal rights.

Gorbachev presided over the Conference, doing his best to appear even-handed between the large majority of communist conservatives and passive middle-of-the-roaders, on the one hand, and the small group of radicals, whose undoubted star was Yeltsin, on the other. Gorbachev now unfolded his radical reform plans for the party. The party Secretariat would no longer supervise government ministries; in this way party and state would be separated. The Supreme Soviet would be abolished, to be replaced by a congress of people's deputies. Two-thirds of its members would be elected from a list of candidates approved by electoral committees; one-third were to be nominated – 100 by the Communist Party, the remainder by a variety of social organisations ranging from the Academy of Sciences, which was allocated twenty seats, to the Society of Stamp Collectors and the Red Cross. It was a huge body of 2250 members. Its main function besides listening to speeches during its meetings (over just two or three days a year) was to elect a (new) Supreme Soviet of 400 to 450 members, chosen from the deputies – a working parliament in session for some eight months a year. The head of state, responsible for the government, foreign policy and defence, as well as for the party, would be the chairman of the Supreme Soviet. Gorbachev persuaded the party conference to approve his plans, which enabled these constitutional reforms to be implemented in time for the Congress of People's Deputies to be elected in the spring of 1989.

The proceedings of the Conference were televised, providing a dramatic illustration of the debate that Gorbachev's democratisation was encouraging in the Soviet Union. It was a spectacle unprecedented in Soviet history. Most notable was the last day of the conference, when the bulky figure of Boris Yeltsin insisted on being heard from the rostrum. Gorbachev, presiding, could have prevented him from speaking, but he chose not to. Yeltsin argued for faster democratic progress, genuine elections and the prosecution of corrupt Communist Party bosses, the 'millionaire bribe-takers'. *Perestroika*, he advocated, should first achieve success in one or two essential areas before it was extended to others; the people, he said, were losing faith, dismayed by the lack of progress. Ligachev, the arch-conservative, rebutted Yeltsin's arguments and tried to ridicule him. He also denied, unconvincingly, that the party bosses enjoyed unwarranted luxuries. But the Soviet peoples listening to the debate throughout the USSR knew who was telling the truth. Through the power of the media and by his courageous confrontation Boris Yeltsin had again catapulted himself to national attention as the 'alternative' reformer to Gorbachev, and his following grew. At its close the Conference tamely approved Gorbachev's constitutional proposals as the lesser of the evils presented to them. Obedience to the General Secretary's will was still the norm. The habits of dictatorship served Gorbachev the reformer.

'Democratisation' was for Gorbachev creating not only a conflict between the communist conservatives like Ligachev, who feared that the party would lose control of the country, and the radicals, who accused Gorbachev of wishing to stop at a halfway stage between the old party system and genuine democracy.

Gorbachev's reforms were also creating a clash with independent republics opposed to the Kremlin's central domination of the Union. In the Baltic republics this independence movement had rapidly gathered strength. The anniversary of the Molotov–Ribbentrop Pact of 1939, which had delivered the three Baltic republics, Latvia, Estonia and Lithuania, into the Soviet sphere, prior to their absorption in 1940 and 1941 into the Soviet Union, became the occasion for denunciation. A human chain linked the three republics in a spectacular demonstration of solidarity. Popular fronts were formed between independent-minded communists and nationalists in the three states, the most forceful being the Lithuanian Sajudis. Tentative declarations of sovereignty in all three countries were condemned by Gorbachev as 'nationalist excesses'. Relations between the Baltic representatives and Moscow continued to deteriorate throughout the year. Gorbachev believed that he could not give way without raising similar claims in the Union's other republics. He would go no further than holding out a promise of a measure of economic autonomy, but this did not satisfy the nationalists.

Nationalism was not confined to the Baltics. In the Caucasus the conflict over Nagorno-Karabakh continued unabated, with Moscow's mediation or threats of force settling nothing. Gorbachev's institutional changes also alarmed the people of Georgia, who feared that they would strengthen the centre at the expense of the republics. In November 1988 there had been demonstrations in Tblisi, the capital of Georgia. The inefficiency of the assistance rushed to the victims of a huge earthquake in Armenia in December 1988 again reflected badly

on the Kremlin's powers in general and on Gorbachev in particular. Much worse followed. In April 1989 there was another peaceful demonstration in Tblisi. Gorbachev was out of the country. The Georgian communist leader appealed to the Kremlin for support and the hardliners led by Ligachev ordered troop reinforcements. Gorbachev returned, expecting a peaceful outcome. Instead the troops went into action, firing on the crowd and using gas to disperse them. The Tblisi 'massacre' left twenty dead and hundreds more injured. The brutality tarnished Gorbachev's image on the eve of the first meeting of the Congress of People's Deputies in May.

The elections, conducted over several weeks, had been chaotic. The party had done its best to influence the outcome, but a sizeable group of radicals was returned. Public pressure now counted for something, especially in the large cities. The attempt to exclude Andrei Sakharov, the most famous of the human-rights dissidents, backfired on the Academy of Sciences and he was elected. But the most spectacular victory was that of Boris Yeltsin in the Moscow constituency, where he defeated the party *apparatchik* by a landslide. With 5 million Moscow votes cast for him, Yeltsin could now claim some democratic credibility, in contrast to Gorbachev, who had never submitted himself to any popular election.

The first session of the Congress of People's Deputies began on 25 May 1989. The lack of respect shown for key leaders of the old regime and the reluctance of large numbers of deputies to conform to rules were a tribute to the atmosphere of freedom and the absence of fear that Gorbachev had done so much to bring about. Gorbachev himself had a tough time controlling the proceedings, which were televised in the spirit of *glasnost*. Remarkably Andrei Sakharov gave his support to the proposition that Gorbachev be elected president of the Supreme Soviet, the smaller working parliament that was to be chosen from among the deputies. He admired the man but had reservations about the pace of reform. The majority of the deputies were silent conformists, but active radicals and militant conservatives, plus some individual eccentrics, ensured a lively forum with many speeches on many subjects, and Gorbachev and his ministers heard many of their policies challenged. When it came to electing the Supreme Soviet, the majority voted in party conservatives, mainly nonentities. Yeltsin and other radicals were left out. The people of Moscow mounted a large demonstration against the exclusion of their hero. The democratic spirit had been truly awakened and could no longer be smothered by old-style KGB and police repression. Even the conservatives now understood this and amended the laws accordingly.

Could the peoples of the Soviet Union be granted fewer political freedoms than their allies and neighbours in the people's republics? Economic crisis at home was hastening Soviet disengagement from what had once been satellites, in Hungary, Poland, Bulgaria, Romania, Czechoslovakia and the German Democratic Republic. From the spring of 1989 to the end of the year communist rulers, no longer protected by the Red Army, were being overthrown one after the other by popular revolutionary movements. These assertions of independence could not fail to make an impact in the Soviet republics. Why should communism survive in the Soviet Union when it was being rejected by people everywhere else? Even China could not entirely isolate herself from this world revolutionary movement. In the Soviet Union improving economic conditions might have reconciled the people a little longer to the reform of communism that Gorbachev was striving to bring about. But material conditions were constantly getting worse. A massive strike by miners in the summer of 1989 was settled only by giving in to all the miners' demands, though the promises made could not all be kept.

Gorbachev believed there was only one answer: to push on with his political and institutional reforms. He thought he could counteract the increasing dangers of a breakdown by gathering more and more power to himself. He had no intention of becoming an autocrat, except in the sense of seeing democratic reforms through to their successful conclusion. At the same time he was afraid to introduce radical economic remedies which would raise prices and create millions of unemployed. The people's anger might then sweep away *perestroika* and *glasnost* and his own humane programme.

At the second session of the Congress of People's Deputies in December 1989 democratic elections took another step forward with the abolition of seats reserved for the Communist Party and communist-dominated 'social organisations'. During the spring session of 1990, the government of the Soviet Union was reshaped once more, giving even greater powers to Gorbachev. He was elected president of the Soviet Union on 15 March 1990. The president's executive functions were supported by two councils, a presidential council of his personal advisers and ministers and a federative council of representatives from the fifteen republics; the two councils would often meet together. These new structures completely marginalised the old party centres of power, the Politburo (renamed Praesidium) and the Central Committee. Even the 'leading role' of the Communist Party, enshrined in Article 6 of the constitution, came under such heavy attack that it had to be abandoned, and the Soviet Union seemed on the threshold of permitting multi-party elections. Yet for Gorbachev the preservation of the Communist Party, as the one cohesive element binding the Union together, remained a crucial objective. If this could no longer be achieved by constitutional law, as he had hoped it could be, then a reformed party would have to win the approval of the people in a contest with others. Gorbachev remained by conviction a communist, albeit a new type of 'humane communist'. But the tide of history was against him.

Nineteen-ninety was the first of the real crisis years. Paradoxically the more constitutional power Gorbachev acquired, the weaker in reality he became. Under the immense strains which the great drama was imposing on him, Gorbachev was tiring; at times he seemed to lose heart and offered to resign. But there was no one among the conservative majority in the party ready to replace him, and the radicals like Yeltsin were anathema to that majority. The nationalist problems also kept mounting. Gorbachev turned to strong-arm tactics to regain control and to preserve the Union. In January a massacre of Armenians by Azeri in Baku led to a showdown, with Red Army units 'retaking' Baku on Gorbachev's orders. The President then visited Lithuania, where he met general hostility. The democratising movement he had set in motion during the spring of 1990 now led to elections for new parliaments in each of the republics, elections which enormously strengthened the nationalists. The Popular Front in Lithuania swept the board and on 11 March 1990 the Lithuanian Parliament declared the country's independence, appointing Vytantas Landsbergis president. The declaration was declared invalid in Moscow, and Soviet tanks and paratroopers appeared in the streets of Vilnius in a vain attempt to overawe the population. Gorbachev next instituted an economic blockade, then made conciliatory gestures. But Estonia and Latvia followed Lithuania's lead during the course of the year. By the end of 1990 negotiations between the Baltic representatives and Gorbachev had reached stalemate. The Western powers hesitated to support the Baltic moves for independence, because they still relied on Gorbachev in international affairs and wished to do nothing to weaken him. But on the economic side the West did little to strengthen him, having no confidence that the economic reforms were going far enough.

The largest of the Soviet Union's republics was the Russian Federation, which contained about half the Soviet Union's population and three-quarters of her territory. The elections in the cities had returned radical deputies, though the countryside was still traditional. Moscow's new mayor was the radical Gavriil Popov, and St Petersburg's (the rechristened Leningrad) mayor was another democrat, Anatoly Sobchak. The Federation's new parliament appeared to be fairly evenly split between conservatives and radicals. Boris Yeltsin, the obvious leader of the radicals, now campaigned for the presidency of parliament, which would make him practically leader of the republic. He made his aim clear: to gain independence for the Russian Federation without leaving the Soviet Union. The powers to be delegated to the Union would become a matter for negotiation. Gorbachev supported a conservative candidate, but Yeltsin won the vote by a comfortable majority. He now emerged as a powerful national leader.

There were great policy differences between Yeltsin and Gorbachev, not least on the best way to handle the nationality conflicts. Yeltsin believed that the republics could be associated only in a voluntary union, preserving independence but handing some joint responsibilities to the Soviet Union. If any wished to leave the Soviet Union altogether, as the Baltic republics did, no obstacles should be placed in their way. He accordingly arranged for the Russian Federation to sign separate agreements with the Baltic republics. This went too far for Gorbachev, who saw a purely voluntary association as a recipe for disintegration and chaos. On the issue of democratisation, Yeltsin was totally disenchanted with the Communist Party and did not wish to see it enjoy any special position in the Soviet Union. For Gorbachev it remained the backbone of unity and the only possible adminis-

trative tool of reform. There was also the question of how to modernise the Soviet economy. Gorbachev hankered after some socialist halfway-house. Yeltsin saw no alternative but a rapid transformation to a market economy at whatever cost in terms of immediate hardship to the Russian people.

The only hope for the Soviet Union in 1990 seemed to be for the old rivals Yeltsin and Gorbachev to work together, and both expressed their willingness to try. At the meeting of the Twenty-Eighth Congress of the Communist Party in July 1990, Gorbachev delivered an address outlining his vision of a truly free society founded on a respect for human rights. He went further than ever before in defining democratisation as involving free elections and a multi-party system. He defended *perestroika* and denied that it was responsible for the lamentable condition of the Soviet economy – yet he had little but words to offer as remedies. He was strong on freedom, on political and party reform, weak and cautious on how best to tackle the crisis in the economy. He was bitterly attacked by Ligachev and the majority of the conservatives. Yeltsin, with an eye, as always, for the dramatic opening, chose the Congress to announce his resignation from the Communist Party. The party was split and demoralised, and most of the Soviet peoples were losing confidence in Gorbachev and his reforms, which seemed only to be increasing the queues, the shortages and the exorbitant black-market profits. Corruption now flourished in low places too. People had got used to freedom and were now taking it for granted.

At this late hour Gorbachev's prime minister Nikolai Ryzhkov produced a cautious proposal for economic reform which postponed any serious move to a market economy and to realistic, unsubsidised prices. But were things about to change? While Ryzhkov tinkered with the economy, Gorbachev in January 1990 turned to a young academic economist, Stanislav Shatalin, as an additional adviser. By the summer Gorbachev and Yeltsin were co-operating, and they set Shatalin to work at the head of a team of like-minded economists to produce a programme which would rapidly introduce a market economy. By the end of August the '500 Days' plan was ready and Gorbachev and Yeltsin agreed to back it.

As summer turned to autumn Gorbachev began to have second thoughts. He saw that all control was slipping from his hands, with the majority of the party in opposition, the republics daily issuing new independence claims and disregarding Kremlin directives. Conditions had become so bad that Gorbachev's public credit was all but exhausted. If he now adopted the shock therapy of the Shatalin plan, which would entail huge price increases and considerable unemployment, he feared that the Soviet Union would slide into anarchy. So he withdrew his backing from Shatalin's radical prescription. To save the crumbling edifice of the Soviet Union, he discussed with Yeltsin and other republican leaders a new treaty which would preserve the Union while making many concessions to the republics' demands for sovereignty. He was trying to gain time.

Significantly he also turned to his hitherto conservative opponents to bolster the Kremlin's failing powers. In yet another change he abolished the Presidential Council, and brought in the KGB, army and police to a new Security Council. New hardliners suddenly became the President's right-hand men. Soon old Cold War rhetoric was heard once again. The fourth session of the Congress of People's Deputies in December 1990 was memorable for one astounding event: Foreign Minister Eduard Shevardnadze publicly announced his resignation in protest against Gorbachev's reliance on reactionary party members. He warned against 'the advance of dictatorship'.

As the new year began, Gorbachev had few ideas left about how to lift the Soviet Union out of her crisis. When the military attempted to suppress the nationalists in Lithuania and Latvia and snuff out their independence movements, the people of Riga and Vilnius rallied to the defence of their new democratic parliaments and governments. The deaths of twenty civilians only strengthened popular defiance as the people erected barricades, and Gorbachev claimed that he had not ordered the bloodshed. His main efforts that spring and summer were to negotiate a new constitution with the republican leaders. Even as Georgia declared her independence in April 1991, Gorbachev's extraordinary negotiating skills scored one final success. In May 1991 the fifteen republican leaders, brought together by the President, agreed to form a new union. Later nine of those republics, including the Russian Federation, approved the 'principles' of such a treaty, which was to be solemnly signed on 20 August 1991. But the hardliners struck back. As the dramatic events unfolded in Moscow on

Monday morning, 19 August, the whole world held its breath.

The coup that should have been foretold caught Gorbachev completely by surprise. It was Sunday, 18 August. Gorbachev was spending the last two days of his vacation in his villa in the Crimea, working on the speech he was to deliver at the ceremony on 20 August marking the signature of the new Union Treaty. That afternoon he was visited by a group who represented, they said, a State Committee for the State of Emergency; they demanded that he should proclaim a state of emergency and hand over power to his vice-president, Gennadi Yanayev. Gorbachev indignantly refused. He was then kept prisoner in his own villa and cut off from all outside contact, while the coup got under way in Moscow. Early the following morning, 19 August, Moscow awoke to the news that Gorbachev was ill and that an eight-member State Committee for the State of Emergency had taken over. Most shocking of all, those men were not members of a reactionary opposition but had been Gorbachev's most recent ministers, leaders and aides, the conservatives he had chosen in 1989: Gennadi Yanayev, Boris Pugo (Minister of the Interior), Dimitri Yazov (Minister of Defence), Vladimir Kryuchkov (head of the KGB since 1988), Valentin Pavlov (Prime Minister) and three others. It was a total betrayal. Gorbachev was imprisoned and powerless for seventy-two hours; he prepared a videotape condemning the coup, while his wife Raisa became ill from the shock.

All the action was in Moscow. The Committee proclaimed a state of emergency and rule by decree; demonstrations were banned; at midday tanks and troops appeared in the streets of Moscow and were placed around key buildings. The junta also issued a decree that the constitution of the Soviet Union took precedence over that of the republics; it was to be the end of any notions of sovereignty for the republics or of a new Union treaty. Boris Yeltsin just escaped arrest and rushed to the Russian parliament building, which was known as the White House because of its white marble frontage. But the coup leaders were inept and failed to act decisively and ruthlessly on that first day. They were out of their depth, and Yanayev, the titular head, was said to be drunk most of the time.

Yeltsin took his life in his hands when he rushed to the White House. The most unforgettable image of the coup was presented by Yeltsin climbing on

to a tank just outside the Russian parliament mid-morning on Monday the 19th. He uncompromisingly denounced the coup and called for a general strike and popular support. But the response was patchy. The miners of the Kuznetsk Basin beyond the Urals said they would strike, but only in St Petersburg did the Mayor Anatoly Sobchak provide decisive support.

The fate of the coup would be decided in Moscow. Yeltsin's call for the people of Moscow to defend the Russian parliament building proved decisive. Before his appeal no more than 200 people had gathered in front of the White House. Millions of Muscovites simply went about their business, fatalistically accepting the coup. But Yeltsin's courage proved infectious. By Monday night there were hundreds more. The hours passed, and it

Left: *The emblematic courage of Boris Yeltsin, seen addressing supporters on a friendly tank outside the Russian White House, thwarted the abortive reactionary Communist putsch in the Soviet Union, August 1991.*

Below: *A symbol of terror falls in Moscow on 22 August 1991. The founder of the Soviet Union's secret police, Felix Dzerzhinsky, is toppled from pride of place in front of the KGB headquarters, the Lubianka.*

became evident that some elements in the army and KGB were not behind the coup. The expected attack on the White House did not materialise that night.

By Tuesday night not thousands but tens of thousands had gathered to protect the White House, and barricades were thrown up. The young conscript tank crews were bewildered. It was clear that, even if ordered to do so, they could not be relied upon to fire on the people. Around one barricade there was a scuffle which claimed three victims, the only deaths in Moscow. Some tanks defected and joined the people in defence of the Russian parliament. Tuesday midnight passed without the expected assault on the White House materialising. Somewhat belatedly the West on Tuesday condemned the coup outright. On Wednesday it was all over. Kryuchkov and Yazov tried to save themselves by fleeing from Moscow to negotiate with Gorbachev in the Crimea; instead they were arrested there. All the principal plotters were soon in prison. Only Boris Pugo escaped – by committing suicide.

On Thursday, early in the morning, Gorbachev returned to Moscow airport, to be met by Yeltsin and a large crowd of well-wishers. But Gorbachev was a defeated man. Yeltsin manoeuvred shrewdly, and made no attempt to replace Gorbachev illegally. Over the next three months he eroded the Soviet Union until there was no job left for its president. After his return Gorbachev had lost the initiative by lining himself up behind the totally discredited Communist Party. Yeltsin had already broken their power in the Russian Federation and he now finished the job, shutting down the party in Moscow altogether. Belatedly on Saturday, 24 August, Gorbachev announced his resignation as general secretary and recommended that the Central Committee dissolve itself, thus decapitating the party. It was finished. Hated party statues were toppled from their pedestals. But one relic survived: no one could bring himself to remove Lenin from the mausoleum.

Yeltsin went on to side-track Gorbachev, who was warning of the dangers facing the Soviet Union if co-operation between the republics could not be secured by a new Union treaty. Yeltsin went ahead on his own, asserting Russian independence of action, and in October 1991 proposed a separate and radical economic reform programme which was to lead to a free-market economy. The plan had been masterminded by the young economist Yegor Gaidar and his team. Yeltsin also began separate negotiations with the Ukraine and Belorussia to ensure economic co-operation between the Republics. The formal preservation of the Soviet Union still had some advantages for Yeltsin's Russian Federation as a framework for essential trade interchange, especially with the Ukraine. But when, on 1 December 1991, the Ukraine in a referendum overwhelmingly voted for independence the old Soviet Union ceased to have much purpose. A week later on 8 December Yeltsin and the leaders of the Ukraine came to an evidently hurried decision to make a complete break with the past and to create a new association, the Commonwealth of Independent States, around the Slavic core of the three republics (the third was Belorussia). They were quickly joined by Kazakhstan, by the four other Asian republics and then by three more republics. As 1992 began, the eleven members of this new Commonwealth still had many problems to sort out, among them the control of nuclear missiles, the future division of military and naval units and what unified structures should remain, their economic relationships and unresolved territorial questions. The most critical issues concerned the Ukraine and Russia, whose presidents had to sort out the futures of the Crimea and of the Black Sea fleet, the transfer of nuclear weapons to Russia and trade between the two republics. The death of the Soviet Union solved a number of old problems, but it also raised many new ones.

On Christmas Day 1991, Gorbachev resigned, having to the last attempted to preserve the Soviet Union. His enormous achievements had been rightly acknowledged with the Nobel Peace Prize. His belief in a humane socialism was sincere, and he knew that without legality in a state there could be no humanity. During his years of power, the Gulags were liquidated, all political prisoners were set free and civil rights and freedoms were returned to the Soviet peoples. His refusal to protect the communist bosses in the former satellites or to use the Red Army to quell popular unrest brought freedom to East Germans, Czechs and Slovaks, Hungarians, Poles, Bulgarians, Romanians. With the freedom came new problems, in part the inheritance of decades of communist misrule. But the nightmare of a nuclear holocaust receded as the Cold War came to an end.

All this was accomplished by one extraordinary

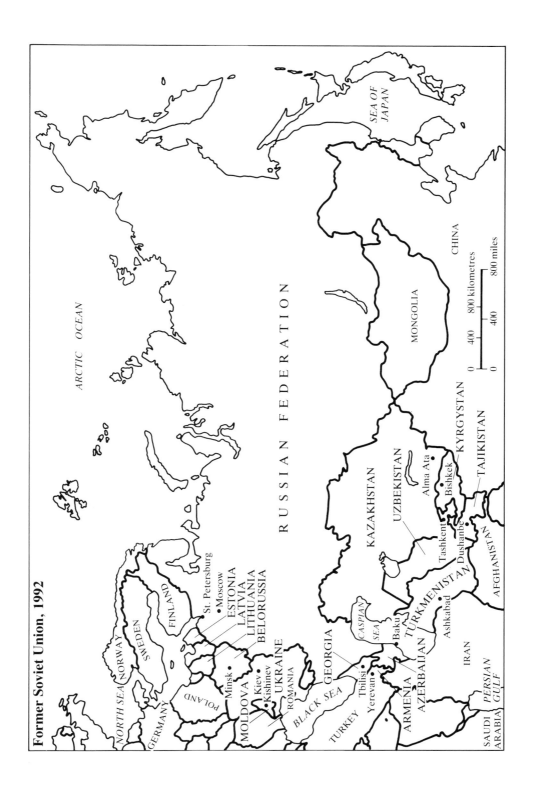

**Former Soviet Union, 1992**

ARCTIC OCEAN

SEA OF JAPAN

NORTH SEA

NORWAY

SWEDEN

FINLAND

GERMANY

POLAND

St. Petersburg

Moscow

ESTONIA

LATVIA

LITHUANIA

BELORUSSIA

Minsk

MOLDOVA

Kiev

Kishinev

UKRAINE

ROMANIA

BLACK SEA

GEORGIA

TURKEY

Tbilisi

Yerevan

ARMENIA

AZERBAIJAN

Baku

CASPIAN SEA

IRAN

PERSIAN GULF

SAUDI ARABIA

R U S S I A N   F E D E R A T I O N

KAZAKHSTAN

UZBEKISTAN

TURKMENISTAN

Ashkabad

Tashkent

Dushanbe

AFGHANISTAN

TAJIKISTAN

KYRGYSTAN

Bishkek

Alma Ata

MONGOLIA

CHINA

0    400    800 kilometres

0    400    800 miles

man, himself the product of a communist upbringing and of a communist system, to which he remained loyal to the end. He attracted able men to support him in his policies and created a mass following in the Soviet Union. At first suspiciously but later with matching openness, the West responded. It was Gorbachev who did most to initiate the biggest change in global relationships since the Second World War. For this alone he will go down as one of the great leaders of the twentieth century, his a crucial role in shaping its history.

We can also begin to understand the reasons for Gorbachev's failures, for they too are embedded in his concept of 'humane democratic socialism'. He chose the opposite course to the Chinese reformers of the 1980s. Gorbachev's priority was the reform of the party, to open the party to democratic influences and competition, which would revive the Soviet economy as the burdens of war and bureaucracy were lifted from the shoulders of the Soviet peoples. The expanded, though still small, private sector of the economy, which had always existed even under Stalin, would be allowed to compete with the revived state sector to increase efficiency without threatening to overtake the socialist economy. But Gorbachev always saw that the most urgent need was for political reform, which he believed would lead to economic improvement.

Six years from March 1985 were not such a long time to bring about a root-and-branch change in party and government after more than sixty years of communist autocracy, whose basic assumptions had never been challenged by Khrushchev or any of his successors. Gorbachev's thinking was revolutionary and opened up the possibility of a better future for the Soviet Union. Neither he nor most of his contemporaries inside and outside the Soviet Union foresaw where these policies were leading to, even while they could not fail to notice the increasing hardships placed on the Soviet peoples during the years of political transition. Gorbachev was blamed by Yeltsin and his supporters, as well as by some economists in the West, for not *simultaneously* pursuing radical economic market reforms as well. Significant Western credit was denied because of their absence. But Gorbachev feared they would have led to anarchy and chaos. Nowhere in the world have *both* drastic political and economic change been attempted successfully at one and the same time. During the 1980s Deng and the Chinese reformers pursued economic reform while maintaining communist political power largely intact. In both China and the former Soviet Union only half of the double transition, to a market economy *and* to democracy, has been attempted – a different half in each country.

Gorbachev's strength and weakness lay in his political instincts, the fertility of a mind that appeared to conjure up compromises out of apparently unbridgeable contradictions. He spoke of democracy, but it was a democracy which was meant to coexist with the role of the Communist Party and its enormous bureaucracy, newspapers, sanatoria, resorts and manifold privileges. He conceded that the republics could leave the Union if they wished, but sent in tanks and guns to intimidate the Baltic republics when they wanted independence without delay. The limited sovereignty he was prepared to grant was far less than the republics were going to take if they did not get their way. Unfulfilled promises lost him the support of the Soviet peoples as the economy spiralled into decline. Compromises here resulted in the worst of two worlds. As he himself put it, at the end 'the old system fell apart even before the new system began to work' – but to what 'new system' was he referring? No new economic structures were established as the old central-planning apparatus disintegrated with the rise of nationalism in the republics. And yet Gorbachev's precarious tightrope act might have lasted a good deal longer if the reactionary conservative leadership had not attempted to topple him in August 1991. Nobody seemed big enough to step into his shoes until Yeltsin emerged as the man of the hour, the saviour of Russia. The coup had so diminished the Communist Party's stature and that of Gorbachev that the one was swept away and Gorbachev himself was legally brought to the point where he was the President of a Union that had ceased to exist.

In the Russian Federation 'democracy' will have little chance of survival without a successful transition to a market economy. The planned start was radical. The policy adopted by the Deputy Prime Minister Yegor Gaidar with Yeltsin's backing was to attempt a rapid transition. Even with Western support, this would have entailed mass unemployment as bloated state industries collapsed. Only a strong government can weather the storm and defeat attempts to revert to the old ways of autocratic rule, which may seem less frightening to millions than the prospects of unemployment and penury. The key, Yeltsin believed, was to make this transition period a short one, even if it made the hardship even greater. Yeltsin, President and Prime Minister of the Russian Federation in 1992, and Gaidar narrowly won the support of the Russian parliament for their policies in April of that year. Yeltsin still enjoyed overwhelming popular support, but he was not likely to be given as long as Gorbachev to deliver tolerable standards of living for the Russian people. The Russian economy continued its catastrophic decline in 1992. The Russian people, despite showing extraordinary patience and fortitude, were becoming evermore disillusioned with their rulers who were unable to deliver a basic standard of living. The beneficial results of Gaidar's reforms failed to make themselves felt in ways the Russian people could see. Gradually the reforms requiring strict financial controls were relaxed. Roubles were printed to pay the wages of workers in inefficient state industries. Without the control of a Central Bank, the republics printed more roubles until the whole country, flooded with paper money, plunged into hyperinflation by the end of the year.

At the heart of Russia's crisis lay not only an economic but also a political problem. Who was in charge of what? Ministries and the Central Bank vied for control. Russia's executive with Yeltsin at its head was subject to parliament, Russia's Congress of People's Deputies. The Congress was still packed with the communist deputies elected in the spring of 1990 (when it was still Supreme Soviet) before the failed *coup* of August 1991. Yeltsin and the communist majority in the Congress who disapproved of his reforms were at loggerheads. Yeltsin showed some readiness to compromise by dropping Gaidar in December 1992 whilst assuring the international financial world that the path of reform would not be abandoned. The conflict between the opposition in the Soviet parliament and the president threatened to paralyse economic reform. On 21 September 1993 Yeltsin simply dismissed parliament and called for new elections in December. A defiant opposition condemned the decree, denounced it as unconstitutional and set up a rival government with Alexander Rutskoi as the new prime minister. Yeltsin reacted by ordering the army to surround the White House, but still attempted to leave the way open for a peaceful resolution of the crisis. Instead the 100-odd hard-core deputies who remained deposed Yeltsin and declared Rutskoi President. Rutskoi and the parliamentary speaker Khasbulatov badly miscalculated in believing that they could swing the army and

people behind them. They attempted a coup and sent out a call to supporters to seize Moscow's television station. On 4 October Yeltsin also responded with force – ordering the tanks to fire on the White House. The spectacle was played out on the world's television screens. It was all over in twenty-four hours and the deputies, Rutskoi and Khasbulatov surrendered. The cost was some 140 dead and many injured. But the struggle between parliament and the president was not over. The December elections proved disappointing for the reformers even though the new constitution proposed by Yeltsin, which strengthened the power of the president, was accepted in a national referendum. The big shock of the elections was the emergence of Vladimir Zhirinovsky, the populist ultra-nationalistic leader of the anti-reform group misnamed the 'Liberal Democratic Party', which gained sixty-four seats. Yegor Gaidar's Russia's Choice, a reformist party, secured a disappointing seventy seats, the Communist party forty-eight, the anti-reform Agrarian party thirty-three, and the Women of Russia twenty-three. The balance of forces is against radical reform even though 129 Independents were also elected. Russia's new democratic institutions are fragile; the workings of democracy are not fully understood in a factional conflict lacking any consensus; the economy with its constantly declining output is only being reformed piecemeal. And added to the difficulties of trying to maintain standards of living is the peripheral but lethal nationalities problem.

As one looks over the eventful years in Soviet history from 1985 to 1994, perhaps the most surprising aspect of the revolution in the Soviet Union herself and in her former central European and Balkan satellite states is that, unlike the first Russian Revolution, it was comparatively bloodless. The upheaval in the lives of many tens of millions of peoples in this vast land-mass was not entirely without casualties, especially in the republics of Central Asia, the Caucasus and Moldova, but they constitute only a tiny percentage of the total populations. Yugoslavia alone has suffered more in one year of civil wars. The communist empire collapsed and her leaders did not plunge her into a bloodbath during her death throes. With the dreadful exceptions of the conflicts in Tajikistan, Armenia, Georgia and Azerbaijan, the former Soviet peoples have demonstrated a degree of self-discipline and humanity rarely matched in similar upheavals before.

# CHAPTER 81

# The United States: Reagan and Bush

Ronald Reagan had many detractors, who directed sneers at the movie actor turned president, the 'great communicator' who failed to grasp the essential details of issues, the hands-off President. When he did stumble into trouble, as in the Iran–Contra affair, he did not appear to realise precisely what or who had gone wrong. Yet he retained his personal popularity throughout his two administrations, as troubles just seemed to slide off him, earning him the nickname the 'Teflon President'. Was Reagan just lucky to be in the White House during a decade most of which brought increasing prosperity to the Western world, in contrast to the difficult 1970s? Was he merely fortunate that the Soviet Union had gained a new leader in the mid-1980s who saw the futility of the Cold War and was determined to end it? Or was there more to it? Perhaps the judgement should be that Reagan spotted opportunities and responded positively to them. He was a likeable, kindly president and he had the skill to project his warmth. The American people were in tune with his optimism; they wanted to put Vietnam behind them. They responded to his upbeat projections of a bright future and rejected Carter's gloomy 'crisis of confidence' diagnosis of what was wrong with America.

Reagan was carried forward across the nation, not just in California, by a revival of the conservative tradition which had already made itself felt in the 1970s. It was a scepticism about the 'nanny state', about government's ability to find solutions to all the country's ills, including the growing and predominantly black underclass, the drug-use, the gun culture and the increasing numbers of one-parent families. The American people would have to accept their responsibilities. Welfare meant taxation. In California in 1978, the state had to obey the results of a referendum called Proposition 13, which cut property taxes and so left the state budget with insufficient funds for all its welfare and social programmes. Reagan recognised that the California tax revolt was not just a local but a national issue. The diagnosis was that taxation fell too heavily on the creators of wealth. There was too much regulation stifling America's natural enterprise. In his inaugural address he coined the slogan, 'Government is not the solution to our problem – government *is* the problem.' The United States needed government, but it should work with the people, not sit on their backs. The United States, he declared with some exaggeration, was the 'last and greatest bastion of freedom'.

But how was America to be restored to greatness and prosperity? An answer was seemingly found. Reagan had been converted before the elections to the theory of supply-side economics, or more precisely to the scientific truth of the 'Laffer curve', the discovery of Professor Arthur Laffer. If Carter was a born-again Christian, Reagan was a born-again economist. On the face of it, supply-side economics was a miracle: it held that if you lowered taxes you actually collected more revenue. The theory was that lower taxes gave firms more profit, and consumers more money in their pockets; this in turn would lead to more investment and greater employment; people would have more incentive to work harder, and with increased economic activity more tax revenue would be collected and unemployment and welfare benefits saved. Reagan grasped that this was an attractive policy to put to the American people. It left out of account, however, the effects of inflation, from which higher taxation inevitably followed as more people's earnings were pushed into higher tax brackets. Without constant rate reductions of tax, taxation would actually become heavier.

The objectives of Reagan's economic policies, as put forward by the administration, were to lower taxes, to reduce government spending, to balance the budget and to restrict money supply so as to lower inflation. Professor Milton Friedman of Chicago University was the money-supply guru; he and Frederick Hayek attacked the notions of the welfare state and socialism, which they taught would lead to a totalitarian state. The correct policy was to deregulate, to remove restrictions on business and to allow free-market competition. The combination of all these ideas became known as Reaganomics. The economic cures for inflation and stagnation had already been tested in Pinochet's Chile with some success. Now they were going to be tried in the United States.

It sounded too good to be true; indeed, before George Bush became vice-president, while he was still competing with Reagan for the Republican nomination, he coined the memorable phrase 'voodoo economics' to describe Reaganomics. And it *was* too good to be true; all the objectives could not be harmonised. The United States did not balance her budget as promised and turned a small national debt into a large one. In other words, the excess of government expenditure over revenue income in the Reagan years injected a significant stimulus to the economy in good old Keynesian fashion at the cost of a ballooning deficit.

Deregulation, too, had its limits. Environmental concerns cannot be completely ignored. And there were instances where only one-half of a business's activities were deregulated. This stored up for the 1990s the Savings and Loans Association disaster. While depositors were federally insured (up to $100,000 in any one Savings and Loans account), the financial managers could now operate without the severe restrictions on their activities of previous years. To attract customers they vied with each other to offer higher savings interest rates and so had to engage in more risky investments themselves to be able to pay them. With the collapse of real-estate markets at the close of the 1980s, the insolvency of many of them and of some banks involved the federal authorities in a huge financial bail-out to compensate the investors. This is one important example of how deregulation has not always led to the expected good results.

There was little sign that Reaganomics was really working during the first two years of the administration. Reagan wanted a 10 per cent reduction in corporate and personal taxes in each of the first three years but this meant cutting the federal budget too. Compensating completely for the tax cuts would have been an exceedingly painful process, though Reagan undertook not to cut any essential welfare benefits to the needy and elderly. There was much waste, 'pork barrel' expenditure, that could have been cut, but members of Congress fiercely defended their electors' favourite subsidies. Getting his budget proposals substantially unaltered through both Houses of Congress in 1981 despite the Democrat majority in the House of Representatives was a major triumph for Reagan personally.

In the end, Congress modified the biggest tax cut in US history only slightly; in the first year the cut would be 5 per cent instead of the 10 per cent originally proposed, so as not to increase the budget deficit to inordinate heights, but accepted 10 per cent in each of the following two years. But the budget director, David Stockman, had presented an incomplete financial prospectus. It would have got any company director into severe trouble. In his very critical inside story of his years in the administration, published after his resignation in 1985, Stockman depicts an almost unbelievable blindness to the realities of financial arithmetic. The budget could not be balanced given the large tax cuts *and* an increase of defence expenditure of 10 per cent per year. Caspar Weinberger, previously renowned for his cost-cutting ways, was in charge of defence. A miscalculation had the consequence that instead of a hefty 7 per cent per year real growth of expenditure on defence, it actually came out at 10 per cent per year from 1980 to 1986, that is rising from $142 billion in 1980 to a planned $368 billion by 1986. As it turned out, defence spending was trimmed so that by 1986 it had 'only' doubled to $273.4 billion.

How then were the budget figures to add up to

produce a balanced budget by 1984? The computer provided a simple answer. The supply-side economic stimulus would increase output by some 5 per cent a year. Instead the economy went into recession in 1981 and 1982, thus creating a burgeoning deficit. The recession brought inflation under control, but unemployment increased to 10 per cent – more than 11 million Americans were out of work across the country. In some regions unemployment was far worse than in others, and blacks and other ethnic minorities were especially hard-hit. The ability of trade unions to defend their members was weakened by Reagan's policies. The most dramatic showdown came in 1981 when the air-traffic controllers' union called a strike. Reagan took the tough decision to dismiss all the strikers after they had refused to return to work. Military air-traffic controllers filled the gap until new personnel had been trained. It was an example that Mrs Thatcher was to bear in mind during her confrontation with the miners in 1984. With defence spending protected by Reagan on the ground that it was essential for facing down the Russians, and with his insistence on persevering with tax cuts, reductions in the growth of welfare spending took the brunt of the economies, but they were quite insufficient to halt the growth of the budget deficit. Some tax increases, implemented despite the fashionable economic theories, proved too small to bring the deficit under control, and the tax cuts turned out to have benefited the rich far more than the middle-income families and the poor. Wealth had failed to trickle down to the bottom 20 per cent, as the theories had predicted it would.

Reagan persisted with his unpopular policies. The economic turnaround began in 1983. There followed six years of economic growth, despite temporary blips (as in 1987), and the creation of 17 million jobs, though many of these were in low-paying service industries. But was this due to the virtuous effects of supply-side economics? Federal spending increased instead of declining on all the major items, including social security and various welfare payments. As the national debt increased, so interest on it doubled, adding $68 billion in just five years. Easy credit and the deficits put more money in people's pockets and they spent more. The supply-side economists' prediction that investment would increase proved wrong.

By the end of the 1980s the United States also had the largest trade deficit of any major industrialised

country. Even the proportion of Gross National Product collected in taxes did not significantly decrease from the post-war average. So was Reaganomics all smoke and mirrors? Was the US prosperity of the years 1983 to 1990 simply based on borrowed time, on credits that have to be paid for in the future? There is no simple answer. The United States is immensely rich in resources. By West European standards, outlays on welfare were woefully inadequate before 1981 and even increased federal spending has not brought it proportionally to the same level as in Germany, Britain or France. That the US deficit was not allowed to soar out of control for a time owed much to a reform enacted by the Senate and proposed by two Republican senators, Phil Gramm and Warren Rudman. This required the implementation of phased reductions of the deficit and automatic spending cuts (to fall equally on military and non-military provision) when deficit targets were exceeded. Pension and poverty programmes were excluded from the cuts. Reagan reluctantly signed the measure in December 1985. It held back the growth of the deficits until the slow down in the economy later in the decade.

The Reagan revolution was not as revolutionary as it seemed. But the American people, who had overwhelmingly re-elected him in November 1984, gave the 'old Gipper' the benefit of the doubt. He remained throughout his latter years of office one of the most popular presidents in American history. The economy continued to respond and unemployment did not rise above 7 per cent; people felt good – at least, most of them did. The darker side was there too: ethnic discrimination and poverty, crime and drugs, the decay of big cities, increasing indebtedness and an adverse trade balance. Despite the Laffer curve, there is no miracle cure. Reagan, in fact, was a big spender on programmes other than defence. The only way to bring the budget into balance was by raising taxes. Reagan would not hear of it, nor would George 'read my lips' Bush during the presidential election of 1988. It was one important reason for Bush's election victory that November over the Democratic candidate, who had been too frank. Yet the spending spree of the mid-1980s came to haunt his successor in the White House when the economy once more turned down.

During the Reagan–Bush era the United States' northern neighbour Canada faced serious constitutional problems. The Liberal Party, in power since

1963 except for a period of nine months, was swept out of office in the general election of 1984 by the Progressive Conservative Party led by Brian Mulroney. It was the end of the Trudeau era; Pierre Trudeau himself gave up the leadership of the Liberal Party. Canada thus followed the sea-change of Western politics, adopting policies to roll back the frontiers of the state, cut government spending and encourage business enterprise. Mulroney also promised to solve Canada's long-standing constitutional problems, especially the question of French-speaking Quebec. His approach was conciliatory, though he was soon perceived as too irresolute.

Canada benefited from the upswing which lifted Western economies after 1982, and her Gross National Produce grew strongly until 1990. A major plank of Mulroney's strategy was a drive for free trade. After fierce debate about the threat to her independence, Canada in 1988 concluded a treaty with the United States which came into force in January 1989 and provided for the dismantling of all trade barriers over a ten-year period. Already 70 per cent of Canada's trade was with the Americans. The satisfactory state of the economy enabled Mulroney's Progressive Conservative Party in the federal election of 1988 to retain power with an overall majority. But the constitutional issue raised by the passionate desire of French-speaking Quebec to preserve her identity was becoming the burning question in Canadian politics. For the first time Canadians were talking of the unthinkable, namely that the Canadian federation could break up.

A new constitution designed to regulate relations between the provincial and federal governments, devised by Trudeau in 1982, had foundered on the objections put forward by Quebec. Nonetheless, Mulroney and the prime ministers of the ten provinces reached an agreement in June 1987 known as the Meech Lake Accord, which accepted French-speaking Quebec's demand to be recognised as a 'distinct society'. The agreement next required ratification by the parliaments of the provinces. In December 1988 Quebec's Prime Minister Robert Bourassa insisted that in Quebec only external signs in French would henceforth be permissible. That infringed the rights of the 12 per cent of the province's population who were English-speaking. The language issue was symbolic of deeper intentions and aroused a storm in the English community. Two English-speaking provinces now put off decisions to

*Pierre Trudeau was the third French-speaking Prime Minister of Canada. He stood for broad tolerance and the maintenance of the federation, and he dominated Canadian politics from 1968 to 1984.*

approve the Meech Lake Accord. If it was to come into force, it required the unanimous approval of all the provinces by June 1990. In the end only eight, including Quebec, had approved and Manitoba's and Newfoundland's refusal to ratify meant that the Accord lapsed.

Negotiations for a solution had to be begun anew. The pro-independence parties in Quebec gained in strength. The chances of a successful outcome had deteriorated since the abortive Meech Lake Accord. The English-speaking provinces questioned why Quebec, which had already benefited disproportionately from federal economic aid, should be granted special status. Mulroney was further weakened by his personal unpopularity, and that of his government, while Bourassa had to maintain his position in Quebec against the rising tide of sentiment favouring independence. Nevertheless a new agreement was eventually hammered out and announced in September 1991 by the federal government and the provincial prime ministers embodying far-reaching constitutional changes. These included the crucial recognition of Quebec as a 'distinct society' and the granting of self-government to Canada's indigenous peoples, the Amerindians and the Inuit. The referendum throughout Canada in October 1992 saw the rejection of the constitutional proposals. This in part reflected the unpopularity of Mulroney; moreover, the majority of English-speaking Canadians felt that the concessions to French-speaking Canadians went too far, yet for French Canadians they did not go far enough. Canada did not break up as most Canadians tired of the issue.

If there was less of a revolution in US domestic policies than was thought at the time, a real revolution did occur during the Reagan years in America's role and standing in global politics. As recently as 1988 distinguished academics were vying with each other to analyse the reasons for America's terminal decline. 'Overstretch' of America's 'imperial' global responsibilities was the favourite diagnosis. How the picture has changed since then! No doubt academics will catch up.

Reagan certainly began his years in the White House as an outspoken enemy of communism the world over. Russia was an 'evil empire', and the 'focus of evil in the modern world'. The spread of communism, especially in what Reagan perceived as America's backyard, Central America and the Caribbean, he saw as a direct threat to the security of the United States, because communist victories in Nicaragua and El Salvador could spread to Mexico and so to the very borders of the United States. The domino theory was revived. Behind the global dangers, the administration did not doubt, was the hand of the Kremlin. The condemnation of the Soviet Union reached its peak when a Soviet fighter in September 1983 shot down a Korean civilian airliner which had strayed over militarily sensitive Soviet territory. Many lives were lost, including those of Americans.

But there was always a positive side to the administration's and Reagan's policy calculations. The Soviets were rational. If the United States did not flinch from confrontation, from spending whatever was necessary to ensure potential military dominance, the basis would eventually be reached for an accommodation, and for disarmament, especially of the nuclear arsenals. When Reagan launched his Strategic Defence Initiative, or Star Wars as it was popularly known, in March 1983 he knew that the Soviets could not afford to keep pace. SDI would, it was hoped, enable the United States ultimately to defend herself against nuclear attack far more effectively than the Soviet Union could. The thinking was that there was not the remotest possibility that the United States would be the aggressor in a superpower war, so the world would be safe from nuclear war. Once the Soviet Union could also be persuaded to accept that the United States was not likely in the future to become an aggressor, the huge nuclear arsenals would become redundant. Serious disarmament could be given a chance, with nuclear and other weapons serving as a limited deterrent insurance. The great change occurred in the Reagan era of the 1980s.

The transformation in US–Soviet relations would not have happened but for events outside Reagan's control, the changing leadership in the Kremlin and the Soviet Union's worsening economic plight. When Gorbachev became the Soviet leader in March 1985, the scene was set for a *pas de deux* that began with each leader keeping a careful distance from the other and ended in an embrace, with Reagan strolling cheerfully around Red Square in the spring of 1988. Perhaps only a president with Reagan's impeccable anti-communist credentials could have persuaded Congress to accept that the Soviet Union could be trusted to abide by the agreements reached and that she had ceased to be an 'evil empire'.

During his first administration, Reagan's crusading rhetoric castigating communism and the Soviet empire never really matched the administration's actual policies. Although not ratified by the Senate, the SALT II treaty provisions were observed; this in the end proved to be to America's advantage. The scope for using American military forces was limited by a law passed by Congress after the Vietnam War to restrict the president's freedom of action: this was the War Powers Act of 1973. The president as commander-in-chief was still able to use armed force when he thought it necessary, but he had to inform Congress within forty-eight hours of their deployment abroad and would have to withdraw them after sixty days unless Congress specifically directed otherwise. There were other realistic restraints. The Soviet invasion of Afghanistan in December 1979 had led to the retaliatory American grain embargo. But the US farmers came first; their plight induced the Reagan administration to lift Carter's embargo on the sale of wheat in April 1981 and to follow this up with further huge sales in 1983. That in turn made it difficult for the US to dissuade West European firms from supplying the apparatus to the Soviet Union for oil and gas pipelines. Meanwhile public opinion in the United States and Western Europe was becoming ever more hostile to further nuclear escalation. Reagan declared that he was committed to arms control, but negotiations with the Soviet Union made no progress during his first administration. Meanwhile the Russians became increasingly bogged down in Afghanistan. For the US it was a Vietnam in reverse. With Pakistan as an ally, she was able to arm the desperate Mujahideen in Afghanistan, who inflicted casualties on the Soviet troops which proved unacceptable in an unwinnable war.

US involvement in the Lebanon and a Middle East peace process likewise made little headway. The United States was not willing to use all her power to coerce Israel and the Arab nations, and in any case it was extraordinarily difficult to make much progress on the Palestinian question. That part of Carter's Camp David agreements (page 914) remained a dead letter. Reagan sent 800 marines to the Lebanon as part of an international peace-keeping force after Israel's invasion in 1982; in October 1983, 241 marines were killed in their barracks by a fanatical Muslim. There was an outcry in the United States, and after a decent interval the marines were withdrawn in 1984. The Middle Eastern problems were now too great, and US policy too indecisive, for the US Navy in the Mediterranean and a few hundred marines to provide a solution.

The liveliest area of foreign policy was in Central America and the Caribbean. In October 1983 marines were sent into the island of Grenada to remove an illegitimate left-wing regime. Since Grenada was a member of the British Commonwealth, Margaret Thatcher was much annoyed. More serious was US intervention in Central America. Here Reagan and Secretary of State Alexander Haig (and later his successor, George Shultz) were fighting communism most actively. The Sandinista victory in Nicaragua had brought a communist-style government to power, and the United States had cut off aid; in El Salvador there was a left-wing insurrection. The Reagan administration sent increasing quantities of military and economic aid to the El Salvadorian government, despite its appalling human-rights record. A war by proxy was being waged in Nicaragua, with the Soviet Union supplying the Sandinistas, and the CIA from 1981 funding the opposition forces, which became known as the Contras, operating from bases in El Salvador and Honduras. With memories of Vietnam still vivid, however, Reagan faced strong public opposition, which was reflected in Congress. Most Americans cared less about the excesses of the Sandinistas and the left-wing rebels in El Salvador than about the possibility that young US soldiers would be dragged into the conflict, many of them to come home in body-bags.

Reagan's convincing victory in the 1984 election strengthened his hand considerably. In the course of his second term he was to meet the new Soviet leader Mikhail Gorbachev five times. At their very first meeting in Geneva in November 1985, the ice was broken. Reagan was a great believer in the power of personal relations to overcome set ideological positions. He came to share Margaret Thatcher's view that Gorbachev was a new kind of Soviet leader with whom it would be possible to negotiate on a more trusting basis. The various on-and-off arms-reduction negotiations had achieved very little so far. On the table since 1981 was Reagan's 'zero option': if the Soviets withdrew their SS20 and other intermediate-range missiles in Eastern Europe, the US would not counter them by sending over Pershing and Cruise missiles to Britain and other NATO allies. The proposal did not affect missiles outside Europe, that is in the US or Siberia. So far the Soviets had rejected this, and the US had rejected Soviet proposals for deep cuts in both sides' nuclear arsenals. When Gorbachev and Reagan met at Reykjavik in October 1986, the Soviet leader hoped that he could get Reagan to give up Star Wars by tempting him with a spectacular agreement to reduce nuclear arms. Despite his obvious disappointment at the failure of all his efforts, Reagan stood firm (page 822). The setback proved temporary. The Soviet need for Western technological assistance and for defence savings was urgent. In December 1987 the signing of the INF (intermediate-range nuclear forces) Treaty in Washington set the seal on the new US–Soviet relationship, not only in settling direct issues between them but also in the context of regional conflicts all over the world. The treaty banned the production and testing of intermediate-range missiles, and all existing missiles in this class were to be destroyed.

Reagan's policies in Central America were the

*The Nuclear Arms Reduction Treaty is signed in the White House on 8 December 1987, and Gorbachev and Reagan's relationship grows ever warmer.*

most controversial in the administration's conduct of foreign relations. His appeal for support for the Nicaraguan Contras – 'freedom fighters', as he called them – was rejected by Congress, which confined help strictly to non-military aid. Meanwhile the peace initiative undertaken by the Central American presidents was looked upon with suspicion in the White House (page 725). The American economic embargo of Nicaragua, the CIA mining of her ports (1984) and the administration's efforts to keep the Contras in the field did enormous damage to Nicaragua's economy, which had been placed on a war footing. Sandinista mismanagement did the rest. When the Soviet Union and her satellites eventually cut off aid to the Sandinistas, the hardline Marxist–Leninists conceded genuinely free elections, which to their surprise they lost (page 729). For the time being at least, Reagan's victory over communism in Latin America was complete. But most of the conditions which gave rise to communism remain.

The handling of the Middle East was the least successful aspect of the administration's conduct of external relations. It led to the one major scandal

of the Reagan era, the so called Iran–Contra affair. In the Gulf War between Iran and Iraq, there was no doubt which side the United States favoured, though she imposed an arms embargo on both countries. Ayatollah Khomeini's hate campaign against the United States as enemy number one and the fanaticism of Iran's Muslim fundamentalists threatened the conservative Gulf oil states, Kuwait, Saudi Arabia and the Gulf Emirates. Consequently they supported Saddam Hussein's Iraq, even though he had started the Gulf War with his invasion of Iran. When Iran countered by attacking oil shipments from Kuwait, the United States and an international naval force moved in to protect them. Kuwaiti tankers were reflagged in May 1987 so that they came under direct US protection. US warships shelled Iranian oil installations in reprisal for attacks on the oil tankers.

Yet by a twist of fate the scandal that broke concerned illegal arms shipments from the United States by way of Israel to *Iran*. The cause was humanitarian. In the Lebanon imbroglio eight American hostages were taken by Lebanese groups such as the Hezbollah, the 'Party of God', believed to be responsive to Khomeini's commands. Their release was secretly arranged in 1985 in return for secret shipments of desperately needed arms and spare parts to the Iranians. These were paid for handsomely as well. The immediate organiser of the deal was an intelligence operative in Washington, Lieutenant-Colonel Oliver North. It appears to have been his 'neat' idea that the profits from the deal should be illegally channelled to the Contras. One hostage had been released and more releases were in prospect when the deal leaked. The subsequent judicial and Congressional investigations found that the participants in the scheme, and Colonel North's boss Rear Admiral John M. Poindexter, the National Security Adviser, had broken the law. President Reagan accepted responsibility for dealing with Iran, but not for the diversion of funds to the Contras. It does seem unlikely that he fully grasped what was going on. But the Iran–Contra affair tarnished the administration's record. With the Iran–Iraq war ending in the summer of 1988, the immediate urgency for active Gulf diplomacy appeared to have ended. But peace in the Gulf was soon to prove illusory.

When Reagan delivered his farewell address to the American people on 11 January 1989 he could claim with justice that 'America is respected again in the world, and looked to for leadership . . .' It was also true that countries 'across the globe are turning to free markets and free speech – and turning away from the ideologies of the past . . . Democracy, the profoundly good, is also the profoundly productive.' The astonishing changes in Eastern Europe in 1989 and 1990 were suddenly to fulfil Reagan's prophecy.

Americans still felt good when it came to choosing between the two presidential candidates in November 1988. The problems of deregulation, the deficit budgeting, easy credit and junk bonds largely lay in the future. The economy was still going strong, the balance of payments improving and unemployment dropping to around 5 per cent. But the Republican candidate Vice-President George Bush was not very inspiring and early in the summer looked like losing to the Democratic candidate Michael Dukakis, the Governor of Massachusetts, who had greatly improved the economy of his state. More charismatic than either was the Democratic leader, the Reverend Jesse Jackson. But the time was not ripe for a black Democratic vice-presidential running-mate. Bush further handicapped himself by choosing Senator Dan Quayle, a personable conservative politician who was considered too young and too inexperienced. The election turned largely on domestic issues. Dukakis warned of the need for higher taxes. Bush riposted with 'Read my lips, no new taxes'; it became virtually his campaign slogan. The Dukakis campaign, by way of contrast, was inept and lost him his big early lead. 'Contented America', to use Professor Galbraith's phrase, was in the majority and turned to the safety of Bush and to the comforting conclusion that spending more money on welfare and urban deprivation provided no solution to America's social problems. It was enough for Bush to promise help where it was really needed and to express the wish to create a 'kinder, gentler nation'. On 8 November 1988, he won convincingly.

In Congress in 1989 Bush faced Democratic majorities in both Houses. The Democrats were not inclined to vote measures to reduce the large deficit if it meant cutting welfare, social security, medical care for the old or any of the pet 'pork-barrel' projects which gained Democrats and Republicans alike support from their constituencies. The President's policies at home began cautiously in 1989; with an eye on the deficit, he rejected

public-spending increases. But the deregulation of the Savings and Loans institutions during the Reagan years had led to imprudent lending and the imminent bankruptcies that ensued required a large federal bail-out. The deficit grew instead of shrinking, and the economy began to show signs of downturn after the credit expansion and stock-market wheeling and dealing of the 1980s.

A severe recession began in 1990 and continued through 1992. Despite his campaign promises, President Bush was forced to raise indirect taxes and reduce exemptions from tax for the better-off. He was widely blamed for not giving sufficient attention to the state of the economy and the rapidly growing unemployment. Yet for a time his popularity reached extraordinary heights.

The explanation for this lies in 'patriotic' America. Bush's forceful handling of Panama gained him enthusiastic support. The strongman of Panama was the virulently anti-American General Manuel Noriega, who was wanted in the United States for drug dealing. In May 1990 Noriega had forcibly prevented the democratic opposition leader from gaining the presidency: the elections had been accompanied by violence, intimidation and corruption. The US pressed for the removal of Noriega, but without success. Finally on 20 December 1989, a large US military force descended on Panama City, causing some loss of life and destruction. Noriega was cornered, captured and brought to the United States for trial, and the opposition candidate of the previous May was installed as president. But such forceful intervention raised renewed fears in Latin America of 'gunboat diplomacy'.

A much bigger issue was the Gulf crisis after the Iraqi invasion of Kuwait in August 1990 (page 921). President Bush's consistent and decisive response in leading the United Nations and forming a coalition of European and Arab nations to defend Saudi Arabia won him general support. The despatch of ground troops, however, caused considerable anxiety inside and outside Congress. By the end of the year, from the Democratic side of Congress especially, there was opposition to the use of force and an insistence that negotiations and sanctions should be continued and allowed time to work. When the Gulf War was quickly and brilliantly won with few American casualties in 1991, Bush's reputation was at its height.

But Bush's decision to stop the fighting once Kuwait had been liberated without toppling Saddam

Hussein damaged his reputation. Nor did the immense efforts at mediation by Secretary of State James Baker, which brought together Israel and her Arab neighbours to try and negotiate a peace settlement at conferences in Madrid and Washington in the autumn of 1991 and early in 1992 lead to much progress. The Palestinian issue and the future of Jerusalem remain intractable obstacles.

The Bush administration could certainly take credit for responding positively to the changes in the Soviet Union and for recognising that to welcome the reunification of the two Germanys was a more realistic and productive policy than the more hesitant reactions in Western Europe. Nor should Bush or Baker be criticised for not recognising the independence of the Baltic states sooner, which would only have added to Gorbachev's difficulties. Gorbachev's credentials as an international statesman and peacemaker were impeccable, while those of Boris Yeltsin (then only a possible successor) were still untried. Bush remained cautious throughout, preferring what looked like the safer bet. Nor was he ready to commit American resources or to sacrifice the lives of US servicemen for ideological reasons or to engage in war a day longer than was required to meet American objectives. He could claim that his had been a safe pair of hands.

But the election in November 1992, with the Cold War over, no longer turned on foreign issues or defence. Attention focused on domestic problems, the state of the economy, the frustrations of the economically disadvantaged and of the middle class, many of whom were threatened by unemployment.

The nation had become increasingly polarised, not simply between blacks and whites but between the haves and the have-nots, as the destructive Los Angeles riots demonstrated in May 1992. The United States might in this respect prove to be something of a model for the future of other highly industrialised nations. The development of an 'underclass' of the poor, with the black ethnic group its largest but not its only component, could produce further violence, crime and drug-taking and increased dependence on welfare. A vicious circle was set up: inner-city ghettos with deteriorating education and employment opportunities became the derelict homes of the poor. Well-paid employment requires education and skills, and the market economy provided less rather than more jobs for the unskilled. To put them to work, to provide training and education, to revitalise the inner cities, to provide more manual jobs – all this would require more public spending, which in turn would mean higher taxation and sacrifices by the better-off. When the poor and those on low wages constituted a majority they represented political power, as in F. D. Roosevelt's day. In the last quarter of the twentieth century their numbers had shrunk, however, and many were alienated from the democratic process, which they saw as unhelpful to them. They no longer constituted so significant a group among those who vote. Less government interference and lower tax burdens appealed to those who vote, among them a large elderly population who claimed medical and social benefits fully, without regard to their income and wealth.

As long as the violence of the poorest section of society was contained there was little real incentive to 'declare war' on poverty, especially as it was comfortingly argued that past efforts to do so in the 1960s had not been effective. Now that the Cold War was over, would the American people resolve the crisis in many inner urban centres, which at times of eruption could resemble a war? That was one of the large questions of the 1990s.

The November 1992 election was a 'three horse race'. A millionaire, Ross Perot, stood as an independent. It is a measure of America's disenchantment with politics and a tribute to Perot's gutsy television performances that he won 19% of the popular vote. A rather lacklustre Bush, who could not persuade the American people that the recession was over, lost the presidential election but only by a small margin of popular votes. The reforming governor from Arkansas, Bill Clinton, and his vice-presidential running mate Albert Gore, a senator from Tennessee, turned the White House Democrat. The two men, both still in their forties, belong to a new post-war generation. Clinton projected the aura that reminded America and the world of the dynamic Kennedy years with one significant contrast. Unlike Jacqueline, the new First Lady Hillary Rodham Clinton, is a formidable partner actively involved in politics. The question for the nineties is how far a change in direction, and the abandonment of 'Reaganomics', will meet the challenge of guiding the world's largest economy forwards successfully and curing the ills of poverty and deprivation which continue to exist in an avowedly affluent society.

# PART XVII

*Western Europe Gathers
Strength: After 1968*

# CHAPTER 82

# The German Federal Republic: Reaching Maturity

The 1960s mark a dividing point in the history of the Western world. The old generation in government was passing; the welfare state had come to provide a safety net; a university education was no longer the preserve of the privileged few; the young were freed from sexual taboos and fears, and they discovered a new sense of identity and mission: romantic, idealistic, searching for a cause more worthwhile than crass materialism in a secular age. That similar feelings were burgeoning in the Soviet-dominated East becomes clear from events in Poland and from the Prague Spring (pages 798–9), but for the most part repression kept the lid on free expression. In the United States, university students on the eastern seaboard in particular identified themselves in the 1960s with the civil-rights cause of the blacks, though in this context they had the support of a new-generation president in J. F. Kennedy. Elsewhere the old generation was still in control, typified by de Gaulle in the Élysée. In the United States the promise of the Kennedy years ended with the President's assassination. Vietnam increasingly blighted the lives of youth, of the conscripts sent to fight on the other side of the world; the war became the focus of a new student protest movement and aroused general disillusionment with the honesty of those who governed.

For the West German youth there was the added trauma of the question 'What did my parents do during the war?'. The almost total silence in their country about the Nazi past only widened the gulf between the generations. As the active protesters in Berlin, Hamburg and Frankfurt saw it, the 'grand coalition' of Kissinger–Brandt was a cynical closing of the ranks of the establishment. There was a short-lived resurgence of the extreme right, a switch of voters from the CDU, for whom the coalition with the Social Democrats was repugnant. Far more substantial was the movement by those on the left who could not stomach the coalition for exactly the opposite reason and felt disillusioned by Willy Brandt's political manoeuvres.

This discontent was fanned by the stirring news of student riots in Paris and throughout the Western world. Self-styled international student leaders emerged and became cult figures. The protesters were right about some of the causes they espoused – the need for practical reforms in the universities, for example, or the campaign against excessive police repression, which threatened civil liberties – but they were naïve to suppose that they could spearhead a Trotskyist or anarchistic revolutionary movement. They themselves were mainly the offspring of the better-off privileged professional and middle classes, and workers in Germany, France and Britain felt little sympathy for them and less urge to identify with their manifold causes. What gave the student rioting such potency, nevertheless, were the television cameras transmitting into millions of peaceable sitting room scenes of blazing petrol bombs and charging policemen.

The single event that provided the spark and allowed the ultra-left to capture the student organis-

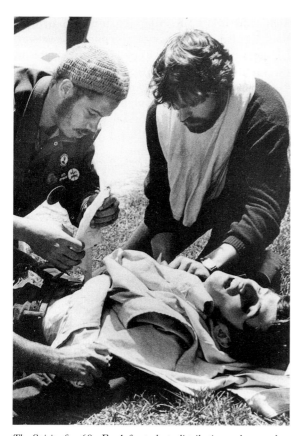

*The Spirit of 1968.* Far left: *students distributing underground literature in Wenceslas Square after the suppression of the Prague Spring.*. Below: *in May students in Paris began a mass protest against authoritarian French institutions; it was a violent affair and rocked de Gaulle's administration.* Left: *in London in October the Vietnam War was the catalyst. The 'Vietnam Solidarity Committee' brought together an alliance of principally leftist groupings and organized a protest outside the US Embassy in Grosvenor Square, London. The police were criticized for using excessive force to maintain order.* Above: *in the United States itself the anti-Vietnam demonstrations ended in tragedy in May 1970 on the campus of Kent State University, where four students were shot dead.*

ations was the brutal reaction of the Berlin police to students demonstrating against the visit of the Shah of Iran. On 2 June 1967, a policeman shot and killed an unarmed student, who at once became a martyr. Street battles followed in several German cities. But the student movement had no alternative to offer to German society; no extreme leftist movement could evoke mass sympathies with the spectacle of communist rule in the East before everyone's eyes. Did the student movement, then, achieve anything beyond the reform of its own nest, the universities? It probably strengthened the feeling that there was a need for change; some politicians like Willy Brandt, leader of the SPD, understood that here was a new electorate, a new generation to be listened to and reconciled to the democratic institutions of the Federal Republic created by the old founding fathers.

By the time the general election was held in September 1969, the grand coalition had fallen apart. The SPD had substantially increased its share of the vote, the German economy having recovered under the guidance of a Social Democratic minister working in tandem with Franz Josef Strauss, thus ridding them of their 'red' image. The CDU/CSU, nevertheless, remained the leading party; its partners, the FDP, lost heavily and now switched its support to the SPD, which under the leadership of Willy Brandt offered a fresh direction in foreign policy. Together they formed the new government. It was the start of a new period of SPD–FDP rule. In this way, the system of proportional representation had in 1969 placed the party with the largest number of votes, the CDU/CSU, into opposition; by far the smallest of the three parties, the FDP, had decided which of the two major parties was placed in power. With less than 2 million votes, and barely passing the 5 per cent threshold necessary to gain representation, the FDP had brought about a decisive change by switching sides. The working

**Bundestag Elections, 1969 and 1972** (*votes in millions*)

|      | CDU/CSU | | | SPD | | | FDP | | | Extreme Right Wing | | |
|------|-------|------|-------|-------|------|-------|-------|------|-------|-------|------|-------|
|      | Votes | % | Seats | Votes | % | Seats | Votes | % | Seats | Votes | % | Seats |
| 1969 | 15.2 | 46.1 | 242 | 14.0 | 42.7 | 224 | 1.9 | 5.8 | 30 | 1.4 | 4.3 | 0 |
| 1972 | 16.8 | 44.8 | 225 | 17.2 | 45.9 | 230 | 3.1 | 8.4 | 41 | 0.2 | 0.6 | 0 |
| 1976 | 18.4 | 48.6 | 244 | 16.1 | 42.6 | 213 | 3.0 | 7.9 | 39 | 0.3 | 0.7 | 0 |

of democracy under proportional representation has its critics, but that a change of government was made possible had strengthened parliamentary government in the Federal Republic.

The Federal Republic now had her Kennedy in the charismatic Willy Brandt, a youthful fifty-five-year old. He had played no part in Nazi Germany, emigrating in 1933 when only nineteen years old. He had lived in Norway and eventually fled to Sweden. In 1947 he resumed his German citizenship and ten years later became a courageous mayor of Berlin, championing the rights of the Berliners. His anti-totalitarian and anti-communist credentials were impeccable. A long period of office appeared to stretch before him especially after the electoral victory in 1972, which for the first time made the SPD the leading party. But his trust in a refugee, Günter Guillaume, originally from East Germany, who served on his staff and was privy to state secrets, proved to be misplaced. Guillaume turned out to be a spy and Brandt, accepting responsibility, resigned in 1974. But it had been a remarkable five years, not least for the new direction he had given to the Federal Republic's relations with the Soviet Union and her Eastern neighbours, a policy known as *Ostpolitik*.

Brandt contributed to the climate of detente between East and West; he was not simply reacting to it. A quarter-century after the end of the war, he believed the time had come to normalise relations in central Europe. The Federal Republic's refusal to recognise the 'other' German state, the German Democratic Republic had prevented all negotiations with the DDR which might ease the hardships inflicted on families by the division of Germany. In 1954 Adenauer had solemnly pledged that the Federal Republic would alter no frontiers by force of arms, but that pledge had been given only to the Western allies. The Federal Republic's claim to speak for all Germans, her refusal to recognise annexations by Poland east of the Oder–Neisse (Silesia), the talk about ultimate reunification and her strident hostility to communism, all made it appear that the Federal Republic was a threat to the security of the German Democratic Republic and Poland if given half a chance. Such views of an aggressive West German state did not reflect reality either.

Periods of detente in East–West relations have succeeded particular crises. The Soviet invasion of Czechoslovakia in 1968 (page 798) was followed by a decade of diminishing tension and bridge-building. Brandt's policy of accepting the existing frontiers of the Federal Republic and recognising the German Democratic Republic required West Germans to overcome a deep psychological barrier and to sever certain links with the past. But, eventually, the eastern territories were juridically abandoned and the legitimacy of the German Democratic Republic accepted.

The foundation of the *Ostpolitik* rested on five treaties. In August 1970, Brandt travelled to Moscow, as he said, 'to turn over a new page of history', and he called for an end to enmity and for a partnership between the peoples of Eastern and Western Europe. After signing the Soviet–German treaty, he visited Warsaw in December 1970 to conclude a Polish–German treaty. Television cameras recorded for all the world to see Brandt's act of repentance, when as the Federal Chancellor he spontaneously sank to his knees before the memorial to the half million Jewish victims of the Warsaw Ghetto. The gesture graphically symbolised the new Germany and her acceptance of responsibility for the Nazi past. A four-power agreement over Berlin (September 1971), a treaty between the Federal Republic and the German Democratic Republic (December 1972) and finally a Czech–German treaty (December 1973) completed the clutch of Eastern treaties.

Visiting the German Democratic Republic in March 1970, Brandt laid the foundations for a new businesslike relationship. The Berlin Wall, constructed in 1961, had stemmed the haemorrhage of population loss from East Germany and in this negative way had created a basis of forced stability for nearly thirty years. But the masters of the German Democratic Republic were alarmed at Brandt's popularity. Even after the treaty was signed, inter-German relations were far from normal. The viability of the East German state rested on Soviet support, specifically on the Soviet veto of union with the West German state. Brezhnev had, nevertheless, responded to Brandt's overtures and forced the East German party boss Ulbricht to reach agreements. Western recognition of the Eastern settlements was worth a great deal to the USSR in stabilising her hold over the East. The boost given to inter-German trade, in addition, supported the ailing Eastern economies; Brandt's Eastern policy also brought international recognition and benefits for the Federal Republic, chief

*During his visit to Poland, German Chancellor Willy Brandt makes a great, impulsive gesture on the steps of the memorial to Jews killed in the Warsaw Ghetto Rising of 1943.*

rebellion, was to be radically changed. The youth rebellion burnt itself out; under Brandt's guidance, the SDP became more tolerant of its young socialists. He also hoped to provide an umbrella under which views from left to right could all shelter, though more often than not left and right fought each other within the party. That was to remain the SPD's abiding problem, the price paid for the wide electoral support necessary to establish itself as the senior party of government.

The Brandt government fell short of fulfilling its high aims at home. Between 1969 and 1975, the business cycle had turned downwards and the annual growth of the German economy fell from 8 to 1 per cent, a fall that was particularly steep after the huge rise in oil prices in 1973–4 (page 484). The 'economic miracle' appeared to be over; the West Germans could not escape the depression of the 1970s.

Brandt's successor was Helmut Schmidt, the most able SPD chancellor of the post-war years. Practical, energetic and decisive in leadership, he provided a vivid contrast to the idealistic and emotional Brandt. But he did not suffer fools gladly and he made many enemies, especially among ideologues. His principle was to find pragmatic solutions to existing problems and to get things done. He inherited the downturn of the economy and the consequences of the oil shock – a severe depression followed in 1974–5. The Schmidt government managed to keep inflation below 6 per cent. To Germans inflation was akin to original sin. But government measures to encourage efficiency and competitiveness to maintain full employment were only partially successful; even so, unemployment was kept down to between 4 and 5 per cent. Falling economic growth did not permit grandiose social-reform schemes to be realised, but budgetary cuts and financial rectitude kept the German economy in much better shape than that of her neighbours. Schmidt, a 'European', recognised the interdependence of the Western world and worked in close collaboration with the French President Valéry Giscard d'Estaing.

The Schmidt years were severely strained by an upsurge of terrorism. A prominent German industrialist, Hans Martin Schleyer, was kidnapped in 1977 and then murdered when Schmidt refused to meet the terrorists' demands. It was just one of a series of abductions and murders. That same year in October a Lufthansa jet with eighty-six passen-

among which was the recognition by the Soviet Union of the permanence of the ties between the Federal Republic and West Berlin. Moreover, movement between the two Germanies was eased.

Brandt had thus extricated his country from the increasingly damaging Hallstein Doctrine whereby the Federal Republic had cut off relations with any state that recognised the German Democratic Republic (except for the Soviet Union. This had increasingly narrowed West Germany's room for manoeuvre; now the way was open again for renewed trade and cultural relations with Eastern and central Europe. By taking the initiative, the Federal Republic was showing the world that she was no longer content with her inferior status, an 'economic giant but a political dwarf'.

Willy Brandt and his FDP partner Walter Scheel also proclaimed a new era at home. Far-reaching reforms were promised which would deepen the attachment of every citizen to the democratic order. The perception of government by a remote elite, leaving the electorate either acquiescent or in open

gers was hijacked by Arab terrorists to Mogadishu, where a specially trained German force spectacularly freed the victims. Fortunately the wave of terrorism abated without having turned the Federal Republic into a police state.

Schmidt's period in office required almost continuous crisis management. In foreign affairs he was particularly concerned about the rapid build-up of Soviet missiles aimed at Western Europe just when the United States and the Soviet Union had reached an agreement on balancing their intercontinental missiles (SALT I, page 802). Schmidt saw two dangers: either that the US might decouple from Europe in the event of a nuclear threat, or, more likely, that a third world war would be fought in Europe. Then there would be nothing left of Germany. Until the Soviet Union disarmed her European missiles, the only response was to build up Western missiles in Europe as a deterrence. But Schmidt had a hard time getting President Carter to pay much attention to the issue.

In December 1979, with Schmidt a leading advocate, NATO took the 'dual track' decision: there would be a period of negotiation designed to persuade the Soviet Union to withdraw her European missiles completely (the zero option) or to reduce them, and if these made no progress NATO would respond by stationing US missiles in Europe; the most dangerous of these, the Pershing missiles, would be based in the Federal Republic. The incoming Reagan administration was not keen on this deal, or any serious negotiations with the Soviet Union. Off-the-cuff remarks by administration spokesmen that a 'limited' nuclear war in Europe was feasible made the situation worse. Schmidt's role and the NATO decision produced a powerful resurgence of protest outside parliament and strong opposition within the party. But Schmidt persevered. Reagan took up the zero option in November 1981, without results. Two years later in 1983 the US began her missiles build-up to match the Russian arsenal, thus setting out on a path that led eventually to the Soviet–US treaty abolishing intermediate- and short-range missiles, signed at the Washington summit in December 1987 by Reagan and Gorbachev. This success owed much to Schmidt's original clarity of vision, steadfastness and courage in following an unpopular policy that at the time was characterised as an irrational twist to the dangerous nuclear-arms build up.

When Schmidt sought a renewal of his mandate as chancellor together with his coalition partner, the FDP, now led by Hans-Dietrich Genscher, the Foreign Minister, in the general election of 1980, he faced as the CDU/CSU candidate the able but mercurial Strauss, whose right-wing politics thoroughly alarmed the liberal reformers. Although the economy showed no signs of improvement – indeed, with rising inflation, rather the reverse – the Schmidt coalition beat the CDU/CSU. The SPD had held its share of the vote at 42.9 per cent, the FDP had increased its share to 10.6 per cent, and Strauss had lost votes compared to the CDU/CSU's results four years earlier. Schmidt seemed set for a long period in office, but his health had been undermined, and the increasingly uneasy coalition with the FDP finally fell apart in 1982. The economic situation had seriously deteriorated throughout Western Europe. In the Federal Republic unemployment rose to over 7 per cent and the FDP was demanding cuts in government spending on unemployment benefit which the SDP could not accept. The FDP now once more switched its support to the CDU/CSU, and with Genscher's support Helmut Kohl became chancellor in October 1982.

It was largely the economic situation that had finally beaten Schmidt, though the fault lay not with his policies but with a world recession, which actually affected the Federal Republic less badly than her neighbours. At times of perceived economic crisis the majority of the electorate turned more conservative. Kohl won the 1983 election by a handsome margin. A new phase of CDU/CSU–FDP government began. Unemployment rapidly increased as the coalition fought the recession with sound money policies, as the rest of Western Europe was doing. The most significant feature of the Federal Republic's condition, however, has proved to be her stability in difficult times. Unlike the Germans under Weimar, the vast majority of today's electorate have no wish for radical change. The new SPD leader, Hans-Jochen Vogel, moved his party slightly to the left but failed to capture the Green constituency. The new protest party, the Greens, who made their debut in 1979 and won an astonishing 5.6 per cent of the vote, giving them twenty-seven seats in the Bundestag, represent a mixture of left-wing causes and concern for the environment. They struck a genuine chord and on environmental issues continue to exert a wholesome influence, despite their eccentric behaviour in and out parliament and their lack of unity. They have added a refreshing touch to the rather staid and mature democratic republic that West Germany has thankfully become. Extremism failed to win sufficient electoral votes to gain any seats. Terrorism remained a worrying feature of social life, but in one form or other it had become common throughout Western Europe, the Middle East and many regions of the world.

### Bundestag Elections, 1983 and 1988
*(percentage of votes)*

|      | CDU/CSU | FDP  | SPD  | Greens |
|------|---------|------|------|--------|
| 1980 | 44.5    | 10.6 | 42.9 | –      |
| 1983 | 48.8    | 6.9  | 38.2 | 5.6    |
| 1988 | 44.4    | 9.1  | 37.0 | 8.3    |

Kohl's chief problem was to satisfy Franz Josef Strauss, his CSU coalition partner and Prime Minister of Bavaria, who on most social issues stood well to his right. Genscher wished to retain the Foreign Ministry and was to become almost a permanent holder of the office, but Strauss also wanted to become foreign minister. In the end Kohl got the upper hand and Strauss was thwarted – but he had no other home to go to. The two issues dominating the administration from 1983 to 1987 were the economy and East–West relations, which centred on the stationing of nuclear missiles in the Federal Republic to match the Soviet build-up and, it was hoped, pave the way to comprehensive disarmament on both sides. But for a while another unexpected political development, the Flick affair, overshadowed politics at home and worryingly raised questions about the health of Germany's democracy. A large group of companies was controlled by a senior manager of the Flick concern. He was accused of bribing the CDU, SPD and FDP parties and individual politicians. The FDP Economics Minister Count Otto Lambsdorff had to resign in June 1984, as did the chairman of the CDU and the Speaker of the Bundestag after accusations of involvement. But, on the positive side, economic recovery began in 1984 and continued steadily until 1987. Inflation fell to its lowest rate in decades; in 1986 there was none at all. Exports boomed and the trade surplus grew

larger. For the great majority in work all this promised continued stable prosperity. But the black spot was unemployment, which hardly improved. Nine per cent of the workforce, more than 2 million people, remained without a job.

### Gross Domestic Product (*US$ millions*)

|                              | 1983    | 1985    | 1987      |
|------------------------------|---------|---------|-----------|
| Federal Republic of Germany  | 654,565 | 622,249 | 1,117,731 |
| Britain                      | 455,995 | 455,740 | 669,572   |

### Gross National Product per head (*US$*)

|                              | 1983   | 1985   | 1987   |
|------------------------------|--------|--------|--------|
| Federal Republic of Germany  | 10,510 | 10,940 | 14,400 |
| Britain                      | 8,186  | 8,460  | 10,420 |

### Unemployment as percentage of workforce

|                              | 1983 | 1985 | 1987 |
|------------------------------|------|------|------|
| Federal Republic of Germany  | 8.9  | 9.0  | 8.9  |
| Britain                      | 12.5 | 11.3 | 10.3 |

What was true of other Western countries was true of West Germany: even as the majority were increasing their standards of living, a heterogeneous underclass was forming. These were the 'classless', below any recognisable class: immigrants who could find no place in Western society, who were either unemployed or illegally employed at sweated wages, the mentally sick without family ties, drug addicts and prostitutes, some little more than children, haunting such areas as Bahnhof Zoo in Berlin. Then there were those sleeping rough in cardboard boxes, for example under the arches of London's Waterloo railway station. Few were aggressive – the squatters in Hafenstrasse in Hamburg were something of an exception. In many cities unemployment was unacceptably high, but the social climate of the 1980s had grown altogether more harsh; economic health was the priority. Governments encouraged enterprise and productivity in industry, and the devil catch the hindmost. So the safety net was beginning to show large holes.

*Communist Europe inflicted savage environmental damage on itself; not the least of the problems facing Europe as she reconstructs herself is how to clean up the pollution caused by industrial plant such as this in Espenhain, in what was East Germany.*

Ecology, the health of the earth, became a growing concern. In Western Germany especially, a sizeable part of the community rebelled against a society which put material interests above all else and was therefore damaging the environment. There were ever more cars, and forests were dying from acid rain. Governments began to take notice and to discuss measures to reduce pollution. The Chernobyl disaster in 1986 (page 819) sensitised people to the dangers of nuclear reactors. The Greens benefited as the anti-nuclear party. There were violent clashes between protesters and police at the sites of two nuclear reactors being built at Wackersdorf and Brokdorf. The government defended the nuclear-energy option, but this was really the end of nuclear expansion in West Germany. France meanwhile took the opposite course.

West Germany was characterised during these years by an altogether more active public ready to join mass protests on issues that moved them. The protesters were no longer only young people and students, as they had been in the 1960s. It was a welcome sign that Germans were no longer awed by authority and bureaucracy, as they had been in the bad old days of the 1930s. The Pershing missiles based in Germany were the cause of continuous and widespread protest. But Genscher's diplomacy maintained West Germany on a steady path, keeping Franco-German relations in good repair, behaving as good Europeans in the European Community and particularly normalising relations with the East German regime. While reunification remained the official line, few at that time believed they would see it happen in their lifetime. So the West German government set itself the task of overcoming the unnatural divisions caused by the Wall and concluded agreements which made travel between the two Germanies easier. The East German regime was much aided by the flourishing trade with West Germany, which also gave her neighbour large credits.

With unemployment high, every legal effort was made to stem the number of asylum-seekers, other

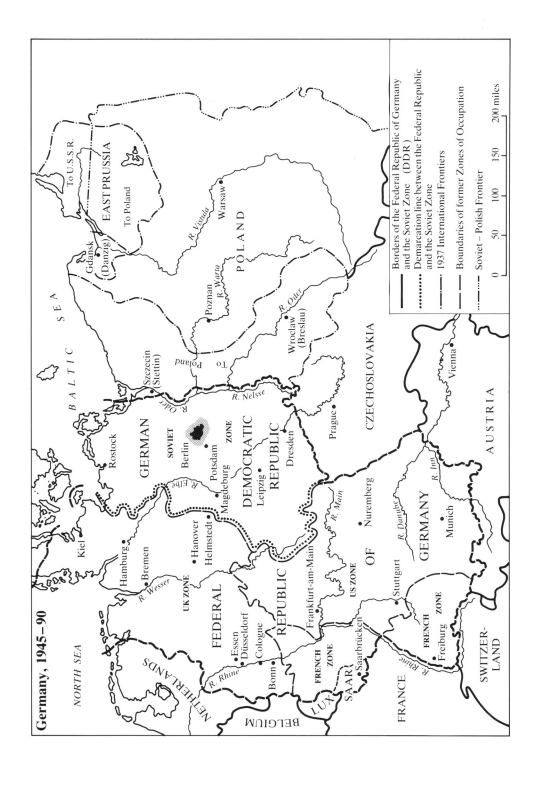

**Germany, 1945–90**

NORTH SEA

BALTIC SEA

NETHERLANDS

BELGIUM

LUX.

FRANCE

SWITZER-LAND

AUSTRIA

CZECHOSLOVAKIA

POLAND

EAST PRUSSIA

To U.S.S.R.

To Poland

To Poland

**GERMAN DEMOCRATIC REPUBLIC**

SOVIET ZONE

**FEDERAL REPUBLIC OF GERMANY**

UK ZONE

US ZONE

FRENCH ZONE

FRENCH ZONE

SAAR

SWITZER-LAND

Kiel
Hamburg
Bremen
Hanover
Helmstedt
Rostock
Berlin
Potsdam
Magdeburg
Leipzig
Dresden
Essen
Düsseldorf
Cologne
Bonn
Saarbrücken
Frankfurt-am-Main
Nuremberg
Stuttgart
Freiburg
Munich
Szczecin (Stettin)
Gdansk (Danzig)
Warsaw
Poznan
Wroclaw (Breslau)
Prague
Vienna

R. Wesser
R. Rhine
R. Elbe
R. Main
R. Danube
R. Inn
R. Rhine
R. Oder
R. Neisse
R. Oder
R. Warta
R. Vistula

Borders of the Federal Republic of Germany and the Soviet Zone (DDR)

Demarcation line between the Federal Republic and the Soviet Zone

1937 International Frontiers

Boundaries of former Zones of Occupation

Soviet – Polish Frontier

0    50    100    150    200 miles

than Germans from the East, wishing to enter the Federal Republic. The *Gastarbeiter* were not as welcome as before, and Turkish families who had lived for years in West Germany were encouraged to return by the offer of a federal grant. Few took advantage of it.

As election day in January 1987 approached, the Kohl administration could count on solid support from the electorate, which was enthused by the expanding economy and prepared to overlook the unemployment. Genscher was popular too; he enjoyed a reputation as a skilful and successful foreign minister who was covering more air-miles than any of his predecessors. Kohl was rather under-rated, as it turned out, and was regarded as stodgy, with an unfortunate flair for putting his foot in it. That the television stations repeated his 1985 Christmas address in 1986 by mistake seemed a typical mishap. A more serious incident occurred during Reagan's visit in May 1985. To mark the anniversary of the ending of the Second World War, as a gesture of reconciliation the US President and the federal Chancellor paid their respects at a German military cemetery, but the choice of Bittsburg was unfortunate, because it contained many SS graves. There were protests, and Reagan was embarrassed. Kohl made another gaffe in 1987 when he likened Gorbachev's propaganda to that of Joseph Goebbels. But in truth these were really just minor embarrassments. No one would have believed how surefootedly the Chancellor, with Genscher's help, would overcome the obstacles of reunification as the decade drew to its close. (See also pages 905–7.)

The election for the Bundestag in January 1987 gave the CDU–CSU 223 seats and a 44.3% share of the votes, the FDP coalition partners secured 46 seats with 9.1% of the vote and the SPD 186 seats and 37% of the votes. The Greens advanced spectacularly with 42 seats and 8.3% of the votes; no other party secured even 1% of the vote. Support for extremist parties such as neoNazis was insignificant before unification. In 1989, West Germany, on the occasion of the fortieth anniversary of the foundation of the Federal Republic could feel it was prosperous, mature, and that democracy was firmly established. They could look confidently to the future unaware of the problems that lay ahead.

# CHAPTER 83

# Contemporary Italy: Progress Despite Politics

In Italy, the protest and turbulence of 1968 were not confined to student groups or to a rebellion of youth, but spawned in their aftermath an upsurge in the militancy of the industrial workers. The divisions and weaknesses of the trade union movement were overcome by local bargaining and by the development of factory organisations – the factory councils. The Marxist student-protest movement struck real roots among the workers, unlike in West Germany and France, where protesting students met with little sympathy from working people, whose taxes gave students time for their sit-ins and endless debates; in Britain, student protest and influence were negligible outside the universities, prompting tolerant amusement or perhaps criticism of the authorities for allowing such disruption. In Italy the protests and the breakdown of order were far more serious.

The 'hot autumn' of 1969 saw the spread of many strikes, supporting demands for higher pay and better working conditions. The Italian people could no longer be easily led; there was a loss of respect for institutions and for the political leadership which extended through all parties and traditions. Labour legislation the following year, in 1970, gave the trade unionist more power. The Italian economy began to suffer from characteristic stress: inflation took off in the mid-1970s; the sudden increase in oil costs hit the Italian economy hard; workers' wages outpaced productivity; the agricultural south lagged ever more behind the industrial north. The expansion of the Italian economy slowed. Although the average annual growth in GNP in the 1970s still exceeded 3 per cent, it gyrated wildly from year to year.

The economic upheavals and the social ferment were reflected in the instability of governments from 1968 to 1976. The Christian Democrats hardly changed in electoral strength, but internal divisions and the continued political jockeying among coalition partners, who agreed on little beyond the need to keep the communists out, produced one crisis government after another. The trend was to form centre–left alignments, and the contemporary legislation reflected this, as did the distancing of politics from the demands of the Church, as Italy became increasingly secularised. In 1970 a civil divorce law finally passed through parliament. Effective implementation, however, required a referendum. The Church continued to oppose divorce vehemently, and so did the leadership of the Christian Democrats, but when the referendum was finally held in 1974 a majority of the Italian population backed divorce. Women's rights too gradually made headway in Italy in the 1970s and the 1980s, as elsewhere in the Western world. And youth gained more influence, with the voting age reduced from twenty-one to eighteen in 1974.

In another attempted reform of the Italian political landscape, decentralisation and regional autonomy were taken further. The first regional elections of 1970 brought only limited progress; they nevertheless made possible communist participation in local government without admitting communists into central government. The Communist Party provided comparatively efficient administration in the 'red' central regions of Emilia Romagna, Umbria and Tuscany, when contrasted with the corruption of the other parties. The communist response to welfare and environmental needs spurred the Christian Democrats and other parties to compete on these issues. But political bargaining and central power in Rome nevertheless predominate, inhibiting the development of genuine regional autonomy as intended by the Italian constitution. What the regional system has not achieved is a levelling out between the wealthiest and the poorest parts of Italy. In 1978 against a Gross National Product per head for Italy as a whole of 100, the poorest region – Calabria in the southern toe – achieved only just over half the average (53) and the wealthiest – the Val d'Aosta in the north-west corner – three times as much (157), while industrial northern Italy has more than twice the GNP of the south. Italy remains divided.

There is a darker side to recent Italian history. The grass-roots political militancy produced a fanatical extremist element, small in number but great in their impact because of the ruthless terrorist tactics they employed; the best known were the Red Brigades. Bombs were set off in railway trains in Milan, in Bologna and elsewhere with considerable loss of life. Their purpose was to destroy the social and democratic political structure. The most spectacular Red Brigade terrorist action was the March 1978 kidnapping of Aldo Moro, the leader of the Christian Democratic Party, when he was on his way to parliament. The terrorists demanded the release from prison of thirteen of their companions. The government held firm, despite heart-rending messages from Moro. Eight weeks later Moro's corpse was left in the trunk of a car in the centre of Rome. The general revulsion was so great that it strengthened rather than weakened Italian democracy. But terrorism continued, reaching an horrific climax in August 1980 when bombs were set off in Bologna railway station, which was crowded with tourists. Eighty-four people were killed.

Italy also experienced common West European problems – she was no longer backward, a nation apart. For a long time Italians had had to emigrate to more prosperous countries to find work. Now Africans were coming to Italy, and, as in the rest of Western Europe, the stream of immigrants – often performing menial functions for poor pay

*Italian Christian Democrat leader Aldo Moro is displayed to the world on television by his captors, the Red Brigades, before they murder him in March 1978.*

which Italians no longer wished to take on – created multi-ethnic communities in the cities with their attendant problems of exploitation, discrimination, poverty, crime and tension. At the general election of 1976 the Communist Party, now led by Enrico Berlinguer, hoped to overtake the Christian Democrats, since Berlinguer's open defiance of Moscow and his leading role in the rise of Eurocommunism had enhanced the party's standing. It came close to succeeding.

The communists demanded full acceptance within the political system, particularly inclusion in a government of national unity. They were supported by parties of the left. Italy's NATO partners were thoroughly alarmed and warned the Christian Democratic leadership against such a step. To avert the danger that no government would be found, that Italy would be virtually ungovernable because the Christian Democrats could form no coalition with the non-communist left which would give them a majority, agreement was reached with the communists in 1976 that they would support a minority Christian Democrat government in return for

## Chamber of Deputies Elections, 1972–1987

|  | 1972 | | 1976 | | 1979 | | 1983 | | 1987 | |
|---|---|---|---|---|---|---|---|---|---|---|
|  | % | Seats | % | Seats | % | Seats | % | Seats | % | Seats |
| Communists (PCI) | 27.2 | 179 | 34.4 | 227 | 30.4 | 201 | 29.9 | 198 | 26.6 | 177 |
| Socialists (PSI) | 9.6 | 61 | 9.7 | 57 | 9.8 | 62 | 11.4 | 73 | 14.3 | 94 |
| Democratic Socialists (PSDI) | 5.1 | 29 | 3.4 | 15 | 3.8 | 20 | 4.1 | 23 | 3.0 | 17 |
| Christian Democrats (DC) | 38.7 | 266 | 38.8 | 263 | 38.3 | 262 | 32.9 | 225 | 34.3 | 234 |
| Liberal Party (PLI) | 3.9 | 20 | 1.3 | 5 | 1.9 | 9 | 2.9 | 16 | 2.1 | 11 |
| Republican Party (PRI) | 2.9 | 15 | 3.1 | 14 | 3.0 | 16 | 5.1 | 29 | 3.7 | 21 |
| Neo-Fascists (MSI) | 8.7 | 56 | 6.1 | 35 | 5.3 | 30 | 6.8 | 49 | 5.9 | 35 |
| Others | 3.8 | 0 | 3.2 | 10 | 7.5 | 24 | 6.9 | 18 | 10.1 | 41 |

consultation. This involvement of the communists in the government of the country, which was called the 'historic compromise', came to an end after the 1979 election, when the Christian Democrats formed a new coalition government with the non-communist left.

Widespread corruption and influence-peddling continues to mar the workings of Italian democracy. Links between Christian Democrats and the Mafia in Sicily have proved highly embarrassing to the party. The scandal of the freemason lodge known as P2, which broke in 1981, was both alarming and sensational. The lodge formed a secret society of nearly 1000 members drawn from political, administrative and military elites, including members of the government and extending to links with high finance and the criminal underworld.

Later investigation uncovered another murky secret underground organisation called Operation Gladio. It was originally set up early in the Cold War as a secret military group to move into action to counter a communist takeover of Italy. Its functioning was known to successive Italian prime ministers, including Giulio Andreotti, and revelations by the judiciary in 1990 caused the ruling political elite considerable embarrassment. It seems to have become an extreme-right terrorist organisation which attempted to incite anti-left reactions. It was rumoured that Gladio was responsible for a number of bombings in the 1970s and 1980s, including the explosion at Bologna railway station. The theory was that Gladio intended thereby to undermine the left, whose terrorists were blamed

for the outrages. If so, Gladio was as much out of control as the Red Brigades. What is clear is that Gladio belonged to the unacceptable side of Italian politics. Yet it was a healthy sign that there were other politicians, civil servants and men with responsibilities in the regions who were willing to bring corruption to light. The mass trials of Mafiosi in Palermo in the mid-1980s attested to their courage and determination. The fight against corruption had not been won, but at least it was being waged.

With a period of political stability, reinforced by the financial reforms of Bettino Craxi, the first Socialist to become prime minister, which he achieved in 1983 with majority Christian Democrat backing, the Italian economy was nursed back to better health. Inflation fell to an acceptable 5 per cent and unemployment fell too. But the fundamental problems of Italy remained. The north–south gap was increasing; northern industry was geared to and competitive within Western Europe; the regions south of Rome, despite thirty years of development aid, remained backward and uncompetitive, with a few remarkable exceptions. The Abruzzo region, west of Rome, with a population of 1.2 million, was no longer tied to poor farming, but had developed modern industry and tourism. Was that a harbinger of things to come? There was little sign of this in Calabria, Sicily or Sardinia. Twenty million Italians lived in the south in the early 1990s; one in five was unemployed. Thirty-six million Italians lived in the northern half, where about one in fourteen was unemployed and standards of living were almost twice as high. As Western Europe integrated in the 1990s, the south could be left increasingly behind. If Italian government remained unstable – and the auguries were not good – the mismanagement of public resources, the growth of the huge public debt and the inefficiency of an army of bureaucrats would carry on unimpeded, and interest groups would continue to be paid off from state funds. It was a considerable burden, mainly carried by the efficient, large-scale private industry of the north. Without political reform, all these problems would intensify.

Craxi managed to remain in office until August 1987, just short of an unprecedented four years. In the election held that month he slightly increased his percentage of the vote at the expense of the Christian Democrats, who nonetheless gained twice as many votes as the Socialists. The alliance of the Socialists and Christian Democrats under the premiership of Craxi had been one of pure electoral convenience rather than common aims or mutual trust. It was replaced by an uneasy five-party coalition headed by a Christian Democrat and including Craxi's Socialists. March 1988 saw another administration formed by a Christian Democratic premier in increasingly uneasy partnership with Craxi. This administration succeeded in passing the long-overdue abolition of secret voting in the Chamber on most issues. When in March 1989, Craxi withdrew his party from the coalition, the Christian Democrat Prime Minister resigned. It took nine weeks to find a new premier. In July 1989, the veteran politician Giulio Andreotti became prime minister for the sixth time, leading the forty-ninth post-war administration, yet another five-party coalition, including Craxi's Socialists. Thus the stability of government continued to rest on the co-operation of the Christian Democrats and Socialists, which allowed Craxi pretty much to name his conditions.

A feature of Italian politics unique in Western Europe was the relatively small change in the shares of the vote on left and right. Majorities in parliament could at times be secured only by striking bargains with the communists, who were thus able to influence the national government without being part of it. In the regions a Socialist–communist alliance was not unusual, so the communists were not entirely excluded from the political coalitions that ran Italy. In the early 1990s the Christian Democrats had been in power as the largest partner in coalition

governments without interruption since the Liberation. Changes of policy had, nevertheless, occurred, changes which roughly mirrored the political swings in the rest of Western Europe. In Italy, however, they were the result not of governments changing hands between opposite parties, but of the parties themselves changing direction. Party policies were pragmatic. The Communist Party had altered course; the Socialist Party was hardly 'socialist'; the Christian Democrats did not always follow policies to the right of centre – all this made changes of direction in government possible. The 1990s brought old problems once more grimly to the surface: the web of Mafia corruption and drug trafficking had spread to the north. The whole of Italy was shocked when in the spring and summer of 1992 two of Italy's most prominent Mafia judges were murdered. Organised crime appeared to be beyond the control of the government. Corruption scandals further alienated the people from the self-serving politicians. The huge deficit caused by government spending had doubled the country's debts during the 1980s. At the same time, Italy's infrastructure – her railways, her roads, her telecommunications – was crumbling.

Somehow Italian politics had managed to defy gravity in the past. A founding member of the European Community, Italy enthusiastically backed the monetary and political union envisaged by the Maastricht Treaty (page 882), but her parlous economic condition made the idea of convergence with the economies of France and Germany within a few years difficult to take seriously.

The general election in 1992 weakened the four-party governing coalition, leaving it with so small a majority that it could not hope to push through any reforming measures. As a result, Giuliano Amato, the deputy leader of the Socialist Party, was asked by the President to form the fifty-first Italian government. Amato was faced with the problem of gaining parliamentary approval for necessary financial reforms, to cut welfare and pension payments. There was no other way to meet Italy's burgeoning deficit. In September 1992 she suffered the indignity, in company with Britain, of having to devalue and leave the Exchange Rate Mechanism. In the early 1990s Italy seemed to have reached a turning point. Political scandal, Mafia criminality and an economic débâcle threatened a continuous national crisis unless fundamental reforms were carried through, and not just talked about.

The criminal investigations begun by members of the judiciary in Milan in 1992 involving Craxi snowballed in 1993 to reveal endemic political and financial corruption throughout the upper echelons of local and national government and in commerce. Even Andreotti, the veteran political survivor, seven times prime minister, was accused of being in the service of the Mafia. The collapse of the Cold War in any case altered the shape of Italian politics. Government coalitions formed around the Christian Democrats and Socialists to keep the Communists out had lost their *raison d'être*. So many party leaders, ministers and deputies were touched by scandal and accusations of corruption moreover, that the political game simply could not continue as before. The electorate was disillusioned; business wished to end government waste; the people of the north baulked at subsidising the south; unemployment ran at over ten per cent. The demand for political change thus became irresistible.

Reforms were passed in time for the March 1994 national elections. Three quarters of the seats were allocated to first-past-the-post winners in constituencies and one quarter on the basis of the old proportional representation but with a new five per cent hurdle. The politicians of the established parties rushed to put on new clothes. The Communist Party, phoenix-like, re-emerged as the Democratic Party of the Left (PDS); a minority of the old orthodox party now called themselves Reconstructed Communists; the disgraced Christian Democrats turned to its pre-fascist past and fought the election as the Popular Party of Italy; but there were also entirely new forces such as the Northern League led by Umberto Bossi, a regional party wishing to break up the centralised state and demanding the right to keep the wealth generated by industry in the region; it had already made a striking debut in the elections of 1992. The real phenomenon of 1994, however, was the emergence of an anti-socialist, free-market, right-wing party, the brainchild of a charismatic business tycoon Silvio Berlusconi, owner of three national TV channels and the Milan football club whose battle cry, *forza*, inspired the name of his party, *Forza Italia*. Formed only a few weeks before the March 1994 elections to stop the expected bandwagon of the Left, Berlusconi scored an unprecedented victory. The elections were fought in alliance groupings of the Left as the 'Progressives', the Right as the 'Alliance for Freedom', and the Centre, 'Pact for Italy'.

But has political stability been brought any nearer? There are serious differences between the parties making up the three alliance groupings and the centre is weak. Italian politics is polarised, yet coalitions have to be formed. Nonetheless, Italian politics changed out of all recognition in 1994, without question.

# CHAPTER 84

# How to Make Britain More Prosperous: Conservative and Labour Remedies

Whatever the rest of the world may have expected, the British people did not spend much energy grieving over their lost empire or hankering after past glories. Apart from crises in which Britain was directly involved, such as Berlin in 1948, Suez in 1956 and the Falklands in 1982, little of what was occurring in the outside world distracted them from domestic concerns. Their attention was overwhelmingly fixed on the economy at home, on wage bargaining and wage restraint, on the trade unions and their growing power, on whether Britain could keep pace with, and later whether she could catch up with, the spectacular progress of her West European neighbours, above all on whether people felt confident about better times ahead. These issues decided elections. Chancellors of the Exchequer had to develop policies which would create the right economic conditions and the right mood on election day. Labour and the Conservatives attacked each other's economic policies, though in practice a consensus prevailed on many aspects of domestic policy at least until 1979: to sustain full employment, to aid declining industry and to promote economic growth. There was, of course, a price to pay; over-manning meant low productivity, sheltered industries became less competitive, and steeply progressive taxation to meet the costs of these policies had to be exacted. Britain slipped further behind, her standard of living advancing more slowly than that of her West European neighbours. Yet economic statistics alone do not accurately reflect

the quality of life. Home ownership, for example, had spread to relatively low-income groups, much further than on the European continent.

Government policies sought a surge in productivity, growth in manufacturing exports and a reduction in imports of consumer goods from cars to refrigerators, from washing machines to television sets, which were coming to be regarded as basic requirements. If these needs could be met from production at home and if Britain could export enough to pay for her necessary imports, the economy could develop healthily. Progress was made but it ran into periodic crises, and what became known as stop–go economic management began to typify Treasury policy.

Up to the early 1950s the British economy was still holding its own in manufacturing, and the City of London was contributing valuable 'invisible' earnings by providing banking and insurance services. Western Europe was still recovering from the war, but the overall trend is made very apparent by the statistics set out in the table.

The British economy suffered from another problem. The average rate of 2 to 3 per cent annual growth hides large variations between the fast-growth 'go' years and the slow-growth 'stop' periods. The average annual growth rates of industrial production in the 'go' years of 1953 to 1955, 1959 to 1960 and 1962 to 1964 were a respectable 5.8 per cent annually, but the 'stop' periods in between, 1955 to 1958, 1960 to 1962 and 1964 to

**Gross National Product, 1951–1978** (*Average annual percentage rates of growth*)

|  | Japan | USA | Britain | West Germany | France | Italy | Netherlands |
|---|---|---|---|---|---|---|---|
| 1951–73 | 9.5 | 3.7 | 2.7 | 5.7 | 5.0 | 5.1 | 5.0 |
| 1973–8 | 3.7 | 2.4 | 0.9 | 1.9 | 2.9 | 2.1 | 2.4 |

1966, raised production by an annual percentage of only 0.9 per cent. During the 1970s and early 1980s the gap between the performance of Britain and her neighbours in manufacturing grew rather than decreased, and her manufacturing output fell steeply, creating large-scale unemployment.

In relative terms, Britain was not doing well; but people compared their living standards with earlier years, not with those of their continental neighbours. During the Conservative years from 1957 to 1964 these standards were rising significantly, with improved housing, more effective social services, a National Health Service that removed financial worries from illness, higher real wages, better education and better provision for the old-age pensioner. The blessings of full employment came to be regarded as the norm. There were more vacancies for the skilled and new openings in the professions and the civil service. More university places and increased provision of grants made it easier to cross class barriers, especially for the ex-servicemen. Complete equality of opportunity did not exist any more then than it does now, but there were no insuperable barriers for the talented, the hardworking and the highly motivated. Compared with before the war, Britain had become a much better country to live in.

Harold Wilson's years as prime minister from 1964 to 1970 were remarkable for new thinking and experimentation to improve Britain's performance in a mixed economy, combining state and private enterprise. Wilson believed that government had to become more interventionist and to copy the indicative planning which had proved so successful in Germany and France. Central to this aim was the attempt to establish a link between higher wages and productivity. Prices and incomes were compulsorily regulated by a government-appointed board set up in 1965. In March 1966 Wilson went to the country and succeeded in massively increasing Labour's majority. But the following year the economy ran into severe trouble, and sterling was belatedly devalued. The attempt to co-ordinate national economic planning with a Department of Economic Affairs (headed by the deputy Labour leader George Brown) was in ruins. Britain's foreign and military commitments 'east of Suez' were cut in 1968. Wilson extended state control and renationalised steel, a move which in the long term cost the taxpayer dear in subsidies. Low wages and workers' discontent led to many strikes. With the Labour Party financially dependent on the trade unions, the government could not put in place effective legislation to curb their power, which was unbalancing industrial relations. That was the biggest hole in Labour's planning for a more efficient Britain. Direct state investment was not always successful, though private industry did not always choose the right path either. The merger of British car manufacturers into Leyland only accelerated the downward path of this once highly competitive and successful industry. Wilson also tried to obtain Britain's entry into the European Economic Community, but was blocked a second time when de Gaulle vetoed the application in November 1967.

Labour paid particular attention to policies designed to equalise opportunities for all Britain's young people. Schools were reorganised into mixed-ability 'comprehensives'; more successful was Labour's continuing commitment to the expansion of university and higher education first launched by the Conservatives. But the continuing flaw was the lack of attention given to technical education: it was not accorded an academic esteem equal to that of other subjects – which it has long received in Germany, for instance. The privileged private 'public schools' were not abolished and so continued to underpin a class-based society, though mobility between the classes did increase significantly. The middle classes widened and so did middle-class culture. More young people aspired to own a house rather than rent; by 1970 half of all houses were owner-occupied. In 1961 only 4 million Britons travelled abroad for their holidays. In 1984 15 million did so. Washing machines, tele-

*Not wartime Britain but Toxteth, a suburb of Liverpool, during the riots of July 1981.*

visions and cars were no longer the preserve of the few. Women began to insist on equal rights: the contraceptive pill gave them full control over their sexuality. Despite continuing hardships, especially in the north of England and Northern Ireland, the 1960s and 1970s were years of expanding horizons and growing freedom.

Among the dark areas were inner-city neglect, unemployment, drugs and racial tension aggravated by youth unemployment. Second- and third-generation immigrants, nurtured on civil rights and protest movements, were not as willing to accept discrimination as their parents and grandparents had been. The race riot in London's Notting Hill in 1958 was a foretaste of what was to come: Bristol, Brixton, Liverpool (Toxteth) in the summer of 1981 and Handsworth in 1985, drew attention to the problems of densely populated, deprived city areas. In the 1970s and 1980s a new phenomenon arose to threaten the strong social cohesion of Britain, that of whole groups becoming alienated from society, such as the unskilled young blacks and whites, whose prospects of employment had become remote and who now sought expression in an alternative society while relying on welfare hand-

outs. To them the politicians in Westminster were distant and unreal. But youth unemployment in the 1970s and 1980s was not just a British problem – it plagued Western European countries. Although the existence of a black economy should be taken into account, the official statistics tell a shocking story of waste and frustration.

Another black spot was Northern Ireland. The partition of Ireland in 1920–1 after the bloody civil war was never fully accepted by the South, while the Protestant majority in the six counties of Ulster in the north insisted on the maintenance of union with Britain. The Catholic minority in Ulster was discriminated against and deprived of political influence. A separate government and parliament at Stormont, under Westminster's ultimate authority, allowed discriminatory practices to continue which would not have been tolerated in the rest of Britain. The Irish Republican Army, or IRA, which aims to coerce the north into a unified Ireland, has successfully resisted the Protestant-dominated Royal Ulster Constabulary, or RUC. Economic decline aggravated the conflict. IRA militancy was revived by the Provisional IRA offshoot, and Protestant militancy by the formation of the Ulster Defence Association. In 1969 British troops were sent to Ireland to reinforce the police, but the number of bombings and sectarian killings rapidly increased.

With firearms on the street, calamitous mistakes were bound to occur. The worst was Bloody Sunday, 30 January 1972, when British troops opened fire on a banned Catholic civil-rights march in Londonderry, killing sixteen. IRA terrorists meanwhile carried out a series of vicious murders: on 21 July 1973 twenty bombs indiscriminately killed eleven people in Belfast; in 1979 Lord Mountbatten and eighteen soldiers were the victims of attacks. By 1992 some 3000 civilians and soldiers had lost their lives since the Troubles began. Catholic and Protestant Church leaders have condemned the killing of innocent people, but in vain. For a whole generation of youngsters violence became the norm. The efforts of British governments to find a solution have failed, even though the province was directly subordinated to Westminster in March 1972, under the day-to-day control of a secretary of state for Northern Ireland.

Attempts to achieve co-operation between London and Dublin made some progress, but they have not ended the cycle of violence. The first attempt was the December 1973 Sunningdale agreement, which proposed Catholic–Protestant power-sharing in the province and the handing back of control to a Northern Irish executive. But there was a backlash from Protestant workers and the agreement was buried. The middle ground of Catholic–Protestant relations – represented, for example, by the non-sectarian Alliance Party – has remained too weak. Hopes of co-operation between London and Dublin were revived by the signing of the Anglo-Irish Agreement in November 1985, by Margaret Thatcher and Garret Fitzgerald. But Protestant opponents in Northern Ireland denounced the idea of giving Dublin any role in Northern Irish politics as 'treachery', although the government of the Republic of Ireland had recognised that Irish unity could be brought about only by the consent of the majority in Northern Ireland. The agreement has also been condemned by the IRA and its political wing Sinn Fein. Nevertheless, the co-operative institution created by the agreement, the Intergovernmental Conference, continues to function, even though its practical achievements have been sparse.

*The Falls Road, South Belfast, 1978. The casualties of violence in Northern Ireland mount ever higher daily.*

Despite the difficulties the Wilson government had experienced economically from 1967 to 1969, Labour was expected to beat the Conservatives when the Prime Minister called the election for June 1970. To most people's surprise, the Conservatives won, and their leader Edward Heath was in 10 Downing Street. Heath, a grammar schoolboy, represented a break with the tradition of grand Tory leaders of the Macmillan and Home school. He had a good record as a minister, and although he had failed to overcome de Gaulle's veto of British entry into the EEC, his handling of the negotiations from 1961 to 1963 had earned him respect.

Now it was Heath's and the Conservatives' turn to try to cure the 'British disease' of economic inertia. The remedy adopted was a market-oriented approach: a vigorous Britain would diminish government subsidies and welfare and reward hard work and enterprise; taxation was to be reduced, the frontiers of the state rolled back; wage control was abandoned. Social programmes were cut, including free school milk. But the doctrine of non-state intervention and bale-outs of industry was quickly reversed, the U-turn beginning in February 1971 when Rolls-Royce was rescued and taken into public ownership. The undoing of the Heath government was its bitter clash with the trade unions. The restriction of their rights by the Industrial Relations Act in 1971 coincided with an economic downturn. In 1973, the rise in oil prices made the situation still worse. The Heath government now resorted to draconian price and wage controls. Government intervention even came to exceed that of Labour. In February 1974 the miners went on strike against the government wages policy. That winter of gloom the lights literally went out and industry was forced to work a three-day week. The government's confrontation with the miners was thoroughly mishandled and when Heath called an election in February 1974 on the issue of 'Who governs Britain?' he narrowly lost.

The major achievement of Heath's administration had been Britain's entry at last into the Common Market in 1973. In this critical area of policy Heath and Wilson were agreed, though both were faced with considerable opposition within their own parties on the issue. Wilson's difficulties were the more serious. In October 1971 the Labour Party Conference had voted against joining the EEC. It was, therefore, fortunate that it was under a Conservative government that the terms Heath had secured were submitted to the Commons for approval.

The terms of accession allowed Britain a transitional period of adjustment for a maximum of six years. By then, with few exceptions, her food prices would rise above world prices as duties would be imposed on food imported from the Commonwealth and the United States. The formula for calculating Britain's contribution to the common budget created such a disproportionate burden that Margaret Thatcher had to negotiate its reduction, amid much acrimony, during her first administration (1979–83).

Support for and opposition to 'joining Europe' aroused great passions, though more so in Parliament than in the country as a whole, where a majority were simply in favour of efforts to find solutions to Britain's problems. The opposition in Parliament could marshal powerful arguments: the loss of sovereignty and submission to the bureaucracy of Brussels; the disadvantage to Britain, with her small and efficient agricultural sector, of the regressive Common Agricultural Policy; and the high cost of membership because of Britain's large budget contributions. The proponents' claim that the advantages of the larger market counterbalanced the cost underestimated the difficulty of making Britain competitive.

The House of Commons majorities were never large, but enough Labour pro-Europeans voted for the bill to cancel out the Conservative anti-marketeers and the majority of Labour Members who voted against. Wilson held his party skilfully together by promising to negotiate better terms and then to submit the decision to the nation in a referendum. The bill passed through the Commons on 13 July 1972 and Britain entered the EEC on 1 January 1973.

In February 1974 it fell to a minority Labour government to try to solve Britain's problems and to halt her economic decline. During the election campaign, Labour had offered the country something new: the so-called Social Contract between the government and the trade unions. In return for repealing Heath's 1971 Industrial Relations Act and so freeing the unions from the threat of legal action, the unions promised *voluntary* wage restraint. By the time Wilson called another election in October 1974 the worst industrial troubles were over. The need to secure a Labour victory acted as a restraint on the unions. The miners' strike had been settled and the country was back to a full working week. This time, in October, Labour gained a small working majority. But by 1975 inflation had rocketed to 24 per cent, and wage settlements were even higher. The Social Contract was not working. Once more Wilson had to resort to what amounted to a virtually compulsory pay policy.

Wilson was also confronted with the divisive European issue. He had promised to renegotiate the terms of entry to the EEC and to submit them to a referendum as the best means to reconcile his divided party. He secured significant concessions in the negotiations and by a two-thirds majority the electorate endorsed Britain's membership of the Community.

In March 1976, Wilson unexpectedly resigned. After a total of eight years at 10 Downing Street trying to manoeuvre between the left and right of his party and the trade unions, he apparently lost his zest for politics. The economic crisis facing the country was the most severe since 1947. His hopes of regenerating British industry from the left had been dashed. But he had provided a steadying influence and in his way he had as unflappable an air as Macmillan. His administration bequeathed the National Enterprise Board, whose purpose was to stimulate growth in profitable new industry through government investment, in return for a share of the profits. The government had also established the British National Oil Corporation, taking a majority stake in it to ensure that the state would profit from the forthcoming bonanza of North Sea oil. But the extension of state intervention in industry was bitterly attacked by the Conservative opposition.

When James Callaghan took over the reins of government in April 1976 he found the Labour majority precarious and the country in deep economic trouble. He secured his parliamentary position by entering into a pact with the Liberal Party, allowing its leader David Steel to exercise a major influence on government legislation without entering the government itself. In this way Callaghan was able to soldier on until 1979.

Once more in the forefront of policy objectives was wage restraint, and fresh negotiations were held with the Trades Union Congress (TUC) in 1976. But in trying to maintain for too long sterling's dollar exchange rate, Britain faced a serious financial crisis in her balance of payments in 1976 and had to take a large loan from the International Monetary Fund on condition that cuts were made in public spending. The economy began to fare better, inflation came down to just below 16 per cent in 1977 and to 8 per cent in 1978, but unemployment stubbornly remained around 1.5 million (about 8 per cent). Working people had taken cuts in their living standards under successive phases of pay restraint; in the winter of 1978/9 pressure mounted to retrieve lost ground in past wage settlements. When Callaghan tried to bring down inflation further by announcing a wage-rise norm of 5 per cent, which would have entailed further cuts in living standards, there was widespread revolt. If Callaghan had gone to the country in the autumn of 1978 when the country appeared to be at last out of crisis and on a steady course, he might have won the election. The pervasive industrial unrest of what became known as the 'winter of discontent' destroyed his chance of victory. Even the grave-diggers struck. It seemed to working people that they were being called upon to 'solve' Britain's problems by depressing their living standards time and time again; a family man could not live on his wages but was forced to collect a whole range of state social benefits. The country was in a mess. Many blamed the unions, others the government.

Having lost the support of the Liberals and of the Scottish nationalists after the failure to push through devolution proposals for Scotland and Wales, the government was forced to hold a general election in May 1979 and was soundly defeated.

A new Conservative prime minister, Margaret Thatcher, who had ousted Heath as party leader in 1975, promised radical change. Like Heath she did not come from a privileged background, but was the proud daughter of a grocer; she was an example of what could be achieved in post-war Britain by hard work, courage and dedication. Describing herself as a 'conviction politician' whose policies and outlook were based on simple values, she gained the support not only of the middle classes but also of the working classes, especially among the skilled workers whose differentials had suffered. With the austere Sir Keith Joseph as her intellectual mentor, she promised to move away from the past compromises of Labour and Conservative, which had shifted the centre of politics constantly to the left.

The new policies were designed to allow market forces to improve Britain's competitiveness. State industries would be made so efficient that they could hold their own without subsidies from the taxpayers; once profitable, some of them would be sold back to private enterprise. The power of the trade unions would be curbed, and they would be made accountable both to their members and to the public. According to Conservative thinking, a better balance between employer and employee would in this way be restored. Individual responsibility and independence had to be encouraged; hard work and enterprise would once again reap their rewards. Direct taxation was reduced. A popular electoral move was to promise that council-house tenants would be able to buy their homes at a reduced price. Social benefits would be restricted to those who, through old age or sickness, were not able to help themselves; they would not be extended to the able-bodied striker for instance. The government would not finance its expenditure by printing money and so fuel inflation; sound money would be its watchword.

During Mrs Thatcher's first year in office, the election promise to honour pay awards led to widespread and substantial wage increases. This, together with the second oil-price rise of 1979–80, knocked the economy sideways, as inflation climbed to over 20 per cent. The government nevertheless carried out part of its programme by shifting the fiscal burden from direct to indirect taxation. The lowering of income tax, and the promise to reduce direct taxation further, proved an election winner over the next decade. The harsh deflation of 1980 and 1981, with a tightly controlled money supply and high interest rates, decimated British manufacturing industry and sent unemployment soaring to over 3 million. Full employment had ceased to be a priority of government policy. By the autumn of 1981, according to opinion polls Margaret Thatcher had become the most unpopular prime minister since Neville Chamberlain in 1940. But she now displayed what was to become her greatest electoral asset: she stuck to her policies. Within the government too she asserted her control, gradually ridding herself of 'wet' ministers – former prominent Heath supporters – and replacing them with loyal followers of her own views. To the country at large she declared that there was no other way to restore the patient to health.

The Labour opposition meanwhile was enfeebled by internal divisions between its militant left, the soft left and the right. Its drift to the left led in 1981 to the formation on the right of an entirely

new party, the Social Democratic Party, which later concluded an electoral pact with the Liberal Party, and the Alliance was born. For a time it appeared uncertain whether the Labour Party would survive as the main opposition. The split in the opposition electoral vote rendered Thatcher's Conservative government unbeatable for almost a decade, although the Conservative share of the vote never exceeded 44 per cent at the general elections of 1979, 1983 or 1987.

In April 1982 Britain was plunged into a most improbable conflict with Argentina. When the Argentinian junta invaded the Falklands islands, Margaret Thatcher did not hesitate. Regardless of the cost of defending a barren island with more sheep on it than people, a principle was at stake: Britain had to respond when her territory was attacked. The Falkland islanders were British and had rejected any form of Argentine sovereignty. If Britain allowed herself to be expelled by the Argentinians her credibility as a significant power would be gravely damaged. Unlike the Suez adventure, this was an enterprise that attracted overwhelming public support.

Just a year later, in June 1983, Margaret Thatcher fought her second election. Helped by the Falklands victory, and by the tough leadership she had displayed, the Conservatives won a landslide victory with a parliamentary majority of 188 over the Labour Party, whose share of the vote had sunk to 27.6 per cent. The Labour Party was severely handicapped by two issues: its promise to take Britain out of the European Community if elected, and its adherence to unilateral nuclear disarmament. The conservatives had a commanding majority of 144 over all other parties combined. The new Alliance, at this, its first test, was closely behind Labour, with 25.4 per cent of the vote, but the electoral system gave them only twenty-three MPs. The question remained open: would a three-party contest now become the norm, or would the Alliance or Labour emerge as the winners in a resumption of two-party politics?

Thatcher's second administration, from 1983 to 1987, saw no let-up in the attempt radically to reshape Britain's economy. Public expenditure and the budget deficit would be reduced. Privatisation of state-run industries would be accelerated: British Telecom, British Airways and British Gas provided a lucrative sales programme. The administration was cautious on defence, increasing expenditure

*The Argentinian disaster in the Falkland Islands.*

and supporting the American Cruise missile instal-lation on bases in Britain. Law and order and strengthening the police were also high on the list, while further restrictions were imposed on the unions in the Trade Union Reform Act. Even so, it was from the National Union of Miners, led by Arthur Scargill, that the government faced its most serious threat. The miners had brought down Heath; could they now bring down Thatcher, who was not only determined to curb the unions in general but ready to take on the miners? The new National Coal Board's head was Ian MacGregor, who had gained a reputation for ruthless efficiency by slimming down and rationalising the steel industry, in the process defeating the steel workers; his appointment to the NCB by the government persuaded the coal miners to strike for fear of pit closures and job losses. The strike began in March 1984 and ended in defeat for the miners a year later. In the course of it, there were many ugly confrontations between miners and police. But the government was fully prepared, with large coal stocks, and in any case the Nottingham and Derby miners refused to strike, so dooming the National Union of Miners to defeat. Despite a great deal of sympathy for the hardship suffered by the miners

and their families, there was little nationwide support for the leadership of the NUM or the trade union bosses.

The government's economic policies, however, continued to be heavily criticised. Unemployment rose to over 3 million, and spending cuts put the government at loggerheads with local authorities. Admiration for Thatcher's composure was again aroused in October 1984, this time after the IRA's bombing of the Grand Hotel in Brighton, where the Cabinet was staying during the Conservative Party Conference. But her personal style of leader-ship was also now meeting mounting criticism, culminating in January 1986 in the walkout from her Cabinet of the popular Defence Secretary Michael Heseltine. The rights and wrongs of their quarrel were less important than Heseltine's accusation that Margaret Thatcher no longer accepted the normal practices of Cabinet government, that her behaviour represented a breakdown of the constitutional process. These were the first warning signals that approval for strong leadership could turn into general resentment of 'bossiness' and 'nannying'. It was also noted that Thatcher had the irritating habit of referring to herself with a royal 'we'.

With an election approaching, public spending

restrictions were eased, a policy made more feasible by the rise in oil-tax revenues and by industrial growth since the low of 1981. Inflation had fallen from 11 per cent in 1981 to an average of 4.4 per cent in 1985–7, and wages for those in work rose much faster than inflation, while mortgage-holders benefited from low interest rates. Council-house sales proved very popular too. But unemployment, at over 3 million, remained stubbornly high, though government training measures had slightly reduced the total. Manufacturing industry had shrunk, and what remained was leaner and more productive; but the 2 million jobs lost added greatly to the numbers of the long-term unemployed.

In foreign affairs Thatcher was equally determined to make her views clearly known. She strongly supported NATO and the American alliance and established an especially close rapport with President Reagan, though that did not inhibit her from making strong protests when she thought he was wrong, as when the United States invaded Grenada in 1983 (page 738). But she permitted the use of US bases in Britain for the American attack on Libya in April 1986, because she regarded it as justified by Gaddafi's support for terrorism. She continued to show that she deserved the sobriquet 'Iron Lady', maintaining her robust opposition to all communist tyrannies. Yet she was the first world leader to recognise that Mikhail Gorbachev was a new phenomenon in Soviet leadership, a man with whom 'one could do business'. At the end of March 1987, she visited Moscow and had long talks with the Soviet President which helped to pave the way for the ending of the Cold War.

The future of the Crown colony of Hong Kong, much of whose territory would return to China in 1997, was another problem her administration tackled. To her it was a practical question of making the best deal possible. At the time of the negotiations in December 1984, China was in a reforming phase, and Britain appeared to have secured at least some safeguards, preserving for Hong Kong a high degree of autonomy (page 679).

Less happy were Thatcher's relations with the rest of the Commonwealth. She opposed any but innocuous sanctions against the *apartheid* policies of South Africa, arguing that they would harm the blacks more than the whites. This placed her in a minority of one. In Western Europe, too, she frequently found herself isolated. She was no friend of the Brussels bureaucracy and was inclined to

The 'Iron Lady' (British Prime Minister Margaret Thatcher) goes to Moscow, 29 March 1987.

resist the claims of the Commission to regulate in detail. As she saw it, she was not about to free Britons from Whitehall only to subordinate them to Brussels. She was a free-trader at heart, believing in the unhindered flow of world trade as the best guarantee of prosperity. Opposed to the interventionism of Brussels and in particular to the featherbedding of French and German farmers, she made unremitting efforts to reduce the cost of the Common Agricultural Policy, which kept food prices artificially high for the people in the Community, partly by accumulating butter mountains and wine lakes. But her tone was often strident and abrasive. It secured results over such issues as the reduction of Britain's excessive contribution to the common Community budget but was counter-productive in other ways. Mrs Thatcher was not regarded by her fellow EC leaders as a 'good European', yet she believed that the policies she pursued were right not only for Britain but for the Community as a whole.

When Margaret Thatcher decided to call her third general election in 1987, the majority in work were better off than ever before. The economy appeared to be progressing steadily and the opposition was split between the Alliance and the Labour Party. Since October 1983, the Labour Party had had a youthful new leader in Neil Kinnock, the son of a Welsh miner. Kinnock, who belonged to the moderate left, had succeeded in uniting the party once again but was handicapped by an electoral pledge to remove all nuclear weapons from Britain. On the nuclear defence issue, the Alliance was also in complete disarray. All three parties made use during the election campaign of slick advertising-agency promotion. Television and media consultants were pressed into the campaign as never before. For Labour, the red rose replaced the red flag. For the Conservatives, Thatcher was bathed in blue with golden hairdos of singular height. The Alliance sported a 'battle bus' vividly decorated with balloons. On polling day in June 1987, the Conservatives achieved almost the same level of support (42.3 per cent of the vote) as in 1983. For Labour and the Alliance the result was decisive: Labour had clearly seen off the Alliance's attempt to replace it (Labour gained 30.8 per cent of the vote and the Alliance dropped to 22.6 per cent). Thatcher's programme to change Britain would continue for a further term. Indeed, there seemed not the remotest possibility that she was even contemplating retirement. She declared that she was ready to go on to a fourth election victory and beyond.

Thatcher was determined to show that though this was her third administration there would be no loss of vigour, no retreat from the Thatcher revolution. The great state-run services – social security, the National Health Service and education – would be shaken up by the introduction of competition, to produce efficiency and responsiveness to the customer, and better value for the taxpayer. This was radical conservatism. Just as a radical Labour administration after 1945 had been ready to take on the establishment, so Mrs Thatcher relished doing the same: the British Medical Association, the National Union of Teachers, university vice-chancellors, lawyers and judges. Reforms were indeed highly desirable. Providing ever more funds was not the answer to dirty hospitals and cross-infection, to poor standards in many state schools, to a higher-education sector unwilling to increase student numbers without additional cash. But the public mood was changing; there was a feeling that it was time to consolidate. Thatcher's philosophy was hurting not only the idle, but also the poor. Benefits from reform were not seen to be coming through. Privatisation of a whole host of state enterprises from British Airways to the water authorities had lost its excitement and seemed only to be

making profits for investors.

The country was split between the rich south and the deprived manufacturing towns of the north. Entering the third industrial revolution, Britain was experiencing much painful readjustment; unemployment remained above the 2 million mark. Britain's industrial base had shrunk but was in a much more competitive position: that was the positive side. The Thatcher government's great achievement was the conquest of inflation – or was it?

The economy began to go wrong in 1988 after six years of unprecedented growth. After the stock-market fall (it was thought at the time to be a crash), the Chancellor of the Exchequer Nigel Lawson had eased money control too much; then in trying to keep sterling from rising too high and hurting exports, he over-compensated and pushed interest rates too low. Difficulties multiplied: the trade balance slipped, a tax-cutting budget in April 1988 proved not to be the right remedy. Income tax cuts had been the most popular strategy of the Thatcher governments, in large measure paid for by raising indirect taxes, reducing central government contributions to local authority spending and increasing National Insurance payments. The total tax burden had not in fact been reduced; and the wealthy benefited far more than the poor. Inflation began to rise again and interest rates also climbed to heights which hurt all homeowners with mortgages. An excessive house-price boom shuddered to a halt.

Pressured by Lawson and Howe, the Prime Minister agreed that Britain should soon join the European Exchange Rate Mechanism (ERM) when a number of conditions had been met. But in October 1989 Lawson resigned, complaining that Mrs Thatcher was undermining his stewardship of the economy by turning to an outside adviser. By then the Thatcher economic miracle was looking tarnished. But what spelt political doom for her was the ill-advised introduction of a new method of financing local government spending, the community charge, or 'poll tax' as it became universally known. If the total revenue the local authorities had to raise because of the declining central government contribution had not been generally so high, the measure might have attracted less odium. But it was seen as patently unfair that the lord in his manor was now paying less than a working-class family crowded into a council house.

During 1990 unease grew among the Conservative faithful. The party was deeply divided between Thatcher loyalists in an increasingly smaller majority and the sceptics who thought that, under Margaret Thatcher, the Conservatives would lose the next election, which could not be held later than 1992. When, in November 1990, Sir Geoffrey Howe became the third senior Conservative minister to resign from the Cabinet, in his case incensed by Thatcher's handling of relations with the European Community, she knew she had a real fight on her hands if she was to remain leader of the party. Although she gained a majority and almost made it on the first ballot, her majority under the party's rules was not quite large enough to assure her of outright victory. Her Cabinet colleagues now warned her that she would lose the second round to Michael Heseltine. On 22 November 1990 she resigned and threw her support behind John Major, the Chancellor of the Exchequer, in a determined bid to stop Heseltine. Major was elected and healed party divisions by immediately asking Heseltine to join the Cabinet.

The trend in Britain in the early 1990s, as in the United States, was to present a more caring social image. The Conservative Party had dropped the longest-serving prime minister in the twentieth century, winner of three elections. Despite obvious flaws as a politician, Margaret Thatcher succeeded in changing the course of British politics. When in 1979 she entered Downing Street it was by no means widely accepted that state socialism was a dismal failure – she altered the political agenda. An impoverished country, after all, cannot care for those in need. The right balance has to be struck between wealth-creation and the provision of health and social services for all those who have a right to expect it.

Fundamentally Thatcherism was about the rejection of socialism in all its manifestations, from the public ownership of industry to curing the problems of poverty through welfare. Margaret Thatcher destroyed trade union power and the cartel restrictions of labour, and poured scorn on the ideal that the care of the individual from 'cradle to grave' was the responsibility of society. She set out to stop the centre of politics swinging every few years a bit more to the left. In socialism's place she held out a different vision, of the able-bodied individuals being masters of their own fate, making their own provision instead of relying on a welfare state. Welfare was to be restricted to those who could

not help themselves. The British people were to recapture the spirit of enterprise, the urge to advance their own fortunes. Inequalities of wealth were to be welcomed, as a necessary consequence of motivation. Conservative governments would therefore lower direct taxation and seek to reduce government expenditure as a proportion of the country's wealth. They proclaimed that people should be able to spend their money themselves and not have the government spend it for them. The free-market economy was the way forward for the country, not state planning and intervention.

In practice many of Mrs Thatcher's policies were modified during the course of her own three administrations. The British people collectively were opposed to any significant tampering with free state education, social security and universal health provision. Spending for these sectors from 1978 to 1990 increased substantially to cope with high unemployment and an ageing population with growing expectations of care. The British on the whole are not given to ideological extremes. In the face of the electorate's suspicions of their aims, Conservative governments, including John Major's since 1990, have attempted through reorganisation and by creating an element of competition, to achieve better value for money in the state sector. Health treatment remains universally free for every patient, while the cost of medicines and ancillary services have been raised for wage-earners. Beveridge's vision of a welfare state is intact. British society has turned against Marxist economic organisation, but socialist ideals of equal opportunity, of a classless society, of progressive taxation, of help for the disadvantaged and the poor continue to permeate all political parties.

The enterprise culture had some successes for a time, especially in the establishment of a record number of small businesses. House ownership rose from just over half to 66 per cent of the population, the highest in Western Europe. The deep recession which began in 1990 dented these achievements, but the trend of increased home ownership over the decade continued. The same is true of small businesses, although a record number failed during the recession of the early 1990s.

Margaret Thatcher also succeeded in increasing inequality. The higher-rate tax of 40 per cent benefited most the very rich, who now paid the same marginal rate as the middle class. Living standards rose for all sections of the community, but unequally – the wealthiest 20 per cent gained by nearly a third, while the bottom 20 per cent secured only 1 per cent more income. The most negative impact of the Thatcher years was the absolute growth of long-term unemployment with real poverty more than trebling from 6 per cent to 19 per cent between 1979 and 1987. And as unemployment and poverty rose, so did crime. With unemployment over 2 million in 1990 and rising, and easy money having fuelled inflation, Thatcher left an unenviable legacy to her successor, John Major. As chancellor of the Exchequer, he had tried to remedy the inflationary policies of 1987 and 1988, when Nigel Lawson had held that post.

Margaret Thatcher's success has to be measured in terms of economic growth. After the recession of 1980–2 there was comparatively rapid growth until the recession that started in 1990, but manufacturing industry overall saw little expansion, in contrast to the experience of other developed nations. It was the service sector that took up some of the slack, helping to account for an increase in Gross Domestic Product of 27 per cent during the years from 1979 to 1990. In 1991 to 1992 output declined, and so lowered the average annual gain. Privatisation was one of the most striking features of the Thatcher years; no less remarkable were the increases in productivity and competitiveness of many industries, which thus came to match the best of Britain's Western neighbours. But the jury is out on privatised monopolies or near-monopolies such as telephones, gas and water and how far their new status benefits the consumer.

Detailed economic and social statistics reveal the uneven successes of the Thatcher years. Trade union power had been reined back, but mobility of labour was still hindered by lack of technical training and by the differentials in housing costs between regions of high and low unemployment. London became unaffordable for the working man from Liverpool, and the quantity of rented accommodation and council houses drastically diminished. Thatcher succeeded in changing the debate within British politics. It was the Conservatives who now forced Labour to move away from certain socialist tenets, such as nationalisation. But John Major, in espousing the classless society stole some of the socialist clothing.

Under Neil Kinnock's leadership the Labour Party entered the April 1992 election with a firmly pro-European Community policy. With the aban-

donment of both unilateral nuclear disarmament and nationalisation, the main socialist plank was the proposal to redistribute taxes so that they fell more heavily on the upper-income groups. This proved to be one reason why Labour lost the election, the voters fearing that in the end the rich would not be the only losers. They were above all concerned with financial prudence, to safeguard their employment and reduce the cost of their mortgages. Redistribution to the poor was not their first priority. There is some parallel here with the United States (page 833).

The post-Thatcher years of British politics were different in style. John Major projected an image of someone who understood the needs of ordinary men and women. Much was made of the fact that he had climbed the social ladder the hard way, and that in his younger years he had experienced unemployment. He immediately began by rectifying the poll-tax disaster, which he and Nigel Lawson (then Chancellor of the Exchequer) had opposed when its introduction was debated in the Cabinet in 1987 and 1988. It was replaced in 1993 with a modified property tax. Poll-tax burdens meanwhile were softened by additional government grants to local authorities paid by a rise in VAT. The Major government, with Norman Lamont continuing as chancellor of the Exchequer, braved the unpopularity after 1990 of having to squeeze inflation once more out of the system by raising interest rates and keeping them high. Britain had entered the European Community Exchange Rate Mechanism (ERM) at a relatively high exchange rate in October 1990, in the hope that this also would bear down on inflation. The fierce squeeze led to rising unemployment again and to an unprecedented drop in house prices after the boom of the late 1980s. This was intended to allow an early end to the recession so that the next election in the early 1990s could be fought with lower interest rates, sound money, a strong economy and a return of confidence.

Norman Lamont began to talk about green shoots of recovery in the summer of 1991, but by the spring of 1992 no recovery had appeared. Thus the Conservatives were left fighting the election in April 1992 in the midst of a recession. The pundits said that the Conservatives would do well just to remain the largest party, with the Liberal Democrats holding the balance and Labour not far behind the Conservatives. It was even possible that Labour would win outright. When all was gloom around him John Major fought an upbeat election campaign, projecting once again a reasonable and likeable personality, the sort of man you can trust. Neil Kinnock, the Labour leader, who had done so much to reunite his party, to expel the militant extremists and to convey a moderate, caring outlook, also campaigned with warmth and verve. But to overturn the huge Conservative majority was a mountain no party had successfully climbed before. When the results of the 9 April election were in, Labour had made large gains but not enough to become the party of government. Surprisingly, the total Conservative vote had not fallen from the number cast for Margaret Thatcher in 1987.

**Parliamentary Elections, 1987 and 1992**

|  | 1987 | | 1992 | |
|---|---|---|---|---|
|  | % | Seats | % | Seats |
| Conservatives | 42.2 | 376 | 41.8 | 336 |
| Labour | 30.8 | 229 | 34.2 | 271 |
| Liberal Democrats | 22.6 | 22 | 27.9 | 20 |

The Liberal Democrats' hopes of forcing through a system of proportional representation were dashed. Neil Kinnock's leadership was over. The new Conservative government expected a long period of political stability.

John Major's Cabinet made it a priority to cure the economy once and for all by reducing inflation to the same low levels as prevailed in France and Germany. The discipline of the ERM with its fixed exchange rates and resulting low pay awards was among the weapons. At the Maastricht summit in December 1991 Major scored a personal triumph in securing for Britain the special terms she wanted. At home after a short period of pain Britain was expected to move out of her longest recession since the war. Inflation came down sharply in 1992, but unemployment continued to rise. The green shoots of recovery had long ago withered and the landscape remained as desolate as before.

The Labour Party in July 1992 under the leadership of the newly elected John Smith gained greater credence by calling for a change of policy. Everyone blamed the Germans, who were financing east German recovery by spending money the government did not have instead of substantially raising

taxes. The result was high interest rates in Germany and misery all around. But Britain's ills ran deeper. Major with his winning personality and nice smile was elected as a less formidable and more flexible replacement for the Iron Lady.

But in economic policy Major attempted to act as the Iron Man. Britain, he declared, would play a role at the 'heart' of Europe. At the centre of the government's policy for defeating inflation and making Britain fully competitive was the decision to link the pound with the least inflationary currency in Europe, the German Mark, through the ERM at a fixed rate of exchange. In September 1992 John Major faced a humiliating retreat. The exchange rate could be held no longer and Britain left the ERM. In practice this led to the devaluation of the pound. It was a political disaster of a magnitude few governments since the war had suffered. The credibility of the Prime Minister, of the Chancellor of the Exchequer and indeed of the whole government was damaged. The issue of closer ties with Europe, of moving towards political and financial union by the end of the century, had already split the Conservative and Labour Parties. But a majority in both had favoured the moves towards this goal embodied in the Maastricht Treaty. Now the anti-Maastricht groups in both parties took heart from the débâcle. It had become clear, and the narrow victory for ratification in France confirmed it, that there were many people throughout Europe who felt deep misgivings about European union and the loss of national sovereignty. Attitudes were hardening against the Conservative government and its whole European strategy.

At home, October 1992 proved another disastrous month for the Prime Minister and his Cabinet. The announcement that thirty-one pits were to be closed and thousands of miners left without work, albeit with some compensation, caused widespread anger well beyond the mining communities. Facing defeat in the House of Commons the government had to draw back. The loss of contact with public feeling, the continuing recession and unemployment rising towards 3 million, more than one in ten of the workforce, brought the public approval rating of the government to a new low. Most damagingly, John Major's leadership and good judgement were being widely questioned. Rarely had a government's fortunes been so quickly reversed after an election victory.

There were close parallels between Reaganomics

and the conduct of the economic policies followed by the conservatives. These parallels included a rising budget deficit as the costs of unemployment increased while tax revenue fell during the years of recession, the longest since the war. House prices dropped steeply, the overhang of the personal credit binge of the 1980's which had showered plastic cards on virtually everyone, and the continuing threat of unemployment undermined the confidence of the man in the street to spend money on anything other than necessities. In 1993 a shift in economic policy had become unavoidable. The number one problem was now unemployment which once again was three million. Special statistical measures and government training schemes disguised the true total which was much higher. This time it affected not just the midland and northern industrial regions but also the conservative heartlands of London, eastern and southern England. The pendulum of economic and social policies was swinging back from 'less government' to the need for more intervention and assistance. Thatcherite conservatism proved to be no more the last word in British politics than Reagonomics was in the United States.

# CHAPTER 85

# The Revival of France

After the high drama of the de Gaulle years, President Georges Pompidou restored calm to France. Pompidou had been closely associated with de Gaulle and had served as his prime minister until the General dismissed him in July 1968. After de Gaulle's resignation in 1969, Pompidou returned to power as his successor. A cautious conservative, Pompidou was nevertheless ready to embark on reforms designed to ease social and regional tensions. His succession to the presidency promised continuity without de Gaulle's autocratic style of government. He was approachable, a symbol of the good life that France provided for her more fortunate citizens. With a background in finance, Pompidou had served as a director of the merchant bank Rothschild Frères. The healing of France's divisions, the President believed, would best be served by putting France once more on the road to prosperity.

An austerity programme that was set in motion in 1969, the devaluation of the franc and a loan from the International Monetary Fund, realistic steps which de Gaulle would have rejected as a slur on French nationalism, provided the springboard for future expansion. But they also provoked a rash of strikes in 1969. In France the archaic and the modern had continued to exist side by side: the small peasant farmer and the large landholder, the department store and multitudes of small shopkeepers, technologically advanced industries and artisans. Exports lagged behind those of other countries – much of French industry was not competitive.

The Sixth Plan set out to modernise France more rapidly by opening her to international competition. It gave priority to industrial development, but gave less scope to central control than previous plans. Pompidou's liberal, free-market approach achieved good results. Until the oil shock of 1973–4, Pompidou helped to accelerate industrialisation, now stimulated by world demand for French goods. The Gross Domestic Product between 1969 and 1973 grew by an annual average of 5.6 per cent, while inflation was contained and unemployment kept low.

As industry became competitive once more in world markets, Pompidou cleverly cushioned French farmers, who could not be competitive. In return for agreeing to abandon de Gaulle's veto on Britain's entry to the EEC, he secured a good deal for France's farmers from her Common Market partners.

Apart from a softer style and a great improvement in Anglo-French relations, France's fundamentally nationalist and independent outlook did not change much in foreign affairs. The pursuit of a European option and of detente with the Soviet Union and the Eastern bloc was only temporarily successful, and not of any lasting consequence. Nor did the more friendly Gaullist policies towards the Arab states save France from the huge oil-price rises which the Arab oil-exporting countries imposed on the rest of the world after the outbreak of the Arab–Israeli War in October 1973.

Pompidou's first prime minister, Jacques

Chaban-Delmas, wanted a more radical programme, a Kennedy-style 'new society', but was able to win the President's consent only to limited reforms. Decentralisation and co-operation between the modern and the traditional sectors of French industry and commerce were furthered in 1969 by creating local commissions and elected chambers of commerce and industry. Indirectly elected regional bodies, created in 1972, to oversee regional development were another half-hearted attempt to broaden participation at the local level. None of these reforms went far enough and Pompidou's last year in office before he died of cancer in April 1974 saw a decline in the economy and in July 1972 the replacement of Chaban-Delmas by the more conservative Pierre Messmer.

French politics were not a straightforward two- or three-party contest, as in Britain and the Federal Republic of Germany. The success of a dominant coalition depended on manoeuvring by the main parties, not least among groups further to their right or left. Two groups made up the right–centre coalition. First were the Gaullists, known after 1968 as the Union Démocrats pour la République (UDR). Many of the UDR's prominent members were powerful former Gaullist resistance leaders, who had accepted de Gaulle's leadership and his emphasis on French independence and nationalism. On other economic and social issues, however, they differed widely, so as soon as the recognised leader, de Gaulle, and his accepted heir, Pompidou, had departed, their cohesion became fragile. They had also inherited the Gaullist tradition of lax discipline, which made their continued cohesion after 1974 even more problematical when the more powerful politicians contested the leadership. Though in decline after 1968, and more so after 1973, they still formed the majority in the coalition of the right.

The other party of the right–centre coalition had been founded by Pompidou's Minister of Finance, Valéry Giscard d'Estaing. More liberal than the UDR, closer to the social-market views of the West German CDU, the Independent Republican Party (RP) was also less nationalistic, more open to European co-operation and more in favour of the American alliance. The excitement aroused by French politics in the 1970s and 1980s was therefore as much due to the rivalries within the right–centre coalition as to its contest with the socialists.

On the left, the traditional division between the political parties and the trade unions dated back all the way to the Tours Congress of 1920, at which they had split. The post-war French Communist Party (PCF) modelled itself closely on its bigger Soviet brother and was loyal to Moscow; but it had in its way become a conservative force too, and was careful to have nothing to do with the students' revolutionary tactics in 1968. It took a more demo-cratic stance in the 1970s and for a time, from 1972 to 1977, once more accepted the popular-front electoral alliance with the Socialist Party, after being wooed by François Mitterrand, the wily Socialist Party leader. But the PCF's rapid decline after 1978 (in the election of 1986 it gained only thirty-five seats, no more than the extreme-right National Front) has effected a radical change in French politics.

The Socialist Party, before 1971 a creature of the centre as much as of the left, had also precipitously lost support. When François Mitterrand became its leader, he undertook to revive it with a more democratic socialist-oriented programme of nationalisation, worker control and decentralisation. He also espoused a reduction of presidential govern-ment, in line with his bitter attacks on de Gaulle's autocratic style. Most important in laying the foun-dation for his eventual triumph in ending the twenty-three-year run of right–centre coalitions was his success in securing the agreement of the Communists to a Common Programme of govern-ment. To this coalition were added other groups, including the new Radical Movement of the Left (MRE). In the presidential elections of 1974 Mitter-rand came close to defeating the man who had finally emerged as the right–centre coalition's presidential candidate, Giscard d'Estaing.

Though Giscard had beaten off a Gaullist chal-lenge in the first ballot of the elections for the presidency, before going on to beat Mitterrand by a whisker, the Gaullists in the National Assembly were not only the largest party but they had more than three times as many seats as Giscard's RP party. Ever since he had broken away from de Gaulle in 1962, Giscard's relations with the Gaullists had been characterised by opposition as much as by co-operation. Yet co-operation between the Gaul-lists and the RP was essential if they were to beat off the combined forces of the left. So Giscard set out to strengthen his government by drawing his ministers from a broad coalition of the right and centre with Jacques Chirac, a Gaullist UDR leader, as prime minister. The intensely ambitious Chirac had, like Giscard, served Pompidou as a minister, but he felt no sympathy for much of Giscard's liberal reforming zeal, nor for his European outlook. Chirac's power base was the UDR, whose influence Giscard was attempting to erode by creating a broad coalition of the right and centre. Giscard, who to begin with had cordially refrained from presidential interference in government affairs, was soon clashing with Chirac over control of policies. But their co-operation in 1974 and 1975 saw the passage of important reforms.

Giscard projected himself as a popular people's president, modelling his fireside television chats on those of Franklin Roosevelt, in an attempt to overcome his elitist disdain for the people. But his desire for a more liberal, modern and just society was both strong and sincere. He was sympathetic to the assertion of women's rights and a number of laws were passed in 1974 and 1975 to help achieve equality of the sexes; greater benefits were allowed to single parents; abortion was legalised; and divorce was made easier if it was mutually desired or if the marriage had broken down. Health programmes received large additional funds. The poorest were helped by increases in the minimum wage, and Giscard also showed his concern for the lot of the immigrants from North Africa. Excessive state controls and administrative intrusions into private lives, such as telephone tapping, were restricted.

These liberal reforms met with much opposition from the Gaullists in the National Assembly and passed only with the help of the left. It was clear to Chirac that his association with these Giscard-inspired policies was bound to alienate him from the Gaullist UDR. His break with the President came in August 1976, when he resigned in protest against Giscard's interference in government and his increasing reliance on his own Élysée staff. The differences between them on social and foreign policies, with Giscard more intent on strengthening Western European co-operation and the institutions of the European Community, were real and deep. And of course an independent Chirac was in a better position to build up a political power base to displace Giscard when the time came. Without Chirac's help, however, Giscard's efforts after 1976 to push through further social reforms were largely frustrated.

On the economic front Giscard was unfortunate to be in office during the difficult 1970s, when the shocks of increasing oil prices in 1973–4 and 1979–

80 seriously damaged world trade. Nothing like this had happened before and governments in the West were uncertain how best to adjust economic policy. Giscard began in 1974 with a policy of austerity and deflation. Industrial production dropped and unemployment rose to 1 million. Then, in the characteristic stop–go pattern of the time, the policy was reversed in 1975 to counteract the recession. The result was inflation and higher wages, which led to an increase in imports and a deteriorating balance of trade. Chirac's successor as prime minister in 1976 was Raymond Barre, who also held the post of finance minister. Barre did not come from the ranks of National Assembly politicians, but was economics professor at the Sorbonne and later vice-president of the European Commission – a background reminiscent of the highly successful German Finance Minister of the 1950s, Ludwig Erhard. Indeed, Barre took the German free-market economy, with its minimum of government regulation, as his own model.

The Barre Plan began with savage austerity, which reduced inflation rapidly but inevitably increased unemployment. This was followed in 1978 by a step-by-step programme to free industry from state regulations and directions. But much tighter controls were exerted over state-sector industries: their subsidies were reduced and industries in trouble were no longer bailed out. The state, however, still directly oversaw the planning of what Giscard and Barre regarded as key sectors of industry. And because the dependence on imported oil had revealed an energy weakness, France embarked on a massive expansion of her nuclear-power resources, the most ambitious programme in Europe. The national budget ceased to be planned with large deficits and continuous devaluation of the franc was no longer taken as the easy option out. The Barre Plan was starting to work in 1978 and early 1979, with a favourable trade balance, growth of industrial output, a stable exchange rate and reduced inflation, but the new Middle Eastern turmoil and the second oil-price rise threw the economy off course. Inflation and unemployment rose; France was sliding again into recession. The second dose of Barre's medicine of deflation, which caused a further rise in unemployment, coincided in May 1981 with the presidential elections.

Politically, May 1981 marked a turning point in French politics: the Socialists finally made the breakthrough and captured not only the presidency but, a month later, a majority in the National Assembly elections as well. François Mitterrand had beaten his rivals to the nomination and put forward a programme designed to attract a combined left vote including that of the communists. He presented a socialist manifesto which promised to reduce unemployment, extend nationalisation, raise minimum wages, impose a tax on wealth and carry through constitutional reforms to reduce the power of an autocratic presidency, which Giscard had been accused of exploiting. The communist leader, Georges Marchais, had contested the first ballot of the presidential elections, but he had had to drop out after failing to gain first or second place, whereupon he had placed his weight behind the remaining socialist candidate Mitterrand in the run-off election.

On the right, President Giscard had beaten off the challenge for the nomination from Jacques Chirac, who led the substantial Gaullist wing of the right coalition. In the second ballot, defections from traditional supporters of the right who were antagonised by Giscard's haughty presidential style, and attracted by Mitterrand's promise to reverse the economic austerity programme, as well as the backing of communist voters, gave Mitterrand a small but decisive majority over Giscard, of 15.7 million votes to 14.6 million.

### National Assembly Election, 1981

|            | %    | Seats |
|------------|------|-------|
| PS and MRG | 37.8 | 286   |
| PC         | 16.1 | 44    |
| RPR        | 20.9 | 83    |
| UDF        | 19.1 | 61    |

The surprise of the National Assembly elections which Mitterrand called in June was the large increase in support for the Socialist Party. The Communist Party lost further ground. With communist support in the National Assembly, Mitterrand commanded a substantial majority. The spectacular decline of Giscard's UDF gave leadership of the combined opposition on the right to the hard-driving but not always predictable Chirac, who was distrusted by the UDF. Thus the right was in considerable disarray.

Mitterrand's honeymoon lasted just over a year.

To maintain the broad support of the left and centre, he included in his government adherents from all groups. For the first time since 1947, four communist ministers were brought into the administration. Michel Rocard as minister for planning represented the market-oriented right wing of the Socialist Party and Prime Minister Pierre Mauroy the traditional socialist soft left. The government passed legislation to strengthen civil liberties, a continuation of the efforts earlier made by Giscard. Mitterrand's electoral promises of taxes on wealth and the raising of minimum wages and welfare payments were fulfilled. Decentralisation, the Deferre Law, gave more power to elected regional councils, while the role of the centrally appointed prefects was reduced. This shifted the balance of control and local government significantly, not that central government was ready to give up its overall controlling power. A large-scale nationalisation programme was another pillar of Mitterrand's rigorous socialist programme. The nationalisation of leading armaments, metallurgical, electrical, computer, chemical, pharmaceutical and insurance companies and banks still in private hands brought almost a third of all industry into public ownership. (Less than 20 per cent had been in public ownership before 1982.)

The most spectacular part of the Mitterrand programme was the attempt to counter the world-wide recession caused by the oil-price rise with a 'socialist' solution: a dash for growth that reversed the Barre austerity plan. Many people in Britain at that time, suffering from the sharp retrenchment of Margaret Thatcher's Conservative government, which cut a swathe through manufacturing industry, looked with admiration on the bold Mitterrand strategy. The 'recovery plan' pumped money into the French economy, created jobs in housebuilding and the civil service, raised the income of the poorest in society and increased investment in the public sector. It was accepted that higher taxes would not pay for this as well as for nationalisation, but it was argued that in a recession a large deficit was acceptable until higher demand expanded the economy again and brought the deficit down.

It did not work. Unemployment rose to 2 million and inflation soared once more above 15 per cent in October 1981; the deficit forced a devaluation of the franc, and the lack of confidence private industry felt for the Socialist government showed up in a shortage of investment and production.

In June 1982 Mitterrand made his famous policy U-turn and switched to austerity and public-spending cuts proposed by the Finance Minister Jacques Delors. Public spending was further curtailed in the spring of 1983. Socialist reforms were downgraded in July 1984, when the able young Industry Minister, the undogmatic, technocrat Laurent Fabius, replaced Mauroy as prime minister. The policy turned to the centre, towards market-oriented reforms and industrial modernisation. Not surprisingly the communist ministers resigned. The French economy recovered, thanks to the application of policies not so very different from those of the Giscard–Barre years. Higher productivity had high unemployment as its trade-off, as it had in the rest of Western Europe. Mitterrand accepted the price of unpopularity in the expectation that an upturn would follow the austerity of 1984–6 in good time for the presidential elections due in 1988. In an effort to improve the chances of the Socialists, whose popularity was plummeting, he pushed through an electoral reform, changing from a 'first past the post' system to proportional representation.

The National Assembly elections in March 1986 turned out better than expected for the Socialists, who remained the largest party, picking up much support from former communist supporters. The Communist Party fared disastrously, losing a third of its votes. The broad-left coalition (including the communists), had it been reconstructed, could command only 251 votes. The right, despite the rivalries between Giscard's UDF and Chirac's RPR, enjoyed a clear majority with 277 votes. What caused a real shock to traditional French politics was the rise of a fascist National Front party led by the barnstorming ex-paratrooper Jean-Marie Le Pen. Almost one in ten voters had voted for this racist, anti-Semitic party, turning their backs on the traditional parties and placing their confidence in a leader who in the name of 'patriotism' attacked the North African immigrants as foreigners who caused white unemployment. Le Pen promised to bring law and order back to France. The immigrants would be forcibly repatriated.

After the elections, the Fifth Republic found herself in an unprecedented condition, with a Socialist president and a National Assembly dominated by the right. Unlike the government of the United States, where the executive president and those he appoints to his administration are separated from

### National Assembly Election, 1986

|  | % | Seats |
|---|---|---|
| PS and MRG | 31.9 | 216 |
| PC | 9.7 | 35 |
| UDF | 42.0 | 129 |
| RPR |  | 148 |
| National Front | 9.7 | 35 |

Congress, the government of France is appointed by the president, but in order to function it must command a majority in the National Assembly.

In March 1986, Mitterrand called on Jacques Chirac, who headed the largest of the parties of the right, to form a government. Chirac did not have an easy task, for ever looking over his shoulder at the Giscard party in the National Assembly, whose members disliked him intensely; they were nevertheless an indispensable part of his majority. He also had in the Élysée a Socialist as his president. The French found a witty way to describe his predicament – cohabitation. Chirac found no room in the government for Giscard, who had hoped to return to the Finance Ministry. Thus, from the start, Chirac exposed himself not only to the opposition of the left but also to jealousy from the UDF, which was largely excluded from power. Part of Chirac's economic recovery programme was not so different from that of the outgoing Socialist government. But there was bound to be a clash over his determination to privatise and denationalise state-owned companies. Though the President tried, he could not stop the privatisations receiving the assent of the National Assembly. Chirac also reversed the system of proportional representation, to which the National Front had owed their spectacular breakthrough nationally. With a return to 'first past the post', the National Front could not hope to gain many seats.

The cutbacks imposed by the government were not popular. In December 1986 a long rail strike paralysed the French railways for nearly a month. Strikes spread in January 1987 in the public sector and Chirac was forced to compromise on pay and conditions. During the period from 1986 to 1988, inflation, however, fell to between 2 and 3 per cent.

Mitterrand was able cleverly to project an image of standing above the parties and so escaped blame for the government's policies. His message was that he represented a solid rallying point for the nation. Meanwhile, students and universities seethed in protest and unemployment remained above 2.5 million. Chirac accused Mitterrand of excessive presidential interference in government. The farmers, once protected by the right, have since the 1980s had to face reductions in subsidies, increased competition and generally harder times. As a 'statesman', Mitterrand maintained a high profile in foreign affairs, in particular playing a leading role at the European Community summits. He also cultivated close relations with the West German Chancellor Helmut Kohl, thus strengthening the Bonn–Paris axis; his relations with Margaret Thatcher, on the other hand, were formal and cool. Mitterrand was just as firm as his predecessors in maintaining France's independent nuclear strike force.

When the time came for the presidential election in the spring of 1988, Mitterrand easily led the first ballot amid nine contenders; Chirac came second. The real shock was that Le Pen had secured over 4 million votes, 14.4 per cent of the votes, running fourth only just behind the respected and popular Barre. The second-ballot run-off was a foregone conclusion, with Mitterrand substantially increasing his percentage share of the votes, attaining 54 per cent to Chirac's 46 per cent (16.7 million votes to 14.2 million). Chirac resigned the premiership and Mitterrand chose the undogmatic market-oriented Michel Rocard as his successor. He then dissolved the National Assembly.

The Socialists had scored a great success, though after the second round of voting for the National

### National Assembly Election, First Round, June 1988

|  | % | Seats |
|---|---|---|
| PS, MRG and affiliated parties | 37.60 | 277 |
| PC | 11.32 | 27 |
| UDF | 37.75 | 130 |
| RPR | | 129 |
| National Front | 9.65 | 0 |
| Other parties of the right | 2.85 | 13 |

Assembly they did not obtain an overall majority, achieving with their affiliated parties 276 seats. In fact, the broad left and right coalitions were fairly evenly divided. With the National Front reduced to one seat thanks to the abandonment of proportional representation, with the communists unlikely to vote with the right, and with the right divided, the centrist Socialist Prime Minister, Rocard, enjoyed comfortable majorities when voting took place in the Assembly. Rocard, who emphasised consensus in politics, was dull compared to Laurent Fabius. He had no grand plans, but he laid stress on solid achievement and won public approval because most people were tired of the right–left confrontations. The economy continued on a 'virtuous' path, with a good rate of growth and low inflation. The Rocard government did not alarm private industry and Mitterrand was clearly steering a more central political course. But a tight control over public sector pay led to renewed strikes in the closing years of the 1980s.

Financial rectitude was accompanied by close on 10 per cent unemployment, which stubbornly persisted into the 1990s. Mitterrand's France was beset by a political malaise. The Socialist Party suffered from the deepening unpopularity of the President, though he had long ceased to follow traditional socialist policies. Meanwhile, rivalry and friction between Chirac and Valéry Giscard d'Estaing tarnished the appeal of the right. Mitterrand hoped that replacing Rocard with Mme Edith Cresson as prime minister would restore the fortunes of the socialist government. But her approval rating sank fast. Essentially, economic policy had not changed and there were no signs of an expansion sufficiently strong to absorb the unemployed.

The issue that provoked most heat was the position of the North African migrants. Jean-Marie Le Pen's National Front based its strong support largely on this widespread hostility to Arab migrants, a community mainly poor and concentrated in a few cities like Marseilles and Paris. In 1991 official figures estimated that 4 million migrants, mainly Muslim Arabs from North Africa, lived in France. Their birthrate is high and about 1 million children have been left out of this census. Racism also extended to a renewal of anti-Semitism among the National Front, which managed to seem the only really dynamic party in a stagnant political scene. In regional elections in March 1992 the Socialist

Party gained only 2 per cent more votes than the National Front (at 14 per cent). In April 1992, after less than a year, Mme Cresson was replaced as prime minister by Pierre Bérégovoy.

The deep malaise in politics was also reflected in the uncertainty over where France should be heading in the 1990s. Once the enthusiastic founding partners of the new Europe in close alliance with the Germans, the French people were deeply divided in September 1992 when asked to approve the Maastricht Treaty (page 882). The 'yes' vote was only just sufficient, and many people had voted in favour not out of a feeling of enthusiasm for Europe but rather for negative reasons. There was a widespread fear of the newly united Germany of 79 million. By a small margin the French people decided that it was safer to keep Germany hemmed in by European institutions, despite her preponderant weight in such a union, instead of leaving France to face an unfettered German colossus alone. But the biggest issue in France in 1993 was the continued recession and unemployment. At the elections for the National Assembly in March 1993 the socialists (in power for twelve years) were swept out of office. The electoral system exaggerated the swing of seats. The socialists lost 212 seats and were left with 70. Chirac's RPR now occupied 247 and Giscard d'Estaing's UDF 213, the communists fell 3 to 23, the National Front lost their only seat. Thus the right has an overwhelming majority in the 577 strong Assembly. Mitterrand chose Edouard Balladur of the RPR as the new prime minister for a new period of *cohabitation*. But the French people and the two rival aspirants, Giscard d'Estaing and Chirac, are waiting for the presidential elections and a chance to unseat Mitterrand himself.

# CHAPTER 86

# The European Community

In the European Community agreement on common goals has frequently been reached only after long-drawn-out negotiations and carefully cobbled-together compromises. But the original aim of the 1957 Treaty of Rome – that all obstacles which impeded the free movement of goods, capital and services, such as insurance and banking, within the Community of 360 million people should be lifted – had still not been entirely met in the early 1990s. The Europe of the twelve members of the Community was still fissured by customs frontiers and blocked by mountains of paper forms as well as hidden obstructions. Nevertheless, the three major continental West European nations – Germany, France and Italy – backed the drive for closer union. Britain was more reluctant to hand over control to the Commission in Brussels, whose president from 1985 was the former French Minister of Finance, Jacques Delors. Margaret Thatcher stood at the forefront of those who believed that to elevate the Commission as the ultimate source of power would be profoundly undemocratic and that the European Parliament was too weak to play the role of existing national parliaments.

Which direction the European Community took depended on the decisions reached by the heads of government of its member states. It had always been so and essentially it remained so in the early 1990s. This was not the intention of the founding fathers, who wanted to move towards the closer integration of Western Europe. They laid down that, after an early stage during which unanimity would be required in the Council of Ministers, the 'qualified majority' voting formula would come into play. This meant that if France, Germany and Italy were agreed, the other three original members – Netherlands, Belgium and Luxembourg – would be outvoted. Moreover, the three smaller powers acting together would not achieve enough votes to get a measure passed unless they could gain the agreement of at least two of the other three. In other words, neither Germany, France nor Italy had enough voting power on her own to veto a decision all the others were agreed upon. De Gaulle scuppered any such notion of diminished sovereignty in 1965: he boycotted the Community for seven months and returned only when the so-called Luxembourg Compromise was agreed on in January 1966. This gave each member the right to veto any decision affecting her vital national interests – and the interpretation of 'vital national interests' was left to the member state and could include such matters as the price of barley.

The successive enlargements of the European Community have altered the mechanics of 'qualified majority' voting, but the national veto was still in place in the early 1990s. The periodic summit meetings of the heads of government – accompanied, since 1974, by their foreign ministers – was given the formal name of European Council. They convene three times a year, and their decisions set the guidelines. At the Council of Ministers, more detailed agreements are reached. The European Commission of civil servant under the president and his 'cabinet' of sixteen nationally appointed commissioners also has a powerful influence. It can initiate proposals and then draw up amendments, but these require the consent of the Council of Ministers, who in turn take their instructions from their national governments. The European Parliament, directly elected for the first time in 1979, has the power to dismiss the Commission but not to appoint one. Its day-to-day powers are limited; it is a consultative rather than a legislative parliament. There is also a court of justice.

The Single European Act of 1987 limited the use of the national veto by requiring that qualified majority voting should be substituted for unanimity in a number of important areas concerned with the creation of a common market. But the national veto was still applicable in other areas.

A chronic Community problem centres around the budget, which is contributed by member nations. The main difficulty was the costly Common Agricultural Policy (CAP), which absorbed two-thirds of total expenditure; a temporary difficulty was the implementation of a 1980 undertaking to reduce Britain's excessive net contribution, which arose because with her small farming sector she received relatively little in the form of CAP subsidies. Since she was one of the poorer countries in the EC, this was patently unfair. Margaret Thatcher insisted in 1983 that the British government would not sanction any increase in the Community's financial resources unless a long-term solution was reached to replace the annual haggling.

In many ways Margaret Thatcher was out of tune with the 'continental' style of the Community, which Britain had entered too late. She abhorred the Brussels bureaucracy and its pettifogging regulations; she opposed the protectionist stance which the EC adopted towards world trade; above all she attacked the absurdities of the CAP, which on the one hand created huge and expensive butter mountains and wine lakes to subsidise the farmers out of taxation raised in member states, and on the other increased EC food prices above world prices generally. A free-trader by conviction, what she did support was the removal of trade barriers between member states. But she remained profoundly suspicious of closer political union. The European Community institutions are undemocratic, and the one democratically elected body, the European Parliament, lacks real power. In any case, Thatcher was not ready to allow European institutions to

override the 700-year-old Parliament at Westminster. She regarded democracy and parliamentary institutions on the continent as too recently established and not rooted in tradition, as they were in Britain. What is more she feared the overwhelming influence Germany would be able to exert in a politically and economically unified Community. All these views she expressed with a passion and directness that made her seem the outsider, even when others might secretly agree with her.

Despite much acrimony and despite often giving an impression of immobility the Community tends to acquire sudden forward movement when continuing crisis threatens its credibility. At the Fontainbleau summit in June 1984, agreement on the principal bones of contention was reached: the British obtained the long-term settlement of their budget contribution and the Community's resources were increased by undertakings to raise the level of Value Added Tax. In a move which was to prove of great significance in the 1990s, the European Parliament in 1984 adopted a report calling for a new treaty to create a European political union.

Much wrangling in 1985 was settled in December at the Luxembourg summit when it was agreed in principle to adopt a Single European Act. This comprised two separate parts, one establishing a treaty for political co-operation, and the other amending the Treaty of Rome to remove all existing obstacles to a free internal market by the end of 1992, thus making the original vision of a common market a reality. Clearly the two parts, 'politics' and 'trade', could move forward at entirely different speeds. It was a far cry from the European union which a majority in the European Parliament wanted – though, as we have seen, the Act also provided for an extension of qualified majority voting.

The dynamic but frequently tactless Jacques Delors, Commission president, had little success in persuading Margaret Thatcher to agree to an increase in the powers of the Commission or to support the closer political integration of the EC members. For her part, Thatcher took the lead in demanding reform of the CAP, though this made slow progress. But in 1987 the Single European Act was ratified by national governments and finally adopted. The Community also accepted compromises on the budget on the basis of proposals put forward by Delors, which involved gradual reductions in the proportion spent on agriculture. Further cuts were in prospect if production of specified agricultural produce exceeded set ceilings.

As the decade drew to a close, the differences between Britain and the rest of the Community once more became accentuated. Britain favoured the dismantling of barriers to trade and the creation of a free market, but she declined to join the European Monetary System (EMS), which had come into force in 1979, and therefore did not participate in the Exchange Rate Mechanism (ERM), which was designed to create currency stability. In September 1988 Delors chaired a committee of experts to discuss European monetary union. The outcome became known as the Delors Plan, which the Commission President submitted to member heads of government in June 1989. It envisaged the creation of monetary union with a single currency. This was to be achieved in three stages. All member states agreed in June 1989 to participate in stage one, the drafting of a treaty on monetary union. But Britain refused to begin the second stage, which – following signature of the treaty – would lay down the conditions to be met by member states that would make possible the attainment of stage three: monetary union with a single currency in use throughout the Community.

In opposing the moves towards monetary union, Margaret Thatcher found herself increasingly isolated not only in Europe but within her own Cabinet. It was her chancellor of the Exchequer and her foreign secretary who insisted at the Madrid summit in July 1989 that Britain should formally accept the whole of the first stage in principle. Margaret Thatcher continued to oppose the goal of monetary union as it would undermine national sovereignty, but in October 1990 she was reluctantly driven to agree to Britain joining the system of fixed exchange rates (the ERM). It transpired that John Major, then Chancellor of the Exchequer, joined at too high a mark exchange rate. As Mrs Thatcher's adviser Sir Alan Walters had warned, the resultant high interest rates in Britain deepened the recession and increased unemployment.

European political and economic union remained a goal for the 1990s, though it was hardly realisable with the members' economies still so widely divergent. This became painfully clear when in September 1992 the Italian lira and the British pound came to be regarded by the currency exchanges as overvalued. Speculation against the two currencies overwhelmed the defences mounted within the ERM and both currencies had to accept the market's judgement and leave the ERM. This meant that in effect they devalued against the previously fixed rate. It was a healthy reminder to politicians that in a free financial world their powers are limited. Nor did the Community nations manage to speak with a common voice on all vital issues of foreign and internal affairs. The realisation that such union might not be attainable within the agreed timetable soon became clear.

Seven smaller but nonetheless prosperous Western European countries which had not joined the European Community – Sweden, Norway, Finland, Iceland, Austria, Switzerland and Liechtenstein, members of the European Free Trade Association – negotiated a treaty with the Community in 1991 to create in 1993 an enlarged European Economic Area of 380 million people. In addition, Austria, Sweden, Norway and Finland hope to join the Community in January 1995; Switzerland too was expected to join those in the antechamber until in a referendum in December 1992 the populace decided by a narrow majority *not* to join. Swiss neutrality had triumphed. Negotiations were likely to be completed before the mid-1990s, each country's special problems having been taken into account. Sweden and Switzerland were reluctant to abandon their traditional neutrality. Sweden, after shedding her socialist policies and government in 1991, embarked on the formation of a market economy to lift the country out of a deep recession. Finland, also in recession in the early 1990s, found herself freed from her dependence on the Soviet Union, whose collapse also meant that she lost her best trade partner. Austria in 1992 replaced a president, Kurt Waldheim, who had become an international embarrassment, and in the same year her international reputation was greatly enhanced by the generous way the small country opened her doors to refugees from the former Yugoslavia. The Community welcomed the possible accession of the wealthier countries, which would help to provide funds for the poorer Mediterranean members and for Portugal.

Fundamental problems remained to be solved. These included the reform of the Community budget, and more particularly the need to curb farm spending; the relationship to be developed with the newly liberated nations of Eastern and central Europe; and trade relations with rest of the world,

**Six Members of EFTA, 1989**

|  | Population (*millions*) | Gross National Product per head (*US$*) |
|---|---|---|
| Sweden | 8.5 | 21,500 |
| Norway | 4.2 | 22,290 |
| Finland | 5.0 | 22,100 |
| Iceland | 0.254 | 21,100 |
| Austria | 7.6 | 17,300 |
| Switzerland (1990) | 6.8 | 37,800 |

especially the United States, which demanded a reduction of the Community's protective barriers. It held up the 'Uruguay' round of negotiations to liberalise world trade through the General Agreement on Tariffs and Trade begun in 1986 and concluded in December 1993. The main remaining obstacle was US Congressional approval before the agreement could come into force in 1995. Agreement also had to be reached on the respective roles of the Community institutions, the relationship between the European Parliament, the Commissioners and national governments. There was a readiness among national governments to relinquish sovereignty to a limited degree.

It appeared that a high point of co-operation had been reached when in December 1991 the leaders of the Community as part of the Delors Plan concluded a new treaty at Maastricht to create an 'ever closer union among the peoples of Europe'. Britain led the opposition to the ideals of a 'federal Europe' and a single common currency. Britain also opted out of the 'Social Chapter', which sought to provide minimum conditions and standards in the workplace for employees. French, Dutch and Belgian support for Maastricht was based to a large extent on a desire to ensure that the power of the recently unified Germany should remain firmly anchored in European institutions. This view had the enthusiastic support of Germany's Chancellor Kohl. John Major agreed, albeit with important reservations, because he wished to keep Britain's place of influence at the 'heart of Europe'.

Within a few months it turned out that the Community's leaders were far ahead of their electorates and had concluded a treaty difficult to ratify and short of obvious popular appeal. The threatened

loss of national identity and objections to giving Brussels more central control underlay misgivings. Denmark only approved the treaty after a second referendum held in May 1993. In the French referendum, there was no resounding approval either – the vote in favour was very slim. At a time of general recession there were widespread misgivings about a commitment to such fundamental changes. In Britain ratification split the Conservatives; only the threat of a general election enabled the government to carry the treaty, without the Social Chapter, through Parliament in 1993.

Three countries – Greece, Spain and Portugal – were for many years barred from applying to join the European Community, not principally on account of the economic difficulties which their membership would arouse but because of their political systems. A fourth country, Turkey, an 'associate' since the 1960s, still awaited a favourable verdict in the early 1990s.

Greece's treaty of accession was concluded in 1979 and she became a full member in 1981. She had only recently returned to democracy after the collapse of the military junta in 1974. Although democratic government had a difficult passage after 1974, membership of the European Community was a strong support.

The Greeks suffered more than any nation in the post-war free world, the civil war from 1946 to 1949 causing widespread devastation. But that conflict was followed by a period of conservative parliamentary government under Field Marshal Papagos and the most durable politician of post-war Greece, Constantine Karamanlis. In 1963, George Papandreou was able to form a liberal reforming coalition until he was dismissed by King Constantine after a dispute over who should control the army. A group of extremist army officers accused Papandreou's Centre Union Party of preparing the way for a communist takeover and organised a coup in April 1967 ahead of the planned general election. The dictatorial rule of the Greek colonels from 1967 to 1974 was a disastrous period for Greece. Abuses of human rights, including torture, were rampant, and so was corruption. The economy, which had been doing well in the 1960s, deteriorated sharply. In 1974, beset by vociferous public demonstrations and resistance following the fiasco of their Cyprus policy and the shambles of army mobilisation, the colonels' junta collapsed.

Cyprus, after a long struggle (pages 562–3),

had been granted independence in August 1960 and placed under the guarantee of Greece, Turkey and Britain. But the power-sharing constitution never worked in the face of Turkish Cypriot and Greek Cypriot animosities. Conflict on the island led to the despatch of a United Nations peacekeeping force in 1964, and Turkey and Greece themselves came close to war. Ten years later, in July 1974, the Greek colonels organised a coup and forced the President of Cyprus, Archbishop Makarios, to flee, preparatory to bringing Cyprus under Greek control; the Turks reacted by invading and occupying the northern portion of the island, defeating the Greek Cypriots. An exchange of populations, with 200,000 Greek Cypriots leaving their homes in the north, and Turkish Cypriots resettling there, effectively partitioned Cyprus. All efforts to unite the two halves and reach a workable compromise between the two communities had failed by the early 1990s, but the partition, with a UN force patrolling the line between the two sides, had ended the bloodshed.

The Cyprus dispute led to strained relations between two NATO allies, Turkey and Greece.

But Greece's attachment to NATO after 1974 was ambivalent, partly because it was widely believed in Greece that the United States had supported the hated colonels. US bases and the US naval presence in Greece were consequently very unpopular, both with the conservative governments headed by Karamanlis, who had opposed the colonels from exile in Paris, and with the liberal centre governments of Andreas Papandreou (son of George Papandreou) in the 1980s.

On his return from exile in 1974, Karamanlis, with true statesmanship, guided Greece back to democracy, only for Andreas Papandreou's Panhellenic Socialist Party to win the election in 1981, though his administration evinced little socialism. Papandreou had gained a reputation as an American-trained economist, but, as elsewhere in the world, the shock of the oil-price rise compounded Greece's economic difficulties in the mid-1980s. In opposition, Papandreou had been stridently anti-Common Market and anti-American; in government he acted with a greater sense of responsibility. But by the end of the 1980s he and his ministers became implicated in financial

*UN peace-keeping troops take time off in the amphitheatre at Salamis, Cyprus.*

884    WESTERN EUROPE GATHERS STRENGTH: AFTER 1968

scandals; his electoral support nevertheless remained solid. Greek politics were also enlivened by his love affair with a former airline stewardess thirty-five years his junior, photographed with a telephoto lens bare-bosomed on the beach. Papandreou was seriously ill with heart trouble at the same time. He subsequently divorced his wife, married his mistress and was narrowly defeated in the general election of 1989. No party emerged as outright winner, and coalition governments were succeeded in 1990 by a conservative administration with a tiny majority led by Prime Minister Konstantinos Mitsotakis. Reforms strengthened the economy after years of socialist profligacy but also caused hardship. The elections in October 1993 returned Papandreou to power. The Cyprus question continued to disrupt her relations with Turkey. But as a member of the Community she had received aid and gained substantial advantages.

Spain joined the Community in 1986, a move made possible by an astonishing decade of change. In November 1975, the old dictator Franco had finally died, wired up to many machines in a vain attempt to prolong his life by a few days. He had given Spain stability and, shrewdly, had not thrown in his lot with his fascist helper Mussolini or with Hitler during the Second World War. It was to his credit too that he had not marched into Gibraltar during Britain's great crisis in 1940. That Spanish volunteers had fought on the Russian front with Hitler was not held against him in the 1950s. He survived the early years of international ostracism and, with the onset of the Cold War he began to be rehabilitated by the United States in 1950. Three years later in September 1953 the US gave aid in return for three bases and a mutual defence pact; international forgiveness was extended when Spain in December 1955 became a full member of the United Nations. (Spain was not admitted into NATO until 1982.)

Franco's Spain remained a repressive regime in the 1950s, but during the 1960s reforms were gradually introduced, military courts were abolished and workers were granted a carefully limited right to strike. Constitutional changes effected in 1966 provided for the election of a minority of members of parliament, though political parties were banned. Franco enjoyed widespread popular support and was seen as standing above the Falange, the Church and the army, which were locked in bitter conflict.

The most serious threat to his rule came from ETA, the independence movement of Basque nationalism. As his successor, Franco had groomed Prince Juan Carlos, grandson of Alfonso XIII; Franco judged that a return to a ruling monarch would be the best guarantee for preserving conservative peace in Spain. Juan Carlos gave no sign during Franco's lifetime of the liberal and democratic role he would crucially play after the Caudillo's death.

During the three decades since the Second World War, Spain had begun to modernise both her agriculture and her industry. The progress made since the 1960s had been considerable, aided by the West European discovery of Spain as a holiday playground. But democratic advance was by no means assured in 1975. King Juan Carlos appointed a moderate socialist, Adolfo Suárez, as prime minister. Suárez restored parliamentary democracy and permitted all parties, including the communists, to compete in the general election of 1977. King Juan Carlos gave his firm backing to democracy, and neither he nor the people would tolerate an army coup, such as was attempted in 1981. A further coup was threatened ahead of the general election in 1982, which the Socialist Party won, Felipe González becoming prime minister. González's biggest success was the signature in June 1985 of the treaty of accession to the European Economic Community, which Spain joined in January 1986. The second half of the 1980s was a period of sustained economic growth, as González followed orthodox economic policies – to the chagrin of his more socialist followers. In 1989 he won the general election for a third time by a narrow margin. The economy has continued to grow. One black spot in Spain's astonishing progress was the continuation into the 1990s of sporadic terrorist attacks by the Basque extremists. But Spain was not alone in the Community in this respect. In the early 1990s she shared the problems of recession with the other members of the Community, including high unemployment, and González's popularity fell.

Portugal joined the European Community at the same time as Spain. But her transition to democracy was far more traumatic. António Salazar was Europe's most enduring dictator, ruling from 1932 to 1968, when a stroke incapacitated him and the right-wing regime of Marcello Caetano took control for six years. As dictators go, he was relatively mild, imprisoning rather than executing his opponents,

*Democracy Returns to Portugal.* Left: *the Portuguese dictator, Salazar, shortly before his death.* Right: *peasants attend a Communist rally prior to the presidential elections of April 1975.*

and during the Second World War he had actively assisted the Allied cause. After 1945, therefore, he remained in relatively good standing, even though he had a secret police and a card-index system concerning his opponents which was borrowed from the Gestapo. In 1970 Salazar died. The revolution which broke out in April 1974 was not democratic in intent but was organised by army officers disillusioned with the wars in Portugal's African colonies of Mozambique and Angola. It took a curious turn when radical army groups entered an alliance with the communists. A general election was held in April 1975 and the Socialist party gained most support; the communists lost out. Mário Soares became prime minister until his replacement in 1979 by a centre–right coalition. By then, democratic parliamentary rule was firmly established – despite their great poverty, the Portuguese people had not turned to the communists. After the election of 1983, Soares again headed a government

coalition of Socialists and the centre, which successfully implemented economic reforms, making state enterprises more efficient and encouraging the private sector; of traditional socialism there was little.

From having no elections, Portugal now had too many. Party manoeuvres led to the fall of Soares in 1985 and another general election. In the following year, the country's kaleidoscopic politics required the election of a new president and, after more party manoeuvrings, the office was won by Soares, who thereupon resigned from the leadership of the Socialist Party. The government of Portugal after 1985 rested on the support of the Social Democratic Party, which once it had gained an overall majority in the election of 1987 set itself the task of reversing socialist state control of industry. Prime Minister Cavaço Silva 'cohabited' amicably with the socialist President Soares, who was re-elected with an overwhelming majority in January 1991. The following

October Cavaço Silva's Social Democratic Party scored a second electoral victory with an impressive overall majority endorsing 'cohabitation'.

During the 1980s Portugal made considerable economic progress, as governments turned from socialism to a market-oriented economy. All pretence that Portugal was in a 'transition to socialism' and was committed to becoming 'classless' was dropped from the new constitution of 1989. Her Gross National Product per head of $2020 in 1978 had tripled by the early 1990s. Since the mid-1980s Portugal had achieved a remarkable degree of political stability and economic progress, and was an enthusiastic member of the European Community.

Turkey applied for full membership of the Community in 1987. Two years later, the Community replied that it was deferring consideration of further applications until after 1993, though it offered the sop that she was eligible. Greece, as a member of the Community, remained deeply suspicious of Turkey, though their relations improved after a low point in 1987. Nevertheless the Cyprus question continued to stand in the way of a normal cordial relationship. Turkey's human-rights record was also suspect and her economy tended to fluctuate wildly between growth and stagnation. The Kurds represent a serious minority problem and the Asia Minor region of the country is not only poverty-stricken but practically under military rule. The economy, too, is backward. Kemal Atatürk had set up State Economic Enterprises in the 1920s and 1930s to modernise Turkish industry, but by the early 1990s they had become outdated and unproductive. With her rapidly increasing population of 57 million in 1990, Turkey's Gross National Product per head, estimated at $1870, was that of a Third World country, far less than Greece's and even that of Portugal, the poorest country in the Community. Nor was parliamentary democracy absolutely secure. The army was faithful to the Atatürk tradition and kept a watchful eye on the civilian politicians, periodically making itself responsible for holding the country together.

In May 1960 the army seized power and the former Prime Minister Adnan Menderes was executed a year later. When a resumption of civilian

*In May 1960, General Gemal Gursel stages a military coup in Turkey.*

politics in the 1960s and 1970s was again accompanied by growing disorder and economic hardship, another army takeover followed in September 1980. In November 1983 there was then a return to semi-civilian parliamentary government, accompanied by much political repression of liberals and socialists; martial law remained in force under the conservative Prime Minister Turgut Özal. He instituted some vigorous economic reforms and privatisations, and gradually returned Turkey to a more normal political state, but the parties contesting for power remained unstable.

Özal sought to lessen tension with Turkey's neighbours, especially Greece. His main aim was to gain full membership of the European Community, to continue the military and economic aid which the United States had steadily sent to a valuable ally during the Cold War. Turkey was also an important player in the Middle East. In November 1989, Özal enhanced his stature by becoming president, but the economy rapidly deteriorated again. Turks fled from Bulgaria in 1989. In April 1993 Özal died. The biggest internal problem that faced his successors was the armed struggle of revolutionary Kurds.

The Democratic German Republic, of course, was barred from the European Community, but West Germany was allowed to extend trading benefits to her. With the death of the DDR and her incorporation into a united Germany in 1990, the territory became a part of the EC without, of course, adding to the number of members.

There was talk, too, in the early 1990s of the new democracies in Eastern and central Europe joining, transforming an essentially West European community into a genuine Europe-wide one. That too remained a distant prospect, particularly at a time when the majority of the EC member states were striving to achieve closer economic and political union.

One of the major achievements of the European Community was the strengthening of democracy in the poorer nations of the West – Spain, Portugal and Greece. Membership of the club is open only to countries which respect civil rights and abjure totalitarian forms of government. Once brought in, no country has suffered a relapse, and such an eventuality is difficult to imagine. Thus not only has the European Community become an association promising greater prosperity to the poorer West European nations, but it is also a powerful bastion of freedom in the world.

The habit of close co-operation and negotiated settlement of differences has become the norm of national relations within the Community. With the removal of trade barriers, 1 January 1993 marked the beginning of a new phase of increasingly close Community co-operation in the sphere of trade to the benefit of the 340 million people whose countries are its members.

Caught up in a general recession during the early years of the 1990s, the Community had to catch its breath, so the aspiration towards a common currency by the end of the decade as agreed in the Maastricht Treaty was soon looking over-ambitious. The harmonisation of the economies with limits on the proportion of their deficits and other conditions appear unlikely to be met by the end of the decade. Progress was not consistent, with the Brussels bureaucracy indulging at times in too much pettifogging interference. But in almost four decades the Community transformed attitudes in Western Europe. National rivals became neighbours – though of course even neighbours fall out with each other from time to time.

**Greece, Cyprus, Spain and Portugal, 1989–1990**

|  | Population (*millions*) | Gross National Product per head (*US$*) |
|---|---|---|
| Greece | 10.0 | 5,350 |
| Greek Cyprus | 0.554 | 9,000 |
| Turkish Cyprus | 0.165 | 3,500 |
| Spain | 39.0 | 8,950 |
| Portugal | 10.3 | 5,680 |

# PART XVIII

*The Cold War and After*

# CHAPTER 87

# The Iron Curtain Disintegrates:
# The Death of Communism in Eastern Europe

In 1989, a wave of popular revolutions transformed eastern and central Europe. Communism was swept away. The Soviet Union withdrew. Only ten years earlier the Warsaw Pact and Soviet domination of central and Eastern Europe had still looked solid and unshakeable. There were difficulties of course. Romania was showing signs of nationalist independence; her communist leader Nicolae Ceauşescu was much admired in the West, which courted him assiduously – much to its later embarrassment. In Bulgaria, the German Democratic Republic, Hungary and Czechoslovakia, the communist regimes had proved durable, though the last two countries had to be brought into conformity with tanks and guns. For two generations now the people of Eastern Europe had known nothing but communism, and those aged forty-five years and older had known only different forms of authoritarian rule before the Iron Curtain descended. The communist leaderships had claimed that they had made great social and economic advances; a golden future beckoned; hardship and suffering were only temporary, the means to greater virtue and prosperity.

One supposed virtue was that worker and peasant solidarity had replaced destructive bourgeois nationalism. The Soviet alliance, people were told, guaranteed their protection from German revanchism. This seemed to justify the stationing of the Red Army in their countries. Only the Romanians in 1958 succeeded in ridding themselves of their unwelcome Soviet guests. But all the

Eastern-bloc national forces relied mainly on Soviet weapons. The economic exploitation of the satellites, a feature of the Stalinist post-war years, had long ceased. Indeed, the Soviet Union was now subsidising the East European economies in the 1980s to a significant extent, at some sacrifice to herself. Oil and raw materials were supplied at less than world prices. The goods manufactured in Eastern Europe, moreover, were of a design and quality that for the most part were unsaleable anywhere else but in the Soviet Union. Of course the USSR, because of her sheer size, dominated trading relationships. It is also notoriously difficult to evaluate the advantages and disadvantages of the Soviet-led Council of Mutual Economic Assistance (Comecon) on the basis of price calculations. And if the Eastern Europeans had not found a ready market for their goods and had to find a market in the West, would that not have made them more competitive? In the end they found themselves linked to a collapsing Soviet economy and, when that link was cut, faced economic collapse themselves. Little reliance can be placed on the statistics of economic 'progress' published by the regimes, although they were carefully analysed by economic experts in the West. In any event, they show a precipitous fall from the 1970s to the end of the 1980s.

What can be measured is the increasing indebtedness of Eastern Europe to the West. With the reduction of East–West tension, loans had become more readily available to accelerate the regimes'

**EUROPE, 1993**

ICELAND

Reykjavik

*NORWEGIAN SEA*

*ATLANTIC OCEAN*  Torshavn FAEROE ISLANDS

NORWAY

SWEDEN

N

Oslo

Stockh

0        400 km

0        200 miles

*NORTH SEA*

IRELAND

Dublin

DENMARK  Copenhagen

B.

UNITED KINGDOM

NETHERLANDS

London

Amsterdam

Berlin

PO

BELGIUM

Brussels

GERMANY

LUXEMBOURG

Prague

CZECH REPUBL

Paris

LIECHTENSTEIN

Bratisla

Vienna

FRANCE

Vaduz

AUSTRIA  Bu

Berne

SWITZERLAND

SLOVENIA

Ljubljana

Zagre

MONACO

CROATIA

PORTUGAL

ANDORRA

SAN MARINO

S

Lisbon

Madrid

Andorra La Vella

ITALY

BOSNIA-HERZEGOV

SPAIN

VATICAN CITY

Rome

*MEDITERRANEAN SEA*

MOROCCO

ALGERIA

MALTA  Valletta

FINLAND

Helsinki

Tallinn
ESTONIA

LATVIA
Riga

THUANIA
Vilnius
Minsk

BELORUSSIA

w

Kiev

UKRAINE

MOLDOVA
Kishinev

A

ROMANIA

Bucharest

IA

BULGARIA
Sofia

NIA

kopje

MACEDONIA

ECE

Athens

RUSSIAN FEDERATION

Moscow

CASPIAN
SEA

GEORGIA

AZERBAIJAN

ARMENIA

BLACK     SEA

TURKEY

IRAN

Nicosia

SYRIA

CYPRUS

IRAQ

plans to catch up with the West industrially. These too failed. The heaviest burdened were the East Germans, whose debt increased from $1.4 billion in 1971 to $20.7 billion in 1988. They were fortunate: their debts were assumed by the Federal Republic. The Poles ($1.1 billion debt in 1971) groaned under a debt of over $48.5 billion in 1991, and the Hungarians suffered from massive foreign debts, the highest amount per head. The only 'virtuous' country was Romania. By draconian measures which drove much of the population below any tolerable living standard Ceauşescu had, by the time of his fall in 1990, paid off his country's debts, which totalled $10 billion in 1981. Neither he nor his family shared the austerity he imposed on his countrymen: they lacked nothing in the way of imported Western luxuries. In this respect he was only an extreme example of Eastern European communist leadership, all of which did very well out of communism and Soviet protection.

The corruption was obvious and open. But the regimes also had a large privileged clientele who benefited from their continuing in power. The host of bureaucrats needed in the central planning ministries, the officers in the army, the secret police and the party and trade union functionaries all had a vested interest in upholding the communist state system. Now and then, at worst, one leader might be replaced by another, but in the 1970s and 1980s there were remarkably few changes in the upper reaches of the communist leadership. Poland, in the wake of the Solidarity crisis of 1979 to 1982, was something of an exception. The election of a Polish cardinal, Karol Wojtyla, as Pope John Paul II in 1978 greatly encouraged the Polish people in their resistance to communism. His visit to Poland in 1983 after the suppression of Solidarity prompted a massive demonstration of resistance and independence. But few foresaw the collapse of communist rule in Eastern Europe much before it happened. The impact of the year of revolution, 1989, was therefore all the greater.

With hindsight it is possible to discern the roots of that revolution, the discontent of the masses that boiled over, and the reason why the communist leaders were afraid to resort to bloody repression – why, had they tried to do so, the forces ready to do their bidding were no longer strong enough. It was the mass of the people who rose against the leadership. Not only intellectuals and dissidents but hundreds of thousands of formerly good communists turned on a system they had previously supported. In the face of realities, of oppression and of falling living standards, they became utterly disillusioned. Once they realised they were no longer a small group which could be harried, beaten and imprisoned, the people began to lose their fear of the state. Increasing contacts with the West in the 1970s and 1980s rendered the contrast in living standards even starker. What fanned discontent, however, were not just poor living standards and dwindling hopes of a better future but the growing recognition that their leaders and the whole communist system of repression and economic management were the cause of their troubles.

The new thinking stimulated by Gorbachev in the Soviet Union spread to the smaller nations of Eastern Europe with electrifying effect after 1987. The communist leaderships could not adjust themselves to realities. They remained cocooned, brainwashed by their own ideology and propaganda. There is no better illustration of this than Ceauşescu's last appearance on 22 December 1989, on the balcony of his palace, unable to make himself heard over the catcalls of the crowd gathered in the square below. The complete bewilderment of a once all-powerful man, whose only experience for years had been hero-worship and the sound of sycophantic clapping in unison, showed on his face in television pictures beamed around the world. Even on the day the opposition stood him and his hated wife Elena against a wall to be shot, they were both convinced that the people loved them. It was Christmas Day. Absolute power not only corrupts, it also blinds.

Until the year of revolution, the communist leaderships had felt sufficiently secure to assert a measure of national independence from Soviet economic and political control. To that extent, the Gorbachev phenomenon was welcome. He promised, in April 1985, a month after coming to power, to accord full respect for the sovereignty of the Eastern European nations which uphold 'socialist internationalism'. That sounded like a softer version of the Brezhnev doctrine, not a repudiation of it. The regimes went on believing that the communist state was safe and would, if the need again arose, be defended by the Red Army, as it had been in East Germany in 1953, Hungary in 1956 and Czechoslovakia in 1968. It dawned on them only slowly, if ever, that Gorbachev was ready to abandon them if that was the will of the people.

By the time of the Twenty-Seventh Party Congress in February and March 1986 Gorbachev had moved on and was urging much more radical political reform in the Soviet Union. By September, he was telling the people of Krasnodar that the 'essence of *perestroika* . . . is for people to feel they are the country's master'. In 1987 and 1988 he reshaped Soviet foreign policy, determined to win the support, trust and economic help of the West. His new foreign minister, Eduard Shevardnadze, gave him his enthusiastic backing and put forward to the Central Committee of the Soviet Communist Party in February 1990 an important reason for this revolution in the Soviet Union's policies: 'It is only through extensive international co-operation that we will be able to solve our most acute domestic problems.' Soviet-led repression in Eastern Europe would irreparably harm the more important new Soviet interests. Like other imperial powers, the Soviet Union had reached the point where the burdens of empire, and its negative effects on Soviet relations with the rest of the world, far outweighed the advantages. In the missile age, territorial buffers no longer provided protection; the 'military imperative' of the immediate post-war years had vanished too.

The prop that had held up national communist regimes in Eastern Europe – the popular belief that their communist leaders were at least better than a Soviet occupation and direct Soviet rule – had been knocked away. In 1989, the possibility of Soviet intervention was no longer feared. And without the Red Army behind them, the national people's armies of conscripts could no longer be relied on to support the regimes against their own people.

One by one the reasons for the revolutions that swept through Eastern Europe in 1989 become clear. The nucleus of a dissident leadership was somewhat uncertainly in place in Hungary, Romania and East Germany; there was a more entrenched one in Czechoslovakia, where the Charter 77 group had a long history of protest; and Solidarity in Poland was already a power in its own right. Crucial also was the disillusionment of the masses with the economic situation and with the whole decaying system. The leadership elite knew that it could no longer save itself simply by changing the man at the top. The revolt began with the young. The feeling soon all pervading, that the Iron Curtain was full of holes, that it could no longer separate the angry people from the centres of power in East Berlin,

Prague, Budapest or Sofia, any more than it could prevent people in the East from contacting the West, was intoxicating. On 9 November 1989, the Berlin Wall, that potent Iron Curtain barrier, fell before an onslaught of the people. It was as symbolic an event as the fall of the Bastille.

The final rot had begun ten years earlier in the Lenin Shipyard in Gdańsk. The Solidarity movement had spread until it had gained the support of half of Poland's adult population. With the Gdańsk agreement concluded between the Solidarity leaders and the government in 1980, the stranglehold of the Polish Communist Party appeared to be broken. The support for Solidarity had a variety of roots; repeated economic failures during thirty-five years of communist rule, working-class and intellectual resistance to a single-party authoritarian state, nationalism and Catholic rejection of atheistic communism – these together provided a fertile soil for the growth of a broad opposition. Solidarity was a party in all but name, and, in the year during which it was allowed to function as a free trade union movement, recruited 10 million members. The morale of the Communist Party collapsed as communists also switched to Solidarity.

As the economy slumped further, General Jaruzelski became the new party leader and declared martial law on 13 December 1981. Fearing Soviet intervention, the conscript Polish army obeyed him. There was some sullen relief, but protest strikes also broke out, harshly suppressed at the cost of a number of deaths and injuries. With the Communist Party now a broken reed, Jaruzelski formed the Military Council of National Salvation. Solidarity was outlawed, hundreds of its members were arrested, including for a short time Lech Wałęsa, and the rest of the leadership was driven underground. Yet the attempt to obliterate Solidarity proved a total failure. The electrician Wałęsa did not sink back into obscurity but was internationally celebrated with the award of the Nobel Peace Prize in 1983. The over-subsidised command economy failed to respond to economic medications applied by the communists, and US economic sanctions and rejection by the West isolated the regime until 1983. The workforce was not to be inspired by military or communist appeals to work harder. A particularly shocking example of the brutality prevailing under the regime was the abduction and murder by the Interior Ministry's security forces of a popular radical priest, Father Jerzy Popieluszko, whose church had become a focus for the opposition.

Gradually Jaruzelski relaxed military rule and the majority of Solidarity activists were released from jail. But attempts by Jaruzelski to improve the economy by cutting subsidies provoked new strikes in 1988. The people were not prepared to accept such measures from a regime which kept itself in power by force. The authorities knew that national malaise and economic crisis could not be overcome without the co-operation of the opposition. And so in February 1989 began the 'round-table talks' between the military communist regime and opposition groups, including Solidarity. The constitutional reforms agreed by April that year ended one-party rule. Solidarity was permitted to emerge as a political party – that was a far-reaching concession. Czechoslovakia had been invaded in 1968 when Dubček had conceded as much. This time, Gorbachev had made it clear that the Eastern European nations could follow their own road of development.

The concession Solidarity made was that in the lower house of the Polish parliament, the Sejm, 65 per cent of the seats would be reserved for the Communist Party and only 35 per cent would be contested. A senate was created as well, which would be freely elected, and the Senate and the Sejm together would elect a president. Solidarity swept the board in the elections held in June 1989: of the 161 seats in the lower chamber which they were able to contest, they and their nominees won 160; in the Senate, they won 92 out of 100 seats. It was a triumph for Wałęsa. With their 299 reserved seats, the communist coalition partners still had a majority in the lower chamber. When it came to the election of the president, Jaruzelski made it by one vote, with some help from Wałęsa, who refused to stand against him for fear that this would push the communists and Moscow too far. The compromise was cemented when, in August 1989, Jaruzelski appointed the first non-communist premier, a Solidarity supporter and close associate of Wałęsa, Tadeusz Mazowiecki; he in turn, with an eye on Moscow, formed a coalition government in which Solidarity ministers formed the largest group but which allocated the crucial ministries of Defence and the Interior to two communists.

Because the leading role of the communists had been removed by compromise and negotiation in Poland, vestiges of entrenched communist power, such as the free elections for only a part of the lower chamber, survived until October 1991 when a 'reserved' communist majority was no longer an option after the revolutions elsewhere in Eastern Europe during 1989. Poland was also the first communist nation to attempt to transform herself from a planned to a Western-style free-market economy. The new government inherited a ruined economy with soaring inflation and falling production. The Finance Minister, Leszek Balcerowicz, inaugurated a harsh programme to restore the value of the currency, cut subsidies, deal with a huge foreign debt and make industry competitive and productive once more. The shops began to fill with stocks in 1990, but at prices few could afford. Standards of living fell more steeply than under the communists. The Solidarity alliance grew weaker as the 'common enemy' vanished, and Wałęsa began attacking Mazowiecki, blaming his government for the hardships of economic reform because it was not acting energetically and speedily enough.

In December 1990, the bewildered Poles came to elect their new president, Jaruzelski's term having been shortened. A hitherto unknown Polish–Canadian gained more votes than Mazowiecki, and Lech Wałęsa won easily. It would be more difficult to deliver what he had promised. Western aid was relatively small. Without the Soviet market, much of Poland's industry was uncompetitive. With such poor business prospects, who would buy shares in privatised industries? Polish shock therapy did bring down inflation and saved the value of the currency, but living standards fell.

The Mazowiecki government in 1990 boldly set in motion policies to achieve a rapid transition to a market economy. Privatisation took off with almost half of all Poland's employees working for the private sector by 1992 and nearly all retail business in private hands. There remained a large state industrial sector which no one wanted to buy. In 1990 Poland suffered from soaring inflation of almost 700 per cent, but in 1991 it fell back to a more manageable 60 per cent. Even so, price rises fuelled popular discontent because wages did not keep pace. Unemployment meanwhile exceeded 11 per cent of the workforce and in 1992 was still rising. The Polish disenchantment with democratic politicians was clearly in evidence when at the general election held in October 1991 less than half the Poles bothered to vote at all and those who did returned twenty different parties to the Sejm with none receiving more than 12 per cent of the vote. The unity Solidarity had enjoyed in opposition did not last long after its victory over communism. The shock therapy of economic reform, applauded by the West, which finally helped to reduce Poland's debt burden, turned the Polish people's enthusiasm for post-communist freedom into disillusionment. The transition to capitalism was proving hard, even though Poland had started early. By 1993 the Polish economy at last showed signs of recovery with output rising. Nearly half of the GDP was produced by the private sector. Poland was even being governed by her first woman prime minister Hanna Suchoka. In the face of political instability Poland made steady progress restructuring her economy. The steep fall in output from 1989 to 1991 began to be reversed in 1992.

Kádár's regime in Hungary had since the late 1960s placed economic reforms, rising living standards, more choice and greater freedoms in the forefront of its policies. The softer image of the Communist Party, whose leading role could not be challenged, reconciled the majority of the people to the limited options it permitted. Kádár projected himself as the leader who knew how far he could go without risking a repeat of the Soviet invasion of 1956. The 1968 New Economic Mechanism, as the mixture of central planning and market-oriented policies was called, seemed to work for a while. Four years later, there was some backtracking to a planned economy. Goulash communism was kept going by increasingly heavy foreign credits – and so debts. By the mid-1980s, Hungary's economy was showing every sign of sickness. Kádár's reforms were too cautious. Communist Party dominance of economic planning blocked any genuine market-oriented course. Kádár at heart was a communist who wanted to make communism work, not a pragmatic market economist or a believer in democracy. Even so, communist power dragged on.

In May 1988, the party itself got rid of Kádár, and the reformist communist Prime Minister Károly Grósz replaced him. Grósz banked on a more efficient authoritarian communist system to pull Hungary out of her economic stagnation. But, for an opposition within the party led by Imre Pozsgay, this did not constitute any real break with Kádárism. Pozsgay raised the ghost of Imre Nagy, who, he

declared, had not led a counter-revolution but had put himself at the head of a national uprising. The issue involved a repudiation of Kádár's claim to legitimacy and to the party's claim that Nagy had been wrong to espouse a multi-party political system. In June 1988, the remains of Nagy were reinterred with honour. Henceforth the Communist Party was deeply divided between reformers and conservatives.

The opposition parties were equally split between the liberal, urban and intellectually led Alliance of Free Democrats and the populist Hungarian Democratic Forum, which claimed to defend the ordinary man and the small farmers and peasants of the countryside. As in Poland, where anti-intellectual and anti-Semitic sentiments during the presidential election were used to discredit Mazow-iecki (he was 'smeared' as being of Jewish descent, though he was not), so the Democratic Forum denigrated the Alliance of Free Democrats for its supposedly intellectual 'Jewish' influences (anti-semitism has remained a flourishing evil in Eastern Europe). When the free elections were held in March 1990, the communists – now calling them-selves the Hungarian Socialist Party – suffered a humiliating defeat, which also sealed the fate of Pozsgay. Thus in Hungary as in Poland, there was a peaceful end to communist rule and a transfer to a Democratic Forum government in May. The Prime Minister, Forum's leader Jozsef Antall, stressed that he would follow a gradual route to a market economy. But Hungarian nationalism was reviving, which threatened to isolate Hungary and exacerbate the problems with her neighbours, Slovakia with 600,000 ethnic Hungarians, Serbia with 150,000 and Romania with 1 million 800 thousand. In 1993 moderation prevailed and neo-fascist appeals for *Lebensraum* were being rejected; prosperity came before conflict.

Hungary in Kádár's later years was positively liberal compared to Czechoslovakia after the crushing of the Prague Spring in 1968. Gustáv Husák was the Communist Party boss who reimposed a strong authoritarian regime.

The Czech and Slovak peoples had to acquiesce in Husák's rule, with the Red Army troops stationed in Czechoslovakia ready to back it. Stability brought a measure of economic improvement in the 1970s and for a time rising standards of living, but by the 1980s the Czech economy was in deep crisis. As was the case throughout Eastern Europe, Czecho-slovakia was relying on increasingly outdated factories and methods of production. Once, in previous years, Czechoslovakia had been a model of economic progress in Eastern Europe, compar-able to Western countries; now she had been turned into a characteristic Soviet-bloc economy – stag-nant, with an over-emphasis on heavy industry, and so unmindful of the environment that industry was creating in parts of the country an ecological disaster, rendering the air so polluted that it made the population sick.

But Czechoslovakia had one positive aspect in common with its heavy-handed Soviet mentor: an immensely lively and distinguished group of dissi-dent writers and intellectuals. Their courageous spokesman was a playwright, Václav Havel. The Helsinki Agreements promising human rights provided the dissidents with a unifying programme with which to attack the communist regime. In January 1977 they formed the Charter 77 move-ment, whose manifesto demanded respect for human rights. Its leaders, who met informally in each other's houses, were arrested, harassed and imprisoned for anti-state activities. But their protests reached a wide audience in the West and kept the spark of resistance alive in Czechoslovakia.

As the 1980s drew to a close, Husak could not isolate Czechoslovakia from the stirrings of freedom in Poland and Hungary or from the reformist impact of Gorbachev's 'new thinking'. The old reactionary communist stance had had its day. But Husak did not give up. He resigned from the leadership of the party in December 1987 only to hand it to another hardline communist, Milos Jakeš, while he himself retained the presidency. In 1988 and during the early months of 1989, Czechoslovakia seemed still to be firmly in the communist grip, out of tune with all the other East European states except Romania which remained obedient to Ceauşescu's dictator-ship. But the Czech communist leadership felt ill at ease and began to make a number of concessions.

Thereafter the collapse of communist rule was both sudden and unexpected. On 17 November 1989 there was a large student demonstration in Prague joined by thousands of people. The brutality of the police attempts to suppress it, which caused many injuries, provoked increasingly large mass protests. Meanwhile, under Havel's leadership, opposition groups, with Charter 77 members at their core, began to organise themselves as the Civic

Forum opposition. Their aim was the overthrow of the communist regime. An emotional open-air meeting was addressed by Alexander Dubček in Prague. In the end the workers' decision to join a national strike brought down the government. Jakeš resigned with his ministers. The Velvet Revolution was completed without violence only a month later when Havel on 29 December 1989 was elected president. High on the agenda for Havel and the government elected in June 1990 was how to deal humanely with the problems of creating an efficient market economy, and with the nationality problem that had beset the state from its birth, the relation-ship between Slovaks and Czechs.

Slovakia was particularly hard hit since most of the heavy industry was located there. Separate reformist parties, the Civic Forum and the Slovak Public Against Violence, gained a clear majority in the multi-party federal election held in June 1990. The Communist Party survived with a large decline in support. The dominant issue in 1991 became whether the country would split. Slovakia, which had most to fear from a rapid move to a market economy, turned to a new leader Vladimír Mečiar, who founded a nationalist party. By the close of 1992, a bloodless separation of the Czech Republic and Slovakia had been agreed. President Havel, still the most popular political leader in the Czech half, had in effect lost his role as federal president. Despite their deep economic problems, the Czech Republic with its proximity to Germany, its earlier industrial tradition and its beautiful capital visited by many tourists was in a position to look to the future with more confidence than Slovakia. With unemployment and inflation low in the Czech Republic production too began to recover in 1992.

Romania's revolution of 1989 was both the bloodiest and the most enigmatic in its outcome. Two commu-nist leaders dominated Romania's post-war history, Gheorge Gheorghiu-Dej from 1945 to his death in 1965, and his successor Nicolae Ceauşescu from 1965 until his ignominious end, shot with his wife beside him against a wall. The savagery of the Romanian revolution was a reaction to the harshly repressive rule of his closing years. Both Gheorghiu-Dej and Ceauşescu were driven by a ruthless nationalism to make Romania independent of the Soviet Union, and to make her strong. They followed the classic Stalinist route of emphasis on the crash development of heavy industry and, under

*The 'Velvet Revolution'. Václav Havel, playwright, political prisoner and the biggest thorn in the Communists' side for years, triumphs with Civic Forum, toppling Gustáv Husák's hardline regime in the autumn of 1989. He and the architect of the 1968 Prague Spring, Alexander Dubček (pictured on the left), address enthusiastic crowds of supporters.*

Ceauşescu, this was done without any regard to the cost of the people's standard of living. Gheorghiu-Dej succeeded in persuading the Kremlin to withdraw the Red Army from Romanian soil in 1958, and thereafter his country was a nominal member of the Warsaw Pact rather than a loyal, subservient ally. In the Kremlin the Romanians' uncomfortable stance was accepted, because there was never any doubt about their communist credentials.

Ceauşescu succeeded Gheorghin-Dej after his death in 1965. He eliminated all his political rivals, courted mass popularity by playing the anti-Soviet card and during his early years manipulated public attitudes by permitting considerable cultural freedom. He also followed an independent foreign policy, allowing openings to the West. Admiration for the 'strong leader' and fear of Soviet intervention buttressed his support at home. It also earned him far too uncritical support in the West – knighted in Britain, he was host to President Nixon in Bucharest in 1969. In 1983, Vice-President George Bush

was sufficiently misled to describe him as 'one of Europe's good communists'. The Cold War blinkered sound judgement.

During the 1970s Western credits helped him to pursue his vision of turning Romania into a modern industrial nation, but in the 1980s his grandiose economic plans ended in disaster. There was no new investment, as the dictator squeezed everything productive for export to repay the international debts. He was not willing to be dependent on Western creditors either. With his wife Elena, Ceauşescu in the end lost all touch with reality and built up a personality cult without parallel. His family exploited and pillaged Romania's scant resources for their own luxurious lifestyles. They lived like potentates. Among his final acts of economic madness was his urbanisation programme, which would have involved simply bulldozing half of Romania's villages and building soulless blocks of flats in their place. A beginning was made, and at last the West was shocked.

The secret police, the Securitate, made sure that

*In Bucharest on 21 December 1989, Nicolae and Elena Ceauşescu make their last public appearance. Within days, the applause has ceased for good and the dictatorial duo are dead.*

any opposition from the cowed people was extinguished; in Romania even the Church leaders made their own peace with the regime. For Ceauşescu the right path to follow during the years of communism's crisis at the end of the 1980s was that of the Chinese leadership in Tiananmen Square, not the Kremlin's *glasnost* and *perestroika*. Until the outbreak of the spontaneous revolution in December 1989, Romania appeared to be as securely in the grip of her leader as Albania. Wishing to stand well with the West, Ceauşescu's solution for the small, brave intellectual opposition was to force them to leave the country. In the 1980s the Securitate behaved more ruthlessly against lesser-known critics of the regime; an unknown number were murdered.

A curtain-raiser for the revolution two years later was the 1987 revolt by the workers of Kronstadt. Some 5000 stormed the party headquarters and shouted 'Down with Ceauşescu!' Their lives had become intolerable. The Securitate put down the rebellion with murderous brutality. Just a few brave individuals continued to protest and demonstrate. Among them was Pastor Laszlo Tokes in Timişoara, who looked after his Hungarian ethnic flock. Timişoara lay in a region in western Romania that had been part of the Austro-Hungarian Empire before 1918; since then it had remained in Romania. The Securitate harassed the pastor, and his bishop under state pressure ordered his removal to another parish. On 15 December 1989, his congregation, Hungarians and Romanians, surrounded his house

to protect him and his family from deportation. Once again, as so often in history, this particular dissent, small and apparently inconsequential, was the spark that started a revolution. The protest spread to the mixed Romanian and Hungarian population of Timişoara. On 17 December 1989, the army moved in. Bloody clashes ensued, and the unequal fight soon ended with many dead. The news spread through Romania and the world. Ceauşescu was losing control.

On 21 December Ceauşescu arranged for the usual adulation to greet him when he addressed a crowd of 100,000 in Bucharest's University Square from the balcony of the Communist Party Central Committee Building. Well-rehearsed expressions of approval arose from the front of the crowd, but from behind followed catcalls and shouts of 'Murderers of Timişoara!' Ceauşescu, bewildered, was hustled back into the building and Romanian television interrupted its broadcast. It was the signal people had been waiting for: in the afternoon and evening they poured into the streets. Securitate and army units started firing indiscriminately at them, killing and wounding many. Defiantly, the crowds gathered again in University Square on 22 December and were ready to storm the Central Committee Building. They sensed that the army was now with them and that only isolated fanatics of the Securitate were still resisting the overthrow of Ceauşescu. That morning the Ceauşescus finally fled from the roof of the building by helicopter, a journey that ended with their summary trial and execution on Christmas Day.

A Council of the Front for National Salvation was formed, and Ion Iliescu, once Ceauşescu's secretary for ideological issues, was chosen by them as president. There was no democratic tradition in Romania. The National Salvation Front was dominated by reformist communists, who disingenuously denied that they were bringing forth the Communist Party in a new guise. Iliescu won working-class support with concessions on wages, and living conditions were rapidly improved. He wanted to avoid plunging Romania into hardship by trying to produce a Western-style market-oriented economy. He also emphasised Romanian nationalism, especially by means of the 'Romanisation' of Transylvania, whose population was now evenly divided between ethnic Hungarians and Romanians. The region had been part of Hungary until 1918; it was then handed to Romania, returned to Hungary by Hitler in 1940 and then given back to Romania by the Allies in 1945 – it had been a football of international diplomacy, which had shown little concern for the protection of the minorities involved.

In May 1990, Iliescu won an overwhelming victory in the presidential elections and the National Salvation Front was no less triumphant in the parliamentary elections. In June, claiming that the Front was in danger, Iliescu let some 20,000 communist miners, who had been transported to Bucharest, loose on the democratic opposition, and they beat up civilians indiscriminately 'to restore order'. Violence also marked dealings with the democratic opposition of the Hungarian Democratic Union Party. Beset by ethnic hatreds, by discrimination against minorities and by the mob's knee-jerk hostility to foreigners, Hungarians and Jews, the political future of Romania, a country which has never known democracy, looked bleak. The terrible legacy of Ceauşescu's rule, including the neglected orphans with Aids and the shattered economy, remained a heavy burden. The intimidation of the opposition during and after the election in May, and the violence of the miners brought to Bucharest in June 1990, revealed the true colours of the National Salvation Front. A rapid drive towards a market economy was launched by Prime Minister Petre Roman. The consequences were dire – falling production and soaring unemployment – and President Iliescu dismissed Roman. In the early 1990s Romania retained links with its communist past;

President Iliescu therefore continued to enjoy support. But there have been economic reforms, though at a much slower pace than in Hungary, Czechoslovakia and Poland. The fall in output continued even in 1992 to about half the level of 1989. In these dire conditions the people fear radical remedies and cling to some of the old guard leadership.

For most of the post-war years, from 1954 to 1989, Todor Zhivkov led the Bulgarian Communist Party as a kind of feudal boss, ruling the country with the assistance of feudal regional bosses in what was industrially the most backward of the Eastern European nations, excepting only Albania. Bulgaria was distinctive too in that she traditionally looked to Russia as her friend. So there was none of the nationalist agitation against the Soviet Union common elsewhere in Eastern Europe. That hatred was reserved for her Turkish neighbour, her bitter foe since the days of the Ottomans.

Zhivkov was as odious a dictator as any, his repressive machinery of state claiming thousands of victims. Prodded by the Kremlin, he proposed reforms in 1987, but nothing came of them. Instead, to bolster his popularity, he turned on the Turkish minority in the summer of 1989. Violent repression of Turkish demonstrations led to a mass exodus of the Turks from Bulgaria into Turkey and badly tarnished Zhivkov's standing both in the West and in the Kremlin. The democratic opposition groups had only recently been formed, so they were too weak to topple him. The job was done by reformist communists from within: in November 1989 Zhivkov, to his astonishment, was dismissed by the Politburo. The reformers won, and in June 1990, in a free election, the communists, now called the Bulgarian Socialist Party, gained a substantial victory over the Western-oriented Union of Democratic Forces, though achieving only a small overall majority of eleven in the 400-member parliament. Anti-Turkish nationalism and fear of the consequences of introducing Western capitalism had swayed the voters. In August 1990, the urban opposition in Sofia turned to violent demonstration, but in the circumstances the response of the ruling communists in the Bulgarian Socialist Party was moderate. With the direct election as president of the incumbent Zheliu Zhelev in January 1992, it was to be hoped that Bulgaria was entering a more stable period. Much of the communist bureaucracy remained in place and economic reform was only halfhearted at best. Not surprisingly foreign investment was slow to appear, and inflation in 1991 reached 600 per cent but adopting IMF designed remedies it fell to 80% in 1992. With Romania, Bulgaria also suffered severely, her output falling to a little over 60% of that in 1987.

Communist rule lasted the longest where Soviet domination ceased decades ago. Enver Hoxha, fervent Stalinist admirer, was fortunate to die in 1985 before the wave of revolution. In Albania, the revolution was delayed. Not until 1991 were statues of the great leader Enver toppled by angry students. That there were students at all, a university and a high degree of literacy was one of the few positive results of Hoxha's forty-year rule. For Albania was the most backward and the poorest country in Europe. Hoxha, Stalinist and repressive, broke with the post-Stalin Soviet Union in the 1960s and with the reformist phase of Chinese communism in the late 1970s. The intense nationalism of his regime and the successful assertion of independence from powerful neighbours, especially Yugoslavia contributed to the popular support he enjoyed during his years in power. His successor, Ramiz Alia, was also a convinced communist but was attempting to adjust Albania to the changing, more liberal climate of Eastern Europe. He was also leading her out of self-imposed isolation. He remained as one of the undiluted communist survivors of the post-revolutionary years. The West, although accustomed to viewing poverty in the Third World, was deeply shocked by the conditions still existing in Albania. Yet refugees trying to flee in boats to Italy were turned back. An Italian relief operation codenamed Pelican launched during the winter of 1991 alone saved Albanians from widespread starvation. The communists were not ousted until 1992 when Sali Berisla was elected the first non-communist president. For the ordinary Albanian the prospects in the 1990s remained grim.

Bloodshed, war and ethnic strife in Eastern Europe reached heights in what was formerly Yugoslavia that exceeded anything witnessed elsewhere, including the Soviet Union. The Western powers and the United Nations sought to mediate, but Serbs, Croats and Muslims – while endlessly talking and concluding ceasefire agreements – went on bloodily fighting each other. The memory of the bitter struggle between Serbs and those Croats who had supported the fascist puppet regime in Croatia during the Second World War was revived. Tito's legacy of a federal state held together by the Communist Party disintegrated with disastrous effect. But after his death in 1980 even his huge prestige and the power of the Communist Party apparatus could not overcome the weakening of the centre. Local party bosses, cultural differences and gross economic discrepancies between comparatively prosperous Slovenia and the poverty of parts of Serbia hastened the separation of the republics. Successive constitutions sought to avoid violent nationality clashes by conceding more power to the communist leadership and its apparatus in each republic. Yugoslavia was open to the West. Indeed, tourism became the most important hard-currency earner with the start of mass air travel in the 1960s. By the 1980s, the Yugoslav economy was in a mess and reached levels of hyperinflation similar to the worst in Latin America. In 1990 the federal Prime Minister's currency reform and economic measures restored financial stability but at the cost of hardship and unemployment which exacerbated the conflict between the nationalities.

The conflict had become very evident in 1987 when the Communist Party of the most powerful republic, Serbia, was taken over by Slobodan Milošević. He gained momentum and popularity by fanning Serbian national fervour. An issue was immediately at hand: the problem presented by the province of Kosovo, one of the poorest regions in the whole country, peopled by a majority of Albanians, but with a large Serbian minority. The proportion of Albanians, with their much higher birthrate, would increase further in any case, but this process was hastened by the mass emigration of Serbians. Without real evidence, Milošević claimed that this was the result of Albanian terrorism. Albanian protest against Serbian repression led to uprisings, demonstrations and bloody conflict. More serious still was the struggle between a revived Croatian nationalism and Serbia.

Serbia sought to dominate the other republics; Croatian nationalism not only resisted Serbian pretensions but had its own designs on the ethnically mixed population of the republic of Bosnia and Herzogovina, while the Serbs in Croatia were protesting against the discrimination practised against them. The Slovenes not only wanted to rid themselves of all communist control but also desired

*In Tirana, Albania, a former political prisoner enjoys his freedom while leaning on a toppled statue of Lenin, 1991.*

virtual independence. Free elections fatally weakened not only the communists, however much they attempted to distance themselves from the past by renaming their party, but also the federal union.

By the close of 1990, in each of the constitutional republics of Serbia, Croatia and Slovenia elections had been held and governments installed. Talks on continuing the federal Yugoslav structure, however, collapsed. During the early months of 1991 Slovenia and Croatia moved towards independence. Serbia denounced the attempt to break up Yugoslavia and declared that she would defend Serbians who would otherwise be forced to live as minorities under hated Croatian rule. In June 1991 Slovenia and Croatia finally declared their independence. At once there was a prospect of bloody conflict between the overwhelmingly Serbian-manned and -officered federal Yugoslav army units stationed in barracks in Slovenia and Croatia and local militias which had been hastily raised. Slovenia had the good fortune to escape civil war and, after much negotiation mediated by the European Community, the Yugoslav troops withdrew from her territory. But Croatia, with her large Serbian minority, was

attacked by the Serbs, who after bitter fighting captured the eastern region of the new country. The European Community and the United States offered mediation, which succeeded only in establishing a truce in the spring of 1992 after Serbia had gained all the territory she sought. A UN peacekeeping force was despatched to keep the two sides apart but without orders to use force as it was far too weak and small to do so.

In March 1992 Bosnia–Herzegovina proclaimed her independence, and an even greater tragedy unfolded. The new republic contained an explosive mixed ethnic population – 44 per cent Muslim, 33 per cent Serb–Christian, 17 per cent Croat–Christian. Some of the Serbs, Croats and Muslims began massacring minorities in their midst. The Croats refused to recognise the frontiers of the republic of Bosnia–Herzegovina and captured regions in the north and east inhabited by a majority of 600,000 Croats. The local Serbian militia meanwhile, supported by Belgrade, brutally attacked their Muslim neighbours, so that the million-odd Serbs living in Bosnia–Herzegovina could consolidate their hold on a large slice of the republic's territory and join it to the rest of Serbia. The Serbs engaged in 'ethnic cleansing', driving out the Muslim population – and so adding a new phrase to the vocabulary of genocide. Many Muslims were killed, others incarcerated in camps. Sarajevo, the capital of Bosnia–Herzegovina, was besieged and indiscriminately shelled. No distinction in this horrific civil war was made between combatants and civilians. Snipers killed at random, shooting women and children, even mourners attending funerals. Such barbarism had not occurred in Europe since the Second World War, and its legacy of hatred was certain to poison relations for generations to come between peoples who had such a short time before been peaceful neighbours in Yugoslavia. Atrocities were committed by all sides but the heaviest responsibility for the bloody wars rests on Serbian shoulders in their aim to 'liberate' all Serbian minorities in Croatia and Bosnia-Herzegovina. Only gradually and sporadically did international relief efforts to bring food and medicine to Sarajevo and to other beleaguered cities get under way.

The countries of the West were reluctant to intervene by force to bring the fighting to an end, but diplomatic efforts and economic sanctions failed to deter the Serbs from pursuing their aggression. The conflicts represented the greatest human tragedy since the Second World War. Tens of thousands lost their lives, though no count was possible while the war raged. 'Ethnic cleansing' drove 2 million penniless refugees, possessing only what they could carry, from one Yugoslav republic to another: in 1992 some 640,000 refugees were in camps in Croatia, 680,000 in Bosnia–Herzegovina, 415,000 in Serbia and the remainder in UN-patrolled areas, and in Montenegro, Slovenia and Macedonia. In addition to the 2 million, another half a million refugees reached the West. Germany accepted the most; in relation to their size both Austria (57,000) and Hungary (50,000) responded generously; Switzerland accepted 70,000 and Sweden 48,000. But the record of other Western countries was abysmal.

The conscience of Europe and the world prompted only a meagre response, no more than limited peacekeeping, humanitarian aid and diplomatic mediation. Everyone talked and talked while the killing went on. By not acting more decisively at the beginning, in the summer of 1991, the extent of the conflicts and the resulting human misery

were immeasurably increased. In Bosnia at least 130,000, most of them Muslims, have been killed; in what was Yugoslavia 100,000 are missing and over 3 million are refugees.

By comparison with their Eastern European neighbours, the Germans living in the now defunct German Democratic Republic appeared to be the lucky ones. They were not simply cast adrift, like those neighbours, cut off from the Soviet Union, having to struggle to transform their countries largely by their own efforts, with relatively little Western help. The Germans in the East were united with the most prosperous country in Europe, their fellow Germans in the West. Both lots of Germans had greeted with jubilation the tearing down of the Berlin Wall on 9 November 1989.

The DDR economy was the most advanced of all the economies in Eastern Europe. With help and investment from the Federal Republic it was expected it would be brought up to Western standards after reunification. The costs of all this, no doubt high temporarily, could be met by increased state borrowing and then repaid from the growth of the German economy as a whole. Just as the Federal Republic was reaching an economic plateau, here was the chance of another *Wirtschafts-wunder*, a happy combination of a moral victory and an economic opportunity. But it all went sour as quickly as the unexpected unification of Germany had been accomplished.

As 1989 began no one in Europe or the rest of the world anticipated a cataclysmic change. Erich Honecker, the DDR head of state, lauded the 'scarcely conceivable' achievements of the 'first socialist state of workers and peasants on German soil'. The dour and dedicated communist Walter Ulbricht was forced in May 1971 to step down as Party Secretary, probably on Moscow's instructions, and was replaced by Erich Honecker. It was Ulbricht who had ordered the Berlin Wall to be built in August 1961 to stem the haemorrhage of the 'workers' and 'peasants' crossing to freedom and a better life in the West. He had also ruthlessly built up East German manufacturing in heavy industry and chemicals, regardless of the ecological cost. The attempt to make the DDR an industrial and independent communist showpiece fell apart under Honecker in the 1970s and 1980s, despite the advantages of a privileged relationship with the European Community: trade between the two

*In the south Slav lands of Serbia, Bosnia and Croatia such grieving was a common sight in 1991–94 in an internecine conflict all too reminiscent, for many, of older forms of ethnic and religious struggle.*

Germanies counted as internal EEC trade, a concession to the Federal Republic which offered automatic West German citizenship to any DDR citizen who wanted it and could get to the West.

It is quite possible that Honecker actually believed all the false statistics put out by his government showing how well things were going. They were certainly going well enough for him and the communist elite, living in the lap of luxury and owning extravagantly appointed holiday villas on land on which ordinary mortals were not allowed to set foot. Control over the people was exercised by the Stasi, the 85,000-strong security police who relied on denunciations to alert them to dissident comrades. As in National Socialist Germany, there was no shortage of friends and neighbours, teachers and managers, who were ready to spy and to report wrong attitudes to the state authorities. The bulging files of the Stasi are now among the most embarrassing legacies of the DDR.

During the spring and summer of 1989, Honecker resisted all pressures for reform, despite the radical changes taking place among two of the DDR's neighbours, Poland and Hungary. In the Kremlin, too, Gorbachev had shown that there was

no alternative to reform, to respect for human rights and to the removal of the corrupt and stultifying party apparatchiks. The DDR Politburo did not welcome this, but the hardline comrades could take heart from the firmness the Czech leadership was showing. And if demonstrations looked like getting out of hand, the Chinese showed that summer how best to deal with them. Honecker even despatched his protégé, Egon Krenz, to Beijing to congratulate the Chinese leadership on its bloody handling of the students in Tiananmen Square. Albania was another stout ally. Honecker, by now totally out of touch, was looking forward to celebrating the fortieth anniversary of the founding of the DDR.

So far the West Germans had done little to encourage ideas of fundamental change in the relationship between the two Germanies. Chancellor Kohl, whose popularity had fallen very low, seemed clumsy and out of depth. Within his coalition government there were tensions with the Free Democratic Party and with the astute Foreign Minister Hans-Dietrich Genscher, who since 1987 had advocated a more flexible policy towards the Soviet Union. The moments of pivotal change in the triangular relationship of East and West

Germany and the USSR can be dated with some precision. The Achilles heel of the Soviet Union's dominance was her own collapsing economy. Gorbachev badly needed Western help, especially West German help. When he arrived in Bonn to a rapturous welcome from the crowds in June 1989, he really came as a supplicant for economic assistance. The price was freedom for the Germans in the DDR. Gorbachev and Kohl signed an accord pledging them to work to end the division of Europe, to respect human rights and to expand economic and cultural co-operation. Gorbachev's spokesman, Gennadi Gerasimov quipped that, for the people of the DDR, 'there was the Brezhnev Doctrine. Now we have the Frank Sinatra Doctrine – let them do it their way.' They very soon did.

The East German regime had to watch with bewilderment the flood of DDR 'tourists' who travelled to neighbouring Hungary, Czechoslovakia and Poland and then camped there in the West German embassies waiting to leave for the West. A trickle turned into a flood. During August and September 1989 tens of thousands left and the Hungarians opened the border to Austria. The Hungarians, heavily in debt to the West, were more anxious to please prosperous West Germany than the bankrupt East. On 7 October, the anniversary celebrations were held in East Berlin. Gorbachev planted a Judas kiss on the seventy-seven-year-old Honecker's cheek. It was the last occasion when regimented loyalists waved their flags and cheered their leader. In the back streets, riot police were trying to keep the protesters in check. Soon, Honecker was urging that the police and army should open fire on the demonstrators who were gathering in Eastern Germany's principal cities – East Berlin, Dresden and above all in Leipzig. This decided leading communists in the Politburo to organise a coup, with the Kremlin's secret approval. On 18 October 1989, Egon Krenz toppled and replaced an astonished Honecker. But, with his wolfish look and smile, Krenz could not quell the spirit of revolt. On 9 November he ordered that the Berlin Wall should be opened.

The Protestant Church in East Germany had played an honourable and courageous role in forming an opposition grouping. It called itself New Forum, a coalition of clergymen, artists, socialists and ordinary men and women who wanted to bring to an end the repression. Soon, hundreds of thousands, many among them former communists, took

*In the shadow of the Reichstag, the Berlin Wall is breached: after 9 November 1989, it was no real barrier to any German.*

to the streets to demonstrate. The call for the gang of communist leaders to go was almost universal. Hundreds of thousands wanted to live and move in freedom, to change their drab lives. The eldorado of the West beckoned. Meanwhile, Chancellor Kohl was becoming alarmed. The East Germans flooding to West Germany, which was trying to cope with her own unemployment and housing problems, were, on second thoughts, not all that welcome. Would it not be better after all if they stayed in their own reformed eastern half of Germany?

In the DDR economic collapse and mounting popular protest were wresting control from the communist leadership. Scandals and corruption were revealed. A reformist communist, Hans Modrow, replaced Krenz early in December 1989. His hold on power was brief and tenuous. The West Germans were in a sense also in danger of losing control. Their fear was that they would be swamped with Germans from the East. Kohl, who had hesitated until the close of 1989, had little alternative in 1990 but to ride the tiger. Once he came to this conclusion he campaigned with increasing gusto. First, in late November 1989, he put forward a plan for a 'confederation' of the two Germanies. This was not well received in Moscow, nor was it much welcomed by Mrs Thatcher's government. The former Second World War Allies would in any case have the last word. Thatcher and Mitterrand advised a cautious approach; Bush, with better judgement, gave his full backing to Kohl.

The German people in the end decided the pace. Once free elections in East Germany had been conceded, the New Forum, with its objective of creating a civilised, socialist East German state, and other spontaneous political groups with odd labels were all swept aside. The West German heavy-weight parties moved in, the CDU, the FDP and the SPD. East German party clones of the Western parties campaigned for control. Kohl and Genscher, Brandt and SPD politicians were rapturously received in the East.

The complete unification of Germany proved unstoppable and happened much faster than anyone expected. Kohl carried all before him on a barn-storming six-city election tour in March 1990, promising currency union and a one-for-one exchange of East German into West German marks. The election on 18 March 1990 gave a landslide victory to the East German CDU, and its chairman, Lothar de Maizière became the new East German prime minister. On 1 July, the currency union was carried through as promised, with the one-to-one exchange for savings up to 4000 marks.

Maizière was still hoping for a gradual process of unification, but the majority of East Germans wanted no delay. Meanwhile in July at a meeting between Kohl and Gorbachev agreement was quickly reached. Gorbachev dropped his objection to united Germany remaining a member of NATO; in return Kohl agreed to cut German troops from 590,000 to 370,000 and renounced nuclear, chemical and biological weapons. Gorbachev agreed to pull the Russian troops out of East Germany by 1994, and Kohl promised to pay for their rehousing in the Soviet Union. With the Soviet Union and the United States now consenting to union, the other two treaty powers France and Britain could no longer delay their formal consent. In the mean-time the bankruptcy of the East German state forced Maizière to give up negotiating for a gradual unifi-cation. On 23 August 1990 the Volkskammer voted to dissolve the state and for East Germany to become part of the Federal Republic. Such a suicide was unique in the history of international politics – but then the patient was terminally ill.

At midnight, 3 October 1990, to the muted tones of 'Deutschland, Deutschland Über Alles' and beneath a sky lit up by fireworks, the most momen-tous change in the transformation of Eastern Europe was consummated. By now, no one in West Germany any longer believed that unification would be an easy or cheap or painless process. Still, Kohl had become the first post-war chancellor of all Germany, and he reaped the reward for his skilful leadership, so ably supported by Genscher, when in the December 1990 all-German election the SPD was soundly beaten and the CDU/CSU and its partner the FDP emerged with a substantially increased majority. Kohl had promised his country's neighbours that Germany would be a good Euro-pean, democratic and peaceful. His sincerity on that point, reflecting the views of the vast majority of the German people, was not in doubt. Germany in any case had enough trouble of her own to discourage even the thought of adventurism.

**Bundestag Elections, December 1990**

|  | % | Seats |
|---|---|---|
| CDU/CSU | 43.8 | 319 |
| SPD | 33.5 | 239 |
| FDP | 11.0 | 79 |
| PDS | 2.4 | 17 |
| Greens East | 1.2 | 8 |

*Note:* The PDS (Party of Democratic Socialism) was the renamed Communist Party of the former DDR. The Greens (West) gained no seats, and the extremist Republican Party, which polled 2.1 per cent of the vote, gained no seats either.

The derelict state of the new federal *Länder* in the eastern half of Germany, an economy that had already faltered in its trade with the communist bloc and then in 1990 was unable to meet Western competition, a German workforce whose productivity was low after decades of the communist command economy – all these created far deeper problems for the western half of Germany than was anticipated by the Kohl government. Kohl had promised to revive the east without raising taxes. The DDR currency was exchanged, within certain limits, on a ratio of one to one with the sound West German Mark. To do otherwise, the Kohl government had feared, would have stimulated a mass migration to the prosperous western *Länder*. Aid had to be poured in speedily to narrow as quickly as possible the gap between the standards of living, pay, salaries and pensions between east and west.

Even so, more than 300,000 Germans moved from the east to the west in the year after unification. The difficulties, the costs and the time it would take to raise the eastern economy to western, free-market standards were badly underestimated. Kohl's forecast during the 1990 election campaign of 'blossoming landscapes' in the east by 1994 was soon regarded as unlikely to be fulfilled. His undertaking that 'nobody after unification will be worse off' was rapidly abandoned.

Despite the billions of Deutsche Marks poured into the eastern *Länder* and despite efforts to privatise state industries, the majority of Germans living in the east continued to face severe problems. Material benefits still lay in the future for 3 million workers, one-third of the workforce in the east, who were unemployed or on special programmes designed to mask the true extent of unemployment. Disillusionment and frustration led to growing support for extremist groups, even for neo-Nazis. Anger was turned on the hapless foreign asylum-seekers who had taken advantage of Germany's hitherto generous immigration provisions – 190,000 had entered in 1990 and 250,000 in 1991. The fire-bombing of hostels and violent demonstrations shocked democratic opinion in Germany and the West, but unemployed eastern Germans continued to resent the help given to foreigners, which they claimed deprived 'fellow Germans' of their due. After half a century of brown and red dictatorships, this was evidence of a distinct deficit in ethical values.

The number of foreign immigrants was actually less than the number of ethnic Germans who had lived for generations in the Soviet Union and Eastern Europe and had now migrated to Germany.

*In Leipzig, the dissolution of Communism and the reunification of Germany flush out a minority of young Germans who glorify their country's Nazi past – throughout Germany, youths like these attack refugee hostels, demonstrate provocatively, hound immigrants and, occasionally, resort to murder.*

They had been encouraged in quite different circumstances, before unification, to come back to the land of their fathers. During 1990 and 1991 alone, almost three-quarters of a million took advantage of this opportunity. One of the consequences of recession and of pressure to enter the West was that efforts to halt the flow began to play an increasingly important role in German and in West European politics.

Former citizens of the DDR in the 1990s had to make many painful adjustments before they could expect living standards comparable with those in the West. Some lessons were psychological, such as not waiting to be told what to do but taking the initiative; others were more practical, such as adapting to the needs of the market, working effectively to raise productivity and learning the skills of market management. Another hurdle was to overcome the corruption of the past, the evidence of which lay in twelve miles of files in the former secret police (Stasi) archives. These preserved denunciations by tens of thousands of informants who had reported on their neighbours, employers, employees, teachers and students. It was not easy to accept that the old system could not be divided into the good (such as the guarantee of employment) and the bad (such as the Berlin Wall), that a government and society have to be judged as a whole. It was difficult for East Germans not to be resentful of the west Germans who came over to patronise them and fill the best managerial posts; and it was hard for them to have to wait for an indefinite number of years for the promised land of plenty. Meanwhile in western Germany there was resentment about the sacrifices necessitated by the transfer of money to the east, the higher taxes and high interest rates. The east Germans were blamed for their own plight, for their unrealistic expectations of achieving overnight what had taken the west Germans decades to accomplish.

The shock to the economic system of providing aid for 17 million east Germans was felt throughout Europe. High interest rates slowed down hopes of recovery in France, Britain and the rest of the European Community. Germany could no longer act as the power-house of trade and lift the Community out of recession. Unemployment in the Community was running at around 10 per cent and in some countries was even higher in 1992. Europe in the early 1990s was mired in recession, instead of enjoying the expected 'peace dividend' from the collapse of communism. The former Soviet Union stood on the edge of an economic abyss. But the enormous German effort to transform had begun to show results, and there could be little doubt that in the longer term – though nobody could be sure how long – the problems would be overcome. Germany, unlike Italy, was not likely to remain a divided country, with a prosperous industrial west and an impoverished east.

# CHAPTER 88

# Continuing Turmoil and War in the Middle East

In the West, the 1980s was a decade of economic problems apparently overcome and one of rising prosperity during the good years. Tensions lessened between the East and West; the Cold War came to an end. In the unstable Middle East the 1980s began a new decade of wars, with huge casualties in the Gulf. The wider world wants peace in the region.

The West cannot accept that any one nation, rabidly hostile to the West, should be able to dominate the whole of the Middle East by force of arms. From the Western economic point of view the region means oil, and oil is the lifeblood of contemporary economic life. Yet this oil lies in less developed countries, ruled feudally, as in Saudi Arabia and the various sheikhdoms of the Gulf, or dictatorially, as in Iraq and Iran. The masses can be aroused by nationalism in inter-Arab conflicts, by hatred for the 'imperialist' West, which in the recent past had practically colonised the region, by the arousal of anti-Western Islamic fundamentalism, and by what is regarded as the Western imperialist Zionist outpost, Israel. The bloodiest war of the twentieth century in the Middle East was fought for eight years by two Muslim Middle Eastern oil nations, Iran and Iraq, one of them Persian, the other Arab. When the decade came to its end, the Arab nations were still pitted against each other: Baathist socialist Iraq, violently nationalist and ruled by Saddam Hussein, was confronted by Baathist socialist Syria, dominated by Hafez Assad and the military; secular Egypt's relations with the feudal and rich Saudi Arabia and the sheikhdoms of the Gulf were hostile. Yet in different degrees the Arab nations together faced Israel in enmity. The factions of the Palestinian Liberation Organisation and the Palestinian rising on the occupied West Bank and Gaza added further destabilising elements. In addition, for the greater part of the 1980s West and East still sought to establish regions of influence, a Cold War policy calculation which did not make for peace.

Into this cauldron of instability the West and the Soviet Union poured in the latest weapons of war. The West supplied these arms to secure some leverage over the policies of Middle Eastern nations and to protect Saudi Arabia and the Gulf sheikhdoms from their more powerful neighbours, Iran and Iraq. The Soviet Union also massively armed Iraq and Syria. To deny arms, the West concluded, would only leave the way open to Soviet supply and influence. Thus the Cold War was partly responsible for the fuelling of deadly conflicts. Not only 'legitimate' weapons were sent; 'merchants of death' in West Germany and other countries have secretly helped to set up poison-gas factories and the technology for the manufacture of nuclear weapons. Weapons came from as far away as Brazil, and were used in Middle Eastern wars to terrible effect. For the majority of abject poor living and struggling in this part of the world the wars further set back any hopes of improvement.

Terrorism is also closely linked to the conflicts of the Middle East. It is a phenomenon that is not amenable to diplomacy and reason; it is difficult to control; a few ruthless men and women can commit spectacular acts of carnage and so capture the world headlines. In this way, the numerically weak draw attention to their causes in the expectation of exercising influence out of all proportion to the support they enjoy. Television carries these crimes graphically into millions of homes the world over. Terrorism is not confined to the Middle East and loose connections were forged between various terrorist groups – German, Japanese, Irish and Arab. A Czech factory supplied the most widely used plastic explosive, Semtex. Colonel Gaddafi of Libya and President Assad of Syria, among others, provided funds and armaments to a number of terrorist organisations fighting for what they regarded as just causes. As a result, terrorism greatly increased from the end of the 1960s. Among the most continuous perpetrators were various Arab groups hostile to Israel and the United States, but also to each other. Car bombs in the Lebanon's capital, Beirut, caused indiscriminate slaughter, planes were hijacked, martyrs even blew themselves up to kill their enemies. The list of terrorist acts is too long to be detailed here. Among the most horrifying was the murder of the Israeli athletes

at the Munich Olympics in September 1972. But sometimes the intended victims could be rescued.

In June 1976 the Popular Front for the Liberation of Palestine hijacked an Air France plane with eighty-three Israelis on board; its final landing place was Entebbe in Uganda, where the Israelis were held as hostages. This set the scene for one of the most dramatic and daring rescue operations. Idi Amin, the crazed dictator of Uganda, appointed himself a mediator – the release of terrorists in the prisons of Israel and other countries was demanded by the hijackers. Instead, Israeli paratroopers landed and, camouflaging their arrival at the airport in a fleet of cars as might be used by Amin and his entourage, broke undetected into the airport building, killed the captors and rescued all but three of the hostages, with the loss of one Israeli officer and an elderly Israeli woman (formerly a hostage) murdered in a Ugandan hospital.

Against suicide attacks defence is difficult. In the Lebanon, sixty-three Americans were killed in April 1983 by a fanatical Shia Muslim driving a car full of explosives into the American Embassy in Beirut; a few months later, in October, another suicide bomber killed 241 US marines at their base close to Beirut airport. An especial horror in December

*The Munich Olympics, September 1972. A glimpse of one of the Black September terrorists who murdered 11 Israeli athletes while the Games went on.*

1988 was the explosion over Scotland of a Pan American jumbo en route from London to New York, causing the deaths of all its crew and passengers. But Western lives lost were but a tiny fraction of the number of people killed almost daily in the Middle East. The Lebanon was in virtual anarchy, from the mid-1970s to 1991, with civilians caught up in the infighting of murderous factions, though in 1992 the kidnapping of foreign hostages ended. Western responses were limited and largely ineffective. The organisers of terror, the men behind the scenes, established their shifting headquarters in Baghdad, Teheran, Damascus and Tripoli, their various factions no more than pawns in Arab struggles for predominance. Only the Arab leaders themselves could control them, and their hold was not absolute.

No country in the Middle East has suffered more from brutal civil conflicts than the Lebanon. The Christian Lebanese merchants and bankers did not long enjoy the prosperity the oil-rich Middle East brought them in the 1960s and 1970s. A power-sharing agreement, known as the National Pact and in operation since the Second World War, guaranteed the presidency to a Maronite Christian, but it fell apart under the pressure of Muslim–Christian and left–right rivalries, resulting in civil war in 1958. Though fighting ceased for a time, the central Lebanese government was unable to overcome the problems presented by the class conflicts, the family loyalties and the various militias of Muslim and Christian groups. In 1967, the Lebanon's predicament was further aggravated by the arrival of uninvited Palestinian refugees following the Arab–Israeli war. Arab enmity towards Israel deepened the gulf between what had become a Muslim majority, which included the poorer part of the Lebanese population, and the wealthier Maronite Christians. 'National' for the Muslims now meant pro-Arab; for the Christians (except the Greek Orthodox), 'national' meant perpetuation of Christian and right-wing predominance in an independent pro-Western Lebanon.

In 1970 the Palestinian militants failed in their attempt to achieve domination over Jordan. Yasser Arafat and the Palestinian Liberation Organisation were forced out and with their militant followers moved into the hapless Lebanon, where they proceeded to build up their last territorial stronghold in the areas controlled by the refugees. The term 'refugee camps' applied to these strongholds is really a misnomer, for the Palestinians created a state within a state. From the Lebanon Palestinian commandos raided Israel, attacking settlements and provoking Israeli counter-strikes against Palestinian targets in the Lebanon.

In 1975 civil war was renewed. The Muslim groups forged an alliance with the Palestinians, the army split and the central government lost control over the country. It could regain it only with outside help. The Lebanon was now divided into warring factions; Christian family clans fought each other for supreme power even as they battled with the Muslim–Palestinian–left alliance. The Israelis sent arms to the Maronite Christians, and the Syrians, responding to pleas for help from the Christian-dominated central Lebanese government, intervened militarily in 1976, driving the Muslim–Palestinian forces back. Yasser Arafat's independent PLO was as little loved in Syria as it was in Jordan. In 1978, to stamp out Palestinian commando raids, the Israelis occupied the southern Lebanon, and before withdrawing installed a 'friendly' Maronite Christian militia under Major Saad Haddad to keep order and prevent further PLO attacks. The Lebanon had long since ceased to be a unitary state and was becoming a quagmire of internecine factions, none of which was sufficiently powerful to control more than a particular area, each with its own stronghold. As if these internal rivalries were not enough, Syrian–Israeli hostility, the Palestinian–Maronite Christian conflict and, after the outbreak of the Gulf War in 1980, pro-Iraqi and pro-Iranian Muslim rivalry accelerated the disintegration and destruction of the Lebanon.

For the Israelis, the continued presence of the PLO in the Lebanon, not to mention the Syrians, represented a serious threat. So the civil strife offered opportunities, but it led them into the ill-fated invasion of the Lebanon in 1982, which was intended to settle once and for all the Palestinian question and to prove that continued Arab enmity towards Israel was unrealistic in view of her military superiority. The militant PLO would be driven from their last land base in a neighbouring country. Israeli prospects seemed favourable, because Syria and the Palestinians were practically isolated and their forces much inferior. Israel had already by concluding peace with Egypt secured her southern border against the only strong army that might have threatened her. Her first war of aggression was the consequence of a fundamental change in her internal politics during the previous five years.

In Israeli politics a major turning point occurred in 1977 with the victory of the right-wing Likud Party over the broad labour grouping led by the Labour Party (Mapai). Labour's support had suffered after the heavy casualties of the Yom Kippur War in 1973, which had found Israel inadequately prepared and had placed the country for a time in real danger. Golda Meir fell from office and was succeeded by Yitzhak Rabin, who had been chief of staff in the Six-Day War of 1967. During Rabin's premiership, the United States made great efforts to mediate a peace between Israel and her neighbours. This introduced the diplomatic world to the new concept of 'shuttle diplomacy', as the American Secretary of State Henry Kissinger carried out negotiations, tirelessly flying between Damascus, Cairo and Jerusalem. Kissinger succeeded at least partially – disengagement agreements were concluded between Israel, Syria and Egypt. What blocked a more comprehensive settlement was the requirement of the Arab states that Israel should withdraw from the territories she had conquered in 1967 – the West Bank, the Gaza Strip and East Jerusalem. This raised the possibility of a hostile Palestinian presence or even state as Israel's new neighbour. Israeli militants were already creating their own settlements, and there was broad support from large sections of the electorate that the West Bank, biblical Judaea and Samaria, must remain a part of an enlarged Israel. With Arab–Israeli talks deadlocked, only Nasser's successor, President Anwar Sadat, was ready to move further, in order to regain the Sinai, lost in 1967.

During 1977, election year, Labour's chances were harmed by government scandals and by the damage inflicted on the economy by the high cost of war and armaments. The oriental Jews in particular regarded the Labour ministers as too ready to compromise with Israel's Arab neighbours. All this contributed to the sea-change in Israeli politics.

The May 1977 elections brought Menachem Begin and Likud to power at the head of a coalition, breaking three decades of uninterrupted Labour predominance. Begin, at sixty-four years of age, was no longer the terrorist he had been during Israel's struggle for independence, but he was convinced that only armed strength, self-reliance and rock-like firmness of purpose would secure

Israel's future. On the question of the West Bank and some possible accommodation with the PLO, he was unyielding: for him the right of the Jewish people to 'Judaea and Samaria' was not negotiable; for him this was not 'occupied' but 'liberated' territory, and so was East Jerusalem, which had been captured from Jordan in 1967. Nor did Begin in 1977 give any indication that he contemplated handing back occupied Sinai in return for peace with Egypt. Yet that was to become the crowning achievement of his first administration. Perhaps only an Israeli prime minister with Begin's uncompromising reputation could have won virtually wholehearted Israeli support for relinquishing the Sinai.

At home, free-enterprise policies soon led the country into economic crisis. Given the realities of Israeli expenditure and the huge foreign indebtedness, Likud eventually had to return to the mixed economic policies of previous governments. Even so, for his supporters – the poor oriental Jews – Begin provided help in housing, and assisted the renewal of poor neighbourhoods by twinning them with Jewish communities abroad; extending free education was a further important social reform.

Abroad the Begin government responded to Sadat's search for peace, with US mediation playing a crucial role. Sadat wanted to modernise Egypt, raise the standard of living of her rapidly expanding population. He turned to Western investment and away from a state-directed economy. Success depended above all on securing a lasting peace with Israel. The crossing by the Egyptian army of the Suez Canal in the 1973 war had removed one major obstacle to peace – Egypt's self-image, pride and self-confidence had been restored; Israel had not won all the battles. The illusion of military prowess in war was enough to turn Sadat into a hero in Egyptian eyes, as Nasser had become a hero after Suez. Sadat cut all links with the Soviet Union and took to relying on US support and US influence in Israel. In 1975 he opened the Suez Canal to shipping again, and allowed cargoes to Israel, though not Israeli ships, to pass through. In 1977 it was because four men occupied crucial positions in their countries which made a peace settlement possible.

In Washington Jimmy Carter entered the White House, like his predecessors, anxious to facilitate a settlement in the Middle East. Begin's priorities were to secure 'Judaea and Samaria', and to defeat the PLO. Peace with Egypt, even at the price of returning most of the occupied Sinai, would isolate Israel's enemies and make her position militarily unchallengeable. It was thus a price worth paying, provided the existing Israeli settlements and air-bases were retained. General Moshe Dayan, Begin's new foreign minister, entirely shared this view. Security for the West Bank was worth the loss of most of the Sinai. Sadat was also eager for peace: the cost of continued hostility was simply too high for the sake of Arab solidarity or the Palestinian cause. In 1977 he expelled the PLO from Cairo. Nicolae Ceauşescu, President of Romania, later to be discredited for his brutal suppressions at home, was an unlikely mediator, having preserved good relations with Israel. Another channel of communication between Egypt and Israel was opened through the good offices of the King of Morocco. Begin also demonstrated goodwill by warning Sadat of a Palestinian assassination plot.

That a new era in Israeli–Egyptian relations had begun became publicly known in a dramatic way. Sadat liked springing surprises. On 9 November 1977 he announced in Cairo's parliament that he was ready in person to go to the Israeli parliament in Jerusalem, the Knesset, to discuss the issues that divided Israel from her Arab neighbours. Begin was amazed, but he recovered quickly and the next day invited Sadat to Jerusalem. The Arab world condemned the visit. It was unprecedented and many in Israel responded warmly and emotionally. A score of the Egyptian national anthem had to be rushed to the Israeli army band drawn up at Ben Gurion airport to receive the Egyptian President and his entourage. As he landed, on 19 November 1977, to a twenty-one gun salute, with Israeli and Egyptian flags fluttering side by side, it was a moving spectacle. Sadat had certainly seized the initiative, catching the world's imagination as peacemaker, and millions of people watched his arrival on television. Sadat spoke to the Knesset on 20 November. Many hard negotiating sessions would be necessary, for Sadat spoke of peace with all the Arabs, including the Palestinians, and of a total Israeli withdrawal from occupied lands.

But he also spoke of accepting Israel in friendship and peace, words no other Arab leader had uttered, at least not publicly, since 1947. Begin's response was conciliatory in form but uncompromising in reality on the issues of the Palestinians and the continued Israeli possession of the West Bank and East Jerusalem. Yet direct personal contact had

been made, the long road to Camp David and peace was at least now open. Begin offered to return the Sinai apart from existing Israeli settlements. Although there and then there could be no talk of formal peace, Sadat and Begin agreed that only by negotiation and not by war could divisive issues be resolved. Yet negotiations between Cairo and Jerusalem dragged on fruitlessly for almost a year, with Washington trying in vain to find a way of resolving their differences. The Palestinian issue, the West Bank, the Gaza Strip and the Israeli settlements were blocking progress. Carter tried again. Finally, Sadat and Begin accepted an invitation to his presidential retreat at Camp David to attempt to break the deadlock. Sadat had been the more accommodating so far; would Begin also compromise?

Sadat, Begin, Carter and their advisers laboured for thirteen days at Camp David until the agreement was signed on 17 September 1978. Carter's role was crucial, as he cajoled and pressurised Sadat and (especially) Begin in turn. To have reached agreement at all in the face of the Israeli leader's obduracy was a personal triumph for the President. The two major issues were the Sinai, and the West Bank and Gaza. Could Begin be made to give up the whole of the Sinai, including the oilwells the Israelis had developed at great cost, and to pull back strategic settlements which he had repeatedly pledged he would never abandon? Secondly, would the Palestinians be allowed to develop in the occupied territories some form of self-government short of statehood, with the bulk of Israelis withdrawing? And would the two issues be linked, as Sadat was insisting: no peace with Egypt without concrete steps towards a solution of the Palestinian problem? Begin at first refused to budge, and Sadat threatened to leave. Carter promised to place the blame for a breakdown on Begin when he came to report to Congress. Reluctantly, Begin gave way – the whole of the Sinai would be handed back in stages. But the procedures leading to Palestinian autonomy, and what that really meant, left practically everything to Israel's readiness and judgement; in practice, there was no linkage. The various compromises were wrapped up in two main agreements and a number of agreed additional letters and documents. At a subsequent news conference, which was televised, Sadat and Begin embraced as a beaming Carter looked on. Even then the road to the definitive peace treaty signed in the White House on 26

March 1979 was strewn with obstacles, overcome only by determined American mediation and financial help.

In Israel most people approved of the peace – the hawks because it strengthened Israel against the other Arab states by leaving her in firm occupation of the West Bank, and the doves because it showed that peace could be concluded with an Arab state, formerly an implacable enemy. But the Palestinian issue festered. The chance to make genuine progress was lost. If Israel had acted speedily to fulfil the spirit of the Camp David Accords, 'autonomy' – a genuine degree of self-determination – might have had a chance. The Palestinians on the West Bank and Gaza were greatly benefiting from a rapid rise in their standard of living as a result of their close association with the Israeli economy – but the military occupation acted as a constant reminder that their status was not that of a self-respecting free people. Inevitably a younger, better-educated generation of Palestinians was radicalised. The prospect of a Palestinian–Israeli reconciliation was thrown away, and the Israelis and Palestinians have been paying the bitter price ever since.

How much better it would have been to follow Sadat's advice. He secured the return of the Sinai but was ostracised and condemned by the rest of the Arab world. US financial help and the resources of the Sinai did not fully compensate Egypt for the loss of aid from the oil-rich Arab states. Her economic problems, with a rapidly increasing population, prevented a quick improvement in living standards for the mass of the poor. But no more young Egyptian lives would be lost in war. Instead, the courageous and far-seeing President paid for peace with his own life. At a military parade on 6 October 1981 a small group of Egyptians recruited by Muslim fundamentalists assassinated Sadat as he took the salute. The Vice-President, Hosni Mubarak, miraculously survived the hail of bullets to become Egypt's new head of state. The peace prevailed, but the sincerity and warmth of feeling, the desire for genuine reconciliation between Egyptian and Israeli, were interred with Sadat's remains.

Begin's first government from 1977 to 1981 had seemed to promise a new peaceful beginning with the Camp David Accords and the Egyptian peace treaty. The soldiers in his Cabinet were cautious men unwilling to be drawn into new confrontations.

Yasser Arafat's PLO and Assad's Syrian regime too were aware of their own vulnerability and were observing truce agreements. But inside the Lebanon the factional struggles sucked in the Syrians in support of the Christian Maronites, who then also made constant appeals to the Israelis. Meanwhile the PLO was strong enough to dominate the southern Lebanon with increasing effectiveness. Begin's ministers continued to urge caution in dealing with the mess in the Lebanon; but they were split on whether a preventive airstrike against Iraq was advisable, some arguing that there could be no justification in international law for such an attack at a time of peace. But Begin won out.

On 7 June 1981 eight Israeli F-16 jet fighters took off and, together with an escort of six F-15s, with surgical precision destroyed the Iraqi Osiraq nuclear reactor. All the Israeli planes returned to the bases safely. The reactor, built with French help, was not yet capable of producing atomic bombs, but given time the Iraqis would undoubtedly have succeeded in acquiring all that was necessary to make the weapons. There was international condemnation of Israel, but at home the Israelis rallied to Begin, which did his coalition no harm in the general election that June. Despite the economic setbacks, Likud strengthened its position, but the new coalition Begin led depended for its tiny majority on the religious parties. His views had always been hardline on the Palestinian and West Bank issues. Now instead of being moderated by the exigencies of coalition government, they were reinforced by the extremist religious groups. The most aggressive of the hawks, Ariel Sharon, the daring military commander who had turned the tide for Israel in the 1973 Yom Kippur War, became minister of defence. The new government's external policies came to be overshadowed by Sharon's 'grand design', which turned out disastrously for Begin personally and for Israel.

On the occupied West Bank new Israeli settlements had sprung up, and more were planned. They clearly indicated Israel's intention of staying. Sharon wanted to go further – a knock-out blow against the Palestinians and Syrians that would once and for all settle the issue of what should constitute the secure land of Israel. Begin's Cabinet was persuaded to back what was innocuously called Operation Peace for the Galilee. In alliance with the Christian Maronite leader Bashir Gemayel, Sharon planned an invasion of the Lebanon as far as Beirut to clear out the Syrians, the PLO and their allies. A Maronite-led Lebanon would then become a friendly non-Arab neighbour. Israel's hold over the West Bank and her denial of Palestinian rights would then be unchallengeable.

The decision to launch the attack came as a consequence of a murderous attack on an Israeli diplomat far away from the Middle East. As Ambassador Shlomo Argov was leaving the Dorchester Hotel in London on the evening of 3 June 1982, a renegade Palestinian group bitterly hostile to Arafat and acting on Iraqi instructions fired a bullet into Argov's head, inflicting critical wounds which left him paralysed. On 4 June, Israeli planes struck at PLO targets in the Lebanon. The PLO responded by shelling Israeli kibbutzim in Galilee. The truce was broken. On the 6th, the Israeli Defence Force began its operation in Lebanon. But instead of confining themselves to the southern Lebanon, as the watching world expected, they knocked out the Syrian Soviet missiles in the Bekaa Valley on 9 June and advanced four days later all the way to the outskirts of West Beirut, where the PLO had established their strongholds.

In the eyes of the world – and in the face of growing opposition at home, as the Labour Party strongly condemned the extension of the war to Beirut – the Israelis were now playing an entirely new role. No longer heroically defending their homeland, the Israeli army and air force seemed to be indiscriminately (though this was actually not so) shelling the districts of West Beirut; half of the city remained under siege for more than a month. This was Sharon's war, the culmination of his grand design, though neither Begin nor the Israeli Cabinet was fully aware of his plans. On 21 August the PLO's fighting force, loyal to Yasser Arafat, began leaving Beirut by sea under the protection of a multinational force, having accepted Israel's terms of surrender. Nearly 15,000 Palestinians and Syrians were evacuated during the next few days by sea and land. But neither the Syrians nor the PLO were crushed or even cowed – they would fight back another day. Sharon's grand design had not succeeded; rather, it had severely damaged Israel's international reputation and her people's confidence in democratic government. Nor could a stable Christian Maronite Lebanon be reconstructed as a friendly neighbour. In mid-September the Lebanon's president-elect, the Christian Maronite Bashir Gemayel, was assassinated on the orders of Syrian intelligence. The Lebanon was lapsing into chaos as warring factions fought each other once again.

The evacuation agreement reached with the PLO contained an important clause stipulating that law-abiding, non-combatant Palestinians who had remained in West Beirut and the southern Lebanon would be guaranteed protection. In the massacre that ensued in two Palestinian refugee camps, Sabra and Shatila, Israel's reputation suffered the most ignominious blow. The sadistic killings were a savage revenge for Bashir's assassination, but the Phalangist Christians who committed the atrocity and who hated the Palestinians had determined on a massacre long before. The Israeli commanders had sent them into the camps to clear out any remaining terrorists, little imagining they would also turn on whole families, including defenceless women and children. They should have known better. The bodies, bloated by the sun, were shown to the world on television. Israel was blamed for the hundreds of dead. At a subsequent inquiry in Israel in 1983, Sharon was judged primarily responsible and his dismissal as minister of defence was urged. It is to Begin's discredit that though Sharon had to quit the defence post he remained a minister in Begin's and successive governments. Massive 'Peace Now' rallies in Israel and mounting Israeli casualties among the forces occupying parts of the Lebanon finally persuaded the government to order their withdrawal.

The Lebanon war had been a disaster for Israel. It achieved fundamentally nothing. The Lebanon remained torn between rival Muslim Iranian and Iraqi factions, the Druse and right-wing Phalangist Christians. Central government was nearly power-less and was dominated by Syria. Killings continued daily in the city, divided between Muslim West Beirut and Christian East Beirut by the so-called Green Line, until the Christian Forces agreed to withdraw in November 1990. The West learnt that it can achieve nothing, by force or by diplomacy, to bring peace to the Lebanon, even though rival Muslim groups held Western hostages. And the Syrians, still controlling parts of the country, were stuck in the quagmire of conflict. The Syrians did not withdraw as promised, but after 1990, under Asad's watchful gaze, Lebanon rediscovered a fragile peace.

Begin accepted the consequences of his failure and, haunted by the many Israeli casualties, resigned in September 1983, to be replaced by another Likud hardliner, Yitzhak Shamir. The election of 1984 ended in a stalemate, with the religious parties holding the balance. Instead of giving in to their demands, Labour and Likud agreed on a 'National Unity' government, shared between Shamir and the Labour leader Shimon Peres. So divided a cabinet could follow no decisive policies. The paralysing division of the Israeli electorate continued, with Likud supporters favouring hardline policies on the West Bank and the Palestinian question, and Labour supporters more ready to find a compromise solution. The result, as a new generation of Palestinians on the West Bank and in Gaza grew to manhood, was a violent challenge to the continued Israeli occupation – the uprising, the *intifada*, which began in December 1987. Israel's young conscripts were ordered in to re-establish control. Civil conflict is brutalising. Inexperienced Israeli soldiers were unequal to the task of dealing with stone-throwing young men and children; in frustration bullets were fired, unarmed Palestinians killed. A military curfew was imposed, which alienated the Palestinians still further.

Yasser Arafat was one of the great political survivors, still a familiar figure on the world's state in the early 1990s who had dedicated his life to creating a Palestinian state. Through terrorism the Palestinians succeeded in drawing global attention to their cause when neither their Arab brethren nor the rest of the world cared. For the Arab nations the Palestinians were pawns to be supported or rejected as their own interests dictated, and the PLO fighters were fractious and rebellious 'guests' of their host nations. Thus the Palestinians were successively expelled from Jordan, Egypt and the Lebanon. But Arafat had succeeded in dominating the mainstream of Palestinians in 1969 as chairman of the Palestine Liberation Organisation. During the 1970s he supported terrorism as the only effective weapon the Palestinians had. In 1974 at the Arab summit in Rabat the Arab nations accepted the PLO as the authentic voice of the Palestinians, a step forward that implied independence not only from Israel but from Jordan's King Hussein. Arafat came to recognise that continued terrorism would now harm his cause, which needed world support. Bitter enmities developed between him and those

*Among the fractious Palestinian factions, Yasser Arafat represents the Palestinian cause to the world, as here at a meeting of non-aligned nations in Havana.*

Palestinian factions which continued their campaign of terrorism. But he would not condemn individual terrorist attacks against Israel either, for fear of losing support among the Palestinians who regarded these fighters as martyrs. So he spoke in two contradictory voices: to the West he gave assurances, which he promptly denied giving when speaking to his own people; until September 1993.

During the 1980s Arafat worked out a 'legitimate' strategy for creating a Palestinian state. It would have been unrealistic to have as its objective the destruction of Israel and the retaking of the whole of Palestine. Instead a mini-state solution emerged. The Palestinian state would comprise the West Bank, Gaza and East Jerusalem. To gain the support of the United States, Arafat in December 1988 publicly renounced terrorism and accepted Israel's right to exist. Talks between the US representatives and the PLO were held sporadically, but ended when Arafat once more appeared to condone terrorism in practice. Meanwhile, in Israel, Shamir resisted all US pressure to consider some form of genuine Palestinian autonomy, exchanging Gaza, the West Bank (or most of it) and East Jerusalem for peace. The Israeli right also rejected any direct negotiations with the PLO. Israeli opinion, however, was deeply divided and the rest of the world was losing patience with what appeared to be Israeli intransigence. The continued killing of Palestinians, and the indiscrimi-

nate shooting on the Temple Mount in October 1990, after Palestinians had hurled stones at praying Jews, further alienated world opinion.

Yitzhak Shamir's coalition with Labour had collapsed the previous March in bitter disagreement over the peace process. With the help of extreme right-wing religious groups, he was able to form a new government in June, offering no hope of concession to the Palestinians. The government would neither negotiate with the PLO nor allow a Palestinian state to be created.

Yasser Arafat's cause was seriously hurt when he sided with Saddam Hussein in the Gulf War after the August 1990 invasion of Kuwait, and he lost his Arab friends in the Gulf who had supported the PLO with money. The Israelis, moreover, could declare that the fears for their own security were not exaggerated, as Scud missiles from Iraq fell on Tel Aviv to the cheers of the Palestinians. In August 1992 the Labour leader Rabin, promising to seek peace, replaced the 'hardline' Shamir. Rabin turned out to be as tough as Shamir in dealing with Palestinian fundamentalist terrorists belonging to Hamas. The 'peace process', begun under the Americans' aegis in Madrid in October 1991, made little progress despite round after round of talks between Palestinian and Israeli representatives. Rabin in total secrecy now authorised Foreign Minister Peres to negotiate directly with the PLO in Norway.

*The Palestinian Intifada makes the Gaza strip a hazardous posting for Israeli conscripts, January 1988.*

The longest and bloodiest war in the Middle East in the 1980s was the Gulf War between Iran and Iraq, which in the course of eight years devastated large areas of both countries and left at least half a million dead and many more crippled. On 22 September 1980, Iraq attacked Iran, counting on a swift victory.

It was just twenty months after Ayatollah Khomeini's return to Teheran in triumph on 1 February 1979. Khomeini had rapidly disposed of the politicians and generals still loyal to the Shah's regime, having them summarily executed by secret revolutionary courts. That conflict between the royalists and revolutionaries had cost thousands of lives and left the economy in ruins, though Khomeini continued to be revered by the mass of the people.

The mosques with their local revolutionary komitehs played a vital role during and after the revolution. Once more, to the outside world Iran appeared to be going through months of turmoil and near anarchy, with radical Muslim groups, Marxist and more moderate opposition politicians struggling for control of the country, with the *ulema*, or clergy, acting independently as a rival faction. Khomeini, the acknowledged leader, at first kept in the background. For a time the state was confusingly divided between a prime minister and a formal government and the Islamic Revolutionary Council. But between 1979 and 1982, the Council gradually took over real power, first by creating its own political party, the Islamic Revolutionary Party, then by setting up an Islamic militia of Revolutionary Guards. During the summer of 1979 the Islamic Revolutionary Party dominated the Assembly, which produced a constitution for the Islamic Republic. This laid down that religious leadership would guide the country. There could be no other leader than the 'Grand Ayatollah Iman Khomeini', who was also the commander-in-chief and head of the Supreme Defence Council. He could declare war and peace; he was empowered to approve and appoint the president on his election by the Assembly; he was the chief justice. The ordinances of Islam were supreme, but the believers of Islam would be free to debate their differences.

Khomeini invariably sided with the radicals. Soon revolutionary Iran was enmeshed in fighting the Kurds, the most nationalistic ethnic minority in the country. The Kurds' success in October 1979 forced Teheran to accept a compromise ceasefire. A new enemy was branded just a short while after – the American 'Satan'. Khomeini, fearing a US-backed attempt to overthrow the Islamic Revolution and restore the Shah to power, demanded the Shah's extradition to stand trial. The Carter administration, which had allowed the Shah to enter a New York hospital, refused. Directly encouraged by Khomeini, militant students thereupon seized the American Embassy on 4 November 1979 in a well-planned operation to capture secret US documents, in a bid to compromise the United States as well as internal opponents. Fifty-two Embassy staff were held hostage for fifteen months until 21 January 1981, the day of Reagan's inauguration. In the meantime, rivalries among clerics and politicians in Iran appeared to present a picture of complete disarray. This is what tempted the Iraqis to invade Iran: the conditions seemed ideal for the defeat of an old rival for predominance in the Gulf.

The immediate cause of conflict was the Shatt al-Arab, the waterway between Iraq and Iran leading out to the Gulf. Should the frontier run in mid-channel or were both banks Iraqi territory? If the latter, Iranian shipping would have to pay tolls to the Iraqis and Iraq would control the waterway through which oil tankers passed. The dispute goes back to the nineteenth century, and a settlement of 1937 favouring Iraq was torn up in 1969 by the Shah, who imposed the median line by a show of force. Relations between Iran and Iraq deteriorated, with each country encouraging national dissident movements in the other – especially of Kurds, who straddled both countries. But between 1975 and 1978 peaceful relations were restored.

The Islamic revolution in Iran, however, alarmed Saddam Hussein's socialist Baathist regime, not least because it was condemned by Khomeini as hostile to Islamic rule. Saddam ruthlessly crushed the internal opposition, executing militant sympathisers of the Iranian Islamic revolutionaries. Khomeini meanwhile called on the Iraqi army to overthrow Saddam.

Full-scale fighting began on 22 September 1980 with an Iraqi invasion. The Iranian air force did well in response. Each side attacked the other's oil centres, but despite advancing rapidly the Iraqi army failed to capture the great refinery at Abadan. Iranian artillery continued throughout the war to deny Iraqi warships passage of Shatt al-Arab, while the Iranian army and the new Revolutionary Guards defended fanatically, inflicting heavy casualties on the Iraqi forces and preventing them from extending their early gains. The conflict became a war of attrition – though one which strengthened the hold of the Iranian clergy. Khomeini declared a holy war which, he said, would end only when Saddam Hussein, the aggressor against the Islamic Republic, had been overthrown. From the spring of 1982, the Iranians, with their much greater reserves of manpower, began to gain the initiative, gradually pushing the Iraqis out of the territories they had captured in the first month of the war. Mediation attempts and offers of a ceasefire were rejected by the Ayatollah because Saddam Hussein remained in power unpunished.

Young Iranians, many barely out of childhood, enlisted in the Revolutionary Guards in response to Khomeini's call to fight evil. To die for the faith brought glorious martyrdom and would ensure a welcome in heaven. In the martyrs' cemetery in Teheran, 'the fountain of blood' graphically symbolised the sacrifice of life. Prayer meetings, attended by thousands in villages and cities, strengthened resolve. Tens of thousands of young volunteers hurled themselves in human-wave attacks against the Iraqi defences.

Saddam Hussein was equally successful in maintaining the war spirit but less so in representing himself as the Pan-Arab champion against the old Persian foe. Syria, Iraq's rival, backed Iran and in 1982 blocked Iraq's oil pipeline to the Mediterranean; even Israel, though Zionism was denounced by the revolutionaries in Iran, appears to have provided some secret technical assistance to the Iranian army and air force. For most of the war the Soviet Union and the United States were anxious to contain Iran and to counter the 'export' of Iranian-style Muslim fundamentalism to the USSR's Central Asian republics or to America's allies in the Gulf, Saudi Arabia and the Gulf states. The leaders of the Gulf states, which were in the direct firing line, feared Iran the most and so supplied money to Iraq. But fears that Iranian-style revolutions would destabilise the Gulf states had not been realised in the early 1990s.

Iran suffered huge losses in driving the Iraqis out. Her forces had no hope of defeating the well-entrenched Iraqi army, whose military supplies were purchased with Saudi Arabian, Kuwaiti and United States help. The US arms embargo, and the international fleet from the West which protected the tankers of the Gulf states from Iranian retaliation after the Iraqi attacks on Iranian oil installations, underlined Teheran's diplomatic isolation. Weapons did reach Iran, despite embargoes – indeed, the bizarre Iran–Contra affair belongs to this chapter of secret arms deals. They were not enough to turn the war in Iran's favour, but they were sufficient to prolong the military stalemate.

Iran's war effort was being worn down by the end of 1987. Long-range Iraqi missile attacks sapped morale in Teheran, and the enthusiasm of recruits was waning as Iran's offensives failed to make much further progress. Iraq's use of poison gas added to the horrors of the war. Once more the Iranian poor suffered the most, while the rich could indulge in imported luxury goods. Nonetheless, Iranians, unlike Iraqis, were allowed a considerable degree of freedom to debate and discuss. The shooting down in July 1988 of an Iranian airliner, mistaken by a US warship as a fighter coming in to attack, helped to convince the Iranian leadership that the American 'imperialists' would stop at nothing. After Khomeini, the most powerful man in Iran was Hojatoleslam Rafsanjani, the adroit Speaker of the Assembly, a cleric and faithful follower of Khomeini. Rafsanjani, a pragmatist, concluded that the war had to be brought to an end. All depended on Khomeini, who had never compromised or given way on a matter of right and wrong. But the sorry state of Iran and the inability of the military to mount any more offensives persuaded him with great reluctance and feelings of bitterness to side with Rafsanjani and with those who wished to end the war. Accordingly Iran accepted the ceasefire resolution of the United Nations. On 18 July 1988, Khomeini's message that after eight years the war had ended without the defeat of Iraq stunned the Iranian masses.

The death of Khomeini a year later, in June 1989, tilted power more to the moderates, and Rafsanjani took over the leading role in the country, though the radicals remained a powerful group. Rafsanjani's efforts to improve relations with the West were obstructed by a bizarre affair, the earlier publication by Salman Rushdie, a British author, of *The Satanic Verses*, which Muslims condemned as blasphemous. Violent protest erupted in many Muslim countries, and Khomeini pronounced a *fatwa*, a religious sentence of death on Rushdie, who had to go into hiding. Even after the Ayatollah's death, Rafsanjani was not able to undo the sentence. But Iran's relations with the West were improving,

*The Iran–Iraq Gulf War demanded unending sacrifice on both sides. In the effort to punish the Iraqi invaders, even Iranian women are called on to train to be revolutionary warriors.*

buttressed by her co-operative behaviour during the Kuwaiti Gulf War. She remained an important factor in any Middle Eastern peace order.

Iraq interpreted Iran's change of heart as a victory. In the aftermath of the war, Iraq decided to crush the dissident Kurds in the north by killing them with poison gas in their villages; 100,000 refugees escaped into Turkey. It was a crime against humanity, but the world did no more than express regret. The West was more concerned with stabilising the Middle East and so removing the dangers to the Gulf and to oil. In Iraq, Saddam Hussein strengthened his own regime's hold over the country and his personality cult reached new heights. In 1990 a subservient Assembly appointed him president for life. The growing power and pretensions of Iraq now began to cause alarm in the West and Israel. Her invasion on 2 August 1990 of her neighbour, Kuwait, over which Saddam had angrily claimed sovereignty, marked the start of a new world crisis.

That Saddam Hussein should start another war so soon after the conclusion of the devastating and fruitless conflict with Iran took the West by surprise. Kuwait had assisted Iraq and now became her victim. The quarrel between the small emirate and her powerful neighbour arose out of a disputed frontier and the oilfield that straddled it. Iraq also accused Kuwait of lowering the price of oil by over-production. Iraq was desperately short of funds, so the oil-rich emirate was a tempting prize to seize. Even the Arab states believed that the dispute could be mediated with their help and accepted Saddam's assurances that he would not attack Kuwait. When he did so, he caught Kuwait, Egypt, Syria and Saudi Arabia entirely off-guard. It was a gamble, but with the most powerful army in the region Saddam believed he was safe. Kuwait was annexed as Iraq's 'nineteenth province', though the plundering by the invading soldiers did not diminish. Iraq's claim to the emirate was in fact historically spurious. Kuwait had existed as an entity (a British protectorate in 1899 and granted independence in 1971) before Iraq was created from the ashes of the Ottoman Empire after the First World War.

The West acted promptly, the lead given by the

Bush administration in Washington. On 6 August 1990 the Security Council passed a resolution that required all member states to cut off trade with Iraq. Iraq's main export earner, oil, was paralysed. In all, twelve resolutions, of increasing severity, were passed at the UN. They required Iraq to quit Kuwait unconditionally, and on the initiative of the United States a deadline was set for 15 January 1991, after which date, if Iraq had not by then left Kuwait, 'all necessary means' to drive Iraqi forces out of Kuwait were authorised. The Security Council was in rare unanimity. The Chinese wished to show their respect for the international rule of law after the world's condemnation of the Tiananmen Square massacre. Gorbachev, who had met Bush in Helsinki on 9 September, was looking for Western assistance to help meet the economic crisis at home and joined the American President in condemning Iraq's invasion. As the deadline drew near, the mediating efforts of the UN Secretary-General Javier Peréz de Cuéllar failed, as did a last-minute attempt by Gorbachev.

Bush acted without hesitation, strongly supported by Margaret Thatcher. Saddam Hussein could not be allowed to get away with his forcible annexation. After Kuwait, Saudi Arabia and the other Gulf emirates would be at his mercy. As controller of the Gulf's oil, he could hold the industrial world to ransom. Syria and Egypt were not prepared to allow Saddam's Iraq such a huge increase of power either. Thus from the beginning the United States and Britain could count on regional Arab allies, including of course the Gulf emirates and Saudi Arabia, whose vast financial reserves were at the disposal of the alliance. A war against Iraq would thus not be another Western 'colonial' drubbing of an Arab nation. The United States mounted a tremendous military effort, the largest since Vietnam, and the speediest build-up of military might since the Second World War. By the time the land war began, half the forces were not American, though the United States had made by far the largest contribution to the fighting forces on land, on the sea and in the air. The command of the allied armies, more than 600,000 strong, was assumed by the US General H. Norman Schwarzkopf, who soon became a swashbuckling television personality. Never before had almost every minute of a war been televised as a worldwide spectacle. War was never formally declared, and media correspondents remained in Baghdad even through the weeks of air attacks which preceded the land war.

Bush was the acknowledged leader of the international effort, which comprised more than thirty nations contributing forces, munitions or cash. Principal among them were Britain, Egypt, Syria, France, Italy, Saudi Arabia and the Gulf emirates, with further troops made up of exiled Kuwaitis. Financial aid was provided by Germany and Japan. Most of the twenty-eight allies had a non-combatant role: for example, just over 200 men were sent from Czechoslovakia, all of them medical and chemical-warfare specialists, while 310 Muslim mujahideen guarded shrines. Bush was careful to keep within the limits set by the UN resolutions. Six months were needed to build up a force considered sufficient to deal with what was said to be the fourth-largest army in the world. Meanwhile diplomacy and increasing pressure failed to move Saddam out of Kuwait. As a gesture of goodwill early in December 1990, he released the 20,000 foreigners working in Iraq, 3000 of them Americans, whom he had held as hostages, as 'human shields'. He indicated a readiness to withdraw from Kuwait if a Middle Eastern conference were called to discuss not only Kuwait but also Israel's occupation of Arab territories and the Palestinian question, a ploy designed to split the Arab nations aligned

*As US firepower is trained on Baghdad during the second Gulf War, amidst the devastation some strive to carve out a normal life, February 1991.*

against him. At worst he would emerge a hero in Arab eyes for having forced a settlement of the Palestinian demands. But Bush would permit no direct linkage of the Palestine issue and Kuwait. Saddam could not be seen to have profited from aggression. The Iraqi leader now threatened 'the mother of battles' for Kuwait and the use of chemical weapons if attacked.

Early in the morning of 17 January 1991 the shooting war, Desert Storm, began with airstrikes on strategic targets in Baghdad. For six weeks thousands of air sorties were mounted against Iraqi military targets, roads, bridges and essential services. New high-technology weapons worked with awesome accuracy. Inevitably there were also innocent civilian casualties, most tragically when an air-raid shelter in Baghdad received a direct hit. Iraqi counter-strikes with Russian Scud missiles were militarily ineffective but the devastating allied airstrikes were beginning to create a popular Arab reaction in North Africa, Jordan and other Muslim countries. By the end of the onslaught, Iraq's fighting morale had been sapped. When the land war opened on 24 February, the high-tech armour sliced through and completely outflanked the Iraqi troops. Their number and fighting readiness had been overestimated – many of those dug in in Kuwait were half starved and only too happy to be taken prisoner. In just 100 hours the whole Iraqi army had been routed. No accurate figures for Iraqi casualties killed has been established; they were probably between 30,000 and 90,000; the United States suffered 389 killed, the British 44 killed, and the total for the allies was about 466 and in all about 1,187 wounded. The only real danger to the Arab-Western coalition, the involvement of Israel in the war in retaliation for the Iraqi Scud missile attacks, was averted by US diplomacy and the stationing of US Patriot defensive missile batteries in Israel. On 26 February Saddam announced withdrawal from Kuwait and on the following day Iraq accepted all the UN resolutions. That same day, 27 February 1991 Bush ordered the suspension of fighting. He saw grave disadvantages to future Arab–Western relations if the defenceless Iraqis continued to be slaughtered as they fled from Kuwait and from the areas in Iraq occupied by allied troops. Bush also concluded that Saddam could no longer resist whatever demands were made and was unlikely to stay in power. Saddam, however, signalled his defiance by setting

alight Kuwait's oil wells as his routed troops pulled back. It was a disaster months of fire-fighting only partially overcame.

An uprising by the people of Iraq was expected, but not the forms it took. The Shia Muslims rebelled in the south of the country, seizing Basra, and the Kurds in the north saw their opportunity for gaining at least autonomy, if not independence. The Kurdish rebels rapidly occupied the principal northern towns, as well as the oil-rich Kirkuk district. Iraq was falling to pieces. The Soviet Union, Syria and Turkey, with restless Kurdish minorities of their own, were all greatly concerned by the Kurdish rebellion. For the US, the possibility of an extension of Shi'ite Iranian influence in southern Iraq was equally unacceptable. And so the Kurds and Shi'ites were left to their fate as the rump of Saddam's forces with tanks and aircraft brutally crushed the risings. It was an inhuman consequence of the Gulf War. For those members of the Security Council with internal repressions of their own on their conscience. China and the Soviet

*Iraqi Kurds flee to the mountains as Saddam Hussein crushes their uprising.*

Union, the principle that the UN could not interfere in the 'internal' affairs of a country was sacrosanct. For the United States, striving for peace and stability, the raising of the Kurdish national question in 1991 seemed likely to add another explosive issue to others already detonated in the Middle East, foremost among them the Israeli–Palestine and Arab conflict.

In the face of the human catastrophe that threatened the Kurdish people as they fled into the inhospitable mountains of northern Iraq the shock the civilized world felt overcame calculations of *Realpolitik*. Britain and the United States declared the region a 'safe haven' and with air bases in Turkey and UN backing enforced their decision to stop any further Iraqi military action. The UN also orchestrated humanitarian aid though there was much criticism at the lack of competence revealed that winter. During the course of 1992 the Kurds established quasi-independence, with their own guerrilla army, government and elected parliament while declaring their aim to be only a federal, democratic Iraq. The Kurds were especially dependent on the toleration of Turkey, their most powerful neighbour, and therefore avoided going as far as stating that their aim was an independent Kurd nation. Iran, Syria and Turkey all have their own Kurdish minorities and had a common interest in crushing any such ambitions. To reassure the Turks, the Iraqi Kurds even made common cause with them, fighting against their own ethnic kin, the Kurdish Marxist guerrillas in Turkey. But even Kurdish autonomy remained precarious and was regarded with suspicion by her neighbours. They wanted a unified Iraq, led by a strong man other than Saddam Hussein.

The fate of the Shias in the south of Iraq initially attracted less attention. But Saddam's brutal repression, when it extended to the ethnic Arab families living primitively in the marshes in the south of the country who made their simple living from fishing, eventually aroused the West. A second 'no fly zone' was declared to cover the south to provide some, far from complete, protection.

Saddam Hussein meanwhile remained in power in Baghdad, surviving an international economic blockade and the humiliations inflicted by the UN. Perhaps these were even proving counter-productive as Iraqis rallied to their leader who was presented as standing up to overwhelming western

hostility. Saddam played a cat-and-mouse game frustrating the fulfillment of UN demands that he throw open his nuclear facilities for inspection destroy his missiles as long as he dared. It remained in the interests of the nations in the region and of the West to maintain Iraq as a unitary state and that helped Saddam to survive for so long after defeat. What appeared to be morally right did not necessarily correspond to what were regarded as the wider interests of peace in the Middle East and the priorities of the world's most powerful nations. General peace in the volatile Middle East remained a distant prospect. But on 13 September 1993 there was one totally unexpected and dramatic turn for the better. On that day on the White House lawn the Israeli prime minister, Rabin, shook the hand of PLO chairman Arafat. Their agreement had been secretly brokered by the Norwegian foreign minister. Arafat signed a letter recognising that Israel must exist in peace and security and Rabin accepted the PLO as the 'representative of the Palestinian people'. Gaza and Jericho were to be handed over to Palestinian self-rule when all the details had been worked out. There was an outcry from opponents – from Hamas and from among the fearful Jewish settlers in 144 settlements on the West Bank and Gaza, who constitute some four per cent of Israel's population. The detailed negotiations dragged on, and the December date for the handover passed. Three months later a fanatical Israeli settler sprayed a mosque in Hebron, the Patriarchs' Tomb, with bullets from the automatic weapon many settlers carry, killing thirty Palestinians; Hamas retaliated in kind. The Israeli army was seen to maintain order one-sidedly – ready to shoot at Palestinians, but not at Jews. It was a setback, but there was no alternative but to try and implement what had already been agreed in principle in Washington. Meanwhile a reluctant Hafez Assad, cajoled by the Americans, had moved a step nearer to normalising relations with Israel. But his prior demand that he recover the Golan Heights remained to be met. In Egypt, Mubarak came under increasing pressure from groups of Muslim fundamentalist terrorists. The fires of conflict thus continued to smoulder under the surface; the future remains unpredictable. But with the end of the Cold War there has been undoubted gain: no nation outside the region any longer fanned strife within it.

# CHAPTER 89

# After The Cold War

The Cold War, reflecting the tensions between the two most powerful nations on earth, dominated the decades from 1945 to 1990. It led to a spate of economic and military engagements in the Middle East, Asia and Africa by the West and by the Soviet Union. Indeed, but for the Cold War, powerful countries outside these regions would have been less likely to intervene.

The Cold War created international conflicts which were superimposed on regional conflicts. The civil war in Korea in the 1950s escalated to a war involving the United States and her allies on the one side and China on the other. In what was formerly Indo-China, the anti-colonial struggle against the French developed into a civil and international war of communism against the free world. The destruction of life and resources these wars caused were so great as to be almost incalculable. Chinese, Russian and American suspicions of each other were partly responsible for the continuation of the civil war in long-suffering Cambodia until 1992. In Africa, the wars in Angola and Mozambique between rival groups received military help from anti-communist and communist forces, including Chinese and Cubans. In the Middle East in the 1980s, Afghanistan became the focus of international intervention from the Soviet Union while the anti-communist mujahideen factions were provided with weapons by the United States via Pakistan. In Central America, El Salvador and Nicaragua similarly suffered from the interaction of their civil wars and the Cold War. Many more examples could be cited. What would follow the Cold War?

Unfortunately, it was not likely to be global peace. The near unanimity of the United Nations in ridding Kuwait, a member of the UN, of the Iraqi occupation forces had created an expectation that the UN would henceforth act to preserve peace and justice everywhere in the world and so live up to its most noble ideals. Such expectations could not be fulfilled. In 1991 an unusual combination of circumstances had created the necessary unanimity on the Security Council. The Soviet Union had been beset by domestic problems and Gorbachev had been seeking the help of the West, while the Chinese had wished to shake off their near-pariah status after the massacre in Tiananmen Square. The West, led by the United States, had been determined to check war and aggression in the Middle East, especially in the Gulf region with its vital oil supplies. The Arab nations had viewed with alarm and hostility the growth of Iraqi military power, ruthlessly employed. Consequently, it had become possible to build up a coalition under the banner of the United Nations. The same could not be expected whenever and wherever aggression or civil wars should occur.

Military intervention is costly. The short Gulf War was estimated to have cost the allied forces some $60 billion. Fortunately it did not lead to heavy allied casualties, though heavy loss of life and wealth were inflicted on Iraq, and nearly all Kuwait's oilwells were set on fire. The war in Vietnam resulted not only in great destruction to the country but also in many deaths at the hands of the intervening US forces. It was the Cold War which justified such a heavy price, the belief that the conflicts were about more than the future of Nicaragua or of Vietnam, that these countries were the front line, the battleground, in the struggle between the slavery of the communist world and the liberty of the free world.

The Yalta scheme of the four policemen worked up to a point and in an unintended fashion from 1945 to the 1980s. The Soviet Union and China each kept her part of the world in order, at the point of the bayonet where necessary. The United States policed the Caribbean and Central America. Western Europe built up its defences and the West safeguarded its vital interests in the Middle East. Without the Cold War, the policemen's roles diminished. A conflict in a country or region not vitally affecting the interests of the West or East was likely to be allowed to find its own bloody solution. Diplomatic good offices, sincere attempts at mediation within or outside the United Nations, and humanitarian aid might well be offered, but there would be reluctance to intervene militarily. Possibly the economic carrot and stick, the granting or withholding of loans, aid and trade, would be the most common non-violent means by which the rich West would seek to influence the outcome of particular struggles.

The impact of international economic relations played a relatively larger role in the 1990s than before. But the aspiration to free trade in the non-communist countries, as envisaged by the General Agreement on Tariffs and Trade (GATT), was difficult to realise. Yet domestically the fate of governments in the longer term depended on the state of their country's economy, and trade relations with tariffs on one side and import restrictions on the other were the cause of bad feelings and of threats of retaliation between the wealthy nations of the West. The European Community with its protection of the farmers was in dispute with the United States. Japan's export drive to sell cars and electronic goods met resistance in the United States and in Europe because her own home market impeded penetration from outside.

To circumvent the difficulties of protectionism international corporations established production and distribution centres not just in their own country but the world over. By 1914, multinational companies were already operating in such industries

as oil, chemicals and aluminium, but compared to national production their output was small. After 1945, there was a huge expansion, led by US companies such as Ford and IBM in Western Europe. One positive result was the transfer of technology from the more to the less advanced economies, but most of this investment went to already developed countries. West European multinationals in return made large investments in the United States. Surging latecomers in the 1980s were the Japanese, opening car plants and electronic assembly plants in Western Europe, the United States and the Pacific rim. The weakness of the dollar meant that the acquisition of property and resources by the Japanese in the United States appeared at the time to be relatively cheap. But with the Japanese economy in trouble in 1991 and 1992 many of these assets were sold at a loss. The multinationals, bounding over national frontiers, were playing an increasingly important role in international trade, one which could not have been envisaged before 1945. Their economies of scale and the vastness of their markets promoted the growth of global trade. In the Third World, although multinational companies could bring desperately needed Western technology, management and capital, they would constitute a much larger proportion of those countries' total economies. This could place them in a commanding economic and sometimes political position.

After the Cold War the triangular relationships between the oil-rich nations, the Third World poor and the West continued to be a global problem. It had not proved possible in the longer term for countries producing mainly commodities – agricultural products, minerals and oil – to form successful cartels to raise prices sufficiently to keep pace with the increased cost of industrial products manufactured by the West. What are called the terms of trade deteriorated for the Third World after 1953, despite temporary fluctuations. In the decade from 1973 to 1983 the oil producers appeared to buck the trend by organising supply through OPEC. But in the early 1990s the world was once more awash in oil, which had become a cheap energy source in real-value terms. In oil-producing nations like Iran with relatively large populations, 'oil riches' did not benefit the ordinary people much and the revenue was diverted into destructive tanks and planes. The Kuwaitis (until 1990), the Saudi Arabians and the inhabitants of the Gulf oil emirates were lucky –

but their total population comprise only some 12 million.

Attempts in Africa and Latin America to escape poverty through modernisation and industrialisation created huge debts whose interest payments outstripped international aid. The enormous task that remained was to discover how the West, in its own interests, could help the Third World to attain more steady growth sufficient at least to cope with the increase of population. The alternative was not only famine but continuing social unrest. Yet it was unlikely that the rich West would make significant sacrifices in its own standards of living to help the millions of poor in the Third World. The 'peace dividend' arising out of the lessening of East–West tensions was more likely to boost social services in Western Europe and the United States. Endemic conflict and wars brought countries like Yugoslavia, Somalia, the Sudan, Afghanistan, Liberia, Mozambique and Sri Lanka, to mention only some, to a state of utter destitution for a majority of their peoples. The rest of the world would not impose peace; peace was likely to come only when the peoples of those countries stopped fighting.

The Cold War fractured the world economy. The advanced Western nations prohibited technological transfer to the communist East in areas which could enhance the military capacity of the Soviet Union. The Soviet Union was in some fields, for instance missile development, able to match the West, but this was not so in general. From the 1970s and the start of the third industrial revolution – the computer, the microchip and information technology – the East was left behind. Communist central planning compounded the East's comparative backwardness, as bureaucracies burgeoned and inefficiency and corruption multiplied. The ending of the Cold War reduced these obstacles, while the eventual integration of the Eastern economies with the Western-dominated global economy opened new vistas in the 1990s.

Population control, by means other than mass famine and disease, was the most urgent need of the Third World. Rising standards of living exerted their own form of population control as families tried to preserve their way of life and that of their offspring. In the Western world the fear was more of inadequate growth and the costs of maintaining an ageing population. But among the poor of the Third World rising standards of living were too slow or non-existent for this self-limiting principle

to work. World population expansion was very uneven; the relative stability of Europe stood in stark contrast to the population explosions of Asia, Africa and South America, which outstripped the availability of food and condemned many millions to malnutrition and famine. Their soaring growth rates could not continue. It was calculated that a world population of over 4000 million was reached by 1980 and that this might double in thirty years unless there were drastic limiting factors. By the year 2150, according to the UN, every fourth person will be an African, and half the world's population will live in Asia. In a democratic free world, family size is left to the individual. In South America the orthodox teaching of the Catholic Church limits the means by which fertility is controlled to natural methods. In much of the developed world artificial barriers and the pill provide effective means of contraception. India made great efforts to educate the poor to adopt birth control, with limited success, while the authoritarian Chinese leaders went further along a semi-coercive policy of restricting the size of family. Globally the problem remained a serious one for the future and was intimately linked to the preservation of the world's environment. If the rainforests were not to disappear, if the ozone layer was to be preserved, the world's population would have to grow more slowly.

The 1980s and the early 1990s saw an increasing popular awareness that the resources of the globe are not infinite and should be husbanded more carefully. But there was little translation of this knowledge into practical policies of conservation as cars multiplied and energy-consumption rose. Here and there a small beginning was made, for instance the Brazilian government's efforts to preserve the rainforest from further depredation. The other side of the coin was the possible harm done by the modern age's wasteful energy use and the carbon emissions into the atmosphere. The 'greenhouse effect' of global warming and the disastrous floods and climatic changes that could ensue were the subject of much inconclusive debate by scientists.

On only one environmental issue was there a significant change of attitude – the proliferation of nuclear power. After the accident at the American nuclear-power plant on Three Mile Island, where radiation of the environment was only just averted, and the catastrophe at Chernobyl, which inflicted extensive damage on the Ukraine, the dangers of nuclear power galvanised people to put pressure on

*The destruction of the primaeval Amazonian forests progresses relentlessly. An ecosystem developed over millennia is destroyed in a few decades by the greed of mankind.*

their governments to halt the spread of nuclear plants. The campaigns were most successful in the 1980s in the United States and West Germany, though nuclear-power plans were slowed down in Britain too. But in the 1990s France continued to rely heavily on nuclear power. The insufficiently safe nuclear-power stations of Eastern and central Europe, built on Soviet models, represented something of a time-bomb. More immediately harmful to human life was the smoke-stack industry of that mismanaged communist region. To begin to clear up their harmful ecological effects was also on the agenda for the 1990s.

The nightmare that a third great war would break out in Europe in the twentieth century was lifted. The Cold War was officially declared at an end in 1990. Negotiations for the diminution of conventional and nuclear arms between the United States, the Soviet Union and its successor states continued to make spectacular progress. The Warsaw Pact military alliance was dissolved in March 1991. NATO remained but was changing its functions. The armed frontier which ran through the middle of

Germany evaporated. Not only was the theoretical Western line of defence pushed eastwards, but to the east of that line were friendly countries, Czechoslovakia and Poland, which were keen to join the European Community. Not military but economic problems dominated this new East–West relationship. It was to be hoped that the need to defend frontiers militarily in Eastern Europe would become as outdated as it was already in Western Europe.

As the threat of a nuclear holocaust started by an American–Soviet superpower war receded and disappeared, so the awareness grew of the danger of a nuclear spread to smaller countries with unstable governments in regions of conflict and tension. There were fears that an impoverished Russia might sell missiles to any country able to pay, that former Soviet nuclear scientists would be lured abroad with high salaries. The barriers against the spread of nuclear weapons had proved inadequate, despite the setting up in 1957 of the International Atomic Energy Agency, which was meant to inspect nuclear-power installations all over the world to ensure they were used only for peaceful purposes.

The Non-Proliferation Treaty of 1968 had by 1990 secured 141 adherents, but a number of countries – including France and China and those with nuclear-weapon ambitions – had not joined; and one, North Korea, tried to withdraw. Among the non-signatories were Pakistan and India; India had demonstrated her capacity for a nuclear explosion and Pakistan, despite a cut-off of US aid, either already had or was close to developing her own weapon in the early 1990s. In 1993, South Africa admitted to possession of nuclear weapons but President de Klerk assured the world that they had all now been destroyed. In Latin America, Argentina and Brazil had nuclear-weapons programmes. In the volatile Middle East, although Israel had never openly acknowledged possession of nuclear weapons, she had in all likelihood stockpiled some atomic weapons, using the plutonium from her reactor at Dimona. Iraq was an early candidate for making her own nuclear bomb under Saddam Hussein, though Israel's destruction of his Osirak reactor in 1981 was a setback. When the UN insisted on dismantling his nuclear installations in 1992, Iraq was revealed to be far advanced once again. Libya was keen to acquire the technology and the enriched uranium to make her own bomb, but probably had not done so by the early 1990s. South Africa acquired uranium and developed a nuclear-weapons capacity. Progress was possible only because of technological assistance and the delivery of uranium for 'peaceful' purposes. Over 340 nuclear reactors supplying electricity functioned in twenty-six countries. China, the former Soviet Union (in 1992 the weapons in Kazakhstan and the Ukraine were supposed to be transferred for destruction to the Russian Federation), France, Britain and the United States had tested nuclear weapons. The uranium and technology was supplied to other countries by some of these and by Belgium and Italy. France sent uranium to Iraq with safeguards for its use. The safeguards proved inadequate. Other uranium consignments reached the recipient countries by devious routes through black-market activities. Where there is money, there is usually a way. It was important to include on the peace agenda of the 1990s better supervision and control of weapons of mass destruction, a category which embraced biological and chemical warfare.

A new form of Western 'defence' had emerged by the early 1990s: stemming the flow of immigrants from the poorer countries of Eastern Europe and the Third World to the West.

Barriers against free immigration were not new, but had become common after the First World War. After 1945, immigrants from her empire were welcome in a Britain short of labour. But she could not sustain a common citizenship with her former empire in the third quarter of the twentieth century. This alone would have made the abandonment of imperial rule a necessity. Similarly Italy could no longer absorb unlimited immigration from her former African colonies nor could France from North Africa. Refugees were attracted to West Germany from all over the world, and she tightened her laws granting rights of asylum, though she remained less multicultural than the rest of Western Europe. The 1990s now placed Germany within a reshaped Europe in the front line of immigration from further east. A formidable backlash against the old and new immigrants had a powerful impact on Germany and France: right-wing neo-Nazi and neo-fascist movements in both countries made startling advances in elections held in 1992.

After reunification west Germany faced a unique immigration problem from 17 million Germans in the former communist East German state. The products of their outdated and inefficient industries geared to exports to the Soviet Union and to the former East European economic community were no longer wanted. Massive unemployment was one consequence. Germany's energies would be absorbed during much of the 1990s coping with the problems of unification. An over-powerful Germany at the heart of Europe resurrected some apprehension among her neighbours. Kohl's government responded by reassuring the world that the Federal Republic desired a strong European Community and would remain a loyal and good partner.

As the 1990s got under way reality was likely to overtake the utopian dream of achieving complete unity within the Community in the near future. Economic union and currency union would probably not be achievable until the economies of the Community converged far more. The objectives set out at the summit in Maastricht in December 1991 would be hard to reach in the short term. The currency crises of 1992 and 1993, Britain's and Italy's departure from the fixed exchange-rate system, the economic recession in 1993, and the destabilising impact of unemployment, were serious impediments to progress.

Throughout the West, economic management and government were swinging back in the early 1990s to the political centre, with governments placing more emphasis on being caring, on providing better social services, education and training. Not only communism. but also democratic socialism, which advocated state-run industries and control of the 'commanding heights of the economy', had been discredited all over the world.

As the era 1945 to the early 1990s was drawing to its close the cries of 'democracy', 'freedom' and 'choice' were taken up by peoples in many different parts of the world, from South Africa to Korea. The words may have had different meanings in different societies, but their power to move people was evident in their demands for government responsive to their wishes. 'People power' was a new concept: it helped to overthrow the Shah in Iran and President Marcos in the Philippines, among others. Authoritarian rulers were put on notice that their assumed right to rule could no longer be taken for granted. Again and again, ordinary people lost their fear. No image conveyed this more movingly than the lone Chinese student halting a whole line of tanks in the streets of Beijing during the pro-democracy demonstrations in Tiananmen Square. Repressive rule was in retreat all over the world, even if in some parts, as in China, it was able to recover authority. This shattered a Western illusion that the change from a command economy to a free market was bound to undermine the political control of a one-party communist state. This might turn out to be true in the long run but there were no immediate signs of it in the China of the early 1990s.

At the beginning of the 1990s revolutionary changes in the world from Eastern Europe to South America, from Nepal to Namibia, were driven by a demand that human rights be respected. In the former Soviet Union the machinery of repression was destroyed, and statues of her founders were smashed. In Chile the human-rights abuses and the killings by the military junta were investigated anew. Apartheid, an affront to human dignity, was dismantled in South Africa. These were but a few of the indications of progress. But human-rights abuses persisted all over the world. In Iraq, where the Kurds and Shias were under constant threat of repression, in Turkey, with her hundreds of political prisoners, with her own repressed Kurds, in practically every country of the world there was abuse.

Saudi Arabian law allowed amputations as a punishment; China had hundreds of political prisoners, and executions for various crimes ran into several thousand in 1990. The reports of Amnesty International make sombre reading.

There was hope, but no guarantee, that the tide against repression would continue to run strongly. But bloody ethnic, religious and racial conflicts also remained virulent. In South Africa in the early 1990s Mandela was the hope of a black majority, despite inter-black fighting. In Sri Lanka ethnic strife inflicted wounds which refused to heal. These kinds of hatred seemed hardest to eradicate and they were not confined to the Third World, as Yugoslavia and Northern Ireland showed.

Eastern and central Europe were confronted with gigantic problems in the 1990s, as they tried to effect the transfer from a communist command to a free-market economy. In Poland the painful transfer was quite advanced, in the Soviet Union it was only beginning. The immediate hardship it inflicted on the people, the threat of mass unemployment and the declining standard of living tarnished the promises of 'new democracy'. People questioned whether leaders such as Poland's Lech Wałęsa, an electrician and trade union boss, or Czechoslovakia's Václav Havel, a writer and intellectual, who had proved such courageous leaders in the struggle against communist autocracy, were the right men to lead their nations in the new and difficult post-communist era.

Economic hardship also undermined the cohesion of nations, whose diverse groups were now allowed much freer expression. Slovaks and Czechs agreed peacefully on separation; in Yugoslavia the bitter ethnic tensions and national ambitions led to bloody civil wars, the stronger carving up the weaker. The diverse ethnic composition of the Balkan nations, no longer suppressed by communist rule, revived historic patterns of conflict. Economic hardship and nationalism are corrosive forces. In the Soviet Union, Gorbachev's careful balancing act between freedom and economic reform on the one hand and the need to preserve the Union became daily more difficult, until it collapsed altogether in December 1991. The Commonwealth of Independent States then had to argue about the division of what had once belonged to the Soviet Union. By 1993 the disintegration of the former Soviet Union was far advanced; Russia still the largest republic by far. The new Commonwealth, the CIS, was leading an increasingly shadowy exist-ence.

In the early 1990s, there were still many conflicts, actual and potential, in Asia, Africa, the Pacific, the Americas and Europe. The Kashmiri issue festered on the Indian sub-continent. With the end of the Cold War, the communist regime in Afghanistan finally, and much later than expected, collapsed in April 1992. The mujahideen victoriously entered Kabul and immediately began to fight each other. In Africa, Somalia was destroying herself and civil war had ravaged Mozambique, Angola and Rwanda and Burundi. In former Yugoslavia the portents of peace were extinguished, as ancient ethnic rivalries led to savage war. In many countries moderate Islam battled with fundamentalism. In Burma (or Myanmar), more isolated than ever, civil rights continued to be denied and ethnic minorities were suppressed. In the Middle East the peace process between Israel, Syria and the Palestinians had only made slow and painful progress. The future of the old Soviet Union was still in doubt, one of the most important uncertainties of the 1990s.

The end of the Cold War removed one great dark shadow. For the first time in the twentieth century, if not indeed in modern history, the most powerful nations on earth no longer expected to fight each other. In the renewed confidence of their relations they rapidly diminished their armaments. That was an immense step forward. Cold war conflicts by proxy have ceased to be fought, a gain for humanity. The deficit remains that civil wars continue as in Afghanistan or break out where communist power collapses as in former Yugoslavia. The world is once more at a stage of great transition

*Russian Federation President Boris Yeltsin meets US President Bill Clinton to discuss how the West will aid Russia's transition to democracy, Vancouver, April 1993.*

just as a century earlier. It would be foolish to deny the dangers that lie ahead or to minimise the uncertainties of the future. Possibilities of peace and progress in the decades ahead nevertheless have opened up, allowing an historian of the world to end by expressing the hope that history's bloodiest century may soon lie behind us.

# SUGGESTIONS FOR FURTHER READING

This bibliography represents only a fraction of the immense, rich and varied literature concerned with the history of the twentieth-century world. On the whole I have concentrated on books available in English – either written in that language or in translation. (English has become something of a universal language but that does not mean of course that *all* the most important works of scholarship are available in English.) It is fortunate that many books have appeared in paperback and these are marked with an asterisk. Hardcover editions of those paperbacks which are out of print are frequently available in libraries. In the first instance I have chosen books which provide an overview of large subjects, as these are likely to be particularly useful to the student and general reader. The main difficulty is to know how many books of detailed scholarship additionally to cite. In compiling not too long a reading list, I have made some pretty arbitrary judgements. The suggestions made here should not, therefore, be regarded as including all the more important books. My aim has been a different one: to provide a list of further reading which will introduce the reader to some of the complexities and controversies of interpretation which syntheses tend to iron out. I should have liked to mention all the books from which I have profited, but unfortunately that is not practicable. This is not so much a bibliography, then, as a useful starting point for further study. (Quotations from the papers of Neville Chamberlain are cited by permission of the University of Birmingham, and quotations from the unpublished Goebbels diaries are from the microfilm at Stanford University.)

## CONTENTS

# 1. GENERAL HISTORIES

Two stimulating world histories are P. Johnson, *Modern Times: History of the World from 1920s to 1990s\**, a revised edition of a book first published in 1983 (Weidenfeld & Nicolson, 1992), and T. E. Vadney, *World since 1945: A Complete History of Global Change from 1945 to the Present\**, revised edn (Penguin, 1992). Older but still useful, D. C. Watt, F. Spencer and N. Brown, *A History of the World in the Twentieth Century*, really three books in one, is a more detailed treatment (Hodder & Stoughton, 1967). G. Barraclough examines some underlying forces in *An Introduction to Contemporary History* (Penguin, 1969). *The New Cambridge Modern History* had two shots at covering the twentieth century, a volume edited by D. Thomson, *The Era of Violence 1898–1945* (Cambridge, 1960), which was incomplete for events after 1933, and C. L. Mowat's *The Shifting Balance of World Forces, 1898–1945* (Cambridge, 1968). Both volumes contain good individual narrative chapters. Two French interpretations are M. Crouzet, *L'Epoque contemporaine: á la recherche d'une civilisation nouvelle* (5th edn, Presses Universitaires, 1969); and a factual overview, J. Bouillon, P. Sorlin and J. Rudel, *Le Monde contemporaine* (13th edn, Bordas, 1968). For a good introduction to the forces shaping culture and society, see M. Biddiss, *The Age of the Masses\** (Penguin, 1977).

EUROPE. J. Joll, *Europe since 1870\** (Penguin, 1990) is outstanding; also excellent is H. S. Hughes, *Contemporary Europe: A History* (4th edn,

Prentice-Hall, 1976). Three volumes of the Rise of Modern Europe series cover the first half-century: O. J. Hale, *The Great Illusion, 1900–1914\**, R. J. Sontag, *A Broken World 1919–1939\**; and G. Wright, *The Ordeal of Total War, 1939–1945\** (Harper & Row, 1971, 1971 and 1968), all well worth reading.

EASTERN ASIA. J. K. Fairbank, E. O. Reischauer and A. M. Craig, *China: Transition and Transformation\** (2nd edn, Unwin & Hyman, 1989); H. Tinker, *South Asia: A Short History\** (Praeger, 1966); D. G. E. Hall, *A History of South-east Asia* (3rd edn, Macmillan, 1968); E. O. Reischauer and A. M. Craig, *Japan: Tradition and Transformation\** (2nd edn, Unwin & Hyman, 1989).

AFRICA. The best one-volume history from origins to independence is J. D. Fage, *A History of Africa\** (2nd edn, Unwin Hyman, 1993).

LATIN AMERICA. B. Keen, *A History of Latin America* (vol. 2, 4th edn, Houghton Mifflin, 1992) provides an excellent survey of the nineteenth and twentieth centuries.

THE MIDDLE EAST. Two good general surveys are P. Mansfield, *The Middle East\** (Penguin, 1992) and W. R. Polk, *The Arab World Today\** (4th edn, Harvard, 1991). A. H. Hourani, *A History of the Arab Peoples\** (Faber & Faber, 1991) and M. E. Yapp, *The Near East since the First World War\** (Longman, 1990) are also useful.

THE WORLD ECONOMY. For a one-volume survey, see H. van der Wee, *Prosperity and Upheaval: The World Economy 1945–1980\** (Penguin, 1991). In the same series the first half of the century is covered in more detail by D. H. Aldcroft, *The European Economy, 1914–1990\** (Routledge, 1989). See also A. S. Milward, *War, Economy and Society, 1939–1945\** (Methuen, 1987). An interesting theory of modernisation and economic development is propounded by W. W. Rostow, *The World Economy: History and Prospect* (Macmillan, 1978). W. Ashworth, *A Short History of the International Economy since 1850\** (4th edn, Longman, 1987); W. M. Scammell, *The International Economy since 1945\** (2nd edn, Macmillan, 1983); and F. B. Tipton and R. Aldrich, *An Economic and Social History of Europe, 1890 to the Present\** (2 vols, Macmillan, 1983) are of value.

WORLD INTERNATIONAL RELATIONS. Two good textbooks are available in paperback: the well-tried P. Calvocoressi, *World Politics since 1945\** (6th edn, Longman, 1991) and W. R. Keylor, *The Twentieth Century World: An International History\** (2nd edn, Oxford, 1992). These can be supplemented by J. A. S. Grenville, *The Major International Treaties, 1914–1945: A History and Guide with Texts*, and J. A. S. Grenville and B. Wasserstein, *The Major International Treaties since 1945: A History and Guide with Texts* (Methuen, 1987). Contemporary problems and their origins are set out in G. Segal, *The World Affairs Companion\** (new edn, Simon & Schuster, 1991).

## 2. SOME GENERAL NATIONAL HISTORIES

FRANCE. From among the rich choice, A. Cobban, *A History of France, 1871–1961** (vol. 3, Penguin, 1961) remains one of the best introductions. It may be supplemented by Georges Dupeux, *French Society, 1789–1970** (Methuen, 1976), a very useful survey with statistics. See also W. L. Shirer, *The Collapse of the Third Republic** (Pan, 1969); T. Zeldin, *France, 1849–1945** (2 vols, Oxford, 1979); and J. Néré, *La Troisième République* (Oxford, 1967). A lucid one-volume survey with a good bibliography is J. F. McMillan, *Twentieth Century France* (Arnold, 1992). For a good social and economic analysis, see C. Flockton and E. Kofman, *France** (Paul Chapman, 1989). For France since the First World War, a sound general treatment is H. Tint, *France since 1918** (2nd edn, Batsford, 1980). M. Larkin, *France since the Popular Front: Government and People 1936–1986** (Oxford, 1988) covers the later years.

GERMANY. There are a number of excellent one-volume histories, including W. Carr, *A History of Germany, 1815–1990** (4th edn, Arnold 1991) and Hajo Holborn, *A History of Modern Germany* (Knopf, 1969). G. Mann, *The History of Germany since 1789** (Penguin, 1974) offers a personal and stimulating view. A well-written survey paying attention to the 'moods' of different periods is Gordon A. Craig, *Germany, 1866–1945* (Oxford, 1978). A critical analytical study is V. R. Berghahn, *Modern Germany: Society, Economy and Politics in the Twentieth Century** (2nd edn, Cambridge, 1988).

ITALY. D. Mack Smith, *Italy: A Modern History* (revised edn, Michigan, 1969); C. J. Lowe and F. Marzari, *Italian Foreign Policy, 1870–1940* (Routledge, 1975); S. B. Clough, *Economic History of Modern Italy* (Columbia, 1968); A. C. Jemolo, *Church and State in Italy, 1850–1950* (Blackwell, 1960); R. A. Webster, *Christian Democracy in Italy, 1860–1960* (Hollis & Carter, 1961); C. Seton-Watson, *Italy from Liberalism to Fascism, 1870–1925* (Methuen, 1967). In addition there are a number of excellent one-volume histories to choose from: P. Ginsborg, *A History of Contemporary Italy: Society and Politics, 1943–1988** (Penguin, 1990); N. Kogan, *A Political History of Postwar Italy** (Praeger, 1983); M. Clark, *Modern Italy, 1871–1982** (Longman, 1985); and H. Hearder, *Italy: A Short History** (Cambridge, 1990).

BRITAIN. There are some very good general histories; among the older, C. L. Mowat, *Britain between the Wars** (Methuen, 1968) has stood the test of time well. For a comprehensive account, among the most reliable and perceptive is W. N. Medlicott, *Contemporary England, 1914–74** (Longman, 1976). A. J. P. Taylor, *English History, 1914–45** (Oxford, 1965) is stimulating. A good recent account is T. O. Lloyd, *Empire to Welfare State: English History, 1906–92** (4th edn, Oxford, 1992); see also W. N. Medlicott, *British Foreign Policy since Versailles, 1919–63** (2nd edn, Methuen, 1968). For brief and perceptive accounts, see D. Thomson, *England in the Twentieth Century** (Penguin, 1965) and H. Pelling, *Modern Britain, 1885–1955* (Nelson, 1960). A fresh approach is offered in A. Marwick, *Britain in the Century of Total War** (Penguin, 1971). The best survey of Britain and her Commonwealth is W. D. McIntyre, *The Commonwealth of Nations: Origins and Impact, 1869–1971* (Minnesota, 1977). R. R. James, *The British Revolution: British Politics, 1880–1939** (Methuen, 1978) is very good. For the period before 1915 there is an outstandingly good paperback, R. Shannon, *The Crisis of Imperialism, 1865–1915** (Paladin, 1976). For post-1945 Britain there are two excellent one-volume histories, K. O. Morgan, *The People's Peace: British History, 1945–1990** (Oxford, 1991) and A. Sked and C. Cook, *Post-War Britain: A Political History, 1945–1992** (4th edn, Penguin, 1993).

TSARIST RUSSIA AND THE SOVIET UNION. A good recent survey is J. N. Westwood, *Endurance and Endeavour: Russian History, 1812–1992** (Oxford, 1993). For the last decades of Tsarist Russia, see L. Kochan, *Russia in Revolution** (Paladin, 1970). An invaluable analysis of Tsarist society is R. Pipes, *Russia under the Old Regime** (Penguin, 1977). M. T. Florinsky, *The End of the Russian Empire** (Collier-Macmillan, 1961); B. Dmytryshyn, *USSR: A Concise History** (3rd edn, Scribner, 1978); and M. McAuley, *Soviet Politics, 1917–1991** (Oxford, 1992) are also useful. A good survey that takes the collapse of the USSR into account is G. Hosking, *A History of the Soviet Union, 1917–1991** (HarperCollins, 1992). The history of the freed Baltic nations can be studied in J. Hiden, *The Baltic Nations and Europe: Estonia, Latvia and Lithuania in the Twentieth Century** (Longman, 1991).

HABSBURG EMPIRE AND AUSTRIA. C. A. Macartney, *The Habsburg Empire, 1790–1918* (Weidenfeld & Nicolson, 1969) is probably the best general survey in any language. For a good study in German, see E. Zöllner, *Geschichte Österreichs* (4th edn, Munich, 1970). See also A. J. P. Taylor, *The Habsburg Monarchy, 1815–1918** (Penguin, 1964); A. J. May, *The Habsburg Monarchy, 1867–1914* (Cambridge, Mass., 1951); R. Kann, *The Multinational Empire* (2 vols, Columbia, 1964). For the history of the Austrian republic, Karl R. Stadler, *Austria* (Benn, 1971) is sympathetic and outstanding.

UNITED STATES. There are many excellent general histories of the United States and many others besides those here mentioned could equally well be commended. In paperback there is William Miller, *A New*

*History of the United States*\* (Paladin, 1970). For a well-written and beautifully produced one-volume history, see M. B. Norton, D. Katzman, P. Escott, T. Patterson, H. Chardacoff and W. Tuttle, *A People and a Nation: A History of the United States* (2nd edn, Houghton Mifflin, 1986); two good surveys are D. Grantham, *Recent America: The United States since 1945*\* (Harlan Davidson, 1987) and W. La Feber, *The American Century: A History of the United States since the 1890s* (4th edn, McGraw-Hill, 1991). A concise economic history is H. N. Scheiber, H. G. Vatter and H. V. Faulkner, *American Economic History* (9th edn, Harper & Row, 1976). See also J. A. Garraty, *The American Nation*\* (7th edn, Harper & Row, 1990). For a broad view, see R. H. Wiebe, *The Search for Order, 1877–1920* (Greenwood, 1980). Foreign policy is carefully surveyed in S. F. Bemis, *A Short History of American Foreign Policy and Diplomacy* (Holt, 1959).

CHINA. J. Chesneaux, F. Le Barbier and M.-C. Bergère, *China from the Opium Wars to the 1911 Revolution*\* (Harvester, 1976) and *China From the 1911 Revolution to Liberation*\* (Harvester, 1977) provide a sound factual survey, though somewhat disjointed. For a stimulating analysis and good narrative, see J. E. Sheridan, *China in Disintegration, 1912–49*\* (Collier-Macmillan, 1977). Brief but informative is M. Gasster, *China's Struggle to Modernize*\* (Knopf, 1972). See also J. Ch'en, *China and the West*\* (Hutchinson, 1979); I. C. Y. Hsü, *The Rise of Modern China* (4th edn, Oxford, 1992); A. Feuerwerker, *The Chinese Economy, 1870–1911* (Michigan, 1969); and *The Chinese Economy, 1912–49* (Michigan, 1977). Information on many aspects is to be found in C. Mackerras and A. Yorke, *The*

*Cambridge Handbook of Contemporary China*\* (2nd edn, Cambridge, 1991) and B. Hook and D. Twitchett, *The Cambridge Encyclopaedia of China* (Cambridge, 1991). The doyen of America's historians of China, J. K. Fairbank, has produced *China: A New History*\* (Harvard, 1992). The authoritative multi-volume history of China is *The Cambridge History of China*, vol. 10 (*1800–1911*, pt 1), ed. J. K. Fairbank; vol. 11 (*1800–1911*, pt 2), ed. J. K. Fairbank and Kwang-Ching Liu; vol. 12 (*1912–1949*, pt 1), ed. J. K. Fairbank; vol. 13 (*1912–1949*, pt 2), ed. J. K. Fairbank and A. Feuerwerker; vol. 14 (*1949–1965*), ed. R. MacFarquar and J. K. Fairbank; vol. 15 (*1966–1982*), ed. R. MacFarquar and J. K. Fairbank (Cambridge, 1978–92). See also S. Karnow, *Mao and China: Inside China's Cultural Revolution*\* (Penguin, 1985); M. Yahuda, *Towards the End of Isolationism: China's Foreign Policy after Mao* (Macmillan, 1985); J. Gittings, *China Changes Face: The Road from Revolution, 1949–1989*\* (Oxford, 1990); C. Riskin, *China's Political Economy: The Quest for Development since 1949* (Oxford, 1987). An account by Chinese scholars of the development of the economy can be found in *China's Socialist Economy: An Outline History (1949–1984)*,\* ed. Liu Suinian and Wu Qungan (Beijing Review, 1986).

JAPAN. Among the best one-volume histories is R. Storry, *A History of Modern Japan*\* (Penguin, 1976). Another good survey is W. G. Beasley, *The Rise of Modern Japan*\* (Weidenfeld & Nicolson, 1990). Full of stimulating insights is E. O. Reischauer, *The Japanese* (Harvard, 1977). On Japan's relations with the West, see R. Storry, *Japan and the Decline of the West in Asia, 1894–1943*\* (Macmillan, 1979). See also K. B.

Pyle, *The New Generation in Meiji Japan* (Stanford, 1969); I. Nish, *Japanese Foreign Policy, 1869–1942* (Routledge, 1977); M. Schaller, *The American Occupation of Japan: The Origins of the Cold War in Asia* (Oxford, 1986). A lively and critical account is J. Woronoff, *Politics the Japanese Way*\* (St Martin's, 1990). For the book of a first-rate BBC Television series, see W. Horsley and R. Buckley, *Nippon New Superpower: Japan since 1945* (BBC Publications, 1990). See also M. Morischima, *Why Has Japan 'Succeeded'?: Western Technology and the Japanese Ethos* (Cambridge, 1982).

SOME OTHER COUNTRIES. R. Carr, *Spain, 1808–1939* (Oxford, 1966); H. V. Livermore, *A New History of Portugal*\* (2nd edn, Cambridge, 1976); J. Rothschild, *East Central Europe between the Two World Wars*\* (Washington, 1975); H. Roos, *History of Modern Poland* (Eyre & Spottiswoode, 1966); A. Polonsky, *Politics in Independent Poland, 1921–39* (Oxford, 1972). H. G. Skilling (ed.), *Czechoslovakia, 1918–88: Seventy Years from Independence* (Macmillan, 1991); H. G. Skilling, *Czechoslovakia's Interrupted Revolution* (Princeton, 1976); B. Lewis, *The Emergence of Modern Turkey* (2nd edn, Oxford, 1968); A. G. Mazour, *Finland between East and West* (Greenwood, 1975); V. S. Vardys and R. J. Misinnas (eds), *The Baltic States in Peace and War, 1917–45* (Pennsylvania, 1978); C. P. Woodhouse, *Modern Greece: A Short History*\* (4th edn, Faber & Faber, 1986); R. Clogg, *A Short History of Modern Greece*\* (2nd edn, Cambridge, 1986); T. B. Millar, *Australia in Peace and War* (Hurst, 1978); P. Mansfield, *The Ottoman Empire and Its Successors*\* (Macmillan, 1973); B. N. Pandey, *The Rise of Modern India* (Macmillan, 1967).

## 3. ORIGINS AND COURSE OF FIRST WORLD WAR

ORIGINS. The classic account is the immensely detailed L. Albertini, *The Origins of the War of 1914* (3 vols, Oxford, 1952–7). A 'revisionist' debate over German war-guilt began with F. Fischer, *Griff nach der Weltmacht* (Droste, 1961), translated as *Germany's Aims in the First World War* (Chatto & Windus, 1967). These ideas were supported and supplemented in V. R. Berghahn's excellent study, *Germany and the Approach of War in 1914*\* (Macmillan, 1973). By far the best book on British policy is Z. Steiner, *Britain and the Origins of the First World War*\* (Macmillan, 1977). For the foreign policy of Austria–Hungary there is the well-researched and sympathetic study by F. R. Bridge, *From Sadowa to Sarajevo* (Routledge, 1972). A good brief introduction is L. C. F. Turner, *Origins of the First World War*\* (Arnold, 1970); see also J. Röhl, *Delusion or Design* (Elek, 1973). For Serbian policies, see V. Dedijer, *The Road to Sarajevo* (MacGibbon & Kee, 1967). For a French view, see P. Renouvin, *La Crise européenne et la Première Guerre Mondiale* (4th edn, Presses Universitaires, 1962). The outstanding account of British relations with Germany is P. Kennedy, *The rise of the Anglo-German Antagonism, 1860–1914* (Allen & Unwin, 1980). The best general synthesis is J. Joll, *The Origins of the First World War*\* (Longman, 1992).

MILITARY. P. M. Kennedy (ed.), *The War Plans of the Great Powers, 1880–1914* (Allen & Unwin, 1979); C. Falls, *The Great War*\* (Putnam, 1961). An older study still useful for the western front is Basil Liddell Hart, *History of the First World War*\*, first published in 1930, also in paperback (Pan, 1972). For links between strategy and politics, see L. L. Farrar, *The Short War Illusion*\* (Clio, 1973) and M. Kitchen, *The Silent Dictatorship* (Croom Helm, 1976). For the conflict between Russia, Germany and Austria–Hungary, see N. Stone's stimulating assessment in *The Eastern Front* (Hodder & Stoughton, 1975). See also J. M. Bourne, *Britain and the Great War, 1914–1918*\* (Arnold, 1989).

GENERAL and DIPLOMATIC. M. Ferro, *The Great War 1914–18*\* (Routledge, 1973); Z. A. B. Zeman, *A Diplomatic History of the First World War* (Macmillan, 1971); E. R. May, *The World War and American Isolation, 1914–17*\* (Times Books, 1966); E. Kedourie, *England and the Middle East: The Destruction of the Ottoman Empire, 1914–21* (Harvester, 1977); V. H. Rothwell, *British War Aims and Peace Diplomacy* (Oxford, 1971); D. Stevenson, *First World War and International Politics* (Oxford, 1987); B. Hunt and A. Preston (eds), *War Aims and Strategic Policy in the Great War, 1914–18* (Croom Helm, 1977); R. A. Kann, B. K. Kiraly and P. S. Fichtner (eds), *The Habsburg Empire in World War I* (Columbia, 1977); A. Marwick, *The Deluge: British Society and the First World War*\* (Macmillan, 1973).

## 4. THE RUSSIAN REVOLUTION 1917

W. H. Chamberlin, *The Russian Revolution, 1917–22*\* (2 vols, Grosset, 1965) was written close to the events it describes, a vivid portrait first published in 1935. See also A. B. Ulam, *Lenin and the Bolsheviks*\* (Fontana, 1969); E. H. Carr, *The Bolshevik Revolution 1917–23*\* (3 vols, Penguin, 1950–3); S. P. Melgunov, *Bolshevik Seizure of Power*\* (Clio, 1972); I. Deutscher, *The Prophet Armed: Trotsky, 1879–1921*\* (Oxford, 1954) and *The Prophet Unarmed: Trotsky, 1921–9*\* (Oxford, 1970). E. H. Carr's classic fourteen-volume *History of Soviet Russia* is likely to be studied only by the specialist; the first three volumes have already been cited under their sub-heading, *The Bolshevik Revolution*; E. H. Carr distilled the multi-volume work into one very readable volume to serve as a general introduction, entitled *The Russian Revolution: From Lenin to Stalin, 1917–29*\* (Macmillan, 1980). See also under national histories. More recent works include E. Acton, *Rethinking the Russian Revolution* (Arnold, 1990); E. Mawdsley, *The Russian Civil War*\* (Allen & Unwin, 1987); and, from the doyen of American historians, R. Pipes, *The Russian Revolution, 1899–1919*\* (Collins Harvill, 1990).

## 5. PEACEMAKING AND DIPLOMACY IN THE 1920s

For a good synthesis, see A. Sharp, *The Versailles Settlement: Peacemaking in Paris, 1919*\* (Macmillan, 1991). For British policy, see E. Goldstein, *Winning the Peace: British Diplomatic Strategy, Peace Planning and the Paris Peace Conference* (Cambridge, 1991). See also S. P. Tillman, *Anglo-American Relations at the Paris Peace Conference of 1919* (Princeton, 1961); H. Nicolson, *Peacemaking, 1919* (Constable, 1934); J. M. Keynes, *The Economic Consequences of the Peace* (reprint, Macmillan, 1976); E. Mantoux, *The Carthaginian Peace* (reprint, Arno, 1978); J. M. Blum, *Woodrow Wilson and the Politics of Morality* (Little, Brown, 1956); A. S. Link, *Wilson the Diplomatist*\* (Johns Hopkins, 1957). For a brief general survey, see G. Schulz, *Revolutions and*

*Peace Treaties, 1917–20*\* (Methuen, 1972). Also of value are H. I. Nelson, *Land and Power: British and Allied Policy on Germany's Frontiers, 1916–19*\* (David & Charles, 1971); and A. Mayer, *Politics and Diplomacy of Peacemaking: Containment and Counter-revolution at Versailles 1918–1919* (Weidenfeld & Nicolson, 1968). A good general survey is S. Marks, *The Illusion of Peace: International Relations in Europe, 1918–33*\*

(Macmillan, 1976). J. Jacobson, *Locarno Diplomacy* (Princeton, 1972) is based on new research. Also important is P. Wandycz, *France and Her Eastern Allies, 1919–25* (Minneapolis, 1962), and *Soviet–Polish Relations, 1917–21* (Harvard, 1969). See also R. Ullman, *Anglo-Soviet Relations, 1917–21* (3 vols, Princeton, 1961–7); F. P. Walters, *A History of the League of Nations* (2 vols, Oxford, 1952); H. A. Turner, *Stresemann and*

*the Politics of the Weimar Republic* (Greenwood, 1979). Interesting contributions are to be found in H. A. Turner (ed.), *European Diplomacy between Two Wars, 1919–1939*\* (Quadrangle, 1972). Also useful are G. A. Craig and F. Gilbert, (eds), *The Diplomats, 1919–39*\* (2 vols, Athenaeum, 1963); and A. Orde, *Great Britain and International Security, 1920–36* (Royal Historical Society, 1978).

## 6. CHINA AND JAPAN AND THE WEST BEFORE THE SECOND WORLD WAR

CHINA. V. Purcell, *The Boxer Uprising* (Cambridge, 1963); Y. C. Wang, *Chinese Intellectuals and the West, 1872–1949* (Carolina, 1966); M. C. Wright, *China in Revolution: The First Phase, 1900–13*\* (Yale, 1971); J. E. Rue, *Mao Tse-tung in Opposition, 1927–35* (Stanford, 1966); Lucien Bianco, *Origins of the Chinese Revolution*\* (Stanford, 1971); C. Tse-tung, *The May Fourth Movement: Intellectual Revolution in Modern China* (Harvard, 1960); R. C. Thornton, *China: The*

*Struggle for Power, 1917–72*\* (Indiana, 1973); J. Gittings, *The World and China, 1922–72* (Eyre Methuen, 1974); J. Ch'en, *Mao and the Chinese Revolution*\* (Oxford, 1968). See also under national histories.

JAPAN. J. Livingston, J. Moore and F. Oldfather, *The Japan Reader: Imperial Japan, 1800–1945*\* (Penguin, 1976); A. Iriye, *After Imperialism*\* (Athenaeum, 1973); R. Storry, *Japan and the Decline of the West in Asia, 1894–*

*1943*\* (Macmillan, 1979); A. D. Coox and H. Conroy (eds), *China and Japan: Search for Balance since World War I* (Clio, 1978); J. B. Crowley, *Japan's Quest for Autonomy: National Security and Foreign Policy, 1930–8* (Princeton, 1966); R. D. Burns and E. M. Bennett (eds), *Diplomats in Crisis*\* (Clio, 1975); *The Cambridge History of Japan: The Twentieth Century*, ed. P. Duus (Cambridge, 1989); W. E. Beasley, *Japanese Imperialism, 1894–1945* (Oxford, 1987).

## 7. THE DEPRESSION YEARS: THE UNITED STATES, BRITAIN AND FRANCE

GENERAL. P. Fearon, *The Origins and Nature of the Great Slump, 1929–32*\* (Macmillan, 1979) surveys the literature and sums up. J. K. Galbraith, *The Great Crash 1929*\* (new edn, Deutsch, 1980) is a stimulating account. More technical are D. H. Aldcroft, *From Versailles to Wall Street: The International Economy, 1919–29* (Allen Lane, 1971); and C. P. Kindleberger, *The World in Depression, 1929–39* (Allen Lane, 1973). See also D. E. Moggridge, *Keynes*\* (Fontana, 1976).

UNITED STATES, DEPRESSION AND NEW DEAL. There is a rich choice of stimulating general treatments. See especially R. Hofstadter, *The Age of Reform: From Bryan to F.D.R.*\* (Vintage, 1973). For a good survey of the period with bibliographical

discussion, see R. S. Kirkendall, *The United States, 1929–45: Years of Crisis and Change*\* (McGraw-Hill, 1974). See also W. E. Leuchtenburg, *The Perils of Prosperity, 1914–32*\* (Chicago, 1958); A. M. Schlesinger's three volumes, *The Age of Roosevelt: The Crisis of the Old Order, 1919–33*, *The Coming of the New Deal* and *The Politics of Upheaval* (Houghton Mifflin, 1957, 1959, 1960); and H. Stein, *The Fiscal Revolution in America*\* (Chicago, 1971). An outstanding treatment is W. E. Leuchtenburg, *Franklin Roosevelt and the New Deal*\* (Harper & Row, 1963). A valuable series of studies of the New Deal can be found in J. Braeman, R. H. Bremner and D. Brody, *The New Deal* (2 vols, Ohio, 1975). See also E. A. Rosen, *Hoover, Roosevelt and the Brains Trust* (Columbia, 1977). A fine

biography of Roosevelt is F. Freidel, *F. D. Roosevelt* (4 vols, Little, Brown, 1952–73). Stimulating analysis in one volume is J. MacGregor Burns, *Roosevelt: The Lion and the Fox* (Harcourt, 1956). A good biography from outstanding New Dealer is S. F. Charles, *Minister of Relief: Harry Hopkins and the Depression* (Syracuse, 1963).

BRITAIN. In addition to books already cited under national histories for the traumatic industrial breakdown of the mid-1920s, see M. Morris, *The General Strike*\* (Penguin, 1976); S. Pollard, *The Development of the British Economy, 1914–67*\* (Arnold, 1969); M. Cowling, *The Impact of Labour* (Cambridge, 1971); T. Wilson, *The Downfall of the Liberal Party, 1914–35*\* (Macmillan, 1975); and P.

Rowland, *Lloyd George* (Barrie & Jenkins, 1975). A recent study of the critical 1929–34 period is D. Marquand, *Ramsay MacDonald* (Cape, 1977). Other biographies of especial value are K. Middlemas and John Barnes, *Baldwin: A Biography* (Weidenfeld & Nicolson, 1969); R. Skidelsky, *Politicians and the Slump\** (Macmillan, 1967); R. Skidelsky, *Oswald Mosley* (Macmillan, 1975); C. Cross, *The Fascists in Britain* (London, 1961); K. Feiling, *The Life of Neville Chamberlain* (Macmillan, 1946); M. Gilbert, vol. 5, *Winston S. Churchill, 1922–1939* (Heinemann, 1976). For a fascinating social history, see N. Branson and M. Heinemann, *Britain in the Nineteen Thirties\** (Panther, 1973). See also D. Winch, *Economics and Policy\** (Hodder & Stoughton, 1969); R. Blake, *The Conservative Party from Peel to Thatcher\** (Fontana, 1985); T. F. Lindsay and M. Harrington, *The Conservative Party, 1918–70\** (Macmillan, 1979); H. Pelling, *A Short History of the Labour Party\** (Macmillan, 1978). Providing a controversial but stimulating link between politics and foreign policy is M. Cowling, *The Impact of Hitler\** (new edn, Chicago, 1977). A provocative and stimulating account is A. J. P. Taylor's *English History, 1914–45\** (Penguin, 1970).

FRANCE. For an overview, see D. Thomson, *Democracy in France since 1870\** (5th edn, Oxford, 1969). See also J. P. T. Bury, *France: The Insecure Peace\** (Macdonald, 1972); J. Lacouture, *Léon Blum* (Seuil, 1977); R. Rémond and J. Bourdin (eds), *Édouard Daladier, Chef de Gouvernement* (Fondation Nationale des Sciences Politiques, 1977); A. Sauvy, *Histoire économique de la France entre les deux guerres, 1918–39* (2 vols, Fayard, 1965–7); J. Plumyène and R. Lasierra, *Les Fascismes français, 1923–63* (Paris, 1963); R. Rémond, *The Right Wing in France from 1815 to de Gaulle* (2nd edn, Pennsylvania, 1966). See also under national histories.

## 8. ITALY AND THE RISE OF FASCISM

Covering not only Italy but fascism in general, is the very useful W. Laqueur (ed.), *Fascism: A Reader's Guide\** (Penguin, 1976). See also R. De Felice, *Interpretations of Fascism* (Harvard, 1977); A. J. Gregor, *Fascism: The Contemporary Interpretations\** (General Learning Press, 1974) and the same author's *Italian Fascism and Developmental Dictatorship* (Princeton, 1979); A. Lyttelton (ed.), *Fascism in Italy, 1919–29\** (Princeton, 1988). A classic study is the same author's *The Seizure of Power, 1919–29* (Scribner's, 1973). A useful overview is G. Carocci, *Italian Fascism\** (Penguin, 1975). See also E. Nolte, *Three Faces of Fascism\** (Mentor, 1970); F. Carsten, *The Rise of Fascism\** (Methuen, 1970); E. Wiskemann, *Fascism in Italy\** (Macmillan, 1972); S. J. Woolf (ed.), *European Fascism* (Weidenfeld & Nicolson, 1968); and A. Cassels, *Fascist Italy\** (Routledge, 1969). P. F. Sugar, *Native Fascism in the Successor States, 1918–45\** (Clio, 1971) is a stimulating collection of essays on the spread of fascism in central and south-east Europe.

For biographies of Mussolini, see L. Fermi, *Mussolini\** (Chicago, 1966); M. Gallo, *Mussolini's Italy* (Macmillan, 1973). is a treatment of the man and his times, and I. Kirkpatrick, *Mussolini* (reprint, Greenwood, 1976). A stimulating book is D. Mack Smith, *Mussolini's Roman Empire* (Longman, 1976). A marvellous study of the last years is F. W. Deakin, *The Brutal Friendship: Mussolini, Hitler and the Fall of the Italian Fascism\** (Penguin, 1966). See also A. J. Gregor, *Young Mussolini and the Intellectual Origins of Fascism* (California, 1980).

## 9. THE SOVIET UNION: GENERAL, AND THE STALIN ERA

(Books additional to those cited under national histories.) There are a number of outstanding biographies, not least I. Deutscher, *Stalin: A Political Biography\** (Penguin, 1970); the leading work for the early period is R. C. Tucker, *Stalin as a Revolutionary, 1879–1929* (Norton, 1973); by the same author is *Stalin in Power: The Revolution from Above, 1928–1941* (Norton, 1990). See also I. Deutscher, *The Prophet Unarmed: Trotsky, 1921–9\** (Oxford, 1970) (two further volumes deal with the remainder of Trotsky's life); for a useful and more brief discussion, see I. Howe, *Trotsky\** (Fontana, 1978); in the same Modern Masters series, see R. Conquest, *Lenin\** (Fontana, 1972). Also valuable is A. B. Ulam, *Lenin and the Bolsheviks\** (Fontana, 1969). The best single overview of the economy is A. Nove, *An Economic History of the USSR\** (2nd edn, Penguin, 1989). On party and politics, see M. Fainsod, *How Russia is Ruled* (revised edn, Harvard, 1965); L. B. Schapiro, *The Communist Party of the Soviet Union* (2nd edn, Eyre & Spottiswoode, 1970); A. Nove, *Stalinism and After\** (Allen & Unwin, 1975); and M. Fainsod, *Smolensk under Soviet Rule* (Harvard, 1958). An outstanding study of the problems of the peasantry and Soviet policies is M. Lewin, *Russian Peasants and Soviet Power\** (Allen & Unwin, 1968). R. W. Davies, provides the authoritative account of collectivisation in two volumes, *The Socialist Offensive, 1929–30* and *The Soviet Collective Farm, 1929–30* (Macmillan, 1980). A condemnation of Stalinism can be found in R. A. Medvedev, *Let History Judge\** (Spokesman, 1976). On the military, see J. Erickson, *The Soviet High Command: A Military–Political*

*History, 1918–41* (St Martin, 1962). An outstanding history of Soviet foreign relations in A. Ulam, *Expansion and Co-existence: A History of Soviet Foreign Policy* (2nd edn, Praeger, 1974). A brief and stimulating survey is G. F. Kennan, *Russia and the West** (Mentor, 1967). J. Haslam, *Soviet Foreign Policy, 1930–41* (5 vols, Macmillan, 1983–91) is a re-examination of Soviet foreign policy in a multi-volume study.

## 10. SPAIN AND THE CIVIL WAR

A good general history is R. Carr, *Spain, 1808–1939* (Oxford, 1966); see also S. G. Payne, *A History of Spain and Portugal* (vol. 2, Wisconsin, 1976), and the same author's *Politics and the Military in Modern Spain* (Stanford, 1967). Stimulating is R. Herr, *Modern Spain** (California, 1971). Other outstanding books dealing more generally with the 1930s, include G. Brenan, *The Spanish Labyrinth** (2nd edn, Cambridge, 1950); G. Jackson, *The Spanish Republic and the Civil War, 1931–9** (Princeton, 1965); S. G. Payne, *The Spanish Revolution** (Norton, 1969); R. A. H. Robinson, *The Origins of Franco's Spain* (Pittsburgh, 1971); S. G. Payne, *Falange History of Spanish Fascism** (Stanford, 1961); H. Thomas, *The Spanish Civil War** (3rd edn, Penguin, 1977). The impact on Britain is discussed in K. W. Watkins, *Britain Divided* (reprint, Greenwood, 1976).

For Portugal, see A. H. De Oliveira Marques, *History of Portugal* (vol. 2, Columbia, 1972).

## 11. GERMANY: THE WEIMAR REPUBLIC AND THE THIRD REICH

An interesting general account is M. Kolinsky, *Continuity and Change in European Society since 1870** (Croom Helm, 1974). On Weimar, the classic account is E. Eyck, *The Weimar Republic* (2 vols, Harvard, 1962–4); see also S. W. Halperin, *Germany Tried Democracy: A Political History of the Reich from 1918 to 1933* (New York, 1946). For the foundation year, see F. L. Carsten, *Revolution in Central Europe, 1917–19* (Temple Smith, 1972); and a crucial aspect of the history of the Republic, *The Reichswehr and Politics 1918 to 1933* (Oxford, 1966). Indispensable for a view of the origins and impact of National Socialism is K. D. Bracher, *The German Dictatorship** (Penguin, 1978); see also M. Broszat, *German National Socialism** (Clio, 1966). Lively but somewhat dated is W. Shirer, *The Rise and Fall of the Third Reich** (Pan, 1960). A brief account of Weimar's collapse is A. J. Nicholls, *Weimar and the Rise of Hitler** (2nd edn, Macmillan, 1979).

Thousands of books have now been written on all aspects of Hitler and the Third Reich. The following are likely to be found especially useful. I. Kershaw, *The Nazi Dictatorship** (2nd edn, Arnold, 1989) is a valuable discussion of problems of interpretation. Also useful for elucidating different approaches is J. Hiden and J. Farquarson, *Explaining Hitler's Germany: Historians and the Third Reich** (2nd edn, Batsford, 1989). Both these books refer to the extensive literature on the subject. The classic biography is A. Bullock, *Hitler: A Study in Tyranny** (Penguin, 1962); see also, by the same author, *Hitler and Stalin: Parallel Lives** (Fontana Press, 1993). A stimulating discussion can be found in W. Carr, *Hitler: A Study in Personality and Politics* (Arnold, 1978). J. P. Stern, *Hitler: The Führer and the People** (Fontana Press, 1975) is outstanding. On more specialised topics, see A. Tyrell, *Vom 'Trommler' zum 'Führer'* (Fink, 1975); J. Gordon, *Hitler and the Beer Hall Putsch* (Princeton, 1972); J. Noakes, *The Nazi Party in Lower Saxony, 1921–33* (Oxford, 1971); and G. Pridham, *Hitler's Rise to Power: The Nazi Movement in Bavaria, 1923–33* (Hart-Davis, 1973). A series of studies of Nazi leaders appears in J. C. Fest, *The Face of the Third Reich** (Penguin, 1970). An excellent survey of the Third Reich is R. Grunberger, *A Social History of the Third Reich** (Penguin, 1974). See also I. Kershaw, *The 'Hitler Myth': Image and Reality in the Third Reich** (Oxford, 1989).

For foreign policy a good synthesis is W. Carr, *Arms, Autarky and Aggression** (Arnold, 1972). The early years are authoritatively analysed by G. L. Weinberg, *The Foreign Policy of Hitler's Germany: Diplomatic Revolution in Europe, 1933–6* and *Starting World War II* (Chicago, 1970 and 1980).

On the SS, see H. Krausnick and M. Broszat, *Anatomy of the SS State** (Paladin, 1973). On the churches in the Third Reich, see J. Conway, *The Nazi Persecution of the Churches* (Weidenfeld & Nicolson, 1968). On relations with the army, see R. O'Neill, *The German Army and the Nazi Party* (Heinemann, 1976). A good survey of the resistance is P. Hoffmann, *The History of the German Resistance, 1933–45* (Macdonald & Jane's, 1977).

## 12. THE ORIGINS OF WAR IN ASIA AND EUROPE

The books on foreign policy mentioned in the previous sections are relevant.

ASIA AND THE PACIFIC. J. W. Morley (ed.), *Japan's Foreign Policy, 1868–1941: A Research Guide* (Columbia, 1974) contains essays and bibliographies. See also I. Nish, *Japanese Foreign Policy, 1869–1942* (Routledge, 1977); S. N. Ogata, *Defiance in Manchuria: The Making of Japanese Foreign Policy, 1869–1942* (London, 1977); and S. E. Pelz, *Race to Pearl Harbor: The Future of the Second London Naval Conference and the Onset of World War II* (Harvard, 1974). J. W. Morley (ed.), *Japan's Road to the Pacific War: Deterrent Diplomacy, 1935–40* (Columbia, 1976) and S. Ienaga, *Japan's Last War* (Blackwell, 1979) offer two very different Japanese views. Also useful is C. Thorne, *The Limits of Foreign Policy: The West, the League and the Far Eastern Crisis of 1931–3* (Hamish Hamilton, 1972). A. Iriye (ed.), *Mutual Images: Essays in American Japanese Relations* (Harvard, 1975) provides a stimulating broader series of excellent essays. By the same author is *The Origins of the Second World War in Asia and the Pacific\** (Longman, 1987). A detailed analysis of aspects of the origins of the war in the Pacific can be found in D. Borg and S. Okamoto, *Pearl Harbor: A History. Japanese–American Relations, 1931–41* (Columbia, 1973). For British policy, see P. Lowe, *Great Britain and the Origins of the Pacific War: A Study of British Far Eastern Policy* (Oxford, 1977). A good analysis appears in R. Dallek, *Franklin D. Roosevelt and American Foreign Policy,*

*1932–45* (Oxford, 1979) which deals not only with eastern Asia, but with the whole range of United States policy. An older classic work on United States foreign policy in Europe and Asia and American entry into the Second World War is W. L. Langer and S. E. Gleason, *Challenge to Isolation, 1937–40* and *The Undeclared War, 1940–1* (Harper & Row, 1952–3). Also valuable is D. Reynolds, *The Creation of the Anglo-American Alliance, 1937–41* (North Carolina, 1981).

EUROPE. A collection of essays on the controversy aroused by A. J. P. Taylor, *Origins of the Second World War\** (Penguin, 1963) is in E. M. Robertson (ed.), *The Origins of the Second World War\** (Macmillan, 1971). A good brief synthesis is P. M. H. Bell, *The Origins of the Second World War in Europe\** (Longman, 1986). The most authoritative treatment of the immediate crisis years is D. C. Watt, *How War Came: The Immediate Origins of the Second World War, 1938–39\** (Mandarin, 1990). A stimulating German survey is K. Hildebrand, *The Foreign Policy of the Third Reich\** (Batsford, 1973). A. Adamthwaite provides a valuable study of *France and the Coming of the Second World War, 1936–9* (Cass, 1977). A French view of the coming of the war can be found in M. Baumont, *The Origins of the Second World War* (Yale, 1978). See also J. Néré, *The Foreign Policy of France, 1914–45* (Routledge, 1974). British foreign policy is well surveyed in F. S. Northedge, *The Troubled Giant* (Bell, 1966). Detailed analysis of British policy on the eve of the

war from 1937 to 1939 appear in K. Middlemas, *The Diplomacy of Illusion* (Weidenfeld & Nicolson, 1972) and S. Aster, *The Making of the Second World War* (Deutsch, 1973). Provocative older books are M. Gilbert and R. Gott, *The Appeasers\** (Weidenfeld & Nicolson, 1967) and N. Thompson, *The Anti-appeasers* (Oxford, 1971). See also D. C. Watt, *Personalities and Policies* (Longman, 1965). Of general importance is M. Howard, *The Continental Commitment\** (Penguin, 1974). Polish policy is set out in A. M. Cienciala, *Poland and the Western Powers, 1938–9* (Routledge, 1968) and in P. Prazmowska, *Britain, Poland and the Eastern Front, 1939* (Cambridge, 1987). Italian policy is discussed in M. Toscano, *The Origins of the Pact of Steel* (Johns Hopkins, 1967); E. Wiskemann, *The Rome–Berlin Axis\** (2nd edn, Fontana, 1966); G. Salvemini, *Prelude to World War II* (Gollancz, 1953); C. J. Lowe and F. Marzari, *Italian Foreign Policy, 1870–1940* (Routledge, 1975); and D. Mack Smith, *Mussolini's Roman Empire* (Longman, 1976). For a Soviet view, see I. Maisky, *Who Helped Hitler?* (Hutchinson, 1964). A good survey of the last two years is C. Thorne, *The Approach of War, 1938–9\** (Macmillan, 1967). Specialist studies include J. T. Emmerson, *The Rhineland Crisis* (Temple Smith, 1977); J. Gehl, *Austria, Germany and the Anschluss* (new edn, Greenwood, 1970); K. Robbins, *Munich, 1938* (Cassell, 1968); the same subject is covered in great detail and at length by T. Taylor, *Munich: The Price of Peace* (Hodder & Stoughton, 1979).

## 13. THE SECOND WORLD WAR

Among the best one-volume histories are P. Calvocoressi and G. Wint, *Total War\** (Penguin, 1974); R. A. C. Parker, *Struggle for Survival: The History of the Second World War\** (Oxford, 1990), an outstanding synthesis; M. Gilbert, *Second World*

*War* (Collins, 1990); G. L. Weinberg, *A World at Arms* (Cambridge, 1994). W. S. Churchill, *The Second World War* (6 vols, Cassell, 1948–54) is indispensable for a feel of the war as seen through Churchill's eyes. For a Soviet view, see P. N. Pospelov and

others, *The Great Patriotic War of the Soviet Union, 1941–5* (Progress, 1974). The classic Western account is J. Erickson, *Stalin's War with Germany* (2 vols, Weidenfeld & Nicolson, 1975–83).

Britain at war is also interestingly

discussed by P. M. H. Bell, *A Certain Eventuality* (London, 1974) and in H. Pelling, *Britain and the Second World War** (Fontana, 1970). A. Calder presents a vivid portrait in *The People's War: Britain, 1939–45** (Panther, 1971). Also good is P. Addison, *The Road to 1945** (Quartet, 1977).

R. Paxton, *Vichy France* (Barrie & Jenkins, 1972); A. S. Milward, *The New Order and the French Economy* (Oxford, 1970); H. R. Kedward, *Resistance in Vichy France, 1940–42* (Oxford, 1978) all reveal important facets of events in France. See also R. Griffiths, *Marshal Pétain* (Constable, 1970); J. Isorni, *Philippe Pétain* (2 vols, Table Ronde, 1972–3); G. Hirschfeld and P. Marsh (eds), *Collaboration in France: Politics and Culture during the Nazi Occupation, 1940–1944* (Berg, 1989).

Important for a study of Germany are A. S. Milward, *The German Economy at War* (Athlone, 1965); M. G. Steinert, *Hitler's War and the Germans* (Ohio, 1977); E. K. Bramsted, *Goebbels and National Socialist Propaganda* (East Lansing, 1965); Z. A. B. Zeman, *Nazi Propaganda** (2nd edn, Oxford, 1973); M. Balfour, *Propaganda in War, 1939–45* (Routledge, 1979).

A perceptive short book on the murder of the Jews considered in its widest setting is Y. Bauer, *The Holocaust in Historical Perspective* (Sheldon, 1979). See also F. H. Littell and H. G. Locke (eds), *The German Church, Struggle and the Holocaust* (Wayne, 1974) and, oustanding, R. Gutteridge, *Open Thy Mouth for the Dumb* (Blackwell, 1976). A magisterial study is R. Hillberg, *The Destruction of the European Jews* (new edn, 3 vols, Holmes & Meier, 1985). Interesting contributions have been made by G. Fleming, *Hitler and the Final Solution* (California, 1984); W. Laqueur, *The Terrible Secret** (Penguin, 1982); C. Browning, *The Path to Genocide: Essays on Launching the Final Solution** (Cambridge, 1992); M. Gilbert, *Auschwitz and the Allies** (Mandarin, 1991). J. Steinberg, *All or Nothing: The Axis and the Holocaust, 1941–43* (Routledge, 1990) compares the humanity of the Italian army on the Adriatic with the barbarity of the German. M. Gilbert, *The Holocaust: The Jewish Tragedy** (Collins, 1987) is an unbearably detailed account of atrocities all over occupied Europe. The Israeli scholar

D. Bankier, in *The Germans and the Final Solution: Public Opinion under Nazism* (Blackwell, 1992), addresses the important question what Germans knew and thought. The best one-volume account is L. Dawidowicz, *The War Against the Jews, 1933–1945** (Penguin, 1990).

For Allied diplomacy during the Second World War, see H. Feis, *Churchill, Roosevelt, Stalin** and *Between War and Peace** (Princeton, 1967 and 1960); L. Giovannitti and F. Freed, *The Decision to Drop the Bomb* (Methuen, 1967); G. Kolko, *The Politics of War: The World and United States Foreign Policy, 1943–5** (Pantheon, 1990); W. R. Louis, *Imperialism at Bay, 1941–5: The United States and the Decolonization of the British Empire* (Oxford, 1978). A critical assessment of Allied policy towards Poland can be found in E. J. Rozek, *Wartime Diplomacy: A Pattern in Poland* (Wiley, 1958). Also useful is R. Edmonds, *The Big Three: Churchill, Roosevelt and Stalin** (Penguin, 1992). For a study of Japan's impact and her occupation policies during the war, an outstanding book is J. Pluvier, *South East Asia from Colonialism to Independence* (Oxford, 1975).

## 14. WESTERN EUROPE: POST-WAR RECOVERY AND GROWTH

W. Laqueur, *Europe in Our Time, 1945–1992** (Penguin, 1993) provides an overview, as does D. Urwin, *Western Europe since 1945: A Political History* (Longman, 1989). M. J. Hogan, *The Marshall Plan: America, Britain, and the Reconstruction of Europe** (Cambridge, 1989) examines American motivation in seeking to integrate a free-market Western Europe; A. S. Milward's classic study, *The Reconstruction of Western Europe, 1945–51** (Routledge, 1987), shows recovery under way before the Marshall Plan could make an impact.

BRITAIN. K. O. Morgan, *The People's Peace: British History, 1945–1990** (Oxford, 1992); the same author has made a special study of the post war

Labour record in *Labour in Power, 1945–51** (Oxford, 1985) and *Labour People** (Oxford, 1990). Of the biographies interesting reading is B. Pimlott's *Hugh Dalton** (Macmillan, 1986) and the same author's *Harold Wilson* (HarperCollins, 1992). See also K. Harris, *Attlee** (Weidenfeld & Nicolson, 1984); A. Horne, *Harold Macmillan** (2 vols, Macmillan, 1988–9); R. Blake, *The Conservative Party from Peel to Thatcher* (Fontana Press, 1985). A good synthesis is A. Sked and C. Cook, *Post-War Britain: A Political History, 1945–1992** (Penguin, 1993). For a stimulating interpretation see P. Calvocoressi, *The British Experience, 1945–75** (Penguin, 1978). See also V. Bogdanor and R. Skidelsky (eds),

*The Age of Affluence, 1951–1964** (Macmillan, 1970); D. Marquand, *The Unprincipled Society: New Demands and Old Politics* (Cape, 1988). Violence, not only that caused by the IRA is discussed in R. Clutterbuck, *Britain in Agony: The Growth of Political Violence** (Penguin, 1978); for a readable and subtle analysis of the British way of life, see A. Marwick, *British Society since 1945** (2nd edn, Penguin, 1990). Two good studies of the Thatcher decade are D. Kavanagh, *Thatcherism and British Politics: The End of Consensus?** (Penguin, 1988) and P. Riddell, *The Thatcher Era and Its Legacy** (Blackwell, 1991). For an antidote to patriotic fervour, see Lieutenant D. Tinker's moving letters, *A Message from the Falklands**, posthumously compiled by H. Tinker (Junction Books, 1982). On the impact and reception of immigrants to Britain, see J. Walvin, *Passage to Britain** (Penguin, 1984). A good overview of Britain's external relations is provided by D. Reynolds, *Britannia Overruled: British Policy and World Power in the 20th Century** (Longman, 1991), with an extensive bibliography.

REPUBLIC OF IRELAND AND NORTHERN IRELAND. F. S. L. Lyons, *Ireland since the Famine* (2nd edn, Fontana Press, 1985); R. F. Foster, *Modern Ireland, 1600–1972** (Penguin, 1989); J. J. Lee, *Ireland, 1912–1985* (Cambridge, 1989). P. Arthur and K. Jeffery, *Northern Ireland since 1968** (Blackwell, 1988) chronicles and analyses the conflict.

FRANCE. One of the best general overviews is J.-P. Rioux, *The Fourth Republic, 1914–1958* (Cambridge, 1987); perhaps the most interesting way to tackle post-war France is through the English version of J. Lacouture's brilliant biography, *De Gaulle: The Ruler, 1945–1970* (Harvill, 1991); see by the same author, *Pierre Mendès-France* (Holmes & Meier, 1984). See also J. R. Frears, *France in the Giscard Presidency* (Allen & Unwin, 1981); D. S. Bell and B. Criddle, *The French Socialist Party: The Emergence of a Party of Government** (2nd edn, Oxford, 1988). Two very readable contributions illuminating French politics and way of life are J. Ardagh, *The New France: A Society in Transition, 1945–1977** (2nd edn, Penguin, 1973) and the same author's *France in the 1980s** (Penguin, 1982). On France's war in Indo-China, see J. Dalloz, *War in Indo-China, 1945–1954* (Gill & Macmillan, 1990). The conflict in Algeria is graphically covered in A. Horne, *A Savage War of Peace: Algeria, 1954–1962** (Penguin, 1979); for French policy in the West, see F. R. Willis, *France, Germany and the New Europe, 1945–1963* (Stanford, 1965); economic and social developments since 1945 are analysed in C. Flockton and E. Kofman, *France** (Chapman, 1989).

GERMANY. A. Grosser, *Germany in Our Time: A Political History of the Post-war Years** (Penguin, 1974) is an interpretative study by the German-born author, who emigrated to France. With a demise of the German Democratic Republic, H. A. Turner had to revise his *The Two Germanies since 1945* published in 1987, and he contrasts and recounts the history of the two Germanies from a new perspective in *Germany from Partition to Reunification* (Yale, 1992). See also T. Prittie, *The Velvet Chancellors: A History of Postwar Germany* (Muller, 1979) and M. Balfour, *West Germany: A Contemporary History* (Croom Helm, 1982). For the American occupation, see J. Gimbel, *The American Occupation of Germany: Politics and the Military* (Stanford, 1968). *The Konrad Adenauer Memoirs, 1945–53*, trans. B. Ruhm von Orpen (Weidenfeld & Nicolson, 1966) make for pretty dry reading and can be supplemented by T. Prittie, *Konrad Adenauer* (Stacey, 1972), by the same author's biography *Willy Brandt: Portrait of a Statesman* (Schocken, 1974) and by G. Pridham, *Christian Democracy in Western Germany* (Croom Helm, 1977). W. Griffith, *The Ostpolitik of the Federal Republic of Germany* (MIT, 1978) traces the changing relationship with the other Germans; see also P. Merkl, *German Foreign Policies East and West* (Clio, 1974). The history of the German Democratic Republic until her dissolution will need to be rewritten; meantime D. Childs, *The GDR: Moscow's German Ally* (2nd edn, Allen & Unwin, 1988) and M. McCauley, *The German Democratic Republic since 1945* (Macmillan, 1983) are useful outlines. A sound German account is T. Vogelsang, *Das geteilte Deutschland** (dtv., 1980) and P.

Bender, *Neue Ostpolitik vom Mauerbau bis zum Moskauer Vertrag** (dtv., 1986)

ITALY. There are several good general histories of post-war Italy, including P. Ginsborg, *A History of Contemporary Italy: Society and Politics, 1943–1988** (Penguin, 1990), with an extensive bibliography, and N. Kogan, *A Political History of Postwar Italy* (Praeger, 1981). The early years can be studied in S. J. Woolf (ed.), *The Rebirth of Italy, 1943–1950* (Longman, 1972); corruption and the political way of life are discussed in J. Chubb, *Patronage, Power and Poverty in Southern Italy: A Tale of Two Cities* (Cambridge, 1982) and J. Walston, *The Mafia and Clientilism: Roads to Rome in Postwar Calabria* (Routledge, 1988).

SPAIN AND PORTUGAL. An overview can be found in R. Carr, *Modern Spain, 1875–1980* (Oxford, 1980); for post-civil-war Spain, see R. Carr and J. P. Fusi, *Spain: Dictatorship to Democracy** (2nd edn, Allen & Unwin, 1981). A biography of Franco in English translation is E. de Blaye, *Franco and the Politics of Spain** (Penguin, 1976). See also P. Preston, *The Triumph of Democracy in Spain* (Methuen, 1986); R. Robinson, *Contemporary Portugal: A History* (Allen & Unwin, 1979).

THE EUROPEAN COMMUNITY. Three good overviews, are J. Lodge (ed.), *The European Community and the Challenge of the Future** (Pinter, 1989); J. Pinder, *European Community: The Building of a Union* (Oxford, 1991); and D. Swann, *The Economics of a Common Market** (6th edn, Penguin, 1988). C. Tugendhat, *Making Sense of Europe** (Penguin, 1986), by a former vice-president of the EC Commission from 1981 to 1985, is a realistic but upbeat appraisal of its achievements and future needs. See also S. de la Mahotière, *Towards One Europe** (Penguin, 1970).

## 15. THE COLD WAR

V. Rothwell, *Britain and the Cold War, 1941–1947* (Routledge, 1982); A. Deighton, *The Impossible Peace: Britain, the Division of Germany and the Origins of the Cold War* (Oxford, 1990). There is a large literature looking especially at the role of the United States in the Cold War: T. H. Anderson, *The United States, Great Britain and the Cold War* (Columbia, 1981); J. L. Gaddis, *The United States and the Origins of the Cold War, 1941–1947** (Columbia, 1972) and, by the same author, *Strategies of Containment: A Critical Appraisal of Post-War American National Security Policy** (Oxford, 1982), which links ideology, diplomacy and strategic thinking, and *The United States and the End of the Cold War: Implications, Reconstructions, Provocations* (Oxford, 1992). See also W. La Feber, *America, Russia and the Cold War, 1945–1992* (7th edn, McGraw, 1992). An excellent overview is D. Yergin's *Shattered Peace: The Origins of the Cold War and the National Security State** (Penguin, 1977).

More detailed studies of special aspects include J. Gimbel, *The American Occupation of Germany: Politics and Military, 1945–1949* (Stanford, 1968); J. O. Iatrides, *Revolt in Athens: The Greek Communist 'Second Round', 1944–45* (Princeton,

1972); W. P. Davison, *The Berlin Blockade: A Study in Cold War Politics* (Princeton, 1958); D. Cook, *Forging the Alliance: The Birth of the Nato Treaty and the Dramatic Transformation of U.S. Foreign Policy between 1945 and 1950** (Secker & Warburg, 1989). The memoirs of one of the principal architects of the alliance should be read: Dean Acheson, *Present at the Creation** (Norton, 1969). See also R. Garthoff, *Detente and Confrontation: American–Soviet Relations from Nixon to Reagan* (Brookings, 1985); A. Grosser, *The Western Alliance: European–American Relations since 1945** (Macmillan, 1980). See also the special issue of the journal *Diplomacy and Statecraft* edited by D. Armstrong and E. Goldstein (Cass) vol. 1, number 3, November 1990, which is devoted to the Cold War. For the Soviet side (which with the opening of the Soviet archives will be reassessed), see V. Mastny, *Russia's Road to the Cold War* (Columbia, 1979). See also section 17, The Soviet Union and Eastern Europe since the Second World War. For early glimpses from the archives of the former Soviet Union, see C. M. Andrew and O. Gordievsky, *KGB: Inside Story** (HarperCollins, 1990).

In Asia, the Cold War moved to real war. A. Iriye, *The Cold War in*

*Asia: A Historical Introduction* (Prentice Hall, 1974); P. Lowe, *The Origins of the Korean War** (Longman, 1986); Max Hastings, *The Korean War** (Pan, 1988); A. Short, *The Origins of the Vietnam War** (Longman, 1989); G. C. Herring, *America's Longest War: The United States and Vietnam, 1950–75** (2nd edn, McGraw, 1986); S. Karnow, *Vietnam: A History** (Penguin, 1984); W. Shawcross, *Sideshow: Kissinger, Nixon and the Destruction of Cambodia** (Simon & Schuster, 1981). The miscalculations of US policymakers in devising policy in Vietnam are analysed in L. Cable, *Unholy Grail: The U.S. and the Wars in Vietnam, 1965–8* (Routledge, 1991).

The Cuban missile crisis is described by an insider in Robert F. Kennedy, *The Cuban Missile Crisis, October 1962: Thirteen Days** (Pan, 1969). The best account is M. R. Beschloss, *The Crisis Years: Kennedy and Khrushchev, 1960–1963* (HarperCollins, 1991). A highly critical account of America's overall policies towards Cuba is M. H. Morley, *Imperial State and Revolution: The United States and Cuba, 1952–1986** (Cambridge, 1987). See also section 16, The United States during the Post-war Years.

## 16. THE UNITED STATES DURING THE POST-WAR YEARS

Interesting overviews are D. J. Boorstin, *The Americans: The Democratic Experience** (Random House, 1974); Carl Degler, *The Democratic Experience: An American History* (vol. 2, 5th edn, Glenview, 1981) and, for the growth of prosperity, W. E. Brownlee, *Dynamics of Ascent A History of the American Economy** (2nd edn, Wadsworth, 1988). See also J. K. Galbraith, *The Affluent Society* (2nd edn, Hamish Hamilton, 1969). A first-rate overview of social history is R. Polenberg, *One Nation Divisible: Class, Race, and Ethnicity in the United States since 1938** (Penguin, 1980). More special-

ised is L. Banner, *Woman in Modern America: A Brief History* (Harcourt Brace, 1974).

For the Truman presidency there is a two-volume study by R. J. Donovan, *Conflict and Crisis: The Presidency of Harry S. Truman, 1945–1948* (Norton, 1977) and *Tumultuous Years: The Presidency of Harry S. Truman, 1949–1953* (Norton, 1982). There is also a new one-volume biography from birth to death, D. McCullough, *Truman* (Simon & Schuster, 1992).

McCarthyism and the Cold War anti-communist drive which took forms subverting civil rights led to an

extensive literature, among them D. Caute, *The Great Fear: The Anti-Communist Purge under Truman and Eisenhower* (Secker & Warburg, 1978). The Eisenhower years can be studied in S. E. Ambrose, *Eisenhower* (2 vols, Simon & Schuster, 1983–4). Two sympathetic studies are A. M. Schlesinger Jr, *A Thousand Days: John F. Kennedy in the White House* (Houghton Mifflin, 1965) and T. C. Sorensen, *Kennedy* (Harper, 1965). See also H. S. Parmet, *J.F.K.: The Presidency of John F. Kennedy** (Penguin, 1984). R. Nixon, *The Memoirs of Richard Nixon** (Touchstone, 1990) are bulky, illuminating and well written. For an historian's assessment, see S. Ambrose, *Nixon: The Education of a Politician, 1913–1962* and *Nixon: The Triumph of a Politician, 1962–1972* (Simon & Schuster, 1987–9).

There is a synthesis available for the Reagan years: D. Mervin, *Ronald Reagan and the American Presidency*\* (Longman, 1990). For an insider's criticism of 'Reaganomics', see D. A. Stockman, *The Triumph of Politics: The Inside Story of the Reagan Revolution*\* (Avon, 1986).

RACE RELATIONS. From the large literature the following are a good starting point: H. Sitkoff, *The Struggle for Black Equality, 1954–1980* (Hill & Wang, 1981); D. M. Katzman, *Before the Ghetto: Black Detroit in the Nineteenth Century* (Urbana, 1977); K. Kusmer, *A Ghetto Takes Shape: Black Cleveland, 1870–1930* (Urbana, 1976); Martin Luther King's own account, *Stride toward Freedom: The Montgomery Story*\* (Harper, 1987); and S. B. Oates's biography of the great moderate black leader, *Let the Trumpet Sound: The Life of Martin Luther King, Jr*\* (Ment, 1988). King and the black struggle are vividly portrayed in the Pulitzer-winning book by T. Branch, *Parting the Waters:*

*America in the King Years, 1954–63*\* (Touchstone, 1989). See also W. H. Chafe, *Civilities and Civil Rights: Greensboro, North Carolina and the Black Struggle for Freedom*\* (Oxford, NY, 1980).

THE UNITED STATES AND THE WORLD. There are some good overviews of US foreign policy: S. E. Ambrose, *Rise to Globalism: American Foreign Policy since 1938*\* (6th edn, Penguin, 1991); Seyom Brown, *The Faces of Power: Constancy and Change in United States Foreign Policy from Truman to Reagan*\* (Columbia, 1983); R. S. Kirkendall, *A Global Power: America since the Age of Roosevelt*\* (2nd edn, Knopf, 1980); J. W. Spanier, *American Foreign Policy since World War II*\* (Praeger, 1985). Policy towards Latin America is critically assessed by W. La Feber, *Inevitable Revolutions*\* (revised edn, Norton, 1984) and by the same author in *The Panama Canal: The Crisis in Historical Perspective* (Oxford, 1978). See also L. Schoultz, *Human Rights and United States Policy toward Latin America*\* (Princeton, 1981). J. W. Fulbright, the distinguished former chairman of the Senate Committee of Foreign Relations, in *The Arrogance of Power* (Random House, 1966), stressed the dangers of over-extension, especially

from US policy in Vietnam. Gaddis Smith examines the Carter period in *Morality, Reason, and Power: American Diplomacy in the Carter Years*\* (Hill & Wang, 1986). For US policy in Iran from the close of the Second World War to the hostage crisis, see B. Rubin, *Paved with Good Intentions: The American Experience in Iran*\* (Penguin, 1981). For the period identified with Henry Kissinger, see his own account, *The White House Years* (Little, 1979). See also M. Mandelbaum, *The Nuclear Question: The United States and Nuclear Weapons, 1946–1976*\* (Cambridge, 1979); L. S. Spector, *Nuclear Proliferation Today*\* (Vintage, 1984).

Finally, for an examination of the large role television has played in shaping public opinion, see R. J. Donovan and R. Scherer, *Unsilent Revolution: Television News and American Public Life, 1948–1991* (Cambridge, 1992).

See also section 15, The Cold War.

CANADA. See R. Bothwell, I. Drummond and J. English, *Canada since 1945: Power Politics and Provincialism* (Toronto, 1989) for a good overview. See also K. McNaught, *The Pelican History of Canada*\* (Penguin, 1985).

## 17. THE SOVIET UNION AND EASTERN EUROPE SINCE THE SECOND WORLD WAR

Two stimulating general accounts explaining the Russian way of life by the *New York Times* correspondent H. Smith: *The Russians*\* (Sphere, 1976) and *The New Russians* (Random House, 1990); for the last years of Stalin, *Khrushchev Remembers*\* (2 vols, Penguin, 1977) can serve as an introduction. On Khrushchev and destalinisation, see R. and Zh. Medvedev, *Khrushchev: The Years in Power* (Oxford, 1977) and C. Linden, *Khrushchev and the Soviet Leadership, 1957–64* (Johns Hopkins, 1966), as well as Khrushchev's memoirs above. A brief account can be found in A.

Nove, *Stalinism and After*\* (Allen & Unwin, 1975). See also A. Brown and M. Kaser (eds), *The Soviet Union since the Fall of Khrushchev* (2nd edn, Macmillan, 1978) and the same editors' *Soviet Policy for the 1980s*, the sequel covers political, economic and social develpments during the Brezhnev years of the old Soviet Union, (Macmillan, 1980). Zh. Medvedev wrote a study of *Andropov* (Blackwell, 1983); see also R. W. Davies, *Soviet History in the Gorbachev Revolution* (Macmillan, 1989).

EASTERN EUROPE. An overview is

provided by J. Held (ed.), *The Columbia History of Eastern Europe in the Twentieth Century* (Columbia, 1992). F. Fetjö, *A History of the People's Democracies and Eastern Europe since Stalin*\* (2nd edn, Penguin, 1974) remains one of the best accounts, told with the inside knowledge of a leading Hungarian newspaper correspondent. For the early years of communist rule, see M. McCauley (ed.), *Communist Power in Europe, 1944–49* (Macmillan, 1977), a collection of essays. There are good studies of individual countries: J. Korbel, *Twentieth Century Czechoslovakia: The Meanings* *of its History* (Columbia, 1977); H. G. Skilling, *Czechoslovakia's Interrupted Revolution* (Princeton, 1976); and Alexander Dubček's own memoirs (HarperCollins, 1992) for the stirring events of the Prague Spring and Soviet intervention in 1968. The origins of the 1989 revolution are recounted in H. G. Skilling, *Charter 77 and Human Rights in Czechoslovakia* (Allen & Unwin, 1981). For Poland see N. Davies, *God's Playground: A History of Poland* (2 vols, Columbia, 1981); N. Ascherson, *The Polish August** (Penguin, 1981), for the workers' protests in 1980–1 and the birth of Solidarity. The years of growing crises are covered in P. G. Lewis, *Political Authority and Party Secretaries in Poland, 1975–1985* (Cambridge, 1989); see also T. Garton-Ash, *The Polish Revolution: Solidarity* (Cape, 1983). For Yugoslavia before the civil war, S. Pavlowitch, *The Improbable Survivor: Yugoslavia and its Problems* (Hurst, 1988).

BREAK-UP OF THE SOVIET UNION AND EASTERN EUROPE. A good starting point is the study by Z. Brzezinski, *The Grand Failure: The Birth and Death of Communism in the Twentieth Century* (Scribner's, 1989). The book, completed in August 1988, foretold that communism was in terminal crisis and that the 'reform' of communism would fail. Even so perceptive an observer, however, could not forecast future events with complete accuracy: he concluded that East Germany, Romania, China and North Korea were not in crisis, which turned out to be true only for North Korea, and for China partially. With East and central European history changing so rapidly, books soon became out of date. Of particular value is Mikhail Gorbachev's *Perestroika: New Thinking for our Country and the World** (Collins, 1988), setting out his hopes and intentions; two especially valuable studies are S. White, *Gorbachev in Power** (Cambridge, 1990) and R. Sakwa, *Gorbachev and his Reforms, 1985–1990** (Philip Alan, 1990), which contains an extensive bibliography. A stimulating overview is the book of the BBC Television series, Angus Roxburgh, *The Second Russian Revolution: The Struggle for Power in the Kremlin* (BBC Publications, 1991). An analysis of issues and problems can be found in A. Jones and D. E. Powell (eds), *Soviet Update, 1989–1990* (Harvard, 1991). Fundamental to an understanding of the Soviet Union is G. Smith (ed.), *The Nationalities Question in the Soviet Union** (Longman, 1990). The revolutions in Eastern and Central Europe are examined in J. Batt, *East Central Europe from Reform to Transformation** (Royal Institute for International Affairs, 1991) and in K. Dawisha, *Eastern Europe, Gorbachev, and Reform** (2nd edn, Cambridge, 1990). M. Glenny, *The Rebirth of History: Eastern Europe in the Age of Democracy** (Penguin, 1990) is an account based on personal experiences by the BBC correspondent. The last period of the unloved German Democratic Republic is chronicled in a collection of documents from secret archives: A. Mitter and S. Wolle, *Ich liebe euch doch alle! Befehle und Lageberichte des MFS Januar–November 1989* (Basis Druck, 1990).

## 18. THE MIDDLE EAST

Good overviews are P. Mansfield, *A History of the Middle East** (Penguin, 1992) and the same author's *The Arabs** (5th edn, Penguin, 1992); M. E. Yapp, *The Near East since the First World War** (Longman, 1991); W. R. Polk, *The Arab World** (4th edn, Harvard, 1980); D. Hiro, *Inside the Middle East** (Routledge & Kegan Paul, 1982); E. Kedourie, *Politics in the Middle East** (Oxford, 1992); A. H. Hourani, *The Emergence of the Modern Middle East* (Macmillan, 1981); and the same author's *A History of the Arab People** (Faber & Faber, 1991).

P. J. Vatikotis, *History of Modern Egypt: From Muhammad Ali to Sadat** (4th edn, Weidenfeld & Nicolson, 1991); D. Hopwood, *Egypt: Politics and Society, 1945–1992* (3rd edn, Routledge, 1992); A. McDermott, *Egypt from Nasser to Mubarak: A Flawed Revolution* (Chapman & Hall, 1988).

Lord Kinross, *Atatürk: The Rebirth of a Nation** (Weidenfeld & Nicolson, 1990), readable and informative; B. Lewis, *The Emergence of Modern Turkey* (2nd edn, Oxford, 1968); I. C. Schick and E. A. Tonak (eds), *Turkey in Transition: New Perspectives, 1923 to the Present* (Oxford, NY, 1986).

N. R. Keddie, *The Roots of Revolution: An Interpretive History of Modern Iran** (Yale, 1981); D. Hiro, *Iran under the Ayatollas** (Routledge & Kegan Paul, 1985); F. Halliday, *Iran: Dictatorship and Development* (2nd edn, Penguin, 1979).

D. Hopwood, *Syria, 1945–1986: Politics and Society** (Routledge, 1991); P. Seale, *The Struggle for Syria: A Study in Post-War Arab Politics* (2nd edn, Yale, 1987); and, by the same author, *Asad of Syria: The Struggle for the Middle East** (California, 1989).

K. Salibi, *The Modern History of Lebanon* (Weidenfeld & Nicolson, 1977); H. Cobban, *The Making of Modern Lebanon** (Hutchinson, 1985).

P. Sluglett and M. Farouk-Sluglett, *Iraq since 1958: From Revolution to Dictatorship** (I. B. Tauris, 1991); R. Lacey, *The Kingdom** (Avon, 1983), a history of Saudi Arabia.

A good history of Israel is H. M. Sachar, *A History of Israel* (2 vols, Oxford, NY, 1987).

ISRAEL AND THE PALESTINE CONFLICTS. N. Bethell, *The Palestine Triangle: The Struggle between the British, the Jews and the Arabs, 1935–1948** (Futura, 1980) is a good introduction. This can be followed by R. Ovendale, *The Origins of the Arab–Israeli Wars** (Longman, 1984). An invaluable collection is W. Laqueur and B. Rubin, *The Israel–Arab Reader: A Documentary History of the Middle East Conflict* (revised edn, Penguin, 1984). Y. Porath, *The Emergence of the Palestinian Arab National Movement* (2 vols, Cass, 1974–7), covers the years 1918 to 1939. B. Wasserstein, *The British in Palestine: The Mandatory Government and the Arab–Jewish Conflict, 1917–1929* (Royal Historical Society, 1978) is good on the origins of the conflict. See also M. J. Cohen, *Palestine: Retreat from the Mandate: The Making of British Policy, 1936–45* (Holmes &

Meier, 1978); M. Rodinson, *Israel and the Arabs*\* (2nd edn, Penguin, 1982). There is a vivid personal account of the conflict in the 1980s by T. Friedman, the *New York Times* correspondent in Beirut and Jerusalem, *From Beirut to Jerusalem*\* (Harper Collins, 1990).

For the great powers and the Middle East a good overview is A. Williams, *Britain and France in the Middle East and North Africa, 1914–1967*\* (Macmillan, 1968). With the opening of the British archives for 1956 a reassessment of the Suez war became possible. Keith Kyle

produced a readable, many-faceted account, *Suez* (Weidenfeld & Nicolson, 1991). W. Scott Lucas, *Divided We Stand: Britain, the U.S. and the Suez Crisis* (Hodder & Stoughton, 1991) is both clear and illuminating. Startling in some of its revelations, Ze'ev Schiff and Ehud Ya'ari, *Israel's Lebanon War* (Allen & Unwin, 1984) explains that tragic conflict. For the bloody war between Iran and Iraq, see J. Bullock and H. Morris, *The Gulf War: Its Origins, History and Consequences* (Methuen, 1989).

## 19. THE INDIAN SUBCONTINENT

INDIA. J. M. Brown, *Modern India: The Origins of an Asian Democracy*\* (Oxford, 1985) is one of the best introductions. There is a sizeable literature on British India and the transfer of power. R. J. Moore covers the period since 1917 in three studies, *The Crisis of Indian Unity, 1917–1940* (Oxford, 1974), *Churchill, Cripps and India* (Oxford, 1979), and *Escape from Empire: The Attlee Government and the Indian Problem* (Oxford, 1983). See also R. B. Tomlinson, *The Indian National Congress and the Raj: The Penultimate Phase* (Macmillan, 1976); and the same author's *The Political Economy of the Raj, 1914–1947* (Macmillan, 1979); C. H. Philips and M. D. Wainwright (eds), *The Partition of India* (Allen & Unwin, 1970). The relevant chapters of P. Ziegler, *Mountbatten* (Collins, 1985) provide a sympathetic picture of the last Viceroy. Still useful are B. P. Lamb, *India: A World in Transition* (3rd edn, Praeger, 1968), and P. Spear, *A*

*History of India* (vol. 2, Penguin, 1970), but both are rather dated. See also S. Wolpert, *A New History of India*\* (4th edn, Oxford, NY, 1992). The problem of separatist movements in India is well covered by a distinguished Indian journalist, M. J. Akbar, *India: The Siege Within: Challenges to a Nation's Unity*\* (Penguin, 1985). P. R. Brass, *The Politics of India since Independence*, vol. iv, 1, of *The Cambridge History of India*, (Cambridge, 1990) provides a thematic political-science approach. D. Hiro, *Inside India Today* (Cambridge, 1976) is a good read and stimulating. Among excellent biographies, possibly the best way to study the history of independent India, are J. M. Brown's *Gandhi: Prisoner of Hope* (Yale, 1989) and S. Gopal, *Jawaharlal Nehru: A Biography* (3 vols, Cape, 1975–84) the latter abridged to a one-volume edition (Oxford, 1990). See also K. Bhatia, *Indira: A Biography of Prime Minister*

*Gandhi* (Angus Robertson, 1974).

PAKISTAN. An excellent one-volume history with an extensive bibliography is Omar Noman, *Pakistan: Political and Economic History since 1947* (Kegan Paul, 1988). The founding father is the subject of S. Wolpert's biography, *Jinnah of Pakistan* (Oxford, NY, 1984). For contemporary Pakistan, see A. Kapur, *Pakistan in Crisis* (Routledge, 1991).

SRI LANKA. K. M. de Silva, *A History of Sri Lanka* (Oxford, 1981); M. Ram, *Sri Lanka*\* (Penguin, 1989).

BANGLADESH. L. Ziring, *Bangladesh: A Political Analysis* (Macmillan, 1992).

BURMA (MYANMAR). J. Silverstein, *Burmese Politics: The Dilemma of National Unity* (Rutgers, 1980); and, by the same author, *Burma: Military Rule and the Politics of Stagnation*\* (Cornell, 1977).

## 20. THE LANDS OF THE PACIFIC

For an overview of south-east and eastern Asia, a good source book is M. Borthwick (ed.), *Pacific Century: The Emergence of Modern Pacific Asia*\* (Westview Press, 1992), with contributions by a number of distinguished scholars. It is inter-disciplinary in

approach; besides brief historical outlines, it contains valuable data on demography, trade relations, economic and social developments, and inter-regional international relations, up to 1990. The reader is referred to this work especially for the recent

development of Taiwan, Korea, the Philippines, Vietnam and Indonesia, as well as of the giants, China and Japan. A good bibliography is provided. The book was written to accompany an Annenberg US college television course. For a useful introduction to the transformation from colonial rule to independence of several Asian nations of India, the Philippines, Indonesia, Vietnam and Malaya, see R. Jeffrey (ed.), *Asia: The Winning of Independence* (Macmillan, 1981), with an extensive bibliography. An excellent survey is D. G. E. Hall, *A History of Southeast Asia* (4th edn, Macmillan, 1981).

JAPAN. P. Duus, *The Rise of Modern Japan* (Houghton Mifflin, 1976), an overview; M. Schaller, *The American Occupation of Japan: The Origins of the Cold War in Asia* (Oxford, 1986); M. Schaller, *Douglas MacArthur: The Far Eastern General* (Oxford, NY, 1989); J. Woronoff, *Politics the Japanese Way* (St Martin's, 1990), a lively and critical account; W. Horsley and R. Buckley, *Nippon New Superpower: Japan since 1945* (BBC Publications, 1990), the book of a first-rate BBC Television series; M. Morischima, *Why Has Japan 'Succeeded'? Western Technology and the Japanese Ethos* (Cambridge, 1982).

CHINA. An excellent overview is J. Spence, *The Search for Modern China* (Norton, 1990). The authoritative multi-volume history of China is *The Cambridge History of China*, vol. 10 (*1800–1911*, pt 1), ed. J. K. Fairbank; vol. 11, (*1800–1911*, pt 2, ed. J. K. Fairbank and Kwang-Ching Liu; vol. 12 *1912–1949*, pt 1), ed. J. K. Fairbank; vol. 13 (*1912–1949*, pt 2) ed.

J. K. Fairbank and A. Feuerwerker; vol. 14 (*1949–1965*, pt 1), ed. R. MacFarquar and J. K. Fairbank; vol. 15 (*1966–1982*), ed. R. MacFarquar and J. K. Fairbank (Cambridge, 1978–92). See also S. Karnow, *Mao and China: Inside China's Cultural Revolution* (Penguin, 1985); M. Yahuda, *Towards the End of Isolationism: China's Foreign Policy after Mao* (Macmillan, 1985); J. Gittings, *China Changes Face: The Road from Revolution, 1949–1989* (Oxford, 1990); C. Riskin, *China's Political Economy: The Quest for Development since 1949* (Oxford, 1987). An account by Chinese scholars of the development of the economy can be found in Liu Juinian and Wu Qungen (eds), *China's Socialist Economy: An Outline History (1949–1984)* (Beijing Review, 1986).

For Japan and China see also section 6, China and Japan and the West.

KOREA. The rise of Korea as an Asian economic power and her location on the front line of the Cold War has led to a large number of academic studies: C. J. Eckert, *Korea Old and New: A History* (Ilchoak Publishers, Seoul, 1990); T. Hatada, *A History of Korea* (ABC-Clio, 1969), an older history stressing Korean traditions and still valuable; D. S. Lewis (ed.), *Korea: Enduring Division* (Longman, 1988); B.-N. Song, *The Rise of the Korean Economy* (Oxford, NY, 1989); J. A.

Kim, *Divided Korea: The Politics of Development, 1945–1972* (Harvard, 1975). More general in coverage is T. W. Robinson, *Democracy and Development in East Asia: Taiwan, South Korea and the Philippines* (AEI Press, 1991).

TAIWAN. S. Long, *Taiwan* (Macmillan, 1991).

VIETNAM. M. Beresford, *National Unification and Economic Development in Vietnam* (St Martin's, 1989).

PHILIPPINES. O. D. Corpuz, *The Philippines* (Prentice-Hall, 1965); E. Lachica, *The Huk Rebellion: A Study of Peasant Revolt in the Philippines* (Praeger, 1971); J. Bresnan (ed.), *Crisis in the Philippines: The Marcos Era and Beyond* (Princeton, 1986).

AUSTRALIA. M. Clark, *A Short History of Australia* (3rd edn, Penguin–Mentor, 1963). A succinctly authoritative account is the *Oxford History of Australia*, vol. 4, J. McIntyre, *1901–42: The Succeeding Age* (Oxford, 1987), and vol. 5, G. Bolton, *1942–88: The Middle Way* (Oxford, 1990).

NEW ZEALAND. K. Sinclair, *A History of New Zealand* (revised edn, Penguin, 1989); W. H. Oliver and B. R. William (eds), *The Oxford History of New Zealand* (2nd edn, revised G. W. Rice, Oxford, NZ, 1993).

## 21. AFRICA

The standard work is the multi-volume *Cambridge History of Africa*; for the twentieth century the relevant volumes are vol. 6 (*From 1870–1905*), ed. R. Oliver and G. N. Sanderson; vol. 7 (*From 1905–1940*), ed. A. Roberts; vol. 8 (*From 1940–1975*), ed. M. Crowder (Cambridge, 1984–6). The overall editors of the history are J. D. Fage and R. Oliver. The best one-volume overviews are J. D. Fage, *A History of Africa* (2nd edn, Unwin Hyman, 1993); B. Davidson,

*Africa in History* (revised edn, Macmillan, 1992); B. Freund, *The Making of Contemporary Africa: The Development of African Society since 1800* (Macmillan, 1984). A stimulating study emphasising the African viewpoint is A. A. Mazrui and M. Tidy, *Nationalism and New States in Africa* (Heinemann, 1984). See also P. Calvocoressi, *Independent Africa and the World* (Longman, 1985). For British imperialism in Africa and the rest of the world, a good overview

is B. Porter, *The Lion's Share: Short History of British Imperialism, 1850–1953* (Longman, 1984). Also of value is J. Gallagher, *The Decline, Revival and Fall of the British Empire* (Cambridge, 1982). The multi-volume *Colonialism in Africa*, 5 vols, ed. L. H. Gann and P. Duignan (Cambridge, 1969–74), is comprehensive. There is also a very good one-volume study, J. D. Hargreaves, *Decolonization in Africa* (Longman, 1988).

For economic and development aspects specifically, D. K. Fieldhouse, *Black Africa, 1945–1980: Economic Decolonization and Arrested Development** (Allen & Unwin, 1987) puts forward reasons for slow progress. See also C. Ake, *A Political Economy of Africa** (Longman, 1981); A. G. Hopkins, *Economic History of West Africa* (Longman, 1973).

EAST AFRICA. R. Oliver (ed.), *Oxford History of East Africa* (3 vols, Oxford, 1963–75); K. Ingham, *The Making of Modern Uganda* (Allen & Unwin, 1958); by the same author, *A History of East Africa* (3rd edn, Longman, 1965);

T. Virginia and R. Adloff, *Djibouti and the Horn* (Stanford, 1968); B. H. Selassie, *Conflict and Intervention in the Horn of Africa** (Monthly Review Press, 1980); M. Meredith, *The Past is Another Country: Rhodesia UDI to Zimbabwe** (Pan, 1980).

WEST AFRICA. M. Crowder, *West Africa under Colonial Rule* (Hutchinson, 1968); J. D. Fage, *History of West Africa** (Cambridge, 1969); by the same author, *Ghana: A Historical Interpretation* (Greenwood, 1983); G. A. Langley, *Pan-Africanism and Nationalism in West Africa* (Oxford, 1973); J. Dunn (ed.), *West African*

*States: Failure and Promise* (Cambridge, 1978).

SOUTH AFRICA. There is a large literature. An excellent overview is T. R. H. Davenport, *South Africa: A Modern History** (3rd edn, Macmillan, 1987). See also G. M. Gerhart, *Black Power in South Africa: The Evolution of an Ideology** (California, 1978); M. Benson, *South Africa: The Struggle for a Birthright* (International Defence Aid, 1985); T. Huddleston, *Naught for Comfort* (Fount, 1977); R. M. Price, *The Apartheid State in Crisis: Political Transformation in South Africa, 1975–90* (Oxford, 1991).

## 22. LATIN AMERICA

Two good overviews are B. Keen, *A History of Latin America** (vol. 2, 4th edn, Houghton Mifflin, 1992) and T. E. Skidmore and P. H. Smith, *Modern Latin America** (Oxford, 1992), which covers the century from the 1880s to the 1980s and also contains an extensive bibliography. An interesting interpretation by the Latin American correspondent of the *Observer*, H. O'Shaughnessy is the book of the BBC radio series *Latin Americans** (BBC–Parkwest, 1988). The monumental *Cambridge History of Latin America*, under its editor L. Bethell, is gradually being completed, volumes 4 and 5 cover the years 1870 to 1930 and volumes 7 and 8 the years since 1930 (Cambridge, 1986–92).

MEXICO. M. C. Meyer and W. L. Sherman, *The Course of Mexican History** (4th edn, Oxford, NY, 1991); A. Knight, *The Mexican Revolution* (2 vols, Cambridge, 1986).

VENEZUELA. J. V. Lombardi, *Venezuela: The Search for Order, the Dream of Progress* (Oxford, NY, 1982).

CENTRAL AMERICA. R. L. Woodward Jr, *Central America: A Nation Divided** (2nd edn, Oxford, NY, 1986). For economic development, see V. Bulmer-Thomas, *The Political Economy of Central America since 1920** (Cambridge, 1987). See also J. Valenta and E. Duran (eds), *Conflict in Nicaragua: A Multidimensional Perspective** (Allen & Unwin, 1987); R. R. Fagen, *Forging Peace: The Challenge of Central America** (Blackwell, 1987).

CUBA. For a general history, see H. Thomas, *Cuba: The Pursuit of Freedom* (Harper & Row, 1971).

ARGENTINA. For overviews, see D. Rock, *Argentina, 1516–1982: From Spanish Colonization to the Falklands War** (California, 1985) and, edited

by the same author, *Argentina in the Twentieth Century* (Pittsburgh, 1975). See also G. I. Blanksten, *Perón's Argentina* (Chicago, 1974).

CHILE. E. Kaufman, *Crisis in Allende's Chile: New Perspectives* (Praeger, 1988). J. Valenzuela and A. Valenzuela, *Military Rule in Chile: Dicatorship and Oppositions* (Johns Hopkins, 1986).

BRAZIL. P. Flynn, *Brazil: A Political Analysis* (Ernest Benn, 1978); T. E. Skidmore, *Politics in Brazil, 1930–1964: An Experiment in Democracy* (Oxford, NY, 1967); and by the same author, *Politics of Military Rule in Brazil, 1964–1985* (Oxford, NY, 1988).

Two studies of general interest are S. Lindquist, *Land and Power in South America** (Penguin, 1979) and T. Beeson and J. Pearce, *A Vision of Hope: The Churches and Change in Latin America** (Collins, 1984).

## 23. THE UNITED NATIONS AND THE EUROPEAN COMMUNITY

See. D. Armstrong, *The Rise of International Organisations* (Macmillan, 1982) for a good general overview of international organisations. See also E. Luard, *The United Nations*

(Macmillan, 1979); H. G. Nicholas *The United Nations as a Political Institution* (Oxford, 1975); S. Bailey, *The United Nations* (Macmillan, 1989).

For a general overview of the

coming together of Western Europe, see D. W. Urwin, *The Community of Europe: A History of European Integration since 1945* (Longman, 1991). See also J. Pinder, *European*

*Community: The Building of a Union* (Oxford, 1991); D. Swann, *The Economics of the Common Market** (6th edn, Penguin, 1988). For an upbeat assessment of the EC's achievements and future needs by a former vice-president of the European Commission from 1981 to 1985, see C. Tugendhat, *Making Sense of Europe** (Penguin, 1986).

## 24. SOME GENERAL REFERENCE WORKS

*The Statesman's Year Book* provides annual updates of pertinent information country by country. It is published by Macmillan and in 1992–3 was in its 129th edition. Another immensely useful reference work providing good factual accounts of a year's events country by country is *The Annual Register: A Record of World Events*, which was first edited by Edmund Burke in 1758 and in 1991 was edited by A. J. Day assisted by V. Hoffman (Longman, 1992). For contemporary events there are the press and documentary programmes on television, but for good consistent reporting *The Economist* is invaluable, as are the US weeklies *Time* and *Newsweek*. The German version is *Der Spiegel*.

A number of compendiums periodically updated provide detailed statistical information and more. The *Europa Publications* are excellent, covering in separate volumes *USA and Canada* (1990), *South America, Central America and the Caribbean* (1993), *The Far East and Australasia* (1993), *The Middle East and North Africa* (1993), *Africa South of the Sahara* (1993), *Eastern Europe and the Commonwealth of Independent States* (1992), *Western Europe* (1993), and the globe in *The Europa World Year Book* (2 vols, 1993). The major encyclopaedias also add annual volumes to their most recent editions. Also available is B. R. Mitchell and B. Redman, *International Historical Statistics. Europe 1750–1988* (rev. edn, Macmillan, 1993).

Convenient brief accounts of political and economic conditions with useful statistical data are published in a handy paperback series, *Spotlight on Politics*, covering a number of countries including Britain, the United States, China, France and West Germany: I. Derbyshire, *Politics in West Germany from Schmidt to Kohl* (Chambers, 1987); I. Derbyshire, *Politics in France from Giscard to Mitterrand* (Chambers, 1987); J. D. Derbyshire and I. Derbyshire, *Politics in Britain from Callaghan to Thatcher* (Chambers, 1990).

An invaluable guide to bibliographies is R. H. Fritze, B. E. Coutts and L. A. Vyhnanek, *Reference Sources in History: An Introductory Guide* (ABC-Clio, 1990).

# INDEX

bold numbers indicate a reference to an illustration